STEPHEN WOLFRAM
A NEW KIND OF SCIENCE

STEPHEN WOLFRAM
A NEW KIND OF SCIENCE

Visit **www.wolframscience.com** for the latest information on the science in this book, related material, software and initiatives.

Send mail to contact@wolframscience.com for questions or comments. Do not send confidential or proprietary material. See www.wolframscience.com/contact for more information.

Author website: **www.stephenwolfram.com**

Publisher: Wolfram Media, Inc.

web: www.wolfram-media.com
email: info@wolfram-media.com
phone: +1-217-398-9090/1-800-943-9626
fax: +1-217-398-9095
mail: 100 Trade Center Drive, Champaign, IL 61820, USA
international: Wolfram Research Europe Ltd.
　　　　　　　 Wolfram Research Asia Ltd.

Subject category: General science

Library of Congress Cataloging-in-Publication Data

Wolfram, Stephen, 1959 –
A New Kind of Science / Stephen Wolfram.
p. cm
Includes index.

ISBN 1-57955-008-8 (alk. paper)
1. Cellular automata. 2. Computational complexity. I. Title.

QA267.5.C45 W67 2001
500—dc21　　　　　　　　　　　　　　　　 2001046603
　　　　　　　　　　　　　　　　　　　　　　 CIP

Permissions information: www.wolframscience.com/nks/permissions
(see below; versions of images suitable for reproduction are available)

Copyright © 2002 by Stephen Wolfram, LLC

STEPHEN
WOLFRAM
A NEW
KIND OF
SCIENCE

Contents

Preface

Just over twenty years ago I made what at first seemed like a small discovery: a computer experiment of mine showed something I did not expect. But the more I investigated, the more I realized that what I had seen was the beginning of a crack in the very foundations of existing science, and a first clue towards a whole new kind of science.

This book is the culmination of nearly twenty years of work that I have done to develop that new kind of science. I had never expected it would take anything like as long, but I have discovered vastly more than I ever thought possible, and in fact what I have done now touches almost every existing area of science, and quite a bit besides.

In the early years, I did as I had done before as a scientist, and published accounts of my ongoing work in the scientific literature. But although what I wrote seemed to be very well received, I gradually came to realize that technical papers scattered across the journals of all sorts of fields could never successfully communicate the kind of major new intellectual structure that I seemed to be beginning to build.

So I resolved just to keep working quietly until I had finished, and was ready to present everything in a single coherent way. Fifteen years later this book is the result. And with it my hope is to share what I have done with as wide a range of scientists and non-scientists as possible.

In modern times it has been almost unheard of for genuinely new science to be presented for the first time in a book that can be read by non-scientists. For progress in science has mostly tended to take place in small steps that cannot reasonably be explained without relying on specialized technical knowledge of what has gone before.

But to develop the new kind of science that I describe in this book I have had no choice but to take several large steps at once, and in doing so I have mostly ended up having to start from scratch—with new ideas and new methods that ultimately depend very little on what has gone before.

In some ways it might have been easier for me to present what I have done in some kind of new technical formalism. But instead I have chosen to spend the effort to take things to the point where they are clear enough to be explained quite fully just in ordinary language and pictures.

Unfortunately, however, this will no doubt mean that there are some—particularly from the existing sciences—who will at first assume that their existing technical knowledge must somehow already cover whatever is in this book. And a few, I fear, will stop at that point, and choose to learn no more. But many, I hope, will at least look at the book long enough to begin to be surprised by what it actually says.

At first probably they will think that parts of it cannot possibly be correct—for they seem so at odds with existing science. And indeed if I myself were just to pick up this book today without having spent the past twenty years thinking about its contents, I have little doubt that I too would not believe many of the things it says.

But the computer experiments on which the science in the book is ultimately based are easy to check on any modern computer. And almost all the arguments in the book—while often not conceptually simple—require no specialized scientific or other knowledge to follow.

Yet it has certainly taken me years to come to terms with the conclusions I have reached. And while I hope that all the effort I have put into presentation in this book will make it easier for others, I do not expect it to be a quick process. For to absorb in any real way what the book has to say requires a fairly major shift in intuition and thinking.

But the most important first step, I believe, is just to recognize what is involved. For though there are connections of all sorts, this book is first and foremost about a fundamentally new intellectual structure, that needs to be understood in its own terms, and cannot reasonably be fit into any existing framework.

It has been a great challenge for me to capture the things I have discovered over the past twenty years in a book of manageable size. And to do so I have often ended up compressing into a page or even a paragraph the essence of what a chapter or even a book could have been written about.

In the quarter million or so words of the main text my emphasis is on communicating the core of my ideas and discoveries—as well as indicating a little of how I came to them. The last three hundred or so pages of the book—themselves another quarter million or so words—supplement the main text with many historical and technical notes, and also summarize more discoveries. The notes that begin on page 849 address some specific issues about reading this book.

Throughout the book my primary concern is with basic science and fundamental issues. But building on the foundations in the book there are a vast array of applications—both conceptual and practical—that can now be developed.

No doubt some will come quickly. But most will probably take decades to emerge. Yet in time I expect that the ideas of this book will come to pervade not only science and technology but also many areas of general thinking. And with this its methods will eventually become a standard part of education—much as mathematics is today. And in the end most of what now seems surprising and remarkable in the book will come to seem familiar and commonplace.

But for me what has always been most important is the actual process of discovery. For I know of nothing as profoundly exciting as to glimpse for the first time some new and basic truth. And now that I have finished building the intellectual structure that I describe in this book it is my hope that those who read these words can share in the excitement I have had in making the discoveries that were involved.

Stephen Wolfram
January 15, 2002

The creation of this book and the science it describes has been a vast personal undertaking, spanning the better part of half my life so far. And for it to all have been even remotely possible has required a series of particular personal circumstances. Foremost among them is that I have lived at the moment in history when technology has first made it possible to do the kinds of things I have done. But also crucial has been that my early successes in science and business have for more than twenty years allowed me to be free to pursue the personal intellectual objectives I have chosen.

That by my late teenage years I had already become established in science was what originally provided the personal confidence and practical situation that made it possible for me to embark on an intellectual project as ambitious as this. My early experiences—particularly in physics and computing—were crucial in pointing me in the basic direction I took. My work in designing and documenting *Mathematica* and its forerunners was central in developing for me a certain definite pattern of clear thinking. My experiences in business were also important in helping me form a capacity for making strategic intellectual decisions. And the fact that for most of my life I have tried to learn as broadly and deeply as possible about science and other fields has provided me a crucial base of knowledge. But more than anything else what has finally allowed me to create the new kind of science in this book is *Mathematica*. For while building *Mathematica* has taken a considerable amount of my time, I would without it as a tool never have been able to do the vast majority of what is now in this book.

In my early years I was very much a part of the traditional scientific community. But had I remained there I have little doubt that I would never have been able to create something of the magnitude that I describe in this book. For even just to spend so many years on a single project outside of existing disciplines—and without publishing anything about it—would likely have become impossible even in the highly favorable academic circumstances in which I found myself.

But with the commercial success of *Mathematica* and Wolfram Research there have for many years not been any such issues for me. And indeed, within my company I have been able to build up a remarkable group of people—who have supported my efforts in all sorts of ways. Over the past fifteen years hundreds of members of our R&D and engineering groups have worked to take my ideas for *Mathematica* and turn them into finished software that I and millions of others rely on every day. And at one time or another almost every major department of my company has provided help that has been crucial to some aspect of the creation or production of this book.

Yet what is probably most striking is that even in my role as CEO of a highly active company I have for more than ten years been able to devote the large amounts of time that have been required to write this book and develop the science it describes. And more than anything else, what has made this possible is the outstanding team that has helped manage the ongoing operations of the company—especially our current executive committee: George Beck, Roger Germundsson, Theodore Gray, Becky Porth, Brenda Skelly, Tom Wickham-Jones and my brother Conrad Wolfram.

To pursue a project of the length and intensity of this book would not have been possible without the great personal support of my family and friends. Particularly crucial have been my wife—who has contributed both directly and indirectly to many aspects of the form and content of this book, and my children—whose excitement about the world has provided continual encouragement and stimulation. Also important—especially in my youth—were my parents, who supported my early interests and direction.

Like almost any highly creative project, the writing of this book has ultimately been a quite solitary and personal matter. But I have been fortunate over the years to employ a variety of talented assistants, who have helped the project in many different ways: Eric Berg (project management, 2000–2001), Jason Cawley (historical and philosophical issues, 2001–2002 and before), Matthew Cook (technical content, particularly constructions and proofs, 1991–1998), Andrew de Laix (technical content and book production systems, 1998–2002), Matthew Frank (mathematical and historical issues, 2001–2002), Andrea Gerlach (fact finding and checking, 1999–2002), David Hillman (constructions and other technical content, 1997–2001), Scott Koranda (book production systems and project management, 1996–1998), Ed Pegg, Jr. (technical content, 2000–2002), Todd Rowland (mathematical issues, 2001–2002), Malgorzata Strzebonska (graphics finishing, 1997–2002), Matthew Szudzik (mathematical issues, 1998–2000, 2001), Øyvind Tafjord (physics and other technical issues, 2001–2002), Kelli Wendt (project management, 2001–2002), Erik Winfree (software development, 1991–1992). Other members of Wolfram Research and Wolfram Media who have made particularly significant contributions include: Larry Adelston (book layout, 2000–2002), George Beck (project management oversight, 2001–2002 and before), John Bonadies (cover design and other issues, 1995, 1991–1999), Cat Boucher (project management, 2001–2002), Jean Buck (library research 1991–1999; many internal and external issues 1999–2002), Jeremy Davis (design, 2000–2002), Deb Forgacs (library research, 2000–2002), Thomasanna Hail (project management assistance, 2001), Yu He (technical issues, 1991–1992), Andy Hunt (font design, 1997–2002), Janice Hunter (book distribution, 2000–2002), André Kuzniarek (book design and production, 1991–2002), Richard Miske (book layout, 2001–2002), Jan Progen (proofreading, 1997–2002), David Reiss (external communications, 2001–2002), Patrick Rice (book build automation, 2001–2002), Brenda Skelly (manufacturing management, 2001–2002 and before), Caroline Small (document quality assurance, 2001), Michael Trott (occasional technical issues, 1994–2002), Allan Wylde (publishing issues, 1998–1999). (See also the colophon at the very end of the book.) My administrative and computer systems assistants have also been crucial in allowing me to maintain the high level of personal productivity needed to pursue and complete this project.

In developing the new kind of science in this book I have benefitted in many ways from the worldwide intellectual community. I have always worked hard to learn as many fields as possible as deeply as I can—and to keep abreast of new developments that emerge. Part of what has allowed me to do this is reading an immense number of books, articles and websites. But over the years what has also been important is that I have interacted personally with a great many individuals, and I have been fortunate that my position in science and technology has brought me into contact at one time or another with the leaders of almost every major technical field.

In the early and mid-1980s I did collaborative work relevant to this book—some published, some unpublished—with several people: Richard Feynman (foundations of physics and computing), Olivier Martin (additive cellular automata), John Milnor (mathematics of cellular automata), Andrew Odlyzko (additive cellular automata), Norman Packard (2D cellular automata) and Jim Salem (cellular automaton fluids).

Over the course of the past twenty years I have learned many things relevant to this book from many people. Sometimes I have asked specific questions and got specific answers. Sometimes discussions separated by months or years have gradually made me come to understand something. Sometimes just a single discussion has caused me to learn an important fact or piece of history—or has clarified limitations of some particular field. And sometimes a question asked of me has led me to discover something or to see how to present something better. In all I recall nearly three hundred people who have helped me in these kinds of ways in the past twenty years (this does not include people—especially from the physics community—with whom my main interactions were before 1981, or those with whom my interactions have mostly been about *Mathematica* or the business of Wolfram Research): Ralph Abraham, Victor Adamchik, Ron Adrian, Guenther Ahlers, Berni Alder, Jan Ambjørn, John Baez, Jim Bailey, Igor Bakshee, Mary Barsony, Andrej Bauer, George Beck, Charles Bennett, Michael Berry, Philippe Binder, Lenore Blum, Manuel Blum, Bruce Boghosian, Enrico Bombieri, Phil Boyland, William Bricken, Bruno Buchberger, Art Burks, David Campbell, John Campbell, Chris Carlson, Pete Carruthers, Forrest Carter, Elise Cawley, Greg Chaitin, Steve Christensen, David Chudnovsky, Gregory Chudnovsky, John Conway, Barbara Cooper, Jack Cowan, Richard Crandall, Jim Crutchfield, Karel Culik, Predrag Cvitanović, Gautam Dasgupta, Roger Dashen, Martin Davis, Richard Dawkins, David Deutsch, Kee Dewdney, Persi Diaconis, Whitfield Diffie, Freeman Dyson, Paul Erdős, Benson Farb, Doyne Farmer, Mitchell Feigenbaum, Carl Feynman, Richard Feynman, David Finkelstein, Michael Fisher, Mike Foale, Joseph Ford, John Franks, Ed Fredkin, Harvey Friedman, Uriel Frisch, Peter Gacs, Jill Gardner, Laurie Gay, Todd Gayley, Richard Gaylord, Murray Gell-Mann, Roger Germundsson, Etienne Ghys, Don Glaser, Nigel Goldenfeld, Shafi Goldwasser, Beatrice Golomb, Solomon Golomb, Bill Gosper, Peter Grassberger, Alfred Gray, Jeremy Gray, John Gray, Theodore Gray, David Griffeath, Misha Gromov, David Gross, John Guckenheimer, Charlie Gunn, Howard Gutowitz, Hyman Hartman, Jeff Harvey, Brosl Hasslacher, David Hawkins, Gustav Hedlund, Danny Hillis, Pierre Hohenberg, John Holland, John Hopfield, Bernardo Huberman, Alfred Hübler, Dominique d'Humières, Lyman Hurd, Ken Iverson, Raymond Jeanloz, Erica Jen, Leo Kadanoff, Dave Kammeyer, Kuni Kaneko, Stuart Kauffman, Karen Kavanagh, Jerry Keiper, Evelyn Fox Keller, Veikko Keränen, Scott Kirkpatrick, Sergiu Klainerman, Rob Knapp, Don Knuth, Rocky Kolb, John Koza, Bob Kraichnan, Yoshi Kuramoto, Jeff Lagarias, Rolf Landauer, Jim Langer, Chris Langton, Joel Lebowitz, David Levermore, Leonid Levin, Silvio Levy, Steven Levy, Debra Lewis, Wentian Li, Albert Libchaber, David Librik, Dan Lichtblau, Doug Lind, Aristid Lindenmayer, Kristian Lindgren, Chris Lindsey, Ed Lorenz, Saunders Mac Lane, Roman Mäder, Janice Malouf, Benoit Mandelbrot, Norman Margolus, Oleg Marichev, Olivier Martin, Yuri Matiyasevich, John Maynard Smith, Curt McMullen, Hans Meinhardt, Michel Mendès France, Nick Metropolis, John Miller, John Milnor, Marvin Minsky, Don Mitchell, Kim Molvig, John Moussouris, Walter Munk, Jim Murray, Lee Neuwirth, Alan Newell, Mats Nordahl, John Novak, Andrew Odlyzko, Steve Orszag, George Oster, Peter Overmann, Norman Packard, Heinz Pagels, Leonard Parker, Roger Payne, Holly Peck, Hans-Otto Peitgen, Roger Penrose, Alan Perelson, Malcolm Perry, Charlie Peskin, David Pines, Simon Plouffe, Yves Pomeau, Bjorn Poonen, Marian Pour-El, Kendall Preston, Lutz Priese, Ilya Prigogine, Itamar Procaccia, Charles Radin, Tom Ray, Jim Reeds, John Reif, David Reiss, Stanley Reiter, Ken Ribet, Jane Richardson, Ron Rivest, Igor Rivin, Terry Robb, Julia Robinson, Raphael Robinson, Robert Rosen, Gian-Carlo Rota, Lee Rubel, Rudy Rucker, David Ruelle, Jim Salem, Len Sander, Dana Scott, Terry Sejnowski, Rob Shaw, Tim Shaw, Steve Shenker, Bev Sher, Tsutomu Shimomura, Peter Shor, Brian Silverman, Karl Sims, Steven Skiena, Steve Smale, Caroline Small, Alvy Ray Smith, Bruce Smith, Lee Smolin, Mark Sofroniou, Gene Stanley, Ken Steiglitz, Dan Stein, Paul Steinhardt, Pat Suppes, Gerry Sussman, Klaus Sutner, Noel Swerdlow, Harry Swinney, Bart Taub, David Terr, René Thom, Bill Thurston, Tom Toffoli, Alar Toomre, Russell Towle, Amos Tversky, Stan Ulam, Leslie Valiant, Léon van Hove, Ilan Vardi, Hal Varian, Geerat Vermeij, Gerard Vichniac, Stan Wagon, Bob Wainwright, Bruce Walker, Denis Weaire, Eric Weinstein, Paul Wellin, Caroline Wickham-Jones, Tom Wickham-Jones, Amie Wilkinson, Stephen Willson, Jack Wisdom, Rob Wolff, Alexander Wolfram, Conrad Wolfram, Sybil Wolfram, Lewis Wolpert, Michael Woodford, Larry Wos, Larry Yaffe, Victor Yakhot, Jim Yorke, John Zerolis, Richard Zippel, George Zweig, Helio Zwi. In addition to those with whom I have had direct contact, other individuals have provided input indirectly through my assistants or others (excluding photograph sources listed in the colophon): Bill Beyer, Sheila Blair, Victor Dan, Brent Daniel, Noam Elkies, Peter Falloon, Erich Friedman, Jochen Gerber, Branko Grünbaum, Richard Guy, Michel Janssen, Martin Kraus, Temur Kutsia, Richard Langley, Bernd Löchner, Crista Malick, Brendan McKay, Thomas Scanlon, Rob Scharein, Marjorie Senechal, Marc Sher, David Singmaster, Neil Sloane, Milton Van Dyke, Bob Veroff, Curtis Wilson, Mirek Wójtowicz. Librarians at many institutions—especially the University of Illinois—have often helped my assistants in locating materials. Many individuals at Wolfram Research have also contributed their collective breadth of knowledge on diverse smaller questions.

I began serious development of ideas that eventually led to this book in 1981, and until 1988 I continued to be a member of various academic institutions: California Institute of Technology (Physics Department, 1978–1982), Institute for Advanced Study, Princeton (School of Natural Sciences, 1982–1986), University of Illinois (Center for Complex Systems Research, and Departments of Physics, Mathematics and Computer Science, 1986–1988). I built up successively larger research groups at these institutions, and both the scientific and other members of these groups made a variety of contributions to my work.

In the early to mid-1980s I was a consultant to a number of organizations. The primary ones at which I pursued projects that helped me in formulating issues for this book were Bell Laboratories, Los Alamos National Laboratory and Thinking Machines Corporation. In the period before 1986 a few of my projects received incidental support from various parts of the U.S. government, and I made use of early workstation computers given to me by Sun Microsystems. The MacArthur Fellowship that I received in May 1981 was an important element of personal support, and in fact it was a few months after this award that I made the decision to focus my work towards what would eventually become the new kind of science in this book.

In the early years of the project—and before I became independent of academia—there were a number of individuals who showed particular foresight in arranging for organizational support or publication of my work, including: George Bell, Bill Brinkman, Roger Dashen, Marvin Denicoff, Herman Feshbach, John Gage, Murray Gell-Mann, Paul Halmos, Sheryl Handler, Danny Hillis, Bob Kraichnan, Oscar Lanford, Joel Lebowitz, Elliott Lieb, John Maddox, K. K. Phua, David Pines, Gian-Carlo Rota, Mike Schlesinger, Ralph Simmons, Larry Smarr, Harry Woolf.

Many influences early in my life are no doubt reflected in one way or another in this book. That my mother was an Oxford philosophy don caused me in my youth to be exposed to a certain amount of academic philosophy. My classical English education—in elementary school (Dragon School) and high school (Eton)—emphasized such pursuits as writing, and exposed me to a certain range of subjects, a remarkable fraction of which have ended up being useful, especially in the historical research for this book. My brief times in college (Oxford) and graduate school (Caltech) enhanced my enthusiasm and confidence in science, and allowed me rapidly to begin life as a professional scientist. In the years that I was a member of the theoretical physics community a great many people provided encouragement, and contributed to my understanding of science and how it should be done. Among those friends, colleagues, teachers and others from before 1981 from whom I learned things relevant for the methods, content or writing of this book were: Ed Berger, Euan Cameron, Chris Cole, Armand D'Angour, Richard Feynman, Rick Field, Geoffrey Fox, Philip Gladstone, Nathan Isgur, Nicholas Kermack, Rocky Kolb, Chris Llewellyn Smith, David Longrigg, Rob Pike, David Politzer, Dick Roberts, Norman Routledge, George Rutter, Ken Spencer, Christopher Stuart-Clark, Tony Terrano, Tini Veltman, Peregrine Williams, Hugo Wolfram, Sybil Wolfram, Larry Yaffe, George Zweig.

To complete a project of the magnitude of this book requires extreme personal focus. And to maintain this, I have for most of the past decade been an almost complete recluse, attending almost no outside events, and interacting mainly just with family, friends, assistants and senior staff at my company. During this period it has nevertheless provided important encouragement to see that even without my personal presence, my earlier work in science—and even more so my work on *Mathematica*—has had an increasingly great impact on the world. It has also been a continuing source of further encouragement to see just how broadly and deeply the worldwide *Mathematica* community has been able to make use of the fundamental ideas that I have embodied in *Mathematica*.

To write this book has taken me more than ten years of almost continuous work, more than a hundred million keystrokes, and more than a hundred mouse miles. I have accumulated tens of gigabytes and hundreds of thousands of pages of *Mathematica* notebooks. I have executed nearly a million lines of *Mathematica* input, and altogether more than a million billion computer operations. But now that the task is finally done—and I have written down at least the main elements of my discoveries so far—I look forward to everything that is now possible.

1

The Foundations for a
New Kind of Science

An Outline of Basic Ideas

Three centuries ago science was transformed by the dramatic new idea that rules based on mathematical equations could be used to describe the natural world. My purpose in this book is to initiate another such transformation, and to introduce a new kind of science that is based on the much more general types of rules that can be embodied in simple computer programs.

It has taken me the better part of twenty years to build the intellectual structure that is needed, but I have been amazed by its results. For what I have found is that with the new kind of science I have developed it suddenly becomes possible to make progress on a remarkable range of fundamental issues that have never successfully been addressed by any of the existing sciences before.

If theoretical science is to be possible at all, then at some level the systems it studies must follow definite rules. Yet in the past throughout the exact sciences it has usually been assumed that these rules must be ones based on traditional mathematics. But the crucial realization that led me to develop the new kind of science in this book is that there is in fact no reason to think that systems like those we see in nature should follow only such traditional mathematical rules.

Earlier in history it might have been difficult to imagine what more general types of rules could be like. But today we are surrounded by computers whose programs in effect implement a huge variety of rules. The programs we use in practice are mostly based on extremely complicated rules specifically designed to perform particular tasks. But a program can in principle follow essentially any definite set of rules. And at the core of the new kind of science that I describe in this book are discoveries I have made about programs with some of the very simplest rules that are possible.

One might have thought—as at first I certainly did—that if the rules for a program were simple then this would mean that its behavior must also be correspondingly simple. For our everyday experience in building things tends to give us the intuition that creating complexity is somehow difficult, and requires rules or plans that are themselves complex. But the pivotal discovery that I made some eighteen years ago is that in the world of programs such intuition is not even close to correct.

I did what is in a sense one of the most elementary imaginable computer experiments: I took a sequence of simple programs and then systematically ran them to see how they behaved. And what I found— to my great surprise—was that despite the simplicity of their rules, the behavior of the programs was often far from simple. Indeed, even some of the very simplest programs that I looked at had behavior that was as complex as anything I had ever seen.

It took me more than a decade to come to terms with this result, and to realize just how fundamental and far-reaching its consequences are. In retrospect there is no reason the result could not have been found centuries ago, but increasingly I have come to view it as one of the more important single discoveries in the whole history of theoretical science. For in addition to opening up vast new domains of exploration, it implies a radical rethinking of how processes in nature and elsewhere work.

Perhaps immediately most dramatic is that it yields a resolution to what has long been considered the single greatest mystery of the natural world: what secret it is that allows nature seemingly so effortlessly to produce so much that appears to us so complex.

It could have been, after all, that in the natural world we would mostly see forms like squares and circles that we consider simple. But in fact one of the most striking features of the natural world is that across a vast range of physical, biological and other systems we are continually confronted with what seems to be immense complexity. And indeed throughout most of history it has been taken almost for granted that such complexity—being so vastly greater than in the works of humans—could only be the work of a supernatural being.

But my discovery that many very simple programs produce great complexity immediately suggests a rather different explanation. For all it takes is that systems in nature operate like typical programs and then it follows that their behavior will often be complex. And the reason that such complexity is not usually seen in human artifacts is just that in building these we tend in effect to use programs that are specially chosen to give only behavior simple enough for us to be able to see that it will achieve the purposes we want.

One might have thought that with all their successes over the past few centuries the existing sciences would long ago have managed to address the issue of complexity. But in fact they have not. And indeed for the most part they have specifically defined their scope in order to avoid direct contact with it. For while their basic idea of describing behavior in terms of mathematical equations works well in cases like planetary motion where the behavior is fairly simple, it almost inevitably fails whenever the behavior is more complex. And more or less the same is true of descriptions based on ideas like natural selection in biology. But by thinking in terms of programs the new kind of science that I develop in this book is for the first time able to make meaningful statements about even immensely complex behavior.

In the existing sciences much of the emphasis over the past century or so has been on breaking systems down to find their underlying parts, then trying to analyze these parts in as much detail as possible. And particularly in physics this approach has been sufficiently successful that the basic components of everyday systems are by now completely known. But just how these components act together to produce even some of the most obvious features of the overall behavior we see has in the past remained an almost complete mystery. Within the framework of the new kind of science that I develop in this book, however, it is finally possible to address such a question.

From the tradition of the existing sciences one might expect that its answer would depend on all sorts of details, and be quite different for different types of physical, biological and other systems. But in the world of simple programs I have discovered that the same basic forms of behavior occur over and over again almost independent of underlying details. And what this suggests is that there are quite universal principles that determine overall behavior and that can be expected to apply not only to simple programs but also to systems throughout the natural world and elsewhere.

In the existing sciences whenever a phenomenon is encountered that seems complex it is taken almost for granted that the phenomenon must be the result of some underlying mechanism that is itself complex. But my discovery that simple programs can produce great complexity makes it clear that this is not in fact correct. And indeed in the later parts of this book I will show that even remarkably simple programs seem to capture the essential mechanisms responsible for all sorts of important phenomena that in the past have always seemed far too complex to allow any simple explanation.

It is not uncommon in the history of science that new ways of thinking are what finally allow longstanding issues to be addressed. But I have been amazed at just how many issues central to the foundations of the existing sciences I have been able to address by using the idea of thinking in terms of simple programs. For more than a century, for example, there has been confusion about how thermodynamic behavior arises in physics. Yet from my discoveries about simple programs I have developed a quite straightforward explanation. And in biology, my discoveries provide for the first time an explicit way to understand just how it is that so many organisms exhibit such great complexity. Indeed, I even have increasing evidence that thinking in terms of simple programs will make it possible to construct a single truly fundamental theory of physics, from which space, time, quantum mechanics and all the other known features of our universe will emerge.

When mathematics was introduced into science it provided for the first time an abstract framework in which scientific conclusions could be drawn without direct reference to physical reality. Yet despite all its development over the past few thousand years mathematics itself has continued to concentrate only on rather specific types of abstract systems—most often ones somehow derived from arithmetic or geometry. But the new kind of science that I describe in this book introduces what are in a sense much more general abstract systems, based on rules of essentially any type whatsoever.

One might have thought that such systems would be too diverse for meaningful general statements to be made about them. But the crucial idea that has allowed me to build a unified framework for the new kind of science that I describe in this book is that just as the rules for any system can be viewed as corresponding to a program, so also its behavior can be viewed as corresponding to a computation.

Traditional intuition might suggest that to do more sophisticated computations would always require more sophisticated underlying rules. But what launched the whole computer revolution is the remarkable fact that universal systems with fixed underlying rules can be built that can in effect perform any possible computation.

The threshold for such universality has however generally been assumed to be high, and to be reached only by elaborate and special systems like typical electronic computers. But one of the surprising discoveries in this book is that in fact there are systems whose rules are simple enough to describe in just one sentence that are nevertheless universal. And this immediately suggests that the phenomenon of universality is vastly more common and important—in both abstract systems and nature—than has ever been imagined before.

But on the basis of many discoveries I have been led to a still more sweeping conclusion, summarized in what I call the Principle of Computational Equivalence: that whenever one sees behavior that is not obviously simple—in essentially any system—it can be thought of as corresponding to a computation of equivalent sophistication. And this one very basic principle has a quite unprecedented array of implications for science and scientific thinking.

For a start, it immediately gives a fundamental explanation for why simple programs can show behavior that seems to us complex. For like other processes our own processes of perception and analysis can be thought of as computations. But though we might have imagined that such computations would always be vastly more sophisticated than those performed by simple programs, the Principle of Computational Equivalence implies that they are not. And it is this equivalence between us as observers and the systems that we observe that makes the behavior of such systems seem to us complex.

One can always in principle find out how a particular system will behave just by running an experiment and watching what happens. But the great historical successes of theoretical science have typically revolved around finding mathematical formulas that instead directly allow one to predict the outcome. Yet in effect this relies on being able to shortcut the computational work that the system itself performs.

And the Principle of Computational Equivalence now implies that this will normally be possible only for rather special systems with simple behavior. For other systems will tend to perform computations that are just as sophisticated as those we can do, even with all our mathematics and computers. And this means that such systems are computationally irreducible—so that in effect the only way to find their behavior is to trace each of their steps, spending about as much computational effort as the systems themselves.

So this implies that there is in a sense a fundamental limitation to theoretical science. But it also shows that there is something irreducible that can be achieved by the passage of time. And it leads to an explanation of how we as humans—even though we may follow definite underlying rules—can still in a meaningful way show free will.

One feature of many of the most important advances in science throughout history is that they show new ways in which we as humans are not special. And at some level the Principle of Computational Equivalence does this as well. For it implies that when it comes to computation—or intelligence—we are in the end no more sophisticated than all sorts of simple programs, and all sorts of systems in nature.

But from the Principle of Computational Equivalence there also emerges a new kind of unity: for across a vast range of systems, from simple programs to brains to our whole universe, the principle implies that there is a basic equivalence that makes the same fundamental phenomena occur, and allows the same basic scientific ideas and methods to be used. And it is this that is ultimately responsible for the great power of the new kind of science that I describe in this book.

Relations to Other Areas

Mathematics. It is usually assumed that mathematics concerns itself with the study of arbitrarily general abstract systems. But this book shows that there are actually a vast range of abstract systems based on simple programs that traditional mathematics has never considered. And because these systems are in many ways simpler in construction than most traditional systems in mathematics it is possible with appropriate methods in effect to go further in investigating them.

Some of what one finds are then just unprecedentedly clear examples of phenomena already known in modern mathematics. But one also finds some dramatic new phenomena. Most immediately obvious is a very high level of complexity in the behavior of many systems whose underlying rules are much simpler than those of most systems in standard mathematics textbooks.

And one of the consequences of this complexity is that it leads to fundamental limitations on the idea of proof that has been central to traditional mathematics. Already in the 1930s Gödel's Theorem gave some indications of such limitations. But in the past they have always seemed irrelevant to most of mathematics as it is actually practiced.

Yet what the discoveries in this book show is that this is largely just a reflection of how small the scope is of what is now considered mathematics. And indeed the core of this book can be viewed as introducing a major generalization of mathematics—with new ideas and methods, and vast new areas to be explored.

The framework I develop in this book also shows that by viewing the process of doing mathematics in fundamentally computational terms it becomes possible to address important issues about the foundations even of existing mathematics.

Physics. The traditional mathematical approach to science has historically had its great success in physics—and by now it has become almost universally assumed that any serious physical theory must be based on mathematical equations. Yet with this approach there are still many common physical phenomena about which physics has had remarkably little to say. But with the approach of thinking in terms of simple programs that I develop in this book it finally seems possible to make some dramatic progress. And indeed in the course of the book we will see that some extremely simple programs seem able to capture the essential mechanisms for a great many physical phenomena that have previously seemed completely mysterious.

Existing methods in theoretical physics tend to revolve around ideas of continuous numbers and calculus—or sometimes probability. Yet most of the systems in this book involve just simple discrete elements with definite rules. And in many ways it is the greater simplicity of this underlying structure that ultimately makes it possible to identify so many fundamentally new phenomena.

Ordinary models for physical systems are idealizations that capture some features and ignore others. And in the past what was most common was to capture certain simple numerical relationships—that could for example be represented by smooth curves. But with the new kinds of models based on simple programs that I explore in this book it becomes possible to capture all sorts of much more complex features that can only really be seen in explicit images of behavior.

In the future of physics the greatest triumph would undoubtedly be to find a truly fundamental theory for our whole universe. Yet despite occasional optimism, traditional approaches do not make this seem close at hand. But with the methods and intuition that I develop in this book there is I believe finally a serious possibility that such a theory can actually be found.

Biology. Vast amounts are now known about the details of biological organisms, but very little in the way of general theory has ever emerged. Classical areas of biology tend to treat evolution by natural selection as a foundation—leading to the notion that general observations about living systems should normally be analyzed on the basis of evolutionary history rather than abstract theories. And part of the reason for this is that traditional mathematical models have never seemed to come even close to capturing the kind of complexity we see in biology. But the discoveries in this book show that simple programs can produce a high level of complexity. And in fact it turns out that such programs can reproduce many features of biological organisms—and for example seem to capture some of the essential mechanisms through which genetic programs manage to generate the actual biological forms we see. So this means that it becomes possible to make a wide range of new models for biological systems—and potentially to see how to emulate the essence of their operation, say for medical purposes. And insofar as there are general principles for simple programs, these principles should also apply to biological organisms—making it possible to imagine constructing new kinds of general abstract theories in biology.

Social Sciences. From economics to psychology there has been a widespread if controversial assumption—no doubt from the success of the physical sciences—that solid theories must always be formulated in terms of numbers, equations and traditional mathematics. But I suspect that one will often have a much better chance of capturing fundamental mechanisms for phenomena in the social sciences by using instead the new kind of science that I develop in this book based on simple programs. No doubt there will quite quickly be all sorts of claims about applications of my ideas to the social sciences. And indeed the new intuition that emerges from this book may well almost immediately explain phenomena that have in the past seemed quite mysterious. But the very results of the book show that there will inevitably be fundamental limits to the application of scientific methods. There will be new questions formulated, but it will take time before it becomes clear when general theories are possible, and when one must instead inevitably rely on the details of judgement for specific cases.

Computer Science. Throughout its brief history computer science has focused almost exclusively on studying specific computational systems set up to perform particular tasks. But one of the core ideas of this book is to consider the more general scientific question of what arbitrary computational systems do. And much of what I have found is vastly different from what one might expect on the basis of existing computer science. For the systems traditionally studied in computer science tend to be fairly complicated in their construction—yet yield fairly simple behavior that recognizably fulfills some particular purpose. But in this book what I show is that even systems with extremely simple construction can yield behavior of immense complexity. And by thinking about this in computational terms one develops a new intuition about the very nature of computation.

One consequence is a dramatic broadening of the domain to which computational ideas can be applied—in particular to include all sorts of fundamental questions about nature and about mathematics. Another consequence is a new perspective on existing questions in computer science—particularly ones related to what ultimate resources are needed to perform general types of computational tasks.

Philosophy. At any period in history there are issues about the universe and our role in it that seem accessible only to the general arguments of philosophy. But often progress in science eventually provides a more definite context. And I believe that the new kind of science in this book will do this for a variety of issues that have been considered fundamental even since antiquity. Among them are questions about ultimate limits to knowledge, free will, the uniqueness of the human condition and the inevitability of mathematics. Much has been said over the course of philosophical history about each of these. Yet inevitably it has been informed only by current intuition about how things are supposed to work. But my discoveries in this book lead to radically new intuition. And with this intuition it turns out that one can for the first time begin to see resolutions to many longstanding issues—typically along rather different lines from those expected on the basis of traditional general arguments in philosophy.

Art. It seems so easy for nature to produce forms of great beauty. Yet in the past art has mostly just had to be content to imitate such forms. But now, with the discovery that simple programs can capture the essential mechanisms for all sorts of complex behavior in nature, one can imagine just sampling such programs to explore generalizations of the forms we see in nature. Traditional scientific intuition—and early computer art—might lead one to assume that simple programs would always produce pictures too simple and rigid to be of artistic interest. But looking through this book it becomes clear that even a program that may have extremely simple rules will often be able to generate pictures that have striking aesthetic qualities—sometimes reminiscent of nature, but often unlike anything ever seen before.

Technology. Despite all its success, there is still much that goes on in nature that seems more complex and sophisticated than anything technology has ever been able to produce. But what the discoveries in this book now show is that by using the types of rules embodied in simple programs one can capture many of the essential mechanisms of nature. And from this it becomes possible to imagine a whole new kind of technology that in effect achieves the same sophistication as nature. Experience with traditional engineering has led to the general assumption that to perform a sophisticated task requires constructing a system whose basic rules are somehow correspondingly complicated. But the discoveries in this book show that this is not the case, and that in fact extremely simple underlying rules—that might for example potentially be implemented directly at the level of atoms—are often all that is needed. My main focus in this book is on matters of basic science. But I have little doubt that within a matter of a few decades what I have done will have led to some dramatic changes in the foundations of technology—and in our basic ability to take what the universe provides and apply it for our own human purposes.

Some Past Initiatives

My goals in this book are sufficiently broad and fundamental that there have inevitably been previous attempts to achieve at least some of them. But without the ideas and methods of this book there have been basic issues that have eventually ended up presenting almost insuperable barriers to every major approach that has been tried.

Artificial Intelligence. When electronic computers were first invented, it was widely believed that it would not be long before they would be capable of human-like thinking. And in the 1960s the field of artificial intelligence grew up with the goal of understanding processes of human thinking and implementing them on computers. But doing this turned out to be much more difficult than expected, and after some spin-offs, little fundamental progress was made. At some level, however, the basic problem has always been to understand how the seemingly simple components in a brain can lead to all the complexities of thinking. But now finally with the framework developed in this book one potentially has a meaningful foundation for doing this. And indeed building on both theoretical and practical ideas in the book I suspect that dramatic progress will eventually be possible in creating technological systems that are capable of human-like thinking.

Artificial Life. Ever since machines have existed, people have wondered to what extent they might be able to imitate living systems. Most active from the mid-1980s to the mid-1990s, the field of artificial life concerned itself mainly with showing that computer programs could be made to emulate various features of biological systems. But normally it was assumed that the necessary programs would have to be quite complex. What the discoveries in this book show, however, is that in fact very simple programs can be sufficient. And such programs make the fundamental mechanisms for behavior clearer—and probably come much closer to what is actually happening in real biological systems.

Catastrophe Theory. Traditional mathematical models are normally based on quantities that vary continuously. Yet in nature discrete changes are often seen. Popular in the 1970s, catastrophe theory was concerned with showing that even in traditional mathematical models, certain simple discrete changes could still occur. In this book I do not start from any assumption of continuity—and the types of behavior I study tend to be vastly more complex than those in catastrophe theory.

Chaos Theory. The field of chaos theory is based on the observation that certain mathematical systems behave in a way that depends arbitrarily sensitively on the details of their initial conditions. First noticed at the end of the 1800s, this came into prominence after computer simulations in the 1960s and 1970s. Its main significance is that it implies that if any detail of the initial conditions is uncertain, then it will eventually become impossible to predict the behavior of the system. But despite some claims to the contrary in popular accounts, this fact alone does not imply that the behavior will necessarily be complex. Indeed, all that it shows is that if there is complexity in the details of the initial conditions, then this complexity will eventually appear in the large-scale behavior of the system. But if the initial conditions are simple, then there is no reason for the behavior not to be correspondingly simple. What I show in this book, however, is that even when their initial conditions are very simple there are many systems that still produce highly complex behavior. And I argue that it is this phenomenon that is for example responsible for most of the obvious complexity we see in nature.

Complexity Theory. My discoveries in the early 1980s led me to the idea that complexity could be studied as a fundamental independent phenomenon. And gradually this became quite popular. But most of the scientific work that was done ended up being based only on my earliest discoveries, and being very much within the framework of one or another of the existing sciences—with the result that it managed to make very little progress on any general and fundamental issues. One feature of the new kind of science that I describe in this book is that it finally makes possible the development of a basic understanding of the general phenomenon of complexity, and its origins.

Computational Complexity Theory. Developed mostly in the 1970s, computational complexity theory attempts to characterize how difficult certain computational tasks are to perform. Its concrete results have tended to be based on fairly specific programs with complicated structure yet rather simple behavior. The new kind of science in this book, however, explores much more general classes of programs—and in doing so begins to shed new light on various longstanding questions in computational complexity theory.

Cybernetics. In the 1940s it was thought that it might be possible to understand biological systems on the basis of analogies with electrical machines. But since essentially the only methods of analysis available were ones from traditional mathematics, very little of the complex behavior of typical biological systems was successfully captured.

Dynamical Systems Theory. A branch of mathematics that began roughly a century ago, the field of dynamical systems theory has been concerned with studying systems that evolve in time according to certain kinds of mathematical equations—and in using traditional geometrical and other mathematical methods to characterize the possible forms of behavior that such systems can produce. But what I argue in this book is that in fact the behavior of many systems is fundamentally too complex to be usefully captured in any such way.

Evolution Theory. The Darwinian theory of evolution by natural selection is often assumed to explain the complexity we see in biological systems—and in fact in recent years the theory has also increasingly been applied outside of biology. But it has never been at all clear just why this theory should imply that complexity is generated. And indeed I will argue in this book that in many respects it tends to oppose complexity. But the discoveries in the book suggest a new and quite different mechanism that I believe is in fact responsible for most of the examples of great complexity that we see in biology.

Experimental Mathematics. The idea of exploring mathematical systems by looking at data from calculations has a long history, and has gradually become more widespread with the advent of computers and

Mathematica. But almost without exception, it has in the past only been applied to systems and questions that have already been investigated by other mathematical means—and that lie very much within the normal tradition of mathematics. My approach in this book, however, is to use computer experiments as a basic way to explore much more general systems—that have never arisen in traditional mathematics, and that are usually far from being accessible by existing mathematical means.

Fractal Geometry. Until recently, the only kinds of shapes widely discussed in science and mathematics were ones that are regular or smooth. But starting in the late 1970s, the field of fractal geometry emphasized the importance of nested shapes that contain arbitrarily intricate pieces, and argued that such shapes are common in nature. In this book we will encounter a fair number of systems that produce such nested shapes. But we will also find many systems that produce shapes which are much more complex, and have no nested structure.

General Systems Theory. Popular especially in the 1960s, general systems theory was concerned mainly with studying large networks of elements—often idealizing human organizations. But a complete lack of anything like the kinds of methods I use in this book made it almost impossible for any definite conclusions to emerge.

Nanotechnology. Growing rapidly since the early 1990s, the goal of nanotechnology is to implement technological systems on atomic scales. But so far nanotechnology has mostly been concerned with shrinking quite familiar mechanical and other devices. Yet what the discoveries in this book now show is that there are all sorts of systems that have much simpler structures, but that can nevertheless perform very sophisticated tasks. And some of these systems seem in many ways much more suitable for direct implementation on an atomic scale.

Nonlinear Dynamics. Mathematical equations that have the property of linearity are usually fairly easy to solve, and so have been used extensively in pure and applied science. The field of nonlinear dynamics is concerned with analyzing more complicated equations. Its greatest success has been with so-called soliton equations for which careful manipulation leads to a property similar to linearity. But the kinds of systems that I discuss in this book typically show much more complex behavior, and have no such simplifying properties.

Scientific Computing. The field of scientific computing has usually been concerned with taking traditional mathematical models—most often for various kinds of fluids and solids—and trying to implement them on computers using numerical approximation schemes. Typically it has been difficult to disentangle anything but fairly simple phenomena from effects associated with the approximations used. The kinds of models that I introduce in this book involve no approximations when implemented on computers, and thus readily allow one to recognize much more complex phenomena.

Self-Organization. In nature it is quite common to see systems that start disordered and featureless, but then spontaneously organize themselves to produce definite structures. The loosely knit field of self-organization has been concerned with understanding this phenomenon. But for the most part it has used traditional mathematical methods, and as a result has only been able to investigate the formation of fairly simple structures. With the ideas in this book, however, it becomes possible to understand how vastly more complex structures can be formed.

Statistical Mechanics. Since its development about a century ago, the branch of physics known as statistical mechanics has mostly concerned itself with understanding the average behavior of systems that consist of large numbers of gas molecules or other components. In any specific instance, such systems often behave in a complex way. But by looking at averages over many instances, statistical mechanics has usually managed to avoid such complexity. To make contact with real situations, however, it has often had to use the so-called Second Law of Thermodynamics, or Principle of Entropy Increase. But for more than a century there have been nagging difficulties in understanding the basis for this principle. With the ideas in this book, however, I believe that there is now a framework in which these can finally be resolved.

The Personal Story of the Science in This Book

I can trace the beginning of my serious interest in the kinds of scientific issues discussed in this book rather accurately to the summer of 1972, when I was twelve years old. I had bought a copy of the physics textbook on the right, and had become very curious about the process of randomization illustrated on its cover. But being far from convinced by the mathematical explanation given in the book, I decided to try to simulate the process for myself on a computer.

The book cover that originally sparked my interest in some of the issues discussed in this book.

The computer to which I had access at that time was by modern standards a very primitive one. And as a result, I had no choice but to study a very simplified version of the process in the book. I suspected from the start that the system I constructed might be too simple to show any of the phenomena I wanted. And after much programming effort I managed to convince myself that these suspicions were correct.

Yet as it turns out, what I looked at was a particular case of one of the main kinds of systems—cellular automata—that I consider in this book. And had it not been for a largely technical point that arose from my desire to make my simulations as physically realistic as possible, it is quite possible that by 1974 I would already have discovered some of the principal phenomena that I now describe in this book.

As it was, however, I decided at that time to devote my energies to what then seemed to be the most fundamental area of science: theoretical particle physics. And over the next several years I did indeed manage to make significant progress in a few areas of particle physics and cosmology. But after a while I began to suspect that many of the most important and fundamental questions that I was encountering were quite independent of the abstruse details of these fields.

And in fact I realized that there were many related questions even about common everyday phenomena that were still completely unanswered. What for example is the fundamental origin of the complicated patterns that one sees in turbulent fluids? How are the intricate patterns of snowflakes produced? What is the basic mechanism that allows plants and animals to grow in such complex ways?

To my surprise, very little seemed to have been done on these kinds of questions. At first I thought it might be possible to make progress just by applying some of the sophisticated mathematical techniques that I had used in theoretical physics. But it soon became clear that for the phenomena I was studying, traditional mathematical results would be very difficult, if not impossible, to find.

So what could I do? It so happened that as an outgrowth of my work in physics I had in 1981 just finished developing a large software system that was in some respects a forerunner to parts of *Mathematica*. And at least at an intellectual level the most difficult part of the project had been designing the symbolic language on which the system was based. But in the development of this language I had seen rather clearly how just a few primitive operations that I had come up with could end up successfully covering a vast range of sophisticated computational tasks.

So I thought that perhaps I could do something similar in natural science: that there might be some appropriate primitives that I could find that would successfully capture a vast range of natural phenomena. My ideas were not so clearly formed at the time, but I believe I implicitly imagined that the way this would work is that such primitives could be used to build up computer programs that would simulate the various natural systems in which I was interested.

There were in many cases well-established mathematical models for the individual components of such systems. But two practical issues stood in the way of using these as a basis for simulations. First, the models were usually quite complicated, so that with realistic computer resources it was very difficult to include enough components for interesting phenomena to occur. And second, even if one did see such phenomena, it was almost impossible to tell whether in fact they were genuine consequences of the underlying models or were just the result of approximations made in implementing the models on a computer.

But what I realized was that at least for many of the phenomena I wanted to study, it was not crucial to use the most accurate possible models for individual components. For among other things there was evidence from nature that in many cases the details of the components did not matter much—so that for example the same complex patterns of flow occur in both air and water. And with this in mind, what I decided was that rather than starting from detailed realistic models, I would instead start from models that were somehow as simple as possible—and were easy to set up as programs on a computer.

At the outset, I did not know how this would work, and how complicated the programs I would need would have to be. And indeed when I looked at various simple programs they always seemed to yield behavior vastly simpler than any of the systems I wanted to study.

But in the summer of 1981 I did what I considered to be a fairly straightforward computer experiment to see how all programs of a particular type behaved. I had not really expected too much from this experiment. But in fact its results were so surprising and dramatic that as I gradually came to understand them, they forced me to change my whole view of science, and in the end to develop the whole intellectual structure of the new kind of science that I now describe in this book.

The picture on the right shows a reproduction of typical output from my original experiment. The graphics are primitive, but the elaborate patterns they contain were like nothing I had ever seen before. At first I did not believe that they could possibly be correct. But after a while I became convinced that they were—and I realized that I had seen a sign of a quite remarkable and unexpected phenomenon: that even from very simple programs behavior of great complexity could emerge.

But how could something as fundamental as this never have been noticed before? I searched the scientific literature, talked to many people, and found out that systems similar to the ones I was studying had been named "cellular automata" some thirty years earlier. But despite a few close approaches, nobody had ever actually tried anything quite like the type of experiment I had.

Yet I still suspected that the basic phenomenon I had seen must somehow be an obvious consequence of some known scientific principle. But while I did find that ideas from areas like chaos theory and fractal geometry helped in explaining some specific features, nothing even close to the phenomenon as a whole seemed to have ever been studied before.

My early discoveries about the behavior of cellular automata stimulated a fair amount of activity in the scientific community. And

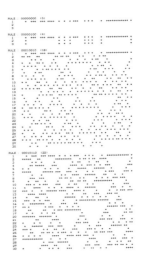

A reproduction of the computer printout that first gave me a hint of some of the central phenomena in this book.

by the mid-1980s, many applications had been found in physics, biology, computer science, mathematics and elsewhere. And indeed some of the phenomena I had discovered were starting to be used as the basis for a new area of research that I called complex systems theory.

Throughout all this, however, I had continued to investigate more basic questions, and by around 1985 I was beginning to realize that what I had seen before was just a hint of something still much more dramatic and fundamental. But to understand what I was discovering was difficult, and required a major shift in intuition.

Yet I could see that there were some remarkable intellectual opportunities ahead. And my first idea was to try to organize the academic community to take advantage of them. So I started a research center and a journal, published a list of problems to attack, and worked hard to communicate the importance of the direction I was defining.

But despite growing excitement—particularly about some of the potential applications—there seemed to be very little success in breaking away from traditional methods and intuition. And after a while I realized that if there was going to be any dramatic progress made, I was the one who was going to have to make it. So I resolved to set up the best tools and infrastructure I could, and then just myself pursue as efficiently as possible the research that I thought should be done.

In the early 1980s my single greatest impediment had been the practical difficulty of doing computer experiments using the various rather low-level tools that were available. But by 1986 I had realized that with a number of new ideas I had it would be possible to build a single coherent system for doing all kinds of technical computing. And since nothing like this seemed likely to exist otherwise, I decided to build it.

The result was *Mathematica*.

For five years the process of building *Mathematica* and the company around it absorbed me. But in 1991—now no longer an academic, but instead the CEO of a successful company—I was able to return to studying the kinds of questions addressed in this book.

And equipped with *Mathematica* I began to try all sorts of new experiments. The results were spectacular—and within the space of a few months I had already made more new discoveries about what simple programs do than in all the previous ten years put together. My earlier work had shown me the beginnings of some unexpected and very remarkable phenomena. But now from my new experiments I began to see the full force and generality of these phenomena.

As my methodology and intuition improved, the pace of my discoveries increased still more, and within just a couple of years I had managed to take my explorations of the world of simple programs to the point where the sheer volume of factual information I had accumulated would be the envy of many long-established fields of science.

Quite early in the process I had begun to formulate several rather general principles. And the further I went, the more these principles were confirmed, and the more I realized just how strong and general they were.

When I first started at the beginning of the 1980s, my goal was mostly just to understand the phenomenon of complexity. But by the mid-1990s I had built up a whole intellectual structure that was capable of much more, and that in fact provided the foundations for what could only be considered a fundamentally new kind of science.

It was for me a most exciting time. For everywhere I turned there were huge untouched new areas that I was able to explore for the first time. Each had its own particular features. But with the overall framework I had developed I was gradually able to answer essentially all of what seemed to be the most obvious questions that I had raised.

At first I was mostly concerned with new questions that had never been particularly central to any existing areas of science. But gradually I realized that the new kind of science I was building should also provide a fundamentally new way to address basic issues in existing areas.

So around 1994 I began systematically investigating each of the various major traditional areas of science. I had long been interested in fundamental questions in many of these areas. But usually I had tended to believe most of the conventional wisdom about them. Yet when I began to study them in the context of my new kind of science I kept on seeing signs that large parts of this conventional wisdom could not be correct.

The typical issue was that there was some core problem that traditional methods or intuition had never successfully been able to address—and which the field had somehow grown to avoid. Yet over and over again I was excited to find that with my new kind of science I could suddenly begin to make great progress—even on problems that in some cases had remained unanswered for centuries.

Given the whole framework I had built, many of the things I discovered seemed in the end disarmingly simple. But to get to them often involved a remarkable amount of scientific work. For it was not enough just to be able to take a few specific technical steps. Rather, in each field, it was necessary to develop a sufficiently broad and deep understanding to be able to identify the truly essential features—that could then be rethought on the basis of my new kind of science.

Doing this certainly required experience in all sorts of different areas of science. But perhaps most crucial for me was that the process was a bit like what I have ended up doing countless times in designing *Mathematica*: start from elaborate technical ideas, then gradually see how to capture their essential features in something amazingly simple. And the fact that I had managed to make this work so many times in *Mathematica* was part of what gave me the confidence to try doing something similar in all sorts of areas of science.

Often it seemed in retrospect almost bizarre that the conclusions I ended up reaching had never been reached before. But studying the history of each field I could in many cases see how it had been led astray by the lack of some crucial piece of methodology or intuition that had now emerged in the new kind of science I had developed.

When I made my first discoveries about cellular automata in the early 1980s I suspected that I had seen the beginning of something important. But I had no idea just how important it would all ultimately turn out to be. And indeed over the past twenty years I have made more discoveries than I ever thought possible. And the new kind of science that I have spent so much effort building has seemed an ever more central and critical direction for future intellectual development.

2

The Crucial Experiment

How Do Simple Programs Behave?

New directions in science have typically been initiated by certain central observations or experiments. And for the kind of science that I describe in this book these concerned the behavior of simple programs.

In our everyday experience with computers, the programs that we encounter are normally set up to perform very definite tasks. But the key idea that I had nearly twenty years ago—and that eventually led to the whole new kind of science in this book—was to ask what happens if one instead just looks at simple arbitrarily chosen programs, created without any specific task in mind. How do such programs typically behave?

The mathematical methods that have in the past dominated theoretical science do not help much with such a question. But with a computer it is straightforward to start doing experiments to investigate it. For all one need do is just set up a sequence of possible simple programs, and then run them and see how they behave.

Any program can at some level be thought of as consisting of a set of rules that specify what it should do at each step. There are many possible ways to set up these rules—and indeed we will study quite a few of them in the course of this book. But for now, I will consider a particular class of examples called cellular automata, that were the very first kinds of simple programs that I investigated in the early 1980s.

An important feature of cellular automata is that their behavior can readily be presented in a visual way. And so the picture below shows what one cellular automaton does over the course of ten steps.

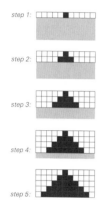

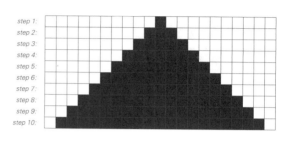

A visual representation of the behavior of a cellular automaton, with each row of cells corresponding to one step. At the first step the cell in the center is black and all other cells are white. Then on each successive step, a particular cell is made black whenever it or either of its neighbors were black on the step before. As the picture shows, this leads to a simple expanding pattern uniformly filled with black.

The cellular automaton consists of a line of cells, each colored either black or white. At every step there is then a definite rule that determines the color of a given cell from the color of that cell and its immediate left and right neighbors on the step before.

For the particular cellular automaton shown here the rule specifies—as in the picture below—that a cell should be black in all cases where it or either of its neighbors were black on the step before.

A representation of the rule for the cellular automaton shown above. The top row in each box gives one of the possible combinations of colors for a cell and its immediate neighbors. The bottom row then specifies what color the center cell should be on the next step in each of these cases. In the numbering scheme described in Chapter 3, this is cellular automaton rule 254.

And the picture at the top of the page shows that starting with a single black cell in the center this rule then leads to a simple growing pattern uniformly filled with black. But modifying the rule just slightly one can immediately get a different pattern.

As a first example, the picture at the top of the facing page shows what happens with a rule that makes a cell white whenever both of its neighbors were white on the step before—even if the cell itself was black before. And rather than producing a pattern that is uniformly filled with black, this rule now instead gives a pattern that repeatedly alternates between black and white like a checkerboard.

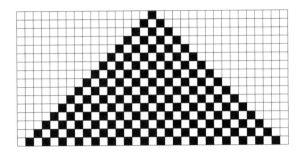

A cellular automaton with a slightly different rule. The rule makes a particular cell black if either of its neighbors was black on the step before, and makes the cell white if both its neighbors were white. Starting from a single black cell, this rule leads to a checkerboard pattern. In the numbering scheme of Chapter 3, this is cellular automaton rule 250.

This pattern is however again fairly simple. And we might assume that at least with the type of cellular automata that we are considering, any rule we might choose would always give a pattern that is quite simple. But now we are in for our first surprise.

The picture below shows the pattern produced by a cellular automaton of the same type as before, but with a slightly different rule.

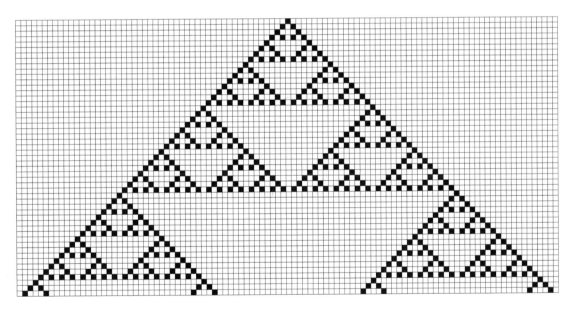

A cellular automaton that produces an intricate nested pattern. The rule in this case is that a cell should be black whenever one or the other, but not both, of its neighbors were black on the step before. Even though the rule is very simple, the picture shows that the overall pattern obtained over the course of 50 steps starting from a single black cell is not so simple. The particular rule used here can be described by the formula $a_i' = Mod[a_{i-1} + a_{i+1}, 2]$. In the numbering scheme of Chapter 3, it is cellular automaton rule 90.

This time the rule specifies that a cell should be black when either its left neighbor or its right neighbor—but not both—were black on the step before. And again this rule is undeniably quite simple. But now the picture shows that the pattern it produces is not so simple.

And if one runs the cellular automaton for more steps, as in the picture below, then a rather intricate pattern emerges. But one can now see that this pattern has very definite regularity. For even though it is intricate, one can see that it actually consists of many nested triangular pieces that all have exactly the same form. And as the picture shows, each of these pieces is essentially just a smaller copy of the whole pattern, with still smaller copies nested in a very regular way inside it.

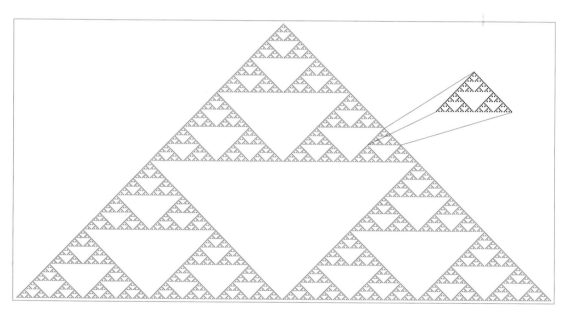

A larger version of the pattern from the previous page, now shown without a grid explicitly indicating each cell. The picture shows five hundred steps of cellular automaton evolution. The pattern obtained is intricate, but has a definite nested structure. Indeed, as the picture illustrates, each triangular section is essentially just a smaller copy of the whole pattern, with still smaller copies nested inside it. Patterns with nested structure of this kind are often called "fractal" or "self-similar".

So of the three cellular automata that we have seen so far, all ultimately yield patterns that are highly regular: the first a simple uniform pattern, the second a repetitive pattern, and the third an intricate but still nested pattern. And we might assume that at least for cellular automata with rules as simple as the ones we have been using these three forms of behavior would be all that we could ever get.

But the remarkable fact is that this turns out to be wrong.

And the picture below shows an example of this. The rule used— that I call rule 30—is of exactly the same kind as before, and can be described as follows. First, look at each cell and its right-hand neighbor. If both of these were white on the previous step, then take the new color of the cell to be whatever the previous color of its left-hand neighbor was. Otherwise, take the new color to be the opposite of that.

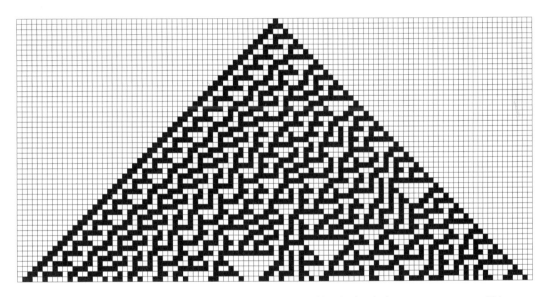

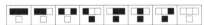

A cellular automaton with a simple rule that generates a pattern which seems in many respects random. The rule used is of the same type as in the previous examples, and the cellular automaton is again started from a single black cell. But now the pattern that is obtained is highly complex, and shows almost no overall regularity. This picture is our first example of the fundamental phenomenon that even with simple underlying rules and simple initial conditions, it is possible to produce behavior of great complexity. In the numbering scheme of Chapter 3, the cellular automaton shown here is rule 30.

The picture shows what happens when one starts with just one black cell and then applies this rule over and over again. And what one sees is something quite startling—and probably the single most surprising scientific discovery I have ever made. Rather than getting a simple regular pattern as we might expect, the cellular automaton instead produces a pattern that seems extremely irregular and complex.

But where does this complexity come from? We certainly did not put it into the system in any direct way when we set it up. For we just used a simple cellular automaton rule, and just started from a simple initial condition containing a single black cell.

Yet the picture shows that despite this, there is great complexity in the behavior that emerges. And indeed what we have seen here is a first example of an extremely general and fundamental phenomenon that is at the very core of the new kind of science that I develop in this book. Over and over again we will see the same kind of thing: that even though the underlying rules for a system are simple, and even though the system is started from simple initial conditions, the behavior that the system shows can nevertheless be highly complex. And I will argue that it is this basic phenomenon that is ultimately responsible for most of the complexity that we see in nature.

The next two pages show progressively more steps in the evolution of the rule 30 cellular automaton from the previous page. One might have thought that after maybe a thousand steps the behavior would eventually resolve into something simple. But the pictures on the next two pages show that nothing of the sort happens.

Some regularities can nevertheless be seen. On the left-hand side, for example, there are obvious diagonal bands. And dotted throughout there are various white triangles and other small structures. Yet given the simplicity of the underlying rule, one would expect vastly more regularities. And perhaps one might imagine that our failure to see any in the pictures on the next two pages is just a reflection of some kind of inadequacy in the human visual system.

But it turns out that even the most sophisticated mathematical and statistical methods of analysis seem to do no better. For example, one can look at the sequence of colors directly below the initial black cell. And in the first million steps in this sequence, for example, it never repeats, and indeed none of the tests I have ever done on it show any meaningful deviation at all from perfect randomness.

In a sense, however, there is a certain simplicity to such perfect randomness. For even though it may be impossible to predict what

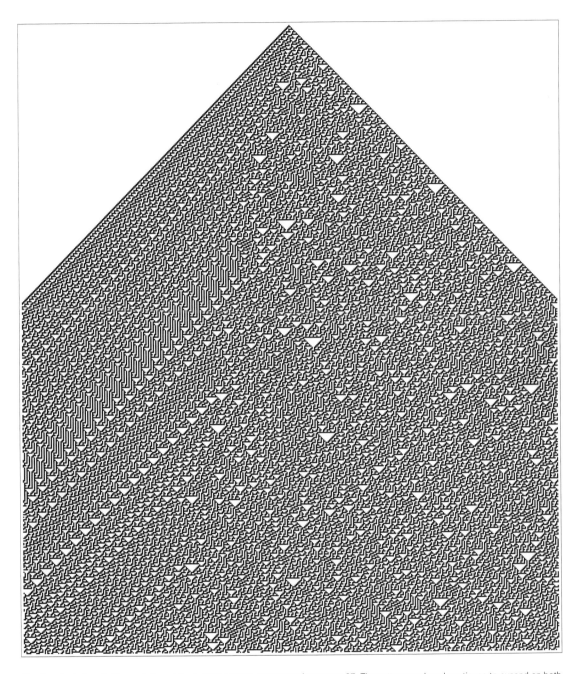

Five hundred steps in the evolution of the rule 30 cellular automaton from page 27. The pattern produced continues to expand on both left and right, but only the part that fits across the page is shown here. The asymmetry between the left and right-hand sides is a direct consequence of asymmetry that exists in the particular underlying cellular automaton rule used.

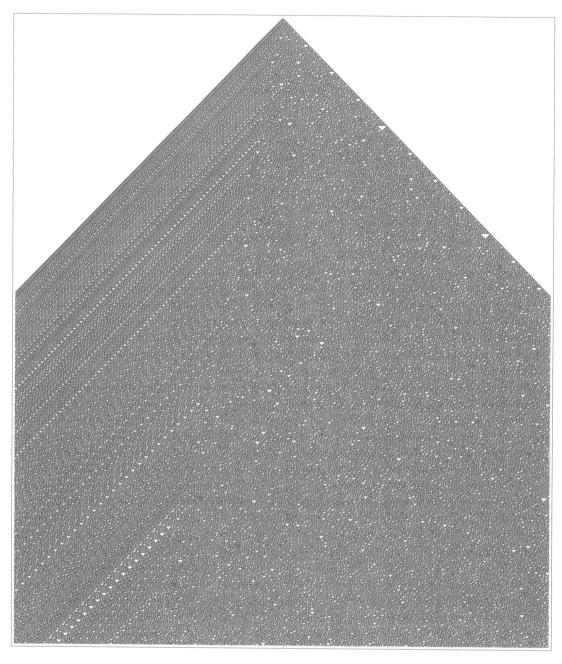

Fifteen hundred steps of rule 30 evolution. Some regularities are evident, particularly on the left. But even after all these steps there are no signs of overall regularity—and indeed even continuing for a million steps many aspects of the pattern obtained seem perfectly random according to standard mathematical and statistical tests. The picture here shows a total of just under two million individual cells.

color will occur at any specific step, one still knows for example that black and white will on average always occur equally often.

But it turns out that there are cellular automata whose behavior is in effect still more complex—and in which even such averages become very difficult to predict. The pictures on the next several pages give a rather dramatic example. The basic form of the rule is just the same as before. But now the specific rule used—that I call rule 110— takes the new color of a cell to be black in every case except when the previous colors of the cell and its two neighbors were all the same, or when the left neighbor was black and the cell and its right neighbor were both white.

The pattern obtained with this rule shows a remarkable mixture of regularity and irregularity. More or less throughout, there is a very regular background texture that consists of an array of small white triangles repeating every 7 steps. And beginning near the left-hand edge, there are diagonal stripes that occur at intervals of exactly 80 steps.

But on the right-hand side, the pattern is much less regular. Indeed, for the first few hundred steps there is a region that seems essentially random. But by the bottom of the first page, all that remains of this region is three copies of a rather simple repetitive structure.

Yet at the top of the next page the arrival of a diagonal stripe from the left sets off more complicated behavior again. And as the system progresses, a variety of definite localized structures are produced.

Some of these structures remain stationary, like those at the bottom of the first page, while others move steadily to the right or left at various speeds. And on their own, each of these structures works in a fairly simple way. But as the pictures illustrate, their various interactions can have very complicated effects.

And as a result it becomes almost impossible to predict—even approximately—what the cellular automaton will do.

Will all the structures that are produced eventually annihilate each other, leaving only a very regular pattern? Or will more and more structures appear until the whole pattern becomes quite random?

The only sure way to answer these questions, it seems, is just to run the cellular automaton for as many steps as are needed, and to

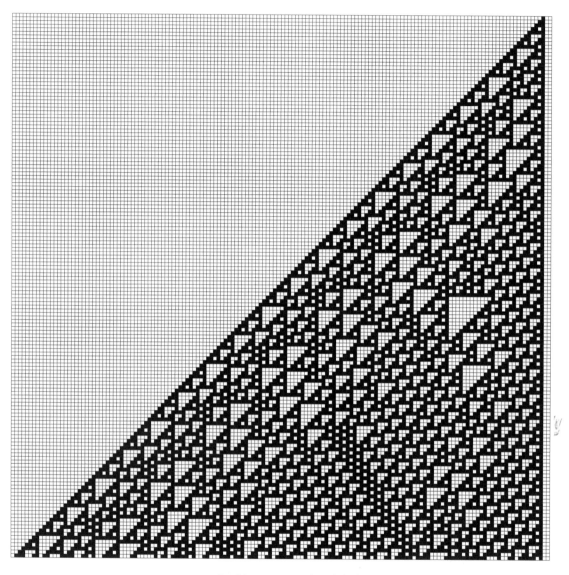

A cellular automaton whose behavior seems neither highly regular nor completely random. The picture is obtained by applying the simple rule shown for a total of 150 steps, starting with a single black cell. Note that the particular rule used here yields a pattern that expands on the left but not on the right. In the scheme defined in Chapter 3, the rule is number 110.

More steps in the pattern shown above. Each successive page shows a total of 700 steps. The pattern continues to expand on the left forever, but only the part that fits across each page is shown. For a long time it is not clear how the right-hand part of the pattern will eventually look. But after 2780 steps, a fairly simple repetitive structure emerges. Note that to generate the pictures that follow requires applying the underlying cellular automaton rule for individual cells a total of about 12 million times. ▶

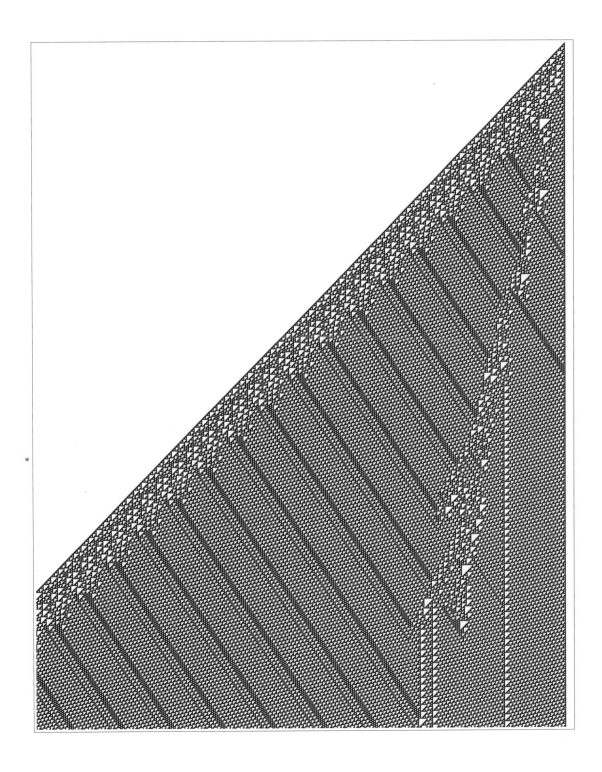

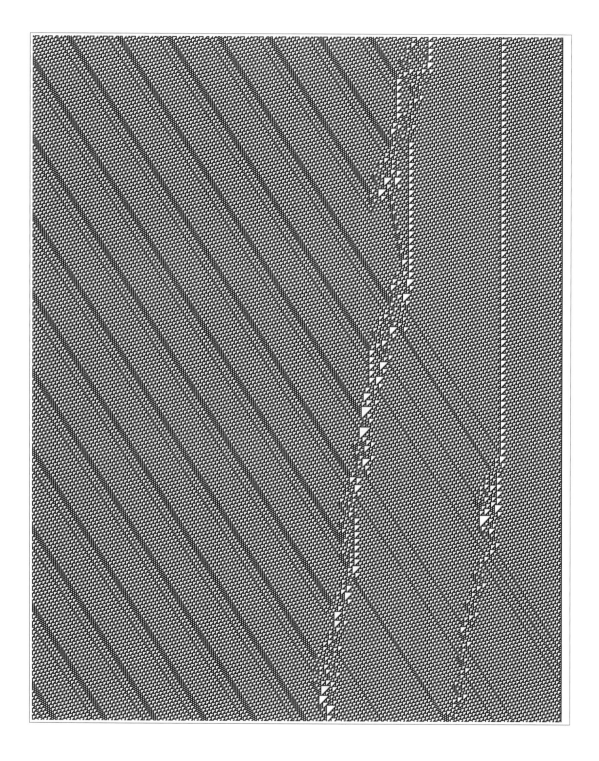

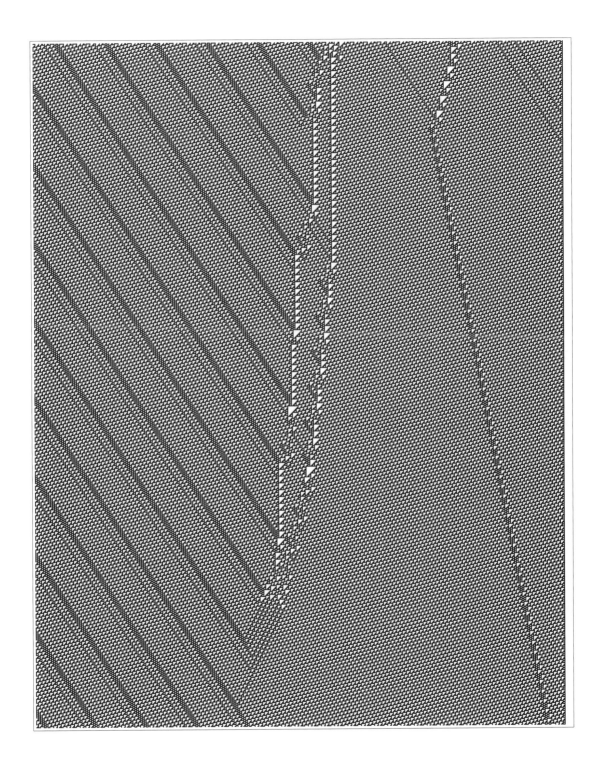

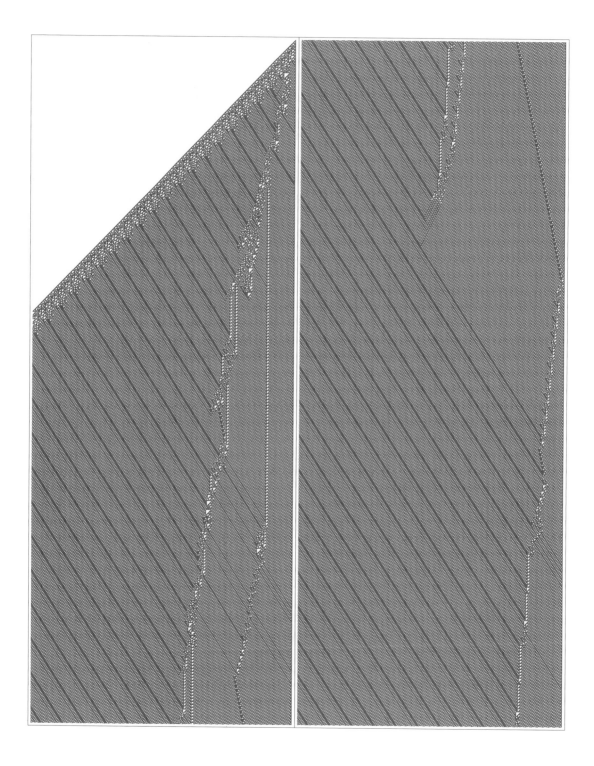

watch what happens. And as it turns out, in the particular case shown here, the outcome is finally clear after about 2780 steps: one structure survives, and that structure interacts with the periodic stripes coming from the left to produce behavior that repeats every 240 steps.

However certain one might be that simple programs could never do more than produce simple behavior, the pictures on the past few pages should forever disabuse one of that notion. And indeed, what is perhaps most bizarre about the pictures is just how little trace they ultimately show of the simplicity of the underlying cellular automaton rule that was used to produce them.

One might think, for example, that the fact that all the cells in a cellular automaton follow exactly the same rule would mean that in pictures like the last few pages all cells would somehow obviously be doing the same thing. But instead, they seem to be doing quite different things. Some of them, for example, are part of the regular background, while others are part of one or another localized structure. And what makes this possible is that even though individual cells follow the same rule, different configurations of cells with different sequences of colors can together produce all sorts of different kinds of behavior.

Looking just at the original cellular automaton rule one would have no realistic way to foresee all of this. But by doing the appropriate computer experiments one can easily find out what actually happens— and in effect begin the process of exploring a whole new world of remarkable phenomena associated with simple programs.

The Need for a New Intuition

The pictures in the previous section plainly show that it takes only very simple rules to produce highly complex behavior. Yet at first this may seem almost impossible to believe. For it goes against some of our most basic intuition about the way things normally work.

◀ A single picture of the behavior from the previous five pages. A total of 3200 steps are shown. Note that this is more than twice as many as in the picture on page 30.

For our everyday experience has led us to expect that an object that looks complicated must have been constructed in a complicated way. And so, for example, if we see a complicated mechanical device, we normally assume that the plans from which the device was built must also somehow be correspondingly complicated.

But the results at the end of the previous section show that at least sometimes such an assumption can be completely wrong. For the patterns we saw are in effect built according to very simple plans—that just tell us to start with a single black cell, and then repeatedly to apply a simple cellular automaton rule. Yet what emerges from these plans shows an immense level of complexity.

So what is it that makes our normal intuition fail? The most important point seems to be that it is mostly derived from experience with building things and doing engineering—where it so happens that one avoids encountering systems like the ones in the previous section.

For normally we start from whatever behavior we want to get, then try to design a system that will produce it. Yet to do this reliably, we have to restrict ourselves to systems whose behavior we can readily understand and predict—for unless we can foresee how a system will behave, we cannot be sure that the system will do what we want.

But unlike engineering, nature operates under no such constraint. So there is nothing to stop systems like those at the end of the previous section from showing up. And in fact one of the important conclusions of this book is that such systems are actually very common in nature.

But because the only situations in which we are routinely aware both of underlying rules and overall behavior are ones in which we are building things or doing engineering, we never normally get any intuition about systems like the ones at the end of the previous section.

So is there then any aspect of everyday experience that should give us a hint about the phenomena that occur in these systems? Probably the closest is thinking about features of practical computing.

For we know that computers can perform many complex tasks. Yet at the level of basic hardware a typical computer is capable of executing just a few tens of kinds of simple logical, arithmetic and other instructions. And to some extent the fact that by executing large numbers of such instructions one can get all sorts of complex behavior is similar to the phenomenon we have seen in cellular automata.

But there is an important difference. For while the individual machine instructions executed by a computer may be quite simple, the sequence of such instructions defined by a program may be long and complicated. And indeed—much as in other areas of engineering—the typical experience in developing software is that to make a computer do something complicated requires setting up a program that is itself somehow correspondingly complicated.

In a system like a cellular automaton the underlying rules can be thought of as rough analogs of the machine instructions for a computer, while the initial conditions can be thought of as rough analogs of the program. Yet what we saw in the previous section is that in cellular automata not only can the underlying rules be simple, but the initial conditions can also be simple—consisting say of just a single black cell—and still the behavior that is produced can be highly complex.

So while practical computing gives a hint of part of what we saw in the previous section, the whole phenomenon is something much larger and stronger. And in a sense the most puzzling aspect of it is that it seems to involve getting something from nothing.

For the cellular automata we set up are by any measure simple to describe. Yet when we ran them we ended with patterns so complex that they seemed to defy any simple description at all.

And one might hope that it would be possible to call on some existing kind of intuition to understand such a fundamental phenomenon. But in fact there seems to be no branch of everyday experience that provides what is needed. And so we have no choice but to try to develop a whole new kind of intuition.

And the only reasonable way to do this is to expose ourselves to a large number of examples. We have seen so far only a few examples, all in cellular automata. But in the next few chapters we will see many more examples, both in cellular automata and in all sorts of other systems. And by absorbing these examples, one is in the end able to develop an intuition that makes the basic phenomena that I have discovered seem somehow almost obvious and inevitable.

Why These Discoveries Were Not Made Before

The main result of this chapter—that programs based on simple rules can produce behavior of great complexity—seems so fundamental that one might assume it must have been discovered long ago. But it was not, and it is useful to understand some of the reasons why it was not.

In the history of science it is fairly common that new technologies are ultimately what make new areas of basic science develop. And thus, for example, telescope technology was what led to modern astronomy, and microscope technology to modern biology. And now, in much the same way, it is computer technology that has led to the new kind of science that I describe in this book.

Indeed, this chapter and several of those that follow can in a sense be viewed as an account of some of the very simplest experiments that can be done using computers. But why is it that such simple experiments were never done before?

One reason is just that they were not in the mainstream of any existing field of science or mathematics. But a more important reason is that standard intuition in traditional science gave no reason to think that their results would be interesting.

And indeed, if it had been known that they were worthwhile, many of the experiments could actually have been done even long before computers existed. For while it may be somewhat tedious, it is certainly possible to work out the behavior of something like a cellular automaton by hand. And in fact, to do so requires absolutely no sophisticated ideas from mathematics or elsewhere: all it takes is an understanding of how to apply simple rules repeatedly.

And looking at the historical examples of ornamental art on the facing page, there seems little reason to think that the behavior of many cellular automata could not have been worked out many centuries or even millennia ago. And perhaps one day some Babylonian artifact created using the rule 30 cellular automaton from page 27 will be unearthed. But I very much doubt it. For I tend to think that if pictures like the one on page 27 had ever in fact been seen in ancient times then science would have been led down a very different path from the one it actually took.

22,000 BC (Paleolithic)   *3500 BC (Sumerian)*   *1200 BC (Greek)*   *9th century BC (Phoenician)*

1st century BC (Celtic)   *2nd century (Roman)*   *8th century (Islamic)*   *8th century (Celtic)*

12th century (Italian)   *13th century (English)*   *13th century (Italian)*   *13th century (Italian)*

13th century (Italian)   *13th century (Italian)*   *14th century (Islamic)*   *14th century (Islamic)*

Historical examples of ornamental art. Repetitive patterns are common and some nested patterns are seen, but the more complicated kinds of patterns discussed in this chapter do not ever appear to have been used. Note that the second-to-last picture is not an abstract design, but is instead text written in a highly stylized form of Arabic script.

Even early in antiquity attempts were presumably made to see whether simple abstract rules could reproduce the behavior of natural systems. But so far as one can tell the only types of rules that were tried were ones associated with standard geometry and arithmetic. And using these kinds of rules, only rather simple behavior could be obtained—adequate to explain some of the regularities observed in astronomy, but unable to capture much of what is seen elsewhere in nature.

And perhaps because of this, it typically came to be assumed that a great many aspects of the natural world are simply beyond human understanding. But finally the successes based on calculus in the late 1600s began to overthrow this belief. For with calculus there was finally real success in taking abstract rules created by human thought and using them to reproduce all sorts of phenomena in the natural world.

But the particular rules that were found to work were fairly sophisticated ones based on particular kinds of mathematical equations. And from seeing the sophistication of these rules there began to develop an implicit belief that in almost no important cases would simpler rules be useful in reproducing the behavior of natural systems.

During the 1700s and 1800s there was ever-increasing success in using rules based on mathematical equations to analyze physical phenomena. And after the spectacular results achieved in physics in the early 1900s with mathematical equations there emerged an almost universal belief that absolutely every aspect of the natural world would in the end be explained by using such equations.

Needless to say, there were many phenomena that did not readily yield to this approach, but it was generally assumed that if only the necessary calculations could be done, then an explanation in terms of mathematical equations would eventually be found.

Beginning in the 1940s, the development of electronic computers greatly broadened the range of calculations that could be done. But disappointingly enough, most of the actual calculations that were tried yielded no fundamentally new insights. And as a result many people came to believe—and in some cases still believe today—that computers could never make a real contribution to issues of basic science.

But the crucial point that was missed is that computers are not just limited to working out consequences of mathematical equations. And indeed, what we have seen in this chapter is that there are fundamental discoveries that can be made if one just studies directly the behavior of even some of the very simplest computer programs.

In retrospect it is perhaps ironic that the idea of using simple programs as models for natural systems did not surface in the early days of computing. For systems like cellular automata would have been immensely easier to handle on early computers than mathematical equations were. But the issue was that computer time was an expensive commodity, and so it was not thought worth taking the risk of trying anything but well-established mathematical models.

By the end of the 1970s, however, the situation had changed, and large amounts of computer time were becoming readily available. And this is what allowed me in 1981 to begin my experiments on cellular automata.

There is, as I mentioned above, nothing in principle that requires one to use a computer to study cellular automata. But as a practical matter, it is difficult to imagine that anyone in modern times would have the patience to generate many pictures of cellular automata by hand. For it takes roughly an hour to make the picture on page 27 by hand, and it would take a few weeks to make the picture on page 29.

Yet even with early mainframe computers, the data for these pictures could have been generated in a matter of a few seconds and a few minutes respectively. But the point is that one would be very unlikely to discover the kinds of fundamental phenomena discussed in this chapter just by looking at one or two pictures. And indeed for me to do it certainly took carrying out quite large-scale computer experiments on a considerable number of different cellular automata.

If one already has a clear idea about the basic features of a particular phenomenon, then one can often get more details by doing fairly specific experiments. But in my experience the only way to find phenomena that one does not already know exist is to do very systematic and general experiments, and then to look at the results with as few preconceptions as possible. And while it takes only rather basic computer technology to make single pictures of cellular automata, it requires considerably more to do large-scale systematic experiments.

Indeed, many of my discoveries about cellular automata came as direct consequences of using progressively better computer technology.

As one example, I discovered the classification scheme for cellular automata with random initial conditions described at the beginning of Chapter 6 when I first looked at large numbers of different cellular automata together on high-resolution graphics displays. Similarly, I discovered the randomness of rule 30 (page 27) when I was in the process of setting up large simulations for an early parallel-processing computer. And in more recent years, I have discovered a vast range of new phenomena as a result of easily being able to set up large numbers of computer experiments in *Mathematica*.

Undoubtedly, therefore, one of the main reasons that the discoveries I describe in this chapter were not made before the 1980s is just that computer technology did not yet exist powerful enough to do the kinds of exploratory experiments that were needed.

But beyond the practicalities of carrying out such experiments, it was also necessary to have the idea that the experiments might be worth doing in the first place. And here again computer technology played a crucial role. For it was from practical experience in using computers that I developed much of the necessary intuition.

As a simple example, one might have imagined that systems like cellular automata, being made up of discrete cells, would never be able to reproduce realistic natural shapes. But knowing about computer displays it is clear that this is not the case. For a computer display, like a cellular automaton, consists of a regular array of discrete cells or pixels. Yet practical experience shows that such displays can produce quite realistic images, even with fairly small numbers of pixels.

And as a more significant example, one might have imagined that the simple structure of cellular automaton programs would make it straightforward to foresee their behavior. But from experience in practical computing one knows that it is usually very difficult to foresee what even a simple program will do. Indeed, that is exactly why bugs in programs are so common. For if one could just look at a program and immediately know what it would do, then it would be an easy matter to check that the program did not contain any bugs.

Notions like the difficulty of finding bugs have no obvious connection to traditional ideas in science. And perhaps as a result of this, even after computers had been in use for several decades, essentially none of this type of intuition from practical computing had found its way into basic science. But in 1981 it so happened that I had for some years been deeply involved in both practical computing and basic science, and I was therefore in an almost unique position to apply ideas derived from practical computing to basic science.

Yet despite this, my discoveries about cellular automata still involved a substantial element of luck. For as I mentioned on page 19, my very first experiments on cellular automata showed only very simple behavior, and it was only because doing further experiments was technically very easy for me that I persisted.

And even after I had seen the first signs of complexity in cellular automata, it was several more years before I discovered the full range of examples given in this chapter, and realized just how easily complexity could be generated in systems like cellular automata.

Part of the reason that this took so long is that it involved experiments with progressively more sophisticated computer technology. But the more important reason is that it required the development of new intuition. And at almost every stage, intuition from traditional science took me in the wrong direction. But I found that intuition from practical computing did better. And even though it was sometimes misleading, it was in the end fairly important in putting me on the right track.

Thus there are two quite different reasons why it would have been difficult for the results in this chapter to be discovered much before computer technology reached the point it did in the 1980s. First, the necessary computer experiments could not be done with sufficient ease that they were likely to be tried. And second, the kinds of intuition about computation that were needed could not readily have been developed without extensive exposure to practical computing.

But now that the results of this chapter are known, one can go back and see quite a number of times in the past when they came at least somewhat close to being discovered.

It turns out that two-dimensional versions of cellular automata were already considered in the early 1950s as possible idealized models for biological systems. But until my work in the 1980s the actual investigations of cellular automata that were done consisted mainly in constructions of rather complicated sets of rules that could be shown to lead to specific kinds of fairly simple behavior.

The question of whether complex behavior could occur in cellular automata was occasionally raised, but on the basis of intuition from engineering it was generally assumed that to get any substantial complexity, one would have to have very complicated underlying rules. And as a result, the idea of studying cellular automata with simple rules never surfaced, with the result that nothing like the experiments described in this chapter were ever done.

In other areas, however, systems that are effectively based on simple rules were quite often studied, and in fact complex behavior was sometimes seen. But without a framework to understand its significance, such behavior tended either to be ignored entirely or to be treated as some kind of curiosity of no particular fundamental significance.

Indeed, even very early in the history of traditional mathematics there were already signs of the basic phenomenon of complexity. One example known for well over two thousand years concerns the distribution of prime numbers (see page 132). The rules for generating primes are simple, yet their distribution seems in many respects random. But almost without exception mathematical work on primes has concentrated not on this randomness, but rather on proving the presence of various regularities in the distribution.

Another early sign of the phenomenon of complexity could have been seen in the digit sequence of a number like $\pi \simeq 3.141592653 \dots$ (see page 136). By the 1700s more than a hundred digits of π had been computed, and they appeared quite random. But this fact was treated essentially as a curiosity, and the idea never appears to have arisen that there might be a general phenomenon whereby simple rules like those for computing π could produce complex results.

In the early 1900s various explicit examples were constructed in several areas of mathematics in which simple rules were repeatedly applied to numbers, sequences or geometrical patterns. And sometimes nested or fractal behavior was seen. And in a few cases substantially more complex behavior was also seen. But the very complexity of this behavior was usually taken to show that it could not be relevant for real mathematical work—and could only be of recreational interest.

When electronic computers began to be used in the 1940s, there were many more opportunities for the phenomenon of complexity to be seen. And indeed, looking back, significant complexity probably did occur in many scientific calculations. But these calculations were almost always based on traditional mathematical models, and since previous analyses of these models had not revealed complexity, it tended to be assumed that any complexity in the computer calculations was just a spurious consequence of the approximations used in them.

One class of systems where some types of complexity were noticed in the 1950s are so-called iterated maps. But as I will discuss on page 149, the traditional mathematics that was used to analyze such systems ended up concentrating only on certain specific features, and completely missed the main phenomenon discovered in this chapter.

It is often useful in practical computing to produce sequences of numbers that seem random. And starting in the 1940s, several simple procedures for generating such sequences were invented. But perhaps because these procedures always seemed quite ad hoc, no general conclusions about randomness and complexity were drawn from them.

Along similar lines, systems not unlike the cellular automata discussed in this chapter were studied in the late 1950s for generating random sequences to be used in cryptography. Almost all the results that were obtained are still military secrets, but I do not believe that any phenomena like the ones described in this chapter were discovered.

And in general, within the context of mainstream science, the standard intuition that had been developed made it very difficult for anyone to imagine that it would be worth studying the behavior of the very simple kinds of computer programs discussed in this chapter. But outside of mainstream science, some work along such lines was done. And for example in the 1960s early computer enthusiasts tried running various simple programs, and found that in certain cases these programs could succeed in producing nested patterns.

Then in the early 1970s, considerable recreational computing interest developed in a specific two-dimensional cellular automaton known as the Game of Life, whose behavior is in some respects similar to the rule 110 cellular automaton discussed in this chapter. Great effort was spent trying to find structures that would be sufficiently simple and predictable that they could be used as idealized components for engineering. And although complex behavior was seen it was generally treated as a nuisance, to be avoided whenever possible.

In a sense it is surprising that so much could be done on the Game of Life without the much simpler one-dimensional cellular automata in this chapter ever being investigated. And no doubt the lack of a connection to basic science was at least in part responsible.

But whatever the reasons, the fact remains that, despite many hints over the course of several centuries, the basic phenomenon that I have described in this chapter was never discovered before.

It is not uncommon in the history of science that once a general new phenomenon has been identified, one can see that there was already evidence of it much earlier. But the point is that without the framework that comes from knowing the general phenomenon, it is almost inevitable that such evidence will have been ignored.

It is also one of the ironies of progress in science that results which at one time were so unexpected that they were missed despite many hints eventually come to seem almost obvious. And having lived with the results of this chapter for nearly two decades, it is now difficult for me to imagine that things could possibly work in any other way. But the history that I have outlined in this section—like the history of many other scientific discoveries—provides a sobering reminder of just how easy it is to miss what will later seem obvious.

The World of Simple Programs

The Search for General Features

At the beginning of the last chapter we asked the basic question of what simple programs typically do. And as a first step towards answering this question we looked at several specific examples of a class of programs known as cellular automata.

The basic types of behavior that we found are illustrated in the pictures on the next page. In the first of these there is pure repetition, and a very simple pattern is formed. In the second, there are many intricate details, but at an overall level there is still a very regular nested structure that emerges.

In the third picture, however, one no longer sees such regularity, and instead there is behavior that seems in many respects random. And finally in the fourth picture there is what appears to be still more complex behavior—with elaborate localized structures being generated that interact in complex ways.

At the outset there was no indication that simple programs could ever produce behavior so diverse and often complex. But having now seen these examples, the question becomes how typical they are. Is it only cellular automata with very specific underlying rules that produce such behavior? Or is it in fact common in all sorts of simple programs?

My purpose in this chapter is to answer this question by looking at a wide range of different kinds of programs. And in a sense my

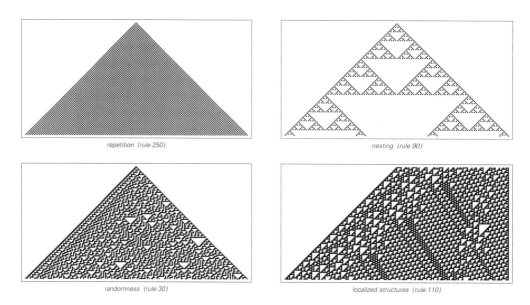

repetition (rule 250)

nesting (rule 90)

randomness (rule 30)

localized structures (rule 110)

Four basic examples from the previous chapter of behavior produced by cellular automata with simple underlying rules. In each case, the most obvious features that are seen are different. Note that all the pictures are shown on the same scale; the last picture appears coarser because the structures it contains are larger.

approach is to work like a naturalist—exploring and studying the various forms that exist in the world of simple programs.

I start by considering more general cellular automata, and then I go on to consider a whole sequence of other kinds of programs—with underlying structures further and further away from the array of black and white cells in the cellular automata of the previous chapter.

And what I discover is that whatever kind of underlying rules one uses, the behavior that emerges turns out to be remarkably similar to the basic examples that we have already seen in cellular automata.

Throughout the world of simple programs, it seems, there is great universality in the types of overall behavior that can be produced. And in a sense it is ultimately this that makes it possible for me to construct the coherent new kind of science that I describe in this book—and to use it to elucidate a large number of phenomena, independent of the particular details of the systems in which they occur.

More Cellular Automata

The pictures below show the rules used in the four cellular automata on the facing page. The overall structure of these rules is the same in each case; what differs is the specific choice of new colors for each possible combination of previous colors for a cell and its two neighbors.

rule 250   *rule 90*

rule 30   *rule 110*

The rules used for the four examples of cellular automata on the facing page. In each case, these specify the new color of a cell for each possible combination of colors of that cell and its immediate neighbors on the previous step. The rules are numbered according to the scheme described below.

There turn out to be a total of 256 possible sets of choices that can be made. And following my original work on cellular automata these choices can be numbered from 0 to 255, as in the picture below.

The sequence of 256 possible cellular automaton rules of the kind shown above. As indicated, the rules can conveniently be numbered from 0 to 255. The number assigned is such that when written in base 2, it gives a sequence of 0's and 1's that correspond to the sequence of new colors chosen for each of the eight possible cases covered by the rule.

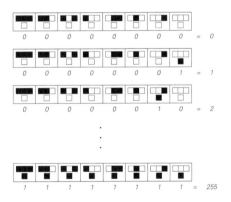

But so how do cellular automata with all these different rules behave? The next page shows a few examples in detail, while the following two pages show what happens in all 256 possible cases.

At first, the diversity of what one sees is a little overwhelming. But on closer investigation, definite themes begin to emerge.

In the very simplest cases, all the cells in the cellular automaton end up just having the same color after one step. Thus, for example, in

Evolution of cellular automata with a sequence of different possible rules, starting in all cases from a single black cell.

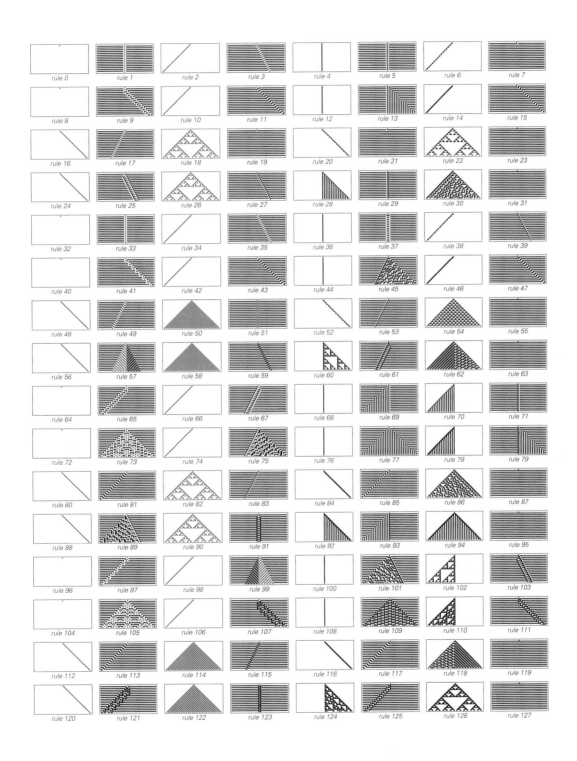

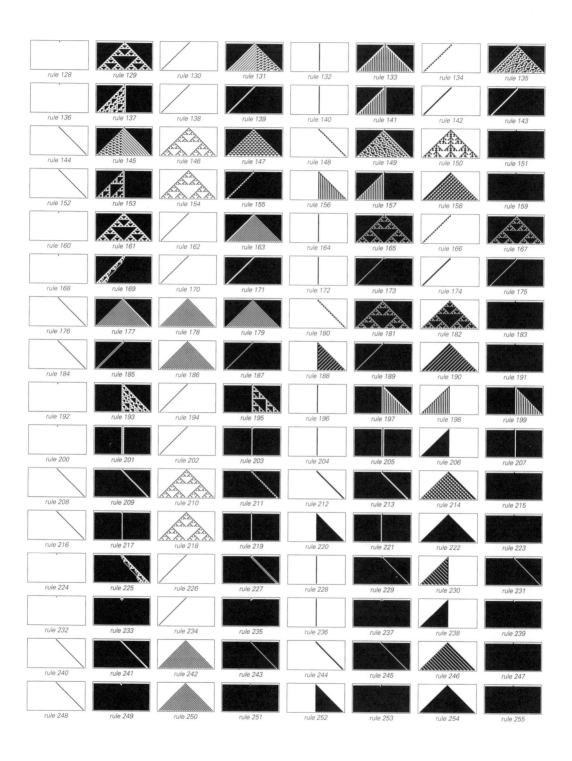

rules 0 and 128 all the cells become white, while in rule 255 all of them become black. There are also rules such as 7 and 127 in which all cells alternate between black and white on successive steps.

But among the rules shown on the last few pages, the single most common kind of behavior is one in which a pattern consisting of a single cell or a small group of cells persists. Sometimes this pattern remains stationary, as in rules 4 and 123. But in other cases, such as rules 2 and 103, it moves to the left or right.

It turns out that the basic structure of the cellular automata discussed here implies that the maximum speed of any such motion must be one cell per step. And in many rules, this maximum speed is achieved—although in rules such as 3 and 103 the average speed is instead only half a cell per step.

In about two-thirds of all the cellular automata shown on the last few pages, the patterns produced remain of a fixed size. But in about one-third of cases, the patterns instead grow forever. Of such growing patterns, the simplest kind are purely repetitive ones, such as those seen in rules 50 and 109. But while repetitive patterns are by a small margin the most common kind, about 14% of all the cellular automata shown yield more complicated kinds of patterns.

The most common of these are nested patterns, like those on the next page. And it turns out that although 24 rules in all yield such nested patterns, there are only three fundamentally different forms that occur. The simplest and by far the most common is the one exemplified by rules 22 and 60. But as the pictures on the next page show, other nested forms are also possible. (In the case of rule 225, the width of the overall pattern does not grow at a fixed rate, but instead is on average proportional to the square root of the number of steps.)

◀ The behavior of all 256 possible cellular automata with rules involving two colors and nearest neighbors. In each case, thirty steps of evolution are shown, starting from a single black cell. Note that some of the rules are related just by interchange of left and right or black and white (e.g. rules 2 and 16 or rules 126 and 129). There are 88 fundamentally inequivalent such elementary rules.

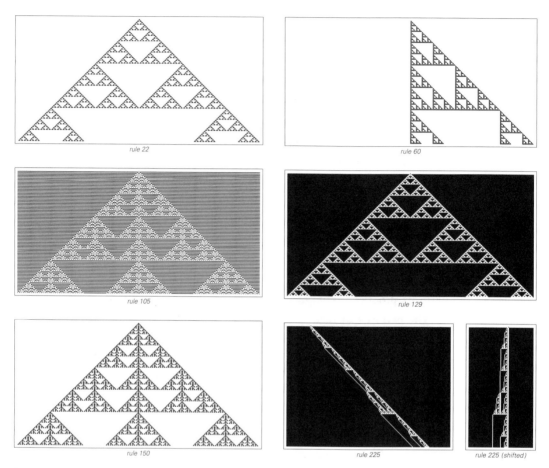

rule 22

rule 60

rule 105

rule 129

rule 150

rule 225

rule 225 (shifted)

Examples of cellular automata that produce nested or fractal patterns. Rule 22—like rule 90 from page 26—gives a pattern with fractal dimension $Log[2, 3] \simeq 1.59$; rule 150 gives one with fractal dimension $Log[2, 1 + \sqrt{5}\,] \simeq 1.69$. The width of the pattern obtained from rule 225 increases like the square root of the number of steps.

Repetition and nesting are widespread themes in many cellular automata. But as we saw in the previous chapter, it is also possible for cellular automata to produce patterns that seem in many respects random. And out of the 256 rules discussed here, it turns out that 10 yield such apparent randomness. There are three basic forms, as illustrated on the facing page.

Examples of cellular automata that produce patterns with many apparently random features. Three hundred steps of evolution are shown, starting in each case from a single black cell. ▶

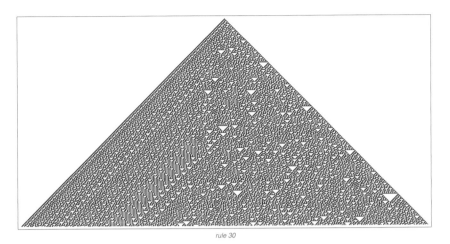

rule 30

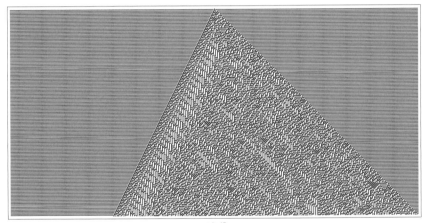

rule 45

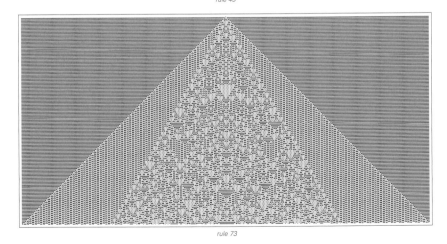

rule 73

Beyond randomness, the last example in the previous chapter was rule 110: a cellular automaton whose behavior becomes partitioned into a complex mixture of regular and irregular parts. This particular cellular automaton is essentially unique among the 256 rules considered here: of the four cases in which such behavior is seen, all are equivalent if one just interchanges the roles of left and right or black and white.

So what about more complicated cellular automaton rules?

The 256 "elementary" rules that we have discussed so far are by most measures the simplest possible—and were the first ones I studied. But one can for example also look at rules that involve three colors, rather than two, so that cells can not only be black and white, but also gray. The total number of possible rules of this kind turns out to be immense—7,625,597,484,987 in all—but by considering only so-called "totalistic" ones, the number becomes much more manageable.

The idea of a totalistic rule is to take the new color of each cell to depend only on the average color of neighboring cells, and not on their individual colors. The picture below shows one example of how this works. And with three possible colors for each cell, there are 2187 possible totalistic rules, each of which can conveniently be identified by a code number as illustrated in the picture. The facing page shows a representative sequence of such rules.

Example of a totalistic cellular automaton with three possible colors for each cell. The rule is set up so that the new color of every cell is determined by the average of the previous colors of the cell and its immediate neighbors. With 0 representing white, 1 gray and 2 black, the rightmost element of the rule gives the result for average color 0, while the element immediately to its left gives the result for average color 1/3—and so on. Interpreting the sequence of new colors as a sequence of base 3 digits, one can assign a code number to each totalistic rule.

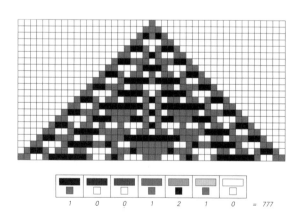

We might have expected that by allowing three colors rather than two we would immediately get noticeably more complicated behavior.

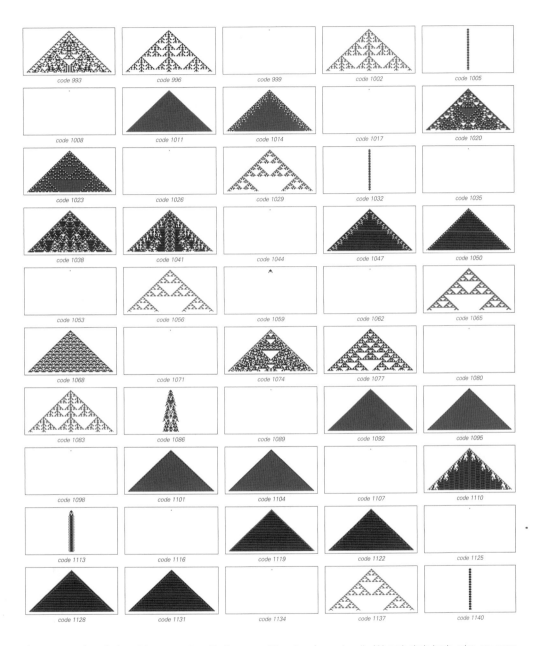

code 993 code 996 code 999 code 1002 code 1005

code 1008 code 1011 code 1014 code 1017 code 1020

code 1023 code 1026 code 1029 code 1032 code 1035

code 1038 code 1041 code 1044 code 1047 code 1050

code 1053 code 1056 code 1059 code 1062 code 1065

code 1068 code 1071 code 1074 code 1077 code 1080

code 1083 code 1086 code 1089 code 1092 code 1095

code 1098 code 1101 code 1104 code 1107 code 1110

code 1113 code 1116 code 1119 code 1122 code 1125

code 1128 code 1131 code 1134 code 1137 code 1140

A sequence of totalistic cellular automata with three possible colors for each cell. Although their basic rules are more complicated, the cellular automata shown here do not seem to have fundamentally more complicated behavior than the two-color cellular automata shown on previous pages. Note that in the sequence of rules shown here, those that change the white background are not included. The symmetry of all the patterns is a consequence of the basic structure of totalistic rules.

But in fact the behavior we see on the previous page is not unlike what we already saw in many elementary cellular automata a few pages back. Having more complicated underlying rules has not, it seems, led to much greater complexity in overall behavior.

And indeed, this is a first indication of an important general phenomenon: that at least beyond a certain point, adding complexity to the underlying rules for a system does not ultimately lead to more complex overall behavior. And so for example, in the case of cellular automata, it seems that all the essential ingredients needed to produce even the most complex behavior already exist in elementary rules.

Using more complicated rules may be convenient if one wants, say, to reproduce the details of particular natural systems, but it does not add fundamentally new features. Indeed, looking at the pictures on the previous page one sees exactly the same basic themes as in elementary cellular automata. There are some patterns that attain a definite size, then repeat forever, as shown below, others that continue to grow, but have a repetitive form, as at the top of the facing page, and still others that produce nested or fractal patterns, as at the bottom of the page.

Examples of three-color totalistic rules that yield patterns which attain a certain size, then repeat forever. The maximum repetition period is found to be 78 steps, and is achieved by the rule with code number 1329. In the pictures shown here and on the following pages, the initial condition used contains a single gray cell.

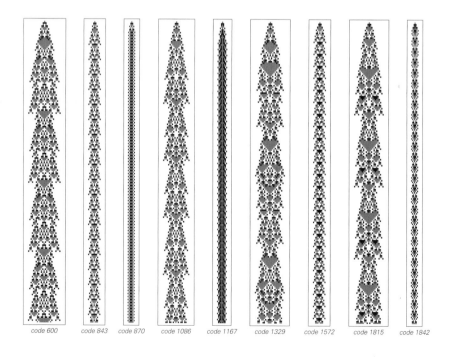

code 600   code 843   code 870   code 1086   code 1167   code 1329   code 1572   code 1815   code 1842

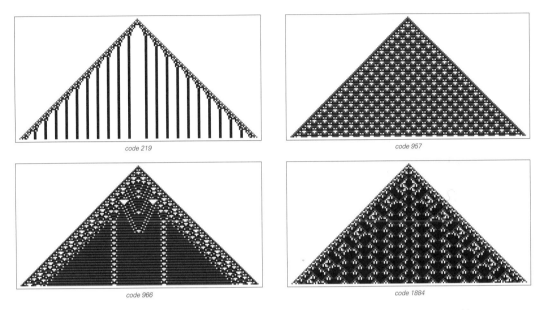

code 219 *code 957*

code 966 *code 1884*

Examples of three-color totalistic rules that yield patterns which grow forever but have a fundamentally repetitive structure.

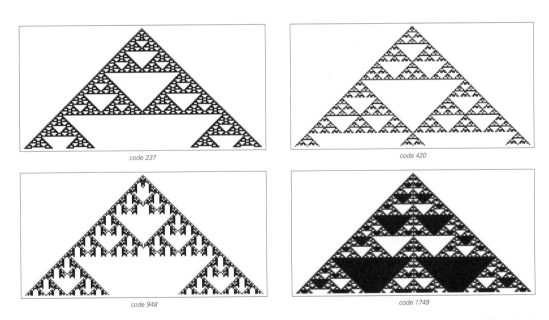

code 237 *code 420*

code 948 *code 1749*

Examples of three-color totalistic rules which yield nested patterns. In most cases, these patterns have an overall form that is similar to what was found with two-color rules. But code 420, for example, yields a pattern with a slightly different structure.

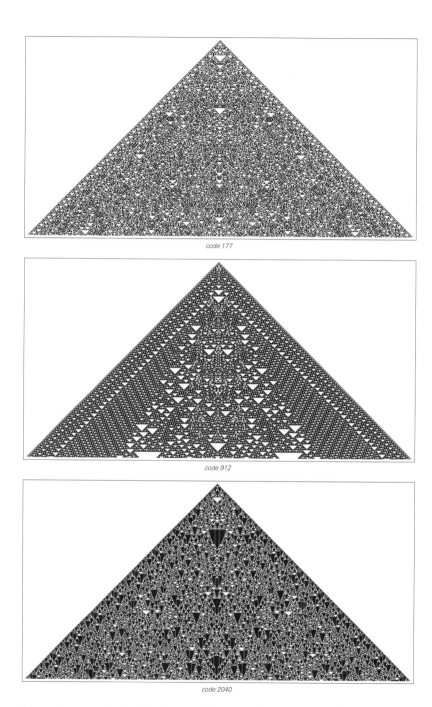

code 177

code 912

code 2040

Examples of three-color totalistic rules that yield patterns with seemingly random features. Three hundred steps of evolution are shown in each case.

In detail, some of the patterns are definitely more complicated than those seen in elementary rules. But at the level of overall behavior, there are no fundamental differences. And in the case of nested patterns even the specific structures seen are usually the same as for elementary rules. Thus, for example, the structure in codes 237 and 948 is the most common, followed by the one in code 1749. The only new structure not already seen in elementary rules is the one in code 420—but this occurs only quite rarely.

About 85% of all three-color totalistic cellular automata produce behavior that is ultimately quite regular. But just as in elementary cellular automata, there are some rules that yield behavior that seems in many respects random. A few examples of this are given on the facing page.

Beyond fairly uniform random behavior, there are also cases similar to elementary rule 110 in which definite structures are produced that interact in complicated ways. The next page gives a few examples. In the first case shown, the pattern becomes repetitive after about 150 steps. In the other two cases, however, it is much less clear what will ultimately happen. The following pages continue these patterns for 3000 steps. But even after this many steps it is still quite unclear what the final behavior will be.

Looking at pictures like these, it is at first difficult to believe that they can be generated just by following very simple underlying cellular automaton rules. And indeed, even if one accepts this, there is still a tendency to assume that somehow what one sees must be a consequence of some very special feature of cellular automata.

As it turns out, complexity is particularly widespread in cellular automata, and for this reason it is fortunate that cellular automata were the very first systems that I originally decided to study.

But as we will see in the remainder of this chapter, the fundamental phenomena that we discovered in the previous chapter are in no way restricted to cellular automata. And although cellular automata remain some of the very best examples, we will see that a vast range of utterly different systems all in the end turn out to exhibit extremely similar types of behavior.

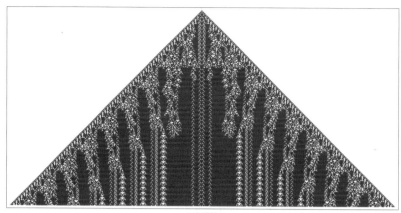

code 1041

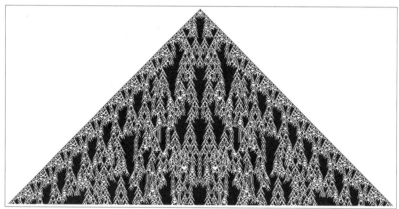

code 1635

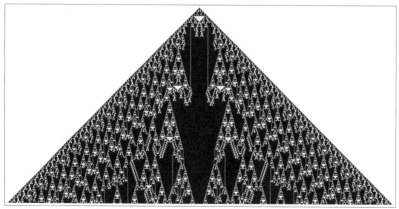

code 2049

Examples of three-color totalistic rules with highly complex behavior showing a mixture of regularity and irregularity. The partitioning into identifiable structures is similar to what we saw in rule 110 on page 32.

code 1635

code 2049

The pictures below show totalistic cellular automata whose overall patterns of growth seem, at least at first, quite complicated. But it turns out that after only about 100 steps, three out of four of these patterns have resolved into simple forms.

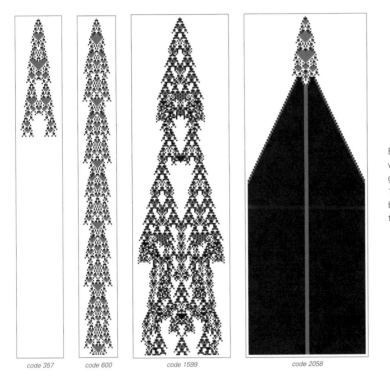

code 357   code 600   code 1599   code 2058

Examples of rules that yield patterns which seem to be on the edge between growth and extinction. For all but code 1599, the fate of these patterns in fact becomes clear after less than 100 steps. A total of 250 steps are shown here.

The one remaining pattern is, however, much more complicated. As shown on the next page, for several thousand steps it simply grows, albeit somewhat irregularly. But then its growth becomes slower. And inside the pattern parts begin to die out. Yet there continue to be occasional bursts of growth. But finally, after a total of 8282 steps, the pattern resolves into 31 simple repetitive structures.

◀ Three thousand steps in the evolution of the last two cellular automata from page 66. Despite the simplicity of their underlying rules, the final patterns produced show immense complexity. In neither case is it clear what the final outcome will be—whether apparent randomness will take over, or whether a simple repetitive form will emerge.

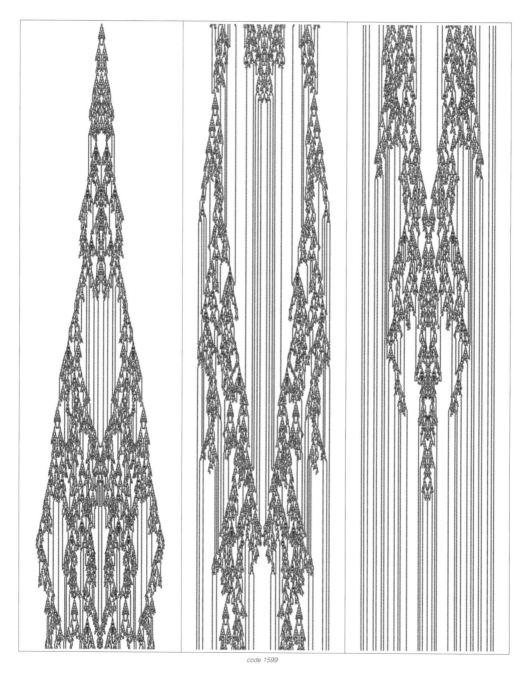

code 1599

Nine thousand steps in the evolution of the three-color totalistic cellular automaton with code number 1599. Starting from a single gray cell, each column corresponds to 3000 steps. The outcome of the evolution finally becomes clear after 8282 steps, when the pattern resolves into 31 simple repetitive structures.

Mobile Automata

One of the basic features of a cellular automaton is that the colors of all the cells it contains are updated in parallel at every step in its evolution.

But how important is this feature in determining the overall behavior that occurs? To address this question, I consider in this section a class of systems that I call "mobile automata".

Mobile automata are similar to cellular automata except that instead of updating all cells in parallel, they have just a single "active cell" that gets updated at each step—and then they have rules that specify how this active cell should move from one step to the next.

The picture below shows an example of a mobile automaton. The active cell is indicated by a black dot. The rule applies only to this active cell. It looks at the color of the active cell and its immediate neighbors, then specifies what the new color of the active cell should be, and whether the active cell should move left or right.

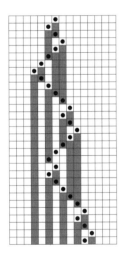

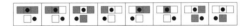

An example of a mobile automaton. Like a cellular automaton, a mobile automaton consists of a line of cells, with each cell having two possible colors. But unlike a cellular automaton, a mobile automaton has only one "active cell" (indicated here by a black dot) at any particular step. The rule for the mobile automaton specifies both how the color of this active cell should be updated, and whether it should move to the left or right. The result of evolution for a larger number of steps with the particular rule shown here is given as example (f) on the next page.

Much as for cellular automata, one can enumerate all possible rules of this kind; it turns out that there are 65,536 of them. The pictures at the top of the next page show typical behavior obtained with such rules. In cases (a) and (b), the active cell remains localized to a small region, and the behavior is very simple and repetitive. Cases (c) through (f) are similar,

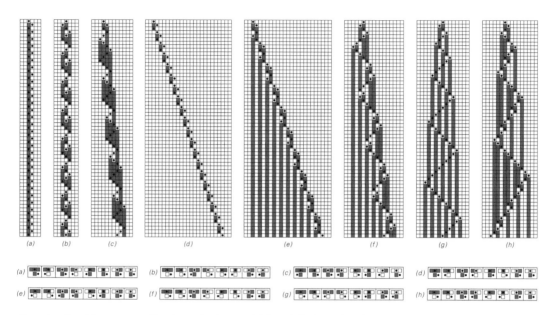

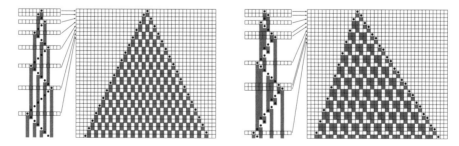

Examples of mobile automata with various rules. In cases (a) through (f) the motion of the active cell is purely repetitive. In cases (g) and (h) it is not. The width of the pattern in these cases after t steps grows roughly like $\sqrt{2t}$.

except that the whole pattern shifts systematically to the right, and in cases (e) and (f) a sequence of stripes is left behind.

But with a total of 218 out of the 65,536 possible rules, one gets somewhat different behavior, as cases (g) and (h) above show. The active cell in these cases does not move in a strictly repetitive way, but instead sweeps backwards and forwards, going progressively further every time.

The overall pattern produced is still quite simple, however. And indeed in the compressed form below, it is purely repetitive.

Compressed versions of the evolution of mobile automata (g) and (h) above, obtained by showing only those steps at which the active cell is further to the left or right than it has ever been before.

Of the 65,536 possible mobile automata with rules of the kind discussed so far it turns out that not a single one shows more complex behavior. So can such behavior then ever occur in mobile automata?

One can extend the set of rules one considers by allowing not only the color of the active cell itself but also the colors of its immediate neighbors to be updated at each step. And with this extension, there are a total of 4,294,967,296 possible rules.

If one samples these rules at random, one finds that more than 99% of them just yield simple repetitive behavior. But once in every few thousand rules, one sees behavior of the kind shown below—that is not purely repetitive, but instead has a kind of nested structure.

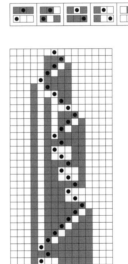

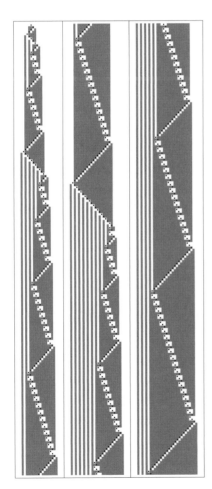

A mobile automaton with slightly more complicated rules that yields a nested pattern. Each column on the left shows 200 steps in the mobile automaton evolution. The compressed form of the pattern is based on a total of 8000 steps.

compressed

The overall pattern is nevertheless still very regular. But after searching through perhaps 50,000 rules, one finally comes across a rule of the kind shown below—in which the compressed pattern exhibits very much the same kind of apparent randomness that we saw in cellular automata like rule 30.

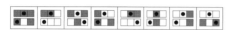

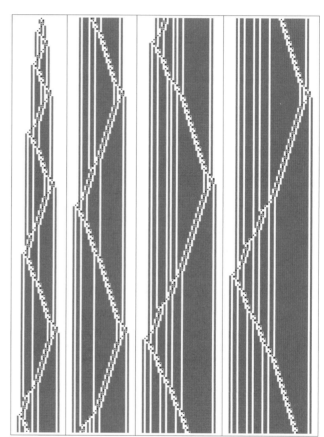

A mobile automaton that yields a pattern with seemingly random features. The motion of the active cell is still quite regular, as the picture on the right shows. But when viewed in compressed form, as below, the overall pattern of colors seems in many respects random. Each column on the right shows 200 steps of evolution; the compressed form below corresponds to 50,000 steps.

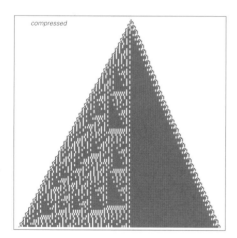

compressed

But even though the final pattern left behind by the active cell in the picture above seems in many respects random, the motion of the active cell itself is still quite regular. So are there mobile automata in which the motion of the active cell is also seemingly random? At first, I believed that there might not be. But after searching through a few million rules, I finally found the example shown on the facing page.

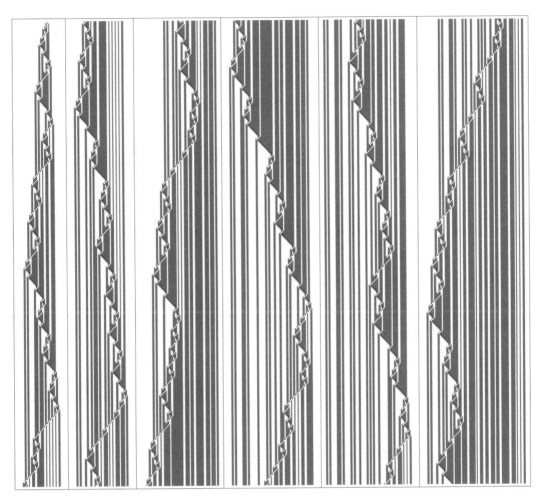

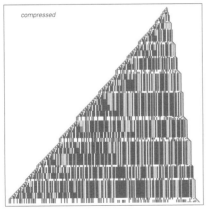

compressed

A mobile automaton in which the position of the active cell moves in a seemingly random way. Each column above shows 400 steps; the compressed form corresponds to 50,000 steps. It took searching through a few million mobile automata to find one with behavior as complex as what we see here.

Despite the fact that mobile automata update only one cell at a time, it is thus still possible for them to produce behavior of great complexity. But while we found that such behavior is quite common in cellular automata, what we have seen in this section indicates that it is rather rare in mobile automata.

One can get some insight into the origin of this difference by studying a class of generalized mobile automata, that in a sense interpolate between ordinary mobile automata and cellular automata.

The basic idea of such generalized mobile automata is to allow more than one cell to be active at a time. And the underlying rule is then typically set up so that under certain circumstances an active cell can split in two, or can disappear entirely.

Thus in the picture below, for example, new active cells end up being created every few steps.

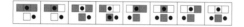

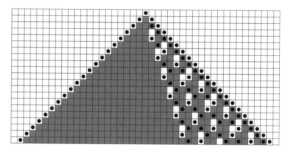

A generalized mobile automaton in which any number of cells can be active at a time. The rule given above is applied to every cell that is active at a particular step. In many cases, the rule specifies just that the active cell should move to the left or right. But in some cases, it specifies that the active cell should split in two, thereby creating an additional active cell.

If one chooses generalized mobile automata at random, most of them will produce simple behavior, as shown in the first few pictures on the facing page. But in a few percent of all cases, the behavior is much more complicated. Often the arrangement of active cells is still quite regular, although sometimes it is not.

But looking at many examples, a certain theme emerges: complex behavior almost never occurs except when large numbers of cells are active at the same time. Indeed there is, it seems, a significant correlation between overall activity and the likelihood of complex behavior. And this is part of why complex behavior is so much more common in cellular automata than in mobile automata.

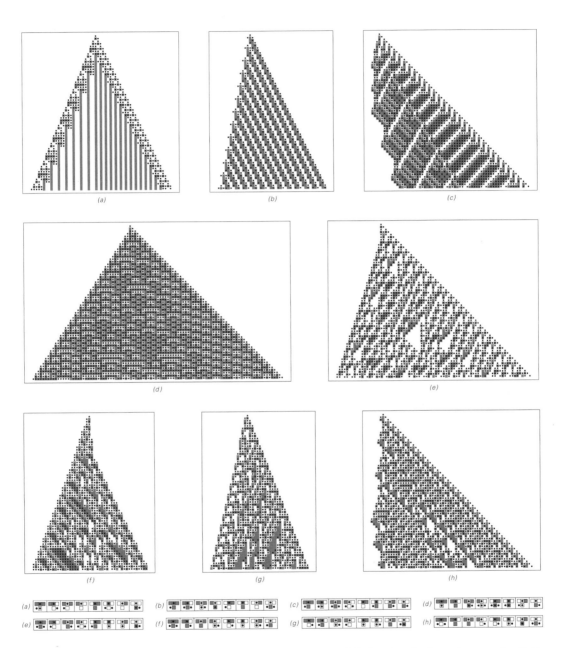

Examples of generalized mobile automata with various rules. In case (a), only a limited number of cells ever become active. But in all the other cases shown active cells proliferate forever. In case (d), almost all cells are active, and the system operates essentially like a cellular automaton. In the remaining cases somewhat complicated patterns of cells are active. Note that unlike in ordinary mobile automata, examples of complex behavior like those shown here are comparatively easy to find.

Turing Machines

In the history of computing, the first widely understood theoretical computer programs ever constructed were based on a class of systems now called Turing machines.

Turing machines are similar to mobile automata in that they consist of a line of cells, known as the "tape", together with a single active cell, known as the "head". But unlike in a mobile automaton, the head in a Turing machine can have several possible states, represented by several possible arrow directions in the picture below.

And in addition, the rule for a Turing machine can depend on the state of the head, and on the color of the cell at the position of the head, but not on the colors of any neighboring cells.

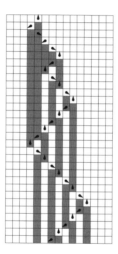

An example of a Turing machine. Like a mobile automaton, the Turing machine has one active cell or "head", but now the head has several possible states, indicated by the directions of the arrows in this picture.

Turing machines are still widely used in theoretical computer science. But in almost all cases, one imagines constructing examples to perform particular tasks, with a huge number of possible states and a huge number of possible colors for each cell.

But in fact there are non-trivial Turing machines that have just two possible states and two possible colors for each cell. The pictures on the facing page show examples of some of the 4096 machines of this kind. Both repetitive and nested behavior are seen to occur, though nothing more complicated is found.

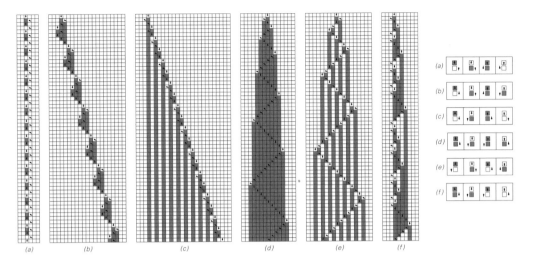

Examples of Turing machines with two possible states for the head. There are a total of 4096 rules of this kind. Repetitive and nested patterns are seen, but nothing more complicated ever occurs.

From our experience with mobile automata, however, we expect that there should be Turing machines that have more complex behavior.

With three states for the head, there are about three million possible Turing machines. But while some of these give behavior that looks slightly more complicated in detail, as in cases (a) and (b) on the next page, all ultimately turn out to yield just repetitive or nested patterns—at least if they are started with all cells white.

With four states, however, more complicated behavior immediately becomes possible. Indeed, in about five out of every million rules of this kind, one gets patterns with features that seem in many respects random, as in the pictures on the next two pages.

So what happens if one allows more than four states for the head? It turns out that there is almost no change in the kind of behavior one sees. Apparent randomness becomes slightly more common, but otherwise the results are essentially the same.

Once again, it seems that there is a threshold for complex behavior—that is reached as soon as one has at least four states. And just as in cellular automata, adding more complexity to the underlying rules does not yield behavior that is ultimately any more complex.

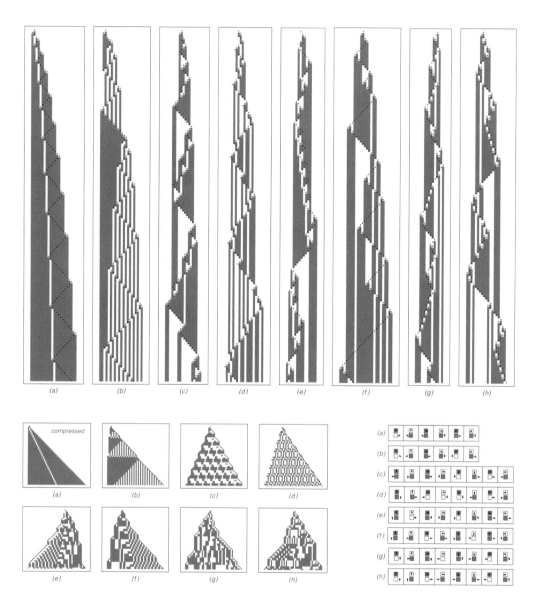

Examples of Turing machines with three and four possible states. With three possible states, only repetitive and nested patterns are ever ultimately produced, at least starting with all cells white. But with four states, more complicated patterns are generated. The top set of pictures show the first 150 steps of evolution according to various different rules, starting with the head in the first state (arrow pointing up), and all cells white. The bottom set of pictures show the evolution in each case in a compressed form. Each of these pictures includes the first 50 steps at which the head is further to the left or right than it has ever been before.

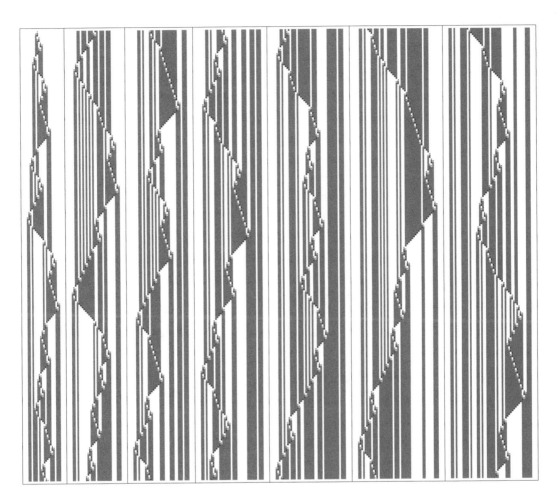

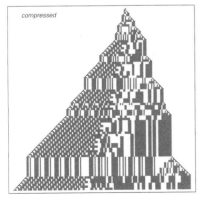

compressed

A Turing machine that exhibits behavior which seems in many respects random. The Turing machine has four possible states for its head, and two possible colors for each cell on its tape. It starts with all cells white, corresponding to a blank tape. Each column above shows 250 steps of evolution; the compressed form on the left corresponds to a total of 20,000 steps.

Substitution Systems

One of the features that cellular automata, mobile automata and Turing machines all have in common is that at the lowest level they consist of a fixed array of cells. And this means that while the colors of these cells can be updated according to a wide range of different possible rules, the underlying number and organization of cells always stays the same.

Substitution systems, however, are set up so that the number of elements can change. In the typical case illustrated below, one has a sequence of elements—each colored say black or white—and at each step each one of these elements is replaced by a new block of elements.

In the simple cases shown, the rules specify that each element of a particular color should be replaced by a fixed block of new elements, independent of the colors of any neighboring elements.

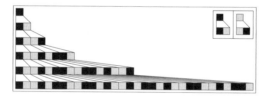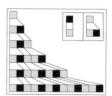

Examples of substitution systems with two possible kinds of elements, in which at every step each kind of element is replaced by a fixed block of new elements. In the first case shown, the total number of elements obtained doubles at every step; in the second case, it follows a Fibonacci sequence, and increases by a factor of roughly $(1 + \sqrt{5})/2 \approx 1.618$ at every step. The two substitution systems shown here correspond to the second and third examples in the pictures on the following two pages.

And with these kinds of rules, the total number of elements typically grows very rapidly, so that pictures like those above quickly become rather unwieldy. But at least for these kinds of rules, one can make clearer pictures by thinking of each step not as replacing every element by a sequence of elements that are drawn the same size, but rather of subdividing each element into several that are drawn smaller.

In the cases on the facing page, I start from a single element represented by a long box going all the way across the picture. Then on successive steps the rules for the substitution system specify how each box should be subdivided into a sequence of shorter and shorter boxes.

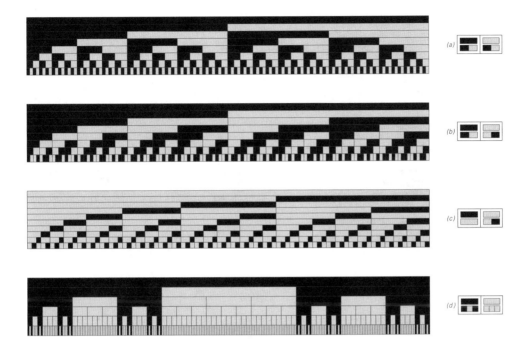

Examples of substitution systems in which every element is drawn as being subdivided into a sequence of new elements at each step. In all cases the overall patterns obtained can be seen to have a very regular nested form. Rule (b) gives the so-called Thue-Morse sequence, which we will encounter many times in this book. Rule (c) is related to the Fibonacci sequence. Rule (d) gives a version of the Cantor set.

The pictures at the top of the next page show a few more examples. And what we see is that in all cases there is obvious regularity in the patterns produced. Indeed, if one looks carefully, one can see that every pattern just consists of a collection of identical nested pieces.

And ultimately this is not surprising. After all, the basic rules for these substitution systems specify that any time an element of a particular color appears it will always get subdivided in the same way.

The nested structure becomes even clearer if one represents elements not as boxes, but instead as branches on a tree. And with this setup the idea is to start from the trunk of the tree, and then at each step to use the rules for the substitution system to determine how every branch should be split into smaller branches.

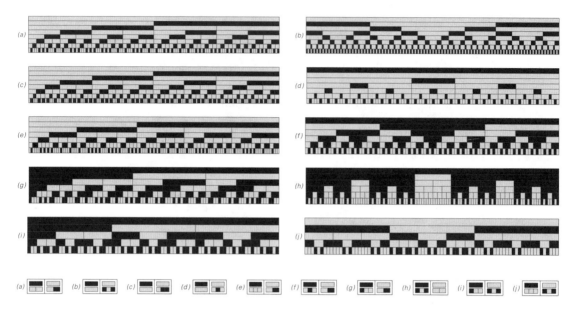

More examples of neighbor-independent substitution systems like those on the previous page. Each rule yields a different sequence of elements, but all of them ultimately have simple nested forms.

Then the point is that because the rules depend only on the color of a particular branch, and not on the colors of any neighboring branches, the subtrees that are generated from all the branches of the same color must have exactly the same structure, as in the pictures below.

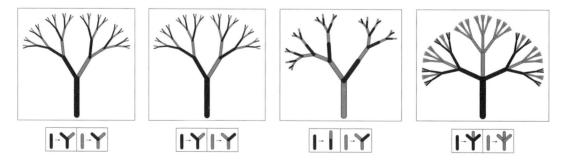

The evolution of the same substitution systems as on the previous page, but now shown in terms of trees. Starting from the trunk at the bottom, the rules specify that at each step every branch of a particular color should split into smaller branches in the same way. The result is that each tree consists of a collection of progressively smaller subtrees with the same structure. On page 400 I will use similar systems to discuss the growth of actual trees and leaves.

To get behavior that is more complicated than simple nesting, it follows therefore that one must consider substitution systems whose rules depend not only on the color of a single element, but also on the color of at least one of its neighbors. The pictures below show examples in which the rules for replacing an element depend not only on its own color, but also on the color of the element immediately to its right.

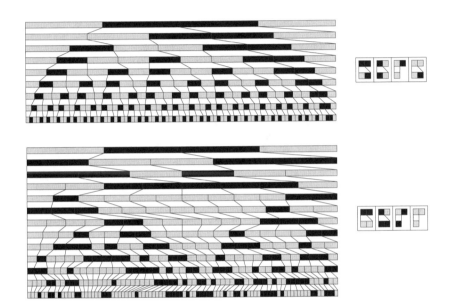

Examples of substitution systems whose rules depend not just on the color of an element itself, but also on the color of the element immediately to its right. Rules of this kind cannot readily be interpreted in terms of simple subdivision of one element into several. And as a result, there is no obvious way to choose what size of box should be used to represent each element in the picture. What I do here is simply to divide the whole width of the picture equally among all elements that appear at each step. Note that on every step the rightmost element is always dropped, since no rule is given for how to replace it.

In the first example, the pattern obtained still has a simple nested structure. But in the second example, the behavior is more complicated, and there is no obvious nested structure.

One feature of both examples, however, is that the total number of elements never decreases from one step to the next. The reason for this is that the basic rules we used specify that every single element should be replaced by at least one new element.

It is, however, also possible to consider substitution systems in which elements can simply disappear. If the rate of such disappearances is too large, then almost any pattern will quickly die out. And if there are too few disappearances, then most patterns will grow very rapidly.

But there is always a small fraction of rules in which the creation and destruction of elements is almost perfectly balanced.

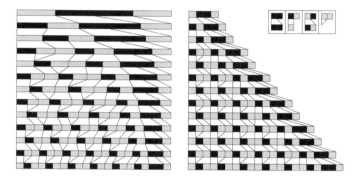

Two views of a substitution system whose rules allow both creation and destruction of elements. In the view on the left, the boxes representing each element are scaled to keep the total width the same, whereas on the right each box has a fixed size, as in our original pictures of substitution systems on page 82. The right-hand view shows that the rates of creation and destruction of elements are balanced closely enough that the total number of elements grows by only a fixed amount at each step.

The picture above shows one example. The number of elements does end up increasing in this particular example, but only by a fixed amount at each step. And with such slow growth, we can again represent each element by a box of the same size, just as in our original pictures of substitution systems on page 82.

When viewed in this way, however, the pattern produced by the substitution system shown above is seen to have a simple repetitive form. And as it turns out, among substitution systems with the same type of rules, all those which yield slow growth also seem to produce only such simple repetitive patterns.

Knowing this, we might conclude that somehow substitution systems just cannot produce the kind of complexity that we have seen in systems like cellular automata. But as with mobile automata and with Turing machines, we would again be wrong. Indeed, as the pictures on the facing page demonstrate, allowing elements to have three or four colors rather than just two immediately makes much more complicated behavior possible.

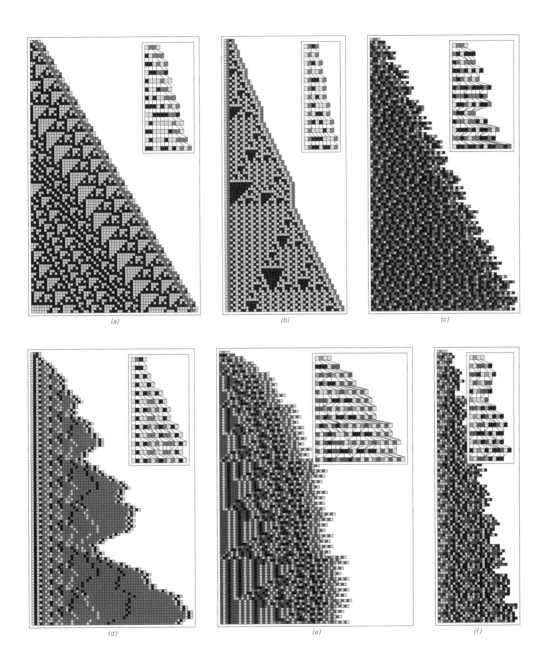

Examples of substitution systems that have three and four possible colors for each element. The particular rules shown are ones that lead to slow growth in the total number of elements. Note that on each line in each picture, only the order of elements is ever significant: as the insets show, a particular element may change its position as a result of the addition or subtraction of elements to its left. Note that the pattern in case (a) does eventually repeat, while the one in case (b) eventually shows a nested structure.

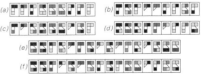

As it turns out, the first substitution system shown works almost exactly like a cellular automaton. Indeed, away from the right-hand edge, all the elements effectively behave as if they were lying on a regular grid, with the color of each element depending only on the previous color of that element and the element immediately to its right.

The second substitution system shown again has patches that exhibit a regular grid structure. But between these patches, there are regions in which elements are created and destroyed. And in the other substitution systems shown, elements are created and destroyed throughout, leaving no trace of any simple grid structure. So in the end the patterns we obtain can look just as random as what we have seen in systems like cellular automata.

Sequential Substitution Systems

None of the systems we have discussed so far in this chapter might at first seem much like computer programs of the kind we typically use in practice. But it turns out that there are for example variants of substitution systems that work essentially just like standard text editors.

The first step in understanding this correspondence is to think of substitution systems as operating not on sequences of colored elements but rather on strings of elements or letters. Thus for example the state of a substitution system at a particular step can be represented by the string ABBBABA, where the A's correspond to white elements and the B's to black ones.

The substitution systems that we discussed in the previous section work by replacing each element in such a string by a new sequence of elements—so that in a sense these systems operate in parallel on all the elements that exist in the string at each step.

But it is also possible to consider sequential substitution systems, in which the idea is instead to scan the string from left to right, looking for a particular sequence of elements, and then to perform a replacement for the first such sequence that is found. And this setup is now directly analogous to the search-and-replace function of a typical text editor.

The picture below shows an example of a sequential substitution system in which the rule specifies simply that the first sequence of the form BA found at each step should be replaced with the sequence ABA.

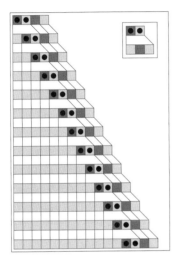

An example of a very simple sequential substitution system. The light squares can be thought of as corresponding to the element A, and the dark squares to the element B. At each step, the rule then specifies that the string which exists at that step should be scanned from left to right, and the first sequence BA that is found should be replaced by ABA. In the picture, the black dots indicate which elements are being replaced at each step. In the case shown, the initial string is BABA. At each step, the rule then has the effect of adding an A inside the string.

The behavior in this case is very simple, with longer and longer strings of the same form being produced at each step. But one can get more complicated behavior if one uses rules that involve more than just one possible replacement. The idea in this case is at each step to scan the string repeatedly, trying successive replacements on successive scans, and stopping as soon as a replacement that can be used is found.

The picture on the next page shows a sequential substitution system with rule {ABA → AAB, A → ABA} involving two possible replacements. Since the sequence ABA occurs in the initial string that is given, the first replacement is used on the first step. But the string BAAB that is produced at the second step does not contain ABA, so now the first replacement cannot be used. Nevertheless, since the string does contain the single element A, the second replacement can still be used.

Despite such alternation between different replacements, however, the final pattern that emerges is very regular. Indeed, if one allows only two possible replacements—and two possible elements—

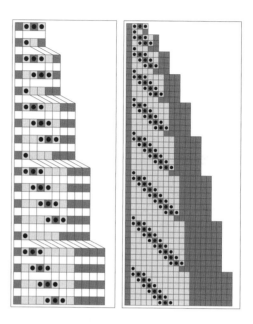

A sequential substitution system whose rule involves two possible replacements. At each step, the whole string is scanned once to try to apply the first replacement, and is then scanned again if necessary to try to apply the second replacement.

then it seems that no rule ever gives behavior that is much more complicated than in the picture above.

And from this one might be led to conclude that sequential substitution systems could never produce behavior of any substantial complexity. But having now seen complexity in many other kinds of systems, one might suspect that it should also be possible in sequential substitution systems.

And it turns out that if one allows more than two possible replacements then one can indeed immediately get more complex behavior. The pictures on the facing page show a few examples. In many cases, fairly regular repetitive or nested patterns are still produced.

But about once in every 10,000 randomly selected rules, rather different behavior is obtained. Indeed, as the picture on the following page demonstrates, patterns can be produced that seem in many respects random, much like patterns we have seen in cellular automata and other systems.

So this leads to the rather remarkable conclusion that just by using the simple operations available even in a very basic text editor, it is still ultimately possible to produce behavior of great complexity.

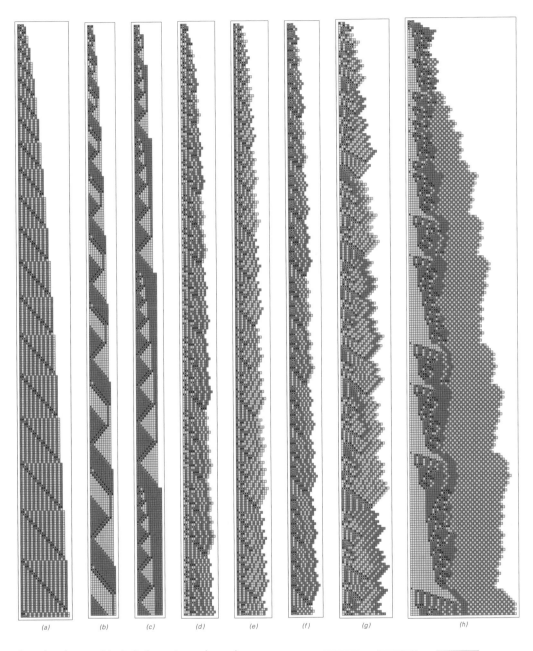

Examples of sequential substitution systems whose rules involve three possible replacements. In all cases, the systems are started from the initial string *BAB*. The black dots indicate the elements that are replaced at each step.

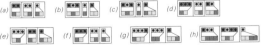

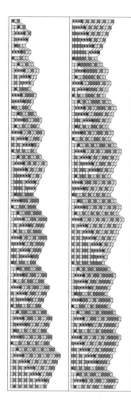

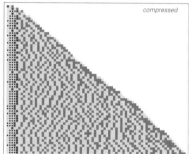

compressed

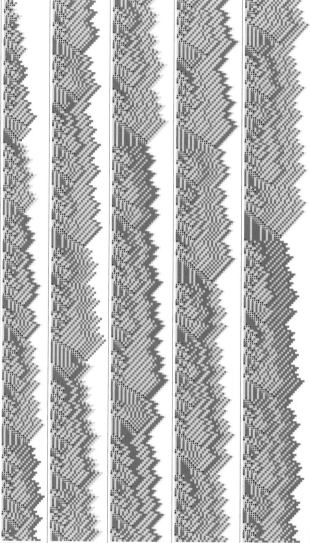

An example of a sequential substitution system that yields apparently random behavior. Each column on the right-hand side shows the evolution of the system for 250 steps. The compressed picture on the left is made by evolving for a million steps, but showing only steps at which the string becomes longer than it has ever been before. (The rule is the same as (g) on the previous page.)

Tag Systems

One of the goals of this chapter is to find out just how simple the underlying structure of a system can be while the system as a whole is still capable of producing complex behavior. And as one example of a class of systems with a particularly simple underlying structure, I consider here what are sometimes known as tag systems.

A tag system consists of a sequence of elements, each colored say black or white. The rules for the system specify that at each step a fixed number of elements should be removed from the beginning of the sequence. And then, depending on the colors of these elements, one of several possible blocks is tagged onto the end of the sequence.

The pictures below show examples of tag systems in which just one element is removed at each step. And already in these systems one sometimes sees behavior that looks somewhat complicated.

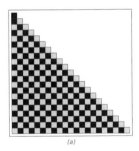
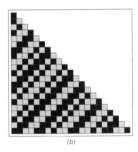
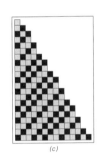
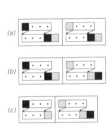

Examples of tag systems in which a single element is removed from the beginning of the sequence at each step, and a new block of elements is added to the end of the sequence according to the rules shown. Because only a single element is removed at each step, the systems effectively just cycle through all elements, replacing each one in turn. And after every complete cycle, the sequences obtained correspond exactly to the sequences produced on successive steps in the first three ordinary neighbor-independent substitution systems shown on page 83.

But in fact it turns out that if only one element is removed at each step, then a tag system always effectively acts just like a slow version of a neighbor-independent substitution system of the kind we discussed on page 83. And as a result, the pattern it produces must ultimately have a simple repetitive or nested form.

If two elements are removed at each step, however, then this is no longer true. And indeed, as the pictures on the next page demonstrate, the behavior that is obtained in this case can often be very complicated.

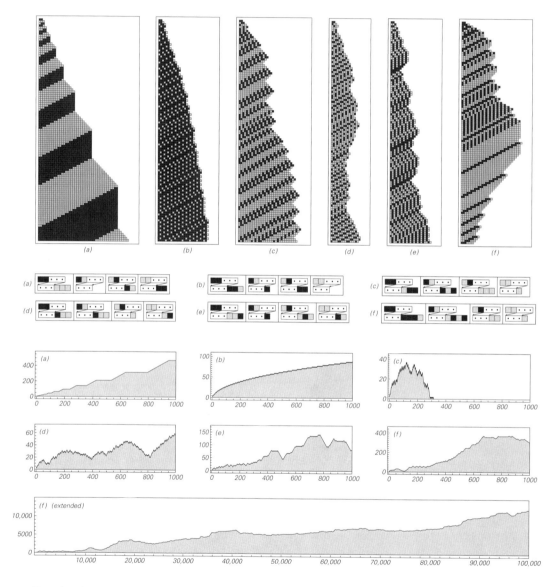

Examples of tag systems in which at each step two elements are removed from the beginning of the sequence and then, based on what these elements are, a specified block of new elements is added to the end of the sequence. (The three dots in the representation of each rule stand for the rest of the elements in the sequence.) The pictures at the top show the first hundred steps in evolution according to various rules starting from a pair of black elements. The plots show the total lengths of the sequences obtained in each case. Note that in case (c), all the elements are eventually removed from the sequence.

Cyclic Tag Systems

The basic operation of the tag systems that we discussed in the previous section is extremely simple. But it turns out that by using a slightly different setup one can construct systems whose operation is in some ways even simpler. In an ordinary tag system, one does not know in advance which of several possible blocks will be added at each step. But the idea of a cyclic tag system is to make the underlying rule already specify exactly what block can be added at each step.

In the simplest case there are two possible blocks, and the rule simply alternates on successive steps between these blocks, adding a block at a particular step when the first element in the sequence at that step is black. The picture below shows an example of how this works.

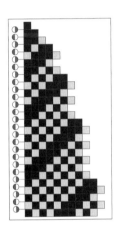 

An example of a cyclic tag system. There are two cases in the rule, and these cases are used on alternate steps, as indicated by the circle icons on the left. In each case a single element is removed from the beginning of the sequence, and then a new block is added at the end whenever the element removed is black. The rule can be summarized just by giving the blocks to be used in each case, as shown below.

rule summary:

The next page shows examples of several cyclic tag systems. In cases (a) and (b) simple behavior is obtained. In case (c) the behavior is slightly more complicated, but if the pattern is viewed in the appropriate way then it turns out to have the same nested form as the third neighbor-independent substitution system shown on page 83.

So what about cases (d) and (e)? In both of these, the sequences obtained at successive steps grow on average progressively longer. But if one looks at the fluctuations in this growth, as in the plots on the next page, then one finds that these fluctuations are in many respects random.

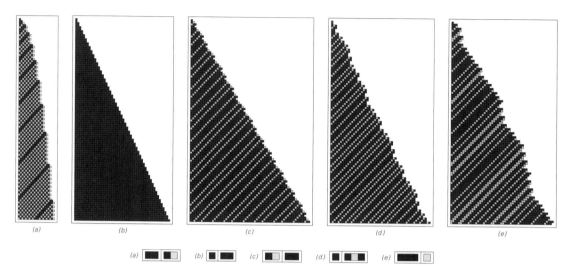

Examples of cyclic tag systems. In each case the initial condition consists of a single black element. In case (c), alternate steps in the leftmost column (which in all cyclic tag systems determines the overall behavior) have the same nested form as the third neighbor-independent substitution system shown on page 83.

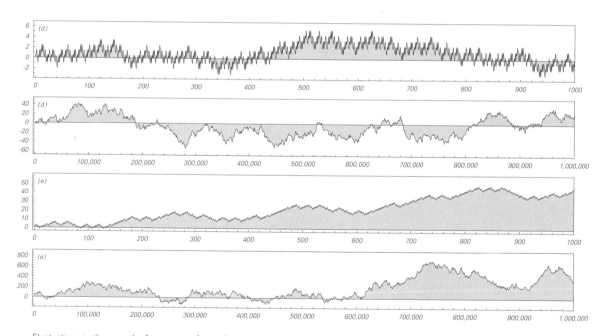

Fluctuations in the growth of sequences for cyclic tag systems (d) and (e) above. The fluctuations are shown with respect to growth at an average rate of half an element per step.

Register Machines

All of the various kinds of systems that we have discussed so far in this chapter can readily be implemented on practical computers. But none of them at an underlying level actually work very much like typical computers. Register machines are however specifically designed to be very simple idealizations of present-day computers.

Under most everyday circumstances, the hardware construction of the computers we use is hidden from us by many layers of software. But at the lowest level, the CPUs of all standard computers have registers that store numbers, and any program we write is ultimately converted into a sequence of simple instructions that specify operations to be performed on these registers.

Most practical computers have quite a few registers, and support perhaps tens of different kinds of instructions. But as a simple idealization one can consider register machines with just two registers—each storing a number of any size—and just two kinds of instructions: "increments" and "decrement-jumps". The rules for such register machines are then idealizations of practical programs, and are taken to consist of fixed sequences of instructions, to be executed in turn.

Increment instructions are set up just to increase by one the number stored in a particular register. Decrement-jump instructions, on the other hand, do two things. First, they decrease by one the number in a particular register. But then, instead of just going on to execute the next instruction in the program, they jump to some specified other point in the program, and begin executing again from there.

Since we assume that the numbers in our registers cannot be negative, however, a register that is already zero cannot be decremented. And decrement-jump instructions are then set up so that if they are applied to a register containing zero, they just do essentially nothing: they leave the register unchanged, and then they go on to execute the next instruction in the program, without jumping anywhere.

This feature of decrement-jump instructions may seem like a detail, but in fact it is crucial—for it is what makes it possible for our register machines to take different paths depending on values in registers through the programs they are given.

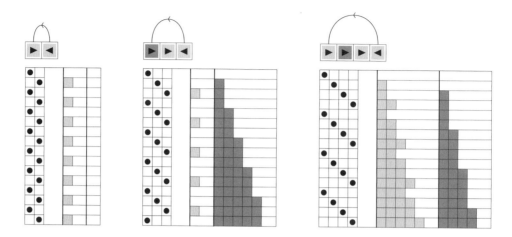

Examples of simple register machines, set up to mimic the low-level operation of practical computers. The machines shown have two registers, whose values on successive steps are given on successive lines down the page. Each machine follows a fixed program given at the top. The program consists of a sequence of increment ▶ and decrement-jump ◀ instructions. Instructions that are shown as light gray boxes refer to the first register; those shown as dark gray boxes refer to the second one. On each line going down the page, the black dot on the left indicates which instruction in the program is being executed at the corresponding step. With the particular programs shown here, each machine just executes successive instructions in turn, jumping to the beginning again when it reaches the end of the program.

And with this setup, the pictures above show three very simple examples of register machines with two registers. The programs for each of the machines are given at the top, with ▶ representing an increment instruction, and ◀ a decrement-jump. The successive steps in the evolution of each machine are shown on successive lines down the page. The instruction being executed is indicated at each step by the position of the dot on the left, while the numbers in each of the two registers are indicated by the gray blocks on the right.

All the register machines shown start by executing the first instruction in their programs. And with the particular programs used here, the machines are then set up just to execute all the other instructions in their programs in turn, jumping back to the beginning of their programs whenever they reach the end.

Both registers in each machine are initially zero. And in the first machine, the first register alternates between 0 and 1, while the second remains zero. In the second machine, however, the first register again alternates between 0 and 1, but the second register progressively grows. And finally, in the third machine both registers grow.

But in all these three examples, the overall behavior is essentially repetitive. And indeed it turns out that among the 10,552 possible register machines with programs that are four or fewer instructions long, not a single one exhibits more complicated behavior.

However, with five instructions, slightly more complicated behavior becomes possible, as the picture below shows. But even in this example, there is still a highly regular nested structure.

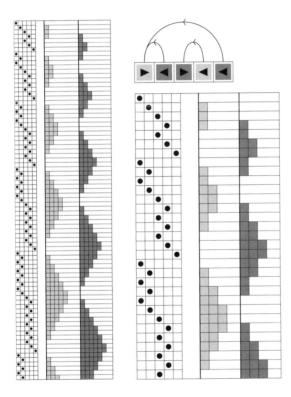

A register machine that shows nested rather than strictly repetitive behavior. The register machine has a program which is five instructions long. It turns out that this program is one of only two (which differ just by interchange of the first and second registers) out of the 248,832 possible programs with five instructions that yield anything other than strictly repetitive behavior.

And it turns out that even with up to seven instructions, none of the 276,224,376 programs that are possible lead to substantially more complicated behavior. But with eight instructions, 126 out of the 11,019,960,576 possible programs finally do show more complicated behavior. The next page gives an example.

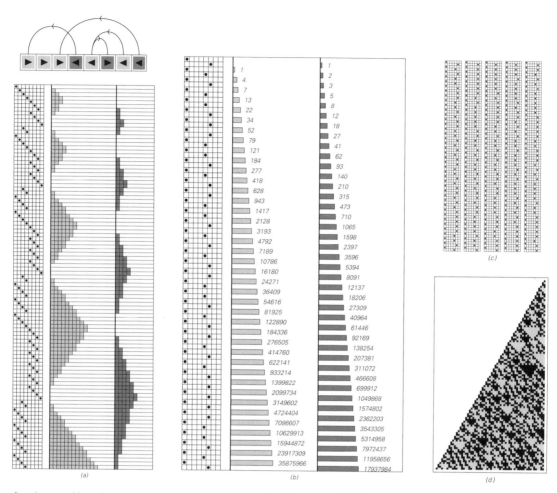

A register machine whose behavior seems in some ways random. The program for this register machine is eight instructions long. Testing all 11,019,960,576 possible programs of length eight revealed just this and 125 similar cases of complex behavior. Part (b) shows the evolution in compressed form, with only those steps included at which either of the registers has just decreased to zero. The values of the nonzero registers are shown using a logarithmic scale. Part (c) shows the instructions that are executed for the first 400 times that one of the registers is decreased to zero. Finally, part (d) gives the successive values attained by the second register at steps where the first register has just decreased to zero. These values are given here as binary digit sequences. As discussed on page 122, the values can in fact be obtained by a simple arithmetic rule, without explicitly following each step in the evolution of the register machine. If one value is n, then the next value is $3n/2$ if n is even, and $(3n + 1)/2$ if n is odd. The initial condition is $n = 1$.

Looking just at the ordinary evolution labelled (a), however, the system might still appear to have quite simple and regular behavior. But a closer examination turns out to reveal irregularities. Part (b) of the picture shows a version of the evolution compressed to include only those steps at which one of the two registers has just decreased to zero. And in this picture one immediately sees some apparently random variation in the instructions that are executed.

Part (c) of the picture then shows which instructions are executed for the first 400 times one of the registers has just decreased to zero. And part (d) finally shows the base 2 digits of the successive values attained by the second register when the first register has just decreased to zero. The results appear to show considerable randomness.

So even though it may not be as obvious as in some of the other systems we have studied, the simple register machine on the facing page can still generate complex and seemingly quite random behavior.

So what about more complicated register machines?

An obvious possibility is to allow more than two registers. But it turns out that very little is normally gained by doing this. With three registers, for example, seemingly random behavior can be obtained with a program that is seven rather than eight instructions long. But the actual behavior of the program is almost indistinguishable from what we have already seen with two registers.

Another way to set up more complicated register machines is to extend the kinds of underlying instructions one allows. One can for example introduce instructions that refer to two registers at a time, adding, subtracting or comparing their contents. But it turns out that the presence of instructions like these rarely seems to have much effect on either the form of complex behavior that can occur, or how common it is.

Yet particularly when such extended instruction sets are used, register machines can provide fairly accurate idealizations of the low-level operations of real computers. And as a result, programs for register machines are often very much like programs written in actual low-level computer languages such as C, BASIC, Java or assembler.

In a typical case, each variable in such a program simply corresponds to one of the registers in the register machine, with no arrays or pointers being allowed. And with this correspondence, our general results on register machines can also be expected to apply to simple programs written in actual low-level computer languages.

Practical details make it somewhat difficult to do systematic experiments on such programs. But the experiments I have carried out do suggest that, just as with simple register machines, searching through many millions of short programs typically yields at least a few that exhibit complex and seemingly random behavior.

Symbolic Systems

Register machines provide simple idealizations of typical low-level computer languages. But what about *Mathematica*? How can one set up a simple idealization of the transformations on symbolic expressions that *Mathematica* does? One approach suggested by the idea of combinators from the 1920s is to consider expressions with forms such as $e[e[e][e]][e][e]$ and then to make transformations on these by repeatedly applying rules such as $e[x\_][y\_] \to x[x[y]]$, where $x\_$ and $y\_$ stand for any expression.

The picture below shows an example of this. At each step the transformation is done by scanning once from left to right, and applying the rule wherever possible without overlapping.

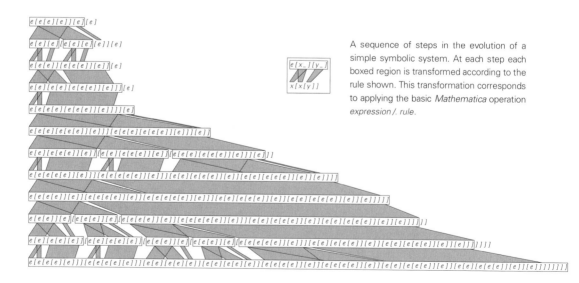

A sequence of steps in the evolution of a simple symbolic system. At each step each boxed region is transformed according to the rule shown. This transformation corresponds to applying the basic *Mathematica* operation *expression /. rule*.

The structure of expressions like those on the facing page is determined just by their sequence of opening and closing brackets. And representing these brackets by dark and light squares respectively, the picture below shows the overall pattern of behavior generated.

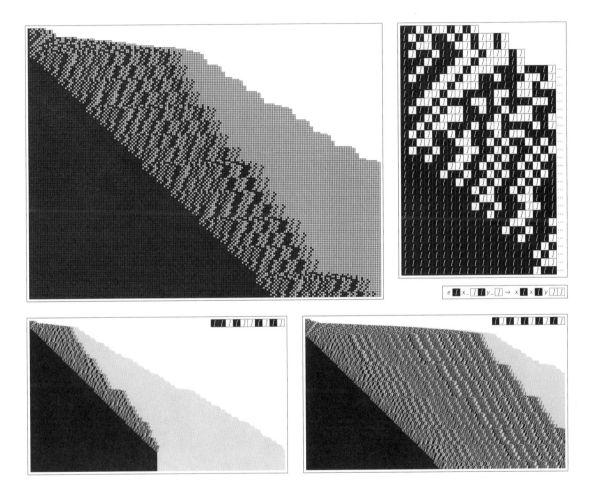

More steps in the evolution on the previous page, with opening brackets represented by dark squares and closing brackets by light ones. In each case configurations wider than the picture are cut off on the right. For the initial condition from the previous page, the system evolves after 264 steps to a fixed configuration involving 256 opening brackets followed by 256 closing brackets. For the initial condition on the bottom right, the system again evolves to a fixed configuration, but now this takes 65,555 steps, and the configuration involves 65,536 opening and closing brackets. Note that the evolution rules are highly non-local, and are rather unlike those, say, in a cellular automaton. It turns out that this particular system always evolves to a fixed configuration, but for initial conditions of size n can take roughly n iterated powers of 2 (or $2^{2^{2}}$) to do so.

With the particular rule shown, the behavior always eventually stabilizes—though sometimes only after an astronomically long time.

But it is quite possible to find symbolic systems where this does not happen, as illustrated in the pictures below. Sometimes the behavior that is generated in such systems has a simple repetitive or nested form. But often—just as in so many other kinds of systems—the behavior is instead complex and seemingly quite random.

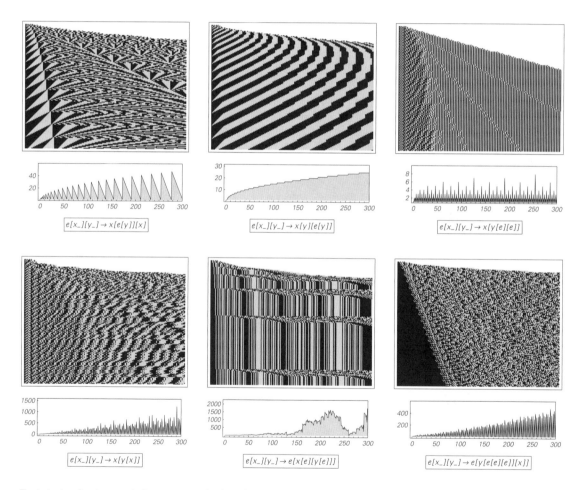

The behavior of various symbolic systems starting from the initial condition $e[e[e][e]][e][e]$. The plots at the bottom show the difference in size of the expressions obtained on successive steps.

Some Conclusions

In the chapter before this one, we discovered the remarkable fact that even though their underlying rules are extremely simple, certain cellular automata can nevertheless produce behavior of great complexity.

Yet at first, this seems so surprising and so outside our normal experience that we may tend to assume that it must be a consequence of some rare and special feature of cellular automata, and must not occur in other kinds of systems.

For it is certainly true that cellular automata have many special features. All their elements, for example, are always arranged in a rigid array, and are always updated in parallel at each step. And one might think that features like these could be crucial in making it possible to produce complex behavior from simple underlying rules.

But from our study of substitution systems earlier in this chapter we know, for example, that in fact it is not necessary to have elements that are arranged in a rigid array. And from studying mobile automata, we know that updating in parallel is also not critical.

Indeed, I specifically chose the sequence of systems in this chapter to see what would happen when each of the various special features of cellular automata were taken away. And the remarkable conclusion is that in the end none of these features actually matter much at all. For every single type of system in this chapter has ultimately proved capable of producing very much the same kind of complexity that we saw in cellular automata.

So this suggests that in fact the phenomenon of complexity is quite universal—and quite independent of the details of particular systems.

But when in general does complexity occur?

The examples in this chapter suggest that if the rules for a particular system are sufficiently simple, then the system will only ever exhibit purely repetitive behavior. If the rules are slightly more complicated, then nesting will also often appear. But to get complexity in the overall behavior of a system one needs to go beyond some threshold in the complexity of its underlying rules.

The remarkable discovery that we have made, however, is that this threshold is typically extremely low. And indeed in the course of this chapter we have seen that in every single one of the general kinds of systems that we have discussed, it ultimately takes only very simple rules to produce behavior of great complexity.

One might nevertheless have thought that if one were to increase the complexity of the rules, then the behavior one would get would also become correspondingly more complex. But as the pictures on the facing page illustrate, this is not typically what happens.

Instead, once the threshold for complex behavior has been reached, what one usually finds is that adding complexity to the underlying rules does not lead to any perceptible increase at all in the overall complexity of the behavior that is produced.

The crucial ingredients that are needed for complex behavior are, it seems, already present in systems with very simple rules, and as a result, nothing fundamentally new typically happens when the rules are made more complex. Indeed, as the picture on the facing page demonstrates, there is often no clear correlation between the complexity of rules and the complexity of behavior they produce. And this means, for example, that even with highly complex rules, very simple behavior still often occurs.

One observation that can be made from the examples in this chapter is that when the behavior of a system does not look complex, it tends to be dominated by either repetition or nesting. And indeed, it seems that the basic themes of repetition, nesting, randomness and localized structures that we already saw in specific cellular automata in the previous chapter are actually very general, and in fact represent the dominant themes in the behavior of a vast range of different systems.

The details of the underlying rules for a specific system can certainly affect the details of the behavior it produces. But what we have seen in this chapter is that at an overall level the typical types of behavior that occur are quite universal, and are almost completely independent of the details of underlying rules.

And this fact has been crucial in my efforts to develop a coherent science of the kind I describe in this book. For it is what implies that

Examples of cellular automata with rules of varying complexity. The rules used are of the so-called totalistic type described on page 60. With two possible colors, just 4 cases need to be specified in such rules, and there are 16 possible rules in all. But as the number of colors increases, the rules rapidly become more complex. With three colors, there are 7 cases to be specified, and 2187 possible rules; with five colors, there are 13 cases to be specified, and 1,220,703,125 possible rules. But even though the underlying rules increase rapidly in complexity, the overall forms of behavior that we see do not change much. With two colors, it turns out that no totalistic rules yield anything other than repetitive or nested behavior. But as soon as three colors are allowed, much more complex behavior is immediately possible. Allowing four or more colors, however, does not further increase the complexity of the behavior, and, as the picture shows, even with five colors, simple repetitive and nested behavior can still occur.

there are general principles that govern the behavior of a wide range of systems, independent of the precise details of each system.

And it is this that means that even if we do not know all the details of what is inside some specific system in nature, we can still potentially make fundamental statements about its overall behavior. Indeed, in most cases, the important features of this behavior will actually turn out to be ones that we have already seen with the various kinds of very simple rules that we have discussed in this chapter.

How the Discoveries in This Chapter Were Made

This chapter—and the last—have described a series of surprising discoveries that I have made about what simple programs typically do. And in making these discoveries I have ended up developing a somewhat new methodology—that I expect will be central to almost any fundamental investigation in the new kind of science that I describe in this book.

Traditional mathematics and the existing theoretical sciences would have suggested using a basic methodology in which one starts from whatever behavior one wants to study, then tries to construct examples that show this behavior. But I am sure that had I used this approach, I would not have got very far. For I would have looked only for types of behavior that I already believed might exist. And in studying cellular automata, this would for example probably have meant that I would only have looked for repetition and nesting.

But what allowed me to discover much more was that I used instead a methodology fundamentally based on doing computer experiments.

In a traditional scientific experiment, one sets up a system in nature and then watches to see how it behaves. And in much the same way, one can set up a program on a computer and then watch how it behaves. And the great advantage of such an experimental approach is that it does not require one to know in advance exactly what kinds of behavior can occur. And this is what makes it possible to discover genuinely new phenomena that one did not expect.

Experience in the traditional experimental sciences might suggest, however, that experiments are somehow always fundamentally imprecise.

For when one deals with systems in nature it is normally impossible to set up or measure them with perfect precision—and indeed it can be a challenge even to make a traditional experiment be at all repeatable.

But for the kinds of computer experiments I do in this book, there is no such issue. For in almost all cases they involve programs whose rules and initial conditions can be specified with perfect precision—so that they work exactly the same whenever and wherever they are run.

In many ways these kinds of computer experiments thus manage to combine the best of both theoretical and experimental approaches to science. For their results have the kind of precision and clarity that one expects of theoretical or mathematical statements. Yet these results can nevertheless be found purely by making observations.

Yet as with all types of experiments it requires considerable skill and judgement to know how to set up a computer experiment that will yield meaningful results. And indeed, over the past twenty years or so my own methodology for doing such experiments has become vastly better.

Over and over again the single most important principle that I have learned is that the best computer experiments are ones that are as simple and straightforward as possible. And this principle applies both to the structure of the actual systems one studies—and to the procedures that one uses for studying them.

At some level the principle of looking at systems with the simplest possible structure can be viewed as an abstract aesthetic one. But it turns out also to have some very concrete consequences.

For a start, the simpler a structure is, the more likely it is that it will show up in a wide diversity of different places. And this means that by studying systems with the simplest possible structure one will tend to get results that have the broadest and most fundamental significance.

In addition, looking at systems with simpler underlying structures gives one a better chance of being able to tell what is really responsible for any phenomenon one sees—for there are fewer features that have been put into the system and that could lead one astray.

At a purely practical level, there is also an advantage to studying systems with simpler structures; for these systems are usually easier to implement on a computer, and can thus typically be investigated more extensively with given computational resources.

But an obvious issue with saying that one should study systems with the simplest possible structure is that such systems might just not be capable of exhibiting the kinds of behavior that one might consider interesting—or that actually occurs in nature.

And in fact, intuition from traditional science and mathematics has always tended to suggest that unless one adds all sorts of complications, most systems will never be able to exhibit any very relevant behavior. But the results so far in this book have shown that such intuition is far from correct, and that in reality even systems with extremely simple rules can give rise to behavior of great complexity.

The consequences of this fact for computer experiments are quite profound. For it implies that there is never an immediate reason to go beyond studying systems with rather simple underlying rules. But to absorb this point is not an easy matter. And indeed, in my experience the single most common mistake in doing computer experiments is to look at systems that are vastly more complicated than is necessary.

Typically the reason this happens is that one just cannot imagine any way in which a simpler system could exhibit interesting behavior. And so one decides to look at a more complicated system—usually with features specifically inserted to produce some specific form of behavior.

Much later one may go back and look at the simpler system again. And this is often a humbling experience, for it is common to find that the system does in fact manage to produce interesting behavior— but just in a way that one was not imaginative enough to guess.

So having seen this many times I now always try to follow the principle that one can never start with too simple a system. For at worst, one will just establish a lower limit on what is needed for interesting behavior to occur. But much more often, one will instead discover behavior that one never thought was possible.

It should however be emphasized that even in an experiment it is never entirely straightforward to discover phenomena one did not expect. For in setting up the experiment, one inevitably has to make assumptions about the kinds of behavior that can occur. And if it turns out that there is behavior which does not happen to fit in with these assumptions, then typically the experiment will fail to notice it.

In my experience, however, the way to have the best chance of discovering new phenomena in a computer experiment is to make the design of the experiment as simple and direct as possible. It is usually much better, for example, to do a mindless search of a large number of possible cases than to do a carefully crafted search of a smaller number. For in narrowing the search one inevitably makes assumptions, and these assumptions may end up missing the cases of greatest interest.

Along similar lines, I have always found it much better to look explicitly at the actual behavior of systems, than to work from some kind of summary. For in making a summary one inevitably has to pick out only certain features, and in doing this one can remove or obscure the most interesting effects.

But one of the problems with very direct experiments is that they often generate huge amounts of raw data. Yet what I have typically found is that if one manages to present this data in the form of pictures then it effectively becomes possible to analyze very quickly just with one's eyes. And indeed, in my experience it is typically much easier to recognize unexpected phenomena in this way than by using any kind of automated procedure for data analysis.

It was in a certain sense lucky that one-dimensional cellular automata were the first examples of simple programs that I investigated. For it so happens that in these systems one can usually get a good idea of overall behavior just by looking at an array of perhaps 10,000 cells—which can easily be displayed in few square inches.

And since several of the 256 elementary cellular automaton rules already generate great complexity, just studying a couple of pages of pictures like the ones at the beginning of this chapter should in principle have allowed one to discover the basic phenomenon of complexity in cellular automata.

But in fact I did not make this discovery in such a straightforward way. I had the idea of looking at pictures of cellular automaton evolution at the very beginning. But the technological difficulty of producing these pictures made me want to reduce their number as much as possible. And so at first I looked only at the 32 rules which had left-right symmetry and made blank backgrounds stay unchanged.

Among these rules I found examples of repetition and nesting. And with random initial conditions, I found more complicated behavior. But since I did not expect that any complicated behavior would be possible with simple initial conditions, I did not try looking at other rules in an attempt to find it. Nevertheless, as it happens, the first paper that I published about cellular automata—in 1983—did in fact include a picture of rule 30 from page 27, as an example of a non-symmetric rule. But the picture showed only 20 steps of evolution, and at the time I did not look carefully at it, and certainly did not appreciate its significance.

For several years, I did progressively more sophisticated computer experiments on cellular automata, and in the process I managed to elucidate many of their properties. But finally, when technology had advanced to the point where it became almost trivial for me to do so, I went back and generated some straightforward pages of pictures of all 256 elementary rules evolving from simple initial conditions. And it was upon seeing these pictures that I finally began to appreciate the remarkable phenomenon that occurs in systems like rule 30.

Seven years later, after I had absorbed some basic intuition from looking at cellular automata like rule 30, I resolved to find out whether similar phenomena also occurred in other kinds of systems. And the first such systems that I investigated were mobile automata.

Mobile automata in a sense evolve very slowly relative to cellular automata, so to make more efficient pictures I came up with a scheme for showing their evolution in compressed form. I then started off by generating pictures of the first hundred, then the first thousand, then the first ten thousand, mobile automata. But in all of these pictures I found nothing beyond repetitive and nested behavior.

Yet being convinced that more complicated behavior must be possible, I decided to persist, and so I wrote a program that would automatically search through large numbers of mobile automata. I set up various criteria for the search, based on how I expected mobile automata could behave. And quite soon, I had made the program search a million mobile automata, then ten million.

But still I found nothing.

So then I went back and started looking by eye at mobile automata with large numbers of randomly chosen rules. And after some time what I realized was that with the compression scheme I was using there could be mobile automata that would be discarded according to my search criteria, but which nevertheless still had interesting behavior. And within an hour of modifying my search program to account for this, I found the example shown on page 74.

Yet even after this, there were still many assumptions implicit in my search program. And it took some time longer to identify and remove them. But having done so, it was then rather straightforward to find the example shown on page 75.

A somewhat similar pattern has been repeated for most of the other systems described in this chapter. The main challenge was always to avoid assumptions and set up experiments that were simple and direct enough that they did not miss important new phenomena.

In many cases it took a large number of iterations to work out the right experiments to do. And had it not been for the ease with which I could set up new experiments using *Mathematica*, it is likely that I would never have gotten very far in investigating most of the systems discussed in this chapter. But in the end, after running programs for a total of several years of computer time—corresponding to more than a million billion logical operations—and creating the equivalent of tens of thousands of pages of pictures, I was finally able to find all of the various examples shown in this chapter and the ones that follow.

4

Systems Based on Numbers

The Notion of Numbers

Much of science has in the past ultimately been concerned with trying to find ways to describe natural systems in terms of numbers.

Yet so far in this book I have said almost nothing about numbers. The purpose of this chapter, however, is to investigate a range of systems that are based on numbers, and to see how their behavior compares with what we have found in other kinds of systems.

The main reason that systems based on numbers have been so popular in traditional science is that so much mathematics has been developed for dealing with them. Indeed, there are certain kinds of systems based on numbers whose behavior has been analyzed almost completely using mathematical methods such as calculus.

Inevitably, however, when such complete analysis is possible, the final behavior that is found is fairly simple.

So can systems that are based on numbers ever in fact yield complex behavior? Looking at most textbooks of science and mathematics, one might well conclude that they cannot. But what one must realize is that the systems discussed in these textbooks are usually ones that are specifically chosen to be amenable to fairly complete analysis, and whose behavior is therefore necessarily quite simple.

And indeed, as we shall see in this chapter, if one ignores the need for analysis and instead just looks at the results of computer experiments, then one quickly finds that even rather simple systems based on numbers can lead to highly complex behavior.

But what is the origin of this complexity? And how does it relate to the complexity we have seen in systems like cellular automata?

One might think that with all the mathematics developed for studying systems based on numbers it would be easy to answer these kinds of questions. But in fact traditional mathematics seems for the most part to lead to more confusion than help.

One basic problem is that numbers are handled very differently in traditional mathematics from the way they are handled in computers and computer programs. For in a sense, traditional mathematics makes a fundamental idealization: it assumes that numbers are elementary objects whose only relevant attribute is their size. But in a computer, numbers are not elementary objects. Instead, they must be represented explicitly, typically by giving a sequence of digits.

The idea of representing a number by a sequence of digits is familiar from everyday life: indeed, our standard way of writing numbers corresponds exactly to giving their digit sequences in base 10. What base 10 means is that for each digit there are 10 possible choices:

Representations of the number 3829 in various bases. The most familiar case is base 10, where starting from the right successive digits correspond to units, tens, hundreds and so on. In base 10, there are 10 possible digits: 0 through 9. In other bases, there are a different number of possible digits. In base 2, as used in practical computers, there are just two possible digits: 0 and 1. And in this base, successive digits starting from the right have coefficients 1, 2, $4 = 2 \times 2$, $8 = 2 \times 2 \times 2$, etc.

$3829 = 3 \times 1000 + 8 \times 100 + 2 \times 10 + 9 \times 1$

| 3 | 8 | 2 | 9 | (base 10) |

$3829 = 5 \times 729 + 2 \times 81 + 2 \times 9 + 4 \times 1$

| 5 | 2 | 2 | 4 | (base 9) |

$3829 = 7 \times 512 + 3 \times 64 + 6 \times 8 + 5 \times 1$

| 7 | 3 | 6 | 5 | (base 8) |

$3829 = 1 \times 2401 + 4 \times 343 + 1 \times 49 + 1 \times 7 + 0 \times 1$

| 1 | 4 | 1 | 1 | 0 | (base 7) |

$3829 = 2 \times 1296 + 5 \times 216 + 4 \times 36 + 2 \times 6 + 1 \times 1$

| 2 | 5 | 4 | 2 | 1 | (base 6) |

$3829 = 1 \times 3125 + 1 \times 625 + 0 \times 125 + 3 \times 25 + 0 \times 5 + 4 \times 1$

| 1 | 1 | 0 | 3 | 0 | 4 | (base 5) |

$3829 = 3 \times 1024 + 2 \times 256 + 3 \times 64 + 3 \times 16 + 1 \times 4 + 1 \times 1$

| 3 | 2 | 3 | 3 | 1 | 1 | (base 4) |

$3829 = 1 \times 2187 + 2 \times 729 + 0 \times 243 + 2 \times 81 + 0 \times 27 + 2 \times 9 + 1 \times 3 + 1 \times 1$

| 1 | 2 | 0 | 2 | 0 | 2 | 1 | 1 | (base 3) |

$3829 = 1 \times 2048 + 1 \times 1024 + 1 \times 512 + 0 \times 256 + 1 \times 128 + 1 \times 64 + 1 \times 32 + 1 \times 16 + 0 \times 8 + 1 \times 4 + 0 \times 2 + 1 \times 1$

| 1 | 1 | 1 | 0 | 1 | 1 | 1 | 1 | 0 | 1 | 0 | 1 | (base 2) |

0 through 9. But as the picture at the bottom of the facing page shows, one can equally well use other bases. And in practical computers, for example, base 2 is almost always what is used.

So what this means is that in a computer numbers are represented by sequences of 0's and 1's, much like sequences of white and black cells in systems like cellular automata. And operations on numbers then correspond to ways of updating sequences of 0's and 1's.

In traditional mathematics, the details of how operations performed on numbers affect sequences of digits are usually considered quite irrelevant. But what we will find in this chapter is that precisely by looking at such details, we will be able to see more clearly how complexity develops in systems based on numbers.

In many cases, the behavior we find looks remarkably similar to what we saw in the previous chapter. Indeed, in the end, despite some confusing suggestions from traditional mathematics, we will discover that the general behavior of systems based on numbers is very similar to the general behavior of simple programs that we have already discussed.

Elementary Arithmetic

The operations of elementary arithmetic are so simple that it seems impossible that they could ever lead to behavior of any great complexity. But what we will find in this section is that in fact they can.

To begin, consider what is perhaps the simplest conceivable arithmetic process: start with the number 1 and then just progressively add 1 at each of a sequence of steps.

The result of this process is to generate the successive numbers 1, 2, 3, 4, 5, 6, 7, 8, … The sizes of these numbers obviously form a very simple progression.

But if one looks not at these overall sizes, but rather at digit sequences, then what one sees is considerably more complicated. And in fact, as the picture on the right demonstrates, these successive digit sequences form a pattern that shows an intricate nested structure.

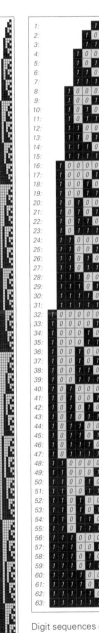

Digit sequences of successive numbers written in base 2. The overall pattern has an intricate nested form.

The pictures below show what happens if one adds a number other than 1 at each step. Near the right-hand edge, each pattern is somewhat different. But at an overall level, all the patterns have exactly the same basic nested structure.

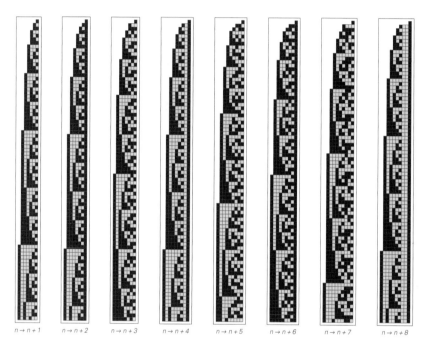

| $n \to n+1$ | $n \to n+2$ | $n \to n+3$ | $n \to n+4$ | $n \to n+5$ | $n \to n+6$ | $n \to n+7$ | $n \to n+8$ |

Digit sequences in base 2 of numbers obtained by starting with 1 and then successively adding a constant at each step. All these patterns ultimately have the same overall nested form.

If instead of addition one uses multiplication, however, then the results one gets can be very different. The first picture at the top of the facing page shows what happens if one starts with 1 and then successively multiplies by 2 at each step.

It turns out that if one represents numbers as digit sequences in base 2, then the operation of multiplying by 2 has a very simple effect: it just shifts the digit sequence one place to the left, adding a 0 digit on the right. And as a result, the overall pattern obtained by successive multiplication by 2 has a very simple form.

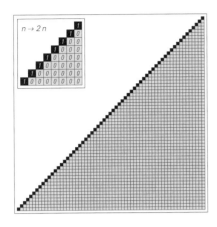 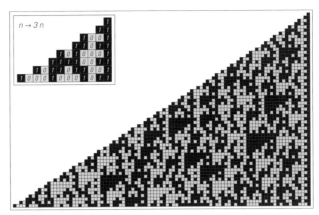

Patterns produced by starting with the number 1, and then successively multiplying by a factor of 2, and a factor of 3. In each case, the digit sequence of the number obtained at each step is shown in base 2. Multiplication by 2 turns out to correspond just to shifting all digits in base 2 one position to the left, so that the overall pattern produced in this case is very simple. But multiplication by 3 yields a much more complicated pattern, as the picture on the right shows. Note that in these pictures the complete numbers obtained at each step correspond respectively to the successive integer powers of 2 and of 3.

But if the multiplication factor at each step is 3, rather than 2, then the pattern obtained is quite different, as the second picture above shows. Indeed, even though the only operation used was just simple multiplication, the final pattern obtained in this case is highly complex.

The picture on the next page shows more steps in the evolution of the system. At a small scale, there are some obvious triangular and other structures, but beyond these the pattern looks essentially random.

So just as in simple programs like cellular automata, it seems that simple systems based on numbers can also yield behavior that is highly complex and apparently random.

But we might imagine that the complexity we see in pictures like the one on the next page must somehow be a consequence of the fact that we are looking at numbers in terms of their digit sequences—and would not occur if we just looked at numbers in terms of their overall size.

A few examples, however, will show that this is not the case.

To begin the first example, consider what happens if one multiplies by $3/2$, or 1.5, at each step. Starting with 1, the successive numbers that one obtains in this way are 1, $3/2 = 1.5$, $9/4 = 2.25$, $27/8 = 3.375$, $81/16 = 5.0625$, $243/32 = 7.59375$, $729/64 = 11.390625$, ...

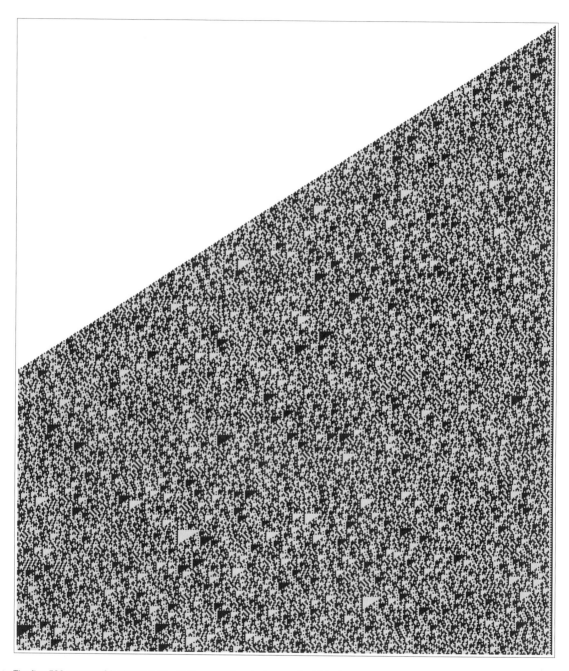

The first 500 powers of 3, shown in base 2. Some small-scale structure is visible, but on a larger scale the pattern seems for all practical purposes random. Note that the pattern shown here has been truncated at the edge of the page on the left, although in fact the whole pattern continues to expand to the left forever with an average slope of $Log[2, 3] \simeq 1.58$.

The picture below shows the digit sequences for these numbers given in base 2. The digits that lie directly below and to the left of the original 1 at the top of the pattern correspond to the whole number part of each successive number (e.g. 3 in 3.375), while the digits that lie to the right correspond to the fractional part (e.g. 0.375 in 3.375).

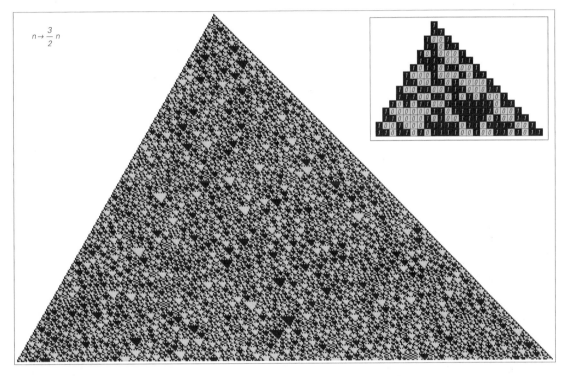

Successive powers of 3/2, shown in base 2. Multiplication by 3/2 can be thought of as multiplication by 3 combined with division by 2. But division by 2 just does the opposite of multiplication by 2, so in base 2 it simply shifts all digits one position to the right. The overall pattern is thus a shifted version of the pattern shown on the facing page.

And instead of looking explicitly at the complete pattern of digits, one can consider just finding the size of the fractional part of each successive number. These sizes are plotted at the top of the next page. And the picture shows that they too exhibit the kind of complexity and apparent randomness that is evident at the level of digits.

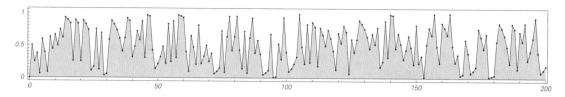

Sizes of the fractional parts of successive powers of 3/2. These sizes are completely independent of what base is used to represent the numbers. Only the dots are significant; the shading and lines between them are just included to make the plot easier to read.

The example just given involves numbers with fractional parts. But it turns out that similar phenomena can also be found in systems that involve only whole numbers.

As a first example, consider a slight variation on the operation of multiplying by 3/2 used above: if the number at a particular step is even (divisible by 2), then simply multiply that number by 3/2, getting a whole number as the result. But if the number is odd, then first add 1— so as to get an even number—and only then multiply by 3/2.

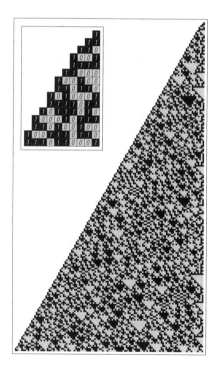

Results of starting with the number 1, then applying the following rule: if the number at a particular step is even, multiply by 3/2; otherwise, add 1, then multiply by 3/2. This procedure yields a succession of whole numbers whose digit sequences in base 2 are shown at the right. The rightmost digits obtained at each step are shown above. The digit is 0 when the number is even and 1 when it is odd, and, as shown, the digits alternate in a seemingly random way. It turns out that the system described here is closely related to one that arose in studying the register machine shown on page 100. The system here can be represented by the rule $n \rightarrow If[EvenQ[n], 3n/2, 3(n+1)/2]$, while the one on page 100 follows the rule $n \rightarrow If[EvenQ[n], 3n/2, (3n+1)/2]$. After the first step these systems give the same sequence of numbers, except for an overall factor of 3.

This procedure is always guaranteed to give a whole number. And starting with 1, the sequence of numbers one gets is 1, 3, 6, 9, 15, 24, 36, 54, 81, 123, 186, 279, 420, 630, 945, 1419, 2130, 3195, 4794, ...

Some of these numbers are even, while some are odd. But as the results at the bottom of the facing page illustrate, the sequence of which numbers are even and which are odd seems to be completely random.

Despite this randomness, however, the overall sizes of the numbers obtained still grow in a rather regular way. But by changing the procedure just slightly, one can get much less regular growth.

As an example, consider the following procedure: if the number obtained at a particular step is even, then multiply this number by $5/2$; otherwise, add 1 and then multiply the result by $1/2$.

If one starts with 1, then this procedure simply gives 1 at every step. And indeed with many starting numbers, the procedure yields purely repetitive behavior. But as the picture below shows, it can also give more complicated behavior.

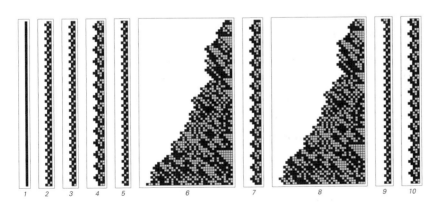

Results of applying the rule $n \rightarrow If[EvenQ[n], 5n/2, (n+1)/2]$, starting with different initial choices of n. In many cases, the behavior obtained is purely repetitive. But in some cases it is not.

Starting for example with the number 6, the sizes of the numbers obtained on successive steps show a generally increasing trend, but there are considerable fluctuations, and these fluctuations seem to be essentially random. Indeed, even after a million steps, when the

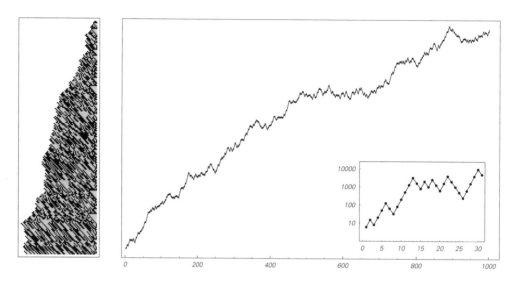

The results of following the same rule as on the previous page, starting from the value 6. Plotted on the right are the overall sizes of the numbers obtained for the first thousand steps. The plot is on a logarithmic scale, so the height of each point is essentially the length of the digit sequence for the number that it represents—or the width of the row on the left.

number obtained has 48,554 (base 10) digits, there is still no sign of repetition or of any other significant regularity.

So even if one just looks at overall sizes of whole numbers it is still possible to get great complexity in systems based on numbers.

But while complexity is visible at this level, it is usually necessary to go to a more detailed level in order to get any real idea of why it occurs. And indeed what we have found in this section is that if one looks at digit sequences, then one sees complex patterns that are remarkably similar to those produced by systems like cellular automata.

The underlying rules for systems like cellular automata are however usually rather different from those for systems based on numbers. The main point is that the rules for cellular automata are always local: the new color of any particular cell depends only on the previous color of that cell and its immediate neighbors. But in systems based on numbers there is usually no such locality.

One knows from hand calculation that even an operation such as addition can lead to "carry" digits which propagate arbitrarily far to the left. And in fact most simple arithmetic operations have the property that a digit which appears at a particular position in their result can depend on digits that were originally far away from it.

But despite fundamental differences like this in underlying rules, the overall behavior produced by systems based on numbers is still very similar to what one sees for example in cellular automata.

So just like for the various kinds of programs that we discussed in the previous chapter, the details of underlying rules again do not seem to have a crucial effect on the kinds of behavior that can occur.

Indeed, despite the lack of locality in their underlying rules, the pictures below and on the pages that follow show that it is even possible to find systems based on numbers that exhibit something like the localized structures that we saw in cellular automata on page 32.

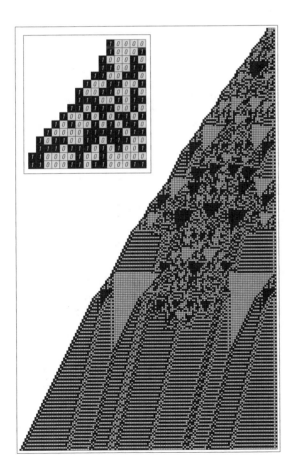

An example of a system defined by the following rule: at each step, take the number obtained at that step and write its base 2 digits in reverse order, then add the resulting number to the original one. For many possible starting numbers, the behavior obtained is very simple. This picture shows what happens when one starts with the number 16. After 180 steps, it turns out that all that survives are a few objects that one can view as localized structures.

A thousand steps in the evolution of a system with the same rule as on the previous page, but now starting with the number 512. Localized structures are visible, but the overall pattern never seems to take on any kind of simple repetitive form.

Continuation of the pattern on the facing page, starting at the millionth step. The picture shows the right-hand edge of the pattern; the complete pattern extends about 700 times the width of the page to the left.

Recursive Sequences

In the previous section, we saw that it is possible to get behavior of considerable complexity just by applying a variety of operations based on simple arithmetic. In this section what I will show is that with the appropriate setup just addition and subtraction turn out to be in a sense the only operations that one needs.

The basic idea is to consider a sequence of numbers in which there is a definite rule for getting the next number in the sequence from previous ones. It is convenient to refer to the first number in each sequence as $f[1]$, the second as $f[2]$, and so on, so that the nth number is denoted $f[n]$. And with this notation, what the rule does is to specify how $f[n]$ should be calculated from previous numbers in the sequence.

In the simplest cases, $f[n]$ depends only on the number immediately before it in the sequence, denoted $f[n-1]$. But it is also possible to set up rules in which $f[n]$ depends not only on $f[n-1]$, but also on $f[n-2]$, as well as on numbers still earlier in the sequence.

The table below gives results obtained with a few specific rules. In all the cases shown, these results are quite simple, consisting of sequences that increase uniformly or fluctuate in a purely repetitive way.

$f[n] = 1 + f[n-1], \; f[1] = 1$

(a)

| 1 | 2 | 3 | 4 | 5 | 6 | 7 | 8 | 9 | 10 | 11 | 12 | 13 | 14 | 15 | 16 | 17 | 18 | 19 | 20 | 21 | 22 | 23 | 24 | 25 | 26 | 27 | 28 | 29 | 30 | 31 | 32 | 33 | 34 | 35 | 36 | 37 | 38 | ... |

$f[n] = 1 - f[n-1], \; f[1] = 1$

(b)

| 1 | 0 | 1 | 0 | 1 | 0 | 1 | 0 | 1 | 0 | 1 | 0 | 1 | 0 | 1 | 0 | 1 | 0 | 1 | 0 | 1 | 0 | 1 | 0 | 1 | 0 | 1 | 0 | 1 | 0 | 1 | 0 | 1 | 0 | 1 | 0 | 1 | 0 | 1 | 0 | 1 | 0 | 1 | 0 | 1 | 0 | 1 | 0 | 1 | 0 | ... |

$f[n] = 2 f[n-1], \; f[1] = 1$

(c)

| 1 | 2 | 4 | 8 | 16 | 32 | 64 | 128 | 256 | 512 | 1024 | 2048 | 4096 | 8192 | 16384 | 32768 | 65536 | 131072 | 262144 | 524288 | 1048576 | 2097152 | ... |

$f[n] = f[n-1] + f[n-2], \; f[1] = 1, \; f[2] = 1$

(d)

| 1 | 1 | 2 | 3 | 5 | 8 | 13 | 21 | 34 | 55 | 89 | 144 | 233 | 377 | 610 | 987 | 1597 | 2584 | 4181 | 6765 | 10946 | 17711 | 28657 | 46368 | 75025 | 121393 | ... |

$f[n] = f[n-1] - f[n-2], \; f[1] = 1, \; f[2] = 1$

(e)

| 1 | 1 | 0 | -1 | -1 | 0 | 1 | 1 | 0 | -1 | -1 | 0 | 1 | 1 | 0 | -1 | -1 | 0 | 1 | 1 | 0 | -1 | -1 | 0 | 1 | 1 | 0 | -1 | -1 | 0 | 1 | 1 | 0 | -1 | -1 | 0 | 1 | 1 | 0 | -1 | -1 | 0 | 1 | 1 | ... |

$f[n] = -f[n-1] + f[n-2], \; f[1] = 1, \; f[2] = 1$

(f)

| 1 | 1 | 0 | 1 | -1 | 2 | -3 | 5 | -8 | 13 | -21 | 34 | -55 | 89 | -144 | 233 | -377 | 610 | -987 | 1597 | -2584 | 4181 | -6765 | 10946 | -17711 | 28657 | -46368 | ... |

Examples of some simple recursive sequences. The nth element in each sequence is denoted $f[n]$, and the rule specifies how this element is determined from previous ones. With all the rules shown here, successive elements either increase smoothly or fluctuate in a purely repetitive way. Sequence (c) is the powers of two; (d) is the so-called Fibonacci sequence, related to powers of the golden ratio $(1 + \sqrt{5})/2 \approx 1.618$. All rules of the kind shown here lead to sequences where $f[n]$ can be expressed in terms of a simple sum of powers of the form a^n.

But it turns out that with slightly more complicated rules it is possible to get much more complicated behavior. The key idea is to consider rules which look at numbers that are not just a fixed distance back in the sequence. And what this means is that instead of depending only on quantities like $f[n-1]$ and $f[n-2]$, the rule for $f[n]$ can also for example depend on a quantity like $f[n-f[n-1]]$.

There is some subtlety here because in the abstract nothing guarantees that $n-f[n-1]$ will necessarily be a positive number. And if it is not, then results obtained by applying the rule can involve meaningless quantities such as $f[0]$, $f[-1]$ and $f[-2]$.

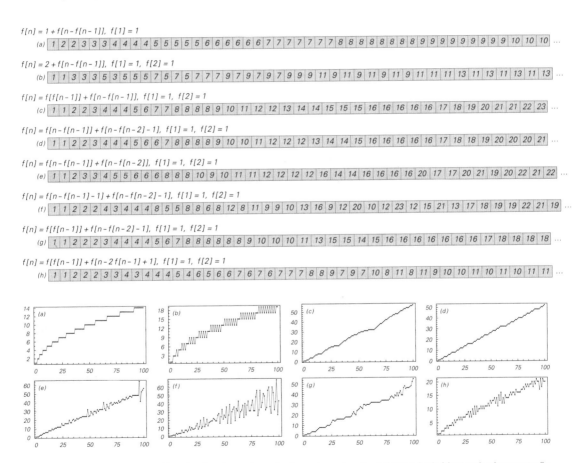

Examples of sequences generated by rules that do not depend only on elements a fixed distance back. Most such rules eventually end up involving meaningless quantities such as $f[0]$ and $f[-1]$, but the particular rules shown here all avoid this problem.

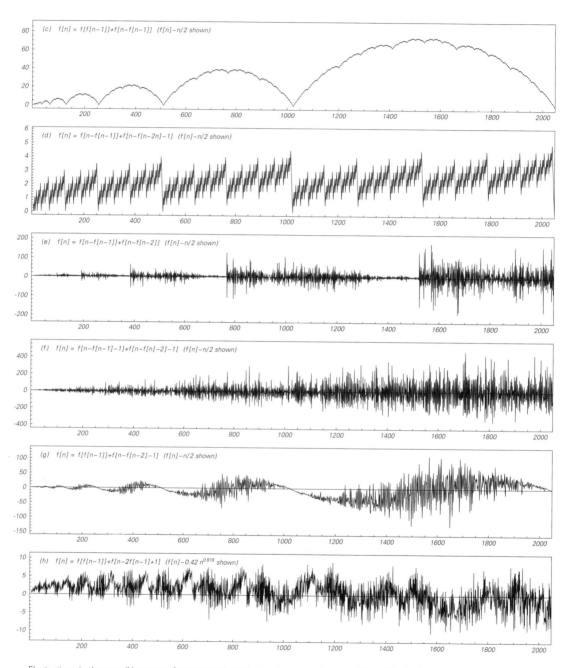

Fluctuations in the overall increase of sequences from the previous page. In cases (c) and (d), the fluctuations have a regular nested form, and turn out to be directly related to the base 2 digit sequence of n. In the other cases, the fluctuations are more complicated, and seem in many respects random. All the rules shown start with $f[1] = f[2] = 1$.

For the vast majority of rules written down at random, such problems do indeed occur. But it is possible to find rules in which they do not, and the pictures on the previous two pages show a few examples I have found of such rules. In cases (a) and (b), the behavior is fairly simple. But in the other cases, it is considerably more complicated.

There is a steady overall increase, but superimposed on this increase are fluctuations, as shown in the pictures on the facing page.

In cases (c) and (d), these fluctuations turn out to have a very regular nested form. But in the other cases, the fluctuations seem instead in many respects random. Thus in case (f), for example, the number of positive and negative fluctuations appears on average to be equal even after a million steps.

But in a sense one of the most surprising features of the facing page is that the fluctuations it shows are so violent. One might have thought that in going say from $f[2000]$ to $f[2001]$ there would only ever be a small change. After all, between $n = 2000$ and 2001 there is only a 0.05% change in the size of n.

But much as we saw in the previous section it turns out that it is not so much the size of n that seems to matter as various aspects of its representation. And indeed, in cases (c) and (d), for example, it so happens that there is a direct relationship between the fluctuations in $f[n]$ and the base 2 digit sequence of n.

In case (d), the fluctuation in each $f[n]$ turns out to be essentially just the number of 1's that occur in the base 2 digit sequence for n. And in case (c), the fluctuations are determined by the total number of 1's that occur in the digit sequences of all numbers less than n.

There are no such simple relationships for the other rules shown on the facing page. But in general one suspects that all these rules can be thought of as being like simple computer programs that take some representation of n as their input.

And what we have discovered in this section is that even though the rules ultimately involve only addition and subtraction, they nevertheless correspond to programs that are capable of producing behavior of great complexity.

The Sequence of Primes

In the sequence of all possible numbers 1, 2, 3, 4, 5, 6, 7, 8, … most are divisible by others—so that for example 6 is divisible by 2 and 3. But this is not true of every number. And so for example 5 and 7 are not divisible by any other numbers (except trivially by 1). And in fact it has been known for more than two thousand years that there are an infinite sequence of so-called prime numbers which are not divisible by other numbers, the first few being 2, 3, 5, 7, 11, 13, 17, 19, 23, 29, 31, 37, …

The picture below shows a simple rule by which such primes can be obtained. The idea is to start out on the top line with all possible numbers. Then on the second line, one removes all numbers larger than 2 that are divisible by 2. On the third line one removes numbers divisible by 3, and so on. As one goes on, fewer and fewer numbers remain. But some numbers always remain, and these numbers are exactly the primes.

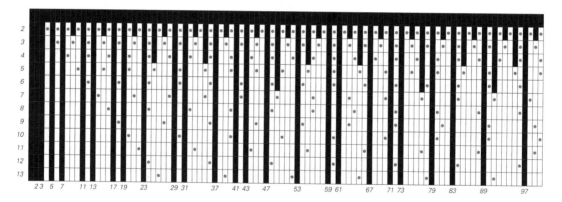

A filtering process that yields the prime numbers. One starts on the top line with all numbers between 1 and 100. Then on the second line, one removes numbers larger than 2 that are divisible by 2—as indicated by the gray dots. On the third line, one removes numbers larger than 3 that are divisible by 3. If one then continues forever, there are some numbers that always remain, and these are exactly the primes. The process shown is essentially the sieve of Eratosthenes, already known in 200 BC.

Given the simplicity of this rule, one might imagine that the sequence of primes it generates would also be correspondingly simple. But just as in so many other examples in this book, in fact it is not. And indeed the plots on the facing page show various features of this sequence which indicate that it is in many respects quite random.

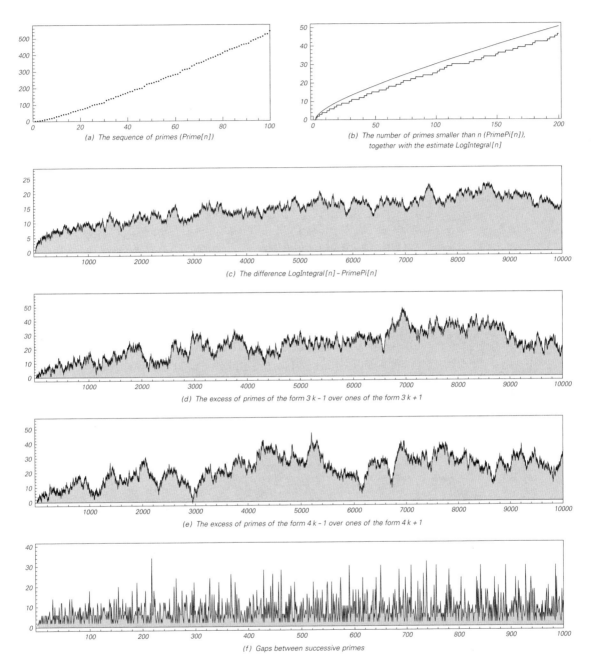

(a) The sequence of primes (Prime[n])

(b) The number of primes smaller than n (PrimePi[n]),
together with the estimate LogIntegral[n]

(c) The difference LogIntegral[n] – PrimePi[n]

(d) The excess of primes of the form 3 k – 1 over ones of the form 3 k + 1

(e) The excess of primes of the form 4 k – 1 over ones of the form 4 k + 1

(f) Gaps between successive primes

Features of the sequence of primes. Despite the simplicity of the rule on the facing page that generates the primes, the actual sequence of primes that is obtained seems in many respects remarkably random.

The examples of complexity that I have shown so far in this book are almost all completely new. But the first few hundred primes were no doubt known even in antiquity, and it must have been evident that there was at least some complexity in their distribution.

However, without the whole intellectual structure that I have developed in this book, the implications of this observation—and its potential connection, for example, to phenomena in nature—were not recognized. And even though there has been a vast amount of mathematical work done on the sequence of primes over the course of many centuries, almost without exception it has been concerned not with basic issues of complexity but instead with trying to find specific kinds of regularities.

Yet as it turns out, few regularities have in fact been found, and often the results that have been established tend only to support the idea that the sequence has many features of randomness. And so, as one example, it might appear from the pictures on the previous page that (c), (d) and (e) always stay systematically above the axis. But in fact with considerable effort it has been proved that all of them are in a sense more random—and eventually cross the axis an infinite number of times, and indeed go any distance up or down.

So is the complexity that we have seen in the sequence of primes somehow unusual among sequences based on numbers? The pictures on the facing page show a few other examples of sequences generated according to simple rules based on properties of numbers.

And in each case we again see a remarkable level of complexity.

Some of this complexity can be understood if we look at each number not in terms of its overall size, but rather in terms of its digit sequence or set of possible divisors. But in most cases—often despite centuries of work in number theory—considerable complexity remains.

And indeed the only reasonable conclusion seems to be that just as in so many other systems in this book, such sequences of numbers exhibit complexity that somehow arises as a fundamental consequence of the rules by which the sequences are generated.

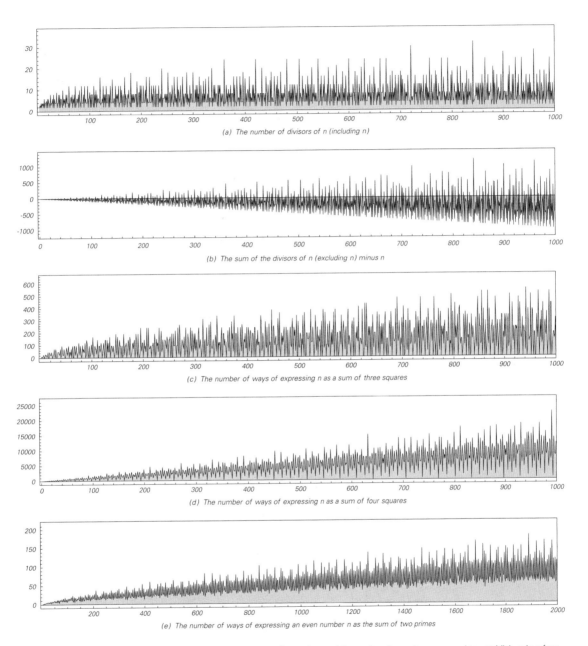

(a) The number of divisors of n (including n)

(b) The sum of the divisors of n (excluding n) minus n

(c) The number of ways of expressing n as a sum of three squares

(d) The number of ways of expressing n as a sum of four squares

(e) The number of ways of expressing an even number n as the sum of two primes

Sequences based on various simple properties of numbers. Extensive work in number theory has managed to establish only a few properties of these. It is for example known that (d) never reaches zero, while curve (c) reaches zero only for numbers of the form $4^r (8 s + 7)$. Sequence (b) is zero at so-called perfect numbers. Even perfect numbers always have a known form, but whether any odd perfect numbers exist is a question that has remained unresolved for more than two thousand years. The claim that sequence (e) never reaches zero is known as Goldbach's Conjecture. It was made in 1742 but no proof or counterexample has ever been found.

Mathematical Constants

The last few sections have shown that one can set up all sorts of systems based on numbers in which great complexity can occur. But it turns out that the possibility of such complexity is already suggested by some well-known facts in elementary mathematics.

The facts in question concern the sequences of digits in numbers like π (pi). To a very rough approximation, π is 3.14. A more accurate approximation is 3.141592653589793238462643383279502088.

But how does this sequence of digits continue?

One might suppose that at some level it must be quite simple and regular. For the value of π is specified by the simple definition of being the ratio of the circumference of any circle to its diameter.

But it turns out that even though this definition is simple, the digit sequence of π is not simple at all. The facing page shows the first 4000 digits in the sequence, both in the usual case of base 10, and in base 2. And the picture below shows a pictorial representation of the first 20,000 digits in the sequence.

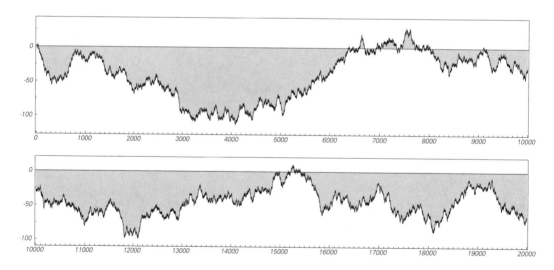

A pictorial representation of the first 20,000 digits of π in base 2. The curve drawn goes up every time a digit is 1, and down every time it is 0. Great complexity is evident. If the curve were continued further, it would spend more time above the axis, and no aspect of what is seen provides any evidence that the digit sequence is anything but perfectly random.

```
3.14159265358979323846264338327950288419716939937510582097494459230781640628620899862803482534211706798214808651328230664709384
4609550582231725359408128481117450284102701938521105559644622948954930381964428810975665933446128475648233786783165271201909145
6485669234603486104543266482133936072602491412737245870066063155881748815209209628292540917153643678925903600113305305488204666
5213841469519415116094330572703657595919530921861173819326117931051185480744623799627495673518857527248912279381830119491298336
7336244065664308602139494639522473719070217986094370277053921717629317675238467481846766940513200056812714526356082778571342575
7789609173637178721468440901224953430146549585371050792279689258923542019956112129021960864034418159813629177477130996051870721
1349999998372978049951059731732816096318595024459455346908302642522308253344685035261931188171010003137838752886587533208381420
6171766914730359825349042875546873115956286388235378759375195778185778053217122680661300192787661119590921642019893809525720106
5485863278865936153381827968230301952035301852968995773622599413891249721775283479131515574857242454150695950829533116861727855
8890750983817546374649393192550604009277016711390098488240128583616035637076601047101819429555961989467678374494482553797747268
4710404753464620804668425906949129331367702898915210475216205696602405803815019351125338243003558764024749647326391419927260426
9922796782354781636009341721641219924586315030286182974555706749838505049458586926995690927210797509302955321165344987202755960
2364806654991198818347977535366369807426542522786255181841757467289097777279380008164706001614524919217321721477235014144197356
8548161361157352552133475741849468438523323907394143334547762416862518983569485562099219222184272550254256887671790494601653466
8049886272327917860857843838279679976681454100953883786360950680064225125205117392984896084128488626945604241965285022210661186
3067442786220391949450471237137869609563643719128746776465757339624413890865832645995813390478027590094657640789512694683983525
9597098258226205224894077267194782684826014769909026401639443745530506820349662524517493996514314298091906592509372216964615157
0985838741059788595977297549893016175392846813826868386894277415599185592524595395943104997252468084598727364469584865383673622
2626099124608051243884390451244136549767628079771569143599770012961608944169486855584840635342207225582848864815845602850601684
2739452267467678889525213852254995466672783239864565961163548862305774564980355936345681743241125150760694794510965960940252288
7971089314566913686722847489405601015033086170288668617928680920872476091782493858590071490967597585261365549781893129784821682
9989487226588048575640142704755513237964145152374623436454285844479526586782105114135473573952311342716610213596953623144295248
4937187110145765405902799344037420070310578539062198384476040845298683334159114540421092250154026975
```

```
11.0010010000111111011010101000100010000101101000110000100010110100110010011001100110010100010111000000110111100000111001101000
100101001000000010010011100000010000100010011001111001100110101000000000100011101111110010100010010010001110010001100110110
0010010100001010010000010000111110011100110100000000010011010111011111001000110111101011101101110110010010101110010101101010
00110110010010000001010100001010010110111110010010111100001010000110111010111110000100110101011010101101010101000111000001
001000011110010000100001011010101110110010110011110111111100100011011110100011011100110001011110011111110010000100010110101
01101011011010111010011011010111011011100011000011010111011101111101011001011011110011011000111000100100100100010001111011001
11001000101101100111101101110000000000001111100101110100001110011001110110111110010010010100110110110110101011010110001011101
01011010100110110111110011011011011001101110011110000101110010101110101001101000001000111110001000101010110101110100001010110
10010010010111100010110100110110100101100011001000110011111001101011110001100000001001010100010011011011000110111001011010100
000100101110101101011001101101011001110000110000110101010101110010010101011001010010101011100100100011000001010100010001110111
0100000100101101001010110011011010100010110000100000100010101111001101011010001111010001111011011100001100101011100100100111001
001010000110100000010110101001101010101010101010100011000100101101010110010101101010100011000100111011000010110000011010001011
011101001001100001100001001110100001010101010111000110000011011010100010111011011001001000000001110010100010011000111011001111
000011010101010111011111100010110010011010011001001101100111101111000010000010000100010100011011011111101111000010101000101011
100110011010101101110110000111100011110001101001000110011100111001011000100010001000011110011001011110000001110110101111110111
001010110001101010101000010000100011011011100000010110111011010111011000100000101100000001001000001110010010000001100100110010
1101110000010011001110000000011101001010000101010001010110100100000101010010100000000100000001000011011001010111010111010101101
011111011110011110010101101111001001001110111010011011011110000011011110110111000011000010010111001101110100100101010011011000
1100100001111010101111100100010001110011010100010110101111010011111101010111011011111011000010011011010010000011011000100100111
000101001010101010100001000110100001001000010001100101101111011010100101010110010011011100110110101010100000100000100010001110
000100011100011000010010010111101000000111010011001010101010011001100110011011001010010101011010101101010101010010001110111010
010100010101010010101010111000010001011011010101010010100110001001011001011000011010100001011101010101110111011100010101101011
```

The first 4000 digits of π in bases 10 and 2. Despite the simple definition of π as the ratio of the circumference to the diameter of a circle, its digit sequence is sufficiently complicated as to seem for practical purposes random.

In no case are there any obvious regularities. Indeed, in all the more than two hundred billion digits of π that have so far been computed, no significant regularity of any kind has ever been found. Despite the simplicity of its definition, the digit sequence of π seems for practical purposes completely random.

But what about other numbers? Is π a special case, or are there other familiar mathematical constants that have complicated digit sequences? There are some numbers whose digit sequences effectively have limited length. Thus, for example, the digit sequence of 3/8 in base 10 is 0.375. (Strictly, the digit sequence is 0.3750000000..., but the 0's do not affect the value of the number, so are normally suppressed.)

It is however easy to find numbers whose digit sequences do not terminate. Thus, for example, the exact value of 1/3 in base 10 is 0.3333333333333..., where the 3's repeat forever. And similarly, 1/7 is 0.142857142857142857142857142857..., where now the block of digits 142857 repeats forever. The table below gives the digit sequences for several rational numbers obtained by dividing pairs of whole numbers. In all cases what we see is that the digit sequences of such numbers have a simple repetitive form. And in fact, it turns out that absolutely all rational numbers have digit sequences that eventually repeat.

1/3 = 0.333333333333333333333333333333333333333333333333333333333333333333333333333333333333333333333333333...
1/7 = 0.142857142857142857142857142857142857142857142857142857142857142857142857142857142857142857142857142...
1/9 = 0.111111111111111111111111111111111111111111111111111111111111111111111111111111111111111111111111111...
1/11 = 0.090909090909090909090909090909090909090909090909090909090909090909090909090909090909090909090909090...
1/81 = 0.012345679012345679012345679012345679012345679012345679012345679012345679012345679012345679012345679...

1/3 = 0.010101010101010101010101010101010101010101010101010101010101010101010101010101010101010101010101010...
1/7 = 0.001001001001001001001001001001001001001001001001001001001001001001001001001001001001001001001001001...
1/9 = 0.000111000111000111000111000111000111000111000111000111000111000111000111000111000111000111000111000...
1/11 = 0.000101110100010111010001011101000101110100010111010001011101000101110100010111010001011101000101110...
1/81 = 0.000000011001010010001011000011111100110101011011101001110000001100101001000101100000...

Digit sequences for various rational numbers, given in base 10 (above) and base 2 (below). For a number of the form p/q, the digit sequence always repeats with a period of at most q – 1 steps.

We can get some understanding of why this is so by looking at the details of how processes for performing division work. The pictures below show successive steps in a particular method for computing the base 2 digit sequence for the rational numbers p/q.

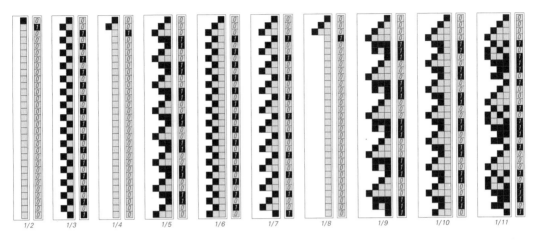

Successive steps in the computation of various rational numbers. In each case, the column on the right shows the sequence of base 2 digits in the number, while the box on the left shows the remainder at each of the steps in the computation.

The method is essentially standard long division, although it is somewhat simpler in base 2 than in the usual case of base 10. The idea is to have a number r which essentially keeps track of the remainder at each step in the division. One starts by setting r equal to p. Then at each step, one compares the values of $2r$ and q. If $2r$ is less than q, the digit generated at that step is 0, and r is replaced by $2r$. Otherwise, r is replaced by $2r - q$. With this procedure, the value of r is always less than q. And as a result, the digit sequence obtained always repeats at most every $q - 1$ steps.

It turns out, however, that rational numbers are very unusual in having such simple digit sequences. And indeed, if one looks for example at square roots the story is completely different.

Perfect squares such as $4 = 2 \times 2$ and $9 = 3 \times 3$ are specifically set up to have square roots that are just whole numbers. But as the table at the top of the next page shows, other square roots have much more complicated digit sequences. In fact, so far as one can tell, all whole numbers other than perfect squares have square roots whose digit sequences appear completely random.

$\sqrt{2}$ =	1.41421356237309504880168872420969807856967187537694807317667973799073247846210 7039...
$\sqrt{3}$ =	1.73205080756887729352744634150587236694280525381038062805580697945193301690880 0037...
$\sqrt{5}$ =	2.23606797749978969640917366873127623544061835961152572427089724541052092563780 4899...
$\sqrt{6}$ =	2.44948974278317809819728407470589139196594748065667012843269256725096037745731 5027...
$\sqrt{7}$ =	2.64575131106459059050161575363926042571025918308245018036833445920106882323028 3628...
$\sqrt{8}$ =	2.82842712474619009760337744841939615713934375075389614635335947598146495692421 4078...
$\sqrt{10}$ =	3.16227766016837933199889354443271853371955513932521682685750485279259443863923 8221...
$\sqrt{11}$ =	3.31662479035539984911493273667068668392708854558935359705868214611648464262609 043847...

$\sqrt{2}$ =	1.0110101000001001111001100110011111110011101111001100100100010001011001011110110...
$\sqrt{3}$ =	1.1011101101100111101011101000010110000100110010101001100111011011001001010111 01000...
$\sqrt{5}$ =	10.0011110001101110111100110110110010111111101001010011110000010101111001110011 1001...
$\sqrt{6}$ =	10.0111001100010001110000101000000100100100010010110011111011010000001100100001 10010...
$\sqrt{7}$ =	10.1010010101001111111010100111010010111110001110100110110111100011100111010100111...
$\sqrt{8}$ =	10.1101010000010011110011001100111111100111011110011001001000010001011001011110110...
$\sqrt{10}$ =	11.00101001100010110000011101011011010010101101101010010100100100000010010100010101 11...
$\sqrt{11}$ =	11.0101000100001100101001001111111101011011110011010000010110100011101111001001001...

Digit sequences for various square roots, given at the top in base 10 and at the bottom in base 2. Despite their simple definition, all these sequences seem for practical purposes random.

But how is such randomness produced? The picture at the top of the facing page shows an example of a procedure for generating the base 2 digit sequence for the square root of a given number n.

The procedure is only slightly more complicated than the one for division discussed above. It involves two numbers r and s, which are initially set to be n and 0, respectively. At each step it compares the values of r and s, and if r is larger than s it replaces r and s by $4(r-s-1)$ and $2(s+2)$ respectively; otherwise it replaces them just by $4r$ and $2s$. And it then turns out that the base 2 digits of s correspond exactly to the base 2 digits of $\sqrt{n}$ —with one new digit being generated at each step.

As the picture shows, the results of the procedure exhibit considerable complexity. And indeed, it seems that just like so many other examples that we have discussed in this book, the procedure for generating square roots is based on simple rules but nevertheless yields behavior of great complexity.

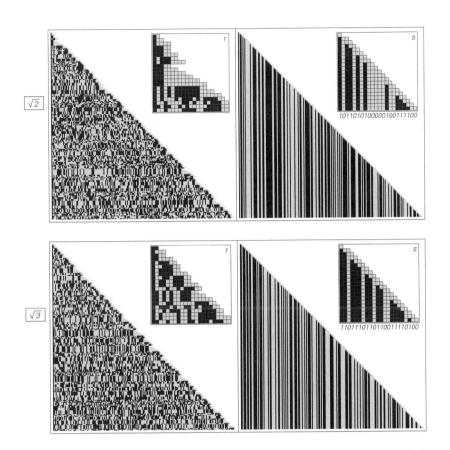

A procedure for generating the digit sequences of square roots. Two numbers, r and s, are involved. To find $\sqrt{n}$ one starts by setting $r = n$ and $s = 0$. Then at each step one applies the rule $\{r, s\} \to If[r > s, \{4(r - s - 1), 2(s + 2)\}, \{4r, 2s\}]$. The result is that the digits of s in base 2 turn out to correspond exactly to the digits of $\sqrt{n}$. Note that if n is not between 1 and 4, it must be multiplied or divided by an appropriate power of 4 before starting this procedure.

It turns out that square roots are certainly not alone in having apparently random digit sequences. As an example, the table on the next page gives the digit sequences for some cube roots and fourth roots, as well as for some logarithms and exponentials. And so far as one can tell, almost all these kinds of numbers also have apparently random digit sequences.

In fact, rational numbers turn out to be the only kinds of numbers that have repetitive digit sequences. And at least in square roots, cube roots, and so on, it is known that no nested digit sequences

$\sqrt[3]{2}$ =	1.2599210498948731647672106072782283505702514647015079800819751121552996765139594837293965624362550941543102560…
$\sqrt[3]{3}$ =	1.4422495703074083823216383107801095883918692534993505775464161945416875968299973398547554797056452566868350808…
$\sqrt[4]{2}$ =	1.1892071150027210667174999705604759152929720924638174130190022247194666682269171598707813445381376737160373947…
$\sqrt[4]{3}$ =	1.3160740129524924608192189017969990551600685902058221767319226585958667951973021330507431502466019315200477423…
Log[2] =	0.6931471805599453094172321214581765680755001343602552541206800094933936219696947156058633269964186875420014810…
Log[3] =	1.0986122886681096913952452369225257046474905578227494517346943336374942932186089668736157548137320887879700290…
e =	2.7182818284590452353602874713526624977572470936999595749669676277240766303535475945713821785251664274274663919…
e^2 =	7.3890560989306502272304274605750078131803155705518473240871278225225737960790577633843124850791217947737531612…

$\sqrt[3]{2}$ =	1.010000010100010100010111110011000110101110010100010101110001000100011101101101010101101100010101101111100010 01…
$\sqrt[3]{3}$ =	1.011100010011011101000100100100010001111101111011001011100110111011110011111110001011011000101011011000110 0…
$\sqrt[4]{2}$ =	1.001100000110111111000001010001100011011011100010101001011011111010001101010110100100011000110000010111001000 01…
$\sqrt[4]{3}$ =	1.010100001110101000110011111110010111110001011001100101111101101101110000110011001111100010100000110100110 11…
Log[2] =	0.101100010111001000010111111101111101000111001111011110011010101110010011100011011100110011000000000011111100…
Log[3] =	1.0001100100111110101001111010101011010000001100001010100101110101010010000011001100011010101010100000101001110…
e =	10.1011011111100001010100010110001010001010111011010010101001101010101011111101110001010110001000000010011100111 10…
e^2 =	111.011000111001100100101110001101010011011101101011011001100001100111010001110111010001000000110101101101000 10…

Digit sequences for cube roots, fourth roots, logarithms and exponentials, given at the top in base 10 and the bottom in base 2. Once again, these sequences seem for practical purposes random.

ever occur. It is straightforward to construct a nested digit sequence using for example the substitution systems on page 83, but the point is that such a digit sequence never corresponds to a number that can be obtained by the mathematical operation of taking roots.

So far in this chapter we have always used digit sequences as our way of representing numbers. But one might imagine that perhaps this representation is somehow perverse, and that if we were just to choose another one, then numbers generated by simple mathematical operations would no longer seem complex.

Any representation for a number can in a sense be thought of as specifying a procedure for constructing that number. Thus, for example, the pictures at the top of the facing page show how the base 10 and base 2 digit sequence representations of π can be used to construct the number π.

$$3.141592653 \ldots = 3 + \frac{1}{10}\,(1 + \frac{1}{10}\,(4 + \frac{1}{10}\,(1 + \frac{1}{10}\,(5 + \frac{1}{10}\,(9 + \frac{1}{10}\,(2 + \frac{1}{10}\,(6 + \frac{1}{10}\,(5 + \frac{1}{10}\,(3 + \ldots\,)))))))))$$

$$11.001001000 \ldots = 2 + 1 + \frac{1}{2}\,(0 + \frac{1}{2}\,(0 + \frac{1}{2}\,(1 + \frac{1}{2}\,(0 + \frac{1}{2}\,(0 + \frac{1}{2}\,(1 + \frac{1}{2}\,(0 + \frac{1}{2}\,(0 + \frac{1}{2}\,(0 + \ldots\,)))))))))$$

Procedures for building up π from its base 10 and base 2 digit sequence representations.

By replacing the addition and multiplication that appear above by other operations one can then get other representations for numbers. A common example are so-called continued fraction representations, in which the operations of addition and division are used, as shown below.

$$3 + 1/(7 + 1/(15 + 1/(1 + 1/(292 + 1/(1 + 1/(1 + 1/(1 + 1/(2 + 1/(1 + 1/(3 + 1/(1 + 1/(14 + \ldots\,)))))))))))$$

$$\{3, 7, 15, 1, 292, 1, 1, 1, 2, 1, 3, 1, 14, 2, 1, 1, 2, 2, 2, 2, 1, 84, 2, 1, 1, 15, 3, 13, 1, 4, 2, 6, 6, 99, 1, 2, 2, 6, 3, 5, 1, \ldots\,\}$$

The continued fraction representation of π. In this representation the value of π is built up by successive additions and divisions, rather than successive additions and multiplications.

The table on the next page gives the continued fraction representations for various numbers. In the case of rational numbers, the results are always of limited length. But for other numbers, they go on forever. Square roots turn out to have purely repetitive continued fraction representations. And the representations of $e \simeq 2.718$ and all its roots also show definite regularity. But for π, as well as for cube roots, fourth roots, and so on, the continued fraction representations one gets seem essentially random.

What about other representations of numbers? At some level, one can always use symbolic expressions like $\sqrt{2} + e^{\sqrt{3}}$ to represent numbers. And almost by definition, numbers that can be obtained by simple mathematical operations will correspond to simple such expressions. But the problem is that there is no telling how difficult it may be to compute the actual value of a number from the symbolic expression that is used to represent it.

And in thinking about representations of numbers, it seems appropriate to restrict oneself to cases where the effort required to find the value of a number from its representation is essentially the same for

$1/7$	$= \{0, 7\}$
$7/11$	$= \{0, 1, 1, 1, 3\}$
$\sqrt{2}$	$= \{1, 2, 2, 2, 2, 2, 2, 2, 2, 2, 2, 2, 2, 2, 2, 2, 2, 2, 2, 2, 2, 2, 2, 2, 2, 2, 2, 2, 2, 2, 2, 2, 2, 2, 2, 2, 2, 2, 2, 2, 2, 2, 2, 2, 2, 2, 2, 2, 2, 2, \ldots\}$
$\sqrt{3}$	$= \{1, 1, 2, 1, \ldots\}$
$\sqrt{5}$	$= \{2, 4, 4, 4, 4, 4, 4, 4, 4, 4, 4, 4, 4, 4, 4, 4, 4, 4, 4, 4, 4, 4, 4, 4, 4, 4, 4, 4, 4, 4, 4, 4, 4, 4, 4, 4, 4, 4, 4, 4, 4, 4, 4, 4, 4, 4, 4, 4, 4, \ldots\}$
$\sqrt{7}$	$= \{2, 1, 1, 1, 4, 1, 1, 1, 4, 1, 1, 1, 4, 1, 1, 1, 4, 1, 1, 1, 4, 1, 1, 1, 4, 1, 1, 1, 4, 1, 1, 1, 4, 1, 1, 1, 4, 1, 1, 1, 4, 1, 1, 1, 4, 1, 1, 1, \ldots\}$
$(1+\sqrt{5})/2$	$= \{1, 1, 1, 1, 1, 1, 1, 1, 1, 1, 1, 1, 1, 1, 1, 1, 1, 1, 1, 1, 1, 1, 1, 1, 1, 1, 1, 1, 1, 1, 1, 1, 1, 1, 1, 1, 1, 1, 1, 1, 1, 1, 1, 1, 1, 1, 1, 1, 1, 1, \ldots\}$
$\sqrt[3]{2}$	$= \{1, 3, 1, 5, 1, 1, 4, 1, 1, 8, 1, 14, 1, 10, 2, 1, 4, 12, 2, 3, 2, 1, 3, 4, 1, 1, 2, 14, 3, 12, 1, 15, 3, 1, 4, 534, 1, 1, 5, 1, 1, 121, 1, 2, 2, 4, 10, 3, 2, 2, \ldots\}$
$\sqrt[3]{3}$	$= \{1, 2, 3, 1, 4, 1, 5, 1, 1, 6, 2, 5, 8, 3, 3, 4, 2, 6, 4, 4, 1, 3, 2, 3, 4, 1, 4, 9, 1, 8, 4, 3, 1, 3, 2, 6, 1, 6, 1, 3, 1, 1, 1, 1, 12, 3, 1, 3, 1, 1, 4, 1, 6, 1, 5, \ldots\}$
$\sqrt[4]{2}$	$= \{1, 5, 3, 1, 1, 40, 5, 1, 1, 25, 2, 3, 1, 6, 2, 1, 1, 2, 1, 2, 1, 1, 1, 2, 2, 1, 7, 2, 7, 1, 1, 1, 2, 1, 1, 32, 4, 1, 6, 2, 1, 1, 1, 15, 1, 5, 1, 4, 1, 1, 1, 3, 1, 3, \ldots\}$
$\sqrt[4]{3}$	$= \{1, 3, 6, 9, 1, 1, 2, 1, 2, 1, 2, 5, 1, 12, 5, 1, 4, 1, 13, 1, 6, 1, 22, 1, 8, 21, 3, 142, 1, 1, 2, 1, 2, 2, 7, 1, 2, 1, 1, 5, 3, 1, 1, 2, 1, 1, 3, 1, 1, 1, \ldots\}$
$Log[2]$	$= \{0, 1, 2, 3, 1, 6, 3, 1, 1, 2, 1, 1, 1, 1, 3, 10, 1, 1, 1, 2, 1, 1, 1, 1, 3, 2, 3, 1, 13, 7, 4, 1, 1, 1, 7, 2, 4, 1, 1, 2, 5, 14, 1, 10, 1, 4, 2, 18, 3, 1, 4, 1, 6, \ldots\}$
$Log[3]$	$= \{1, 10, 7, 9, 2, 2, 1, 3, 1, 32, 2, 17, 1, 15, 1, 1, 7, 3, 1, 35, 1, 1, 1, 2, 5, 3, 2, 1, 4, 2, 1, 3, 1, 5, 3, 13, 1, 1, 1, 6, 2, 3, 1, 152, 1, 2, 3, 1, 7, 9, 2, \ldots\}$
e	$= \{2, 1, 2, 1, 1, 4, 1, 1, 6, 1, 1, 8, 1, 1, 10, 1, 1, 12, 1, 1, 14, 1, 1, 16, 1, 1, 18, 1, 1, 20, 1, 1, 22, 1, 1, 24, 1, 1, 26, 1, 1, 28, 1, 1, 30, 1, 1, 32, 1, \ldots\}$
$\sqrt{e}$	$= \{1, 1, 1, 1, 5, 1, 1, 9, 1, 1, 13, 1, 1, 17, 1, 1, 21, 1, 1, 25, 1, 1, 29, 1, 1, 33, 1, 1, 37, 1, 1, 41, 1, 1, 45, 1, 1, 49, 1, 1, 53, 1, 1, 57, 1, 1, 61, 1, 1, \ldots\}$
$\sqrt[3]{e}$	$= \{1, 2, 1, 1, 8, 1, 1, 14, 1, 1, 20, 1, 1, 26, 1, 1, 32, 1, 1, 38, 1, 1, 44, 1, 1, 50, 1, 1, 56, 1, 1, 62, 1, 1, 68, 1, 1, 74, 1, 1, 80, 1, 1, 86, 1, 1, 92, 1, 1, \ldots\}$
e^2	$= \{7, 2, 1, 1, 3, 18, 5, 1, 1, 6, 30, 8, 1, 1, 9, 42, 11, 1, 1, 12, 54, 14, 1, 1, 15, 66, 17, 1, 1, 18, 78, 20, 1, 1, 21, 90, 23, 1, 1, 24, 102, 26, 1, 1, 27, \ldots\}$
e^3	$= \{20, 11, 1, 2, 4, 3, 1, 5, 1, 2, 16, 1, 1, 16, 2, 13, 14, 4, 6, 2, 1, 1, 2, 2, 2, 3, 5, 1, 3, 1, 1, 68, 7, 5, 1, 4, 2, 1, 1, 1, 1, 1, 7, 3, 1, 6, 1, 2, 5, 4, 7, \ldots\}$
π	$= \{3, 7, 15, 1, 292, 1, 1, 1, 2, 1, 3, 1, 14, 2, 1, 1, 2, 2, 2, 2, 1, 84, 2, 1, 1, 15, 3, 13, 1, 4, 2, 6, 6, 99, 1, 2, 2, 6, 3, 5, 1, 1, 6, 8, 1, 7, 1, 2, 3, 7, 1, 2, \ldots\}$
π^2	$= \{9, 1, 6, 1, 2, 47, 1, 8, 1, 1, 2, 2, 1, 1, 8, 3, 1, 10, 5, 1, 3, 1, 2, 1, 1, 3, 15, 1, 1, 2, 2, 1, 3, 2, 7, 1, 9, 18, 30, 2, 145, 1, 1, 17, 9, 1, 1, 1, 1, 7, 12, 1, \ldots\}$
$Sinh[1]$	$= \{1, 5, 1, 2, 2, 1, 2, 7, 5, 1, 1, 1, 2, 2, 19, 1, 2, 1, 7, 1, 1, 9, 1, 3, 1, 1, 2, 1, 1, 1, 1, 3, 1, 2, 4, 5, 3, 5, 1, 3, 1, 1, 1, 2, 7, 1, 9, 1, 1, 2, 1, 21, 1, \ldots\}$
$Tanh[1]$	$= \{0, 1, 3, 5, 7, 9, 11, 13, 15, 17, 19, 21, 23, 25, 27, 29, 31, 33, 35, 37, 39, 41, 43, 45, 47, 49, 51, 53, 55, 57, 59, 61, 63, 65, 67, 69, 71, 73, \ldots\}$

Continued fraction representations for several numbers. Square roots yield repetitive sequences in this representation, but cube roots and higher roots yield seemingly random sequences.

all numbers. If one does this, then the typical experience is that in any particular representation, some class of numbers will have simple forms. But other numbers, even though they may be the result of simple mathematical operations, tend to have seemingly random forms.

And from this it seems appropriate to conclude that numbers generated by simple mathematical operations are often in some intrinsic sense complex, independent of the particular representation that one uses to look at them.

Mathematical Functions

The last section showed that individual numbers obtained by applying various simple mathematical functions can have features that are quite complex. But what about the functions themselves?

The pictures below show curves obtained by plotting standard mathematical functions. All of these curves have fairly simple, essentially repetitive forms. And indeed it turns out that almost all the standard mathematical functions that are defined, for example, in *Mathematica*, yield similarly simple curves.

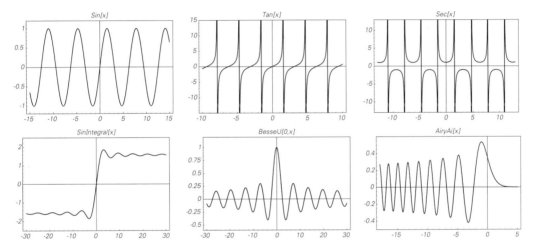

Plots of some standard mathematical functions. The top row shows three trigonometric functions. The bottom row shows three so-called special functions that are commonly encountered in mathematical physics and other areas of traditional science. In all cases the curves shown have fairly simple repetitive forms.

But if one looks at combinations of these standard functions, it is fairly easy to get more complicated results. The pictures on the next page show what happens, for example, if one adds together various sine functions. In the first picture, the curve one gets has a fairly simple repetitive structure. In the second picture, the curve is more complicated, but still has an overall repetitive structure. But in the third and fourth pictures, there is no such repetitive structure, and indeed the curves look in many respects random.

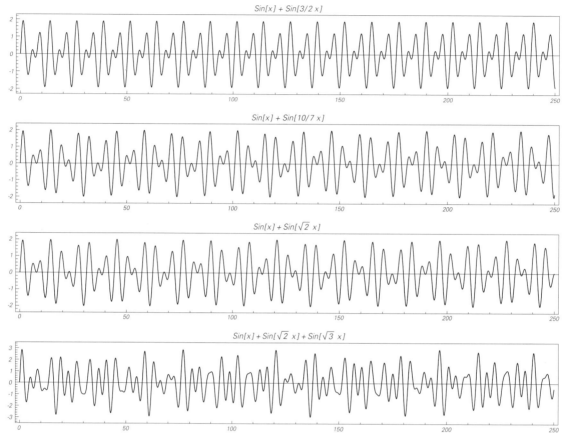

Curves obtained by adding together various sine functions. In the first two cases, the curves are ultimately repetitive; in the second two cases they are not. If viewed as waveforms for sounds, then these curves correspond to chords. The first curve yields a perfect fifth, while the third curve yields a diminished fifth (or tritone) in an equal temperament scale.

In the third picture, however, the points where the curve crosses the axis come in two regularly spaced families. And as the pictures on the facing page indicate, for any curve like $Sin[x] + Sin[\alpha x]$ the relative arrangements of these crossing points turn out to be related to the output of a generalized substitution system in which the rule at each step is obtained from a term in the continued fraction representation of $(\alpha - 1)/(\alpha + 1)$.

When α is a square root, then as discussed in the previous section, the continued fraction representation is purely repetitive,

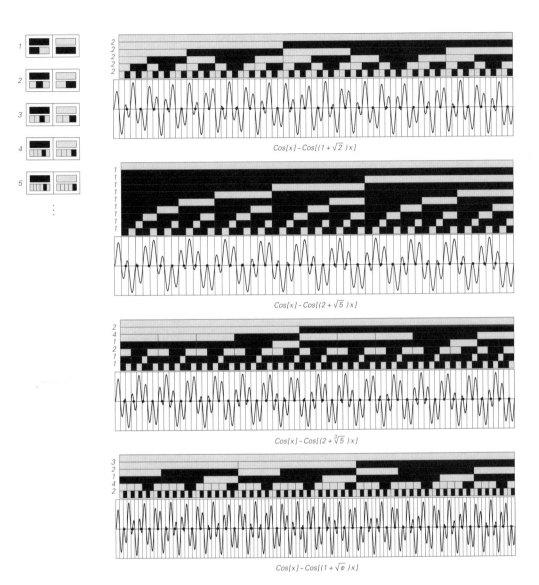

$Cos[x] - Cos[(1 + \sqrt{2}\,)x]$

$Cos[x] - Cos[(2 + \sqrt{5}\,)x]$

$Cos[x] - Cos[(2 + \sqrt[3]{5}\,)x]$

$Cos[x] - Cos[(1 + \sqrt{e}\,)x]$

Curves obtained by adding or subtracting exactly two sine or cosine functions turn out to have a pattern of axis crossings that can be reproduced by a generalized substitution system. In general there is an axis crossing within an interval when the corresponding element in the generalized substitution system is black, and there is not when the element is white. In the case of $Cos[x] - Cos[\alpha x]$ each step in the generalized substitution system has a rule determined as shown on the left from a term in the continued fraction representation of $(\alpha - 1)/(\alpha + 1)$. In the first two examples shown α is a quadratic irrational, so that the continued fraction is repetitive, and the pattern obtained is purely nested. (The second example is analogous to the Fibonacci substitution system on page 83.) In the last two examples, however, there is no such regularity. Note that successive terms in each continued fraction are shown alongside successive steps in the substitution system going up the page.

making the generated pattern nested. But when α is not a square root the pattern can be more complicated. And if more than two sine functions are involved there no longer seems to be any particular connection to generalized substitution systems or continued fractions.

Among all the various mathematical functions defined, say, in *Mathematica* it turns out that there are also a few—not traditionally common in natural science—which yield complex curves but which do not appear to have any explicit dependence on representations of individual numbers. Many of these are related to the so-called Riemann zeta function, a version of which is shown in the picture below.

The basic definition of this function is fairly simple. But in the end the function turns out to be related to the distribution of primes— and the curve it generates is quite complicated. Indeed, despite immense mathematical effort for over a century, it has so far been impossible even to establish for example the so-called Riemann Hypothesis, which in effect just states that all the peaks in the curve lie above the axis, and all the valleys below.

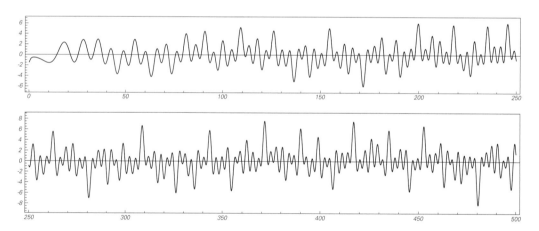

A curve associated with the so-called Riemann zeta function. The zeta function *Zeta[s]* is defined as *Sum[1/k^s, {k, ∞}]*. The curve shown here is the so-called Riemann-Siegel Z function, which is essentially *Zeta[1/2 + i̇ t]*. The celebrated Riemann Hypothesis in effect states that all peaks after the first one in this curve must lie above the axis.

Iterated Maps and the Chaos Phenomenon

The basic idea of an iterated map is to take a number between 0 and 1, and then in a sequence of steps to update this number according to a fixed rule or "map". Many of the maps I will consider can be expressed in terms of standard mathematical functions, but in general all that is needed is that the map take any possible number between 0 and 1 and yield some definite number that is also between 0 and 1.

The pictures on the next two pages show examples of behavior obtained with four different possible choices of maps.

Cases (a) and (b) on the first page show much the same kind of complexity that we have seen in many other systems in this chapter— in both digit sequences and sizes of numbers. Case (c) shows complexity in digit sequences, but the sizes of the numbers it generates rapidly tend to 0. Case (d), however, seems essentially trivial—and shows no complexity in either digit sequences or sizes of numbers.

On the first of the next two pages all the examples start with the number $1/2$—which has a simple digit sequence. But the examples on the second of the next two pages instead start with the number $\pi/4$— which has a seemingly random digit sequence.

Cases (a), (b) and (c) look very similar on both pages, particularly in terms of sizes of numbers. But case (d) looks quite different. For on the first page it just yields 0's. But on the second page, it yields numbers whose sizes continually vary in a seemingly random way.

If one looks at digit sequences, it is rather clear why this happens. For as the picture illustrates, the so-called shift map used in case (d) simply serves to shift all digits one position to the left at each step. And this means that over the course of the evolution of the system, digits further to the right in the original number will progressively end up all the way to the left—so that insofar as these digits show randomness, this will lead to randomness in the sizes of the numbers generated.

It is important to realize, however, that in no real sense is any randomness actually being generated by the evolution of this system. Instead, it is just that randomness that was inserted in the digit sequence of the original number shows up in the results one gets.

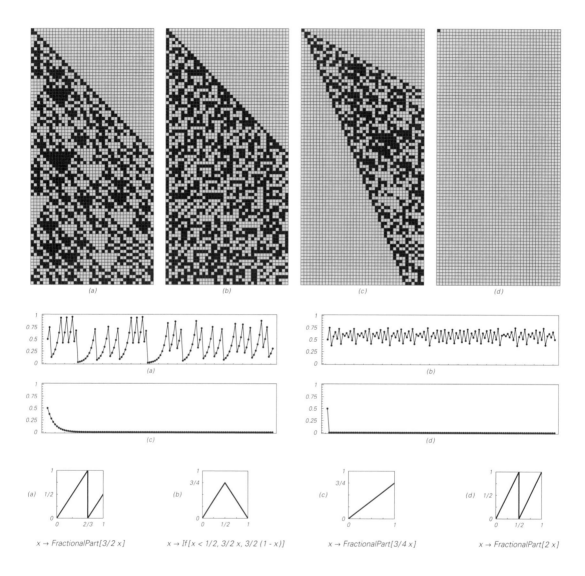

$x \rightarrow FractionalPart[3/2\ x]$ $x \rightarrow If[x < 1/2, 3/2\ x, 3/2\ (1 - x)]$ $x \rightarrow FractionalPart[3/4\ x]$ $x \rightarrow FractionalPart[2\ x]$

Examples of iterated maps starting from simple initial conditions. At each step there is a number *x* between 0 and 1 that is updated by applying a fixed mapping. The four mappings considered here are given above both as formulas and in terms of plots. The pictures at the top of the page show the base 2 digit sequences of successive numbers obtained by iterating this mapping, while the pictures in the middle of the page plot the sizes of these numbers. In all cases, the initial conditions consist of the number 1/2—which has a very simple digit sequence. Yet despite this simplicity, cases (a) and (b) show considerable complexity in both the digit sequences and the sizes of the numbers produced (compare page 122). In case (c), the digit sequences are complicated but the sizes of the numbers tend rapidly to zero. And finally, in case (d), neither the digit sequences nor the sizes of numbers are anything but trivial. Note that in the pictures above each horizontal row of digits corresponds to a number, and that digits further to the left contribute progressively more to the size of this number.

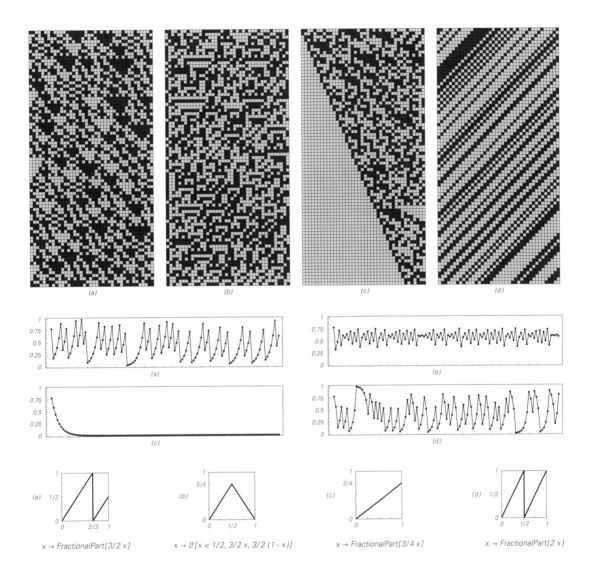

(a)   (b)   (c)   (d)

(a)

(b)

(c)

(d)

(a) $x \rightarrow FractionalPart[3/2\ x]$

(b) $x \rightarrow If[x < 1/2,\ 3/2\ x,\ 3/2\ (1 - x)]$

(c) $x \rightarrow FractionalPart[3/4\ x]$

(d) $x \rightarrow FractionalPart[2\ x]$

The same iterated maps as on the facing page, but now started from the initial condition $\pi/4$—a number with a seemingly random digit sequence. After fairly few steps, cases (a) and (b) yield behavior that is almost indistinguishable from what was seen with simple initial conditions on the facing page. And in case (c), the same exponential decay in the sizes of numbers occurs as before. But in case (d), the behavior is much more complicated. Indeed, if one just looked at the sizes of numbers produced, then one sees the same kind of complexity as in cases (a) and (b). But looking at digit sequences one realizes that this complexity is actually just a direct transcription of complexity introduced by giving an initial condition with a seemingly random digit sequence. Case (d) is the so-called shift map—a classic example of a system that exhibits the sensitive dependence on initial conditions often known as chaos.

This is very different from what happens in cases (a) and (b). For in these cases complex and seemingly random results are obtained even on the first of the previous two pages—when the original number has a very simple digit sequence. And the point is that these maps actually do intrinsically generate complexity and randomness; they do not just transcribe it when it is inserted in their initial conditions.

In the context of the approach I have developed in this book this distinction is easy to understand. But with the traditional mathematical approach, things can get quite confused. The main issue—already mentioned at the beginning of this chapter—is that in this approach the only attribute of numbers that is usually considered significant is their size. And this means that any issue based on discussing explicit digit sequences for numbers—and whether for example they are simple or complicated—tends to seem at best bizarre.

Indeed, thinking about numbers purely in terms of size, one might imagine that as soon as any two numbers are sufficiently close in size they would inevitably lead to results that are somehow also close. And in fact this is for example the basis for much of the formalism of calculus in traditional mathematics.

But the essence of the so-called chaos phenomenon is that there are some systems where arbitrarily small changes in the size of a number can end up having large effects on the results that are produced. And the shift map shown as case (d) on the previous two pages turns out to be a classic example of this.

The pictures at the top of the facing page show what happens if one uses as the initial conditions for this system two numbers whose sizes differ by just one part in a billion billion. And looking at the plots of sizes of numbers produced, one sees that for quite a while these two different initial conditions lead to results that are indistinguishably close. But at some point they diverge and soon become quite different.

And at least if one looks only at the sizes of numbers, this seems rather mysterious. But as soon as one looks at digit sequences, it immediately becomes much clearer. For as the pictures at the top of the facing page show, the fact that the numbers which are used as initial conditions differ only by a very small amount in size just means that their first several digits are the same. And for a while these digits are

initial condition 0.785398163397448310   *initial condition 0.785398163397448311*   *difference*

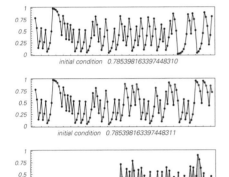

initial condition 0.785398163397448310

initial condition 0.785398163397448311

difference

The effect of making a small change in the initial conditions for the shift map—shown as case (d) on pages 150 and 151. The first picture shows results for the same initial condition as on page 151. The second picture shows what happens if one changes the size of the number in this initial condition by just one part in a billion billion. The plots to the left indicate that for a while the sizes of numbers obtained by the evolution of the system in these two cases are indistinguishable. But suddenly the results diverge and become completely different. Looking at the digit sequences above shows why this happens. The point is that a small change in the size of the number in the initial conditions corresponds to a change in digits far to the right. But the evolution of the system progressively shifts digits to the left, so that the digits which differ eventually become important. The much-investigated chaos phenomenon consists essentially of this effect.

what is important. But since the evolution of the system continually shifts digits to the left, it is inevitable that the differences that exist in later digits will eventually become important.

The fact that small changes in initial conditions can lead to large changes in results is a somewhat interesting phenomenon. But as I will discuss at length in Chapter 7 one must realize that on its own this cannot explain why randomness—or complexity—should occur in any particular case. And indeed, for the shift map what we have seen is that randomness will occur only when the initial conditions that are given happen to be a number whose digit sequence is random.

But in the past what has often been confusing is that traditional mathematics implicitly tends to assume that initial conditions of this kind are in some sense inevitable. For if one thinks about numbers purely in terms of size, one should make no distinction between numbers that are sufficiently close in size. And this implies that in choosing initial conditions for a system like the shift map, one should therefore make no distinction between the exact number $1/2$ and numbers that are sufficiently close in size to $1/2$.

But it turns out that if one picks a number at random subject only to the constraint that its size be in a certain range, then it is overwhelmingly likely that the number one gets will have a digit sequence that is essentially random. And if one then uses this number as the initial condition for a shift map, the results will also be correspondingly random—just like those on the previous page.

In the past this fact has sometimes been taken to indicate that the shift map somehow fundamentally produces randomness. But as I have discussed above, the only randomness that can actually come out of such a system is randomness that was explicitly put in through the details of its initial conditions. And this means that any claim that the system produces randomness must really be a claim about the details of what initial conditions are typically given for it.

I suppose in principle it could be that nature would effectively follow the same idealization as in traditional mathematics, and would end up picking numbers purely according to their size. And if this were so, then it would mean that the initial conditions for systems like the shift map would naturally have digit sequences that are almost always random.

But this line of reasoning can ultimately never be too useful. For what it says is that the randomness we see somehow comes from randomness that is already present—but it does not explain where that randomness comes from. And indeed—as I will discuss in Chapter 7—if one looks only at systems like the shift map then it is not clear any new randomness can ever actually be generated.

But a crucial discovery in this book is that systems like (a) and (b) on pages 150 and 151 can show behavior that seems in many respects random even when their initial conditions show no sign of randomness and are in fact extremely simple.

Yet the fact that systems like (a) and (b) can intrinsically generate randomness even from simple initial conditions does not mean that they do not also show sensitive dependence on initial conditions. And indeed the pictures below illustrate that even in such cases changes in digit sequences are progressively amplified—just like in the shift map case (d).

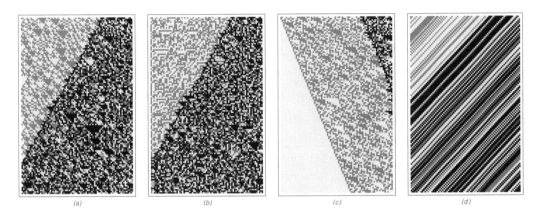

Differences in digit sequences produced by a small change in initial conditions for the four iterated maps discussed in this section. Cases (a), (b) and (d) exhibit sensitive dependence on initial conditions, in the sense that a change in insignificant digits far to the right eventually grows to affect all digits. Case (c) does not show such sensitivity to initial conditions, but instead always evolves to 0, independent of its initial conditions.

But the crucial point that I will discuss more in Chapter 7 is that the presence of sensitive dependence on initial conditions in systems like (a) and (b) in no way implies that it is what is responsible for the randomness and complexity we see in these systems. And indeed, what looking at the shift map in terms of digit sequences shows us is that this phenomenon on its own can make no contribution at all to what we can reasonably consider the ultimate production of randomness.

Continuous Cellular Automata

Despite all their differences, the various kinds of programs discussed in the previous chapter have one thing in common: they are all based on elements that can take on only a discrete set of possible forms, typically just colors black and white. And in this chapter, we have introduced a similar kind of discreteness into our study of systems based on numbers by considering digit sequences in which each digit can again have only a discrete set of possible values, typically just 0 and 1.

So now a question that arises is whether all the complexity we have seen in the past three chapters somehow depends on the discreteness of the elements in the systems we have looked at.

And to address this question, what I will do in this section is to consider a generalization of cellular automata in which each cell is not just black or white, but instead can have any of a continuous range of possible levels of gray. One can update the gray level of each cell by using rules that are in a sense a cross between the totalistic cellular automaton rules that we discussed at the beginning of the last chapter and the iterated maps that we just discussed in the previous section.

The idea is to look at the average gray level of a cell and its immediate neighbors, and then to get the gray level for that cell at the next step by applying a fixed mapping to the result. The picture below shows a very simple case in which the new gray level of each cell is exactly the average of the one for that cell and its immediate neighbors. Starting from a single black cell, what happens in this case is that the gray essentially just diffuses away, leaving in the end a uniform pattern.

A continuous cellular automaton in which each cell can have any level of gray between white (0) and black (1). The rule shown here takes the new gray level of each cell to be the average of its own gray level and those of its immediate neighbors.

0	0	0	0	0	1	0	0	0	0	0
0	0	0	0	0.333	0.333	0.333	0	0	0	0
0	0	0	0.111	0.222	0.333	0.222	0.111	0	0	0
0	0	0.037	0.111	0.222	0.259	0.222	0.111	0.037	0	0
0	0.012	0.049	0.123	0.198	0.235	0.198	0.123	0.049	0.012	0
0.004	0.021	0.062	0.123	0.185	0.21	0.185	0.123	0.062	0.021	0.004

The picture on the facing page shows what happens with a slightly more complicated rule in which the average gray level is multiplied by $3/2$, and then only the fractional part is kept if the result of this is greater than 1.

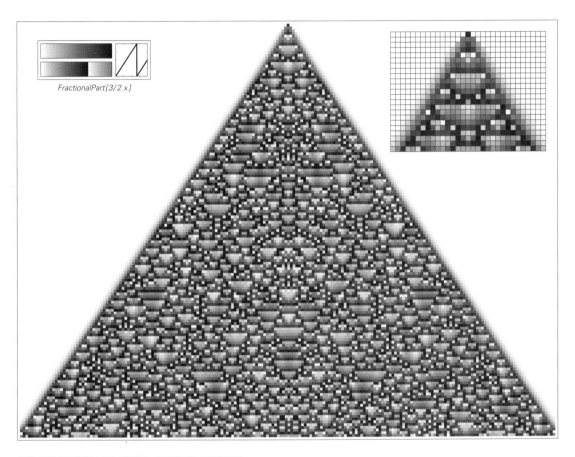

FractionalPart[3/2 x]

0	0	0	0	0	1	0	0	0	0	0
0	0	0	0	0.5	0.5	0.5	0	0	0	0
0	0	0	0.25	0.5	0.75	0.5	0.25	0	0	0
0	0	0.125	0.375	0.75	0.875	0.75	0.375	0.125	0	0
0	0.063	0.25	0.625	0	0.188	0	0.625	0.25	0.063	0
0.031	0.156	0.469	0.438	0.406	0.094	0.406	0.438	0.469	0.156	0.031

A continuous cellular automaton with a slightly more complicated rule. The rule takes the new gray level of each cell to be the fractional part of the average gray level of the cell and its neighbors multiplied by 3/2. The picture shows that starting from a single black cell, this rule yields behavior of considerable complexity. Note that the operation performed on individual average gray levels is exactly iterated map (a) from page 150.

And what we see is that despite the presence of continuous gray levels, the behavior that is produced exhibits the same kind of complexity that we have seen in many ordinary cellular automata and other systems with discrete underlying elements.

In fact, it turns out that in continuous cellular automata it takes only extremely simple rules to generate behavior of considerable complexity. So as an example the picture below shows a rule that determines the new gray level for a cell by just adding the constant 1/4 to the average gray level for the cell and its immediate neighbors, and then taking the fractional part of the result.

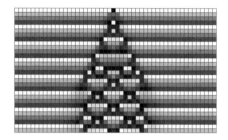

FractionalPart[x+1/4]

A continuous cellular automaton whose rule adds the constant 1/4 to the average gray level for a cell and its immediate neighbors, and takes the fractional part of the result. The background simply repeats every 4 steps, but the main pattern has a complex and in many respects random form.

The facing page and the one after show what happens when one chooses different values for the constant that is added. A remarkable diversity of behavior is seen. Sometimes the behavior is purely repetitive, but often it has features that seem effectively random.

And in fact, as the picture in the middle of page 160 shows, it is even possible to find cases that exhibit localized structures very much like those occasionally seen in ordinary cellular automata.

Continuous cellular automata with the same kind of rules as in the picture above, but with a variety of different constants being added. Note that it is not so much the size of the constant as properties like its digit sequence that seem to determine the overall form of behavior produced in each case. ▶

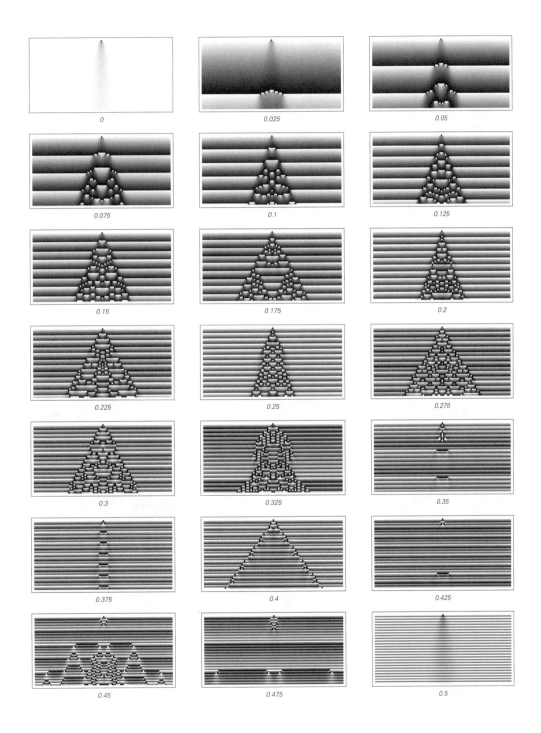

0.1

0.3

0.325

0.3299

0.3299 (differences)

0.35

0.475

0.495

0.9

More steps in the evolution of continuous cellular automata with the same kind of rules as on the previous page. In order to remove the uniform stripes, the picture in the middle shows the difference between the gray level of each cell and its immediate neighbor. Note the presence of discrete localized structures even though the underlying rules for the system involve continuous gray levels.

Partial Differential Equations

By introducing continuous cellular automata with a continuous range of gray levels, we have successfully removed some of the discreteness that exists in ordinary cellular automata. But there is nevertheless much discreteness that remains: for a continuous cellular automaton is still made up of discrete cells that are updated in discrete time steps.

So can one in fact construct systems in which there is absolutely no such discreteness? The answer, it turns out, is that at least in principle one can, although to do so requires a somewhat higher level of mathematical abstraction than has so far been necessary in this book.

The basic idea is to imagine that a quantity such as gray level can be set up to vary continuously in space and time. And what this means is that instead of just having gray levels in discrete cells at discrete time steps, one supposes that there exists a definite gray level at absolutely every point in space and every moment in time—as if one took the limit of an infinite collection of cells and time steps, with each cell being an infinitesimal size, and each time step lasting an infinitesimal time.

But how does one give rules for the evolution of such a system? Having no explicit time steps to work with, one must instead just specify the rate at which the gray level changes with time at every point in space. And typically one gives this rate as a simple formula that depends on the gray level at each point in space, and on the rate at which that gray level changes with position.

Such rules are known in mathematics as partial differential equations, and in fact they have been widely studied for about two hundred years. Indeed, it turns out that almost all the traditional mathematical models that have been used in physics and other areas of science are ultimately based on partial differential equations. Thus, for example, Maxwell's equations for electromagnetism, Einstein's equations for gravity, Schrödinger's equation for quantum mechanics and the Hodgkin-Huxley equation for the electrochemistry of nerve cells are all examples of partial differential equations.

It is in a sense surprising that systems which involve such a high level of mathematical abstraction should have become so widely used in practice. For as we shall see later in this book, it is certainly not that nature fundamentally follows these abstractions.

And I suspect that in fact the current predominance of partial differential equations is in many respects a historical accident—and that had computer technology been developed earlier in the history of mathematics, the situation would probably now be very different.

But particularly before computers, the great attraction of partial differential equations was that at least in simple cases explicit mathematical formulas could be found for their behavior. And this meant that it was possible to work out, for example, the gray level at a particular point in space and time just by evaluating a single mathematical formula, without having in a sense to follow the complete evolution of the partial differential equation.

The pictures on the facing page show three common partial differential equations that have been studied over the years.

The first picture shows the diffusion equation, which can be viewed as a limiting case of the continuous cellular automaton on page 156. Its behavior is always very simple: any initial gray progressively diffuses away, so that in the end only uniform white is left.

The second picture shows the wave equation. And with this equation, the initial lump of gray shown just breaks into two identical pieces which propagate to the left and right without change.

The third picture shows the sine-Gordon equation. This leads to slightly more complicated behavior than the other equations—though the pattern it generates still has a simple repetitive form.

Considering the amount of mathematical work that has been done on partial differential equations, one might have thought that a vast range of different equations would by now have been studied. But in fact almost all the work—at least in one dimension—has concentrated on just the three specific equations on the facing page, together with a few others that are essentially equivalent to them.

And as we have seen, these equations yield only simple behavior.

So is it in fact possible to get more complicated behavior in partial differential equations? The results in this book on other kinds of systems strongly suggest that it should be. But traditional

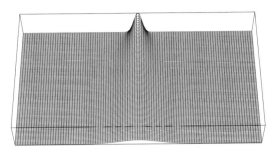

diffusion equation: $\partial_t u[t, x] = 1/4\, \partial_{xx} u[t, x]$

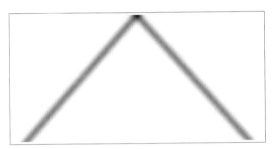

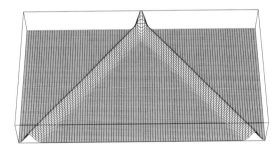

wave equation: $\partial_{tt} u[t, x] = \partial_{xx} u[t, x]$

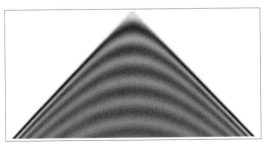

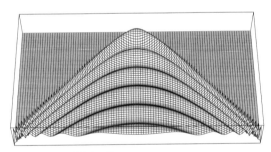

sine-Gordon soliton equation: $\partial_{tt} u[t, x] = \partial_{xx} u[t, x] + Sin[u[t, x]]$

Three partial differential equations that have historically been studied extensively. Just like in other pictures in this book, position goes across the page, and time down the page. In each equation u is the gray level at a particular point, $\partial_t u$ is the rate of change (derivative) of the gray level with time, and $\partial_{tt} u$ is the rate of change of that rate of change (second derivative). Similarly, $\partial_x u$ is the rate of change with position in space, and $\partial_{xx} u$ is the rate of change of that rate of change. On this page and the ones that follow the initial conditions used are $u = e^{-x^2}$, $\partial_t u = 0$.

mathematical methods give very little guidance about how to find such behavior. Indeed, it seems that the best approach is essentially just to search through many different partial differential equations, looking for ones that turn out to show complex behavior.

But an immediate difficulty is that there is no obvious way to sample possible partial differential equations. In discrete systems such as cellular automata there are always a discrete set of possible rules. But in partial differential equations any mathematical formula can appear.

Nevertheless, by representing formulas as symbolic expressions with discrete sets of possible components, one can devise at least some schemes for sampling partial differential equations.

But even given a particular partial differential equation, there is no guarantee that the equation will yield self-consistent results. Indeed, for a very large fraction of randomly chosen partial differential equations what one finds is that after just a small amount of time, the gray level one gets either becomes infinitely large or starts to vary infinitely quickly in space or time. And whenever such phenomena occur, the original equation can no longer be used to determine future behavior.

But despite these difficulties I was eventually able to find the partial differential equations shown on the next two pages.

The mathematical statement of these equations is fairly simple. But as the pictures show, their behavior is highly complex.

Indeed, strangely enough, even though the underlying equations are continuous, the patterns they produce seem to involve patches that have a somewhat discrete structure.

But the main point that the pictures on the next two pages make is that the kind of complex behavior that we have seen in this book is in no way restricted to systems that are based on discrete elements. It is certainly much easier to find and to study such behavior in these discrete systems, but from what we have learned in this section, we now know that the same kind of behavior can also occur in completely continuous systems such as partial differential equations.

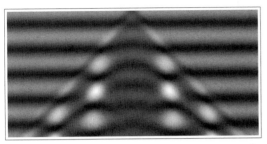
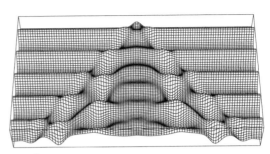

$$\partial_{tt} u[t, x] = \partial_{xx} u[t, x] + (1 - u[t, x]^2)(1 + u[t, x])$$

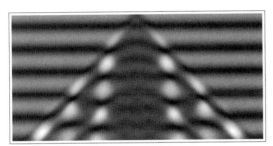
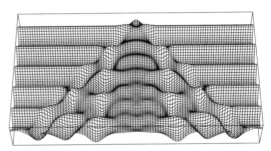

$$\partial_{tt} u[t, x] = \partial_{xx} u[t, x] + (1 - u[t, x]^2)(1 + 2 u[t, x])$$

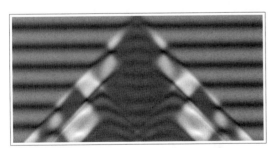
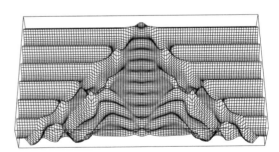

$$\partial_{tt} u[t, x] = \partial_{xx} u[t, x] + (1 - u[t, x]^2)(1 + 4 u[t, x])$$

Examples of partial differential equations I have found that have more complicated behavior. The background in each case purely is repetitive, but the main part of the pattern is complex, and reminiscent of what is produced by continuous cellular automata and many other kinds of systems discussed in this book.

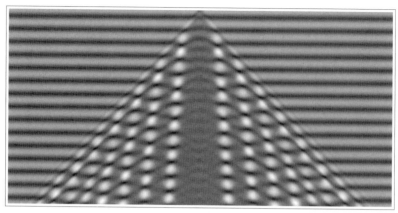

$$\partial_{tt}\, u[t, x] = \partial_{xx}\, u[t, x] + (1 - u[t, x]^2)(1 + u[t, x])$$

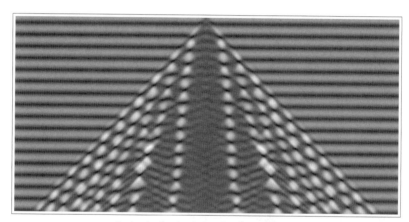

$$\partial_{tt}\, u[t, x] = \partial_{xx}\, u[t, x] + (1 - u[t, x]^2)(1 + 2\, u[t, x])$$

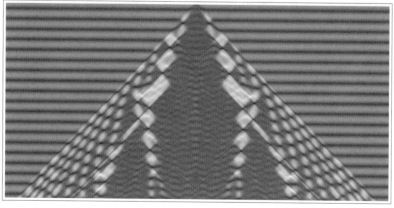

$$\partial_{tt}\, u[t, x] = \partial_{xx}\, u[t, x] + (1 - u[t, x]^2)(1 + 4\, u[t, x])$$

Continuous Versus Discrete Systems

One of the most obvious differences between my approach to science based on simple programs and the traditional approach based on mathematical equations is that programs tend to involve discrete elements while equations tend to involve continuous quantities.

But how significant is this difference in the end?

One might have thought that perhaps the basic phenomenon of complexity that I have identified could only occur in discrete systems. But from the results of the last few sections, we know that this is not the case.

What is true, however, is that the phenomenon was immensely easier to discover in discrete systems than it would have been in continuous ones. Probably complexity is not in any fundamental sense rarer in continuous systems than in discrete ones. But the point is that discrete systems can typically be investigated in a much more direct way than continuous ones.

Indeed, given the rules for a discrete system, it is usually a rather straightforward matter to do a computer experiment to find out how the system will behave. But given an equation for a continuous system, it often requires considerable analysis to work out even approximately how the system will behave. And in fact, in the end one typically has rather little idea which aspects of what one sees are actually genuine features of the system, and which are just artifacts of the particular methods and approximations that one is using to study it.

With all the work that was done on continuous systems in the history of traditional science and mathematics, there were undoubtedly many cases in which effects related to the phenomenon of complexity were seen. But because the basic phenomenon of complexity was not known and was not expected, such effects were probably always dismissed as somehow not being genuine features of the systems being studied. Yet when I came to investigate discrete systems there was no

◀ Solutions to the same equations as on the previous page over a longer period of time. Note the appearance of discrete structures. Particularly in the last picture some details are sensitive to the numerical approximation scheme used in computing the solution to the equation.

possibility of dismissing what I saw in such a way. And as a result I was in a sense forced into recognizing the basic phenomenon of complexity.

But now, armed with the knowledge that this phenomenon exists, it is possible to go back and look again at continuous systems.

And although there are significant technical difficulties, one finds as the last few sections have shown that the phenomenon of complexity can occur in continuous systems just as it does in discrete ones.

It remains much easier to be sure of what is going on in a discrete system than in a continuous one. But I suspect that essentially all of the various phenomena that we have observed in discrete systems in the past several chapters can in fact also be found even in continuous systems with fairly simple rules.

5

Two Dimensions and Beyond

Introduction

The physical world in which we live involves three dimensions of space. Yet so far in this book all the systems we have discussed have effectively been limited to just one dimension.

The purpose of this chapter, therefore, is to see how much of a difference it makes to allow more than one dimension.

At least in simple cases, the basic idea—as illustrated in the pictures below—is to consider systems whose elements do not just lie along a one-dimensional line, but instead are arranged for example on a two-dimensional grid.

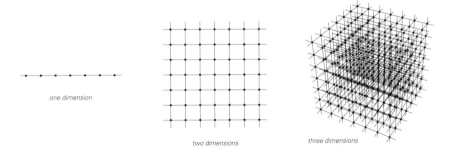

one dimension

two dimensions

three dimensions

Examples of simple arrangements of elements in one, two and three dimensions. In two dimensions, what is shown is a square grid; triangular and hexagonal grids are also possible. In three dimensions, what is shown is a cubic lattice; various other lattices, analogous to those for regular crystals, are also possible—as are arrangements that are not repetitive.

Traditional science tends to suggest that allowing more than one dimension will have very important consequences. Indeed, it turns out that many of the phenomena that have been most studied in traditional science simply do not occur in just one dimension.

Phenomena that involve geometrical shapes, for example, usually require at least two dimensions, while phenomena that rely on the existence of knotted structures require three dimensions. But what about the phenomenon of complexity? How much does it depend on dimension?

It could be that in going beyond one dimension the character of the behavior that we would see would immediately change. And indeed in the course of this chapter, we will come across many examples of specific effects that depend on having more than one dimension.

But what we will discover in the end is that at an overall level the behavior we see is not fundamentally much different in two or more dimensions than in one dimension. Indeed, despite what we might expect from traditional science, adding more dimensions does not ultimately seem to have much effect on the occurrence of behavior of any significant complexity.

Cellular Automata

The cellular automata that we have discussed so far in this book are all purely one-dimensional, so that at each step, they involve only a single line of cells. But one can also consider two-dimensional cellular automata that involve a whole grid of cells, with the color of each cell being updated according to a rule that depends on its neighbors in all four directions on the grid, as in the picture below.

The form of the rule for a typical two-dimensional cellular automaton. In the cases discussed in this section, each cell is either black or white. Usually I consider so-called totalistic rules in which the new color of the center cell depends only on the average of the previous colors of its four neighbors, as well as on its own previous color.

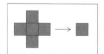

The pictures below show what happens with an especially simple rule in which a particular cell is taken to become black if any of its four neighbors were black on the previous step.

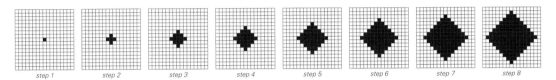

Successive steps in the evolution of a two-dimensional cellular automaton whose rule specifies that a particular cell should become black if any of its neighbors were black on the previous step. (In the numbering scheme described on page 173 this rule is code 1022.)

Starting from a single black cell, this rule just yields a uniformly expanding diamond-shaped region of black cells. But by changing the rule slightly, one can obtain more complicated patterns of growth. The pictures below show what happens, for example, with a rule in which each cell becomes black if just one or all four of its neighbors were black on the previous step, but otherwise stays the same color as it was before.

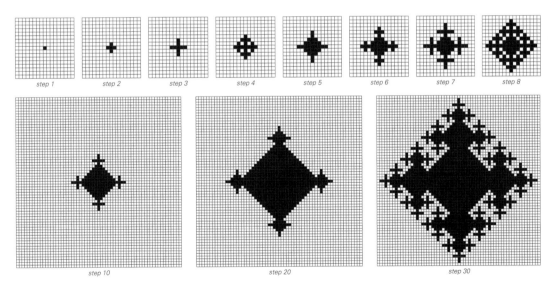

Steps in the evolution of a two-dimensional cellular automaton whose rule specifies that a particular cell should become black if exactly one or all four of its neighbors were black on the previous step, but should otherwise stay the same color. Starting with a single black cell, this rule yields an intricate, if very regular, pattern of growth. (In the numbering scheme on page 173, the rule is code 942.)

The patterns produced in this case no longer have a simple geometrical form, but instead often exhibit an intricate structure somewhat reminiscent of a snowflake. Yet despite this intricacy, the patterns still show great regularity. And indeed, if one takes the patterns from successive steps and stacks them on top of each other to form a three-dimensional object, as in the picture below, then this object has a very regular nested structure.

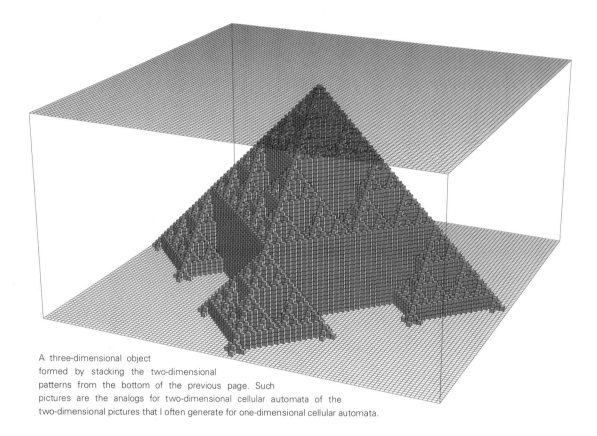

A three-dimensional object formed by stacking the two-dimensional patterns from the bottom of the previous page. Such pictures are the analogs for two-dimensional cellular automata of the two-dimensional pictures that I often generate for one-dimensional cellular automata.

But what about other rules? The facing page and the one that follows show patterns produced by two-dimensional cellular automata with a sequence of different rules. Within each pattern there is often considerable complexity. But this complexity turns out to be very similar to the complexity we have already seen in one-dimensional

code 450 · code 451 · code 452 · code 453 · code 454 · code 455 · code 456
code 457 · code 458 · code 459 · code 460 · code 461 · code 462 · code 463
code 464 · code 465 · code 466 · code 467 · code 468 · code 469 · code 470
code 471 · code 472 · code 473 · code 474 · code 475 · code 476 · code 477
code 478 · code 479 · code 480 · code 481 · code 482 · code 483 · code 484
code 485 · code 486 · code 487 · code 488 · code 489 · code 490 · code 491
code 492 · code 493 · code 494 · code 495 · code 496 · code 497 · code 498

Patterns generated by a sequence of two-dimensional cellular automaton rules. The patterns are produced by starting from a single black square and then running for 22 steps. In each case the base 2 digit sequence for the code number specifies the rule as follows. The last digit specifies what color the center cell should be if all its neighbors were white on the previous step, and it too was white. The second-to-last digit specifies what happens if all the neighbors are white, but the center cell itself is black. And each earlier digit then specifies what should happen if progressively more neighbors are black. (Compare page 60.)

Patterns generated by two-dimensional cellular automata from the previous page, but now after twice as many steps.

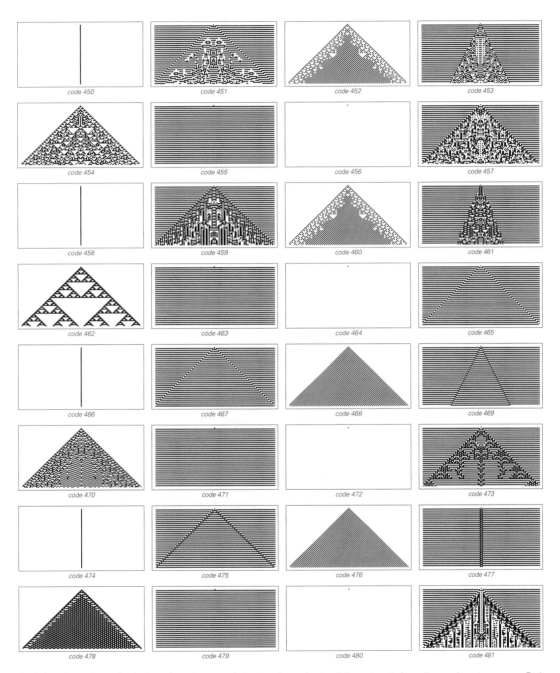

Evolution of one-dimensional slices through some of the two-dimensional cellular automata from the previous two pages. Each picture shows the colors of cells that lie on the one-dimensional line that goes through the middle of each two-dimensional pattern. The results are strikingly similar to ones we saw in previous chapters in purely one-dimensional cellular automata.

cellular automata. And indeed the previous page shows that if one looks at the evolution of a one-dimensional slice through each two-dimensional pattern the results one gets are strikingly similar to what we have seen in ordinary one-dimensional cellular automata.

But looking at such slices cannot reveal much about the overall shapes of the two-dimensional patterns. And in fact it turns out that for all the two-dimensional cellular automata shown on the last few pages, these shapes are always very regular.

But it is nevertheless possible to find two-dimensional cellular automata that yield less regular shapes. And as a first example, the picture on the facing page shows a rule that produces a pattern whose surface has seemingly random irregularities, at least on a small scale.

In this particular case, however, it turns out that on a larger scale the surface follows a rather smooth curve. And indeed, as the picture on page 178 shows, it is even possible to find cellular automata that yield overall shapes that closely approximate perfect circles.

But it is certainly not the case that all two-dimensional cellular automata produce only simple overall shapes. The pictures on pages 179–181 show one rule, for example, that does not. The rule is actually rather simple: it just states that a particular cell should become black whenever exactly three of its eight neighbors—including diagonals—are black, and otherwise it should stay the same color as it was before.

In order to get any kind of growth with this rule one must start with at least three black cells. The picture at the top of page 179 shows what happens with various numbers of black cells. In some cases the patterns produced are fairly simple—and typically stop growing after just a few steps. But in other cases, much more complicated patterns are produced, which often apparently go on growing forever.

The pictures on page 181 show the behavior produced by starting from a row of eleven black cells, and then evolving for several hundred steps. The shapes obtained seem continually to go on changing, with no simple overall form ever being produced.

And so it seems that there can be great complexity not only in the detailed arrangement of black and white cells in a two-dimensional cellular automaton pattern, but also in the overall shape of the pattern.

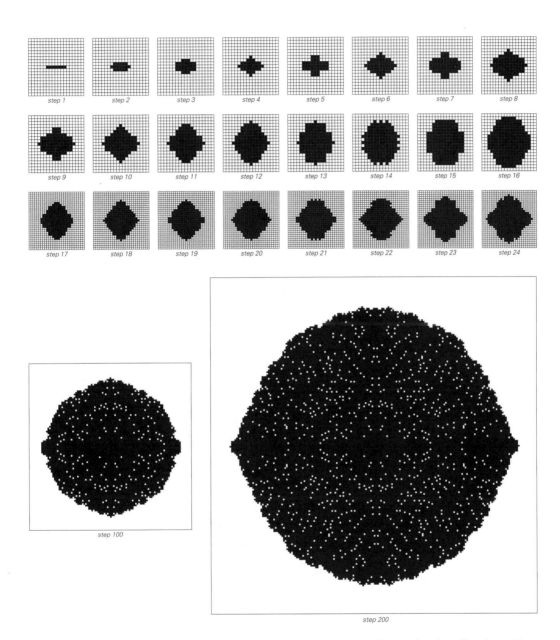

step 1 *step 2* *step 3* *step 4* *step 5* *step 6* *step 7* *step 8*

step 9 *step 10* *step 11* *step 12* *step 13* *step 14* *step 15* *step 16*

step 17 *step 18* *step 19* *step 20* *step 21* *step 22* *step 23* *step 24*

step 100

step 200

A two-dimensional cellular automaton that yields a pattern with a rough surface. The rule used here includes diagonal neighbors, and so involves a total of 8 neighbors for each cell, as indicated in the icon on the left. The rule specifies that the center cell should become black if either 3 or 5 of its 8 neighbors were black on the step before, and should otherwise stay the same color as it was before. The initial condition in the case shown consists of a row of 7 black cells. In an extension to 8 neighbors of the scheme used in the pictures a few pages back, the rule has code number 175850.

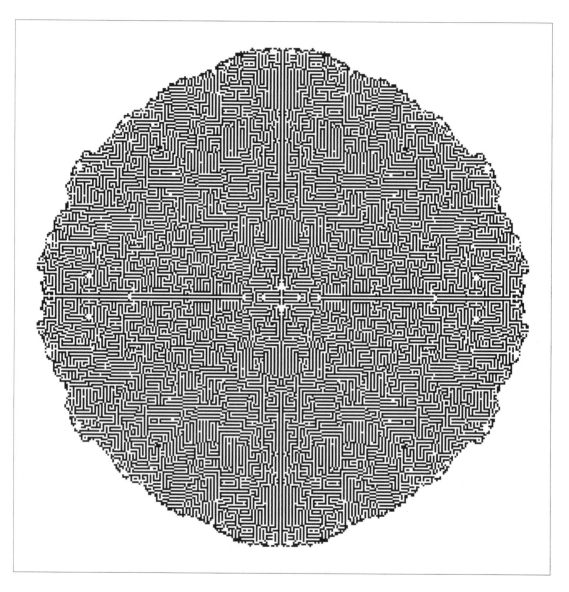

A cellular automaton that yields a pattern whose shape closely approximates a circle. The rule used is of the same kind as on the previous page, but now takes the center cell to become black only if it has exactly 3 black neighbors. If it has 1, 2 or 4 black neighbors then it stays the same color as it was before, and if it has 5 or more black neighbors, then it becomes white on the next step (code number 746). The initial condition consists of a row of 7 black cells, just as in the picture on the previous page. The pattern shown here is the result of 400 steps in the evolution of the system. After t steps, the radius of the approximate circle is about $0.37\,t$.

Patterns produced by evolution according to a simple two-dimensional cellular automaton rule starting from rows of black cells of various lengths. The rule used specifies that a particular cell should become black if exactly three out of its eight neighbors (with diagonal neighbors included) are black (code number 174826). The patterns in the picture are obtained by 60 steps of evolution according to this rule. The smaller patterns above have all stopped growing after this number of steps, but many of the other patterns apparently go on growing forever.

So what about three-dimensional cellular automata? It is straightforward to generalize the setup for two-dimensional rules to the three-dimensional case. But particularly on a printed page it is fairly difficult to display the evolution of a three-dimensional cellular automaton in a way that can readily be assimilated.

Pages 182 and 183 do however show a few examples of three-dimensional cellular automata. And just as in the two-dimensional case, there are some specific new phenomena that can be seen. But overall it seems that the basic kinds of behavior produced are just the same as in one and two dimensions. And in particular, the basic phenomenon of complexity does not seem to depend in any crucial way on the dimensionality of the system one looks at.

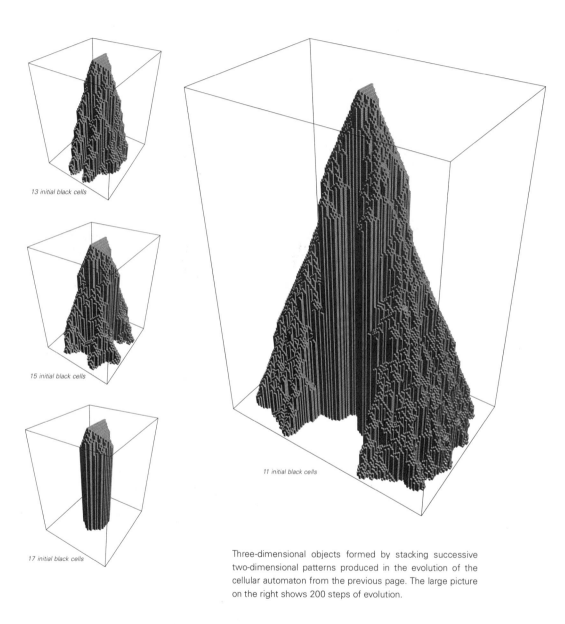

13 initial black cells

15 initial black cells

17 initial black cells

11 initial black cells

Three-dimensional objects formed by stacking successive two-dimensional patterns produced in the evolution of the cellular automaton from the previous page. The large picture on the right shows 200 steps of evolution.

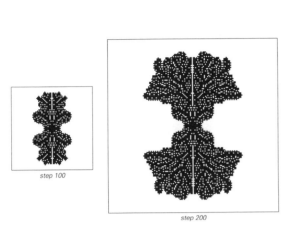

step 100

step 200

step 300

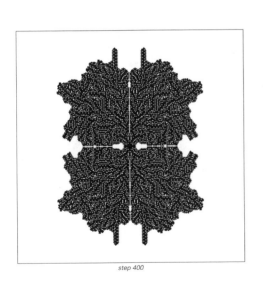

step 400

step 500

Stages in the evolution of the cellular automaton from the facing page, starting with an initial condition consisting of a row of 11 black cells.

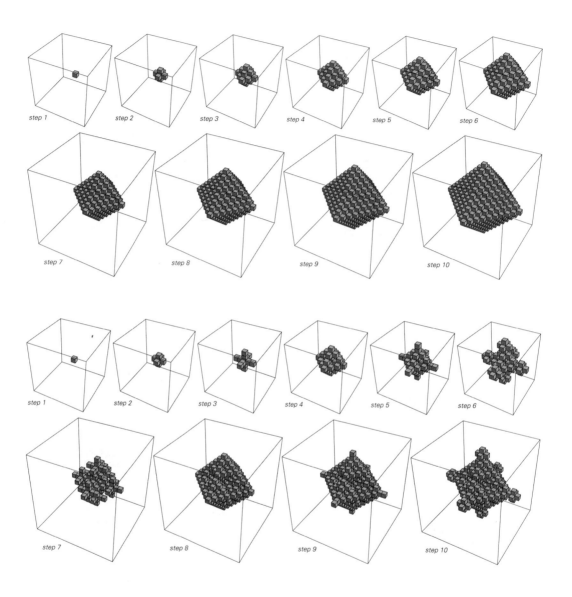

Examples of three-dimensional cellular automata. In the top set of pictures, the rule specifies that a cell should become black whenever any of the six neighbors with which it shares a face were black on the step before. In the bottom pictures, the rule specifies that a cell should become black only when exactly one of its six neighbors was black on the step before. In both cases, the initial condition contains a single black cell. In the top pictures, the limiting shape obtained is a regular octahedron. In the bottom pictures, it is a nested pattern analogous to the two-dimensional one on page 171.

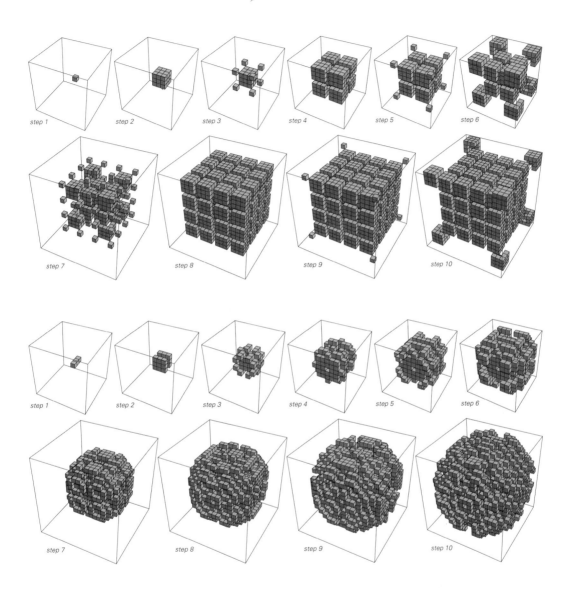

Further examples of three-dimensional cellular automata, but now with rules that depend on all 26 neighbors that share either a face or a corner with a particular cell. In the top pictures, the rule specifies that a cell should become black when exactly one of its 26 neighbors was black on the step before. In the bottom pictures, the rule specifies that a cell should become black only when exactly two of its 26 neighbors were black on the step before. In the top pictures, the initial condition contains a single black cell; in the bottom pictures, it contains a line of three black cells.

Turing Machines

Much as for cellular automata, it is straightforward to generalize Turing machines to two dimensions. The basic idea—shown in the picture below—is to allow the head of the Turing machine to move around on a two-dimensional grid rather than just going backwards and forwards on a one-dimensional tape.

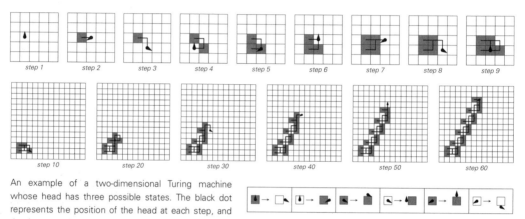

step 1   step 2   step 3   step 4   step 5   step 6   step 7   step 8   step 9

step 10   step 20   step 30   step 40   step 50   step 60

An example of a two-dimensional Turing machine whose head has three possible states. The black dot represents the position of the head at each step, and the three possible orientations of the arrow on this dot correspond to the three possible states of the head. The rule specifies in which of the four possible directions the head should move at each step. Note that the orientation of the arrow representing the state of the head has no direct relationship to directions on the grid—or to which way the head will move at the next step.

When we looked at one-dimensional Turing machines earlier in this book, we found that it was possible for them to exhibit complex behavior, but that such behavior was rather rare.

In going to two dimensions we might expect that complex behavior would somehow immediately become more common. But in fact what we find is that the situation is remarkably similar to one dimension.

For Turing machines with two or three possible states, only repetitive and nested behavior normally seem to occur. With four states, more complex behavior is possible, but it is still rather rare.

The facing page shows some examples of two-dimensional Turing machines with four states. Simple behavior is overwhelmingly the most common. But out of a million randomly chosen rules, there will typically be a few that show complex behavior. Page 186 shows one example where the behavior seems in many respects completely random.

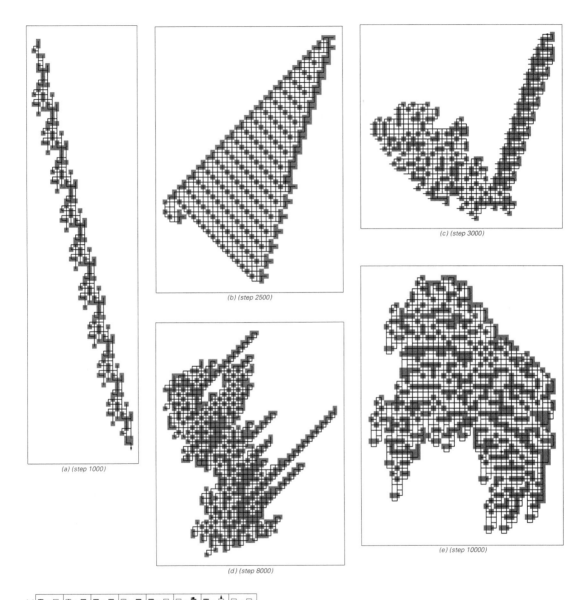

(a) (step 1000)

(b) (step 2500)

(c) (step 3000)

(d) (step 8000)

(e) (step 10000)

Examples of patterns produced by two-dimensional Turing machines whose heads have four possible states. In each case, all cells are initially white, and one of the rules given on the left is applied for the specified number of steps. Note that in the later cases shown, the head often visits the same position on the grid many times.

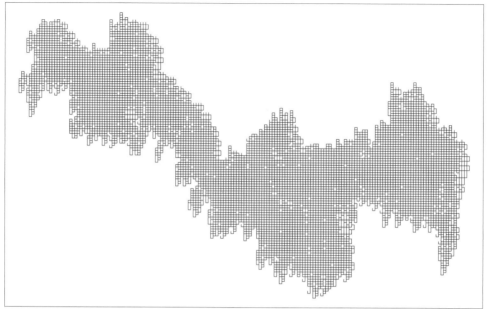

100,000 steps

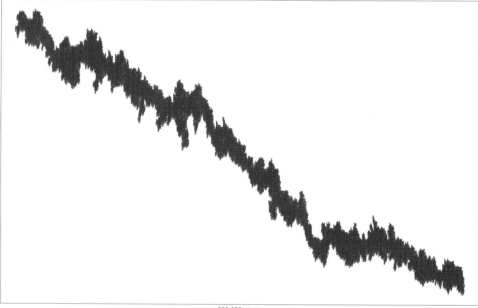

500,000 steps

The path traced out by the head of the two-dimensional Turing machine with rule (e) from the previous page. There are many seemingly random fluctuations in this path, though in general it tends to grow to the right.

Substitution Systems and Fractals

One-dimensional substitution systems of the kind we discussed on page 82 can be thought of as working by progressively subdividing each element they contain into several smaller elements.

One can construct two-dimensional substitution systems that work in essentially the same way, as shown in the pictures below.

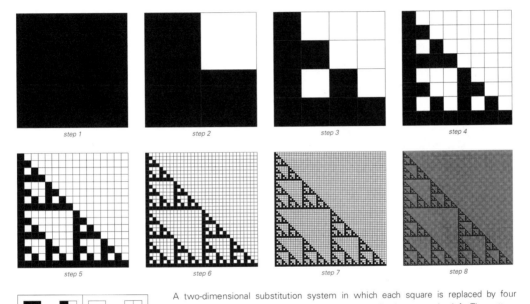

A two-dimensional substitution system in which each square is replaced by four smaller squares at every step according to the rule shown on the left. The pattern generated has a nested form.

The next page gives some more examples of two-dimensional substitution systems. The patterns that are produced are certainly quite intricate. But there is nevertheless great regularity in their overall forms. Indeed, just like patterns produced by one-dimensional substitution systems on page 83, all the patterns shown here ultimately have a simple nested structure.

Why does such nesting occur? The basic reason is that at every step the rules for the substitution system simply replace each black square with several smaller black squares. And on subsequent steps, each of these new black squares is then in turn replaced in exactly the

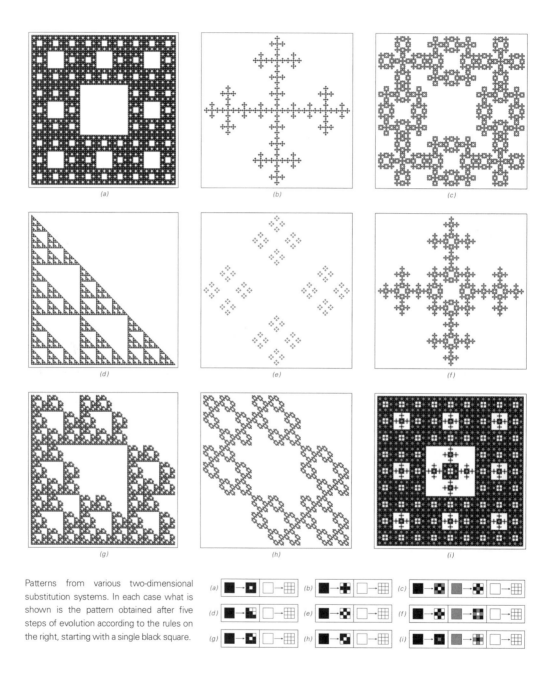

Patterns from various two-dimensional substitution systems. In each case what is shown is the pattern obtained after five steps of evolution according to the rules on the right, starting with a single black square.

same way, so that it ultimately evolves to produce an identical copy of the whole pattern.

But in fact there is nothing about this basic process that depends on the squares being arranged in any kind of rigid grid. And the picture below shows what happens if one just uses a simple geometrical rule to replace each black square by two smaller black squares. The result, once again, is that one gets an intricate but highly regular nested pattern.

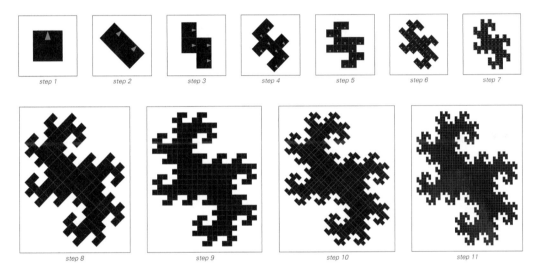

| step 1 | step 2 | step 3 | step 4 | step 5 | step 6 | step 7 |

| step 8 | step 9 | step 10 | step 11 |

The pattern obtained by starting with a single black square and then at every step replacing each black cell with two smaller black cells according to the simple geometrical rule shown on the left. Note that in applying the rule to a particular square, one must take account of the orientation of that square. The final pattern obtained has an intricate nested structure.

In a substitution system where black squares are arranged on a grid, one can be sure that different squares will never overlap. But if there is just a geometrical rule that is used to replace each black square, then it is possible for the squares produced to overlap, as in the picture on the next page. Yet at least in this example, the overall pattern that is ultimately obtained still has a purely nested structure.

The general idea of building up patterns by repeatedly applying geometrical rules is at the heart of so-called fractal geometry. And the

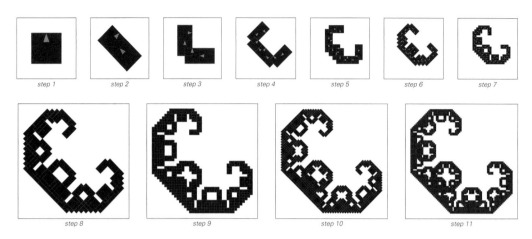

| step 1 | step 2 | step 3 | step 4 | step 5 | step 6 | step 7 |

| step 8 | step 9 | step 10 | step 11 |

The pattern obtained by repeatedly applying the simple geometrical rule shown on the right. Even though this basic rule does not involve overlapping squares, the pattern obtained even by step 3 already has squares that overlap. But the overall pattern obtained after a large number of steps still has a nested form.

pictures on the facing page show several more examples of fractal patterns produced in this way.

The details of the geometrical rules used are different in each case. But what all the rules have in common is that they involve replacing one black square by two or more smaller black squares. And with this kind of setup, it is ultimately inevitable that all the patterns produced must have a completely regular nested structure.

So what does it take to get patterns with more complicated structure? The basic answer, much as we saw in one-dimensional substitution systems on page 85, is some form of interaction between different elements—so that the replacement for a particular element at a given step can depend not only on the characteristics of that element itself, but also on the characteristics of other neighboring elements.

But with geometrical replacement rules of the kind shown on the facing page there is a problem with this. For elements can end up anywhere in the plane, making it difficult to define an obvious notion of neighbors. And the result of this has been that in traditional fractal geometry the idea of interaction between elements is not considered— so that all patterns that are produced have a purely nested form.

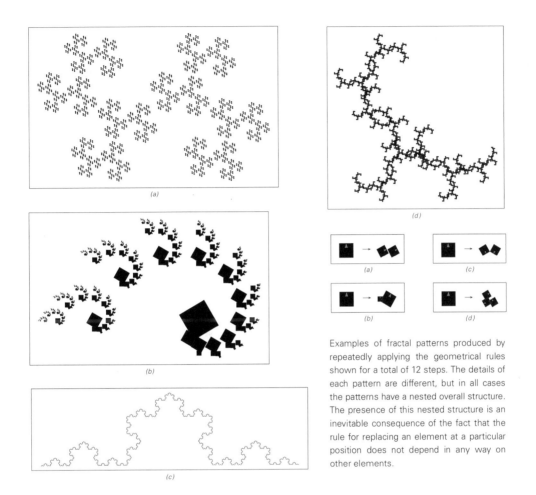

Examples of fractal patterns produced by repeatedly applying the geometrical rules shown for a total of 12 steps. The details of each pattern are different, but in all cases the patterns have a nested overall structure. The presence of this nested structure is an inevitable consequence of the fact that the rule for replacing an element at a particular position does not depend in any way on other elements.

Yet if one sets up elements on a grid it is straightforward to allow the replacements for a given element to depend on its neighbors, as in the picture at the top of the next page. And if one does this, one immediately gets all sorts of fairly complicated patterns that are often not just purely nested—as illustrated in the pictures on the next page.

In Chapter 3 we discussed both ordinary one-dimensional substitution systems, in which every element is replaced at each step, and sequential substitution systems, in which just a single block of elements are replaced at each step. And what we did to find which block of elements should be replaced at a given step was to scan the whole sequence of elements from left to right.

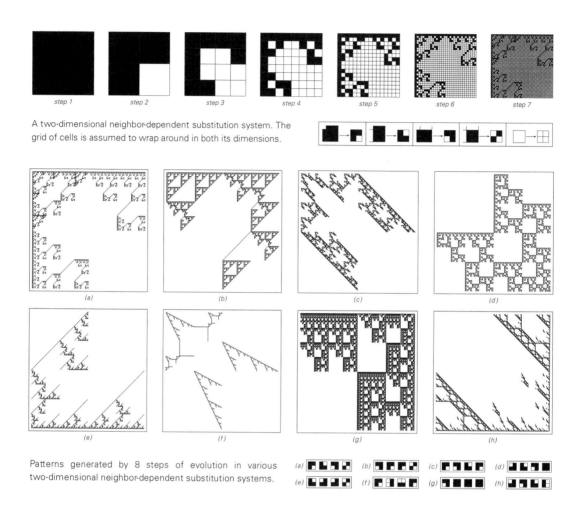

A two-dimensional neighbor-dependent substitution system. The grid of cells is assumed to wrap around in both its dimensions.

Patterns generated by 8 steps of evolution in various two-dimensional neighbor-dependent substitution systems.

So how can this be generalized to higher dimensions? On a two-dimensional grid one can certainly imagine snaking backwards and forwards or spiralling outwards to scan all the elements. But as soon as one defines any particular order for elements—however they may be laid out—this in effect reduces one to dealing with a one-dimensional system.

And indeed there seems to be no immediate way to generalize sequential substitution systems to two or more dimensions. In Chapter 9, however, we will see that with more sophisticated ideas it is in fact possible in any number of dimensions to set up substitution systems in which elements are scanned in order—but whatever order is used, the results are in some sense always the same.

Network Systems

One feature of systems like cellular automata is that their elements are always set up in a regular array that remains the same from one step to the next. In substitution systems with geometrical replacement rules there is slightly more freedom, but still the elements are ultimately constrained to lie in a two-dimensional plane.

Indeed, in all the systems that we have discussed so far there is in effect always a fixed underlying geometrical structure which remains unchanged throughout the evolution of the system.

It turns out, however, that it is possible to construct systems in which there is no such invariance in basic structure, and in this section I discuss as an example one version of what I will call network systems.

A network system is fundamentally just a collection of nodes with various connections between these nodes, and rules that specify how these connections should change from one step to the next.

At any particular step in its evolution, a network system can be thought of a little like an electric circuit, with the nodes of the network corresponding to the components in the circuit, and the connections to the wires joining these components together.

And as in an electric circuit, the properties of the system depend only on the way in which the nodes are connected together, and not on any specific layout for the nodes that may happen to be used.

Of course, to make a picture of a network system, one has to choose particular positions for each of its nodes. But the crucial point is that these positions have no fundamental significance: they are introduced solely for the purpose of visual representation.

In constructing network systems one could in general allow each node to have any number of connections coming from it. But at least for the purposes of this section nothing fundamental turns out to be lost if one restricts oneself to the case in which every node has exactly two outgoing connections—each of which can then either go to another node, or can loop back to the original node itself.

With this setup the very simplest possible network consists of just one node, with both connections from the node looping back, as in the top picture below. With two nodes, there are already three possible patterns of connections, as shown on the second line below. And as the number of nodes increases, the number of possible different networks grows very rapidly.

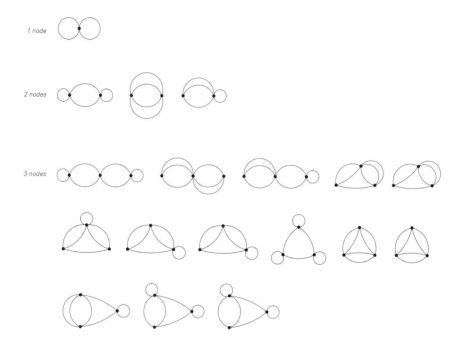

Possible networks formed by having one, two or three nodes, with two connections coming out of each node. The picture shows all inequivalent cases ignoring labels, but excludes networks in which there are nodes which cannot be reached by connections from other nodes.

For most of these networks there is no way of laying out their nodes so as to get a picture that looks like anything much more than a random jumble of wires. But it is nevertheless possible to construct many specific networks that have easily recognizable forms, as shown in the pictures on the facing page.

Each of the networks illustrated at the top of the facing page consists at the lowest level of a collection of identical nodes. But the remarkable fact that we see is that just by changing the pattern of

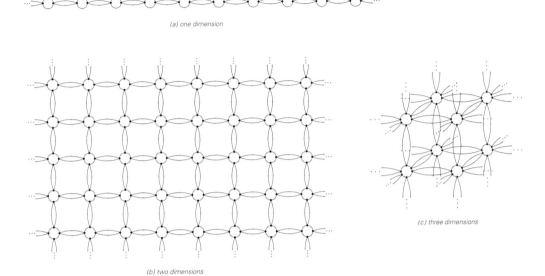

(a) one dimension

(c) three dimensions

(b) two dimensions

Examples of networks that correspond to arrays in one, two and three dimensions. At an underlying level, each network consists just of a collection of nodes with two connections coming from each node. But by setting up appropriate patterns for these connections, one can get networks with very different effective geometrical structures.

connections between these nodes it is possible to get structures that effectively correspond to arrays with different numbers of dimensions.

Example (a) shows a network that is effectively one-dimensional. The network consists of pairs of nodes that can be arranged in a sequence in which each pair is connected to one other pair on the left and another pair on the right.

But there is nothing intrinsically one-dimensional about the structure of network systems. And as example (b) demonstrates, it is just a matter of rearranging connections to get a network that looks like a two-dimensional rather than a one-dimensional array. Each individual node in example (b) still has exactly two connections coming out of it, but now the overall pattern of connections is such that every block of nodes is connected to four rather than two neighboring blocks, so that the network effectively forms a two-dimensional square grid.

Example (c) then shows that with appropriate connections, it is also possible to get a three-dimensional array, and indeed using the same principles an array with any number of dimensions can easily be obtained.

The pictures below show examples of networks that form infinite trees rather than arrays. Notice that the first and last networks shown actually have an identical pattern of connections, but they look different here because the nodes are arranged in a different way on the page.

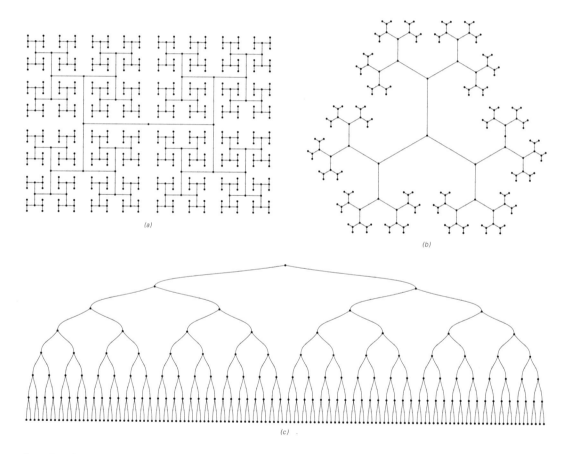

Examples of networks that correspond to infinite trees. Note that networks (a) and (c) are identical, though they look different because the nodes are laid out differently on the page. All the networks shown are truncated at the leaves of each tree.

In general, there is great variety in the possible structures that can be set up in network systems, and as one further example the picture below shows a network that forms a nested pattern.

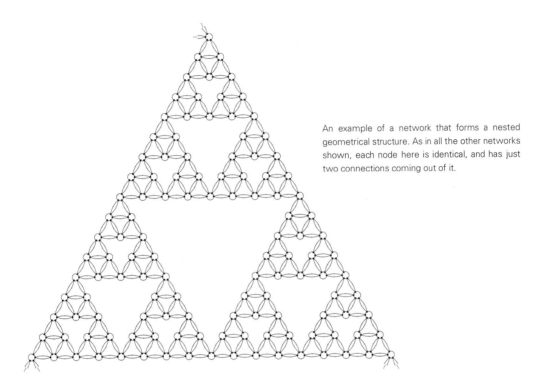

An example of a network that forms a nested geometrical structure. As in all the other networks shown, each node here is identical, and has just two connections coming out of it.

In the pictures above we have seen various examples of individual networks that might exist at a particular step in the evolution of a network system. But now we must consider how such networks are transformed from one step in evolution to the next.

The basic idea is to have rules that specify how the connections coming out of each node should be rerouted on the basis of the local structure of the network around that node.

But to see the effect of any such rules, one must first find a uniform way of displaying the networks that can be produced. The pictures at the top of the next page show one possible approach based on always arranging the nodes in each network in a line across the page. And although this representation can obscure the geometrical structure

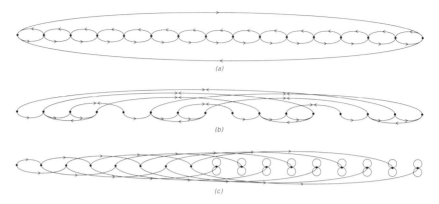

Networks from previous pictures laid out in a uniform way. Network (a) corresponds to a one-dimensional array, (b) to a two-dimensional array, and (c) to a tree. In the layout shown here, all the networks have their nodes arranged along a line. Note that in cases (a) and (b) the connections are arranged so that the arrays effectively wrap around; in case (c) the leaves of the tree are taken to have connections that loop back to themselves.

of a particular network, as in the second and third cases above, it more readily allows comparison between different networks.

In setting up rules for network systems, it is convenient to distinguish the two connections that come out of each node. And in the pictures above one connection is therefore always shown going above the line of nodes, while the other is always shown going below.

The pictures on the facing page show examples of evolution obtained with four different choices of underlying rules. In the first case, the rule specifies that the "above" connection from each node should be rerouted so that it leads to the node obtained by following the "below" connection and then the "above" connection from that node. The "below" connection is left unchanged.

The other rules shown are similar in structure, except that in cases (c) and (d), the "above" connection from each node is rerouted so that it simply loops back to the node itself.

In case (d), the result of this is that the network breaks up into several disconnected pieces. And it turns out that none of the rules I consider here can ever reconnect these pieces again. So as a consequence, what I do in the remainder of this section is to track only the piece that includes the first node shown in pictures such as those

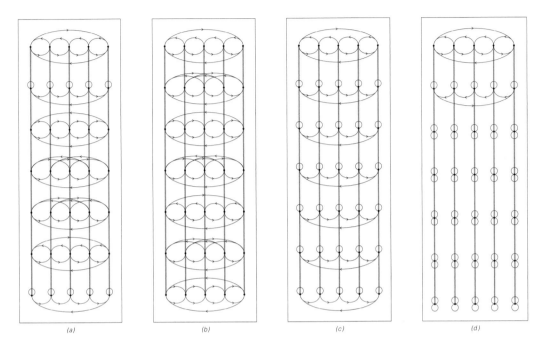

The evolution of network systems with four different choices of underlying rules. Successive steps in the evolution are shown on successive lines down the page. In case (a), the "above" connection of each node is rerouted at each step to lead to the node reached by following first the below connection and then the above connection from that node; the below connection is left unchanged. In case (b), the above connection of each node is rerouted to the node reached by following the above connection and then the above connection again; the below connection is left unchanged. In case (c), the above connection of each node is rerouted so as to loop back to the node itself, while the below connection is left unchanged. And in case (d), the above connection is rerouted so as to loop back, while the below connection is rerouted to lead to the node reached by following the above connection. With the "above" connection labelled as 1 and the "below" connection as 2, these rules correspond to replacing connections $\{\{1\}, \{2\}\}$ at each node by (a) $\{\{2, 1\}, \{2\}\}$, (b) $\{\{1, 1\}, \{2\}\}$, (c) $\{\{\}, \{2\}\}$, and (d) $\{\{\}, \{1\}\}$.

above. And in effect, this then means that other nodes are dropped from the network, so that the total size of the network decreases.

By changing the underlying rules, however, the number of nodes in a network can also be made to increase. The basic way this can be done is by breaking a connection coming from a particular node by inserting a new node and then connecting that new node to nodes obtained by following connections from the original node.

The pictures on the next page show examples of behavior produced by two rules that use this mechanism. In both cases, a new node is inserted in the "above" connection from each existing node in the network. In the first case, the connections from the new node are exactly the same as the connections from the existing node, while in the second case, the "above" and "below" connections are reversed.

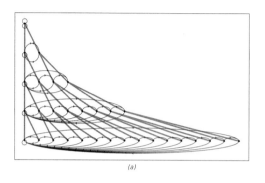
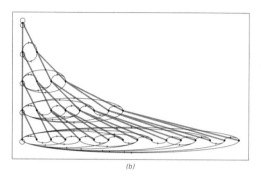

(a)   *(b)*

Evolution of network systems whose rules involve the addition of new nodes. In both cases, the new nodes are inserted in the "above" connection from each node. In case (a), the connections from the new node lead to the same nodes as the connections from the original node. In case (b), the above and below connections for the new node are reversed. In the pictures above, new nodes are placed immediately after the nodes that give rise to them, and gray lines are used to indicate the origin of each node. Note that the initial conditions consist of a network that contains only a single node.

But in both cases the behavior obtained is quite simple. Yet much like neighbor-independent substitution systems these network systems have the property that exactly the same operation is always performed at each node on every step.

In general, however, one can set up network systems that have rules in which different operations are performed at different nodes, depending on the local structure of the network near each node.

One simple scheme for doing this is based on looking at the two connections that come out of each node, and then performing one operation if these two connections lead to the same node, and another if the connections lead to different nodes.

The pictures on the facing page show some examples of what can happen with this scheme. And again it turns out that the behavior is always quite simple—with the network having a structure that inevitably grows in an essentially repetitive way.

But as soon as one allows dependence on slightly longer-range features of the network, much more complicated behavior immediately

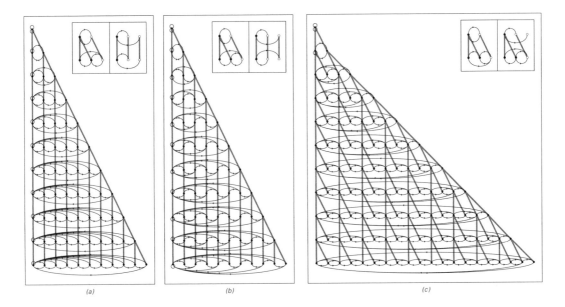

Examples of network systems with rules that cause different operations to be performed at different nodes. Each rule contains two cases, as shown above. The first case specifies what to do if both connections from a particular node lead to the same node; the second case specifies what to do when they lead to different nodes. In the rules shown, the connections from a particular node (indicated by a solid circle) and from new nodes created from this node always go to the nodes indicated by open circles that are reached by following just a single above or below connection from the original node. Even if this restriction is removed, however, more complicated behavior does not appear to be seen.

becomes possible. And indeed, the pictures on the next two pages show examples of what can happen if the rules are allowed to depend on the number of distinct nodes reached by following not just one but up to two successive connections from each node.

With such rules, the sequence of networks obtained no longer needs to form any kind of simple progression, and indeed one finds that even the total number of nodes at each step can vary in a way that seems in many respects completely random.

When we discuss issues of fundamental physics in Chapter 9 we will encounter a variety of other types of network systems—and I suspect that some of these systems will in the end turn out to be closely related to the basic structure of space and spacetime in our universe.

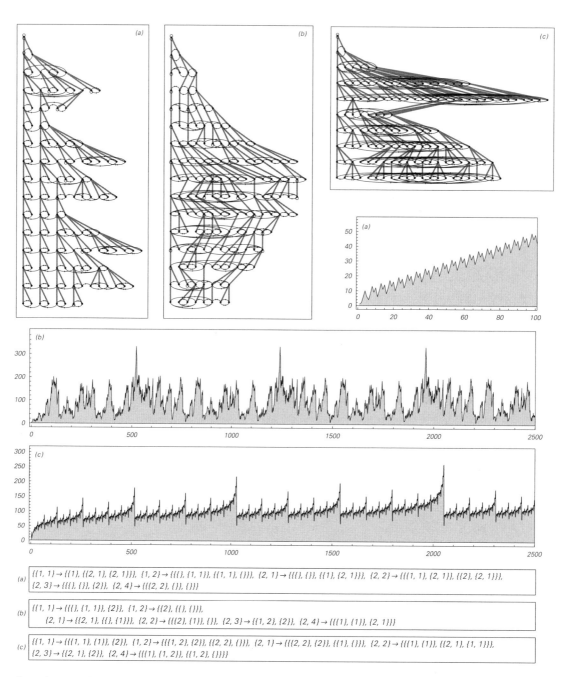

(a) {{1, 1} → {{1}, {{2, 1}, {2, 1}}}, {1, 2} → {{{}, {1, 1}}, {{1, 1}, {}}}, {2, 1} → {{{}, {}}, {{1}, {2, 1}}}, {2, 2} → {{{1, 1}, {2, 1}}, {{2}, {2, 1}}},
{2, 3} → {{{}, {}}, {2}}, {2, 4} → {{{2, 2}, {}}, {}}}

(b) {{1, 1} → {{{}, {1, 1}}, {2}}, {1, 2} → {{2}, {}}, {}},
{2, 1} → {{2, 1}, {{}, {1}}}, {2, 2} → {{{2}, {1}}, {}}, {2, 3} → {{1, 2}, {2}}, {2, 4} → {{{1}, {1}}, {2, 1}}}

(c) {{1, 1} → {{{1, 1}, {1}}, {2}}, {1, 2} → {{{1, 2}, {2}}, {{2, 2}, {}}}, {2, 1} → {{{2, 2}, {2}}, {{1}, {}}}, {2, 2} → {{{1}, {1}}, {2, 1}, {1, 1}}},
{2, 3} → {{2, 1}, {2}}, {2, 4} → {{{1}, {1, 2}}, {{1, 2}, {}}}}

Network systems in which the rule depends on the number of distinct nodes reached by going up to distance two away from each node. The plots show the total number of nodes obtained at each step. In cases (a) and (b), the behavior of the system is eventually repetitive. In case (c), it is nested—the size of the network at step t is related to the number of 1's in the base 2 digit sequence of t.

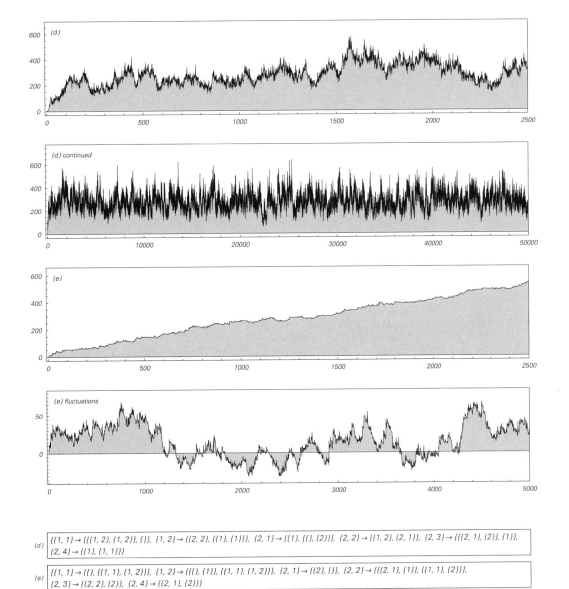

(d) $\{\{1, 1\} \rightarrow \{\{\{1, 2\}, \{1, 2\}\}, \{\}\}, \{1, 2\} \rightarrow \{\{2, 2\}, \{\{1\}, \{1\}\}\}, \{2, 1\} \rightarrow \{\{1\}, \{\}, \{2\}\}\}, \{2, 2\} \rightarrow \{\{1, 2\}, \{2, 1\}\}, \{2, 3\} \rightarrow \{\{\{2, 1\}, \{2\}\}, \{1\}\},$
$\{2, 4\} \rightarrow \{\{1\}, \{1, 1\}\}\}$

(e) $\{\{1, 1\} \rightarrow \{\{\}, \{\{1, 1\}, \{1, 2\}\}\}, \{1, 2\} \rightarrow \{\{\{\}, \{1\}\}, \{\{1, 1\}, \{1, 2\}\}\}, \{2, 1\} \rightarrow \{\{2\}, \{\}\}, \{2, 2\} \rightarrow \{\{\{2, 1\}, \{1\}\}, \{\{1, 1\}, \{2\}\}\},$
$\{2, 3\} \rightarrow \{\{2, 2\}, \{2\}\}, \{2, 4\} \rightarrow \{\{2, 1\}, \{2\}\}\}$

Network systems in which the total number of nodes obtained on successive steps appears to vary in a largely random way forever. About one in 10,000 randomly chosen network systems seem to exhibit the kind of behavior shown here.

Multiway Systems

The network systems that we discussed in the previous section do not have any underlying grid of elements in space. But they still in a sense have a simple one-dimensional arrangement of states in time. And in fact, all the systems that we have considered so far in this book can be thought of as having the same simple structure in time. For all of them are ultimately set up just to evolve progressively from one state to the next.

Multiway systems, however, are defined so that they can have not just a single state, but a whole collection of possible states at any given step.

The picture below shows a very simple example of such a system.

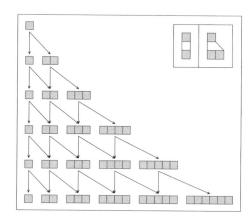

A very simple multiway system in which one element in each sequence is replaced at each step by either one or two elements. The main feature of multiway systems is that all the distinct sequences that result are kept.

Each state in the system consists of a sequence of elements, and in the particular case of the picture above, the rule specifies that at each step each of these elements either remains the same or is replaced by a pair of elements. Starting with a single state consisting of one element, the picture then shows that applying these rules immediately gives two possible states: one with a single element, and the other with two.

Multiway systems can in general use any sets of rules that define replacements for blocks of elements in sequences. We already saw exactly these kinds of rules when we discussed sequential substitution systems on page 88. But in sequential substitution systems the idea was to do just one replacement at each step. In multiway systems, however, the idea is to do all possible replacements at each step—and then to keep all the possible different sequences that are generated.

The pictures below show what happens with some very simple rules. In each of these examples the behavior turns out to be rather simple—with for example the number of possible sequences always increasing uniformly from one step to the next.

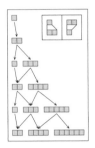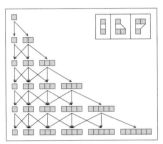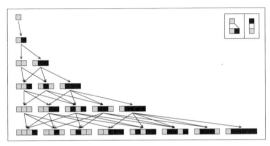

Examples of simple multiway systems. The number of distinct sequences at step *t* in these three systems is respectively *Ceiling[t/2]*, *t* and *Fibonacci[t + 1]* (which increases approximately like *1.618^t*).

In general, however, this number need not exhibit such uniform growth, and the pictures below show examples where fluctuations occur.

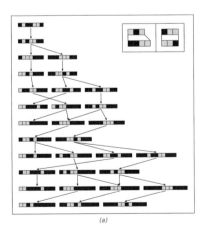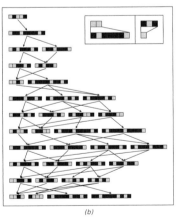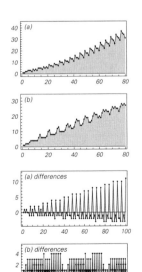

(a)   (b)

Examples of multiway systems with slightly more complicated behavior. The plots on the right show the total number of possible states obtained at each step, and the differences of these numbers from one step to the next. In both cases, essentially repetitive behavior is seen, every 40 and 161 steps respectively. Note that in case (a), the total number of possible states at step *t* increases roughly like *t^2*, while in case (b) it increases only like *t*.

But in both these cases it turns out to be not too long before these fluctuations essentially repeat. The picture below shows an example where a larger amount of apparent randomness is seen. Yet even in this case one finds that there ends up again being essential repetition—although now only every 1071 steps.

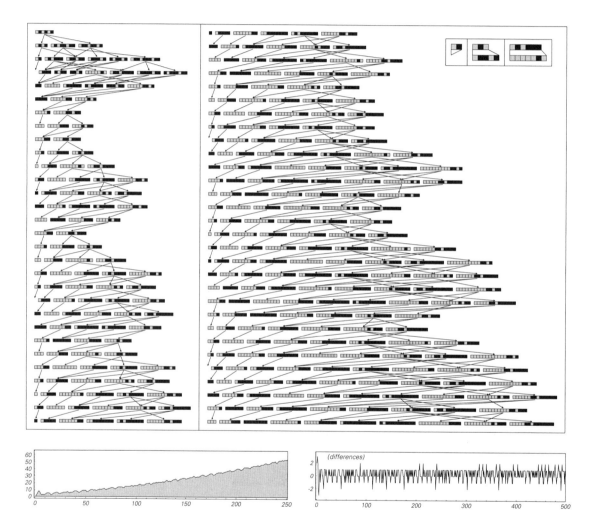

A multiway system with behavior that shows some signs of apparent randomness. The rule for this system involves three possible replacements. Note that the first replacement only removes elements and does not insert new ones. In the pictures sequences containing zero elements therefore sometimes appear. At least with the initial condition used here, despite considerable early apparent randomness, the differences in number of elements do repeat (shifted by 1) every 1071 steps.

If one looks at many multiway systems, most either grow exponentially quickly, or not at all; slow growth of the kind seen on the facing page is rather rare. And indeed even when such growth leads to a certain amount of apparent randomness it typically in the end seems to exhibit some form of repetition. If one allows more rapid growth, however, then there presumably start to be all sorts of multiway systems that never show any such regularity. But in practice it tends to be rather difficult to study these kinds of multiway systems—since the number of states they generate quickly becomes too large to handle.

One can get some idea about how such systems behave, however, just by looking at the states that occur at early steps. The picture below shows an example—with ultimately fairly simple nested behavior.

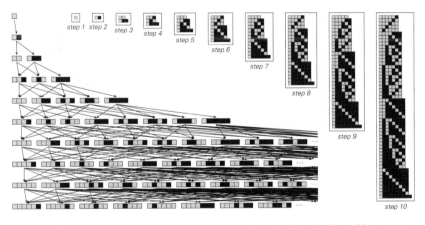

The collections of states generated on successive steps by a simple multiway system with rapid growth shown on page 205. The particular rule used here eventually generates all states beginning with a white cell. At step t there are $Fibonacci[t+1]$ states; a given state with m white cells and n black cells appears at step $2m+n-1$.

The pictures on the next page show some more examples. Sometimes the set of states that get generated at a particular step show essential repetition—though often with a long period. Sometimes this set in effect includes a large fraction of the possible digit sequences of a given length—and so essentially shows nesting. But in other cases there is at least a hint of considerably more complexity—even though the total number of states may still end up growing quite smoothly.

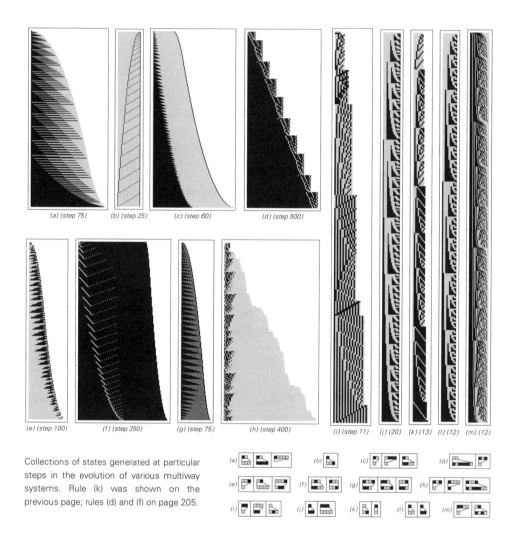

Collections of states generated at particular steps in the evolution of various multiway systems. Rule (k) was shown on the previous page; rules (d) and (f) on page 205.

Looking carefully at the pictures of multiway system evolution on previous pages, a feature one notices is that the same sequences often occur on several different steps. Yet it is a consequence of the basic setup for multiway systems that whenever any particular sequence occurs, it must always lead to exactly the same behavior.

So this means that the complete evolution can be represented as in the picture at the top of the facing page, with each sequence shown explicitly only once, and any sequence generated more than once indicated just by an arrow going back to its first occurrence.

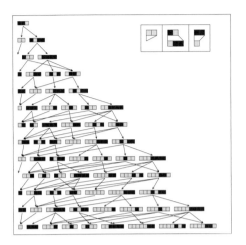 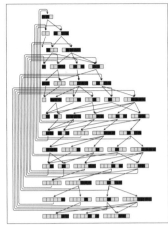

The evolution of a multiway system, first with every sequence explicitly shown at each step, and then with every sequence only ever shown once.

But there is no need to arrange the picture like this: for the whole behavior of the multiway system can in a sense be captured just by giving the network of what sequence leads to what other. The picture below shows stages in building up such a network. And what we see is that just as the network systems that we discussed in the previous section can build up their own pattern of connections in space, so also multiway systems can in effect build up their own pattern of connections in time—and this pattern can often be quite complicated.

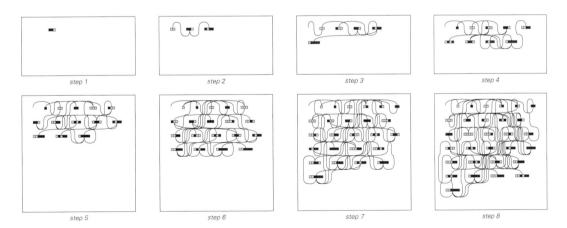

The network built up by the evolution of the multiway system from the top of the page. This network in effect represents a network of connections in time between states of the multiway system.

Systems Based on Constraints

In the course of this book we have looked at many different kinds of systems. But in one respect all these systems have ultimately been set up in the same basic way: they are all based on explicit rules that specify how the system evolves from step to step.

In traditional science, however, it is common to consider systems that are set up in a rather different way: instead of having explicit rules for evolution, the systems are just given constraints to satisfy.

As a simple example, consider a line of cells in which each cell is colored black or white, and in which the arrangement of colors is subject to the constraint that every cell should have exactly one black and one white neighbor. Knowing only this constraint gives no explicit procedure for working out the color of each cell. And in fact it may at first not be clear that there will be any arrangement of colors that can satisfy the constraint. But it turns out that there is—as shown below.

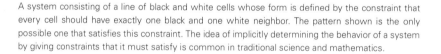

A system consisting of a line of black and white cells whose form is defined by the constraint that every cell should have exactly one black and one white neighbor. The pattern shown is the only possible one that satisfies this constraint. The idea of implicitly determining the behavior of a system by giving constraints that it must satisfy is common in traditional science and mathematics.

And having seen this picture, one might then imagine that there must be many other patterns that would also satisfy the constraint. After all, the constraint is local to neighboring cells, so one might suppose that parts of the pattern sufficiently far apart should always be independent. But in fact this is not true, and instead the system works a bit like a puzzle in which there is only one way to fit in each piece. And in the end it is only the perfectly repetitive pattern shown above that can satisfy the required constraint at every cell.

Other constraints, however, can allow more freedom. Thus, for example, with the constraint that every cell must have at least one neighbor whose color is different from its own, any of the patterns in the picture at the top of the facing page are allowed, as indeed is any pattern that involves no more than two successive cells of the same color.

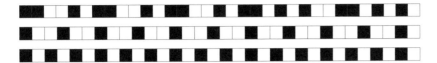

A system consisting of a line of black and white cells whose form is defined by the constraint that every cell should have at least one neighbor whose color is different from its own. There are many possible arrangements of colors that satisfy this constraint. Some, like the first arrangement above, look quite random. But others, like the second two arrangements above, are simple and repetitive. It turns out that in a one-dimensional system no set of local constraints can force arrangements of more complicated types.

But while the first arrangement of colors shown above looks somewhat random, the last two are simple and purely repetitive.

So what about other choices of constraints? We have seen in this book many examples of systems where simple sets of rules give rise to highly complex behavior. But what about systems based on constraints? Are there simple sets of constraints that can force complex patterns?

It turns out that in one-dimensional systems there are not. For in one dimension it is possible to prove that any local set of constraints that can be satisfied at all can always be satisfied by some simple and purely repetitive arrangement of colors.

But what about two dimensions? The proof for one dimension breaks down in two dimensions, and so it becomes at least conceivable that a simple set of constraints could force a complex pattern to occur.

As a first example of a two-dimensional system, consider an array of black and white cells in which the constraint is imposed that every black cell should have exactly one black neighbor, and every white cell should have exactly two white neighbors.

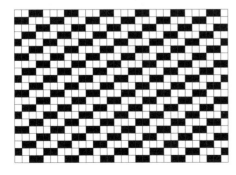

A system consisting of a grid of black and white cells defined by the constraint that every black cell should have exactly one black neighbor among its four neighbors, and every white cell should have exactly two white neighbors. The infinite repetitive pattern shown here, together with its rotations and reflections, is the only one that satisfies this constraint. (The picture is assumed to wrap around at each edge.) The pattern can be viewed as a tessellation of 5 × 5 blocks of cells.

As in one dimension, knowing the constraint does not immediately provide a procedure for finding a pattern which satisfies it. But a little experimentation reveals that the simple repetitive pattern above satisfies the constraint, and in fact it is the only pattern to do so.

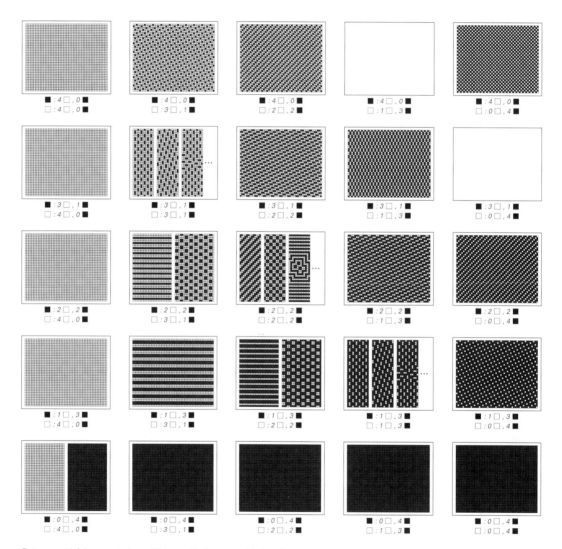

Patterns satisfying constraints which specify that every black cell and every white cell must have a certain fixed number of black and white neighbors. The blank rectangles in the upper right indicate constraints that cannot be satisfied by any pattern whatsoever. Most of the constraints are satisfied by a single pattern, together with its rotations and reflections. In some cases, two distinct patterns are possible, and in a few cases, an infinite set of patterns are possible. In all cases where the constraints can be satisfied at all, a simple repetitive pattern nevertheless suffices.

What about other constraints? The pictures on the facing page show schematically what happens with constraints that require each cell to have various numbers of black and white neighbors.

Several kinds of results are seen. In the two cases shown as blank rectangles on the upper right, there are no patterns at all that satisfy the constraints. But in every other case the constraints can be satisfied, though typically by just one or sometimes two simple infinite repetitive patterns. In the three cases shown in the center a whole range of mixtures of different repetitive patterns are possible. But ultimately, in every case where some pattern can work, a simple repetitive pattern is all that is needed.

So what about more complicated constraints? The pictures below show examples based on constraints that require the local arrangement of colors around every cell to match a fixed set of possible templates.

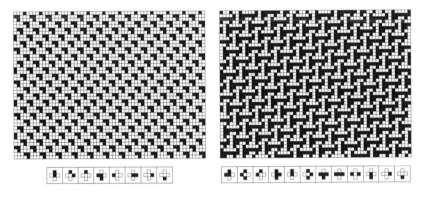

Systems specified by the constraint that the local arrangement of colors around every cell must match the fixed set of possible templates shown. Note that these templates apply to every cell, with templates of neighboring cells overlapping. Pattern (a) can be viewed as formed from a tessellation of 5 × 10 blocks of cells; pattern (b) from a tessellation of 24 × 24 blocks. With the numbering scheme for constraints used on the next two pages the cases shown here correspond to 1384774 and 328778790.

There are a total of 4,294,967,296 possible sets of such templates. And of these, 766,979,044 lead to constraints that cannot be satisfied by any pattern. But among the 3,527,988,252 that remain, it turns out that every single one can be satisfied by a simple repetitive pattern. In fact the number of different repetitive patterns that are ever needed is quite small: if a particular constraint can be satisfied by any pattern, then one of the set of 171 repetitive patterns on the next two pages is always sufficient.

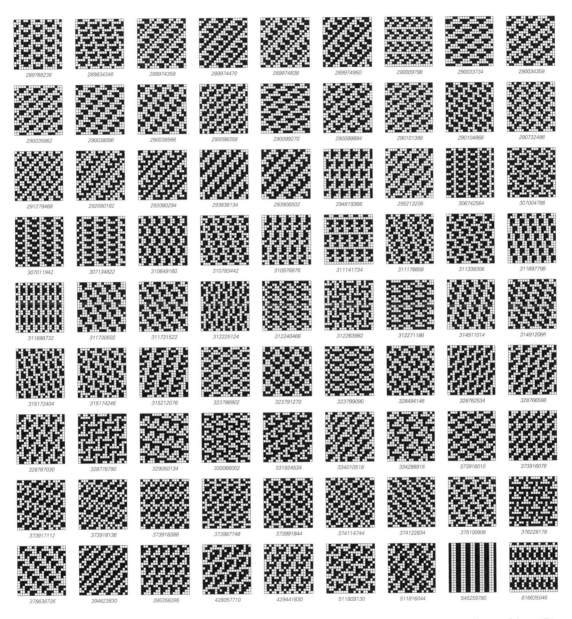

The complete collection of all 171 patterns needed to satisfy constraints of the type shown on the previous page. If none of these 171 patterns satisfy a particular constraint, then it follows that no pattern at all will satisfy the constraint. The patterns are labelled by numbers which specify the minimal constraint which requires the given pattern. Patterns differing by overall reflection, rotation or interchange of black and white are not shown.

So how can one force more complex patterns to occur?

The basic answer is that one must extend at least slightly the kinds of constraints that one considers. And one way to do this is to require not only that the colors around each cell match a set of templates, but also that a particular template from this set must appear at least somewhere in the array of cells.

The pictures below show a few examples of patterns determined by constraints of this kind. A typical feature is that the patterns are divided into several separate regions, often emanating from some kind of center. But at least in all the examples below, the patterns that occur in each individual region are still simple and repetitive.

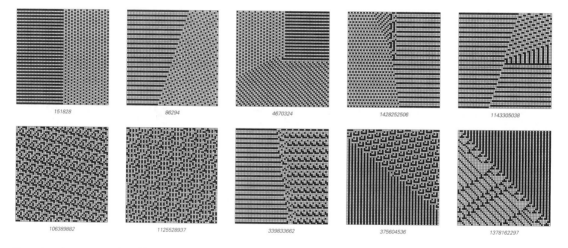

151828
86294
4670324
1428252506
1143305038

106389882
1125528937
339833662
375604536
1378162297

Examples of patterns produced by systems in which not only must the arrangement of colors in each neighborhood match one of a fixed set of templates, but also a certain template from this set must occur at least once in the pattern. The constraints are numbered as before, and in each picture the template that must occur is shown at the center. Constraint 1125528937 leads to a pattern that repeats in 98 × 98 blocks. The last pattern shown is also repetitive, repeating every 56 cells on the diagonal.

So how can one find constraints that force more complex patterns? To do so has been fairly difficult, and in fact has taken almost as much computational effort as any other single result in this book.

The basic problem is that given a constraint it can be extremely difficult to find out what pattern—if any—will satisfy the constraint.

In a system like a cellular automaton that is based on explicit rules, it is always straightforward to take the rule and apply it to see what pattern is produced. But in a system that is based on constraints, there is no such direct procedure, and instead one must in effect always go outside of the system to work out what patterns can occur.

The most straightforward approach might just be to enumerate every single possible pattern and then see which, if any, of them satisfy a particular constraint. But in systems containing more than just a few cells, the total number of possible patterns is absolutely astronomical, and so enumerating them becomes completely impractical.

A more practical alternative is to build up patterns iteratively, starting with a small region, and then adding new cells in essentially all possible ways, at each stage backtracking if the constraint for the system does not end up being satisfied.

The pictures on the next page show a few sequences of patterns produced by this method. In some cases, there emerge quite quickly simple repetitive patterns that satisfy the constraint. But in other cases, a huge number of possibilities have to be examined in order to find any suitable pattern.

And what if there is no pattern at all that can satisfy a particular constraint? One might think that to demonstrate this would effectively require examining every conceivable pattern on the infinite grid of cells. But in fact, if one can show that there is no pattern that satisfies the constraint in a limited region, then this proves that no pattern can satisfy the constraint on the whole grid. And indeed for many constraints, there are already quite small regions for which it is possible to establish that no pattern can be found.

But occasionally, as in the third picture on the next page, one runs into constraints that can be satisfied for regions containing thousands of cells, but not for the whole grid. And to analyze such cases inevitably requires examining huge numbers of possible patterns.

But with an appropriate collection of tricks, it is in the end feasible to take almost any system of the type discussed here, and determine what pattern, if any, satisfies its constraint.

So what kinds of patterns can be needed? In the vast majority of cases, simple repetitive patterns, or mixtures of such patterns, are the only ones that are needed.

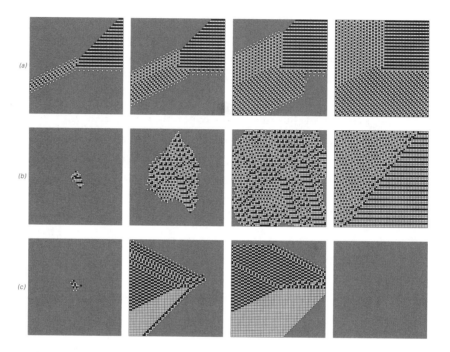

Stages in finding patterns that satisfy constraints (a) 4670324, (b) 373384574, and (c) 387520105. Gray is used to indicate cells whose colors have not yet been determined. The first stage shown in each case corresponds to cells whose colors can be deduced immediately from the presence of a particular template at the center. In case (a) choices for additional cells can be made straightforwardly, and an infinite regular pattern can be built up without any backtracking. In case (b), many choices for additional cells have to be tried, with much backtracking, and in the end the automatic procedure fails to find a repetitive pattern. Nevertheless, as the last stage demonstrates, a repetitive pattern does in fact exist. In case (c), the automatic procedure finds a fairly large and almost regular pattern that satisfies the constraints, but in this case it turns out that no infinite pattern exists.

But if one systematically examines possible constraints in the order shown on pages 214 and 215, then it turns out that after examining more than 18 million of them, one finally discovers the system shown on the facing page. And in this system, unlike all others before it, no repetitive pattern is possible; the only pattern that satisfies the constraint is the non-repetitive nested pattern shown in the picture.

After testing millions of constraints, and tens of billions of candidate patterns, therefore, it is finally possible to establish that a system based on simple constraints of the type discussed here can be forced to exhibit behavior more complex than pure repetition.

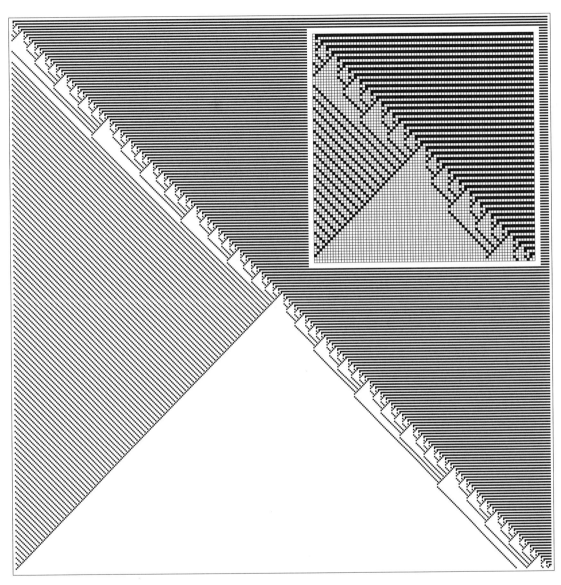

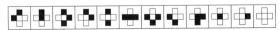

The simplest system based on constraints that is forced to exhibit a non-repetitive pattern. The constraint requires that the arrangement of colors around each cell must match one of the 12 templates shown, and that at least somewhere in the pattern a template containing a pair of stacked black cells must occur. In the numbering scheme used on preceding pages, the constraint is number 18762389. The pattern shown is unique, in that no variations of it, except for trivial translations, will satisfy the constraints. The nested structure on the diagonal essentially corresponds to a progression of base 2 digit sequences for positive and negative numbers.

What about still more complex behavior?

There are altogether 137,438,953,472 constraints of the type shown on page 216. And of the millions of these that I have tested, none have forced anything more complicated than the kind of nested behavior seen on the previous page. But if one extends again the type of constraints one considers, it turns out to become possible to construct examples that force more complex behavior.

The idea is to set up templates that involve complete 3 × 3 blocks of cells, including diagonal neighbors. The picture below then shows an example of such a system, in which by allowing only a specific set of 33 templates, a nested pattern is forced to occur.

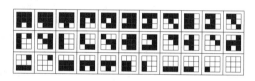

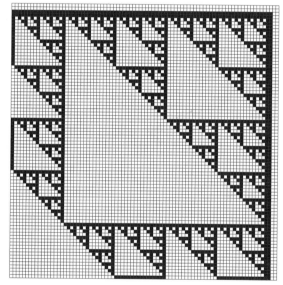

An example of a system based on a constraint involving 3 × 3 templates of cells. In this particular system, only the 33 templates shown above (out of the 512 possible ones) are allowed to occur. This constraint, together with the requirement that the first template must appear at least somewhere, then turns out to force a nested pattern to occur. The system shown was specifically constructed in correspondence with the rule 60 elementary one-dimensional cellular automaton.

What about more complex patterns? Searches have not succeeded in finding anything. But explicit construction, based on correspondence with one-dimensional cellular automata, leads to the example shown at the top of the facing page: a system with 56 allowed templates in which the only pattern satisfying the constraint is a complex and largely random one, derived from the rule 30 cellular automaton.

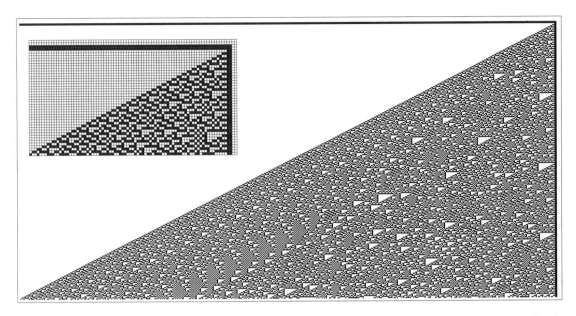

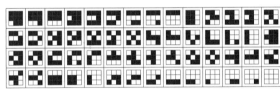

A system based on a constraint, in which a complex and largely random pattern is forced to occur. The constraint specifies that only the 56 3 × 3 templates shown at left can occur anywhere in the pattern, with the first template appearing at least once. The pattern required to satisfy this constraint corresponds to a shifted version of the one generated by the evolution of the rule 30 elementary one-dimensional cellular automaton.

So finally this shows that it is indeed possible to force complex behavior to occur in systems based on constraints. But from what we have seen in this section such behavior appears to be quite rare: unlike many of the simple rules that we have discussed in this book, it seems that almost all simple constraints lead only to fairly simple patterns.

Any phenomenon based on rules can always ultimately also be described in terms of constraints. But the results of this section indicate that these descriptions can have to be fairly complicated for complex behavior to occur. So the fact that traditional science and mathematics tends to concentrate on equations that operate like constraints provides yet another reason for their failure to identify the fundamental phenomenon of complexity that I discuss in this book.

6

Starting from Randomness

The Emergence of Order

In the past several chapters, we have seen many examples of behavior that simple programs can produce. But while we have discussed a whole range of different kinds of underlying rules, we have for the most part considered only the simplest possible initial conditions—so that for example we have usually started with just a single black cell.

My purpose in this chapter is to go to the opposite extreme, and to consider completely random initial conditions, in which, for example, every cell is chosen to be black or white at random.

One might think that starting from such randomness no order would ever emerge. But in fact what we will find in this chapter is that many systems spontaneously tend to organize themselves, so that even with completely random initial conditions they end up producing behavior that has many features that are not at all random.

The picture at the top of the next page shows as a simple first example a cellular automaton which starts from a typical random initial condition, then evolves down the page according to the very simple rule that a cell becomes black if either of its neighbors are black.

What the picture then shows is that every region of white that exists in the initial conditions progressively gets filled in with black, so that in the end all that remains is a uniform state with every cell black.

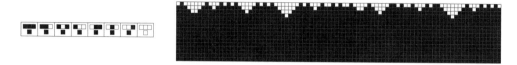

A cellular automaton that evolves to a simple uniform state when started from any random initial condition. The rule in this case was first shown on page 24, and is number 254 in the scheme described on page 53. It specifies that a cell should become black whenever either of its neighbors is already black.

The pictures below show examples of other cellular automata that exhibit the same basic phenomenon. In each case the initial conditions are random, but the system nevertheless quickly organizes itself to become either uniformly white or uniformly black.

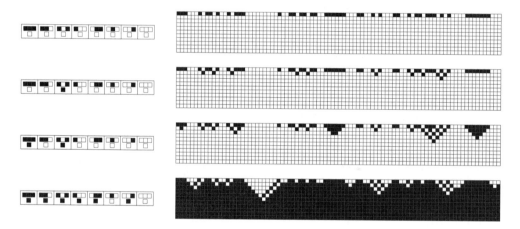

Four more examples of cellular automata that evolve from random initial conditions to completely uniform states. The rules shown here correspond to numbers 0, 32, 160 and 250.

The facing page shows cellular automata that exhibit slightly more complicated behavior. Starting from random initial conditions, these cellular automata again quickly settle down to stable states. But now these stable states are not just uniform in color, but instead involve a collection of definite structures that either remain fixed on successive steps, or repeat periodically.

So if they have simple underlying rules, do all cellular automata started from random initial conditions eventually settle down to give stable states that somehow look simple?

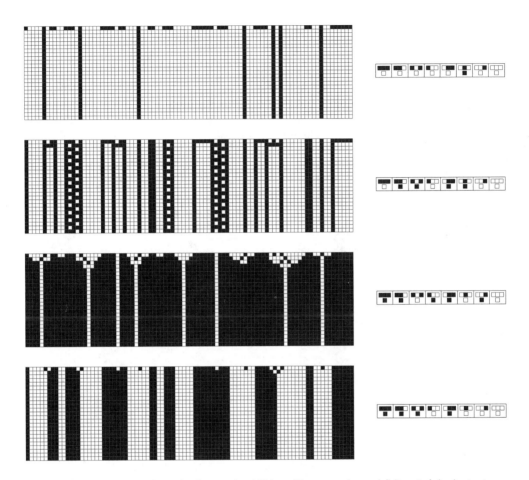

Examples of cellular automata that evolve from random initial conditions to produce a definite set of simple structures. For any particular rule, the form of these structures is always the same. But their positions depend on the details of the initial conditions given, and in many cases the final arrangement of structures can be thought of as a kind of filtered version of the initial conditions. Thus for example in the first rule shown here a structure consisting of a black cell occurs wherever there was an isolated black cell in the initial conditions. The rules shown are numbers 4, 108, 218 and 232.

It turns out that they do not. And indeed the picture on the next page shows one of many examples in which starting from random initial conditions there continues to be very complicated behavior forever. And indeed the behavior that is produced appears in many respects completely random. But dotted around the picture one sees many definite white triangles and other small structures that indicate at least a certain degree of organization.

A cellular automaton that never settles down to a stable state, but instead continues to show behavior that seems in many respects random. The rule is number 126.

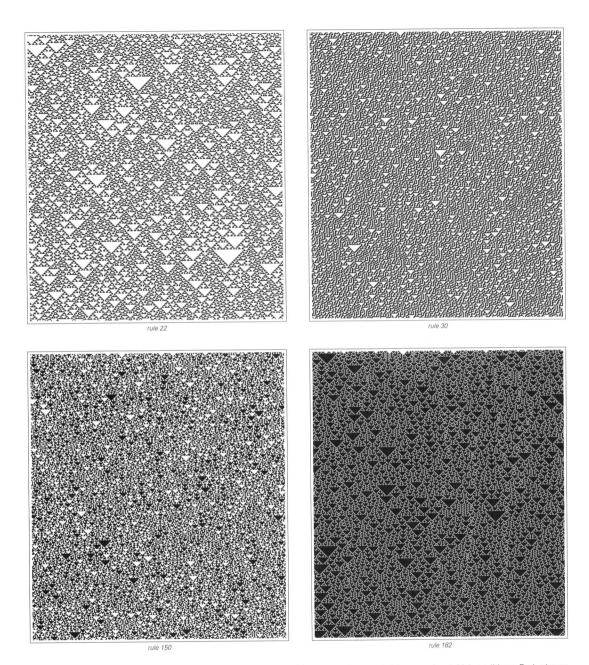

rule 22

rule 30

rule 150

rule 182

Other examples of cellular automata that never settle down to stable states when started from random initial conditions. Each picture is a total of 300 cells across. Note the presence of triangles and other small structures dotted throughout all of the pictures.

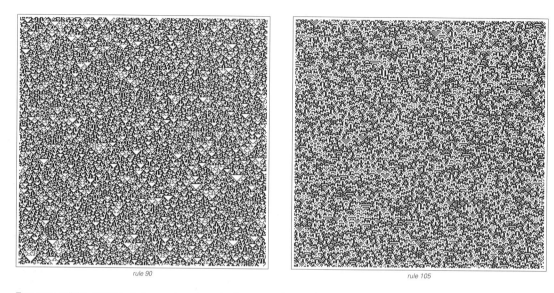

rule 90   rule 105

Two more cellular automata that generate various small structures but continue to show seemingly quite random behavior forever.

The pictures above and on the previous page show more examples of cellular automata with similar behavior. There is considerable randomness in the patterns produced in each case. But despite this randomness there are always triangles and other small structures that emerge in the evolution of the system.

So just how complex can the behavior of a cellular automaton that starts from random initial conditions be? We have seen some examples where the behavior quickly stabilizes, and others where it continues to be quite random forever. But in a sense the greatest complexity lies between these extremes—in systems that neither stabilize completely, nor exhibit close to uniform randomness forever.

The facing page and the one that follows show as an example the cellular automaton that we first discussed on page 32. The initial conditions used are again completely random. But the cellular automaton quickly organizes itself into a set of definite localized structures. Yet now these structures do not just remain fixed, but instead move around and interact with each other in complicated ways. And the result of this is an elaborate pattern that mixes order and randomness—and is as complex as anything we have seen in this book.

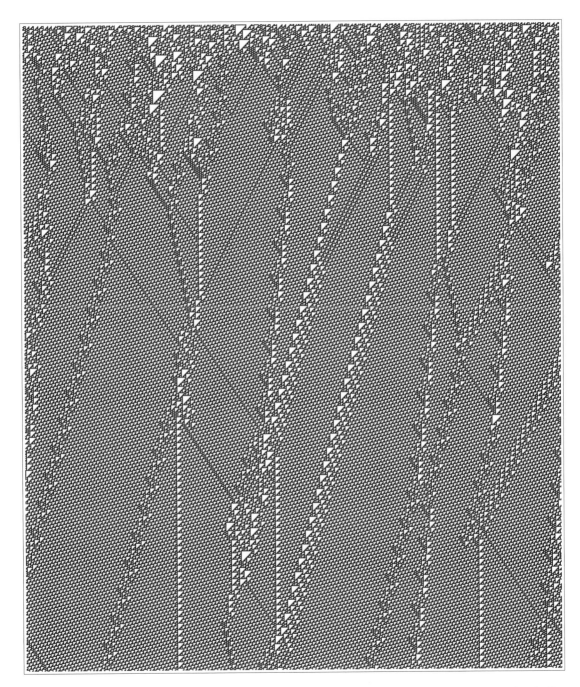

Complex behavior in the rule 110 cellular automaton starting from a random initial condition. The system quickly organizes itself to produce a set of definite localized structures, which then move around and interact with each other in complicated ways.

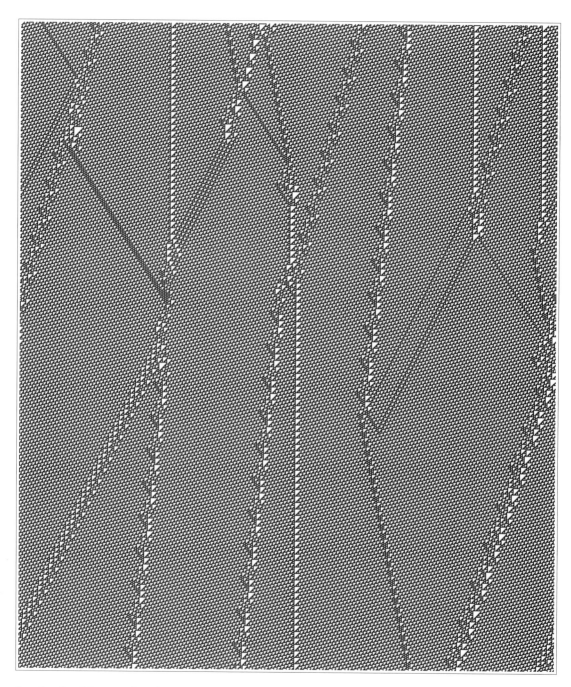

A continuation of the pattern from the previous page. Each page shows 700 steps in the evolution of the cellular automaton.

Four Classes of Behavior

In the previous section we saw what a number of specific cellular automata do if one starts them from random initial conditions. But in this section I want to ask the more general question of what arbitrary cellular automata do when started from random initial conditions.

One might at first assume that such a general question could never have a useful answer. For every single cellular automaton after all ultimately has a different underlying rule, with different properties and potentially different consequences.

But the next few pages show various sequences of cellular automata, all starting from random initial conditions.

And while it is indeed true that for almost every rule the specific pattern produced is at least somewhat different, when one looks at all the rules together, one sees something quite remarkable: that even though each pattern is different in detail, the number of fundamentally different types of patterns is very limited.

Indeed, among all kinds of cellular automata, it seems that the patterns which arise can almost always be assigned quite easily to one of just four basic classes illustrated below.

class 1   *class 2*   *class 3*   *class 4*

Examples of the four basic classes of behavior seen in the evolution of cellular automata from random initial conditions. I first developed this classification in 1983.

These classes are conveniently numbered in order of increasing complexity, and each one has certain immediate distinctive features.

In class 1, the behavior is very simple, and almost all initial conditions lead to exactly the same uniform final state.

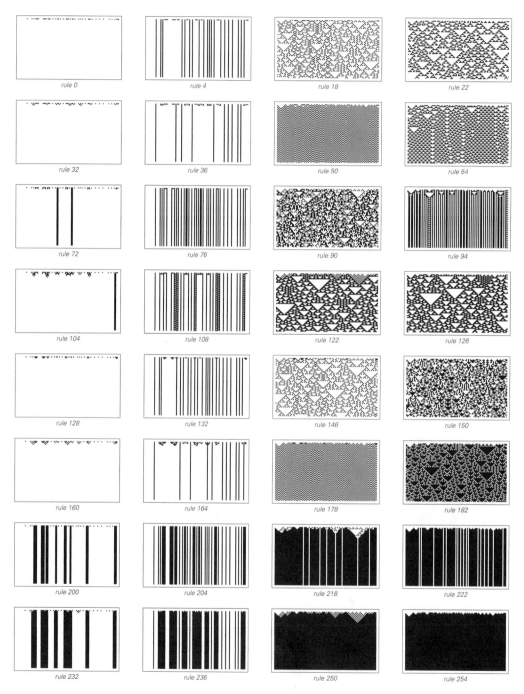

The behavior of all cellular automata that involve only nearest neighbors in a symmetrical way, have two possible colors for each cell, and leave states consisting only of white cells unchanged.

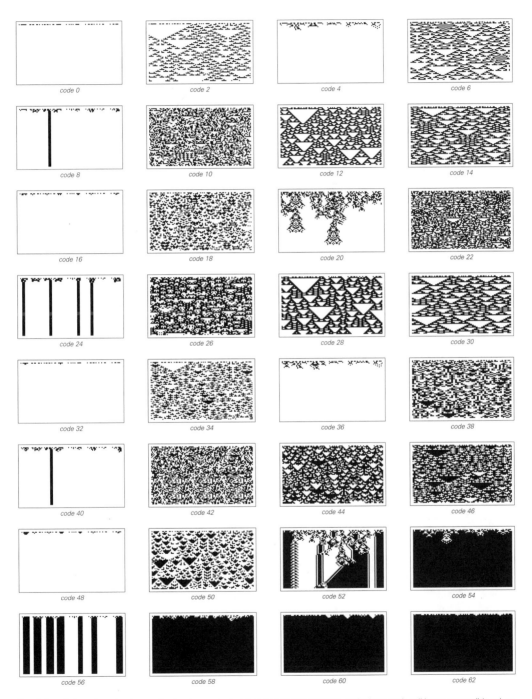

Totalistic cellular automata whose rules involve nearest and next-nearest neighbors, and where each cell has two possible colors.

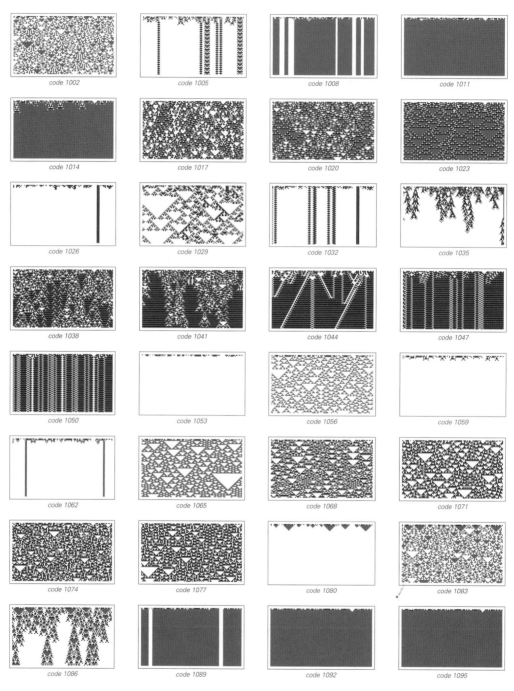

code 1002   code 1005   code 1008   code 1011

code 1014   code 1017   code 1020   code 1023

code 1026   code 1029   code 1032   code 1035

code 1038   code 1041   code 1044   code 1047

code 1050   code 1053   code 1056   code 1059

code 1062   code 1065   code 1068   code 1071

code 1074   code 1077   code 1080   code 1083

code 1086   code 1089   code 1092   code 1095

A sequence of totalistic cellular automata with rules that involve only nearest neighbors, but where each cell can have three possible colors.

In class 2, there are many different possible final states, but all of them consist just of a certain set of simple structures that either remain the same forever or repeat every few steps.

In class 3, the behavior is more complicated, and seems in many respects random, although triangles and other small-scale structures are essentially always at some level seen.

And finally, as illustrated on the next few pages, class 4 involves a mixture of order and randomness: localized structures are produced which on their own are fairly simple, but these structures move around and interact with each other in very complicated ways.

I originally discovered these four classes of behavior some seventeen years ago by looking at thousands of pictures similar to those on the last few pages. And at first, much as I have done here, I based my classification purely on the general visual appearance of the patterns I saw.

But when I studied more detailed properties of cellular automata, what I found was that most of these properties were closely correlated with the classes that I had already identified. Indeed, in trying to predict detailed properties of a particular cellular automaton, it was often enough just to know what class the cellular automaton was in.

And in a sense the situation was similar to what is seen, say, with the classification of materials into solids, liquids and gases, or of living organisms into plants and animals. At first, a classification is made purely on the basis of general appearance. But later, when more detailed properties become known, these properties turn out to be correlated with the classes that have already been identified.

Often it is possible to use such detailed properties to make more precise definitions of the original classes. And typically all reasonable definitions will then assign any particular system to the same class.

Examples of class 4 cellular automata with totalistic rules involving nearest neighbors and three possible colors for each cell. Each picture shows 1500 steps of evolution from random initial conditions. ▶

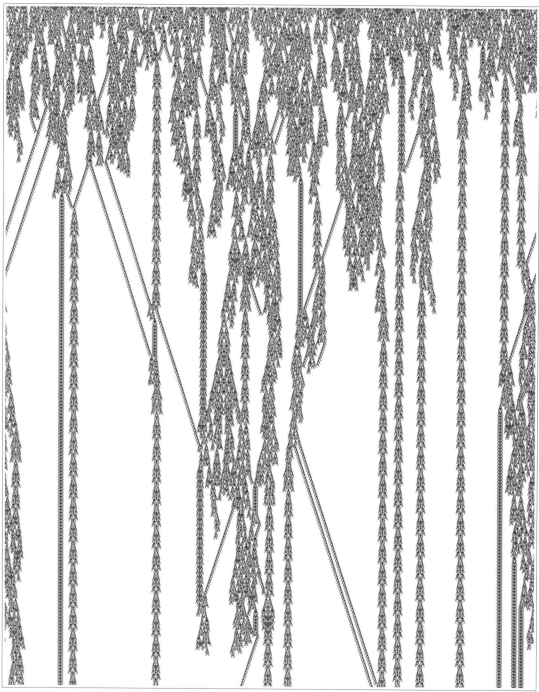

code 1815

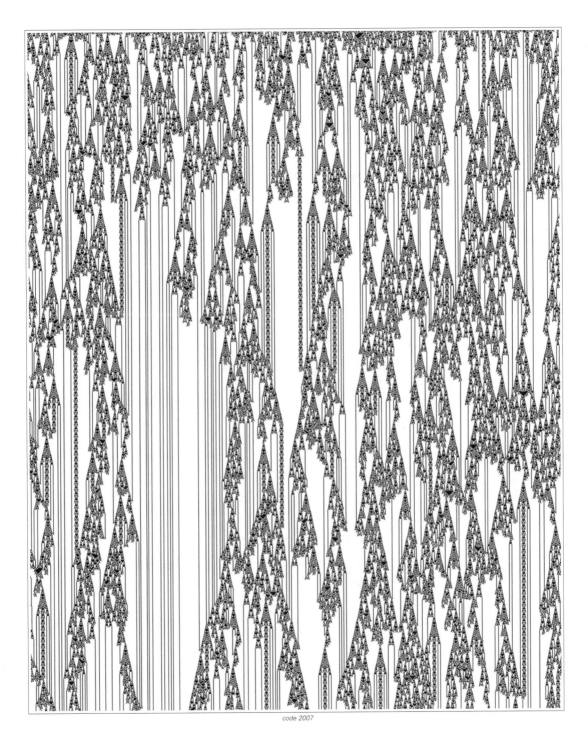

code 2007

code 1659

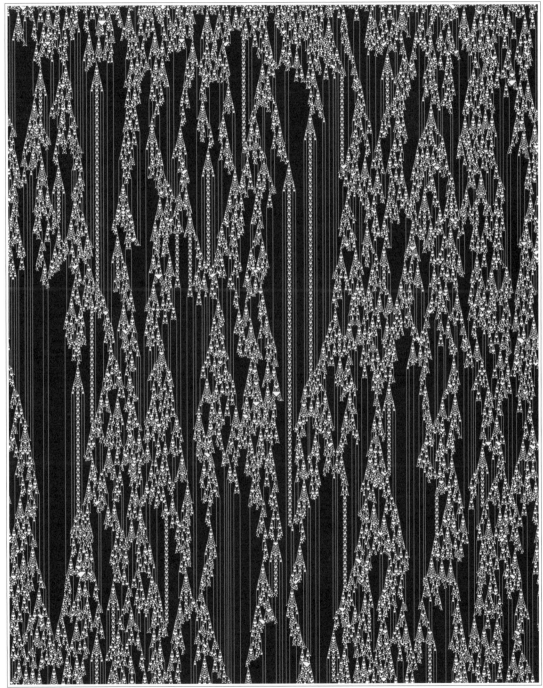

code 2043

But with almost any general classification scheme there are inevitably borderline cases which get assigned to one class by one definition and another class by another definition. And so it is with cellular automata: there are occasionally rules like those in the pictures below that show some features of one class and some of another.

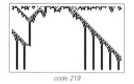  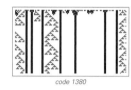 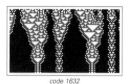

code 219   code 438   code 1380   code 1632

Rare examples of borderline cellular automata that do not fit squarely into any one of the four basic classes described in the text. Different definitions based on different specific properties will place these cellular automata into different classes. The rules shown are totalistic ones involving nearest neighbors and three possible colors for each cell. The first rule can be either class 2 or class 4, the second class 3 or 4, the third class 2 or 3 and the fourth class 1, 2 or 3.

But such rules are quite unusual, and in most cases the behavior one sees instead falls squarely into one of the four classes described above.

So given the underlying rule for a particular cellular automaton, can one tell what class of behavior the cellular automaton will produce?

In most cases there is no easy way to do this, and in fact there is little choice but just to run the cellular automaton and see what it does.

But sometimes one can tell at least a certain amount simply from the form of the underlying rule. And so for example all rules that lie in the first two columns on page 232 can be shown to be unable ever to produce anything besides class 1 or class 2 behavior.

In addition, even when one can tell rather little from a single rule, it is often the case that rules which occur next to each other in some sequence have similar behavior. This can be seen for example in the pictures on the facing page. The top row of rules all have class 1 behavior. But then class 2 behavior is seen, followed by class 4 and then class 3. And after that, the remainder of the rules are mostly class 3.

The fact that class 4 appears between class 2 and class 3 in the pictures on the facing page is not uncommon. For while class 4 is above class 3 in terms of apparent complexity, it is in a sense intermediate

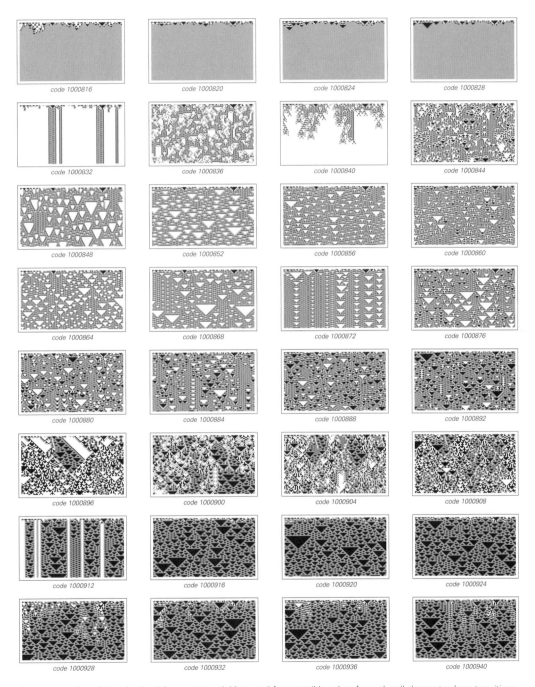

code 1000816   *code 1000820*   *code 1000824*   *code 1000828*

code 1000832   *code 1000836*   *code 1000840*   *code 1000844*

code 1000848   *code 1000852*   *code 1000856*   *code 1000860*

code 1000864   *code 1000868*   *code 1000872*   *code 1000876*

code 1000880   *code 1000884*   *code 1000888*   *code 1000892*

code 1000896   *code 1000900*   *code 1000904*   *code 1000908*

code 1000912   *code 1000916*   *code 1000920*   *code 1000924*

code 1000928   *code 1000932*   *code 1000936*   *code 1000940*

A sequence of totalistic rules involving nearest neighbors and four possible colors for each cell chosen to show transitions between rules with different classes of behavior. Note that class 4 seems to occur between class 2 and class 3.

between class 2 and class 3 in terms of what one might think of as overall activity.

The point is that class 1 and 2 systems rapidly settle down to states in which there is essentially no further activity. But class 3 systems continue to have many cells that change at every step, so that they in a sense maintain a high level of activity forever. Class 4 systems are then in the middle: for the activity that they show neither dies out completely, as in class 2, nor remains at the high level seen in class 3.

And indeed when one looks at a particular class 4 system, it often seems to waver between class 2 and class 3 behavior, never firmly settling on either of them.

In some respects it is not surprising that among all possible cellular automata one can identify some that are effectively on the boundary between class 2 and class 3. But what is remarkable about actual class 4 systems that one finds in practice is that they have definite characteristics of their own—most notably the presence of localized structures—that seem to have no direct relation to being somehow on the boundary between class 2 and class 3.

And it turns out that class 4 systems with the same general characteristics are seen for example not only in ordinary cellular automata but also in such systems as continuous cellular automata.

The facing page shows a sequence of continuous cellular automata of the kind we discussed on page 155. The underlying rules in such systems involve a parameter that can vary smoothly from 0 to 1.

For different values of this parameter, the behavior one sees is different. But it seems that this behavior falls into essentially the same four classes that we have already seen in ordinary cellular automata. And indeed there are even quite direct analogs of for example the triangle structures that we saw in ordinary class 3 cellular automata.

But since continuous cellular automata have underlying rules based on a continuous parameter, one can ask what happens if one smoothly varies this parameter—and in particular one can ask what sequence of classes of behavior one ends up seeing.

The answer is that there are normally some stretches of class 1 or 2 behavior, and some stretches of class 3 behavior. But at the transitions

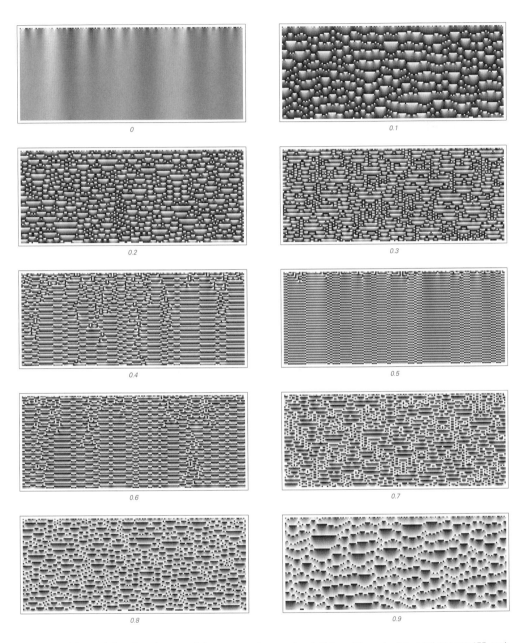

Examples of the evolution of continuous cellular automata from random initial conditions. As discussed on page 155, each cell here can have any gray level between 0 and 1, and at each step the gray level of a given cell is determined by averaging the gray levels of the cell and its two neighbors, adding the specified constant, and then keeping only the fractional part of the result. The behavior produced once again falls into distinct classes that correspond well to the four classes seen on previous pages in ordinary cellular automata.

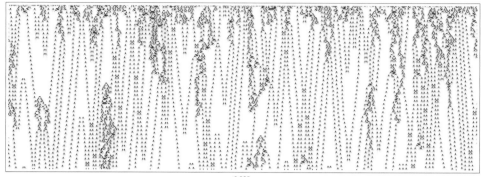

0.398

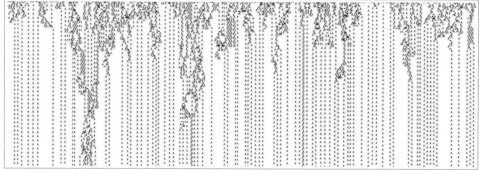

0.4

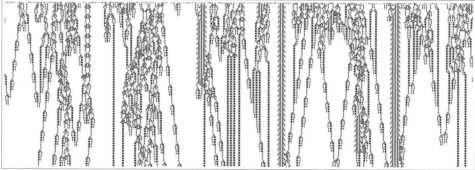

{0.5, 1.13}

Examples of continuous cellular automata that exhibit class 4 behavior. The rules are of the same kind as in the previous picture, except that in the third case shown here, the gray level of each neighboring cell is multiplied by 1.13 before the average is done. In addition, the actual gray levels in these pictures are obtained by taking the difference between the gray level of each cell and its neighbor, thus removing the uniform stripes visible in the previous picture. It is remarkable that class 4 behavior with discrete localized structures can still occur in the continuous systems shown here.

it turns out that class 4 behavior is typically seen—as illustrated on the facing page. And what is particularly remarkable is that this behavior involves the same kinds of localized structures and other features that we saw in ordinary discrete class 4 cellular automata.

So what about two-dimensional cellular automata? Do these also exhibit the same four classes of behavior that we have seen in one dimension? The pictures on the next two pages show various steps in the evolution of some simple two-dimensional cellular automata starting from random initial conditions. And just as in one dimension a few distinct classes of behavior can immediately be seen.

But the correspondence with one dimension becomes much more obvious if one looks not at the complete state of a two-dimensional cellular automaton at a few specific steps, but rather at a one-dimensional slice through the system for a whole sequence of steps.

The pictures on page 248 show examples of such slices. And what we see is that the patterns in these slices look remarkably similar to the patterns we already saw in ordinary one-dimensional cellular automata. Indeed, by looking at such slices one can readily identify the very same four classes of behavior as in one-dimensional cellular automata.

So in particular one sees class 4 behavior. In the examples on page 248, however, such behavior always seems to occur superimposed on some kind of repetitive background—much as in the case of the rule 110 one-dimensional cellular automaton on page 229.

So can one get class 4 behavior with a simple white background? Much as in one dimension this does not seem to happen with the very simplest possible kinds of rules. But as soon as one goes to slightly more complicated rules—though still very simple—one can find examples.

And so as one example page 249 shows a two-dimensional cellular automaton often called the Game of Life in which all sorts of localized structures occur even on a white background. If one watches a movie of the behavior of this cellular automaton its correspondence to a one-dimensional class 4 system is not particularly obvious. But as soon as one looks at a one-dimensional slice—as on page 249—what one sees is immediately strikingly similar to what we have seen in many one-dimensional class 4 cellular automata.

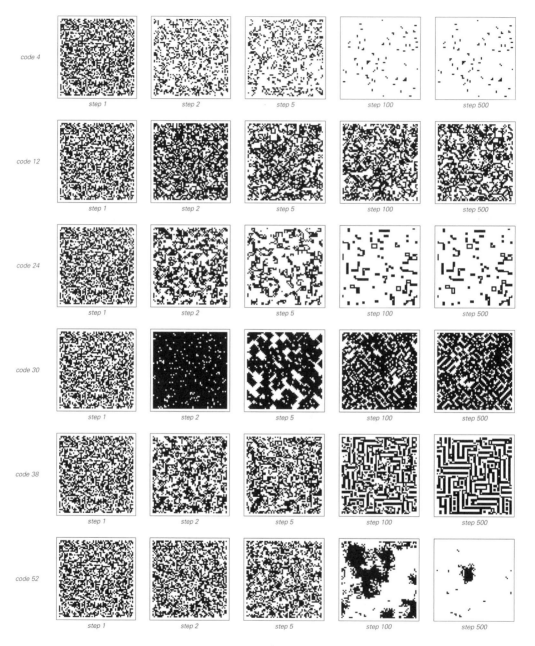

Examples of the evolution of two-dimensional cellular automata with various totalistic rules starting from random initial conditions. The rules involve a cell and its four immediate neighbors. Each successive base 2 digit in the code number for the rule gives the outcome when the total of the cell and its four neighbors runs from 5 down to 0.

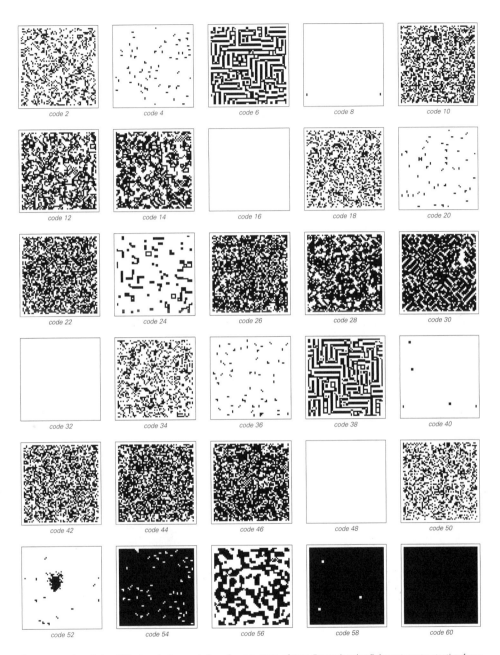

Patterns produced after 500 steps in the evolution of a sequence of two-dimensional cellular automata starting from random initial conditions. The rules shown are of the same kind as on the facing page, and include most of the 64 possibilities that leave a state that contains only white cells unchanged.

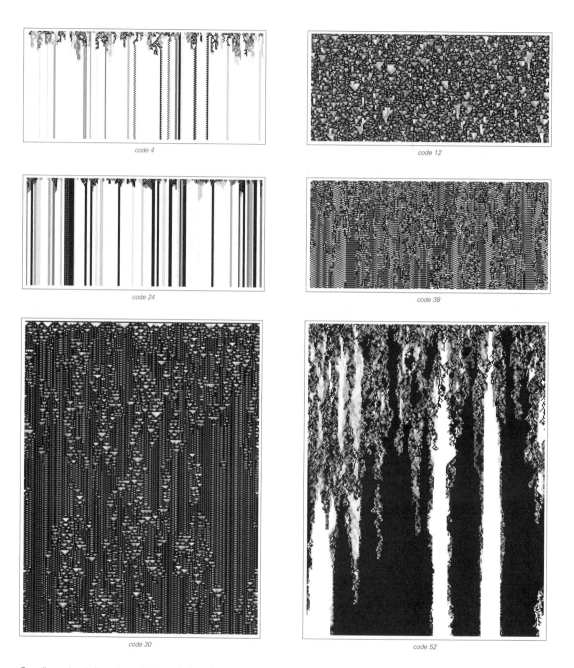

code 4

code 12

code 24

code 38

code 30

code 52

One-dimensional slices through the evolution of various two-dimensional cellular automata. In each picture black cells further back from the position of the slice are shown in progressively lighter shades of gray, as if they were receding into a kind of fog. Note the presence of examples of both class 3 and class 4 behavior that look strikingly similar to examples in one dimension.

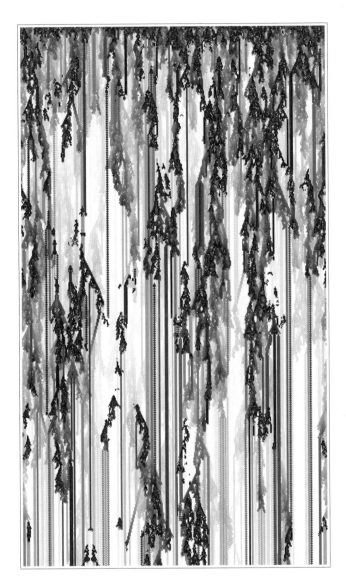

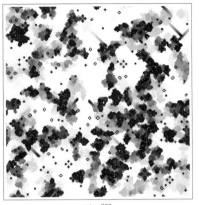

step 200

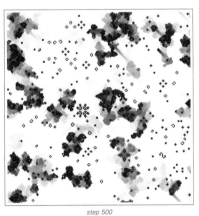

step 500

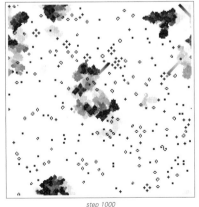

step 1000

The behavior of a class 4 two-dimensional cellular automaton often known in recreational computing as the Game of Life. Localized structures that move (so-called gliders) show up as streaks in the pictures given here. The rule for this cellular automaton considers the 8 neighbors of a cell (including diagonals): if two of these neighbors are black, then the cell stays the same color as before; if three are black, then the cell becomes black; and if any other number of neighbors are black, then the cell becomes white. This rule is outer totalistic 9-neighbor code 224. The pictures on the right show cells that were black on preceding steps in progressively lighter shades of gray.

Sensitivity to Initial Conditions

In the previous section we identified four basic classes of cellular automata by looking at the overall appearance of patterns they produce. But these four classes also have other significant distinguishing features—and one important example of these is their sensitivity to small changes in initial conditions.

The pictures below show the effect of changing the initial color of a single cell in a typical cellular automaton from each of the four classes of cellular automata identified in the previous section.

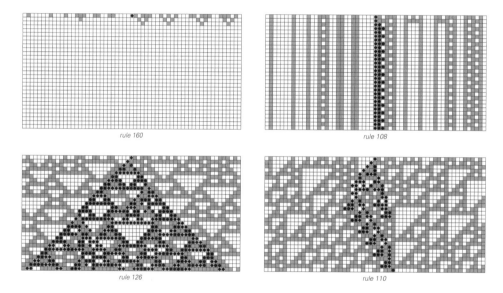

rule 160   *rule 108*

rule 126   *rule 110*

The effect of changing the color of a single cell in the initial conditions for typical cellular automata from each of the four classes identified in the previous section. The black dots indicate all the cells that change. The way that such changes behave is characteristically different for each of the four classes of systems.

The results are rather different for each class.

In class 1, changes always die out, and in fact exactly the same final state is reached regardless of what initial conditions were used. In class 2, changes may persist, but they always remain localized in a small region of the system. In class 3, however, the behavior is quite different. For as the facing page shows, any change that is made

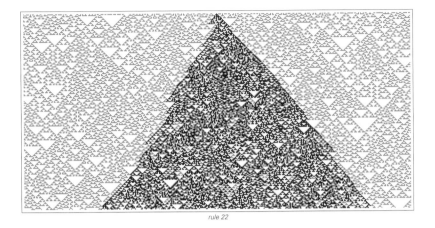

rule 22

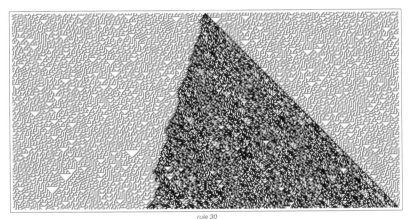

rule 30

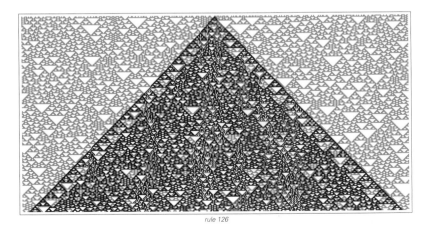

rule 126

The effect of changing the color of a single initial cell in three typical class 3 cellular automata.

typically spreads at a uniform rate, eventually affecting every part of the system. In class 4, changes can also spread, but only in a sporadic way—as illustrated on the facing page and the one that follows.

So what is the real significance of these different responses to changes in initial conditions? In a sense what they reveal are basic differences in the way that each class of systems handles information.

In class 1, information about initial conditions is always rapidly forgotten—for whatever the initial conditions were, the system quickly evolves to a single final state that shows no trace of them.

In class 2, some information about initial conditions is retained in the final configuration of structures, but this information always remains completely localized, and is never in any way communicated from one part of the system to another.

A characteristic feature of class 3 systems, on the other hand, is that they show long-range communication of information—so that any change made anywhere in the system will almost always eventually be communicated even to the most distant parts of the system.

Class 4 systems are once again somewhat intermediate between class 2 and class 3. Long-range communication of information is in principle possible, but it does not always occur—for any particular change is only communicated to other parts of the system if it happens to affect one of the localized structures that moves across the system.

There are many characteristic differences between the four classes of systems that we identified in the previous section. But their differences in the handling of information are in some respects particularly fundamental. And indeed, as we will see later in this book, it is often possible to understand some of the most important features of systems that occur in nature just by looking at how their handling of information corresponds to what we have seen in the basic classes of systems that we have identified here.

The effect of small changes in initial conditions in the rule 110 class 4 cellular automaton. The changes spread only when they are in effect carried by localized structures that propagates across the system. ▶

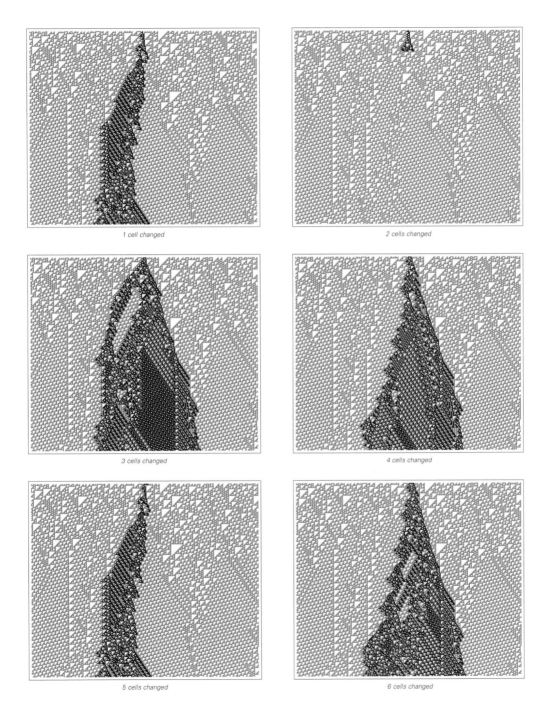

1 cell changed

2 cells changed

3 cells changed

4 cells changed

5 cells changed

6 cells changed

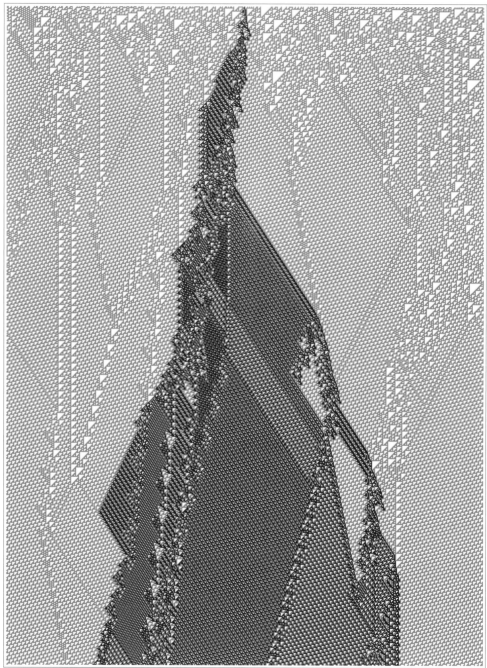

1 cell changed

Systems of Limited Size and Class 2 Behavior

In the past two sections we have seen two important features of class 2 systems: first, that their behavior is always eventually repetitive, and second, that they do not support any kind of long-range communication.

So what is the connection between these two features?

The answer is that the absence of long-range communication effectively forces each part of a class 2 system to behave as if it were a system of limited size. And it is then a general result that any system of limited size that involves discrete elements and follows definite rules must always eventually exhibit repetitive behavior. Indeed, as we will discuss in the next chapter, it is this phenomenon that is ultimately responsible for much of the repetitive behavior that we see in nature.

The pictures below show a very simple example of the basic phenomenon. In each case there is a dot that can be in one of six possible positions. And at every step the dot moves a fixed number of positions to the right, wrapping around as soon as it reaches the right-hand end.

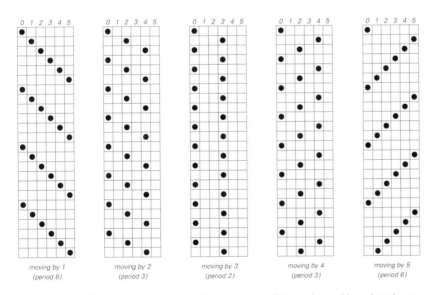

| moving by 1 (period 6) | moving by 2 (period 3) | moving by 3 (period 2) | moving by 4 (period 3) | moving by 5 (period 6) |

A simple system that contains a single dot which can be in one of six possible positions. At each step, the dot moves some number of positions to the right, wrapping around as soon as it reaches the right-hand end. The behavior of this system, like other systems of limited size, is always repetitive.

Looking at the pictures we then see that the behavior which results is always purely repetitive—though the period of repetition is different in different cases. And the basic reason for the repetitive behavior is that whenever the dot ends up in a particular position, it must always repeat whatever it did when it was last in that position.

But since there are only six possible positions in all, it is inevitable that after at most six steps the dot will always get to a position where it has been before. And this means that the behavior must repeat with a period of at most six steps.

The pictures below show more examples of the same setup, where now the number of possible positions is 10 and 11. In all cases, the behavior is repetitive, and the maximum repetition period is equal to the number of possible positions.

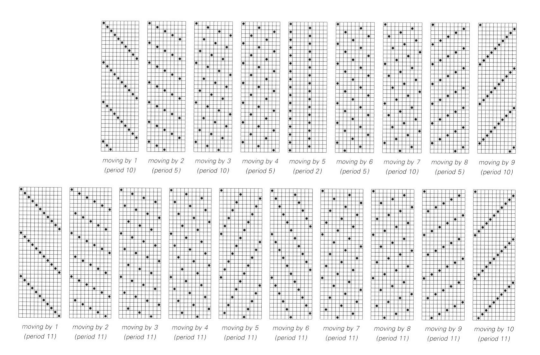

More examples of the type of system shown on the previous page, but now with 10 and 11 possible positions for the dot. The behavior always repeats itself in at most 10 or 11 steps. But the exact number of steps in each case depends on the prime factors of the numbers that define the system.

Sometimes the actual repetition period is equal to this maximum value. But often it is smaller. And indeed it is a common feature of systems of limited size that the repetition period one sees can depend greatly on the exact size of the system and the exact rule that it follows.

In the type of system shown on the facing page, it turns out that the repetition period is maximal whenever the number of positions moved at each step shares no common factor with the total number of possible positions—and this is achieved for example whenever either of these quantities is a prime number.

The pictures below show another example of a system of limited size based on a simple rule. The particular rule is at each step to double the number that represents the position of the dot, wrapping around as soon as this goes past the right-hand end.

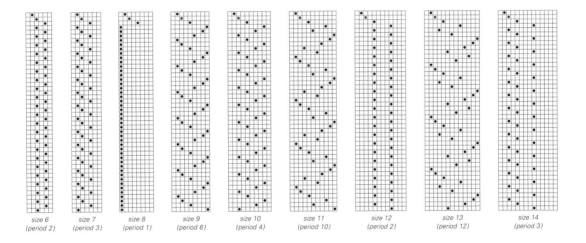

| size 6 (period 2) | size 7 (period 3) | size 8 (period 1) | size 9 (period 6) | size 10 (period 4) | size 11 (period 10) | size 12 (period 2) | size 13 (period 12) | size 14 (period 3) |

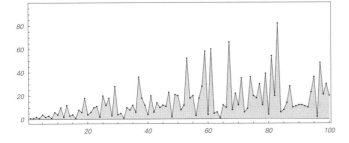

A system where the number that represents the position of the dot doubles at each step, wrapping around whenever it reaches the right-hand end. (After t steps the dot is thus at position $Mod[2^t, n]$ in a size n system.) The plot at left gives the repetition period for this system as a function of its size; for odd n this period is equal to $MultiplicativeOrder[2, n]$.

257

Once again, the behavior that results is always repetitive, and the repetition period can never be greater than the total number of possible positions for the dot. But as the picture shows, the actual repetition period jumps around considerably as the size of the system is changed. And as it turns out, the repetition period is again related to the factors of the number of possible positions for the dot—and tends to be maximal in those cases where this number is prime.

So what happens in systems like cellular automata?

The pictures on the facing page show some examples of cellular automata that have a limited number of cells. In each case the cells are in effect arranged around a circle, so that the right neighbor of the rightmost cell is the leftmost cell and vice versa.

And once again, the behavior of these systems is ultimately repetitive. But the period of repetition is often quite large.

The maximum possible repetition period for any system is always equal to the total number of possible states of the system.

For the systems involving a single dot that we discussed above, the possible states correspond just to possible positions for the dot, and the number of states is therefore equal to the size of the system.

But in a cellular automaton, every possible arrangement of black and white cells corresponds to a possible state of the system. With n cells there are thus 2^n possible states. And this number increases very rapidly with the size n: for 5 cells there are already 32 states, for 10 cells 1024 states, for 20 cells 1,048,576 states, and for 30 cells 1,073,741,824 states.

The pictures on the next page show the actual repetition periods for various cellular automata. In general, a rapid increase with size is characteristic of class 3 behavior. Of the elementary rules, however, only rule 45 seems to yield periods that always stay close to the maximum of 2^n. And in all cases, there are considerable fluctuations in the periods that occur as the size changes.

So how does all of this relate to class 2 behavior? In the examples we have just discussed, we have explicitly set up systems that have limited size. But even when a system in principle contains an infinite number of cells it is still possible that a particular pattern in that system will only grow to occupy a limited number of cells. And in any

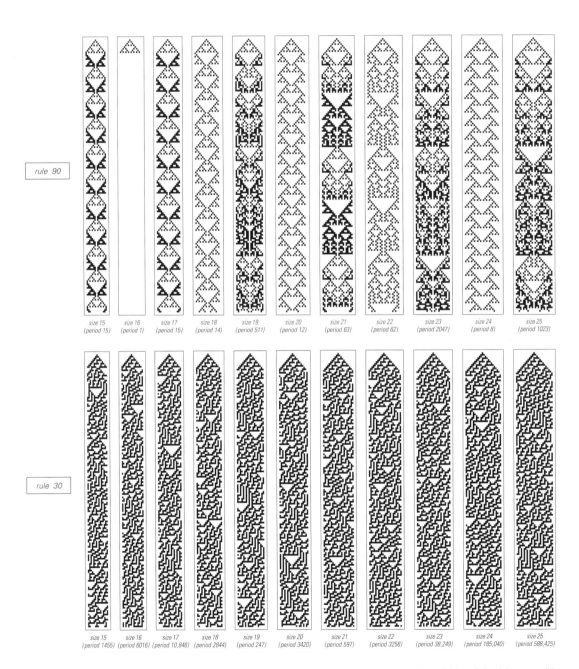

rule 90

size 15 (period 15) | size 16 (period 1) | size 17 (period 15) | size 18 (period 14) | size 19 (period 511) | size 20 (period 12) | size 21 (period 63) | size 22 (period 62) | size 23 (period 2047) | size 24 (period 8) | size 25 (period 1023)

rule 30

size 15 (period 1455) | size 16 (period 6016) | size 17 (period 10,846) | size 18 (period 2844) | size 19 (period 247) | size 20 (period 3420) | size 21 (period 597) | size 22 (period 3256) | size 23 (period 38,249) | size 24 (period 185,040) | size 25 (period 588,425)

The behavior of cellular automata with a limited number of cells. In each case the right neighbor of the rightmost cell is taken to be the leftmost cell and vice versa. The pattern produced always eventually repeats, but the period of repetition can increase rapidly with the size of the system.

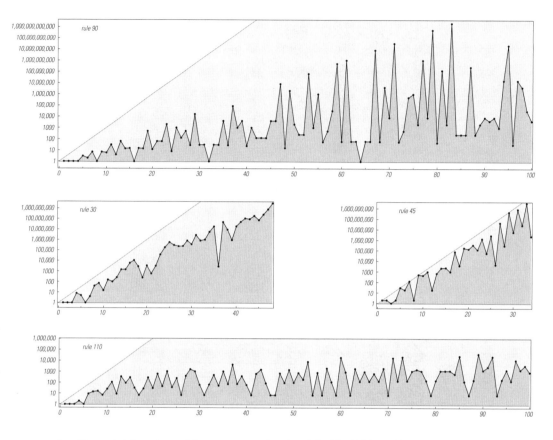

Repetition periods for various cellular automata as a function of size. The initial conditions used in each case consist of a single black cell, as in the pictures on the previous page. The dashed gray line indicates the maximum possible repetition period of 2^n. The maximum repetition period for rule 90 is $2^{(n-1)/2} - 1$. For rule 30, the peak repetition periods are of order $2^{0.63n}$, while for rule 45, they are close to 2^n (for $n = 29$, for example, the period is 463,347,935, which is 86% of the maximum possible). For rule 110, the peaks seem to increase roughly like n^3.

such case, the pattern must repeat itself with a period of at most 2^n steps, where n is the size of the pattern.

In a class 2 system with random initial conditions, a similar thing happens: since different parts of the system do not communicate with each other, they all behave like separate patterns of limited size. And in fact in most class 2 cellular automata these patterns are effectively only a few cells across, so that their repetition periods are necessarily quite short.

Randomness in Class 3 Systems

When one looks at class 3 systems the most obvious feature of their behavior is its apparent randomness. But where does this randomness ultimately come from? And is it perhaps all somehow just a reflection of randomness that was inserted in the initial conditions?

The presence of randomness in initial conditions—together with sensitive dependence on initial conditions—does imply at least some degree of randomness in the behavior of any class 3 system. And indeed when I first saw class 3 cellular automata I assumed that this was the basic origin of their randomness.

But the crucial point that I discovered only some time later is that random behavior can also occur even when there is no randomness in initial conditions. And indeed, in earlier chapters of this book we have already seen many examples of this fundamental phenomenon.

The pictures below now compare what happens in the rule 30 cellular automaton from page 27 if one starts from random initial conditions and from initial conditions involving just a single black cell.

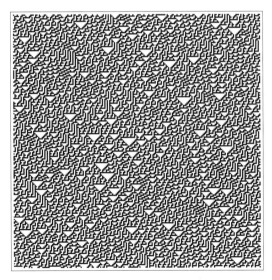 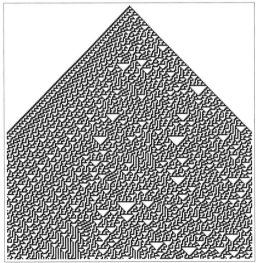

Comparison of the patterns produced by the rule 30 cellular automaton starting from random initial conditions and from simple initial conditions involving just a single black cell. Away from the edge of the second picture, the patterns look remarkably similar.

The behavior we see in the two cases rapidly becomes almost indistinguishable. In the first picture the random initial conditions certainly affect the detailed pattern that is obtained. But the crucial point is that even without any initial randomness much of what we see in the second picture still looks like typical random class 3 behavior.

So what about other class 3 cellular automata? Do such systems always produce randomness even with simple initial conditions?

The pictures below show an example in which random class 3 behavior is obtained when the initial conditions are random, but where the pattern produced by starting with a single black cell has just a simple nested form.

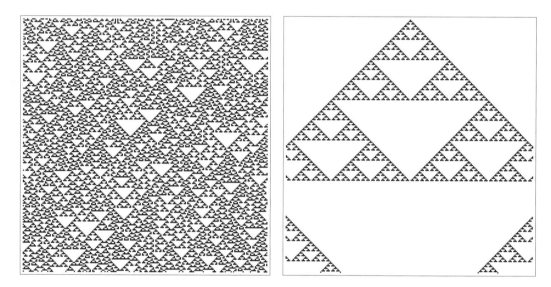

Patterns produced by the rule 22 cellular automaton starting from random initial conditions and from an initial condition containing a single black cell. With random initial conditions typical class 3 behavior is seen. But with the specific initial condition shown on the right, a simple nested pattern is produced.

Nevertheless, the pictures on the facing page demonstrate that if one uses initial conditions that are slightly different—though still simple—then one can still see randomness in the behavior of this particular cellular automaton.

Rule 22 with various different simple initial conditions. In the top four cases, the pattern produced ultimately has a simple nested form. But in the bottom case, it is instead in many respects random, much like rule 30.

There are however a few cellular automata in which class 3 behavior is obtained with random initial conditions, but in which no significant randomness is ever produced with simple initial conditions.

The pictures below show one example. And in this case it turns out that all patterns are in effect just simple superpositions of the basic nested pattern that is obtained by starting with a single black cell.

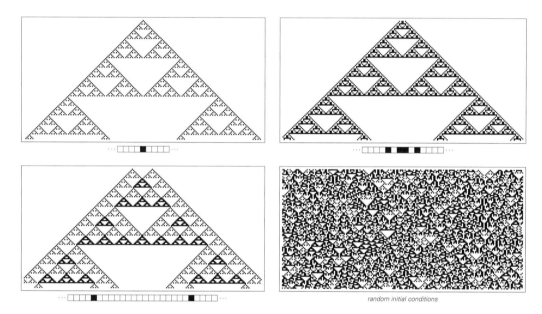

Patterns generated by rule 90 with various initial conditions. This particular cellular automaton rule has the special property of additivity which implies that with any initial conditions the patterns that it produces can be obtained as simple superpositions of the first pattern shown above. Any initial condition that contains black cells only in a limited region will thus lead to a pattern that ultimately has a simple nested form. Unlike rule 30 or rule 22 therefore, rule 90 cannot intrinsically generate randomness starting from simple initial conditions. The randomness in the last picture shown here is thus purely a consequence of the randomness in its initial conditions. Note that the pictures above show only half as many steps of evolution as the corresponding pictures of rule 22 on the previous page.

As a result, when the initial conditions involve only a limited region of black cells, the overall pattern produced always ultimately has a simple nested form. Indeed, at each of the steps where a new white triangle starts in the center, the whole pattern consists just of two copies of the region of black cells from the initial conditions.

The only way to get a random pattern therefore is to have an infinite number of randomly placed black cells in the initial conditions.

And indeed when random initial conditions are used, rule 90 does manage to produce random behavior of the kind expected in class 3.

But if there are deviations from perfect randomness in the initial conditions, then these will almost inevitably show up in the evolution of the system. And thus, for example, if the initial density of black cells is low, then correspondingly low densities will occur again at various later steps, as in the second picture below.

With rule 22, on the other hand, there is no such effect, and instead after just a few steps no visible trace remains of the low density of initial black cells.

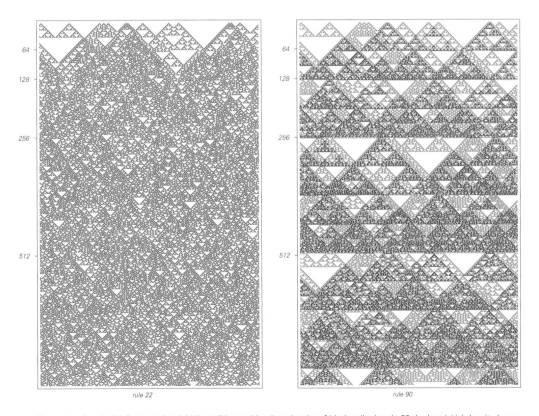

rule 22   rule 90

Examples of evolution from random initial conditions with a low density of black cells. In rule 22 the low initial density has no long-term effect. But in rule 90 its effect continues forever. The reason for this difference is that in rule 22 the randomness we see is intrinsically generated by the evolution of the system, while in rule 90 it comes from randomness in the initial conditions.

A couple of sections ago we saw that all class 3 systems have the property that the detailed patterns they produce are highly sensitive to detailed changes in initial conditions. But despite this sensitivity at the level of details, the point is that any system like rule 22 or rule 30 yields patterns whose overall properties depend very little on the form of the initial conditions that are given.

By intrinsically generating randomness such systems in a sense have a certain fundamental stability: for whatever is done to their initial conditions, they still give the same overall random behavior, with the same large-scale properties. And as we shall see in the next few chapters, there are in fact many systems in nature whose apparent stability is ultimately a consequence of just this kind of phenomenon.

Special Initial Conditions

We have seen that cellular automata such as rule 30 generate seemingly random behavior when they are started both from random initial conditions and from simple ones. So one may wonder whether there are in fact any initial conditions that make rule 30 behave in a simple way.

As a rather trivial example, one certainly knows that if its initial state is uniformly white, then rule 30 will just yield uniform white forever. But as the pictures below demonstrate, it is also possible to find less trivial initial conditions that still make rule 30 behave in a simple way.

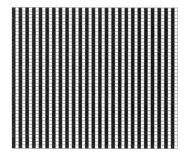  

Examples of special initial conditions that make the rule 30 cellular automaton yield simple repetitive behavior. Small patches with the same structures as shown here can be seen embedded in typical random patterns produced by rule 30. At left is a representation of rule 30. Finding initial conditions that make cellular automata yield behavior with certain repetition periods is closely related to the problem of satisfying constraints discussed on page 210.

In fact, it turns out that in any cellular automaton it is inevitable that initial conditions which consist just of a fixed block of cells repeated forever will lead to simple repetitive behavior.

For what happens is that each block in effect independently acts like a system of limited size. The right-hand neighbor of the rightmost cell in any particular block is the leftmost cell in the next block, but since all the blocks are identical, this cell always has the same color as the leftmost cell in the block itself. And as a result, the block evolves just like one of the systems of limited size that we discussed on page 255. So this means that given a block that is n cells wide, the repetition period that is obtained must be at most 2^n steps.

But if one wants a short repetition period, then there is a question of whether there is a block of any size which can produce it. The pictures on the next page show the blocks that are needed to get repetition periods of up to ten steps in rule 30. It turns out that no block of any size gives a period of exactly two steps, but blocks can be found for all larger periods at least up to 15 steps.

But what about initial conditions that do not just consist of a single block repeated forever? It turns out that for rule 30, no other kind of initial conditions can ever yield repetitive behavior.

But for many rules—including a fair number of class 3 ones—the situation is different. And as one example the picture on the right below shows an initial condition for rule 126 that involves two different blocks but which nevertheless yields repetitive behavior.

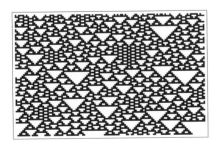 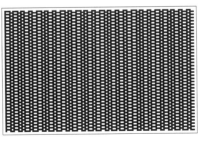

Rule 126 with a typical random initial condition, and with an initial condition that consists of a random sequence of the blocks ■■□ and ■■■□. Rule 126 in general shows class 3 behavior, as on the left. But with the special initial condition on the right it acts like a simple class 2 rule. Note the patches of class 2 behavior even in the picture on the left.

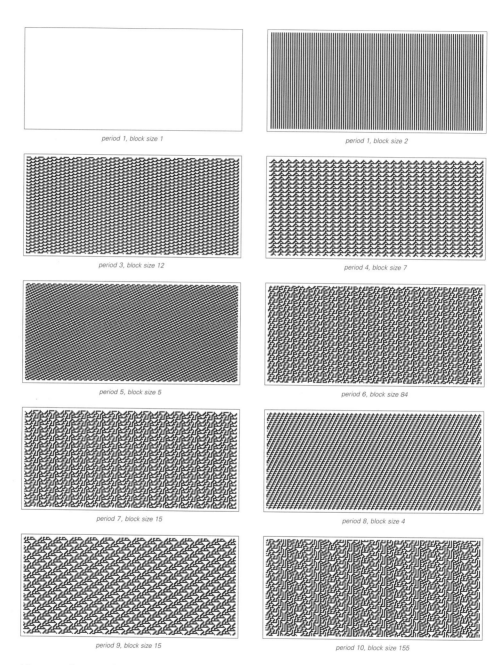

period 1, block size 1

period 1, block size 2

period 3, block size 12

period 4, block size 7

period 5, block size 5

period 6, block size 84

period 7, block size 15

period 8, block size 4

period 9, block size 15

period 10, block size 155

All patterns that repeat in 10 or less steps under evolution according to rule 30. In each case the initial conditions consist of a fixed block of cells that is repeated over and over again. Note that there are no initial conditions that yield a repetition period of exactly 2 steps. To get period 11, a block that contains 275 cells is required.

In a sense what is happening here is that even though rule 126 usually shows class 3 behavior, it is possible to find special initial conditions that make it behave like a simple class 2 rule.

And in fact it turns out to be quite common for there to exist special initial conditions for one cellular automaton that make it behave just like some other cellular automaton.

Rule 126 will for example behave just like rule 90 if one starts it from special initial conditions that contain only blocks consisting of pairs of black and white cells.

The pictures below show how this works: on alternate steps the arrangement of blocks in rule 126 corresponds exactly to the arrangement of individual cells in rule 90. And among other things this explains why it is that with simple initial conditions rule 126 produces exactly the same kind of nested pattern as rule 90.

rule 126   *rule 90*

Two examples of the fact that with special initial conditions rule 126 behaves exactly like rule 90. The initial conditions that are used consist of blocks of cells where each block contains either two black cells or two white cells. If one looks only on every other step, then the blocks behave exactly like individual cells in rule 90. This correspondence is the basic reason that rule 126 produces the same kind of nested patterns as rule 90 when it is started from simple initial conditions.

The point is that these initial conditions in effect contain only blocks for which rule 126 behaves like rule 90. And as a result, the overall patterns produced by rule 126 in this case are inevitably exactly like those produced by rule 90.

So what about other cellular automata that can yield similar patterns? In every example in this book where nested patterns like those from rule 90 are obtained it turns out that the underlying rules that are responsible can be set up to behave exactly like rule 90. Sometimes this will happen, say, for any initial condition that has black cells only in a limited region. But in other cases—like the example of rule 22 on page 263—rule 90 behavior is obtained only with rather specific initial conditions.

So what about rule 90 itself? Why does it yield nested patterns?

The basic reason can be thought of as being that just as other rules can emulate rule 90 when their initial conditions contain only certain blocks, so also rule 90 is able to emulate itself in this way.

The picture below shows how this works. The idea is to consider the initial conditions not as a sequence of individual cells, but rather as a sequence of blocks each containing two adjacent cells. And with an appropriate form for these blocks what one finds is that the configuration of blocks evolves exactly according to rule 90.

The fact that both individual cells and whole blocks of cells evolve according to the same rule then means that whatever pattern is

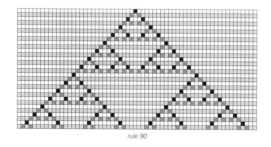

rule 90

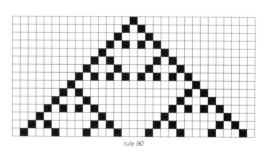

rule 90

A demonstration of the fact that in rule 90 blocks of cells can behave just like individual cells. One consequence of this is that the patterns produced by rule 90 have a nested or self-similar form.

produced must have exactly the same structure whether it is looked at in terms of individual cells or in terms of blocks of cells. And this can be achieved in only two ways: either the pattern must be essentially uniform, or it must have a nested structure—just like we see in rule 90.

So what happens with other rules? It turns out that the property of self-emulation is rather rare among cellular automaton rules. But one other example is rule 150—as illustrated in the picture below.

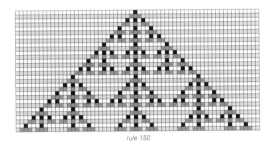

rule 150

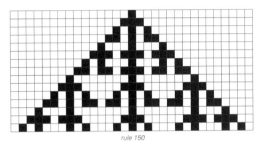

rule 150

Another example of a rule in which blocks of cells can behave just like individual cells. Rule 90 and rule 150 are also essentially the only fundamentally different elementary cellular automaton rules that have the property of being additive (see page 264).

So what else is there in common between rule 90 and rule 150? It turns out that they are both additive rules, implying that the patterns they produce can be superimposed in the way we discussed on page 264. And in fact one can show that any rule that is additive will be able to emulate itself and will thus yield nested patterns. But there are rather few additive rules, and indeed with two colors and nearest neighbors the only fundamentally different ones are precisely rules 90 and 150.

Ultimately, however, additive rules are not the only ones that can emulate themselves. An example of another kind is rule 184, in which blocks of three cells can act like a single cell, as shown below.

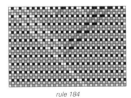

rule 184

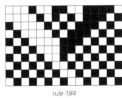

rule 184

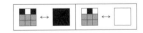

A rule that is not additive, but in which blocks of cells can again behave just like individual cells.

With simple initial conditions of the type we have used so far this rule will always produce essentially trivial behavior. But one way to see the properties of the rule is to use nested initial conditions, obtained for example from substitution systems of the kind we discussed on page 82.

With most rules, including 90 and 150, such nested initial conditions typically yield results that are ultimately indistinguishable from those obtained with typical random initial conditions. But for rule 184, an appropriate choice of nested initial conditions yields the highly regular pattern shown below.

The pattern produced by rule 184 (shown at left) evolving from a nested initial condition. The particular initial condition shown can be obtained by applying the substitution system ■ → ■■, □ → □□■, starting from a single black element ■ (see page 83). With this initial condition, rule 184 exhibits an equal number of black and white stripes, which annihilate in pairs so as to yield a regular nested pattern.

The nested structure seen in this pattern can then be viewed as a consequence of the fact that rule 184 is able to emulate itself. And the picture below shows that rule 184—unlike any of the additive rules—still produces recognizably nested patterns even when the initial conditions that are used are random.

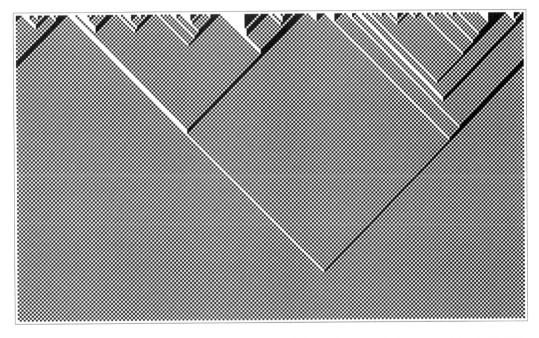

Rule 184 evolving from a random initial condition. Nested structure similar to what we saw in the previous picture is still visible. The presence of such structure is most obvious when there are equal numbers of black and white cells in the initial conditions, but it does not rely on any regularity in the arrangement of these cells.

As we will see on page 338 the presence of such patterns is particularly clear when there are equal numbers of black and white cells in the initial conditions—but how these cells are arranged does not usually matter much at all. And in general it is possible to find quite a few cellular automata that yield nested patterns like rule 184 even from random initial conditions. The picture on the next page shows a particularly striking example in which explicit regions are formed that contain patterns with the same overall structure as rule 90.

Another example of a cellular automaton that produces a nested pattern even from random initial conditions. The particular rule shown involves next-nearest as well as nearest neighbors and has rule number 4067213884. As in rule 184, the nested behavior seen here is most obvious when the density of black and white cells in the initial conditions is equal.

The Notion of Attractors

In this chapter we have seen many examples of patterns that can be produced by starting from random initial conditions and then following the evolution of cellular automata for many steps.

But what can be said about the individual configurations of black and white cells that appear at each step? In random initial conditions, absolutely any sequence of black and white cells can be present. But it is a feature of most cellular automata that on subsequent steps the sequences that can be produced become progressively more restricted.

The first picture below shows an extreme example of a class 1 cellular automaton in which after just one step the only sequences that can occur are those that contain only black cells.

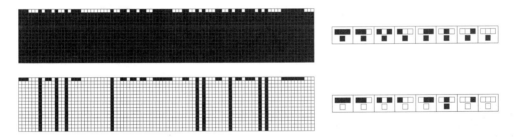

Examples of simple cellular automata that evolve after just one step to attractors in which only certain sequences of black and white cells can occur. In the first case, the sequences that can occur are ones that involve only black cells. In the second case, the sequences are ones in which every black cell is surrounded by white cells. The rules shown are numbers 255 and 4.

The resulting configuration can be thought of as a so-called attractor for the cellular automaton evolution. It does not matter what initial conditions one starts from: one always reaches the same all-black attractor in the end. The situation is somewhat similar to what happens in a mechanical system like a physical pendulum. One can start the pendulum swinging in any configuration, but it will always tend to evolve to the configuration in which it is hanging straight down.

The second picture above shows a class 2 cellular automaton that once again evolves to an attractor after just one step. But now the attractor does not just consist of a single configuration, but instead consists of all configurations in which black cells occur only when they are surrounded on each side by at least one white cell.

The picture below shows that for any particular configuration of this kind, there are in general many different initial conditions that can lead to it. In a mechanical analogy each possible final configuration is like the lowest point in a basin—and a ball started anywhere in the basin will then always roll to that lowest point.

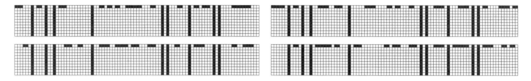

Four different initial conditions that all lead to the same final state in the rule 4 cellular automaton shown on the previous page. The final state can be thought of as one of the possible attractors for the evolution of the cellular automaton; the initial conditions shown then represent different elements in the basin of attraction for this attractor.

For one-dimensional cellular automata, it turns out that there is a rather compact way to summarize all the possible sequences of black and white cells that can occur at any given step in their evolution.

The basic idea is to construct a network in which each such sequence of black and white cells corresponds to a possible path.

In the pictures at the top of the facing page, the first network in each case represents random initial conditions in which any possible sequence of black and white cells can occur. Starting from the node in the middle, one can go around either the left or the right loop in the network any number of times in any order—representing the fact that black and white cells can appear any number of times in any order.

At step 2 in the rule 255 example on the facing page, however, the network has only one loop—representing the fact that at this step the only sequences which can occur with this rule are ones that consist purely of black cells, just as we saw on the previous page.

The case of rule 4 is slightly more complicated: at step 2, the possible sequences that can occur are now represented by a network with two nodes. Starting at the right-hand node one can go around the loop to the right any number of times, corresponding to sequences of

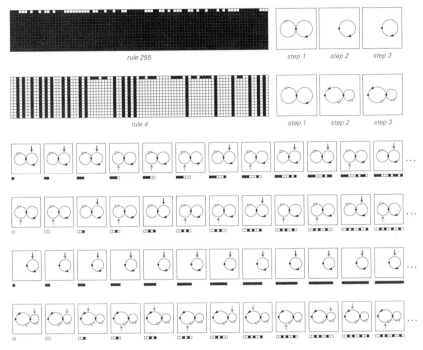

Networks representing possible sequences of black and white cells that can occur at successive steps in the evolution of the two cellular automata shown on the left. In each case the possible sequences correspond to possible paths through the network. Both rules start on step 1 from random initial conditions in which all sequences of black and white cells are allowed. On subsequent steps, rule 255 allows only sequences containing just black cells, while rule 4 allows sequences that contain both black and white cells, but requires that every black cell be surrounded by white cells.

any number of white cells. At any point one can follow the arrow to the left to get a black cell, but the form of the network implies that this black cell must always be followed by at least one white cell.

The pictures on the next page show more examples of class 1 and 2 cellular automata. Unlike in the picture above, these rules do not reach their final states after one step, but instead just progressively evolve towards these states. And in the course of this evolution, the set of sequences that can occur becomes progressively smaller.

In rule 128, for example, the fact that regions of black shrink by one cell on each side at each step means that any region of black that exists after t steps must have at least t white cells on either side of it.

The networks shown on the next page capture all effects like this. And to do this we see that on successive steps they become somewhat more complicated. But at least for these class 1 and 2 examples, the progression of networks always continues to have a fairly simple form.

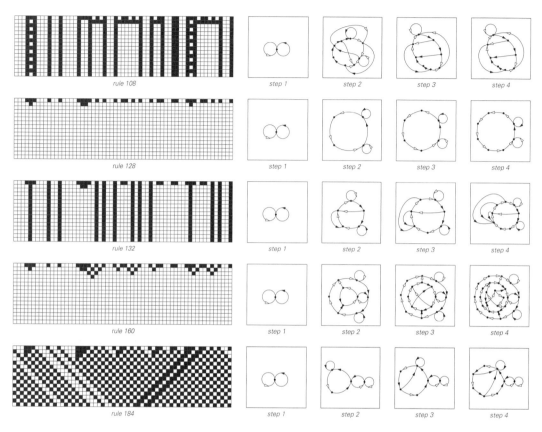

Networks representing possible sequences of black and white cells that can occur at successive steps in the evolution of several class 1 and 2 cellular automata. These networks never have more than about t^2 nodes after t steps.

So what happens with class 3 and 4 systems? The pictures on the facing page show a couple of examples. In rule 126, the only effect at step 2 is that black cells can no longer appear on their own: they must always be in groups of two or more. By step 3, it becomes difficult to see any change if one just looks at an explicit picture of the cellular automaton evolution. But from the network, one finds that now an infinite collection of other blocks are forbidden, beginning with the length 12 block ▭■■■▭■■■▭. And on later steps, the set of sequences that are allowed rapidly becomes more complicated—as reflected in a rapid increase in the complexity of the corresponding networks.

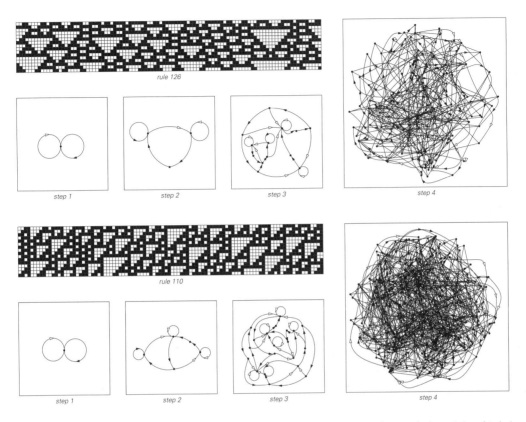

rule 126

step 1   *step 2*   *step 3*   *step 4*

rule 110

step 1   *step 2*   *step 3*   *step 4*

Networks representing possible sequences of black and white cells that can occur at successive steps in the evolution of typical class 3 and 4 cellular automata. The number of nodes in these networks seems to increase at a rate that is at least exponential.

Indeed, this kind of rapid increase in network complexity is a general characteristic of most class 3 and 4 rules. But it turns out that there are a few rules which at first appear to be exceptions.

The pictures at the top of the next page show four different rules that each have the property that if started from initial conditions in which all possible sequences of cells are allowed, these same sequences can all still occur at any subsequent step in the evolution.

The first two rules that are shown exhibit very simple class 2 behavior. But the last two show typical class 3 behavior.

What is going on, however, is that in a sense the particular initial conditions that allow all possible sequences are special for these rules.

Examples of cellular automata which continue to allow all possible sequences of black and white cells at any step in their evolution. Such cellular automata in effect define what are known as surjective or onto mappings.

And indeed if one starts with almost any other initial conditions—say for example ones that do not allow any pair of black cells together, then as the pictures below illustrate, rapidly increasing complexity in the sets of sequences that are allowed is again observed.

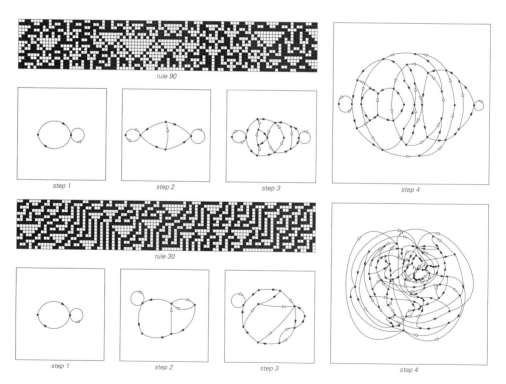

Networks representing possible sequences that can occur in the evolution of the cellular automata at the top of the page, starting from initial conditions in which black cells are only allowed to appear in pairs.

Structures in Class 4 Systems

The next page shows three typical examples of class 4 cellular automata. In each case the initial conditions that are used are completely random. But after just a few steps, the systems organize themselves to the point where definite structures become visible.

Most of these structures eventually die out, sometimes in rather complicated ways. But a crucial feature of any class 4 systems is that there must always be certain structures that can persist forever in it.

So how can one find out what these structures are for a particular cellular automaton? One approach is just to try each possible initial condition in turn, looking to see whether it leads to a new persistent structure. And taking the code 20 cellular automaton from the top of the next page, the page that follows shows what happens in this system with each of the first couple of hundred possible initial conditions.

In most cases everything just dies out. But when we reach initial condition number 151 we finally see a structure that persists.

This particular structure is fairly simple: it just remains fixed in position and repeats every two steps. But not all persistent structures are that simple. And indeed at initial condition 187 we see a considerably more complicated structure, that instead of staying still moves systematically to the right, repeating its basic form only every 9 steps.

The existence of structures that move is a fundamental feature of class 4 systems. For as we discussed on page 252, it is these kinds of structures that make it possible for information to be communicated from one part of a class 4 system to another—and that ultimately allow the complex behavior characteristic of class 4 to occur.

But having now seen the structure obtained with initial condition 187, we might assume that all subsequent structures that arise in the code 20 cellular automaton must be at least as complicated. It turns out, however, that initial condition 189 suddenly yields a much simpler structure—that just stays unchanged in one position at every step.

But going on to initial condition 195, we again find a more complicated structure—this time one that repeats only every 22 steps.

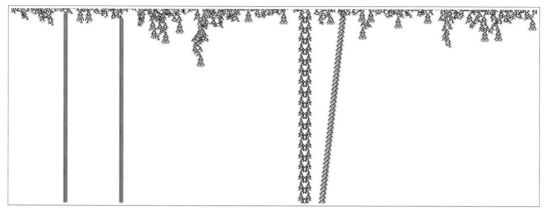

2 colors, next-nearest neighbors, code 20

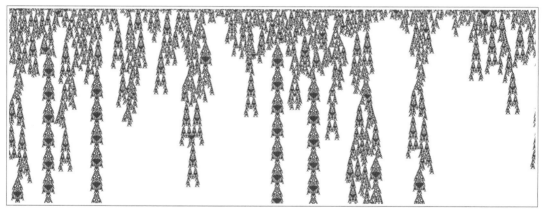

3 colors, nearest neighbors, code 357

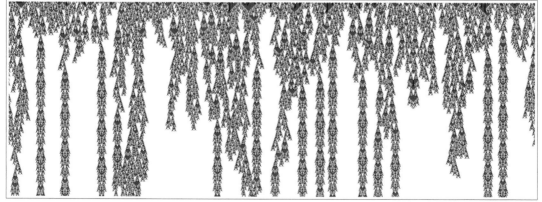

3 colors, nearest neighbors, code 1329

Three typical examples of class 4 cellular automata. In each case various kinds of persistent structures are seen.

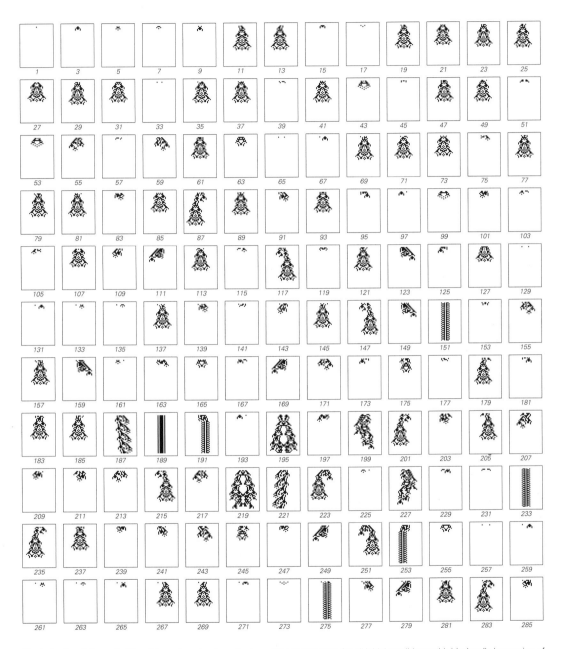

The behavior of the code 20 cellular automaton from the top of the facing page for all initial conditions with black cells in a region of size less than nine. In most cases the patterns produced simply die out. But with some initial conditions, persistent structures are formed. Each initial condition is assigned a number whose base 2 digit sequence gives the configuration of black and white cells in that initial condition. Note that initial conditions 195 and 219 both yield the period 22 persistent structure shown on the next page.

So just what set of structures does the code 20 cellular automaton ultimately support? There seems to be no easy way to tell, but the picture below shows all the structures that I found by explicitly looking at evolution from the first twenty-five billion possible initial conditions.

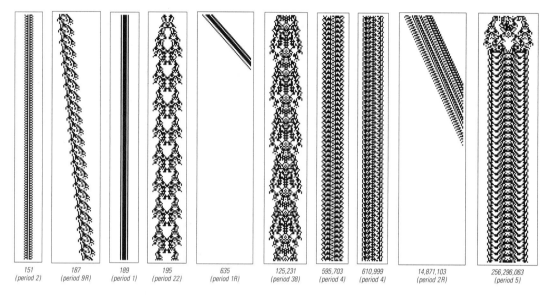

| 151 | 187 | 189 | 195 | 635 | 125,231 | 595,703 | 610,999 | 14,871,103 | 256,296,063 |
| (period 2) | (period 9R) | (period 1) | (period 22) | (period 1R) | (period 38) | (period 4) | (period 4) | (period 2R) | (period 5) |

Persistent structures found by testing the first twenty-five billion possible initial conditions for the code 20 cellular automaton shown on the previous page. Note that reflected versions of the structures shown are also possible. The base 2 digit sequences of the numbers given correspond to the initial conditions in each case, as on the previous page.

Are other structures possible? The largest structure in the picture above starts from a block that is 30 cells wide. And with the more than ten billion blocks between 30 and 34 cells wide, no new structures at all appear. Yet in fact other structures are possible. And the way to tell this is that for small repetition periods there is a systematic procedure that allows one to find absolutely all structures with a given period.

The picture on the facing page shows the results of using this procedure for repetition periods up to 15. And for all repetition periods up to 10—with the exception of 7—at least one fixed or moving structure ultimately turns out to exist. Often, however, the smallest structures for a given period are quite large, so that for example in the case of period 6 the smallest possible structure is 64 cells wide.

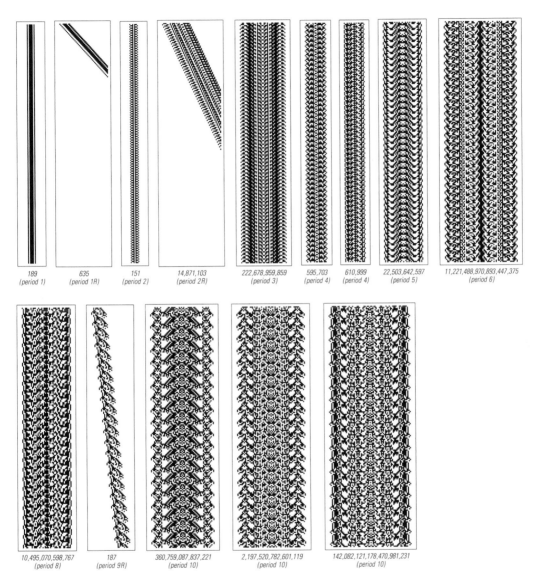

189
(period 1)

635
(period 1R)

151
(period 2)

14,871,103
(period 2R)

222,678,959,859
(period 3)

595,703
(period 4)

610,999
(period 4)

22,503,642,597
(period 5)

11,221,488,970,893,447,375
(period 6)

10,495,070,598,767
(period 8)

187
(period 9R)

360,759,087,837,221
(period 10)

2,197,520,782,601,119
(period 10)

142,082,121,178,470,981,231
(period 10)

All the persistent structures with repetition periods up to 15 steps in the code 20 cellular automaton. The structures shown were found by a systematic method similar to the one used to find all sequences that satisfy the constraints on page 268.

So what about other class 4 cellular automata—like the ones I showed at the beginning of this section? Do they also end up having complicated sets of possible persistent structures?

The picture below shows the structures one finds by explicitly testing the first two billion possible initial conditions for the code 357 cellular automaton from page 282.

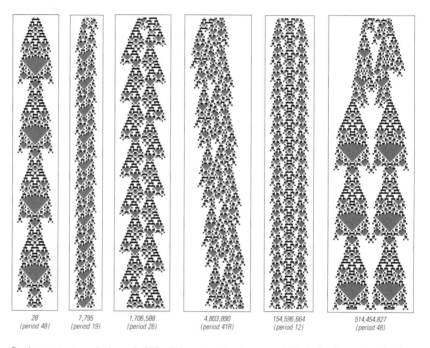

| 28 (period 48) | 7,795 (period 19) | 1,706,588 (period 26) | 4,803,890 (period 41R) | 154,596,664 (period 12) | 514,454,827 (period 48) |

Persistent structures in the code 357 cellular automaton from page 282 obtained by testing the first two billion possible initial conditions. This cellular automaton allows three possible colors for each cell; the initial conditions thus correspond to the base 3 digits of the numbers given. No persistent structures of any size exist in this cellular automaton with repetition periods of less than 5 steps.

Already with initial condition number 28 a fairly complicated structure with repetition period 48 is seen. But with all the first million initial conditions, only one other structure is produced, and this structure is again one that does not move.

So are moving structures in fact possible in the code 357 cellular automaton? My experience with many different rules is that whenever sufficiently complicated persistent structures occur, structures that move can eventually be found. And indeed with code 357, initial condition 4,803,890 yields just such a structure.

So if moving structures are inevitable in class 4 systems, what other fundamentally different kinds of structures might one see if one were to look at sufficiently many large initial conditions?

The picture below shows the first few persistent structures found in the code 1329 cellular automaton from the bottom of page 282. The smallest structures are stationary, but at initial condition 916 a structure is found that moves—all much the same as in the two other class 4 cellular automata that we have just discussed.

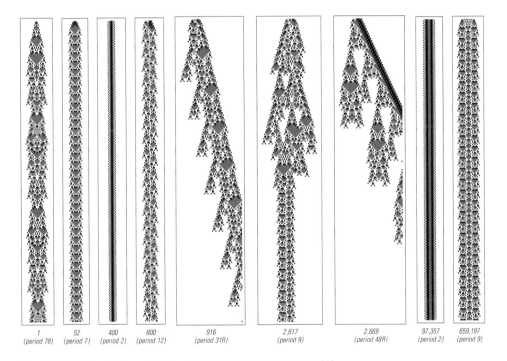

| 1
(period 78) | 52
(period 7) | 400
(period 2) | 800
(period 12) | 916
(period 31R) | 2,617
(period 9) | 2,669
(period 48R) | 97,357
(period 2) | 659,197
(period 9) |

Persistent structures in the code 1329 cellular automaton shown on page 282.

But when initial condition 54,889 is reached, one suddenly sees the rather different kind of structure shown on the next page. The right-hand part of this structure just repeats with a period of 256 steps, but as this part moves, it leaves behind a sequence of other persistent structures. And the result is that the whole structure continues to grow forever, adding progressively more and more cells.

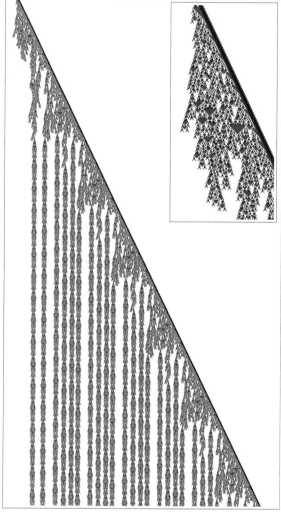

Unbounded growth in code 1329. The initial condition contains a block of 10 cells. The right-hand side of the pattern repeats every 256 steps, and as it moves it leaves behind an infinite sequence of persistent structures.

initial condition number 54,889

Yet looking at the picture above, one might suppose that when unlimited growth occurs, the pattern produced must be fairly complicated. But once again code 1329 has a surprise in store. For the facing page shows that when one reaches initial condition 97,439 there is again unlimited growth—but now the pattern that is produced is very simple. And in fact if one were just to see this pattern, one would probably assume that it came from a rule whose typical behavior is vastly simpler than code 1329.

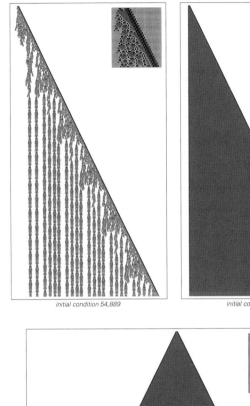

initial condition 54,889

initial condition 97,439

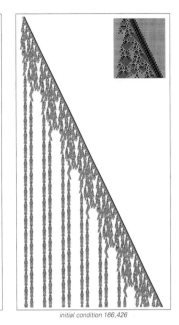

initial condition 166,426

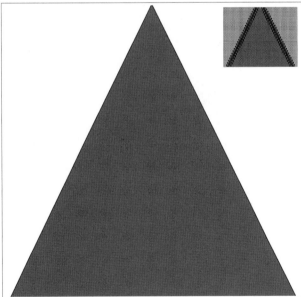

initial condition 115,396

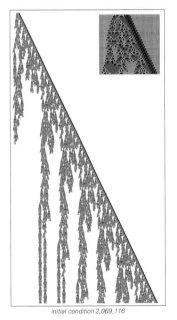

initial condition 2,069,116

Further examples of unbounded growth in code 1329. Most of the patterns produced are complex—but some are simple.

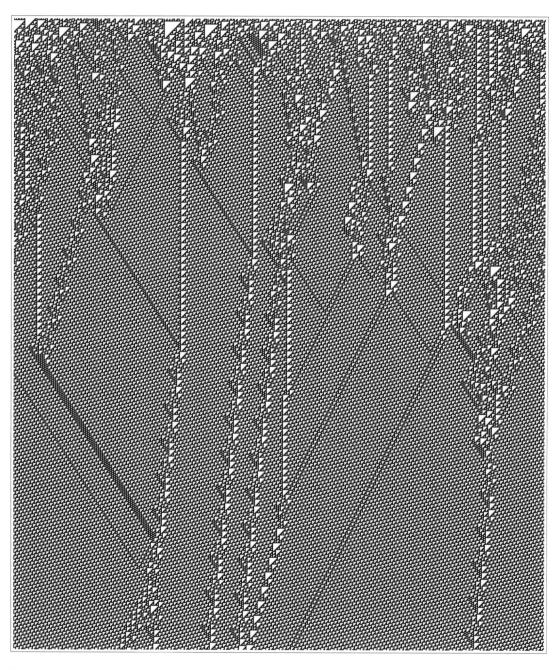

A typical example of the behavior of the rule 110 cellular automaton with random initial conditions. The background pattern consists of blocks of 14 cells that repeat every 7 steps.

Indeed, it is a general feature of class 4 cellular automata that with appropriate initial conditions they can mimic the behavior of all sorts of other systems. And when we discuss computation and the notion of universality in Chapter 11 we will see the fundamental reason this ends up being so. But for now the main point is just how diverse and complex the behavior of class 4 cellular automata can be—even when their underlying rules are very simple.

And perhaps the most striking example is the rule 110 cellular automaton that we first saw on page 32. Its rule is extremely simple—involving just nearest neighbors and two colors of cells. But its overall behavior is as complex as any system we have seen.

The facing page shows a typical example with random initial conditions. And one immediate slight difference from other class 4 rules that we have discussed is that structures in rule 110 do not exist on a blank background: instead, they appear as disruptions in a regular repetitive pattern that consists of blocks of 14 cells repeating every 7 steps.

The next page shows the kinds of persistent structures that can be generated in rule 110 from blocks less than 40 cells wide. And just like in other class 4 rules, there are stationary structures and moving structures—as well as structures that can be extended by repeating blocks they contain.

So are there also structures in rule 110 that exhibit unbounded growth? It is certainly not easy to find them. But if one looks at blocks of width 41, then such structures do eventually show up, as the picture on page 293 demonstrates.

So how do the various structures in rule 110 interact? The answer, as pages 294–296 demonstrate, can be very complicated.

In some cases, one structure essentially just passes through another with a slight delay. But often a collision between two structures produces a whole cascade of new structures. Sometimes the outcome of a collision is evident after a few steps. But quite often it takes a very large number of steps before one can tell for sure what is going to happen.

So even though the individual structures in class 4 systems like rule 110 may behave in fairly repetitive ways, interactions between these structures can lead to behavior of immense complexity.

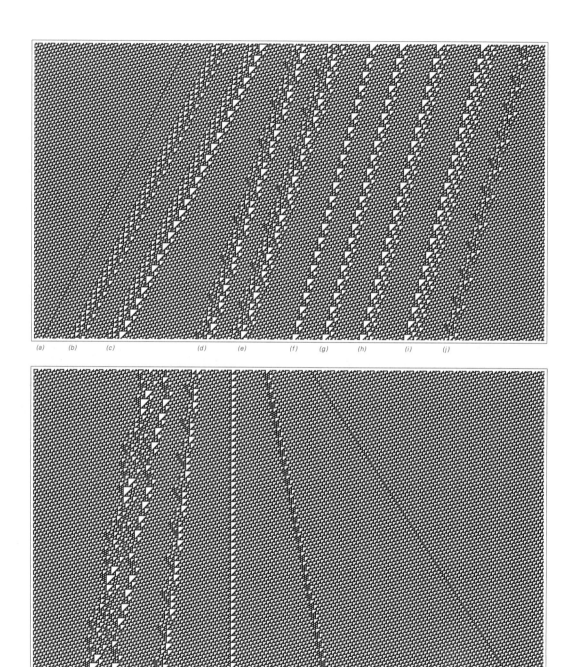

(a)   (b)   (c)   (d)   (e)   (f) (g) (h)   (i)   (j)

        (k)   (l)   (m)   (n)   (o)

Persistent structures found in rule 110. Extended versions exist of all but structures (a) and (j). Structures (m) and (n) also exist in alternate forms shifted with respect to the background.

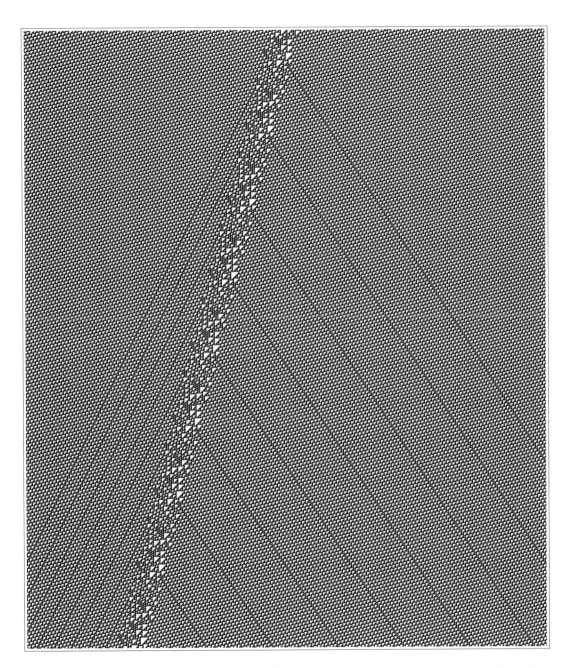

An example of unbounded growth in rule 110. The initial condition consists of a block of length 41 inserted between blocks of the background. New structures on both left and right are produced every 77 steps; the central structure moves 20 cells to the left during each cycle so that the structures on the left are separated by 37 steps while those on the right are separated by 107 steps.

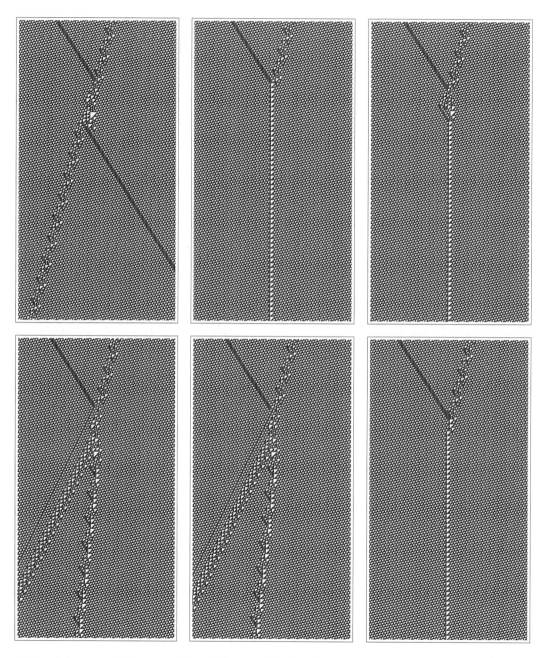

Collisions between persistent structures (o) and (j) from page 292. (The first structure is actually an extended form containing four copies of structure (o) from page 292.) Each successive picture shows what happens when the original structures are started progressively further apart.

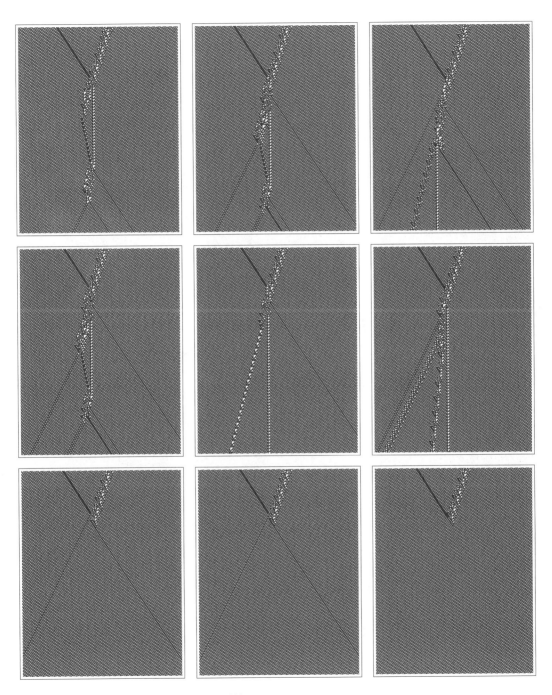

Collisions between structures (e) and (o) from page 292.

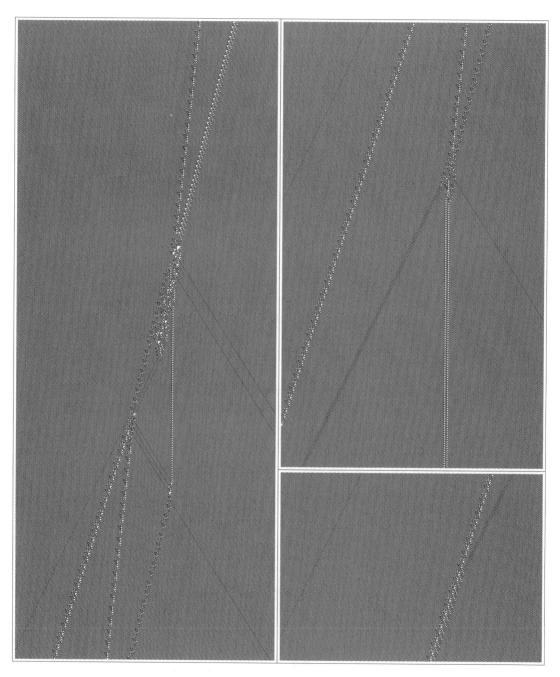

A collision between structures (l) and (i) from page 292. It takes more than 4000 steps for the final outcome involving 8 separate structures to become clear. The height of the picture corresponds to 2000 steps, and the third picture ends at step 4300.

7

Mechanisms in Programs and Nature

Universality of Behavior

In the past several chapters my main purpose has been to address the fundamental question of how simple programs behave. In this chapter my purpose is now to take what we have learned and begin applying it to the study of actual phenomena in nature.

At the outset one might have thought this would never work. For one might have assumed that any program based on simple rules would always lead to behavior that was much too simple to be relevant to most of what we see in nature. But one of the main discoveries of this book is that programs based on simple rules do not always produce simple behavior.

And indeed in the past several chapters we have seen many examples where remarkably simple rules give rise to behavior of great complexity. But to what extent is the behavior obtained from simple programs similar to behavior we see in nature?

One way to get some idea of this is just to look at pictures of natural systems and compare them with pictures of simple programs.

At the level of details there are certainly differences. But at an overall level there are striking similarities. And indeed it is quite remarkable just how often systems in nature end up showing behavior that looks almost identical to what we have seen in some simple program or another somewhere in this book.

So why might this be? It is not, I believe, any kind of coincidence, or trick of perception. And instead what I suspect is that it reflects a deep correspondence between simple programs and systems in nature.

When one looks at systems in nature, one of the striking things one notices is that even when systems have quite different underlying physical, biological or other components their overall patterns of behavior can often seem remarkably similar.

And in my study of simple programs I have seen essentially the same phenomenon: that even when programs have quite different underlying rules, their overall behavior can be remarkably similar.

So this suggests that a kind of universality exists in the types of behavior that can occur, independent of the details of underlying rules.

And the crucial point is that I believe that this universality extends not only across simple programs, but also to systems in nature. So this means that it should not matter much whether the components of a system are real molecules or idealized black and white cells; the overall behavior produced should show the same universal features.

And if this is the case, then it means that one can indeed expect to get insight into the behavior of natural systems by studying the behavior of simple programs. For it suggests that the basic mechanisms responsible for phenomena that we see in nature are somehow the same as those responsible for phenomena that we see in simple programs.

In this chapter my purpose is to discuss some of the most common phenomena that we see in nature, and to study how they correspond with phenomena that occur in simple programs.

Some of the phenomena I discuss have at least to some extent already been analyzed by traditional science. But we will find that by thinking in terms of simple programs it usually becomes possible to see the basic mechanisms at work with much greater clarity than before.

And more important, many of the phenomena that I consider—particularly those that involve significant complexity—have never been satisfactorily explained in the context of traditional science. But what we will find in this chapter is that by making use of my discoveries about simple programs a great many of these phenomena can now for the first time successfully be explained.

Three Mechanisms for Randomness

In nature one of the single most common things one sees is apparent randomness. And indeed, there are a great many different kinds of systems that all exhibit randomness. And it could be that in each case the cause of randomness is different. But from my investigations of simple programs I have come to the conclusion that one can in fact identify just three basic mechanisms for randomness, as illustrated in the pictures below.

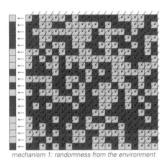
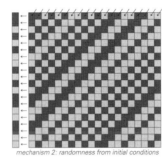
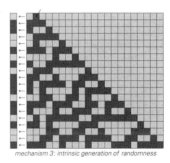

mechanism 1: randomness from the environment   mechanism 2: randomness from initial conditions   mechanism 3: intrinsic generation of randomness

Three possible mechanisms that can be responsible for randomness. The diagonal arrows represent external input. In the first case, there is random input from the environment at every step. In the second case, there is random input only in the initial conditions. And in the third case, there is effectively no random input at all. Yet despite their different underlying structure, each of these mechanisms leads to randomness in the column shown at the left. The first mechanism corresponds to randomness produced by external noise, as captured in so-called stochastic models. The second mechanism is essentially the one suggested by chaos theory. The third mechanism is new, and is suggested by the results on the behavior of simple programs in this book. I will give evidence that this third mechanism is the most common one in nature.

In the first mechanism, randomness is explicitly introduced into the underlying rules for the system, so that a random color is chosen for every cell at each step.

This mechanism is the one most commonly considered in the traditional sciences. It corresponds essentially to assuming that there is a random external environment which continually affects the system one is looking at, and continually injects randomness into it.

In the second mechanism shown above, there is no such interaction with the environment. The initial conditions for the system are chosen randomly, but then the subsequent evolution of the system is assumed to follow definite rules that involve no randomness.

A crucial feature of these rules, however, is that they make the system behave in a way that depends sensitively on the details of its initial conditions. In the particular case shown, the rules are simply set up to shift every color one position to the left at each step.

And what this does is to make the sequence of colors taken on by any particular cell depend on the colors of cells progressively further and further to the right in the initial conditions. Insofar as the initial conditions are random, therefore, so also will the sequence of colors of any particular cell be correspondingly random.

In general, the rules can be more complicated than those shown in the example on the previous page. But the basic idea of this mechanism for randomness is that the randomness one sees arises from some kind of transcription of randomness that is present in the initial conditions.

The two mechanisms for randomness just discussed have one important feature in common: they both assume that the randomness one sees in any particular system must ultimately come from outside of that system. In a sense, therefore, neither of these mechanisms takes any real responsibility for explaining the origins of randomness: they both in the end just say that randomness comes from outside whatever system one happens to be looking at.

Yet for quite a few years, this rather unsatisfactory type of statement has been the best that one could make. But the discoveries about simple programs in this book finally allow new progress to be made.

The crucial point that we first saw on page 27 is that simple programs can produce apparently random behavior even when they are given no random input whatsoever. And what this means is that there is a third possible mechanism for randomness, which this time does not rely in any way on randomness already being present outside the system one is looking at.

If we had found only a few examples of programs that could generate randomness in this way, then we might think that this third mechanism was a rare and special one. But in fact over the past few chapters we have seen that practically every kind of simple program that we can construct is capable of generating such randomness.

And as a result, it is reasonable to expect that this same mechanism should also occur in many systems in nature. Indeed, as I will discuss in this chapter and the chapters that follow, I believe that this mechanism is in fact ultimately responsible for a large fraction, if not essentially all, of the randomness that we see in the natural world.

But that is not to say that the other two mechanisms are never relevant in practice. For even though they may not be able to explain how randomness is produced at the lowest level, they can still be useful in describing observations about randomness in particular systems.

And in the next few sections, I will discuss various kinds of systems where the randomness that is seen can be best described by each of the three mechanisms for randomness identified here.

Randomness from the Environment

With the first mechanism for randomness discussed in the previous section, the randomness of any particular system is taken to be the result of continual interaction between that system and randomness in its environment.

As an everyday example, we can consider a boat bobbing up and down on a rough ocean. There is nothing intrinsically random about the boat itself. But the point is that there is randomness in the continually changing ocean surface that forms the environment for the boat. And since the motion of the boat follows this ocean surface, it also seems random.

But what is the real origin of this apparent randomness? In a sense it is that there are innumerable details about an ocean that it is very difficult to know, but which can nevertheless affect the motion of the boat. Thus, for example, a particular wave that hits the boat could be the result of a nearby squall, of an undersea ridge, or perhaps even of a storm that happened the day before several hundred miles away. But since one realistically cannot keep track of all these things, the ocean will inevitably seem in many respects unpredictable and random.

This same basic effect can be even more pronounced when one looks at smaller-scale systems. A classic example is so-called Brownian motion, in which one takes a small grain, say of pollen, puts it in a liquid, and then looks at its motion under a microscope.

What one finds is that the grain jumps around in an apparently random way. And as was suspected when this was first noticed in the 1820s, what is going on is that molecules in the liquid are continually hitting the grain and causing it to move. But even in a tiny volume of liquid there are already an immense number of molecules. And since one certainly does not even know at any given time exactly where all these molecules are, the details of their effect on the motion of the grain will inevitably seem quite random.

But to observe random Brownian motion, one needs a microscope. And one might imagine that randomness produced by any similar molecular process would also be too small to be of relevance in everyday life. But in fact such randomness is quite obvious in the operation of many kinds of electronic devices.

As an example, consider a radio receiver that is tuned to the wrong frequency or has no antenna connected. The radio receiver is built to amplify any signal that it receives. But what happens when there is no signal for it to amplify?

The answer is that the receiver produces noise. And it turns out that in most cases this noise is nothing other than a highly amplified version of microscopic processes going on inside the receiver.

In practice, such noise is usually considered a nuisance, and indeed modern digital electronics systems are typically designed to get rid of it at every stage. But since at least the 1940s, there have been various devices built for the specific purpose of generating randomness using electronic noise.

Typically these devices work by operating fairly standard electronic components in extreme conditions where there is usually no output signal, but where microscopic fluctuations can cause breakdown processes to occur which yield large output signals.

A large-scale example is a pair of metal plates with air in between. Usually no current flows across this air gap, but when the voltage between the plates is large enough, the air can break down, sparks can be generated, and spikes of current can occur. But exactly when and where the sparks occur depends on the detailed microscopic motion of the molecules in the gas, and is therefore potentially quite random.

In an effort to obtain as much randomness as possible, actual devices that work along these lines have typically used progressively smaller components: first vacuum tubes and later semiconductors. And indeed, in a modern semiconductor diode, for example, a breakdown event can be initiated by the motion of just one electron.

But despite such sensitivity to microscopic effects, what has consistently been found in practice is that the output from such devices has significant deviations from perfect randomness.

At first, this is quite surprising. For one might think that microscopic physical processes would always produce the best possible randomness. But there are two important effects which tend to limit this randomness, or indeed any randomness that is obtained through the mechanism of interaction with the environment.

The first of these concerns the internal details of whatever device is used to sample the randomness in the environment.

Every time the device receives a piece of input, its internal state changes. But in order for successive pieces of input to be treated in an independent and uncorrelated way, the device must be in exactly the same state when it receives each piece of input. And the problem is that while practical devices may eventually relax to what is essentially the same state, they can do this only at a certain rate.

In a device that produces a spark, for example, it inevitably takes some time for the hot gas in the path of the spark to be cleared out. And if another spark is generated before this has happened, the path of the second spark will not be independent of the first.

One might think that such effects could be avoided by allowing a certain "dead time" between successive events. But in fact, as we will also see in connection with quantum mechanics, it is a rather general feature of systems that perform amplification that relaxation to a normal state can effectively occur only gradually, so that one would have to wait an infinite time for such relaxation to be absolutely complete.

But even when the device used to sample the environment does no amplification and has no relevant internal structure, one may still not see perfect randomness. And the reason for this is that there are almost inevitably correlations even in the supposedly random environment.

In an ocean for example, the inertia of the water essentially forces there to be waves on the surface of certain sizes. And during the time that a boat is caught up in a particular one of these waves, its motion will always be quite regular; it is only when one watches the effect of a sequence of waves that one sees behavior that appears in any way random.

In a sense, though, this point just emphasizes the incomplete nature of the mechanism for randomness that we have been discussing in this section. For to know in any real way why the motion of the boat is random, we must inevitably ask more about the randomness of the ocean surface. And indeed, it is only at a fairly superficial level of description that it is useful to say that the randomness in the motion of the boat comes from interaction with an environment about which one will say nothing more than that it is random.

Chaos Theory and Randomness from Initial Conditions

At the beginning of this chapter I outlined three basic mechanisms that can lead to apparent randomness. And in the previous section I discussed the first of these mechanisms—based on the idea that the evolution of a system is continually affected by randomness from its environment.

But to get randomness in a particular system it turns out that there is no need for continual interaction between the system and an external random environment. And in the second mechanism for randomness discussed at the beginning of this chapter, no explicit randomness is inserted during the evolution of a system. But there is still randomness in the initial conditions, and the point is that as the system evolves, it samples more and more of this randomness, and as a result produces behavior that is correspondingly random.

As a rather simple example one can think of a car driving along a bumpy road. Unlike waves on an ocean, all the bumps on the road are already present when the car starts driving, and as a result, one can consider these bumps to be part of the initial conditions for the system. But the point is that as time goes on, the car samples more and more of the bumps, and if there is randomness in these bumps it leads to corresponding randomness in the motion of the car.

A somewhat similar example is a ball rolled along a rough surface. A question such as where the ball comes to rest will depend on the pattern of bumps on the surface. But now another feature of the initial conditions is also important: the initial speed of the ball.

And somewhat surprisingly there is already in practice some apparent randomness in the behavior of such a system even when there are no significant bumps on the surface. Indeed, games of chance based on rolling dice, tossing coins and so on all rely on just such randomness.

As a simple example, consider a ball that has one hemisphere white and the other black. One can roll this ball like a die, and then look to see which color is on top when the ball comes to rest. And if one does this in practice, what one will typically find is that the outcome seems quite random. But where does this randomness come from?

The answer is that it comes from randomness in the initial speed with which the ball is rolled. The picture below shows the motion of a ball with a sequence of different initial speeds. And what one sees is that it takes only a small change in the initial speed to make the ball come to rest in a completely different orientation.

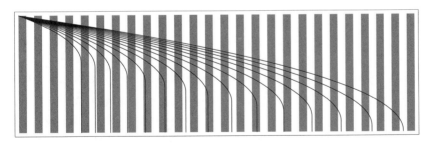

A plot of the position of a ball rolled with various initial speeds. Time goes down the page. The ball starts on the left, with an initial speed given by the initial slope of the curve. The ball slows down as a result of friction, and eventually stops. The ball is half white and half black, and the stripes in the picture indicate which color is on top when the ball is at a particular position. The divergence of the curves in the picture indicate the sensitivity of the motion to the exact initial speed of the ball. Small changes in this speed are seen to make the ball stop with a different color on top. It is such sensitivity to randomness in the initial conditions that makes processes such as rolling dice or tossing coins yield seemingly random output.

The point then is that a human rolling the ball will typically not be able to control this speed with sufficient accuracy to determine whether black or white will end up on top. And indeed on successive trials there will usually be sufficiently large random variations in the initial speed that the outcomes will seem completely random.

Coin tossing, wheels of fortune, roulette wheels, and similar generators of randomness all work in essentially the same way. And in each case the basic mechanism that leads to the randomness we see is a sensitive dependence on randomness that is present in the typical initial conditions that are provided.

Without randomness in the initial conditions, however, there is no randomness in the output from these systems. And indeed it is quite feasible to build precise machines for tossing coins, rolling balls and so on that always produce a definite outcome with no randomness at all.

But the discovery which launched what has become known as chaos theory is that at least in principle there can be systems whose sensitivity to their initial conditions is so great that no machine with fixed tolerances can ever be expected to yield repeatable results.

A classic example is an idealized version of the kneading process which is used for instance to make noodles or taffy. The basic idea is to take a lump of dough-like material, and repeatedly to stretch this material to twice its original length, cut it in two, then stack the pieces on top of each other. The picture at the top of the facing page shows a few steps in this process. And the important point to notice is that every time the material is stretched, the distance between neighboring points is doubled.

The result of this is that any change in the initial position of a point will be amplified by a factor of two at each step. And while a particular machine may be able to control the initial position of a point to a certain accuracy, such repeated amplification will eventually lead to sensitivity to still smaller changes.

But what does this actually mean for the motion of a point in the material? The bottom pictures on the facing page show what happens to two sets of points that start very close together. The most obvious effect is that these points diverge rapidly on successive steps. But after a while, they reach the edge of the material and cannot diverge any

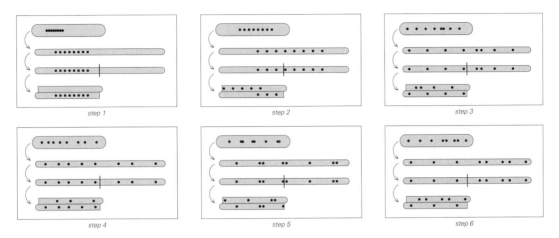

A kneading process similar to ones used to make noodles or taffy, which exhibits very sensitive dependence on initial conditions. In the first part of each step, the material is stretched to twice its original length. Then it is cut in two, and the two halves are stacked on top of each other. The picture demonstrates that dots which are initially close together rapidly separate. (A more realistic kneading process would fold material rather than cutting it, but the same sensitive dependence on initial conditions would occur.)

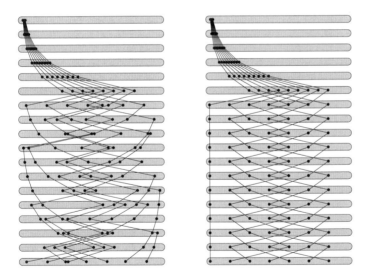

Two examples of what can happen when the kneading process above is applied to nearby collections of points. In both cases the points initially diverge exponentially, as implied by chaos theory. But after a while they reach the edge of the material, and although in the first case they then show quite random behavior, in the second case they instead just show simple repetitive behavior. What differs between the two cases is the detailed digit sequences of the positions of the points: in the first case these digit sequences are quite random, while in the second case they have a simple repetitive form.

further. And then in the first case, the subsequent motion looks quite random. But in the second case it is fairly regular. So why is this?

A little analysis shows what is going on. The basic idea is to represent the position of each point at each step as a number, say *x*, which runs from 0 to 1. When the material is stretched, the number is doubled. And when the material is cut and stacked, the effect on the number is then to extract its fractional part.

But it turns out that this process is exactly the same as the one we discussed on page 153 in the chapter on systems based on numbers.

And what we found there was that it is crucial to think not in terms of the sizes of the numbers x, but rather in terms of their digit sequences represented in base 2. And in fact, in terms of such digit sequences, the kneading process consists simply in shifting all digits one place to the left at each step, as shown in the pictures below.

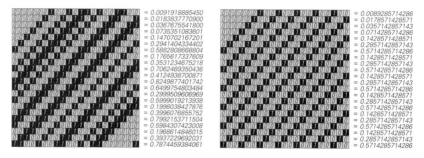

The digit sequences of positions of points on successive steps in the two examples of kneading processes at the bottom of the previous page. At each step these digit sequences are shifted one place to the left. So if the initial digit sequence is random, as in the first example, then the subsequent behavior will also be correspondingly random. But if the initial digit sequence is simple, as in the second example, then the behavior will be correspondingly simple. In general, a point at position x on a particular step will move to position *FractionalPart[2 x]* on the next step.

The way digit sequences work, digits further to the right in a number always make smaller contributions to its overall size. And as a result, one might think that digits which lie far to the right in the initial conditions would never be important. But what the pictures above show is that these digits will always be shifted to the left, so that eventually they will in fact be important. As time goes on, therefore, what is effectively happening is that the system is sampling digits further and further to the right in the initial conditions.

And in a sense this is not unlike what happens in the example of a car driving along a bumpy road discussed at the beginning of this section. Indeed in many ways the only real difference is that instead of being able to see a sequence of explicit bumps in the road, the initial conditions for the position of a point in the kneading process are encoded in a more abstract form as a sequence of digits.

But the crucial point is that the behavior we see will only ever be as random as the sequence of digits in the initial conditions. And in the first case on the facing page, it so happens that the sequence of digits for each of the initial points shown is indeed quite random, so the behavior we see is correspondingly random. But in the second case, the sequence of digits is regular, and so the behavior is correspondingly regular.

Sensitive dependence on initial conditions thus does not in and of itself imply that a system will behave in a random way. Indeed, all it does is to cause digits which make an arbitrarily small contribution to the size of numbers in the initial conditions eventually to have a significant effect. But in order for the behavior of the system to be random, it is necessary in addition that the sequence of digits be random. And indeed, the whole idea of the mechanism for randomness in this section is precisely that any randomness we see must come from randomness in the initial conditions for the system we are looking at.

It is then a separate question why there should be randomness in these initial conditions. And ultimately this question can only be answered by going outside of the system one is looking at, and studying whatever it was that set up its initial conditions.

Accounts of chaos theory in recent years have, however, often introduced confusion about this point. For what has happened is that from an implicit assumption made in the mathematics of chaos theory, the conclusion has been drawn that random digit sequences should be almost inevitable among the numbers that occur in practice.

The basis for this is the traditional mathematical idealization that the only relevant attribute of any number is its size. And as discussed on page 152, what this idealization suggests is that all numbers which are sufficiently close in size should somehow be equally common. And indeed if this were true, then it would imply that typical initial conditions would inevitably involve random digit sequences.

But there is no particular reason to believe that an idealization which happens to be convenient for mathematical analysis should apply in the natural world. And indeed to assume that it does is effectively just to ignore the fundamental question of where randomness in nature comes from.

But beyond even such matters of principle, there are serious practical problems with the idea of getting randomness from initial conditions, at least in the case of the kneading process discussed above.

The issue is that the description of the kneading process that we have used ignores certain obvious physical realities. Most important among these is that any material one works with will presumably be made of atoms. And as a result, the notion of being able to make arbitrarily small changes in the position of a point is unrealistic.

One might think that atoms would always be so small that their size would in practice be irrelevant. But the whole point is that the kneading process continually amplifies distances. And indeed after just thirty steps, the description of the kneading process given above would imply that two points initially only one atom apart would end up nearly a meter apart.

Yet long before this would ever happen in practice other effects not accounted for in our simple description of the kneading process would inevitably also become important. And often such effects will tend to introduce new randomness from the environment. So the idea that randomness comes purely from initial conditions can be realistic only for a fairly small number of steps; randomness which is seen after that must therefore typically be attributed to other mechanisms.

One might think that the kneading process we have been discussing is just a bad example, and that in other cases, randomness from initial conditions would be more significant.

The picture on the facing page shows a system in which a beam of light repeatedly bounces off a sequence of mirrors. The system is set up so that every time the light goes around, its position is modified in exactly the same way as the position of a point in the kneading process. And just as in the kneading process, there is very sensitive dependence on the details of the initial conditions, and the behavior that is seen reflects the digit sequence of these initial conditions.

But once again, in any practical implementation, the light would go around only a few tens of times before being affected by microscopic

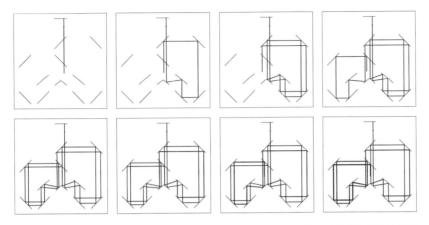

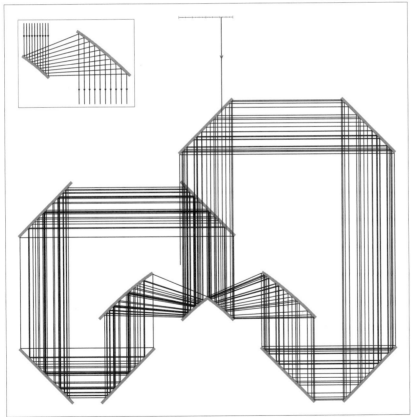

An arrangement of mirrors set up to exhibit randomness arising from sensitive dependence on initial conditions. The initial condition for the system is specified by the position of the incoming light ray in the gray region at the top of each picture. Whether the light ray goes to the left or to the right at each step is then determined by successive digits in the base 2 representation for the number that gives the initial condition. The heart of the system is the "amplifier" shown on the left which uses a pair of parabolic mirrors to double the displacement of each incoming ray. The initial condition used here is $\pi/4$, which has digit sequence 0.1100100100001111111.

perturbations in the mirrors and by other phenomena that are not accounted for in the simple description we have given.

At the heart of the system shown on the previous page is a slightly complicated arrangement of parabolic mirrors. But it turns out that almost any convex reflector will lead to the divergence of trajectories necessary to get sensitive dependence on initial conditions.

Indeed, the simple pegboard shown below exhibits the same phenomenon, with balls dropped at even infinitesimally different initial positions eventually following very different trajectories.

The details of these trajectories cannot be deduced quite as directly as before from the digit sequences of initial positions, but

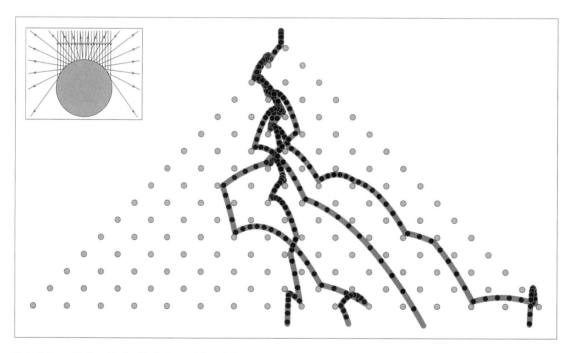

Paths followed by four idealized balls dropped from initial positions differing by one part in a thousand into an array of identical circular pegs. The balls are taken to fall under gravity, and to bounce elastically whenever they hit a peg. As illustrated in the inset, small differences in direction are amplified—roughly doubling—at each bounce, with the result that after a few bounces the trajectories of the three balls are quite different. In a physical version of the system with balls of the same actual size as on this page perturbations from the environment will inevitably be amplified to have a significant effect on the trajectories after roughly the number of bounces shown. Versions of the system illustrated here—particularly with smaller peg spacings—are sometimes known as Galton or quincunx boards, and have been used since the late 1800s to demonstrate principles of probability theory. If balls are assumed to fall randomly on each side of each peg then with a large number of balls the final positions will approximate a binomial distribution.

exactly the same phenomenon of successively sampling less and less significant digits still occurs. And once again, at least for a while, any randomness in the motion of the ball can be attributed to randomness in this initial digit sequence.

But after at most ten or so collisions, many other effects, mostly associated with continual interaction with the environment, will always in practice become important, so that any subsequent randomness cannot solely be attributed to initial conditions.

And indeed in any system, the amount of time over which the details of initial conditions can ever be considered the dominant source of randomness will inevitably be limited by the level of separation that exists between the large-scale features that one observes and small-scale features that one cannot readily control.

So in what kinds of systems do the largest such separations occur? The answer tends to be systems in astronomy. And as it turns out, the so-called three-body problem in astronomy was the very first place where sensitive dependence on initial conditions was extensively studied.

The three-body problem consists in determining the motion of three bodies—such as the Earth, Sun and Moon—that interact through gravitational attraction. With just two bodies, it has been known for nearly four hundred years that the orbits that occur are simple ellipses or hyperbolas. But with three bodies, the motion can be much more complicated, and—as was shown at the end of the 1800s—can be sensitively dependent on the initial conditions that are given.

The pictures on the next page show a particular case of the three-body problem, in which there are two large masses in a simple elliptical orbit, together with an infinitesimally small mass moving up and down through the plane of this orbit. And what the pictures demonstrate is that even if the initial position of this mass is changed by just one part in a hundred million, then within 50 revolutions of the large masses the trajectory of the small mass will end up being almost completely different.

So what happens in practice with planets and other bodies in our solar system? Observations suggest that at least on human timescales most of their motion is quite regular. And in fact this regularity was in

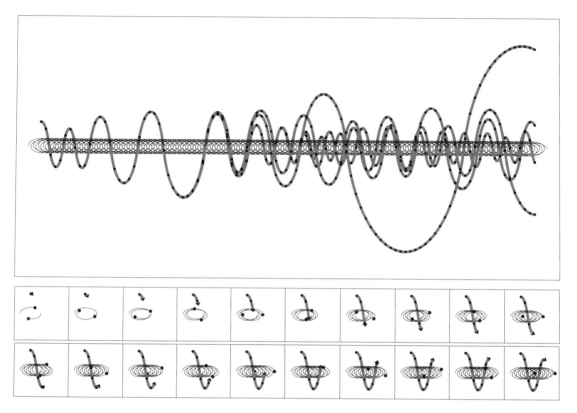

An example of the three-body problem, in which an idealized planet moves up and down through the plane of two equal-mass idealized stars in a perfect elliptical orbit. The trajectories obtained with four possible initial positions for the planet—differing by 10^{-8}—are shown. The pictures are made assuming the system to be in uniform motion from left to right. Successive black dots indicate where the planets are on each revolution of the stars. The main picture shows what happens over the course of 100 revolutions. The planet is assumed to be of negligible mass relative to the stars, and to start with zero vertical velocity at exactly an equal distance between the stars. The divergence of trajectories with slightly different initial vertical positions indicates sensitive dependence on initial conditions.

the past taken as one of the key pieces of evidence for the idea that simple laws of nature could exist.

But calculations imply that sensitive dependence on initial conditions should ultimately occur even in our solar system. Needless to say, we do not have the option of explicitly setting up different initial conditions. But if we could watch the solar system for a few million years, then there should be significant randomness that could be attributed to sensitive dependence on the digit sequences of initial conditions—and whose presence in the past may explain some observed present-day features of our solar system.

The Intrinsic Generation of Randomness

In the past two sections, we have studied two possible mechanisms that can lead to observed randomness. But as we have discussed, neither of these in any real sense themselves generate randomness. Instead, what they essentially do is just to take random input that comes from outside, and transfer it to whatever system one is looking at.

One of the important results of this book, however, is that there is also a third possible mechanism for randomness, in which no random input from outside is needed, and in which randomness is instead generated intrinsically inside the systems one is looking at.

The picture below shows the rule 30 cellular automaton in which I first identified this mechanism for randomness. The basic rule for the system is very simple. And the initial condition is also very simple.

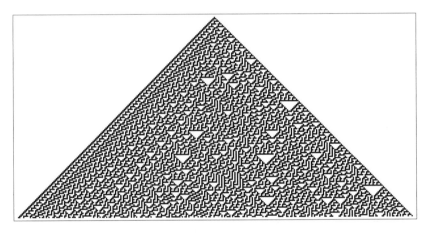

The rule 30 cellular automaton from page 27 that was the first example I found of intrinsic randomness generation. There is no random input to this system, yet its behavior seems in many respects random. I suspect that this is how much of the randomness that we see in nature arises.

Yet despite the lack of anything that can reasonably be considered random input, the evolution of the system nevertheless intrinsically yields behavior which seems in many respects random.

As we have discussed before, traditional intuition makes it hard to believe that such complexity could arise from such a simple underlying process. But the past several chapters have demonstrated that this is not only possible, but actually quite common.

Yet looking at the cellular automaton on the previous page there are clearly at least some regularities in the pattern it produces—like the diagonal stripes on the left. But if, say, one specifically picks out the color of the center cell on successive steps, then what one gets seems like a completely random sequence.

But just how random is this sequence really?

For our purposes here the most relevant point is that so far as one can tell the sequence is at least as random as sequences one gets from any of the phenomena in nature that we typically consider random.

When one says that something seems random, what one usually means in practice is that one cannot see any regularities in it. So when we say that a particular phenomenon in nature seems random, what we mean is that none of our standard methods of analysis have succeeded in finding regularities in it. To assess the randomness of a sequence produced by something like a cellular automaton, therefore, what we must do is to apply to it the same methods of analysis as we do to natural systems.

As I will discuss in Chapter 10, some of these methods have been well codified in standard mathematics and statistics, while others are effectively implicit in our processes of visual and other perception. But the remarkable fact is that none of these methods seem to reveal any real regularities whatsoever in the rule 30 cellular automaton sequence. And thus, so far as one can tell, this sequence is at least as random as anything we see in nature.

But is it truly random?

Over the past century or so, a variety of definitions of true randomness have been proposed. And according to most of these definitions, the sequence is indeed truly random. But there are a certain class of definitions which do not consider it truly random.

For these definitions are based on the notion of classifying as truly random only sequences which can never be generated by any simple procedure whatsoever. Yet starting with a simple initial condition and then applying a simple cellular automaton rule constitutes a simple procedure. And as a result, the center column of rule 30 cannot be considered truly random according to such definitions.

But while definitions of this type have a certain conceptual appeal, they are not likely to be useful in discussions of randomness in nature. For as we will see later in this book, it is almost certainly impossible for any natural process ever to generate a sequence which is guaranteed to be truly random according to such definitions.

For our purposes more useful definitions tend to concentrate not so much on whether there exists in principle a simple way to generate a particular sequence, but rather on whether such a way can realistically be recognized by applying various kinds of analysis to the sequence. And as discussed above, there is good evidence that the center column of rule 30 is indeed random according to all reasonable definitions of this kind.

So whether or not one chooses to say that the sequence is truly random, it is, as far as one can tell, at least random for all practical purposes. And in fact sequences closely related to it have been used very successfully as sources of randomness in practical computing.

For many years, most kinds of computer systems and languages have had facilities for generating what they usually call random numbers. And in *Mathematica*—ever since it was first released—Random[Integer] has generated 0's and 1's using exactly the rule 30 cellular automaton.

The way this works is that every time Random[Integer] is called, another step in the cellular automaton evolution is performed, and the value of the cell in the center is returned. But one difference from the picture two pages ago is that for practical reasons the pattern is not allowed to grow wider and wider forever. Instead, it is wrapped around in a region that is a few hundred cells wide.

One consequence of this, as discussed on page 259, is that the sequence of 0's and 1's that is generated must then eventually repeat. But even with the fastest foreseeable computers, the actual period of repetition will typically be more than a billion billion times the age of the universe.

Another issue is that if one always ran the cellular automaton from page 315 with the particular initial condition shown there, then one would always get exactly the same sequence of 0's and 1's. But by using different initial conditions one can get completely different sequences. And in practice if the initial conditions are not explicitly specified, what *Mathematica* does, for example, is to use as an initial condition a representation of various features of the exact state of the computer system at the time when Random was first called.

The rule 30 cellular automaton provides a particularly clear and good example of intrinsic randomness generation. But in previous chapters we have seen many other examples of systems that also intrinsically produce apparent randomness. And it turns out that one of these is related to the method used since the late 1940s for generating random numbers in almost all practical computer systems.

The pictures on the facing page show what happens if one successively multiplies a number by various constant factors, and then looks at the digit sequences of the numbers that result. As we first saw on page 119, the patterns of digits obtained in this way seem quite random. And the idea of so-called linear congruential random number generators is precisely to make use of this randomness.

For practical reasons, such generators typically keep only, say, the rightmost 31 digits in the numbers at each step. Yet even with this restriction, the sequences generated are random enough that at least until recently they were almost universally what was used as a source of randomness in practical computing.

So in a sense linear congruential generators are another example of the general phenomenon of intrinsic randomness generation. But it turns out that in some respects they are rather unusual and misleading.

Keeping only a limited number of digits at each step makes it inevitable that the sequences produced will eventually repeat. And one of the reasons for the popularity of linear congruential generators is that with fairly straightforward mathematical analysis it is possible to tell exactly what multiplication factors will maximize this repetition period.

It has then often been assumed that having maximal repetition period will somehow imply maximum randomness in all aspects of the sequence one gets. But in practice over the years, one after another linear congruential generator that has been constructed to have maximal repetition period has turned out to exhibit very substantial deviations from perfect randomness.

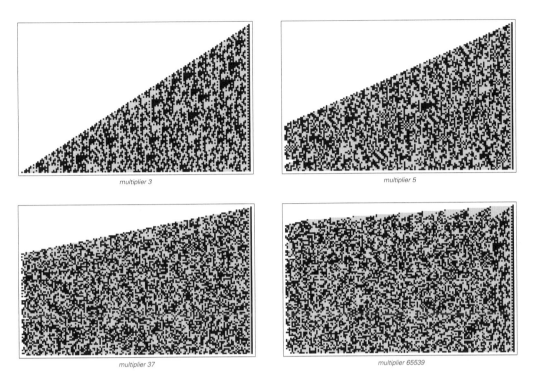

multiplier 3 *multiplier 5*

multiplier 37 *multiplier 65539*

Patterns of digits in base 2 produced by starting with the number 1 and then repeatedly multiplying by various fixed constants. In all cases, the complete pattern has a triangular form, but except in the first case, it is truncated on the left here. The mathematical structure of these systems is nevertheless such that digits further to the left do not affect those shown: at each step the number obtained is effectively reduced modulo 2^n, where n is the width of the picture.

A typical kind of failure, illustrated in the pictures on the next page, is that points with coordinates determined by successive numbers from the generator turn out to be distributed in an embarrassingly regular way. At first, such failures might suggest that more complicated schemes must be needed if one is to get good randomness. And indeed with this thought in mind all sorts of elaborate combinations of linear congruential and other generators have been proposed. But although some aspects of the behavior of such systems can be made quite random, deviations from perfect randomness are still often found.

And seeing this one might conclude that it must be essentially impossible to produce good randomness with any kind of system that has reasonably simple rules. But the rule 30 cellular automaton that we discussed above demonstrates that in fact this is absolutely not the case.

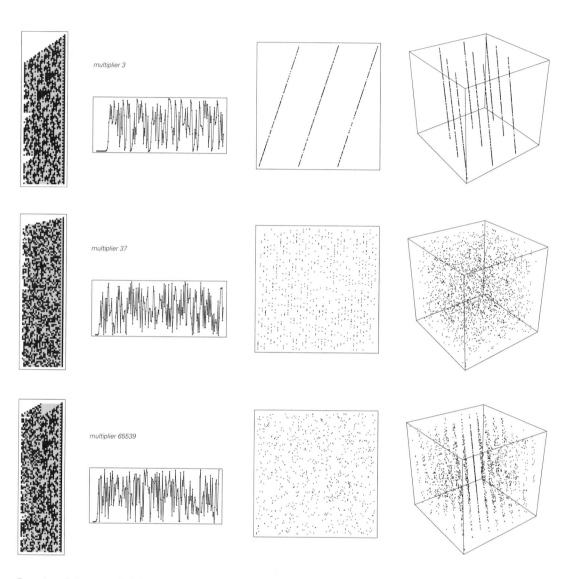

multiplier 3

multiplier 37

multiplier 65539

Examples of three so-called linear congruential random number generators. In each case they start with the number 1, then successively multiply by the specified multiplier, keeping only the rightmost 31 digits in the base 2 representation of the number obtained at each step. A version of the case with multiplier 3 was already shown on page 120. Multiplier 65539 was used as the random number generator on many computer systems, starting with mainframes in the 1960s. The last two pictures in each row above give the distribution of points whose coordinates in two and three dimensions are obtained by taking successive numbers from the linear congruential generator. If the output from the generator was perfectly random, then in each case these points would be uniformly distributed. But as the pictures demonstrate, stripes are visible in either two or three dimensions, or both.

Indeed, the rules for this cellular automaton are in some respects much simpler than for even a rather basic linear congruential generator. Yet the sequences it produces seem perfectly random, and do not suffer from any of the problems that are typically found in linear congruential generators.

So why do linear congruential generators not produce better randomness? Ironically, the basic reason is also the reason for their popularity. The point is that unlike the rule 30 cellular automaton that we discussed above, linear congruential generators are readily amenable to detailed mathematical analysis. And as a result, it is possible for example to guarantee that a particular generator will indeed have a maximal repetition period.

Almost inevitably, however, having such a maximal period implies a certain regularity. And in fact, as we shall see later in this book, the very possibility of any detailed mathematical analysis tends to imply the presence of at least some deviations from perfect randomness.

But if one is not constrained by the need for such analysis, then as we saw in the cellular automaton example above, remarkably simple rules can successfully generate highly random behavior.

And indeed the existence of such simple rules is crucial in making it plausible that the general mechanism of intrinsic randomness generations can be widespread in nature. For if the only way for intrinsic randomness generation to occur was through very complicated sets of rules, then one would expect that this mechanism would be seen in practice only in a few very special cases.

But the fact that simple cellular automaton rules are sufficient to give rise to intrinsic randomness generation suggests that in reality it is rather easy for this mechanism to occur. And as a result, one can expect that the mechanism will be found often in nature.

So how does the occurrence of this mechanism compare to the previous two mechanisms for randomness that we have discussed?

The basic answer, I believe, is that whenever a large amount of randomness is produced in a short time, intrinsic randomness generation is overwhelmingly likely to be the mechanism responsible.

We saw in the previous section that random details of the initial conditions for a system can lead to a certain amount of randomness in the behavior of a system. But as we discussed, there is in most practical situations a limit on the lengths of sequences whose randomness can realistically be attributed to such a mechanism. With intrinsic randomness generation, however, there is no such limit: in the cellular automaton above, for example, all one need do to get a longer random sequence is to run the cellular automaton for more steps.

But it is also possible to get long random sequences by continual interaction with a random external environment, as in the first mechanism for randomness discussed in this chapter.

The issue with this mechanism, however, is that it can take a long time to get a given amount of good-quality randomness from it. And the point is that in most cases, intrinsic randomness generation can produce similar randomness in a much shorter time.

Indeed, in general, intrinsic randomness generation tends to be much more efficient than getting randomness from the environment. The basic reason is that intrinsic randomness generation in a sense puts all the components in a system to work in producing new randomness, while getting randomness from the environment does not.

Thus, for example, in the rule 30 cellular automaton discussed above, every cell in effect actively contributes to the randomness we see. But in a system that just amplifies randomness from the environment, none of the components inside the system itself ever contribute any new randomness at all. Indeed, ironically enough, the more components that are involved in the process of amplification, the slower it will typically be to get each new piece of random output. For as we discussed two sections ago, each component in a sense adds what one can consider to be more inertia to the amplification process.

But with a larger number of components it becomes progressively easier for randomness to be generated through intrinsic randomness generation. And indeed unless the underlying rules for the system somehow explicitly prevent it, it turns out in the end that intrinsic randomness generation will almost inevitably occur—often producing so much randomness that it completely swamps any randomness that might be produced from either of the other two mechanisms.

Yet having said this, one can ask how one can tell in an actual experiment on some particular system in nature to what extent intrinsic randomness generation is really the mechanism responsible for whatever seemingly random behavior one observed.

The clearest sign is a somewhat unexpected phenomenon: that details of the random behavior can be repeatable from one run of the experiment to another. It is not surprising that general features of the behavior will be the same. But what is remarkable is that if intrinsic randomness generation is the mechanism at work, then the precise details of the behavior can also be repeatable.

In the mechanism where randomness comes from continual interaction with the environment, no repeatability can be expected. For every time the experiment is run, the state of the environment will be different, and so the behavior one sees will also be correspondingly different. And similarly, in the mechanism where randomness comes from the details of initial conditions, there will again be little, if any, repeatability. For the details of the initial conditions are typically affected by the environment of the system, and cannot realistically be kept the same from one run to another.

But the point is that with the mechanism of intrinsic randomness generation, there is no dependence on the environment. And as a result, so long as the setup of the system one is looking at remains the same, the behavior it produces will be exactly the same. Thus for example, however many times one runs a rule 30 cellular automaton, starting with a single black cell, the behavior one gets will always be exactly the same. And so for example the sequence of colors of the center cell, while seemingly random, will also be exactly the same.

But how easy is it to disturb this sequence? If one makes a fairly drastic perturbation, such as changing the colors of cells all the way from white to black, then the sequence will indeed often change, as illustrated in the pictures at the top of the next page.

But with less drastic perturbations, the sequence can be quite robust. As an example, one can consider allowing each cell to be not just black or white, but any shade of gray, as in the continuous cellular automata we discussed on page 155. And in such systems, one can

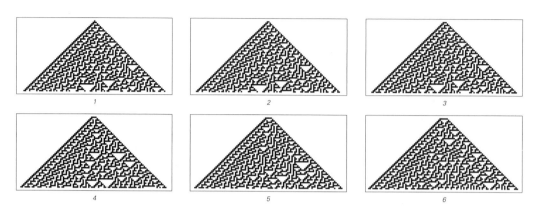

The effect of changing the number of initial black cells in the rule 30 cellular automaton shown above. With only 2 or 3 black cells, the sequence in the center of the pattern does not change. But as soon as more black cells are added, it does change.

investigate what happens if at every step one randomly perturbs the gray level of each cell by a small amount.

The pictures on the facing page show results for perturbations of various sizes. What one sees is that when the perturbations are sufficiently large, the sequence of colors of the center cell does indeed change. But the crucial point is that for perturbations below a certain critical size, the sequence always remains essentially unchanged.

Even though small perturbations are continually being made, the evolution of the system causes these perturbations to be damped out, and produces behavior that is in practice indistinguishable from what would be seen if there were no perturbations.

The question of what size of perturbations can be tolerated without significant effect depends on the details of the underlying rules. And as the pictures suggest, rules which yield more complex behavior tend to be able to tolerate only smaller sizes of perturbations. But the crucial point is that even when the behavior involves intrinsic randomness generation, perturbations of at least some size can still be tolerated.

And the reason this is important is that in any real experiment, there are inevitably perturbations on the system one is looking at.

With more care in setting up the experiment, a higher degree of isolation from the environment can usually be achieved. But it is never possible to eliminate absolutely all interaction with the environment.

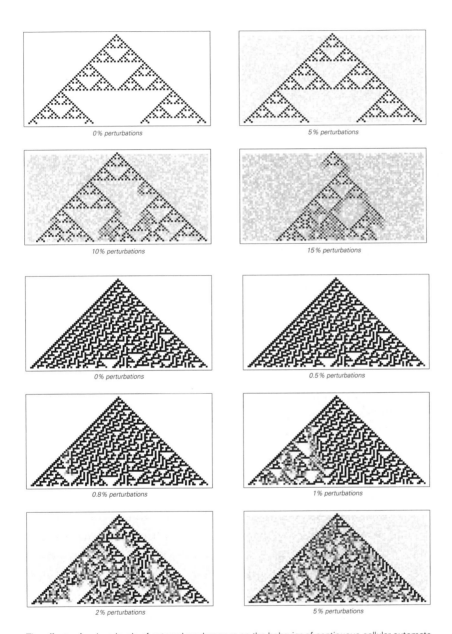

The effects of various levels of external randomness on the behavior of continuous cellular automata with generalizations of rules 90 and 30. The value of each cell can be any gray level between 0 and 1. For the generalization of rule 90, the values of the left and right cells are added together, and the value of the cell on the next step is then found by applying the continuous generalization of the modulo 2 function shown at the right. For the generalization of rule 30, a similar scheme based on an algebraic representation of the rule is used. In both cases, every value at each step is also perturbed by a random amount up to the percentage indicated for each picture.

And as a result, the system one is looking at will be subjected to at least some level of random perturbations from the environment.

But what the pictures on the previous page demonstrate is that when such perturbations are small enough, they will have essentially no effect. And what this means is that when intrinsic randomness generation is the dominant mechanism it is indeed realistic to expect at least some level of repeatability in the random behavior one sees in real experiments.

So has such repeatability actually been seen in practice?

Unfortunately there is so far very little good information on this point, since without the idea of intrinsic randomness generation there was never any reason to look for such repeatability when behavior that seemed random was observed in an experiment.

But scattered around the scientific literature—in various corners of physics, chemistry, biology and elsewhere—I have managed to find at least some cases where multiple runs of the same carefully controlled experiment are reported, and in which there are clear hints of repeatability even in behavior that looks quite random.

If one goes beyond pure numerical data of the kind traditionally collected in scientific experiments, and instead looks for example at the visual appearance of systems, then sometimes the phenomenon of repeatability becomes more obvious. Indeed, for example, as I will discuss in Chapter 8, different members of the same biological species often have many detailed visual similarities—even in features that on their own seem complex and apparently quite random.

And when there are, for example, two symmetrical sides to a particular system, it is often possible to compare the visual patterns produced on each side, and see what similarities exist. And as various examples in Chapter 8 demonstrate, across a whole range of physical, biological and other systems there can indeed be remarkable similarities.

So in all of these cases the randomness one sees cannot reasonably be attributed to randomness that is introduced from the environment—either continually or through initial conditions. And instead, there is no choice but to conclude that the randomness must in fact come from the mechanism of intrinsic randomness generation that I have discovered in simple programs, and discussed in this section.

The Phenomenon of Continuity

Many systems that we encounter in nature have behavior that seems in some way smooth or continuous. Yet cellular automata and most of the other programs that we have discussed involve only discrete elements. So how can such systems ever reproduce what we see in nature?

The crucial point is that even though the individual components in a system may be discrete, the average behavior that is obtained by looking at a large number of these components may still appear to be smooth and continuous. And indeed, there are many familiar systems in nature where exactly this happens.

Thus, for example, air and water seem like continuous fluids, even though we know that at a microscopic level they are both in fact made up of discrete molecules. And in a similar way, sand flows much like a continuous fluid, even though we can easily see that it is actually made up of discrete grains. So what is the basic mechanism that allows systems with discrete components to produce behavior that seems smooth and continuous?

Most often, the key ingredient is randomness.

If there is no randomness, then the overall forms that one sees tend to reflect the discreteness of the underlying components. Thus, for example, the faceted shape of a crystal reflects the regular microscopic arrangement of discrete atoms in the crystal.

But when randomness is present, such microscopic details often get averaged out, so that in the end no trace of discreteness is left, and the results appear to be smooth and continuous. The next page shows a classic example of this phenomenon, based on so-called random walks.

Each random walk is made by taking a discrete particle, and then at each step randomly moving the particle one position to the left or right. If one starts off with several particles, then at any particular time, each particle will be at a definite discrete position. But what happens if one looks not at the position of each individual particle, but rather at the overall distribution of all particles?

The answer, as illustrated on the next page, is that if there are enough particles, then the distribution one sees takes on a smooth and

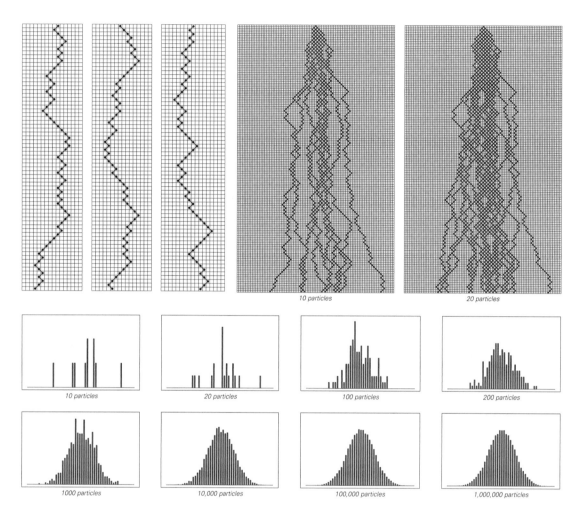

The distribution of positions by reached particles that follow random walks. The top left shows three individual examples of random walks, in which each particle randomly moves one position to the left or right. Even though the individual particles are discrete, the pictures show that when a large number of particles are considered, the overall behavior obtained seems smooth and continuous.

continuous form, and shows no trace of the underlying discreteness of the system; the randomness has in a sense successfully washed out essentially all the microscopic details of the system.

The pictures at the top of the facing page show what happens if one uses several different underlying rules for the motion of each particle. And what one sees is that despite differences at a microscopic level, the overall distribution obtained in each case has exactly the same continuous form.

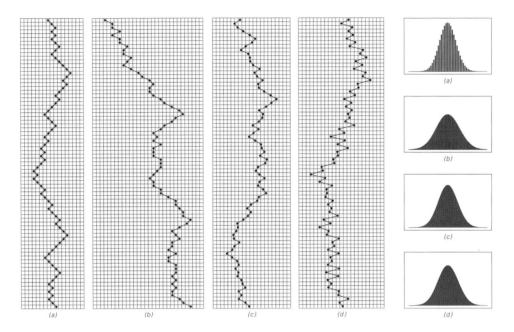

A demonstration of the fact that for a wide range of underlying rules for each step in a random walk, the overall distribution obtained always has the same continuous form. In case (a), each particle moves just one position to the left or right at each step. In case (b), it can move between 0, 1 or 2 positions, while in case (c) it can move any distance between 0 and 1 at each step. Finally, in case (d), on alternate steps the particle moves either always to the right or always to the left.

Indeed, in the particular case of systems such as random walks, the Central Limit Theorem suggested over two centuries ago ensures that for a very wide range of underlying microscopic rules, the same continuous so-called Gaussian distribution will always be obtained.

This kind of independence of microscopic details has many important consequences. The pictures on the next page show, for example, what happens if one looks at two-dimensional random walks on square and hexagonal lattices.

One might expect that the different underlying forms of these lattices would lead to different shapes in overall distributions. But the remarkable fact illustrated on the next page is that when enough particles are considered, one gets in the end distributions that have a purely circular shape that shows no trace of the different discrete structures of the underlying lattices.

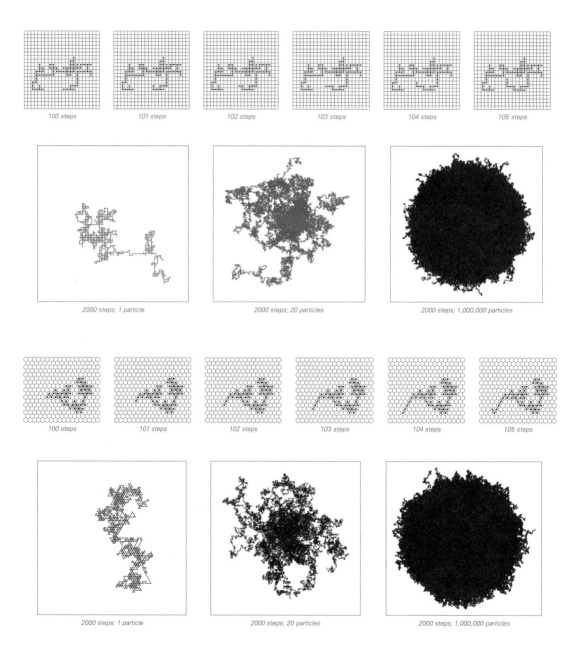

100 steps   *101 steps*   *102 steps*   *103 steps*   *104 steps*   *105 steps*

2000 steps; 1 particle   *2000 steps; 20 particles*   *2000 steps; 1,000,000 particles*

100 steps   *101 steps*   *102 steps*   *103 steps*   *104 steps*   *105 steps*

2000 steps; 1 particle   *2000 steps; 20 particles*   *2000 steps; 1,000,000 particles*

Examples of random walks on square and hexagonal lattices. Despite the different underlying lattices the average of sufficiently many particles yields ultimately circular behavior in both cases—as implied by the Central Limit Theorem.

Beyond random walks, there are many other systems based on discrete components in which randomness at a microscopic level also leads to continuous behavior on a large scale. The picture below shows as one example what happens in a simple aggregation model.

Behavior of a simple aggregation model, in which a single new black cell is added at each step at a randomly chosen position adjacent to the existing cluster of black cells. The system is a version of the so-called Eden model. The shape obtained is ultimately an almost perfect circle.

The idea of this model is to build up a cluster of black cells by adding just one new cell at each step. The position of this cell is chosen entirely at random, with the only constraint being that it should be adjacent to an existing cell in the cluster.

At early stages, clusters that are grown in this way look quite irregular. But after a few thousand steps, a smooth overall roughly circular shape begins to emerge. Unlike for the case of random walks, there is as yet no known way to make a rigorous mathematical analysis of this process. But just as for random walks, it appears once again that the details of the underlying rules for the system do not have much effect on the main features of the behavior that is seen.

The pictures below, for example, show generalizations of the aggregation model in which new cells are added only at positions that have certain numbers of existing neighbors. And despite such changes

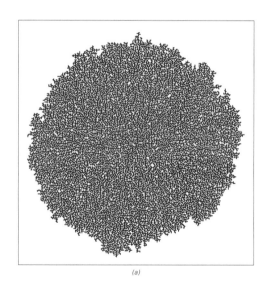

(a)

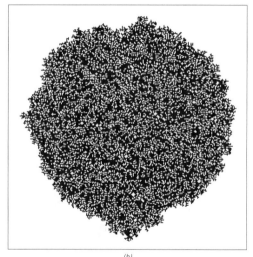

(b)

Patterns produced by generalized aggregation models in which a new cell is added only if (a) it would have only one immediate neighbor (out of four), or (b) it would have either one or four neighbors. The pictures above show step 30,000, while those on the right show step 200. Despite the difference in underlying rules, the same basic overall shape of pattern is eventually produced.

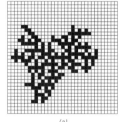

(a)

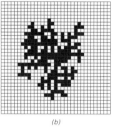

(b)

in underlying rules, the overall shapes of the clusters produced remain very much the same.

In all these examples, however, the randomness that is involved comes from the same basic mechanism: it is explicitly inserted from outside at each step in the evolution of the system.

But it turns out that all that really seems to matter is that randomness is present: the mechanism through which it arises appears to be largely irrelevant. And in particular what this means is that randomness which comes from the mechanism of intrinsic randomness generation discussed in the previous section is able to make systems with discrete components behave in seemingly continuous ways.

The picture on the next page shows a two-dimensional cellular automaton where this happens. There is no randomness in the rules or the initial conditions for this system. But through the mechanism of intrinsic randomness generation, the behavior of the system exhibits considerable randomness. And this randomness turns out to lead to an overall pattern of growth that yields the same basic kind of smooth roughly circular form as in the aggregation model.

Having seen this, one might then wonder whether in fact any system that involves randomness will ultimately produce smooth overall patterns of growth. The answer is definitely no. In discussing two-dimensional cellular automata in Chapter 5, for example, we saw many examples where randomness occurs, but where the overall forms of growth that are produced have a complicated structure with no particular smoothness or continuity.

As a rough guide, it seems that continuous patterns of growth are possible only when the rate at which small-scale random changes occur is substantially greater than the overall rate of growth. For in a sense it is only then that there is enough time for randomness to average out the effects of the underlying discrete structure.

And indeed this same issue also exists for processes other than growth. In general the point is that continuous behavior can arise in systems with discrete components only when there are features that evolve slowly relative to the rate of small-scale random changes.

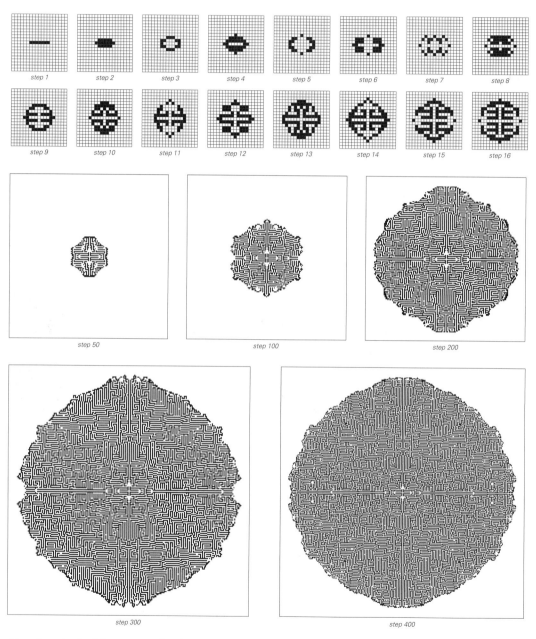

A two-dimensional cellular automaton first shown on page 178 with the rule that if out of the eight neighbors (including diagonals) around a given cell, there are exactly three black cells, then the cell itself becomes black on the next step. If the cell has 1, 2 or 4 black neighbors, then it stays the same color as before, and if it has 5 or more black neighbors, then it becomes white on the next step. (Outer totalistic code 746.) This simple rule produces randomness through the mechanism of intrinsic randomness generation, and this randomness in turn leads to a pattern of growth that takes on an increasingly smooth more-or-less circular form.

The pictures on the next page show an example where this happens. The detailed pattern of black and white cells in these pictures changes at every step. But the point is that the large domains of black and white that form have boundaries which move only rather slowly. And at an overall level these boundaries then behave in a way that looks quite smooth and continuous.

It is still true, however, that at a small scale the boundaries consist of discrete cells. But as the picture below shows, the detailed configuration of these cells changes rapidly in a seemingly random way. And just as in the other systems we have discussed, what then emerges on average from all these small-scale random changes is overall behavior that again seems in many ways smooth and continuous.

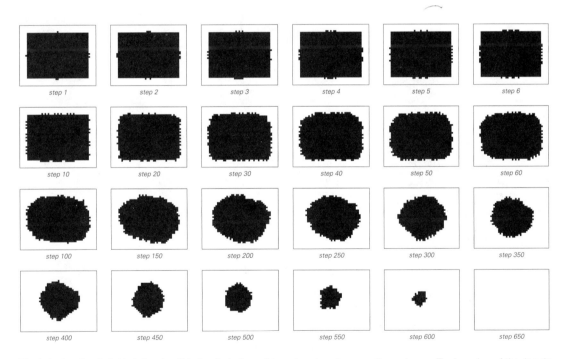

The behavior of an individual domain of black cells in the cellular automaton shown on the next page. The boundary of the domain exhibits seemingly random fluctuations. But at an overall level, the behavior that is produced seems in many respects quite smooth and continuous. The domain effectively behaves as if it has a surface tension, so that it first evolves to a roughly circular shape, then shrinks eventually to nothing. The main black rectangle is initially 39 × 29 cells in size.

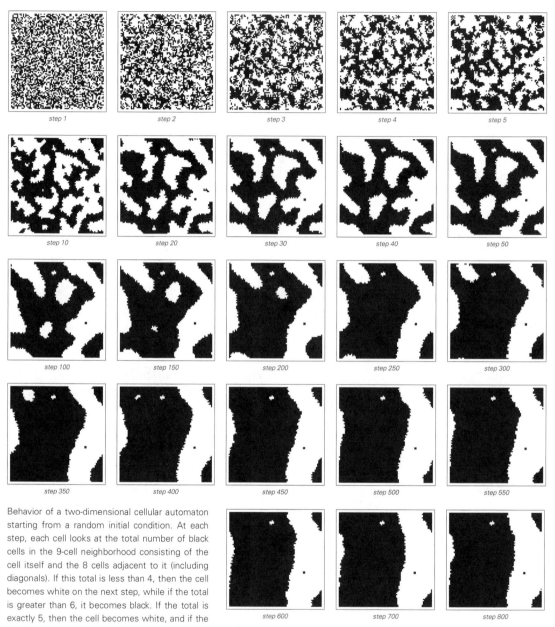

step 1   step 2   step 3   step 4   step 5

step 10   step 20   step 30   step 40   step 50

step 100   step 150   step 200   step 250   step 300

step 350   step 400   step 450   step 500   step 550

step 600   step 700   step 800

Behavior of a two-dimensional cellular automaton starting from a random initial condition. At each step, each cell looks at the total number of black cells in the 9-cell neighborhood consisting of the cell itself and the 8 cells adjacent to it (including diagonals). If this total is less than 4, then the cell becomes white on the next step, while if the total is greater than 6, it becomes black. If the total is exactly 5, then the cell becomes white, and if the total is exactly 4, then it becomes black. (The rule has totalistic code 976.) The pictures show that on a large scale, the rule leads to regions of black and white whose boundaries behave in a seemingly smooth and continuous way. Note that each picture is 80 cells across, and is effectively wrapped around so that the left neighbor of the leftmost cell is the rightmost cell, and so on.

Origins of Discreteness

In the previous section we saw that even though a system may on a small scale consist of discrete components, it is still possible for the system overall to exhibit behavior that seems smooth and continuous. And as we have discussed before, the vast majority of traditional mathematical models have in fact been based on just such continuity.

But when one looks at actual systems in nature, it turns out that one often sees discrete behavior—so that, for example, the coat of a zebra has discrete black and white stripes, not continuous shades of gray. And in fact many systems that exhibit complex behavior show at least some level of overall discreteness.

So what does this mean for continuous models? In the previous section we found that discrete models could yield continuous behavior. And what we will find in this section is that the reverse is also true: continuous models can sometimes yield behavior that appears discrete.

Needless to say, if one wants to study phenomena that are based on discreteness, it usually makes more sense to start with a model that is fundamentally discrete. But in making contact with existing scientific models and results, it is useful to see how discrete behavior can emerge from continuous processes.

The boiling of water provides a classic example. If one takes some water and continuously increases its temperature, then for a while nothing much happens. But when the temperature reaches 100°C, a discrete transition occurs, and all the water evaporates into steam.

It turns out that there are many kinds of systems in which continuous changes can lead to such discrete transitions.

The pictures at the top of the next page show a simple example based on a one-dimensional cellular automaton. The idea is to make continuous changes in the initial density of black cells, and then to see what effect these have on the overall behavior of the system.

One might think that if the changes one makes are always continuous, then effects would be correspondingly continuous. But the pictures on the next page demonstrate that this is not so.

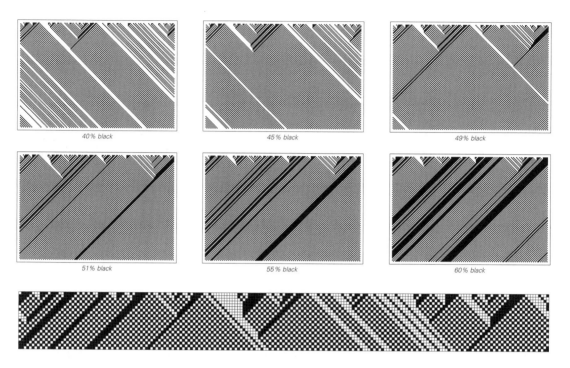

A one-dimensional cellular automaton that shows a discrete change in behavior when the properties of its initial conditions are continuously changed. If the initial density of black cells is less than 50%, then only white stripes ultimately survive. But as soon as the density increases above 50%, the white stripes disappear, and black stripes dominate. The underlying rule for the cellular automaton shown takes the new color of a cell to be the color of its right neighbor if the cell is black and its left neighbor if the cell is white. (This corresponds to rule 184 in the scheme described on page 53.)

When the initial density of black cells has any value less than 50%, only white stripes ever survive. But as soon as the initial density increases above 50%, a discrete transition occurs, and it is black stripes, rather than white, that survive.

The pictures on the facing page show another example of the same basic phenomenon. When the initial density of black cells is less than 50%, all regions of black eventually disappear, and the system becomes completely white. But as soon as the density increases above 50%, the behavior suddenly changes, and the system eventually becomes completely black.

It turns out that such discrete transitions are fairly rare among one-dimensional cellular automata, but in two and more dimensions

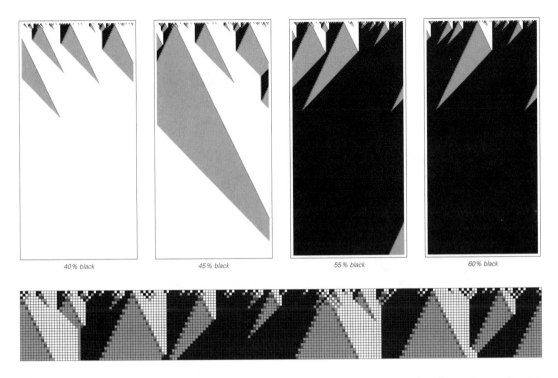

40% black   45% black   55% black   60% black

A one-dimensional cellular automaton in which the density of black cells obtained after a large number of steps changes discretely when the initial density of black cells is continuously increased. With an initial density below 50%, regions of black always eventually disappear. But as soon as the density is increased above 50%, regions of black progressively expand, eventually taking over the whole system. The underlying rule allows four possible colors for each cell. The rule is set up so that whenever a region of black occurs to the left of a region of white, an expanding region of gray appears in between. The crucial point is then that if the region of white is narrower than the region of black, then the gray will reach the edge of the white before it reaches the edge of the black. And when this happens, the black expands and the gray gradually tapers away.

they become increasingly common. The pictures on the next page show two examples—the second corresponding to a rule that we saw in a different context at the end of the previous section.

In both examples, what essentially happens is that in regions where there is an excess of black over white, an increasingly large fraction of cells become black, while in regions where there is an excess of white over black, the reverse happens. And so long as the boundaries of the regions do not get stuck—as happens in many one-dimensional cellular automata—the result is that whichever color was initially more common eventually takes over the whole system.

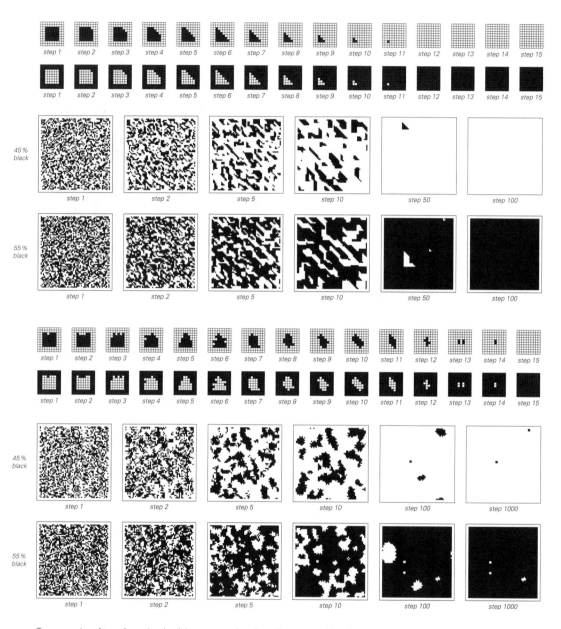

Two examples of two-dimensional cellular automata that show discrete transitions in behavior when the density of initial black cells is continuously varied. In the top rule, the new color of a particular cell is found simply by looking at that cell and its immediate neighbors above and to the right. If two or more of these three cells are black, then the new color is black; otherwise it is white. The pictures in the middle above show that with this rule blocks of opposite color are progressively destroyed, so that whichever color was initially more common eventually dominates completely. The bottom rule above is exactly the same as was shown on page 336. Whichever color was initially more common again eventually dominates, though with this rule it takes somewhat longer for this to occur.

In most cellular automata, the behavior obtained after a long time is either largely independent of the initial density, or varies quite smoothly with it. But the special feature of the cellular automata shown on the facing page is that they have two very different stable states—either all white or all black—and when one changes the initial density a discrete transition occurs between these two states.

One might think that the existence of such a discrete transition must somehow be associated with the discrete nature of the underlying cellular automaton rules. But it turns out that it is also possible to get such transitions in systems that have continuous underlying rules.

The pictures below show a standard very simple example of how this can happen. If one starts to the left of the center hump, then the ball will always roll into the left-hand minimum. But if one progressively changes the initial position of the ball, then when one passes the center a discrete transition occurs, and the ball instead rolls into the right-hand minimum.

A standard simple example of a continuous system in which there is a discrete change in behavior as a consequence of a continuous change in initial conditions. When the ball starts anywhere to the left of the center line, it rolls into the left-hand minimum. But if instead it starts on the right, then it rolls into the right-hand minimum. There are many systems in nature that follow the same general form of mathematical equations as those that describe the energy and motion of the ball.

Thus even though the mathematical equations which govern the motion of the ball have a simple continuous form, the behavior they produce still involves a discrete transition. And while this particular example may seem contrived, it turns out that essentially the same mathematical equations also occur in many other situations—such as the evolution of chemical concentrations in various chemical reactions.

And whenever such equations arise, they inevitably lead to a limited number of stable states for the system, with discrete transitions occurring between these states when the parameters of the system are varied.

So even if a system at some level follows continuous rules it is still possible for the system to exhibit discrete overall behavior. And in fact it is quite common for such behavior to be one of the most obvious features of a system—which is why discrete systems like cellular automata end up often being the most appropriate models.

The Problem of Satisfying Constraints

One feature of programs is that they immediately provide explicit rules that can be followed to determine how a system will behave. But in traditional science it is common to try to work instead with constraints that are merely supposed implicitly to force certain behavior to occur.

At the end of Chapter 5 I gave some examples of constraints, and I showed that constraints do exist that can force quite complex behavior to occur. But despite this, my strong suspicion is that of all the examples of complex behavior that we see in nature almost none can in the end best be explained in terms of constraints.

The basic reason for this is that to work out what pattern of behavior will satisfy a given constraint usually seems far too difficult for it to be something that happens routinely in nature.

Many types of constraints—including those in Chapter 5—have the property that given a specific pattern it is fairly easy to check whether the pattern satisfies the constraints. But the crucial point is that this fact by no means implies that it is necessarily easy to go from the constraints to find a pattern that satisfies them.

The situation is quite different from what happens with explicit evolution rules. For if one knows such rules then these rules immediately yield a procedure for working out what behavior will occur. Yet if one only knows constraints then such constraints do not on their own immediately yield any specific procedure for working out what behavior will occur.

In principle one could imagine looking at every possible pattern, and then picking out the ones that satisfy the constraints. But even with a 10×10 array of black and white squares, the number of possible patterns is already 1,267,650,600,228,229,401,496,703,205,376. And with a

20 × 20 array this number is larger than the total number of particles in the universe. So it seems quite inconceivable that systems in nature could ever carry out such an exhaustive search.

One might imagine, however, that if such systems were just to try patterns at random, then even though incredibly few of these patterns would satisfy any given constraint exactly, a reasonable number might at least still come close. But typically it turns out that even this is not the case. And as an example, the pictures below show what fraction of patterns chosen at random have a given percentage of squares that violate the constraints described on page 211.

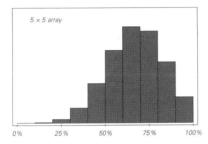
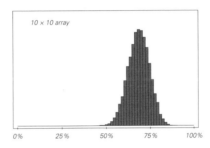

The fraction of all possible patterns in which a certain percentage of squares violate the constraints discussed on page 211. Only a handful of patterns satisfy the constraints exactly (so that 0% of the squares are wrong). For large arrays, the vast majority of possible patterns have about 70% of the squares wrong.

For the majority of patterns around 70% of the squares turn out to violate the constraints. And in a 10 × 10 array the chance of finding a pattern where the fraction of squares that violate the constraints is even less than 50% is only one in a thousand, while the chance of finding a pattern where the fraction is less than 25% is one in four trillion.

And what this means is that a process based on picking patterns at random will be incredibly unlikely to yield results that are even close to satisfying the constraints.

So how can one do better? A common approach used both in natural systems and in practical computing is to have some form of iterative procedure, in which one starts from a pattern chosen at random, then progressively modifies the pattern so as to make it closer to satisfying the constraints.

As a specific example consider taking a series of steps, and at each step picking a square in the array discussed above at random, then reversing the color of this square whenever doing so will not increase the total number of squares in the array that violate the constraints.

The picture below shows results obtained with this procedure. For the first few steps, there is rapid improvement. But as one goes on, one sees that the rate of improvement gets slower and slower. And even after a million steps, it turns out that 15% of the squares in a 10×10 array will on average still not satisfy the constraints.

In practical situations this kind of approximate result can sometimes be useful, but the pictures at the top of the facing page show that the actual patterns obtained do not look much at all like the exact results that we saw for this system in Chapter 5.

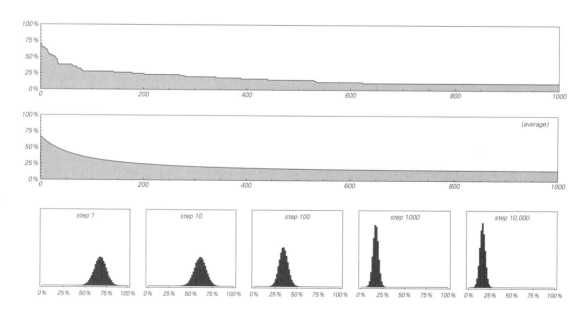

The results of a procedure intended to produce patterns that get progressively closer to satisfying the constraints described on page 211. The procedure starts with a randomly chosen pattern, then at each step picks a square in the pattern at random, and reverses the color of this square whenever doing so does not increase the total number of squares in the pattern that violate the constraints. The top picture shows one particular run of this procedure. The second picture shows the average behavior obtained from many runs. And finally, the bottom picture shows how the fraction of patterns with different percentages of squares violating the constraints changes as the procedure progresses. In all cases 10×10 patterns are used.

Patterns generated by using the same procedure as in the previous picture but with three different sets of constraints. Case (a) uses the same constraints as in the previous picture, (b) requires every black square and every white square to have exactly two adjacent black squares, and (c) requires every black square to have 3 adjacent black squares and 1 white square, and every white square to have 4 adjacent white squares. In cases (a) and (b) it is possible to satisfy the constraints exactly; in case (c) it is not. The pictures show the evolution of a 30 × 30 array, which is nearly 10 times the area of the array shown in the previous picture. Although the fraction of squares that violate the constraints is less than 20% after 100,000 steps, the overall patterns still do not look much like the exact results.

So why does the procedure not work better? The problem turns out to be a rather general one. And as a simple example, consider a line of black and white squares, together with the constraint that each square should have the same color as its right-hand neighbor. This constraint will be satisfied only if every square has the same color— either black or white. But to what extent will an iterative procedure succeed in finding this solution?

As a first example, consider a procedure that at each step picks a square at random, then reverses its color whenever doing so reduces the total number of squares that violate the constraint. The pictures at the top of the next page show what happens in this case. The results are

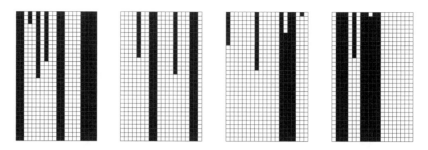

Results of four tries at applying an iterative procedure to find configurations which satisfy the simple constraint that every square should be the same color as the square to its right. (The squares are assumed to be arranged cyclically, so that the right neighbor of the rightmost square is the leftmost square.) The procedure starts from a random configuration of squares, and then at each step picks a square at random, then reverses the color of this square whenever doing so reduces the total number of squares that violate the constraint. The only configurations that ultimately satisfy the constraints are all white and all black. But the procedure gets stuck long before it reaches these configurations. The problem is that for any block more than one square across changing the color of a square at either end will not reduce the total number of squares that violate the constraint. And as a result, such blocks remain fixed and cannot disappear.

remarkably poor: instead of steadily evolving to all black or all white, the system quickly gets stuck in a state that contains regions of different colors.

And as it turns out, this kind of behavior is not uncommon among iterative procedures; indeed it is even seen in such simple cases as trying to find the lowest point on a curve. The most obvious iterative procedure to use for such a problem involves taking a series of small steps, with the direction of each step being chosen so as locally to go downhill.

And indeed for the first curve shown below, this procedure works just fine, and quickly leads to the lowest point. But for the second

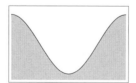
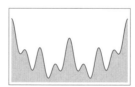
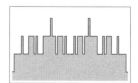

Three examples of curves. In the first case, the most obvious mechanical or mathematical procedure of continually going downhill will successfully lead one to the lowest point. But in the other two cases, this procedure will usually end up getting stuck at a local minimum. This is the basic phenomenon which makes it difficult to find patterns that satisfy constraints exactly using a procedure that is based on progressive improvement. The third picture above is a representation of the kind of curve that arises in almost all discrete systems based on constraints.

curve, the procedure will already typically not work; it will usually get stuck in one of the local minima and never reach a global minimum.

And for discrete systems involving, say, just black and white squares, it turns out to be almost inevitable that the curves which arise have the kind of jagged form shown in the third picture at the bottom of the facing page. So this has the consequence that a simple iterative procedure that always tries to go downhill will almost invariably get stuck.

How can one avoid this? One general strategy is to add randomness, so that in essence one continually shakes the system to prevent it from getting stuck. But the details of how one does this tend to have a great effect on the results one gets.

The procedure at the top of the facing page already in a sense involved randomness, for it picked a square at random at each step. But as we saw, with this particular procedure the system can still get stuck.

Modifying the procedure slightly, however, can avoid this. And as an example the pictures below show what happens if at each step one reverses the color of a random square not only if this will decrease the total number of squares violating the constraints, but also if it leaves this number the same. In this case the system never gets permanently stuck, and instead will always eventually evolve to satisfy the constraints.

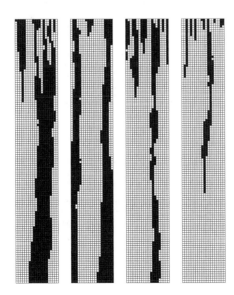

Results from a slight modification to the procedure used in the picture at the top of the facing page. A random square is again picked at each step. But now the color of that square is reversed not only if doing so actually changes the total number of squares that violate the constraint, but also if it leaves this number the same. With this procedure, evolution from any initial condition can visit every possible configuration, so that the configurations which satisfy the constraints will at least eventually be reached.

But this process may still take a very long time. And indeed in the two-dimensional case discussed earlier in this section, the number of steps required can be quite astronomically long.

So can one speed this up? The more one knows about a particular system, the more one can invent tricks that work for that system. But usually these turn out to lead only to modest speedups, and despite various hopes over the years there seem in the end to be no techniques that work well across any very broad range of systems.

So what this suggests is that even if in some idealized sense a system in nature might be expected to satisfy certain constraints, it is likely that in practice the system will actually not have a way to come even close to doing this.

In traditional science the notion of constraints is often introduced in an attempt to summarize the effects of evolution rules. Typically the idea is that after a sufficiently long time a system should be found only in states that are invariant under the application of its evolution rules. And quite often it turns out that one can show that any states that are invariant in this way must satisfy fairly simple constraints. But the problem is that except in cases where the behavior as a whole is very simple it tends not to be true that systems in fact evolve to strictly invariant states.

The two cellular automata on the left both have all white and all black as invariant states. And in the first case, starting from random initial conditions, the system quickly settles down to the all black invariant state. But in the second case, nothing like this happens, and instead the system continues to exhibit complicated and seemingly random behavior forever.

The two-dimensional patterns that arise from the constraints at the end of Chapter 5 all turn out to correspond to invariant states of various two-dimensional cellular automata. And so for example the pattern of page 211 is found to be the unique invariant state for 572,522 of the 4,294,967,296 possible five-neighbor cellular automaton rules. But if one starts these rules from random initial conditions, one typically never gets the pattern of page 211. Instead, as the pictures at the top of the facing page show, one sees a variety of patterns that very

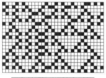

Two of the 28 elementary cellular automata whose only invariant states are uniform in color. In the first case one of these invariant states is always reached; in the second it is not.

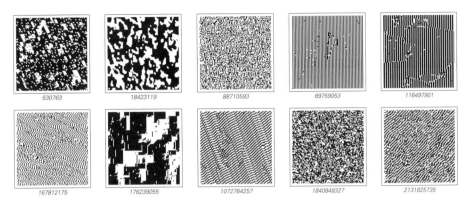

530763	18423119	88710593	89759053	116497901

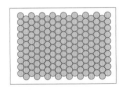

invariant state

167812175	176239055	1072764257	1840848327	2131825735

Typical behavior of two-dimensional cellular automata that leave only the pattern on the right invariant. The results shown come from 500 steps of evolution starting from random initial conditions. In no case does the global behavior seen come even close to satisfying the simple constraints that determine the invariant state.

much more reflect explicit rules of evolution than the constraint associated with the invariant state.

So what about actual systems in physics? Do they behave any differently? As one example, consider a large number of circular coins pushed together on a table. One can think of such a system as having an invariant state that satisfies the constraint that the coins should be packed as densely as possible. For identical coins this constraint is satisfied by the simple repetitive pattern shown on the right. And it turns out that in this particular case this pattern is quickly produced if one actually pushes coins together on a table.

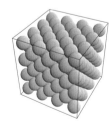

The densest packing of identical circles in the plane. Each circle is surrounded by six others.

But with balls in three dimensions the situation is quite different. In this case the constraint of densest packing is known to be satisfied when the balls are laid out in the simple repetitive way shown on the right. But if one just tries pushing balls together they almost always get stuck, and never take on anything like the arrangement shown. And if one jiggles the balls around one still essentially never gets this arrangement. Indeed, the only way to do it seems to be to lay the balls down carefully one after another.

In two dimensions similar issues arise as soon as one has coins of more than one size. Indeed, even with just two sizes, working out how to satisfy the constraint of densest packing is already so difficult that in most cases it is still not known what configuration does it.

The densest packing of identical spheres in three-dimensional space. Each sphere is surrounded by 12 others.

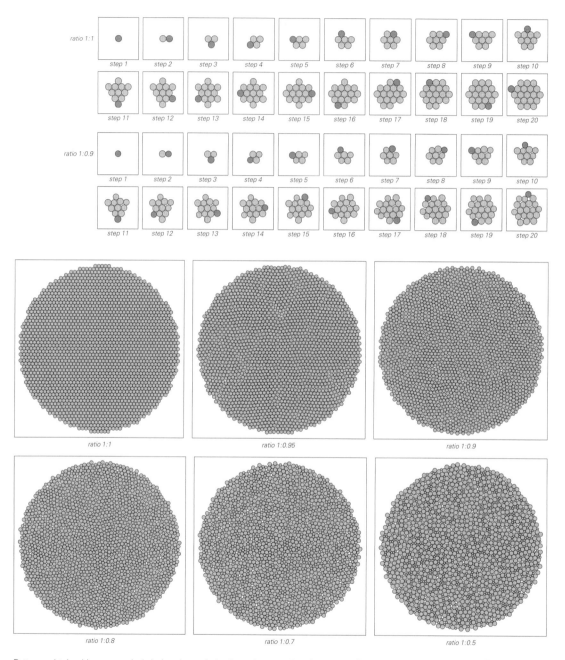

Patterns obtained by successively laying down circles in such a way that the center of each new circle is as close as possible to the center of the first circle. Except in the very first case, the extent to which these represent the densest possible packings is not clear, and indeed it is quite possible that in most such actual packings circles of different sizes are just separated into several uniform regions.

The pictures on the facing page show what happens if one starts with a single circle, then successively adds new circles in such a way that the center of each one is as close to the center of the first circle as possible. When all circles are the same size, this procedure yields a simple repetitive pattern. But as soon as the circles have significantly different sizes, the pictures on the facing page show that this procedure tends to produce much more complicated patterns—which in the end may or may not have much to do with the constraint of densest packing.

One can look at all sorts of other physical systems, but so far as I can tell the story is always more or less the same: whenever there is behavior of significant complexity its most plausible explanation tends to be some explicit process of evolution, not the implicit satisfaction of constraints.

One might still suppose, however, that the situation could be different in biological systems, and that somehow the process of natural selection might produce forms that are successfully determined by the satisfaction of constraints.

But what I strongly believe, as I discuss in the next chapter, is that in the end, much as in physical systems, only rather simple forms can actually be obtained in this way, and that when more complex forms are seen they once again tend to be associated not with constraints but rather with the effects of explicit evolution rules—mostly those governing the growth of an individual organism.

Origins of Simple Behavior

There are many systems in nature that show highly complex behavior. But there are also many systems that show rather simple behavior—most often either complete uniformity, or repetition, or nesting.

And what we have found in this book is that programs are very much the same: some show highly complex behavior, while others show only rather simple behavior.

Traditional intuition might have made one assume that there must be a direct correspondence between the complexity of observed behavior and the complexity of underlying rules. But one of the central discoveries of this book is that in fact there is not.

For even programs with some of the very simplest possible rules yield highly complex behavior, while programs with fairly complicated rules often yield only rather simple behavior. And indeed, as we have seen many times in this book, and as the pictures below illustrate, even rules that are extremely similar can produce quite different behavior.

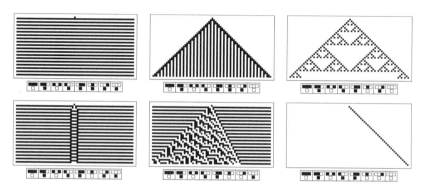

A sequence of elementary cellular automata whose rules differ from one to the next only at one position (a Gray code sequence). Despite the similarity of their rules, the overall behavior of these cellular automata differs considerably.

If one just looks at a rule in its raw form, it is usually almost impossible to tell much about the overall behavior it will produce. But in cases where this behavior ends up being simple, one can often recognize in it specific mechanisms that seem to be at work.

If the behavior of a system is simple, then this inevitably means that it will have many regularities. And usually there is no definite way to say which of these regularities should be considered causes of what one sees, and which should be considered effects.

But it is still often useful to identify simple mechanisms that can at least serve as descriptions of the behavior of a system.

In many respects the very simplest possible type of behavior in any system is pure uniformity. And uniformity in time is particularly straightforward, for it corresponds just to no change occurring in the evolution of a system. But uniformity in space is already slightly more complicated, and indeed there are several different mechanisms that can be involved in it. A rather straightforward one, illustrated in the pictures below, is that some process can start at one point in space and then progressively spread, doing the same thing at every point it reaches.

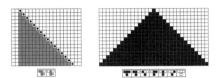

Homogenous growth from a single point is one straightforward way that uniformity in space can be produced, here illustrated in a mobile automaton and a cellular automaton.

Another mechanism is that every part of a system can evolve completely independently to the same state, as in the pictures below.

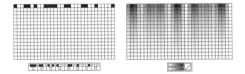

Uniformity in space can be achieved almost trivially if each element in a system independently evolves to the same state.

A slightly less straightforward mechanism is illustrated in the pictures below. Here different elements in the system do interact, but the result is still that all of them evolve to the same state.

Class 1 cellular automata that exhibit evolution to a uniform state, as discussed in Chapter 6.

So far all the mechanisms for uniformity I have mentioned involve behavior that is in a sense simple at every level. But in nature uniformity often seems to be associated with quite complex microscopic behavior. Most often what happens is that on a small scale a system exhibits randomness, but on a larger scale this randomness averages out to leave apparent uniformity, as in the pictures below.

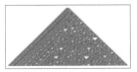

Averaging out small-scale randomness yields apparent uniformity, as shown here for a rule 30 pattern.

It is common for uniform behavior to be quite independent of initial conditions or other input to a system. But sometimes different uniform behavior can be obtained with different input.

One way this can happen, illustrated in the pictures below, is for the system to conserve some quantity—such as total density of black—and for this quantity to end up being spread uniformly throughout the system by its evolution.

With each cell at each step having a gray level that is the average of its predecessor and its two neighbors the total amount of black is conserved, but eventually becomes spread uniformly throughout the system.

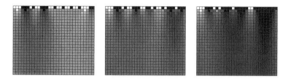

An alternative is that the system may always evolve to certain specific uniform phases, but the choice of which phase may depend on the total value of some quantity, as in the pictures below.

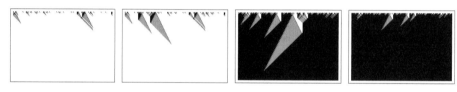

With different initial conditions this cellular automaton from page 339 can evolve either to uniform white or uniform black. Such discrete transitions are somewhat less common in one dimension than elsewhere.

Constraints are yet another basis for uniformity. And as a trivial example, the constraint in a line of black or white cells that every cell should be the same color as both its neighbors immediately implies that the whole line must be either uniformly black or uniformly white.

Beyond uniformity, repetition can be considered the next-simplest form of behavior. Repetition in time corresponds just to a system repeatedly returning to a particular state.

This can happen if, for example, the behavior of a system in effect follows some closed curve such as a circle which always leads back to the same point. And in general, in any system with definite rules that only ever visits a limited number of states, it is

The behavior of a system will be repetitive in time whenever it effectively follows a closed curve—either literally in space, or in terms of states that it visits.

inevitable—as discussed on page 255 and illustrated above—that the behavior of the system will eventually repeat.

In some cases the basic structure of a system may allow only a limited number of possible states. But in other cases what happens is instead just that the actual evolution of a system never reaches more than a limited number of states.

Often it is very difficult to predict whether this will be so just by looking at the underlying rules. But in a system like a cellular automaton the typical reason for it is just that in the end effects never spread beyond a limited region, as in the examples shown below.

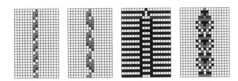

Examples of behavior in mobile automata and cellular automata that remains localized to a limited region and thus always eventually repeats.

Given repetition in time, repetition in space will follow whenever elements that repeat systematically move in space. The pictures below show two cases of this, with the second picture illustrating the notion of waves that is common in traditional physics.

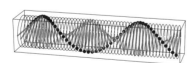

Examples where repetition in time leads directly to repetition in space. The second picture shows standard wave motion.

Growth from a simple seed can also readily lead to repetition in both space and time, as in the pictures below.

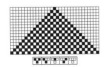

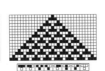

Cellular automata in which a repetitive pattern in both space and time is generated by evolution from a simple seed.

But what about random initial conditions? Repetition in time is still easy to achieve—say just by different parts of a system behaving independently. But repetition in space is slightly more difficult to achieve. For even if localized domains of repetition form, they need to have some mechanism for combining together.

And the walls between different domains often end up not being mobile enough to allow this to happen, as in the examples below.

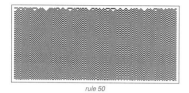
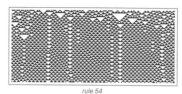
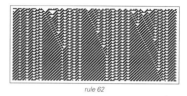

rule 50   *rule 54*   *rule 62*

Cellular automata in which domains of repetitive behavior form, but in which walls typically remain forever between these domains.

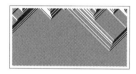

A cellular automaton (rule 184) in which domains quickly combine to make the whole system repetitive in space.

But there are certainly cases—in one dimension and particularly above—where different domains do combine, and exact repetition is achieved. Sometimes this happens quickly, as in the picture on the left.

But in other cases it happens only rather slowly. An example is rule 110, in which repetitive domains form with period 14 in space and 7 in time, but as the picture below illustrates, the localized structures which separate these domains take a very long time to disappear.

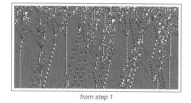
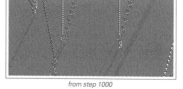
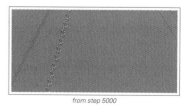

from step 1   *from step 1000*   *from step 5000*

The behavior of rule 110 starting from random initial conditions. Domains of repetitive behavior are formed, which in most cases gradually combine as the localized structures which separate them disappear.

As we saw at the end of Chapter 5, many systems based on constraints also in principle yield repetition—though from the discussion of the previous section it seems likely that this is rarely a good explanation for actual repetition that we see in nature.

Beyond uniformity and repetition, the one further type of simple behavior that we have often encountered in this book is nesting. And as with uniformity and repetition, there are several quite different ways that nesting seems to arise.

Nesting can be defined by thinking in terms of splitting into smaller and smaller elements according to some fixed rule. And as the pictures below illustrate, nested patterns are generated very directly in substitution systems by each element successively splitting explicitly into blocks of smaller and smaller elements.

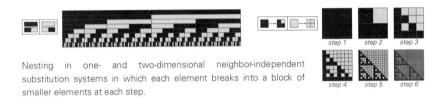

Nesting in one- and two-dimensional neighbor-independent substitution systems in which each element breaks into a block of smaller elements at each step.

An essentially equivalent process involves every element branching into smaller and smaller elements and eventually forming a tree-like structure, as in the pictures below.

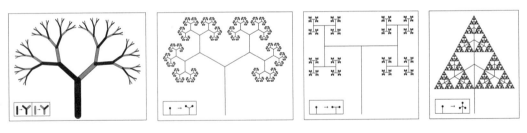

Nested patterns generated by simple branching processes. (Compare page 406.)

So what makes a system in nature operate in this way? Part of it is that the same basic rules must apply regardless of physical scale. But on its own this would be quite consistent with various kinds of uniform or spiral growth, and does not imply that there will be what we usually think of as nesting. And indeed to get nesting seems to require that there also be some type of discrete splitting or branching process in which several distinct elements arise from an individual element.

A somewhat related source of nesting relevant in many mathematical systems is the nested pattern formed by the digit sequences of successive numbers, as illustrated on page 117.

But in general nesting need not just arise from larger elements being broken down into smaller ones: for as we have discovered in this book it can also arise when larger elements are built up from smaller ones—and indeed I suspect that this is its more common origin in nature.

As an example, the pictures below show how nested patterns with larger and larger features can be built up by starting with a single black cell, and then following simple additive cellular automaton rules.

Nested patterns built by the evolution of the rule 90 and rule 150 additive cellular automata starting from a single black cell.

It turns out that the very same patterns can also be produced—as the pictures below illustrate—by processes in which new branches form at regular intervals, and annihilate when any pair of them collide.

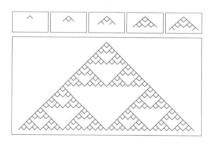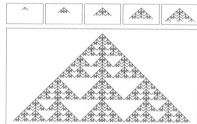

Nested patterns obtained by processes in which either two or three branches are formed at regular intervals, and annihilate when any pair of them collide.

But what about random initial conditions? Can nesting also arise from these? It turns out that it can. And the basic mechanism is typically some kind of progressive annihilation of elements that are initially distributed randomly.

The pictures below show an example, based on the rule 184 cellular automaton. Starting from random initial conditions this rule yields a collection of stripes which annihilate whenever they meet, leading to a sequence of progressively larger nested regions.

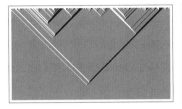 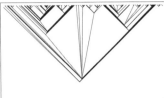 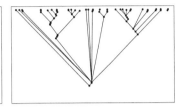

The generation of a nested pattern by rule 184 starting from random initial conditions. The pattern consists of a collection of stripes, highlighted in the second picture, which form the tree-like structure shown in the third picture. The initial condition used has exactly equal numbers of black and white cells, causing all the stripes eventually to annihilate.

And as the pictures show, these regions form a pattern that corresponds to a random tree that builds up from its smallest branches, much in the way that a river builds up from its tributaries.

Nesting in rule 184 is easiest to see when the initial conditions contain exactly equal numbers of black and white cells, so that the numbers of left and right stripes exactly balance, and all stripes eventually annihilate. But even when the initial conditions are such that some stripes survive, nested regions are still formed by the stripes that do annihilate. And indeed in essentially any system where there are domains that grow fairly independently and then progressively merge the same basic overall nesting will be seen.

As an example, the picture below shows the rule 110 cellular automaton evolving from random initial conditions. The picture

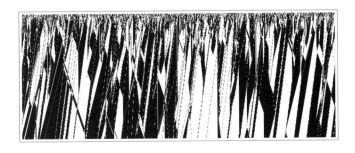

A highly compressed representation of the evolution of rule 110 from random initial conditions in which only the first cell in every 14 × 7 block is sampled.

samples just the first cell in every 14 × 7 block of cells, making each domain of repetitive behavior stand out as having a uniform color.

In the detailed behavior of the various localized structures that separate these domains of repetitive behavior there is all sorts of complexity. But what the picture suggests is that at some rough overall level these structures progressively tend to annihilate each other, and in doing so form an approximate nested pattern.

It turns out that this basic process is not restricted to systems which produce simple uniform or repetitive domains. And the pictures below show for example cases where the behavior inside each domain is quite random.

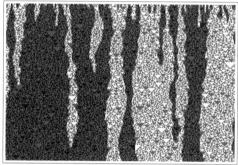

k=3 totalistic code 1893

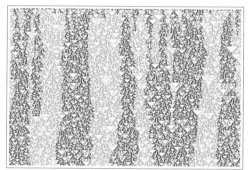

elementary rule 18 (compressed)

Examples involving domains containing apparent randomness. In the second picture, each element shown represents a 2 × 2 block of original cells. In both cases, the boundaries between domains appear to follow random walks, annihilating when they meet and thus forming a nested overall pattern.

Instead of following simple straight lines, the boundaries of these domains now execute seemingly random walks. But the fact that they annihilate whenever they meet once again tends to lead to an overall nested pattern of behavior.

So what about systems based on constraints? Can these also lead to nesting? In Chapter 5 I showed that they can. But what I found is that whereas at least in principle both uniformity and repetition can be forced fairly easily by constraints, nesting usually cannot be.

At the outset, one might have thought that there would be just one definite mechanism for each type of simple behavior. But what we have seen in this section is that in fact there are usually several apparently quite different mechanisms possible.

Often one can identify features in common between the various mechanisms for any particular kind of behavior. But typically these end up just being inevitable consequences of the fact that some specific kind of behavior is being produced.

And so, for example, one might notice that most mechanisms for nesting can at some level be viewed as involving hierarchies in which higher components affect lower ones, but not the other way around. But in a sense this observation is nothing more than a restatement of a property of nesting itself.

So in the end one can indeed view most of the mechanisms that I have discussed in this section as being in some sense genuinely different. Yet as we have seen all of them can be captured by quite simple programs. And in Chapter 12 I will discuss how this is related to the fact that so few fundamentally different types of overall behavior ultimately seem to occur.

Implications for Everyday Systems

Issues of Modelling

In the previous chapter I showed how various general forms of behavior that are common in nature can be understood by thinking in terms of simple programs. In this chapter what I will do is to take what we have learned, and look at a sequence of fairly specific kinds of systems in nature and elsewhere, and in each case discuss how the most obvious features of their behavior arise.

The majority of the systems I consider are quite familiar from everyday life, and at first one might assume that the origins of their behavior would long ago have been discovered. But in fact, in almost all cases, rather little turns out to be known, and indeed at any fundamental level the behavior that is observed has often in the past seemed quite mysterious. But what we will discover in this chapter is that by thinking in terms of simple programs, the fundamental origins of this behavior become much less mysterious.

It should be said at the outset that it is not my purpose to explain every detail of all the various kinds of systems that I discuss. And in fact, to do this for even just one kind of system would most likely take at least another whole book, if not much more.

But what I do want to do is to identify the basic mechanisms that are responsible for the most obvious features of the behavior of each kind of system. I want to understand, for example, how in general snowflakes come to have the intricate shapes they do. But I am not concerned, for example, with details such as what the precise curvature of the tips of the arms of the snowflake will be.

In most cases the basic approach I take is to try to construct the very simplest possible model for each system. From the intuition of traditional science we might think that if the behavior of a system is complex, then any model for the system must also somehow be correspondingly complex.

But one of the central discoveries of this book is that this is not in fact the case, and that at least if one thinks in terms of programs rather than traditional mathematical equations, then even models that are based on extremely simple underlying rules can yield behavior of great complexity. And in fact in the course of this chapter, I will construct a whole sequence of remarkably simple models that do rather well at reproducing the main features of complex behavior in a wide range of everyday natural and other systems.

Any model is ultimately an idealization in which only certain aspects of a system are captured, and others are ignored. And certainly in each kind of system that I consider here there are many details that the models I discuss do not address. But in most cases there have in the past never really been models that can even reproduce the most obvious features of the behavior we see. So it is already major progress that the models I discuss yield pictures that look even roughly right.

In many traditional fields of science any model which could yield such pictures would immediately be considered highly successful. But in some fields—especially those where traditional mathematics has been used the most extensively—it has come to be believed that in a sense the only truly objective or scientific way to test a model is to look at certain rather specific details.

Most often what is done is to extract a small set of numbers from the observed behavior of a system, and then to see how accurately these numbers can be reproduced by the model. And for systems whose overall behavior is fairly simple, this approach indeed often works quite well. But when the overall behavior is complex, it becomes impossible to characterize it in any complete way by just a few numbers.

And indeed in the literature of traditional science I have quite often seen models which were taken very seriously because they could be made to reproduce a few specific numbers, but which are shown up as completely wrong if one works out the overall behavior that they imply. And in my experience by far the best first step in assessing a model is not to look at numbers or other details, but rather just to use one's eyes, and to compare overall pictures of a system with pictures from the model.

If there are almost no similarities then one can reasonably conclude that the model is wrong. But if there are some similarities and some differences, then one must decide whether or not the differences are crucial. Quite often this will depend, at least in part, on how one intends to use the model. But with appropriate judgement it is usually not too difficult from looking at overall behavior to get at least some sense of whether a particular model is on the right track.

Typically it is not a good sign if the model ends up being almost as complicated as the phenomenon it purports to describe. And it is an even worse sign if when new observations are made the model constantly needs to be patched in order to account for them.

It is usually a good sign on the other hand if a model is simple, yet still manages to reproduce, even quite roughly, a large number of features of a particular system. And it is an even better sign if a fair fraction of these features are ones that were not known, or at least not explicitly considered, when the model was first constructed.

One might perhaps think that in the end one could always tell whether a model was correct by explicitly looking at sufficiently low-level underlying elements in a system and comparing them with elements in the model. But one must realize that a model is only ever supposed to provide an abstract representation of a system—and there is nothing to say that the various elements in this representation need have any direct correspondence with the elements of the system itself.

Thus, for example, a traditional mathematical model might say that the motion of a planet is governed by a set of differential equations. But one does not imagine that this means that the planet itself contains a device that explicitly solves such equations. Rather, the idea is that the equations provide some kind of abstract representation for the physical effects that actually determine the motion of the planet.

When I have discussed models like the ones in this chapter with other scientists I have however often encountered great confusion about such issues. Perhaps it is because in a simple program it is so easy to see the underlying elements and the rules that govern them. But countless times I have been asked how models based on simple programs can possibly be correct, since even though they may successfully reproduce the behavior of some system, one can plainly see that the system itself does not, for example, actually consist of discrete cells that, say, follow the rules of a cellular automaton.

But the whole point is that all any model is supposed to do— whether it is a cellular automaton, a differential equation, or anything else—is to provide an abstract representation of effects that are important in determining the behavior of a system. And below the level of these effects there is no reason that the model should actually operate like the system itself.

Thus, for example, a cellular automaton can readily be set up to represent the effect of an inhibition on growth at points on the surface of a snowflake where new material has recently been added. But in the cellular automaton this effect is just implemented by some rule for certain configurations of cells—and there is no need for the rule to correspond in any way to the detailed dynamics of water molecules.

So even though there need not be any correspondence between elements in a system and in a model, one might imagine that there must still be some kind of complete correspondence between effects. But the whole point of a model is to have a simplified representation of a system, from which those features in which one is interested can readily be deduced or understood. And the only way to achieve this is to pick out only certain effects that are important, and to ignore all others.

Indeed, in practice, the main challenge in constructing models is precisely to identify which effects are important enough that they have to be kept, and which are not. In some simple situations, it is sometimes possible to set up experiments in which one can essentially isolate each individual effect and explicitly measure its importance. But in the majority of cases the best evidence that some particular set of effects are in fact the important ones ultimately comes just from the success of models that are based on these effects.

The systems that I discuss in this chapter are mostly complicated enough that there are at least tens of quite different effects that could contribute to their overall behavior. But in trying to construct the simplest possible models, I have always picked out just a few effects that I believe will be the most important. Inevitably there will be phenomena that depend on other effects, and which are therefore not correctly reproduced by the models I consider. So if these phenomena are crucial to some particular application, then there will be no choice but to extend the model for that application.

But insofar as the goal is to understand the basic mechanisms that are responsible for the most obvious features of overall behavior, it is important to keep the underlying model as simple as possible. For even with just a few extensions models usually become so complicated that it is almost impossible to tell where any particular feature of behavior really comes from.

Over the years I have been able to watch the progress of perhaps a dozen significant models that I have constructed—though in most cases never published—for a variety of kinds of systems with complex behavior. My original models have typically been extremely simple. And the initial response to them has usually been great surprise that such simple models could ever yield behavior that has even roughly the right features. But experts in the particular types of systems involved have usually been quick to point out that there are many details that my models do not correctly reproduce.

Then after an initial period where the models are often said to be too simplistic to be worth considering, there begin to be all sorts of extensions added that attempt to capture more effects and more details. The result of this is that after a few years my original models have evolved into models that are almost unrecognizably complex. But these models have often then been used with great success for many practical purposes. And at that point, with their success established, it sometimes happens that the models are examined more carefully—and it is then discovered that many of the extensions that were added were in fact quite unnecessary, so that in the end, after perhaps a decade has passed, it becomes recognized that models equivalent to the simple ones I originally proposed do indeed work quite well.

One might have thought that in the literature of traditional science new models would be proposed all the time. But in fact the vast majority of what is done in practically every field of science involves not developing new models but rather accumulating experimental data or working out consequences of existing models.

And among the models that have been used, almost all those that have gone beyond the level of being purely descriptive have ended up being formulated in very much the same kind of way: typically as collections of mathematical equations. Yet as I emphasized at the very beginning of this book, this is, I believe, the main reason that in the past it has been so difficult to find workable models for systems whose behavior is complex. And indeed it is one of the central ideas of this book to go beyond mathematical equations, and to consider models that are based on programs which can effectively involve rules of any kind.

It is in many respects easier to work with programs than with equations. For once one has a program, one can always find out what its behavior will be just by running it. Yet with an equation one may need to do elaborate mathematical analysis in order to find out what behavior it can lead to. It does not help that models based on equations are often stated in a purely implicit form, so that rather than giving an actual procedure for determining how a system will behave—as a program does—they just give constraints on what the behavior must be, and provide no particular guidance about finding out what, if any, behavior will in fact satisfy these constraints.

And even when models based on equations can be written in an explicit form, they still typically involve continuous variables which cannot for example be handled directly by a practical computer. When their overall behavior is sufficiently simple, complete mathematical formulas to describe this behavior can sometimes be found. But as soon as the behavior is more complex there is usually no choice but to use some form of approximation. And despite many attempts over the past fifty or so years, it has almost never been possible to demonstrate that results obtained from such approximations even correctly reproduce what the original mathematical equations would imply.

Models based on simple programs, however, suffer from no such problems. For essentially all of them involve only discrete elements which can be handled quite directly on a practical computer. And this means that it becomes straightforward in principle—and often highly efficient in practice—to work out at least the basic consequences of such models.

Many of the models that I discuss in this chapter are actually based on some of the very simplest kinds of programs that I consider anywhere in this book. But as we shall see, even these models appear quite sufficient to capture the behavior of a remarkably wide range of systems from nature and elsewhere—establishing beyond any doubt, I believe, the practical value of thinking in terms of simple programs.

The Growth of Crystals

At a microscopic level crystals consist of regular arrays of atoms laid out much like the cells in a cellular automaton. A crystal forms when a liquid or gas is cooled below its freezing point. Crystals always start from a seed—often a foreign object such as a grain of dust—and then grow by progressively adding more atoms to their surface.

As an idealization of this process, one can consider a cellular automaton in which black cells represent regions of solid and white cells represent regions of liquid or gas. If one assumes that any cell which is adjacent to a black cell will itself become black on the next step, then one gets the patterns of growth shown below.

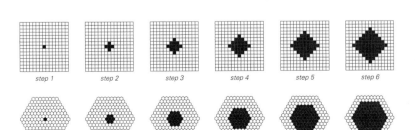

step 1   step 2   step 3   step 4   step 5   step 6

step 1   step 2   step 3   step 4   step 5   step 6

Cellular automata with rules that specify that a cell should become black if any of its neighbors are already black. The patterns produced have a simple faceted form that reflects directly the structure of the underlying lattice of cells.

The shapes produced in each case are very simple, and ultimately consist just of flat facets arranged in a way that reflects directly the structure of the underlying lattice of cells. And many crystals in nature—including for example most gemstones—have similarly simple faceted forms. But some do not. And as one well-known example, snowflakes can have highly intricate forms, as illustrated below.

Examples of typical forms of snowflakes. Note that the scales for different pictures are different.

To a good approximation, all the molecules in a snowflake ultimately lie on a simple hexagonal grid. But in the actual process of snowflake growth, not every possible part of this grid ends up being filled with ice. The main effect responsible for this is that whenever a piece of ice is added to the snowflake, there is some heat released, which then tends to inhibit the addition of further pieces of ice nearby.

One can capture this basic effect by having a cellular automaton with rules in which cells become black if they have exactly one black neighbor, but stay white whenever they have more than one black neighbor. The pictures on the facing page show a sequence of steps in the evolution of such a cellular automaton. And despite the simplicity of its underlying rules, what one sees is that the patterns it produces are strikingly similar to those seen in real snowflakes.

From looking at the behavior of the cellular automaton, one can immediately make various predictions about snowflakes. For example,

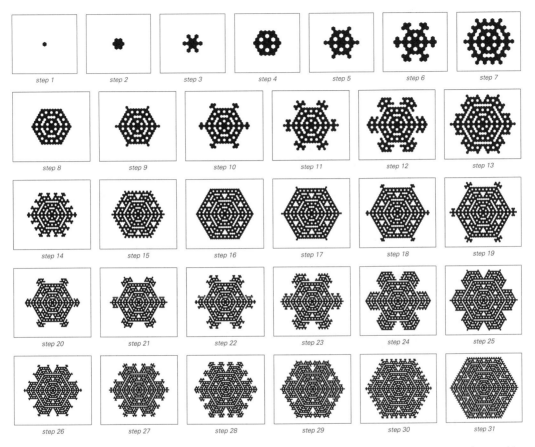

step 1　step 2　step 3　step 4　step 5　step 6　step 7

step 8　step 9　step 10　step 11　step 12　step 13

step 14　step 15　step 16　step 17　step 18　step 19

step 20　step 21　step 22　step 23　step 24　step 25

step 26　step 27　step 28　step 29　step 30　step 31

The evolution of a cellular automaton in which each cell on a hexagonal grid becomes black whenever exactly one of its neighbors was black on the step before. This rule captures the basic growth inhibition effect that occurs in snowflakes. The resulting patterns obtained at different steps look remarkably similar to many real snowflakes.

one expects that during the growth of a particular snowflake there should be alternation between tree-like and faceted shapes, as new branches grow but then collide with each other.

And if one looks at real snowflakes, there is every indication that this is exactly what happens. And in fact, in general the simple cellular automaton shown above seems remarkably successful at reproducing all sorts of obvious features of snowflake growth. But inevitably there are many details that it does not capture. And indeed some of the photographs on the facing page do not in the end look much like patterns produced at any step in the evolution shown above.

But it turns out that as soon as one tries to make a more complete model, there are immediately an immense number of issues that arise, and it is difficult to know which are really important and which are not. At a basic level, one knows that snowflakes are formed when water vapor in a cloud freezes into ice, and that the structure of a given snowflake is determined by the temperature and humidity of the environment in which it grows, and the length of time it spends there.

The growth inhibition mentioned above is a result of the fact that when water or water vapor freezes into ice, it releases a certain amount of latent heat—as the reverse of the phenomenon that when ice is warmed to 0°C it still needs heat applied before it will actually melt.

But there are also many effects. The freezing temperature, for example, effectively varies with the curvature of the surface. The rate of heat conduction differs in different directions on the hexagonal grid. Convection currents develop in the water vapor around the snowflake. Mechanical stresses are produced in the crystal as it grows.

Various models of snowflake growth exist in the standard scientific literature, typically focusing on one or two of these effects. But in most cases the models have at some basic level been rather unsuccessful. For being based on traditional mathematical equations they have tended to be able to deal only with what amount to fairly simple smooth shapes—and so have never really been able to address the kind of intricate structure that is so striking in real snowflakes.

But with models based on simple programs such as cellular automata, there is no problem in dealing with more complicated shapes, and indeed, as we have seen, it is actually quite easy to reproduce the basic features of the overall behavior that occurs in real snowflakes.

So what about other types of crystals?

In nature a variety of forms are seen. And as the pictures on the facing page demonstrate, the same is true even in cellular automata with very simple rules. Indeed, much as in nature, the diversity of behavior is striking. Sometimes simple faceted forms are produced. But in other cases there are needle-like forms, tree-like or dendritic forms, as well as rounded forms, and forms that seem in many respects random.

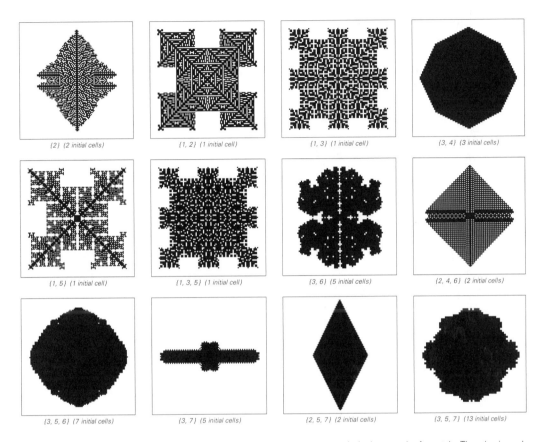

Examples of patterns produced by two-dimensional cellular automata set up to mimic the growth of crystals. The rules in each case take a cell to become black if the specified number of its neighbors (including diagonals) on a square grid are black on the step before. These rules are such that once a cell has become black, corresponding to solid, it never reverts to white again. In each case a row of initial black cells of the specified length was used.

The occurrence of these last forms is at first especially surprising. For one might have assumed that any apparent randomness in the final shape of something like a crystal must always be a consequence of randomness in its original seed, or in the environment in which it grew.

But in fact, as the pictures above show—and as we have seen many times in this book—it is also possible for randomness to arise intrinsically just through the application of simple underlying rules. And contrary to what has always been assumed, I suspect that this is actually how the apparent randomness that one sometimes sees in shapes formed by crystalline materials often comes about.

The Breaking of Materials

In everyday life one of the most familiar ways to generate randomness is to break a solid object. For although the details vary from one material to another it is almost universally the case that the line or surface along which fracture actually occurs seems rough and in many respects random.

So what is the origin of this randomness? At first one might think that it must be a reflection of random small-scale irregularities within the material. And indeed it is true that in materials that consist of many separate crystals or grains, fractures often tend to follow the boundaries between such elements.

But what happens if one takes for example a perfect single crystal—say a standard highly pure industrial silicon crystal—and breaks it? The answer is that except in a few special cases the pattern of fracture one gets seems to look just as random as in other materials.

And what this suggests is that whatever basic mechanism is responsible for such randomness, it cannot depend on the details of particular materials. Indeed, the fact that almost indistinguishable patterns of fracture are seen both at microscopic scales and in geological systems on scales of order kilometers is another clue that there must be a more general mechanism at work.

So what might this mechanism be?

When a solid material breaks what typically happens is that a crack forms—usually at the edge of the material—and then spreads. Experience with systems from hand-held objects to engineering structures and earthquakes suggests that it can take a while for a crack to get started, but that once it does, the crack tends to move quickly and violently, usually producing a lot of noise in the process.

One can think of the components of a solid—whether at the level of atoms, molecules, or pieces of rock—as being bound together by forces that act a little like springs. And when a crack propagates through the solid, this in effect sets up an elaborate pattern of vibrations in these springs. The path of the crack is then in turn determined by where the springs get stretched so far that they break.

There are many factors which affect the details of displacements and vibrations in a solid. But as a rough approximation one can perhaps assume that each element of a solid is either displaced or not, and that the displacements of neighboring elements interact by some definite rule—say a simple cellular automaton rule.

The pictures below show the behavior that one gets with a simple model of this kind. And even though there is no explicit randomness inserted into the model in any way, the paths of the cracks that emerge nevertheless appear to be quite random.

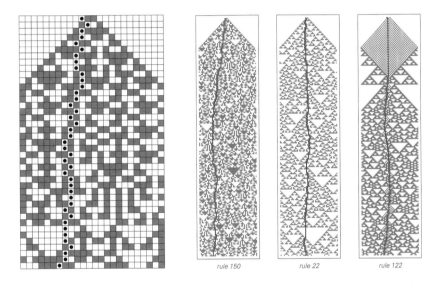

rule 150   rule 22   rule 122

A very simple cellular automaton model for fracture. At each step, the color of each cell, which roughly represents the displacement of an element of the solid, is updated according to a cellular automaton rule. The black dot, representing the location of a crack, moves from one cell to another based on the displacements of neighboring cells, at each step setting the cell it reaches to be white. Even though no randomness is inserted from outside, the paths of the cracks that emerge from this model nevertheless appear to a large extent random. There is some evidence from physical experiments that dislocations around cracks can form patterns that look similar to the gray and white backgrounds above.

There are certainly many aspects of real materials that this model does not even come close to capturing. But I nevertheless suspect that even when much more realistic models for specific materials are used, the fundamental mechanisms responsible for randomness will still be very much the same as in the extremely simple model shown here.

Fluid Flow

A great many striking phenomena in nature involve the flow of fluids like air and water—as illustrated on the facing page. Typical of what happens is what one sees when water flows around a solid object. At sufficiently slow speeds, the water in effect just slides smoothly around, yielding a very simple laminar pattern of flow. But at higher speeds, there starts to be a region of slow-moving water behind the object, and a pair of eddies are formed as the water swirls into this region.

As the speed increases, these eddies become progressively more elongated. And then suddenly, when a critical speed is reached, the eddies in effect start breaking off, and getting carried downstream. But every time one eddy breaks off, another starts to form, so that in the end a whole street of eddies are seen in the wake behind the object.

At first, these eddies are arranged in a very regular way. But as the speed of the flow is increased, glitches begin to appear, at first far behind the object, but eventually throughout the wake. Even at the highest speeds, some overall regularity nevertheless remains. But superimposed on this is all sorts of elaborate and seemingly quite random behavior.

But this is just one example of the very widespread phenomenon of fluid turbulence. For as the pictures on the facing page indicate—and as common experience suggests—almost any time a fluid is made to flow rapidly, it tends to form complex patterns that seem in many ways random.

So why fundamentally does this happen?

Traditional science, with its basis in mathematical equations, has never really been able to provide any convincing underlying explanation. But from my discovery that complex and seemingly random behavior is in a sense easy to get even with very simple programs, the phenomenon of fluid turbulence immediately begins to seem much less surprising.

But can simple programs really reproduce the particular kinds of behavior we see in fluids? At a microscopic level, physical fluids consist of large numbers of molecules moving around and colliding with each other. So as a simple idealization, one can consider having a large number of particles move around on a fixed discrete grid, and undergo collisions governed by simple cellular-automaton-like rules.

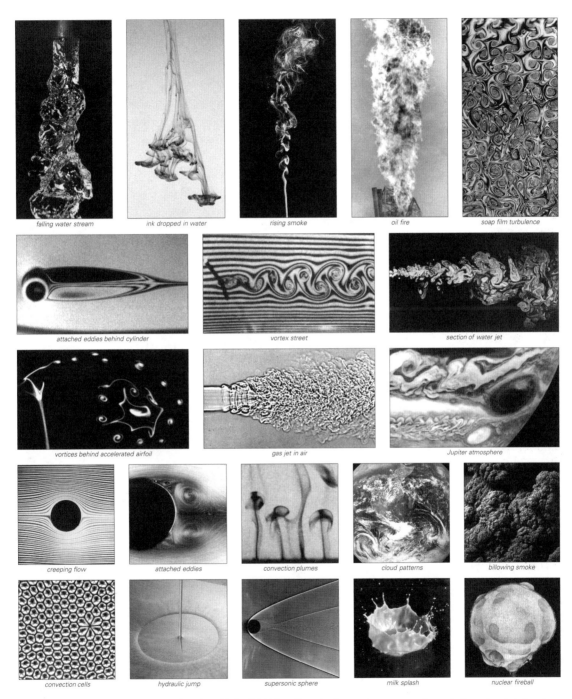

Examples of typical patterns generated in various kinds of fluid flow. Note the frequent occurrence of seemingly random turbulence.

The pictures below give an example of such a system. In the top row of pictures—as well as picture (a)—all one sees is a collection of discrete particles bouncing around. But if one zooms out, and looks at average motion of increasingly large blocks of particles—as in pictures (b) and (c)—then what begins to emerge is behavior that seems smooth and continuous—just like one expects to see in a fluid.

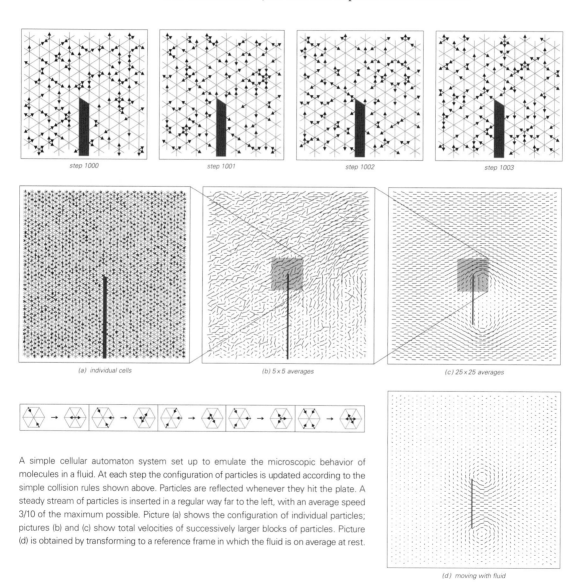

step 1000   step 1001   step 1002   step 1003

(a) individual cells   (b) 5 x 5 averages   (c) 25 x 25 averages

A simple cellular automaton system set up to emulate the microscopic behavior of molecules in a fluid. At each step the configuration of particles is updated according to the simple collision rules shown above. Particles are reflected whenever they hit the plate. A steady stream of particles is inserted in a regular way far to the left, with an average speed 3/10 of the maximum possible. Picture (a) shows the configuration of individual particles; pictures (b) and (c) show total velocities of successively larger blocks of particles. Picture (d) is obtained by transforming to a reference frame in which the fluid is on average at rest.

(d) moving with fluid

This happens for exactly the same reason as in a real fluid, or, for that matter, in various examples that we saw in Chapter 7: even though at an underlying level the system consists of discrete particles, the effective randomness of the detailed microscopic motions of these particles makes their large-scale average behavior seem smooth and continuous.

We know from physical experiments that the characteristics of fluid flow are almost exactly the same for air, water, and all other ordinary fluids. Yet at an underlying level these different fluids consist of very different kinds of molecules, with very different properties. But somehow the details of such microscopic structure gets washed out if one looks at large-scale fluid-like behavior.

Many times in this book we have seen examples where different systems can yield very much the same overall behavior, even though the details of their underlying rules are quite different. But in the particular case of systems like fluids, it turns out that one can show—as I will discuss in the next chapter—that so long as certain physical quantities such as particle number and momentum are conserved, then whenever there is sufficient microscopic randomness, it is almost inevitable that the same overall fluid behavior will be obtained.

So what this means is that to reproduce the observed properties of physical fluids one should not need to make a model that involves realistic molecules: even the highly idealized particles on the facing page should give rise to essentially the same overall fluid behavior.

And indeed in pictures (c) and (d) one can already see the formation of a pair of eddies, just as in one of the pictures on page 377.

So what happens if one increases the speed of the flow? Does one see the same kinds of phenomena as on page 377? The pictures on the next page suggest that indeed one does. Below a certain critical speed, a completely regular array of eddies is formed. But at the speed used in the pictures on the next page, the array of eddies has begun to show random irregularities just like those associated with turbulence in real fluids.

So where does this randomness come from?

In the past couple of decades it has come to be widely believed that randomness in turbulent fluids must somehow be associated with

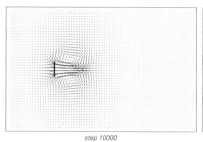

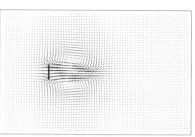

step 10000

step 20000

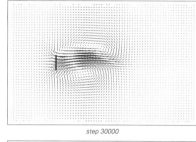

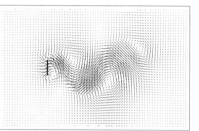

step 30000

step 40000

A larger example of the cellular automaton system shown on the previous page. In each picture there are a total of 30 million underlying cells. The individual velocity vectors drawn correspond to averages over 20 × 20 blocks of cells. Particles are inserted in a regular way at the left-hand end so as to maintain an overall flow speed equal to about 0.4 of the maximum possible. To make the patterns of flow easier to see, the velocities shown are transformed so that the fluid is on average at rest, and the plate is moving. The underlying density of particles is approximately 1 per cell, or 1/6 the maximum possible—a density which more or less minimizes the viscosity of the fluid. The Reynolds number of the flow shown is then approximately 100. The agreement with experimental results on actual fluid flows is striking.

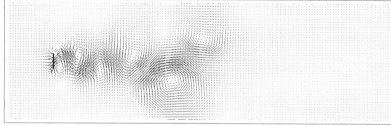

step 50000

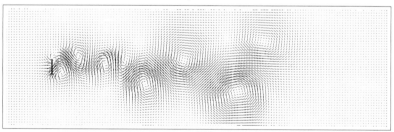

step 60000

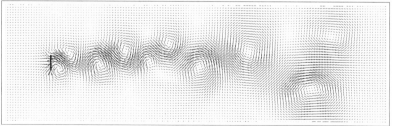

step 70000

sensitive dependence on initial conditions, and with the chaos phenomenon that we discussed in Chapter 4.

But while there are certainly mathematical equations that exhibit this phenomenon, none of those typically investigated have any close connection to realistic descriptions of fluid flow.

And in the model on the facing page it turns out that there is essentially no sensitive dependence on initial conditions, at least at the level of overall fluid behavior. If one looks at individual particles, then changing the position of even one particle will typically have an effect that spreads rapidly. But if one looks instead at the average behavior of many particles, such effects get completely washed out. And indeed when it comes to large-scale fluid behavior, it seems to be true that in almost all cases there is no discernible difference between what happens with different detailed initial conditions.

So is there ever sensitive dependence on initial conditions?

Presumably there do exist situations in which there is some kind of delicate balance—say of whether the first eddy is shed at the top or bottom of an object—and in which small changes in initial conditions can have a substantial effect. But such situations appear to be very much the exception rather than the rule. And in the vast majority of cases, small changes instead seem to damp out rapidly—just as one might expect from everyday experience with viscosity in fluids.

So what this means is that the randomness we observe in fluid flow cannot simply be a reflection of randomness that is inserted through the details of initial conditions. And as it turns out, in the pictures on the facing page, the initial conditions were specifically set up to be very simple. Yet despite this, there is still apparent randomness in the overall behavior that is seen.

And so, once again, just as for many other systems that we have studied in this book, there is little choice but to conclude that in a turbulent fluid most of the randomness we see is not in any way inserted from outside but is instead intrinsically generated inside the system itself. In the pictures on page 378 considerable randomness was already evident at the level of individual particles. But since changes in the configurations of such particles do not seem to have any discernible

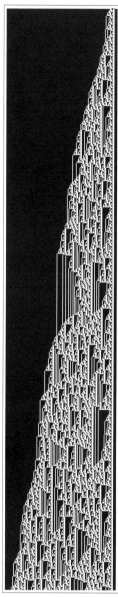

A cellular automaton (rule 225) whose behavior is reminiscent of turbulent fluid flow.

effect on overall patterns of flow, one cannot realistically attribute the large-scale randomness that one sees in a turbulent fluid to randomness that exists at the level of individual particles.

Instead, what seems to be happening is that intrinsic randomness generation occurs directly at the level of large-scale fluid motion. And as an example of a simple approach to modelling this, one can consider having a collection of discrete eddies that occur at discrete positions in the fluid, and interact through simple cellular automaton rules.

The picture on the left shows an example of what can happen. And although many details are different from what one sees in real fluids, the overall mixture of regularity and randomness is strikingly similar.

One consequence of the idea that there is intrinsic randomness generation in fluids and that it occurs at the level of large-scale fluid motion is that with sufficiently careful preparation it should be possible to produce patterns of flow that seem quite random but that are nevertheless effectively repeatable—so that they look essentially the same on every successive run of an experiment.

And even if one looks at existing experiments on fluid flow, there turn out to be quite a few instances—particularly for example involving interactions between small numbers of vortices—where there are known patterns of fluid flow that look intricate, but are nevertheless essentially repeatable. And while none of these yet look complicated enough that they might reasonably be called random, I suspect that in time similar but vastly more complex examples will be found.

Among the patterns of fluid flow on page 377 each has its own particular details and characteristics. But while some of the simpler ones have been captured quite completely by methods based on traditional mathematical equations, the more complex ones have not. And in fact from the perspective of this book this is not surprising.

But now from the experience and intuition developed from the discoveries in this book, I expect that there will in fact be remarkably simple programs that can be found that will successfully manage to reproduce the main features of even the most intricate and apparently random forms of fluid flow.

Fundamental Issues in Biology

Biological systems are often cited as supreme examples of complexity in nature, and it is not uncommon for it to be assumed that their complexity must be somehow of a fundamentally higher order than other systems.

And typically it is thought that this must be a consequence of the rather unique processes of adaptation and natural selection that operate in biological systems. But despite all sorts of discussion over the years, no clear understanding has ever emerged of just why such processes should in the end actually lead to much complexity at all.

And in fact what I have come to believe is that many of the most obvious examples of complexity in biological systems actually have very little to do with adaptation or natural selection. And instead what I suspect is that they are mainly just another consequence of the very basic phenomenon that I have discovered in this book in the context of simple programs: that in almost any kind of system many choices of underlying rules inevitably lead to behavior of great complexity.

The general idea of thinking in terms of programs is, if anything, even more obvious for biological systems than for physical ones. For in a physical system the rules of a program must normally be deduced indirectly from the laws of physics. But in a biological organism there is genetic material which can be thought of quite directly as providing a program for the development of the organism.

Most of the programs that I have discussed in this book, however, have been very simple. Yet the genetic program for every biological organism known today is long and complicated: in humans, for example, it presumably involves millions of separate rules—making it by most measures as complex as large practical software systems like *Mathematica*.

So from this one might think that the complexity we see in biological organisms must all just be a reflection of complexity in their underlying rules—making discoveries about simple programs not really relevant. And certainly the presence of many different types of organs and other elements in a typical complete organism seems likely to be related to the presence of many separate sets of rules in the underlying program. But what if one looks not at a complete organism but instead just at some part of an organism?

Particularly on a microscopic scale, the forms one sees are often highly regular and quite simple, as in the pictures on the facing page. And when one looks at these, it seems perfectly reasonable to suppose that they are in effect produced by fairly simple programs.

But what about the much more complicated forms that one sees in biological systems? On the basis of traditional intuition one might assume that such forms could never be produced by simple programs. But from the discoveries in this book we now know that in fact it is possible to get remarkable complexity even from very simple programs.

So is this what actually happens in biological systems?

There is certainly no dramatic difference between the underlying types of cells or other elements that occur in complex biological forms and in the forms on the facing page. And from this one might begin to suspect that in the end the kinds of programs which generate all these forms are quite similar—and all potentially rather simple.

For even though the complete genetic program for an organism is long and complicated, the subprograms which govern individual aspects of an organism can still be simple—and there are now plenty of specific simple examples where this is known to be the case. But still one might assume that to get significant complexity would require something more. And indeed at first one might think that it would never really be possible to say much at all about complexity just by looking at parts of organisms.

But in fact, as it turns out, a rather large fraction of the most obvious examples of biological complexity seem to involve only surprisingly limited parts of the organisms. Elaborate pigmentation patterns, for instance, typically exist just on an outer skin, and are made up of only a few types of cells. And the vast majority of complicated

Examples of highly regular forms occurring in biological systems. Most of these forms are simple enough that it seems immediately plausible that they could in effect be generated by simple programs. The majority show either simple geometrical shapes, or repetition of identical elements. A few, however, show various types of nesting. Note that there seems to be no obvious correlation between the sophistication of a form and when in geological time it first appeared. ▶

protist microspine section

alga

chloroplast

diatom

coccolithophorid

heliozoan axopod

radiolarian

thallus

cactus

chickweed pollen

romanesco broccoli

heather pollen

cow parsley

carrot leaf

tobacco mosaic viruses

daisy

corn

insect muscle section

Burgess Shale fossil

trilobite

barnacle

fly eye

wasp nest

fossil ammonite septa

nautilus shell section

octopus tentacle

opened brachiopod

starfish

sea urchin

armadillo skin

morphological structures get their forms from arrangements of very limited numbers of types of cells or other elements.

But just how are the programs for these and other features of organisms actually determined? Over the past century or so it has become almost universally believed that at some level these programs must end up being the ones that maximize the fitness of the organism, and the number of viable offspring it produces.

The notion is that if a line of organisms with a particular program typically produce more offspring, then after a few generations there will inevitably be vastly more organisms with this program than with other programs. And if one assumes that the program for each new offspring involves small random mutations then this means that over the course of many generations biological evolution will in effect carry out a random search for programs that maximize the fitness of an organism.

But how successful can one expect such a search to be?

The problem of maximizing fitness is essentially the same as the problem of satisfying constraints that we discussed at the end of Chapter 7. And what we found there is that for sufficiently simple constraints—particularly continuous ones—iterative random searches can converge fairly quickly to an optimal solution. But as soon as the constraints are more complicated this is no longer the case. And indeed even when the optimal solution is comparatively simple it can require an astronomically large number of steps to get even anywhere close to it.

Biological systems do appear to have some tricks for speeding up the search process. Sexual reproduction, for example, allows large-scale mixing of similar programs, rather than just small-scale mutation. And differentiation into organs in effect allows different parts of a program to be updated separately. But even with a whole array of such tricks, it is still completely implausible that the trillion or so generations of organisms since the beginning of life on Earth would be sufficient to allow optimal solutions to be found to constraints of any significant complexity.

And indeed one suspects that in fact the vast majority of features of biological organisms do not correspond to anything close to optimal solutions: rather, they represent solutions that were fairly easy to find, but are good enough not to cause fatal problems for the organism.

The basic notion that organisms tend to evolve to achieve a maximum fitness has certainly in the past been very useful in providing a general framework for understanding the historical progression of species, and in yielding specific explanations for various fairly simple properties of particular species.

But in present-day thinking about biology the notion has tended to be taken to an extreme, so that especially among those not in daily contact with detailed data on biological systems it has come to be assumed that essentially every feature of every organism can be explained on the basis of it somehow maximizing the fitness of the organism.

It is certainly recognized that some aspects of current organisms are in effect holdovers from earlier stages in biological evolution. And there is also increasing awareness that the actual process of growth and development within an individual organism can make it easier or more difficult for particular kinds of structures to occur.

But beyond this there is a surprisingly universal conviction that any significant property that one sees in any organism must be there because it in essence serves a purpose in maximizing the fitness of the organism.

Often it is at first quite unclear what this purpose might be, but at least in fairly simple cases, some kind of hypothesis can usually be constructed. And having settled on a supposed purpose it often seems quite marvellous how ingenious biology has been in finding a solution that achieves that purpose.

Thus, for example, the golden ratio spiral of branches on a plant stem can be viewed as a marvellous way to minimize the shading of leaves, while the elaborate patterns on certain mollusc shells can be viewed as marvellous ways to confuse the visual systems of supposed predators.

But it is my strong suspicion that such purposes in fact have very little to do with the real reasons that these particular features exist. For instead, as I will discuss in the next couple of sections, what I believe is that these features actually arise in essence just because they are easy to produce with fairly simple programs. And indeed as one looks at more and more complex features of biological organisms—notably texture and pigmentation patterns—it becomes increasingly difficult to find any credible purpose at all that would be served by the details of what one sees.

In the past, the idea of optimization for some sophisticated purpose seemed to be the only conceivable explanation for the level of complexity that is seen in many biological systems. But with the discovery in this book that it takes only a simple program to produce behavior of great complexity, a quite different—and ultimately much more predictive—kind of explanation immediately becomes possible.

In the course of biological evolution random mutations will in effect cause a whole sequence of programs to be tried. And the point is that from what we have discovered in this book, we now know that it is almost inevitable that a fair fraction of these programs will yield complex behavior.

Some programs will presumably lead to organisms that are more successful than others, and natural selection will cause these programs eventually to dominate. But in most cases I strongly suspect that it is comparatively coarse features that tend to determine the success of an organism—not all the details of any complex behavior that may occur.

Thus in a very simple case it is easy to imagine for example that an organism might be more likely to go unnoticed by its predators, and thus survive and be more successful, if its skin was a mixture of brown and white, rather than, say, uniformly bright orange. But it could then be that most programs which yield any mixture of colors also happen to be such that they make the colors occur in a highly complex pattern.

And if this is so, then in the course of random mutation, the chances are that the first program encountered that is successful enough to survive will also, quite coincidentally, exhibit complex behavior.

On the basis of traditional biological thinking one would tend to assume that whatever complexity one saw must in the end be carefully crafted to satisfy some elaborate set of constraints. But what I believe instead is that the vast majority of the complexity we see in biological systems actually has its origin in the purely abstract fact that among randomly chosen programs many give rise to complex behavior.

In the past it tends to have been implicitly assumed that to get substantial complexity in a biological system must somehow be fundamentally very difficult. But from the discoveries in this book I have come to the conclusion that instead it is actually rather easy.

So how can one tell if this is really the case?

One circumstantial piece of evidence is that one already sees considerable complexity even in very early fossil organisms. Over the course of the past billion or so years, more and more organs and other devices have appeared. But the most obvious outward signs of complexity, manifest for example in textures and other morphological features, seem to have already been present even from very early times.

And indeed there is every indication that the level of complexity of individual parts of organisms has not changed much in at least several hundred million years. So this suggests that somehow the complexity we see must arise from some straightforward and general mechanism—and not, for example, from a mechanism that relies on elaborate refinement through a long process of biological evolution.

Another circumstantial piece of evidence that complexity is in a sense easy to get in biological systems comes from the observation that among otherwise very similar present-day organisms features such as pigmentation patterns often vary from quite simple to highly complex.

Whether one looks at fishes, butterflies, molluscs or practically any other kind of organism, it is common to find that across species or even within species organisms that live in the same environment and have essentially the same internal structure can nevertheless exhibit radically different pigmentation patterns. In some cases the patterns may be simple, but in other cases they are highly complex.

And the point is that no elaborate structural changes and no sophisticated processes of adaptation seem to be needed in order to get these more complex patterns. And in the end it is, I suspect, just that some of the possible underlying genetic programs happen to produce complex patterns, while others do not.

Two sections from now I will discuss a rather striking potential example of this: if one looks at molluscs of various types, then it turns out that the range of pigmentation patterns on their shells corresponds remarkably closely with the range of patterns that are produced by simple randomly chosen programs based on cellular automata.

And examples like this—together with many others in the next couple of sections—provide evidence that the kind of complexity we see in biological organisms can indeed successfully be reproduced by short and simple underlying programs. But there still remains the question of whether actual biological organisms really use such programs, or whether somehow they instead use much more complicated programs.

Modern molecular biology should soon be able to isolate the specific programs responsible, say, for the patterns on mollusc shells, and see explicitly how long they are. But there are already indications that these programs are quite short.

For one of the consequences of a program being short is that it has little room for inessential elements. And this means that almost any mutation or change in the program—however small—will tend to have a significant effect on at least the details of patterns it produces.

Sometimes it is hard to tell whether changes in patterns between organisms within a species are truly of genetic origin. But in cases where they appear to be it is common to find that different organisms show a considerable variety of different patterns—supporting the idea that the programs responsible for these patterns are indeed short.

So what about the actual process of biological evolution? How does it pick out which programs to use? As a very simple idealization of biological evolution, one can consider a sequence of cellular automaton programs in which each successive program is obtained from the previous one by a random mutation that adds or modifies a single element.

The pictures on the facing page then show a typical example of what happens with such a setup. If one starts from extremely short programs, the behavior one gets is at first quite simple. But as soon as the underlying programs become even slightly longer, one immediately sees highly complex behavior.

Traditional intuition would suggest that if the programs were to become still longer, the behavior would get ever richer and more complex. But from the discoveries in this book we know that this will not in general be the case: above a fairly low threshold, adding complexity to an underlying program does not fundamentally change the kind of behavior that it can produce.

And from this one concludes that biological systems should in a sense be capable of generating essentially arbitrary complexity by using short programs formed by just a few mutations.

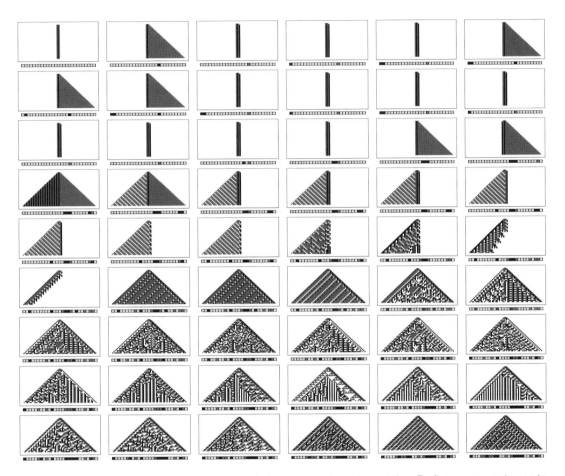

The behavior of a sequence of cellular automaton programs obtained by successive random mutations. The first program contains no rules for changing the color of a cell with any neighborhood. Mutations in successive programs add rules for changing the colors of cells with specific neighborhoods, or modify these rules. Each program in the sequence differs from the previous one by a single mutation, made completely at random. The sequence provides a very simple idealization of biological evolution without explicit natural selection. The cellular automata shown here all have 3 possible colors and nearest-neighbor rules. The label for each picture gives a representation of the rules for each of the 27 possible 3-cell neighborhoods. A dot signifies that the rule does not change the color of the center cell in the neighborhood.

But if complexity is this easy to get, why is it not even more widespread in biology? For while there are certainly many examples of elaborate forms and patterns in biological systems, the overall shapes and many of the most obvious features of typical organisms are usually quite simple.

So why should this be? My guess is that in essence it reflects limitations associated with the process of natural selection. For while natural selection is often touted as a force of almost arbitrary power, I have increasingly come to believe that in fact its power is remarkably limited. And indeed, what I suspect is that in the end natural selection can only operate in a meaningful way on systems or parts of systems whose behavior is in some sense quite simple.

If a particular part of an organism always grows, say, in a simple straight line, then it is fairly easy to imagine that natural selection could succeed in picking out the optimal length for any given environment. But what if an organism can grow in a more complex way, say like in the pictures on the previous page? My strong suspicion is that in such a case natural selection will normally be able to achieve very little.

There are several reasons for this, all somewhat related.

First, with more complex behavior, there are typically a huge number of possible variations, and in a realistic population of organisms it becomes infeasible for any significant fraction of these variations to be explored.

Second, complex behavior inevitably involves many elaborate details, and since different ones of these details may happen to be the deciding factors in the fates of individual organisms, it becomes very difficult for natural selection to act in a consistent and definitive way.

Third, whenever the overall behavior of a system is more complex than its underlying program, almost any mutation in the program will lead to a whole collection of detailed changes in the behavior, so that natural selection has no opportunity to pick out changes which are beneficial from those which are not.

Fourth, if random mutations can only, say, increase or decrease a length, then even if one mutation goes in the wrong direction, it is easy for another mutation to recover by going in the opposite direction. But if there are in effect many possible directions, it becomes much more difficult to recover from missteps, and to exhibit any form of systematic convergence.

And finally, as the results in Chapter 7 suggest, for anything beyond the very simplest forms of behavior, iterative random searches rapidly tend to get stuck, and make at best excruciatingly slow progress towards any kind of global optimum.

In a sense it is not surprising that natural selection can achieve little when confronted with complex behavior. For in effect it is being asked to predict what changes would need to be made in an underlying program in order to produce or enhance a certain form of overall behavior. Yet one of the main conclusions of this book is that even given a particular program, it can be very difficult to see what the behavior of the program will be. And to go backwards from behavior to programs is a still much more difficult task.

In writing this book it would certainly have been convenient to have had a systematic way to be able to find examples of programs that exhibit specified forms of complex behavior. And indeed I have tried hard to develop iterative search procedures that would do this. But even using a whole range of tricks suggested by biology—as well as quite a number that are not—I have never been successful. And in fact in every single case I have in the end reverted either to exhaustive or to purely random searches, with no attempt at iterative improvement.

So what does this mean for biological organisms? It suggests that if a particular feature of an organism is successfully going to be optimized for different environments by natural selection, then this feature must somehow be quite simple.

And no doubt that is a large part of the reason that biological organisms always tend to consist of separate organs or other parts, each of which has at least some attributes that are fairly simple. For in this way there end up being components that are simple enough to be adjusted in a meaningful fashion by natural selection.

It has often been claimed that natural selection is what makes systems in biology able to exhibit so much more complexity than systems that we explicitly construct in engineering. But my strong suspicion is that in fact the main effect of natural selection is almost exactly the opposite: it tends to make biological systems avoid complexity, and be more like systems in engineering.

When one does engineering, one normally operates under the constraint that the systems one builds must behave in a way that is readily predictable and understandable. And in order to achieve this one typically limits oneself to constructing systems out of fairly small numbers of components whose behavior and interactions are somehow simple.

But systems in nature need not in general operate under the constraint that their behavior should be predictable or understandable. And what this means is that in a sense they can use any number of components of any kind—with the result, as we have seen in this book, that the behavior they produce can often be highly complex.

However, if natural selection is to be successful at systematically molding the properties of a system then once again there are limitations on the kinds of components that the system can have. And indeed, it seems that what is needed are components that behave in simple and somewhat independent ways—much as in traditional engineering.

At some level it is not surprising that there should be an analogy between engineering and natural selection. For both cases can be viewed as trying to create systems that will achieve or optimize some goal.

Indeed, the main difference is just that in engineering explicit human effort is expended to find an appropriate form for the system, whereas in natural selection an iterative random search process is used instead. But the point is that the conditions under which these two approaches work turn out to be not so different.

In fact, there are even, I suspect, similarities in quite detailed issues such as the kinds of adjustments that can be made to individual components. In engineering it is common to work with components whose properties can somehow be varied smoothly, and which can therefore be analyzed using the methods of calculus and traditional continuous mathematics.

And as it turns out, much as we saw in Chapter 7, this same kind of smooth variation is also what tends to make iterative search methods such as natural selection be successful.

In biological systems based on discrete genetic programs, it is far from clear how smooth variation can emerge. Presumably in some cases it can be approximated by the presence of varying numbers of repeats in the underlying program. And more often it is probably the result of combinations of large numbers of elements that each produce fairly random behavior.

But the possibility of smooth variation seems to be important enough to the effectiveness of natural selection that it is extremely common in actual biological systems. And indeed, while there are some traits—such as eye color and blood type in humans—that are more or less discrete, the vast majority of traits seen, say, in the breeding of plants and animals, show quite smooth variation.

So to what extent does the actual history of biological evolution reflect the kinds of simple characteristics that I have argued one should expect from natural selection?

If one looks at species that exist today, and at the fossil record of past species, then one of the most striking features is just how much is in common across vast ranges of different organisms. The basic body plans for animals, for example, have been almost the same for hundreds of millions of years, and many organs and developmental pathways are probably even still older.

In fact, the vast majority of structurally important features seem to have changed only quite slowly and gradually in the course of evolution—just as one would expect from a process of natural selection that is based on smooth variations in fairly simple properties.

But despite this it is still clear that there is considerable diversity, at least at the level of visual appearance, in the actual forms of biological organisms that occur. So how then does such diversity arise?

One effect, to be discussed at greater length in the next section, is essentially just a matter of geometry. If the relative rates of growth of different parts of an organism change even slightly, then it turns out that this can sometimes have dramatic consequences for the overall shape of the organism, as well as for its mechanical operation.

And what this means is that just by making gradual changes in quantities such as relative rates of growth, natural selection can succeed in producing organisms that at least in some respects look very different.

But what about other differences between organisms? To what extent are all of them systematically determined by natural selection?

Following the discussion earlier in this section, it is my strong suspicion that at least many of the visually most striking differences—

associated for example with texture and pigmentation patterns—in the end have almost nothing to do with natural selection.

And instead what I believe is that such differences are in essence just reflections of completely random changes in underlying genetic programs, with no systematic effects from natural selection.

Particularly among closely related species of organisms there is certainly quite a contrast between the dramatic differences often seen in features such as pigmentation patterns and the amazing constancy of other features. And most likely those features in which a great degree of constancy is seen are precisely the ones that have successfully been molded by natural selection.

But as I mentioned earlier, it is almost always those features which change most rapidly between species that show the most obvious signs of complexity. And this observation fits precisely with the idea that complexity is easy to get by randomly sampling simple programs, but is hard for natural selection to handle in any kind of systematic way.

So in the end, therefore, what I conclude is that many of the most obvious features of complexity in biological organisms arise in a sense not because of natural selection, but rather in spite of it.

No doubt it will for many people be difficult to abandon the idea that natural selection is somehow crucial to the presence of complexity in biological organisms. For traditional intuition makes one think that to get the level of complexity that one sees in biological systems must require great effort—and the long and ponderous course of evolution revealed in the fossil record seems like just the kind of process that should be involved.

But the point is that what I have discovered in this book shows that in fact if one just chooses programs at random, then it is easy to get behavior of great complexity. And it is this that I believe lies at the heart of most of the complexity that we see in nature, both in biological and non-biological systems.

Whenever natural selection is an important determining factor, I suspect that one will inevitably see many of the same simplifying features as in systems created through engineering. And only when natural selection is not crucial, therefore, will biological systems be able to exhibit the same level of complexity that one observes for example in many systems in physics.

In biology the presence of long programs with many separate parts can lead to a certain rather straightforward complexity analogous to having many physical objects of different kinds collected together. But the most dramatic examples of complexity in biology tend to occur in individual parts of systems—and often involve patterns or structures that look remarkably like those in physics.

Yet if biology samples underlying genetic programs essentially at random, why should these programs behave anything like programs that are derived from specific laws of physics?

The answer, as we have seen many times in this book, is that across a very wide range of programs there is great universality in the behavior that occurs. The details depend on the exact rules for each program, but the overall characteristics remain very much the same.

And one of the important consequences of this is that it suggests that it might be possible to develop a rather general predictive theory of biology that would tell one, for example, what basic forms are and are not likely to occur in biological systems.

One might have thought that the traditional idea that organisms are selected to be optimal for their environment would already long ago have led to some kind of predictive theory. And indeed it has for example allowed some simple numerical ratios associated with populations of organisms to be successfully derived. But about a question such as what forms of organisms are likely to occur it has much less to say.

There are a number of situations where fairly complicated structures appear to have arisen independently in several very different types of organisms. And it is sometimes claimed that this kind of convergent evolution occurs because these structures are in some ultimate sense optimal, making it inevitable that they will eventually be produced.

But I would be very surprised if this explanation were correct. And instead what I strongly suspect is that the reason certain structures appear repeatedly is just that they are somehow common among programs of certain kinds—just as, for example, we have seen that the

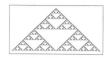

An example of a basic pattern that is produced in several variants by a wide range of simple programs.

intricate nested pattern shown on the left arises from many different simple programs.

Ever since the original development of the theory of evolution, there has been a widespread belief that the general trend seen in the fossil record towards the formation of progressively more complicated types of organisms must somehow be related to an overall increase in optimality.

Needless to say, we do not know what a truly optimal organism would be like. But if optimality is associated with having as many offspring as possible, then very simple organisms such as viruses and protozoa already seem to do very well.

So why then do higher organisms exist at all? My guess is that it has almost nothing to do with optimality, and that instead it is essentially just a consequence of strings of random mutations that happened to add more and more features without introducing fatal flaws.

It is certainly not the case—as is often assumed—that natural selection somehow inevitably leads to organisms with progressively more elaborate structures and progressively larger numbers of parts.

For a start, some kinds of organisms have been subject to natural selection for more than a billion years, but have never ended up becoming much more complicated. And although there are situations where organisms do end up becoming more complicated, they also often become simpler.

A typical pattern—remarkably similar, as it happens, to what occurs in the history of technology—is that at some point in the fossil record some major new capability or feature is suddenly seen. At first there is then rapid expansion, with many new species trying out all sorts of possibilities that have been opened up. And usually some of these possibilities get quite ornate and elaborate. But after a while it becomes clear what makes sense and what does not. And typically things then get simpler again.

So what is the role of natural selection in all of this? My guess is that as in other situations, its main systematic contribution is to make things simpler, and that insofar as things do end up getting more complicated, this is almost always the result of essentially random sampling of underlying programs—without any systematic effect of natural selection.

For the more superficial aspects of organisms—such as pigmentation patterns—it seems likely that among programs sampled at random a fair fraction will produce results that are not disastrous for the organism. But when one is dealing with the basic structure of organisms, the vast majority of programs sampled at random will no doubt have immediate disastrous consequences. And in a sense it is natural selection that is responsible for the fact that such programs do not survive.

But the point is that in such a case its effect is not systematic or cumulative. And indeed it is my strong suspicion that for essentially all purposes the only reasonable model for important new features of organisms is that they come from programs selected purely at random.

So does this then mean that there can never be any kind of general theory for all the features of higher organisms? Presumably the pattern of exactly which new features were added when in the history of biological evolution is no more amenable to general theory than the specific course of events in human history. But I strongly suspect that the vast majority of significant new features that appear in organisms are at least at first associated with fairly short underlying programs. And insofar as this is the case the results of this book should allow one to develop some fairly general characterizations of what can happen.

So what all this means is that much of what we see in biology should correspond quite closely to the typical behavior of simple programs as we have studied them in this book—with the main caveat being just that certain aspects will be smoothed and simplified by the effects of natural selection. Seeing in earlier chapters of this book all the diverse things that simple programs can do, it is easy to be struck by analogies to books of biological flora and fauna. Yet what we now see is that in fact such analogies may be quite direct—and that many of the most obvious features of actual biological organisms may in effect be direct reflections of typical behavior that one sees in simple programs.

Growth of Plants and Animals

Looking at all the elaborate forms of plants and animals one might at first assume that the underlying rules for their growth must be highly complex. But in this book we have discovered that even by following very simple rules it is possible to obtain forms of great complexity. And what I have come to believe is that in fact most aspects of the growth of plants and animals are in the end governed by remarkably simple rules.

As a first example of biological growth, consider the stem of a plant. It is usually only at the tip of a stem that growth can occur, and much of the time all that ever happens is that the stem just gets progressively longer. But the crucial phenomenon that ultimately leads to much of the structure we see in many kinds of plants is that at the tip of a stem it is possible for new stems to form and branch off. And in the simplest cases these new stems are in essence just smaller copies of the original stem, with the same basic rules for growth and branching.

With this setup the succession of branchings can then be represented by steps in the evolution of a neighbor-independent substitution system in which the tip of each stem is at each step replaced by a collection of smaller stems in some fixed configuration.

Two examples of such substitution systems are shown in the pictures below. In both cases the rules are set up so that every stem in effect just branches into exactly three new stems at each step. And this

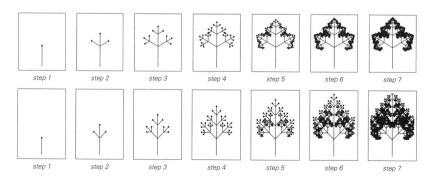

Steps in the evolution of substitution systems that provide simple models for the growth of plants. At each step every growing stem is replaced by a collection of three new stems according to the rules shown. For individual stems this type of branching is known in botany as monopodial.

means that the network of connections between stems necessarily has a very simple nested form. But if one looks at the actual geometrical arrangement of stems there is no longer such simplicity; indeed, despite the great simplicity of the underlying rules, considerable complexity is immediately evident even in the pictures at the bottom of the facing page.

The pictures on the next page show patterns obtained with various sequences of choices for the lengths and angles of new stems. In a few cases the patterns are quite simple; but in most cases they turn out to be highly complex—and remarkably diverse.

The pictures immediately remind one of the overall branching patterns of all sorts of plants—from algae to ferns to trees to many kinds of flowering plants. And no doubt it is from such simple rules of growth that most such overall branching patterns come.

But what about more detailed features of plants? Can they also be thought of as consequences of simple underlying rules of growth?

For many years I wondered in particular about the shapes of leaves. For among different plants there is tremendous diversity in such shapes—as illustrated in the pictures on page 403. Some plants have leaves with simple smooth boundaries that one might imagine could be described by traditional mathematical functions. Others have leaves with various configurations of sharp points. And still others have leaves with complex and seemingly somewhat random boundaries.

So given this diversity one might at first suppose that no single kind of underlying rule could be responsible for what is seen. But looking at arrays of pictures like the ones on the next page one makes a remarkable discovery: among the patterns that can be generated by simple substitution systems are ones whose outlines look extremely similar to those of a wide variety of types of leaves.

There are patterns with smooth edges that look like lily pads. There are patterns with sharp points that look like prickly leaves of various kinds. And there are patterns with intricate and seemingly somewhat random shapes that look like sycamore or grape leaves.

It has never in the past been at all clear how leaves get the shapes they do. Presumably most of the processes that are important take place while leaves are still folded up inside buds, and are not yet very solid.

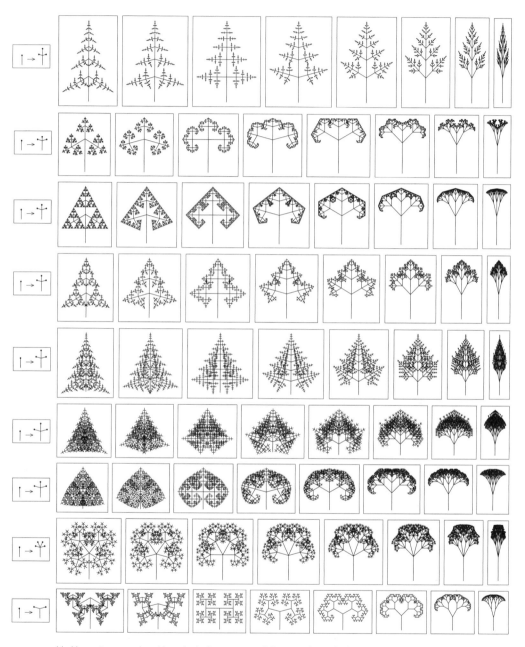

Limiting patterns produced by substitution systems of the type shown in the previous picture. The patterns on each row are obtained from rules that are set up to give branches with particular relative lengths. The angles between the branches are taken to increase by 15° in successive pictures across the row. Note that pictures shown on different rows are scaled differently—so that the initial vertical stem does not always appear with the same height. The similarity between pictures on this page and overall branching patterns and shapes of leaves in many kinds of plants is striking.

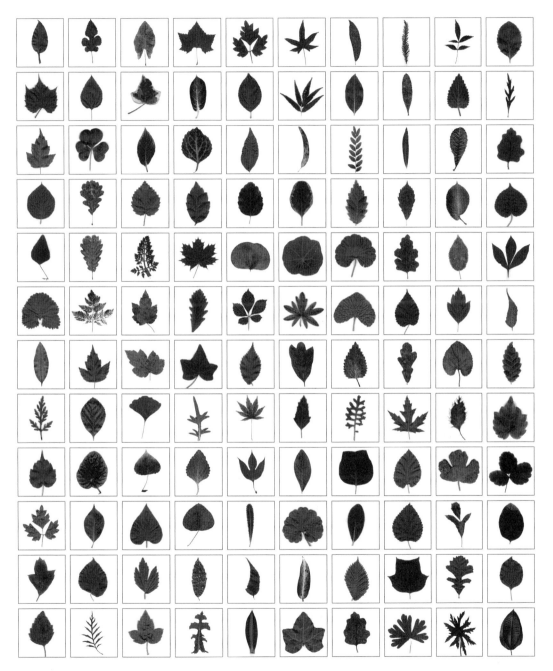

Examples of different kinds of leaves, mostly from common flowering plants. The diversity of shapes is remarkable, as is the similarity to the forms shown on the facing page. The leaves range in size from under an inch to many feet.

For although leaves typically expand significantly after they come out, the basic features of their shapes almost never seem to change.

There is some evidence that at least some aspects of the pattern of veins in a leaf are laid down before the main surface of the leaf is filled in, and perhaps the stems in the branching process I describe here correspond to precursors of structures related to veins. Indeed, the criss-crossing of veins in the leaves of higher plants may be not unrelated to the fact that stems in the pictures two pages ago often cross over—although certainly many of the veins in actual full-grown leaves are probably added long after the shapes of the leaves are determined.

One might at the outset have thought that leaves would get their shapes through some mechanism quite unrelated to other aspects of plant growth. But I strongly suspect that in fact the very same simple process of branching is ultimately responsible both for the overall forms of plants, and for the shapes of their leaves.

Quite possibly there will sometimes be at least some correspondence between the lengths and angles that appear in the rules for overall growth and for the growth of leaves. But in general the details of all these rules will no doubt depend on very specific characteristics of individual plants.

The distance before a new stem appears is, for example, probably determined by the rates of production and diffusion of plant hormones and related substances, and these rates will inevitably depend both on the thickness and mechanical structure of the stem, as well as on all kinds of biochemical properties of the plant. And when it comes to the angles between old and new stems I would not be surprised if these were governed by such microscopic details as individual shapes of cells and individual sequences of cell divisions.

The traditional intuition of biology would suggest that whenever one sees complexity—say in the shape of a leaf—it must have been generated for some particular purpose by some sophisticated process of natural selection. But what the pictures on the previous pages demonstrate is that in fact a high degree of complexity can arise in a sense quite effortlessly just as a consequence of following certain simple rules of growth.

No doubt some of the underlying properties of plants are indeed guided by natural selection. But what I strongly suspect is that in the vast majority of cases the occurrence of complexity—say in the shapes of leaves—is in essence just a side effect of the particular rules of growth that happen to result from the underlying properties of the plant.

The pictures on the next page show the array of possible forms that can be produced by rules in which each stem splits into exactly two new stems at each step. The vertical black line on the left-hand side of the page represents in effect the original stem at each step, and the pictures are arranged so that the one which appears at a given position on the page shows the pattern that is generated when the tip of the right-hand new stem goes to that position relative to the original stem shown on the left.

In some cases the patterns obtained are fairly simple. But even in these cases the pictures show that comparatively small changes in underlying rules can lead to much more complex patterns. And so if in the course of biological evolution gradual changes occur in the rules, it is almost inevitable that complex patterns will sometimes be seen.

But just how suddenly can the patterns change? To get some idea of this one can construct a kind of limit of the array on the next page in which the total number of pictures is in effect infinite, but only a specific infinitesimal region of each picture is shown. Page 407 gives results for four choices of the position of this region relative to the original stem. And instead of just displaying black or white depending on whether any part of the pattern lies in the region, the picture uses gray levels to indicate how close it comes.

The areas of solid black thus correspond to ranges of parameters in the underlying rule for which the patterns obtained always reach a particular position. But what we see is that at the edges of these areas there are often intricate structures with an essentially nested form. And the presence of such structures implies that at least with some ranges of parameters, even very small changes in underlying rules can lead to large changes in certain aspects of the patterns that are produced.

So what this suggests is that it is almost inevitable that features such as the shapes of leaves can sometimes change greatly even when the underlying properties of plants change only slightly. And I suspect

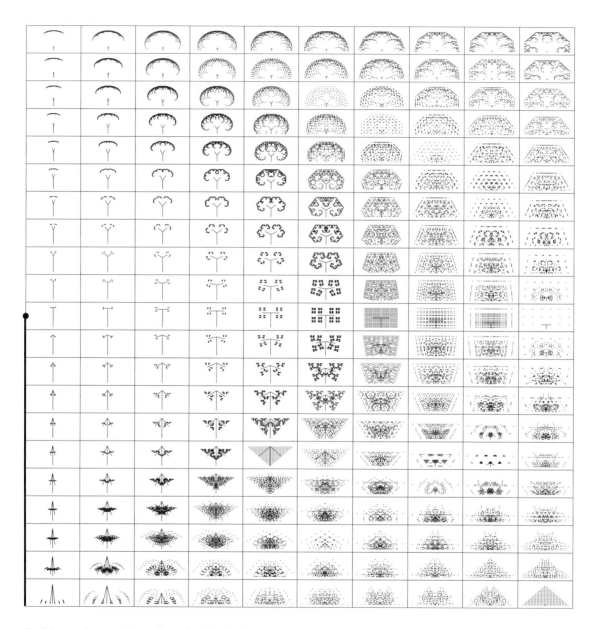

The full array of patterns that can be produced by simple substitution systems in which each stem branches into exactly two symmetrical stems at each step. The patterns are arranged on the page so that the pattern shown at a particular position corresponds to what is obtained with a rule in which the tip of the right-hand stem goes to that position (corrected for the aspect ratio of the array) relative to the original stem shown as a vertical line on the left-hand side of the page. In each case the result of 10 steps of evolution is shown, and the pictures are scaled so that all points above the bottom of the original stem can be included. Note that for rules outside of a distorted semicircle centered on the dot at the left-hand side of the page, and touching the three other sides of the page, the patterns generated grow at each step, rather than tending to a limit of fixed size.

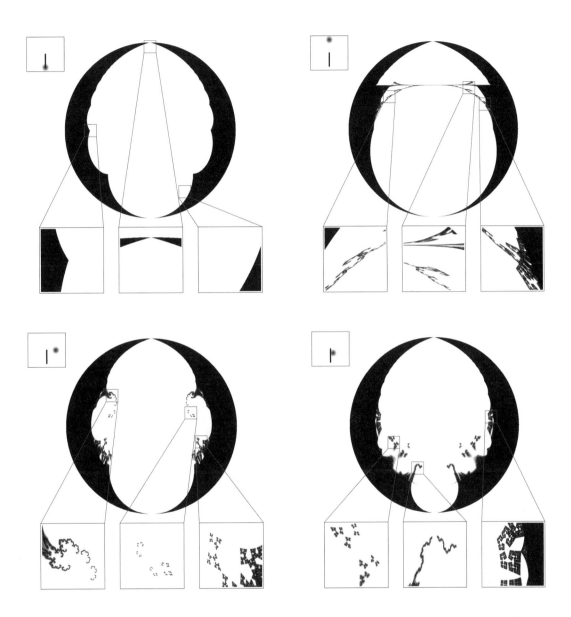

Maps of where in the space of parameters for the substitution systems on the facing page the patterns obtained overlap the region indicated in the icon at the top left of each picture. Black corresponds to complete overlap, while white corresponds to no overlap. The maps shown can be thought of as being made by taking an infinitely dense limit of the array of pictures on the facing page, but keeping only what one sees in each picture by looking through a peephole at a particular position relative to the original stem.

that this is precisely why such diverse shapes of leaves are occasionally seen even in plants that otherwise appear very similar.

But while features such as the shapes of leaves typically differ greatly between different plants, there are also some seemingly quite sophisticated aspects of plants that typically remain almost exactly the same across a huge range of species.

One example is the arrangement of sequences of plant organs or other elements around a stem. In some cases successive leaves, say, will always come out on opposite sides of a stem—180° apart. But considerably more common is for leaves to come out less than 180° apart, and in most plants the angle turns out to be essentially the same, and equal to almost exactly 137.5°.

It is already remarkable that such a definite angle arises in the arrangement of leaves—or so-called phyllotaxis—of so many plants. But it turns out that this very same angle also shows up in all sorts of other features of plants, as shown in the pictures at the top of the facing page. And although the geometry is different in different cases, the presence of a fixed angle close to 137.5° always leads to remarkably regular spiral patterns.

Over the years, much has been written about such patterns, and about their mathematical properties. For it turns out that an angle between successive elements of about 137.5° is equivalent to a rotation by a number of turns equal to the so-called golden ratio $(1 + \sqrt{5})/2 \simeq 1.618$ which arises in a wide variety of mathematical contexts—notably as the limiting ratio of Fibonacci numbers.

And no doubt in large part because of this elegant mathematical connection, it has usually come to be assumed that the 137.5° angle and the spiral patterns to which it leads must correspond to some kind of sophisticated optimization found by an elaborate process of natural selection.

But I do not believe that this is in fact the case. And instead what I strongly suspect is that the patterns are just inevitable consequences of a rather simple process of growth not unlike one that was already discussed, at least in general terms, nearly a century ago.

Examples of spiral arrangements of elements in various plant systems. The details of the final geometry are different in different cases. But in all cases it turns out that the original angle between successive elements is almost exactly 137.5°. The first row shows red cabbage (cut open), artichoke, asparagus, raspberry and strawberry. The first two objects on the last row are a pinecone and an acorn.

The positions of new plant organs or other elements around a stem are presumably determined by what happens in a small ring of material near the tip of the growing stem. And what I suspect is that a new element will typically form at a particular position around the ring if at that position the concentration of some chemical has reached a certain critical level.

But as soon as an element is formed, one can expect that it will deplete the concentration of the chemical in its local neighborhood, and thus inhibit further elements from forming nearby. Nevertheless, general processes in the growing stem will presumably make the concentration steadily rise throughout the ring of active material, and eventually this concentration will again get high enough at some position that it will cause another element to be formed.

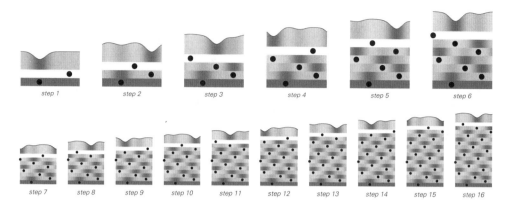

step 1   step 2   step 3   step 4   step 5   step 6

step 7 step 8 step 9 step 10 step 11 step 12 step 13 step 14 step 15 step 16

A simple model for the arrangement of leaves or other elements produced at the growing tip of a plant stem. The stem is taken to grow up the page, and for purposes of display it is unrolled into a line. The positions of leaves or other elements are indicated by black dots. The concentration of a chemical is indicated by gray level, and for the top line at each step, it is also plotted. The rule for the system places a new black dot at whatever position this concentration is largest. The black dot is then assumed to deplete the concentration around it, but the overall concentration is uniformly increased before the next step. It turns out that successive black dots rapidly become spaced at almost exactly 137.5°.

The pictures above show an example of this type of process. For purposes of display the ring of active material is unrolled into a line, and successive states of this line are shown one on top of each other going up the page. At each step a new element, indicated by a black dot, is taken to be generated at whatever position the concentration is maximal. And around this position the new element is then taken to produce a dip in concentration that is gradually washed out over the course of several steps.

The way the pictures are drawn, the angles between successive elements correspond to the horizontal distances between them. And although these distances vary somewhat for the first few steps, what we see in general is remarkably rapid convergence to a fixed distance—which turns out to correspond to an angle of almost exactly 137.5°.

So what happens if one changes the details of the model? In the extreme case where all memory of previous behavior is immediately damped out the first picture at the top of the facing page shows that successive elements form at 180° angles. And in the case where there is very little damping the last two pictures show that at least for a while elements can form at fairly random angles. But in the majority of cases one sees rather rapid convergence to almost precisely 137.5°.

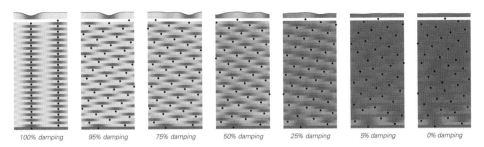

100% damping	95% damping	75% damping	50% damping	25% damping	5% damping	0% damping

Examples of changing the amount of damping used in the model on the facing page. 100% damping corresponds to increasing the overall concentration at each step so much that no memory of previous steps remains. 0% corresponds to no increase in overall concentration at each step. Away from these extreme cases, rapid convergence is seen to a spacing between black dots of almost exactly 137.5°.

So just how does this angle show up in actual plant systems? As the top pictures below demonstrate, the details depend on the geometry and relative growth rates of new elements and of the original stem. But in all cases very characteristic patterns are produced.

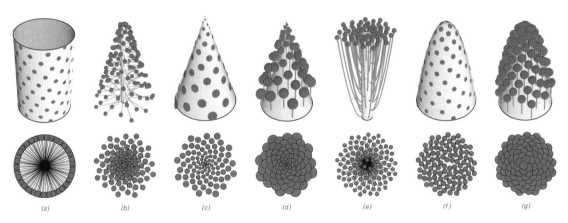

(a)	(b)	(c)	(d)	(e)	(f)	(g)

Examples of structures formed in various geometries by successively adding elements at a golden ratio angle 137.5°. Each of these structures is seen in one type of plant growth or another, as illustrated on page 409.

120°	130°	137°	137.5°	138°	140°	150°

Overall patterns formed by successively adding elements at a variety of different angles. In each case the nth element appears at coordinates $\sqrt{n}\ \{Cos[n\,\theta],\ Sin[n\,\theta]\}$. Stripes are seen if θ/π (with θ in radians) is easy to approximate by a rational number. (The size of the region before stripes appear depends on $Length[ContinuedFraction[\theta/\pi]]$.)

And as the bottom pictures on the previous page demonstrate, the forms of these patterns are very sensitive to the precise angle of successive elements: indeed, even a small deviation leads to patterns that are visually quite different. At first one might have assumed that to get a precise angle like 137.5° would require some kind of elaborate and highly detailed process. But just as in so many other situations that we have seen in this book, what we have seen is that in fact a very simple rule is all that is in the end needed.

One of the general features of plants is that most of their cells tend to develop fairly rigid cellulose walls which make it essentially impossible for new material to be added inside the volume of the plant, and so typically force new growth to occur only on the outside of the plant—most importantly at the tips of stems.

But when plants form sheets of material as in leaves or petals there is usually some flexibility for growth to occur within the sheet. And the pictures below show examples of what can happen if one starts with a flat disk and then adds different amounts of material in different places.

If more material is added near the center than near the edge, as in case (b), then the disk is forced to take on a cup shape similar to many

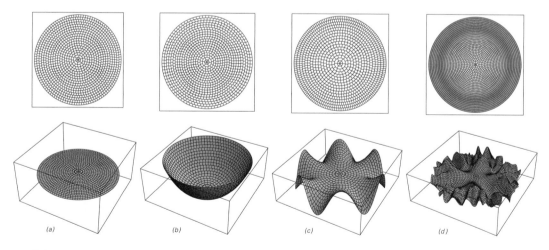

(a)   (b)   (c)   (d)

Disks with varying amounts of material at different distances from their centers. In the top row the disks are always flat, forcing the cells of material to vary in size and shape. In the bottom row, the disks form shapes in three dimensions in which all cells are the same size and shape. Relative to case (a), the amount of material going out from the center decreases linearly in case (b), increases linearly in case (c), and increases exponentially in case (d).

flowers. But if more material is added near the edge than near the center, as in case (c), then the sheet will become wavy at the edge, much like some leaves. And if the amount of material increases sufficiently rapidly from the center to the edge, as in case (d), then the disk will be forced to become highly corrugated, somewhat like a lettuce leaf.

So what about animals? To what extent are their mechanisms of growth the same as plants? If one looks at air passages or small blood vessels in higher animals then the patterns of branching one sees look similar to those in plants. But in most of their obvious structural features animals do not typically look much like plants at all. And in fact their mechanisms of growth mostly turn out to be rather different.

As a first example, consider a horn. One might have thought that, like a stem in a plant, a horn would grow by adding material at its tip. But in fact, like nails and hair, a horn instead grows by adding material at its base. And an immediate consequence of this is that the kind of branching that one sees in plants does not normally occur in horns.

But on the other hand coiling is common. For in order to get a structure that is perfectly straight, the rate at which material is added must be exactly the same on each side of the base. And if there is any difference, one edge of the structure that is produced will always end up being longer than the other, so that coiling will inevitably result, as in the pictures below.

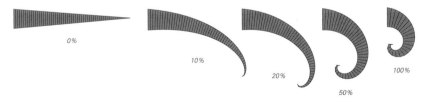

Idealized horns generated by progressively adding new material, with the amount of material on the upper edge of the base always being the specified percentage larger than the amount on the lower edge. These pictures can be viewed as one-dimensional analogs of those on the facing page.

And as has been thought for several centuries, it turns out that a three-dimensional version of this phenomenon is essentially what leads to the elaborate coiled structures that one sees in mollusc shells. For in a typical case, the animal which lives at the open end of the shell secretes new shell material faster on one side than the other, causing the shell to grow in a spiral. The rates at which shell material is secreted at different points around the opening are presumably determined by details of the anatomy of the animal. And it turns out that—much as we saw in the case of branching structures earlier in this section—even fairly small changes in such rates can have quite dramatic effects on the overall shape of the shell.

The pictures below show three examples of what can happen, while the facing page shows the effects of systematically varying certain growth rates. And what one sees is that even though the same very simple underlying model is used, there are all sorts of visually very different geometrical forms that can nevertheless be produced.

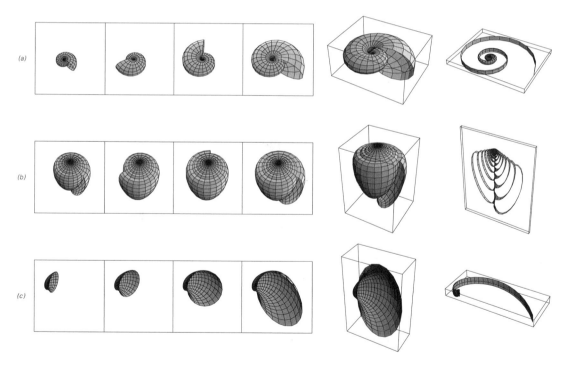

A simple model for the growth of mollusc shells. In each case new shell material is progressively added at the open end of the shell. The rule on the left shows the amount of material added at each stage at different points around the opening; the line from the center indicates the progressive lateral displacement of the opening. Case (a) is typical of a nautilus shell, (b) of a cone shell and (c) of one-half of a clam shell. All shells produced by adding material according to fixed rules of the kind shown here have the property that throughout their growth they maintain the same overall shape.

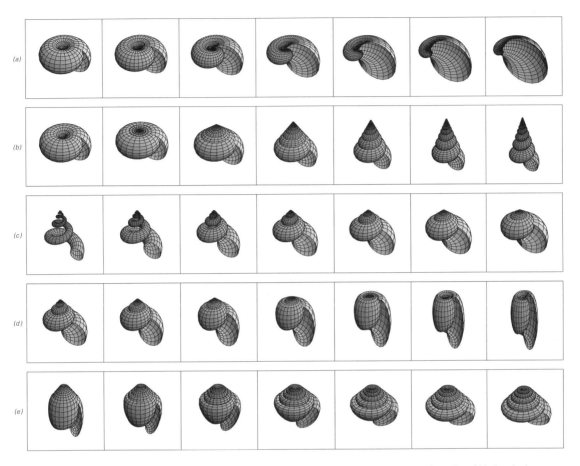

The effects of varying five simple features of the rule for the growth of a mollusc shell: (a) the overall factor by which the size increases in the course of each revolution; (b) the relative amount by which the opening is displaced downward at each revolution; (c) the size of the opening relative to the overall size of the shell; (d) the elongation of the opening; (e) the orientation of elongation in the opening. The pictures at the beginning and end of each row correspond roughly to the following: (a) pond snail shell, cockle shell; (b) pond snail shell, horn shell; (c) worm shell, bonnet shell; (d) periwinkle shell, cowrie shell; (e) olive shell, sundial shell.

So out of all the possible forms, which ones actually occur in real molluscs? The remarkable fact illustrated on the next page is that essentially all of them are found in some kind of mollusc or another.

If one just saw a single mollusc shell, one might well think that its elaborate form must have been carefully crafted by some long process of natural selection. But what we now see is that in fact all the different forms that are observed are in effect just consequences of the

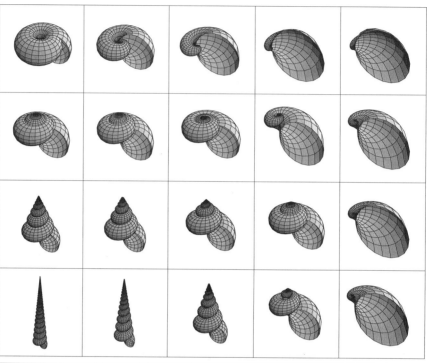

Shell shapes generated by the simple model and found in nature. The array shows systematic variation of the first two parameters from the previous page. Similar arrays could be made for the other parameters.

application of three-dimensional geometry to very simple underlying rules of growth. And so once again therefore natural selection cannot reasonably be considered the source of the elaborate forms we see.

Away from mollusc shells, coiled structures—like branched ones—are not especially common in animals. Indeed, the vast majority of animals do not tend to have overall forms that are dominated by any single kind of structure. Rather, they are usually made up of a collection of separate identifiable parts, like heads, tails, legs, eyes and so on, all with their own specific structure.

Sometimes some of these parts are repeated, perhaps in a sequence of segments, or perhaps in some kind of two-dimensional array. And very often the whole animal is covered by a fairly uniform outer skin. But the presence of many different kinds of parts is in the end one of the most obvious features of many animals.

So how do all these parts get produced? The basic mechanism seems to be that at different places and different times inside a developing animal different sections of its genetic program end up getting used—causing different kinds of growth to occur, and different structures to be produced. And part of what makes this possible is that particularly at the stage of the embryo most cells in an animal are not extremely rigid—so that even when different pieces of the animal grow quite differently they can still deform so as to fit together.

Usually there are some elements—such as bones—that eventually do become rigid. But the crucial point is that at the stage when the basic form of an animal is determined most of these elements are not yet rigid. And this allows various processes to occur that would otherwise be impossible.

Probably the most important of these is folding. For folding is not only involved in producing shapes such as teeth surfaces and human ear lobes, but is also critical in allowing flat sheets of tissue to form the kinds of pockets and tubes that are so common inside animals.

Folding seems to occur for a variety of reasons. Sometimes it is most likely the direct result of tugging by microscopic fibers. And in other cases it is probably a consequence of growth occurring at different rates in different places, as in the pictures on page 412.

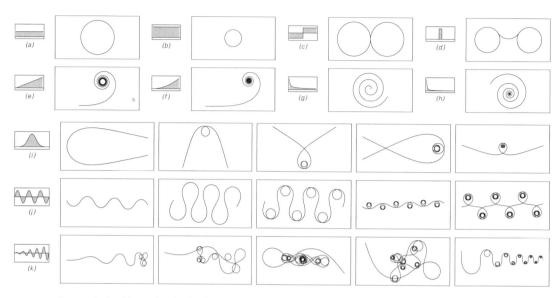

Curves obtained by varying the local curvature according to definite rules as one goes from one end to the other. Each sequence of curves shows what happens when the local curvature is multiplied by a progressively larger factor. The local curvature at any particular point is defined to be the reciprocal of the radius of a circle that approximates the curve at that point. The formulas for local curvature as a function of arc length for each set of pictures are as follows: 1 (circle); s (Cornu spiral or clothoid); s^2; $1/\sqrt{s}$ (involute of circle); $1/s$ (logarithmic or equiangular spiral); $1/s^2$; e^{-s^2}; $Sin[s]$; $s\,Sin[s]$. The curvature functions $f[s]$ can be thought of as specifying how much to turn a vehicle at every moment in order to keep it driving along the curve. The curves have been rotated so as to fit into the frames provided.

But what kinds of shapes can folding produce? The pictures above show what happens when the local curvature—which is essentially the local rate of folding—is taken to vary according to several simple rules as one goes along a curve. In a few cases the shapes produced are rather simple. But in most cases they are fairly complicated. And it takes only very simple rules to generate shapes that look like the villi and other corrugated structures one often sees in animals.

In addition to folding, there are other kinds of processes that are made possible by the lack of rigidity in a developing animal. One is furrowing or tearing of tissue through a loss of adhesion between cells. And another is explicit migration of individual cells based on chemical or immunological affinities.

But how do all these various processes get organized to produce an actual animal? If one looks at the sequence of events that take place in a typical ánimal embryo they at first seem remarkably haphazard. But presumably the main thing that is going on—as mentioned above—is that at different places and different times different sections of the underlying genetic program are being used, and these different sections can lead to very different kinds of behavior. Some may produce just uniform growth. Others may lead to various kinds of local folding. And still others may cause regions of tissue to die—thereby for example allowing separate fingers and toes to emerge from a single sheet of tissue.

But just how is it determined what section of the underlying genetic program should be used at what point in the development of the animal? At first, one might think that each individual cell that comes into existence might use a different section of the underlying genetic program. And in very simple animals with just a few hundred cells this is most likely what in effect happens.

But in general it seems to be not so much individual cells as regions of the developing animal that end up using different sections of the underlying program. Indeed, the typical pattern seems to be that whenever a part of an animal has grown to be a few tenths of a millimeter across, that part can break up into a handful of smaller regions which each use a different section of the underlying genetic program.

So how does this work? What appears to be the case is that there are cells which produce chemicals whose concentrations decrease over distances of a few tenths of a millimeter. And what has been discovered in the past decade or so is that in all animals—as well as plants—there are a handful of so-called homeobox genes which seem to become active or inactive at particular concentration levels and which control what section of the underlying genetic program will be used.

The existence of a fixed length scale at which such processes occur then almost inevitably implies that an embryo must develop in a somewhat hierarchical fashion. For at a sufficiently early stage, the whole embryo will be so small that it can contain only a handful of regions that use different sections of the genetic program. And at this stage there may, for example, be a leg region, but there will not yet be a distinct foot region.

As the embryo grows, however, the leg region will eventually become large enough that it can differentiate into several separate regions. And at this point, a distinct foot region can appear. Then, when the foot region becomes large enough, it too can break into separate regions that will, say, turn into bone or soft tissue. And when a region that will turn into bone becomes large enough, it can break into further regions that will, say, yield separate individual bones.

If at every stage the tissue in each region produced grows at the same rate, and all that differs is what final type of cells will exist in each region, then inevitably a simple and highly regular overall structure will emerge, as in the idealized picture below. With different substitution rules for each type of cell, the structure will in general be nested. And in fact there are, for example, some parts of the skeletons of animals that do seem to exhibit, at least roughly, a few levels of nesting of this kind.

A schematic illustration of the successive subdivisions which presumably occur in the growth of animals. Here the subdivisions are taken to occur in two directions, always giving three simple rectangles which all grow at the same rate. In practice, the geometry will usually be much more complex.

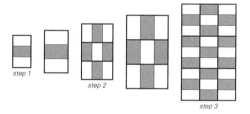

step 1

step 2

step 3

But in most cases there is no such obvious nesting of this kind. One reason for this is that a region may break not into a simple line of smaller regions, but into concentric circles or into some collection of regions in a much more complicated arrangement—say of the kind that I discuss in the next section. And perhaps even more important, a region may break into smaller regions that grow at different rates, and that potentially fold over or deform in other ways. And when this happens, the geometry that develops will in turn affect the way that subsequent regions break up.

The idea that the basic mechanism for producing different parts of animals is that regions a few tenths of a millimeter across break into separate smaller regions turns out in the end to be strangely similar to the idea that stems of plants whose tips are perhaps a millimeter across grow by splitting off smaller stems. And indeed it is even known that some of the genetic phenomena involved are extremely similar.

But the point is that because of the comparative rigidity of plants during their most important period of growth, only structures that involve fairly explicit branching can be produced. In animals, however, the lack of rigidity allows a vastly wider range of structures to appear, since now tissue in different regions need not just grow uniformly, but can change shape in a whole variety of ways.

By the time an animal hatches or is born, its basic form is usually determined, and there are bones or other rigid elements in place to maintain this form. But in most animals there is still a significant further increase in size. So how does this work?

Some bones in effect just expand by adding material to their outer surface. But in many cases, bones are in effect divided into sections, and growth occurs between these sections. Thus, for example, the long bones in the arms and legs have regions of growth at each end of their main shafts. And the skull is divided into a collection of pieces that each grow around their edges.

Typically there are somewhat different rates of growth for different parts of an animal—leading, for example, to the decrease in relative head size usually seen from birth to adulthood. And this inevitably means that there will be at least some changes in the shapes of animals as they mature.

But what if one compares different breeds or species of animals? At first, their shapes may seem quite different. But it turns out that among animals of a particular family or even order, it is very common to find that their overall shapes are in fact related by fairly simple and smooth geometrical transformations.

And indeed it seems likely that—much like the leaves and shells that we discussed earlier in this section—differences between the shapes and forms of animals may often be due in large part merely to different patterns in the rates of growth for their different parts.

Needless to say, just like with leaves and shells, such differences can have effects that are quite dramatic both visually and mechanically— turning, say, an animal that walks on four legs into one that walks on two. And, again just like with leaves and shells, it seems likely that among the animals we see are ones that correspond to a fair fraction of the possible choices for relative rates of growth.

We began this section by asking what underlying rules of growth would be needed to produce the kind of diversity and complexity that we see in the forms of plants and animals. And in each case that we have examined what we have found is that remarkably simple rules seem to suffice. Indeed, in most cases the basic rules actually seem to be somewhat simpler than those that operate in many non-biological systems. But what allows the striking diversity that we see in biological systems is that different organisms and different species of organisms are always based on at least slightly different rules.

In the previous section I argued that for the most part such rules will not be carefully chosen by natural selection, but instead will just be picked almost at random from among the possibilities. From experience with traditional mathematical models, however, one might then assume that this would inevitably imply that all plants and animals would have forms that look quite similar.

But what we have discovered in this book is that when one uses rules that correspond to simple programs, rather than, say, traditional mathematical equations, it is very common to find that different rules lead to quite different—and often highly complex—patterns of behavior. And it is this basic phenomenon that I suspect is responsible for most of the diversity and complexity that we see in the forms of plants and animals.

Biological Pigmentation Patterns

At a visual level, pigmentation patterns represent some of the most obvious examples of complexity in biological organisms. And in the past it has usually been assumed that to get the kind of complexity that one sees in such patterns there must be some highly complex underlying mechanism, presumably related to optimization through natural selection.

Following the discoveries in this book, however, what I strongly suspect is that in fact the vast majority of pigmentation patterns in biological organisms are instead generated by processes whose basic rules are extremely simple—and are often chosen essentially at random.

The pictures below shows some typical examples of patterns found on mollusc shells. Many of these patterns are quite simple. But some are highly complex. Yet looking at these patterns one notices a remarkable similarity to patterns that we have seen many times before in this book—generated by simple one-dimensional cellular automata.

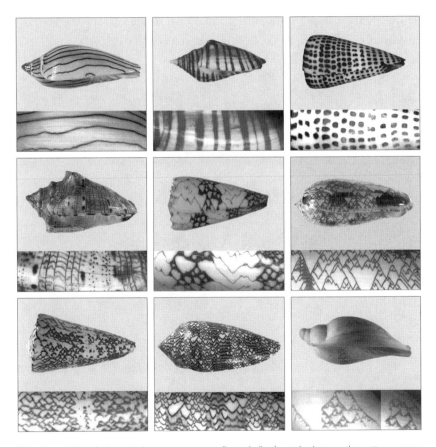

Typical examples of pigmentation patterns on mollusc shells. In each close-up the pattern grows from top to bottom, just like in a one-dimensional cellular automaton. Patterns with triangles are often said to have a "tent" or "divaricate" form. The shell on the bottom right is a slightly rare specimen where something close to an explicit nested pattern can be seen. Most of the shells are between one and four inches long; the one on the bottom right is nine inches long. The patterns are all various shades of brown on roughly white backgrounds. The shells are the following types: first row: Elliot's volute, vexillate volute, lettered cone; second row: music volute, banded marble cone, tent olive; third row: bough cone, textile cone, false melon volute (*Livonia mammilla*).

This similarity is, I believe, no coincidence. A mollusc shell, like a one-dimensional cellular automaton, in effect grows one line at a time, with new shell material being produced by a lip of soft tissue at the edge of the animal inside the shell. Quite how the pigment on the shell is laid down is not completely clear. There are undoubtedly elements in the soft tissue that at any point either will or will not secrete pigment. And presumably these elements have certain interactions with each other. And given this, the simplest hypothesis in a sense is that the new state of the element is determined from the previous state of its neighbors— just as in a one-dimensional cellular automaton.

Examples of patterns produced by the evolution of each of the simplest possible symmetrical one-dimensional cellular automaton rules, starting from a random initial condition. The types of patterns obtained show striking similarities to those seen on mollusc shells from the previous page.

But which specific cellular automaton rule will any given mollusc use? The pictures at the bottom of the facing page show all the possible symmetrical rules that involve two colors and nearest neighbors. And comparing the patterns in these pictures with patterns on actual mollusc shells, one notices the remarkable fact that the range of patterns that occur in the two cases is extremely similar.

Traditional ideas might have suggested that each kind of mollusc would carefully optimize the pattern on its shell so as to avoid predators or to attract mates or prey. But what I think is much more likely is that these patterns are instead generated by rules that are in effect chosen at random from among a collection of the simplest possibilities. And what this means is that insofar as complexity occurs in such patterns it is in a sense a coincidence. It is not that some elaborate mechanism has specially developed to produce it. Rather, it just arises as an inevitable consequence of the basic phenomenon discovered in this book that simple rules will often yield complex behavior.

And indeed it turns out that in many species of molluscs the patterns on their shells—both simple and complex—are completely hidden by an opaque skin throughout the life of the animal, and so presumably cannot possibly have been determined by any careful process of optimization or natural selection.

So what about pigmentation patterns on other kinds of animals? Mollusc shells are almost unique in having patterns that are built up one line at a time; much more common is for patterns to develop all at once all over a surface.

Most often what seems to happen is that at some point in the growth of an embryo, precursors of pigment-producing cells appear on its surface, and groups of these cells associated with pigments of different colors then become arranged in a definite pattern. Typically each individual group of cells is initially some fraction of a tenth of a millimeter across. But since different parts of an animal usually grow at different rates, the final pattern that one sees on an adult animal ends up being scaled differently in different places—so that, for example, the pattern is smaller in scale on the head of an animal, since the head grows more slowly.

Typical examples of pigmentation patterns on animals. Note that many very different animals end up having remarkably similar patterns.

The pictures on the facing page show typical examples of pigmentation patterns in animals, and demonstrate that even across a vast range of different types of animals just a few kinds of patterns occur over and over again. So how are these patterns produced? Even though some of them seem quite complex, it turns out that once again there is a rather simple kind of rule that can account for them.

The idea is that when a pattern forms, the color of each element will tend to be the same as the average color of nearby elements, and opposite to the average color of elements further away. Such an effect could have its origin in the production and diffusion of activator and inhibitor chemicals, or, for example, in actual motion of different types of cells. But regardless of its origin, the effect itself can readily be captured just by setting up a two-dimensional cellular automaton with appropriate rules.

The pictures below show what happens with two slightly different choices for the relative importance of elements that are further away. In both cases, starting from a random distribution of black and white elements there quickly emerge definite patterns—in the first case a collection of spots, and in the second case a maze-like or labyrinthine structure.

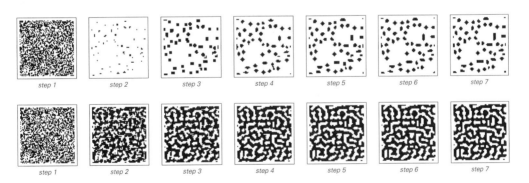

Evolution of simple two-dimensional cellular automata in which the color of each cell at each step is determined by looking at a weighted sum of the average colors of cells up to distance 3 away. In both rules shown the cell itself and its nearest neighbors enter with weight 1. Cells at distances 2 and 3 enter with negative weights— -0.4 per cell for the first rule, and -0.2 for the second. A cell becomes black if the weighted sum is positive, and white otherwise. Starting from random initial conditions, both rules quickly evolve to stationary states that look very much like pigmentation patterns seen in animals.

The next page shows the final patterns obtained with a whole array of different choices of weightings for elements at different distances. A certain range of patterns emerges—almost all of which turn out to be quite similar to patterns that one sees on actual animals.

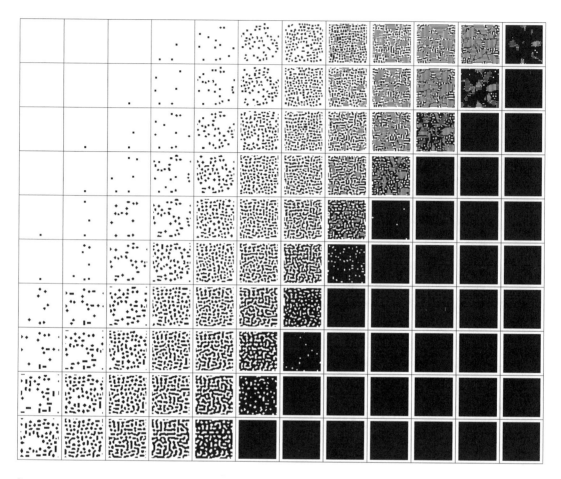

Patterns generated by rules of the type shown on the previous page, with a range of choices for the weights of cells at distances 2 and 3. Weights vary from -0.9 to 0 down the page for distance 2, and from -0.7 to 0.4 across the page for distance 3. In all cases the evolution starts from the same random initial condition, and is continued until it stabilizes. Note that pigmentation patterns for actual animals may contain either larger or smaller numbers of elements than the patterns shown here.

But all of these patterns in a sense have the same basic form in every direction. Yet there are many animals whose pigmentation patterns exhibit stripes with a definite orientation. Sometimes these stripes are highly regular, and can potentially arise from any of the possible mechanisms that yield repetitive behavior. But in cases where the stripes are less regular they typically look very much like the patterns generated in the pictures at the top of the facing page using a version of the simple mechanism described above.

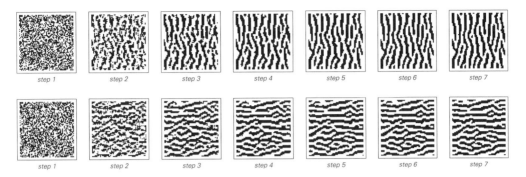

step 1   step 2   step 3   step 4   step 5   step 6   step 7

step 1   step 2   step 3   step 4   step 5   step 6   step 7

Examples of rules in which cells in the horizontal and vertical directions are weighted differently. In the first case, cells at distances 2 and 3 only have an effect in the vertical direction; in the second case, they only have an effect in the horizontal direction. The result is the formation of either vertical or horizontal stripes.

Financial Systems

During the development of the ideas in this book I have been asked many times whether they might apply to financial systems. There is no doubt that they do, and as one example I will briefly discuss here what is probably the most obvious feature of essentially all financial markets: the apparent randomness with which prices tend to fluctuate.

Whether one looks at stocks, bonds, commodities, currencies, derivatives or essentially any other kind of financial instrument, the sequences of prices that one sees at successive times show some overall trends, but also exhibit varying amounts of apparent randomness.

So what is the origin of this randomness?

In the most naive economic theory, price is a reflection of value, and the value of an asset is equal to the total of all future earnings—such as dividends—which will be obtained from it, discounted for the interest that will be lost from having to wait to get these earnings.

With this view, however, it seems hard to understand why there should be any significant fluctuations in prices at all. What is usually said is that prices are in fact determined not by true value, but rather by the best estimates of that value that can be obtained at any given time. And it is then assumed that these estimates are ultimately affected by all sorts of events that go on in the world, making random movements in prices in a sense just reflections of random changes going on in the outside environment.

But while this may be a dominant effect on timescales of order weeks or months—and in some cases perhaps even hours or days—it is difficult to believe that it can account for the apparent randomness that is often seen on timescales as short as minutes or even seconds.

In addition, occasionally one can identify situations of seemingly pure speculation in which trading occurs without the possibility of any significant external input—and in such situations prices tend to show more, rather than less, seemingly random fluctuations.

And knowing this, one might then think that perhaps random fluctuations are just an inevitable feature of the way that prices adjust to their correct values. But in negotiations between two parties, it is common to see fairly smooth convergence to a final price. And certainly one can construct algorithms that operate between larger numbers of parties that would also lead to fairly smooth behavior.

So in actual markets there is presumably something else going on. And no doubt part of it is just that the sequence of trades whose prices are recorded are typically executed by a sequence of different entities—whether they be humans, organizations or programs—each of which has its own detailed ways of deciding on an appropriate price.

But just as in so many other systems that we have studied in this book, once there are sufficiently many separate elements in a system, it is reasonable to expect that the overall collective behavior that one sees will go beyond the details of individual elements.

It is sometimes claimed that it is somehow inevitable that markets must be random, since otherwise money could be made by predicting them. Yet many people believe that they make money in just this way every day. And beyond certain simple situations, it is difficult to see how feedback mechanisms could exist that would systematically remove predictable elements whenever they were used.

No doubt randomness helps in maintaining some degree of stability in markets—just as it helps in maintaining stability in many other kinds of systems that we have discussed in this book. Indeed, most markets are set up so that extreme instabilities associated with certain kinds of loss of randomness are prevented—sometimes by explicit suspension of trading.

But why is there randomness in markets in the first place?

Practical experience suggests that particularly on short timescales much of the randomness that one sees is purely a consequence of internal dynamics in the market, and has little if anything to do with the nature or value of what is being traded.

So how can one understand what is going on? One needs a basic model for the operation and interaction of a large number of entities in a market. But traditional mathematics, with its emphasis on reducing everything to a small number of continuous numerical functions, has rather little to offer along these lines.

The idea of thinking in terms of programs seems, however, much more promising. Indeed, as a first approximation one can imagine that much as in a cellular automaton entities in a market could follow simple rules based on the behavior of other entities.

To be at all realistic one would have to set up an elaborate network to represent the flow of information between different entities. And one would have to assign fairly complicated rules to each entity— certainly as complicated as the rules in a typical programmed trading system. But from what we have learned in this book it seems likely that this kind of complexity in the underlying structure of the system will not have a crucial effect on its overall behavior.

And so as a minimal idealization one can for example try viewing a market as being like a simple one-dimensional cellular automaton. Each cell then corresponds to a single trading entity, and the color of the cell at a particular step specifies whether that entity chooses to buy or sell at that step. One can imagine all sorts of schemes by which such colors could be updated. But as a very simple idealization of the way that information flows in a market, one can, for example, take each color to be given by a fixed rule that is based on each entity looking at the actions of its neighbors on the previous step.

With traditional intuition one would assume that such a simple model must have extremely simple behavior, and certainly nothing like what is seen in a real market. But as we have discovered in this book, simple models do not necessarily have simple behavior. And indeed the picture below shows an example of the behavior that can occur.

An example of a very simple idealized model of a market. Each cell corresponds to an entity that either buys or sells on each step. The behavior of a given cell is determined by looking at the behavior of its two neighbors on the step before according to the rule shown. The plot below gives as a rough analog of a market price the running difference of the total numbers of black and white cells at successive steps. And although there are patches of predictability that can be seen in the complete behavior of the system the plot on the right looks in many respects random.

In real markets, it is usually impossible to see in detail what each entity is doing. Indeed, often all that one knows is the sequence of prices at which trades are executed. And in a simple cellular automaton the rough analog of this is the running difference of the total numbers of black and white cells obtained on successive steps.

And as soon as the underlying rule for the cellular automaton is such that information will eventually propagate from one entity to all others—in effect a minimal version of an efficient market hypothesis—it is essentially inevitable that running totals of numbers of cells will exhibit significant randomness.

One can always make the underlying system more complicated—say by having a network of cells, or by allowing different cells to have different and perhaps changing rules. But although this will make it more difficult to recognize definite rules even if one looks at the complete behavior of every element in the system, it does not affect the basic point that there is randomness that can intrinsically be generated by the evolution of the system.

9

Fundamental Physics

The Problems of Physics

In the previous chapter, we saw that many important aspects of a wide variety of everyday systems can be understood by thinking in terms of simple programs. But what about fundamental physics? Can ideas derived from studying simple programs also be applied there?

Fundamental physics is the area in which traditional mathematical approaches to science have had their greatest success. But despite this success, there are still many central issues that remain quite unresolved. And in this chapter my purpose is to consider some of these issues in the light of what we have learned from studying simple programs.

It might at first not seem sensible to try to use simple programs as a basis for understanding fundamental physics. For some of the best established features of physical systems—such as conservation of energy or equivalence of directions in space—seem to have no obvious analogs in most of the programs we have discussed so far in this book.

As we will see, it is in fact possible for simple programs to show these kinds of features. But it turns out that some of the most important unresolved issues in physics concern phenomena that are in a sense more general—and do not depend much on such features.

And indeed what we will see in this chapter is that remarkably simple programs are often able to capture the essence of what is going on—even though traditional efforts have been quite unsuccessful.

Thus, for example, in the early part of this chapter I will discuss the so-called Second Law of Thermodynamics or Principle of Entropy Increase: the observation that many physical systems tend to become irreversibly more random as time progresses. And I will show that the essence of such behavior can readily be seen in simple programs.

More than a century has gone by since the Second Law was first formulated. Yet despite many detailed results in traditional physics, its origins have remained quite mysterious. But what we will see in this chapter is that by studying the Second Law in the context of simple programs, we will finally be able to get a clear understanding of why it so often holds—as well as of when it may not.

My approach in investigating issues like the Second Law is in effect to use simple programs as metaphors for physical systems. But can such programs in fact be more than that? And for example is it conceivable that at some level physical systems actually operate directly according to the rules of a simple program?

Looking at the laws of physics as we know them today, this might seem absurd. For at first the laws might seem much too complicated to correspond to any simple program. But one of the crucial discoveries of this book is that even programs with very simple underlying rules can yield great complexity.

And so it could be with fundamental physics. Underneath the laws of physics as we know them today it could be that there lies a very simple program from which all the known laws—and ultimately all the complexity we see in the universe—emerges.

To suppose that our universe is in essence just a simple program is certainly a bold hypothesis. But in the second part of this chapter I will describe some significant progress that I have made in investigating this hypothesis, and in working out the details of what kinds of simple programs might be involved.

There is still some distance to go. But from what I have found so far I am extremely optimistic that by using the ideas of this book the most fundamental problem of physics—and one of the ultimate problems of all of science—may finally be within sight of being solved.

The Notion of Reversibility

At any particular step in the evolution of a system like a cellular automaton the underlying rule for the system tells one how to proceed to the next step. But what if one wants to go backwards? Can one deduce from the arrangement of black and white cells at a particular step what the arrangement of cells must have been on previous steps?

All current evidence suggests that the underlying laws of physics have this kind of reversibility. So this means that given a sufficiently precise knowledge of the state of a physical system at the present time, it is therefore possible to deduce not only what the system will do in the future, but also what it did in the past.

In the first cellular automaton shown below it is also straightforward to do this. For any cell that has one color at a particular step must always have had the opposite color on the step before.

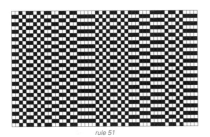
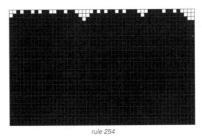

rule 51   *rule 254*

Examples of cellular automata that are and are not reversible. Rule 51 is reversible, so that it preserves enough information to allow one to go backwards from any particular step as well as forwards. Rule 254 is not reversible, since it always evolves to uniform black and preserves no information about the arrangement of cells on earlier steps.

But the second cellular automaton works differently, and does not allow one to go backwards. For after just a few steps, it makes every cell black, regardless of what it was before—with the result that there is no way to tell what color might have occurred on previous steps.

There are many examples of systems in nature which seem to organize themselves a little like the second case above. And indeed the conflict between this and the known reversibility of underlying laws of physics is related to the subject of the next section in this chapter.

But my purpose here is to explore what kinds of systems can be reversible. And of the 256 elementary cellular automata with two colors and nearest-neighbor rules, only the six shown below turn out to be reversible. And as the pictures demonstrate, all of these exhibit fairly trivial behavior, in which only rather simple transformations are ever made to the initial configuration of cells.

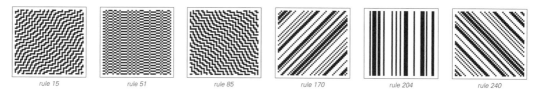

| rule 15 | rule 51 | rule 85 | rule 170 | rule 204 | rule 240 |

Examples of the behavior of the six elementary cellular automata that are reversible. In all cases the transformations made to the initial conditions are simple enough that it is straightforward to go backwards as well as forwards in the evolution.

So is it possible to get more complex behavior while maintaining reversibility? There are a total of 7,625,597,484,987 cellular automata with three colors and nearest-neighbor rules, and searching through these one finds just 1800 that are reversible. Of these 1800, many again exhibit simple behavior, much like the pictures above. But some exhibit more complex behavior, as in the pictures below.

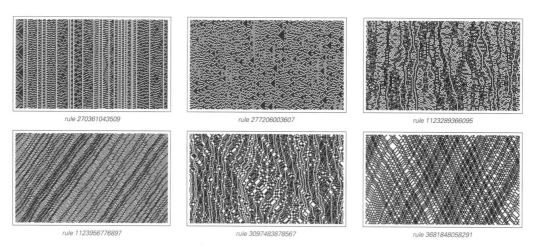

| rule 270361043509 | rule 277206003607 | rule 1123289366095 |
| rule 1123956776897 | rule 3097483878567 | rule 3681848058291 |

Examples of some of the 1800 reversible cellular automata with three colors and nearest-neighbor rules. Even though these systems exhibit complex behavior that scrambles the initial conditions, all of them are still reversible, so that starting from the configuration of cells at the bottom of each picture, it is always possible to deduce the configurations on all previous steps.

How can one now tell that such systems are reversible? It is no longer true that their evolution leads only to simple transformations of the initial conditions. But one can still check that starting with the specific configuration of cells at the bottom of each picture, one can evolve backwards to get to the top of the picture. And given a particular rule it turns out to be fairly straightforward to do a detailed analysis that allows one to prove or disprove its reversibility.

But in trying to understand the range of behavior that can occur in reversible systems it is often convenient to consider classes of cellular automata with rules that are specifically constructed to be reversible. One such class is illustrated below. The idea is to have rules that explicitly remain the same even if they are turned upside-down, thereby interchanging the roles of past and future.

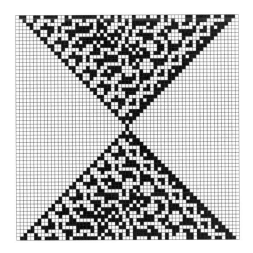

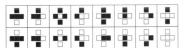

An example of a cellular automaton that is explicitly set up to be reversible. The rule for the system remains unchanged if all its elements are turned upside-down— effectively interchanging the roles of past and future. Patterns produced by the rule must exhibit the same time reversal symmetry, as shown on the left. The specific rule used here is based on taking elementary rule 214, then adding the specification that the new color of a cell should be inverted whenever the cell was black two steps back. Note that by allowing a total of four rather than two colors, a version of the rule that depends only on the immediately preceding step can be constructed.

Such rules can be constructed by taking ordinary cellular automata and adding dependence on colors two steps back.

The resulting rules can be run both forwards and backwards. In each case they require knowledge of the colors of cells on not one but two successive steps. Given this knowledge, however, the rules can be used to determine the configuration of cells on either future or past steps.

The next two pages show examples of the behavior of such cellular automata with both random and simple initial conditions.

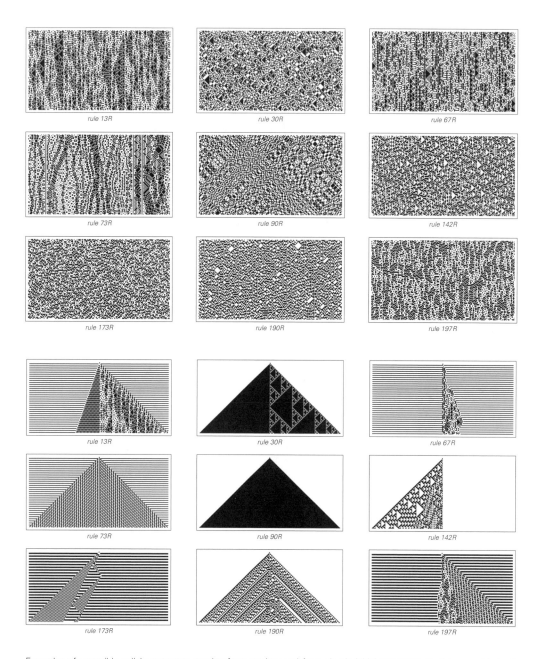

Examples of reversible cellular automata starting from random and from simple initial conditions. In the upper block of pictures, every cell is chosen to be black or white with equal probability on the two successive first steps. In the lower block of pictures, only the center cell is taken to be black on these steps.

rule 150R

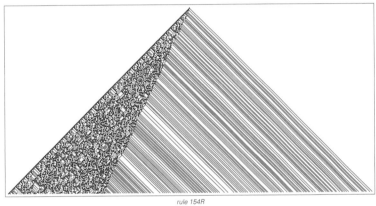

rule 154R

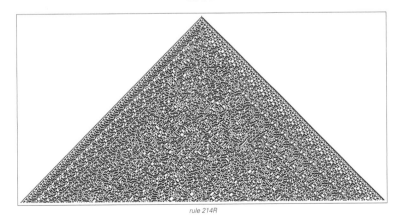

rule 214R

The evolution of three reversible cellular automata for 300 steps. In the first case, a regular nested pattern is obtained. In the other cases, the patterns show many features of randomness.

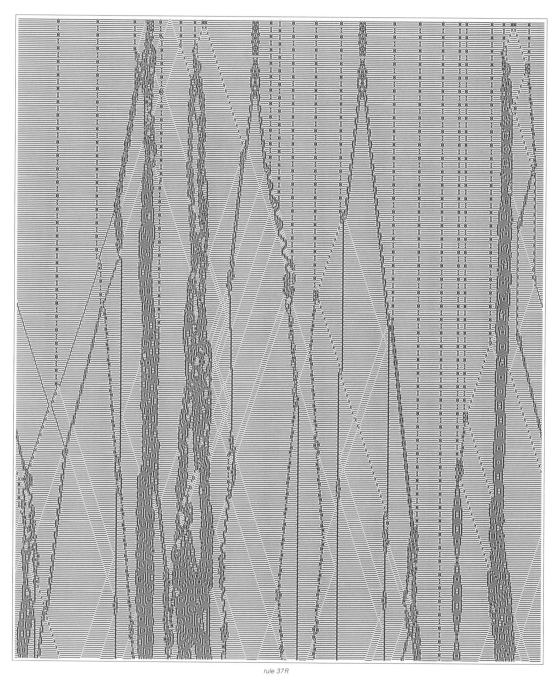

rule 37R

An example of a reversible cellular automaton whose evolution supports localized structures. Because of the reversibility of the underlying rule, every collision must be able to occur equally well when its initial and final states are interchanged.

In some cases, the behavior is fairly simple, and the patterns obtained have simple repetitive or nested structures. But in many cases, even with simple initial conditions, the patterns produced are highly complex, and seem in many respects random.

The reversibility of the underlying rules has some obvious consequences, such as the presence of triangles pointing sideways but not down. But despite their reversibility, the rules still manage to produce the kinds of complex behavior that we have seen in cellular automata and many other systems throughout this book.

So what about localized structures?

The picture on the facing page demonstrates that these can also occur in reversible systems. There are some constraints on the details of the kinds of collisions that are possible, but reversible rules typically tend to work very much like ordinary ones.

So in the end it seems that even though only a very small fraction of possible systems have the property of being reversible, such systems can still exhibit behavior just as complex as one sees anywhere else.

Irreversibility and the Second Law of Thermodynamics

All the evidence we have from particle physics and elsewhere suggests that at a fundamental level the laws of physics are precisely reversible. Yet our everyday experience is full of examples of seemingly irreversible phenomena. Most often, what happens is that a system which starts in a fairly regular or organized state becomes progressively more and more random and disorganized. And it turns out that this phenomenon can already be seen in many simple programs.

The picture at the top of the next page shows an example based on a reversible cellular automaton of the type discussed in the previous section. The black cells in this system act a little like particles which bounce around inside a box and interact with each other when they collide.

At the beginning the particles are placed in a simple arrangement at the center of the box. But over the course of time the picture shows that the arrangement of particles becomes progressively more random.

A reversible cellular automaton that exhibits seemingly irreversible behavior. Starting from an initial condition in which all black cells or particles lie at the center of a box, the distribution becomes progressively more random. Such behavior appears to be the central phenomenon responsible for the Second Law of Thermodynamics. The specific cellular automaton used here is rule 122R. The system is restricted to a region of size 100 cells.

Typical intuition from traditional science makes it difficult to understand how such randomness could possibly arise. But the discovery in this book that a wide range of systems can generate randomness even with very simple initial conditions makes it seem considerably less surprising.

But what about reversibility? The underlying rules for the cellular automaton used in the picture above are precisely reversible. Yet the picture itself does not at first appear to be at all reversible. For there appears to be an irreversible increase in randomness as one goes down successive panels on the page.

The resolution of this apparent conflict is however fairly straightforward. For as the picture on the facing page demonstrates, if the

An extended version of the picture on the facing page, in which the reversibility of the underlying cellular automaton is more clearly manifest. An initial condition is carefully constructed so that halfway through the evolution shown a simple arrangement of particles will be produced. If one starts with this arrangement, then the randomness of the system will effectively increase whether one goes forwards or backwards in time from that point.

simple arrangement of particles occurs in the middle of the evolution, then one can readily see that randomness increases in exactly the same way—whether one goes forwards or backwards from that point.

Yet there is still something of a mystery. For our everyday experience is full of examples in which randomness increases much as in the second half of the picture above. But we essentially never see the kind of systematic decrease in randomness that occurs in the first half.

By setting up the precise initial conditions that exist at the beginning of the whole picture it would certainly in principle be possible to get such behavior. But somehow it seems that initial conditions like these essentially never actually occur in practice.

There has in the past been considerable confusion about why this might be the case. But the key to understanding what is going on is simply to realize that one has to think not only about the systems one is studying, but also about the types of experiments and observations that one uses in the process of studying them.

The crucial point then turns out to be that practical experiments almost inevitably end up involving only initial conditions that are fairly simple for us to describe and construct. And with these types of initial conditions, systems like the one on the previous page always tend to exhibit increasing randomness.

But what exactly is it that determines the types of initial conditions that one can use in an experiment? It seems reasonable to suppose that in any meaningful experiment the process of setting up the experiment should somehow be simpler than the process that the experiment is intended to observe.

But how can one compare such processes? The answer that I will develop in considerable detail later in this book is to view all such processes as computations. The conclusion is then that the computation involved in setting up an experiment should be simpler than the computation involved in the evolution of the system that is to be studied by the experiment.

It is clear that by starting with a simple state and then tracing backwards through the actual evolution of a reversible system one can find initial conditions that will lead to decreasing randomness. But if one looks for example at the pictures on the last couple of pages the complexity of the behavior seems to preclude any less arduous way of finding such initial conditions. And indeed I will argue in Chapter 12 that the Principle of Computational Equivalence suggests that in general no such reduced procedure should exist.

The consequence of this is that no reasonable experiment can ever involve setting up the kind of initial conditions that will lead to decreases in randomness, and that therefore all practical experiments will tend to show only increases in randomness.

It is this basic argument that I believe explains the observed validity of what in physics is known as the Second Law of Thermodynamics. The law was first formulated more than a century ago, but despite many related technical results, the basic reasons for its validity have until now remained rather mysterious.

The field of thermodynamics is generally concerned with issues of heat and energy in physical systems. A fundamental fact known since the mid-1800s is that heat is a form of energy associated with the random microscopic motions of large numbers of atoms or other particles.

One formulation of the Second Law then states that any energy associated with organized motions of such particles tends to degrade irreversibly into heat. And the pictures at the beginning of this section show essentially just such a phenomenon. Initially there are particles which move in a fairly regular and organized way. But as time goes on, the motion that occurs becomes progressively more random.

There are several details of the cellular automaton used above that differ from actual physical systems of the kind usually studied in thermodynamics. But at the cost of some additional technical complication, it is fairly straightforward to set up a more realistic system.

The pictures on the next two pages show a particular two-dimensional cellular automaton in which black squares representing particles move around and collide with each other, essentially like particles in an ideal gas. This cellular automaton shares with the cellular automaton at the beginning of the section the property of being reversible. But it also has the additional feature that in every collision the total number of particles in it remains unchanged. And since each particle can be thought of as having a certain energy, it follows that the total energy of the system is therefore conserved.

In the first case shown, the particles are taken to bounce around in an empty square box. And it turns out that in this particular case only very simple repetitive behavior is ever obtained. But almost any change destroys this simplicity.

And in the second case, for example, the presence of a small fixed obstacle leads to rapid randomization in the arrangement of particles—very much like the randomization we saw in the one-dimensional cellular automaton that we discussed earlier in this section.

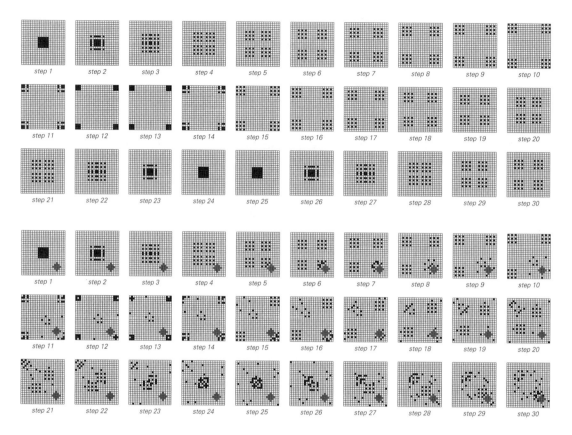

step 1 | step 2 | step 3 | step 4 | step 5 | step 6 | step 7 | step 8 | step 9 | step 10

step 11 | step 12 | step 13 | step 14 | step 15 | step 16 | step 17 | step 18 | step 19 | step 20

step 21 | step 22 | step 23 | step 24 | step 25 | step 26 | step 27 | step 28 | step 29 | step 30

step 1 | step 2 | step 3 | step 4 | step 5 | step 6 | step 7 | step 8 | step 9 | step 10

step 11 | step 12 | step 13 | step 14 | step 15 | step 16 | step 17 | step 18 | step 19 | step 20

step 21 | step 22 | step 23 | step 24 | step 25 | step 26 | step 27 | step 28 | step 29 | step 30

The behavior of a simple two-dimensional cellular automaton that emulates an ideal gas of particles. In the top group of pictures, the particles bounce around in an empty square box. In the bottom group of pictures, the box contains a small fixed obstacle. In the top group of pictures, the arrangement of particles shows simple repetitive behavior. In the bottom group, however, it becomes progressively more random with time. The underlying rules for the cellular automaton used here are reversible, and conserve the total number of particles. The specific rules are based on 2 × 2 blocks—a two-dimensional generalization of the block cellular automata to be discussed in the next section. For each 2 × 2 block the configuration of particles is taken to remain the same at a particular step unless there are exactly two particles arranged diagonally within the block, in which case the particles move to the opposite diagonal.

So even though the total of the energy of all particles remains the same, the distribution of this energy becomes progressively more random, just as the usual Second Law implies.

An important practical consequence of this is that it becomes increasingly difficult to extract energy from the system in the form of systematic mechanical work. At an idealized level one might imagine trying to do this by inserting into the system some kind of paddle which would experience force as a result of impacts from particles.

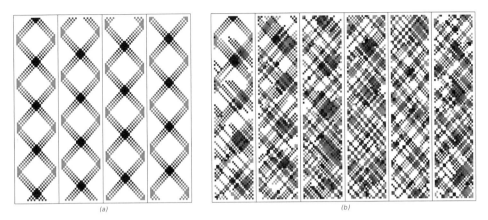

Time histories of the cellular automata from the facing page. In each case a slice is taken through the midline of the box. Black cells that are further from the midline are shown in progressively lighter shades of gray. Case (a) corresponds to an empty square box, and shows simple repetitive behavior. Case (b) corresponds to a box containing a fixed obstacle, and in this case rapid randomization is seen. Each panel corresponds to 100 steps in the evolution of the system; the box is 24 cells across.

The pictures below show how such force might vary with time in cases (a) and (b) above. In case (a), where no randomization occurs, the force can readily be predicted, and it is easy to imagine harnessing it to produce systematic mechanical work. But in case (b), the force quickly randomizes, and there is no obvious way to obtain systematic mechanical work from it.

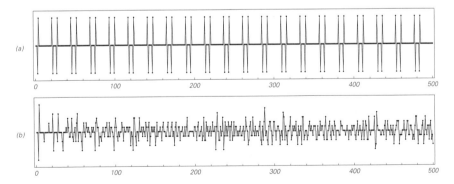

The force on an idealized paddle placed on the midline of the systems shown above. The force reflects an imbalance in the number of particles at each step arriving at the midline from above and below. In case (a) this imbalance is readily predictable. In case (b), however, it rapidly becomes for most practical purposes random. This randomness is essentially what makes it impossible to build a physical perpetual motion machine which continually turns heat into mechanical work.

One might nevertheless imagine that it would be possible to devise a complicated machine, perhaps with an elaborate arrangement of paddles, that would still be able to extract systematic mechanical work even from an apparently random distribution of particles. But it turns out that in order to do this the machine would effectively have to be able to predict where every particle would be at every step in time.

And as we shall discuss in Chapter 12, this would mean that the machine would have to perform computations that are as sophisticated as those that correspond to the actual evolution of the system itself. The result is that in practice it is never possible to build perpetual motion machines that continually take energy in the form of heat—or randomized particle motions—and convert it into useful mechanical work.

The impossibility of such perpetual motion machines is one common statement of the Second Law of Thermodynamics. Another is that a quantity known as entropy tends to increase with time.

Entropy is defined as the amount of information about a system that is still unknown after one has made a certain set of measurements on the system. The specific value of the entropy will depend on what measurements one makes, but the content of the Second Law is that if one repeats the same measurements at different times, then the entropy deduced from them will tend to increase with time.

If one managed to find the positions and properties of all the particles in the system, then no information about the system would remain unknown, and the entropy of the system would just be zero. But in a practical experiment, one cannot expect to be able to make anything like such complete measurements.

And more realistically, the measurements one makes might for example give the total numbers of particles in certain regions inside the box. There are then a large number of possible detailed arrangements of particles that are all consistent with the results of such measurements. The entropy is defined as the amount of additional information that would be needed in order to pick out the specific arrangement that actually occurs.

We will discuss in more detail in Chapter 10 the notion of amount of information. But here we can imagine numbering all the possible arrangements of particles that are consistent with the results of our measurements, so that the amount of information needed to pick out a single arrangement is essentially the length in digits of one such number.

The pictures below show the behavior of the entropy calculated in this way for systems like the one discussed above. And what we see is that the entropy does indeed tend to increase, just as the Second Law implies.

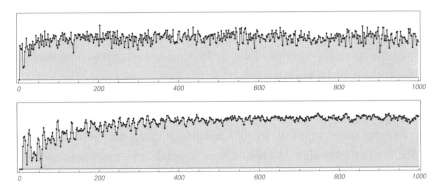

The entropy as a function of time for systems of the type shown in case (b) from page 447. The top plot is exactly for case (b); the bottom one is for a system three times larger in size. The entropy is found in each case by working out how many possible configurations of particles are consistent with measurements of the total numbers of particles in a 6 × 6 grid of regions within the system. Just as the Second Law of Thermodynamics suggests, the entropy tends to increase with time. Note that the plots above would be exactly symmetrical if they were continued to the left: the entropy would increase in the same way going both forwards and backwards from the simple initial conditions used.

In effect what is going on is that the measurements we make represent an attempt to determine the state of the system. But as the arrangement of particles in the system becomes more random, this attempt becomes less and less successful.

One might imagine that there could be a more elaborate set of measurements that would somehow avoid these problems, and would not lead to increasing entropy. But as we shall discuss in Chapter 12, it again turns out that setting up such measurements would have to involve the same level of computational effort as the actual evolution of the system itself. And as a result, one concludes that the entropy associated with measurements done in practical experiments will always tend to increase, as the Second Law suggests.

In Chapter 12 we will discuss in more detail some of the key ideas involved in coming to this conclusion. But the basic point is that the phenomenon of entropy increase implied by the Second Law is a more or less direct consequence of the phenomenon discovered in this book that even with simple initial conditions many systems can produce complex and seemingly random behavior.

One aspect of the generation of randomness that we have noted several times in earlier chapters is that once significant randomness has been produced in a system, the overall properties of that system tend to become largely independent of the details of its initial conditions.

In any system that is reversible it must always be the case that different initial conditions lead to at least slightly different states— otherwise there would be no unique way of going backwards. But the point is that even though the outcomes from different initial conditions differ in detail, their overall properties can still be very much the same.

The pictures on the facing page show an example of what can happen. Every individual picture has different initial conditions. But whenever randomness is produced the overall patterns that are obtained look in the end almost indistinguishable.

The reversibility of the underlying rules implies that at some level it must be possible to recognize outcomes from different kinds of initial conditions. But the point is that to do so would require a computation far more sophisticated than any that could meaningfully be done as part of a practical measurement process.

So this means that if a system generates sufficient randomness, one can think of it as evolving towards a unique equilibrium whose properties are for practical purposes independent of its initial conditions.

This fact turns out in a sense to be implicit in many everyday applications of physics. For it is what allows us to characterize all sorts of physical systems by just specifying a few parameters such as temperature and chemical composition—and avoids us always having to know the details of the initial conditions and history of each system.

The existence of a unique equilibrium to which any particular system tends to evolve is also a common statement of the Second Law of

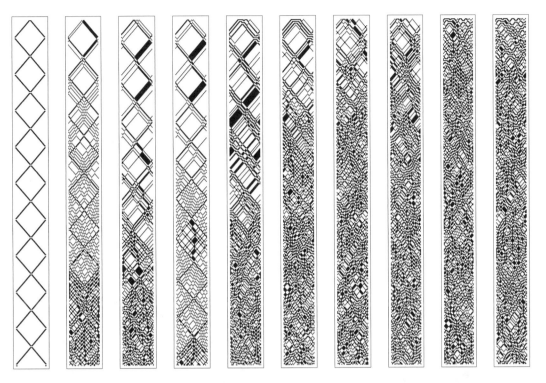

The approach to equilibrium in a reversible cellular automaton with a variety of different initial conditions. Apart from exceptional cases where no randomization occurs, the behavior obtained with different initial conditions is eventually quite indistinguishable in its overall properties. Because the underlying rule is reversible, however, the details with different initial conditions are always at least slightly different—otherwise it would not be possible to go backwards in a unique way. The rule used here is 122R. Successive pairs of pictures have initial conditions that differ only in the color of a single cell at the center.

Thermodynamics. And once again, therefore, we find that the Second Law is associated with basic phenomena that we already saw early in this book.

But just how general is the Second Law? And does it really apply to all of the various kinds of systems that we see in nature?

Starting nearly a century ago it came to be widely believed that the Second Law is an almost universal principle. But in reality there is surprisingly little evidence for this.

Indeed, almost all of the detailed applications ever made of the full Second Law have been concerned with just one specific area: the behavior of gases. By now there is therefore good evidence that gases obey the Second Law—just as the idealized model earlier in this section suggests. But what about other kinds of systems?

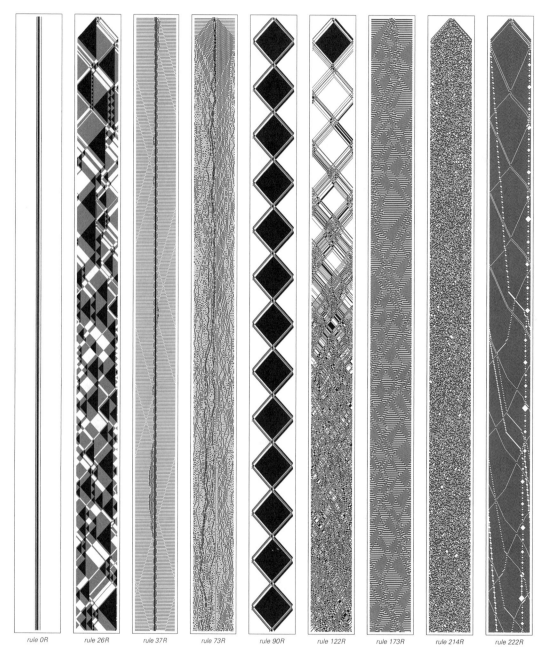

rule 0R   rule 26R   rule 37R   rule 73R   rule 90R   rule 122R   rule 173R   rule 214R   rule 222R

Examples of reversible cellular automata with various rules. Some quickly randomize, as the Second Law of Thermodynamics would suggest. But others do not—and thus in effect do not obey the Second Law of Thermodynamics.

The pictures on the facing page show examples of various reversible cellular automata. And what we see immediately from these pictures is that while some systems exhibit exactly the kind of randomization implied by the Second Law, others do not.

The most obvious exceptions are cases like rule 0R and rule 90R, where the behavior that is produced has only a very simple fixed or repetitive form. And existing mathematical studies have indeed identified these simple exceptions to the Second Law. But they have somehow implicitly assumed that no other kinds of exceptions can exist.

The picture on the next page, however, shows the behavior of rule 37R over the course of many steps. And in looking at this picture, we see a remarkable phenomenon: there is neither a systematic trend towards increasing randomness, nor any form of simple predictable behavior. Indeed, it seems that the system just never settles down, but rather continues to fluctuate forever, sometimes becoming less orderly, and sometimes more so.

So how can such behavior be understood in the context of the Second Law? There is, I believe, no choice but to conclude that for practical purposes rule 37R simply does not obey the Second Law.

And as it turns out, what happens in rule 37R is not so different from what seems to happen in many systems in nature. If the Second Law was always obeyed, then one might expect that by now every part of our universe would have evolved to completely random equilibrium.

Yet it is quite obvious that this has not happened. And indeed there are many kinds of systems, notably biological ones, that seem to show, at least temporarily, a trend towards increasing order rather than increasing randomness.

How do such systems work? A common feature appears to be the presence of some kind of partitioning: the systems effectively break up into parts that evolve at least somewhat independently for long periods of time.

The picture on page 456 shows what happens if one starts rule 37R with a single small region of randomness. And for a while what one sees is that the randomness that has been inserted persists. But eventually the system instead seems to organize itself to yield just a small number of simple repetitive structures.

steps 0-3000   steps 5000-8000   steps 10000-13000   steps 20000-23000   steps 100000-103000   steps 200000-203000

More steps in the evolution of the reversible cellular automaton with rule 37R. This system is an example of one that does not in any meaningful way obey the Second Law of Thermodynamics. Instead of exhibiting progressively more random behavior, it appears to fluctuate between quite ordered and quite disordered states.

This kind of self-organization is quite opposite to what one would expect from the Second Law. And at first it also seems inconsistent with the reversibility of the system. For if all that is left at the end are a few simple structures, how can there be enough information to go backwards and reconstruct the initial conditions?

The answer is that one has to consider not only the stationary structures that stay in the middle of the system, but also all various small structures that were emitted in the course of the evolution. To go backwards one would need to set things up so that one absorbs exactly the sequence of structures that were emitted going forwards.

If, however, one just lets the emitted structures escape, and never absorbs any other structures, then one is effectively losing information. The result is that the evolution one sees can be intrinsically not reversible, so that all of the various forms of self-organization that we saw earlier in this book in cellular automata that do not have reversible rules can potentially occur.

If we look at the universe on a large scale, then it turns out that in a certain sense there is more radiation emitted than absorbed. Indeed, this is related to the fact that the night sky appears dark, rather than having bright starlight coming from every direction. But ultimately the asymmetry between emission and absorption is a consequence of the fact that the universe is expanding, rather than contracting, with time.

The result is that it is possible for regions of the universe to become progressively more organized, despite the Second Law, and despite the reversibility of their underlying rules. And this is a large part of the reason that organized galaxies, stars and planets can form.

Allowing information to escape is a rather straightforward way to evade the Second Law. But what the pictures on the facing page demonstrate is that even in a completely closed system, where no information at all is allowed to escape, a system like rule 37R still does not follow the uniform trend towards increasing randomness that is suggested by the Second Law.

What instead happens is that kinds of membranes form between different regions of the system, and within each region orderly behavior can then occur, at least while the membrane survives.

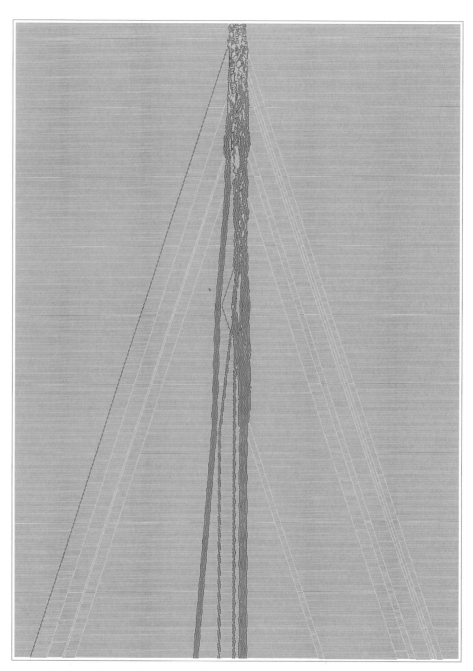

An example of evolution according to rule 37R from an initial condition containing a fairly random region. Even though the system is reversible, this region tends to organize itself so as to take on a much simpler form. Information on the initial conditions ends up being carried by localized structures which radiate outwards.

This basic mechanism may well be the main one at work in many biological systems: each cell or each organism becomes separated from others, and while it survives, it can exhibit organized behavior.

But looking at the pictures of rule 37R on page 454 one may ask whether perhaps the effects we see are just transients, and that if we waited long enough something different would happen.

It is an inevitable feature of having a closed system of limited size that in the end the behavior one gets must repeat itself. And in rules like 0R and 90R shown on page 452 the period of repetition is always very short. But for rule 37R it usually turns out to be rather long. Indeed, for the specific example shown on page 454, the period is 293,216,266.

In general, however, the maximum possible period for a system containing a certain number of cells can be achieved only if the evolution of the system from any initial condition eventually visits all the possible states of the system, as discussed on page 258. And if this in fact happens, then at least eventually the system will inevitably spend most of its time in states that seem quite random.

But in rule 37R there is no such ergodicity. And instead, starting from any particular initial condition, the system will only ever visit a tiny fraction of all possible states. Yet since the total number of states is astronomically large—about 10^{60} for size 100—the number of states visited by rule 37R, and therefore the repetition period, can still be extremely long.

There are various subtleties involved in making a formal study of the limiting behavior of rule 37R after a very long time. But irrespective of these subtleties, the basic fact remains that so far as I can tell, rule 37R simply does not follow the predictions of the Second Law.

And indeed I strongly suspect that there are many systems in nature which behave in more or less the same way. The Second Law is an important and quite general principle—but it is not universally valid. And by thinking in terms of simple programs we have thus been able in this section not only to understand why the Second Law is often true, but also to see some of its limitations.

Conserved Quantities and Continuum Phenomena

Reversibility is one general feature that appears to exist in the basic laws of physics. Another is conservation of various quantities—so that for example in the evolution of any closed physical system, total values of quantities like energy and electric charge appear always to stay the same.

With most rules, systems like cellular automata do not usually exhibit such conservation laws. But just as with reversibility, it turns out to be possible to find rules that for example conserve the total number of black cells appearing on each step.

Among elementary cellular automata with just two colors and nearest-neighbor rules, the only types of examples are the fairly trivial ones shown in the pictures below.

rule 170 (25% black)   *rule 170 (50% black)*   *rule 170 (75% black)*

rule 184 (25% black)   *rule 184 (50% black)*   *rule 184 (75% black)*

rule 204 (25% black)   *rule 204 (50% black)*   *rule 204 (75% black)*

Elementary cellular automata whose evolution conserves the total number of black cells. The behavior of the rules shown here is simple enough that in each case it is fairly obvious how the number of black cells manages to stay the same on every step.

But with next-nearest-neighbor rules, more complicated examples become possible, as the pictures below demonstrate.

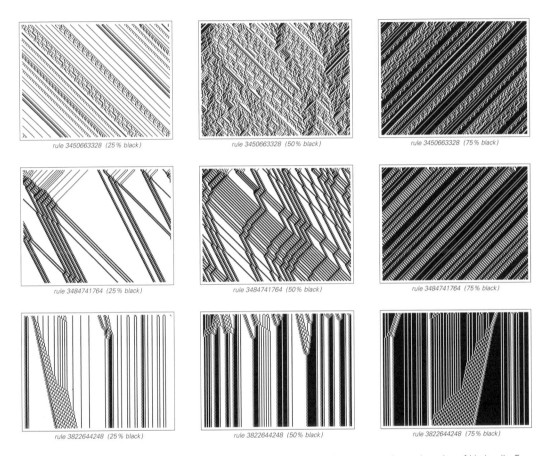

rule 3450663328 (25% black)   *rule 3450663328 (50% black)*   *rule 3450663328 (75% black)*

rule 3484741764 (25% black)   *rule 3484741764 (50% black)*   *rule 3484741764 (75% black)*

rule 3822644248 (25% black)   *rule 3822644248 (50% black)*   *rule 3822644248 (75% black)*

Examples of cellular automata with next-nearest-neighbor rules whose evolution conserves the total number of black cells. Even though it is not immediately obvious by eye, the total number of black cells stays exactly the same on each successive step in each picture. Among the 4,294,967,296 possible next-neighbor rules, only 428 exhibit the kind of conservation property shown here.

One straightforward way to generate collections of systems that will inevitably exhibit conserved quantities is to work not with ordinary cellular automata but instead with block cellular automata. The basic idea of a block cellular automaton is illustrated at the top of the next page. At each step what happens is that blocks of adjacent cells are replaced by other blocks of the same size according to some definite rule. And then on successive steps the alignment of these blocks shifts by one cell.

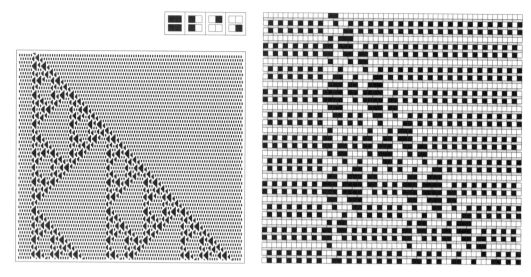

An example of a block cellular automaton. The system works by partitioning the sequence of cells that exists at each step into pairs, then replacing these pairs by other pairs according to the rule shown. The choice of whether to pair a cell with its left or right neighbor alternates on successive steps. Like many block cellular automata, the system shown is reversible, since in the rule each pair has a unique predecessor. It does not, however, conserve the total number of black cells.

And with this setup, if the underlying rules replace each block by one that contains the same number of black cells, it is inevitable that the system as a whole will conserve the total number of black cells.

With two possible colors and blocks of size two the only kinds of block cellular automata that conserve the total number of black cells are the ones shown below—and all of these exhibit rather trivial behavior.

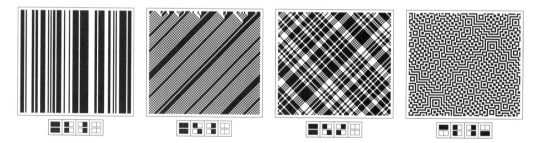

Block cellular automata with two possible colors and blocks of size two that conserve the total number of black cells (the last example has this property only on alternate steps). It so happens that all but the second of the rules shown here not only conserve the total number of black cells but also turn out to be reversible.

But if one allows three possible colors, and requires, say, that the total number of black and gray cells together be conserved, then more complicated behavior can occur, as in the pictures below.

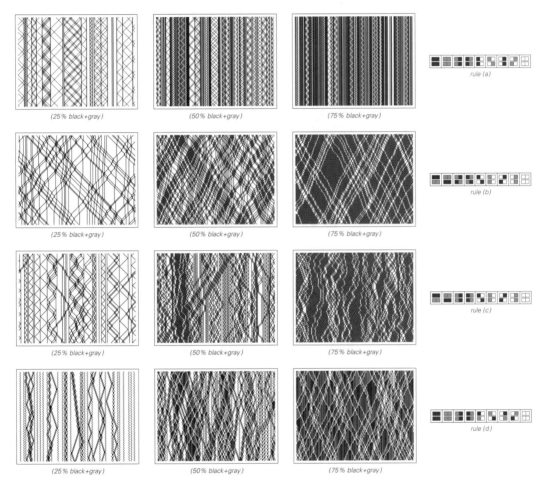

Block cellular automata with three possible colors which conserve the combined number of black and gray cells. In rule (a), black and gray cells remain in localized regions. In rule (b), they move in fairly simple ways, and in rules (c) and (d), they move in a seemingly somewhat random way. The rules shown here are reversible, although their behavior is similar to that of non-reversible rules, at least after a few steps.

Indeed, as the pictures on the next page demonstrate, such systems can produce considerable randomness even when starting from very simple initial conditions.

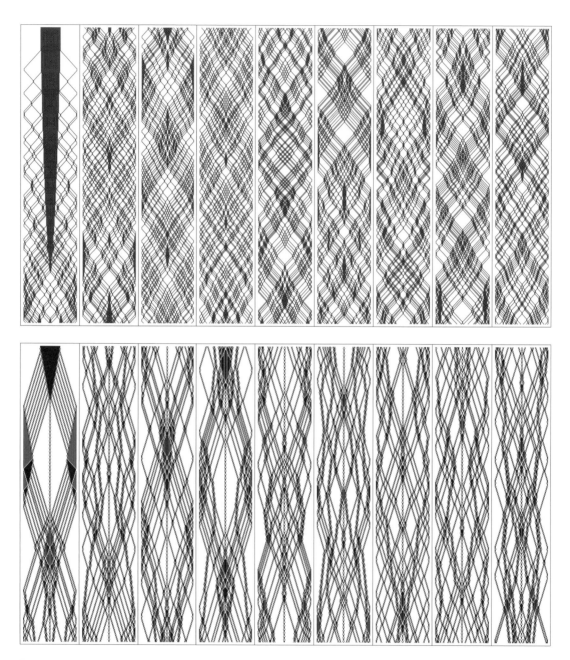

The behavior of rules (c) and (d) from the previous page, starting with very simple initial conditions. Each panel shows 500 steps of evolution, and rapid randomization is evident. The black and gray cells behave much like physical particles: their total number is conserved, and with the particular rules used here, their interactions are reversible. Note that the presence of boundaries is crucial; for without them there would in a sense be no collisions between particles, and the behavior of both systems would be rather trivial.

But there is still an important constraint on the behavior: even though black and gray cells may in effect move around randomly, their total number must always be conserved. And this means that if one looks at the total average density of colored cells throughout the system, it must always remain the same. But local densities in different parts of the system need not—and in general they will change as colored cells flow in and out.

The pictures below show what happens with four different rules, starting with higher density in the middle and lower density on the sides. With rules (a) and (b), each different region effectively remains separated forever. But with rules (c) and (d) the regions gradually mix.

As in many kinds of systems, the details of the initial arrangement of cells will normally have an effect on the details of the behavior that occurs. But what the pictures below suggest is that if one looks only at the overall distribution of density, then these details will become largely irrelevant—so that a given initial distribution of density will always tend to evolve in the same overall way, regardless of what particular arrangement of cells happened to make up that distribution.

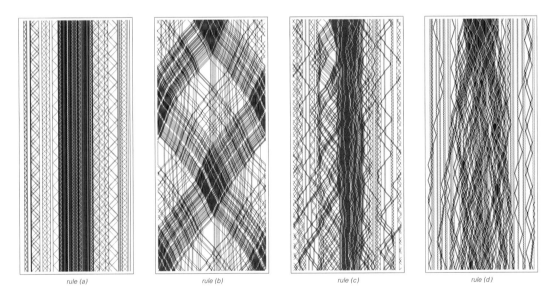

rule (a)   rule (b)   rule (c)   rule (d)

The block cellular automata from previous pages started from initial conditions containing regions of different density. In rules (a) and (b) the regions remain separated forever, but in rules (c) and (d) they gradually diffuse into each other.

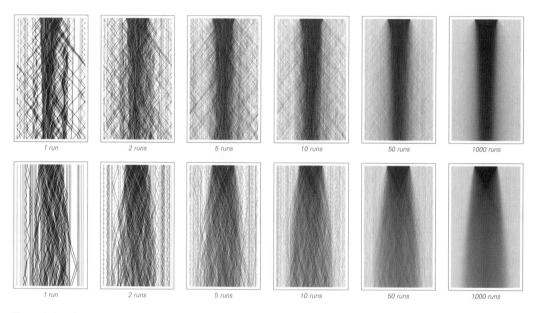

The evolution of overall density for block cellular automata (c) and (d) from the previous page. Even though at an underlying level these systems consist of discrete cells, their overall behavior seems smooth and continuous. The results shown here are obtained by averaging over progressively larger numbers of runs with initial conditions that differ in detail, but have the same overall density distribution. In the limit of an infinite number of runs (or infinite number of cells), the behavior in the second case approaches the form implied by the continuum diffusion equation. (In the first case correlations in effect last too long to yield exactly such behavior.)

The pictures above then show how the average density evolves in systems (c) and (d). And what is striking is that even though at the lowest level both of these systems consist of discrete cells, the overall distribution of density that emerges in both cases shows smooth continuous behavior.

And much as in physical systems like fluids, what ultimately leads to this is the presence of small-scale apparent randomness that washes out details of individual cells or molecules—as well as of conserved quantities that force certain overall features not to change too quickly. And in fact, given just these properties it turns out that essentially the same overall continuum behavior always tends to be obtained.

One might have thought that continuum behavior would somehow rely on special features of actual systems in physics. But in fact what we have seen here is that once again the fundamental mechanisms responsible already occur in a much more minimal way in programs that have some remarkably simple underlying rules.

Ultimate Models for the Universe

The history of physics has seen the development of a sequence of progressively more accurate models for the universe—from classical mechanics, through quantum mechanics, to quantum field theory, and beyond. And one may wonder whether this process will go on forever, or whether at some point it will come to an end, and one will reach a final ultimate model for the universe.

Experience with actual results in physics would probably not make one think so. For it has seemed that whenever one tries to get to another level of accuracy, one encounters more complex phenomena. And at least with traditional scientific intuition, this fact suggests that models of progressively greater complexity will be needed.

But one of the crucial points discovered in this book is that more complex phenomena do not always require more complex models. And indeed I have shown that even models based on remarkably simple programs can produce behavior that is in a sense arbitrarily complex.

So could this be what happens in the universe? And could it even be that underneath all the complex phenomena we see in physics there lies some simple program which, if run for long enough, would reproduce our universe in every detail?

The discovery of such a program would certainly be an exciting event—as well as a dramatic endorsement for the new kind of science that I have developed in this book.

For among other things, with such a program one would finally have a model of nature that was not in any sense an approximation or idealization. Instead, it would be a complete and precise representation of the actual operation of the universe—but all reduced to readily stated rules.

In a sense, the existence of such a program would be the ultimate validation of the idea that human thought can comprehend the construction of the universe. But just knowing the underlying program does not mean that one can immediately deduce every aspect of how the universe will behave. For as we have seen many times in this book, there is often a great distance between underlying rules and overall behavior. And in fact, this is precisely why it is conceivable that a simple program could reproduce all the complexity we see in physics.

Given a particular underlying program, it is always in principle possible to work out what it will do just by running it. But for the whole universe, doing this kind of explicit simulation is almost by definition out of the question. So how then can one even expect to tell whether a particular program is a correct model for the universe? Small-scale simulation will certainly be possible. And I expect that by combining this with a certain amount of perhaps fairly sophisticated mathematical and logical deduction, it will be possible to get at least as far as reproducing the known laws of physics—and thus of determining whether a particular model has the potential to be correct.

So if there is indeed a definite ultimate model for the universe, how might one set about finding it? For those familiar with existing science, there is at first a tremendous tendency to try to work backwards from the known laws of physics, and in essence to try to "engineer" a universe that will have particular features that we observe.

But if there is in fact an ultimate model that is quite simple, then from what we have seen in this book, I strongly believe that such an approach will never realistically be successful. For human thinking— even supplemented by the most sophisticated ideas of current mathematics and logic—is far from being able to do what is needed.

Imagine for example trying to work backwards from a knowledge of the overall features of the picture on the facing page to construct a rule that would reproduce it. With great effort one might perhaps come up with some immensely complex rule that would work in most cases. But there is no serious possibility that starting from overall features one would ever arrive at the extremely simple rule that was actually used.

It is already difficult enough to work out from an underlying rule what behavior it will produce. But to invert this in any systematic way is probably even in principle beyond what any realistic computation can do.

So how then could one ever expect to find the underlying rule in such a case? Almost always, it seems that the best strategy is a simple one: to come up with an appropriate general class of rules, and then just

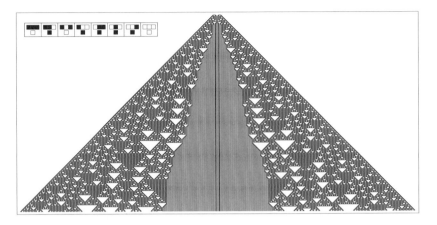

A typical example of a situation where it would be very difficult to deduce the underlying rule from a description of the overall behavior that it produces. There is in a sense too great a distance between the simple rule shown and the behavior that emerges from it. I suspect that the same will be true of the basic rule for the universe. The particular rule shown here is the elementary cellular automaton with rule number 94, and with initial condition ▄▄▄▄▄□□□□▄▄▄▄ .

to search through these rules, trying each one in turn, and looking to see if it produces the behavior one wants.

But what about the rules for the universe? Surely we cannot simply search through possible rules of certain kinds, looking for one whose behavior happens to fit what we see in physics?

With the intuition of traditional science, such an approach seems absurd. But the point is that if the rule for the universe is sufficiently simple—and the results of this book suggest that it might be—then it becomes not so unreasonable to imagine systematically searching for it.

To start performing such a search, however, one first needs to work out what kinds of rules to consider. And my suspicion is that none of the specific types of rules that we have discussed so far in this book will turn out to be adequate. For I believe that all these types of rules in some sense probably already have too much structure built in.

Thus, for example, cellular automata probably already have too rigid a built-in notion of space. For a defining feature of cellular automata is that their cells are always arranged in a rigid array in space. Yet I strongly suspect that in the underlying rule for our universe there will be no such built-in structure. Rather, as I discuss in the sections that follow, my guess is that at the lowest level there will just be certain patterns of connectivity that tend to exist, and that space as we know it will then emerge from these patterns as a kind of large-scale limit.

And indeed in general what I expect is that remarkably few familiar features of our universe will actually be reflected in any direct way in its ultimate underlying rule. For if all these features were somehow explicitly and separately included, the rule would necessarily have to be very complicated to fit them all in.

So if the rule is indeed simple, it almost inevitably follows that we will not be able to recognize directly in it most features of the universe as we normally perceive them. And this means that the rule—or at least its behavior—will necessarily seem to us unfamiliar and abstract.

Most likely for example there will be no easy way to visualize what the rule does by looking at a collection of elements laid out in space. Nor will there probably be any immediate trace of even such basic phenomena as motion.

But despite the lack of these familiar features, I still expect that the actual rule itself will not be too difficult for us to represent. For I am fairly certain that the kinds of logical and computational constructs that we have discussed in this book will be general enough to cover what is needed. And indeed my guess is that in terms of the kinds of pictures—or *Mathematica* programs—that we have used in this book, the ultimate rule for the universe will turn out to look quite simple.

No doubt there will be many different possible formulations— some quite unrecognizably different from others. And no doubt a formulation will eventually be found in which the rule somehow comes to seem quite obvious and inevitable.

But I believe that it will be essentially impossible to find such a formulation without already knowing the rule. And as a result, my guess is that the only realistic way to find the rule in the first place will be to start from some very straightforward representation, and then just to search through large numbers of possible rules in this representation.

Presumably the vast majority of rules will lead to utterly unworkable universes, in which there is for example no reasonable notion of space or no reasonable notion of time.

But my guess is that among appropriate classes of rules there will actually be quite a large number that lead to universes which share at least some features with our own. Much as the same laws of continuum fluid mechanics can emerge in systems with different underlying rules for molecular interactions, so also I suspect that properties such as the existence of seemingly continuous space, as well as certain features of gravitation and quantum mechanics, will emerge with many different possible underlying rules for the universe.

But my guess is that when it comes to something like the spectrum of masses of elementary particles—or perhaps even the overall dimensionality of space—such properties will be quite specific to particular underlying rules.

In traditional approaches to modelling, one usually tries first to reproduce some features of a system, then goes on to reproduce others. But if the ultimate rule for the universe is at all simple, then it follows that every part of this rule must in a sense be responsible for a great many different features of the universe. And as a result, it is not likely to be possible to adjust individual parts of the rule without having an effect on a whole collection of disparate features of the universe.

So this means that one cannot reasonably expect to use some kind of incremental procedure to find the ultimate rule for the universe. But it also means that if one once discovers a rule that reproduces sufficiently many features of the universe, then it becomes extremely likely that this rule is indeed the final and correct one for the whole universe.

And I strongly suspect that even in many of the most basic everyday physical processes, every element of the underlying rule for the universe will be very extensively exercised. And as a result, if these basic processes are reproduced correctly, then I believe that one can have considerable confidence that one in fact has the complete rule for the universe.

Looking at the history of physics, one might think that it would be completely inadequate just to reproduce everyday physical processes. For one might expect that there would always be some other esoteric phenomenon, say in particle physics, that would be discovered and would show that whatever rule one has found is somehow incomplete.

But I do not think so. For if the rule for our universe is at all simple, then I expect that to introduce a new phenomenon, however esoteric, will involve modifying some basic part of the rule, which will also affect even common everyday phenomena.

But why should we believe that the rule for our universe is in fact simple? Certainly among all possible rules of a particular kind only a limited number can ever be considered simple, and these rules are by definition somehow special. Yet looking at the history of science, one might expect that in the end there would turn out to be nothing special about the rule for our universe—just as there has turned out to be nothing special about our position in the solar system or the galaxy.

Indeed, one might assume that there are in fact an infinite number of universes, each with a different rule, and that we simply live in a particular—and essentially arbitrary—one of them.

It is unlikely to be possible to show for certain that such a theory is not correct. But one of its consequences is that it gives us no reason to think that the rule for our particular universe should be in any way simple. For among all possible rules, the overwhelming majority will not be simple; in fact, they will instead tend to be almost infinitely complex.

Yet we know, I think, that the rule for our universe is not too complex. For if the number of different parts of the rule were, for example, comparable to the number of different situations that have ever arisen in the history of the universe, then we would not expect ever to be able to describe the behavior of the universe using only a limited number of physical laws.

And in fact if one looks at present-day physics, there are not only a limited number of physical laws, but also the individual laws often seem to have the simplest forms out of various alternatives. And knowing this, one might be led to believe that for some reason the universe is set up to have the simplest rules throughout.

But, unfortunately perhaps, I do not think that this conclusion necessarily follows. For as I have discussed above, I strongly suspect that the vast majority of physical laws discovered so far are not truly fundamental, but are instead merely emergent features of the large-scale behavior of some ultimate underlying rule. And what this means is that any simplicity observed in known physical laws may have little connection with simplicity in the underlying rule.

Indeed, it turns out that simple overall laws can emerge almost regardless of underlying rules. And thus, for example, essentially as a consequence of randomness generation, a wide range of cellular automata show the simple density diffusion law on page 464—whether or not their underlying rules happen to be simple.

So it could be that the laws that we have formulated in existing physics are simple not because of simplicity in an ultimate underlying rule, but rather because of some general property of emergent behavior for the kinds of overall features of the universe that we readily perceive.

Indeed, with this kind of argument, one could be led to think that there might be no single ultimate rule for the universe at all, but that instead there might somehow be an infinite sequence of levels of rules, with each level having a certain simplicity that becomes increasingly independent of the details of the levels below it.

But one should not imagine that such a setup would make it unnecessary to ask why our universe is the way it is: for even though certain features might be inevitable from the general properties of emergent behavior, there will, I believe, still be many seemingly arbitrary choices that have to be made in arriving at the universe in which we live. And once again, therefore, one will have to ask why it was these choices, and not others, that were made.

So perhaps in the end there is the least to explain if I am correct that the universe just follows a single, simple, underlying rule.

There will certainly be questions about why it is this particular rule, and not another one. And I am doubtful that such questions will ever have meaningful answers.

But to find the ultimate rule will be a major triumph for science, and a clear demonstration that at least in some direction, human thought has reached the edge of what is possible.

The Nature of Space

In the effort to develop an ultimate model for the universe, a crucial first step is to think about the nature of space—for inevitably it is in space that the processes in our universe occur.

Present-day physics almost always assumes that space is a perfect continuum, in which objects can be placed at absolutely any position. But one can certainly imagine that space could work very differently. And for example in a cellular automaton, space is not a continuum but instead consists just of discrete cells.

In our everyday experience space nevertheless appears to be continuous. But then so, for example, do fluids like air and water. And yet in the case of these fluids we know that at an underlying level they are composed of discrete molecules. And in fact over the course of the past century a great many aspects of the physical world that at first seemed continuous have in the end been discovered to be built up from discrete elements. And I very strongly suspect that this will also be true of space.

Particle physics experiments have shown that space acts as a continuum down to distances of around 10^{-20} meters—or a hundred thousandth the radius of a proton. But there is absolutely no reason to think that discrete elements will not be found at still smaller distances.

And indeed, in the past one of the main reasons that space has been assumed to be a perfect continuum is that this makes it easier to handle in the context of traditional mathematics. But when one thinks in terms of programs and the kinds of systems I have discussed in this book, it no longer seems nearly as attractive to assume that space is a perfect continuum.

So if space is not in fact a continuum, what might it be? Could it, for example, be a regular array of cells like in a cellular automaton?

At first, one might think that this would be completely inconsistent with everyday observations. For even though the individual cells in the array might be extremely small, one might still imagine that one would for example see all sorts of signs of the overall orientation of the array.

The pictures below show three different cellular automata, all set up on the same two-dimensional grid. And to see the effect of the grid, I show what happens when each of these cellular automata is started from blocks of black cells arranged at three different angles.

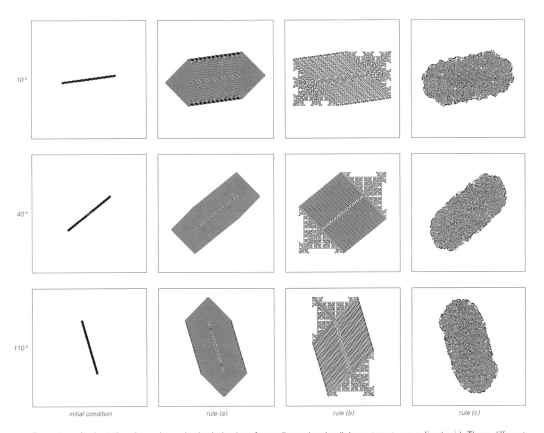

Examples of orientation dependence in the behavior of two-dimensional cellular automata on a fixed grid. Three different initial conditions, consisting of blocks at three different angles, are shown. For rules (a) and (b) the patterns produced always exhibit features that remain aligned with directions in the underlying grid. But with rule (c) essentially the same rounded pattern is obtained regardless of orientation. The rules shown here are outer totalistic: (a) 4-neighbor code 468, (b) 4-neighbor code 686 and (c) 8-neighbor code 746. In cases (a) and (b) 40 steps of evolution are used; in case (c) 100 steps are used.

In all cases the patterns produced follow at least to some extent the orientation of the initial block. But in cases (a) and (b) the effects of the underlying grid remain quite obvious—for the patterns produced always have facets aligned with the directions in this grid. But in case (c) the situation is different, and now the patterns produced turn out always to have the same overall rounded form, essentially independent of their orientation with respect to the underlying grid.

And indeed what happens is similar to what we have seen many times in this book: the evolution of the cellular automaton generates enough randomness that the effects of the underlying grid tend to be washed out, with the result that the overall behavior produced ends up showing essentially no distinction between different directions in space.

So should one conclude from this that the universe is in fact a giant cellular automaton with rules like those of case (c)?

It is perhaps not impossible, but I very much doubt it.

For there are immediately simple issues like what one imagines happens at the edges of the cellular automaton array. But much more important is the fact that I do not believe in the distinction between space and its contents implied by the basic construction of a cellular automaton.

For when one builds a cellular automaton one is in a sense always first setting up an array of cells to represent space itself, and then only subsequently considering the contents of space, as represented by the arrangement of colors assigned to the cells in this array.

But if the ultimate model for the universe is to be as simple as possible, then it seems much more plausible that both space and its contents should somehow be made of the same stuff—so that in a sense space becomes the only thing in the universe.

Several times in the past ideas like this have been explored. And indeed the standard theory for gravity introduced in 1915 is precisely based on the notion that gravity can be viewed merely as a feature of space. But despite various attempts in the 1930s and more recently it has never seemed possible to extend this to cover the whole elaborate collection of forces and particles that we actually see in our universe.

Yet my suspicion is that a large part of the reason for this is just the assumption that space is a perfect continuum—described by traditional mathematics. For as we have seen many times in this book, if one looks at systems like programs with discrete elements then it immediately becomes much easier for highly complex behavior to emerge. And this is fundamentally what I believe is happening at the lowest level in space throughout our universe.

Space as a Network

In the last section I argued that if the ultimate model of physics is to be as simple as possible, then one should expect that all the features of our universe must at some level emerge purely from properties of space. But what should space be like if this is going to be the case?

The discussion in the section before last suggests that for the richest properties to emerge there should in a sense be as little rigid underlying structure built in as possible. And with this in mind I believe that what is by far the most likely is that at the lowest level space is in effect a giant network of nodes.

In an array of cells like in a cellular automaton each cell is always assigned some definite position. But in a network of nodes, the nodes are not intrinsically assigned any position. And indeed, the only thing that is defined about each node is what other nodes it is connected to.

Yet despite this rather abstract setup, we will see that with a sufficiently large number of nodes it is possible for the familiar properties of space to emerge—together with other phenomena seen in physics.

I already introduced in Chapter 5 a particular type of network in which each node has exactly two outgoing connections to other nodes, together with any number of incoming connections. The reason I chose this kind of network in Chapter 5 is that there happens to be a fairly easy way to set up evolution rules for such networks. But in trying to find an ultimate model of space, it seems best to start by considering networks that are somehow as simple as possible in basic structure— and it turns out that the networks of Chapter 5 are somewhat more complicated than is necessary.

For one thing, there is no need to distinguish between incoming and outgoing connections, or indeed to associate any direction with each connection. And in addition, nothing fundamental is lost by requiring that all the nodes in a network have exactly the same total number of connections to other nodes.

With two connections, only very trivial networks can ever be made. But if one uses three connections, a vast range of networks immediately become possible. One might think that one could get a

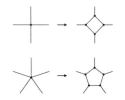

Examples of how nodes with more than three connections can be decomposed into collections of nodes with exactly three connections.

fundamentally larger range if one allowed, say, four or five connections rather than just three. But in fact one cannot, since any node with more than three connections can in effect always be broken into a collection of nodes with exactly three connections, as in the pictures on the left.

So what this means is that it is in a sense always sufficient to consider networks with exactly three connections at each node. And it is therefore these networks that I will use here in discussing fundamental models of space.

The pictures below show a few small examples of such networks. And already considerable diversity is evident. But none of the networks shown seem to have many properties familiar from ordinary space.

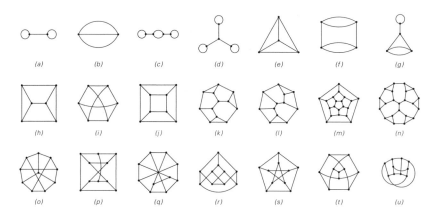

Examples of small networks with exactly three connections at each node. The first line shows all possible networks with up to four nodes. In what follows I consider only non-degenerate networks, in which there is at most one connection between any two nodes. Example (i) is the smallest network that cannot be drawn in two dimensions without lines crossing. Examples (k) and (l) are the smallest networks that have no symmetries between different nodes. Example (e) corresponds to the net of a tetrahedron, (j) to the net of a cube, and (m) to the net of a dodecahedron. Examples (o) through (u) show seven ways of drawing the same network, in this case the so-called Petersen network.

So how then can one get networks that correspond to ordinary space? The first step is to consider networks that have much larger numbers of nodes. And as examples of these, the pictures at the top of the facing page show networks that are specifically constructed to correspond to ordinary one-, two- and three-dimensional space.

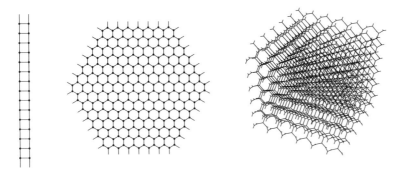

Examples of networks with three connections at each node that are effectively one, two and three-dimensional. These networks can be continued forever, and all have the property of being homogeneous, in the sense that every node has an environment identical to every other node.

Each of these networks is at the lowest level just a collection of nodes with certain connections. But the point is that the overall pattern of these connections is such that on a large scale there emerges a clear correspondence to ordinary space of a particular dimension.

The pictures above are drawn so as to make this correspondence obvious. But what if one was just presented with the raw pattern of connections for some network? How could one see whether the network could correspond to ordinary space of a particular dimension?

The pictures below illustrate the main difficulty: given only its pattern of connections, a particular network can be laid out in many completely different ways, most of which tell one very little about its potential correspondence with ordinary space.

(a) (b) (c) (d) (e) (f)

Six different ways of laying out the same network. (a) nodes arranged around a circle; (b) nodes arranged along a line; (c) nodes arranged across the page according to distance from a particular node; (d) 2D layout with network and spatial distances as close as possible; (e) planar layout; (f) 3D layout.

So how then can one proceed? The fundamental idea is to look at properties of networks that can both readily be deduced from their pattern of connections and can also be identified, at least in some large-scale limit, with properties of ordinary space. And the notion of distance is perhaps the most fundamental of such properties.

A simple way to define the distance between two points is to say that it is the length of the shortest path between them. And in ordinary space, this is normally calculated by subtracting the numerical coordinates of the positions of the points. But on a network things become more direct, and the distance between two nodes can be taken to be simply the minimum number of connections that one has to follow in order to get from one node to the other.

But can one tell just by looking at such distances whether a particular network corresponds to ordinary space of a certain dimension?

To a large extent one can. And a test is to see whether there is a way to lay out the nodes in the network in ordinary space so that the distances between nodes computed from their positions in space agree—at least in some approximation—with the distances computed directly by following connections in the network.

The three networks at the top of the previous page were laid out precisely so as to make this the case respectively for one, two and three-dimensional space. But why for example can the second network not be laid out equally well in one-dimensional rather than two-dimensional space? One way to see this is to count the number of nodes that appear at a given distance from a particular node in the network.

And for this specific network, the answer for this is very simple: at distance r there are exactly $3r$ nodes—so that the total number of nodes out to distance r grows like r^2. But now if one tried to lay out all these nodes in one dimension it is inevitable that the network would have to bulge out in order to fit in all the nodes. And it turns out that it is uniquely in two dimensions that this particular network can be laid out in a regular way so that distances based on following connections in it agree with ordinary distances in space.

For the other two networks at the top of the previous page similar arguments can be given. And in fact in general the condition for a network to correspond to ordinary d-dimensional space is precisely that the total number of nodes that appear in it out to distance r grows in some limiting sense like r^d—a result analogous to the standard mathematical fact that the area of a two-dimensional circle is πr^2, while the volume of a three-dimensional sphere is $4/3\,\pi\,r^3$, the volume of a four-dimensional hypersphere is $1/2\,\pi^2\,r^4$, and so on.

Below I show pictures of various networks. In each case the first picture is drawn to emphasize obvious regularities in the network. But the second picture is drawn in a more systematic way—by picking a specific starting node, and then laying out other nodes so that those at

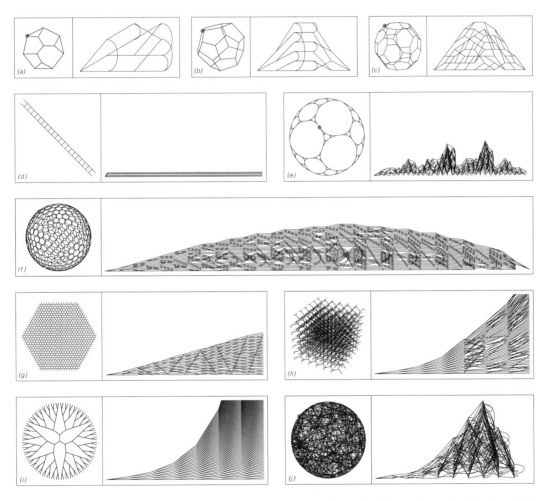

Examples of various networks, shown first to emphasize their regularities, and second to illustrate the number of nodes reached by going successively more steps from a given node. For networks that in a limiting sense correspond to ordinary d-dimensional space, this number grows like r^{d-1}. All the larger networks shown are approximately uniform, in the sense that similar results are obtained starting from any node. Network (e) effectively has limiting dimension $Log[2, 3] \simeq 1.58$.

successively greater network distances appear in successive columns across the page. And this setup has the feature that the height of column r gives the number of nodes that are at network distance r.

So by looking at how these heights grow across the page, one can see whether there is a correspondence with the r^{d-1} form that one expects for ordinary d-dimensional space. And indeed in case (g), for example, one sees exactly r^1 linear growth, reflecting dimension 2.

Similarly, in case (d) one sees r^0 growth, reflecting dimension 1, while in case (h) one sees r^2 growth, reflecting dimension 3.

Case (f) illustrates slightly more complicated behavior. The basic network in this case locally has an essentially two-dimensional form—but at large scales it is curved by being wrapped around a sphere. And what therefore happens is that for fairly small r one sees r^1 growth—reflecting the local two-dimensional form—but then for larger r there is slower growth, reflecting the presence of curvature.

Later in this chapter we will see how such curvature is related to the phenomenon of gravity. But for now the point is just that network (f) again behaves very much like ordinary space with a definite dimension.

So do all sufficiently large networks somehow correspond to ordinary space in a certain number of dimensions? The answer is definitely no. And as an example, network (i) from the previous page has a tree-like structure with 3^r nodes at distance r. But this number grows faster than r^d for any d—implying that the network has no correspondence to ordinary space in any finite number of dimensions.

If the connections in a network are chosen at random—as in case (j)—then again there will almost never be the kind of locality that is needed to get something that corresponds to ordinary finite-dimensional space.

So what might an actual network for space in our universe be like?

It will certainly not be as simple and regular as most of the networks on the previous page. For within its pattern of connections must be encoded everything we see in our universe.

And so at the level of individual connections, the network will most likely at first look quite random. But on a larger scale, it must be arranged so as to correspond to ordinary three-dimensional space. And somehow whatever rules update the network must preserve this feature.

The Relationship of Space and Time

To make an ultimate theory of physics one needs to understand the true nature not only of space but also of time. And I believe that here again the idea of thinking in terms of programs provides some crucial insights.

In our everyday experience space and time seem very different. For example, we can move from one point in space to another in more or less any way we choose. But we seem to be forced to progress through time in a very specific way. Yet despite such obvious apparent differences, almost all models in present-day fundamental physics have been built on the idea that space and time somehow work fundamentally the same.

But for most of the systems based on programs that I have discussed in this book this is certainly not true. And thus for example in a cellular automaton moving from one point in space to another just corresponds to shifting from one cell to another. But moving from one point in time to another involves actually applying the cellular automaton rule.

When we make a picture of the behavior of a cellular automaton, however, we do nevertheless tend to represent space and time in the same visual kind of way—with space going across the page and time going down. And in fact the basic notion of extending the idea of position in space to an idea of position in time has been common in scientific thought for more than five centuries.

But in the past century what has happened is that space and time have come to be thought of as being much more fundamentally similar. As we will discuss later in this chapter, the main origin of this is that in relativity theory certain aspects of space and time seem to become interchangeable. And from this there emerged the idea of thinking in terms of a spacetime continuum in which time appears merely as a fourth dimension just like the three ordinary dimensions of space.

So while in a system like a cellular automaton one typically imagines that a new and separate state of the system is somehow produced at each step in time, present-day physics more tends to think of the complete history of the universe throughout time as being just a single structure laid out in the four dimensions of spacetime.

So what then might determine the form of this structure?

The laws of physics in effect provide a collection of constraints on the structure. And while these laws are traditionally stated in terms of sophisticated mathematical equations, their basic character is similar to the simple constraints on arrays of black and white cells that I discussed at the end of Chapter 5. But now instead of defining constraints just in space, the laws of physics can be thought of as defining constraints on what can happen in both space and time.

Just as for space, it is my strong belief that time is fundamentally discrete. And from the discussion of networks for space in the previous section, one might imagine that perhaps the whole history of the universe in spacetime could be represented by a giant four-dimensional network.

By analogy with the systems at the end of Chapter 5 a simple model would then be that this network is determined by the constraint that around every one of its nodes the overall arrangement of other nodes must match some particular template or set of templates.

Yet much as in Chapter 5 it turns out often not to be especially easy to find out which networks, if any, satisfy specific constraints of this kind. The pictures on the facing page nevertheless show results for quite a few choices of templates—where in each case the dangling connections in a template are taken to go to nodes that are not part of the template itself.

Pictures (a) and (b) show what happens with the two very simplest possible templates—involving just a single node. In case (a), all networks are allowed except for ones in which a node is connected directly to itself. In case (b), only the single network shown is allowed.

With templates that involve nodes out to distance one there are a total of 11 distinct non-trivial cases. And of these, 8 allow no complete networks to be formed, as in picture (e). But there turn out to be three cases—shown as pictures (c), (d) and (f)—in which complete networks can be formed, and in each of these one discovers that a fairly simple infinite set of networks are actually allowed.

In order to have a meaningful model for the universe, however, what must presumably happen is that essentially just one network can satisfy whatever constraints there are, and this one network must then represent all of the complex spacetime history of our universe.

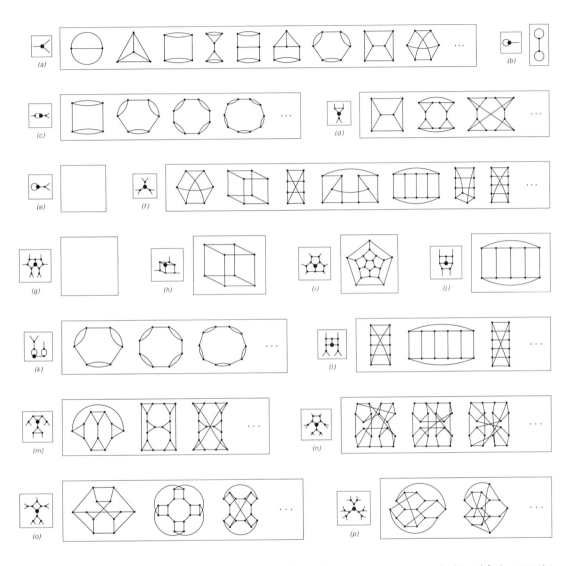

Examples of networks determined by constraints. In each case the networks shown are required to satisfy the constraint that around every node their form must correspond to the template shown, in such a way that no dangling connections in the template are joined to each other. The pictures include all 14 templates that involve nodes out to distance at most two for which complete networks can be formed. In most cases where any such network can be formed, an infinite sequence of networks is allowed. But in cases (b), (h), (i) and (j) just a single network turns out to be allowed. The network constraint systems shown here are analogs of the two-dimensional systems based on constraints discussed at the end of Chapter 5.

So what does one find if one allows templates that include nodes out to distance two? There are a total of 690 distinct non-trivial such templates—and of these, 681 allow no complete networks to be formed, as in case (g). Six of the remaining templates then again allow an infinite sequence of networks. But there are three templates—shown as cases (h), (i) and (j)—that turn out to allow just single networks. These networks are however rather simple, and indeed the most complicated of them—case (i)—has just 20 nodes, and corresponds to a dodecahedron.

So are there in fact reasonably simple sets of constraints that in the end allow just one highly complex network, or perhaps a family of similar networks? I tend to doubt it. For our experience in Chapter 5 was that even in the much more rigid case of arrays of black and white squares, it was rather difficult to find constraints that would succeed in forcing anything but very simple patterns to occur.

So what does this mean for getting the kind of complexity that we see in our universe? We have not had difficulty in getting remarkable complexity from systems like cellular automata that we have discussed in this book. But such systems work not by being required to satisfy constraints, but instead by just repeatedly applying explicit rules.

So is it in the end sensible to think of the universe as a single structure in spacetime whose form is determined by a set of constraints? Should we really imagine that the complete spacetime history of the universe somehow always exists, and that as time progresses, we are merely exploring different parts of it? Or should we instead think that the universe—more like systems such as cellular automata—explicitly evolves in time, so that at each moment a new state of the universe is in effect created, and the old one is lost?

Models based on traditional mathematical equations—in which space and time appear just as abstract symbolic variables—have never had to make much distinction between these two views. But in trying to understand the ultimate underlying mechanisms of the universe, I believe that one must inevitably distinguish between these views.

And I strongly believe that the second view is the one most likely to provide a meaningful underlying model for our universe. But while this view is closer to our everyday perception of time, it seems to contradict the correspondence between space and time that is built into most of present-day physics. So one might wonder how then it could be consistent with experiments that have been done in physics?

One possibility, illustrated in the pictures below, is to have a system that evolves in time according to explicit rules, but for these rules to have built into them a symmetry between space and time.

Examples of one-dimensional cellular automata which exhibit a symmetry between space and time. Each picture can be generated by starting from initial conditions at the top, and then just evolving down the page repeatedly applying the cellular automaton rule. The particular rules shown are reversible second-order ones with numbers 90R and 150R.

But I very much doubt that any such obvious symmetry between space and time exists in the fundamental rules for our universe. And instead what I expect is much like we have seen many times before in this book: that even though at the lowest level there is no direct correspondence between space and time, such a correspondence nevertheless emerges when one looks in the appropriate way at larger scales of the kind probed by practical experiments.

As I will discuss in the next several sections, I suspect that for many purposes the history of the universe can in fact be represented by a certain kind of spacetime network. But the way this network is formed in effect treats space and time rather differently. And in particular—just as in a system like a cellular automaton—the network can be built up incrementally by starting with certain initial conditions and then applying appropriate underlying rules over and over again.

Any such rules can in principle be thought of as providing a set of constraints for the spacetime network. But the important point is that there is no need to do a separate search to find networks that satisfy such constraints—for the rules themselves instead immediately define a procedure for building up the necessary network.

Time and Causal Networks

I argued in the last section that the progress of time should be viewed at a fundamental level much like the evolution of a system like a cellular automaton. But one of the features of a cellular automaton is that it is set up to update all of its cells together, as if at each tick of some global clock. Yet just as it seems unreasonable to imagine that the universe consists of a rigid grid of cells in space, so also it seems unreasonable to imagine that there is a global clock which defines the updating of every element in the universe synchronized in time.

But what is the alternative? At first it may seem bizarre, but one possibility that I believe is ultimately not too far from correct is that the universe might work not like a cellular automaton in which all cells get updated at once, but instead like a mobile automaton or Turing machine, in which just a single cell gets updated at each step.

As discussed in Chapter 3—and illustrated in the picture on the right—a mobile automaton has just a single active cell which moves around from one step to the next. And because this active cell is the only one that ever gets updated, there is never any issue about synchronizing behavior of different elements at a given step.

Yet at first it might seem absurd to think that our universe could work like a mobile automaton. For certainly we do not notice any kind of active cell visiting different places in the universe in sequence. And indeed, to the contrary, our perception is that different parts of the universe seem to evolve in parallel and progress through time together.

But it turns out that what one perceives as happening in a system like a mobile automaton can depend greatly on whether one is looking at the system from outside, or whether one is oneself somehow part of the system. For from the outside, one can readily see each individual step in the evolution of a mobile automaton, and one can tell that there is just a single active cell that visits different parts of the system in sequence. But to an observer who is actually part of the mobile automaton, the perception can be quite different.

For in order to recognize that time has passed, or indeed that anything has happened, the state of the observer must somehow change. But if the observer itself just consists of a collection of cells inside a mobile automaton, then no such change can occur except on steps when the active cell in the mobile automaton visits this collection of cells.

And what this means is that between any two successive moments of time as perceived by an observer inside the mobile automaton, there can be a great many steps of underlying mobile automaton evolution.

If an observer could tell what was happening on every step, then it would be easy to recognize the sequential way in which cells are updated. But because an observer who is part of a mobile automaton can in effect only occasionally tell what has happened, then as far as such an observer is concerned, many cells can appear to have been updated in parallel between successive moments of time.

To see in more detail how this works it could be that it would be necessary to make a specific model for the observer. But in fact, it turns out that it is sufficient just to look at the evolution of the mobile

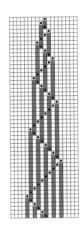

A mobile automaton in which only the single active cell indicated by a dot is updated at each step, thereby avoiding the issue of global synchronization.

automaton not in terms of individual steps, but rather in terms of updating events and the causal relationships between them.

The pictures on the facing page show an example of how this works. Picture (a) is a version of the standard representation that I have used for mobile automaton evolution elsewhere in the book—in which successive lines give the colors of cells on successive steps, and the position of the active cell is indicated at each step by a gray dot. The subsequent pictures on the facing page all ultimately give essentially the same information, but gradually present it to emphasize more a representation in terms of updating events and causal relationships.

Picture (b) is very similar to (a), but shows successive steps of mobile automaton evolution separated, with gray blobs in between indicating "updating events" corresponding to each application of the underlying mobile automaton rule. Picture (b) still has a definite row of cells for each individual step of mobile automaton evolution. But in picture (c) cells not updated on a given step are merged together, yielding vertical stripes of color that extend from one updating event to another.

So what is the significance of these stripes? In essence they serve to carry the information needed to determine what the next updating event will be. And as picture (d) begins to emphasize, one can think of these stripes as indicating what causal relationships or connections exist between updating events.

And this notion then suggests a quite different representation for the whole evolution of the mobile automaton. For rather than having a picture based on successive individual steps of evolution, one can instead form a network of the various causal relationships between updating events, with each updating event being a node in this network, and each stripe being a connection from one node to another.

A sequence of views of the evolution of a mobile automaton, showing how a network of causal relationships between updating events can be created. This network provides a very simple model for spacetime in the universe. Picture (a) is essentially the standard representation of mobile automaton evolution that I have used in this book. Picture (b) includes gray blobs to indicate updating events. Picture (c) merges cells that are not being updated. Picture (d) emphasizes the role of vertical stripes as connections between updating events. Pictures (e) through (g) show how a network can be formed with nodes corresponding to updating events. Pictures (h) and (i) demonstrate that with the particular underlying rule used here, a highly regular network is produced. ▶

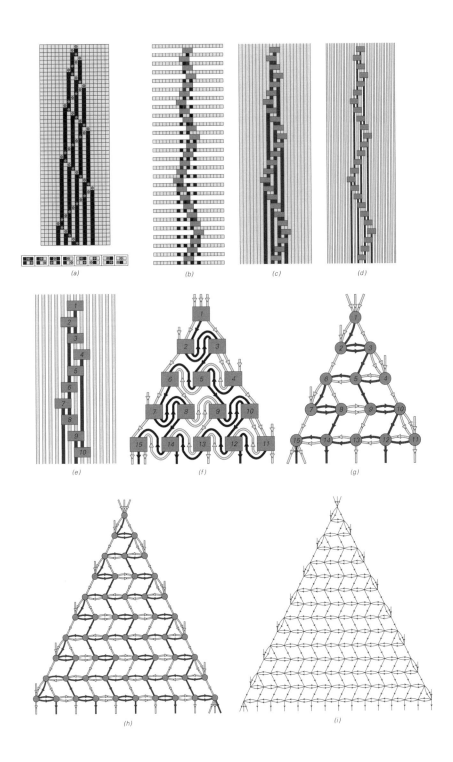

(a)

(b)

(c)

(d)

(e)

(f)

(g)

(h)

(i)

Picture (e) shows the updating events and stripes from the top of picture (d), with the updating events now explicitly numbered. Pictures (f) and (g) then show how one can take the pattern of connectivity from picture (e) and lay out the updating events as nodes so as to produce an orderly network. And for the particular mobile automaton rule used here, the network one gets ends up being highly regular, as illustrated in pictures (h) and (i).

So what is the significance of this network? It turns out that it can be thought of as defining a structure for spacetime as perceived by an observer inside the mobile automaton—in much the same way as the networks we discussed two sections ago could be thought of as defining a structure for space. Each updating event, corresponding to each node in the network, can be imagined to take place at some point in spacetime. And the connections between nodes in the network can then be thought of as defining the pattern of neighbors for points in spacetime.

But unlike in the space networks that we discussed two sections ago, the connections in the causal networks we consider here always go only one way: each connection corresponds to a causal relationship in which one event leads to another, but not the other way around.

This kind of directionality, however, is exactly what is needed if a meaningful notion of time is to emerge. For the progress of time can be defined by saying that only those events that occur later in time than a particular event can be affected by that event.

And indeed the networks in pictures (g) through (i) on the previous page were specifically laid out so that successive rows of nodes going down the page would correspond, at least roughly, to events occurring at successively later times.

As the numbering in pictures (e) through (g) illustrates, there is no direct correspondence between this notion of time and the sequence of updating events that occur in the underlying evolution of the mobile automaton. For the point is that an observer who is part of the mobile automaton will never see all the individual steps in this evolution. The most they will be able to tell is that a certain network of causal relationships exists—and their perception of time must therefore derive purely from the properties of this network.

So does the notion of time that emerges actually have the familiar features of time as we know it? One might think for example that in a network there could be loops that would lead to a deviation from the linear progression of time that we appear to experience. But in fact, with a causal network constructed from an underlying evolution process in the way we have done it here no such loops can ever occur.

So what about traces of the sequential character of evolution in the original mobile automaton? One might imagine that with only a single active cell being updated at each step different parts of the system would inevitably be perceived to progress through time one after another. But what the pictures on page 489 demonstrate is that this need not be the case. Indeed, in the networks shown there all the nodes on each row are in effect connected in parallel to the nodes on the row below. So even though the underlying rules for the mobile automaton involve no global synchronization, it is nevertheless possible for an observer inside the mobile automaton to perceive time as progressing in a synchronized way.

Later in this chapter I will discuss how space works in the context of causal networks—and how ideas of relativity theory emerge. But for now one can just think of networks like those on page 489 as being laid out so that time goes down the page and space goes across. And one can then see that if one follows connections in the network, one is always forced to go progressively down the page, even though one is able to move both backwards and forwards across the page—thus agreeing with our everyday experience of being able to move in more or less any direction in space, but always being forced to move onward in time.

So what happens with other mobile automata?

The pictures on the next two pages show a few examples.

Rules (a) and (b) yield very simple repetitive networks in which there is in effect a notion of time but not of space. The underlying way any mobile automaton works forces time to continue forever. But with rules (a) and (b) only a limited number of points in space can ever be reached.

The other rules shown do not, however, suffer from this problem: in all of them progressively more points are reached in space as time goes on. Rules (c) and (d) yield networks that can be laid out in a quite

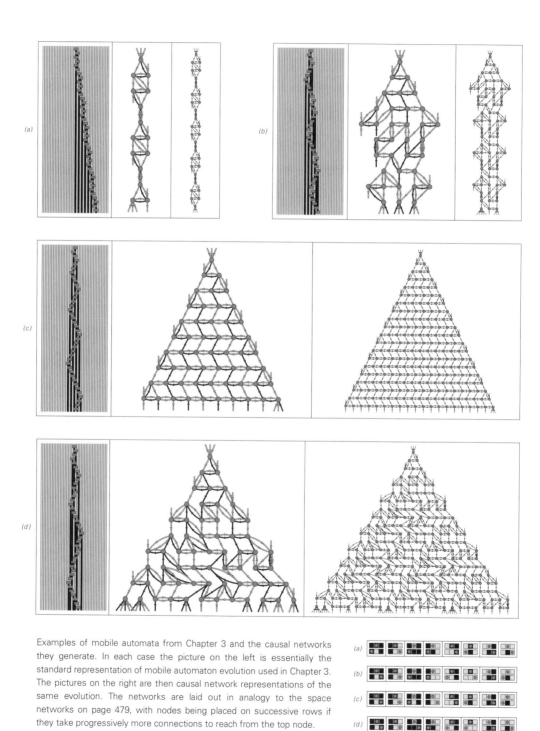

Examples of mobile automata from Chapter 3 and the causal networks they generate. In each case the picture on the left is essentially the standard representation of mobile automaton evolution used in Chapter 3. The pictures on the right are then causal network representations of the same evolution. The networks are laid out in analogy to the space networks on page 479, with nodes being placed on successive rows if they take progressively more connections to reach from the top node.

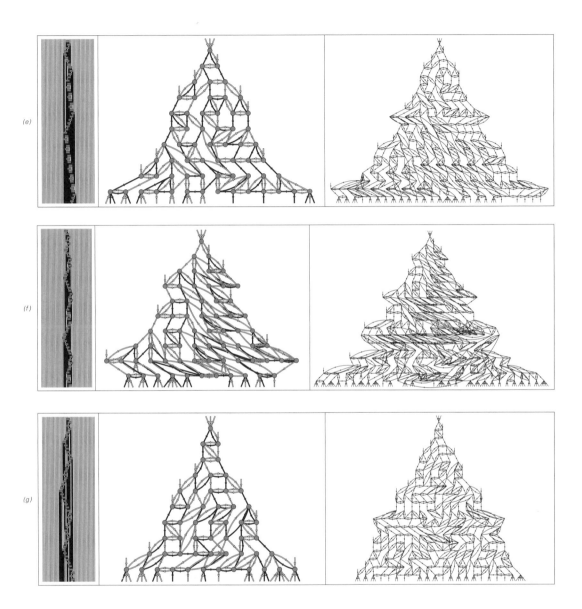

Note that a single connection can join events that occur at very different steps in the evolution of the underlying mobile automaton. And indeed to construct even a small part of the causal network can require an arbitrarily long computation in the underlying mobile automaton. Thus for example to make the causal networks in pictures (e), (f) and (g) requires looking respectively at 2447, 731 and 322 steps of mobile automaton evolution. And indeed in some cases there can be connections that are in effect never resolved. And thus for example in picture (a) there are downward connections that never reach any other node—reflecting the presence of positions on the left in the mobile automata evolution to which the active cell never returns.

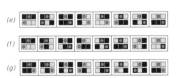

regular manner. But with rules (e), (f) and (g) the networks are more complicated, and begin to seem somewhat random.

The procedure that is used to lay out the networks on the previous two pages is a direct analog of the procedure used for space networks on page 479: the row in which a particular node will be placed is determined by the minimum number of connections that have to be followed in order to reach that node starting from the node at the top.

In cases (a) and (c) the networks obtained in this way have the property that all connections between nodes go either across or down the page. But in every other case shown, at least some connections also go up the page. So what does this mean for our notion of time? As mentioned earlier, there can never be a loop in any causal network that comes from an evolution process. But if one identifies time with position down the page, the presence of connections that go up as well as down the page implies that in some sense time does not always progress in the same direction. Yet at least in the cases shown here there is still a strong average flow down the page—agreeing with our everyday perception that time progresses only in one direction.

Like in so many other systems that we have studied in this book, the randomness that we find in causal networks will inevitably tend to wash out details of how the networks are constructed. And thus, for example, even though the underlying rules for a mobile automaton always treat space and time very differently, the causal networks that emerge nevertheless often exhibit a kind of uniform randomness in which space and time somehow work in many respects the same.

But despite this uniformity at the level of causal networks, the transformation from mobile automaton evolution to causal network is often far from uniform. And for example the pictures at the top of the facing page show the causal networks for rules (e) and (f) from the previous page—but now with each node numbered to specify the step of mobile automaton evolution from which it was derived.

And what we see is that even nodes that are close to the top of the causal network can correspond to events which occur after a large number of steps of mobile automaton evolution. Indeed, to fill in just twenty rows

Causal networks corresponding to rules (e) and (f) from page 493, with each node explicitly labelled to specify from which step of mobile automaton evolution it is derived. Even to fill in the first few rows of such causal networks, many steps of underlying mobile automaton evolution must be traced.

of the causal networks for rules (e) and (f) requires following the underlying mobile automaton evolution for 2447 and 731 steps respectively.

One feature of causal networks is that they tell one not only what the consequences of a particular event will be, but also in a sense what its causes were. Thus, for example, if one starts, say, with event 17 in the first causal network above, then to find out that its causes were events 11 and 16 one simply has to trace backwards along the connections which lead to it.

With the specific type of underlying mobile automaton used here, every node has exactly three incoming and three outgoing connections. And at least when there is overall apparent randomness, the networks that one gets by going forwards and backwards from a particular node will look very similar. In most cases there will still be small differences; but the causal network on the right above is specifically constructed to be exactly reversible—much like the cellular automata we discussed near the beginning of this chapter.

Looking at the causal networks we have seen so far, one may wonder to what extent their form depends on the particular properties of the underlying mobile automata that were used to produce them.

For example, one might think that the fact that all the networks we have seen so far grow at most linearly with time must be an inevitable consequence of the one-dimensional character of the mobile automaton rules we have used. But the picture below demonstrates that even with such one-dimensional rules, it is actually possible to get causal networks that grow more rapidly. And in fact in the case shown below there are roughly a factor 1.22 more nodes on each successive row—corresponding to overall approximate exponential growth.

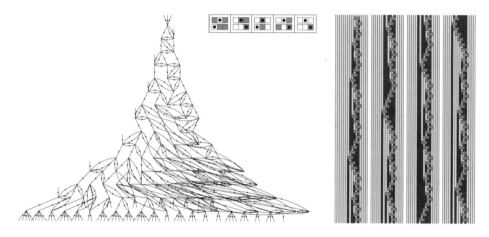

A one-dimensional mobile automaton which yields a causal network that in effect grows exponentially with time. The underlying mobile automaton acts like a binary counter, yielding a pattern whose width grows logarithmically with the number of steps. The three cases not shown in the rule are never used with the initial conditions given here.

The causal network for a system is always in some sense dual to the underlying evolution of the system. And in the case shown here the slow growth of the region visited by the active cell in the underlying evolution is reflected in rapid growth of the corresponding causal network.

As we will see later in this chapter there are in the end some limitations on the kinds of causal networks that one-dimensional mobile automata and systems like them can produce. But with different mobile automaton rules one can still already get tremendous diversity.

And even though when viewed from outside, systems like mobile automata might seem to have almost none of the familiar features of our universe, what we see is that if we as observers are in a sense part of such systems then immediately some major features quite similar to those of our universe can emerge.

The Sequencing of Events in the Universe

In the last section I discussed one type of model in which familiar notions of time can emerge without any kind of built-in global clock. The particular models I used were based on mobile automata—in which the presence of a single active cell forces only one event ever to occur in the universe at once. But as we will see in this section, there is actually no need for the setup to be so rigid, or indeed for there to be any kind of construct like an active cell.

One can think of mobile automata as being special cases of substitution systems of the type I introduced in Chapter 3. Such systems in general take a string of elements and at each step replace blocks of these elements with other elements according to some definite rule.

The picture below shows an example of one such system, and illustrates how—just like in a mobile automaton—relations between updating events can be represented by a causal network.

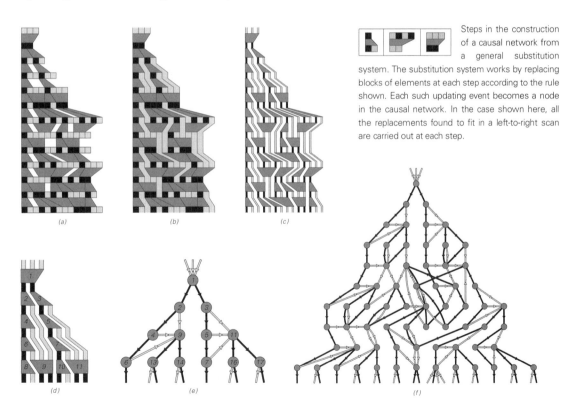

Steps in the construction of a causal network from a general substitution system. The substitution system works by replacing blocks of elements at each step according to the rule shown. Each such updating event becomes a node in the causal network. In the case shown here, all the replacements found to fit in a left-to-right scan are carried out at each step.

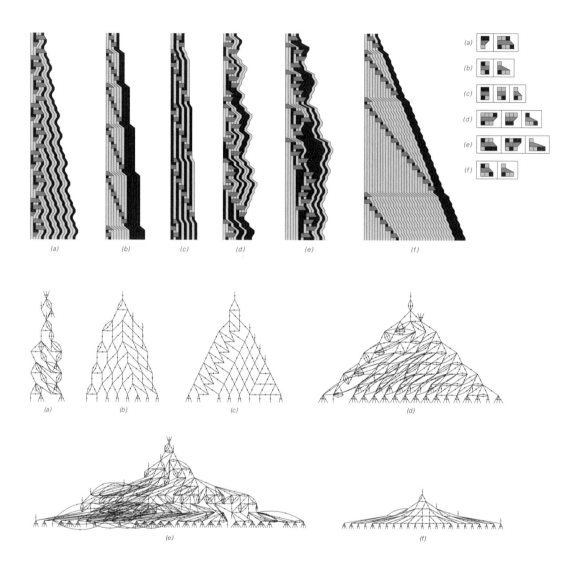

Examples of sequential substitution systems of the type discussed on page 88, and the causal networks that emerge from them. In a sequential substitution system only the first replacement that is found to apply in a left-to-right scan is ever performed at any step. Rule (a) above yields a causal network that is purely repetitive and thus yields no meaningful notion of space. Rules (b), (c) and (d) yield causal networks that in effect grow roughly linearly with time. In rule (f) the causal network grows exponentially, while in rule (e) the causal network also grows quite rapidly, though its overall growth properties are not clear. Note that to obtain the 10 levels shown here in the causal network for rule (e), it was necessary to follow the evolution of the underlying substitution system for a total of 258 steps.

Substitution systems that correspond to mobile automata can be thought of as having rules and initial conditions that are specially set up so that only one updating event can ever occur on any particular step. But with most rules—including the one shown on the previous page—there are usually several possible replacements that can be made at each step.

One scheme for deciding which replacement to make is just to scan the string from left to right and then pick the first replacement that applies. This scheme corresponds exactly to the sequential substitution systems we discussed in Chapter 3.

The pictures on the facing page show a few examples of what can happen. The behavior one gets is often fairly simple, but in some cases it can end up being highly complex. And just as in mobile automata, the causal networks that emerge typically in effect grow linearly with time. But, again as in mobile automata, there are rules such as (a) in which there is no growth—and effectively no notion of space. And there are also rules such as (f)—which turn out to be much more common in general substitution systems than in mobile automata—in which the causal network in effect grows exponentially with time.

But why do only one replacement at each step? The pictures on the next page show what happens if one again scans from left to right, but now one performs all replacements that fit, rather than just the first one.

In the case of rules (a) and (b) the result is to update every single element at every step. But since the replacements in these particular rules involve only one element at a time, one in effect has a neighbor-independent substitution system of the kind we discussed on page 82. And as we discovered there, such systems can only ever produce rather simple behavior: each element repeatedly branches into several others, yielding a causal network that has the form of a regular tree.

So what happens with replacements that involve more than just one element? In many cases, the behavior is still quite simple. But as several of the pictures on the next page demonstrate, fairly simple rules are sufficient—as in so many other systems that we have discussed in this book—to obtain highly complex behavior.

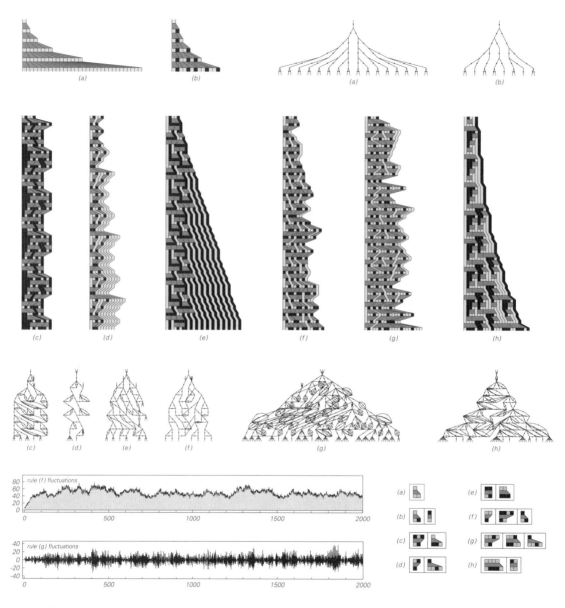

Examples of general substitution systems and the causal networks that emerge from them. In the pictures shown here, every replacement that is found to fit in a left-to-right scan is performed at each step. Rules (a) and (b) act like neighbor-independent substitution systems of the type discussed on page 84, and yield exponentially growing tree-like causal networks. The plots at the bottom show the growth rates of the patterns produced by rules (f) and (g). In the case of rule (f) the pattern turns out to be repetitive, with a period of 796 steps.

One may wonder, however, to what extent the behavior one sees depends on the exact scheme that one uses to pick which replacements to apply at each step. The answer is that for the vast majority of rules—including rules (c) through (g) in the picture on the facing page—using different schemes yields quite different behavior—and a quite different causal network.

But remarkably enough there do exist rules for which exactly the same causal network is obtained regardless of what scheme is used. And as it turns out, rules (a) and (b) from the picture on the facing page provide simple examples of this phenomenon, as illustrated in the pictures below.

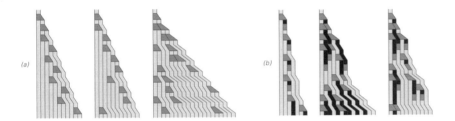

The behavior of rules (a) and (b) from the facing page when replacements are performed at random. Even though the detailed patterns obtained are different, the causal networks in these particular rules that represent relationships between replacement events are always exactly the same.

For each rule, the three different pictures shown above correspond to three different ways that replacements can be made. And while the positions of particular updating events are different in every picture, the point is that the network of causal connections between these events is always exactly the same.

This is certainly not true for every substitution system. Indeed, the pictures on the right show how it can fail, for example, for rule (e) from the facing page. What one sees in these pictures is that after event 4, different choices of replacements are made in the two cases, and the causal relationships implied by these replacements are different.

So what could ensure that no such situation would ever arise in a particular substitution system? Essentially what needs to be true is that the sequence of elements alone must always uniquely determine what replacements can be made in every part of the system. One still has a

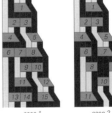

case 1   case 2

Examples of two different ways of performing replacements in rule (e) from the facing page, yielding two different causal networks.

choice of whether actually to perform a given replacement at a particular step, or whether to delay that replacement until a subsequent step. But what must be true is that there can never be any ambiguity about what replacement will eventually be made in any given part of the system.

In rules like the ones at the top of page 500 where each replacement involves just a single element this is inevitably how things must work. But what about rules that have replacements involving blocks of more than one element? Can such rules still have the necessary properties?

The pictures below show two examples of rules that do. In the first picture for each rule, replacements are made at randomly chosen steps, while in the second picture, they are in a sense always made at the earliest possible step. But the point is that in no case is there any ambiguity about what replacement will eventually be made at any particular place in the system. And as a result, the causal network that represents the relationships between different updating events is always exactly the same.

(a) 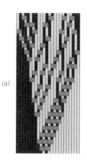    (b)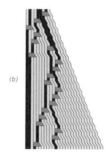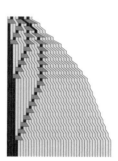

(a) (b) Examples of substitution systems in which the same causal networks are obtained regardless of the way in which replacements are performed. In the first picture for each rule, the replacements are performed essentially at random. In the second picture they are performed on the earliest possible step. Note that rule (a) effectively sorts the elements in its initial conditions, always placing black before white.

So what underlying property must the rules for a substitution system have in order to make the system as a whole operate in this way? The basic answer is that somehow different replacements must never be able to interfere with each other. And one way to guarantee this is if the blocks involved in replacements can never overlap.

In both the rules shown on the facing page, the only replacement specified is for the block ▫■. And it is inevitably the case that in any sequence of ▫'s and ■'s different blocks of the form ▫■ do not overlap. If one had replacements for blocks such as ■■, ▫▫ or ■▫■ then these could overlap. But there is an infinite sequence of blocks such as ■▫, ■▫▫ or ■▫▫▫ for which no overlap is possible, and thus for which different replacements can never interfere.

If a rule involves replacements for several distinct blocks, then to avoid the possibility of interference one must require that these blocks can never overlap either themselves or each other. The simplest non-trivial pair of blocks that has this property is ■■▫▫, ■■▫▫, while the simplest triple is ■■▫▫, ■▫▫▫, ■▫■▫. And any substitution system whose rules specify replacements only for blocks such as these is guaranteed to yield the same causal network regardless of the order in which replacements are performed.

In general the condition is in fact somewhat weaker. For it is not necessary that no overlaps exist at all in the replacements—only that no overlaps occur in whatever sequences of elements can actually be generated by the evolution of the substitution systems.

And in the end there are then all sorts of substitution systems which have the property that the causal networks they generate are always independent of the order in which their rules are applied.

So what does this mean for models of the universe?

In a system like a cellular automaton, the same underlying rule is in a sense always applied in exact synchrony to every cell at every step. But what we have seen in this section is that there also exist systems in which rules can in effect be applied whenever and wherever one wants—but the same definite causal network always emerges.

So what this means is that there is no need for any built-in global clock, or even for any mechanism like an active cell. Simply by choosing the appropriate underlying rules it is possible to ensure that any sequence of events consistent with these rules will yield the same causal network and thus in effect the same perceived history for the universe.

Uniqueness and Branching in Time

If our universe has no built-in global clock and no construct like an active cell, then it is almost inevitable that at the lowest level there will be at least some arbitrariness in how its rules can be applied.

Yet in the previous section we discovered the rather remarkable fact that there exist rules with the property that essentially regardless of how they are applied, the same causal network—and thus the same perceived history for the universe—will always emerge.

But must it in the end actually be true that the underlying rules for our universe force there to be a unique perceived history? Near the end of Chapter 5 I introduced multiway systems as examples of systems that allow multiple histories. And it turns out that multiway systems are actually extremely similar in basic structure to the substitution systems that I discussed in the previous section.

Both types of systems perform the same type of replacements on strings of elements. But while in a substitution system one always carries out just a single set of replacements at each step, getting a single new string, in a multiway system one instead carries out every possible replacement, thereby typically generating many new strings.

The picture below shows a simple example of how this works. On the first step in this particular picture, there happens to be only one replacement that can be performed consistent with the rules, so only a single string is produced. But on subsequent steps several different replacements are possible, so several strings are produced. And in general every path through a picture like this corresponds to a possible history that exists in the evolution of the multiway system.

A simple example of a multiway system in which replacements are applied in all possible ways to each string at each step.

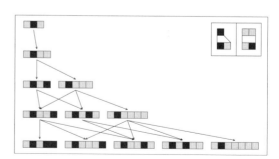

So is it conceivable that the ultimate model for our universe could be based on a multiway system? At first one might not think so. For our everyday impression is that our universe has just one definite history, not some kind of whole collection of different histories. And assuming that one is able to look at a multiway system from the outside, one will immediately see that different paths exist corresponding to different histories.

But the crucial point is that if the complete state of our universe is in effect like a single string in a multiway system, then there is no way for us ever to look at the multiway system from the outside. And as entities inside the multiway system, our perception will inevitably be that just a single path was followed, corresponding to a single history.

If one were able to look at the multiway system from the outside, this path would seem quite arbitrary. But for us inside the multiway system it is the unique path that represents the thread of experience we have had.

Up until a few centuries ago, it was widely believed that the Earth had some kind of fundamentally unique position in space. But gradually it became clear that this was not so, and that in a sense it was merely our own presence that made our particular location in space seem in any way unique. Yet for time the belief still exists that we—and our universe—somehow have a unique history. But if in fact our universe is part of a multiway system, then this will not be true. And indeed the only thing that will be unique about the particular history that our universe has had will be that it is the one we have experienced.

At a purely human level I find it rather disappointing to think that essentially none of the details of our existence are in any way unique, and that there might be other paths in the multiway system on which everything would be different. And scientifically it is also unsatisfying to have to say that there are features of our universe which are not determined by any finite set of underlying rules, but are instead in a sense just pure accidents of history associated with the particular path that we have happened to follow in a multiway system.

In the early parts of Chapter 7 we discussed various possible origins for the apparent randomness that we see in many natural systems. And if the universe is described by a multiway system, then there will be an additional source of randomness: the arbitrariness of the path corresponding to the history that we have experienced.

In many respects this randomness is similar to the randomness from the environment that we discussed at the beginning of Chapter 7. But an important difference is that it would occur even if one could in effect perfectly isolate a system from the rest of the universe. If in the past one had seen apparent randomness in such a system there might have seemed to be no choice but to assume something like an underlying multiway system. But one of the discoveries of this book is that it is actually quite possible to generate what appears to be almost perfect randomness just by following definite underlying rules.

And indeed I would not expect that observations of randomness could ever reasonably be used to show that our universe is part of a multiway system. And in fact my guess is that the only way to show this with any certainty would be actually to find a specific set of multiway system rules with the property that regardless of the path that gets followed these rules would always yield behavior that agrees with the various observed features of our universe.

At some level it might seem surprising that a multiway system could ever consistently exhibit any particular form of behavior. For one might imagine that with so many different paths to choose from it would often be the case that almost any behavior would be able to occur on some path or another. And indeed, as the picture on the left shows, it is not difficult to construct multiway systems in which all possible strings of a particular kind are produced.

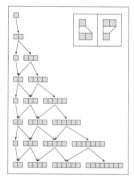

A multiway system in which strings of any length can be generated—but in which only specific sequences of lengths actually occur on any path.

But if one looks not just at individual strings but rather at the sequences of strings that exist along paths in the multiway system, then one finds that these can no longer be so arbitrary. And indeed, in any multiway system with a limited set of rules, such sequences must necessarily be subject to all sorts of constraints.

In general, each path in a multiway system can be thought of as being defined by a possible sequence of ways in which the replacements specified by a multiway system rule can be applied. And each such path in turn then defines a causal network of the kind we discussed in the previous section. But as we saw there, certain underlying rules have the property that the form of this causal network ends up being the same regardless of the order in which replacements are applied—and thus regardless of the path that is followed in the multiway system.

The pictures below show some simple examples of rules with this property. And as it turns out, it is fairly easy to recognize the presence of the property from the overall pattern of multiway system paths that occur.

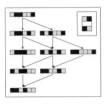 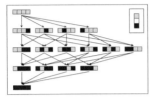

Examples of multiway systems in which the causal network associated with every path is exactly the same. All such multiway systems have the property that every pair of paths which diverge at a particular step can converge again on the following step. The first rule shown has the effect of sorting the elements in the string.

 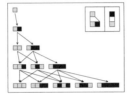

If one starts from a given initial string, then typically one will generate different strings by applying different replacements. But if one is going to get the same causal network, then it must always be the case that there are replacements one can apply to the strings one has generated that yield the same final string. So what this means is that any pair of paths in the multiway system that diverge must be able to converge again within just one step—so that all the arrows in pictures like the ones above must lie on the edges of quadrilaterals.

Most multiway systems, however, do not have exactly this property, and as a result the causal networks that are obtained by following different paths in them will not be absolutely identical. But it still turns out that whenever paths can always eventually converge—even if not in a fixed number of steps—there will necessarily be similarities on a sufficiently large scale in the causal networks that are obtained.

At the level of individual events, the structure of the causal networks will typically vary greatly. But if one looks at large enough collections of events, these details will tend to be washed out, and regardless of the path one chooses, the overall form of causal network will be essentially the same. And what this means is that on a sufficiently large scale, the universe will appear to have a unique history, even though at the level of individual events there will be considerable arbitrariness.

If there is not enough convergence in the multiway system it will still be possible to get stuck with different types of strings that never lead to each other. And if this happens, then it means that the history of the universe can in effect follow many truly separate branches. But whenever there is significant randomness produced by the evolution of the multiway system, this does not typically appear to occur.

So this suggests that in fact it is at some level not too difficult for multiway systems to reproduce our everyday perception that more or less definite things happen in the universe. But while this means that it might be possible for there to be arbitrariness in the causal network for the universe, it still tends to be my suspicion that there is not—and that in fact the particular rules followed by the universe do in the end have the property that they always yield the same causal network.

Evolution of Networks

Earlier in this chapter, I suggested that at the lowest level space might consist of a giant network of nodes. But how might such a network evolve?

The most straightforward possibility is that it could work much like the substitution systems that we have discussed in the past few sections—and that at each step some piece or pieces of the network could be replaced by others according to some fixed rule.

The pictures at the top of the facing page show two very simple examples. Starting with a network whose connections are like the edges of a tetrahedron, both the rules shown work by replacing each node at each step by a certain fixed cluster of nodes.

This setup is very much similar to the neighbor-independent substitution systems that we discussed on pages 83 and 187. And just as in these systems, it is possible for intricate structures to be produced, but the structures always turn out to have a highly regular nested form.

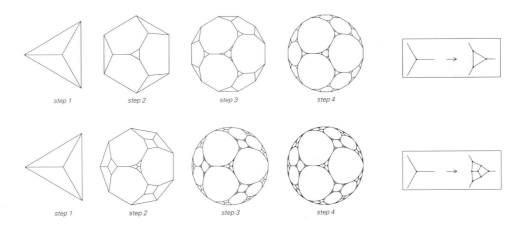

Network evolution in which each node is replaced at each step by a fixed cluster of nodes. The resulting networks have a regular nested form. The dimensions of the limiting networks are respectively *Log[2, 3]* ≈ *1.58* and *Log[3, 7]* ≈ *1.77*.

So what about more general substitution systems? Are there analogs of these for networks? The answer is that there are, and they are based on making replacements not just for individual nodes, but rather for clusters of nodes, as shown in the pictures below.

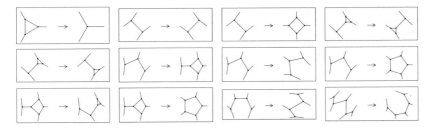

Examples of rules that involve replacing clusters of nodes in a network by other clusters of nodes. All these rules preserve the planarity of a network. Notice that some of them cannot be reversed since their right-hand sides are too symmetrical to determine which orientation of the left-hand side should be used.

In the substitution systems for strings discussed in previous sections, the rules that are given can involve replacing any block of elements by any other. But in networks there are inevitably some restrictions. For example, if a cluster of nodes has a certain number of connections to the rest of the network, then it cannot be replaced by a cluster which has a different number of connections. And in addition, one cannot have replacements

A replacement whose outcome orientation cannot be determined.

like the one on the left that go from a symmetrical cluster to one for which a particular orientation has to be chosen.

But despite these restrictions a fairly large number of replacements are still possible; for example, there are a total of 419 distinct ones that exist involving clusters with no more than five nodes.

So given a replacement for a cluster of a particular form, how should such a replacement actually be applied to a network? At first one might think that one could set up some kind of analog of a cellular automaton and just replace all relevant clusters of nodes at once.

But in general this will not work. For as the picture below illustrates, a particular form of cluster can in general appear in many overlapping ways within a given network.

 The 12 ways in which the cluster of nodes on the left occurs in a particular network. In the particular case shown, each way turns out to overlap with nodes in exactly four others.

The issue is essentially no different from the one that we encountered in previous sections for blocks of elements in substitution systems on strings. But an additional complication is that in networks, unlike strings, there is no immediately obvious ordering of elements.

Nevertheless, it is still possible to devise schemes for deciding where in a network replacements should be carried out. One fairly simple scheme, illustrated on the facing page, allows only a single replacement to be performed at each step, and picks the location of this replacement so as to affect the least recently updated nodes.

In each pair of pictures in the upper part of the page, the top one shows the form of the network before the replacement, and the bottom one shows the result after doing the replacement—with the cluster of nodes involved in the replacement being highlighted in both cases. In the 3D pictures in the lower part of the page, networks that arise on successive steps are shown stacked one on top of the other, with the nodes involved in each replacement joined by gray lines.

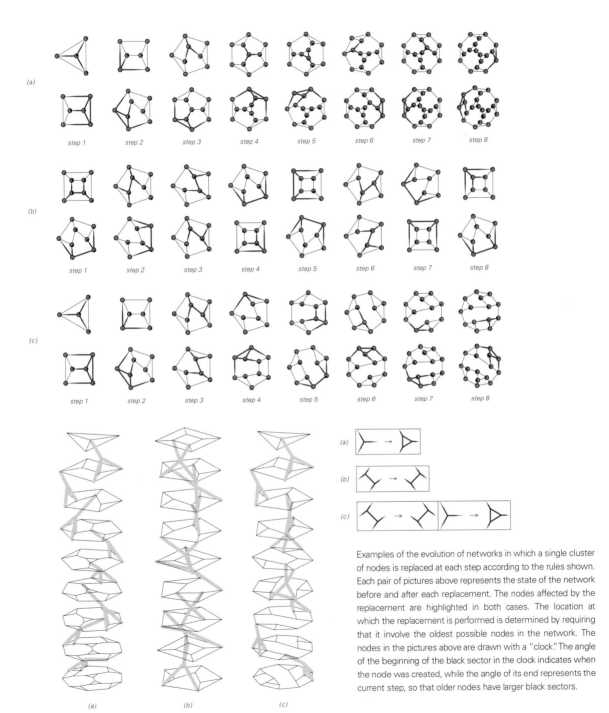

step 1   step 2   step 3   step 4   step 5   step 6   step 7   step 8

(b)

step 1   step 2   step 3   step 4   step 5   step 6   step 7   step 8

(c)

step 1   step 2   step 3   step 4   step 5   step 6   step 7   step 8

(a)

(b)

(c)

(a)

(b)

(c)

Examples of the evolution of networks in which a single cluster of nodes is replaced at each step according to the rules shown. Each pair of pictures above represents the state of the network before and after each replacement. The nodes affected by the replacement are highlighted in both cases. The location at which the replacement is performed is determined by requiring that it involve the oldest possible nodes in the network. The nodes in the pictures above are drawn with a "clock". The angle of the beginning of the black sector in the clock indicates when the node was created, while the angle of its end represents the current step, so that older nodes have larger black sectors.

Inevitably there is a certain arbitrariness in the way these pictures are drawn. For the underlying rules specify only what the pattern of connections in a network should be—not how its nodes should be laid out on the page. And in the effort to make clear the relationship between networks obtained on different steps, even identical networks can potentially be drawn somewhat differently.

With rule (a), however, it is fairly easy to see that a simple nested structure is produced, directly analogous to the one shown on page 509. And with rule (b), obvious repetitive behavior is obtained.

So what about more complicated behavior? It turns out that even with rule (c), which is essentially just a combination of rules (a) and (b), significantly more complicated behavior can already occur.

The picture below shows a few more steps in the evolution of this rule. And the behavior obtained never seems to repeat, nor do the networks produced exhibit any kind of obvious nested form.

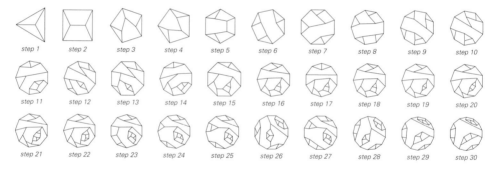

More steps in the evolution of rule (c) from the previous page. The number of nodes increases irregularly (though roughly linearly) with successive steps.

What about other schemes for applying replacements? The pictures on the facing page show what happens if at each step one allows not just a single replacement, but all replacements that do not overlap.

It takes fewer steps for networks to be built up, but the results are qualitatively similar to those on the previous page: rule (a) yields a nested structure, rule (b) gives repetitive behavior, while rule (c) produces behavior that seems complicated and in some respects random.

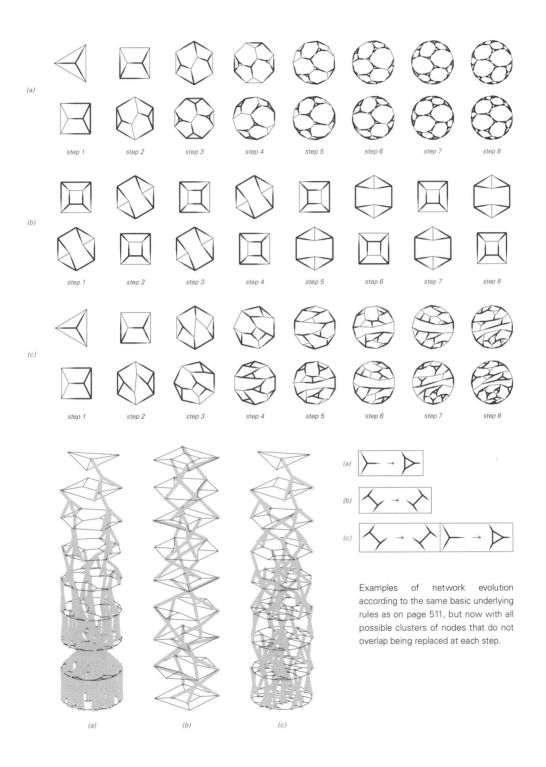

Examples of network evolution according to the same basic underlying rules as on page 511, but now with all possible clusters of nodes that do not overlap being replaced at each step.

Just as for substitution systems on strings, one can find causal networks that represent the causal connections between different updating events on networks. And as an example the pictures below show such causal networks for the evolution processes on the previous page.

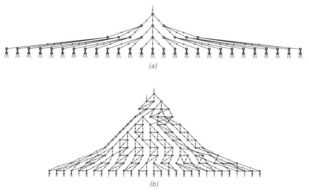

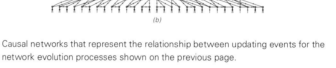

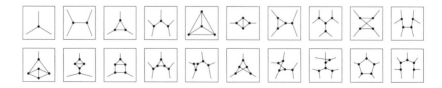

Causal networks that represent the relationship between updating events for the network evolution processes shown on the previous page.

In the rather simple case of rule (a) the results turn out to be independent of the updating scheme that was used. But for rules (b) and (c), different schemes in general yield different causal networks.

So what kinds of underlying replacement rules lead to causal networks that are independent of how the rules are applied? The situation is much the same as for strings—with the basic criterion just being that all replacements that appear in the rules should be for clusters of nodes that can never overlap themselves or each other.

The pictures below show all possible distinct clusters with up to five nodes—and all but three of these already can overlap themselves.

All possible distinct clusters containing up to five nodes, with planarity not required.

But among slightly larger clusters there turn out to be many that do not overlap themselves—and indeed this becomes common as soon as there are at least two connections between each dangling one.

The first few examples are shown below. And in almost all of these, there is no overlap not only within a single cluster, but also between different clusters. And this means that rules based on replacements for collections of these clusters will have the property that the causal networks they produce are independent of the updating scheme used.

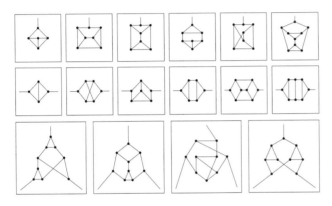

The simplest clusters that have no overlaps with themselves—and mostly have no overlaps with each other. Replacements for sets of clusters that do not overlap have the property of causal invariance.

One feature of the various rules I showed earlier is that they all maintain planarity of networks—so that if one starts with a network that can be laid out in the plane without any lines crossing, then every subsequent network one gets will also have this property.

Yet in our everyday experience space certainly does not seem to have this property. But beyond the practical problem of displaying what happens, there is actually no fundamental difficulty in setting up rules that can generate non-planarity—and indeed many rules based on the clusters above will for example do this.

So in the end, if one manages to find the ultimate rules for the universe, my expectation is that they will give rise to networks that on a small scale look largely random. But this very randomness will most likely be what for example allows a definite and robust value of 3 to emerge for the dimensionality of space—even though all of the many complicated phenomena in our universe must also somehow be represented within the structure of the same network.

Space, Time and Relativity

Several sections ago I argued that as observers within the universe everything we can observe must at some level be associated purely with the network of causal connections between events in the universe. And in the past few sections I have outlined a series of types of models for how such a causal network might actually get built up.

But how do the properties of causal networks relate to our normal notions of space and time? There turn out to be some slight subtleties—but these seem to be exactly what end up yielding the theory of relativity.

As we saw in earlier sections, if one has an explicit evolution history for a system it is straightforward to deduce a causal network from it. But given only a causal network, what can one say about the evolution history?

The picture below shows an example of how successive steps in a particular evolution history can be recovered from a particular set of slices through the causal network derived from it. But what if one were to choose a different set of slices? In general, the sequence of strings that one would get would not correspond to anything that could arise from the same underlying substitution system.

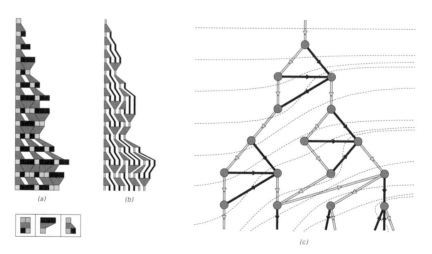

(a)   (b)

(c)

An example of how the succession of states in an evolution history can be recovered by taking appropriate slices through a causal network. Any consistent choice of such slices will correspond to a possible evolution history—with the same underlying rules, but potentially a different scheme for determining the order in which to apply replacements.

But if one has a system that yields the same causal network independent of the scheme used to apply its underlying rules, then the situation is different. And in this case any slice that consistently divides the causal network into a past and a future must correspond to a possible state of the underlying system—and any non-overlapping sequence of such slices must represent a possible evolution history for the system.

If we could explicitly see the particular underlying evolution history for the system that corresponds to our universe then this would in a sense immediately provide absolute information about space and time in the universe. But if we can observe only the causal network for the universe then our information about space and time must inevitably be deduced indirectly from looking at slices of causal networks.

And indeed only some causal networks even yield a reasonable notion of space at all. For one can think of successive slices through a causal network as corresponding to states at successive moments in time. But for there to be something one can reasonably think of as space one has to be able to identify some background features that stay more or less the same—which means that the causal network must yield consistent similarities between states it generates at successive moments in time.

One might have thought that if one just had an underlying system which did not change on successive steps then this would immediately yield a fixed structure for space. But in fact, without updating events, no causal network at all gets built up. And so a system like the one at the top of the next page is about the simplest that can yield something even vaguely reminiscent of ordinary space.

In practice I certainly do not expect that even parts of our universe where nothing much seems to be going on will actually have causal networks as simple as at the top of the next page. And in fact, as I mentioned at the end of the previous section, what I expect instead is that there will always tend to be all sorts of complicated and seemingly random behavior at small scales—though at larger scales this will typically get washed out to yield the kind of consistent average properties that we ordinarily associate with space.

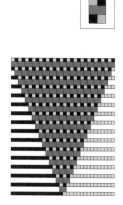

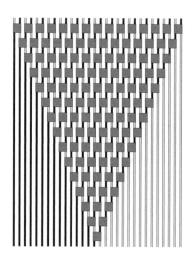

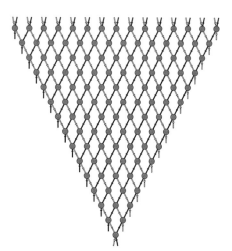

A very simple substitution system whose causal network has slices that can be thought of as corresponding to a highly regular idealization of one-dimensional ordinary space. The rule effectively just sorts elements so that black ones come first, and yields the same causal network regardless of what updating scheme is used.

One of the defining features of space as we normally experience it is a certain locality that leads most things that happen at some particular position to be able at first to affect only things very near them.

Such locality is built into the basic structure of systems like cellular automata. For in such systems the underlying rules allow the color of a particular cell to affect only its immediate neighbors at each step. And this has the consequence that effects in such systems can spread only at a limited rate, as manifest for example in a maximum slope for the edges of patterns like those in the pictures below.

Examples of patterns produced by cellular automata, illustrating the fact discussed in Chapter 6 that the edge of each pattern has a maximum slope equal to one cell per step, corresponding to an absolute upper limit on the rate of information transmission—similar to the speed of light in physics.

In physics there also seems to be a maximum speed at which the effects of any event can spread: the speed of light, equal to about 300 million meters per second. And it is common in spacetime physics to draw "light cones" of the kind shown at the right to indicate the region that will be reached by a light signal emitted from a particular position in space at a particular time. So what is the analog of this in a causal network?

The answer is straightforward, for the very definition of a causal network shows that to see how the effects of a particular event spread one just has to follow the successive connections from it in the causal network.

But in the abstract there is no reason that these connections should lead to points that can in any way be viewed as nearby in space. Among the various kinds of underlying systems that I have studied in this book many have no particular locality in their basic rules. But the particular kinds of systems I have discussed for both strings and networks in the past few sections do have a certain locality, in that each individual replacement they make involves only a few nearby elements.

One might choose to consider systems like these just because it seems easier to specify their rules. But their locality also seems important in giving rise to anything that one can reasonably recognize as space.

For without it there will tend to be no particular way to match up corresponding parts in successive slices through the causal networks that are produced. And as a result there will not be the consistency between successive slices necessary to have a stable notion of space.

In the case of substitution systems for strings, locality of underlying replacement rules immediately implies overall locality of effects in the system. For the different elements in the system are always just laid out in a one-dimensional string, with the result that local replacement rules can only ever propagate effects to nearby elements in the string—much like in a one-dimensional cellular automaton.

If one is dealing with an underlying system based on networks, however, then the situation can be somewhat more complicated. For as we discussed several sections ago—and will discuss again in the final sections of this chapter—there will typically be only an approximate correspondence between the structure of the network and the structure of ordinary space. And so for example—as we will discuss later in connection with quantum phenomena—there may sometimes be a kind of thread that connects parts of the network that would not

Schematic illustration of a light cone in physics. Light emitted at a point in space will normally spread out with time into a cone, whose cross-section is shown schematically here.

normally be considered nearby in three-dimensional space. And so when clusters of nodes that are nearby with respect to connections on the network get updated, they can potentially propagate effects to what might be considered distant points in space.

Nevertheless, if a network is going to correspond to space as it seems to exist in our universe, such phenomena must not be too important—and in the end there must to a good approximation be the kind of straightforward locality that exists for example in the simple causal network of page 518.

In the next section I will discuss how actual physical entities like particles propagate in systems represented by causal networks. But ultimately the whole point of causal networks is that their connections represent all possible ways that effects propagate. Yet these connections are also what end up defining our notions of space and time in a system. And particularly in a causal network as regular as the one on page 518 one can then immediately view each connection in the causal network as corresponding to an effect propagating a certain distance in space during a certain interval in time.

So what about a more complicated causal network? One might imagine that its connections could perhaps represent varying distances in space and varying intervals in time. But there is no independent way to work out distance in space or interval in time beyond looking at the connections in the causal network. So the only thing that ultimately makes sense is to measure space and time taking each connection in the causal network to correspond to an identical elementary distance in space and elementary interval in time.

One may guess that this elementary distance is around 10^{-35} meters, and that the elementary time interval is around 10^{-43} seconds. But whatever these values are, a crucial point is that their ratio must be a fixed speed, and we can identify this with the speed of light. So this means that in a sense every connection in a causal network can be viewed as representing the propagation of an effect at the speed of light.

And with this realization we are now close to being able to see how the kinds of systems I have discussed must almost inevitably succeed in reproducing the fundamental features of relativity theory.

But first we must consider the concept of motion.

To say that one is not moving means that one imagines one is in a sense sampling the same region of space throughout time. But if one is moving—say at a fixed speed—then this means that one imagines that the region of space one is sampling systematically shifts with time, as illustrated schematically in the simple pictures on the right.

Graphical representation in space and time of motion at fixed speeds.

But as we have seen in discussing causal networks, it is in general quite arbitrary how one chooses to match up space at different times. And in fact one can just view different states of motion as corresponding to different such choices: in each case one matches up space so as to treat the point one is at as being the same throughout time.

Motion at a fixed speed is then the simplest case—and the one emphasized in the so-called special theory of relativity. And at least in the context of a highly regular causal network like the one in the picture on page 518 there is a simple interpretation to this: it just corresponds to looking at slices at different angles through the causal network.

Successive parallel slices through the causal network in general correspond to successive states of the underlying system at successive moments in time. But there is nothing that determines in any absolute way the overall angle of these slices in pictures like those on page 518. And the point is that in fact one can interpret slices at different angles as corresponding to motion at different fixed speeds.

If the angle is so great that there are connections going up as well as down between slices, then there will be a problem. But otherwise it will always be the case that regardless of angle, successive slices must correspond to possible evolution histories for the underlying system.

One might have thought that states obtained from slices at different angles would inevitably be consistent only with different sets of underlying rules. But in fact this is not the case, and instead the exact same rules can reproduce slices at all angles. And this is a consequence of the fact that the substitution system on page 518 has the property of causal invariance—so that it gives the same causal network independent of the scheme used to apply its underlying rules.

It is slightly more complicated to represent uniform motion in causal networks that are not as regular as the one on page 518. But whenever there is sufficient uniformity to give a stable structure to space one can still think of something like parallel slices at different angles as representing motion at different fixed speeds.

And the crucial point is that whenever the underlying system is causal invariant the exact same underlying rules will account for what one sees in slices at different angles. And what this means is that in effect the same rules will apply regardless of how fast one is going.

And the remarkable point is then that this is also what seems to happen in physics. For everyday experience—together with all sorts of detailed experiments—strongly support the idea that so long as there are no effects from acceleration or external forces, physical systems work exactly the same regardless of how fast they are moving.

At the outset it might not have seemed conceivable that any system which at some level just applies a fixed program to various underlying elements could successfully capture the phenomenon of motion. For certainly a system like a typical cellular automaton does not—since for example its effective rules for evolution at different angles will usually be quite different. But there are two crucial ideas that make motion work in the kinds of systems I am discussing here. First, that causal networks can represent everything that can be observed. And second, that with causal invariance different slices through a causal network can be produced by the same underlying rules.

Historically, the idea that physical processes should always be independent of overall motion goes back at least three hundred years. And from this idea one expects for example that light should always travel at its usual speed with respect to whatever emitted it. But what if one happens to be moving with respect to this emitter? Will the light then appear to be travelling at a different speed? In the case of sound it would. But what was discovered around the end of the 1800s is that in the case of light it does not. And it was essentially to explain this surprising fact that the special theory of relativity was developed.

In the past, however, there seemed to be no obvious underlying mechanism that could account for the validity of this basic theory. But now it turns out that the kinds of discrete causal network models that I have described almost inevitably end up being able to do this.

And essentially the reason for this is that—as I discussed above—each individual connection in any causal network must almost by definition represent propagation of effects at the speed of light. The overall structure of space that emerges may be complicated, and there may be objects that end up moving at all sorts of speeds. But at least locally the individual connections basically define the speed of light as a fixed maximum rate of propagation of any effect. And the point is that they do this regardless of how fast the source of an effect may be moving.

So from this one can use essentially standard arguments to derive all the various phenomena familiar from ordinary relativity theory. A typical example is time dilation, in which a fixed time interval for a system moving at some speed seems to correspond to a longer time interval for a system at rest. The picture on the next page shows schematically how this at first unexpected result arises.

The basic idea is to consider what happens when a system that can act as a simple clock moves at different speeds. At a traditional physics level one can think of the clock as having a photon of light bouncing backwards and forwards between mirrors a fixed distance apart. But more generally one can think of following criss-crossing connections that exist in some fixed fragment of a causal network.

In the picture on the next page time goes down the page. The internal mechanism of the clock is shown as a zig-zag black line—with each sweep of this line corresponding to the passage of one unit of time.

The black line is always assumed to be moving at the speed of light—so that it always lies on the surface of a light cone, as indicated in the top row of pictures. But then in successive pictures the whole clock is taken to move at increasing fractions of the speed of light.

The dark gray region in each picture represents a fixed amount of time for the clock—corresponding to a fixed number of sweeps of the black line. But as the pictures indicate, it is then essentially just a matter of geometry to see that this dark gray region will correspond to progressively larger amounts of time for a system at rest—in just the way predicted by the standard formula of relativistic time dilation.

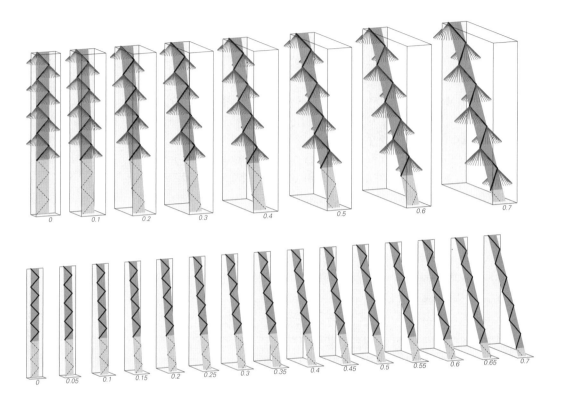

A simple derivation of the classic phenomenon of relativistic time dilation. The pictures show the behavior of a very simple idealized clock going at different fractions of the speed of light. The clock can be thought of as consisting of a photon of light bouncing backwards and forwards between mirrors a fixed distance apart. (At a more general level in my approach it can also be thought of as a fragment of a causal network.) Time is shown going down the page, so that the photon in the clock traces out a zig-zag path. The fundamental assumption—that in my approach is just a consequence of basic properties of causal networks—is that the photon always goes at the speed of light, so that its path always lies on the surface of light cones like the ones in the top row of pictures. A fixed interval of time for the clock—as indicated by the length of the darker gray regions—corresponds to a progressively longer interval of time at rest. The amount of this time dilation is given by the classic relativistic formula $1/\sqrt{1 - v^2/c^2}$, where v/c is the ratio of the speed of the clock to the speed of light. Such time dilation is routinely observed in particle accelerators—and has to be corrected for in GPS satellites. It leads to the so-called twin paradox in which less time will pass for a member of a twin going at high speed in a spacecraft than one staying at rest. The fact that time dilation is a general phenomenon not restricted to something like the simple clock shown relies in my approach on general properties of causal networks. Once the basic assumptions are established, the derivation of time dilation given here is no different in principle from the original one given in 1905, though I believe it is in many ways considerably clearer. Note that it is necessary to consider motion in two dimensions—so that the clock as a whole can be moving perpendicular to the path of the photon inside it. If these were parallel, one would inevitably get not just pure time dilation, but a mixture of it and length contraction.

Elementary Particles

There are some aspects of the universe—notably the structure of space and time—that present-day physics tends to assume are continuous. But over the past century it has at least become universally accepted that all matter is made up of identifiable discrete particles.

Experiments have found a fairly small number of fundamentally different kinds of particles, with electrons, photons, muons and the six basic types of quarks being a few examples. And it is one of the striking observed regularities of the universe that all particles of a given kind—say electrons—seem to be absolutely identical in their properties.

But what actually are particles? As far as present-day experiments can tell, electrons, for example, have zero size and no substructure. But particularly if space is discrete, it seems almost inevitable that electrons and other particles must be made up of more fundamental elements.

So how might this work? An immediate possibility that I suspect is actually not too far from the mark is that such particles are analogs of the localized structures that we saw earlier in this book in systems like the class 4 cellular automata shown on the right. And if this is so, then it means that at the lowest level, the rules for the universe need make no reference to particular particles. Instead, all the particles we see would just emerge as structures formed from more basic elements.

In networks it can be somewhat difficult to visualize localized structures. But the picture below nevertheless shows a simple example of how a localized structure can move across a regular planar network.

Both the examples on this page show structures that exist on very regular backgrounds. But to get any kind of realistic model for actual

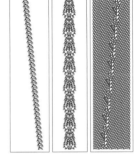

Typical examples of particle-like localized structures in class 4 cellular automata.

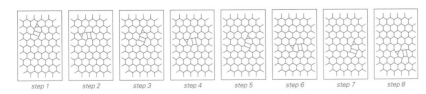

step 1   step 2   step 3   step 4   step 5   step 6   step 7   step 8

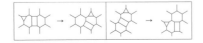

A particle-like localized structure in a network.

particles in physics one must consider structures on much more complicated and random backgrounds. For any network that has a serious chance of representing actual space—even a supposedly empty part—will no doubt show all sorts of seemingly random activity. So any localized structure that might represent a particle will somehow have to persist even on this kind of random background.

Yet at first one might think that such randomness would inevitably disrupt any kind of definite persistent structure. But the pictures below show two simple examples where it does not. In the first case, there are localized cracks that persist. And in the second case, there are two different types of regions, separated by boundaries that act like localized structures with definite properties, and persist until they annihilate.

 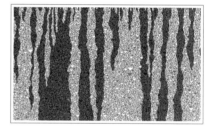

Examples of one-dimensional cellular automata that support various forms of persistent structures even on largely random backgrounds. These are 3-color totalistic rules with codes 294 and 1893.

So what about networks? It turns out that here again it is possible to get definite structures that persist even in the presence of randomness. And to see an example of this consider setting up rules like those on page 509 that preserve the planarity of networks.

Starting off with a network that is planar—so that it can be drawn flat on a page without any lines crossing—such rules can certainly give all sorts of complex and apparently random behavior. But the way the rules are set up, all the networks they produce must still be planar.

And if one starts off with a network like the one on the left that can only be drawn with lines crossing, then what will happen is that the non-planarity of the network will be preserved. But to what extent does this non-planarity correspond to a definite structure in the network?

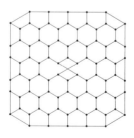

A network with a single irreducible crossing of lines.

There are typically many different ways to draw a non-planar network, each with lines crossing in different places. But there is a fundamental result in graph theory that shows that if a network is not planar, then it must always be possible to identify in it a specific part that can be reduced to one of the two forms shown on the right—or just the second form for a network with three connections at each node.

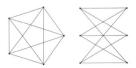

The K_5 and $K_{3,3}$ forms that lead to non-planarity in networks.

So this implies that one can in fact meaningfully associate a definite structure with non-planarity. And while at some level the structure can be spread out in the network, the point is that it must always in effect have a localized core with the form shown on the right.

In general one can imagine having several pieces of non-planarity in a network—perhaps each pictured like a carrying handle. But if the underlying rules for the network preserve planarity then each of these pieces of non-planarity must on their own be persistent—and can in a sense only disappear through processes like annihilating with each other.

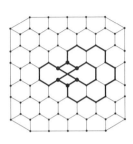

How $K_{3,3}$ is embedded in the network from the facing page.

So might these be like actual particles in physics?

In the realistic case of network rules for the universe, planarity as such is presumably not preserved. But observations in physics suggest that there are several quantities like electric charge that are conserved. And ultimately the values of these quantities must reflect properties of underlying networks that are preserved by network evolution rules.

And if these rules satisfy the constraint of causal invariance that I discussed in previous sections, then I suspect that this means that they will inevitably exhibit various additional features—perhaps notably including for example what is usually known as local gauge invariance.

But what is most relevant here is that it seems likely that—much as for non-planarity—nonzero values of quantities conserved by network evolution rules can be thought of as being associated with some sort of local structures or tangles of connections in the network. And I suspect that it is essentially such structures that define the cores of the various types of elementary particles that are seen in physics.

Before the results of this book it might have seemed completely implausible that anything like this could be correct. For independent of any specific arguments about networks and their evolution, traditional intuition would tend to make one think that the elaborate properties of particles must inevitably be the result of an elaborate underlying setup. But what we have now seen over and over again in this book is that in fact it is perfectly possible to get phenomena of great complexity even with a remarkably simple underlying setup. And I suspect that particles in physics—with all their various properties and interactions—are just yet another example of this very general phenomenon.

One immediate thing that might seem to suggest that elementary particles must somehow be based on simple discrete structures is the fact that their values of quantities like electric charge always seem to be in simple rational ratios. In traditional particle physics this is explained by saying that many if not all particles are somehow just manifestations of the same underlying abstract object, related by a simple fixed group of symmetry operations. But in terms of networks one can imagine a much more explicit explanation: that there are just a simple discrete set of possible structures for the cores of particles—each perhaps related in some quite mechanical way by the group of symmetry operations.

But in addition to quantities like electric charge, another important intrinsic property of all particles is mass. And unlike for example electric charge the observed masses of elementary particles never seem to be in simple ratios—so that for example the muon is about 206.7683 times the mass of the electron, while the tau lepton is about 16.819 times the mass of the muon. But despite such results, it is still conceivable that there could in the end be simple relations between truly fundamental particle masses—since it turns out that the masses that have actually been observed in effect also include varying amounts of interaction energy.

A defining feature of any particle is that it can somehow move in space while maintaining its identity. In traditional physics, such motion has a straightforward mathematical representation, and it has not usually seemed meaningful to ask what might underlie it. But in the approach that I take here, motion is no longer such an intrinsic concept, and the motion of a particle must be thought of as a process that is made up of a whole sequence of explicit lower-level steps.

So at first, it might seem surprising that one can even set up a particular type of particle to move at different speeds. But from the discussion in the previous section it follows that this is actually an almost inevitable consequence of having underlying rules that show causal invariance. For assuming that around the particle there is some kind of uniformity in the causal network—and thus in the apparent structure of space—taking slices through the causal network at an appropriate angle will always make any particle appear to be at rest. And the point is that causal invariance then implies that the same underlying rules can be used to update the network in all such cases.

But what happens if one has two particles that are moving with different velocities? What will the events associated with the second particle look like if one takes slices through the causal network so that the first particle appears to be at rest? The answer is that the more the second particle moves between successive slices, the more updating events must be involved. For in effect any node that was associated with the particle on either one slice or the next must be updated—and the more the particle moves, the less these will overlap. And in addition, there will inevitably appear to be an asymmetry in the pattern of events relative to whatever direction the particle is moving.

There are many subtleties here, and indeed to explain the details of what is going on will no doubt require quite a few new and rather abstract concepts. But the general picture that I believe will emerge is that when particles move faster they will appear to have more nodes associated with them.

Most likely the intrinsic properties of a particle—like its electric charge—will be associated with some sort of core that corresponds to a definite network structure involving a roughly fixed number of nodes. But I suspect that the apparent motion of the particle will be associated with a kind of coat that somehow interpolates from the core to the uniform background of surrounding space. With different slices through the causal network, the apparent size of this coat can change. But I suspect that the size of the coat in a particular case will somehow be related to the apparent energy and momentum of a particle in that case.

An important fact in traditional physics is that interactions between particles seem to conserve total energy and momentum. And conceivably the reason for this is that such interactions somehow tend to preserve the total number of network nodes. Indeed, perhaps in most situations—save those associated with the overall expansion of the universe—the basic rules for the network at least on average just rearrange nodes and never change their number.

In traditional physics energy and momentum are always assumed to have continuous values. But just as in the case of position there is no contradiction with sufficiently small underlying discrete elements.

As I will discuss in the last section of this chapter, quantum mechanics tends to make one think of particles with higher momenta as being somehow progressively less spread out in space. So how can this be consistent with the idea that higher momentum is associated with having more nodes? Part of the answer probably has to do with the fact that outside the piece of the network that corresponds to the particle, the network presumably matches up to yield uniform space in much the same way as without the particle. And within the piece of the network corresponding to the particle, the effective structure of space may be very different—with for example more long-range connections added to reduce the effective overall distance.

The Phenomenon of Gravity

At an opposite extreme from elementary particles one can ask how the universe behaves on the largest possible scales. And the most obvious effect on such scales is the phenomenon of gravity. So how then might this emerge from the kinds of models I have discussed here?

The standard theory of gravity for nearly a century has been general relativity—which is based on the idea of associating gravity with curvature in space, then specifying how this curvature relates to the energy and momentum of whatever matter is present.

Something like a magnetic field in general has different effects on objects made of different materials. But a key observation verified experimentally to considerable accuracy is that gravity has exactly the same effect on the motion of different objects, regardless of what those objects are made of. And it is this that allows one to think of gravity as a general feature of space—rather than for example as some type of force that acts specifically on different objects.

In the absence of any gravity or forces, our normal definition of space implies that when an object moves from one point to another, it always goes along a straight line, which corresponds to the shortest path. But when gravity is present, objects in general move on curved paths. Yet these paths can still be the shortest—or so-called geodesics— if one takes space to be curved. And indeed if space has appropriate curvature one can get all sorts of paths, as in the pictures below.

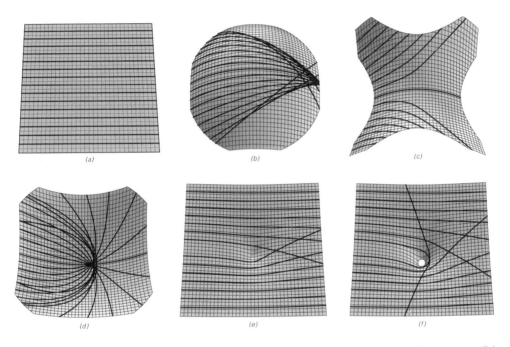

Examples of the effect of curvature in space on paths taken by objects. In each case all the paths shown start parallel, but do not remain so when there is curvature. The paths are geodesics which go the minimum distance on the surface to get to all the points they reach. (In general, the minimum may only be local.) Case (b) shows the top of a sphere, which is a surface of positive curvature. Case (c) shows the negatively curved surface $z = x^2 - y^2$, (d) a paraboloid $z = x^2 + y^2$, and (e,f) $z = 1/(r + \delta)$—a rough analog of curvature in space produced by a sphere of mass.

But in our actual universe what determines the curvature of space? The answer from general relativity is that the Einstein equations give conditions for the value of a particular kind of curvature in terms of the energy and momentum of matter that is present. And the point then is that the shortest paths in space with this curvature seem to be consistent with those followed by objects moving under the influence of gravity associated with the given distribution of matter.

For a continuous surface—or in general a continuous space—the idea of curvature is a familiar one in traditional geometry. But if the universe is at an underlying level just a discrete network of nodes then how does curvature work? At some level the answer is that on large scales the discrete network must approximate continuous space.

But it turns out that one can actually also recognize curvature in the basic structure of a network. If one has a simple array of hexagons—as in the picture on the left—then this can readily be laid out flat on a two-dimensional plane. But what if one replaces some of these hexagons by pentagons? One still has a fundamentally two-dimensional surface. But if one tries to keep all edges the same length the surface will inevitably become curved—like a soccer ball or a geodesic dome.

So what this suggests is that in a network just changing the pattern of connections can in effect change the overall curvature. And indeed the pictures below show a succession of networks that in effect have curvatures with a range of negative and positive values.

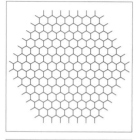
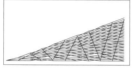

A hexagonal array corresponding to flat two-dimensional space.

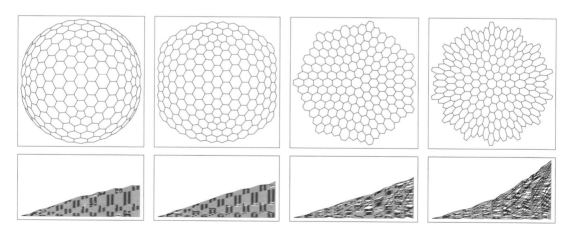

Networks with various limiting curvatures. If every region in the network is in effect a hexagon—as in the picture at the top of the page—then the network will behave as if it is flat. But if pentagons are introduced, as in the cases on the left, the network will increasingly behave as if it has positive curvature—like part of a sphere. And if heptagons are introduced, as in the cases on the right, the network will behave as if it has negative curvature. In the bottom row of pictures, the networks are laid out as on page 479, so that successive heights give the number of nodes at successive distances r from a particular node. In the limit of large r, this number is approximately $r^2 (1 - k r^2 + ...)$ where k turns out to be exactly proportional to the curvature.

But how can we determine the curvature from the structure of each network? Earlier in this chapter we saw that if a network is going to correspond to ordinary space in some number of dimensions d, then this means that by going r connections from any given node one must reach about r^{d-1} nodes. But it turns out that when curvature is present it leads to a systematic correction to this.

In each of the pictures on the facing page the network shown can be thought of as corresponding to two-dimensional space. And this means that to a first approximation the number of nodes reached must increase linearly with r. But the bottom row of pictures show that there are corrections to this. And what happens is that when there is positive curvature—as in the pictures on the left—progressively fewer than r nodes end up being reached. But when there is negative curvature—as on the right—progressively more nodes end up being reached. And in general the leading correction to the number of nodes reached turns out to be proportional to the curvature multiplied by r^{d+1}.

So what happens in more than two dimensions? In general the result could be very complicated, and could for example involve all sorts of different forms of curvature and other characteristics of space. But in fact the leading correction to the number of nodes reached is always quite simple: it is just proportional to what is called the Ricci scalar curvature, multiplied by r^{d+1}. And already here this is some suggestion of general relativity—for the Ricci scalar curvature also turns out to be a central quantity in the Einstein equations.

But in trying to see a more detailed correspondence there are immediately a variety of complications. Perhaps the most obvious is that the traditional mathematical formulation of general relativity seems to rely on many detailed properties of continuous space. And while one expects that sufficiently large networks should in some sense act on average like continuous space, it is far from clear at first how the kinds of properties of relevance to general relativity will emerge.

If one starts, say, from an ordinary continuous surface, then it is straightforward to approximate it as in the picture on the right by a collection of flat faces. And one might think that the edges of these faces would define a network of the kind I have been discussing.

A surface approximated by flat faces whose edges form a trivalent network.

But in fact, such a network has vastly less information. For given just a set of connections between nodes, there is no obvious way even to know which of these connections should be associated with the same face—let alone to work out anything like angles between faces.

Yet despite this, it turns out that all the geometrical features that are ultimately of relevance to general relativity can actually be determined in large networks just from the connectivity of nodes.

One of these is the value of the so-called Ricci tensor, which in effect specifies how the Ricci scalar curvature is made up from different curvature components associated with different directions.

As indicated above, the scalar curvature associated with a network is directly related to how many nodes lie within successive distances r of a given node on the network—or in effect how many nodes lie within successive generalized spheres around that node. And it turns out that the projection of the Ricci tensor along a particular direction is then just related to the number of nodes that lie within a cylinder oriented in that direction. But even just defining a consistent direction in a network is not entirely straightforward. But one way to do it is simply to pick two points in the network, then to say that paths in the network are going in the same direction if they are segments of the same shortest path between those points. And with this definition, a region that approximates a cylinder can be formed just by setting up spheres with centers at every point on the path.

But there is now another issue to address: at least in its standard formulation general relativity is set up in terms of properties not of three-dimensional space but rather of four-dimensional spacetime. And this means that what is relevant are properties not so much of specific networks representing space, but rather of complete causal networks.

And one immediate feature of causal networks that differs from space networks is that their connections go only one way. But it turns out that this is exactly what one needs in order to set up the analog of a spacetime Ricci tensor. The idea is to start at a particular event in the causal network, then to form what is in effect a cone of events that can be reached from there. To define the spacetime Ricci tensor, one considers—as on page 516—a sequence of spacelike slices through this cone and asks how the number of events that lie within the cone increases as one goes to successive slices. After t steps, the number of events reached will be proportional to t^d. But there is then a correction proportional to t^{d+2}, that has a coefficient that is a combination of the spacetime Ricci scalar and a projection of the spacetime Ricci tensor along what is in effect the time direction defined by the sequence of spacelike slices chosen.

So how does this relate to general relativity? It turns out that when there is no matter present the Einstein equations simply state that the spacetime Ricci tensor—and thus all of its projections—are exactly zero. There can still for example be higher-order curvature, but there can be no curvature at the level described by the Ricci tensor.

So what this means is that any causal network whose behavior obeys the Einstein equations must at the level of counting nodes in a cone have the same uniform structure as it would if it were going to correspond to ordinary flat space. As we saw a few sections ago, many underlying replacement rules end up producing networks that are for example too extensively connected to correspond to ordinary space in any finite number of dimensions. But I suspect that if one has replacement rules that are causal invariant and that in effect successfully maintain a fixed number of dimensions they will almost inevitably lead to behavior that follows something close to the Einstein equations.

Probably the situation is somewhat analogous to what we saw with fluid behavior in cellular automata in Chapter 8—that at least if there are underlying rules whose behavior is complicated enough to generate significant effective randomness, then almost whenever the rules lead to conservation of total particle number and momentum something close to the ordinary Navier-Stokes equation behavior emerges.

So what about matter?

As a first step, one can ask what effect the structure of space has on something like a particle—assuming that one can ignore the effect of the particle back on space. In traditional general relativity it is always assumed that a particle which is not interacting with anything else will move along a shortest path—or so-called geodesic—in space.

But what about an explicit particle of the kind we discussed in the previous section that exists as a structure in a network? Given two nodes in a network, one can always identify a shortest path from one to the other that goes along a sequence of individual connections in the network. But in a sense a structure that corresponds to a particle will normally not fit through this path. For usually the structure will involve many nodes, and thus typically require many connections going in more or less the same direction in order to be able to move across the network.

But if one assumes a certain uniformity in networks—and in particular in the causal network—then it still follows that particles of the kind that we discussed in the previous section will tend to move along geodesics. And whereas in traditional general relativity the idea of motion along geodesics is essentially an assumption, this can now in principle be derived explicitly from an underlying network model.

One might have thought that in the absence of matter there would be little to say about gravity—since after all the Einstein equations then say that there can be no curvature in space, at least of the kind described by the Ricci tensor. But it turns out that there can still be other kinds of curvature—described for example by the so-called Riemann tensor—and these can in fact lead to all sorts of phenomena. Examples include familiar ones like inverse-square gravitational fields around massive objects, as well as unfamiliar ones like gravitational waves.

But while the mathematical structure of general relativity is complicated enough that it is often difficult to see just where in spacetime effects come from, it is usually assumed that matter is somehow ultimately required to provide a source for gravity. And in the full Einstein equations the Ricci tensor need not be zero; instead it is specified at every point in space as being equal to a certain combination of energy and momentum density for matter at that point. So this means that to know what will happen even in phenomena primarily associated with gravity one typically has to know all sorts of properties of matter.

But why exactly does matter have to be introduced explicitly at all? It has been the assumption of traditional physics that even though gravity can be represented in terms of properties of space, other elements of our universe cannot. But in my approach everything just emerges from the same underlying network—or in effect from the structure of space. And indeed even in traditional general relativity one can try avoiding introducing matter explicitly—for example by imagining that everything we call matter is actually made up of pure gravitational energy, or of something like gravitational waves.

But so far as one can tell, the details of this do not work out—so that at the level of general relativity there is no choice but to introduce matter explicitly. Yet I suspect that this is in effect just a sign of limitations in the Einstein equations and general relativity.

For while at a large scale these may provide a reasonable description of average behavior in a network, it is almost inevitable that closer to the scale of individual connections they will have to be modified. Yet presumably one can still use the Einstein equations on large scales if one introduces matter with appropriate properties as a way to represent small-scale effects in the network.

In the previous section I suggested that energy and momentum might in effect be associated with the presence of excess nodes in a network. And this now potentially seems to fit quite well with what we have seen in this section. For if the underlying rule for a network is going to maintain to a certain approximation the same average number of nodes as flat space, then it follows that wherever there are more nodes corresponding to energy and momentum, this must be balanced by something reducing the number of nodes. But such a reduction is exactly what is needed to correspond to positive curvature of the kind implied by the Einstein equations in the presence of ordinary matter.

Quantum Phenomena

From our everyday experience with objects that we can see and touch we develop a certain intuition about how things work. But nearly a century ago it became clear that when it comes to things like electrons some of this intuition is no longer correct. Yet there has developed an elaborate mathematical formalism in quantum theory that successfully reproduces much of what is observed. And while some aspects of this formalism remain mysterious, it has increasingly come to be believed that any fundamental theory of physics must somehow be based on it.

Yet the kinds of programs I have discussed in this book are not in any obvious way set up to fit in with this formalism. But as we have seen a great many times in the course of the book, what emerges from a program can be very different from what is obvious in its underlying rules. And in fact it is my strong suspicion that the kinds of programs that I have discussed in the past few sections will actually in the end turn out to show many if not all the key features of quantum theory.

To see this, however, will not be easy. For the kinds of constructs that are emphasized in the standard formalism of quantum theory are very different from those immediately visible in the programs I have discussed. And ultimately the only reliable way to make contact will probably be to set up rather complete and realistic models of experiments—then gradually to see how limits and idealizations of these manage to match what is expected from the standard formalism. Yet from what we have seen in this chapter and earlier in this book there are already some encouraging signs that one can identify.

At first, though, things might not seem promising. For my model of particles such as electrons being persistent structures in a network might initially seem to imply that such particles are somehow definite objects just like ones familiar from everyday experience. But there are all sorts of phenomena in quantum theory that seem to indicate that electrons do not in fact behave like ordinary objects that have definite properties independent of us making observations of them.

So how can this be consistent? The basic answer is just that a network which represents our whole universe must also include us as observers. And this means that there is no way that we can look at the network from the outside and see the electron as a definite object. Instead, anything we deduce about the electron must come from processes that explicitly go on inside the network.

But this is not just an issue in studying things like electrons: it is actually a completely general feature of the models I have discussed. And in fact, as we saw earlier in this chapter, it is what allows them to support meaningful notions of even such basic concepts as time. At a more formal level, it also implies that everything we can observe can be captured by a causal network. And as I will discuss a little below, I suspect that the idea of causal invariance for such a network will then be what turns out to account for some key features of quantum theory.

The basic picture of our universe that I have outlined in the past few sections is a network whose connections are continually updated according to some simple set of underlying rules. In the past one might have assumed that a system like this would be far too simple to correspond to our universe. But from the discoveries in this book we now know that even when the underlying rules for a system are simple, its overall behavior can still be immensely complex.

And at the lowest level what I expect is that even though the rules being applied are perfectly definite, the overall pattern of connections that will exist in the network corresponding to our universe will continually be rearranged in ways complicated enough to seem effectively random.

Yet on a slightly larger scale such randomness will then lead to a certain average uniformity. And it is then essentially this that I believe is responsible for maintaining something like ordinary space—with gradual variations giving rise to the phenomenon of gravity.

But superimposed on this effectively random background will then presumably also be some definite structures that persist through many updatings of the network. And it is these, I believe, that are what correspond to particles like electrons.

As I discussed in the last two sections, causal invariance of the underlying rules implies that such structures should be able to move at a range of uniform speeds through the background. Typically properties like charge will be associated with some specific pattern of connections at the core of the structure corresponding to a particle, while the energy and momentum of the particle will be associated with roughly the number of nodes in some outer region around the core.

So what about interactions? If the structures corresponding to different particles are isolated, then the underlying rules will make them persist. But if they somehow overlap, these same rules will usually make some different configuration of particles be produced.

A collision between localized structures in the rule 110 class 4 cellular automaton.

At some level the situation will no doubt be a little like in the evolution of a typical class 4 cellular automaton, as illustrated on the left. Given some initial set of persistent structures, these can interact to produce some intermediate pattern of behavior, which then eventually resolves into a final set of structures that again persist.

In the intermediate pattern of behavior one may also be able to identify some definite structures. Ones that do not last long can be very different from ones that would persist forever. But ones that last longer will tend to have properties progressively closer to genuinely persistent structures. And while persistent structures can be thought of as corresponding to real particles, intermediate structures are in many ways like the virtual particles of traditional particle physics.

So this means that a picture like the one on the left above can be viewed in a remarkably literal sense as being a spacetime diagram of particle interactions—a bit like a Feynman diagram from particle physics.

One immediate difference, however, is that in traditional particle physics one does not imagine a pattern of behavior as definite and determined as in the picture above. And indeed in my model for the universe it is already clear that there is more going on. For any process like the one in the picture above must occur on top of a background of apparently random small-scale rearrangements of the network. And in effect what this background does is to introduce a kind of random environment that can make many different detailed patterns of behavior occur with certain probabilities even with the same initial configuration of particles.

The idea that even a vacuum without particles will have a complicated and in some ways random form also exists in standard quantum field theory in traditional physics. The full mathematical structure of quantum field theory is far from completely worked out. But the basic notion is that for each possible type of particle there is some kind of continuous field that exists throughout space—with the presence of a particle corresponding to a simple type of structure in this field.

In general, the equations of quantum field theory seem to imply that there can be all sorts of complicated configurations in the field, even in the absence of actual particles. But as a first approximation, one can consider just short-lived pairs of virtual particles and antiparticles. And in fact one can often do something similar for networks. For even in the planar networks discussed on page 527 a great many different arrangements of connections can be viewed as being formed from different configurations of nearby pairs of non-planar persistent structures.

Talking about a random background affecting processes in the universe immediately tends to suggest certain definite relations between probabilities for different processes. Thus for example, if there are two different ways that some process can occur, it suggests that the total probability for the whole process should be just the sum of the probabilities for the process to occur in the two different ways.

But the standard formalism of quantum theory says that this is not correct, and that in fact one has to look at so-called probability amplitudes, not ordinary probabilities. At a mathematical level, such amplitudes are analogous to ones for things like waves, and are in effect just numbers with directions. And what quantum theory says is that the probability for a whole process can be obtained by linearly combining the amplitudes for the different ways the process can occur, then looking at the square of the magnitude of the result—or the analog of intensity for something like a wave.

So how might this kind of mathematical procedure emerge from the types of models I have discussed? The answer seems complicated. For even though the procedure itself may sound straightforward, the constructs on which it operates are actually far from easy to define just on the basis of an underlying network—and I have seen no easy way to unravel the various limits and idealizations that have to be made.

Nevertheless, a potentially important point is that it is in some ways misleading to think of particles in a network as just interacting according to some definite rule, and being perturbed by what is in essence a random background. For this suggests that there is in effect a unique history to every particle interaction—determined by the initial conditions and the configuration that exists in the random background.

But the true picture is more complicated. For the sequence of updates to the underlying network can be made in any order—yet each order in effect gives a different detailed history for the network. But if there is causal invariance, then ultimately all these different histories must in a sense be equivalent. And with this constraint, if one breaks some process into parts, there will typically be no simple way to describe how the effect of these parts combines together.

And for at least some purposes it may well make sense to think explicitly about different possible histories, combining something like amplitudes that one assigns to each of them. Yet quite how this might work will certainly depend on what feature of the network one tries to look at.

It has always been a major issue in quantum theory just how one tells what is happening with a particular particle like an electron. From our experience with everyday objects we might think that it should somehow be possible to do this without affecting the electron. But if the only things we have are particles, then to find out something about a given particle we inevitably have to have some other particle—say a photon of light—explicitly interact with it. And in this interaction the original particle will inevitably be affected in some way.

And in fact just one interaction will certainly not be enough. For we as humans cannot normally perceive individual particles. And indeed there usually have to be a huge number of particles doing more or less the same thing before we successfully register it.

Most often the way this is made to happen is by setting up some kind of detector that is initially in a state that is sufficiently unstable that just a single particle can initiate a whole cascade of consequences. And usually such a detector is arranged so that it evolves to one or another stable state that has sufficiently uniform properties that we can recognize it as corresponding to a definite outcome of a measurement.

At first, however, such evolution to an organized state might seem inconsistent with microscopic reversibility. But in fact—just as in so many other seemingly irreversible processes—all that is needed to preserve reversibility is that if one looks at sufficient details of the system there can be arbitrary and seemingly random behavior. And the point is just that in making conclusions about the result of a measurement we choose to ignore such details.

So even though the actual result that we take away from a measurement may be quite simple, many particles—and many events—

will always be involved in getting it. And in fact in traditional quantum theory no measurement can ultimately end up giving a definite result unless in effect an infinite number of particles are involved.

As I mentioned above, ordinary quantum processes can appear to follow different histories depending on what scheme is used to decide the order in which underlying rules are applied. But taking the idealized limit of a measurement in which an infinite number of particles are involved will probably in effect establish a single history.

And this implies that if one knew all of the underlying details of the network that makes up our universe, it should always be possible to work out the result of any measurement. I strongly believe that the initial conditions for the universe were quite simple. But like many of the processes we have seen in this book, the evolution of the universe no doubt intrinsically generates apparent randomness.

And the result is that most aspects of the network that represents the current state of our universe will seem essentially random. So this means that to know its form we would in essence have to sample every one of its details—which is certainly not possible if we have to use measurements that each involve a huge number of particles.

One might however imagine that as a first approximation one could take account of underlying apparent randomness just by saying that there are certain probabilities for particles to behave in particular ways. But one of the most often quoted results about foundations of quantum theory is that in practice there can be correlations observed between particles that seem impossible to account for in at least the most obvious kind of such a so-called hidden-variables theory.

For in particular, if one takes two particles that have come from a single source, then the result of a measurement on one of them is found in a sense to depend too much on what measurement gets done on the other—even if there is not enough time for information travelling at the speed of light to get from one to the other. And indeed this fact has often been taken to imply that quantum phenomena can ultimately never be the result of any definite underlying process of evolution.

But this conclusion depends greatly on traditional assumptions about the nature of space and of particles. And it turns out that for the kinds of models I have discussed here it in general no longer holds.

And the basic reason for this is that if the universe is a network then it can in a sense easily contain threads that continue to connect particles even when the particles get far apart in terms of ordinary space.

The picture that emerges is then of a background containing a very large number of connections that maintain an approximation to three-dimensional space, together with a few threads that in effect go outside of that space to make direct connections between particles.

If two particles get created together, it is reasonable to expect that the tangles that represent their cores will tend to have a few connections in common—and indeed this for example happens for lumps of non-planarity of the kind we discussed on page 527. But until there are interactions that change the structure of the cores, these common connections will then remain—and will continue to define a thread that goes directly from one particle to the other.

But there is immediately a slight subtlety here. For earlier in this chapter I discussed measuring distance on a network just by counting the minimum number of successive individual connections that one has to follow in order to get from one point to another. Yet if one uses this measure of distance then the distance between two particles will always tend to remain fixed as the number of connections in the thread.

But the point is that this measure of distance is in reality just a simple idealization of what is relevant in practice. For the only way we end up actually being able to measure physical distances is in effect by looking at the propagation of photons or other particles. Yet such particles always involve many nodes. And while they can get from one point to another through the large number of connections that define the background space, they cannot in a sense fit through a small number of connections in a thread. So this means that distance as we normally experience it is typically not affected by threads.

But it does not mean that threads can have no effect at all. And indeed what I suspect is that it is precisely the presence of threads that leads to the correlations that are seen in measurements on particles.

It so happens that the standard formalism of quantum theory provides a rather simple mathematical description of these correlations. And it is certainly far from obvious how this might emerge from detailed mechanisms associated with threads in a network. But the fact that this and other results seem simple in the standard formalism of quantum theory should not be taken to imply that they are in any sense particularly fundamental. And indeed my guess is that most of them will actually in the end turn out to depend on all sorts of limits and idealizations in quantum theory—and will emerge just as simple approximations to much more complex underlying behavior.

In its development since the early 1900s quantum theory has produced all sorts of elaborate results. And to try to derive them all from the kinds of models I have outlined here will certainly take an immense amount of work. But I consider it very encouraging that some of the most basic quantum phenomena seem to be connected to properties like causal invariance and the network structure of space that already arose in our discussion of quite different fundamental issues in physics.

And all of this supports my strong belief that in the end it will turn out that every detail of our universe does indeed follow rules that can be represented by a very simple program—and that everything we see will ultimately emerge just from running this program.

10

Processes of Perception and Analysis

Introduction

In the course of the past several chapters, we have discussed the basic mechanisms responsible for a variety of phenomena that occur in nature. But in trying to explain our actual experience of the natural world, we need to consider not only how phenomena are produced in nature, but also how we perceive and analyze these phenomena. For inevitably our experience of the natural world is based in the end not directly on behavior that occurs in nature, but rather on the results of our perception and analysis of this behavior.

Thus, for example, when we look at the behavior of a particular natural system, there will be certain features that we notice with our eyes, and certain features, perhaps different, that we can detect by doing various kinds of mathematical or other analysis.

In previous chapters, I have argued that the basic mechanisms responsible for many processes that occur in nature can be captured by simple computer programs based on simple rules. But what about the processes that are involved in perception and analysis?

Particularly when it comes to the higher levels of perception, there is much that we do not know for certain about this. But what I will argue in this chapter is that the evidence we have suggests that the basic mechanisms at work can once again successfully be captured by simple programs based on simple rules.

In the traditional sciences, it has rarely been thought necessary to discuss in any explicit kind of way the processes that are involved in perception and analysis. For in most cases all that one studies are rather simple features that can readily be extracted by very straightforward processes—and which can for example be described by just a few numbers or by a simple mathematical formula.

But as soon as one tries to investigate behavior of any substantial complexity, the processes of perception and analysis that one needs to use are no longer so straightforward. And the results one gets can then depend on these processes.

In the traditional sciences it has usually been assumed that any result that is not essentially independent of the processes of perception and analysis used to obtain it cannot be definite or objective enough to be of much scientific value. But the point is that if one explicitly studies processes of perception and analysis, then it becomes possible to make quite definite and objective statements even in such cases.

And indeed some of the most significant conclusions that I will reach at the end of this book are based precisely on comparing the processes that are involved in the production of certain forms of behavior with the processes involved in their perception and analysis.

What Perception and Analysis Do

In everyday life we are continually bombarded by huge amounts of data, in the form of images, sounds, and so on. To be able to make use of this data we must reduce it to more manageable proportions. And this is what perception and analysis attempt to do. Their role in effect is to take large volumes of raw data and extract from it summaries that we can use.

At the level of raw data the picture at the top of the facing page, for example, can be thought of as consisting of many thousands of individual black and white cells. But with our powers of visual perception and analysis we can immediately see that the picture can be summarized just by saying that it consists essentially of an array of repeated black diamond shapes.

An example of a picture that our powers of perception and analysis readily allow us to summarize quite succinctly in simple geometrical terms. At the lowest level, however, the picture consists of 24,000 black and white cells.

There are in general two ways in which data can be reduced by perception and analysis. First, those aspects of data that are not relevant for whatever purpose one has can simply be ignored. And second, one can avoid explicitly having to specify every element in the data by making use of regularities that one sees.

Thus, for example, in summarizing the picture above, we choose to ignore some details, and then to describe what remains in terms of its simple repetitive overall geometrical structure.

Whenever there are regularities in data, it effectively means that some of the data is redundant. For example, if a particular pattern is repeated, then one need not specify the form of this pattern more than once—for the original data can be reproduced just by repeating a copy of the pattern. And in general, the presence of regularities makes it possible to replace literal descriptions of data by shorter descriptions that are based on procedures for reproducing the data.

There are many forms of perception and analysis. Some happen quite automatically in our eyes, ears and brains—and these we usually call perception. Others require explicit conscious effort and mathematical or computational work—and these we usually call analysis. But the basic goal in all cases is the same: to reduce raw data to a useful summary form.

Such a summary is important whenever one wants to store or communicate data efficiently. It is also important if one wants to compare new data with old, or make meaningful extrapolations or predictions based on data. And in modern information technology the problems of data compression, feature detection, pattern recognition and system identification all in effect revolve around finding useful summaries of data.

In traditional science statistical analysis has been the most common way of trying to find summaries of data. And in general perception and analysis can be viewed as equivalent to finding models that reproduce whatever aspects of data one considers relevant.

Perception and analysis correspond in many respects to the inverse of most of what we have studied in this book. For typically what we have done is to start from a simple computer program, and then seen what behavior this program produces. But in perception and analysis we start from behavior that we observe, then try to deduce what procedure or program will reproduce this data.

So how easy is it to do this? It turns out that for most of the kinds of rules used in traditional mathematics, it is in fact fairly easy. But for the more general rules that I discuss in this book it appears to often be extremely difficult. For even though the rules may be simple, the behavior they produce is often highly complex, and shows absolutely no obvious trace of its simple origins.

As one example, the pictures on the facing page were all generated by starting from a single black cell and then applying very simple two-dimensional cellular automaton rules. Yet if one looks just at these final pictures, there is no easy way to tell how they were made. Our standard methods of perception and analysis can certainly determine that the pictures are for example symmetrical. But none of these methods typically get even close to being able to recognize just how simple a procedure can in fact be used to produce the pictures.

One might think that our inability to find such a procedure could just be a consequence of limitations in the particular methods of perception and analysis that we, as humans, happen to have developed. And one might therefore suppose that an alien intelligence could exist which would be able to look at our pictures and immediately tell that they were produced by a very simple procedure.

But in fact I very much doubt that this will ever be the case. For I suspect that there are fundamental limitations on what perception and analysis can ever be expected to do. For there seem to be many kinds of

Patterns produced by taking a single black cell, then evolving for 50 and 100 steps according to outer totalistic cellular automaton rules 54, 222 and 374. Despite the simple description that can be given of this procedure, our standard methods of perception and analysis cannot readily deduce this description given just the final pictures shown here.

systems in which it is overwhelmingly easier to generate highly complex behavior than to recognize the origins of this behavior.

As I have discovered in this book, it is rather easy to generate complex behavior by starting from simple initial conditions and then following simple sets of rules. But the point is that if one starts from some particular piece of behavior there are in general no such simple rules that allow one to go backwards and find out how this behavior can be produced. Typically the problem is similar to trying to find solutions that will satisfy certain constraints. And as we have seen several times in this book, such problems can be extremely difficult.

So insofar as the actual processes of perception and analysis that end up being used are fairly simple, it is inevitable that there will be situations where one cannot recognize the origins of behavior that one sees—even when this behavior is in fact produced by very simple rules.

Defining the Notion of Randomness

Many times in this book I have said that the behavior of some system or another seems random. But so far I have given no precise definition of what I mean by randomness. And what we will discover in this section is that to come up with an appropriate definition one has no choice but to consider issues of perception and analysis.

One might have thought that from traditional mathematics and statistics there would long ago have emerged some standard definition of randomness. But despite occasional claims for particular definitions, the concept of randomness has in fact remained quite obscure. And indeed I believe that it is only with the discoveries in this book that one is finally now in a position to develop a real understanding of what randomness is.

At the level of everyday language, when we say that something seems random what we usually mean is that there are no significant regularities in it that we can discern—at least with whatever methods of perception and analysis we use.

We would not usually say, therefore, that either of the first two pictures at the top of the facing page seem random, since we can readily recognize highly regular repetitive and nested patterns in them. But the third picture we would probably say does seem random, since at least at the level of ordinary visual perception we cannot recognize any significant regularities in it.

So given this everyday notion of randomness, how can we build on it to develop more precise definitions? The first step is to clarify what it means not to be able to recognize regularities in something. Following the discussion in the previous section, we know that whenever we find regularities, it implies that redundancy is present, and this in turn means that a shorter description can be given. So when we say that we cannot recognize any regularities, this is equivalent to saying that we cannot find a shorter description.

The three pictures on the facing page can always be described by explicitly giving a list of the colors of each of the 6561 cells that they contain. But by using the regularities that we can see in the first two

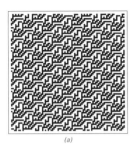 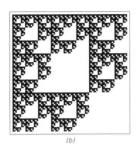 

(a) (b) (c)

Pictures exhibiting different degrees of apparent randomness. Pictures (a) and (b) have obvious regularities, and would never be considered particularly random. But picture (c) has almost no obvious regularities, and would typically be considered quite random. As it turns out, picture (c), like (a) and (b), can actually be generated by a quite simple process. But the point is that the simplicity of this process does not affect the fact that with our standard methods of perception and analysis picture (c) is for practical purposes random.

pictures, we can readily construct much shorter—yet still complete—descriptions of these pictures.

The repetitive structure of picture (a) implies that to reproduce this picture all we need do is to specify the colors in a 49×2 block, and then say that this block should be repeated an appropriate number of times. Similarly, the nested structure of picture (b) implies that to reproduce this picture, all we need do is to specify the colors in a 3×3 block, and then say that as in a two-dimensional substitution system each black cell should repeatedly be replaced by this block.

But what about picture (c)? Is there any short description that can be given of this picture? Or do we have no choice but just to specify explicitly the color of every one of the cells it contains?

Our powers of visual perception certainly do not reveal any significant regularities that would allow us to construct a shorter description. And neither, it turns out, do any standard methods of mathematical or statistical analysis. And so for practical purposes we have little choice but just to specify explicitly the color of each cell.

But the fact that no short description can be found by our usual processes of perception and analysis does not in any sense mean that no such description exists at all. And indeed, as it happens, picture (c) in fact allows a very short description. For it can be generated just by starting with a single black cell and then applying a simple two-dimensional cellular automaton rule 250 times.

But does the existence of this short description mean that picture (c) should not be considered random? From a practical point of view the fact that a short description may exist is presumably not too relevant if we can never find this description by any of the methods of perception and analysis that are available to us. But from a conceptual point of view it may seem unsatisfactory to have a definition of randomness that depends on our methods of perception and analysis, and is not somehow absolute.

So one possibility is to define randomness so that something is considered random only if no short description whatsoever exists of it. And before the discoveries in this book such a definition might have seemed not far from our everyday notion of randomness. For we would probably have assumed that anything generated from a sufficiently short description would necessarily look fairly simple. But what we have discovered in this book is that this is absolutely not the case, and that in fact even from rules with very short descriptions it is easy to generate behavior in which our standard methods of perception and analysis recognize no significant regularities.

So to say that something is random only if no short description whatsoever exists of it turns out to be a highly restrictive definition of randomness. And in fact, as I mentioned in Chapter 7, it essentially implies that no process based on definite rules can ever manage to generate randomness when there is no randomness before. For since the rules themselves have a short description, anything generated by following them will also have a correspondingly short description, and will therefore not be considered random according to this definition.

And even if one is not concerned about where randomness might come from, there is still a further problem: it turns out in general to be impossible to determine in any finite way whether any particular thing can ever be generated from a short description. One might imagine that one could always just try running all programs with progressively longer descriptions, and see whether any of them ever generate what one wants. But the problem is that one can never in general tell in advance how many steps of evolution one will need to look at in order to be sure that any particular piece of behavior will not occur. And as a result, no finite process can in general be used to guarantee that there is no short description that exists of a particular thing.

By setting up various restrictions, say on the number of steps of evolution that will be allowed, it is possible to obtain slightly more tractable definitions of randomness. But even in such cases the amount of computational work required to determine whether something should be considered random is typically astronomically large. And more important, while such definitions may perhaps be of some conceptual interest, they correspond very poorly with our intuitive notion of randomness. In fact, if one followed such a definition most of the pictures in this book that I have said look random—including for example picture (c) on page 553—would be considered not random. And following the discussion of Chapter 7, so would at least many of the phenomena in nature that we normally think of as random.

Indeed, what I suspect is that ultimately no useful definition of randomness can be based solely on the issue of what short descriptions of something may in principle exist. Rather, any useful definition must, I believe, make at least some reference to how such short descriptions are supposed to be found.

Over the years, a variety of definitions of randomness have been proposed that are based on the absence of certain specific regularities. Often these definitions are presented as somehow being fundamental. But in fact they typically correspond just to seeing whether some particular process—and usually a rather simple one—succeeds in recognizing regularities and thus in generating a shorter description.

A common example—to be discussed further two sections from now—involves taking, say, a sequence of black and white cells, and then counting the frequency with which each color and each block of colors occurs. Any deviation from equality among these frequencies represents a regularity in the sequence and reveals nonrandomness. But despite some confusion in the past it is certainly not true that just checking equality of frequencies of blocks of colors—even arbitrarily long ones—is sufficient to ensure that no regularities at all exist. This procedure can indeed be used to check that no purely repetitive pattern exists, but as we will see later in this chapter, it does not successfully detect the presence of even certain highly regular nested patterns.

So how then can we develop a useful yet precise definition of randomness? What we need is essentially just a precise version of the statement at the beginning of this section: that something should be considered random if none of our standard methods of perception and analysis succeed in detecting any regularities in it. But how can we ever expect to find any kind of precise general characterization of what all our various standard methods of perception and analysis do?

The key point that will emerge in this chapter is that in the end essentially all these methods can be viewed as being based on rather simple programs. So this suggests a definition that can be given of randomness: something should be considered to be random whenever there is essentially no simple program that can succeed in detecting regularities in it.

Usually if what one is studying was itself created by a simple program then there will be a few closely related programs that always succeed in detecting regularities. But if something can reasonably be considered random, then the point is that the vast majority of simple programs should not be able to detect any regularities in it.

So does one really need to try essentially all sufficiently simple programs in order to determine this? In my experience, the answer tends to be no. For once a few simple programs corresponding to a few standard methods of perception and analysis have failed to detect regularities, it is extremely rare for any other simple program to succeed in detecting them.

So this means that the everyday definition of randomness that we discussed at the very beginning of this section is in the end already quite unambiguous. For it typically will not matter much which of the standard methods of perception and analysis we use: after trying a few of them we will almost always be in a position to come to a quite definite conclusion about whether or not something should be considered random.

Defining Complexity

Much of what I have done in this book has been concerned in one way or another with phenomena associated with complexity. But just as one does not need a formal definition of life in order to study biology, so also it has not turned out to be necessary so far in this book to have a formal definition of complexity. Nevertheless, following our discussion of randomness in the previous section, we are now in a position to consider how the notion of complexity might be formally defined.

In everyday language, when we say that something seems complex what we typically mean is that we have not managed to find any simple description of it—or at least of those features of it in which we happen to be interested. But the goal of perception and analysis is precisely to find such descriptions, so when we say that something seems complex, what we are effectively saying is that our powers of perception and analysis have failed on it.

As we discussed two sections ago, there are two ways in which perception and analysis can typically operate. First, they can just throw away details in which we are not interested. And second, they can remove redundancy that is associated with any regularities that they manage to recognize.

The definition of randomness that we discussed in the previous section was based on the failure of the second of these two functions. For what it said was that something should be considered random if our standard methods of perception and analysis could not find any short description from which the thing could faithfully be reproduced.

But in defining complexity we need to consider both functions of perception and analysis. For what we want to know is not whether a simple or short description can be found of every detail of something, but merely whether such a description can be found of those features in which we happen to be interested.

In everyday language, the terms "complexity" and "randomness" are sometimes used almost interchangeably. And for example any of the three pictures at the top of the next page could potentially be referred to as either "quite random" or "quite complex". But if one chooses to look only at overall features, then typically one would tend to say that the third picture seems more complex than the other two.

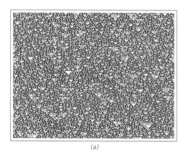 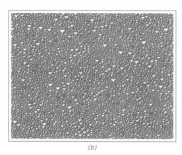 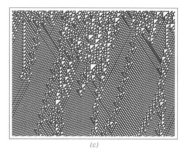

(a) (b) (c)

Examples of pictures that at an everyday level one might typically describe either as being "quite random" or as being "quite complex".

For even though the detailed placement of black and white cells in the first two pictures does not seem simple to describe, at an overall level these pictures still admit a quite simple description: in essence they just involve a kind of uniform randomness in which every region looks more or less the same as every other. But the third picture shows no such uniformity, even at an overall level. And as a result, we cannot give a short description of it even if we ignore its small-scale details.

Of course, if one goes to an extreme and looks, say, only at how big each picture is, then all three pictures have very short descriptions. And in general how short a description of something one can find will depend on what features of it one wants to capture—which is why one may end up ascribing a different complexity to something when one looks at it for different purposes.

But if one uses a particular method of perception or analysis, then one can always see how short a description this manages to produce. And the shorter the description is, the lower one considers the complexity to be.

But to what extent is it possible to define a notion of complexity that is independent of the details of specific methods of perception and analysis? In this chapter I argue that essentially all common forms of perception and analysis correspond to rather simple programs. And if one is interested in descriptions in which no information is lost—as in the discussion of randomness in the previous section—then as I mentioned in the previous section, it seems in practice that different simple programs usually agree quite well in their ability or inability to find short descriptions.

But this seems to be considerably less true when one is dealing with descriptions in which information can be lost. For it is rather common to see cases in which only a few features of a system may be difficult to describe—and depending on whether or not a given program happens to be sensitive to these features it can ascribe either a quite high or a quite low complexity to the system.

Nevertheless, as a practical matter, by far the most common way in which we determine levels of complexity is by using our eyes and our powers of visual perception. So in practice what we most often mean when we say that something seems complex is that the particular processes that are involved in human visual perception have failed to extract a short description.

And indeed I suspect that even below the level of conscious thought our brains already have a rather definite notion of complexity. For when we are presented with a complex image, our eyes tend to dwell on it, presumably in an effort to give our brains a chance to extract a simple description.

If we can find no simple features whatsoever—as in the case of perfect randomness—then we tend to lose interest. But somehow the images that draw us in the most—and typically that we find the most aesthetically pleasing—are those for which some features are simple for us to describe, but others have no short description that can be found by any of our standard processes of visual perception.

Before the discoveries in this book, one might have thought that to create anything with a significant level of apparent complexity would necessarily require a procedure which itself had significant complexity. But what we have discovered in this book is that in fact there are remarkably simple programs that produce behavior of great complexity. And what this means—as the images in this book repeatedly demonstrate—is that in the end it is rather easy to make pictures for which our visual system can find no simple overall description.

Data Compression

One usually thinks of perception and analysis as being done mainly in order to provide material for direct human consumption. But in most modern computer and communications systems there are processes equivalent to perception and analysis that happen all the time when data is compressed for more efficient storage or transmission.

One simple example of such a process is run-length encoding—a method widely used in practice to compress data that involves long sequences of identical elements, such as bitmap images of pages of text with large areas of white.

The basic idea of run-length encoding is to break data into runs of identical elements, and then to specify the data just by giving the lengths of these runs. This means, for example, that instead of having to list explicitly all the cells in a run of, say, 53 identical cells, one instead just gives the number "53". And the point is that even if the "53" is itself represented in terms of black and white cells, this representation can be much shorter than 53 cells.

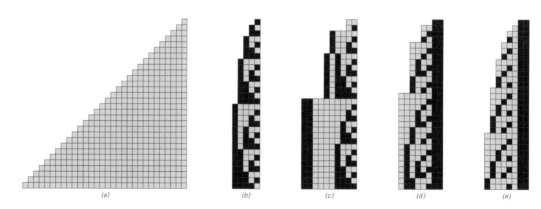

(a) (b) (c) (d) (e)

Various representations of numbers from 1 to 30. (a) is unary, in which any given number is represented by a sequence of cells whose length is equal to that number. (b) is ordinary binary or base 2 representation. (c), (d) and (e) are set up to be self-delimiting, so that the end of a number can be recognized purely by looking at the cells within it. (c) is like (b), except that it has a specification of the number of digits at the front. (d) is essentially binary-coded-ternary, with the end of the number indicated by a pair of black cells. (e) uses a non-integer base derived from the Fibonacci sequence, with the property that a pair of black cells can appear only at the end of each number.

Indeed, any digit sequence can be thought of as providing a short representation for a number. But for run-length encoding it turns out that ordinary base 2 digit sequences do not quite work. For if the numbers corresponding to the lengths of successive runs are given one after another then there is no way to tell where the digits of one number end and the next begin.

Several approaches can be used, however, to avoid this problem. One, illustrated in picture (c) at the bottom of the facing page, is to insert at the beginning of each number a specification of how many digits the number contains. Another approach, illustrated in picture (d), is in effect to have two cells representing each digit, and then to indicate the end of the number by a pair of black cells. A variant on this approach, illustrated in picture (e), uses a non-integer base in which pairs of black cells can occur only at the end of a number.

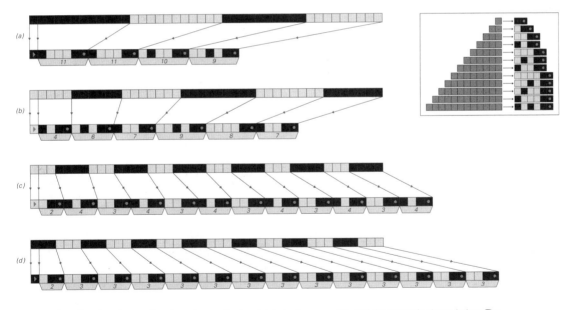

Examples of run-length encoding. In each case the input data is shown on top, and the output is shown below. The arrows between input and output show how the data is broken into runs of identical elements. Each run is then specified by a number, represented as a sequence ending with two black cells, as indicated in the inset picture, and in picture (e) on the facing page. For the first two sets of input data there are enough long runs present that compression is achieved. But for the other two sets no compression is achieved. Note that the first cell in the output is used to specify whether the first run is black or white. In this picture and those that follow, the output consists purely of black and white cells; the gray annotations are included purely as aids to interpretation.

For small numbers, all these approaches yield representations that are at least somewhat longer than the explicit sequences shown in picture (a). But for larger numbers, the representations quickly become much shorter. And this means that they can potentially be used to achieve compression in run-length encoding.

The pictures at the bottom of the previous page show what happens when one applies run-length encoding using representation (e) from page 560 to various sequences of data. In the first two cases, there are sufficiently many long runs that compression is achieved. But in the last two cases, there are too many short runs, and the output from run-length encoding is actually longer than the input.

The pictures below show the results of applying run-length encoding to typical patterns produced by cellular automata. When the patterns contain enough regions of uniform color, compression is achieved. But when the patterns are more intricate—even in a simple repetitive way—little or no compression is achieved.

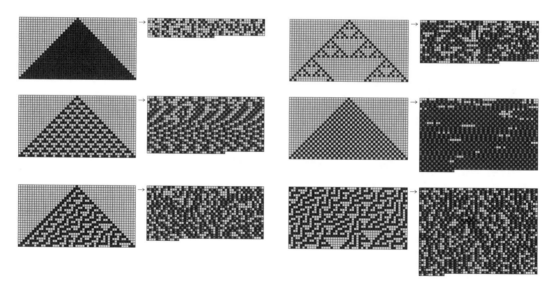

Examples of applying run-length encoding to patterns produced by cellular automata. Successive rows in each original image are placed end to end so as to give a one-dimensional sequence, then run-length encoded, and then chopped into rows again. Compression is typically achieved whenever most of the image consists of regions of uniform color.

Run-length encoding is based on the idea of breaking data up into runs of identical elements of varying lengths. Another common approach to data compression is based on forming blocks of fixed length, and then representing whatever distinct blocks occur by specific codewords.

The pictures below show a few examples of how this works. In each case the input is taken to be broken into blocks of length 3. In the first two cases, there are then only two distinct blocks that occur, so each of these can be represented by a codeword consisting of a single cell, with the result that substantial compression is achieved.

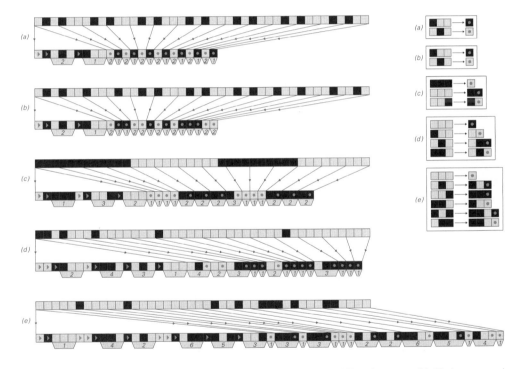

Examples of Huffman coding based on blocks of length 3. In cases (a) and (b), only two possible blocks occur, and these are assigned codewords consisting of a single black cell and a single white cell. In case (c), 3 possible blocks occur; the most common is assigned a codeword consisting of a single white cell, while the others are assigned codewords consisting of two cells. In case (d) 4 out of the 8 possible blocks occur, while in case (e) 6 occur. In all cases, the output begins with a preamble specifying which block is to be represented by which codeword. The blocks appear explicitly in this preamble, and are indicated by numbered tabs. The codewords are represented implicitly by the arrangement of cells shown with arrows. The preamble is followed by the actual codewords representing the data. The codewords are self-delimiting, so that they can be given one after another, with no separator in between.

When a larger number of distinct blocks occur, longer codewords must inevitably be used. But compression can still be achieved if the codewords for common blocks are sufficiently much shorter than the blocks themselves.

One simple strategy for assigning codewords is to number all distinct blocks in order of decreasing frequency, and then just to use the resulting numbers—given, say, in one of the representations discussed above—as the codewords. But if one takes into account the actual frequencies of different blocks, as well as their ranking, then it turns out that there are better ways to assign codewords.

The pictures below show examples based on a method known as Huffman coding. In each case the first part of the output specifies which blocks are to be represented by which codewords, and then the remainder of the output gives the actual succession of codewords that correspond to the blocks appearing in the data. And as the pictures below illustrate, whenever there are fairly few distinct blocks that occur with high frequency, substantial compression is achieved.

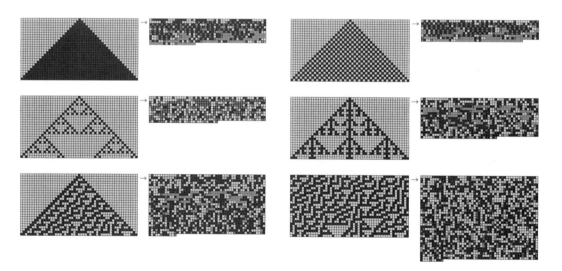

Huffman encoding with blocks of length 6 applied to patterns produced by cellular automata. The maximum possible compression is by a factor of 6; the maximum achieved here is roughly a factor of 3. The difference between the size of the results for the last two examples is mostly a consequence of the presence of large areas of white in the first of them.

But ultimately there is a limit to the degree of compression that can be obtained with this method. For even in the very best case any block of cells in the input can never be compressed to less than one cell in the output.

So how can one achieve greater compression? One approach—which turns out to be similar to what is used in practice in most current high-performance general-purpose compression systems—is to set up an encoding in which any particular sequence of elements above some length is given explicitly only once, and all subsequent occurrences of the same sequence are specified by pointers back to the first one.

The pictures below show what happens when this approach is applied to a few short sequences. In each case, the output consists of two kinds of objects, one giving sequences that are occurring for the first time, and the other giving pointers to sequences that have occurred before. Both kinds of objects start with a single cell that specifies their type. This is

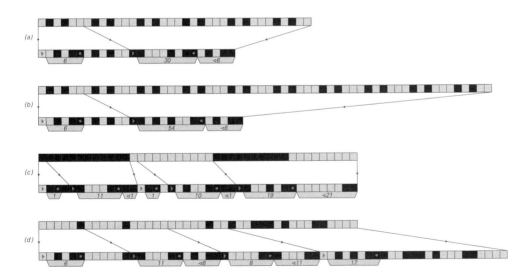

Examples of pointer-based encoding, in which sequences that have occurred once in the data are subsequently specified just by pointers. Each section of output starts with an element which indicates whether what follows is a new sequence, or a pointer to a previous one. After this comes a specification of the length of sequence represented by this section of output, with the number given in the form used for run-length encoding above. Then comes either a literal sequence, or a number giving the offset to where the required sequence last occurred in the data. In the examples shown, pointers are used only for sequences of length at least 6. Pointer-based encoding is similar to the Lempel-Ziv algorithm widely used in practical high-performance general-purpose compression systems.

followed by a specification of the length of the sequence that the object describes. In the first kind of object, the actual sequence is then given, while in the second kind of object what is given is a specification of how far back in the data the required sequence can be found.

With data that is purely repetitive this method achieves quite dramatic compression. For having once specified the basic sequence to be repeated, all that then needs to be given is a pointer to this sequence, together with a representation of the total length of the data.

Purely nested data can also be compressed nearly as much. For as the pictures below illustrate, each whole level of nesting can be viewed just as adding a fixed number of repeated sequences.

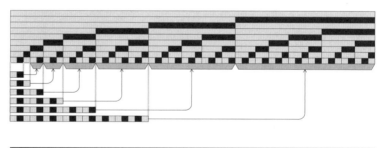

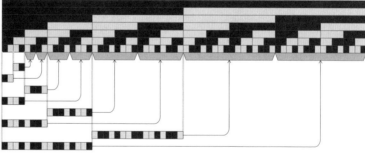

Examples of the pattern of repeats found in purely nested data. As indicated in these pictures, any such data must correspond to the output of a neighbor-independent substitution system (see page 83). In pointer-based encoding, the number of pointers required to represent the data increases essentially like the number of steps in the evolution of the substitution system. Taking into account the length of the representation for each pointer, the compressed form of a nested sequence of length n will typically grow in length like $Log[n]^2$. (This can be compared with $Log[n]$ growth for a purely repetitive sequence.) Note that actual algorithms for pointer-based encoding will typically find a slightly less regular pattern of repeats than is shown in the pictures here.

So what about two-dimensional patterns? The pictures below show what happens if one takes various patterns, arranges their rows one after another in a long line, and then applies pointer-based encoding to the resulting sequences. When there are obvious regularities in the original pattern, some compression is normally achieved—but in most cases the amount is not spectacular.

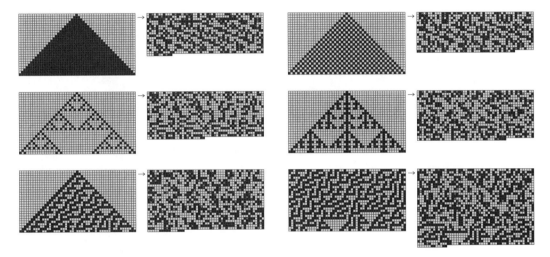

Examples of one-dimensional pointer-based encoding applied to patterns produced by cellular automata. Successive rows in each image are placed end to end so as to get a sequence to which the encoding can be applied. Pointers are used only for repeats that are of length at least 4. In the last example, large regions contain no such repeats, and therefore appear in the output just as they do in the input.

So how can one do better? The basic answer is that one needs to take account of the two-dimensional nature of the patterns. Most compression schemes used in practice have in the past primarily been set up just to handle one-dimensional sequences. But it is not difficult to set up schemes that operate directly on two-dimensional data.

The picture on the next page shows one approach based on the idea of breaking images up into collections of nested pieces, each with a uniform color. In some respects this scheme is a two-dimensional analog of run-length encoding, and when there are large regions of uniform color it yields significant compression.

It is also easy to extend block-based encoding to two dimensions: all one need do is to assign codewords to two-dimensional rather than

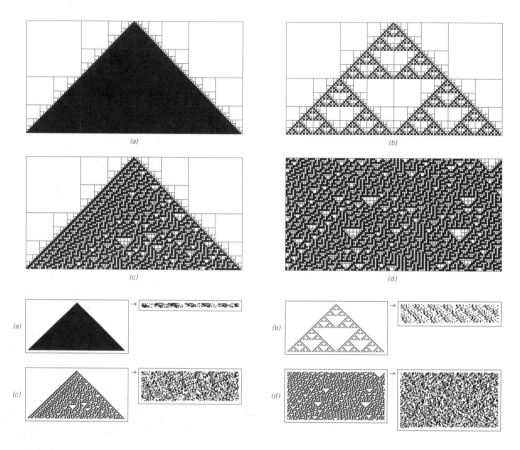

Examples of encoding by two-dimensional recursive subdivision. The idea is to use a generalization of a two-dimensional substitution system, in which at each step a square either remains the same or is subdivided into four small squares. The encoding specifies which choice is made at each step for each square. The method is analogous to the quadtree representation sometimes used in computer graphics. The substantial compression seen even in case (c) is a consequence of the large areas of uniform white that are present.

one-dimensional blocks. And as the pictures at the top of the facing page demonstrate, this procedure can lead to substantial compression. Particularly notable is what happens in case (d). For even though this pattern is produced by a simple one-dimensional cellular automaton rule, and even though one can see by eye that it contains at least some small-scale regularities, none of the schemes we have discussed up till now have succeeded in compressing it at all.

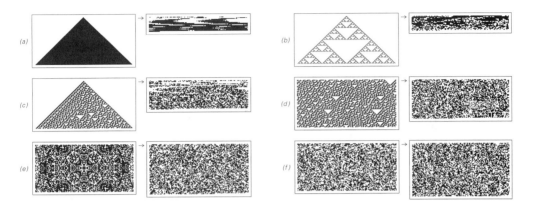

Examples of two-dimensional block-based encoding. Each image is broken into 3 × 2 blocks, and codewords are then assigned to these blocks using the Huffman scheme. Note the presence of compression even in case (d). This is a consequence of the fact that the cellular automaton rule allows only certain blocks to appear in the pattern, as illustrated in the picture below. (e) is generated by a two-dimensional cellular automaton; (f) is the sequence that appears on the center column of rule 30.

The picture below demonstrates why two-dimensional block encoding does, however, manage to compress it. The point is that the two-dimensional blocks that one forms always contain cells whose colors are connected by the cellular automaton rule—and this greatly reduces the number of different arrangements of colors that can occur.

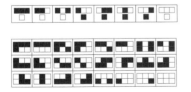

Cellular automaton rule 30, and the 3 × 2 blocks which appear in large patterns generated by it. There are a total of $2^6 = 64$ possible 3 × 2 blocks of black and white cells; the fact that only 24 of them appear in patterns generated by rule 30 is what makes it possible for two-dimensional block-based encoding to compress such patterns.

In cases (e) and (f), however, there is no simple rule for going from one row to the next, and two-dimensional block encoding—like all the other encoding schemes we have discussed so far—does not yield any substantial compression.

Like block encoding, pointer-based encoding can also be extended to two dimensions. The basic idea is just to scan two-dimensional data looking for repeats not of one-dimensional sequences, but instead of two-dimensional regions. And although such a procedure does not in the past appear to have been used in practice, it is quite straightforward to implement. The pictures on the facing page show some examples of the results one gets. And in many cases it turns out that the overall level of compression obtained is considerably greater than with any of the other schemes discussed in this section. But what is perhaps still more striking is that the patterns of repeated regions seem to capture almost every regularity that we readily notice by eye—as well as some that we do not. In pictures (c) and (d), for example, fairly subtle repetition on the left-hand side is captured, as is fourfold symmetry in picture (e).

One might have thought that to capture all these kinds of regularities would require a whole collection of complicated procedures. But what the pictures on the facing page demonstrate is that in fact just a single rather straightforward procedure is quite sufficient. And indeed the amount of compression achieved by this procedure in different cases seems to agree rather well with our intuitive impression of how much regularity is present.

All of the methods of data compression that we have discussed in this section can be thought of as corresponding to fairly simple programs. But each method involves a program with a rather different structure, and so one might think that it would inevitably be sensitive to rather different kinds of regularities.

But what we have seen in this section is that in fact different methods of data compression have remarkably similar characteristics. Essentially every method, for example, will successfully compress large regions of uniform color. And most methods manage to compress behavior that is repetitive, and at least to some extent behavior that is nested—exactly the two kinds of simple behavior that we have noted many times in this book.

For more complicated behavior, however, none of the methods seem capable of substantial compression. It is not that no compression is ever in principle possible. Indeed, as it happens, every single one of the pictures on the facing page can for example be generated from very short cellular automaton programs.

But the point is that except when the overall behavior shows repetition or nesting none of the standard methods of data compression

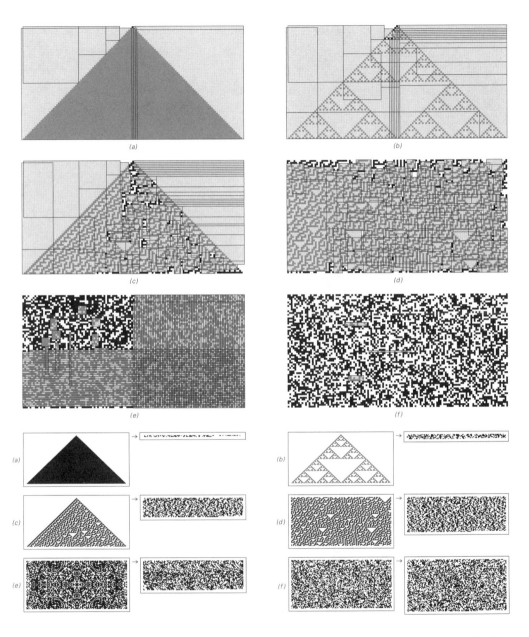

Examples of two-dimensional pointer-based encoding. The gray rectangles in the upper pictures indicate repeated regions that are encoded using pointers. In the particular scheme used here, each of these regions is required to contain at least 25 cells that have not already been encoded using pointers. The images are scanned sequentially and at every point the maximal rectangle extending to the right and down is found that is a repeat of a rectangle previously encountered, and contains the largest number of cells not already encoded using pointers. In many cases this maximal rectangle overlaps those found at subsequent points.

as we have discussed them in this section come even close to finding such short descriptions. And as a result, at least with respect to any of these methods all we can reasonably say is that the behavior we see seems for practical purposes random.

Irreversible Data Compression

All the methods of data compression that we discussed in the previous section are set up to be reversible, in the sense that from the encoded version of any piece of data it is always possible to recover every detail of the original. And if one is dealing with data that corresponds to text or programs such reversibility is typically essential. But with images or sounds it is typically no longer so necessary: for in such cases all that in the end usually matters is that one be able to recover something that looks or sounds right. And by being able to drop details that have little or no perceptible effect one can often achieve much higher levels of compression.

In the case of images a simple approach is just to ignore features that are smaller than some minimum size. The pictures below show

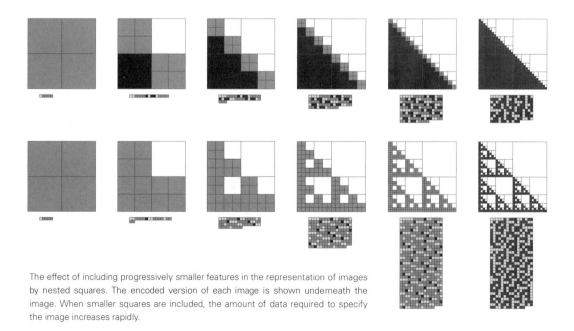

The effect of including progressively smaller features in the representation of images by nested squares. The encoded version of each image is shown underneath the image. When smaller squares are included, the amount of data required to specify the image increases rapidly.

basic forms

ranked basic forms

(a)

(b)

Examples of how images can be built up by adding together basic forms consisting of so-called two-dimensional Walsh functions. On the top left the basic forms are given in so-called sequency order. On the top right they are reordered roughly so as to go systematically from coarser to finer. In the bottom arrays of pictures each successive picture is obtained by adding in the corresponding basic form with an appropriate weight. The basic forms shown here have the property of being orthogonal, so that the weight for each form can be deduced simply by multiplying the original image by that form. Note that the forms involve numerical values -1 and +1, corresponding to cells colored white and black. The images shown here are all rescaled so that smallest values are white and largest black. The JPEG method of image compression uses an approach similar to the one shown here, though with basic forms that have continuous levels of gray, rather than just black and white.

what happens if one divides an image into a collection of nested squares, but imposes a lower limit on the size of these squares. And what one sees is that as the lower limit is increased, the amount of compression increases rapidly—though at the cost of a correspondingly rapid decrease in the quality of the image.

So can one do better at maintaining the quality of the image? Various schemes are used in practice, and almost all of them are based on the idea from traditional mathematics that by viewing data in terms of numbers it becomes possible to decompose the data into sums of fixed basic forms—some of which can be dropped in order to achieve compression.

The pictures on the previous page show an example of how this works. On the top left is a set of basic forms which have the property that any two-dimensional image can be built up simply by adding together these forms with appropriate weights. On the top right these forms are then ranked roughly from coarsest to finest. And given this ranking, the arrays of pictures at the bottom show how two different images can be built up by progressively adding in more and more of the basic forms.

If all the basic forms are included, then the original image is faithfully reproduced. But if one drops some of the later forms—thereby reducing the number of weights that have to be specified—one gets only an approximation to the image. The facing page shows what happens to a variety of images when different fractions of the forms are kept.

Images that are sufficiently simple can already be recognized even when only a very small fraction of the forms are included—corresponding to a very high level of compression. But most other images typically require more forms to be included—and thus do not allow such high levels of compression.

Indeed the situation is very much what one would expect from the definition of complexity that I gave two sections ago. The relevant features of both simple and completely random images can readily be recognized even at quite high levels of compression. But images that one would normally consider complex tend to have features that cannot be recognized except at significantly lower levels of compression.

All the pictures on the facing page, however, were generated from the specific ordering of basic forms shown on the previous page. And

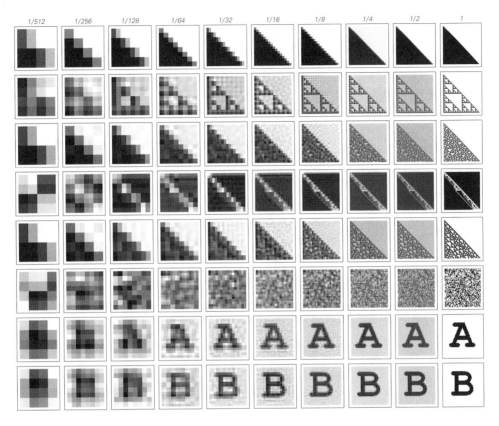

Examples of images obtained by keeping only certain fractions of the complete set of basic forms. In the case of both simple and completely random images, many features are recognizable even with fairly few basic forms—implying that a highly compressed representation can be given.

one might wonder whether perhaps some other ordering would make it easier to compress more complex images.

One simple approach is just to assemble a large collection of images typical of the ones that one wants to compress, and then to order the basic forms so that those which on average occur with larger weights in this collection appear first. The pictures on the next page show what happens if one does this first with images of cellular automata and then with images of letters. And indeed slightly higher levels of compression are achieved. But whatever ordering is used the fact seems to remain that images that we would normally consider complex still cannot systematically be compressed more than a small amount.

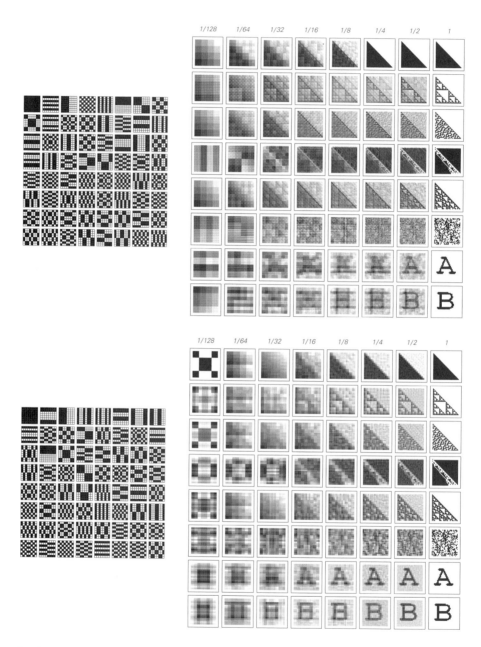

Results obtained by deducing optimal orderings of basic forms from collections of images of cellular automata (top) and letters (bottom). The orderings of basic forms are shown on the left, in each case starting with those whose weights are largest in absolute value when averaged over the collection of images. Note that the orderings are shown for 8 × 8 basic forms, while the actual images are 32 × 32. The orderings are deduced respectively from images of the 256 elementary cellular automata, and the 52 upper and lower case letters.

Visual Perception

In modern times it has usually come to be considered quite unscientific to base very much just on how things look to our eyes. But the fact remains that despite all the various methods of mathematical and other analysis that have been developed, our visual system still represents one of the most powerful and reliable tools we have. And certainly in writing this book I have relied heavily on our ability to make all sorts of deductions on the basis of looking at visual representations.

So how does the human visual system actually work? And what are its limitations? There are many details yet to be resolved, but over the past couple of decades, it has begun to become fairly clear how at least the lowest levels of the system work. And it turns out—just as in so many other cases that we have seen in this book—that much of what goes on can be thought of in terms of remarkably simple programs.

In fact, across essentially every kind of human perception, the basic scheme that seems to be used over and over again is to have particular kinds of cells set up to respond to specific fixed features in the data, and then to ignore all other features.

Color perception provides a classic example. On the retina of our eye are three kinds of color-sensitive cells, with each kind responding essentially to the level of either red, green or blue. Light from an object typically involves a whole spectrum of wavelengths. But the fact that we have only three kinds of color-sensitive cells means that our eyes essentially sample only three features of this spectrum. And this is why, for example, we have the impression that mixtures of just three fixed colors can successfully reproduce all other colors.

So what about patterns and textures? Does our visual system also work by picking out specific features of these? Everyday experience suggests that indeed it does. For if we look, say, at the picture on the next page we do not immediately notice every detail. And instead what our visual system seems to do is just to pick out certain features which quickly make us see the picture as a collection of patches with definite textures.

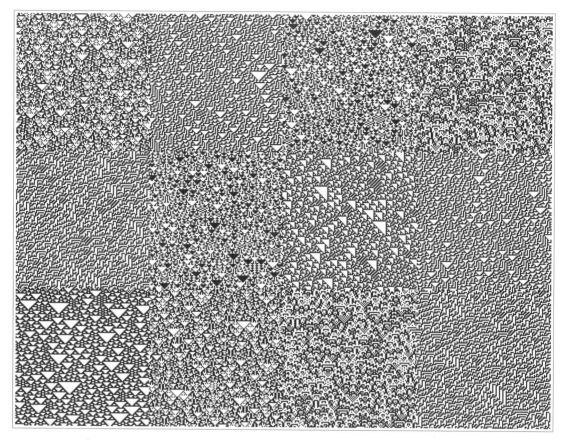

Patches generated by a variety of one-dimensional cellular automaton rules. Each patch is set up to have a roughly equal number of black and white squares. But despite this, our visual system quickly notices that different patches have different textures. And presumably this is because the visual system is automatically identifying particular features in each patch. Everyone appears immediately to be able to see some patches when shown this picture. But after looking at the picture for a while, the boundaries between the patches seem to get somewhat clearer.

So how does this work? The basic answer seems to be that there are nerve cells in our eyes and brains which are set up to respond to particular local patterns in the image formed on the retina of our eye.

The way this comes about appears to be surprisingly direct. Behind the 100 million or so light-sensitive cells on our retina are a sequence of layers of nerve cells, first in the eye and then in the brain. The connections between these cells are set up so that a given cell in the visual cortex will typically receive inputs only from cells in a fairly small area on our retina. Some of these inputs will be positive if the image in a certain part of the area is, say, colored white, while others will be positive if it is colored black. And the cell in the visual cortex will then respond only if enough of its inputs are positive, corresponding to a specific pattern being present in the image.

In practice many details of this setup are quite complicated. But as a simple idealization, one can consider an array of squares on the retina, each colored either black or white. And one can then assume that in the visual cortex there is a corresponding array of cells, with each cell receiving input from, say, a 2×2 block of squares, and following the rule that it responds whenever the colors of these squares form some particular pattern.

The pictures below show a simple example. In each case the first picture shows the image on the retina, while the second picture shows which cells respond to it. And with the specific choice of rule used here, what effectively happens is that the vertical black edges in the original image get picked out.

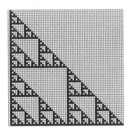 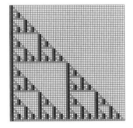 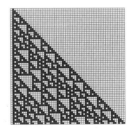 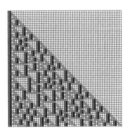

Responses to two sample images of cells sensitive to the 2 × 2 template shown on the left. The cells that respond are indicated by darker squares in the second picture in each pair. Such responses occur whenever the 2 × 2 template on the left appears, corresponding to the presence of a vertical black edge. The extraction of features by this kind of simple template matching appears to be a key element in human visual perception—as well as being common in technological image processing. The sample images used here are ones generated by the evolution of elementary one-dimensional cellular automata with rules 60 and 124 respectively.

Neurophysiological experiments suggest that cells in the visual cortex respond to a variety of specific kinds of patterns. And as a simple idealization, the pictures on the next page show what happens with cells that respond to each of the 16 possible 2×2 arrangements of black and white squares. In each case, one can think of the results as corresponding to picking out some specific local feature in the original image.

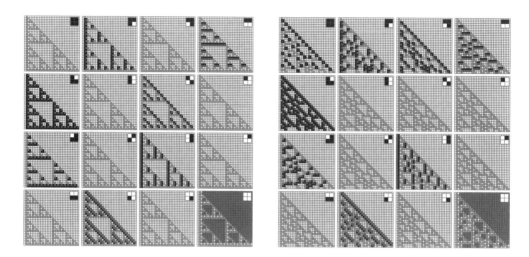

Responses to the sample images from the previous page by types of cells sensitive to each of the local arrangements of black and white squares shown. In each case, one can think of the resulting patterns as being filtered versions of the original images in which only parts that exhibit particular features are kept. The patterns can also be viewed as outputs from a single step in the evolution of two-dimensional block cellular automata in which the rules specify that a block becomes dark if it has the arrangement of cells shown, and becomes light otherwise. The comparative sparsity of dark blocks is a consequence of the fact that at any given position a dark block can occur in only one of the 16 cases shown. The absence of any dark blocks in many of the cases shown can be viewed as a reflection of constraints introduced by the construction of the images from one-dimensional cellular automaton rules.

So is this very simple kind of process really what underlies our seemingly sophisticated perception of patterns and textures? I strongly suspect that to a large extent it is. An important detail, however, is that there are cells in the visual cortex which in effect receive input from larger regions on the retina. But as a simple idealization one can assume that such cells in the end just respond to repeated versions of the basic 2×2 patterns.

So with this setup, the pictures on the facing page show what happens with an image like the one from page 578. The results are somewhat remarkable. For even though the average density of black and white squares is exactly the same across the whole image, what we see is that in different patches the features that end up being picked out have different densities. And it is this, I suspect, that makes us see different patches as having different textures.

For much as we distinguish colors by their densities of red, green and blue, so also it seems likely that we distinguish textures by their

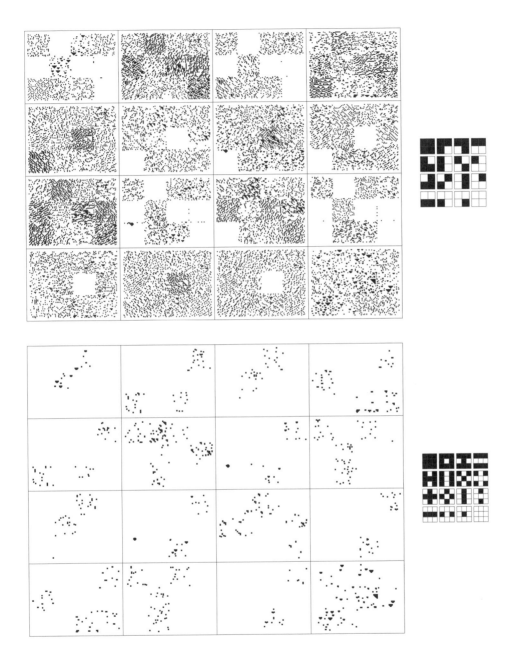

Responses to a smaller version of the image from page 578 by cells sensitive to all 16 possible 2 × 2 blocks, as well as their repetitive 3 × 3 extensions. Patches which appear to have different textures in the original image are seen to contain characteristically different densities of these various blocks. I strongly suspect that it is density differences such as these that allow our visual system to distinguish textures.

densities of certain local features. And the reason that this happens so quickly when we look at an image is no doubt that the procedure for picking out such features is a very simple one that can readily be carried out in parallel by large numbers of separate cells in our eyes and brains.

For patterns and textures, however, unlike for colors, we can always get beyond the immediate impression that our visual system provides. And so for example, by making a conscious effort, we can scan an image with our eyes, scrutinizing different parts in turn and comparing whatever details we want.

But what kinds of things can we expect to tell in this way? As the pictures below suggest, it is usually quite easy to see if an image is purely repetitive—even in cases where the block that repeats is fairly large.

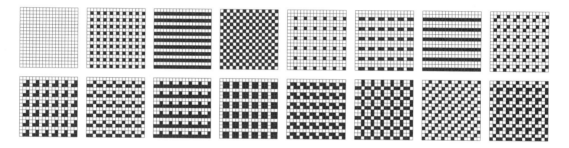

Examples of all the distinct repetitive patterns that can be formed from arrays of 2 × 2 and 3 × 3 blocks. In every single case the presence of pure repetition is easy to recognize by eye. Note that in a pattern generated by repeating one particular block, there will normally be other blocks that occur with other alignments. Page 215 shows patterns obtained in systems based on constraints in which one effectively requires that only certain blocks or sets of blocks occur.

But with nesting the story is quite different. All eight pictures on the facing page were generated from the two-dimensional substitution systems shown, and thus correspond to purely nested patterns. But except for the last picture on each row—which happen to be dominated by large areas of essentially uniform color—it is remarkably difficult for us to tell that the patterns are nested. And this can be viewed as a clear example of a limitation in our powers of visual perception.

As we found two sections ago, many standard methods of data compression have the same limitation. But at the end of that section I showed that the fairly simple procedure of two-dimensional pointer

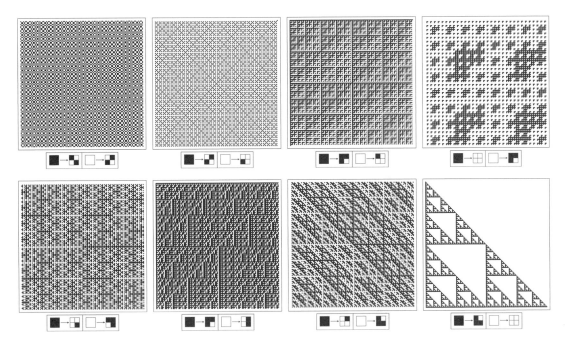

Examples of nested patterns created by following the two-dimensional substitution rules shown. Except for the last examples on each row, it is remarkably difficult to recognize the nested structure in these patterns by eye, even with quite careful scrutiny. The two-dimensional pointer-based encoding scheme from page 571 does however manage to recognize the structure in all cases.

encoding will succeed in recognizing nesting. So it is not that nesting is somehow fundamentally difficult to recognize; it is just that the particular processes that happen to occur in human visual perception do not in general manage to do it.

So what about randomness? The pictures on the next page show a few examples of images with various degrees of randomness. And just by looking at these images it is remarkably difficult to tell which of them is in fact the most random.

The basic problem is that our visual system makes us notice local features—such as clumps of black squares—even if their density is consistent with what it should be in a completely random array. And as a result, much as with constellations of stars, we tend to identify what seem to be regularities even in completely random patterns.

In principle it could be that there would be images in which our visual system would notice essentially no local features. And indeed in

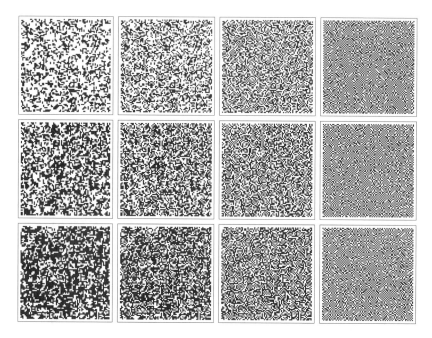

Examples of images that approximate perfect randomness. The second image on each row has squares chosen independently to be black with probabilities 0.4, 0.5 and 0.6 respectively. In the other images various features are added or removed. In the first image on each row, if any square is surrounded by four squares with identical colors, then the square is forced to have the same color. In the third image, any clump of squares with the same color is broken up by reversing the color of the center square. And in the fourth image, the same is done with lines of squares of the same color.

the last two images on each row above all clumps of squares of the same color, and then all lines of squares of the same color, have explicitly been removed. At first glance, these images do in some respects look more random. But insofar as our visual system contains elements that respond to each of the possible local arrangements of squares, it is inevitable that we will identify features of some kind or another in absolutely any image.

In practice there are presumably some types of local patterns to which our visual system responds more strongly than others. And knowing such a hierarchy, one should be able to produce images that in a sense seem as random as possible to us. But inevitably such images would reflect much more the details of our process of visual perception than they would anything about actual underlying randomness.

Auditory Perception

In the course of this book I have made extensive use of pictures. So why not also sounds? One issue—beyond the obvious fact that sounds cannot be included directly in a printed book—is that while one can study the details of a picture at whatever pace one wants, a sound is in a sense gone as soon as it has finished playing.

But everyday experience makes it quite clear that one can still learn a lot by listening to sounds. So what then are the features of sounds that our auditory system manages to pick out?

At a fundamental level all sounds consist of patterns of rapid vibrations. And the way that we hear sounds is by such vibrations being transmitted to the array of hair cells in our inner ear. The mechanics of the inner ear are set up so that each row of hair cells ends up being particularly sensitive to vibrations at some specific frequency. So what this means is that what we tend to perceive most about sounds are the frequencies they contain.

Musical notes usually have just one basic frequency, while voiced speech sounds have two or three. But what about sounds from systems in nature, or from systems of the kinds we have studied in this book?

There are a number of ways in which one can imagine such systems being used to generate sounds. One simple approach illustrated on the right is to consider a sequence of elements produced by the system, and then to take each element to correspond to a vibration for a brief time—say a thousandth of a second—in one of two directions.

A sequence of discrete elements and a possible corresponding waveform for a sound.

So what are such sounds like? If the sequence of elements is repetitive then what one hears is in essence a pure tone at a specific frequency—much like a musical note. But if the sequence is random then what one hears is just an amorphous hiss.

So what happens between these extremes? If the properties of a sequence gradually change in a definite way over time then one can often hear this in the corresponding sound. But what about sequences that have more or less uniform properties? What kinds of regularities does our auditory system manage to detect in these?

The answer, it seems, is surprisingly simple: we readily recognize exact or approximate repetition at definite frequencies, and essentially nothing else. So if we listen to nested sequences, for example, we have no direct way to tell that they are nested, and indeed all we seem sensitive to are some rather simple features of the spectrum of frequencies that occur.

The pictures below show spectra obtained from nested sequences produced by various simple one-dimensional substitution systems. The diversity of these spectra is quite striking: some have simple nested forms dominated by a few isolated peaks at specific frequencies, while others have quite complex forms that cover large ranges of frequencies.

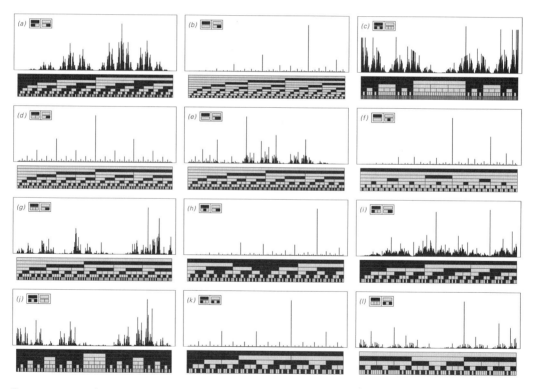

Frequency spectra of nested sequences generated by one-dimensional neighbor-independent substitution systems. The rules are the same as shown on pages 83 and 84. Note the presence of both isolated peaks and complicated background patterns. If a sequence corresponds to a pure tone and repeats every n elements then its spectrum will consist of $n/2$ equally spaced peaks. Sequences whose spectra contain no dominant peaks typically sound like random noise, although sometimes explicit time variation can be heard, and indeed sequence (c) just sounds like a succession of idealized frog ribbets. Intensity or power spectra are obtained by squaring the quantities shown.

And given only the underlying rule for a substitution system, it turns out to be fairly difficult to tell even roughly what the spectrum will be like. But given the spectrum, one can immediately tell how we will perceive the sound. When the spectrum is dominated by just one large peak, we hear a definite tone. And when there are two large peaks we also typically hear definite tones. But as the number of peaks increases it rapidly becomes impossible to keep track of them, and we end up just hearing random noise—even in cases where the peaks happen to have frequencies that are in the ratios of common musical chords.

So the result is that our ears are not sensitive to most of the elaborate structure that we see in the spectra of many nested sequences. Indeed, it seems that as soon as the spectrum covers any broad range of frequencies all but very large peaks tend to be completely masked, just as in everyday life a sound needs to be loud if it is to be heard over background noise.

So what about other kinds of regularities in sequences? If a sequence is basically random but contains some short-range correlations then these will lead to smooth variations in the spectrum. And for example sequences that consist of random successions of specific blocks can yield any of the types of spectra shown below—and can sound variously like hisses, growls or gurgles.

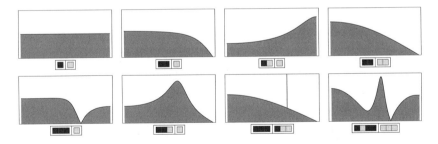

Frequency spectra for long sequences obtained by concatenating blocks in random orders. Such spectra can be calculated by fairly standard methods from stochastic analysis. The first case shown corresponds to white noise. The second-to-last case always has a black element at every third position, so exhibits a peak at the corresponding repetition frequency.

To get a spectrum with a more elaborate structure requires long-range correlations—as exist in nested sequences. But so far as I can tell, the only kinds of correlations that are ultimately important to our auditory system are those that lead to some form of repetition.

So in the end, any features of the behavior of a system that go beyond pure repetition will tend to seem to our ears essentially random.

Statistical Analysis

When it comes to studying large volumes of data the method almost exclusively used in present-day science is statistical analysis. So what kinds of processes does such analysis involve? What is typically done in practice is to compute from raw data various fairly simple quantities whose values can then be used to assess models which could provide summaries of the data.

Most kinds of statistical analysis are fundamentally based on the assumption that such models must be probabilistic, in the sense that they give only probabilities for behavior, and do not specifically say what the behavior will be. In different situations the reasons for using such probabilistic models have been somewhat different, but before the discoveries in this book one of the key points was that it seemed inconceivable that there could be deterministic models that would reproduce the kinds of complexity and apparent randomness that were so often seen in practice.

If one has a deterministic model then it is at least in principle quite straightforward to find out whether the model is correct: for all one has to do is to compare whatever specific behavior the model predicts with behavior that one observes. But if one has a probabilistic model then it is a much more difficult matter to assess its validity—and indeed much of the technical development of the field of statistics, as well as many of its well-publicized problems, can be traced to this issue.

As one simple example, consider a model in which all possible sequences of black and white squares are supposed to occur with equal probability. By effectively enumerating all such sequences, it is easy to see that such a model predicts that in any particular sequence the fraction of black squares is most likely to be $1/2$.

But what if a sequence one actually observes has 9 black squares out of 10? Even though this is not the most likely thing to see, one certainly cannot conclude from seeing it that the model is wrong. For the model does not say that such sequences are impossible—it merely says that they should occur only about 1% of the time.

And indeed there is no meaningful way without more information to deduce any kind of absolute probability for the model to be correct. So in practice what almost universally ends up being done is to consider not just an individual model, but rather a whole class of models, and then to try to identify which model from this class is the best one—as measured, say, by the criterion that its likelihood of generating the observed data is as large as possible.

For sequences of black and white squares a simple class of models to consider are those in which each square is taken to be black with some fixed independent probability p. Given a set of raw data the procedure for finding which model in this class is best—according, say, to the criterion of maximum likelihood—is extremely straightforward: all one does is to compute what fraction of squares in the data are black, and this value then immediately gives the value of p for the best model.

So what about more complicated models? Instead of taking each square to have a color that is chosen completely independently, one can for example take blocks of squares of some given length to have their colors chosen together. And in this case the best model is again straightforward to find: it simply takes the probabilities for different blocks to be equal to the frequencies with which these blocks occur in the data.

If one does not decide in advance how long the blocks are going to be, however, then things can become more complicated. For in such a case one can always just make up an extreme model in which only one very long block is allowed, with this block being precisely the sequence that is observed in the data.

Needless to say, such a model would for most purposes not be considered particularly useful—and certainly it does not succeed in providing any kind of short summary of the data. But to exclude models like this in a systematic way requires going beyond criteria such as maximum likelihood, and somehow explicitly taking into account the complexity of the model itself.

For specific types of models it is possible to come up with various criteria based for example on the number of separate numerical parameters that the models contain. But in general the problem of working out what model is most appropriate for any given set of data is an extremely difficult one. Indeed, as discussed at the beginning of Chapter 8, it is in some sense the core issue in any kind of empirical approach to science.

But traditional statistical analysis is usually far from having to confront such issues. For typically it restricts itself to very specific classes of models—and usually ones which even by the standards of this book are extremely simple. For sequences of black and white squares, for example, models that work as above by just assigning probabilities to fixed blocks of squares are by far the most common. An alternative, typically viewed as quite advanced, is to assign probabilities to sequences by looking at the paths that correspond to these sequences in networks of the kind shown below.

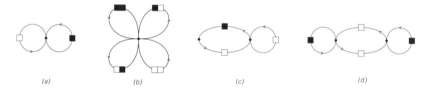

(a)   (b)   (c)   (d)

Networks defining probabilistic models. Each connection in each network has a certain probability associated with it, and the model takes sequences of black and white squares to be generated by tracing paths through the networks according to these probabilities. Cases (a) and (b) are so-called Markov models that in effect involve no memory and are equivalent to models discussed above. Cases (c) and (d) correspond to so-called hidden Markov models, with some short-term memory.

Networks (a) and (b) represent cases already discussed above. Network (a) specifies that the colors of successive squares should be chosen independently, while network (b) specifies that this should be done for successive pairs of squares. Network (c), however, specifies that different probabilities should be used depending on whether the path has reached the left or the right node in the network. But at least so long as the structure of the network is kept the same, it is fairly easy even in this case to deduce from a given set of data what probabilities in the network provide the best model for the data—for essentially all one need do is to follow the path corresponding to the data, and see with what frequency each connection from each node ends up being used.

So what about two-dimensional data? From the discussion in Chapter 5 it follows that no straightforward analogs of the types of probabilistic models described above can be constructed in such a case. But as an alternative it turns out that one can use probabilistic versions of one-dimensional cellular automata, as in the pictures below.

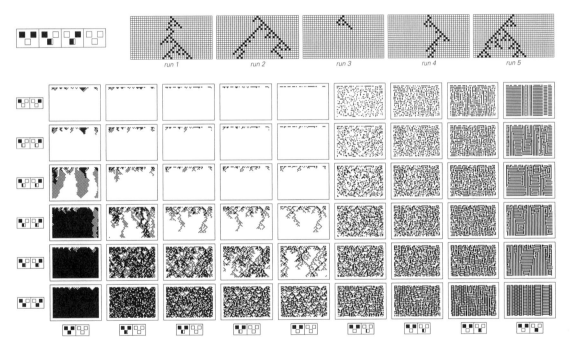

Examples of probabilistic cellular automata, in which the rule specifies the probabilities for each color of cell to be generated given what the colors of its two neighbors were on the previous step. Because the rule is probabilistic a different detailed pattern of evolution will in general be obtained each time the cellular automaton is run—as in the top row of pictures above. Despite this, however, any particular probabilistic cellular automaton will typically exhibit some characteristic overall pattern of behavior, as illustrated in the array of pictures above. Note that it is fairly common for phase transitions to occur, in which continuous changes in underlying probabilities lead to discrete changes in typical behavior. Probabilistic cellular automata can be viewed as generalizations of so-called directed percolation models.

The rules for such cellular automata work by assigning to each possible neighborhood of cells a certain probability to generate a cell of each color. And for any particular form of neighborhood, it is once again quite straightforward to find the best model for any given set of data. For essentially all one need do is to work out with what frequency each color of cell appears below each possible neighborhood in the data.

But how good are the results one then gets? If one looks at quantities such as the overall density of black cells that were in effect used in finding the model in the first place then inevitably the results one gets seem quite good. But as soon as one looks at explicit pictures like the ones below, one immediately sees dramatic differences between the original data and what one gets from the model.

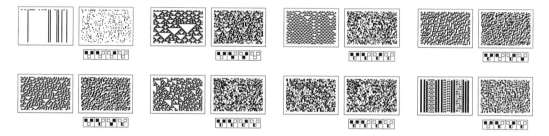

A comparison between data generated by ordinary cellular automata and the probabilistic cellular automata that are considered the best fit to it. While properties such as the density of black cells are typically set up to agree between the data and the model, the pictures make it clear that more detailed features do not.

In most cases, the typical behavior produced by the model looks considerably more random than the data. And indeed at some level this is hardly surprising: for by using a probabilistic model one is in a sense starting from an assumption of randomness.

The model can introduce certain regularities, but these almost never seem sufficient to force anything other than rather simple features of data to be correctly reproduced.

Needless to say, just as for most other forms of perception and analysis, it is typically not the goal of statistical analysis to find precise and complete representations of data. Rather, the purpose is usually just to extract certain features that are relevant for drawing specific conclusions about the data.

And a fundamental example is to try to determine whether a given sequence can be considered perfectly random—or whether instead it contains obvious regularities of some kind.

From the point of view of statistical analysis, a sequence is perfectly random if it is somehow consistent with a model in which all possible sequences occur with equal probability.

But how can one tell if this is so? What is typically done in practice is to take a sequence that is given and compute from it the values of various specific quantities, and then to compare these values with averages obtained by looking at all possible sequences.

Thus, for example, one might compute the fraction of squares in a given sequence that are black, and compare this to $1/2$. Or one might compute the frequency with which more than two consecutive black squares occur together, and compare this with the value $1/4$ obtained by averaging over all possible sequences.

And if one finds that a value computed from a particular sequence lies close to the average for all possible sequences then one can take this as evidence that the sequence is indeed random. But if one finds that the value lies far from the average then one can take this as evidence that the sequence is not random.

The pictures at the top of the next page show the results of computing the frequencies of different blocks in various sequences, and in each case each successive row shows results for all possible blocks of a given length. The gray levels on every row are set up so that the average of all possible sequences corresponds to the pattern of uniform gray shown below. So any deviation from such uniform gray potentially provides evidence for a deviation from randomness.

And what we see is that in the first three pictures, there are many obvious such deviations, while in the remaining pictures there are no obvious deviations. So from this it is fairly easy to conclude that the first three sequences are definitely not random, while the remaining sequences could still be random.

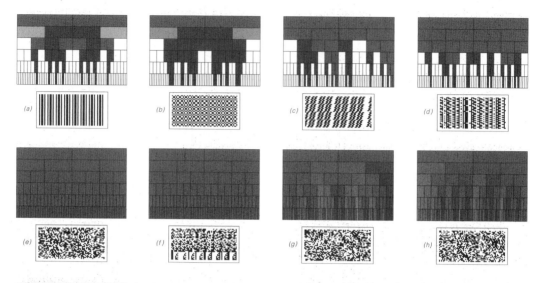

Statistics of block frequencies for various sequences. In each case the frequency of a particular block is represented by gray level, with results for blocks of successively greater lengths being shown on successive rows as indicated on the left. The original sequences are shown broken into lines and arranged in two dimensions. Sequences (b), (c) and (d) are generated by substitution systems with rules (b) ■ → ■□, □ → □■, (c) ■ → ■■□, □ → □ and (d) ■ → ■■□□□, □ → ■□ respectively. (Note that these substitution systems are the simplest ones that yield equal frequencies of all blocks up to lengths 1, 2 and 3 respectively.) Sequence (e) is generated by a linear feedback shift register (essentially an additive cellular automaton) with tap positions {2, 11}. Sequence (f) is formed by concatenating base 2 digits of successive integers. Sequence (g) is the center column of the pattern generated by the rule 30 cellular automaton. Sequence (h) is the base 2 digits of π.

And indeed sequence (a) is certainly not random; in fact it is purely repetitive. And in general it is fairly easy to see that in any sequence that is purely repetitive there must beyond a certain length be many blocks whose frequencies are far from equal.

It turns out that the same is true for nested sequences. And in the picture above, sequences (b), (c) and (d) are all nested.

But what about the remaining sequences? Sequences (e) and (f) seem to yield frequencies that in every case correspond accurately to those obtained by averaging over all possible sequences. Sequences (g) and (h) yield results that are fairly similar, but exhibit some definite fluctuations.

So do these fluctuations represent evidence that sequences (g) and (h) are not in fact random? If one looks at the set of all possible sequences, one can fairly easily calculate the distribution of frequencies for any particular block. And from this distribution one can tell with what probability a given deviation from the average should occur for a sequence that is genuinely chosen at random.

The result turns out to be quite consistent with what we see in pictures (g) and (h). But it is far from what we see in pictures (e) and (f). So even though individual block frequencies seem to suggest that sequences (d) and (e) are random, the lack of any spread in these frequencies provides evidence that in fact they are not.

So are sequences (g) and (h) in the end truly random? Just like other sequences discussed in this chapter they are in some sense not, since they can both be generated by simple underlying rules. But what the picture on the facing page demonstrates is that if one just does statistical analysis by computing frequencies of blocks one will see no evidence of any such underlying simplicity.

One might imagine that if one were to compute other quantities one could immediately find such evidence. But it turns out that many of the obvious quantities one might consider computing are in the end equivalent to various combinations of block frequencies. And perhaps as a result of this, it has sometimes been thought that if one could just compute frequencies of blocks of all lengths one would have a kind of universal test for randomness. But sequences like (e) and (f) on the facing page make it clear that this is not the case.

So what kinds of quantities can one in the end use in doing statistical analysis? The answer is that at least in principle one can use any quantity whatsoever, and in particular one can use quantities that arise from any of the processes of perception and analysis that I have discussed so far in this chapter. For in each case all one has to do is to compute the value of a quantity from a particular sequence of data, and then compare this value with what would be obtained by averaging over all possible sequences. In practice, however, the kinds of quantities actually used in statistical analysis of sequences tend to be rather limited. Indeed, beyond block frequencies, the only other ones that are common are those based on correlations, spectra, and occasionally run lengths—all of which we already discussed earlier in this chapter.

Nevertheless, one can in general imagine taking absolutely any process and using it as the basis for statistical analysis. For given some specific process one can apply it to a piece of raw data, and then see how the results compare with those obtained from all possible sequences.

If the process is sufficiently simple then by using traditional mathematics one can sometimes work out fairly completely what will happen with all possible sequences. But in the vast majority of cases this cannot be done, and so in practice one has no choice but just to compare with results obtained by sampling some fairly limited collection of possible sequences.

Under these circumstances therefore it becomes quite unrealistic to notice subtle deviations from average behavior. And indeed the only reliable strategy is usually just to look for cases in which there are huge differences between results for particular pieces of data and for typical sequences. For any such differences provide clear evidence that the data cannot in fact be considered random.

As an example of what can happen when simple processes are applied to data, the pictures on the facing page show the results of evolution according to various cellular automaton rules, with initial conditions given by the sequences from page 594. On each row the first picture illustrates the typical behavior of each cellular automaton. And the point is that if the sequences used as initial conditions for the other pictures are to be considered random then the behavior they yield should be similar.

But what we see is that in many cases the behavior actually obtained is dramatically different. And what this means is that in such cases statistical analysis based on simple cellular automata succeeds in recognizing that the sequences are not in fact random.

But what about sequences like (g) and (h)? With these sequences none of the simple cellular automaton rules shown here yield behavior that can readily be distinguished from what is typical. And indeed this is what I have found for all simple cellular automata that I have searched.

So from this we must conclude that—just as with all the other methods of perception and analysis discussed in this chapter—statistical analysis, even with some generalization, cannot readily recognize that sequences like (g) and (h) are anything but completely random—even though at an underlying level these sequences were generated by quite simple rules.

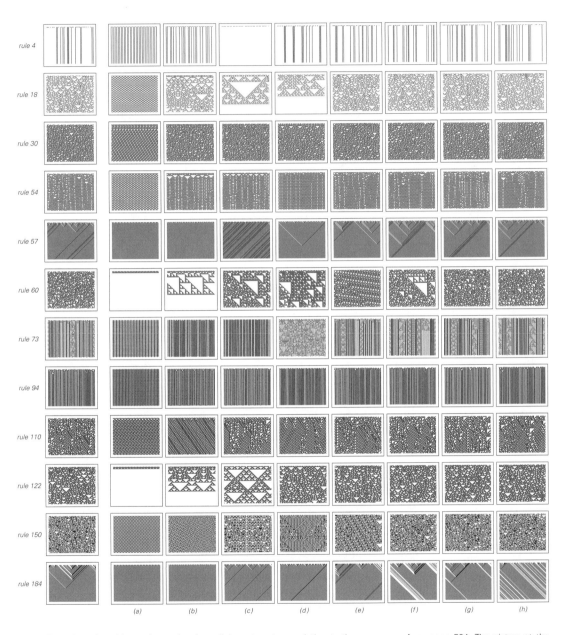

Examples of applying various rules for cellular automaton evolution to the sequences from page 594. The picture at the left-hand end of each row is chosen to show the typical behavior of each cellular automaton, given arbitrary initial conditions. Each cellular automaton rule in effect corresponds to a different statistical analysis procedure. Rule 4 picks out isolated black cells. Rule 60 essentially constructs a difference table for the sequence of elements. Rules 57 and 184 test for the overall density of black cells. (As indicated by page 136 the preponderance of white stripes with rule 184 in case (h) is a fluctuation.)

Cryptography and Cryptanalysis

The purpose of cryptography is to hide the contents of messages by encrypting them so as to make them unrecognizable except by someone who has been given a special decryption key. The purpose of cryptanalysis is then to defeat this by finding ways to decrypt messages without being given the key.

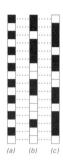

(a) (b) (c)

Example of a scheme for encryption. From the original message (a) an encrypted message (c) is generated by reversing the color of each square for which the corresponding square in the encrypting sequence (b) is black. This scheme is the basis for essentially all practical stream ciphers.

The picture on the left shows a standard method of encrypting messages represented by sequences of black and white squares. The basic idea is to have an encrypting sequence, shown as column (b) on the left, and from the original message (a) to get an encrypted version of the message (c) by reversing the color of every square for which the corresponding square in the encrypting sequence (b) is black.

So if one receives the encrypted message (c), how can one recover the original message (a)? If one knows the encrypting sequence (b) then it is straightforward. For all one need do is to repeat the process that was used for encryption, and reverse the color of every square in (c) for which the corresponding square in (b) is black.

But how can one arrange that only the intended recipient of the message knows the encrypting sequence (b)? In some situations it may be feasible to transmit the whole encrypting sequence in some secure way. But much more common is to be able to transmit only some short key in a secure way, and then to have to generate the encrypting sequence from this key.

So what kind of procedure might one use to get an encrypting sequence from a key? The picture at the top of the facing page shows an extremely simple approach that was widely used in practical cryptography until less than a century ago. The idea is just to form an encrypting sequence by repeatedly cycling through the elements in the key. And as the picture demonstrates, combining this with the original message leads to an encrypted message in which at least some of the structure in the original message is obscured.

But perhaps not surprisingly it is fairly easy to do cryptanalysis in such a case. For if one can find out what any sufficiently long segment in the encrypting sequence was, then this immediately gives the key,

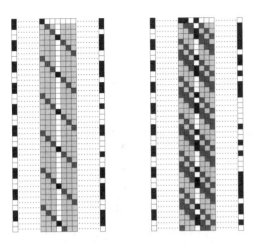

A simple example of an encryption system in which the encrypting sequence is obtained by repetitively cycling through the elements of the key. Encryption with two different keys is shown. In each case the original message is on the left, the encrypted message is on the right, and the encrypting sequence corresponds to the highlighted column of cells. The system is essentially a Vigenère cipher of the kind widely used between the 1500s and the early 1900s.

and from the key the whole of the rest of the encrypting sequence can immediately be generated.

So what kind of analysis is needed to find a segment of the encrypting sequence? In an extreme but in practice common case one might happen to know what certain parts of the original message were—perhaps standardized greetings or some such—and by comparing the original and encrypted forms of these parts one can immediately deduce what the corresponding parts of the encrypting sequence must have been.

And even if all one knows is that the original message was in some definite language this is still typically good enough. For it means that there will be certain blocks—say corresponding to words like "the" in English—that occur much more often than others in the original message. And since such blocks must be encrypted in the same way whenever they occur at the same point in the repetition period of the encrypting sequence they will lead to occasional repeats in the encrypted message—with the spacing of such repeats always being some multiple of the repetition period. So this means that just by looking at the distribution of spacings between repeats one can expect to determine the repetition period of the encrypting sequence.

And once this is known, it is usually fairly straightforward to find the actual key. For one can pick out of the encrypted message all the squares that occur at a certain point in the repetition period of the encrypting sequence, and which are therefore encrypted using a particular element of the key. Then one can ask whether such squares are more often black or more often white, and one can compare this with the result obtained by looking at the frequencies of letters in the language of the original message. If these two results are the same, then it suggests that the corresponding element in the key is white, and if they are different then it suggests that it is black. And once one has found a candidate key it is easy to check whether the key is correct by trying to use it to recover some reasonably long part of the original message. For unless one has the correct key, the chance that what one recovers will be meaningful in the language of the original message is absolutely negligible.

So what happens if one uses a more complicated rule for generating an encrypting sequence from a key? Methods like the ones above still turn out to allow features of the encrypting sequence to be found. And so to make cryptography work it must be the case that even if one knows certain features or parts of the encrypting sequence it is still difficult to deduce the original key or otherwise to generate the rest of the sequence.

The picture below shows one way of generating encrypting sequences that was widely used in the early years of electronic cryptography, and is still sometimes used today. The basic idea is to look at the evolution of an additive cellular automaton in a register of limited width. The key then gives the initial condition for the cellular automaton, and the encrypting sequence is extracted, for example, by sampling a particular cell on successive steps.

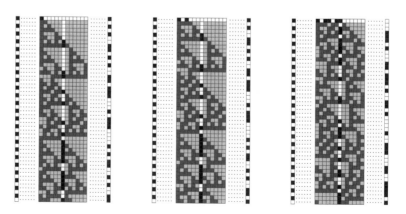

Encryption using the rule 60 additive cellular automaton. This is essentially equivalent to a linear feedback shift register.

So given such an encrypting sequence, is there any easy way to do cryptanalysis and go backwards and work out the key?

It turns out that there is. For as the picture below demonstrates, in an additive cellular automaton like the one considered here the underlying rule is such that it allows one not only to deduce the form of a particular row from the row above it, but also to deduce the form of a particular column from the column to its right. And what this means is that if one has some segment of the encrypting sequence, corresponding to part of a column, then one can immediately use this to deduce the forms of a sequence of other columns, and thus to find the form of a row in the cellular automaton—and hence the original key.

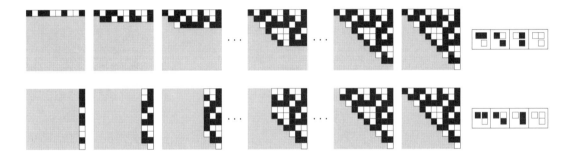

An example of the basis for cryptanalysis of an additive cellular automaton. The first set of pictures show the ordinary evolution of the rule 60 cellular automaton, in which each successive row is deduced from the one above. The second set of pictures show a kind of sideways evolution in which the rule is reinterpreted so as to allow a column of cells to be deduced from the column immediately to its right. Note that in both cases the colors of cells in the area on the lower right cannot be determined without knowing the colors of more initial cells than are shown.

But what happens if the encrypting sequence does not include every single cell in a particular column? One cannot then immediately use the method described above. But it turns out that the additive nature of the underlying rule still makes comparatively straightforward cryptanalysis possible.

The picture on the next page shows how this works. Because of additivity it turns out that one can deduce whether or not some cell a certain number of steps down a given column is black just by seeing whether there are an odd or even number of black cells in certain specific positions in the row at the top. And one can then immediately invert this to get a way to deduce the colors of cells on a given row from the colors of certain combinations of cells in a given column.

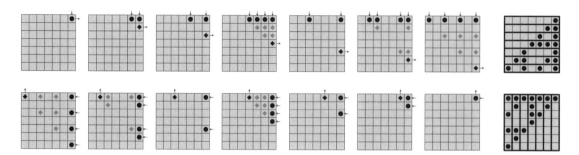

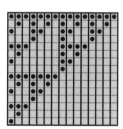

Another consequence of additivity: the correspondence between colors of cells on rows and columns in the rule 60 cellular automaton. In each case specifying the colors of the cells that are marked with dots immediately determines the colors of the cells that are marked with diamonds. The final diamond cell is black if an odd number of the dotted cells are black, and is white otherwise. The pictures on the right show which cells in the top row and which cells in the right-hand column determine the cells at successive positions in the right-hand column and in the top row respectively. These pictures can be thought of as matrices with 1's at the position of each black dot, and 0's elsewhere. Multiplying these matrices modulo 2 by vectors corresponding to a row of the cellular automaton gives a column, and vice versa. This means that the matrix on the second row of pictures is the inverse modulo 2 of the one on the first row.

Which cells in a column are known will depend on how the encrypting sequence was formed. But with almost any scheme it will eventually be possible to determine the colors of cells at each of the positions across any register of limited width. So once again a fairly simple process is sufficient to allow the original key to be found.

So how then can one make a system that is not so vulnerable to cryptanalysis? One approach often used in practice is to form combinations of rules of the kind described above, and then to hope that the complexity of such rules will somehow have the effect of making cryptanalysis difficult.

But as we have seen many times in this book, more complicated rules do not necessarily produce behavior that is fundamentally any more complicated. And instead what we have discovered is that even among extremely simple rules there are ones which seem to yield behavior that is in a sense as complicated as anything.

So can such rules be used for cryptography? I strongly suspect that they can, and that in fact they allow one to construct systems that are at least as secure to cryptanalysis as any that are known.

The picture below shows a simple example based on the rule 30 cellular automaton that I have discussed several times before in this book. The idea is to generate an encrypting sequence by sampling the evolution of the cellular automaton, starting from initial conditions that are defined by a key.

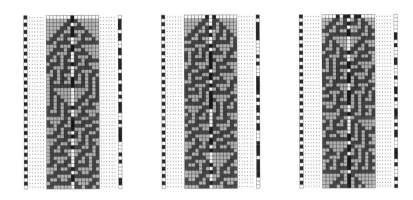

Encryption using a column of rule 30 as the encrypting sequence. I first suggested this method in 1985.

In the case of the additive cellular automaton shown on the previous page its nested structure makes it possible to recognize regularities using many of the methods of perception and analysis discussed in this chapter. But with rule 30 most sequences that are generated—even from simple initial conditions—appear completely random with respect to all of the methods of perception and analysis discussed so far.

So what about cryptanalysis? Does this also fail to find regularities, or does it provide some special way—at least within the context of a setup like the one shown above—to recognize whatever regularities are necessary for one to be able to deduce the initial condition and thus determine the key?

There is one approach that will always in principle work: one can just enumerate every possible initial condition, and then see which of them yields the sequence one wants. But as the width of the cellular automaton increases, the total number of possible initial conditions rapidly becomes astronomical, and to test all of them becomes completely infeasible.

So are there other approaches that can be used? It turns out that as illustrated in the picture below rule 30 has a property somewhat like the additive cellular automaton discussed two pages ago: in addition to allowing one row to be deduced from the row above, it allows columns to be deduced from columns to their right. But unlike for the additive cellular automaton, it takes not just one column but instead two adjacent columns to make this possible.

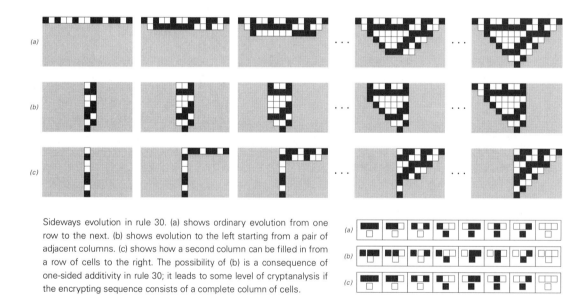

Sideways evolution in rule 30. (a) shows ordinary evolution from one row to the next. (b) shows evolution to the left starting from a pair of adjacent columns. (c) shows how a second column can be filled in from a row of cells to the right. The possibility of (b) is a consequence of one-sided additivity in rule 30; it leads to some level of cryptanalysis if the encrypting sequence consists of a complete column of cells.

So if the encrypting sequence corresponds to a single column, how can one find an adjacent column? The last row of pictures above show a way to do this. One picks some sequence of cells for the right half of the top row, then evolves down the page. And somewhat surprisingly, it turns out that given the cells in one column, there are fairly few possibilities for what the neighboring column can be. So by sampling a limited number of sequences on the top row, one can often find a second column that then allows columns to the left to be determined, and thus for a candidate key to be found.

But it is rather easy to foil this particular approach to cryptanalysis: all one need do is not sample every single cell in a given column in forming the encrypting sequence. For without every cell there does not appear to be enough information for any kind of local rule to be able to deduce one column from others.

The picture below shows evidence for this. The cells marked by dots have colors that are taken as given, and then the colors of other cells are filled in according to the average that is obtained by starting from all possible initial conditions.

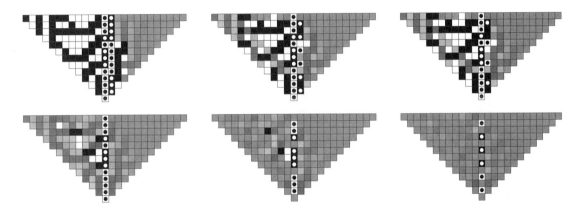

Patterns generated by rule 30 after averaging over all possible initial conditions that reproduce the arrangements of colors in the cells indicated by dots. If a cell is completely black or completely white then this means that its color is uniquely determined by the constraints given. If the cell is shown as gray then this means that it has some probability of being black and some probability of being white. Note that when two complete adjacent columns are specified all the cells on the left-hand side are determined. But when fewer cells are specified, the number of cells that are determined decreases rapidly, indicating that cryptanalysis is likely to become difficult.

With two complete columns given, all cells to the left are determined to be either black or white. And with one complete column given, significant patches of cells still have determined colors. But if only every other cell in a column is given, almost nothing definite follows about the colors of other cells.

So what about the approach on page 602? Could this not be used here? It turns out that the approach relies crucially on the additivity of the underlying rules. And since rule 30 is not additive, it simply does not work. What happens is that the function that determines the color of a particular cell from the colors of cells in a nearby column rapidly becomes extremely complicated—so that the approach probably ends up essentially being no better than just enumerating possible initial conditions.

The conclusion therefore is that at least with standard methods of cryptanalysis—as well as a few others—there appears to be no easy way to deduce the key for rule 30 from any suitably chosen encrypting sequence. But how can one be sure that there really is absolutely no easy way to do this? In Chapter 12 I will discuss some fundamental approaches to such a question. But as a practical matter one can say that not only have direct attempts to find easy ways to deduce the key in rule 30 failed, but also—despite some considerable effort—little progress has been made in solving any of various problems that turn out to be equivalent to this one.

Traditional Mathematics and Mathematical Formulas

Traditional mathematics has for a long time been the primary method of analysis used throughout the theoretical sciences. Its goal can usually be thought of as trying to find a mathematical formula that summarizes the behavior of a system. So in a simple case if one has an array of black and white squares, what one would typically look for is a formula that takes the numbers which specify the position of a particular square and from these tells one whether the square is black or white.

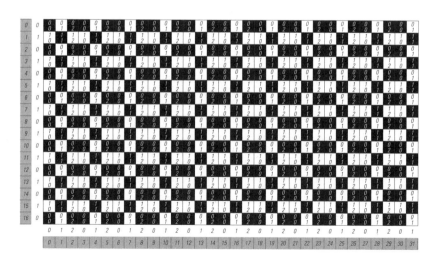

With a pattern that is purely repetitive, the formula is always straightforward, as the picture at the bottom of the facing page illustrates. For all one ever need do is to work out the remainder from dividing the position of a particular square by the size of the basic repeating block, and this then immediately tells one how to look up the color one wants.

So what about nested patterns? It turns out that in most of traditional mathematics such patterns are already viewed as quite advanced. But with the right approach, it is in the end still fairly straightforward to find formulas for them.

The crucial idea—much as in Chapter 4—is to think about numbers not in terms of their size but instead in terms of their digit sequences. And with this idea the picture on the next page shows an example of how what is in effect a formula can be constructed for a nested pattern.

What one does is to look at the digit sequences for the numbers that give the vertical and horizontal positions of a certain square. And then in the specific case shown one compares corresponding digits in these two sequences, and if these digits are ever respectively 0 and 1, then the square is white; otherwise it is black.

So why does this procedure work?

As we have discussed several times in this book, any nested pattern must—almost by definition—be able to be reproduced by a neighbor-independent substitution system. And in the case shown on the next page the rules for this system are such that they replace each square at each step by a 2×2 block of new squares. So as the picture illustrates this means that new squares always have positions that involve numbers containing one extra digit. With the particular rules shown, the new squares always have the same color as the old one, except in one specific case: when a black square is replaced, the new square that appears in the upper right is always white. But this square

◀ An example of how the color of any square in a repetitive pattern can be found from its coordinates by a simple mathematical procedure. The procedure takes the x and y coordinates of the square, and computes their remainders after division by 3 and 2 respectively. Using these remainders—which are shown inside each square—the color of a particular square can be determined by a simple lookup in the repeating block shown on the left. The whole procedure can be represented using a mathematical formula that involves either functions like *Mod* or more traditional functions like *Sin*.

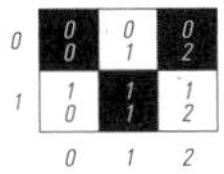

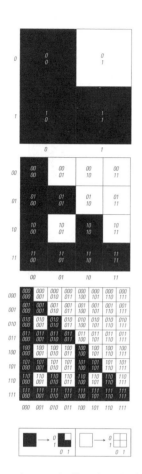

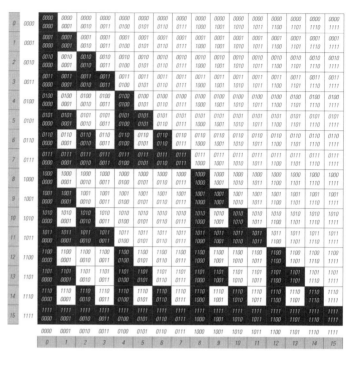

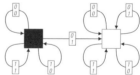

An example of how the color of any square in a nested pattern can be found from its coordinates by a fairly simple mathematical procedure. The procedure works by looking at the base 2 digit sequences of the coordinates. If any digit in the y coordinate of a particular square is 0 when the corresponding digit in the x coordinate is 1 then the square is white; otherwise it is black. The finite automaton at the bottom right gives a representation of this rule. Starting from the black square, one follows the sequence of connections that corresponds to the successive digits that one encounters in the y and x coordinates. Whatever square one lands up at in the finite automaton then gives the color one wants. Why this procedure works is illustrated by the pictures on the left. The nested pattern can be built up by a 2D substitution system with the rules shown. At each step in the evolution of this substitution system one gets a finer grid of squares, each specified in effect by one more digit in their coordinates.

has the property that its vertical position ends with a 0, and its horizontal position ends with a 1. So if the numbers that correspond to the position of a particular square contain this combination of digits at any point, it follows that the square must be white.

So what about other nested patterns? It turns out that using an extension of the argument above it is always possible to take the rules for the substitution system that generates a particular nested pattern, and from these construct a procedure for finding the color of a square in the pattern given its position. The pictures below show several examples, and in all cases the procedures are fairly straightforward.

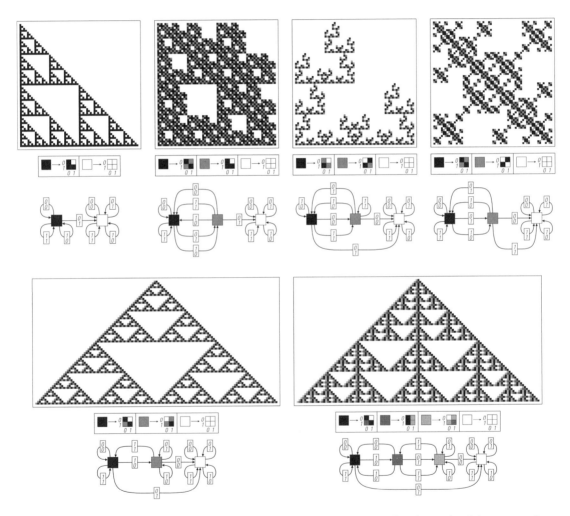

Procedures for determining the color of a square at a given position in various nested patterns. In each case the whole pattern can be generated by repeatedly applying the substitution system rule shown. The color of any particular square can also be found by feeding the digit sequences of its *y* and *x* coordinates to the finite automaton shown. The first example shown corresponds to cellular automaton rule 60; the last two examples correspond respectively to rules 90 and 150. In the top row of examples, the initial condition for the substitution system is a single black square, and the start state for the finite automaton is also its black state. In the second row of examples, the initial condition consists of a light gray square next to a black square. In these cases, the colors of squares to the left of the center can be found by starting from the light gray state in the finite automaton; the colors of squares to the right can be found by starting from the black state.

But while these procedures could easily be implemented as programs, they are in a sense not based on what are traditionally thought of as ordinary mathematical functions. So is it in fact possible to get formulas for the colors of squares that involve only such functions?

In the one specific case shown at the top of the facing page it turns out to be fairly easy. For it so happens that this particular pattern—which is equivalent to the patterns at the beginning of each row on the previous page—can be obtained just by adding together pairs of numbers in the format of Pascal's triangle and then putting a black square whenever there is an entry that is an odd number.

And as the table below illustrates, the entries in Pascal's triangle are simply the binomial coefficients that appear when one expands out the powers of $1 + x$. So to determine whether a particular square in the pattern is black or white, all one need do is to compute the corresponding binomial coefficient, and see whether or not it is an odd number. And this means that if black is represented by 1 and white by 0, one can then give an explicit formula for the color of the square at position x on row y: it is simply $(1 - (-1)\wedge \text{Binomial}[y, x])/2$.

1		1	
$1 + x$	$1 + x$	$1 + x + x^2$	$1 + x + x^2$
$(1+x)^2$	$1 + 2x + x^2$	$(1+x+x^2)^2$	$1 + 2x + 3x^2 + 2x^3 + x^4$
$(1+x)^3$	$1 + 3x + 3x^2 + x^3$	$(1+x+x^2)^3$	$1 + 3x + 6x^2 + 7x^3 + 6x^4 + 3x^5 + x^6$
$(1+x)^4$	$1 + 4x + 6x^2 + 4x^3 + x^4$	$(1+x+x^2)^4$	$1 + 4x + 10x^2 + 16x^3 + 19x^4 + 16x^5 + 10x^6 + 4x^7 + x^8$
$(1+x)^5$	$1 + 5x + 10x^2 + 10x^3 + 5x^4 + x^5$	$(1+x+x^2)^5$	$1 + 5x + 15x^2 + 30x^3 + 45x^4 + 51x^5 + 45x^6 + 30x^7 + 15x^8 + 5x^9 + x^{10}$
	Binomial[t, n]		*GegenbauerC[n, -t, -1/2]*

Algebraic representations of the patterns on the facing page. The coefficient of x^n on each row gives the value of each square. These coefficients can also be obtained from the formulas in terms of *Binomial* and *GegenbauerC* given. A particular square is colored black if its value *a* is odd. This can be determined either from *Mod[a, 2]* or equivalently from $(1 - (-1)^a)/2$ or $Sin[\pi a/2]^2$. The succession of polynomials above can be obtained by expanding the generating functions $1/(1 - (1 + x)y)$ and $1/(1 - (1 + x + x^2)y)$. *Binomial[m, n]* is the ordinary binomial coefficient $m!/(n!(m-n)!)$. *GegenbauerC* is a so-called orthogonal polynomial—a higher mathematical function.

So what about the bottom picture on the facing page? Much as in the top picture numbers can be assigned to each square, but now these numbers are computed by successively adding together triples rather

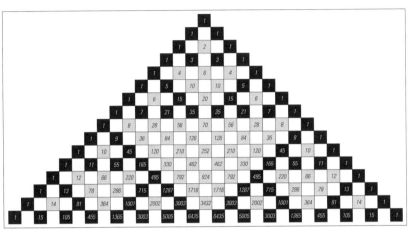

Nested patterns constructed using arithmetic operations. The example at the top is Pascal's triangle, formed by making each number be the sum of the numbers immediately to its left and right on the row above. The example at the bottom is a generalization of Pascal's triangle in which each number is the sum of the numbers above it and to its left and right on the row above. In both cases squares are colored black when the numbers that appear in them are odd. The limiting arrangements of colors correspond to nested patterns. For the top picture the pattern is what would be generated by an additive cellular automaton following rule 90; for the bottom picture it is what would be generated by one following rule 150. The numbers in the top picture are binomial coefficients; those in the bottom picture are particular trinomial coefficients.

than pairs. And once again the numbers appear as coefficients, but now in the expansion of powers of $1 + x + x^2$ rather than of $1 + x$.

So is there an explicit formula for these coefficients? If one restricts oneself to a fixed number of elementary mathematical functions together with factorials and multinomial coefficients then it appears that there is not. But if one also allows higher mathematical functions then it turns out that such a formula can in fact be found: as indicated in the table above each coefficient is given by a particular value of a so-called Gegenbauer or ultraspherical function.

So what about other nested patterns? Both of the patterns shown on the previous page are rather special in that as well as being generated by substitution systems they can also be produced one row at a time by the evolution of one-dimensional cellular automata with simple additive rules. And in fact the approaches used above can be viewed as direct generalizations of such additive rules to the domain of ordinary numbers.

For a few other nested patterns there exist fairly simple connections with additive cellular automata and similar systems— though usually in more dimensions or with more neighbors. But for most nested patterns there seems to be no obvious way to relate them to ordinary mathematical functions. Nevertheless, despite this, it is my guess that in the end it will in fact turn out to be possible to get a formula for any nested pattern in terms of suitably generalized hypergeometric functions, or perhaps other functions that are direct generalizations of ones used in traditional mathematics.

Yet given how simple and regular nested patterns tend to look it may come as something of a surprise that it should be so difficult to represent them as traditional mathematical formulas. And certainly if this example is anything to go by, it begins to seem unlikely that the more complex kinds of patterns that we have seen so many times in this book could ever realistically be represented by such formulas.

But it turns out that there are at least some cases where traditional mathematical formulas can be found even though to the eye or with respect to other methods of perception and analysis a pattern may seem highly complex.

The picture at the top of the facing page is one example. A pattern is built up by superimposing a sequence of repetitive grids, and to the eye this pattern seems highly complex. But in fact there is a simple formula for the color of each square: given the largest factor in common between the

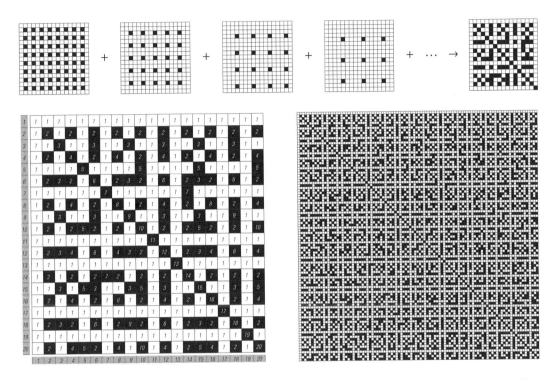

An example of a pattern that looks complex, but can nevertheless still be represented by a simple mathematical formula. Given the horizontal and vertical positions *x* and *y* a square is white when *GCD[x, y] = 1* and is black otherwise. The condition *GCD[x, y] = 1* is equivalent to the statement that *x* and *y* are relatively prime, or that no reduction is required to bring the fraction *x/y* to lowest terms. It can be shown that if the pattern is extended sufficiently far, then any possible local arrangement of black squares will eventually appear—though not necessarily with equal frequency.

numbers that specify the horizontal and vertical positions of the square, the square is white whenever this factor is 1, and is black otherwise.

So what about systems like cellular automata that have definite rules for evolution? Are there ever cases in which patterns generated by such systems seem complex to the eye but can in fact be described by simple mathematical formulas?

I know of one class of examples where this happens, illustrated in the pictures on the next page. The idea is to set up a row of cells corresponding to the digits of a number in a certain base, and then at each step to multiply this number by some fixed factor.

Such a system has many features immediately reminiscent of a cellular automaton. But at least in the case of multiplication by 3 in

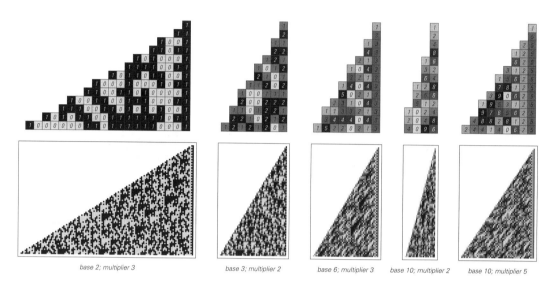

base 2; multiplier 3   base 3; multiplier 2   base 6; multiplier 3   base 10; multiplier 2   base 10; multiplier 5

Patterns of digits in various bases generated by successive multiplication by a fixed factor. Such systems were discussed on page 120. With multiplier m row t corresponds to the power m^t. The value of the cell at position n from the end of row t is thus the nth digit of m^t, or $Mod[Quotient[m^t, k^n], k]$. Despite the apparent complexity of the patterns, a fairly simple mathematical formula thus exists for the color of each square they contain.

base 2, the presence of carry digits in the multiplication process makes the system not quite an ordinary cellular automaton. It turns out, however, that multiplication by 3 in base 6, or by 2 or 5 in base 10, never leads to carry digits, with the result that in such cases the system can be thought of as following a purely local cellular automaton rule of the kind illustrated below.

Cellular automaton rules equivalent to multiplication of digit sequences in various bases. The left part of the picture shows the explicit form of the rule for base 6 and multiplier 3. The arrays of numbers summarize the rule for this case and other cases. Note that only certain specific choices of base and multiplier lead to ordinary cellular automata; with other choices there are carries that propagate arbitrarily far. (See page 661.)

As the pictures at the top of the facing page demonstrate, the overall patterns produced in all cases tend to look complex, and in many respects random. But the crucial point is that because of the way the system was constructed there is nevertheless a simple formula for the color of each cell: it is given just by a particular digit in the number obtained by raising the multiplier to a power equal to the number of steps. So despite their apparent complexity, all the patterns on the facing page can in effect be described by simple traditional mathematical formulas.

But if one thinks about actually using such formulas one might at first wonder what good they really are. For if one was to work out the value of a power m^t by explicitly performing t multiplications, this would be very similar to explicitly following t steps of cellular automaton evolution. But the point is that because of certain mathematical features of powers it turns out to be possible—as indicated in the table below—to find m^t with many fewer than t operations; indeed, one or two operations for every base 2 digit in t is always for example sufficient.

m^1	m	m
m^2	$m \times m$	m^2
m^3	$m \times m \times m$	$m^2 \times m$
m^4	$m \times m \times m \times m$	$(m^2)^2$
m^5	$m \times m \times m \times m \times m$	$(m^2)^2 \times m$
m^6	$m \times m \times m \times m \times m \times m$	$(m^2 \times m)^2$
m^7	$m \times m \times m \times m \times m \times m \times m$	$(m^2 \times m)^2 \times m$
m^8	$m \times m \times m \times m \times m \times m \times m \times m$	$((m^2)^2)^2$
m^9	$m \times m \times m \times m \times m \times m \times m \times m \times m$	$((m^2)^2)^2 \times m$
m^{10}	$m \times m \times m \times m \times m \times m \times m \times m \times m \times m$	$((m^2)^2 \times m)^2$

Examples of how powers can be computed more efficiently than by successive multiplications. In the cases shown, the choice of whether to square or multiply by an additional factor of m at each step in computing m^t is made on the basis of the successive digits in the base 2 representation of the number t.

So what about other patterns produced by cellular automata and similar systems? Is it possible that in the end all such patterns could just be described by simple mathematical formulas? I do not think so. In fact, as I will argue in Chapter 12, my strong belief is that in the vast majority of cases it will be impossible for quite fundamental reasons to find any such simple formula. But even though no simple formula may exist, it is still always in principle possible to represent the outcome of any process of cellular automaton evolution by at least some kind of formula.

The picture below shows how this can be done for a single step in the evolution of three elementary cellular automata. The basic idea is to translate the rule for a given cellular automaton into a formula that depends on three variables a_1, a_2 and a_3 whose values correspond to the colors of the three initial cells. The formula consists of a sum of terms, with each term being zero unless the colors of the three cells match a situation in which the rule yields a black cell.

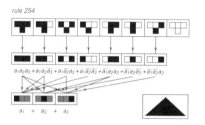

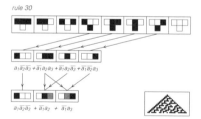

Boolean expression representations of the rules for three elementary cellular automata. The first row shows the original cellular automaton rules. The second row shows those combinations of cells that yield a black cell according to each of the rules. The third row shows a minimized version in which gray cells are introduced to indicate either black or white. In the formulas under the second and third rows the variable a_i represents the color of the ith cell. $e_i\, e_j$ is analogous to $e_i \wedge e_j$, $e_i + e_j$ to $e_i \vee e_j$, and $\overline{e_i}$ to $\neg e_i$. The formulas given are in so-called disjunctive normal form (DNF). They are set up so that only at most one term in each formula is ever relevant for any particular configuration of colors.

In the first instance, each term can be set up to correspond directly to one of the cases in the original rule. But in general this will lead to a more complicated formula than is necessary. For as the picture demonstrates, it is often possible to combine several cases into one term by ignoring the values of some of the variables.

The picture at the top of the facing page shows what happens if one considers two steps of cellular automaton evolution. There are now altogether five variables, but at least for rules like rules 254 and 90 the individual terms end up not depending on most of these variables.

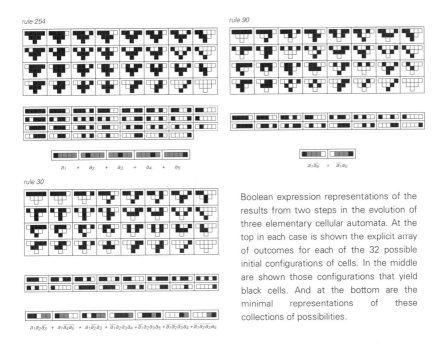

rule 254

rule 90

$$a_1 \quad + \quad a_2 \quad + \quad a_3 \quad + \quad a_4 \quad + \quad a_5$$

$$a_1\overline{a_5} \quad + \quad \overline{a_1}a_5$$

rule 30

$$a_1\overline{a_2}\,\overline{a_3} \; + \; a_1\overline{a_4}\,\overline{a_5} \; + \; a_1\overline{a_2}a_3 \; + \; \overline{a_1}\overline{a_2}a_3a_4 + \overline{a_1}a_2a_3a_5 + \overline{a_1}\overline{a_2}a_3a_4 + \overline{a_1}\overline{a_2}a_3a_5$$

Boolean expression representations of the results from two steps in the evolution of three elementary cellular automata. At the top in each case is shown the explicit array of outcomes for each of the 32 possible initial configurations of cells. In the middle are shown those configurations that yield black cells. And at the bottom are the minimal representations of these collections of possibilities.

So what happens if one considers more steps? As the pictures on the next page demonstrate, rules like 254 and 90 that have fairly simple behavior lead to formulas that stay fairly simple. But for rule 30 the formulas rapidly get much more complicated.

So this strongly suggests that no simple formula exists—at least of the type used here—that can describe patterns generated by any significant number of steps of evolution in a system like rule 30.

But what about formulas of other types? The formulas we have used so far can be thought of as always consisting of sums of products of variables. But what if we allow formulas with more general structure, not just two fixed levels of operations?

It turns out that any rule for blocks of black and white cells can be represented as some combination of just a single type of operation—for example a so-called NAND function of the kind often used in digital electronics. And given this, one can imagine finding for any particular rule the formula that involves the smallest number of NAND functions.

Minimal Boolean expression representations for the results of steps 1 through 5 in the evolution of three elementary cellular automata. Both rules 254 and 90 have fairly simple overall behavior, and yield comparatively small Boolean expressions. Rule 30 has much more complicated behavior and yields Boolean expressions whose size grows rapidly from one step to the next. (For steps 1 through 6, the expressions involve 3, 7, 17, 41, 102 and 261 terms respectively.) In each case the Boolean expressions given are the smallest possible in the disjunctive normal form (DNF) used.

The picture below shows some examples of the results. And once again what we see is that for rules with fairly simple behavior the formulas are usually fairly simple. But in cases like rule 30, the formulas one gets are already quite complicated even after just two steps.

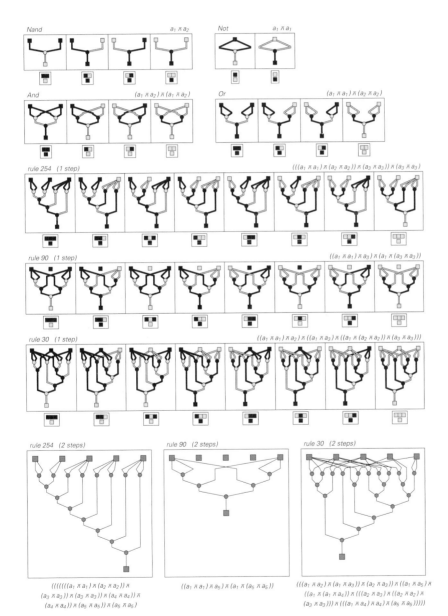

Minimal representations in terms of NAND functions of the first two steps in the evolution of the same cellular automata as on the facing page. In each case, the network and formula shown are ones that involve the absolute minimum number of operations. Finding these effectively required searching through billions of possibilities. The picture at the top left shows the action of a single NAND function. The next three pictures show how the operations used in DNF formulas can be built up from NANDs.

So even if one allows rather general structure, the evidence is that in the end there is no way to set up any simple formula that will describe the outcome of evolution for a system like rule 30.

And even if one settles for complicated formulas, just finding the least complicated one in a particular case rapidly becomes extremely difficult. Indeed, for formulas of the type shown on page 618 the difficulty can already perhaps double at each step. And for the more general formulas shown on the previous page it may increase by a factor that is itself almost exponential at each step.

So what this means is that just like for every other method of analysis that we have considered, we have little choice but to conclude that traditional mathematics and mathematical formulas cannot in the end realistically be expected to tell us very much about patterns generated by systems like rule 30.

Human Thinking

When we are presented with new data one thing we can always do is just apply our general powers of human thinking to it. And certainly this allows us with rather modest effort to do quite well in handling all sorts of data that we choose to interact with in everyday life. But what about data generated by the kinds of systems that I have discussed in this book? How does general human thinking do with this?

There are definitely some limitations, since after all, if general human thinking could easily find simple descriptions of, for example, all the various pictures in this book, then we would never have considered any of them complex.

One might in the past have assumed that if a simple description existed of some piece of data, then with appropriate thinking and intelligence it would usually not be too difficult to find it. But what the results in this book establish is that in fact this is far from true. For in the course of this book we have seen a great many systems whose underlying rules are extremely simple, yet whose overall behavior is sufficiently complex that even by thinking quite hard we cannot recognize its simple origins.

Usually a small amount of thinking allows us to identify at least some regularities. But typically these regularities are ones that can also be found quite easily by many of the standard methods of perception and analysis discussed earlier in this chapter.

So what then does human thinking in the end have to contribute? The most obvious way in which it stands out from other methods of perception and analysis is in its large-scale use of memory.

For all the other methods that we have discussed effectively operate by taking each new piece of data and separately applying some fixed procedure to it. But in human thinking we routinely make use of the huge amount of memory that we have built up from being exposed to billions of previous pieces of data.

And sometimes the results can be quite impressive. For it is quite common to find that even though no other method has much to say about a particular piece of data, we can immediately come up with a description for it by remembering some similar piece of data that we have encountered before.

And thus, for example, having myself seen thousands of pictures produced by cellular automata, I can recognize immediately from memory almost any pattern generated by any of the elementary rules— even though none of the other methods of perception and analysis can get very far whenever such patterns are at all complex.

But insofar as there is sophistication in what can be done with human memory, does this sophistication come merely from the experiences that are stored in memory, or somehow from the actual mechanism of memory itself?

The idea of storing large amounts of data and retrieving it according to various criteria is certainly quite familiar from databases in practical computing. But there is at least one important difference between the way typical databases operate, and the way human memory operates. For in a standard database one tends to be able to find only data that meets some precise specification, such as containing an exact match to a particular string of text. Yet with human memory we routinely seem to be able to retrieve data on the basis of much more general notions of similarity.

In general, if one wants to find a piece of data that has a certain property—either exact or approximate—then one way to do this is just to scan all the pieces of data that one has stored, and test each of them in turn. But even if one does all sorts of parallel processing this approach presumably in the end becomes quite impractical.

So what can one then do? In the case of exact matches there are a couple of approaches that are widely used in practice.

Probably the most familiar is what is done in typical dictionaries: all the entries are arranged in alphabetical order, so that when one looks something up one does not need to scan every single entry but instead one can quickly home in on just the entry one wants.

Practical database systems almost universally use a slightly more efficient scheme known as hashing. The basic idea is to have some definite procedure that takes any word or other piece of data and derives from it a so-called hash code which is used to determine where the data will be stored. And the point is that if one is looking for a particular piece of data, one can then apply this same procedure to that data, get the hash code for the data, and immediately determine where the data would have been stored.

But to make this work, does one need a complex hashing procedure that is carefully tuned to the particular kind of data one is dealing with? It turns out that one does not. And in fact, all that is really necessary is that the hashing procedure generate enough randomness that even though there may be regularities in the original data, the hash codes that are produced still end up being distributed roughly uniformly across all possibilities.

And as one might expect from the results in this book, it is easy to achieve this even with extremely simple programs—either based on numbers, as in most practical database systems, or based on systems like cellular automata.

So what this means is that regardless of what kind of data one is storing, it takes only a very simple program to set up a hashing scheme that lets one retrieve pieces of data very efficiently. And I suspect that at least some aspects of this kind of mechanism are involved in the operation of human memory.

But what about the fact that we routinely retrieve from our memory not just data that matches exactly, but also data that is merely similar? Ordinary hashing would not let us do this. For a hashing procedure will normally put different pieces of data at quite different locations—even if the pieces of data happen in some sense to be similar.

So is it possible to set up forms of hashing that will in fact keep similar pieces of data together? In a sense what one needs is a hashing procedure in which the hash codes that are generated depend only on features of the data that really make a difference, and not on others.

One practical example where this is done is a simple procedure often used for looking up names by sound rather than spelling. In its typical form this procedure works by dropping all vowels and grouping together letters like "d" and "t" that sound similar, with the result that at least in some approximation the only features that are kept are ones that make a difference in the way a word sounds.

So how can one achieve this in general?

In many respects one of the primary goals of all forms of perception and analysis is precisely to pick out those features of data that are considered relevant, and to discard all others.

And so, as we discussed earlier in this chapter, the human visual system, for example, appears to be based on having nerve cells that respond only to certain specific features of images. And this means that if one looks only at the output from these nerve cells, then one gets a representation of visual images in which two images that differ only in certain kinds of details will be assigned the same representation.

So if it is a representation like this that is used as the basis for storing data in memory, the result is that one will readily be able to retrieve not only data that matches exactly, but also data that is merely similar enough to have the same representation.

In actual brains it is fairly clear that input received by all the various sensory systems is first processed by assemblies of nerve cells that in effect extract certain specific features. And it seems likely that especially in lower organisms it is often representations formed quite directly from such features that are what is stored in memory.

But at least in humans there is presumably more going on. For it is quite common that we can immediately recognize that we have encountered some particular object before even if it is superficially presented in a quite different way. And what this suggests is that quite different patterns of raw data from our sensory systems can at least in some cases still lead to essentially the same representation in memory.

So how might this be achieved? One possibility is that our brains might be set up to extract certain specific high-level features—such as, say, topological structure in three-dimensional space—that happen to successfully characterize particular kinds of objects that we traditionally deal with.

But my strong suspicion is that in fact there is some much simpler and more general mechanism at work, that operates essentially just at the level of arbitrary data elements, without any direct reference to the origin or meaning of these data elements.

And one can imagine quite a few ways that such a mechanism could potentially be set up with nerve cells.

One step in a particularly simple scheme is illustrated in the picture below. The basic idea is to have a sequence of layers of nerve cells—much as one knows exist in the brain—with each cell in each successive layer responding only if the inputs it gets from some fixed random set of cells in the layer above form some definite pattern.

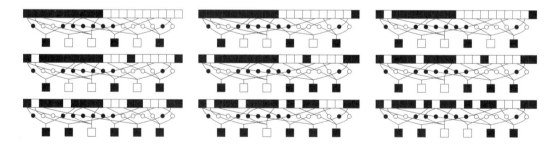

One step in a very simple model of the way hash codes for arbitrary data might be generated by layers of nerve cells in the brain. The response of a single layer of idealized nerve cells to a sequence of progressively different inputs is shown. Each nerve cell fires and yields black output only if the inputs it gets from certain fixed positions match a particular template. The sequence of outputs from all the nerve cells can be used as a hash code, whose value tends to be the same for inputs that differ only by small changes.

In a sense this is a straightforward generalization of the scheme for visual perception that we discussed earlier in this chapter. But the point is that with such a setup detailed changes in the input to the first layer of cells only rarely end up having an effect on output from the last layer of cells.

It is not difficult to find systems in which different inputs often yield the same output. In fact, this is the essence of the very general phenomenon of attractors that we discussed in Chapter 6—and it is seen in the vast majority of cellular automata, and in fact in almost any kind of system that follows definite rules.

But what is somewhat special about the setup above is that inputs which yield the same output tend to be ones that might reasonably be considered similar, while inputs that yield different outputs tend to be significantly different.

And thus, for example, a change in a single input cell typically will not have a high probability of affecting the output, while a change in a large fraction of the input cells will.

So quite independent of precisely which features of the original data correspond to which input cells, this basic mechanism provides a simple way to get a representation—and thus a hash code—that will tend to be the same for pieces of data that somehow have enough features that are similar.

So how would such a representation in the end be used? In a scheme like the one above the output cells would presumably be connected to cells that actually perform actions of some kind—perhaps causing muscles to move, or perhaps just providing inputs to further nerve cells.

But so where in all of this would the actual content of our memory reside? Almost certainly at some level it is encoded in the details of connections between nerve cells.

But how then might such details get set up?

There is evidence that permanent changes can be produced in individual nerve cells as a result of the behavior of nerve cells around them. And as data gets received by the brain such changes presumably do occur at least in some cells. But if one looks, say, at nerve cells involved in the early stages of the visual system, then once the brain has matured past some point these never seem to change their properties much. And quite probably the same is true of many nerve cells involved in the general process of doing the analog of producing hash codes.

The reason for such a lack of change could conceivably be simply that at the relevant level the overall properties of the stream of data corresponding to typical experience remain fairly constant. But it might also be that if one expects to retrieve elements of memory reliably then there is no choice but to set things up so that the hashing procedure one uses always stays essentially the same.

And if there is a fixed such scheme, then this implies that while certain similarities between pieces of data will immediately be recognized, others will not.

So how does this compare to what we know of actual human memory? There are many kinds of similarities that we recognize quite effortlessly. But there are also ones that we do not. And thus, for example, given a somewhat complicated visual image—say of a face or a cellular automaton pattern—we can often not even immediately recognize similarity to the same image turned upside-down.

So are such limitations in the end intrinsic to the underlying mechanism of human memory, or do they somehow merely reflect characteristics of the memory that we happen to build up from our typical actual experience of the world?

My guess is that it is to some extent a mixture. But insofar as more important limitations tend to be the result of quite low-level aspects of our memory system it seems likely that even if these aspects could in principle be changed it would in practice be essentially impossible to do so. For the low levels of our memory system are exposed to an immense stream of data. And so to cause any substantial change one would presumably have to insert a comparable amount of data with the special properties one wants. But for a human interacting with anything like a normal environment this would in practice be absolutely impossible.

So in the end I strongly suspect that the basic rules by which human memory operates can almost always be viewed as being essentially fixed—and, I believe, fairly simple.

But what about the whole process of human thinking? What does it ultimately involve? My strong suspicion is that the use of memory is what in fact underlies almost every major aspect of human thinking.

Capabilities like generalization, analogy and intuition immediately seem very closely related to the ability to retrieve data from memory on the basis of similarity. But what about capabilities like logical reasoning? Do these perhaps correspond to a higher-level type of human thinking?

In the past it was often thought that logic might be an appropriate idealization for all of human thinking. And largely as a result of this, practical computer systems have always treated logic as something quite fundamental. But it is my strong suspicion that in fact logic is very far from fundamental, particularly in human thinking.

For among other things, whereas in the process of thinking we routinely manage to retrieve remarkable connections almost instantaneously from memory, we tend to be able to carry out logical reasoning only by laboriously going from one step to the next. And my strong suspicion is that when we do this we are in effect again just using memory, and retrieving patterns of logical argument that we have learned from experience.

In modern times computer languages have often been thought of as providing precise ways to represent processes that might otherwise be carried out by human thinking. But it turns out that almost all of the major languages in use today are based on setting up procedures that are in essence direct analogs of step-by-step logical arguments.

As it happens, however, one notable exception is *Mathematica*. And indeed, in designing *Mathematica*, I specifically tried to imitate the way that humans seem to think about many kinds of computations. And the structure that I ended up coming up with for *Mathematica* can be viewed as being not unlike a precise idealization of the operation of human memory.

For at the core of *Mathematica* is the notion of storing collections of rules in which each rule specifies how to transform all pieces of data that are similar enough to match a single *Mathematica* pattern. And the success of *Mathematica* provides considerable evidence for the power of this kind of approach.

But ultimately—like other computer languages—*Mathematica* tends to be concerned mostly with setting up fairly short specifications for quite definite computations. Yet in everyday human thinking we seem instead to use vast amounts of stored data to perform tasks whose definitions and objectives are often quite vague.

There has in the past been a great tendency to assume that given all its apparent complexity, human thinking must somehow be an altogether fundamentally complex process, not amenable at any level to simple explanation or meaningful theory.

But from the discoveries in this book we now know that highly complex behavior can in fact arise even from very simple basic rules. And from this it immediately becomes conceivable that there could in reality be quite simple mechanisms that underlie human thinking.

Certainly there are many complicated details to the construction of the brain, and no doubt there are specific aspects of human thinking that depend on some of these details. But I strongly suspect that there is a definite core to the phenomenon of human thinking that is largely independent of such details—and that will in the end turn out to be based on rules that are rather simple.

So how will we be able to tell if this is in fact the case? Detailed direct studies of the brain and its operation may give some clues. But my guess is that the only way that really convincing evidence will be obtained is if actual technological systems are constructed that can successfully be seen to emulate human thinking.

And indeed as of now our experience with practical computing provides rather little encouragement that this will ever be possible. There are certainly some tasks—such as playing chess or doing algebra—that at one time were considered indicative of human-like thinking, but which are now routinely done by computer. Yet when it comes to seemingly much more mundane and everyday types of thinking the computers and programs that exist at present tend to be almost farcically inadequate.

So why have we not done better? No doubt part of the answer has to do with various practicalities of computers and storage systems. But a more important part, I suspect, has to do with issues of methodology.

For it has almost always been assumed that to emulate in any generality a process as sophisticated as human thinking would necessarily require an extremely complicated system. So what has mostly been done is to try to construct systems that perform only rather specific tasks.

But then in order to be sure that the appropriate tasks will actually be performed the systems tend to be set up—as in traditional engineering—so that their behavior can readily be foreseen, typically by standard mathematical or logical methods. And what this almost invariably means is that their behavior is forced to be fairly simple. Indeed, even when the systems are set up with some ability to learn they usually tend to act—much like the robots of classical fiction—with far too much simplicity and predictability to correspond to realistic typical human thinking.

So on the basis of traditional intuition, one might then assume that the way to solve this problem must be to use systems with more complicated underlying rules, perhaps more closely based on details of human psychology or neurophysiology. But from the discoveries in this book we know that this is not the case, and that in fact very simple rules are quite sufficient to produce highly complex behavior.

Nevertheless, if one maintains the goal of performing specific well-defined tasks, there may still be a problem. For insofar as the behavior that one gets is complex, it will usually be difficult to direct it to specific tasks—an issue rather familiar from dealing with actual humans. So what this means is that most likely it will at some level be much easier to reproduce general human-like thinking than to set up some special version of human-like thinking only for specific tasks.

And it is in the end my strong suspicion that most of the core processes needed for general human-like thinking will be able to be implemented with rather simple rules.

But a crucial point is that on their own such processes will most likely not be sufficient to create a system that one would readily recognize as exhibiting human-like thinking. For in order to be able to relate in a meaningful way to actual humans, the system would almost certainly have to have built up a human-like base of experience.

No doubt as a practical matter this could to some extent be done just by large-scale recording of experiences of actual humans. But it seems not unlikely that to get a sufficiently accurate experience base, the system would itself have to interact with the world in very much the same way as an actual human—and so would have to have elements that emulate many elaborate details of human biological and other structure.

Once one has an explicit system that successfully emulates human thinking, however, one can imagine progressively removing some of this complexity, and seeing just which features of human thinking end up being preserved.

So what about human language, for example? Is this purely learned from the details of human experience? Or are there features of it that reflect more fundamental aspects of human thinking?

When one learns a language—at least as a young child—one implicitly tends to deduce simple grammatical rules that are in effect specific generalizations of examples one has encountered. And I suspect that in doing this the types of generalizations that one makes are essentially those that correspond to the types of similarities that one readily recognizes in retrieving data from memory.

Actual human languages normally have many exceptions to any simple grammatical rules. And it seems that with sufficient effort we can in fact learn languages with almost any structure. But the fact that most modern computer languages are specifically set up to follow simple grammatical rules seems to make their structures particularly easy for us to learn—perhaps because they fit in well with low-level processes of human thinking.

But to what extent is the notion of a language even ultimately necessary in a system that does human-like thinking? Certainly in actual humans, languages seem to be crucial for communication. But one might imagine that if the underlying details of different individuals from some class of systems were sufficiently identical then communication could instead be achieved just by directly transferring low-level patterns of activity. My guess, however, is that as soon as the experiences of different individuals become different, this will not work, and that therefore some form of general intermediate representation or language will be required.

But does one really need a language that has the kind of sequential grammatical structure of ordinary human language? Graphical user interfaces for computer systems certainly often use somewhat different schemes. And in simple situations these can work well. But my uniform experience has been that if one wants to specify processes of any significant complexity in a fashion that can reasonably be understood then the only realistic way to do this is to use a language—like *Mathematica*—that has essentially an ordinary sequential grammatical structure.

Quite why this is I am not certain. Perhaps it is merely a consequence of our familiarity with traditional human languages. Or perhaps it is a consequence of our apparent ability to pay attention only to one thing at a time. But I would not be surprised if in the end it is a reflection of fairly fundamental features of human thinking.

And indeed our difficulty in thinking about many of the patterns produced by systems in this book may be not unrelated. For while ordinary human language has little trouble describing repetitive and even nested patterns, it seems to be able to do very little with more complex patterns—which is in a sense why this book, for example, depends so heavily on visual presentation.

At the outset, one might have imagined that human thinking must involve fundamentally special processes, utterly different from all other processes that we have discussed. But just as it has become clear over the past few centuries that the basic physical constituents of human beings are not particularly special, so also—especially after the discoveries in this book—I am quite certain that in the end there will turn out to be nothing particularly special about the basic processes that are involved in human thinking.

And indeed, my strong suspicion is that despite the apparent sophistication of human thinking most of the important processes that underlie it are actually very simple—much like the processes that seem to be involved in all the other kinds of perception and analysis that we have discussed in this chapter.

Higher Forms of Perception and Analysis

In the course of this chapter we have discussed in turn each of the major methods of perception and analysis that we in practice use. And if our goal is to understand the actual experience that we get of the world then there is no reason to go further. But as a matter of principle one can ask whether the methods of perception and analysis that we have discussed in a sense cover what is ultimately possible—or whether instead there are higher and fundamentally more powerful forms of perception and analysis that for some reason we do not at present use.

As we discussed early in this chapter, any method of perception or analysis can at some level be viewed as a way of trying to find simple descriptions for pieces of data. And what we might have assumed in the past is that if a piece of data could be generated from a sufficiently simple description then the data itself would necessarily seem to us quite simple—and would therefore have many regularities that could be recognized by our standard methods of perception and analysis.

But one of the central discoveries of this book is that this is far from true—and that actually it is rather common for rules that have extremely simple descriptions to give rise to data that is highly complex, and that has no regularities that can be recognized by any of our standard methods.

But as we discussed earlier in this chapter the fact that a simple rule can ultimately be responsible for such data means that at some level the data must contain regularities. So the point is that these regularities are just not ones that can be detected by our standard methods of perception and analysis.

Yet the fact that there are in the end regularities means that at least in principle there could exist higher forms of perception and analysis that would succeed in recognizing them.

So might one day some new method of perception and analysis be invented that would in a sense manage to recognize all possible regularities, and thus be able to tell immediately if any particular piece of data could be generated from any kind of simple description?

My strong belief—as I will argue in Chapter 12—is that at least in complete generality this will never be possible. But that does not mean that there cannot exist higher forms of perception and analysis that succeed in recognizing at least some regularities that our existing methods do not.

The results of this chapter, however, might seem to provide some circumstantial evidence that in practice even this might not be possible. For in the course of the chapter we have discussed a whole range of different kinds of perception and analysis, yet in essentially all cases we have found that the overall capabilities they exhibit are rather similar. Most of them, for example, recognize repetition, and some also recognize nesting. But almost none recognize anything more complex.

So what this perhaps suggests is that in the end there might be only certain specific capabilities that can be realized in practical methods of perception and analysis. And certainly it seems not inconceivable that there could be a fundamental result that the only kinds of regularities that both occur frequently in actual systems and can be recognized quickly enough to provide a basis for practical methods of perception and analysis are ones like repetition and nesting.

But there is another possible explanation for what we have seen in this chapter: perhaps it is just that we, as humans, are always very narrow in the methods of perception and analysis that we use. For certainly it is remarkable that none of the methods that we normally use ever in the end seem to manage to get much further than we can already get with our own built-in powers of perception. And what this perhaps suggests is that we choose the methods we use to be essentially those that pick out only regularities with which we are somehow already very familiar from our own built-in powers of perception.

For there is no difficulty in principle in constructing procedures that have capabilities very different from those of our standard methods of perception and analysis. Indeed, as one example, one could imagine just enumerating all possible simple descriptions of some particular type, and then testing in each case to see whether what one gets matches a piece of data that one has.

And in some specific cases, this might well succeed in finding extremely simple descriptions for the data. But to use such a method in any generality almost inevitably requires computational resources far greater than one would normally consider reasonable in a practical method of perception or analysis.

And in fact there is really no reason to consider such a sophisticated procedure. For in a sense any program—including one that is very simple and runs very quickly—can be thought of as implementing a method of perception or analysis. For if one gives a piece of data as the input to the program, then the output one gets— whatever it may be—can be viewed as corresponding to some kind of description of the data.

But the problem is that under most circumstances this description will not be particularly useful. And indeed what typically seems to be necessary to make it useful is that somehow one is already familiar with similar descriptions, and knows their significance.

A description based on output from a cellular automaton rule that one has never seen before is thus for example not likely to be useful. But a description that picks out a feature like repetition that is already very familiar to us will typically be much more useful.

And potentially therefore our lack of higher forms of perception and analysis might in the end have nothing to do with any difficulty in implementing such forms, but instead may just be a reflection of the fact that we only have enough context to make descriptions of data useful when these descriptions are fairly close to the ones we get from our own built-in human methods of perception.

But why is it then that these methods themselves are not more powerful? After all, one might think that biological evolution would inevitably have made us as good as possible at handling data associated with any of the systems that we commonly encounter in nature.

Yet as we have seen in this book almost whenever there is significant complexity our powers of human perception end up being far from adequate to find any kind of minimal summaries of data.

And with the traditional view that biological evolution is somehow a process of infinite power this seems to leave one little choice but to conclude that there must be fundamental limitations on possible methods of perception that can be useful.

One might imagine perhaps that while there could in principle be methods of perception that would recognize features beyond, say, repetition and nesting, any single such feature might never occur in a sufficiently wide range of systems to make its recognition generally useful to a biological organism.

But as of now I do not know of any fundamental reason why this might be so, and following my arguments in Chapter 8 I would not be at all surprised if the process of biological evolution had simply missed even methods of perception that are, in some sense, fairly obvious.

So what about an extraterrestrial intelligence? Free from any effects of terrestrial biological evolution might it have developed all sorts of higher forms of perception and analysis?

Of course we have no direct information on this. But the very fact that we have so far failed to discover any evidence for extraterrestrial intelligence may itself conceivably already be a sign that higher forms of perception and analysis may be in use.

For as I will discuss in Chapter 12 it seems far from inconceivable that some of the extraterrestrial radio and other signals that we pick up and assume to be random noise could in fact be meaningful messages—but just encoded in a way that can be recognized only by higher forms of perception and analysis than those we have so far applied to them.

Yet whether or not this is so, the capabilities of extraterrestrial intelligence are not in the end directly relevant to an understanding of our own experience of the world. In the future we may well manage to use higher forms of perception and analysis, and as a result our experience of the world will change—no doubt along with certain aspects of our science and mathematics. But for now it is the kinds of methods of perception and analysis that we have discussed in most of this chapter that must form the basis for the conclusions we make about the world.

11

The Notion of Computation

Computation as a Framework

In earlier parts of this book we saw many examples of the kinds of behavior that can be produced by cellular automata and other systems with simple underlying rules. And in this chapter and the next my goal is to develop a general framework for thinking about such behavior.

Experience from traditional science might suggest that standard mathematical analysis should provide the appropriate basis for any such framework. But as we saw in the previous chapter, such analysis tends to be useful only when the overall behavior one is studying is fairly simple.

So what can one do when the behavior is more complex?

If traditional science was our only guide, then at this point we would probably be quite stuck. But my purpose in this book is precisely to develop a new kind of science that allows progress to be made in such cases. And in many respects the single most important idea that underlies this new science is the notion of computation.

Throughout this book I have referred to systems such as cellular automata as simple computer programs. So now the point is actually to think of these systems in terms of the computations they can perform.

In a typical case, the initial conditions for a system like a cellular automaton can be viewed as corresponding to the input to a computation, while the state of the system after some number of steps corresponds to the output. And the key idea is then to think in purely abstract terms about the computation that is performed, without necessarily looking at all the details of how it actually works.

Why is such an abstraction useful? The main reason is that it potentially allows one to discuss in a unified way systems that have completely different underlying rules. For even though the internal workings of two systems may have very little in common, the computations the systems perform may nevertheless be very similar.

And by thinking in terms of such computations, it then becomes possible to imagine formulating principles that apply to a very wide variety of different systems—quite independent of the detailed structure of their underlying rules.

Computations in Cellular Automata

I have said that the evolution of a system like a cellular automaton can be viewed as a computation. But what kind of computation is it, and how does it compare to computations that we typically do in practice?

The pictures below show an example of a cellular automaton whose evolution can be viewed as performing a particular simple computation.

If one starts this cellular automaton with an even number of black cells, then after a few steps of evolution, no black cells are left. But if instead one starts it with an odd number of black cells, then a single black cell survives forever. So in effect this cellular automaton can be viewed as computing whether a given number is even or odd.

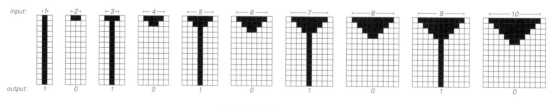

A simple cellular automaton whose evolution effectively computes the remainder after division of a number by 2. Starting from a row of n black cells, 0 black cells survive if n is even, and 1 black cell survives if n is odd. The cellular automaton follows elementary rule 132, as shown on the left.

One specifies the input to the computation by setting up an appropriate number of initial black cells. And then one determines the result of the computation by looking at how many black cells survive in the end.

Testing whether a number is even or odd is by most measures a rather simple computation. But one can also get cellular automata to do more complicated computations. And as an example the pictures below show a cellular automaton that computes the square of any number. If one starts say with 5 black squares, then after a certain number of steps the cellular automaton will produce a block of exactly 5×5 = 25 black squares.

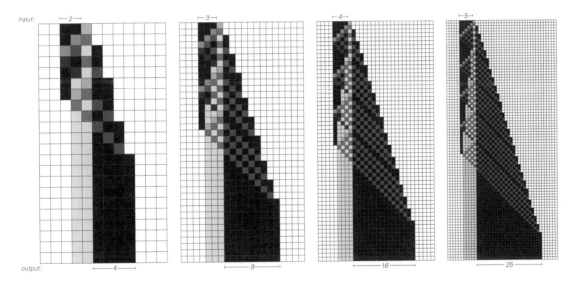

A cellular automaton that computes the square of any number. The cellular automaton effectively works by adding the original number *n* together *n* times. The underlying rule used here involves eight possible colors for each cell.

At first it might seem surprising that a system with the simple underlying structure of a cellular automaton could ever be made to perform such a computation. But as we shall see later in this chapter, cellular automata can in fact perform what are in effect arbitrarily sophisticated computations. And as one example of a somewhat more sophisticated computation, the picture on the next page shows a cellular automaton that computes the successive prime numbers: 2, 3, 5, 7, 11, 13, 17, etc.

The rule for this cellular automaton is somewhat complicated—it involves a total of sixteen colors possible for each cell—but the example demonstrates the point that in principle a cellular automaton can compute the primes.

A cellular automaton constructed to compute the prime numbers. The system generates a dark gray stripe on the left at all positions that correspond to any product of numbers other than 1. White gaps then remain at positions that correspond to the prime numbers 2, 3, 5, 7, 11, 13, 17, etc. The cellular automaton effectively does its computation using the standard sieve of Eratosthenes method. The structures on the right bounce backwards and forwards with repetition periods corresponding to successive odd numbers. Once in each period they produce a gray stripe which propagates to the left, so that in the end there is a gray stripe corresponding to every multiple of every number. The rule for the cellular automaton shown here involves 16 possible colors for each cell.

So what about the cellular automata that we discussed earlier in this book? What kinds of computations can they perform?

At some level, any cellular automaton—or for that matter, any system whatsoever—can be viewed as performing a computation that determines what its future behavior will be.

But for the cellular automata that I have discussed in this section, it so happens that the computations they perform can also conveniently be described in terms of traditional mathematical notions.

And this turns out to be possible for some of the cellular automata that I discussed earlier in this book. Thus, for example, as shown below, rule 94 can effectively be described as enumerating even numbers. Similarly, rule 62 can be thought of as enumerating numbers that are multiples of 3, while rule 190 enumerates numbers that are multiples of 4. And if one looks down the center column of the pattern it produces, rule 129 can be thought of as enumerating numbers that are powers of 2.

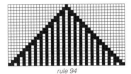
rule 94
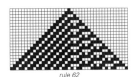
rule 62
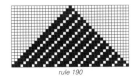
rule 190
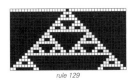
rule 129

Examples of simple cellular automata whose evolution corresponds to computations that can easily be described in traditional mathematical terms. In analogy to the previous page, the positions of white cells at the bottom of the rule 94 picture correspond to even numbers, on the left in rule 62 to multiples of 3, in rule 190 to multiples of 4, and in the center column of rule 129 to powers of 2.

But what kinds of computations are cellular automata like the ones on the right performing? If we compare the patterns they produce to the patterns we have seen so far in this section, then immediately we suspect that we cannot describe these computations by anything as simple as saying, for example, that they generate primes.

So how then can we ever expect to describe these computations? Traditional mathematics is not much help, but what we will see is that there are a collection of ideas familiar from practical computing that provide at least the beginnings of the framework that is needed.

rule 30

rule 45

Examples of cellular automata that have simple underlying rules but whose overall behavior does not seem to correspond to computations with any kind of simple description in standard mathematical or other terms. ▶

rule 73

The Phenomenon of Universality

In the previous section we saw that it is possible to get cellular automata to perform some fairly sophisticated computations. But for each specific computation we wanted to do, we always set up a cellular automaton with a different set of underlying rules. And indeed our everyday experience with mechanical and other devices might lead us to assume that in general in order to perform different kinds of tasks we must always use systems that have different underlying constructions.

But the remarkable discovery that launched the computer revolution is that this is not in fact the case. And instead, it is possible to build universal systems whose underlying construction remains fixed, but which can be made to perform different tasks just by being programmed in different ways.

And indeed, this is exactly how practical computers work: the hardware of the computer remains fixed, but the computer can be programmed for different tasks by loading different pieces of software.

The idea of universality is also the basis for computer languages. For in each language, there are a certain set of primitive operations, which are then strung together in different ways to create programs for different tasks.

The details of a particular computer system or computer language will certainly affect how easy it is to perform a particular task. But the crucial fact that is by now a matter of common knowledge is that with appropriate programming any computer system or computer language can ultimately be made to perform exactly the same set of tasks.

One way to see that this must be true is to note that any particular computer system or computer language can always be set up by appropriate programming to emulate any other one.

Typically the way this is done is by having each individual action in the system that is to be emulated be reproduced by some sequence of actions in the other system. And indeed this is ultimately how, for example, *Mathematica* works. For when one enters a command such as Log[15], what actually happens is that the program which implements the *Mathematica* language interprets this command by executing the appropriate sequence of machine instructions on whatever computer system one is using.

And having now identified the phenomenon of universality in the context of practical computing, one can immediately see various analogs of it in other areas of common experience. Human languages provide an example. For one knows that given a single fixed underlying language, it is possible to describe an almost arbitrarily wide range of things. And given any two languages, it is for the most part always possible to translate between them.

So what about natural science? Is the phenomenon of universality also relevant there? Despite its great importance in computing and elsewhere, it turns out that universality has in the past never been considered seriously in relation to natural science.

But what I will show in this chapter and the next is that in fact universality is for example quite crucial in finding general ways to characterize and understand the complexity we see in natural systems.

The basic point is that if a system is universal, then it must effectively be capable of emulating any other system, and as a result it must be able to produce behavior that is as complex as the behavior of any other system. So knowing that a particular system is universal thus immediately implies that the system can produce behavior that is in a sense arbitrarily complex.

But now the question is what kinds of systems are in fact universal.

Most present-day mechanical devices, for example, are built only for rather specific tasks, and are not universal. And among electronic devices there are examples such as simple calculators and electronic address books that are not universal. But by now the vast majority of practical electronic devices, despite all their apparent differences, are based on computers that are universal.

At some level, however, these computers tend to be extremely similar. Indeed, essentially all of them are based on the same kinds of logic circuits, the same basic layout of data paths, and so on. And knowing this, one might conclude that any system which was universal must include direct analogs of these specific elements. But from experience with computer languages, there is already an indication that the range of systems that are universal might be somewhat broader.

Indeed, *Mathematica* turns out to be a particularly good example, in which one can pick very different sets of operations to use, and yet still be able to implement exactly the same kinds of programs.

So what about cellular automata and other systems with simple rules? Is it possible for these kinds of systems to be universal?

At first, it seems quite implausible that they could be. For the intuition that one gets from practical computers and computer languages seems to suggest that to achieve universality there must be some fundamentally fairly sophisticated elements present.

But just as we found that the intuition which suggests that simple rules cannot lead to complex behavior is wrong, so also the intuition that simple rules cannot be universal also turns out to be wrong. And indeed, later in this chapter, I will show an example of a cellular automaton with an extremely simple underlying rule that can nevertheless in the end be seen to be universal.

In the past it has tended to be assumed that universality is somehow a rare and special quality, usually possessed only by systems that are specifically constructed to have it. But one of the results of this chapter is that in fact universality is a much more widespread phenomenon. And in the next chapter I will argue that for example it also occurs in a wide range of important systems that we see in nature.

A Universal Cellular Automaton

As our first specific example of a system that exhibits universality, I discuss in this section a particular universal cellular automaton that has been set up to make its operation as easy to follow as possible.

The rules for this cellular automaton itself are always the same. But the fact that it is universal means that if it is given appropriate initial conditions it can effectively be programmed to emulate for example any possible cellular automaton—with any set of rules.

The next three pages show three examples of this.

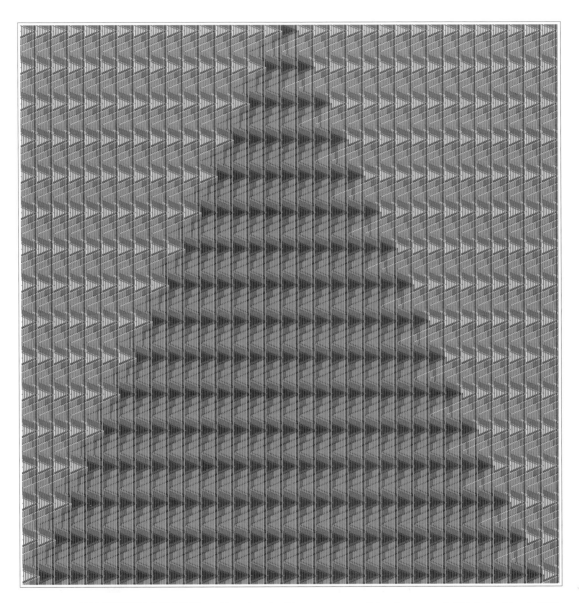

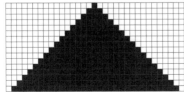

The universal cellular automaton emulating elementary rule 254. Each cell in rule 254 is represented by a block of 20 cells in the universal cellular automaton. Each of these blocks encodes both the color of the cell it represents, and the rule for updating this color.

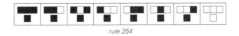

rule 254

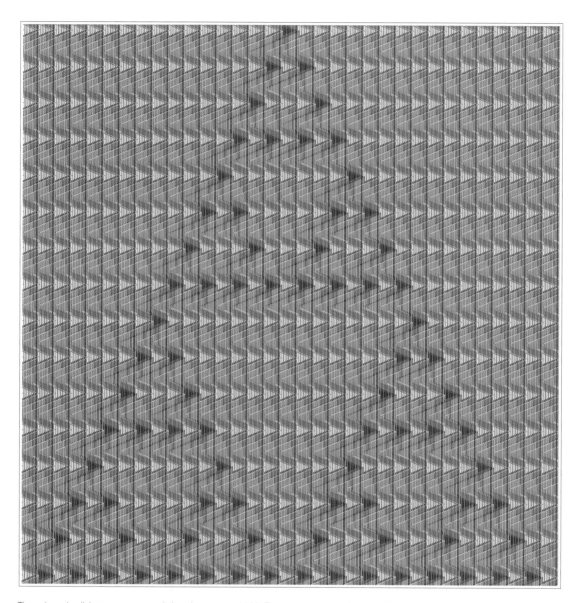

The universal cellular automaton emulating elementary rule 90. The underlying rules for the universal cellular automaton are exactly the same as on the previous page. But each block in the initial conditions now contains a representation of rule 90 rather than rule 254.

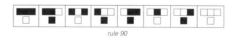

rule 90

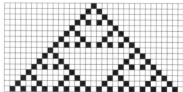

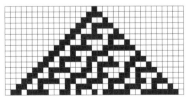

The universal cellular automaton emulating rule 30. A total of 848 steps in the evolution of the universal cellular automaton are shown, corresponding to 16 steps in the evolution of rule 30.

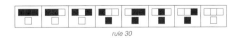

rule 30

On each page the underlying rules for the universal cellular automaton are exactly the same. But on the first page, the initial conditions are set up so as to make the universal cellular automaton emulate rule 254, while on the second page they are set up to make it emulate rule 90, and on the third page rule 30.

The pages that follow show how this works. The basic idea is that a block of 20 cells in the universal cellular automaton is used to represent each single cell in the cellular automaton that is being emulated. And within this block of 20 cells is encoded both a specification of the current color of the cell that is being represented, as well as the rule by which that color is to be updated.

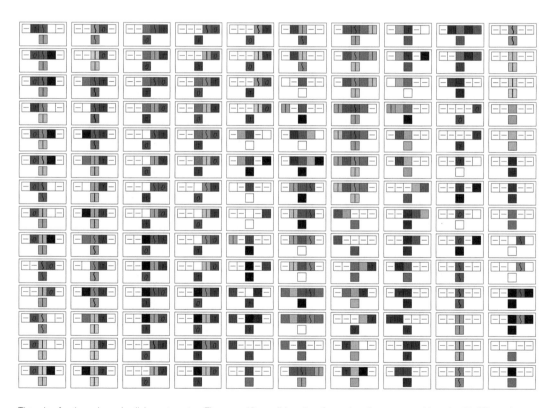

The rules for the universal cellular automaton. There are 19 possible colors for each cell, represented here by 19 different icons. Since the new color of each cell depends on the previous colors of a total of five cells, there are in principle 2,476,099 cases to cover. But by using ⊟ to stand for a cell with any possible color, many cases are combined. Note that the cases shown are in a definite order reading down successive columns, with special cases given before more general ones. With the initial conditions used, there are some combinations of cells that can never occur, and these are not covered in the rules shown.

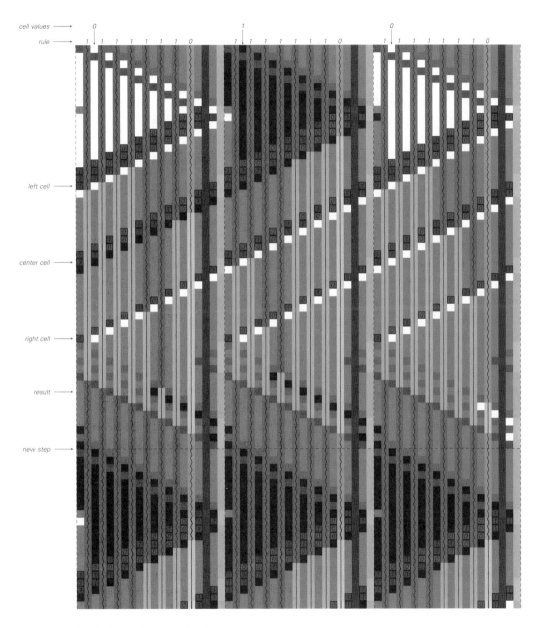

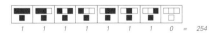

Details of how the universal cellular automaton emulates rule 254. Each of the blocks in the universal cellular automaton represents a single cell in rule 254, and encodes both the current color of the cell and the form of the rule used to update it.

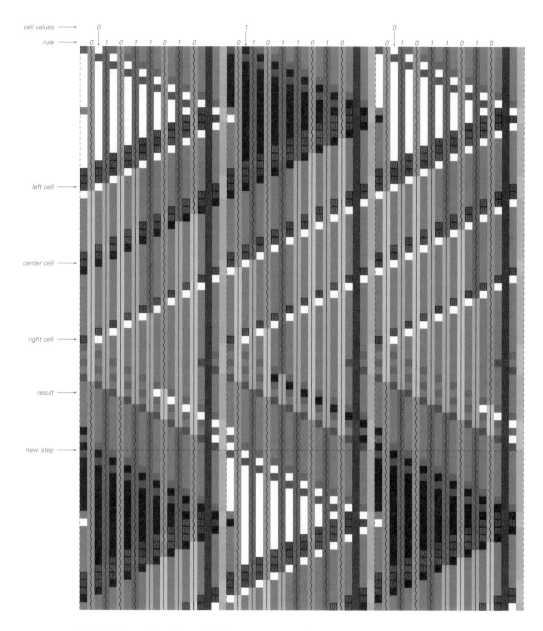

Details of how the universal cellular automaton emulates rule 90. The only difference in initial conditions from the picture on the previous page is that each block now encodes rule 90 instead of rule 254.

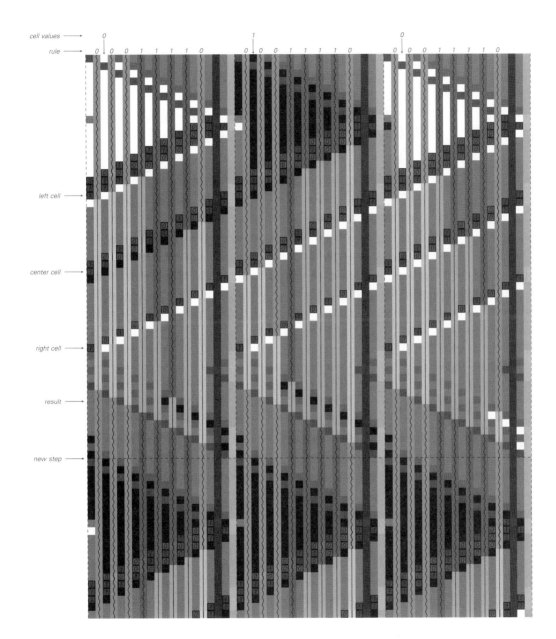

cell values

rule

left cell

center cell

right cell

result

new step

Details of how the universal cellular automaton emulates rule 30. Once again, the only difference in initial conditions from the facing page is that each block now encodes rule 30 instead of rule 90.

0   0   0   1   1   1   1   0   =   30

In the examples shown, the cellular automata being emulated have 8 cases in their rules, with each case giving the outcome for one of the 8 possible combinations of colors of a cell and its immediate neighbors. In every block of 20 cells in the universal cellular automaton, these rules are encoded in a very straightforward way, by listing in order the outcomes for each of the 8 possible cases.

To update the color of the cell represented by a particular block, what the universal cellular automaton must then do is to determine which of the 8 cases applies to that cell. And it does this by successively eliminating cases that do not apply, until eventually only one case remains. This process of elimination can be seen quite directly in the pictures on the previous pages. Below each large black or white triangle, there are initially 8 vertical dark lines. Each of these lines corresponds to one of the 8 cases in the rule, and the system is set up so that a particular line ends as soon as the case to which it corresponds has been eliminated.

It so happens that in the universal cellular automaton discussed here the elimination process for a given cell always occurs in the block immediately to the left of the one that represents that cell. But the process itself is not too difficult to understand, and indeed it works in much the way one might expect of a practical electronic logic circuit.

There are three basic stages, visible in the pictures as three stripes moving to the left across each block. The first stripe carries the color of the left-hand neighbor, and causes all cases in the rule where that neighbor does not have the appropriate color to be eliminated. The next two stripes then carry the color of the cell itself and of its right-hand neighbor. And after all three stripes have passed, only one of the 8 cases ever survives, and this case is then the one that gives the new color for the cell.

The pictures on the last few pages have shown how the universal cellular automaton can in effect be programmed to emulate any cellular automaton whose rules involve nearest neighbors and two possible colors for each cell. But the universal cellular automaton is in no way restricted to emulating only rules that involve nearest neighbors. And thus on the facing page, for example, it is shown emulating a rule that involves next-nearest as well as nearest neighbors.

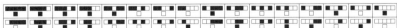

The universal cellular automaton emulating one step in the evolution of the rule shown above, which involves next-nearest as well as nearest-neighbor cells. The rule now covers a total of 32 cases, corresponding to the possible arrangements of colors of a cell and its nearest and next-nearest neighbors. The picture shows the evolution of five cells according to the rule shown, with each cell now being represented by a block of 70 cells in the universal cellular automaton.

The blocks needed to represent each cell are now larger, since they must include all 32 cases in the rule. There are also five elimination stages rather than three. But despite these differences, the underlying rule for the universal cellular automaton remains exactly the same.

What about rules that have more than two possible colors for each cell? It turns out that there is a general way of emulating such rules by using rules that have just two colors but a larger number of neighbors. The picture on the facing page shows an example. The idea is that each cell in the three-color cellular automaton is represented by a block of three cells in the two-color cellular automaton. And by looking at neighbors out to distance five on each side, the two-color cellular automaton can update these blocks at each step in direct correspondence with the rules of the three-color cellular automaton.

The same basic scheme can be used for rules with any number of colors. And the conclusion is therefore that the universal cellular automaton can ultimately emulate a cellular automaton with absolutely any set of rules, regardless of how many neighbors and how many colors they may involve.

This is an important and at first surprising result. For among other things, it implies that the universal cellular automaton can emulate cellular automata whose rules are more complicated than its own. If one did not know about the basic phenomenon of universality, then one would most likely assume that by using more complicated rules one would always be able to produce new and different kinds of behavior.

But from studying the universal cellular automaton in this section, we now know that this is not in fact the case. For given the universal cellular automaton, it is always in effect possible to program this cellular automaton to emulate any other cellular automaton, and therefore to produce whatever behavior the other cellular automaton could produce.

In a sense, therefore, what we can now see is that nothing fundamental can ever be gained by using rules that are more complicated than those for the universal cellular automaton. For given the universal cellular automaton, more complicated rules can always be emulated just by setting up appropriate initial conditions.

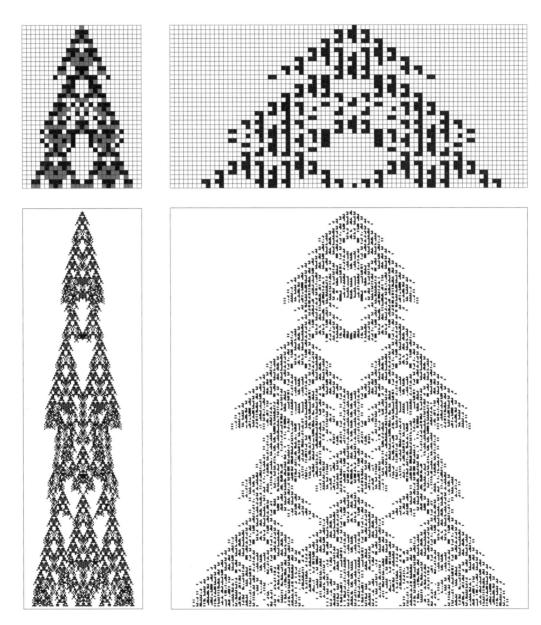

An example of how a cellular automaton with three possible colors and nearest-neighbor rules can be emulated by a cellular automaton with only two possible colors but a larger number of neighbors (in this case five on each side). The basic idea is to represent each cell in the three-color rule by a block of three cells in the two-color rule, according to the correspondence given on the left. The three-color rule illustrated here is totalistic code 1599 from page 70.

Looking at the specific universal cellular automaton that we have discussed in this section, however, we would probably be led to assume that while the phenomenon of universality might be important in principle, it would rarely be relevant in practice. For the rules of the universal cellular automaton in this section are quite complicated—involving 19 possible colors for each cell, and next-nearest as well as nearest neighbors. And if such complication was indeed necessary in order to achieve universality, then one would not expect that universality would be common, for example, in the systems we see in nature.

But what we will discover later in this chapter is that such complication in underlying rules is in fact not needed. Indeed, in the end we will see that universality can actually occur in cellular automata with just two colors and nearest neighbors. The operation of such cellular automata is considerably more difficult to follow than the operation of the universal cellular automaton discussed in this section. But the existence of universal cellular automata with such simple underlying rules makes it clear that the basic results we have obtained in this section are potentially of very broad significance.

Emulating Other Systems with Cellular Automata

The previous section showed that a particular universal cellular automaton could emulate any possible cellular automaton. But what about other types of systems? Can cellular automata also emulate these?

With their simple and rather specific underlying structure one might think that cellular automata would never be capable of emulating a very wide range of other systems. But what I will show in this section is that in fact this is not the case, and that in the end cellular automata can actually be made to emulate almost every single type of system that we have discussed in this book.

As a first example of this, the picture on the facing page shows how a cellular automaton can be made to emulate a mobile automaton.

The main difference between a mobile automaton and a cellular automaton is that in a mobile automaton there is a special active cell that moves around from one step to the next, while in a cellular

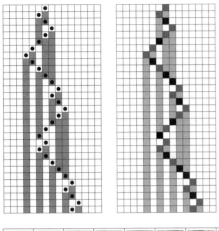

An example of a mobile automaton (see page 71) being emulated by a cellular automaton. In the mobile automaton shown on the left each cell has two possible colors. In the cellular automaton shown on the right, the cells have four possible colors, with two darker colors corresponding to the active cell in the mobile automaton. The rules for the mobile automaton and the cellular automaton are shown below. In the rules for the cellular automaton, ⊟ indicates a cell of any color.

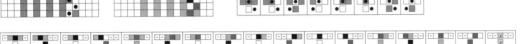

automaton all cells are always effectively treated as being exactly the same. And to emulate a mobile automaton with a cellular automaton it turns out that all one need do is to divide the possible colors of cells in the cellular automaton into two sets: lighter ones that correspond to ordinary cells in the mobile automaton, and darker ones that correspond to active cells. And then by setting up appropriate rules and choosing initial conditions that contain only one darker cell, one can produce in the cellular automaton an exact emulation of every step in the evolution of a mobile automaton—as in the picture above.

The same basic approach can be used to construct a cellular automaton that emulates a Turing machine, as illustrated on the next page. Once again, lighter colors in the cellular automaton represent ordinary cells in the Turing machine, while darker colors represent the cell under the head, with a specific darker color corresponding to each possible state of the head.

One might think that the reason that mobile automata and Turing machines can be emulated by cellular automata is that they both consist of fixed arrays of cells, just like cellular automata. So then one may wonder what happens with substitution systems, for example, where there is no fixed array of elements.

An example of a Turing machine being emulated by a cellular automaton. In the Turing machine on the left each cell has two possible colors, and the head has three possible states. In the cellular automaton, the cells have eight possible colors, with the lightest two colors being used for cells not at the position of the head. The rules for the Turing machine and the cellular automaton are shown below. In the rules for the cellular automaton, ⊟ indicates a cell of any color.

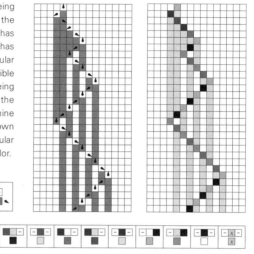

The pictures on the facing page demonstrate that in fact these can also be emulated by cellular automata. But while one can emulate each step in the evolution of a mobile automaton or a Turing machine with a single step of cellular automaton evolution, this is no longer in general true for substitution systems.

That this must ultimately be the case one can see from the fact that the total number of elements in a substitution system can be multiplied by a factor from one step to the next, while in a cellular automaton the size of a pattern can only ever increase by a fixed amount at each step. And what this means is that it can take progressively larger numbers of cellular automaton steps to reproduce each successive step in the evolution of the substitution system—as illustrated in the pictures on the facing page.

The same kind of problem occurs in sequential substitution systems—as well as in tag systems. But once again, as the pictures on page 660 demonstrate, it is still perfectly possible to emulate systems like these using cellular automata.

But just how broad is the set of systems that cellular automata can ultimately emulate? All the examples of systems that I have shown so far can at some level be thought of as involving sequences of elements that are fairly directly analogous to the cells in a cellular automaton.

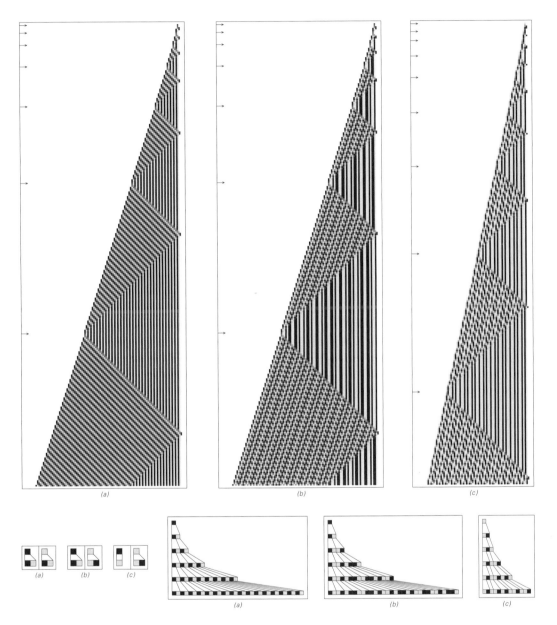

Examples of cellular automata that emulate substitution systems. The successive steps in the evolution of each substitution system are obtained at the points indicated by arrows. Note that the sequences of elements generated by the cellular automata are aligned at the right, while in the pictures of the substitution systems shown they are aligned at the left. The rules for the three cellular automata involve only nearest neighbors, and allow 12 possible colors for each cell.

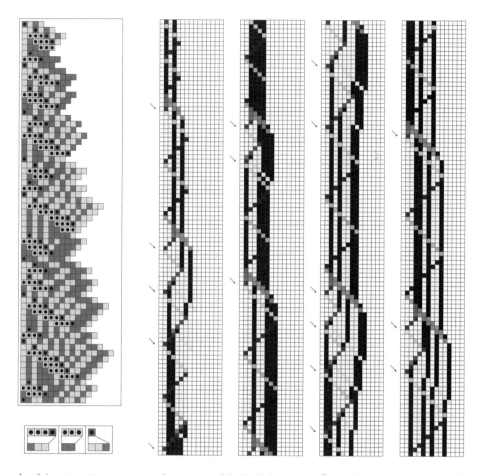

A cellular automaton set up to emulate a sequential substitution system. The cellular automaton involves 28 colors and nearest-neighbor rules. The strings produced by the sequential substitution system appear on successive diagonal stripes indicated by arrows in the evolution of the cellular automaton on the right.

But one example where there is no such direct analogy is a register machine. And at the outset one might not imagine that such a system could ever readily be emulated by a cellular automaton.

But in fact it turns out to be fairly straightforward to do so, as illustrated at the top of the facing page. The basic idea is to have the cellular automaton produce a pattern that expands and contracts on each side in a way that corresponds to the incrementing and decrementing of the sizes of numbers in the first and second registers of

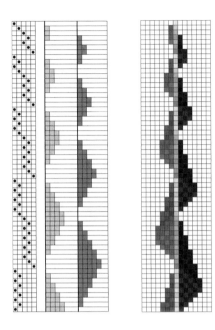

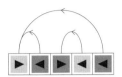

An example of a register machine being emulated by a cellular automaton. The cellular automaton has 12 possible colors for each cell. Of these, 5 are used by the center cell to represent the point that has been reached in the register machine program. The other 7 are used to implement signals that propagate out to the left and right to do the analog of incrementing and decrementing each register.

the register machine. In the center of the cellular automaton is then a cell whose possible colors correspond to possible points in the program for the register machine. And as the cell makes transitions from one color to another, it effectively emits signals that move to the left or right modifying the pattern in the cellular automaton in a way that follows each instruction in the register machine program.

So what about systems based on numbers? Can these also be emulated by cellular automata? As one example the picture on the right shows how a cellular automaton can be set up to perform repeated multiplication by 3 of numbers in base 2. And the only real difficulty in this case is that carries generated in the process of multiplication may need to be propagated from one end of the number to the other.

So what about practical computers? Can these also be emulated by cellular automata? From the examples just discussed of register machines and systems based on numbers, we already know that cellular automata can emulate some of the low-level operations typically found in computers. And the pictures on the next two pages show how cellular automata can also be made to emulate two other important aspects of practical computers.

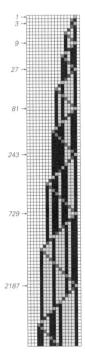

Repeated multiplication by 3 in base 2 being performed by a cellular automaton with 11 colors.

The pictures below show how a cellular automaton can evaluate any logic expression that is given in a certain form. And the picture on the facing page then shows how a cellular automaton can retrieve data from a numbered location in what is effectively a random-access memory.

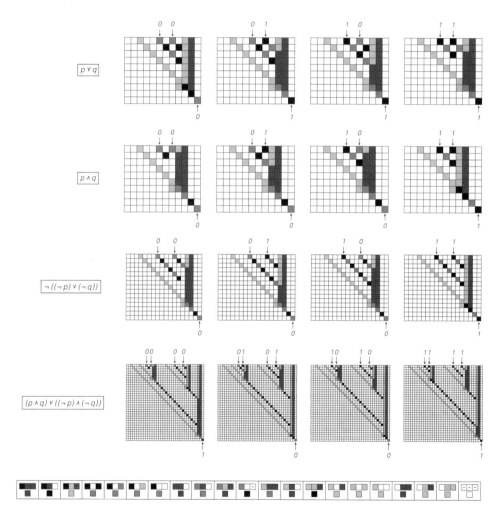

A cellular automaton which emulates basic logic circuits. The underlying rules for the cellular automaton are exactly the same in each case, and involve nearest neighbors and five possible colors for each cell. But the initial condition can represent a logic expression that involves any number of variables together with the operations of AND, OR and NOT. In the examples above, two variables, p and q, are used, and in each case the behavior obtained with all four possible combinations of values for p and q are shown.

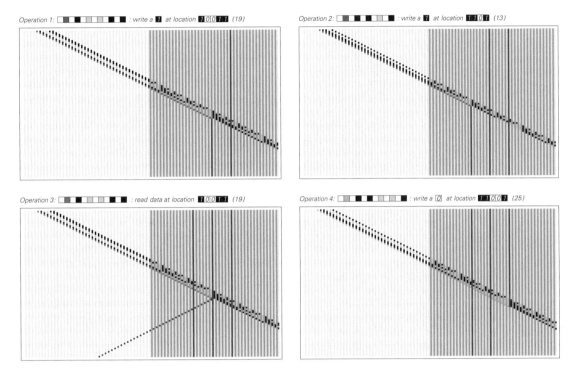

A cellular automaton set up to emulate random-access memory in a computer. The memory is on the right, and can be of any size. Instructions come in from the left, with memory locations specified by addresses consisting of binary digits.

The details for any particular case are quite complicated, but in the end it turns out that it is in principle possible to construct a cellular automaton that emulates a practical computer in its entirety.

And as a result, one can conclude that any of the very wide range of computations that can be performed by practical computers can also be done by cellular automata.

From the previous section we know that any cellular automaton can be emulated by a universal cellular automaton. But now we see that a universal cellular automaton is actually much more universal than we saw in the previous section. For not only can it emulate any cellular automaton: it can also emulate any of a wide range of other systems, including practical computers.

Emulating Cellular Automata with Other Systems

In the previous section we discovered the rather remarkable fact that cellular automata can be set up to emulate an extremely wide range of other types of systems. But is this somehow a special feature of cellular automata, or do other systems also have similar capabilities?

In this section we will discover that in fact almost all of the systems that we considered in the previous section—and in Chapter 3— have the same capabilities. And indeed just as we showed that each of these various systems could be emulated by cellular automata, so now we will show that these systems can emulate cellular automata.

As a first example, the pictures below show how mobile automata can be set up to emulate cellular automata. The basic idea is to have the active cell in the mobile automaton sweep backwards and forwards, updating cells as it goes, in such a way that after each complete sweep it has effectively performed one step of cellular automaton evolution.

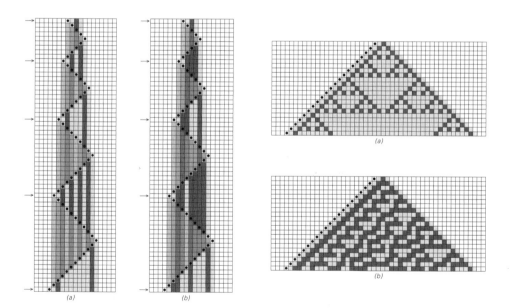

Examples of mobile automata emulating cellular automata. In case (a) the rules for the mobile automaton are set up to emulate the rule 90 elementary cellular automaton; in case (b) they are set up to emulate rule 30. The pictures on the right are obtained by keeping only the steps indicated by arrows on the left, corresponding to times when the active cell in the mobile automaton is further to the left than it has ever been before. The mobile automata used here involve 7 possible colors for each cell.

The specific pictures at the bottom of the facing page are for elementary cellular automata with two possible colors for each cell and nearest-neighbor rules. But the same basic idea can be used for cellular automata with rules of any kind. And this implies that it is possible to construct for example a mobile automaton which emulates the universal cellular automata that we discussed a couple of sections ago.

Such a mobile automaton must then itself be universal, since the universal cellular automaton that it emulates can in turn emulate a wide range of other systems, including all possible mobile automata.

A similar scheme to the one for mobile automata can also be used for Turing machines, as illustrated in the pictures below. And once again, by emulating the universal cellular automaton, it is then possible to construct a universal Turing machine.

But as it turns out, a universal Turing machine was already constructed in 1936, using somewhat different methods. And in fact that universal Turing machine provided what was historically the very first clear example of universality seen in any system.

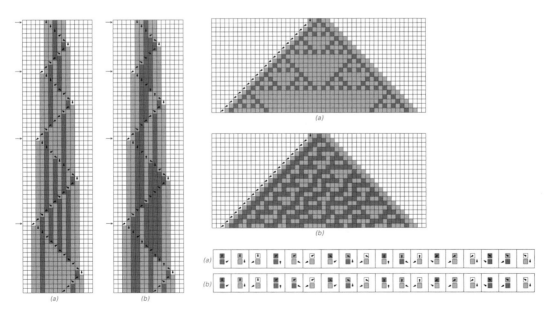

Examples of Turing machines that emulate cellular automata with rules 90 and 30. The pictures on the right are obtained by keeping only the steps indicated by arrows on the left. The Turing machines have 6 states and 3 possible colors for each cell.

Continuing with the types of systems from the previous section, we come next to substitution systems. And here, for once, we find that at least at first we cannot in general emulate cellular automata. For as we discussed on page 83, neighbor-independent substitution systems can generate only patterns that are either repetitive or nested—so they can never yield the more complicated patterns that are, for example, needed to emulate rule 30.

But if one generalizes to neighbor-dependent substitution systems then it immediately becomes very straightforward to emulate cellular automata, as in the pictures below.

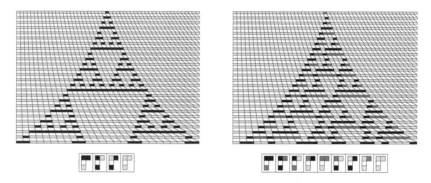

Neighbor-dependent substitution systems that emulate cellular automata with rules 90 and 30. The systems shown are simple examples of neighbor-dependent substitution systems with highly uniform rules always yielding just one cell and corresponding quite directly to cellular automata.

What about sequential substitution systems? Here again it turns out to be fairly easy to emulate cellular automata—as the pictures at the top of the facing page demonstrate.

Perhaps more surprisingly, the same is also true for ordinary tag systems. And even though such systems operate in an extremely simple underlying way, the pictures at the bottom of the facing page demonstrate that they can still quite easily emulate cellular automata.

What about symbolic systems? The structure of these systems is certainly vastly different from cellular automata. But once again—as the picture at the top of page 668 shows—it is quite easy to get these systems to emulate cellular automata.

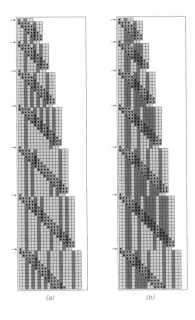

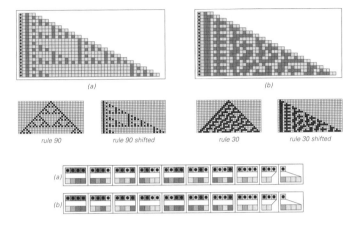

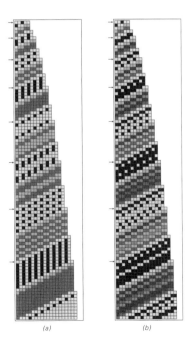

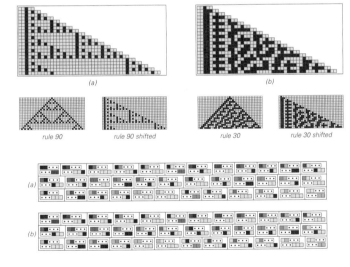

Sequential substitution systems that emulate cellular automata with rules 90 and 30. The pictures at the top above are obtained by keeping only the steps indicated by arrows on the left. The sequential substitution systems involve elements with 3 possible colors.

Tag systems that emulate the rule 90 and rule 30 cellular automata. The pictures at the top above are obtained by keeping only the steps indicated by arrows on the left. Both tag systems involve 6 colors.

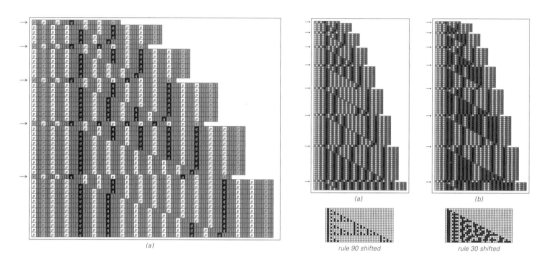

(a)

(a) $p[x\_][p][p][p] \rightarrow p[x[p]][p][p]$, $p[x\_][p][p][q] \rightarrow p[x[q]][p][q]$, $p[x\_][p][q][p] \rightarrow p[x[p]][q][p]$, $p[x\_][p][q][q] \rightarrow p[x[q]][q][q]$, $p[x\_][q][p][p] \rightarrow p[x[q]][p][p]$,
$p[x\_][q][p][q] \rightarrow p[x[p]][p][q]$, $p[x\_][q][q][p] \rightarrow p[x[q]][q][p]$, $p[x\_][q][q][q] \rightarrow p[x[p]][q][q]$, $r[x\_] \rightarrow p[r[p][p]][x]$, $p[x\_][p][p][r] \rightarrow x[p][p][r]$

(b) $p[x\_][p][p][p] \rightarrow p[x[p]][p][p]$, $p[x\_][p][p][q] \rightarrow p[x[q]][p][q]$, $p[x\_][p][q][p] \rightarrow p[x[q]][q][p]$, $p[x\_][p][q][q] \rightarrow p[x[q]][q][q]$, $p[x\_][q][p][p] \rightarrow p[x[q]][p][p]$,
$p[x\_][q][p][q] \rightarrow p[x[p]][p][q]$, $p[x\_][q][q][p] \rightarrow p[x[p]][q][p]$, $p[x\_][q][q][q] \rightarrow p[x[p]][q][q]$, $r[x\_] \rightarrow p[r[p][p]][x]$, $p[x\_][p][p][r] \rightarrow x[p][p][r]$

Symbolic systems set up to emulate cellular automata that have rules 90 and 30. Unlike the examples of symbolic systems in Chapter 3, which involve only one symbol, these symbolic systems involve three symbols, *p*, *q* and *r*.

And as soon as one knows that any particular type of system is capable of emulating any cellular automaton, it immediately follows that there must be examples of that type of system that are universal.

So what about the other types of systems that we considered in Chapter 3? One that we have not yet discussed here are cyclic tag systems. And as it turns out, we will end up using just such systems later in this chapter as part of establishing a dramatic example of universality.

But to demonstrate that cyclic tag systems can manage to emulate cellular automata is not quite as straightforward as to do this for the various kinds of systems we have discussed so far. And indeed we will end up doing it in several stages. The first stage, illustrated in the picture at the top of the facing page, is to get a cyclic tag system to emulate an ordinary tag system with the property that its rules depend only on the very first element that appears at each step.

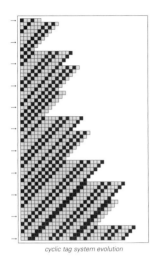

tag system evolution

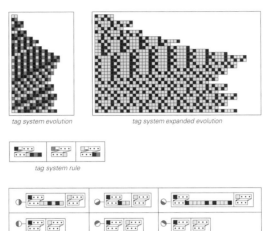

tag system expanded evolution

tag system rule

cyclic tag system evolution

cyclic tag system rule

A cyclic tag system emulating a tag system that depends only on the first element at each step. In the expanded tag system evolution, successive colors of elements are encoded by having a black cell at successive positions inside a fixed block of white cells.

And having done this, the next stage is to get such a tag system to emulate a Turing machine. The pictures on the next page illustrate how this can be done. But at least with the particular construction shown, the resulting Turing machine can only have cells with two possible colors. The pictures below demonstrate, however, that such a Turing

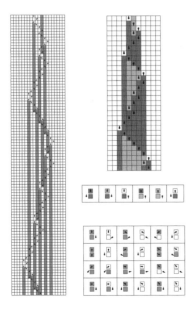

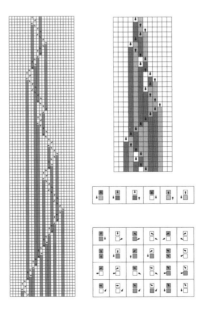

Turing machines with two colors emulating ones with more colors.

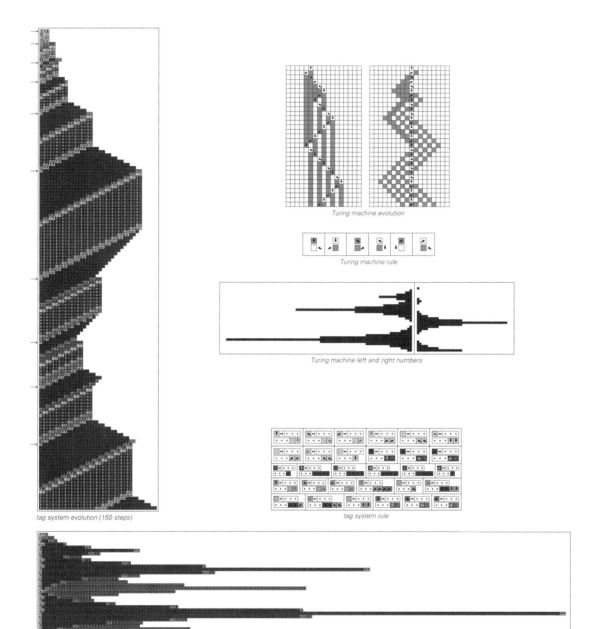

tag system evolution (150 steps)

Turing machine evolution

Turing machine rule

Turing machine left and right numbers

tag system rule

tag system compressed evolution (1500 steps)

Emulating a Turing machine with a tag system that depends only on the first element at each step. The configuration of cells on each side of the head in the Turing machine is treated as a base 2 number. At the steps indicated by arrows the tag system yields sequences of dark cells with lengths that correspond to each of these numbers.

machine can readily be made to emulate a Turing machine with any number of colors. And through the construction of page 665 this then finally shows that a cyclic tag system can successfully emulate any cellular automaton—and can thus be universal.

This leaves only one remaining type of system from Chapter 3: register machines. And although it is again slightly complicated, the pictures on the next page—and below—show how even these systems can be made to emulate Turing machines and thus cellular automata.

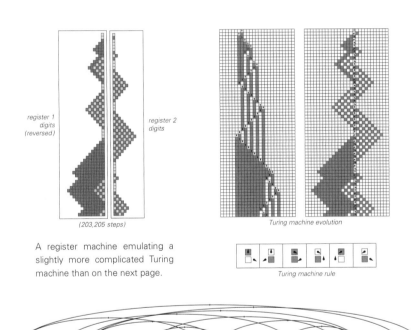

register 1 digits (reversed)

register 2 digits

(203,205 steps)

A register machine emulating a slightly more complicated Turing machine than on the next page.

Turing machine evolution

Turing machine rule

register machine program

So what about systems based on numbers, like those we discussed in Chapter 4? As an example, one can consider a generalization of the arithmetic systems discussed on page 122—in which one has a whole number n, and at each step one finds the remainder after dividing by a constant, and based on the value of this remainder one then applies some specified arithmetic operation to n.

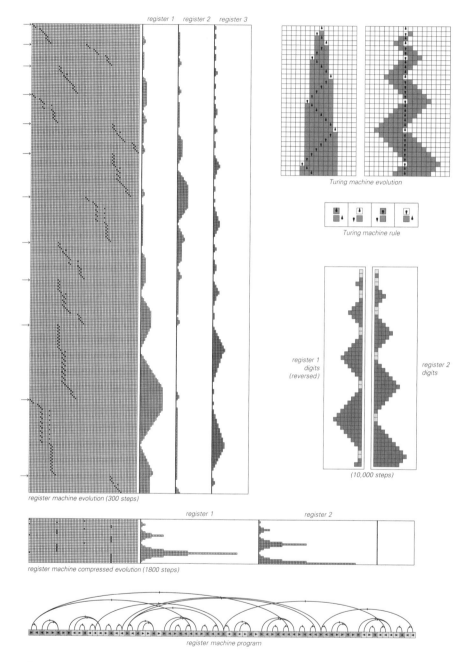

register 1   register 2   register 3

Turing machine evolution

Turing machine rule

register 1
digits
(reversed)

register 2
digits

(10,000 steps)

register machine evolution (300 steps)

register 1   register 2

register machine compressed evolution (1800 steps)

register machine program

An example of a register machine set up to emulate a Turing machine. The Turing machine used here has two states for the head; the register machine program has 72 instructions and uses three registers. The register machine compressed evolution keeps only steps corresponding to every other time the third register gets incremented from zero.

The picture below shows that such a system can be set up to emulate a register machine. And from the fact that register machines are universal it follows that so too are such arithmetic systems.

And indeed the fact that it is possible to set up a universal system using essentially just the operations of ordinary arithmetic is closely related to the proof of Gödel's Theorem discussed on page 784.

But from what we have learned in this chapter, it no longer seems surprising that arithmetic should be capable of achieving universality. Indeed, considering all the kinds of systems that we have found can exhibit universality, it would have been quite peculiar if arithmetic had somehow not been able to support it.

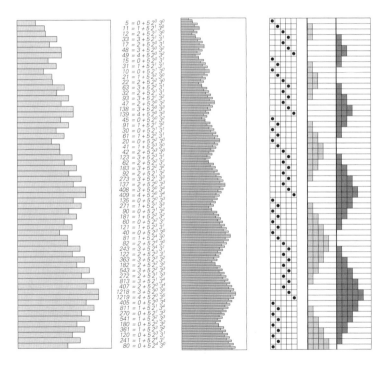

An example of how a simple arithmetic system can emulate a register machine. The arithmetic system takes the value n that it obtains at each step, computes $Mod[n, 30]$, and then depending on the result applies to n one of the arithmetic operations specified by the rule on the left below. The rule is set up so that if the value of n is written in the form $i + 5, 2^a, 3^b$ then the values of i, a and b on successive steps correspond respectively to the position of the register machine in its program, and to the values of the two registers (2 and 3 appear because they are the first two primes; 5 appears because it is the length of the register machine program). The values of n in the pictures on the left are indicated on a logarithmic scale.

$2n+1$	$(n-1)/3$	$3(n-1)$	$(n+1)/2$	$(n-4)/3$	$2n+1$	$n+1$	$3(n-1)$	$n+1$	$n+1$
0	1	2	3	4	5	6	7	8	9
$2n+1$	$n+1$	$3(n-1)$	$(n+1)/2$	$n+1$	$2n+1$	$(n-1)/3$	$3(n-1)$	$n+1$	$(n-4)/3$
10	11	12	13	14	15	16	17	18	19
$2n+1$	$n+1$	$3(n-1)$	$(n+1)/2$	$n+1$	$2n+1$	$n+1$	$3(n-1)$	$n+1$	$n+1$
20	21	22	23	24	25	26	27	28	29

Implications of Universality

When we first discussed cellular automata, Turing machines, substitution systems, register machines and so on in Chapter 3, each of these kinds of systems seemed rather different. But already in Chapter 3 we discovered that at the level of overall behavior, all of them had certain features in common. And now, finally, by thinking in terms of computation, we can begin to see why this might be the case.

The main point, as the previous two sections have demonstrated, is that essentially all of these various kinds of systems—despite their great differences in underlying structure—can ultimately be made to emulate each other.

This is a very remarkable result, and one which will turn out to be crucial to the new kind of science that I develop in this book.

In a sense its most important consequence is that it implies that from a computational point of view a very wide variety of systems, with very different underlying structures, are at some level fundamentally equivalent. For one might have thought that every different kind of system that we discussed for example in Chapter 3 would be able to perform completely different kinds of computations.

But what we have discovered here is that this is not the case. And instead it has turned out that essentially every single one of these systems is ultimately capable of exactly the same kinds of computations.

And among other things, this means that it really does make sense to discuss the notion of computation in purely abstract terms, without referring to any specific type of system. For we now know that it ultimately does not matter what kind of system we use: in the end essentially any kind of system can be programmed to perform the same computations. And so if we study computation at an abstract level, we can expect that the results we get will apply to a very wide range of actual systems.

But it should be emphasized that among systems of any particular type—say cellular automata—not all possible underlying rules are capable of supporting the same kinds of computations.

Indeed, as we saw at the beginning of this chapter, some cellular automata can perform only very simple computations, always yielding for example purely repetitive patterns. But the crucial point is that as one looks at cellular automata with progressively greater computational capabilities, one will eventually pass the threshold of universality. And once past this threshold, the set of computations that can be performed will always be exactly the same.

One might assume that by using more and more sophisticated underlying rules, one would always be able to construct systems with ever greater computational capabilities. But the phenomenon of universality implies that this is not the case, and that as soon as one has passed the threshold of universality, nothing more can in a sense ever be gained.

In fact, once one has a system that is universal, its properties are remarkably independent of the details of its construction. For at least as far as the computations that it can perform are concerned, it does not matter how sophisticated the underlying rules for the system are, or even whether the system is a cellular automaton, a Turing machine, or something else. And as we shall see, this rather remarkable fact forms the basis for explaining many of the observations we made in Chapter 3, and indeed for developing much of the conceptual framework that is needed for the new kind of science in this book.

The Rule 110 Cellular Automaton

In previous sections I have shown that a wide variety of different kinds of systems can in principle be made to exhibit the phenomenon of universality. But how complicated do the underlying rules need to be in a specific case in order actually to achieve universality?

The universal cellular automaton that I described earlier in this chapter had rather complicated underlying rules, involving 19 possible colors for each cell, depending on next-nearest as well as nearest neighbors. But this cellular automaton was specifically constructed so as to make its operation easy to understand. And by not imposing this constraint, one might expect that one would be able to find universal cellular automata that have at least somewhat simpler underlying rules.

Fairly straightforward modifications to the universal cellular automaton shown earlier in this chapter allow one to reduce the number of colors from 19 to 17. And in fact in the early 1970s, it was already known that cellular automata with 18 colors and nearest-neighbor rules could be universal. In the late 1980s—with some ingenuity—examples of universal cellular automata with 7 colors were also constructed.

But such rules still involve 343 distinct cases and are by almost any measure very complicated. And certainly rules this complicated could not reasonably be expected to be common in the types of systems that we typically see in nature. Yet from my experiments on cellular automata in the early 1980s I became convinced that very much simpler rules should also show universality. And by the mid-1980s I began to suspect that even among the very simplest possible rules—with just two colors and nearest neighbors—there might be examples of universality.

The leading candidate was what I called rule 110—a cellular automaton that we have in fact discussed several times before in this book. Like any of the 256 so-called elementary rules, rule 110 can be specified as below by giving the outcome for each of the eight possible combinations of colors of a cell and its nearest neighbors.

The underlying rules for the rule 110 cellular automaton discussed in this section. As elsewhere in the book, each of the eight cases shows what the new color of a cell should be based on its own previous color, and on the previous colors of its neighbors. Despite the extreme simplicity of its underlying rules, what this section will demonstrate is that the rule 110 cellular automaton is in fact universal, and is thus in a sense capable of arbitrarily complex behavior. If the values of the cells in each block are labelled p, q and r, then rule 110 can be written as $Mod[(1 + p) q r + q + r, 2]$ or $\neg (p \wedge q \wedge r) \wedge (q \vee r)$.

Looking just at this very simple specification, however, it seems at first quite absurd to think that rule 110 might be universal. But as soon as one looks at a picture of how rule 110 actually behaves, the idea that it could be universal starts to seem much less absurd. For despite the simplicity of its underlying rules, rule 110 supports a whole variety of localized structures—that move around and interact in many complicated ways. And from pictures like the one on the facing page, it begins to seem not unreasonable that perhaps these localized structures could be arranged so as to perform meaningful computations.

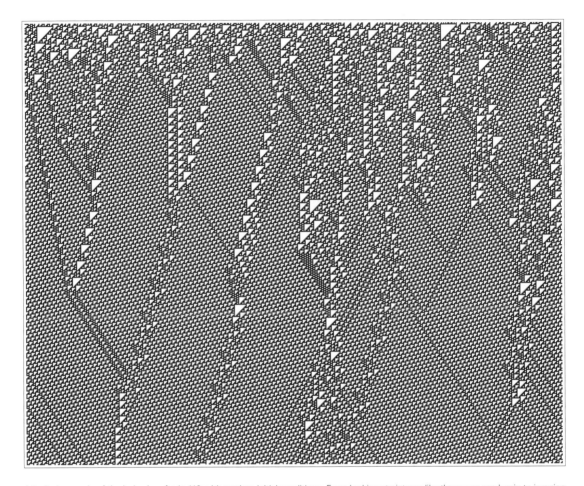

A typical example of the behavior of rule 110 with random initial conditions. From looking at pictures like these one can begin to imagine that it could be possible to arrange localized structures in rule 110 so as to be able to perform meaningful computations. Note that page 292 already showed many of the types of localized structures that can occur in rule 110.

In the universal cellular automaton that we discussed earlier in this chapter, each of the various kinds of components involved in its operation had properties that were explicitly built into the underlying rules. Indeed, in most cases each different type of component was simply represented by a different color of cell. But in rule 110 there are only two possible colors for each cell. So one may wonder how one could ever expect to represent different kinds of components.

The crucial idea is to build up components from combinations of localized structures that the rule in a sense already produces. And if this works, then it is in effect a very economical solution. For it potentially allows one to get a large number of different kinds of components without ever needing to increase the complexity of the underlying rules at all.

But the problem with this approach is that it is typically very difficult to see how the various structures that happen to occur in a particular cellular automaton can be assembled into useful components.

And indeed in the case of rule 110 it took several years of work to develop the necessary ideas and tools. But finally it has turned out to be possible to show that the rule 110 cellular automaton is in fact universal.

It is truly remarkable that a system with such simple underlying rules should be able to perform what are in effect computations of arbitrary sophistication, but that is what its universality implies.

So how then does the proof of universality proceed?

The basic idea is to show that rule 110 can emulate any possible system in some class of systems where there is already known to be universality. And it turns out that a convenient such class of systems are the cyclic tag systems that we introduced on page 95.

Earlier in this chapter we saw that it is possible to construct a cyclic tag system that can emulate any given Turing machine. And since we know that at least some Turing machines are universal, this fact then establishes that universal cyclic tag systems are possible.

So if we can succeed in demonstrating that rule 110 can emulate any cyclic tag system, then we will have managed to prove that rule 110 is itself universal. The sequence of pictures on the facing page shows the beginnings of what is needed. The basic idea is to start from the usual representation of a cyclic tag system, and then progressively to change this representation so as to get closer and closer to what can actually be emulated directly by rule 110.

Picture (a) shows an example of the evolution of a cyclic tag system in the standard representation from pages 95 and 96. Picture (b) then shows another version of this same evolution, but now rearranged so that each element stays in the same position, rather than always shifting to the left at each step.

(a)

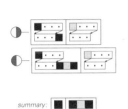

summary:

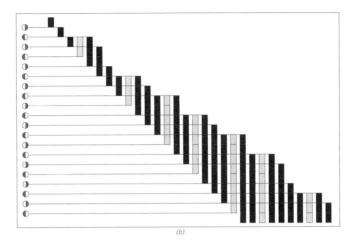

(b)

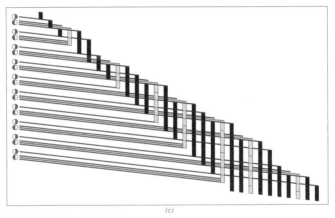

(c)

Four views of a cyclic tag system with rules as shown above, drawn so as to be progressively closer to what can be emulated directly in rule 110. Picture (a) shows the cyclic tag system in the same form as on pages 95 and 96. Picture (b) shows the system with sequences on successive steps rearranged so that they do not shift to the left when the first element is removed. Picture (c) is a skewed version of (b) in which the way information is used from the underlying rules at each step is explicitly indicated. Picture (d) shows a more definite mechanism for the evolution of the system in which different lines effectively indicate the motions of different pieces of information.

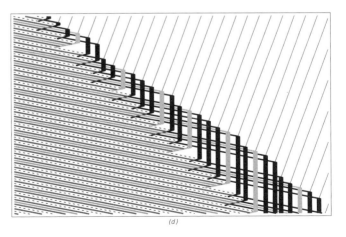

(d)

A cyclic tag system in general operates by removing the first element from the sequence that exists at each step, and then adding a new block of elements to the end of the sequence if this element is black. A crucial feature of cyclic tag systems is that the choice of what block of elements can be added does not depend in any way on the form of the sequence. So, for example, on the previous page, there are just two possibilities, and these possibilities alternate on successive steps.

Pictures (a) and (b) on the previous page illustrate the consequences of applying the rules for a cyclic tag system, but in a sense give no indication of an explicit mechanism by which these rules might be applied. In picture (c), however, we see the beginnings of such a mechanism.

The basic idea is that at each step in the evolution of the system, there is a stripe that comes in from the left carrying information about the block that can be added at that step. Then when the stripe hits the first element in the sequence that exists at that step, it is allowed to pass only if the element is black. And once past, the stripe continues to the right, finally adding the block it represents to the end of the sequence.

But while picture (c) shows the effects of various lines carrying information around the system, it gives no indication of why the lines should behave in the way they do. Picture (d), however, shows a much more explicit mechanism. The collections of lines coming in from the left represent the blocks that can be added at successive steps. The beginning of each block is indicated by a dashed line, while the elements within the block are indicated by solid black and gray lines.

When a dashed line hits the first element in the sequence that exists at a particular step, it effectively bounces back in the form of a line propagating to the left that carries the color of the first element.

When this line is gray, it then absorbs all other lines coming from the left until the next dashed line arrives. But when the line is black, it lets lines coming from the left through. These lines then continue until they collide with gray lines coming from the right, at which point they generate a new element with the same color as their own.

By looking at picture (d), one can begin to see how it might be possible for a cyclic tag system to be emulated by rule 110: the basic

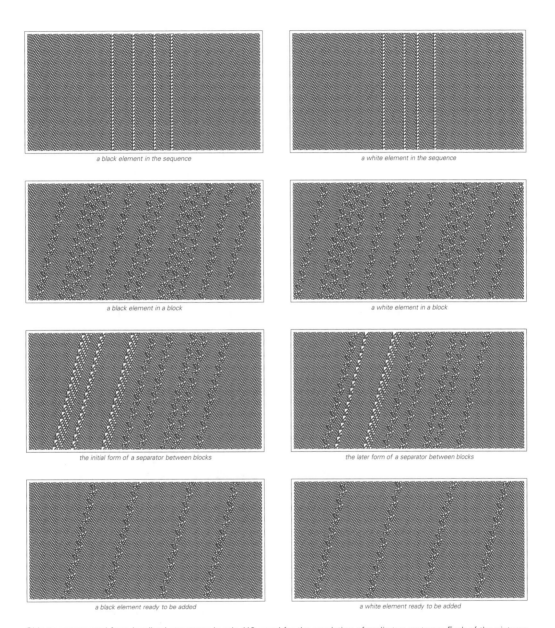

a black element in the sequence

a white element in the sequence

a black element in a block

a white element in a block

the initial form of a separator between blocks

the later form of a separator between blocks

a black element ready to be added

a white element ready to be added

Objects constructed from localized structures in rule 110, used for the emulation of cyclic tag systems. Each of the pictures shown is 500 cells wide. The objects in the top two pictures correspond to the thick vertical black and gray lines in picture (d) on page 679. The objects in the next two pictures correspond to the dark and light gray lines that come in from the left in picture (d). (Note that all the structures are left-right reversed in rule 110.) The third pair of pictures correspond to two versions of the dashed lines in picture (d). And the fourth pair of pictures correspond to right-going lines on the right-hand side of picture (d). All the localized structures involved in the pictures above were shown individually on page 292. Note that the spacings between structures are crucial in determining the objects they represent.

idea is to have each of the various kinds of lines in the picture be emulated by some collection of localized structures in rule 110.

But at the outset it is by no means clear that collections of localized structures can be found that will behave in appropriate ways.

With some effort, however, it turns out to be possible to find the necessary constructs, and indeed the previous page shows various objects formed from localized structures in rule 110 that can be used to emulate most of the types of lines in picture (d) on page 679.

The first two pictures show objects that correspond to the black and white elements indicated by thick vertical lines in picture (d). Both of these objects happen to consist of the same four localized structures, but the objects are distinguished by the spacings between these structures.

The second two pictures on the previous page use the same idea of different spacings between localized structures to represent the black and gray lines shown coming in from the left in picture (d) on page 679.

Note that because of the particular form of rule 110, the objects in the second two pictures on the previous page move to the left rather than to the right. And indeed in setting up a correspondence with rule 110, it is convenient to left-right reverse all pictures of cyclic tag systems. But using the various objects from the previous page, together with a few others, it is then possible to set up a complete emulation of a cyclic tag system using rule 110.

The diagram on the facing page shows schematically how this can be done. Every line in the diagram corresponds to a single localized structure in rule 110, and although the whole diagram cannot be drawn completely to scale, the collisions between lines correctly show all the basic interactions that occur between structures.

The next several pages then give details of what happens in each of the regions indicated by circles in the schematic diagram.

Region (a) shows a block separator—corresponding to a dashed line in picture (d) on page 679—hitting the single black element in the sequence that exists at the first step. Because the element hit is black, an object must be produced that allows information from the block at this step to pass through. Most of the activity in region (a) is concerned with producing such an object. But it turns out that as a side-effect two

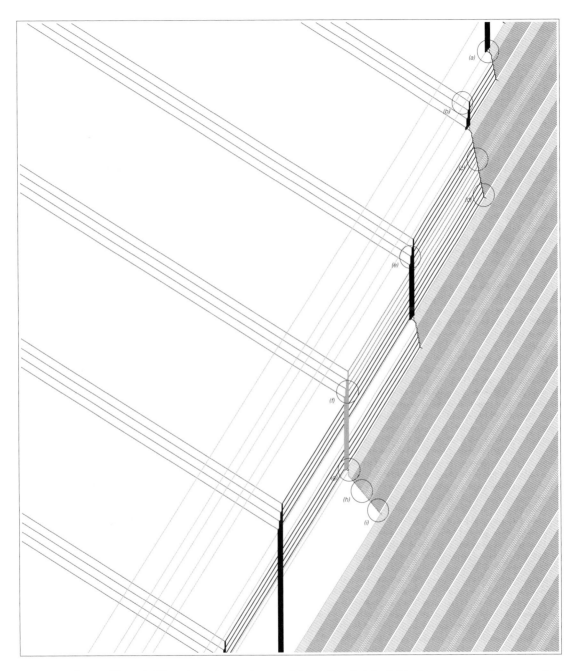

A schematic diagram of how rule 110 can be made to emulate a cyclic tag system. Each line in this diagram corresponds to one localized structure in rule 110. Note that the relative slopes of the structures are reproduced faithfully here, but their spacings are not. Note also that lines shown in different colors here often correspond to the same structure in rule 110.

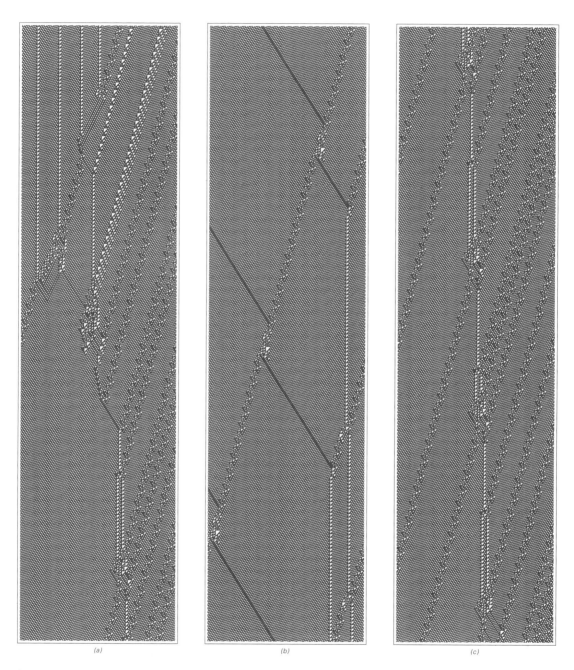

(a)　　　　　　　　　　　(b)　　　　　　　　　　　(c)

Close-ups of circled regions shown schematically on the previous page. Each picture is 320 cells wide and shows 1200 evolution steps.

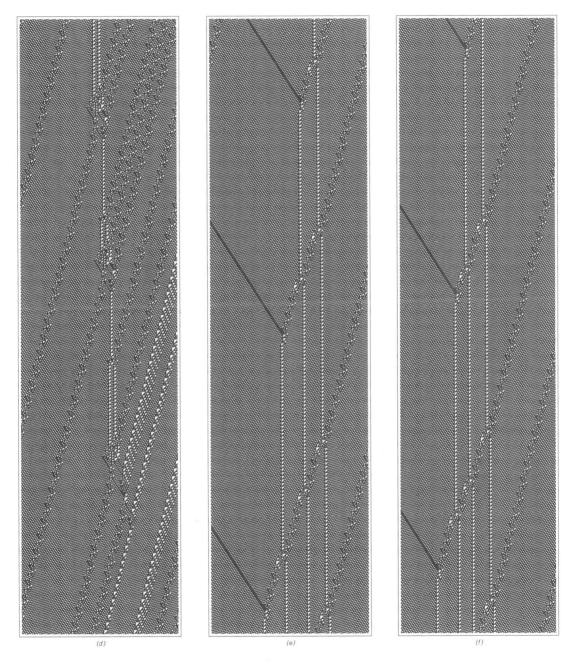

(d)   (e)   (f)

Close-ups (continued).

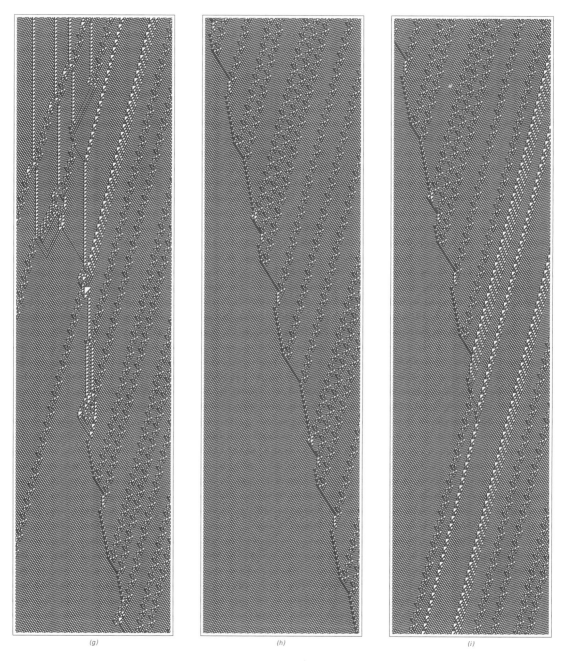

(g) (h) (i)

Close-ups (continued).

additional localized structures are produced that can be seen propagating to the left. These structures could later cause trouble, but looking at region (b) we see that in fact they just pass through other structures that they meet without any adverse effect.

Region (c) shows what happens when the information corresponding to one element in a block passes through the kind of object produced in region (a). The number of localized structures that represent the element is reduced from twelve to four, but the spacings of these structures continue to specify its color. Region (d) then shows how the object in region (c) comes to an end when the beginning of the block separator from the next step arrives.

Region (e) shows how the information corresponding to a black element in a block is actually converted to a new black element in the sequence produced by the cyclic tag system. What happens is that the four localized structures corresponding to the element in the block collide with four other localized structures travelling in the opposite direction, and the result is four stationary structures that correspond to the new element in the sequence.

Region (f) shows the same process as region (e) but for a white element. The fact that the element is white is encoded in the wider spacing of the structures coming from the right, which results in narrower spacing of the stationary structures.

Region (g) shows the analog of region (a), but now for a white element instead of a black one. The region begins much like region (a), except that the four localized structures at the top are more narrowly spaced. Starting around the middle of the region, however, the behavior becomes quite different from region (a): while region (a) yields an object that allows information to pass through, region (g) yields one that stops all information, as shown in regions (h) and (i).

Note that even though they begin very differently, regions (d) and (i) end in the same way, reflecting the fact that in both cases the system is ready to handle a new block, whatever that block may be.

The pictures on the last few pages were all made for a cyclic tag system with a specific underlying rule. But exactly the same principles can be used whatever the underlying rule is. And the pictures below show schematically what happens with a few other choices of rules.

The way that the lines interact in the interior of each picture is always exactly the same. But what changes when one goes from one rule to another is the arrangement of lines entering the picture.

In the way that the pictures are drawn below, the blocks that appear in each rule are encoded in the pattern of lines coming in from the left edge of the picture. But if each picture were extended sufficiently far to the left, then all these lines would eventually be seen to start from the top. And what this means is that the arrangement of lines can therefore always be viewed as an initial condition for the system.

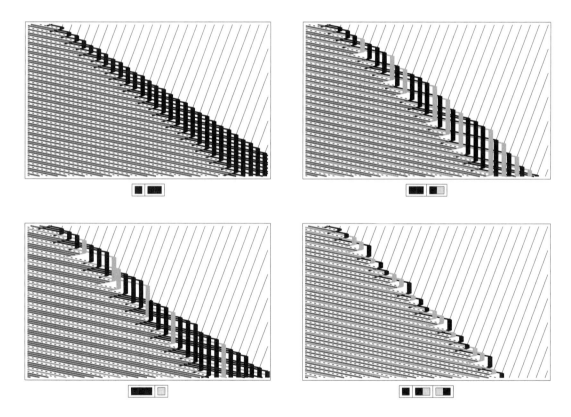

Schematic diagrams of how cyclic tag systems with four different underlying rules can be emulated. The lines in each diagram correspond essentially to collections of localized structures in rule 110. The processes that occur in the interior of each picture are always the same; the different cyclic tag system rules are implemented by different arrangements of lines entering each picture.

This is then finally how universality is achieved in rule 110. The idea is just to set up initial conditions that correspond to the blocks that appear in the rule for whatever cyclic tag system one wants to emulate.

The necessary initial conditions consist of repetitions of blocks of cells, where each of these blocks contains a pattern of localized structures that corresponds to the block of elements that appear in the rule for the cyclic tag system. The blocks of cells are always quite complicated—for the cyclic tag system discussed in most of this section they are each more than 3000 cells wide—but the crucial point is that such blocks can be constructed for any cyclic tag system. And what this means is that with suitable initial conditions, rule 110 can in fact be made to emulate any cyclic tag system.

It should be mentioned at this point however that there are a few additional complications involved in setting up appropriate initial conditions to make rule 110 emulate many cyclic tag systems. For as the pictures earlier in this section demonstrate, the way we have made rule 110 emulate cyclic tag systems relies on many details of the interactions between localized structures in rule 110. And it turns out that to make sure that with the specific construction used the appropriate interactions continue to occur at every step, one must put some constraints on the cyclic tag systems being emulated.

In essence, these constraints end up being that the blocks that appear in the rule for the cyclic tag system must always be a multiple of six elements long, and that there must be some bound on the number of steps that can elapse between the addition of successive new elements to the cyclic tag system sequence.

Using the ideas discussed on page 669, it is not difficult, however, to make a cyclic tag system that satisfies these constraints, but that emulates any other cyclic tag system. And as a result, we may therefore conclude that rule 110 can in fact successfully emulate absolutely any cyclic tag system. And this means that rule 110 is indeed universal.

The Significance of Universality in Rule 110

Practical computers and computer languages have traditionally been the only common examples of universality that we ever encounter. And from the fact that these kinds of systems tend to be fairly complicated in their construction, the general intuition has developed that any system that manages to be universal must somehow also be based on quite complicated underlying rules.

But the result of the previous section shows in a rather spectacular way that this is not the case. It would have been one thing if we had found an example of a cellular automaton with say four or five colors that turned out to be universal. But what in fact we have seen is that a cellular automaton with one of the very simplest possible 256 rules manages to be universal.

So what are the implications of this result? Most important is that it suggests that universality is an immensely more common phenomenon than one might otherwise have thought. For if one knew only about practical computers and about systems like the universal cellular automaton discussed early in this chapter, then one would probably assume that universality would rarely if ever be seen outside of systems that were specifically constructed to exhibit it.

But knowing that a system like rule 110 is universal, the whole picture changes, and now it seems likely that instead universality should actually be seen in a very wide range of systems, including many with rather simple rules.

A couple of sections ago we discussed the fact that as soon as one has a system that is universal, adding further complication to its rules cannot have any fundamental effect. For by virtue of its universality the system can always ultimately just emulate the behavior that would be obtained with any more complicated set of rules.

So what this means is that if one looks at a sequence of systems with progressively more complicated rules, one should expect that the overall behavior they produce will become more complex only until the threshold of universality is reached. And as soon as this threshold is passed, there should then be no further fundamental changes in what one sees.

The practical importance of this phenomenon depends greatly however on how far one has to go to get to the threshold of universality.

But knowing that a system like rule 110 is universal, one now suspects that this threshold is remarkably easy to reach. And what this means is that beyond the very simplest rules of any particular kind, the behavior that one sees should quickly become as complex as it will ever be.

Remarkably enough, it turns out that this is essentially what we already observed in Chapter 3. Indeed, not only for cellular automata but also for essentially all of the other kinds of systems that we studied, we found that highly complex behavior could be obtained even with rather simple rules, and that adding further complication to these rules did not in most cases noticeably affect the level of complexity that was produced.

So in retrospect the results of Chapter 3 should already have suggested that simple underlying rules such as rule 110 might be able to achieve universality. But what the elaborate construction in the previous section has done is to show for certain that this is the case.

Class 4 Behavior and Universality

If one looks at the typical behavior of rule 110 with random initial conditions, then the most obvious feature of what one sees is that there are a large number of localized structures that move around and interact with each other in complicated ways. But as we saw in Chapter 6, such behavior is by no means unique to rule 110. Indeed, it is in fact characteristic of all cellular automata that lie in what I called class 4.

The pictures on the next page show a few examples of such class 4 systems. And while the details are different in each case, the general features of the behavior are always rather similar.

So what does this mean about the computational capabilities of such systems? I strongly suspect that it is true in general that any cellular automaton which shows overall class 4 behavior will turn out—like rule 110—to be universal.

We saw at the end of Chapter 6 that class 4 rules always seem to yield a range of progressively more complicated localized structures. And my expectation is that if one looks sufficiently hard at any

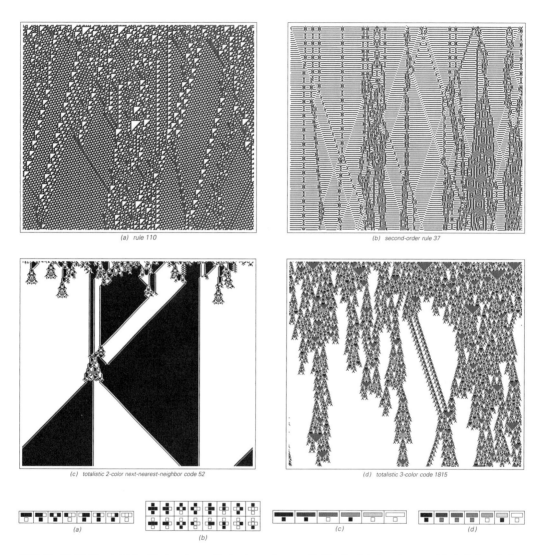

(a) rule 110

(b) second-order rule 37

(c) totalistic 2-color next-nearest-neighbor code 52

(d) totalistic 3-color code 1815

(a)   *(b)*   *(c)*   *(d)*

Examples of cellular automata with class 4 overall behavior, as discussed in Chapter 6. I strongly suspect that all class 4 rules, like rule 110, will turn out to be universal.

particular rule, then one will always eventually be able to find a set of localized structures that is rich enough to support universality.

The final demonstration that a given rule is universal will no doubt involve the same kind of elaborate construction as for rule 110.

But the point is that all the evidence I have so far suggests that for any class 4 rule such a construction will eventually turn out to be possible.

So what kinds of rules show class 4 behavior?

Among the 256 so-called elementary cellular automata that allow only two possible colors for each cell and depend only on nearest neighbors, the only clear immediate example is rule 110—together with rules 124, 137 and 193 obtained by trivially reversing left and right or black and white. But as soon as one allows more than two possible colors, or allows dependence on more than just nearest neighbors, one immediately finds all sorts of further examples of class 4 behavior.

In fact, as illustrated in the pictures on the facing page, it is sufficient in such cases just to use so-called totalistic rules in which the new color of a cell depends only on the average color of cells in its neighborhood, and not on their individual colors.

In two dimensions class 4 behavior can occur with rules that involve only two colors and only nearest neighbors—as shown on page 249. And indeed one example of such a rule is the so-called Game of Life that has been popular in recreational computing since the 1970s.

The strategy for demonstrating universality in a two-dimensional cellular automaton is in general very much the same as in one dimension. But in practice the comparative ease with which streams of localized structures can be made to cross in two dimensions can reduce some of the technical difficulties involved. And as it turns out there was already an outline of a proof given even in the 1970s that the Game of Life two-dimensional cellular automaton is universal.

Returning to one dimension, one can ask whether among the 256 elementary cellular automata there are any apart from rule 110 that show even signs of class 4 behavior. As we will see in the next section, one possibility is rule 54. And if this rule is in fact class 4 then it is my expectation that by looking at interactions between the localized structures it supports it will in the end—with enough effort—be possible to show that it too exhibits the phenomenon of universality.

The Threshold of Universality in Cellular Automata

By showing that rule 110 is universal, we have established that universality is possible even among cellular automata with the very simplest kinds of underlying rules. But there remains the question of what is ultimately needed for a cellular automaton—or any other kind of system—to be able to achieve universality.

In general, if a system is to be universal, then this means that by setting up an appropriate choice of initial conditions it is possible to get the system to emulate any type of behavior that can occur in any other system. And as a consequence, cellular automata like the ones in the pictures below are definitely not universal, since they always produce just simple uniform or repetitive patterns of behavior, whatever initial conditions one uses.

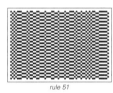

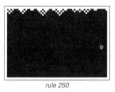

rule 4   rule 51   rule 108   rule 250

Examples of elementary cellular automata which only ever show purely uniform or purely repetitive behavior, and which therefore definitely cannot be universal. These cellular automata are necessarily all class 1 or class 2 systems.

In a sense the fundamental reason for this—as we discussed on page 252—is that such class 1 and class 2 cellular automata never allow any transmission of information except over limited distances. And the result of this is that they can only support processes that involve the correlated action of a limited number of cells.

In cellular automata like the ones at the top of the facing page some information can be transmitted over larger distances. But the way this occurs is highly constrained, and in the end these systems can only produce patterns that are in essence purely nested—so that it is again not possible for universality to be achieved.

What about additive rules such as 90 and 150?

With simple initial conditions these rules always yield very regular nested patterns. But with more complicated initial conditions, they produce more complicated patterns of behavior—as the pictures at

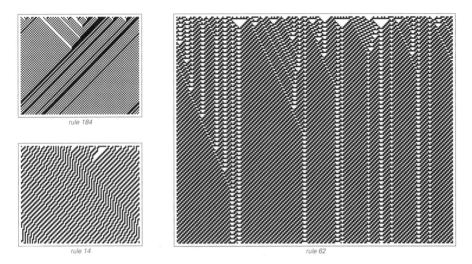

Examples of cellular automata that do allow information to be transmitted over large distances, but only in very restricted ways. The overall patterns produced by such cellular automata are essentially nested. No cellular automata of this kind can ever be universal.

the bottom of this page illustrate. As we saw on page 264, however, these patterns never in fact really correspond to more than rather simple transformations of the initial conditions. Indeed, even after say 1,048,576 steps—or any number of steps that is a power of two—the array of cells produced always turns out to correspond just to a simple superposition of two or three shifted copies of the initial conditions.

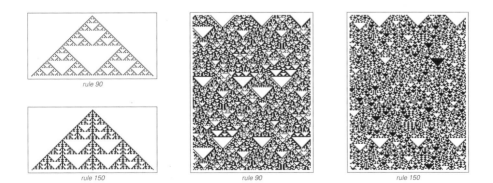

Examples of cellular automata with additive rules. The repetitive occurrence of states that correspond to simple transformations of the initial conditions prevent such cellular automata from ever being universal.

And since there are many kinds of behavior that do not return to such predictable forms after any limited number of steps, one must conclude that additive rules cannot be universal.

At the end of the last section I mentioned rule 54 as another elementary cellular automaton besides rule 110 that might be class 4. The pictures below show examples of the typical behavior of rule 54.

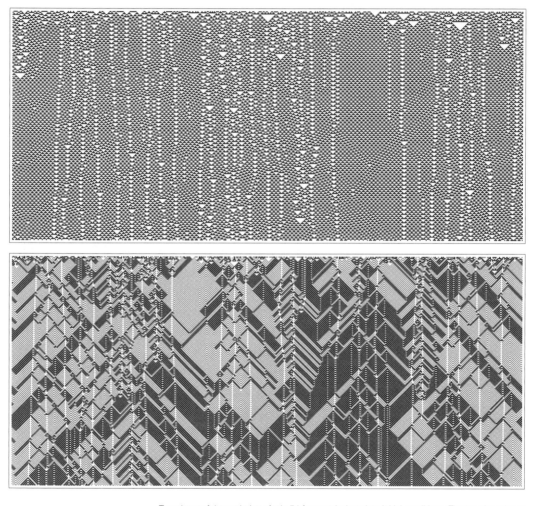

Two views of the evolution of rule 54 from typical random initial conditions. The top view shows the color of every cell at every step. The bottom groups together pairs of cells, and shows only every other step. There are various localized structures—and hints of class 4 behavior.

Some localized structures are definitely seen. But are they enough to support class 4 behavior and universality? The pictures below show what happens if one starts looking in turn at each of the possible initial conditions for rule 54. At first one sees only simple repetitive behavior. At initial condition 291 one sees a very simple form of nesting. And as one continues one sees various other repetitive and nested forms. But at least up to the hundred millionth initial condition one sees nothing that is fundamentally any more complicated.

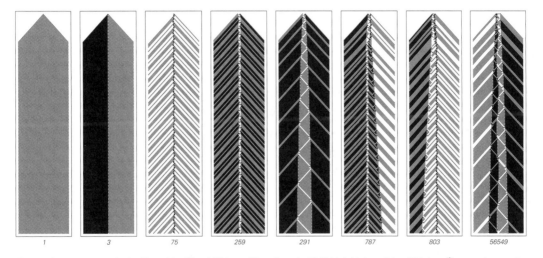

Forms of behavior seen in the first 100 million initial conditions for rule 54. With initial condition 291 the nth new stripe on the right is produced at step $2n^2 + 8n - 9$. Even in the last case shown, the arrangement of stripes eventually becomes completely regular, with the nth new stripe being produced at step $n^2 + 21n/2 - \{6, 5, -4, 3\}[[Mod[n, 4] + 1]]/2$. Pairs of cells are grouped together in each picture, as at the bottom of the facing page.

So can rule 54 achieve universality? I am not sure. It could be that if one went just a little further in looking at initial conditions one would see more complicated behavior. And it could be that even the structures shown above can be combined to produce all the richness that is needed for universality. But it could also be that whatever one does rule 54 will always in the end just show purely repetitive or nested behavior—which cannot on its own support universality.

What about other elementary cellular automata?

As I will discuss in the next chapter, my general expectation is that more or less any system whose behavior is not somehow fundamentally repetitive or nested will in the end turn out to be universal. But I suspect that this fact will be very much easier to establish for some systems than for others—with rule 110 being one of the easiest cases.

In general what one needs to do in order to prove universality is to find a procedure for setting up initial conditions in one system so as to make it emulate some general class of other systems. And at some level the main challenge is that our experience from programming and engineering tends to provide us with only a limited set of methods for coming up with such a procedure. Typically what we are used to doing is constructing things in stages. Usually we start by building components, and then we progressively assemble these into larger and larger structures. And the point is that at each stage, we need think directly only about the scale of structures that we are currently handling—and not for example about all the pieces that make up these structures.

In proving the universality of rule 110, we were able to follow essentially the same basic approach. We started by identifying various localized structures, and then we used these structures as components in building up the progressively larger structures that we needed.

What was in a sense crucial to our approach was therefore that we could readily control the transmission of information in the system. For this is what allowed us to treat different localized structures as being separate and independent objects.

And indeed in any system with class 4 behavior, things will typically always work in more or less the same way. But in class 3 systems they will not. For what usually happens in such systems is that a change made even to a single cell will eventually spread to affect all other cells. And this kind of uncontrolled transmission of information makes it very difficult to identify pieces that could be used as definite components in a construction.

So what can be done in such cases? The most obvious possibility is that one might be able to find special classes of initial conditions in which transmission of information could be controlled. And an example where this can be potentially done is rule 73.

The pictures below show the typical behavior of rule 73—first with completely random initial conditions, and then with initial conditions in which no run of an even number of black squares occurs.

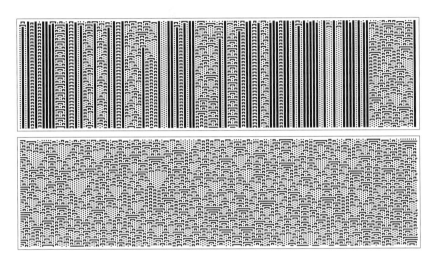

Two examples of rule 73. The top example uses completely random initial conditions; the bottom example uses initial conditions in which no run of an even number of black squares ever occurs. The bottom example is actually part of the pattern obtained from a single black cell—just to the right of the center column, starting with step 1000.

In the second case rule 73 exhibits typical class 3 behavior—with the usual uncontrolled transmission of information. In the first case, however, the black walls that are present seem to prevent any long-range transmission of information at all.

So can one then achieve something intermediate in rule 73—in which information is transmitted, but only in a controlled way?

The pictures at the top of the next page give some indication of how this might be done. For they show that with an appropriate background rule 73 supports various localized structures, some of which move. And while these structures may at first seem more like those in rule 54 than rule 110, I strongly suspect that the complexity of the typical behavior of rule 73 will be reflected in more sophisticated interactions between the structures—and will eventually provide what is needed to allow universality to be demonstrated in much the same way as in rule 110.

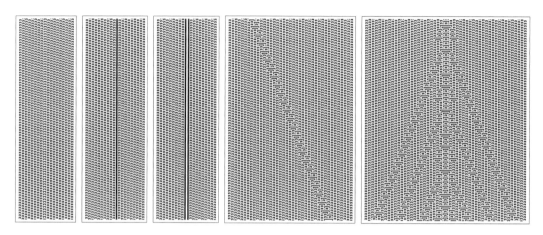

Examples of localized structures in rule 73. Note that in the last case shown, the background patterns on either side are mirror images.

So what about a case like rule 30? With strictly repetitive initial conditions—like any cellular automaton—this must yield purely repetitive behavior. But as soon as one perturbs such initial conditions, one normally seems to get only complicated and seemingly random behavior, as in the top row of pictures below.

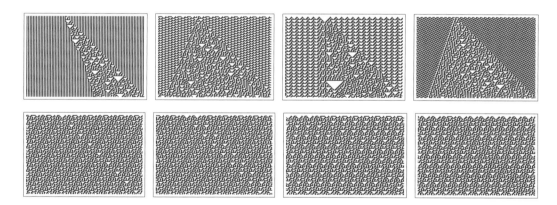

Examples of patterns produced by rule 30 with repetitive backgrounds. The top row shows the effect of inserting a single extra black cell into various backgrounds. The bottom row shows all localized structures involving up to 25 cells supported by rule 30 on repetitive backgrounds with blocks of up to 25 cells. Note that these localized structures always move one cell to the right at each step—making it impossible for them to interact in non-trivial ways.

Yet it turns out still to be possible to get localized structures—as the bottom row of pictures above demonstrate. But these structures always seem to move at the same speed, and so can never interact. And even after searching many billions of cases, I have never succeeded in finding any useful set of localized structures in rule 30.

The picture below shows what happens in rule 45. Many possible perturbations to repetitive initial conditions again yield seemingly random behavior. But in one case a nested pattern is produced. And structures that remain localized are now fairly common—but just as in rule 30 always seem to move at the same speed.

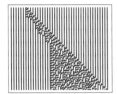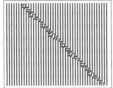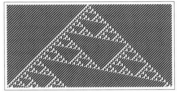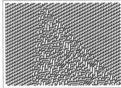

Examples of patterns produced by inserting a single extra black cell into repetitive backgrounds for rule 45. Note the appearance of a slanted version of the nested pattern from rule 90. In rule 45, localized structures turn out to be fairly common—but as in rule 30 they always seem to move at the same speed, and so presumably cannot interact to produce any kind of class 4 behavior.

So although this means that the particular type of approach we used to demonstrate the universality of rule 110 cannot immediately be used for rule 30 or rule 45, it certainly does not mean that these rules are not in the end universal. And as I will discuss in the next chapter, it is my very strong belief that in fact they will turn out to be.

So how might we get evidence for this?

If a system is universal, then this means that with a suitable encoding of initial conditions its evolution must emulate the evolution of any other system. So this suggests that one might be able to get evidence about universality just by trying different possible encodings, and then seeing what range of other systems they allow one to emulate.

In the case of the 19-color universal cellular automaton on page 645 it turns out that encodings in which individual black and white cells are represented by particular 20-cell blocks are sufficient to allow the universal cellular automaton to emulate all 256 possible elementary cellular automata—with one step in the evolution of each of these corresponding to 53 steps in the evolution of the original system.

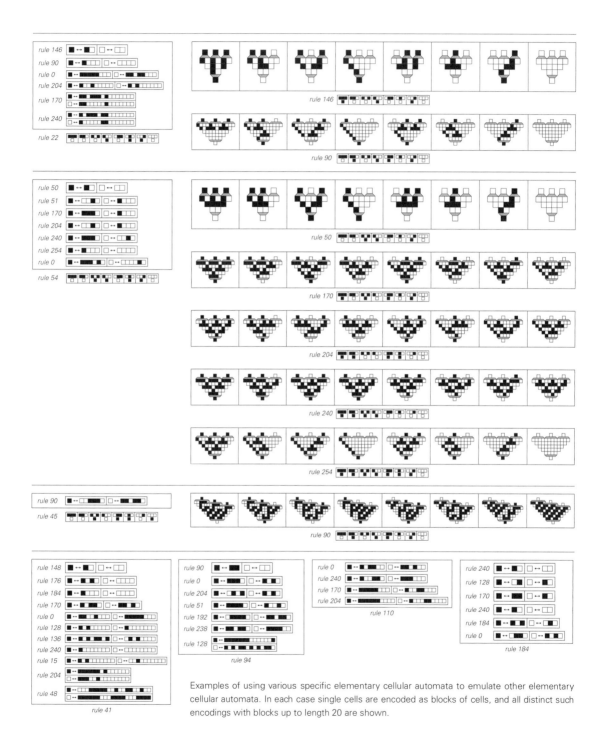

Examples of using various specific elementary cellular automata to emulate other elementary cellular automata. In each case single cells are encoded as blocks of cells, and all distinct such encodings with blocks up to length 20 are shown.

So given a particular elementary cellular automaton one can then ask what other elementary cellular automata it can emulate using blocks up to a certain length.

The pictures on the facing page show a few examples.

The results are not particularly dramatic. No single rule is able to emulate many others—and the rules that are emulated tend to be rather simple. An example of a slight surprise is that rule 45 ends up being able to emulate rule 90. But at least with blocks up to length 25, rule 30 for example is not able to emulate any non-trivial rules at all.

From the proof of universality that we gave it follows that rule 110 must be able to emulate any other elementary cellular automaton with blocks of some size—but with the actual construction we discussed this size will be quite astronomical. And certainly in the picture on the facing page rule 110 does not seem to stand out.

But although it seems somewhat difficult to emulate the complete evolution of one cellular automaton with another, it turns out to be much easier to emulate fragments of evolution for limited numbers of steps. And as an example the picture below shows how rule 30 can be made to emulate the basic action of one step in rule 90.

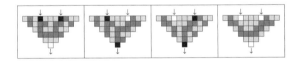 

Rule 30 set up to emulate a single XOR operation—as used in a step of rule 90 evolution. The initial conditions for rule 30 are fixed except at the two positions indicated, where input can effectively be given. The picture shows that for each possible combination of inputs, the result from the rule 30 evolution corresponds exactly to the output from the XOR.

The idea is to set up a configuration in rule 30 so that if one inserts input at particular positions the output from the underlying rule 30 evolution corresponds exactly to what one would get from a single step of rule 90 evolution. And in the particular case shown, this is achieved by having blocks 3 cells wide between each input position.

But as the picture on the next page indicates, by having appropriate blocks 5 cells wide rule 30 can actually be made to emulate

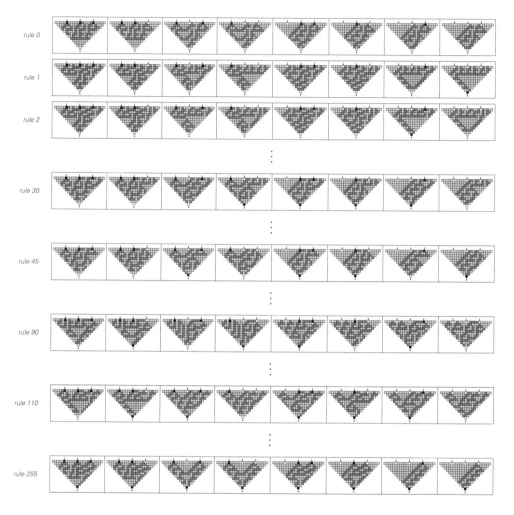

rule 0

rule 1

rule 2

rule 30

rule 45

rule 90

rule 110

rule 255

Illustrations of how rule 30 can be set up to emulate a single step in the evolution of all elementary cellular automata.

one step in the evolution of every single one of the 256 possible elementary cellular automata.

So what about other underlying rules?

The picture on the facing page shows for several different underlying rules which of the 256 possible elementary rules can successfully be emulated with successively wider blocks. In cases where the underlying rules have only rather simple behavior—as with rules 90 and 184—it turns out that it is never possible to emulate more than a few of the 256 possible elementary rules. But for underlying rules that have more complex behavior—like rules 22, 30, or 110—it turns out that in the end it is always possible to emulate all 256 elementary rules.

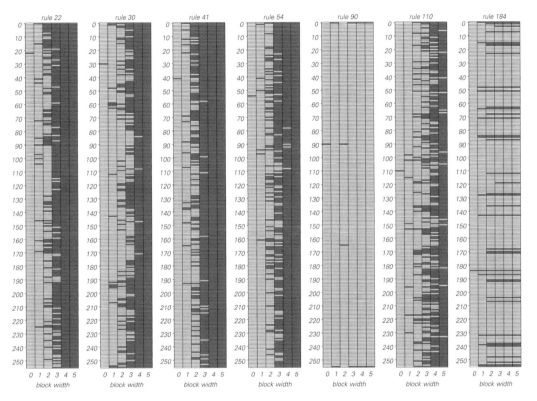

Summaries of how various underlying cellular automata do in emulating a single step in the evolution of each of the 256 possible elementary cellular automata using the scheme from the facing page with blocks of successively greater widths.

The emulation here is, however, only for a single step. So the fact that it is possible does not immediately establish universality in any ordinary sense. But it does once again support the idea that almost any cellular automaton whose behavior seems to us complex can be made to do computations that are in a sense as sophisticated as one wants.

And this suggests that such cellular automata will in the end turn out to be universal—with the result that out of the 256 elementary rules one expects that perhaps as many as 27 will in fact be universal.

Universality in Turing Machines and Other Systems

From the results of the previous few sections, we now have some idea where the threshold for universality lies in cellular automata. But what about other kinds of systems—like Turing machines? How complicated do the rules need to be in order to get universality?

In the 1950s and early 1960s a certain amount of work was done on trying to construct small Turing machines that would be universal. The main achievement of this work was the construction of the universal machine with 7 states and 4 possible colors shown below.

The rule for a universal Turing machine with 7 states and 4 colors constructed in 1962. Until now, this was essentially the simplest known universal Turing machine. Note that one element of the rule can be considered as specifying that the Turing machine should "halt" with the head staying in the same location and same state.

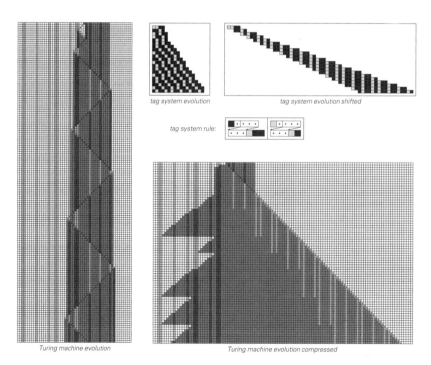

tag system evolution

tag system evolution shifted

tag system rule:

Turing machine evolution

Turing machine evolution compressed

An example of how the Turing machine above can emulate a tag system. A black element in the tag system is set up to correspond to a block of four cells in the Turing machine, while a white element corresponds to a single cell.

The picture at the bottom of the facing page shows how universality can be proved in this case. The basic idea is that by setting up appropriate initial conditions on the left, the Turing machine can be made to emulate any tag system of a certain kind. But it then turns out from the discussion of page 667 that there are tag systems of this kind that are universal.

It is already an achievement to find a universal Turing machine as comparatively simple as the one on the facing page. And indeed in the forty years since this example was found, no significantly simpler one has been found. So one might conclude from this that the machine on the facing page is somehow at the threshold for universality in Turing machines.

But as one might expect from the discoveries in this book, this is far from correct. And in fact, by using the universality of rule 110 it turns out to be possible to come up with the vastly simpler universal Turing machine shown below—with just 2 states and 5 possible colors.

The rule for the simplest Turing machine currently known to be universal, based on discoveries in this book. The machine has 2 states and 5 possible colors.

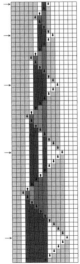

Turing machine evolution

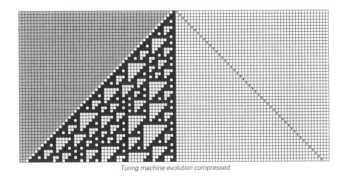

Turing machine evolution compressed

An example of how the Turing machine above manages to emulate rule 110. The compressed picture is made by keeping only the steps indicated at which the head is further to the right than ever before. To get the picture shown requires running the Turing machine for a total of 5000 steps.

As the picture at the bottom of the previous page illustrates, this Turing machine emulates rule 110 in a quite straightforward way: its head moves systematically backwards and forwards, at each complete sweep updating all cells according to a single step of rule 110 evolution. And knowing from earlier in this chapter that rule 110 is universal, it then follows that the 2-state 5-color Turing machine must also be universal.

So is this then the simplest possible universal Turing machine?

I am quite certain that it is not. And in fact I expect that there are some significantly simpler ones. But just how simple can they actually be?

If one looks at the 4096 Turing machines with 2 states and 2 colors it is fairly easy to see that their behavior is in all cases too simple to support universality. So between 2 states and 2 colors and 2 states and 5 colors, where does the threshold for universality in Turing machines lie?

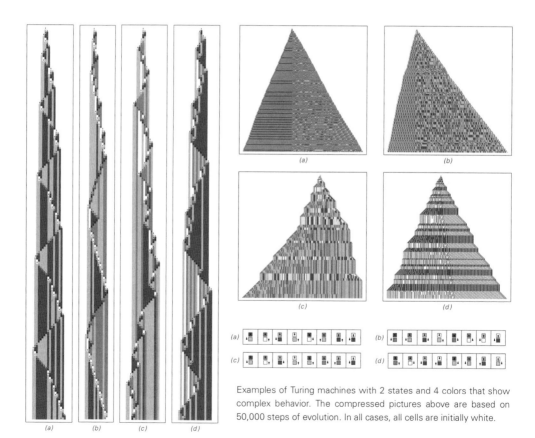

Examples of Turing machines with 2 states and 4 colors that show complex behavior. The compressed pictures above are based on 50,000 steps of evolution. In all cases, all cells are initially white.

The pictures at the bottom of the facing page give examples of some 2-state 4-color Turing machines that show complex behavior. And I have little doubt that most if not all of these are universal.

Among such 2-state 4-color Turing machines perhaps one in 50,000 shows complex behavior when started from a blank tape. Among 4-state 2-color Turing machines the same kind of complex behavior is also seen—as discussed on page 81—but now it occurs only in perhaps one out of 200,000 cases.

So what about Turing machines with 2 states and 3 colors? There are a total of 2,985,984 of these. And most of them yield fairly simple behavior. But it turns out that 14 of them—all essentially equivalent—produce considerable complexity, even when started from a blank tape.

The picture below shows an example.

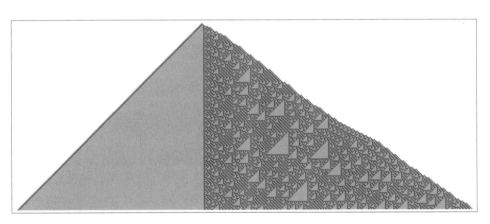

One of the 14 essentially equivalent 2-state 3-color Turing machines that yield complicated behavior when started from a blank tape. The compressed picture above is made by taking the first 100,000 steps, and keeping only those at which the head is further to the left than ever before. The interior of the pattern that emerges is like an inverted version of the rule 60 additive cellular automaton; the boundary, however, is more complicated. In the numbering scheme of page 761 this is machine 596,440 out of the total of 2,985,984 with 2 states and 3 colors.

And although it will no doubt be very difficult to prove, it seems likely that this Turing machine will in the end turn out to be universal. And if so, then presumably it will by most measures be the very simplest Turing machine that is universal.

With 3 states and 2 colors it turns out that with blank initial conditions all of the 2,985,984 possible Turing machines of this type quickly evolve to produce simple repetitive or nested behavior. With more complicated initial conditions the behavior one sees can sometimes be more complicated, at least for a while—as in the pictures below. But in the end it still always seems to resolve into a simple form.

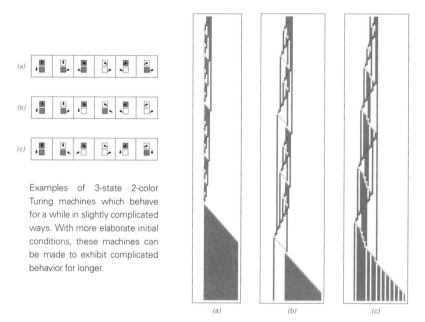

Examples of 3-state 2-color Turing machines which behave for a while in slightly complicated ways. With more elaborate initial conditions, these machines can be made to exhibit complicated behavior for longer.

Yet despite this, it still seems conceivable that with appropriate initial conditions significantly more complex behavior might occur—and might ultimately allow universality in 3-state 2-color Turing machines.

From the universality of rule 110 we know that if one just starts enumerating cellular automata in a particular order, then after going through at most 110 rules, one will definitely see universality. And from other results earlier in this chapter it seems likely that in fact one would tend to see universality even somewhat earlier—after going through only perhaps just ten or twenty rules.

Among Turing machines, the universal 2-state 5-color rule on page 707 can be assigned the number 8,679,752,795,626. So this means that after going through perhaps nine trillion Turing machines one will definitely tend to find an example that is universal. But presumably one will actually find examples much earlier—since for example the 2-state 3-color machine on page 709 is only number 596,440.

And although these numbers are larger than for cellular automata, the fact remains that the simplest potentially universal Turing machines are still very simple in structure, suggesting that the threshold for universality in Turing machines—just like in cellular automata—is in many respects very low.

So what about other types of systems?

I suspect that in almost any case where we have seen complex behavior earlier in this book it will eventually be possible to show that there is universality. And indeed, as I will discuss at length in the next chapter, I believe that in general there is a close connection between universality and the appearance of complex behavior.

Previous examples of systems that are known to be universal have typically had rules that are far too complicated to see this with any clarity. But an almost unique instance where it could potentially have been seen even long ago are what are known as combinators.

Combinators are a particular case of the symbolic systems that we discussed on page 102 of Chapter 3. Originally intended as an idealized way to represent structures of functions defined in logic, combinators were actually first introduced in 1920—sixteen years before Turing machines. But although they have been investigated somewhat over the past eighty years, they have for the most part been viewed as rather obscure and irrelevant constructs.

The basic rules for combinators are given below.

$$s[x\_][y\_][z\_] \rightarrow x[z][y[z]]$$
$$k[x\_][y\_] \rightarrow x$$

Rules for symbolic systems known as combinators, first introduced in 1920, and proved universal by the mid-1930s.

With short initial conditions, the pictures at the top of the next page demonstrate that combinators tend to evolve quickly to simple fixed points. But with initial condition (e) of length 8 the pictures show

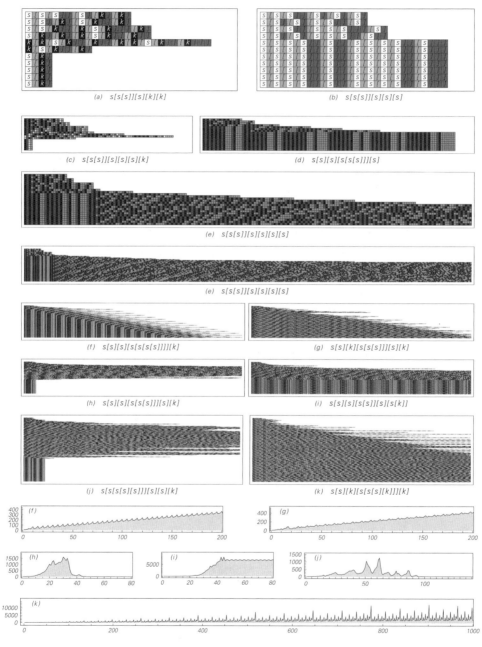

Examples of combinator evolution. The expression in case (e) is the shortest that leads to unlimited growth. The plots at the bottom show the total sizes of expressions reached on successive steps. Note that the detailed pattern of evolution—though not any final fixed point reached—can depend on the fact that the combinator rules are applied at each step in *Mathematica* /. order.

that no fixed point is reached, and instead there is exponential growth in total size—with apparently rather random internal behavior.

Other combinators yield still more complicated behavior—sometimes with overall repetition or nesting, but often not.

There are features of combinators that are not easy to capture directly in pictures. But from pictures like the ones on the facing page it is rather clear that despite their fairly simple underlying rules, the behavior of combinators can be highly complex.

And while issues of typical behavior have not really been studied before, it has been known that combinators are universal almost since the concept of universality was first introduced in the 1930s.

One way that we can now show this is to demonstrate that combinators can emulate rule 110. And as the pictures on the next page illustrate, it turns out that just repeatedly applying the combinator expression below reproduces successive steps in the evolution of rule 110.

```
s[s[k[s]][s[k[s[s[k][k]]]][s[k[k]][s[s[s[s[k][k]][k[s[k]]]][k[s[s[k[s]][s[k[s[s[k][k]]]][s[k[k]][s[s[k[
s]][s[k[s[s[k][k]]]][s[k[k]][s[s[k][k]][k[k]]]]]][s[k[k]][s[s[k][k]][k[s[k]]][k[s[k]]]]]]]][s[k[k]][s[s[
s[k][k]][k[s[k]]]]][k[k]]]]]][s[k[s[s[k][k]][k[s[s[k][k]][k[s[s[k][k]]][k[k]]]][k[k]]]]]][s[k[
k]]][s[s[s[s[k][k]]][k[s[k]]][k[s[s[k][k]]][s[k[s[k][k]]]][s[k[k]][s[s[k][k]][k[k]]][k[k]]]]][s[k[k]]][
s[s[k[s]][s[k[s[s[k][k]]]][s[k[k]][s[s[k][k]][k[s[k]]]]]]][s[k[k]][s[s[s[s[k][k]][k[k]]][k[s[k]]]]][s[s[s[
s[k][k]]][k[k]]]][k[k]]]][k[s[k]]]]][s[s[s[s[s[k][k]][k[k]]][k[k]]]][k[s[k]]]]][k[s[k]]]]][s[s[s[s[s[k][
k]]][k[k]]]][k[s[k]]]]][k[s[k]]]][k[k]]]]]]]][s[s[k[s]]][s[k[s[s[k][k]]]][s[k[k]][s[s[s[s[k]][
k[s[k][k]]]]][s[k[k]]][s[s[k][k]][k[k]]]]]]]][k[k[k]]]]]][k[k[k]]]][k[s[k]]]]]]]][k[k]]]]]][s[k[k]]][s[k[s[s[
k[s]]][k]]]][s[s[k][k]][k[s[k]]]]]]]]
```

A combinator expression that corresponds to the operation of doing one step of rule 110 evolution.

There has in the past been no overall context for understanding universality in combinators. But now what we have seen suggests that such universality is in a sense just associated with general complex behavior.

Yet we saw in Chapter 3 that there are symbolic systems with rules even simpler than combinators that still show complex behavior. And so now I suspect that these too are universal.

And in fact wherever one looks, the threshold for universality seems to be much lower than one would ever have imagined. And this is one of the important basic observations that led me to formulate the Principle of Computational Equivalence that I discuss in the next chapter.

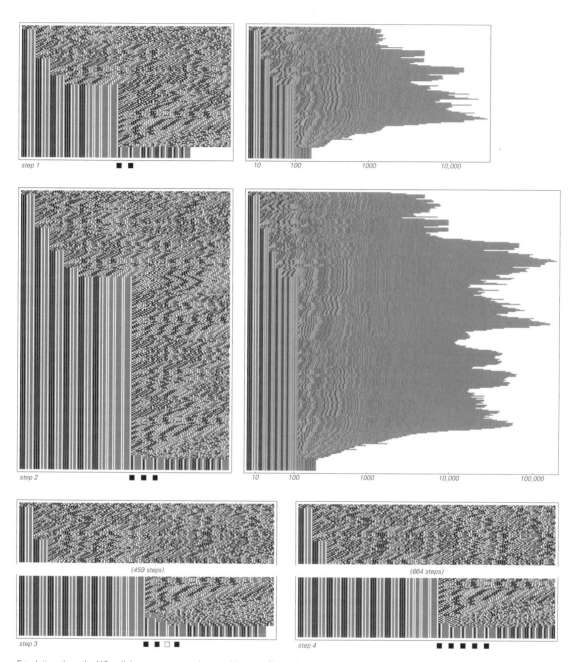

Emulating the rule 110 cellular automaton using combinators. The rule 110 combinator from the previous page is applied once for each step of rule 110 evolution. The initial state is taken to consist of a single black cell.

12

The Principle of
Computational Equivalence

Basic Framework

Following the discussion of the notion of computation in the previous chapter, I am now ready in this chapter to describe a bold hypothesis that I have developed on the basis of the discoveries in this book, and that I call the Principle of Computational Equivalence.

Among principles in science the Principle of Computational Equivalence is almost unprecedentedly broad—for it applies to essentially any process of any kind, either natural or artificial. And its implications are both broad and deep, addressing a host of longstanding issues not only in science, but also in mathematics, philosophy and elsewhere.

The key unifying idea that has allowed me to formulate the Principle of Computational Equivalence is a simple but immensely powerful one: that all processes, whether they are produced by human effort or occur spontaneously in nature, can be viewed as computations.

In our practical experience with computers, we are mostly concerned with computations that have been set up specifically to perform particular tasks. But as I discussed at the beginning of this book there is nothing fundamental that requires a computation to have any such definite purpose. And as I discussed in the previous chapter the process of evolution of a system like a cellular automaton can for example perfectly well be viewed as a computation, even though in a sense all the computation does is generate the behavior of the system.

But what about processes in nature? Can these also be viewed as computations? Or does the notion of computation somehow apply only to systems with abstract elements like, say, the black and white cells in a cellular automaton?

Before the advent of modern computer applications one might have assumed that it did. But now every day we see computations being done with a vast range of different kinds of data—from numbers to text to images to almost anything else. And what this suggests is that it is possible to think of any process that follows definite rules as being a computation—regardless of the kinds of elements it involves.

So in particular this implies that it should be possible to think of processes in nature as computations. And indeed in the end the only unfamiliar aspect of this is that the rules such processes follow are defined not by some computer program that we as humans construct but rather by the basic laws of nature.

But whatever the details of the rules involved the crucial point is that it is possible to view every process that occurs in nature or elsewhere as a computation. And it is this remarkable uniformity that makes it possible to formulate a principle as broad and powerful as the Principle of Computational Equivalence.

Outline of the Principle

Across all the vastly different processes that we see in nature and in systems that we construct one might at first think that there could be very little in common. But the idea that any process whatsoever can be viewed as a computation immediately provides at least a uniform framework in which to discuss different processes.

And it is by using this framework that the Principle of Computational Equivalence is formulated. For what the principle does is to assert that when viewed in computational terms there is a fundamental equivalence between many different kinds of processes.

There are various ways to state the Principle of Computational Equivalence, but probably the most general is just to say that almost all processes that are not obviously simple can be viewed as computations of equivalent sophistication.

And although at first this statement might seem vague and perhaps almost inconsequential, we will see in the course of this chapter that in fact it has many very specific and dramatic implications.

One might have assumed that among different processes there would be a vast range of different levels of computational sophistication. But the remarkable assertion that the Principle of Computational Equivalence makes is that in practice this is not the case, and that instead there is essentially just one highest level of computational sophistication, and this is achieved by almost all processes that do not seem obviously simple.

So what might lead one to this rather surprising idea? An important clue comes from the phenomenon of universality that I discussed in the previous chapter and that has been responsible for much of the success of modern computer technology. For the essence of this phenomenon is that it is possible to construct universal systems that can perform essentially any computation—and which must therefore all in a sense be capable of exhibiting the highest level of computational sophistication.

The most familiar examples of universal systems today are practical computers and general-purpose computer languages. But in the fifty or so years since the phenomenon of universality was first identified, all sorts of types of systems have been found to be able to exhibit universality. Indeed, as I showed in the previous chapter, it is possible for example to get universality in cellular automata, Turing machines, register machines—or in fact in practically every kind of system that I have considered in this book.

So this implies that from a computational point of view even systems with quite different underlying structures will still usually show a certain kind of equivalence, in that rules can be found for them that achieve universality—and that therefore can always exhibit the same level of computational sophistication.

But while this is already a remarkable result, it represents only a first step in the direction of the Principle of Computational

Equivalence. For what the result implies is that in many kinds of systems particular rules can be found that achieve universality and thus show the same level of computational sophistication. But the result says nothing about whether such rules are somehow typical, or are instead very rare and special.

And in practice, almost without exception, the actual rules that have been established to be universal have tended to be quite complex. Indeed, most often they have in effect been engineered out of all sorts of components that are direct idealizations of various elaborate structures that exist in practical digital electronic computers.

And on the basis of traditional intuition it has almost always been assumed that this is somehow inevitable, and that in order to get something as sophisticated as universality there must be no choice but to set up rules that are themselves special and sophisticated.

One of the dramatic discoveries of this book, however, is that this is not the case, and that in fact even extremely simple rules can be universal. Indeed, from our discussion in the previous chapter, we already know that among the 256 very simplest possible cellular automaton rules at least rule 110 and three others like it are universal.

And my strong suspicion is that this is just the beginning, and that in time a fair fraction of other simple rules will also be shown to be universal. For one of the implications of the Principle of Computational Equivalence is that almost any rule whose behavior is not obviously simple should ultimately be capable of achieving the same level of computational sophistication and should thus in effect be universal.

So far from universality being some rare and special property that exists only in systems that have carefully been built to exhibit it, the Principle of Computational Equivalence implies that instead this property should be extremely common. And among other things this means that universality can be expected to occur not only in many kinds of abstract systems but also in all sorts of systems in nature.

And as we shall see in this chapter, this idea already has many important and surprising consequences. But still it is far short of what the full Principle of Computational Equivalence has to say.

For knowing that a particular rule is universal just tells one that it is possible to set up initial conditions that will cause a sophisticated computation to occur. But it does not tell one what will happen if, for example, one starts from typical simple initial conditions.

Yet the Principle of Computational Equivalence asserts that even in such a case, whenever the behavior one sees is not obviously simple, it will almost always correspond to a computation of equivalent sophistication.

So what this means is that even, say, in cellular automata that start from very simple initial conditions, one can expect that those aspects of their behavior that do not look obviously simple will usually correspond to computations of equivalent sophistication.

According to the Principle of Computational Equivalence therefore it does not matter how simple or complicated either the rules or the initial conditions for a process are: so long as the process itself does not look obviously simple, then it will almost always correspond to a computation of equivalent sophistication.

And what this suggests is that a fundamental unity exists across a vast range of processes in nature and elsewhere: despite all their detailed differences every process can be viewed as corresponding to a computation that is ultimately equivalent in its sophistication.

The Content of the Principle

Like many other fundamental principles in science, the Principle of Computational Equivalence can be viewed in part as a new law of nature, in part as an abstract fact and in part as a definition. For in one sense it tells us what kinds of computations can and cannot happen in our universe, yet it also summarizes purely abstract deductions about possible computations, and provides foundations for more general definitions of the very concept of computation.

Without the Principle of Computational Equivalence one might assume that different systems would always be able to perform completely different computations, and that in particular there would be no upper limit on the sophistication of computations that systems with sufficiently complicated structures would be able to perform.

But the discussion of universality in the previous chapter already suggests that this is not the case. For it implies that at least across the kinds of systems that we considered in that chapter there is in fact an upper limit on the sophistication of computations that can be done.

For as we discussed, once one has a universal system such a system can emulate any of the kinds of systems that we considered—even ones whose construction is more complicated than its own. So this means that whatever kinds of computations can be done by the universal system, none of the other systems will ever be able to do computations that have any higher level of sophistication.

And as a result it has often seemed reasonable to define what one means by a computation as being precisely something that can be done by a universal system of the kind we discussed in the previous chapter.

But despite this, at an abstract level one can always imagine having systems that do computations beyond what any of the cellular automata, Turing machines or other types of systems in the previous chapter can do. For as soon as one identifies any such class of computations, one can imagine setting up a system which includes an infinite table of their results.

But even though one can perfectly well imagine such a system, the Principle of Computational Equivalence makes the assertion that no such system could ever in fact be constructed in our actual universe.

In essence, therefore, the Principle of Computational Equivalence introduces a new law of nature to the effect that no system can ever carry out explicit computations that are more sophisticated than those carried out by systems like cellular automata and Turing machines.

So what might make one think that this is true? One important piece of evidence is the success of the various models of natural systems that I have discussed in this book based on systems like cellular automata. But despite these successes, one might still imagine that other systems could exist in nature that are based, say, on continuous mathematics, and which would allow computations more sophisticated than those in systems like cellular automata to be done.

Needless to say, I do not believe that this is the case, and in fact if one could find a truly fundamental theory of physics along the lines I discussed in Chapter 9 it would actually be possible to establish this with complete certainty. For such a theory would have the feature that it could be emulated by a universal system of the type I discussed in the previous chapter—with the result that nowhere in our universe could computations ever occur that are more sophisticated than those carried out by the universal systems we have discussed.

So what about computations that we perform abstractly with computers or in our brains? Can these perhaps be more sophisticated? Presumably they cannot, at least if we want actual results, and not just generalities. For if a computation is to be carried out explicitly, then it must ultimately be implemented as a physical process, and must therefore be subject to the same limitations as any such process.

But as I discussed in the previous section, beyond asserting that there is an upper limit to computational sophistication, the Principle of Computational Equivalence also makes the much stronger statement that almost all processes except those that are obviously simple actually achieve this limit.

And this is related to what I believe is a very fundamental abstract fact: that among all possible systems with behavior that is not obviously simple an overwhelming fraction are universal.

So what would be involved in establishing this fact?

One could imagine doing much as I did early in this book and successively looking at every possible rule for some type of system like a cellular automaton. And if one did this what one would find is that many of the rules exhibit obviously simple repetitive or nested behavior. But as I discovered early in this book, many also do not, and instead exhibit behavior that is often vastly more complex.

And what the Principle of Computational Equivalence then asserts is that the vast majority of such rules will be universal.

If one starts from scratch then it is not particularly difficult to construct rules—though usually fairly complicated ones—that one knows are universal. And from the result in the previous chapter that rule 110 is universal it follows for example that any rule containing this one must also be universal. But if one is just given an arbitrary rule—

and especially a simple one—then it can be extremely difficult to determine whether or not the rule is universal.

As we discussed in the previous chapter, the usual way to demonstrate that a rule is universal is to find a scheme for setting up initial conditions and for decoding output that makes the rule emulate some other rule that is already known to be universal.

But the problem is that in any particular case there is almost no limit on how complicated such a scheme might need to be. In fact, about the only restriction is that the scheme itself should not exhibit universality just in setting up initial conditions and decoding output.

And indeed it is almost inevitable that the scheme will have to be at least somewhat complicated: for if a system is to be universal then it must be able to emulate any of the huge range of other systems that are universal—with the result that specifying which particular such system it is going to emulate for the purposes of a proof will typically require giving a fair amount of information, all of which must somehow be part of the encoding scheme.

It is often even more difficult to prove that a system is not universal than to prove that it is. For what one needs to show is that no possible scheme can be devised that will allow the system to emulate any other universal system. And usually the only way to be sure of this is to have a more or less complete analysis of all possible behavior that the system can exhibit.

If this behavior always has an obvious repetitive or nested form then it will often be quite straightforward to analyze. But as we saw in Chapter 10, in almost no other case do standard methods of perception and analysis allow one to make much progress at all.

As mentioned in Chapter 10, however, I do know of a few systems based on numbers for which a fairly complete analysis can be given even though the overall behavior is not repetitive or nested or otherwise obviously simple. And no doubt some other examples like this do exist. But it is my strong belief—as embodied in the Principle of Computational Equivalence—that in the end the vast majority of systems whose behavior is not obviously simple will turn out to be universal.

If one tries to use some kind of systematic procedure to test whether systems are universal then inevitably there will be three types of outcomes. Sometimes the procedure will successfully prove that a system is universal, and sometimes it will prove that it is not. But very often the procedure will simply come to no definite conclusion, even after spending a large amount of effort.

Yet in almost all such cases the Principle of Computational Equivalence asserts that the systems are in fact universal. And although almost inevitably it will never be easy to prove this in any great generality, my guess is that, as the decades go by, more and more specific rules will end up being proved to exhibit universality.

But even if one becomes convinced of the abstract fact that out of all possible rules that do not yield obviously simple behavior the vast majority are universal, this still does not quite establish the assertion made by the Principle of Computational Equivalence that rules of this kind that appear in nature and elsewhere are almost always universal.

For it could still be that the particular rules that appear are somehow specially selected to be ones that are not universal. And certainly there are all sorts of situations in which rules are constrained to have behavior that is too simple to support universality. Thus, for example, in most kinds of engineering one tends to pick rules whose behavior is simple enough that one can readily predict it. And as I discussed in Chapter 8, something similar seems to happen with rules in biology that are determined by natural selection.

But when there are no constraints that force simple overall behavior, my guess is that most rules that appear in nature can be viewed as being selected in no special way—save perhaps for the fact that the structure of the rules themselves tends to be fairly simple.

And what this means is that such rules will typically show the same features as rules chosen at random from all possibilities—with the result that presumably they do in the end exhibit universality in almost all cases where their overall behavior is not obviously simple.

But even if a wide range of systems can indeed be shown to be universal this is still not enough to establish the full Principle of Computational Equivalence. For the Principle of Computational

Equivalence is concerned not only with the computational sophistication of complete systems but also with the computational sophistication of specific processes that occur within systems.

And when one says that a particular system is universal what one means is that it is possible by choosing appropriate initial conditions to make the system perform computations of essentially any sophistication. But from this there is no guarantee that the vast majority of initial conditions—including perhaps all those that could readily arise in nature—will not just yield behavior that corresponds only to very simple computations.

And indeed in the proof of the universality of rule 110 in the previous chapter extremely complicated initial conditions were used to perform even rather simple computations.

But the Principle of Computational Equivalence asserts that in fact even if it comes from simple initial conditions almost all behavior that is not obviously simple will in the end correspond to computations of equivalent sophistication.

And certainly there are all sorts of pictures in this book that lend support to this idea. For over and over again we have seen that simple initial conditions are quite sufficient to produce behavior of immense complexity, and that making the initial conditions more complicated typically does not lead to behavior that looks any different.

Quite often part of the reason for this, as illustrated in the pictures on the facing page, is that even with a single very simple initial condition the actual evolution of a system will generate blocks that correspond to essentially all possible initial conditions. And this means that whatever behavior would be seen with a given overall initial condition, that same behavior will also be seen at appropriate places in the single pattern generated from a specific initial condition.

So this suggests a way of having something analogous to universality in a single pattern instead of in a complete system. The idea would be that a pattern that is universal could serve as a kind of directory of possible computations—with different regions in the pattern giving results for all possible different initial conditions.

Occurrences of progressively longer blocks in the pattern generated by rule 30 starting from a single black cell. So far as I can tell, all possible blocks eventually appear, potentially letting the pattern serve as a kind of directory of all possible computations.

So as a simple example one could imagine having a pattern laid out on a three-dimensional array with each successive vertical plane giving the evolution of some one-dimensional universal system from each of its successive possible initial conditions. And with this setup any computation, regardless of its sophistication, must appear somewhere in the pattern.

In a pattern like the one obtained from rule 30 above different computations are presumably not arranged in any such straightforward way. But I strongly suspect that even though it may be quite impractical to find particular computations that one wants, it is still the case that essentially any possible computation exists somewhere in the pattern.

Much as in the case of universality for complete systems, however, the Principle of Computational Equivalence does not just say that a sophisticated computation will be found somewhere in a pattern produced by a system like rule 30. Rather, it asserts that unless it is obviously simple essentially any behavior that one sees should correspond to a computation of equivalent sophistication.

And in a sense this can be viewed as providing a new way to define the very notion of computation. For it implies that essentially any piece of complex behavior that we see corresponds to a kind of lump of computation that is at some level equivalent.

It is a little like what happens in thermodynamics, where all sorts of complicated microscopic motions are identified as corresponding in some uniform way to a notion of heat.

But computation is both a much more general and much more powerful notion than heat. And as a result, the Principle of Computational Equivalence has vastly richer implications than the laws of thermodynamics—or for that matter, than essentially any single collection of laws in science.

The Validity of the Principle

With the intuition of traditional science the Principle of Computational Equivalence—and particularly many of its implications—might seem almost absurd. But as I have developed more and more new intuition from the discoveries in this book so I have become more and more certain that the Principle of Computational Equivalence must be valid.

But like any principle in science with real content it could in the future always be found that at least some aspect of the Principle of Computational Equivalence is not valid. For as a law of nature the principle could turn out to disagree with what is observed in our universe, while as an abstract fact it could simply represent an incorrect deduction, and even as a definition it could prove not useful or relevant.

But as more and more evidence is accumulated for phenomena that would follow from the principle, so it becomes more and more reasonable to expect that at least in some formulation or another the principle itself must be valid.

As with many fundamental principles the most general statement of the Principle of Computational Equivalence may at first seem quite vague. But almost any specific application of the principle will tend to suggest more specific and precise statements.

Needless to say, it will always be possible to come up with statements that might seem related to the Principle of Computational Equivalence but are not in fact the same. And indeed I suspect this will happen many times over the years to come. For if one tries to use methods from traditional science and mathematics it is almost inevitable that one will be led to statements that are rather different from the actual Principle of Computational Equivalence.

Indeed, my guess is that there is basically no way to formulate an accurate statement of the principle except by using methods from the kind of science introduced in this book. And what this means is that almost any statement that can, for example, readily be investigated by the traditional methods of mathematical proof will tend to be largely irrelevant to the true Principle of Computational Equivalence.

In the course of this book I have made a variety of discoveries that can be interpreted as limited versions of the Principle of Computational Equivalence. And as the years and decades go by, it is my expectation that many more such discoveries will be made. And as these discoveries are absorbed, I suspect that general intuition in science will gradually shift, until in the end the Principle of Computational Equivalence will come to seem almost obvious.

But as of now the principle is far from obvious to most of those whose intuition is derived from traditional science. And as a result all sorts of objections to the principle will no doubt be raised. Some of them will presumably be based on believing that actual systems have less computational sophistication than is implied by the principle, while others will be based on believing that they have more.

But at an underlying level I suspect that the single most common cause of objections will be confusion about various idealizations that are made in traditional models for systems. For even though a system itself may follow the Principle of Computational Equivalence, there is no guarantee that this will also be true of idealizations of the system.

As I discussed at the beginning of Chapter 8, finding a good model for a system is mostly about finding idealizations that are as simple as possible, but that nevertheless still capture the important features of the system. And the point is that in the past there was never a clear idea that computational capabilities of systems might be important, so these were usually not captured correctly when models were made.

Yet one of the characteristics of the kinds of models based on simple programs that I have developed in this book is that they do appear successfully to capture the computational capabilities of a wide range of systems in nature and elsewhere. And in the context of such models what I have discovered is that there is indeed all sorts of evidence for the Principle of Computational Equivalence.

But if one uses the kinds of traditional mathematical models that have in the past been common, things can seem rather different.

For example, many such models idealize systems to the point where their complete behavior can be described just by some simple mathematical formula that relates a few overall numerical quantities. And if one thinks only about this idealization one almost inevitably concludes that the system has very little computational sophistication.

It is also common for traditional mathematical models to suggest too much computational sophistication. For example, as I discussed at the end of Chapter 7, models based on traditional mathematical equations often give constraints on behavior rather than explicit rules for generating behavior.

And if one assumes that actual systems somehow always manage to find ways to satisfy such constraints, one will be led to conclude that these systems must be computationally more sophisticated than any of the universal systems I have discussed—and must thus violate the Principle of Computational Equivalence.

For as I will describe in more detail later in this chapter, an ordinary universal system cannot in any finite number of steps guarantee to be able to tell whether, say, there is any pattern of black and white squares that satisfies some constraint of the type I discussed at the end of Chapter 5. Yet traditional mathematical models often in effect imply that systems in nature can do things like this.

But I explained at the end of Chapter 7 this is presumably just an idealization. For while in simple cases complicated molecules may for example arrange themselves in configurations that minimize energy, the evidence is that in more complicated cases they typically do not. And in fact, what they actually seem to do is instead to explore different configurations by an explicit process of evolution that is quite consistent with the Principle of Computational Equivalence.

One of the features of cellular automata and most of the other computational systems that I have discussed in this book is that they are in some fundamental sense discrete. Yet traditional mathematical models almost always involve continuous quantities. And this has in the past often been taken to imply that systems in nature are able to do computations that are somehow fundamentally more sophisticated than standard computational systems.

But for several reasons I do not believe this conclusion.

For a start, the experience has been that if one actually tries to build analog computers that make use of continuous physical processes they usually end up being less powerful than ordinary digital computers, rather than more so.

And indeed, as I have discussed several times in this book, it is in many cases clear that the whole notion of continuity is just an idealization—although one that happens to be almost required if one wants to make use of traditional mathematical methods.

Fluids provide one obvious example. For usually they are thought of as being described by continuous mathematical equations. But at an underlying level real fluids consist of discrete particles. And this means that whatever the mathematical equations may suggest, the actual ultimate computational capabilities of fluids must be those of a system of discrete particles.

But while it is known that many systems in nature are made up of discrete elements, it is still almost universally believed that there are some things that are fundamentally continuous—notably positions in space and values of quantum mechanical probability amplitudes.

Yet as I discussed in Chapter 9 my strong suspicion is that at a fundamental level absolutely every aspect of our universe will in the end turn out to be discrete. And if this is so, then it immediately implies that there cannot ever ultimately be any form of continuity in our universe that violates the Principle of Computational Equivalence.

But what if one somehow restricts oneself to a domain where some particular system seems continuous? Can one even at this level perform more sophisticated computations than in a discrete system?

My guess is that for all practical purposes one cannot. Indeed, it is my suspicion that with almost any reasonable set of assumptions even idealized perfectly continuous systems will never in fact be able to perform fundamentally more sophisticated computations.

In a sense the most basic defining characteristic of continuous systems is that they operate on arbitrary continuous numbers. But just to represent every such number in general requires something like an infinite sequence of digits. And so this implies that continuous systems must always in effect be able to operate on infinite sequences.

But in itself this is not particularly remarkable. For even a one-dimensional cellular automaton can be viewed as updating an infinite sequence of cells at every step in its evolution. But one feature of this process is that it is fundamentally local: each cell behaves in a way that is determined purely by cells in a local neighborhood around it.

Yet even the most basic arithmetic operations on continuous numbers typically involve significant non-locality. Thus, for example, when one adds two numbers together there can be carries in the digit sequence that propagate arbitrarily far. And if one computes even a function like $1/x$ almost any digit in x will typically have an effect on almost any digit in the result, as the pictures on the facing page indicate.

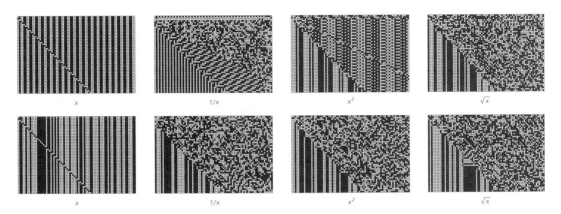

Results from mathematical operations on numbers with similar digit sequences. Each successive line in each picture gives the digit sequence obtained by using a value of x in which one successive digit has been reversed. The top row of pictures start from the repetitive base 2 digit sequence of $x = 3/5$; the bottom row of pictures from $x = \pi/4$. The lack of coherence between successive digit sequences in each picture reflects the non-locality of mathematical operations when applied to digit sequences.

But can this detailed kind of phenomenon really be used as the basis for doing fundamentally more sophisticated computations? To compare the general computational capabilities of continuous and discrete systems one needs to find some basic scheme for constructing inputs and decoding outputs that one can use in both types of systems. And the most obvious and practical approach is to require that this always be done by finite discrete processes.

But at least in this case it seems fairly clear that none of the simple functions shown above can for example ever lead to results that go beyond ones that could readily be generated by the evolution of ordinary discrete systems. And the same is presumably true if one works with essentially any of what are normally considered standard mathematical functions. But what happens if one assumes that one can set up a system that not only finds values of such functions but also finds solutions to arbitrary equations involving them?

With pure polynomial equations one can deduce from results in algebra that no fundamentally more sophisticated computations become possible. But as soon as one even allows trigonometric functions, for example, it turns out that it becomes possible to construct equations for which finding a solution is equivalent to finding the outcome of an infinite number of steps in the evolution of a system like a cellular automaton.

And while these particular types of equations have never seriously been proposed as idealizations of actual processes in nature or elsewhere, it turns out that a related phenomenon can presumably occur in differential equations—which represent the most common basis for mathematical models in most areas of traditional science.

Differential equations of the kind we discussed at the end of Chapter 4 work at some level a little like cellular automata. For given the state of a system, they provide rules for determining its state at subsequent times. But whereas cellular automata always evolve only in discrete steps, differential equations instead go through a continuous process of evolution in which time appears just as a parameter.

And by making simple algebraic changes to the way that time enters a differential equation one can often arrange, as in the pictures below, that processes that would normally take an infinite time will actually always occur over only a finite time.

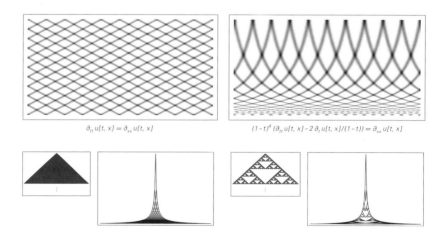

$$\partial_{tt}\, u[t, x] = \partial_{xx}\, u[t, x]$$

$$(1 - t)^4\, (\partial_{tt}\, u[t, x] - 2\, \partial_t\, u[t, x]/(1 - t)) = \partial_{xx}\, u[t, x]$$

Indications of how an infinite amount of computational work can in principle be performed in a finite time in continuous systems like partial differential equations. The top left picture shows a solution to the wave equation. The top right picture shows a solution to an equation obtained from the wave equation by transforming the time variable according to $t \rightarrow 1 - 1/t$. The bottom row shows what the same transformation does to patterns of the kind that are generated by simple cellular automata. It is presumably possible to construct partial differential equations that give both the original and transformed versions of these patterns.

So if such processes can correspond to the evolution of systems like cellular automata, then it follows at least formally that differential equations should be able to do in finite time computations that would take a discrete system like a cellular automaton an infinite time to do.

But just as it is difficult to make an analog computer faithfully reproduce many steps in a discrete computation, so also it seems likely that it will be difficult to set up differential equations that for arbitrarily long times successfully manage to emulate the precise behavior of systems like cellular automata. And in fact my suspicion is that to make this work will require taking limits that are rather similar to following the evolution of the differential equations for an infinite time.

So my guess is that even within the formalism of traditional continuous mathematics realistic idealizations of actual processes will never ultimately be able to perform computations that are more sophisticated than the Principle of Computational Equivalence implies.

But what about the process of human thinking? Does it also follow the Principle of Computational Equivalence? Or does it somehow manage to do computations that are more sophisticated than the Principle of Computational Equivalence implies?

There is a great tendency for us to assume that there must be something extremely sophisticated about human thinking. And certainly the fact that present-day computer systems do not emulate even some of its most obvious features might seem to support this view. But as I discussed in Chapter 10, particularly following the discoveries in this book, it is my strong belief that the basic mechanisms of human thinking will in the end turn out to correspond to rather simple computational processes.

So what all of this suggests is that systems in nature do not perform computations that are more sophisticated than the Principle of Computational Equivalence allows. But on its own this is not enough to establish the complete Principle of Computational Equivalence. For the principle also implies a lower limit on computational sophistication— making the assertion that almost any process that is not obviously simple will tend to be equivalent in its computational sophistication.

And one of the consequences of this is that it implies that most systems whose behavior seems complex should be universal. Yet as of now we only know for certain about fairly few systems that are universal, albeit including ones like rule 110 that have remarkably simple rules. And no doubt the objection will be raised that other systems whose behavior seems complex may not in fact be universal.

In particular, it might be thought that the behavior of systems like rule 30—while obviously at least somewhat computationally sophisticated—might somehow be too random to be harnessed to allow complete universality. And although in Chapter 11 I did give a few pieces of evidence that point towards rule 30 being universal, there can still be doubts until this has been proved for certain.

And in fact there is a particularly abstruse result in mathematical logic that might be thought to show that systems can exist that exhibit some features of arbitrarily sophisticated computation, but which are nevertheless not universal. For in the late 1950s a whole hierarchy of systems with so-called intermediate degrees were constructed with the property that questions about the ultimate output from their evolution could not in general be answered by finite computation, but for which the actual form of this output was not flexible enough to be able to emulate a full range of other systems, and thus support universality.

But when one examines the known examples of such systems—all of which have very intricate underlying rules—one finds that even though the particular part of their behavior that is identified as output is sufficiently restricted to avoid universality, almost every other part of their behavior nevertheless does exhibit universality—just as one would expect from the Principle of Computational Equivalence.

So why else might systems like rule 30 fail to be universal? We know from Chapter 11 that systems whose behavior is purely repetitive or purely nested cannot be universal. And so we might wonder whether perhaps some other form of regularity could be present that would prevent systems like rule 30 from being universal.

When we look at the patterns produced by such systems they certainly do not seem to have any great regularity; indeed in most respects they seem far more random than patterns produced by systems like rule 110 that we already know are universal.

But how can we be sure that we are not being misled by limitations in our powers of perception and analysis—and that an extraterrestrial intelligence, for example, might not immediately recognize regularity that would show that universality is impossible?

For as we saw in Chapter 10 the methods of perception and analysis that we normally use cannot detect any form of regularity much beyond repetition or at most nesting. So this means that even if some higher form of regularity is in fact present, we as humans might never be able to tell.

In the history of science and mathematics both repetition and nesting feature prominently. And if there was some common higher form of regularity its discovery would no doubt lead to all sorts of important new advances in science and mathematics.

And when I first started looking at systems like cellular automata I in effect implicitly assumed that some such form of regularity must exist. For I was quite certain that even though I saw behavior that seemed to me complex the simplicity of the underlying rules must somehow ultimately lead to great regularity in it.

But as the years have gone by—and as I have investigated more and more systems and tried more and more methods of analysis—I have gradually come to the conclusion that there is no hidden regularity in any large class of systems, and that instead what the Principle of Computational Equivalence suggests is correct: that beyond systems with obvious regularities like repetition and nesting most systems are universal, and are equivalent in their computational sophistication.

Explaining the Phenomenon of Complexity

Early in this book I described the remarkable discovery that even systems with extremely simple underlying rules can produce behavior that seems to us immensely complex. And in the course of this book, I have shown a great many examples of this phenomenon, and have argued that it is responsible for much of the complexity we see in nature and elsewhere.

Yet so far I have given no fundamental explanation for the phenomenon. But now, by making use of the Principle of Computational Equivalence, I am finally able to do this.

And the crucial point is to think of comparing the computational sophistication of systems that we study with the computational sophistication of the systems that we use to study them.

At first we might assume that our brains and mathematical methods would always be capable of vastly greater computational sophistication than systems based on simple rules—and that as a result the behavior of such systems would inevitably seem to us fairly simple.

But the Principle of Computational Equivalence implies that this is not the case. For it asserts that essentially any processes that are not obviously simple are equivalent in their computational sophistication. So this means that even though a system may have simple underlying rules its process of evolution can still computationally be just as sophisticated as any of the processes we use for perception and analysis.

And this is the fundamental reason that systems with simple rules are able to show behavior that seems to us complex.

At first, one might think that this explanation would depend on the particular methods of perception and analysis that we as humans happen to use. But one of the consequences of the Principle of Computational Equivalence is that it does not. For the principle asserts that the same computational equivalence exists for absolutely any method of perception and analysis that can actually be used.

In traditional science the idealization is usually made that perception and analysis are in a sense infinitely powerful, so that they need not be taken into account when one draws conclusions about a system. But as soon as one tries to deal with systems whose behavior is anything but fairly simple one finds that this idealization breaks down, and it becomes necessary to consider perception and analysis as explicit processes in their own right.

If one studies systems in nature it is inevitable that both the evolution of the systems themselves and the methods of perception and analysis used to study them must be processes based on natural laws. But at least in the recent history of science it has normally been assumed that the evolution of typical systems in nature is somehow much less sophisticated a process than perception and analysis.

Yet what the Principle of Computational Equivalence now asserts is that this is not the case, and that once a rather low threshold has been reached, any real system must exhibit essentially the same level of computational sophistication. So this means that observers will tend to be computationally equivalent to the systems they observe—with the inevitable consequence that they will consider the behavior of such systems complex.

So in the end the fact that we see so much complexity can be attributed quite directly to the Principle of Computational Equivalence, and to the fact that so many of the systems we encounter in practice turn out to be computationally equivalent.

Computational Irreducibility

When viewed in computational terms most of the great historical triumphs of theoretical science turn out to be remarkably similar in their basic character. For at some level almost all of them are based on finding ways to reduce the amount of computational work that has to be done in order to predict how some particular system will behave.

Most of the time the idea is to derive a mathematical formula that allows one to determine what the outcome of the evolution of the system will be without explicitly having to trace its steps.

And thus, for example, an early triumph of theoretical science was the derivation of a formula for the position of a single idealized planet orbiting a star. For given this formula one can just plug in numbers to work out where the planet will be at any point in the future, without ever explicitly having to trace the steps in its motion.

But part of what started my whole effort to develop the new kind of science in this book was the realization that there are many common systems for which no traditional mathematical formulas have ever been found that readily describe their overall behavior.

At first one might have thought this must be some kind of temporary issue, that could be overcome with sufficient cleverness. But from the discoveries in this book I have come to the conclusion that in fact it is not, and that instead it is one of the consequences of a very fundamental phenomenon that follows from the Principle of Computational Equivalence and that I call computational irreducibility.

If one views the evolution of a system as a computation, then each step in this evolution can be thought of as taking a certain amount of computational effort on the part of the system. But what traditional theoretical science in a sense implicitly relies on is that much of this effort is somehow unnecessary—and that in fact it should be possible to find the outcome of the evolution with much less effort.

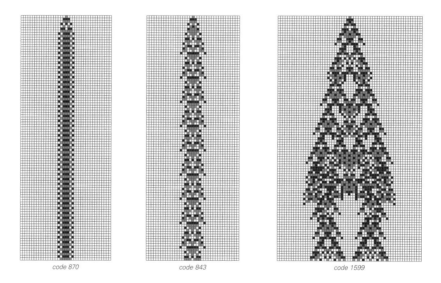

code 870   code 843   code 1599

Examples of computational reducibility and irreducibility in the evolution of cellular automata. The first two rules yield simple repetitive computationally reducible behavior in which the outcome after many steps can readily be deduced without tracing each step. The third rule yields behavior that appears to be computationally irreducible, so that its outcome can effectively be found only by explicitly tracing each step. The cellular automata shown here all have 3-color totalistic rules.

And certainly in the first two examples above this is the case. For just as with the orbit of an idealized planet there is in effect a straightforward formula that gives the state of each system after any number of steps. So even though the systems themselves generate their behavior by going through a whole sequence of steps, we can readily shortcut this process and find the outcome with much less effort.

But what about the third example on the facing page? What does it take to find the outcome in this case? It is always possible to do an experiment and explicitly run the system for a certain number of steps and see how it behaves. But to have any kind of traditional theory one must find a shortcut that involves much less computation.

Yet from the picture on the facing page it is certainly not obvious how one might do this. And looking at the pictures on the next page it begins to seem quite implausible that there could ever in fact be any way to find a significant shortcut in the evolution of this system.

So while the behavior of the first two systems on the facing page is readily seen to be computationally reducible, the behavior of the third system appears instead to be computationally irreducible.

In traditional science it has usually been assumed that if one can succeed in finding definite underlying rules for a system then this means that ultimately there will always be a fairly easy way to predict how the system will behave.

Several decades ago chaos theory pointed out that to have enough information to make complete predictions one must in general know not only the rules for a system but also its complete initial conditions.

But now computational irreducibility leads to a much more fundamental problem with prediction. For it implies that even if in principle one has all the information one needs to work out how some particular system will behave, it can still take an irreducible amount of computational work actually to do this.

Indeed, whenever computational irreducibility exists in a system it means that in effect there can be no way to predict how the system will behave except by going through almost as many steps of computation as the evolution of the system itself.

In traditional science it has rarely even been recognized that there is a need to consider how systems that are used to make predictions actually operate. But what leads to the phenomenon of computational irreducibility is that there is in fact always a fundamental competition

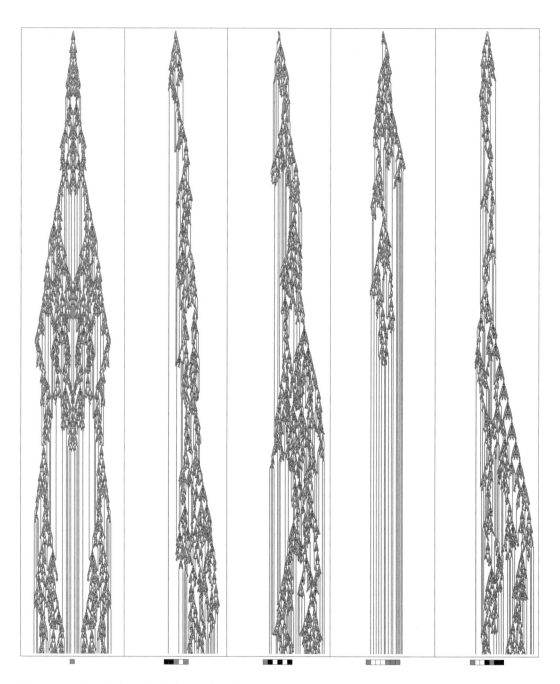

5000 steps in the evolution of the third system from the previous page, starting from several initial conditions. The complexity of the behavior makes it seem inconceivable that there could ever be a procedure that would always immediately find its outcome.

between systems used to make predictions and systems whose behavior one tries to predict.

For if meaningful general predictions are to be possible, it must at some level be the case that the system making the predictions be able to outrun the system it is trying to predict. But for this to happen the system making the predictions must be able to perform more sophisticated computations than the system it is trying to predict.

In traditional science there has never seemed to be much problem with this. For it has normally been implicitly assumed that with our powers of mathematics and general thinking the computations we use to make predictions must be almost infinitely more sophisticated than those that occur in most systems in nature and elsewhere whose behavior we try to predict.

But the remarkable assertion that the Principle of Computational Equivalence makes is that this assumption is not correct, and that in fact almost any system whose behavior is not obviously simple performs computations that are in the end exactly equivalent in their sophistication.

So what this means is that systems one uses to make predictions cannot be expected to do computations that are any more sophisticated than the computations that occur in all sorts of systems whose behavior we might try to predict. And from this it follows that for many systems no systematic prediction can be done, so that there is no general way to shortcut their process of evolution, and as a result their behavior must be considered computationally irreducible.

If the behavior of a system is obviously simple—and is say either repetitive or nested—then it will always be computationally reducible. But it follows from the Principle of Computational Equivalence that in practically all other cases it will be computationally irreducible.

And this, I believe, is the fundamental reason that traditional theoretical science has never managed to get far in studying most types of systems whose behavior is not ultimately quite simple.

For the point is that at an underlying level this kind of science has always tried to rely on computational reducibility. And for example its whole idea of using mathematical formulas to describe behavior makes sense only when the behavior is computationally reducible.

So when computational irreducibility is present it is inevitable that the usual methods of traditional theoretical science will not work. And indeed I suspect the only reason that their failure has not been more obvious in the past is that theoretical science has typically tended to define its domain specifically in order to avoid phenomena that do not happen to be simple enough to be computationally reducible.

But one of the major features of the new kind of science that I have developed is that it does not have to make any such restriction. And indeed many of the systems that I study in this book are no doubt computationally irreducible. And that is why—unlike most traditional works of theoretical science—this book has very few mathematical formulas but a great many explicit pictures of the evolution of systems.

It has in the past couple of decades become increasingly common in practice to study systems by doing explicit computer simulations of their behavior. But normally it has been assumed that such simulations are ultimately just a convenient way to do what could otherwise be done with mathematical formulas.

But what my discoveries about computational irreducibility now imply is that this is not in fact the case, and that instead there are many common systems whose behavior cannot in the end be determined at all except by something like an explicit simulation.

Knowing that universal systems exist already tells one that this must be true at least in some situations. For consider trying to outrun the evolution of a universal system. Since such a system can emulate any system, it can in particular emulate any system that is trying to outrun it. And from this it follows that nothing can systematically outrun the universal system. For any system that could would in effect also have to be able to outrun itself.

But before the discoveries in this book one might have thought that this could be of little practical relevance. For it was believed that except among specially constructed systems universality was rare. And it was also assumed that even when universality was present, very special initial conditions would be needed if one was ever going to perform computations at anything like the level of sophistication involved in most methods of prediction.

But the Principle of Computational Equivalence asserts that this is not the case, and that in fact almost any system whose behavior is not obviously simple will exhibit universality and will perform sophisticated computations even with typical simple initial conditions.

So the result is that computational irreducibility can in the end be expected to be common, so that it should indeed be effectively impossible to outrun the evolution of all sorts of systems.

One slightly subtle issue in thinking about computational irreducibility is that given absolutely any system one can always at least nominally imagine speeding up its evolution by setting up a rule that for example just executes several steps of evolution at once.

But insofar as such a rule is itself more complicated it may in the end achieve no real reduction in computational effort. And what is more important, it turns out that when there is true computational reducibility its effect is usually much more dramatic.

The pictures on the next page show typical examples based on cellular automata that exhibit repetitive and nested behavior. In the patterns on the left the color of each cell at any given step is in effect found by tracing the explicit evolution of the cellular automaton up to that step. But in the pictures on the right the results for particular cells are instead found by procedures that take much less computational effort.

These procedures are again based on cellular automata. But now what the cellular automata do is to take specifications of positions of cells, and then in effect compute directly from these the colors of cells.

The way things are set up the initial conditions for these cellular automata consist of digit sequences of numbers that give positions. The color of a particular cell is then found by evolving for a number of steps equal to the length of these input digit sequences.

And this means for example that the outcome of a million steps of evolution for either of the cellular automata on the left is now determined by just 20 steps of evolution, where 20 is the length of the base 2 digit sequence of the number 1,000,000.

And this turns out to be quite similar to what happens with typical mathematical formulas in traditional theoretical science. For the point of such formulas is usually to allow one to give a number as

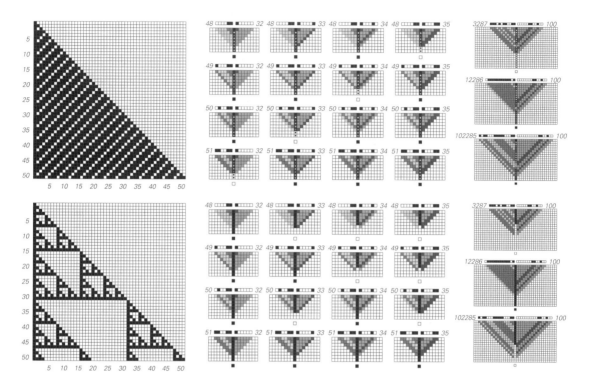

Examples of computational reducibility in action. The pictures on the left show patterns produced by the ordinary evolution of cellular automata with elementary rules 188 and 60. The pictures on the right show how colors of particular cells in these patterns can be found with much less computational effort. In each case the position of a cell is specified by a pair of numbers given as base 2 digit sequences in the initial conditions for a cellular automaton. The evolution of the cellular automaton then quickly determines what the color of the cell at that position in the pattern on the left will be. For rule 188 the cellular automaton that does this involves 12 colors; for rule 60 it involves 6. In general, to find the color of a cell after t steps of rule 188 or rule 60 evolution takes about $Log[2, t]$ steps. Compare page 608.

input, and then to compute directly something that corresponds, say, to the outcome of that number of steps in the evolution of a system.

In traditional mathematics it is normally assumed that once one has an explicit formula involving standard mathematical functions then one can in effect always evaluate this formula immediately.

But evaluating a formula—like anything else—is a computational process. And unless some digits effectively never matter, this process cannot normally take less steps than there are digits in its input.

Indeed, it could in principle be that the process could take a number of steps proportional to the numerical value of its input. But if this were so, then it would mean that evaluating the formula would require as much effort as just tracing each step in the original process whose outcome the formula was supposed to give.

And the crucial point that turns out to be the basis for much of the success of traditional theoretical science is that in fact most standard mathematical functions can be evaluated in a number of steps that is far smaller than the numerical value of their input, and that instead normally grows only slowly with the length of the digit sequence of their input.

So the result of this is that if there is a traditional mathematical formula for the outcome of a process then almost always this means that the process must show great computational reducibility.

In practice, however, the vast majority of cases for which traditional mathematical formulas are known involve behavior that is ultimately either uniform or repetitive. And indeed, as we saw in Chapter 10, if one uses just standard mathematical functions then it is rather difficult even to reproduce many simple examples of nesting.

But as the pictures on the facing page and in Chapter 10 illustrate, if one allows more general kinds of underlying rules then it becomes quite straightforward to set up procedures that with very little computational effort can find the color of any element in any nested pattern.

So what about more complex patterns, like the rule 30 cellular automaton pattern at the bottom of the page?

When I first generated such patterns I spent a huge amount of time trying to analyze them and trying to find a procedure that would allow me to compute directly the color of each cell. And indeed it was the fact that I was never able to make much progress in doing this that first led me to consider the possibility that there could be a phenomenon like computational irreducibility.

And now, what the Principle of Computational Equivalence implies is that in fact almost any system whose behavior is not obviously simple will tend to exhibit computational irreducibility.

But particularly when the underlying rules are simple there is often still some superficial computational reducibility. And so, for example, in the rule 30 pattern on the right one can tell whether a cell at a given position has any chance of not being white just by doing a

An example of a pattern where it is difficult to compute directly the color of a particular cell.

very short computation that tests whether that position lies outside the center triangular region of the pattern. And in a class 4 cellular automaton such as rule 110 one can readily shortcut the process of evolution for at least a limited number of steps in places where there happen to be only a few well-separated localized structures present.

And indeed in general almost any regularities that we manage to recognize in the behavior of a system will tend to reflect some kind of computational reducibility in this behavior.

If one views the pattern of behavior as a piece of data, then as we discussed in Chapter 10 regularities in it allow a compressed description to be found. But the existence of a compressed description does not on its own imply computational reducibility. For any system that has simple rules and simple initial conditions—including for example rule 30—will always have such a description.

But what makes there be computational reducibility is when only a short computation is needed to find from the compressed description any feature of the actual behavior.

And it turns out that the kinds of compressed descriptions that can be obtained by the methods of perception and analysis that we use in practice and that we discussed in Chapter 10 all essentially have this property. So this is why regularities that we recognize by these methods do indeed reflect the presence of computational reducibility.

But as we saw in Chapter 10, in almost any case where there is not just repetitive or nested behavior, our normal powers of perception and analysis recognize very few regularities—even though at some level the behavior we see may still be generated by extremely simple rules.

And this supports the assertion that beyond perhaps some small superficial amount of computational reducibility a great many systems are in the end computationally irreducible. And indeed this assertion explains, at least in part, why our methods of perception and analysis cannot be expected to go further in recognizing regularities.

But if behavior that we see looks complex to us, does this necessarily mean that it can exhibit no computational reducibility? One way to try to get an idea about this is just to construct patterns

(a) If[Mod[Log[x y], 1] > 1/2, 1, 0]

(b) If[Mod[Sqrt[x y], 1] > 1/2, 1, 0]

(c) If[Mod[Sin[x y], 1] > 1/2, 1, 0]

(d) If[Mod[Sin[x] + Sin[y], 1] > 1/2, 1, 0]

(e) Mod[Quotient[y, x], 2]

(f) Mod[Quotient[y^3, x^2], 2]

(g) Mod[Quotient[2^y, x], 2]

(h) Mod[Quotient[3^y, 2^x], 2]

(i) Mod[Mod[y, x], 2]

(j) Mod[Binomial[y, x], 2]

(k) Mod[DigitCount[x y, 2, 1], 2]

(l) If[GCD[x, y] = 1, 1, 0]

(m) Mod[d[x].d[y], 2]

(n) If[Count[d[y] - d[x], 1] = 1, 1, 0]

(o) If[Count[d[y] - d[x], 0] = 3, 1, 0]

(p) If[Count[d[y] - d[x], 0] > 3, 1, 0]

Examples of patterns set up so that a short computation can be used to determine the color of each cell from the numbers representing its position. Most such patterns look to us quite simple, but the examples shown here were specifically chosen to be ones that look more complicated. In most of them fairly standard mathematical functions are used, but in unusual combinations. In every picture both x and y run from 1 to 127. d[n] stands for IntegerDigits[n, 2, 7]. (h) is equivalent to digit sequences of powers of 3 in base 2 (see page 120). (j) is essentially Pascal's triangle (see page 611). (l) was discussed on page 613. (m) is a nested pattern seen on page 583. The only pattern that is known to be obtainable by evolving down the page according to a simple local rule is (j), which corresponds to the rule 60 elementary cellular automaton.

where we explicitly set up the color of each cell to be determined by some short computation from the numbers that represent its position.

When we look at such patterns most of them appear to us quite simple. But as the pictures on the previous page demonstrate, it turns out to be possible to find examples where this is not so, and where instead the patterns appear to us at least somewhat complex.

But for such patterns to yield meaningful examples of computational reducibility it must also be possible to produce them by some process of evolution—say by repeated application of a cellular automaton rule. Yet for the majority of cases shown here there is at least no obvious way to do this.

I have however found one class of systems—already mentioned in Chapter 10—whose behavior does not appear simple, but nevertheless turns out to be computationally reducible, as in the pictures on the facing page. However, I strongly suspect that systems like this are very rare, and that in the vast majority of cases where the behavior that we see in nature and elsewhere appears to us complex it is in the end indeed associated with computational irreducibility.

So what does this mean for science?

In the past it has normally been assumed that there is no ultimate limit on what science can be expected to do. And certainly the progress of science in recent centuries has been so impressive that it has become common to think that eventually it should yield an easy theory—perhaps a mathematical formula—for almost anything.

But the discovery of computational irreducibility now implies that this can fundamentally never happen, and that in fact there can be no easy theory for almost any behavior that seems to us complex.

It is not that one cannot find underlying rules for such behavior. Indeed, as I have argued in this book, particularly when they are formulated in terms of programs I suspect that such rules are often extremely simple. But the point is that to deduce the consequences of these rules can require irreducible amounts of computational effort.

One can always in effect do an experiment, and just watch the actual behavior of whatever system one wants to study. But what one

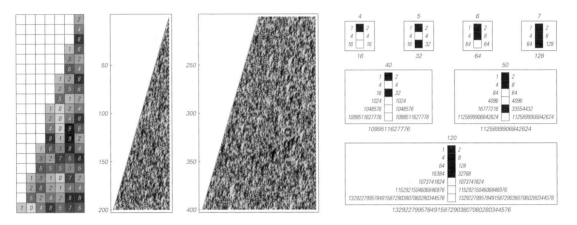

A system whose behavior looks complex but still turns out to be computationally reducible. The system is a cellular automaton with 10 possible colors for each cell. But it can also be viewed as a system based on numbers, in which successive rows are the base 10 digit sequences of successive powers of 2. And it turns out that there is a fast way to compute row *n* just from the base 2 digit sequence of *n*, as the pictures on the right illustrate. This procedure is based on the standard repeated squaring method of finding 2^n by starting from 2, and then successively squaring the numbers one gets, multiplying by 2 if the corresponding base 2 digit in *n* is 1. Using this procedure one can certainly compute the color of any cell on row *n* by doing about $n Log[n]^3$ operations—instead of the n^2 needed if one carried out the cellular automaton evolution explicitly.

cannot in general do is to find an easy theory that will tell one without much effort what every aspect of this behavior will be.

So given this, can theoretical science still be useful at all?

The answer is definitely yes. For even in its most traditional form it can often deal quite well with those aspects of behavior that happen to be simple enough to be computationally reducible. And since one can never know in advance how far computational reducibility will go in a particular system it is always worthwhile at least to try applying the traditional methods of theoretical science.

But ultimately if computational irreducibility is present then these methods will fail. Yet there are still often many reasons to want to use abstract theoretical models rather than just doing experiments on actual systems in nature and elsewhere. And as the results in this book suggest, by using the right kinds of models much can be achieved.

Any accurate model for a system that exhibits computational irreducibility must at some level inevitably involve computations that are as sophisticated as those in the system itself. But as I have shown in

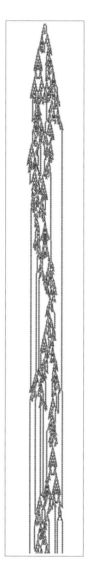

this book even systems with very simple underlying rules can still perform computations that are as sophisticated as in any system.

And what this means is that to capture the essential features even of systems with very complex behavior it can be sufficient to use models that have an extremely simple basic structure. Given these models the only way to find out what they do will usually be just to run them. But the point is that if the structure of the models is simple enough, and fits in well enough with what can be implemented efficiently on a practical computer, then it will often still be perfectly possible to find out many consequences of the model.

And that, in a sense, is what much of this book has been about.

The Phenomenon of Free Will

Ever since antiquity it has been a great mystery how the universe can follow definite laws while we as humans still often manage to make decisions about how to act in ways that seem quite free of obvious laws.

But from the discoveries in this book it finally now seems possible to give an explanation for this. And the key, I believe, is the phenomenon of computational irreducibility.

For what this phenomenon implies is that even though a system may follow definite underlying laws its overall behavior can still have aspects that fundamentally cannot be described by reasonable laws.

For if the evolution of a system corresponds to an irreducible computation then this means that the only way to work out how the system will behave is essentially to perform this computation—with the result that there can fundamentally be no laws that allow one to work out the behavior more directly.

And it is this, I believe, that is the ultimate origin of the apparent freedom of human will. For even though all the components of our brains presumably follow definite laws, I strongly suspect that their overall behavior corresponds to an irreducible computation whose outcome can never in effect be found by reasonable laws.

And indeed one can already see very much the same kind of thing going on in a simple system like the cellular automaton on the left. For

A cellular automaton whose behavior seems to show an analog of free will. Even though its underlying laws are definite—and simple— the behavior is complicated enough that many aspects of it seem to follow no definite laws. (The rule used is the same as on page 740.)

even though the underlying laws for this system are perfectly definite, its overall behavior ends up being sufficiently complicated that many aspects of it seem to follow no obvious laws at all.

And indeed if one were to talk about how the cellular automaton seems to behave one might well say that it just decides to do this or that—thereby effectively attributing to it some sort of free will.

But can this possibly be reasonable? For if one looks at the individual cells in the cellular automaton one can plainly see that they just follow definite rules, with absolutely no freedom at all.

But at some level the same is probably true of the individual nerve cells in our brains. Yet somehow as a whole our brains still manage to behave with a certain apparent freedom.

Traditional science has made it very difficult to understand how this can possibly happen. For normally it has assumed that if one can only find the underlying rules for the components of a system then in a sense these tell one everything important about the system.

But what we have seen over and over again in this book is that this is not even close to correct, and that in fact there can be vastly more to the behavior of a system than one could ever foresee just by looking at its underlying rules. And fundamentally this is a consequence of the phenomenon of computational irreducibility.

For if a system is computationally irreducible this means that there is in effect a tangible separation between the underlying rules for the system and its overall behavior associated with the irreducible amount of computational work needed to go from one to the other.

And it is in this separation, I believe, that the basic origin of the apparent freedom we see in all sorts of systems lies—whether those systems are abstract cellular automata or actual living brains.

But so in the end what makes us think that there is freedom in what a system does? In practice the main criterion seems to be that we cannot readily make predictions about the behavior of the system.

For certainly if we could, then this would show us that the behavior must be determined in a definite way, and so cannot be free. But at least with our normal methods of perception and analysis one typically needs rather simple behavior for us actually to be able to identify overall rules that let us make reasonable predictions about it.

Yet in fact even in living organisms such behavior is quite common. And for example particularly in lower animals there are all sorts of cases where very simple and predictable responses to stimuli are seen. But the point is that these are normally just considered to be unavoidable reflexes that leave no room for decisions or freedom.

Yet as soon as the behavior we see becomes more complex we quickly tend to imagine that it must be associated with some kind of underlying freedom. For at least with traditional intuition it has always seemed quite implausible that any real unpredictability could arise in a system that just follows definite underlying rules.

And so to explain the behavior that we as humans exhibit it has often been assumed that there must be something fundamentally more going on—and perhaps something unique to humans.

In the past the most common belief has been that there must be some form of external influence from fate—associated perhaps with the intervention of a supernatural being or perhaps with configurations of celestial bodies. And in more recent times sensitivity to initial conditions and quantum randomness have been proposed as more appropriate scientific explanations.

But much as in our discussion of randomness in Chapter 6 nothing like this is actually needed. For as we have seen many times in this book even systems with quite simple and definite underlying rules can produce behavior so complex that it seems free of obvious rules.

And the crucial point is that this happens just through the intrinsic evolution of the system—without the need for any additional input from outside or from any sort of explicit source of randomness.

And I believe that it is this kind of intrinsic process—that we now know occurs in a vast range of systems—that is primarily responsible for the apparent freedom in the operation of our brains.

But this is not to say that everything that goes on in our brains has an intrinsic origin. Indeed, as a practical matter what usually seems to happen is that we receive external input that leads to some train of thought which continues for a while, but then dies out until we get more input. And often the actual form of this train of thought is influenced by memory we have developed from inputs in the past—making it not necessarily repeatable even with exactly the same input.

But it seems likely that the individual steps in each train of thought follow quite definite underlying rules. And the crucial point is then that I suspect that the computation performed by applying these rules is often sophisticated enough to be computationally irreducible—with the result that it must intrinsically produce behavior that seems to us free of obvious laws.

Undecidability and Intractability

Computational irreducibility is a very general phenomenon with many consequences. And among these consequences are various phenomena that have been widely studied in the abstract theory of computation.

In the past it has normally been assumed that these phenomena occur only in quite special systems, and not, for example, in typical systems with simple rules or of the kind that might be seen in nature. But what my discoveries about computational irreducibility now suggest is that such phenomena should in fact be very widespread, and should for example occur in many systems in nature and elsewhere.

In this chapter so far I have mostly been concerned with ongoing processes of computation, analogous to ongoing behavior of systems in nature and elsewhere. But as a theoretical matter one can ask what the final outcome of a computation will be, after perhaps an infinite number of steps. And if one does this then one encounters the phenomenon of undecidability that was identified in the 1930s.

The pictures on the next page show an example. In each case knowing the final outcome is equivalent to deciding what will eventually happen to the pattern generated by the cellular automaton evolution. Will it die out? Will it stabilize and become repetitive? Or will it somehow continue to grow forever?

One can try to find out by running the system for a certain number of steps and seeing what happens. And indeed in example (a) this approach works well: in only 36 steps one finds that the pattern

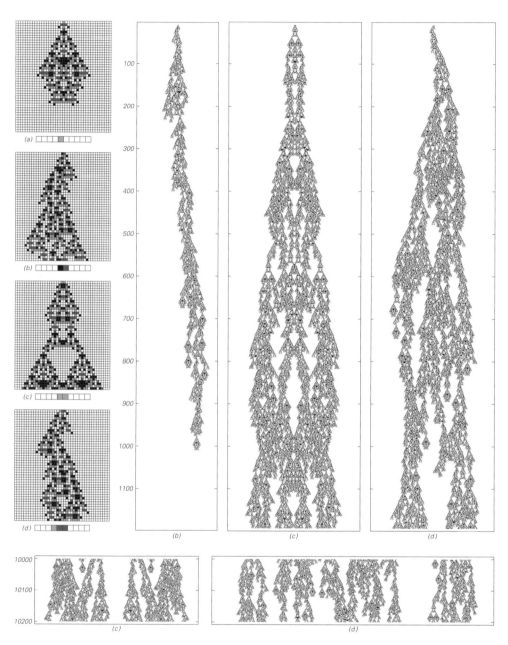

Cellular automaton evolution illustrating the phenomenon of undecidability. Pattern (a) dies out after 36 steps; pattern (b) takes 1017 steps. But what the final outcome in cases (c) and (d) will be is not clear after even a million steps. And in general there appears to be no finite computation that can guarantee to determine the final outcome of the evolution after an infinite number of steps. The cellular automaton rule used is a 4-color totalistic one with code 1004600. Whether a pattern in a cellular automaton ever dies out can be viewed as analogous to a version of the halting problem for Turing machines.

dies out. But already in example (b) it is not so easy. One can go for 1000 steps and still not know what is going to happen. And only after 1017 steps does it finally become clear that the pattern in fact dies out.

So what about examples (c) and (d)? What happens to these? After a million steps neither has died out; in fact they are respectively 31,000 and 39,718 cells wide. And after 10 million steps both are still going, now 339,028 and 390,023 cells wide. But even having traced the evolution this far, one still has no idea what its final outcome will be.

And in any system the only way to be able to guarantee to know this in general is to have some way to shortcut the evolution of the system, and to be able to reduce to a finite computation what takes the system an infinite number of steps to do.

But if the behavior of the system is computationally irreducible— as I suspect is so for the cellular automaton on the facing page and for many other systems with simple underlying rules—then the point is that ultimately no such shortcut is possible. And this means that the general question of what the system will ultimately do can be considered formally undecidable, in the sense there can be no finite computation that will guarantee to decide it.

For any particular initial condition it may be that if one just runs the system for a certain number of steps then one will be able to tell what it will do. But the crucial point is that there is no guarantee that this will work: indeed there is no finite amount of computation that one can always be certain will be enough to answer the question of what the system does after an infinite number of steps.

That this is the case has been known since the 1930s. But it has normally been assumed that the effects of such undecidability will rarely be seen except in special and complicated circumstances. Yet what the picture on the facing page illustrates is that in fact undecidability can have quite obvious effects even with a very simple underlying rule and very simple initial conditions.

And what I suspect is that for almost any system whose behavior seems to us complex almost any non-trivial question about what the system does after an infinite number of steps will be undecidable. So, for example, it will typically be undecidable whether the evolution of the system from some particular initial condition will ever generate a specific arrangement of cell colors—or whether it will yield a pattern that is, say, ultimately repetitive or ultimately nested.

And if one asks whether any initial conditions exist that lead, for example, to a pattern that does not die out, then this too will in general be undecidable—though in a sense this is just an immediate consequence of the fact that given a particular initial condition one cannot tell whether or not the pattern it produces will ever die out.

But what if one just looks at possible sequences—as might be used for initial conditions—and asks whether any of them satisfy some constraint? Even if the constraint is easy to test it turns out that there can again be undecidability. For there may be no limit on how far one has to go to be sure that out of the infinite number of possible sequences there are really none that satisfy the constraint.

The pictures on the facing page show a simple example of this. The idea is to pick a set of pairs of upper and lower blocks, and then to ask whether there is any sequence of such pairs that satisfies the constraint that the upper and lower strings formed end up being in exact correspondence.

When there are just two kinds of pairs it turns out to be quite straightforward to answer this question. For if any sequence is going to satisfy the constraint one can show that there must already be a sequence of limited length that does so—and if necessary one can find this sequence by explicitly looking at all possibilities.

But as soon as there are more than two pairs things become much more complicated, and as the pictures on the facing page demonstrate, even with very short blocks remarkably long and seemingly quite random sequences can be required in order to satisfy the constraints.

And in fact I strongly suspect that even with just three pairs there is already computational irreducibility, so that in effect the only way to answer the question of whether the constraints can be satisfied is explicitly to trace through some fraction of all arbitrarily long sequences—making this question in general undecidable.

And indeed whenever the question one has can somehow involve looking at an infinite number of steps, or elements, or other things, it

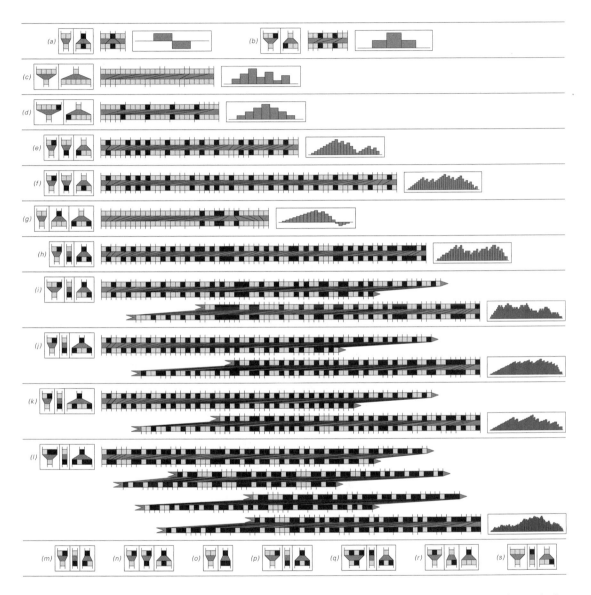

Examples of a class of one-dimensional constraints where it is in general undecidable whether they can be satisfied. The constraints require that concatenating in some order the blocks shown should yield identical upper and lower strings. In cases (a)–(l) the constraints can be satisfied, and the minimal strings which do so are shown. The plots to the right give the successive differences in length between upper and lower strings when each new block is added; that this difference reaches zero reflects the fact that the constraint is satisfied. Cases (m)–(s) show constraints that cannot be satisfied by strings of any finite length. When the constraints involve more than two blocks there seems in general to be no upper limit on how long a string one may need to consider to tell whether the constraints can be satisfied. Pictures (a), (b), (h) and (j) show the longest minimal strings needed for any of the 4096, 16384, 65536 and 262144 constraints involving blocks with totals of 7, 8, 9 and 10 elements. The general problem of satisfying constraints of the kind shown here is known as the Post Correspondence Problem. Finding the systems on this page required constructing—by computer and otherwise—an immense number of proofs of the impossibility of satisfying particular constraints.

turns out that such a question is almost inevitably undecidable if it is asked about a system that exhibits computational irreducibility.

So what about finite questions?

Such questions can ultimately always be answered by finite computations. But when computational irreducibility is present such computations can be forced to have a certain level of difficulty which sometimes makes them quite intractable.

When one does practical computing one tends to assess the difficulty of a computation by seeing how much time it takes and perhaps how big a program it involves and how much memory it needs.

But normally one has no way to tell whether the scheme one has for doing a particular computation is the most efficient possible. And in the past there have certainly been several instances when new algorithms have suddenly allowed all sorts of computations to be done much more efficiently than had ever been thought possible before.

Indeed, despite great efforts in the field of computational complexity theory over the course of several decades almost no firm lower bounds on the difficulty of computations have ever been established. But using the methods of this book it turns out to be possible to begin to get at least a few results.

The key is to consider very small programs. For with such programs it becomes realistic to enumerate every single one of a particular kind, and then just to see explicitly which is the most efficient at performing some specific computation.

In the past such an approach would not have seemed sensible, for it was normally assumed that programs small enough to make it work would only ever be able to do rather trivial computations. But what my discoveries have shown is that in fact even very small programs can be quite capable of doing all sorts of sophisticated computations.

As a first example—based on a rather simple computation—the picture at the top of the facing page shows a Turing machine set up to add 1 to any number. The input to the Turing machine is the base 2 digit sequence for the number. The head of the machine starts at the right-hand end of this sequence, and the machine runs until its head first goes further to the right—at which point the machine stops, with

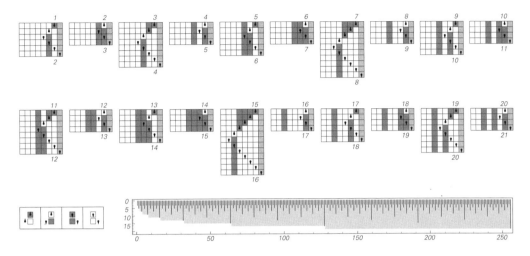

Examples of the behavior of a simple Turing machine that does the computation of adding 1 to a number. The number is given as a base 2 digit sequence; the Turing machine runs until its head hits the gray stripe on the right. The plot shows the number of steps that this takes as a function of the input number x. The result turns out to be given by $2\,IntegerExponent[x + 1, 2] + 3$, which has a maximum of $2\,n + 3$, where n is the length of the digit sequence of x, or $Floor[Log[2, x]]$. The average for a given length of input does not increase with n, and is always precisely 5.

whatever sequence of digits are left behind being taken to be the output of the computation.

And what the pictures above show is that with this particular machine the number of steps needed to finish the computation varies greatly between different inputs. But if one looks just at the absolute maximum number of steps for any given length of input one finds an exactly linear increase with this length.

So are there other ways to do the same computation in a different number of steps? One can readily enumerate all 4096 possible Turing machines with 2 states and 2 colors. And it turns out that of these exactly 17 perform the computation of adding 1 to a number.

Each of them works in a slightly different way, but all of them follow one of the three schemes shown at the top of the next page— and all of them end up exhibiting the same overall linear increase in number of steps with length of input.

So what about other computations?

It turns out that there are 351 different functions that can be computed by one or more of the 4096 Turing machines with 2 states

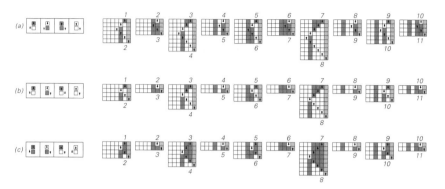

The three schemes for adding 1 to a number that are used by Turing machines with 2 states and 2 colors. All show the same linear growth in maximum number of steps as their size of input increases. This growth can be viewed as a consequence of potentially having to propagate carry digits from one end of the input number to the other. The machines shown are numbered 445, 461 and 1512.

and 2 colors. And as the pictures on the facing page show, different Turing machines can take very different numbers of steps to do the computations they do.

Turing machine (a), for example, always finishes its computation after at most 5 steps, independent of the length of its input. But in most of the other Turing machines shown, the maximum number of steps needed generally increases with the length of the input.

Turing machines (b), (c) and (d) are ones that always compute the same function. But while this means that for a given input each of them yields the same output, the pictures demonstrate that they usually take a different number of steps to do so. Nevertheless, if one looks at the maximum number of steps needed for any given length of input one finds that this still always increases exactly linearly—just as for the Turing machines that add 1 shown at the top of this page.

So are there cases in which there is more rapid growth? Turing machine (e) shows an example in which the maximum number of steps grows like the square of the length of the input. And it turns out that at least among 2-state 2-color Turing machines this is the only one that computes the function it computes—so that at least if one wants to use a program this simple there is no faster way to do the computation.

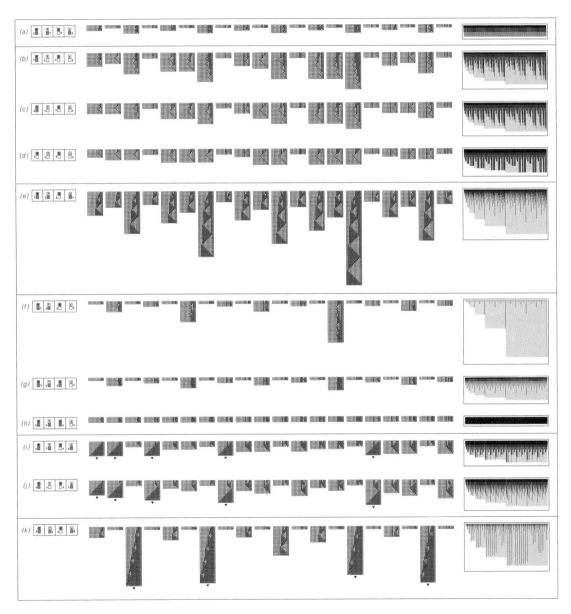

Examples of computations being done by Turing machines with two states and two colors. Evolution from a succession of initial conditions is shown corresponding to inputs of numbers from 1 to 20. Each block of Turing machines yields the same output for a given input. A computation is taken to be complete when the head of the Turing machine goes further to the right than it was at the beginning. The plots show how many steps this takes for successive inputs with lengths up to 9. The maximum for input of length n is (a) 5, (b) $6n+3$, (c) $4n+3$, (d) $2n+3$, (e) $2n^2+8n+7$, (f) $2^{n+1}-1$ (though the average is $n+2$), (g) $2n+1$, (h) 3, (i) $2n+1$, (j) $4n-1$, (k) roughly $2.5n^2$. In cases (i), (j) and (k) there are some inputs for which the head goes further and further to the left, and the Turing machine never halts. The machines shown are numbered 3279, 1285, 3333, 261, 1447, 1953, 1969, 3517, 3246, 3374, 1507.

So are there computations that take still longer to do? In Turing machine (f) the maximum number of steps increases exponentially with the length of the input. But unlike in example (e), this Turing machine is not the only one that computes the function it computes. And in fact both (g) and (h) compute the same function—but in a linearly increasing and constant number of steps respectively.

So what about other Turing machines? In general there is no guarantee that a particular Turing machine will ever even complete a computation in a finite number of steps. For as happens with several inputs in examples (i) and (j) the head may end up simply going further and further to the left—and never get to the point on the right that is needed for the computation to be considered complete.

But if one ignores inputs where this happens, then at least in examples (i) and (j) the maximum number of steps still grows in a very systematic linear way with the length of the input.

In example (k), however, there is more irregular growth. But once again the maximum number of steps in the end just increases like the square of the length of the input. And indeed if one looks at all 4096 Turing machines with 2 states and 2 colors it turns out that the only rates of growth that one ever sees are linear, square and exponential.

And of the six examples where exponential growth occurs, all of them are like example (f) above—so that there is another 2-state 2-color Turing machine that computes the same function, but without the maximum number of steps increasing at all with input length.

So what happens if one considers more complicated Turing machines? With 3 states and 2 colors there are a total of 2,985,984 possible machines. And it turns out that there are about 33,000 distinct functions that one or more of these machines computes.

Most of the time the fastest machine at computing a given function again exhibits linear or at most quadratic growth. But the facing page shows some cases where instead it exhibits exponential growth.

And indeed in a few cases the growth seems to be even faster. Example (h) is the most extreme among 3-state 2-color Turing machines: with the size 7 input 106 it already takes 1,978,213,883 steps

Examples of Turing machines with 3 and 4 states in which the maximum number of steps before a computation is finished grows at least exponentially with the length of the input. In all cases no Turing machines with the same number of states compute the same functions in fewer steps. In case (h) the number of steps grows so rapidly that only two peaks are seen in the plot. The top row of pictures are all scaled to be exactly the same height, even though the initial conditions cannot be chosen to make the number of steps in each case anything more than roughly the same. The machines have numbers: 582285, 657939, 2018806, 2868668, 2138664, 2139050, 132527, 600720, 3374234978, 1806221583, 1232059922, 3238044559. Cases like (c) and (d) show nested behavior reminiscent of a counter which generates digit sequences of successive integers.

to generate its output, and in general with size n input it may be able to take more than 2^{2^n} steps.

But what if one allows Turing machines with more complicated rules? With 4-state 2-color rules it turns out to be possible to generate the same output as examples (c) and (d) in just a fixed number of steps. But for none of the other 3-state 2-color Turing machines shown do 4-state rules offer any speedup.

Nevertheless, if one looks carefully at examples (a) through (h) each of them shows large regions of either repetitive or nested behavior. And it seems likely that this reflects computational reducibility that should make it possible for sufficiently complicated programs to generate the same output in fewer than exponentially many steps.

But looking at 4-state 2-color Turing machines examples (i) through (l) again appear to exhibit roughly exponential growth. Yet now—much as for the 4-state Turing machines in Chapter 3—the actual behavior seen does not show any obvious computational reducibility.

So this suggests that even though they may be specified by very simple rules there are indeed Turing machine computations that cannot actually be carried out except by spending an amount of computational effort that can increase exponentially with the length of input.

And certainly if one allows no more than 4-state 2-color Turing machines I have been able to establish by explicitly searching all 4 billion or so possible rules that there is absolutely no way to speed up the computations in pictures (i) through (l).

But what about with other kinds of systems?

Once one has a system that is universal it can in principle be made to do any computation. But the question is at what rate. And without special optimization a universal Turing machine will for example typically just operate at some fixed fraction of the speed of any specific Turing machine that it is set up to emulate.

And if one looks at different computers and computer languages practical experience tends to suggest that at least at the level of issues like exponential growth the rate at which a given computation can be done is ultimately rather similar in almost every such system.

But one might imagine that across the much broader range of computational systems that I have considered in this book—and that presumably occur in nature—there could nevertheless still be great differences in the rates at which given computations can be done.

Yet from what we saw in Chapter 11 one suspects that in fact there are not. For in the course of that chapter it became clear that almost all the very varied systems in this book can actually be made to emulate each other in a quite comparable number of steps.

Indeed often we found that it was possible to emulate every step in a particular system by just a fixed sequence of steps in another system. But if the number of elements that can be updated in one step is sufficiently different this tends to become impossible.

And thus for example the picture on the right shows that it can take t^2 steps for a Turing machine that updates just one cell at each step to build up the same pattern as a one-dimensional cellular automaton builds up in t steps by updating every cell in parallel.

And in d dimensions it is common for it to take, say, t^{d+1} steps for one system to emulate t steps of evolution of another.

But can it take an exponential number of steps? Certainly if one has a substitution system that yields exponentially many elements then to reproduce all these elements with an ordinary Turing machine will take exponentially many steps. And similarly if one has a multiway system that yields exponentially many strings then to reproduce all these will again take exponentially many steps.

But what if one asks only about some limited feature of the output—say whether some particular string appears after t steps of evolution of the multiway system? Given a specific path like the one in the picture on the right it takes an ordinary Turing machine not much more than t steps to test whether the path yields the desired string.

But how long can it take for a Turing machine to find out whether any path in the multiway system manages to produce the string? If the Turing machine in effect had to examine each of the perhaps exponentially many paths in turn then this could take exponentially many steps. But the celebrated P=NP question in computational complexity theory asks whether in general there is some

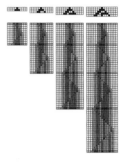

To emulate t steps in the evolution of the cellular automaton takes the Turing machine $2\,t^2 + 5\,t - 6$ steps.

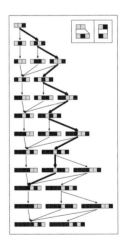

A Turing machine can quickly test the highlighted path but could take exponentially long to test all paths.

way to get such an answer in a number of steps that increases not exponentially but only like a power.

And although it has never been established for certain it seems by now likely that in most meaningful senses there is not. So what this implies is that to answer questions about the t-step behavior of a multiway system can take any ordinary Turing machine a number of steps that increases faster than any power of t.

So how common is this kind of phenomenon? One can view asking about possible outcomes in a multiway system as like asking about possible ways to satisfy a constraint. And certainly a great many practical problems can be formulated in terms of constraints.

But how do such problems compare to each other? The Principle of Computational Equivalence suggests that those that seem difficult should somehow tend to be equivalent. And indeed it turns out that over the course of the past few decades a rather large number of such problems have in fact all been found to be so-called NP-complete.

What this means is that these problems exhibit a kind of analog of universality which makes it possible with less than exponential effort to translate any instance of any one of them into an instance of any other. So as an example the picture on the facing page shows how one type of problem about a so-called non-deterministic Turing machine can be translated to a different type of problem about a cellular automaton.

Much like a multiway system, a non-deterministic Turing machine has rules that allow multiple choices to be made at each step, leading to multiple possible paths of evolution. And an example of an NP-complete problem is then whether any of these paths satisfy the constraint that, say, after a particular number of steps, the head of the Turing machine has ever gone further to the right than it starts.

The top row in the picture on the facing page shows the first few of the exponentially many possible paths obtained by making successive sequences of choices in a particular non-deterministic Turing machine. And in the example shown, one sees that for two of these paths the head goes to the right, so that the overall constraint is satisfied.

So what about the cellular automaton below in the picture? Given a particular initial condition its evolution is completely

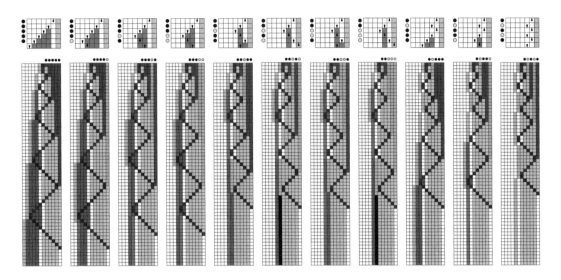

Translation between an NP-complete problem about non-deterministic Turing machines and about cellular automata. The top row shows how a particular non-deterministic Turing machine behaves with successive sequences of choices for rules to apply. The bottom row shows how a cellular automaton can be made to emulate this behavior when given a succession of different initial conditions. The cellular automaton is set up to produce a vertical black stripe if the head of the Turing machine ever goes further to the right than it starts—as it does in cases 6 and 8. The left part of each cellular automaton configuration emulates the actual evolution of the Turing machine; a specification of which rules should be applied at each step is progressively fetched from the right and delivered to the position of the head. Given particular initial conditions for the Turing machine the problem of whether the head ever goes further to the right than it starts is thus equivalent to the problem of whether the cellular automaton ever produces a vertical black stripe given particular initial conditions on its left. The cellular automaton takes $2t^2 + t$ steps to emulate t steps of evolution in the Turing machine. It involves a total of 19 colors.

deterministic. But what the picture shows is that with successive initial conditions it emulates each possible path in the non-deterministic Turing machine.

And so what this means is that the problem of finding whether initial conditions exist that make the cellular automaton produce a certain outcome is equivalent to the non-deterministic Turing machine problem above—and is therefore in general NP-complete.

So what about other kinds of problems?

The picture on the next page shows the equivalence between the classic problem of satisfiability and the non-deterministic Turing machine problem at the top of this page. In satisfiability what one does is to start with a collection of rows of black, white and gray squares. And then what one asks is whether any sequence of just black and

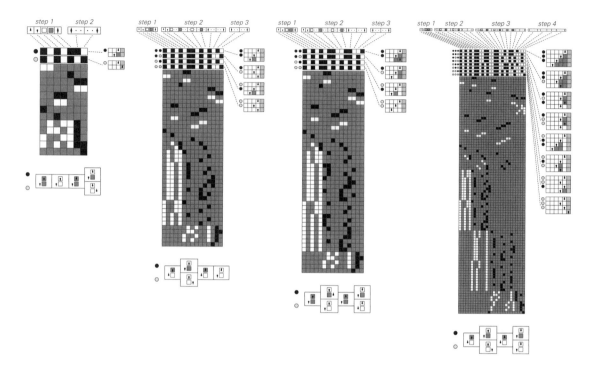

Translation between the NP-complete problem of halting in a non-deterministic Turing machine and the classic NP-complete problem of satisfiability. In satisfiability one sets up a collection of rows of black, white and gray squares, then asks whether there exists any sequence of black and white squares that satisfies the constraint that on every row the color of at least one square agrees with the color of the corresponding square in the sequence. Each row can be viewed as a term in a conjunctive normal form Boolean expression, with each column corresponding to a different variable. When a given square on a particular row is black or white it indicates that a variable or its negation appear in that term. The translation from the Turing machine problem is achieved by representing the behavior of the Turing machine by saying which of a sequence of elementary statements are true about it at each step: whether the head is in one state or another, whether the cell under the head is black or white, and whether the head is at each of the possible positions it can be in. The Boolean expression then gives constraints on which of these statements can simultaneously be true. In the first two pictures, for example, the first row corresponds to the constraint that on the first step of Turing machine evolution, the head cannot simultaneously be in an up and a down state. About the first half of the terms in each Boolean expression correspond to similar general constraints about the operation of Turing machines. There are then a few terms that specify the particular initial conditions used here, followed by terms that give the rule for the Turing machine that is used. The very last term makes the statement that the Turing machine halts. As the pictures indicate, each possible path of evolution for the Turing machine then corresponds to a possible assignment of truth values to the variables associated with each elementary statement. And if there is any path that leads the Turing machine to halt the Boolean expression will be satisfiable. This is the case in the first and fourth examples shown, but not in the other two. In general, it is possible to represent t steps in the evolution of a non-deterministic Turing machine by a Boolean expression with at most t^3 terms in t^2 variables. A version of the translation shown here was what launched the study of NP completeness in the early 1970s.

white squares exists that satisfies the constraint that on every row there is at least one square whose color agrees with the color of the corresponding square in the sequence.

To see the equivalence to questions about Turing machines one imagines breaking the description of the behavior of a Turing machine into a sequence of elementary statements: whether the head is in a particular state on a particular step, whether a certain cell has a particular color, and so on. The underlying rules for the Turing machine then define constraints on which sequences of such statements can be true. And in the picture on the facing page almost every row of black, white and gray squares corresponds to one such constraint.

The last row, however, represents the further constraint that the head of the Turing machine must at some point go further to the right than it starts. And this means that to ask whether there is any sequence in the satisfiability problem that obeys all the constraints is equivalent to finding the answer to the Turing machine problem described above.

Starting from satisfiability it is possible to show that all sorts of well-known computational problems in discrete mathematics are NP-complete. And in addition almost any undecidable problem that involves simple constraints—such as the correspondence problem on page 757—turns out to be NP-complete if restricted to finite cases.

In studying the phenomenon of NP completeness what has mostly been done in the past is to try to construct particular instances of rather general problems that exhibit equivalence to other problems. But almost always what is actually constructed is quite complicated—and certainly not something one would expect to occur at all often.

Yet on the basis of intuition from the Principle of Computational Equivalence I strongly suspect that in most cases there are already quite simple instances of general NP-complete problems that are just as difficult as any NP-complete problem. And so, for example, I suspect that it does not take a cellular automaton nearly as complicated as the one on page 767 for it to be an NP-complete problem to determine whether initial conditions exist that lead to particular behavior.

Indeed, my expectation is that asking about possible outcomes of t steps of evolution will already be NP-complete even for the rule 30 cellular automaton, as illustrated below.

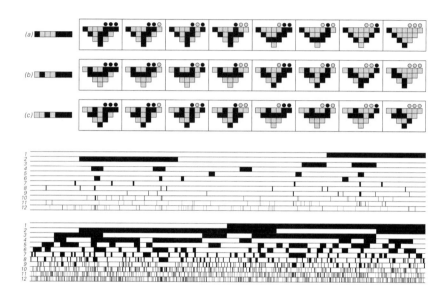

Example of a simple problem that I suspect is NP-complete. The problem is to determine whether right-hand cells in the initial conditions for rule 30 can be filled in so as to produce a vertical black stripe of a certain height at the bottom of the center column formed after t steps of evolution. The pictures at the top show that in case (a) stripes up to height 3 can be produced, in case (b) up to height 2, and in case (c) only up to height 1. The pictures at the bottom indicate in black for which of the 2^{t+1} successive left-hand sequences of $t + 1$ cells it is impossible to get stripes of respectively heights 1 and 2. The apparent randomness of these patterns reflects the likely difficulty of the problem. The problem is related to issues of rule 30 cryptanalysis discussed on page 603.

Just as with the Turing machines of pages 761 and 763 there will be a certain density of cases where the problem is fairly easy to solve. But it seems likely that as one increases t, no ordinary Turing machine or cellular automaton will ever be able to guarantee to solve the problem in a number of steps that grows only like some power of t.

Yet even so, there could still in principle exist in nature some other kind of system that would be able to do this. And for example one might imagine that this would be possible if one were able to use exponentially small components. But almost all the evidence we have suggests that in our actual universe there are limits on the sizes and densities of components that we can ever expect to manipulate.

In present-day physics the standard mathematical formalism of quantum mechanics is often interpreted as suggesting that quantum systems work like multiway systems, potentially following many paths in parallel. And indeed within the usual formalism one can construct quantum computers that may be able to solve at least a few specific problems exponentially faster than ordinary Turing machines.

But particularly after my discoveries in Chapter 9, I strongly suspect that even if this is formally the case, it will still not turn out to be a true representation of ultimate physical reality, but will instead just be found to reflect various idealizations made in the models used so far.

And so in the end it seems likely that there really can in some fundamental sense be an almost exponential difference in the amount of computational effort needed to find the behavior of a system with given particular initial conditions, and to solve the inverse problem of determining which if any initial conditions yield particular behavior.

In fact, my suspicion is that such a difference will exist in almost any system whose behavior seems to us complex. And among other things this then implies many fundamental limits on the processes of perception and analysis that we discussed in Chapter 10.

Such limits can ultimately be viewed as being consequences of the phenomenon of computational irreducibility. But a much more direct consequence is one that we have discussed before: that even given a particular initial condition it can require an irreducible amount of computational work to find the outcome after a given number of steps of evolution.

One can specify the number of steps t that one wants by giving the sequence of digits in t. And for systems with sufficiently simple behavior—say repetitive or nested—the pictures on page 744 indicate that one can typically determine the outcome with an amount of effort that is essentially proportional to the length of this digit sequence.

But the point is that when computational irreducibility is present, one may in effect explicitly have to follow each of the t steps of evolution—again requiring exponentially more computational work.

Implications for Mathematics and Its Foundations

Much of what I have done in this book has been motivated by trying to understand phenomena in nature. But the ideas that I have developed are general enough that they do not apply just to nature. And indeed in this section what I will do is to show that they can also be used to provide important new insights on fundamental issues in mathematics.

At some rather abstract level one can immediately recognize a basic similarity between nature and mathematics: for in nature one knows that fairly simple underlying laws somehow lead to the rich and complex behavior we see, while in mathematics the whole field is in a sense based on the notion that fairly simple axioms like those on the facing page can lead to all sorts of rich and complex results.

So where does this similarity come from? At first one might think that it must be a consequence of nature somehow intrinsically following mathematics. For certainly early in its history mathematics was specifically set up to capture certain simple aspects of nature.

But one of the starting points for the science in this book is that when it comes to more complex behavior mathematics has never in fact done well at explaining most of what we see every day in nature.

Yet at some level there is still all sorts of complexity in mathematics. And indeed if one looks at a presentation of almost any piece of modern mathematics it will tend to seem quite complex. But the point is that this complexity typically has no obvious relationship to anything we see in nature. And in fact over the past century what has been done in mathematics has mostly taken increasing pains to distance itself from any particular correspondence with nature.

So this suggests that the overall similarity between mathematics and nature must have a deeper origin. And what I believe is that in the end it is just another consequence of the very general Principle of Computational Equivalence that I discuss in this chapter.

For both mathematics and nature involve processes that can be thought of as computations. And then the point is that all these computations follow the Principle of Computational Equivalence, so

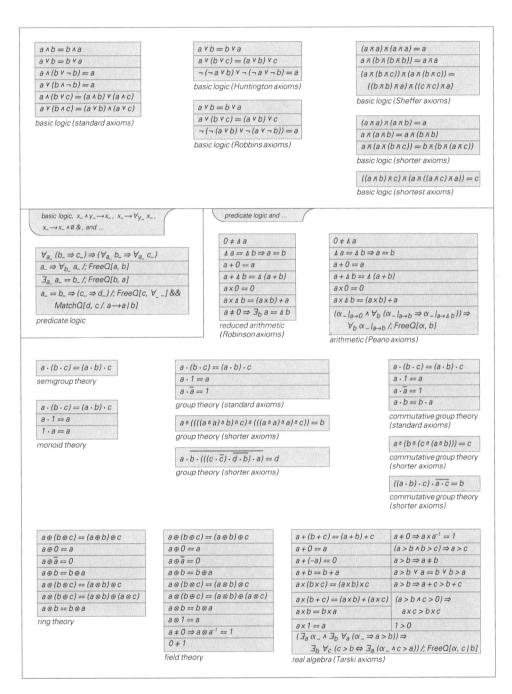

Axiom systems for traditional mathematics. It is from the axiom systems on this page and the next that most of the millions of theorems in the literature of mathematics have ultimately been derived. Note that in several cases axiom systems are given here in much shorter forms than in standard mathematics textbooks. (See also the definitions on the next page.)

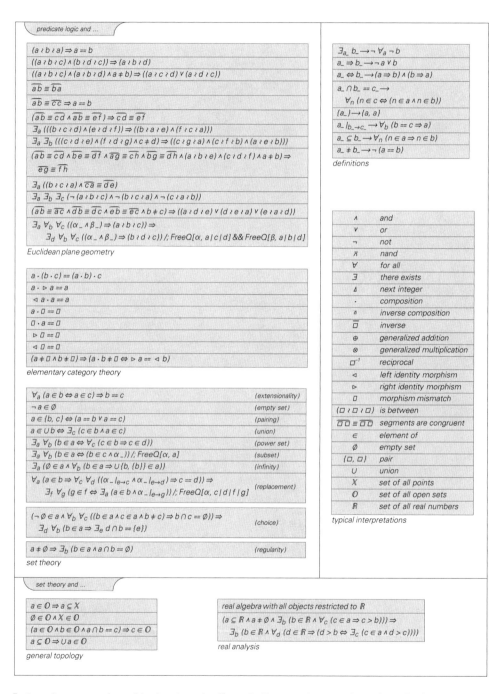

predicate logic and ...

$(a \wr b \wr a) \Rightarrow a == b$

$((a \wr b \wr c) \wedge (b \wr d \wr c)) \Rightarrow (a \wr b \wr d)$

$((a \wr b \wr c) \wedge (a \wr b \wr d) \wedge a \neq b) \Rightarrow ((a \wr c \wr d) \vee (a \wr d \wr c))$

$\overline{ab} \equiv \overline{ba}$

$\overline{ab} \equiv \overline{cc} \Rightarrow a == b$

$(\overline{ab} \equiv \overline{cd} \wedge \overline{ab} \equiv \overline{ef}) \Rightarrow \overline{cd} \equiv \overline{ef}$

$\exists_a ((b \wr c \wr d) \wedge (e \wr d \wr f)) \Rightarrow ((b \wr a \wr e) \wedge (f \wr c \wr a)))$

$\exists_b \exists_c (((c \wr d \wr e) \wedge (f \wr d \wr g) \wedge c \neq d) \Rightarrow ((c \wr g \wr a) \wedge (c \wr f \wr b) \wedge (a \wr e \wr b)))$

$(\overline{ab} \equiv \overline{cd} \wedge \overline{be} \equiv \overline{df} \wedge \overline{ag} \equiv \overline{ch} \wedge \overline{bg} \equiv \overline{dh} \wedge (a \wr b \wr e) \wedge (c \wr d \wr f) \wedge a \neq b) \Rightarrow$
$\overline{eg} \equiv \overline{fh}$

$\exists_a ((b \wr c \wr a) \wedge \overline{ca} \equiv \overline{de})$

$\exists_b \exists_c \exists_c (\neg (a \wr b \wr c) \wedge \neg (b \wr c \wr a) \wedge \neg (c \wr a \wr b))$

$(\overline{ab} \equiv \overline{ac} \wedge \overline{db} \equiv \overline{dc} \wedge \overline{eb} \equiv \overline{ec} \wedge b \neq c) \Rightarrow ((a \wr d \wr e) \vee (d \wr e \wr a) \vee (e \wr a \wr d))$

$\exists_b \forall_c ((\alpha_- \wedge \beta_-) \Rightarrow (a \wr b \wr c)) \Rightarrow$
$\exists_d \forall_b \forall_c ((\alpha_- \wedge \beta_-) \Rightarrow (b \wr d \wr c)) /; \text{FreeQ}[\alpha, a \mid c \mid d] \&\& \text{FreeQ}[\beta, a \mid b \mid d]$

Euclidean plane geometry

$a \cdot (b \cdot c) == (a \cdot b) \cdot c$

$a \rhd a == a$

$\lhd a \cdot a == a$

$a \cdot \Box == \Box$

$\Box \cdot a == \Box$

$\rhd \Box == \Box$

$\lhd \Box == \Box$

$(a \neq \Box \wedge b \neq \Box) \Rightarrow (a \cdot b \neq \Box \Leftrightarrow \rhd a == \lhd b)$

elementary category theory

$\forall_a (a \in b \Leftrightarrow a \in c) \Rightarrow b == c$ *(extensionality)*

$\neg a \in \emptyset$ *(empty set)*

$a \in \{b, c\} \Leftrightarrow (a == b \vee a == c)$ *(pairing)*

$a \in \cup b \Leftrightarrow \exists_c (c \in b \wedge a \in c)$ *(union)*

$\exists_a \forall_b (b \in a \Leftrightarrow \forall_c (c \in b \Rightarrow c \in d))$ *(power set)*

$\exists_a \forall_b (b \in a \Leftrightarrow (b \in c \wedge \alpha_-)) /; \text{FreeQ}[\alpha, a]$ *(subset)*

$\exists_a (\emptyset \in a \wedge \forall_b (b \in a \Rightarrow \cup \{b, \{b\}\} \in a))$ *(infinity)*

$\forall_a (a \in b \Leftrightarrow \forall_c \forall_d ((\alpha_{-|e \to c} \wedge \alpha_{-|e \to d}) \Rightarrow c == d)) \Rightarrow$
$\exists_f \forall_g (g \in f \Leftrightarrow \exists_a (a \in b \wedge \alpha_{-|e \to g})) /; \text{FreeQ}[\alpha, c \mid d \mid f \mid g]$ *(replacement)*

$(\neg \emptyset \in a \wedge \forall_b \forall_c ((b \in a \wedge c \in a \wedge b \neq c) \Rightarrow b \cap c == \emptyset)) \Rightarrow$
$\exists_d \forall_b (b \in a \Rightarrow \exists_e d \cap b == \{e\})$ *(choice)*

$a \neq \emptyset \Rightarrow \exists_b (b \in a \wedge a \cap b == \emptyset)$ *(regularity)*

set theory

$\exists_a b_- \longrightarrow \neg \forall_a \neg b$

$a_- \Rightarrow b_- \longrightarrow \neg a \vee b$

$a_- \Leftrightarrow b_- \longrightarrow (a \Rightarrow b) \wedge (b \Rightarrow a)$

$a_- \cap b_- == c_- \longrightarrow$
$\forall_n (n \in c \Leftrightarrow (n \in a \wedge n \in b))$

$\{a_-\} \longrightarrow \{a, a\}$

$a_- \mid_{b_- \to c_-} \longrightarrow \forall_b (b == c \Rightarrow a)$

$a_- \subseteq b_- \longrightarrow \forall_n (n \in a \Rightarrow n \in b)$

$a_- \neq b_- \longrightarrow \neg (a == b)$

definitions

$\wedge$	and
$\vee$	or
$\neg$	not
$\barwedge$	nand
$\forall$	for all
$\exists$	there exists
$\triangle$	next integer
$\cdot$	composition
δ	inverse composition
$\overline{\Box}$	inverse
$\oplus$	generalized addition
$\otimes$	generalized multiplication
$\Box^{-1}$	reciprocal
$\lhd$	left identity morphism
$\rhd$	right identity morphism
$\Box$	morphism mismatch
$(\Box \wr \Box \wr \Box)$	is between
$\overline{\Box\Box} \equiv \overline{\Box\Box}$	segments are congruent
$\in$	element of
$\emptyset$	empty set
$\{\Box, \Box\}$	pair
$\cup$	union
X	set of all points
O	set of all open sets
$\mathbb{R}$	set of all real numbers

typical interpretations

set theory and ...

$a \in O \Rightarrow a \subseteq X$

$\emptyset \in O \wedge X \in O$

$(a \in O \wedge b \in O \wedge a \cap b == c) \Rightarrow c \in O$

$a \subseteq O \Rightarrow \cup a \in O$

general topology

real algebra with all objects restricted to $\mathbb{R}$

$(a \subseteq \mathbb{R} \wedge a \neq \emptyset \wedge \exists_b (b \in \mathbb{R} \wedge \forall_c (c \in a \Rightarrow c > b))) \Rightarrow$
$\exists_b (b \in \mathbb{R} \wedge \forall_d (d \in \mathbb{R} \Rightarrow (d > b \Leftrightarrow \exists_c (c \in a \wedge d > c))))$

real analysis

Further axiom systems for traditional mathematics. The typical interpretations are relevant for applications, though not for formal derivation of theorems. The last two axioms listed for set theory are usually considered optional.

that they ultimately tend to be equivalent in their computational sophistication—and thus show all sorts of similar phenomena.

And what we will see in this section is while some of these phenomena correspond to known features of mathematics—such as Gödel's Theorem—many have never successfully been recognized.

But just what basic processes are involved in mathematics?

Ever since antiquity mathematics has almost defined itself as being concerned with finding theorems and giving their proofs. And in any particular branch of mathematics a proof consists of a sequence of steps ultimately based on axioms like those of the previous two pages.

The picture below gives a simple example of how this works in basic logic. At the top right are axioms specifying certain fundamental equivalences between logic expressions. A proof of the equivalence $p \barwedge q = q \barwedge p$ between logic expressions is then formed by applying these axioms in the particular sequence shown.

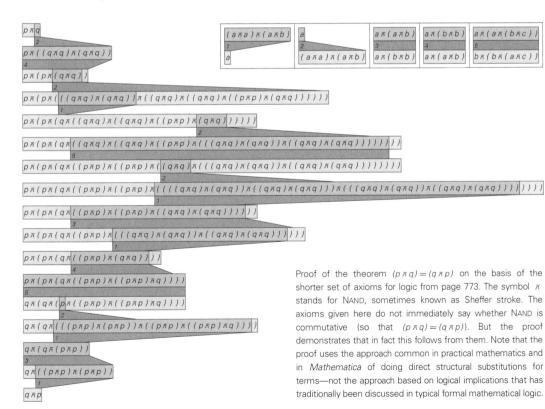

Proof of the theorem $(p \barwedge q) = (q \barwedge p)$ on the basis of the shorter set of axioms for logic from page 773. The symbol $\barwedge$ stands for NAND, sometimes known as Sheffer stroke. The axioms given here do not immediately say whether NAND is commutative (so that $(p \barwedge q) = (q \barwedge p)$). But the proof demonstrates that in fact this follows from them. Note that the proof uses the approach common in practical mathematics and in *Mathematica* of doing direct structural substitutions for terms—not the approach based on logical implications that has traditionally been discussed in typical formal mathematical logic.

In most kinds of mathematics there are all sorts of additional details, particularly about how to determine which parts of one or more previous expressions actually get used at each step in a proof. But much as in our study of systems in nature, one can try to capture the essential features of what can happen by using a simple idealized model.

And so for example one can imagine representing a step in a proof just by a string of simple elements such as black and white squares. And one can then consider the axioms of a system as defining possible transformations from one sequence of these elements to another—just like the rules in the multiway systems we discussed in Chapter 5.

The pictures below show how proofs of theorems work with this setup. Each theorem defines a connection between strings, and proving the theorem consists in finding a series of transformations—each associated with an axiom—that lead from one string to another.

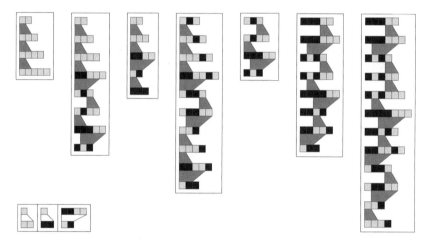

Simple idealizations of proofs in mathematics. The rules on the left in effect correspond to axioms that specify valid transformations between strings of black and white elements. The proofs above then show how one string—say ▫▫—can be transformed into another—say ▫▫▫▫—by using the axioms. Typically there are many different proofs that can be given of a particular theorem; here in each case the ones shown are examples of the shortest possible proofs. The system shown is an example of a general substitution system of the kind discussed on page 497. Note that the fifth theorem ▫■■ → ■■ occurs in effect as a lemma in the second theorem ▫▫ → ■■.

But just as in the multiway systems in Chapter 5 one can also consider an explicit process of evolution, in which one starts from a particular string, then at each successive step one applies all possible transformations, so that in the end one builds up a whole network of connections between strings, as in the pictures below.

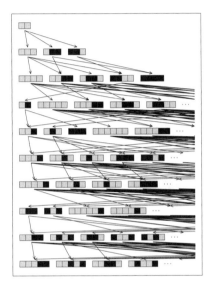 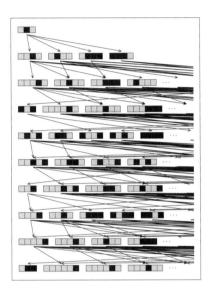

The result of applying the same transformations as on the facing page—but in all possible ways, corresponding to the evolution of a multiway system that represents all possible theorems that can be derived from the axioms. With the axioms used here, the total number of strings grows by a factor of roughly 1.7 at each step; on the last steps shown there are altogether 237 and 973 strings respectively.

In a sense such a network can then be thought of as representing the whole field of mathematics that can be derived from whatever set of axioms one is using—with every connection between strings corresponding to a theorem, and every possible path to a proof.

But can networks like the ones above really reflect mathematics as it is actually practiced? For certainly the usual axioms in every traditional area of mathematics are significantly more complicated than any of the multiway system rules used above.

But just like in so many other cases in this book, it seems that even systems whose underlying rules are remarkably simple are already able to capture many of the essential features of mathematics.

An obvious observation in mathematics is that proofs can be difficult to do. One might at first assume that any theorem that is easy

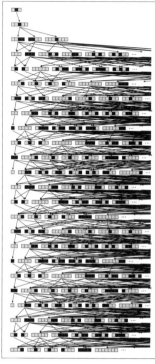

Three examples of multiway systems that show the analog of long proofs. In each case a string consisting of a single white element is eventually generated—but this takes respectively 12, 28 and 34 steps to happen. The first multiway system actually generates all strings in the end (not least since it yields the lemmas ■ → ■■ and ■ → ▫)—and in fact strings of length $n > 2$ appear after at most $2n + 7$ steps. The second multiway system generates only the $n + 1$ strings where black comes before white—and all of these strings appear after at most $7n$ steps. The third multiway system generates a complicated collection of strings; the numbers of lengths up to 8 are 1, 2, 4, 8, 14, 22, 34, 45. All the strings generated have an even number of black elements.

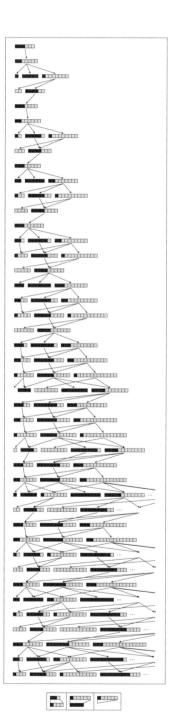

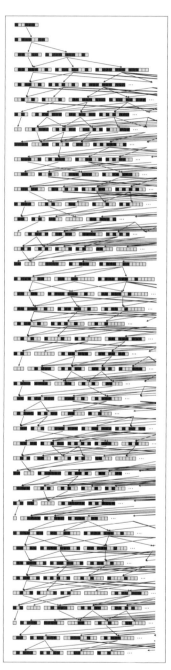

to state will also be easy to prove. But experience suggests that this is far from correct. And indeed there are all sorts of well-known examples—such as Fermat's Last Theorem and the Four-Color Theorem—in which a theorem that is easy to state seems to require a proof that is immensely long.

So is there an analog of this in multiway systems? It turns out that often there is, and it is that even though a string may be short it may nevertheless take a great many steps to reach.

If the rules for a multiway system always increase string length then it is inevitable that any given string that is ever going to be generated must appear after only a limited number of steps. But if the rules can both increase and decrease string length the story is quite different, as the picture on the facing page illustrates. And often one finds that even a short string can take a rather large number of steps to produce.

But are all these steps really necessary? Or is it just that the rule one has used is somehow inefficient, and there are other rules that generate the short strings much more quickly?

Certainly one can take the rules for any multiway system and add transformations that immediately generate particular short strings. But the crucial point is that like so many other systems I have discussed in this book there are many multiway systems that I suspect are computationally irreducible—so that there is no way to shortcut their evolution, and no general way to generate their short strings quickly.

And what I believe is that essentially the same phenomenon operates in almost every area of mathematics. Just like in multiway systems, one can always add axioms to make it easier to prove particular theorems. But I suspect that ultimately there is almost always computational irreducibility, and this makes it essentially inevitable that there will be short theorems that only allow long proofs.

In the previous section we saw that computational irreducibility tends to make infinite questions undecidable. So for example the question of whether a particular string will ever be generated in the evolution of a multiway system—regardless of how long one waits—is in general undecidable. And similarly it can be undecidable whether any proof—regardless of length—exists for a specific result in a mathematical system with particular axioms.

So what are the implications of this?

Probably the most striking arise when one tries to apply traditional ideas of logic—and particularly notions of true and false.

The way I have set things up, one can find all the statements that can be proved true in a particular axiom system just by starting with an expression that represents "true" and then using the rules of the axiom system, as in the picture on the facing page.

In a multiway system, one can imagine identifying "true" with a string consisting of a single black element. And this would mean that every string in networks like the ones below should correspond to a statement that can be proved true in the axiom system used.

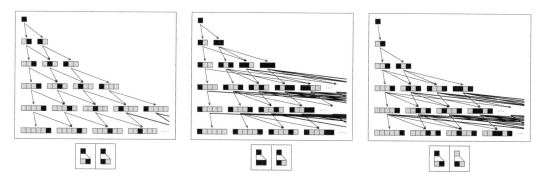

Multiway systems starting from a single black element that represents TRUE. All strings that appear can be thought of as statements that are true according to the axioms represented by the multiway system rules. One can take negation to be the operation that interchanges black and white. This then means that the first multiway system represents an inconsistent axiom system, since on step 2, both ■□ and its negation □■ appear. The other two multiway systems are consistent, so that they never generate both a string and its negation. The third one, however, is incomplete, since for example it never generates either □■ or its negation ■□. The second one, however, is both complete and consistent: it generates all strings that begin with ■, but none that begin with □.

But is this really reasonable? In traditional logic there is always an operation of negation which takes any true statement, and makes it into a false one, and vice versa. And in a multiway system, one possible way negation might work is just to reverse the colors of the elements in a string. But this then leads to a problem in the first picture above.

For the picture implies that both ■□ and its negation □■ can be proved to be true statements. But this cannot be correct. And so what

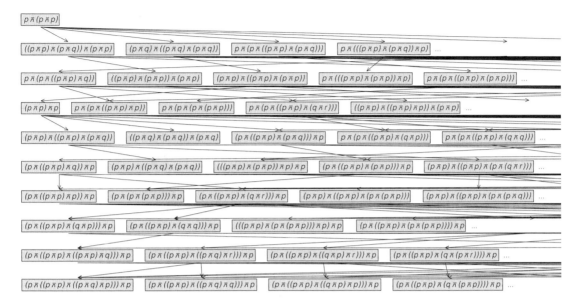

The network of statements that can be proved true using the axiom system for logic from page 775. $p \barwedge (p \barwedge p)$ is the simplest representation for TRUE when logic is set up using the NAND operator $\barwedge$. Each arrow indicates an equivalence established by applying a single axiom. On each row only statements that have not appeared before are given. The statements are sorted so that the simplest are first. Note that some fairly simple statements do not show up for at least several rows. The total number of statements on successive rows grows faster than exponentially; for the first few it is 1, 6, 91, 2180, 76138. If continued forever the network would eventually include all possible true statements (tautologies) of logic (see also page 818). Other simple axiom systems for logic like those on page 808 yield networks similar to the one shown.

this means is that with the setup used the underlying axiom system is inconsistent. So what about the other multiway systems on the facing page? At least with the strings one can see in the pictures there are no inconsistencies. But what about with longer strings? For the particular rules shown it is fairly easy to demonstrate that there are never inconsistencies. But in general it is not possible to do this, for after some given string has appeared, it can for example be undecidable whether the negation of that particular string ever appears.

So what about the axiom systems normally used in actual mathematics? None of those on pages 773 and 774 appear to be inconsistent. And what this means is that the set of statements that can be proved true will never overlap with the set that can be proved false.

But can every possible statement that one might expect to be true or false actually in the end be proved either true or false?

In the early 1900s it was widely believed that this would effectively be the case in all reasonable mathematical axiom systems. For at the time there seemed to be no limit to the power of mathematics, and no end to the theorems that could be proved.

But this all changed in 1931 when Gödel's Theorem showed that at least in any finitely-specified axiom system containing standard arithmetic there must inevitably be statements that cannot be proved either true or false using the rules of the axiom system.

This was a great shock to existing thinking about the foundations of mathematics. And indeed to this day Gödel's Theorem has continued to be widely regarded as a surprising and rather mysterious result.

But the discoveries in this book finally begin to make it seem inevitable and actually almost obvious. For it turns out that at some level it can be viewed as just yet another consequence of the very general Principle of Computational Equivalence.

So what is the analog of Gödel's Theorem for multiway systems? Given the setup on page 780 one can ask whether a particular multiway system is complete in the sense that for every possible string the system eventually generates either that string or its negation.

And one can see that in fact the third multiway system is incomplete, since by following its rules one can never for example generate either ▫▫ or its negation ■■. But what if one extends the rules by adding more transformations, corresponding to more axioms? Can one always in the end make the system complete?

If one is not quite careful, one will generate too many strings, and inevitably get inconsistencies where both a string and its negation appear, as in the second picture on the facing page. But at least if one only has to worry about a limited number of steps, it is always possible to set things up so as to get a system that is both complete and consistent, as in the third picture on the facing page.

And in fact in the particular case shown on the facing page it is fairly straightforward to find rules that make the system always complete and consistent. But knowing how to do this requires having behavior that is in a sense simple enough that one can foresee every aspect of it.

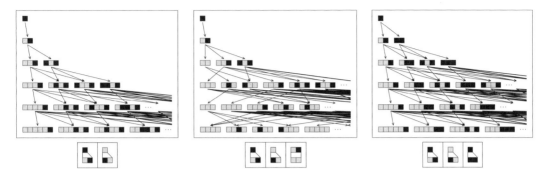

The effect of adding transformations to the rules for a multiway system. The first multiway system is incomplete, in the sense that for some strings, it generates neither the string nor its negation. The second multiway system yields more strings—but introduces inconsistency, since it can generate both ◻◼ and its negation ◼◼. The third multiway system is however both complete and consistent: for every string it eventually generates either that string or its negation.

Yet if a system is computationally irreducible this will inevitably not be possible. For at any point the system will always in effect be able to do more things that one did not expect. And this means that in general one will not be able to construct a finite set of axioms that can be guaranteed to lead to ultimate completeness and consistency.

And in fact it turns out that as soon as the question of whether a particular string can ever be reached is undecidable it immediately follows that there must be either incompleteness or inconsistency. For to say that such a question is undecidable is to say that it cannot in general be answered by any procedure that is guaranteed to finish.

But if one had a system that was complete and consistent then it is easy to come up with such a procedure: one just runs the system until either one reaches the string one is looking for or one reaches its negation. For the completeness of the system guarantees that one must always reach one or the other, while its consistency implies that reaching one allows one to conclude that one will never reach the other.

So the result of this is that if the evolution of a multiway system is computationally irreducible—so that questions about its ultimate behavior are undecidable—the system cannot be both complete and consistent. And if one assumes consistency then it follows that there must be strings where neither the string nor its negation can be reached—corresponding to the fact that statements must exist that cannot be proved either true or false from a given set of axioms.

But what does it take to establish that such incompleteness will actually occur in a specific system?

The basic way to do it is to show that the system is universal.

But what exactly does universality mean for something like an axiom system? In effect what it means is that any question about the behavior of any other universal system can be encoded as a statement in the axiom system—and if the answer to the question can be established by watching the evolution of the other universal system for any finite number of steps then it must also be able to be established by giving a proof of finite length in the axiom system.

So what axiom systems in mathematics are then universal?

Basic logic is not, since at least in principle one can always determine the truth of any statement in this system by the finite—if perhaps exponentially long—procedure of trying all possible combinations of truth values for the variables that appear in it.

And essentially the same turns out to be the case for pure predicate logic, in which one just formally adds "for all" and "there exists" constructs. But as soon as one also puts in an abstract function or relation with more than one argument, one gets universality.

And indeed the basis for Gödel's Theorem is the result that the standard axioms for basic integer arithmetic support universality.

Set theory and several other standard axiom systems can readily be made to reproduce arithmetic, and are therefore also universal. And the same is true of group theory and other algebraic systems like ring theory.

If one puts enough constraints on the axioms one uses, one can eventually prevent universality—and in fact this happens for commutative group theory, and for the simplified versions of both real algebra and geometry on pages 773 and 774.

But of the axiom systems actually used in current mathematics research every single one is now known to be universal.

From page 773 we can see that many of these axiom systems can be stated in quite simple ways. And in the past it might have seemed hard to believe that systems this simple could ever be universal, and thus in a sense be able to emulate essentially any system.

But from the discoveries in this book this now seems almost inevitable. And indeed the Principle of Computational Equivalence implies that beyond some low threshold almost any axiom system should be expected to be universal.

So how does universality actually work in the case of arithmetic?

One approach is illustrated in the picture on the next page. The idea is to set up an arithmetic statement that can be proved true if the evolution of a cellular automaton from a given initial condition makes a given cell be a given color at a given step, and can be proved false if it does not.

By changing numbers in this arithmetic statement one can then in effect sample different aspects of the cellular automaton evolution. And with the cellular automaton being a universal one such as rule 110 this implies that the axioms of arithmetic can support universality.

Such universality then implies Gödel's Theorem and shows that there must exist statements about arithmetic that cannot ever be proved true or false from its normal axioms.

So what are some examples of such statements?

The original proof of Gödel's Theorem was based on considering the particular self-referential statement "this statement is unprovable".

At first it does not seem obvious that such a statement could ever be set up as a statement in arithmetic. But if it could then one can see that it would immediately follow that—as the statement says—it cannot be proved, since otherwise there would be an inconsistency.

And in fact the main technical difficulty in the original proof of Gödel's Theorem had to do with showing—by doing what amounted to establishing the universality of arithmetic—that the statement could indeed meaningfully be encoded as a statement purely in arithmetic.

But at least with the original encoding used, the statement would be astronomically long if written out in the notation of page 773. And from this result, one might imagine that unprovability would never be relevant in any practical situation in mathematics.

But does one really need to have such a complicated statement in order for it to be unprovable from the axioms of arithmetic?

$$(-3x_6 + x_7 + x_8)^2 + (2^{1+x_3(1+x_1+2x_3)}x_2 - 2x_4 - x_{10} + x_{11})^2 + (-2x_8 - x_9 + x_{10} + x_{11})^2 + (1 - 2^{(1+x_3)(x_1+2x_3)} + x_4 + x_{12})^2 +$$

$$(1 - 2^{x_1} + x_2 + x_{13})^2 + (1 - 2^{x_1} + x_5 + x_{14})^2 + (-x_4 + 2^{x_3}x_5 + 2^{x_1+2x_3}x_6 + 2^{x_1+x_3}x_{15} + x_{16})^2 + (1 - 2^{x_3} + x_{15} + x_{17})^2 +$$

$$(1 - 2^{x_3} + x_{16} + x_{18})^2 + (-x_6 - 2x_7 + x_9 + x_{19})^2 + (-(2 + 2^{x_6})^{x_6} + (1 + 2^{x_6})^{x_7}(1 + 2x_{20} + (1 + 2^{x_6})x_{21}) + x_{22})^2 + (1 - (1 + 2^{x_6})^{x_7} + x_{22} + x_{23})^2 +$$

$$(1 - 2^{x_6} + 2x_{20} + x_{24})^2 + (-(2 + 4^{x_6})^{2x_6} + (1 + 4^{x_6})^{x_7}(1 + 2x_{25} + (1 + 4^{x_6})x_{26}) + x_{27})^2 + (1 - (1 + 4^{x_6})^{x_7} + x_{27} + x_{28})^2 +$$

$$(1 - 4^{x_6} + 2x_{25} + x_{29})^2 + (-(2 + 2^{x_8})^{x_8} + (1 + 2^{x_8})^{x_6}(1 + 2x_{30} + (1 + 2^{x_8})x_{31}) + x_{32})^2 + (1 - (1 + 2^{x_8})^{x_6} + x_{32} + x_{33})^2 +$$

$$(1 - 2^{x_8} + 2x_{30} + x_{34})^2 + (-(2 + 2^{x_8})^{x_8} + (1 + 2^{x_8})^{2x_6}(1 + 2x_{35} + (1 + 2^{x_8})x_{36}) + x_{37})^2 + (1 - (1 + 2^{x_8})^{2x_6} + x_{37} + x_{38})^2 +$$

$$(1 - 2^{x_8} + 2x_{35} + x_{39})^2 + (-(2 + 2^{x_6})^{x_6} + (1 + 2^{x_6})^{x_9}(1 + 2x_{40} + (1 + 2^{x_6})x_{41}) + x_{42})^2 + (1 - (1 + 2^{x_6})^{x_9} + x_{42} + x_{43})^2 +$$

$$(1 - 2^{x_6} + 2x_{40} + x_{44})^2 + (-(2 + 4^{x_7})^{2x_7} + (1 + 4^{x_7})^{x_9}(1 + 2x_{45} + (1 + 4^{x_7})x_{46}) + x_{47})^2 + (1 - (1 + 4^{x_7})^{x_9} + x_{47} + x_{48})^2 +$$

$$(1 - 4^{x_7} + 2x_{45} + x_{49})^2 + (-(2 + 2^{x_{19}})^{x_{19}} + (1 + 2^{x_{19}})^{x_6}(1 + 2x_{50} + (1 + 2^{x_{19}})x_{51}) + x_{52})^2 + (1 - (1 + 2^{x_{19}})^{x_6} + x_{52} + x_{53})^2 +$$

$$(1 - 2^{x_{19}} + 2x_{50} + x_{54})^2 + (-(2 + 2^{x_{19}})^{x_{19}} + (1 + 2^{x_{19}})^{2x_7}(1 + 2x_{55} + (1 + 2^{x_{19}})x_{56}) + x_{57})^2 + (1 - (1 + 2^{x_{19}})^{2x_7} + x_{57} + x_{58})^2 +$$

$$(1 - 2^{x_{19}} + 2x_{55} + x_{59})^2 + (-(2 + 2^{x_9})^{x_9} + (1 + 2^{x_9})^{x_{10}}(1 + 2x_{60} + (1 + 2^{x_9})x_{61}) + x_{62})^2 + (1 - (1 + 2^{x_9})^{x_{10}} + x_{62} + x_{63})^2 + (1 - 2^{x_9} + 2x_{60} + x_{64})^2 +$$

$$(-(2 + 4^{x_8})^{2x_8} + (1 + 4^{x_8})^{x_{10}}(1 + 2x_{65} + (1 + 4^{x_8})x_{66}) + x_{67})^2 + (1 - (1 + 4^{x_8})^{x_{10}} + x_{67} + x_{68})^2 + (1 - 4^{x_8} + 2x_{65} + x_{69})^2 +$$

$$(-(2 + 2^{x_{11}})^{x_{11}} + (1 + 2^{x_{11}})^{x_9}(1 + 2x_{70} + (1 + 2^{x_{11}})x_{71}) + x_{72})^2 + (1 - (1 + 2^{x_{11}})^{x_9} + x_{72} + x_{73})^2 + (1 - 2^{x_{11}} + 2x_{70} + x_{74})^2 +$$

$$(-(2 + 2^{x_{11}})^{x_{11}} + (1 + 2^{x_{11}})^{2x_8}(1 + 2x_{75} + (1 + 2^{x_{11}})x_{76}) + x_{77})^2 + (1 - (1 + 2^{x_{11}})^{2x_8} + x_{77} + x_{78})^2 + (1 - 2^{x_{11}} + 2x_{75} + x_{79})^2 = 0$$

x_1 (initial width)	1	x_1 (initial width)	1	x_1 (initial width)	1	x_1 (initial width)	1	x_1 (initial width)	3
x_2 (initial state)	1	x_2 (initial state)	1	x_2 (initial state)	1	x_2 (initial state)	1	x_2 (initial state)	5
x_3 (steps)	1	x_3 (steps)	2	x_3 (steps)	3	x_3 (steps)	4	x_3 (steps)	4
x_4 (evolution)	22	x_4 (evolution)	4508	x_4 (evolution)	17177704	x_4 (evolution)	1105983545840	x_4 (evolution)	1409438147512048
x_5	1	x_5	1	x_5	1	x_5	1	x_5	7
x_6	2	x_6	140	x_6	134200	x_6	2160124112	x_6	688202220464
x_7	0	x_7	8	x_7	2096	x_7	8437888	x_7	940049184
x_8	6	x_8	412	x_8	400504	x_8	6471934448	x_8	2063666612208
x_9	0	x_9	0	x_9	32	x_9	32768	x_9	805306880
x_{10}	0	x_{10}	0	x_{10}	32	x_{10}	32768	x_{10}	805306880
x_{11}	12	x_{11}	824	x_{11}	801008	x_{11}	12943868896	x_{11}	4127333224416
x_{12}	41	x_{12}	28259	x_{12}	251257751	x_{12}	34078388542991	x_{12}	34619358871451919
x_{13}	0	x_{13}	0	x_{13}	0	x_{13}	0	x_{13}	2
x_{14}	0	x_{14}	0	x_{14}	0	x_{14}	0	x_{14}	0
x_{15}	1	x_{15}	3	x_{15}	6	x_{15}	15	x_{15}	13
⋮		⋮		⋮		⋮		⋮	

$x_4 = 22 =$
```
010
110
```

$x_4 = 4508 =$
```
00100
01100
11100
```

$x_4 = 17177704 =$
```
0001000
0011000
0111000
1101000
```

$x_4 = 1105983545840 =$
```
000010000
000110000
001110000
011010000
111110000
```

$x_4 = 1409438147512048 =$
```
00001010000
00011100000
00110010000
01101110000
11011110000
```

Universality in arithmetic, illustrated by an integer equation whose solutions in effect emulate the rule 110 universal cellular automaton from Chapter 11. The equation has many solutions, but all of them satisfy the constraint that the variables x_1 through x_4 must encode possible initial conditions and evolution histories for rule 110. If one fills in fixed values for x_1, x_2 and x_3, then only one value for x_4 is ever possible—corresponding to the evolution history of rule 110 for x_3 steps starting from a width x_1 initial condition given by the digit sequence of x_2. In general any statement about the possible behavior of rule 110 can be encoded as a statement in arithmetic about solutions to the equation. So for example if one fills in values for x_1, x_2 and x_4, but not x_3, then the statement that the equation has no solution for any x_3 corresponds to a statement that rule 110 can never exhibit certain behavior, even after any number of steps. But the universality of rule 110 implies that such statements must in general be undecidable. So from this it follows that in at least some instances the axioms of arithmetic can never be used to give a finite proof of whether or not the statement is true. The construction shown here can be viewed as providing a simple proof of Gödel's Theorem on the existence of unprovable statements in arithmetic. Note that the equation shown is a so-called exponential Diophantine one, in which some variables appear in exponents. At the cost of considerably more complication—and using for example 2154 variables—it is possible to avoid this. The equation above can however already be viewed as capturing the essence of what is needed to demonstrate the general unsolvability of Diophantine equations and Hilbert's Tenth Problem.

Over the past seventy years a few simpler examples have been constructed—mostly with no obviously self-referential character.

But usually these examples have involved rather sophisticated and obscure mathematical constructs—most often functions that are somehow set up to grow extremely rapidly. Yet at least in principle there should be examples that can be constructed based just on statements that no solutions exist to particular integer equations.

If an integer equation such as $x^2 = y^3 + 12$ has a definite solution such as $x = 47$, $y = 13$ in terms of particular finite integers then this fact can certainly be proved using the axioms of arithmetic. For it takes only a finite calculation to check the solution, and this very calculation can always in effect be thought of as a proof.

But what if the equation has no solutions? To test this explicitly one would have to look at an infinite number of possible integers. But the point is that even so, there can still potentially be a finite mathematical proof that none of these integers will work.

And sometimes the proof may be straightforward—say being based on showing that one side of the equation is always odd while the other is always even. In other cases the proof may be more difficult— say being based on establishing some large maximum size for a solution, then checking all integers up to that size.

And the point is that in general there may in fact be absolutely no proof that can be given in terms of the normal axioms of arithmetic.

So how can one see this?

The picture on the facing page shows that one can construct an integer equation whose solutions represent the behavior of a system like a cellular automaton. And the way this works is that for example one variable in the equation gives the number of steps of evolution, while another gives the outcome after that number of steps.

So with this setup, one can specify the number of steps, then solve for the outcome after that number of steps. But what if for example one instead specifies an outcome, then tries to find a solution for the number of steps at which this outcome occurs?

If in general one was able to tell whether such a solution exists then it would mean that one could always answer the question of whether, say, a particular pattern would ever die out in the evolution of a given cellular automaton. But from the discussion of the previous section we know that this in general is undecidable.

So it follows that it must be undecidable whether a given integer equation of some particular general form has a solution. And from the arguments above this in turn implies that there must be specific integer equations that have no solutions but where this fact cannot be proved from the normal axioms of arithmetic.

So how ultimately can this happen?

At some level it is a consequence of the involvement of infinity. For at least in a universal system like arithmetic any question that is entirely finite can in the end always be answered by a finite procedure.

But what about questions that somehow ask, say, about infinite numbers of possible integers? To have a finite way to address questions like these is often in the end the main justification for setting up typical mathematical axiom systems in the first place.

For the point is that instead of handling objects like integers directly, axiom systems can just give abstract rules for manipulating statements about them. And within such statements one can refer, say, to infinite sets of integers just by a symbol like s.

And particularly over the past century there have been many successes in mathematics that can be attributed to this basic kind of approach. But the remarkable fact that follows from Gödel's Theorem is that whatever one does there will always be cases where the approach must ultimately fail. And it turns out that the reason for this is essentially the phenomenon of computational irreducibility.

For while simple infinite quantities like $1/0$ or the total number of integers can readily be summarized in finite ways—often just by using symbols like ∞ and $\aleph_0$—the same is not in general true of all infinite processes. And in particular if an infinite process is computationally irreducible then there cannot in general be any useful finite summary of what it does—since the existence of such a summary would imply computational reducibility.

So among other things this means that there will inevitably be questions that finite proofs based on axioms that operate within ordinary computational systems will never in general be able to answer.

And indeed with integer equations, as soon as one has a general equation that is universal, it typically follows that there will be specific instances in which the absence of solutions—or at least of solutions of some particular kind—can never be proved on the basis of the normal axioms of arithmetic.

For several decades it has been known that universal integer equations exist. But the examples that have actually been constructed are quite complicated—like the one on page 786—with the simplest involving 9 variables and an immense number of terms.

Yet from the discoveries in this book I am quite certain that there are vastly simpler examples that exist—so that in fact there are in the end rather simple integer equations for which the absence of solutions can never be proved from the normal axioms of arithmetic.

If one just starts looking at sequences of integer equations—as on the next page—then in the very simplest cases it is usually fairly easy to tell whether a particular equation will have any solutions. But this rapidly becomes very much more difficult. For there is often no obvious pattern to which equations ultimately have solutions and which do not. And even when equations do have solutions, the integers involved can be quite large. So, for example, the smallest solution to $x^2 = 61\,y^2 + 1$ is $x = 1766319049$, $y = 226153980$, while the smallest solution to $x^3 + y^3 = z^3 + 2$ is $x = 1214928$, $y = 3480205$, $z = 3528875$.

Integer equations such as $a\,x + b\,y + c\,z = d$ that have only linear dependence on any variable were largely understood even in antiquity. Quadratic equations in two variables such as $x^2 = a\,y^2 + b$ were understood by the 1800s. But even equations such as $x^2 = a\,y^3 + b$ were not properly understood until the 1980s. And with equations that have higher powers or more variables questions of whether solutions exist quickly end up being unsolved problems of number theory.

It has certainly been known for centuries that there are questions about integer equations and other aspects of number theory that are easy to state, yet seem very hard to answer. But in practice it has almost

$2x + 3y = 1$ □
$2x + 3y = 2$ □
$2x + 3y = 3$ □
$2x + 3y = 4$ □
$2x + 3y = 5$ — $x = 1$, $y = 1$
$2x + 3y = 6$ □
$2x + 3y = 7$ — $x = 2$, $y = 1$
$2x + 3y = 8$ — $x = 1$, $y = 2$
$2x + 3y = 9$ — $x = 3$, $y = 1$
$2x + 3y = 10$ — $x = 2$, $y = 2$
$2x + 3y = 11$ — $x = 1$, $y = 3$
$2x + 3y = 12$ — $x = 3$, $y = 2$
$2x + 3y = 13$ — $x = 2$, $y = 3$
$2x + 3y = 14$ — $x = 1$, $y = 4$
$2x + 3y = 15$ — $x = 3$, $y = 3$

$x^2 = y^2 + 1$ □
$x^2 = y^2 + 2$ □
$x^2 = y^2 + 3$ — $x = 2$, $y = 1$
$x^2 = y^2 + 4$ □
$x^2 = y^2 + 5$ — $x = 3$, $y = 2$
$x^2 = y^2 + 6$ □
$x^2 = y^2 + 7$ — $x = 4$, $y = 3$
$x^2 = y^2 + 8$ — $x = 3$, $y = 1$
$x^2 = y^2 + 9$ — $x = 5$, $y = 4$
$x^2 = y^2 + 10$ □
$x^2 = y^2 + 11$ — $x = 6$, $y = 5$
$x^2 = y^2 + 12$ — $x = 4$, $y = 2$
$x^2 = y^2 + 13$ — $x = 7$, $y = 6$
$x^2 = y^2 + 14$ □
$x^2 = y^2 + 15$ — $x = 4$, $y = 1$
$x^2 = y^2 + 16$ — $x = 5$, $y = 3$

$x^2 = y^2 + 1$ □
$x^2 = 2y^2 + 1$ — $x = 3$, $y = 2$
$x^2 = 3y^2 + 1$ — $x = 2$, $y = 1$
$x^2 = 4y^2 + 1$ □
$x^2 = 5y^2 + 1$ — $x = 9$, $y = 4$
$x^2 = 6y^2 + 1$ — $x = 5$, $y = 2$
$x^2 = 7y^2 + 1$ — $x = 8$, $y = 3$
$x^2 = 8y^2 + 1$ — $x = 3$, $y = 1$
$x^2 = 9y^2 + 1$ □
$x^2 = 10y^2 + 1$ — $x = 19$, $y = 6$
$x^2 = 11y^2 + 1$ — $x = 10$, $y = 3$
$x^2 = 12y^2 + 1$ — $x = 7$, $y = 2$
$x^2 = 13y^2 + 1$ — $x = 649$, $y = 180$
$x^2 = 14y^2 + 1$ — $x = 15$, $y = 4$
$x^2 = 15y^2 + 1$ — $x = 4$, $y = 1$
$x^2 = 16y^2 + 1$ □
$x^2 = 17y^2 + 1$ — $x = 33$, $y = 8$
$x^2 = 18y^2 + 1$ — $x = 17$, $y = 4$
$x^2 = 19y^2 + 1$ — $x = 170$, $y = 39$
$x^2 = 20y^2 + 1$ — $x = 9$, $y = 2$

$x^2 = y^3 - 20$ — $x = 14$, $y = 6$
$x^2 = y^3 - 19$ — $x = 18$, $y = 7$
$x^2 = y^3 - 18$ — $x = 3$, $y = 3$
$x^2 = y^3 - 17$ □
$x^2 = y^3 - 16$ □
$x^2 = y^3 - 15$ — $x = 7$, $y = 4$
$x^2 = y^3 - 14$ □
$x^2 = y^3 - 13$ — $x = 70$, $y = 17$
$x^2 = y^3 - 12$ □
$x^2 = y^3 - 11$ — $x = 4$, $y = 3$
$x^2 = y^3 - 10$ □
$x^2 = y^3 - 9$ □
$x^2 = y^3 - 8$ □
$x^2 = y^3 - 7$ — $x = 1$, $y = 2$
$x^2 = y^3 - 6$ □
$x^2 = y^3 - 5$ □
$x^2 = y^3 - 4$ — $x = 2$, $y = 2$
$x^2 = y^3 - 3$ □
$x^2 = y^3 - 2$ — $x = 5$, $y = 3$
$x^2 = y^3 - 1$ □
$x^2 = y^3$ — $x = 1$, $y = 1$
$x^2 = y^3 + 1$ — $x = 3$, $y = 2$
$x^2 = y^3 + 2$ □
$x^2 = y^3 + 3$ — $x = 2$, $y = 1$
$x^2 = y^3 + 4$ □
$x^2 = y^3 + 5$ □
$x^2 = y^3 + 6$ □
$x^2 = y^3 + 7$ □
$x^2 = y^3 + 8$ — $x = 3$, $y = 1$
$x^2 = y^3 + 9$ — $x = 6$, $y = 3$
$x^2 = y^3 + 10$ □
$x^2 = y^3 + 11$ □
$x^2 = y^3 + 12$ — $x = 47$, $y = 13$
$x^2 = y^3 + 13$ □
$x^2 = y^3 + 14$ □
$x^2 = y^3 + 15$ — $x = 4$, $y = 1$
$x^2 = y^3 + 16$ □
$x^2 = y^3 + 17$ — $x = 5$, $y = 2$
$x^2 = y^3 + 18$ — $x = 19$, $y = 7$
$x^2 = y^3 + 19$ — $x = 12$, $y = 5$
$x^2 = y^3 + 20$ □

$x^2 = y^3 + 1$ — $x = 3$, $y = 2$
$x^2 = 2y^3 + 1$ □
$x^2 = 3y^3 + 1$ — $x = 2$, $y = 1$
$x^2 = 4y^3 + 1$ □
$x^2 = 5y^3 + 1$ □
$x^2 = 6y^3 + 1$ — $x = 7$, $y = 2$
$x^2 = 7y^3 + 1$ □
$x^2 = 8y^3 + 1$ — $x = 3$, $y = 1$
$x^2 = 9y^3 + 1$ □
$x^2 = 10y^3 + 1$ — $x = 9$, $y = 2$

$x^3 = y^4 - 20xy - 1$ — $x = 10$, $y = 7$
$x^3 = y^4 - 19xy - 1$ — $x = 3$, $y = 4$
$x^3 = y^4 - 18xy - 1$ — $x = 75$, $y = 26$
$x^3 = y^4 - 17xy - 1$ □
$x^3 = y^4 - 16xy - 1$ □
$x^3 = y^4 - 15xy - 1$ — $x = 624$, $y = 125$
$x^3 = y^4 - 14xy - 1$ □
$x^3 = y^4 - 13xy - 1$ □
$x^3 = y^4 - 12xy - 1$ — $x = 3$, $y = 2$
$x^3 = y^4 - 11xy - 1$ □
$x^3 = y^4 - 10xy - 1$ □
$x^3 = y^4 - 9xy - 1$ — $x = 80$, $y = 27$
$x^3 = y^4 - 8xy - 1$ — $x = 12$, $y = 7$
$x^3 = y^4 - 7xy - 1$ — $x = 1$, $y = 2$
$x^3 = y^4 - 6xy - 1$ — $x = 15$, $y = 8$
$x^3 = y^4 - 5xy - 1$ □
$x^3 = y^4 - 4xy - 1$ — $x = 30$, $y = 13$
$x^3 = y^4 - 3xy - 1$ □
$x^3 = y^4 - 2xy - 1$ □
$x^3 = y^4 - xy - 1$ □
$x^3 = y^4 - 1$ □
$x^3 = y^4 + xy - 1$ — $x = 1$, $y = 1$
$x^3 = y^4 + 2xy - 1$ — $x = 3$, $y = 2$
$x^3 = y^4 + 3xy - 1$ — $x = 5$, $y = 3$
$x^3 = y^4 + 4xy - 1$ — $x = 2$, $y = 1$
$x^3 = y^4 + 5xy - 1$ □
$x^3 = y^4 + 6xy - 1$ □
$x^3 = y^4 + 7xy - 1$ □
$x^3 = y^4 + 8xy - 1$ — $x = 20$, $y = 9$
$x^3 = y^4 + 9xy - 1$ — $x = 3$, $y = 1$
$x^3 = y^4 + 10xy - 1$ □
$x^3 = y^4 + 11xy - 1$ — $x = 5$, $y = 2$
$x^3 = y^4 + 12xy - 1$ □
$x^3 = y^4 + 13xy - 1$ □
$x^3 = y^4 + 14xy - 1$ □
$x^3 = y^4 + 15xy - 1$ □
$x^3 = y^4 + 16xy - 1$ — $x = 4$, $y = 1$
$x^3 = y^4 + 17xy - 1$ □
$x^3 = y^4 + 18xy - 1$ — $x = 8$, $y = 3$
$x^3 = y^4 + 19xy - 1$ □
$x^3 = y^4 + 20xy - 1$ □

$x^2 = y^5 + 3$ — $x = 2$, $y = 1$
$x^2 = y^5 + y + 3$ — $x = 2537$, $y = 23$
$x^2 = y^5 + 2y + 3$ □
$x^2 = y^5 + 3y + 3$ □
$x^2 = y^5 + 4y + 3$ □
$x^2 = y^5 + 5y + 3$ — $x = 3$, $y = 1$
$x^2 = y^5 + 6y + 3$ □
$x^2 = y^5 + 7y + 3$ — $x = 7$, $y = 2$
$x^2 = y^5 + 8y + 3$ □
$x^2 = y^5 + 9y + 3$ □

$x^3 + y^3 = z^3 + 1$ — $x = 1$, $y = 1$, $z = 1$
$x^3 + y^3 = z^3 + 2$ — $x = 107$, $y = 232$, $z = 3703$
$x^3 + y^3 = z^3 + 3$ — $x = 1$, $y = 3$, $z = 5$
$x^3 + y^3 = z^3 + 4$ — $x = 5$, $y = 12$, $z = 43$
$x^3 + y^3 = z^3 + 5$ — $x = 1$, $y = 2$, $z = 2$
$x^3 + y^3 = z^3 + 6$ — $x = 7$, $y = 24$, $z = 119$
$x^3 + y^3 = z^3 + 7$ — $x = 2$, $y = 2$, $z = 3$
$x^3 + y^3 = z^3 + 8$ — $x = 1$, $y = 2$, $z = 1$
$x^3 + y^3 = z^3 + 9$ — $x = 3$, $y = 7$, $z = 19$
$x^3 + y^3 = z^3 + 10$ — $x = 2$, $y = 3$, $z = 5$

$x^3 + y^3 = z^3 - 20$ — $x = 107$, $y = 137$, $z = 156$
$x^3 + y^3 = z^3 - 19$ — $x = 14$, $y = 16$, $z = 19$
$x^3 + y^3 = z^3 - 18$ — $x = 1$, $y = 2$, $z = 3$
$x^3 + y^3 = z^3 - 17$ — $x = 103$, $y = 111$, $z = 135$
$x^3 + y^3 = z^3 - 16$ — $x = 10$, $y = 12$, $z = 14$
$x^3 + y^3 = z^3 - 15$ — $x = 262$, $y = 265$, $z = 332$
$x^3 + y^3 = z^3 - 14$ □
$x^3 + y^3 = z^3 - 13$ □
$x^3 + y^3 = z^3 - 12$ — $x = 5725013$, $y = 9019406$, $z = 9730705$
$x^3 + y^3 = z^3 - 11$ — $x = 2$, $y = 2$, $z = 3$
$x^3 + y^3 = z^3 - 10$ — $x = 3$, $y = 3$, $z = 4$
$x^3 + y^3 = z^3 - 9$ — $x = 52$, $y = 216$, $z = 217$
$x^3 + y^3 = z^3 - 8$ — $x = 16$, $y = 12$, $z = 18$
$x^3 + y^3 = z^3 - 7$ — $x = 605809$, $y = 680316$, $z = 812918$
$x^3 + y^3 = z^3 - 6$ — $x = 1$, $y = 1$, $z = 2$
$x^3 + y^3 = z^3 - 5$ □
$x^3 + y^3 = z^3 - 4$ □
$x^3 + y^3 = z^3 - 3$
$x^3 + y^3 = z^3 - 2$ — $x = 5$, $y = 6$, $z = 7$
$x^3 + y^3 = z^3 - 1$ — $x = 6$, $y = 8$, $z = 9$
$x^3 + y^3 = z^3$ □
$x^3 + y^3 = z^3 + 1$ — $x = 1$, $y = 2$, $z = 2$
$x^3 + y^3 = z^3 + 2$ — $x = 1214928$, $y = 3480205$, $z = 3528875$
$x^3 + y^3 = z^3 + 3$ — $x = 4$, $y = 4$, $z = 5$
$x^3 + y^3 = z^3 + 4$
$x^3 + y^3 = z^3 + 5$ □
$x^3 + y^3 = z^3 + 6$ — $x = 10529$, $y = 60248$, $z = 60355$
$x^3 + y^3 = z^3 + 7$ — $x = 32$, $y = 104$, $z = 105$
$x^3 + y^3 = z^3 + 8$ — $x = 1$, $y = 2$, $z = 1$
$x^3 + y^3 = z^3 + 9$ — $x = 2097$, $y = 11305$, $z = 11329$
$x^3 + y^3 = z^3 + 10$ — $x = 130$, $y = 141$, $z = 171$
$x^3 + y^3 = z^3 + 11$ — $x = 297$, $y = 619$, $z = 641$
$x^3 + y^3 = z^3 + 12$ — $x = 7$, $y = 10$, $z = 11$
$x^3 + y^3 = z^3 + 13$ □
$x^3 + y^3 = z^3 + 14$ □
$x^3 + y^3 = z^3 + 15$ — $x = 2$, $y = 2$, $z = 1$
$x^3 + y^3 = z^3 + 16$ — $x = 2429856$, $y = 6960410$, $z = 7057750$
$x^3 + y^3 = z^3 + 17$ — $x = 25$, $y = 50$, $z = 52$
$x^3 + y^3 = z^3 + 18$ — $x = 94$, $y = 101$, $z = 123$
$x^3 + y^3 = z^3 + 19$ — $x = 26$, $y = 76$, $z = 77$
$x^3 + y^3 = z^3 + 20$ — $x = 1$, $y = 3$, $z = 2$

universally been assumed that with the continued development of mathematics any of these questions could in the end be answered.

However, what Gödel's Theorem shows is that there must always exist some questions that cannot ever be answered using the normal axioms of arithmetic. Yet the fact that the few known explicit examples have been extremely complicated has made this seem somehow fundamentally irrelevant for the actual practice of mathematics.

But from the discoveries in this book it now seems quite certain that vastly simpler examples also exist. And it is my strong suspicion that in fact of all the current unsolved problems seriously studied in number theory a fair fraction will in the end turn out to be questions that cannot ever be answered using the normal axioms of arithmetic.

If one looks at recent work in number theory, most of it tends to be based on rather sophisticated methods that do not obviously depend only on the normal axioms of arithmetic. And for example the elaborate proof of Fermat's Last Theorem that has been developed may make at least some use of axioms that come from fields like set theory and go beyond the normal ones for arithmetic.

But so long as one stays within, say, the standard axiom systems of mathematics on pages 773 and 774, and does not in effect just end up implicitly adding as an axiom whatever result one is trying to prove, my strong suspicion is that one will ultimately never be able to go much further than one can purely with the normal axioms of arithmetic.

And indeed from the Principle of Computational Equivalence I strongly believe that in general undecidability and unprovability will start to occur in practically any area of mathematics almost as soon as one goes beyond the level of questions that are always easy to answer.

But if this is so, why then has mathematics managed to get as far as it has? Certainly there are problems in mathematics that have remained unsolved for long periods of time. And I suspect that many of these will in fact in the end turn out to involve undecidability and

◀ Smallest solutions for various sequences of integer (or so-called Diophantine) equations. □ indicates that it can be proved that no solution exists. A blank indicates that I know only that no solution exists below a billion. Methods for resolving some of the equations in the first column were known in antiquity; all had been resolved by the 1800s. Practical methods for resolving the so-called elliptic curve equations in the second column were developed only in the 1980s. No general methods are yet known for most of the other equations given—and some classes of them may in fact show undecidability.

unprovability. But the issue remains why such phenomena have not been much more obvious in everyday work in mathematics.

At some level I suspect the reason is quite straightforward: it is that like most other fields of human inquiry mathematics has tended to define itself to be concerned with just those questions that its methods can successfully address. And since the main methods traditionally used in mathematics have revolved around doing proofs, questions that involve undecidability and unprovability have inevitably been avoided.

But can this really be right? For at least in the past century mathematics has consistently given the impression that it is concerned with questions that are somehow as arbitrary and general as possible.

But one of the important conclusions from what I have done in this book is that this is far from correct. And indeed for example traditional mathematics has for the most part never even considered most of the kinds of systems that I discuss in this book—even though they are based on some of the very simplest rules possible.

So how has this happened? The main point, I believe, is that in both the systems it studies and the questions it asks mathematics is much more a product of its history than is usually realized.

And in fact particularly compared to what I do in this book the vast majority of mathematics practiced today still seems to follow remarkably closely the traditions of arithmetic and geometry that already existed even in Babylonian times.

It is a fairly recent notion that mathematics should even try to address arbitrary or general systems. For until not much more than a century ago mathematics viewed itself essentially just as providing a precise formulation of certain aspects of everyday experience—mainly those related to number and space.

But in the 1800s, with developments such as non-Euclidean geometry, quaternions, group theory and transfinite numbers it began to be assumed that the discipline of mathematics could successfully be applied to any abstract system, however arbitrary or general.

Yet if one looks at the types of systems that are actually studied in mathematics they continue even to this day to be far from as general as possible. Indeed at some level most of them can be viewed as having been arrived at by the single rather specific approach of starting from some known set of theorems, then trying to find systems that are progressively more general, yet still manage to satisfy these theorems.

And given this approach, it tends to be the case that the questions that are considered interesting are ones that revolve around whatever theorems a system was set up to satisfy—making it rather likely that these questions can themselves be addressed by similar theorems, without any confrontation with undecidability or unprovability.

But what if one looks at other kinds of systems?

One of the main things I have done in this book is in a sense to introduce a new approach to generalization in which one considers systems that have simple but completely arbitrary rules—and that are not set up with any constraint about what theorems they should satisfy.

But if one has such a system, how does one decide what questions are interesting to ask about it? Without the guidance of known theorems, the obvious thing to do is just to look explicitly at how the system behaves—perhaps by making some kind of picture.

And if one does this, then what I have found is that one is usually immediately led to ask questions that run into phenomena like undecidability. Indeed, from my experiments it seems that almost as soon as one leaves behind the constraints of mathematical tradition undecidability and unprovability become rather common.

As the picture on the next page indicates, it is quite straightforward to set up an axiom system that deals with logical statements about a system like a cellular automaton. And within such an axiom system one can ask questions such as whether the cellular automaton will ever behave in a particular way after any number of steps.

But as we saw in the previous section, such questions are in general undecidable. And what this means is that there will inevitably be cases of them for which no proof of a particular answer can ever be given within whatever axiom system one is using.

So from this one might conclude that as soon as one looks at cellular automata or other kinds of systems beyond those normally studied in mathematics it must immediately become effectively impossible to make progress using traditional mathematical methods.

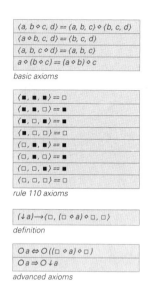

$\langle a, b \diamond c, d \rangle == \langle a, b, c \rangle \diamond \langle b, c, d \rangle$
$\langle a \diamond b, c, d \rangle == \langle b, c, d \rangle$
$\langle a, b, c \diamond d \rangle == \langle a, b, c \rangle$
$a \diamond (b \diamond c) == (a \diamond b) \diamond c$

basic axioms

$\langle \blacksquare, \blacksquare, \blacksquare \rangle == \square$
$\langle \blacksquare, \blacksquare, \square \rangle == \blacksquare$
$\langle \blacksquare, \square, \blacksquare \rangle == \blacksquare$
$\langle \blacksquare, \square, \square \rangle == \square$
$\langle \square, \blacksquare, \blacksquare \rangle == \blacksquare$
$\langle \square, \blacksquare, \square \rangle == \blacksquare$
$\langle \square, \square, \blacksquare \rangle == \blacksquare$
$\langle \square, \square, \square \rangle == \square$

rule 110 axioms

$(\downarrow a) \rightarrow \langle \square, (\square \diamond a) \diamond \square, \square \rangle$

definition

$O a \Leftrightarrow O((\square \diamond a) \diamond \square)$
$O a \Rightarrow O \downarrow a$

advanced axioms

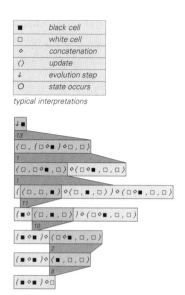

$\blacksquare$	black cell
$\square$	white cell
$\diamond$	concatenation
$\langle\rangle$	update
$\downarrow$	evolution step
O	state occurs

typical interpretations

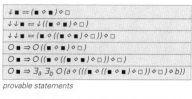

$\downarrow \blacksquare == (\blacksquare \diamond \blacksquare) \diamond \square$
$\downarrow \downarrow \blacksquare == \downarrow ((\blacksquare \diamond \blacksquare) \diamond \square)$
$\downarrow \downarrow \blacksquare == (\blacksquare \diamond ((\blacksquare \diamond \blacksquare) \diamond \square)) \diamond \square$
$O \blacksquare \Rightarrow O((\blacksquare \diamond \blacksquare) \diamond \square)$
$O \blacksquare \Rightarrow O((\blacksquare \diamond ((\blacksquare \diamond \blacksquare) \diamond \square)) \diamond \square)$
$O \blacksquare \Rightarrow \exists_a \exists_b O(a \diamond (((\blacksquare \diamond ((\blacksquare \diamond \blacksquare) \diamond \square)) \diamond \square) \diamond b))$

provable statements

$O \blacksquare \Rightarrow \exists_a \exists_b O(a \diamond (((\square \diamond ((\blacksquare \diamond \square) \diamond \blacksquare)) \diamond \square) \diamond b))$

unprovable statement

An axiom system for statements about the rule 110 cellular automaton. The top statement above makes the assertion that the outcome after one step of evolution from a single black cell has a particular form. A proof of this statement is shown to the left. All the statements in the top block above can be proved true from the axiom system. The statement at the bottom, however, cannot be proved either true or false. The axioms given are set up using predicate logic.

But in fact, in the fifteen years or so since I first emphasized the importance of cellular automata all sorts of traditional mathematical work has actually been done on them. So how has this been possible?

The basic point is that the work has tended to concentrate on particular aspects of cellular automata that are simple enough to avoid undecidability and unprovability. And typically it has achieved this in one of two ways: either by considering only very specific cases that have been observed or constructed to be simple, or by looking at things in so much generality that only rather simple properties ever survive.

So for example when presented with the 256 elementary cellular automaton patterns shown on page 55 mathematicians in my experience have two common responses: either to single out specific patterns that have a simple repetitive or perhaps nested form, or to generalize and look not at individual patterns, but rather at aggregate properties obtained say by evolving from all possible initial conditions.

And about questions that concern, for example, the structure of a pattern that looks to us complex, the almost universal reaction is that such questions can somehow not be of any real mathematical interest.

Needless to say, in the framework of the new kind of science in this book, such questions are now of great interest. And my results suggest that if one is ever going to study many important phenomena that occur in nature one will also inevitably run into them. But to traditional mathematics they seem uninteresting and quite alien.

As I said above, it is at some level not surprising that questions will be considered interesting in a particular field only if the methods of that field can say something useful about them. But this I believe is ultimately why there have historically been so few signs of undecidability or unprovability in mathematics. For any kinds of questions in which such phenomena appear are usually not amenable to standard methods of mathematics based on proof, and as a result such questions have inevitably been viewed as being outside what should be considered interesting for mathematics.

So how then can one set up a reasonable idealization for mathematics as it is actually practiced? The first step—much as I discussed earlier in this section—is to think not so much about systems that might be described by mathematics as about the internal processes associated with proof that go on inside mathematics.

A proof must ultimately be based on an axiom system, and one might have imagined that over the course of time mathematics would have sampled a wide range of possible axiom systems. But in fact in its historical development mathematics has normally stuck to only rather few such systems—each one corresponding essentially to some identifiable field of mathematics, and most given on pages 773 and 774.

So what then happens if one looks at all possible simple axiom systems—much as we looked, say, at all possible simple cellular automata earlier in this book? To what extent does what one sees capture the features of mathematics? With axiom systems idealized as multiway systems the pictures on the next page show some results.

In some cases the total number of theorems that can ever be proved is limited. But often the number of theorems increases rapidly with the length of proof—and in most cases an infinite number of theorems can eventually be proved. And given experience with mathematics an obvious question to ask in such cases is to what extent the system is consistent, or complete, or both.

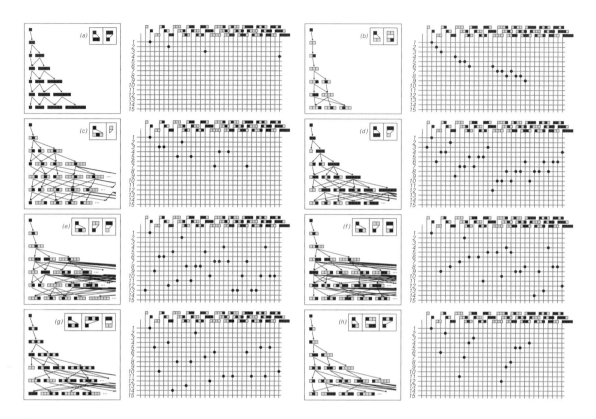

Plots showing which possible strings get generated in the first 15 steps of evolution in various multiway systems. Each string that is generated can be thought of as a theorem derived from the set of axioms represented by the rules of the multiway system. A dot shows at which step a given string first appears—and indicates the shortest proof of the theorem that string represents. In most cases, many strings are never produced—so that there are many possible statements that simply do not follow from the axioms given. Thus for example in first case shown only strings containing nothing but black elements are ever produced.

But to formulate such a question in a meaningful way one needs a notion of negation. In general, negation is just some operation that takes a string and yields another, giving back the original if it is applied a second time. Earlier in this section we discussed cases in which negation simply reverses the color of each element in a string. And as a generalization of this one can consider cases in which negation can be any operation that preserves lengths of strings.

And in this case it turns out that the criterion for whether a system is complete and consistent is simply that exactly half the possible strings of a given length are eventually generated if one starts from the string representing "true".

For if more than half the strings are generated, then somewhere both a string and its negation would have to appear, implying that the system must be inconsistent. And similarly, if less than half the strings are generated, there must be some string for which neither that string nor its negation ever appear, implying that the system is incomplete.

The pictures on the next page show the fractions of strings of given lengths that are generated on successive steps in various multiway systems. In general one might have to wait an arbitrarily large number of steps to find out whether a given string will ever be generated. But in practice after just a few steps one already seems to get a reasonable indication of the overall fraction of strings that will ever be generated.

And what one sees is that there is a broad distribution: from cases in which very few strings can be generated—corresponding to a very incomplete axiom system—to cases in which all or almost all strings can be generated—corresponding to a very inconsistent axiom system.

So where in this distribution do the typical axiom systems of ordinary mathematics lie? Presumably none are inconsistent. And a few—like basic logic and real algebra—are both complete and consistent, so that in effect they lie right in the middle of the distribution. But most are known to be incomplete. And as we discussed above, this is inevitable as soon as universality is present.

But just how incomplete are they? The answer, it seems, is typically not very. For if one looks at axiom systems that are widely used in mathematics they almost all tend to be complete enough to prove at least a fair fraction of statements either true or false.

So why should this be? I suspect that it has to do with the fact that in mathematics one usually wants axiom systems that one can think of as somehow describing definite kinds of objects—about which one then expects to be able to establish all sorts of definite statements.

And certainly if one looks at the history of mathematics most basic axiom systems have been arrived at by starting with objects—such as finite integers or finite sets—then trying to find collections of axioms that somehow capture the relevant properties of these objects.

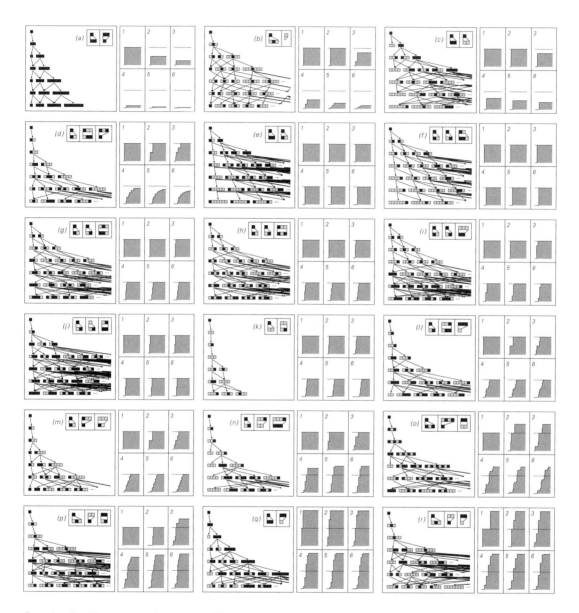

Examples of multiway systems that generate different fractions of possible strings, and in effect range from being highly incomplete to highly inconsistent. The plots show what fraction of strings of a given length have been produced by each of the first 25 steps in the evolution of each multiway system. If less than half the strings of a given length are ever produced, this means that there must be some strings where neither the string nor its negation can be proved, indicating incompleteness. But if more than half the strings are produced, there must be cases where both a string and its negation can be proved, indicating inconsistency. Rules (f) through (i), however, produce exactly half the strings of any given length, and can be considered complete and consistent.

But one feature is that normally the resulting axiom system is in a sense more general than the objects one started from. And this is why for example one can often use the axiom system to extrapolate to infinite situations. But it also means that it is not clear whether the axiom system actually describes only the objects one wants—or whether for example it also describes all sorts of other quite different objects.

One can think of an axiom system—say one of those listed on pages 773 and 774—as giving a set of constraints that any object it describes must satisfy. But as we saw in Chapter 5, it is often possible to satisfy a single set of constraints in several quite different ways.

And when this happens in an axiom system it typically indicates incompleteness. For as soon as there are just two objects that both satisfy the constraints but for which there is some statement that is true about one but false about the other it immediately follows that at least this statement cannot consistently be proved true or false, and that therefore the axiom system must be incomplete.

One might imagine that if one were to add more axioms to an axiom system one could always in the end force there to be only one kind of object that would satisfy the constraints of the system. But as we saw earlier, as soon as there is universality it is normally impossible to avoid incompleteness. And if an axiom system is incomplete there must inevitably be different kinds of objects that satisfy its constraints. For given any statement that cannot be proved from the axioms there must be distinct objects for which it is true, and for which it is false.

If an axiom system is far from complete—so that a large fraction of statements cannot be proved true or false—then there will typically be many different kinds of objects that are easy to specify and all satisfy the constraints of the system but for which there are fairly obvious properties that differ. But if an axiom system is close to complete—so that the vast majority of statements can be proved true or false—then it is almost inevitable that the different kinds of objects that satisfy its constraints must differ only in obscure ways.

And this is presumably the case in the standard axiom system for arithmetic from page 773. Originally this axiom system was intended to describe just ordinary integers. But Gödel's Theorem showed that it is incomplete, so that there must be more than one kind of object that can satisfy its constraints. Yet it is rather close to being complete—since as we saw earlier one has to go through at least millions of statements before finding ones that it cannot prove true or false.

And this means that even though there are objects other than the ordinary integers that satisfy the standard axioms of arithmetic, they are quite obscure—in fact, so much so that none have ever yet actually been constructed with any real degree of explicitness. And this is why it has been reasonable to think of the standard axiom system of arithmetic as being basically just about ordinary integers.

But if instead of this standard axiom system one uses the reduced axiom system from page 773—in which the usual axiom for induction has been weakened—then the story is quite different. There is again incompleteness, but now there is much more of it, for even statements as simple as $x + y = y + x$ and $x + 0 = x$ cannot be proved true or false from the axioms. And while ordinary integers still satisfy all the constraints, the system is sufficiently incomplete that all sorts of other objects with quite different properties also do. So this means that the system is in a sense no longer about any very definite kind of mathematical object—and presumably that is why it is not used in practice in mathematics.

At this juncture it should perhaps be mentioned that in their raw form quite a few well-known axiom systems from mathematics are actually also far from complete. An example of this is the axiom system for group theory given on page 773. But the point is that this axiom system represents in a sense just the beginning of group theory. For it yields only those theorems that hold abstractly for any group.

Yet in doing group theory in practice one normally adds axioms that in effect constrain one to be dealing say with a specific group rather than with all possible groups. And the result of this is that once again one typically has an axiom system that is at least close to complete.

In basic arithmetic and also usually in fields like group theory the underlying objects that one imagines describing can at some level be manipulated—and understood—in fairly concrete ways. But in a field like set theory this is less true. Yet even in this case an attempt has historically been made to get an axiom system that somehow describes definite kinds of objects. But now the main way this has been done is by progressively adding axioms so as to get closer to having a system that is complete—with only a rather vague notion of just what underlying objects one is really expecting to describe.

In studying basic processes of proof multiway systems seem to do well as minimal idealizations. But if one wants to study axiom systems that potentially describe definite objects it seems to be somewhat more convenient to use what I call operator systems. And indeed the version of logic used on page 775—as well as many of the axiom systems on pages 773 and 774—are already set up essentially as operator systems.

The basic idea of an operator system is to work with expressions such as $(p \circ q) \circ ((q \circ r) \circ p)$ built up using some operator $\circ$, and then to consider for example what equivalences may exist between such expressions. If one has an operator whose values are given by some finite table then it is always straightforward to determine whether expressions are equivalent. For all one need do, as in the pictures at the top of the next page, is to evaluate the expressions for all possible values of each variable, and then to see whether the patterns of results one gets are the same.

And in this way one can readily tell, for example, that the first operator shown is idempotent, so that $p \circ p = p$, while both the first two operators are associative, so that $(p \circ q) \circ r = p \circ (q \circ r)$, and all but the third operator are commutative, so that $p \circ q = q \circ p$. And in principle one can use this method to establish any equivalence that exists between any expressions with an operator of any specific form.

But the crucial idea that underlies the traditional approach to mathematical proof is that one should also be able to deduce such results just by manipulating expressions in purely symbolic form, using the rules of an axiom system, without ever having to do anything like filling in explicit values of variables.

And one advantage of this approach is that at least in principle it allows one to handle operators—like those found in many areas of mathematics—that are not based on finite tables. But even for operators given by finite tables it is often difficult to find axiom systems that can successfully reproduce all the results for a particular operator.

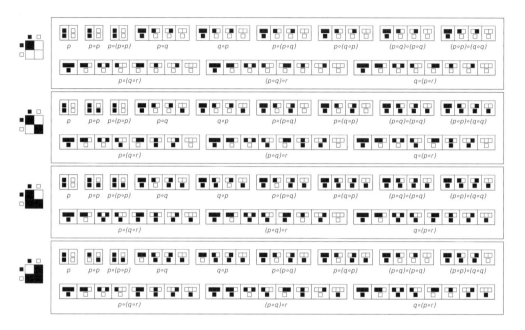

Values of expressions obtained by using operators of various forms. For each expression the sequence of values for every possible combination of values of variables is shown. Two expressions are equivalent when this sequence of values is the same. With black and white interpreted as TRUE and FALSE, the forms of operators shown here correspond respectively to AND, EQUAL, IMPLIES and NAND. (The first argument to each operator is shown on the left; the second on top.) The arrays of values generated can be thought of as being like truth tables.

With the way I have set things up, any axiom system is itself just a collection of equivalence results. So the question is then which equivalence results need to be included in the axiom system in order that all other equivalence results can be deduced just from these.

In general this can be undecidable—for there is no limit on how long even a single proof might need to be. But in some cases it turns out to be possible to establish that a particular set of axioms can successfully generate all equivalence results for a given operator—and indeed the picture at the top of the facing page shows examples of this for each of the four operators in the picture above.

So if two expressions are equivalent then by applying the rules of the appropriate axiom system it must be possible to get from one to the other—and in fact the picture on page 775 shows an example of how

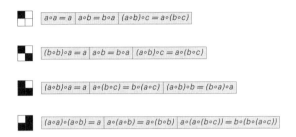

Axiom systems that can be used to derive all the equivalences between expressions that involve operators with the forms shown. Each axiom can be applied in either direction—as in the picture on page 775, with each variable standing for any expression, as in a *Mathematica* pattern. The operators shown are AND, EQUAL, IMPLIES and NAND. They yield respectively junctional, equivalential, implicational and full propositional or sentential calculus (ordinary logic).

this can be done for the fourth axiom system above. But if one removes just a single axiom from any of the axiom systems above then it turns out that they no longer work, and for example they cannot establish the equivalence result stated by whichever axiom one has removed.

In general one can think of axioms for an operator system as giving constraints on the form of the operator. And if one is going to reproduce all the equivalences that hold for a particular form then these constraints must in effect be such as to force that form to occur.

So what happens in general for arbitrary axiom systems? Do they typically force the operator to have a particular form, or not?

The pictures on the next two pages show which forms of operators are allowed by various different axiom systems. The successive blocks of results in each case give the forms allowed with progressively more possible values for each variable.

Indicated by stars near the bottom of the picture are the four axiom systems from the top of this page. And for each of these only a limited number of forms are allowed—all of which ultimately turn out to be equivalent to just the single forms shown on the facing page.

But what about other axiom systems? Every axiom system must allow an operator of at least some form. But what the pictures on the next two pages show is that the vast majority of axiom systems actually allow operators with all sorts of different forms.

And what this means is that these axiom systems are in a sense not really about operators of any particular form. And so in effect they are also far from complete—for they can prove only equivalence results that hold for every single one of the various operators they allow.

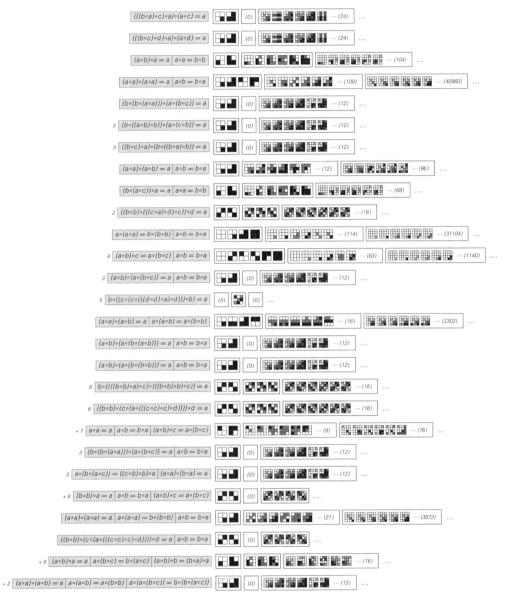

Forms of a binary operator satisfying the constraints of a series of different axiom systems. The successive blocks of results in each case show forms of the operator allowed with 2, 3 and 4 possible elements. Note that with 3 and 4 elements, only forms inequivalent under interchange of element labels are shown. Representations of notable systems in mathematics are: (1) semigroup theory, (2) commutative group theory, (3) basic logic, (4) commutative semigroup theory, (5) squag theory, (6) group theory, (7) junctional calculus, (8) equivalential calculus and (9) implicational calculus. In each case the operator forms shown correspond to possible semigroups, commutative groups, systems of logic (Boolean algebras), etc. with 2, 3 and 4 possible elements. The operator forms shown can be thought of as giving multiplication tables. In model theory, these forms are usually called the models of an axiom system.

So if one makes a list of all possible axiom systems—say starting with the simplest—where in such a list should one expect to see axiom systems that correspond to traditional areas of mathematics?

Most axiom systems as they are given in typical textbooks are sufficiently complicated that they will not show up at all early. And in fact the only immediate exception is the axiom system $\{(a \circ b) \circ c = a \circ (b \circ c)\}$ for what are known as semigroups—which ironically are usually viewed as rather advanced mathematical objects.

But just how complicated do the axiom systems for traditional areas of mathematics really need to be? Often it seems that they can be vastly simpler than their textbook forms. And so, for example, as page 773 indicates, interpreting the $\circ$ operator as division, $\{a \circ (b \circ (c \circ (a \circ b))) = c\}$ is known to be an axiom system for commutative group theory, and $\{a \circ ((((a \circ a) \circ b) \circ c) \circ (((a \circ a) \circ a) \circ c)) = b\}$ for general group theory.

So what about basic logic? How complicated an axiom system does one need for this? Textbook discussions of logic mostly use axiom systems at least as complicated as the first one on page 773. And such axiom systems not only involve several axioms—they also normally involve three separate operators: AND ($\wedge$), OR ($\vee$) and NOT ($\neg$).

But is this in fact the only way to formulate logic?

As the picture below shows, there are 16 different possible operators that take two arguments and allow two values, say true and false. And of these AND, OR and NOT are certainly the most commonly used in both everyday language and most of mathematics.

Logical functions of two arguments and their common names. Black stands for TRUE; white for FALSE. AND, OR, NOT, and IMPLIES are widely used in traditional logic. EQUAL (if and only if) is common in more mathematical settings, while XOR is widespread in discrete mathematics. NAND and NOR are mostly used only in circuit design and in a few foundational studies of logic. The first argument for each function appears on the left in the picture; the second argument on top. The functions are numbered like 2-neighbor analogs of the cellular automaton rules of page 53.

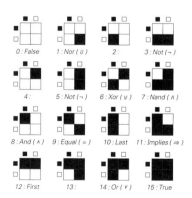

But at least at a formal level, logic can be viewed simply as a theory of functions that take on two possible values given variables with two possible values. And as we discussed on page 616, any such function can be represented as a combination of AND, OR and NOT.

But the table below demonstrates that as soon as one goes beyond the familiar traditions of language and mathematics there are other operators that can also just as well be used as primitives. And indeed it has been known since before 1900 that both NAND and NOR on their own work—a fact I already used on pages 617 and 775.

Block 1 — And, Or, Not (∧) (∨) (¬)

0	$\neg a \wedge a$	1	$\neg(a \vee b)$	2	$\neg a \wedge b$	3	$\neg a$
4	$\neg b \wedge a$	5	$\neg b$	6	$\neg(a \wedge b) \wedge (a \vee b)$	7	$\neg(a \wedge b)$
8	$a \wedge b$	9	$a \wedge b \vee \neg(a \vee b)$	10	b	11	$\neg a \vee b$
12	a	13	$\neg b \vee a$	14	$a \vee b$	15	$\neg a \vee a$

Block 2 — And, Not (∧) (¬)

0	$\neg a \wedge a$	1	$\neg a \wedge \neg b$	2	$\neg a \wedge b$	3	$\neg a$
4	$\neg b \wedge a$	5	$\neg b$	6	$\neg(\neg a \wedge \neg b) \wedge \neg(a \wedge b)$	7	$\neg(a \wedge b)$
8	$a \wedge b$	9	$\neg(\neg a \wedge b) \wedge \neg(\neg b \wedge a)$	10	b	11	$\neg(\neg b \wedge a)$
12	a	13	$\neg(\neg a \wedge b)$	14	$\neg(\neg a \wedge \neg b)$	15	$\neg(\neg a \wedge a)$

Block 3 — Or, Not (∨) (¬)

0	$\neg(\neg a \vee a)$	1	$\neg(a \vee b)$	2	$\neg(\neg b \vee a)$	3	$\neg a$
4	$\neg(\neg a \vee b)$	5	$\neg b$	6	$\neg(\neg a \vee b) \vee \neg(\neg b \vee a)$	7	$\neg a \vee \neg b$
8	$\neg(\neg a \vee \neg b)$	9	$\neg(\neg a \vee b) \vee (a \vee b)$	10	b	11	$\neg a \vee b$
12	a	13	$\neg b \vee a$	14	$a \vee b$	15	$\neg a \vee a$

Block 4 — Implies, Not (⇒) (¬)

0	$\neg(a \Rightarrow a)$	1	$\neg(\neg a \Rightarrow b)$	2	$\neg(b \Rightarrow a)$	3	$\neg a$
4	$\neg(a \Rightarrow b)$	5	$\neg b$	6	$(a \Rightarrow b) \Rightarrow \neg(b \Rightarrow a)$	7	$a \Rightarrow \neg b$
8	$\neg(a \Rightarrow \neg b)$	9	$\neg((a \Rightarrow b) \Rightarrow \neg(b \Rightarrow a))$	10	b	11	$a \Rightarrow b$
12	a	13	$b \Rightarrow a$	14	$\neg a \Rightarrow b$	15	$a \Rightarrow a$

Block 5 — Xor, Implies (⊻) (⇒)

0	$a \veebar a$	1	$(a \Rightarrow b) \veebar b$	2	$((a \Rightarrow b) \Rightarrow b) \veebar a$	3	$(a \Rightarrow a) \veebar a$
4	$((a \Rightarrow b) \Rightarrow b) \veebar b$	5	$(a \Rightarrow a) \veebar b$	6	$a \veebar b$	7	$(a \Rightarrow b) \veebar a$
8	$((a \Rightarrow b) \Rightarrow b) \veebar a) \veebar b$	9	$((a \Rightarrow a) \veebar a) \veebar b$	10	b	11	$a \Rightarrow b$
12	a	13	$b \Rightarrow a$	14	$(a \Rightarrow b) \Rightarrow b$	15	$a \Rightarrow a$

Block 6 — 2 (∘) 13 (∘̇)

0	$a \circ a$	1	$a \circ (a \mathbin{\dot{\circ}} b)$	2	$a \circ b$	3	$a \circ (a \mathbin{\dot{\circ}} a)$
4	$b \circ a$	5	$b \circ (a \mathbin{\dot{\circ}} a)$	6	$a \circ b \circ (b \mathbin{\dot{\circ}} a)$	7	$a \circ b \circ b$
8	$(a \circ b) \circ b$	9	$(a \circ b) \circ (b \mathbin{\dot{\circ}} a)$	10	b	11	$b \mathbin{\dot{\circ}} a$
12	a	13	$a \mathbin{\dot{\circ}} b$	14	$a \circ (a \mathbin{\dot{\circ}} b)$	15	$a \mathbin{\dot{\circ}} a$

Block 7 — Nand (⊼)

0	$((a \barwedge a) \barwedge a) \barwedge ((a \barwedge a) \barwedge a)$	1	$((a \barwedge a) \barwedge (b \barwedge b)) \barwedge ((a \barwedge a) \barwedge a)$	2	$((a \barwedge a) \barwedge a) \barwedge ((a \barwedge a) \barwedge b)$	3	$a \barwedge a$
4	$((a \barwedge a) \barwedge a) \barwedge ((a \barwedge b) \barwedge a)$	5	$b \barwedge b$	6	$((a \barwedge a) \barwedge b) \barwedge ((a \barwedge b) \barwedge a)$	7	$a \barwedge b$
8	$(a \barwedge b) \barwedge (a \barwedge b)$	9	$((a \barwedge a) \barwedge (b \barwedge b)) \barwedge (a \barwedge b)$	10	b	11	$(a \barwedge b) \barwedge a$
12	a	13	$(a \barwedge a) \barwedge b$	14	$(a \barwedge a) \barwedge (b \barwedge b)$	15	$(a \barwedge a) \barwedge a$

Block 8 — Nor (⊽)

0	$(a \veebar a) \veebar a$	1	$a \veebar b$	2	$(a \veebar b) \veebar a$	3	$a \veebar a$
4	$(a \veebar a) \veebar b$	5	$b \veebar b$	6	$((a \veebar a) \veebar (b \veebar b)) \veebar (a \veebar b)$	7	$((a \veebar a) \veebar (b \veebar b)) \veebar ((a \veebar a) \veebar a)$
8	$(a \veebar a) \veebar (b \veebar b)$	9	$((a \veebar a) \veebar b) \veebar ((a \veebar b) \veebar a)$	10	b	11	$((a \veebar a) \veebar a) \veebar ((a \veebar a) \veebar b)$
12	a	13	$((a \veebar a) \veebar a) \veebar ((a \veebar b) \veebar a)$	14	$(a \veebar b) \veebar (a \veebar b)$	15	$((a \veebar a) \veebar a) \veebar ((a \veebar a) \veebar a)$

Functions that can be used to formulate logic. In each case the minimal combinations of primitive functions necessary to reproduce each of the 16 logical functions of two arguments is given. From these any possible logical function with any number of arguments can be obtained. Most textbook treatments of logic use AND, OR, and NOT as primitive functions. NAND and NOR are the only primitive functions that work on their own.

So this means that logic can be set up using just a single operator. But how complicated an axiom system does it then need? The first box in the picture below shows that the direct translation of the standard textbook AND, OR, NOT axiom system from page 773 is very complicated.

(a) $\quad (a \circ b) \circ (a \circ b) = (b \circ a) \circ (b \circ a)$ $\quad (a \circ a) \circ (b \circ b) = (b \circ b) \circ (a \circ a)$ $\quad (a \circ ((b \circ b) \circ ((b \circ b) \circ (b \circ b)))) \circ (a \circ ((b \circ b) \circ ((b \circ b) \circ (b \circ b)))) = a$
$(a \circ a) \circ (((b \circ (b \circ b)) \circ (b \circ (b \circ b))) \circ ((b \circ (b \circ b)) \circ (b \circ (b \circ b)))) = a$ $\quad a \circ b = ((a \circ b) \circ (a \circ b)) \circ ((a \circ b) \circ (a \circ b))$
$(a \circ ((b \circ b) \circ (c \circ c))) \circ (a \circ ((b \circ b) \circ (c \circ c))) = (((a \circ b) \circ (a \circ b)) \circ ((a \circ b) \circ (a \circ b))) \circ (((a \circ c) \circ (a \circ c)) \circ ((a \circ c) \circ (a \circ c)))$
$(a \circ a) \circ (((b \circ c) \circ (b \circ c)) \circ ((b \circ c) \circ (b \circ c))) = (((a \circ a) \circ (b \circ b)) \circ ((a \circ a) \circ (c \circ c))) \circ (((a \circ a) \circ (b \circ b)) \circ ((a \circ a) \circ (c \circ c)))$

(b) $\quad (a \circ a) \circ (a \circ a) = a$ $\quad a \circ b = b \circ a$ $\quad a \circ ((b \circ c) \circ (b \circ c)) = b \circ ((a \circ c) \circ (a \circ c))$ $\quad (a \circ b) \circ (a \circ (b \circ b)) = a$

(c) $\quad (a \circ a) \circ (a \circ a) = a$ $\quad a \circ (b \circ (b \circ b)) = a \circ a$ $\quad (a \circ (b \circ c)) \circ (a \circ (b \circ c)) = ((b \circ b) \circ a) \circ ((c \circ c) \circ a)$

(d) $\quad (a \circ a) \circ (a \circ b) = a$ $\quad a \circ (a \circ b) = a \circ (b \circ b)$ $\quad a \circ (a \circ (b \circ c)) = b \circ (b \circ (a \circ c))$

Axiom systems for basic logic (propositional calculus) formulated in terms of NAND ($\bar{n}$). The number of operators that occur in these axiom systems is respectively 94, 17, 17, 13, 9, 6, 6, 6. System (a) is a translation of the standard textbook one given on page 773 in terms of AND, OR and NOT. (b) is based on the Robbins axioms from page 773. (c) is the Sheffer axiom system. (e) is the Meredith axiom system. The other axiom systems were found for this book. (d) was used on page 775. (g) and (h) are as short as is possible. Each axiom system given applies equally well to NOR as well as NAND.

(e) $\quad a \circ (b \circ (a \circ c)) = ((c \circ b) \circ b) \circ a$ $\quad (a \circ a) \circ (b \circ a) = a$

(f) $\quad (a \circ b) \circ (a \circ (b \circ c)) = a$ $\quad a \circ b = b \circ a$

(g) $\quad ((b \circ c) \circ a) \circ (b \circ ((b \circ a) \circ b)) = a$

(h) $\quad (b \circ ((a \circ b) \circ b)) \circ (a \circ (c \circ b)) = a$

But boxes (b) and (c) show that known alternative axiom systems for logic reduce the size of the axiom system by about a factor of ten. And some further reduction is achieved by manipulating the resulting axioms—leading to the axiom system used above and given in box (d).

But can one go still further? And what happens for example if one just tries to search simple axiom systems for ones that work?

One can potentially test axiom systems by seeing what operators satisfy their constraints, as on page 805. The first non-trivial axiom system that even allows the NAND operator is $\{(a \circ a) \circ (a \circ a) = a\}$. And the first axiom system for which NAND and NOR are the only operators allowed that involve 2 possible values is $\{((b \circ b) \circ a) \circ (a \circ b) = a\}$.

But if one now looks at operators involving 3 possible values then it turns out that this axiom system allows ones not equivalent to NAND

and NOR. And this means that it cannot successfully reproduce all the results of logic. Yet if any axiom system with just a single axiom is going to be able to do this, the axiom must be of the form $\{\ldots = a\}$.

With up to 6 NANDs and 2 variables none of the 16,896 possible axiom systems of this kind work even up to 3-value operators. But with 6 NANDs and 3 variables, 296 of the 288,684 possible axiom systems work up to 3-value operators, and 100 work up to 4-value operators.

And of the 25 of these that are not trivially equivalent, it then turns out that the two given as (g) and (h) on the facing page can actually be proved as on the next two pages to be axiom systems for logic—thus showing that in the end quite remarkable simplification can be achieved relative to ordinary textbook axiom systems.

If one looks at axiom systems of the form $\{\ldots = a, a \circ b = b \circ a\}$ the first one that one finds that allows only NAND and NOR with 2-value operators is $\{(a \circ a) \circ (a \circ a) = a, a \circ b = b \circ a\}$. But as soon as one uses a total of just 6 NANDs, one suddenly finds that out of the 3402 possibilities with 3 variables 32 axiom systems equivalent to case (f) above all end up working all the way up to at least 4-value operators. And in fact it then turns out that (f) indeed works as an axiom system for logic.

So what this means is that if one were just to go through a list of the simplest few thousand axiom systems one would already be quite likely to find one that represents logic.

In human intellectual history logic has had great significance. But if one looks just at axiom systems is there anything obviously special about the ones for logic? My guess is that unless one asks about very specific details there is really not—and that standard logic is in a sense distinguished in the end only by its historical context.

One feature of logic is that its axioms effectively describe a single specific operator. But it turns out that there are all sorts of other axioms that also do this. I gave three examples on page 803, and in the picture on the right I give two more very simple examples. Indeed, given many forms of operator there are always axiom systems that can be found to describe it.

Axiom systems that reproduce equivalence results for the forms of operators shown.

L1 (a((aa)a))(a((aa)a))
= A (((((aa)a)(a((aa)a)))(a((aa)a)))(((aa)a)((((aa)a)(a((aa)a)))((aa)a))))(a((aa)a))
= A (((((aa)a)(a((aa)a)))(a((aa)a)))(((aa)a)(a((aa)a))))(a((aa)a))
= A (((((aa)a)(a((aa)a)))(a((aa)a)))a)(a((aa)a))
= A ((a(a((aa)a)))a)(a((aa)a))
= A a

L2 (aa)((a((aa)a))a)
= A (aa)((a((aa)a))(((a((aa)a))a)(a((aa)a))))
= L1 (aa)((a((aa)a))(((a((aa)a))((a((aa)a))(a((aa)a))))(a((aa)a))))
= L1 (((a((aa)a))(a((aa)a)))((a((aa)a))(a((aa)a))))((a((aa)a))(((a((aa)a))((a((aa)a))(a((aa)a))))(a((aa)a))))
= A (a((aa)a))(a((aa)a))
= L1 a

L3 (ab)((aa)(((aa)b)(aa)))
= L2 (((aa)((a((aa)a))a))b)((aa)(((aa)b)(aa)))
= A b

L4 ((a((ab)a))d)(b((bd)b))
= A ((a((ab)a))d)(b((bd)(((ac)b)(a((ab)a)))))
= A ((a((ab)a))d)(b(((((ac)b)(a((ab)a)))d)(((ac)b)(a((ab)a)))))
= A ((a((ab)a))d)((((ac)b)(a((ab)a)))(((((ac)b)(a((ab)a)))d)(((ac)b)(a((ab)a)))))
= L3 (((((ac)b)(a((ab)a)))((((ac)b)((ac)b))(((((ac)b)((ac)b))(a((ab)a)))(((ac)b)((ac)b)))))d)((((ac)b)(a((ab)a)))(((((ac)b)(a((ab)a)))d)(((ac)b)(a((ab)a)))))
= A d

L5 (a((aa)a))((a((aa)a))a)
= A (a((aa)a))((a((aa)a))(((a((aa)a))a)(a((aa)a))))
= A (((((aa)a)((((aa)a)(a((aa)a)))((aa)a)))(a((aa)a)))(((aa)a)((((aa)a)(a((aa)a)))((aa)a))))((a((aa)a))(((a((aa)a))a)(a((aa)a))))
= A (((((aa)a)((((aa)a)(a((aa)a)))((aa)a)))(a((aa)a)))(((aa)a)(a((aa)a))))((a((aa)a))(((a((aa)a))a)(a((aa)a))))
= A (((((aa)a)((((aa)a)(a((aa)a)))((aa)a)))(a((aa)a)))a)((a((aa)a))(((a((aa)a))a)(a((aa)a))))
= A (((((aa)a)((((aa)a)(a((aa)a)))((aa)a)))(((((aa)a)((((aa)a)(a((aa)a)))((aa)a)))(a((aa)a)))(((aa)a)((((aa)a)(a((aa)a)))((aa)a)))))a)((a((aa)a))(((a((aa)a))a)(a((aa)a))))
= L4 a

L6 (a((aa)a))(a(a((aa)a)))
= L1 (a((aa)a))(((a((aa)a))(a((aa)a)))(a((aa)a)))
= A ((((a((aa)a))((a((aa)a))a))(a((aa)a)))((a((aa)a))(((a((aa)a))(a((aa)a)))(a((aa)a)))))(((a((aa)a))((a((aa)a))a))((((a((aa)a))((a((aa)a))a))((a((aa)a))(((a((aa)a))(a((aa)a)))(a((aa)a)))))((a((aa)a))((a((aa)a))a))))
= A (a((aa)a))(((a((aa)a))((a((aa)a))a))((((a((aa)a))((a((aa)a))a))((a((aa)a))(((a((aa)a))(a((aa)a)))(a((aa)a)))))((a((aa)a))((a((aa)a))a))))
= L5 (a((aa)a))(a((((a((aa)a))((a((aa)a))a))((a((aa)a))(((a((aa)a))(a((aa)a)))(a((aa)a)))))((a((aa)a))((a((aa)a))a))))
= L5 (a((aa)a))(a((a((a((aa)a))(((a((aa)a))(a((aa)a)))(a((aa)a)))))((a((aa)a))((a((aa)a))a))))
= L1 (a((aa)a))(a((a((a((aa)a))(a(a((aa)a)))))((a((aa)a))((a((aa)a))a))))
= L1 (a((aa)a))(a((a((a((aa)a))(((a((aa)a))(a((aa)a)))(a((aa)a)))))((a((aa)a))((a((aa)a))a))))
= L4 (a((aa)a))(a((((a((aa)a))a)(a((aa)a)))((a((aa)a))(((a((aa)a))(a((aa)a)))(a((aa)a)))))((a((aa)a))((a((aa)a))a))))
= A (a((aa)a))(a((a((aa)a))((a((aa)a))((a((aa)a))a))))

L7 (a((aa)a))(a(a((aa)a)))
= L6 (a((aa)a))(a((a((aa)a))((a((aa)a))((a((aa)a))a))))
= L5 (a((aa)a))(a((a((aa)a))a))
= A (a((aa)a))(a(((((aa)a)(a((aa)a)))((aa)(((aa)(a((aa)a)))(aa))))a))
= A (a((aa)a))(a((a((aa)(((aa)(a((aa)a)))(aa))))a))
= L3 ((a(a((aa)a)))((aa)(((aa)(a((aa)a)))(aa))))(a((a((aa)(((aa)(a((aa)a)))(aa))))a))
= A (aa)(((aa)(a((aa)a)))(aa))

L8 ((aa)(((aa)(a((aa)a)))(aa)))((aa)(((aa)(a((aa)a)))(aa)))
= L7 ((a((aa)a))(a(a((aa)a))))((a((aa)a))(a(a((aa)a))))
= L1 ((a((aa)a))(((a((aa)a))(a((aa)a)))(a((aa)a))))((a((aa)a))(((a((aa)a))(a((aa)a)))(a((aa)a))))
= L1 a((aa)a)

L9 (a((aa)a))(a(a((aa)a)))
= L1 (a((aa)a))(((a((aa)a))(a((aa)a)))(a((aa)a)))
= L8 (((a((aa)a))(a((aa)a)))((((a((aa)a))(a((aa)a)))((a((aa)a))(((a((aa)a))(a((aa)a)))(a((aa)a)))))((a((aa)a))(a((aa)a)))))(((a((aa)a))(a((aa)a)))((((a((aa)a))(a((aa)a)))((a((aa)a))(((a((aa)a))(a((aa)a)))(a((aa)a)))))((a((aa)a))(a((aa)a)))))
= L1 (a((((a((aa)a))(a((aa)a)))((a((aa)a))(((a((aa)a))(a((aa)a)))(a((aa)a)))))((a((aa)a))(a((aa)a)))))(a((((a((aa)a))(a((aa)a)))((a((aa)a))(((a((aa)a))(a((aa)a)))(a((aa)a)))))((a((aa)a))(a((aa)a)))))

L10 (aa)(((aa)(a((aa)a)))(aa))
= L7 (a((aa)a))(a(a((aa)a)))
= L9 (a((((a((aa)a))(a((aa)a)))((a((aa)a))(((a((aa)a))(a((aa)a)))(a((aa)a)))))((a((aa)a))(a((aa)a)))))(a((((a((aa)a))(a((aa)a)))((a((aa)a))(((a((aa)a))(a((aa)a)))(a((aa)a)))))((a((aa)a))(a((aa)a)))))
= L1 (a((a((a((aa)a))(((a((aa)a))(a((aa)a)))(a((aa)a)))))((a((aa)a))(a((aa)a)))))(a((a((a((aa)a))(((a((aa)a))(a((aa)a)))(a((aa)a)))))((a((aa)a))(a((aa)a)))))

L11 (aa)(((aa)(a((aa)a)))(aa))
= L10 (a((a((a((aa)a))(((a((aa)a))(a((aa)a)))(a((aa)a)))))((a((aa)a))(a((aa)a)))))(a((a((a((aa)a))(((a((aa)a))(a((aa)a)))(a((aa)a)))))((a((aa)a))(a((aa)a)))))
= L1 (a((a((a((aa)a))(a(a((aa)a)))))((a((aa)a))(a((aa)a)))))(a((a((a((aa)a))(a(a((aa)a)))))((a((aa)a))(a((aa)a)))))
= L7 (a((a((aa)(((aa)(a((aa)a)))(aa))))((a((aa)a))(a((aa)a)))))(a((a((aa)(((aa)(a((aa)a)))(aa))))((a((aa)a))(a((aa)a)))))

L12 (aa)(((aa)(a((aa)a)))(aa))
= L11 (a((a((aa)(((aa)(a((aa)a)))(aa))))((a((aa)a))(a((aa)a)))))(a((a((aa)(((aa)(a((aa)a)))(aa))))((a((aa)a))(a((aa)a)))))
= A (a(((((aa)a)(a((aa)a)))((aa)(((aa)(a((aa)a)))(aa))))((a((aa)a))(a((aa)a)))))(a(((((aa)a)(a((aa)a)))((aa)(((aa)(a((aa)a)))(aa))))((a((aa)a))(a((aa)a)))))
= A (a((a((aa)a))((a((aa)a))(a((aa)a)))))(a((a((aa)a))((a((aa)a))(a((aa)a)))))
= L1 (a((a((aa)a))a))(a((a((aa)a))a))

L13 (a((aa)a))(a(a((aa)a)))
= L7 (aa)(((aa)(a((aa)a)))(aa))
= L12 (a((a((aa)a))a))(a((a((aa)a))a))

L14 (a((a((aa)a))a))(a((a((aa)a))a))
= L13 (a((aa)a))(a(a((aa)a)))
= L1 (a((aa)a))(((a((aa)a))(a((aa)a)))(a((aa)a)))
= A ((((((aa)a)((((aa)a)(a((aa)a)))((aa)a)))(a((aa)a)))(a((aa)a)))((a((aa)a))(((a((aa)a))(a((aa)a)))(a((aa)a)))))(((((aa)a)((((aa)a)(a((aa)a)))((aa)a)))(a((aa)a)))((((((aa)a)((((aa)a)(a((aa)a)))((aa)a)))(a((aa)a)))((a((aa)a))(((a((aa)a))(a((aa)a)))(a((aa)a)))))((((aa)a)((((aa)a)(a((aa)a)))((aa)a)))(a((aa)a)))))
= A ((((((aa)a)((((aa)a)(a((aa)a)))((aa)a)))(((((aa)a)((((aa)a)(a((aa)a)))((aa)a)))(a((aa)a)))(((aa)a)((((aa)a)(a((aa)a)))((aa)a)))))(a((aa)a)))((a((aa)a))(((a((aa)a))(a((aa)a)))(a((aa)a)))))(((((aa)a)((((aa)a)(a((aa)a)))((aa)a)))(a((aa)a)))((((((aa)a)((((aa)a)(a((aa)a)))((aa)a)))(a((aa)a)))((a((aa)a))(((a((aa)a))(a((aa)a)))(a((aa)a)))))((((aa)a)((((aa)a)(a((aa)a)))((aa)a)))(a((aa)a)))))
= L4 (a((aa)a))(((((aa)a)((((aa)a)(a((aa)a)))((aa)a)))(a((aa)a)))((((((aa)a)((((aa)a)(a((aa)a)))((aa)a)))(a((aa)a)))((a((aa)a))(((a((aa)a))(a((aa)a)))(a((aa)a)))))((((aa)a)((((aa)a)(a((aa)a)))((aa)a)))(a((aa)a)))))
= L4 (a((aa)a))(((((aa)a)((((aa)a)(a((aa)a)))((aa)a)))(a((aa)a)))((a((aa)a))((((aa)a)((((aa)a)(a((aa)a)))((aa)a)))(a((aa)a)))))
= A (a((aa)a))(((((aa)a)(a((aa)a)))(a((aa)a)))((a((aa)a))((((aa)a)((((aa)a)(a((aa)a)))((aa)a)))(a((aa)a)))))
= A (a((aa)a))((a(a((aa)a)))((a((aa)a))((((aa)a)((((aa)a)(a((aa)a)))((aa)a)))(a((aa)a)))))
= A (a((aa)a))((a(a((aa)a)))((a((aa)a))((((aa)a)(a((aa)a)))(a((aa)a)))))

L15 (a((a((aa)a))a))(a((a((aa)a))a))
= L14 (a((aa)a))((a(a((aa)a)))((a((aa)a))((((aa)a)(a((aa)a)))(a((aa)a)))))
= A (a((aa)a))((a(a((aa)a)))((a((aa)a))(a(a((aa)a)))))
= L13 (a((aa)a))((a(a((aa)a)))((a((a((aa)a))a))(a((a((aa)a))a))))

L16 (a((a((aa)a))a))(a((a((aa)a))a))
= L15 (a((aa)a))((a(a((aa)a)))((a((a((aa)a))a))(a((a((aa)a))a))))
= L12 (a((aa)a))((a(a((aa)a)))((aa)(((aa)(a((aa)a)))(aa))))
= L3 (a((aa)a))(a((aa)a))

L17 (a((aa)a))(a(a((aa)a)))
= L13 (a((a((aa)a))a))(a((a((aa)a))a))
= L16 (a((aa)a))(a((aa)a))
= L1 a

L18 a((aa)a)
= L1 ((a((aa)a))(((a((aa)a))(a((aa)a)))(a((aa)a))))((a((aa)a))(((a((aa)a))(a((aa)a)))(a((aa)a))))
= L16 ((a((aa)a))(((a((aa)a))(((a((aa)a))(a((aa)a)))(a((aa)a))))(a((aa)a))))((a((aa)a))(((a((aa)a))(((a((aa)a))(a((aa)a)))(a((aa)a))))(a((aa)a))))
= L1 ((a((aa)a))(((a((aa)a))(a(a((aa)a))))(a((aa)a))))((a((aa)a))(((a((aa)a))(a(a((aa)a))))(a((aa)a))))
= L17 ((a((aa)a))(a(a((aa)a))))((a((aa)a))(a(a((aa)a))))
= L17 aa

L19 (aa)(a(aa))
= L18 (aa)(a(a((aa)a)))
= L18 (a((aa)a))(a(a((aa)a)))
= L17 a

L20 a(a((a((aa)a))a))
= L18 a(a((a((a((aa)a))a))a))
= L2 ((aa)((a((aa)a))a))(a((a((a((aa)a))a))a))
= A (a((aa)a))a

L21 a(aa)
= L18 a(a((aa)a))
= L18 a(a((a((aa)a))a))
= L20 (a((aa)a))a

L22 (aa)(aa)
= L18 (a((aa)a))(a((aa)a))
= L1 a

T1 (aa)(aa)
= L22 a

L23 (aa)a
= L18 (a((aa)a))a
= L21 a(aa)

L24 ((ab)a)(aa)
= L18 ((ab)a)(a((aa)a))
= A a

L25 a((a((ab)(ab)))a)
= A (((ab)((ab)(ab)))(a((a((ab)(ab)))a)))((ab)(((ab)(a((a((ab)(ab)))a)))(ab)))
= A ((ab)(ab))((ab)(((ab)(a((a((ab)(ab)))a)))(ab)))
= L19 ((ab)(ab))((ab)(((((ab)(ab))((ab)((ab)(ab))))(a((a((ab)(ab)))a)))(ab)))
= A ((ab)(ab))((ab)(((((ab)(ab))((((ab)(ab))(a((a(ab))a)))((ab)(ab))))(a((a((ab)(ab)))a)))(ab)))
= L24 ((ab)(ab))((ab)((((((((ab)(ab))((((ab)(ab))(a((a(ab))a)))((ab)(ab))))(a((a(ab))a)))(((ab)(ab))((((ab)(ab))(a((a(ab))a)))((ab)(ab)))))((((ab)(ab))((((ab)(ab))(a((a(ab))a)))((ab)(ab))))(((ab)(ab))((((ab)(ab))(a((a(ab))a)))((ab)(ab))))))(a((a((ab)(ab)))a)))(ab)))
= A ((ab)(ab))((ab)((((a((a(ab))a))((((ab)(ab))((((ab)(ab))(a((a(ab))a)))((ab)(ab))))(((ab)(ab))((((ab)(ab))(a((a(ab))a)))((ab)(ab))))))(a((a((ab)(ab)))a)))(ab)))
= A ((ab)(ab))((ab)((((a((a(ab))a))((((ab)(ab))((ab)((ab)(ab))))(((ab)(ab))((ab)((ab)(ab))))))(a((a((ab)(ab)))a)))(ab)))
= L19 ((ab)(ab))((ab)((((a((a(ab))a))((ab)(ab)))(a((a((ab)(ab)))a)))(ab)))
= A ((ab)(ab))((ab)(((ab)(ab))(ab)))

L26 a((a((ab)(ab)))a)
= L25 ((ab)(ab))((ab)(((ab)(ab))(ab)))
= A ((ab)(ab))(((((ab)(ab))(ab))((ab)(((ab)(ab))(ab))))(((ab)(ab))((((ab)(ab))((ab)(((ab)(ab))(ab))))((ab)(ab)))))
= A ((ab)(ab))((ab)(((ab)(ab))((((ab)(ab))((ab)(((ab)(ab))(ab))))((ab)(ab)))))
= L12 ((ab)(ab))((ab)(((ab)(((ab)(((ab)(ab))(ab)))(ab)))((ab)(((ab)(((ab)(ab))(ab)))(ab)))))
= L16 ((ab)(ab))((ab)(((ab)(((ab)(ab))(ab)))((ab)(((ab)(ab))(ab)))))
= L1 ((ab)(ab))((ab)(ab))

L27 a((a((ab)(ab)))a)
= L26 ((ab)(ab))((ab)(ab))
= L22 ab

L28 a
= L24 ((ab)a)(aa)
= L27 ((ab)a)((((ab)a)((((ab)a)(aa))(((ab)a)(aa))))((ab)a))
= L24 ((ab)a)((((ab)a)(aa))((ab)a))

L29 ((ab)a)(a((ab)a))
= L24 ((ab)a)((((ab)a)(aa))((ab)a))
= L28 a

L30 (ab)(aa)
= L27 (a((a((ab)(ab)))a))(aa)
= L29 (a((a((ab)(ab)))a))((((a((ab)(ab)))a)(a((a((ab)(ab)))a)))(((a((ab)(ab)))a)(a((a((ab)(ab)))a))))
= L29 (a((a((ab)(ab)))a))((((a((ab)(ab)))a)((((a((ab)(ab)))a)(a((a((ab)(ab)))a)))((a((ab)(ab)))a)))(((a((ab)(ab)))a)((((a((ab)(ab)))a)(a((a((ab)(ab)))a)))((a((ab)(ab)))a))))
= A (((((a((ab)(ab)))a)((((a((ab)(ab)))a)(a((a((ab)(ab)))a)))((a((ab)(ab)))a)))(a((a((ab)(ab)))a)))(((a((ab)(ab)))a)((((a((ab)(ab)))a)(a((a((ab)(ab)))a)))((a((ab)(ab)))a))))((((a((ab)(ab)))a)((((a((ab)(ab)))a)(a((a((ab)(ab)))a)))((a((ab)(ab)))a)))(((a((ab)(ab)))a)((((a((ab)(ab)))a)(a((a((ab)(ab)))a)))((a((ab)(ab)))a))))
= L24 ((a((ab)(ab)))a)((((a((ab)(ab)))a)(a((a((ab)(ab)))a)))((a((ab)(ab)))a))
= L29 ((a((ab)(ab)))a)(a((a((ab)(ab)))a))
= L29 a

L31 b((ab)(ab))
= L3 ((ab)((aa)(((aa)b)(aa))))((ab)(ab))
= L30 ab

L32 a((ab)(ab))
= L30 ((ab)(aa))((ab)(ab))
= L30 ab

L33 a((ab)a)
= L32 a((a((ab)(ab)))a)
= L27 ab

L34 ((ab)c)(bc)
= L33 ((ab)c)(b((bc)b))
= L33 ((a((ab)a))c)(b((bc)b))
= L4 c

L35 ba
= L31 a((ba)(ba))
= L33 a((a((ba)(ba)))a)
= L31 a((ba)a)

L36 b(b(ab))
= L33 b(b(a((ab)a)))
= L33 b(b((b(a((ab)a)))b))
= A (((a((ab)a))b)(a((ab)a)))(b((b(a((ab)a)))b))
= A (((a((ab)a))(((a((ab)a))b)(a((ab)a))))(a((ab)a)))(b((b(a((ab)a)))b))
= L4 a((ab)a)
= L33 ab

L37 (ab)a
= L36 a(a((ab)a))
= L33 a(ab)

L38 (ba)a
= L36 a(a((ba)a))
= L35 a(ba)

L39 (bb)(b(ab))
= L38 (bb)((ab)b)
= L33 (bb)((ab)(((ab)b)(ab)))
= L3 (bb)((ab)(((ab)((ab)((aa)(((aa)b)(aa)))))(ab)))
= L3 (((ab)((aa)(((aa)b)(aa))))((ab)((aa)(((aa)b)(aa)))))((ab)(((ab)((ab)((aa)(((aa)b)(aa)))))(ab)))
= A (ab)((aa)(((aa)b)(aa)))
= L3 b

L40 a
= L39 (aa)(a((ba)a))
= L38 (aa)(a(a(ba)))
= L36 (aa)(ba)

L41 a
= L39 (aa)(a((ab)a))
= L33 (aa)(ab)

L42 ba
= L41 b((aa)(ab))

```
= L33  b((aa)(a((ab)a)))
= L33  b(((aa)((aa)(a((ab)a)))(aa)))
= A    (((aa)b)(a((ab)a)))((aa)((aa)(a((ab)a)))(aa))
= A    a(a(ab))
= L33  a b
L43  (ac)((ab)c)
= L42  ((ab)c)(ac)
= L33  ((ab)c)(a((ac)a))
= A    c
L44  (bc)((ab)c)
= L42  ((ab)c)(bc)
= L34  c
L45  (ba)((ac)b)
= L42  (ab)((ac)b)
= L43  b
L46  (ba)(a(bc))
= L42  (ab)((bc)a)
= L43  a
L47  b c
= L46  ((ab)(bc))((bc)((ab)c))
= L44  ((ab)(bc))c
= L42  c((ab)(bc))
L48  a b
= L45  ((ab)(ca))(((ca)b)(ab))
= L42  ((ab)(ca))((ab)((ca)b))
= L44  ((ab)(ca))b
L49  b((ab)(ca))
= L42  ((ab)(ca))b
= L48  a b
L50  (ab)c
= L43  ((ab)c)((ac)((ab)c))
= L43  (a((ab)c))c
= L42  c(a((ab)c))
L51  a(b(ab))
= L42  (a(ab))
= L42  ((ab)b)a
= L50  a((ab)(ab)))b)a)
= L42  a((ba)((ab)b)a)
= L44  aa
L52  (ba)(ab)
= L50  (ab)(b((ba)(ab)))
= L47  (ab)(ab)
L53  (aa)((ba)b)
= L44  (aa)((ba)((aa)(ba))((((aa)(ba))(aa))(ba)))
= L50  (aa)(((((aa)(ba))(aa))(ba)))
= L42  (aa)(((aa)(ba))((ba)(aa)))
= L42  (aa)((ba)((aa)(ba)))
= L40  (aa)((ba)((aa)a))
= L42  (aa)((ba)(aaa))
= L47  a(aa)
L54  ((ab)(ab))((ab)(ab))
= L52  ((ba)(ab))((ba)(ab))
= L52  ((ba)(ab))((ab)(ab))
= L52  ((ba)(ab))((ab)(ab))
L55  a b
= L22  ((ab)(ab))((ab)(ab))
= L54  ((ba)(ab))((ab)(ab))
= L52  ((ba)(ab))((ab)(ab))
L56  a(b(bb))
= L53  a((bb)((ab)(bb)))
= L42  a((ab)((bb)(bb)))
= L40  a(((ab)(ab))((bb)(ab))(bb))))
= L53  a((ab)((ab)(bb)))
= L42  a((ab)(ab)(bb))
= L32  a((ab)((ab)(bb)))
= L51  a a
T2  a(b(bb))
= L56  a a
L57  ((aa)(((ab)(ab))c))((aa)(((ab)(ab))c))
= L56  ((aa)(((ab)(d(dd)))c))((aa)(((ab)(d(dd)))c))
= L56  ((a(d(dd))(((ab)(d(dd)))c))((a(d(dd)))(((ab)(d(dd)))c))
= L56  ((a(d(dd)))(((ab)(d(dd)))c))((d(dd))
= L42  ((a(d(dd)))(((ab)(d(dd)))c)(a(d(dd)))
= L42  (d(dd))(((ab)(d(dd)))c)(a(d(dd)))
= L42  ((a(d(dd)))((ab)(d(dd)))c)(a(d(dd)))
= L46  (((ab)(d(dd)))c)(a(d(dd))))((ab)(d(dd)))(d(dd))(((ab)(d(dd)))
= L33  (((ab)(d(dd)))c)(a((a(d(dd)))a)))(((ab)(d(dd)))((d(dd))(((ab)
(d(dd)))))
```

```
= A    ((((ab)(d(dd)))c)(a((a(d(dd)))a)))(((ab)(d(dd)))((((ab)(d(dd)))
(a((a(d(dd)))a)))((ab)(d(dd))))
= A    a(a(d(dd)))
= L33  a(d(dd))
L58  (bb)(((bc)(bc))d)
= L22  ((bb)(((bc)(bc))d))((bb)(((bc)(bc))d))((bb)((((bc)(bc))d))
((bb)((((bc)(bc))d)))
= L57  (b(a(aa)))(b(a(aa)))
= L56  (bb)(bb)
L59  (aa)(((ab)(bb))c)
= L58  (aa)(aa)
= L22  a
L60  (a) a
= L59  (aa)(((a(ba)(cb)))(a(ba)(cb))))((d(a((ba)(cb)))(a(ba)(c
b)))))(ed)))
= L49  (aa)(d((a((ba)(cb)))((a(ba)(cb))))
= L49  (aa)(d((ba)b)))
L61  c((ac)(((ab)c)((ab)c)))
= L42  c((((ab)c)((ab)c))(ac))
= L42  ((((ab)c)((ab)c))(ac))c
= L46  ((((ab)c)((ab)c))(ac))((ac)c((ab)c))
= L33  ((((ab)c)((ab)c))(a((ac)a)))((ab)c)(c((ab)c))
= A    (((ab)c)((ab)c))(a((ac)a)))((ab)c)((((ab)c)(a((ac)a)))((ab)c))
= A    a((ac)a)
= L33  a c
L62  (aa)b
= L61  b(((aa)b)((((a(ac)(ac)))d)b)(((aa)(((ac)(ac))d))b))
= L59  b((aa)b)((ab)(ab)))
= L50  b((ab)b)((aa)(ab)(ab)))
= L45  b((ab)(((ab)((bc)a))(ab)((bc)a))(((aa)b)(ab)(ab))))
= L59  b(ab)
L63  a(ab)
= L42  (ab)a
L64  a(bc)
= L45  ((abc)c)((ca)(abc))
= L42  ((abc)c)((ca)(bca))
= L44  ((abc))c)a
L65  a(bc)
= L64  ((abc)c)a
= L42  a((abc)c)
= L42  a(c(abc))
L66  a c
= L59  ((ac)(ac))(((ac)(ca))((ac)(ca)))b
= L52  ((ac)(ac))(((ca)(ca))((ca)(ca)))b
= L22  ((ac)(ac))((ca)b)
L67  (ab)(ab)
= L59  (((ab)(ab))((ab)(ab)))((((ab)(ab))((ba)(ba)))((ab)(ab))((ba)
(ba)))c)
= L55  (((ab)(ab))((ab)(ab)))((ba)(ba))c
= L22  (ab)(((ba)(ba))c)
L68  ((bc)(ba))((bc)(ba))
= L42  (((bc)(ba))((bc)(ba)))a
= L63  a(a((bc)(ba)))
= L33  a(a((bc)(((bc)(b(ba)(bb)))(bc))))
= A    a((((bc)a)(b((ba)b)))(bc)(((bc)(b((ba)b))))(bc))))
= A    a(b((ba)b))
= L33  a(b(a))
= L62  (bb)a
L69  (bc)a
= L22  (((bc)(bc))(bc))a
= L68  a(((bc)(bc))(cb)((bc)(bc)))a)((((bc)(bc))(cb)(cb)))
(((bc)(bc))a)))
= L55  a(((cb)((bc)(bc))a)((cb)((bc)(bc))a))
= L70  (bc)a
= L69  (bc)a((cb)((bc)(bc)))((cb)((bc)(bc))a)))
= L67  a((cb)(cb))((cb)(bc))a))
= L22  a(cb)
L71  (bc)(bc)a
= L68  a((((bc)(cb))((bc)a)((cb)(cb))((bc)a)))
= L52  a((((bc)(cb))((bc)a)((cb)(cb))((bc)a)))
= L66  a((cb)(cb))
L72  (ba)((bc)a)
= L3   (a(ba(((bc)a)((bc)a)))((aa)((aa)((bc)a)((bc)a))(aa)))
= L33  (a(ba)(((bc)a)((bc)a)))((aa)((ba)((bc)a))((bc)a)))
= L61  (ba)((aa)(((bc)a)((bc)a)))
```

```
= A    ((((ab)(d(dd)))c)(a(a(d(dd)))a)))((ab)(d(dd)))((((ab)(d(dd)))
(a((a(d(dd)))a)))((ab)(d(dd))))
= A    a(a(d(dd)))
= L33  a(d(dd))
L73  (ba)(((bc)a)((bc)a))
= L72  (ba)((aa)(b)((bc)a)((bc)a)))
= L60  (ba)a
= L70  a(ab)
= L63  (bb)a
L74  (aa)c
= L73  (ac)((ab)c)((ab)c)
= L50  ((ab)c)((ab)c)(a((ac)((ab)c))))
= L73  ((ab)c)((ab)c)(a((aa)c))
= L22  (((ab)c)((ab)c))((a((aa)((aa)c)))
= L41  ((ab)c)((ab)c))(aa)
L76  (aa)((c(ab))(ab))
= L71  (((ab)c)((ab)c))(aa)
= L74  (aa)c
L75  b(ac)(aa)
= L22  ((b(ac))(b(ac)))((b(ac))(b(ac)))(aa)
= L63  (aa)((a((b(ac))(b(ac)))))
= L75  ba((aa)b)
L77  ((ab)(ab))(ca)
= L75  ((ab)(ab))((((ab)c)((ca)(ab)c)))
= L45  (ab)(ab)((cc))
L78  ((bc)(bc))a
= L45  ((bc)(bc))(ab)((bc)a))
= L70  ((bc)(bc))(bc)a)
= L22  (((bc)a)(ab))((bc)a)(ab)))(((bc)(a)(ab))(((bc)a)(ab))))((bc)
(bc))
= L63  ((bc)(bc))((bc)(bc))(((bc)a)(ab))((bc)a)))
= L76  ((bc)(a)(ab))((bc)(a(bc)a)))((bc)(bc))
= L70  ((bc)(bc))((bc)(ab))((bc)(a)(ab))((bc)(a))))
= L73  ((bc)(bc))((bc)(ab))((bc)(a(bc)(ab)))
= L63  ((ab)(ab))((bc)(bc))
= L47  ((ab)(ab))((c((ab)(bc)))(c((ab)(bc))))
= L75  ((ab)(ab))c
= L71  c((ba)(ba))
L79  a(c((ba)(ab)))
= L42  a(c((ba)(ba)))
= L78  a(((bc)(bc))a)
= L62  a((((bc)(bc))(bc))a)
= L22  (bc)a
L80  a(ba)c
= L70  (c(ba)a)
= L42  a((((ac)(ac))(ba))
= L77  a((ac)(ac))(ba))
= L78  a(c((a(bb))(a(bb))))
= L79  a((bb)(ca))
L81  ((ca)(bc))((ca)(bc))
= L40  ((((ca)(ab))((ca)(ab)))(((ca)(ab))((ca)(ab)))((aa)((ca)(ab))
((ca)(ab)))
= L75  ((((ca)(ab))((ca)(ab)))((((ca)(ab))((ca)(ab)))((ca)(ca))
= L22  ((ca)(ab)((aa)(ca))
= L70  ((ca)(ca))((aa)(ca))
= L40  a((ab)(ca))
= L70  ((ca)(ab))a
= L79  a(ab)((a(ca))(a(ca)))
= L70  a(((a(ca))(a(ca)))(ba))
= L77  a((((a(ca)(ca)))(bb)))
= L78  a((a((a(bb))(a(bb))))
= L79  a((bb)(ca))a
T3  (bb)a(((c)a
= L42  (bb)a(a(cc))
= L42  (a(cc))((bb)a)
= L22  (((aa)(aa))(cc))a)((bb)a)
= L80  (bb)a(((a((bb)a))(cc)))
= L70  ((cc)(((aa)((bb)a)((bb)a)))
= L81  ((aa)(((bb)a))((bb)a)))((a((bb)a))((bb)a))((bb)a)(c)))
= L40  (a(((bb)a)(c))(a((bb)a)))
= L80  ((((bb)(bb))c)a)((((bb)(bb))c)a)
= L42  (a((bb)(bb))))((cc)((bb)a))
= L40  ((((c((bb)(bb)))(c(bb)(bb))))(bb)(c((bb)(bb)))a)((((c((bb)
(bb)))(c(bb)(bb))))(bb)(c((bb)(bb)))a)))a)
= L60  (((((c((bb)(bb)))(c(bb)(bb)))ba)((((c((bb)(bb)))(c(bb)(b
b))))a)
= L42  ((b(c((bb)(bb)))))(c((bb)(bb))))a)(b(c((bb)(bb)))))(c((bb)(b
b))))a)
= L78  ((((cb)(cb))((bb)(bb)))a)((((cb)(cb))((bb)(bb)))a)
= L40  (((((cb)(cb))((bb)(bb)))(b((cb)(cb))(b((bb)(bb)))))((((cb)(cb))((bb
b)(cb)))(b(bb)(cb)))a
= L65  ((((cb)(cb))((b(cb)(bb(bb)(cb)))))(b(cb)(b(bb)(cb)))a)
(((((cb)(cb))((b(bb)(cb)))(b(cb)(b(bb)(cb))))))a)a
= L75  ((((cb)(cb))b)a)((((cb)(cb))b)a)
= L78  ((b((cb)(cb)))a)((b((cb)(cb)))a)
= L31  ((cb)a)((cb)a)
= L70  (a(bc))(a(bc))
```

A proof that the axiom system $\{((b \circ c) \circ a) \circ (b \circ ((b \circ a) \circ b)) = a\}$ given as example (g) on page 808 can reproduce the Sheffer axiom system (c), and is thus a complete axiom system for logic. The proof involves taking the original axiom [A] and using it to establish a sequence of lemmas [Ln], from which it is eventually possible to prove the three Sheffer axioms [Tn]. In each part of the proof each line can be obtained from the previous one just as on page 775 by applying the axiom or lemma indicated. Explicit π operators have been omitted to allow expressions to be printed more compactly. The proof shown takes a total of 343 steps, and involves intermediate expressions with as many as 128 NANDs. It is quite possible that the proof could be considerably shortened. Note that any proof can always be recast without lemmas, but will usually then be much longer.

So what about patterns of theorems? Does logic somehow stand out when one looks at these? The picture below shows which possible simple equivalence theorems hold in systems from page 805.

And comparing with page 805 one sees that typically the more forms of operator are allowed by the constraints of an axiom system, the fewer equivalence results hold in that axiom system.

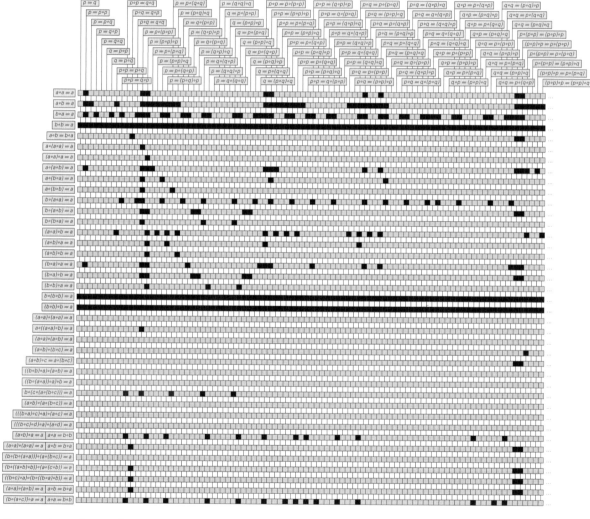

Theorems that can be proved on the basis of simple axiom systems from page 805. A black square indicates that a particular theorem holds in a particular axiom system. In general the question of whether a given theorem holds is undecidable, but the particular theorems given here happen to be simple enough that results for them can with some effort be established with certainty.

So what happens if essentially just a single form of operator is allowed? The pictures below show results for the 16 forms from page 806, and among these one sees that logic yields the fewest theorems.

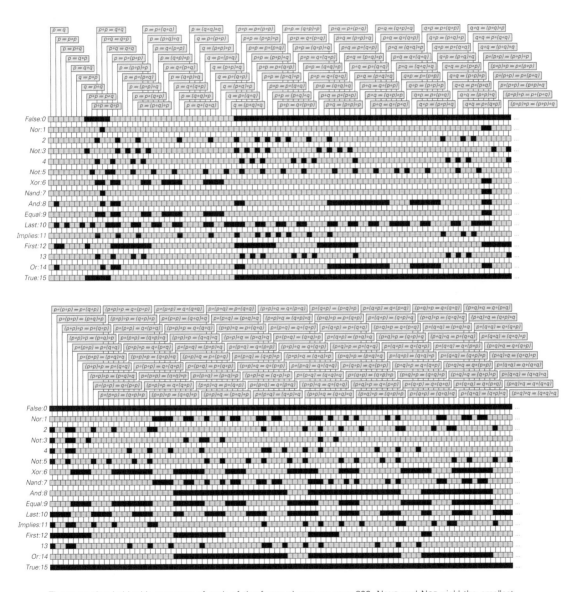

Theorems that hold with operators of each of the forms shown on page 806. NAND and NOR yield the smallest number of theorems.

But if one considers for example analogs of logic for variables with more than two possible values, the picture below shows that one immediately gets systems with still fewer theorems.

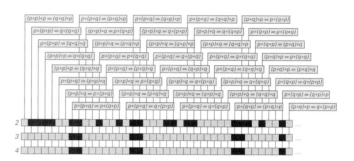

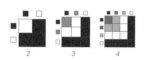

Theorems in analogs of logic that allow different numbers of truth values. Statements like $p = \neg \neg p$ do not hold in general with more than 2 truth values.

So what about proofs? Is there something about these that is somehow special in the case of ordinary logic?

In the axiom systems on page 803 the typical lengths of proofs seem to increase from one system to the next, so that they end up being longest for the last axiom system, which corresponds to logic.

But if one picks a different axiom system for logic—say one of the others on page 808—then the length of a particular proof will usually change. But since one can always just start by proving the new axioms, the change can only be by a fixed amount. And as it turns out, even the simplest axiom system (f) given on page 808 seems to allow fairly short proofs of at least most short theorems.

But as one tries to prove progressively longer theorems it appears that whatever axiom system one uses for logic the lengths of proofs can increase as fast as exponentially. A crucial point, however, is that for theorems of a given length there is always a definite upper limit on the length of proof needed. Yet once again this is not something unique to logic. Indeed, it turns out that this must always be the case for any axiom system—like those on page 803—that ends up allowing essentially only operators of a single form.

So what about other axiom systems?

The very simplest ones on pages 805 and 812 seem to yield proofs that are always comparatively short. But when one looks at axiom systems that are even slightly more complicated the proofs of anything but the simplest results can get much longer—making it in practice often difficult to tell whether a given result can actually even be proved at all.

And this is in a sense just another example of the same basic phenomenon that we already saw early in this section in multiway systems, and that often seems to occur in real mathematics: that even if a theorem is short to state, its proof can be arbitrarily long.

And this I believe is ultimately a reflection of the Principle of Computational Equivalence. For the principle suggests that most axiom systems whose consequences are not obviously simple will tend to be universal. And this means that they will exhibit computational irreducibility and undecidability—and will allow no general upper limit to be placed on how long a proof could be needed for any given result.

As I discussed earlier, most of the common axiom systems in traditional mathematics are known to be universal—basic logic being one of the few exceptions. But one might have assumed that to achieve their universality these axiom systems would have to be specially set up with all sorts of specific sophisticated features.

Yet from the results of this book—as embodied in the Principle of Computational Equivalence—we now know that this is not the case, and that in fact universality should already be rather common even among very simple axiom systems, like those on page 805.

And indeed, while operator systems and multiway systems have many superficial differences, I suspect that when it comes to universality they work very much the same. So in either idealization, one should not have to go far to get axiom systems that exhibit universality—just like most of the ones in traditional mathematics.

But once one has reached an axiom system that is universal, why should one in a sense ever have to go further? After all, what it means for an axiom system to be universal is that by setting up a suitable encoding it must in principle be possible to make that axiom system reproduce any other possible axiom system.

But the point is that the kinds of encodings that are normally used in mathematics are in practice rather limited. For while it is common, say, to take a problem in geometry and reformulate it as a problem in algebra, this is almost always done just by setting up a direct translation between the objects one is describing—usually in effect just by renaming the operators used to manipulate them.

Yet to take full advantage of universality one must consider not only translations between objects but also translations between complete proofs. And if one does this it is indeed perfectly possible, say, to program arithmetic to reproduce any proof in set theory. In fact, all one need do is to encode the axioms of set theory in something like the arithmetic equation system of page 786.

But with the notable exception of Gödel's Theorem these kinds of encodings are not normally used in mathematics. So this means that even when universality is present realistic idealizations of mathematics must still distinguish different axiom systems.

So in the end what is it that determines which axiom systems are actually used in mathematics? In the course of this section I have discussed a few criteria. But in the end history seems to be the only real determining factor. For given almost any general property that one can pick out in axiom systems like those on pages 773 and 774 there typically seem to be all sorts of operator and multiway systems—often including some rather simple ones—that share the exact same property.

So this leads to the conclusion that there is in a sense nothing fundamentally special about the particular axiom systems that have traditionally been used in mathematics—and that in fact there are all sorts of other axiom systems that could perfectly well be used as foundations for what are in effect new fields of mathematics—just as rich as the traditional ones, but without the historical connections.

So what about existing fields of mathematics? As I mentioned earlier in this section, I strongly believe that even within these there are fundamental limitations that have implicitly been imposed on what has actually been studied. And most often what has happened is that there are only certain kinds of questions or statements that have been considered of real mathematical interest.

The picture on the facing page shows a rather straightforward version of this. It lists in order a large number of theorems from basic logic, highlighting just those few that are considered interesting enough by typical textbooks of logic to be given explicit names.

[1] $a = a \wedge a$	[2] $a = a \vee a$	$a \wedge a = a \vee a$	[3] $a \wedge b = b \wedge a$	[4] $a \vee b = b \vee a$	[5] $a = \neg\neg a$
$a \wedge a = \neg\neg a$	$a \vee a = \neg\neg a$	$\neg a = \neg(a \wedge a)$	$\neg a = \neg(a \vee a)$	$a = (a \wedge a) \wedge a$	$a = (a \vee a) \wedge a$
$a = a \wedge (a \wedge a)$	$a = a \wedge (a \vee a)$	$a = a \wedge a \vee a$	$a = (a \vee a) \vee a$	$a = a \vee a \wedge a$	$a = a \vee (a \vee a)$
[6] $a = a \wedge (a \vee b)$	[7] $a = a \vee a \wedge b$	$a = (a \vee b) \wedge a$	$a = a \wedge (b \vee a)$	$a = a \wedge b \vee a$	$a = a \vee b \wedge a$
$a = (b \vee a) \wedge a$	$a = b \wedge a \vee a$	$\neg a = \neg a \wedge \neg a$	$\neg a = \neg a \vee \neg a$	$\neg a \wedge a = a \wedge \neg a$	$\neg a = a \vee \neg a$
$\neg(a \wedge a) = \neg(a \vee a)$	$\neg\neg a = (a \wedge a) \wedge a$	$\neg\neg a = (a \vee a) \wedge a$	$\neg\neg a = a \wedge (a \wedge a)$	$\neg\neg a = a \wedge (a \vee a)$	$\neg\neg a = a \vee (a \vee a)$
$\neg\neg a = a \wedge (b \vee a)$	$\neg\neg a = a \wedge b \vee a$	$\neg\neg a = a \vee (a \vee a)$	$\neg\neg a = a \wedge (a \vee b)$	$\neg\neg a = a \vee a \wedge b$	$\neg\neg a = (a \vee b) \wedge a$
$a \wedge \neg a = b \wedge \neg b$	[9] $\neg a \vee a = \neg b \vee b$	$a \vee \neg a = \neg b \vee b$	[8] $\neg a \wedge a = \neg b \wedge b$	$a \wedge \neg a = \neg b \wedge b$	$\neg a \wedge a = b \wedge \neg b$
$\neg a \wedge a = b \wedge \neg b$	$a \wedge \neg b = \neg b \wedge a$	$\neg a \vee a = b \vee \neg b$	$a \vee \neg a = b \vee \neg b$	$a \vee \neg a = b \vee \neg a$	$\neg\neg a = (b \vee a) \wedge a$
$\neg\neg a = b \wedge a \vee a$	$a \wedge \neg b = \neg b \wedge a$	$\neg a \wedge b = b \wedge \neg a$	$a \vee \neg b = \neg b \vee a$	$\neg a \vee b = b \vee \neg a$	$\neg(a \vee b) = \neg(b \vee a)$
$\neg(a \vee b) = \neg(b \vee a)$	$a \wedge a = (a \wedge a) \wedge a$	$a \vee a = (a \wedge a) \wedge a$	$a \wedge a = (a \vee a) \wedge a$	$a \vee a = (a \vee a) \wedge a$	$a \wedge a = a \wedge (a \wedge a)$
$a \vee a = a \wedge (a \wedge a)$	$a \wedge a = a \wedge (a \vee a)$	$a \vee a = a \wedge (a \vee a)$	$a \wedge a = a \vee (a \vee a)$	$a \vee a = a \vee (a \vee a)$	$a \wedge a = a \wedge (a \vee a)$
$a \vee a = (a \vee a) \vee a$	$a \wedge a = a \vee a \wedge a$	$a \vee a = a \vee a \wedge a$	$a \wedge a = a \vee a \vee a$	$a \vee a = a \vee a \vee a$	$a \wedge a = a \wedge (a \vee b)$
$a \vee a = a \wedge (a \vee b)$	$a \wedge a = a \vee a \wedge b$	$a \vee a = a \vee a \wedge b$	$a \wedge a = (a \vee b) \wedge a$	$a \vee a = (a \vee b) \wedge a$	$a \wedge a = a \wedge (b \vee a)$
$a \vee a = a \wedge (a \vee b)$	$a \wedge a = a \wedge b \vee a$	$a \vee a = a \vee a \wedge b$	$a \wedge a = a \vee b \wedge a$	$a \vee a = a \vee b \wedge a$	$a \wedge a = (b \vee a) \wedge a$
$a \vee a = (b \vee a) \wedge a$	$a \wedge a = b \wedge a \vee a$	$a \vee a = b \wedge a \vee a$	$a \wedge b = (a \wedge a) \wedge b$	$a \vee b = (a \vee a) \wedge b$	$a \wedge b = a \wedge (a \wedge b)$
$a \vee b = a \wedge a \vee b$	$a \vee b = (a \vee a) \vee b$	$a \vee b = a \vee (a \vee b)$	$a \wedge b = (a \wedge a) \wedge b$	$a \wedge b = (a \vee a) \wedge b$	$a \wedge b = a \wedge (a \vee b)$
$a \vee b = a \vee (b \vee b)$	$a \wedge b = (a \wedge b) \wedge b$	$a \wedge b = a \wedge (b \wedge b)$	$a \wedge b = a \wedge (b \vee b)$	$a \vee b = (b \vee b) \vee b$	$a \vee b = a \vee b \wedge a$
$a \vee b = a \vee (b \vee b)$	$a \wedge b = (b \wedge a) \wedge a$	$a \wedge b = b \wedge (a \wedge a)$	$a \vee b = (b \wedge a) \vee a$	$a \vee b = b \vee (b \wedge a)$	$a \wedge b = (b \wedge b) \wedge a$
$a \vee b = b \vee (b \vee b)$	$a \wedge b = b \wedge (a \wedge b)$	$a \wedge b = b \wedge (a \wedge b)$	$a \vee b = (b \vee a) \vee a$	$a \vee b = b \vee (b \vee a)$	$a \wedge b = (b \wedge b) \wedge a$
$a \wedge b = (b \vee b) \wedge a$	$a \wedge b = b \wedge (b \wedge a)$	$a \vee b = b \wedge b \vee a$	$a \vee b = (b \vee b) \vee a$	$\neg(a \wedge a) = \neg a \wedge \neg a$	$\neg(a \vee b) = \neg b \wedge \neg a$
$\neg(a \wedge a) = \neg a \wedge \neg a$	$\neg(a \wedge a) = \neg a \vee \neg a$	$\neg(a \vee a) = \neg a \vee \neg a$	[10] $\neg(a \vee b) = \neg a \wedge \neg b$	$\neg(a \wedge b) = \neg a \vee \neg b$	$\neg(a \vee b) = \neg b \wedge \neg a$
$\neg(a \wedge b) = \neg b \vee \neg a$	$\neg a \wedge \neg a = \neg a \vee \neg a$	$\neg a \wedge \neg b = \neg b \wedge \neg a$	$\neg a \vee \neg b = \neg b \vee \neg a$	$(a \wedge a) \wedge a = (a \vee a) \wedge a$	$(a \wedge a) \wedge a = a \wedge (a \wedge a)$
$(a \vee a) \wedge a = a \wedge (a \wedge a)$	$(a \wedge a) \wedge a = a \wedge (a \vee a)$	$(a \vee a) \wedge a = a \wedge (a \vee a)$	$a \wedge (a \wedge a) = a \wedge (a \vee a)$	$(a \wedge a) \wedge a = a \vee a \wedge a$	$(a \vee a) \wedge a = a \vee a \wedge a$
$a \wedge (a \wedge a) = a \vee a \wedge a$	$a \wedge (a \vee a) = a \wedge a \vee a$	$(a \vee a) \wedge a = (a \vee a) \vee a$	$(a \vee a) \wedge a = (a \vee a) \vee a$	$(a \vee a) \wedge a = a \vee (a \vee a)$	$a \wedge (a \vee a) = (a \vee a) \vee a$
$a \wedge a \vee a = (a \vee a) \vee a$	$(a \wedge a) \wedge a = a \vee a \wedge a$	$(a \vee a) \wedge a = a \vee a \wedge a$	$(a \vee a) \wedge a = a \vee (a \vee a)$	$(a \wedge a) \wedge a = a \vee a \vee a$	$(a \vee a) \wedge a = a \vee a \vee a$
$(a \vee a) \vee a = a \vee (a \vee a)$	$(a \wedge a) \wedge a = a \vee (a \vee a)$	$(a \vee a) \wedge a = a \vee (a \vee a)$	$a \wedge (a \wedge a) = a \vee (a \vee b)$	$(a \wedge a) \wedge a = a \vee a \wedge b$	$a \wedge (a \wedge a) = a \vee a \wedge b$
$a \wedge (a \wedge a) = a \vee a \wedge b$	$a \wedge (a \vee a) = a \vee a \wedge b$	$a \wedge a \vee a = a \vee a \wedge b$	$(a \vee a) \vee a = a \vee a \wedge b$	$a \vee a \wedge a = a \vee a \wedge b$	$a \vee (a \vee a) = a \vee a \wedge b$

: 50 lines

$a \wedge b \vee b = b \wedge (b \vee a)$	$(a \vee b) \vee b = b \wedge b \vee a$	$a \vee b \wedge b = b \wedge b \vee a$	$a \vee (b \vee b) = b \wedge b \vee a$	$(a \vee b) \vee b = (b \vee b) \vee a$	$a \vee b \wedge b = (b \vee b) \vee a$
$a \vee (b \vee c) = (b \vee b) \vee a$	$(a \vee b) \wedge b = b \vee b \wedge a$	$a \wedge b \vee b = b \vee b \wedge a$	$(a \vee b) \vee b = b \vee b \wedge a$	$a \vee b \wedge b = b \vee (b \vee a)$	$a \vee (b \vee b) = b \vee (b \vee a)$
$(a \vee b) \wedge b = (b \wedge b) \wedge b$	$a \wedge b \vee b = (b \wedge b) \wedge b$	$(a \vee b) \wedge b = (b \vee b) \wedge b$	$a \wedge b \vee b = (b \vee b) \wedge b$	$(a \vee b) \wedge b = b \wedge (b \wedge b)$	$a \wedge b \vee b = b \wedge (b \wedge b)$
$(a \vee b) \wedge b = b \wedge (b \vee b)$	$a \wedge b \vee b = b \wedge (b \vee b)$	$(a \vee b) \wedge b = (b \vee b) \wedge b$	$a \wedge b \vee b = b \wedge b \vee b$	$(a \vee b) \wedge b = (b \vee b) \vee b$	$a \wedge b \vee b = (b \vee b) \vee b$
$(a \vee b) \wedge b = b \vee b \wedge c$	$a \wedge b \vee b = b \vee b \wedge c$	$(a \vee b) \wedge b = b \vee (b \vee c)$	$a \wedge b \vee b = b \vee (b \vee c)$	$(a \vee b) \wedge b = b \wedge (b \vee c)$	$a \wedge b \vee b = b \wedge (b \vee c)$
$(a \vee b) \wedge b = b \vee b \wedge c$	$a \wedge b \vee b = b \vee b \wedge c$	$(a \vee b) \wedge b = b \vee (b \vee c)$	$a \wedge b \vee b = b \vee (b \vee c)$	$(a \vee b) \wedge b = b \wedge (b \vee c)$	$a \wedge b \vee b = b \wedge (c \vee b)$
$(a \vee b) \wedge b = b \vee b \wedge c$	$a \wedge b \vee b = b \vee b \wedge c$	$(a \vee b) \wedge b = b \vee (c \vee b)$	$a \wedge b \vee b = b \vee (c \vee b)$	$(a \vee b) \wedge b = b \wedge (c \vee b)$	$a \wedge b \vee b = b \wedge (c \vee b)$
$(a \vee b) \wedge b = c \wedge b \vee b$	$a \wedge b \vee b = c \wedge b \vee b$	[11] $(a \wedge b) \wedge c = a \wedge (b \wedge c)$	[12] $(a \vee b) \vee c = a \vee (b \vee c)$	$(a \wedge b) \wedge c = (a \wedge c) \wedge b$	$a \wedge (b \wedge c) = (a \wedge c) \wedge b$
$(a \vee b) \vee c = a \vee (c \vee b)$	$a \vee (b \vee c) = a \vee (c \vee b)$	$(a \wedge b) \wedge c = (b \wedge a) \wedge c$	$a \wedge (b \wedge c) = (b \wedge a) \wedge c$	$(a \vee b) \vee c = (b \vee a) \vee c$	$(a \wedge b) \wedge c = b \wedge (a \wedge c)$

: 392 lines

$a \wedge (b \vee c) = (a \wedge a) \wedge (c \vee b)$	$a \wedge (b \vee c) = (a \vee a) \wedge (c \vee b)$	$a \vee b \wedge c = a \wedge a \vee c \wedge b$	$a \vee b \wedge c = (a \vee a) \vee c \wedge b$	$(a \vee b) \vee c = a \vee a \vee (c \vee b)$
$(a \vee b) \vee c = (a \vee a) \vee (c \vee b)$	$a \vee (b \vee c) = (a \vee a) \vee (c \vee b)$	$a \vee (b \vee c) = a \vee a \vee (c \vee b)$	$(a \wedge b) \wedge c = (a \wedge b) \wedge (a \wedge c)$	$a \wedge (b \wedge c) = (a \wedge b) \wedge (a \wedge c)$
[13] $a \wedge (b \vee c) = a \wedge b \vee a \wedge c$	[14] $a \vee b \wedge c = (a \vee b) \wedge (a \vee c)$	$(a \vee b) \vee c = (a \vee b) \vee (a \vee c)$	$a \vee (b \wedge c) = (a \vee b) \wedge (a \vee c)$	$(a \wedge b) \wedge c = (a \wedge b) \wedge (b \wedge c)$
$a \wedge (b \wedge c) = (a \wedge b) \wedge (b \wedge c)$	$(a \vee b) \vee c = (a \vee b) \vee (b \vee c)$	$a \vee (b \vee c) = (a \vee b) \vee (b \vee c)$	$(a \wedge b) \wedge c = (a \wedge b) \wedge (c \wedge a)$	$a \wedge (b \wedge c) = (a \wedge b) \wedge (c \wedge a)$

: ⋮

The theorems of basic logic written out in order of increasing complexity. Those considered interesting enough to name in typical textbooks are highlighted. The theorems are respectively: (1), (2) idempotence (laws of tautology) of AND and OR, (3), (4) commutativity of AND and OR, (5) law of double negation, (6), (7) absorption (redundancy) laws, (8) law of noncontradiction (definition of FALSE), (9) law of excluded middle (definition of TRUE), (10) de Morgan's law, (11), (12) associativity of AND and OR, (13), (14) distributive laws. With the exception of the second distributive law, it turns out that the highlighted theorems are exactly the ones that cannot be derived from preceding theorems in the list. The distributive laws appear at positions 2813 and 2814 in the list; it takes a long proof to obtain the second one from preceding theorems.

But what determines which theorems these will be? One might have thought that it would be purely a matter of history. But actually looking at the list of theorems it always seems that the interesting ones are in a sense those that show the least unnecessary complication.

And indeed if one starts from the beginning of the list one finds that most of the theorems can readily be derived from simpler ones earlier in the list. But there are a few that cannot—and that therefore provide in a sense the simplest statements of genuinely new information. And remarkably enough what I have found is that these theorems are almost exactly the ones highlighted on the previous page that have traditionally been identified as interesting.

So what happens if one applies the same criterion in other settings? The picture below shows as an example theorems from the formulation of logic discussed above based on NAND.

a⊼b = b⊼a	a = (a⊼a)⊼(a⊼a)	a = (a⊼a)⊼(a⊼b)	a = (a⊼a)⊼(b⊼a)
a = (a⊼b)⊼(a⊼a)	a = (b⊼a)⊼(a⊼a)	(a⊼a)⊼a = a⊼(a⊼a)	(a⊼a)⊼a = (b⊼b)⊼b
a⊼(a⊼a) = (b⊼b)⊼b	(a⊼a)⊼a = b⊼(b⊼b)	a⊼(a⊼a) = b⊼(b⊼b)	a⊼(a⊼b) = (a⊼b)⊼a
a⊼(a⊼b) = a⊼(b⊼a)	(a⊼a)⊼b = (a⊼b)⊼b	a⊼(a⊼b) = a⊼(b⊼b)	a⊼(a⊼b) = (b⊼a)⊼a
(a⊼a)⊼b = b⊼(a⊼a)	(a⊼a)⊼b = (b⊼a)⊼b	(a⊼a)⊼b = b⊼(a⊼b)	a⊼(a⊼b) = (b⊼b)⊼a
(a⊼a)⊼b = b⊼(b⊼a)	(a⊼b)⊼a = a⊼(b⊼a)	(a⊼b)⊼a = a⊼(b⊼b)	a⊼(b⊼a) = a⊼(b⊼a)
a⊼(b⊼b) = (b⊼b)⊼a	(a⊼b)⊼a = (b⊼a)⊼a	(a⊼b)⊼a = (b⊼b)⊼a	a⊼(b⊼a) = (b⊼b)⊼a
a⊼(b⊼b) = (b⊼b)⊼a	(a⊼b)⊼b = b⊼(a⊼a)	(a⊼b)⊼b = (b⊼a)⊼b	(a⊼b)⊼b = b⊼(a⊼b)
a⊼(b⊼c) = (b⊼c)⊼a	(a⊼b)⊼b = b⊼(b⊼a)	a⊼(b⊼c) = a⊼(c⊼b)	(a⊼b)⊼c = b⊼(a⊼c)
a⊼(b⊼c) = (b⊼c)⊼a	(a⊼b)⊼c = c⊼(a⊼b)	a⊼(b⊼c) = (c⊼b)⊼a	(a⊼b)⊼c = c⊼(b⊼a)
(a⊼a)⊼(a⊼a) = (a⊼a)⊼(a⊼b)	(a⊼a)⊼(a⊼a) = (a⊼a)⊼(b⊼a)	(a⊼a)⊼(a⊼a) = (a⊼b)⊼(a⊼a)	(a⊼a)⊼(a⊼a) = (b⊼a)⊼(a⊼a)
(a⊼a)⊼(a⊼b) = (a⊼a)⊼(a⊼c)	(a⊼a)⊼(a⊼b) = (a⊼a)⊼(b⊼a)	(a⊼a)⊼(a⊼b) = (a⊼a)⊼(c⊼a)	(a⊼a)⊼(a⊼b) = (a⊼b)⊼(a⊼a)

⋮ *118 lines*

a⊼((a⊼b)⊼b) = (c⊼(a⊼a))⊼a	a⊼((a⊼b)⊼b) = ((c⊼a)⊼c)⊼a	a⊼((a⊼b)⊼b) = (c⊼(a⊼c))⊼a	(a⊼(a⊼b))⊼b = (c⊼(b⊼b))⊼b
(a⊼(a⊼b))⊼b = ((c⊼b)⊼c)⊼b	(a⊼(a⊼b))⊼b = (c⊼(b⊼c))⊼b	a⊼((a⊼b)⊼b) = (c⊼(c⊼a))⊼a	(a⊼(a⊼b))⊼b = (c⊼(c⊼b))⊼b
a⊼((a⊼b)⊼b) = ((c⊼c)⊼c)⊼a	a⊼((a⊼b)⊼b) = (c⊼(c⊼c))⊼a	(a⊼(a⊼b))⊼b = ((c⊼c)⊼c)⊼b	(a⊼(a⊼b))⊼b = (c⊼(c⊼c))⊼b
a⊼(a⊼(b⊼c)) = a⊼(a⊼(c⊼b))	(a⊼(a⊼b))⊼c = ((a⊼b)⊼a)⊼c	(a⊼(a⊼b))⊼c = (a⊼(b⊼a))⊼c	a⊼((a⊼b)⊼c) = a⊼((b⊼a)⊼c)
((a⊼a)⊼b)⊼c = ((a⊼b)⊼b)⊼c	(a⊼(a⊼b))⊼c = a⊼((b⊼b)⊼c)	a⊼((a⊼b)⊼c) = a⊼((b⊼b)⊼c)	(a⊼(a⊼b))⊼c = ((b⊼b)⊼c)⊼a
a⊼(a⊼(b⊼c)) = (a⊼(b⊼c))⊼a	a⊼(a⊼(b⊼c)) = a⊼((b⊼c)⊼a)	a⊼(a⊼(b⊼c)) = ((a⊼b)⊼c)⊼c	(a⊼(a⊼b))⊼c = (a⊼(b⊼c))⊼c
a⊼((a⊼b)⊼c) = a⊼((b⊼c)⊼c)	a⊼((a⊼b)⊼c) = a⊼(c⊼(a⊼b))	a⊼(a⊼(b⊼c)) = (a⊼(c⊼b))⊼a	(a⊼(a⊼b))⊼c = (a⊼(b⊼c))⊼c
a⊼((a⊼b)⊼c) = a⊼(c⊼(b⊼a))	a⊼(a⊼(b⊼c)) = ((a⊼c)⊼b)⊼b	a⊼((a⊼b)⊼c) = a⊼(c⊼(b⊼a))	((a⊼a)⊼b)⊼c = ((a⊼c)⊼b)⊼c
(a⊼(a⊼b))⊼c = (a⊼(c⊼b))⊼c	a⊼((a⊼b)⊼c) = a⊼((c⊼b)⊼c)	a⊼((a⊼b)⊼c) = a⊼((c⊼b)⊼c)	a⊼((a⊼b)⊼c) = a⊼(c⊼(c⊼b))

⋮

The theorems of logic formulated in terms of NAND. Theorems which cannot be derived from ones earlier in the list are highlighted. The last highlighted theorem is 539th in the list. No later theorems would be highlighted since the ones shown form a complete axiom system from which any theorem of logic can be derived. The last highlighted theorem is however an example of one that follows from the axioms, but is hard to prove.

818

Now there is no particular historical tradition to rely on. But the criterion nevertheless still seems to agree rather well with judgements a human might make. And much as in the picture on page 817, what one sees is that right at the beginning of the list there are several theorems that are identified as interesting. But after these one has to go a long way before one finds other ones.

So if one were to go still further, would one eventually find yet more? It turns out that with the criterion we have used one would not. And the reason is that just the six theorems highlighted already happen to form an axiom system from which any possible theorem about NANDs can ultimately be derived.

And indeed, whenever one is dealing with theorems that can be derived from a finite axiom system the criterion implies that only a finite number of theorems should ever be considered interesting— ending as soon as one has in a sense got enough theorems to be able to reproduce some formulation of the axiom system.

But this is essentially like saying that once one knows the rules for a system nothing else about it should ever be considered interesting. Yet most of this book is concerned precisely with all the interesting behavior that can emerge even if one knows the rules for a system.

And the point is that if computational irreducibility is present, then there is in a sense all sorts of information about the behavior of a system that can only be found from its rules by doing an irreducibly large amount of computational work. And the analog of this in an axiom system is that there are theorems that can be reached only by proofs that are somehow irreducibly long.

So what this suggests is that a theorem might be considered interesting not only if it cannot be derived at all from simpler theorems but also if it cannot be derived from them except by some long proof. And indeed in basic logic the last theorem identified as interesting on page 817—the distributivity of OR—is an example of one that can in principle be derived from earlier theorems, but only by a proof that seems to be much longer than other theorems of comparable size.

In logic, however, all proofs are in effect ultimately of limited length. But in any axiom system where there is universality—and thus undecidability—this is no longer the case, and as I discussed above I suspect that it will actually be quite common for there to be all sorts of short theorems that have only extremely long proofs.

No doubt many such theorems are much too difficult ever to prove in practice. But even if they could be proved, would they be considered interesting? Certainly they would provide what is in essence new information, but my strong suspicion is that in mathematics as it is currently practiced they would only rarely be considered interesting.

And most often the stated reason for this would be that they do not seem to fit into any general framework of mathematical results, but instead just seem like isolated random mathematical facts.

In doing mathematics, it is common to use terms like difficult, powerful, surprising and deep to describe theorems. But what do these really mean? As I mentioned above, any field of mathematics can at some level be viewed as a giant network of statements in which the connections correspond to theorems. And my suspicion is that our intuitive characterizations of theorems are in effect just reflections of our perception of various features of the structure of this network.

And indeed I suspect that by looking at issues such as how easy a given theorem makes it to get from one part of a network to another it will be possible to formalize many intuitive notions about the practice of mathematics—much as earlier in this book we were able to formalize notions of everyday experience such as complexity and randomness.

Different fields of mathematics may well have networks with characteristically different features. And so, for example, what are usually viewed as more successful areas of pure mathematics may have more compact networks, while areas that seem to involve all sorts of isolated facts—like elementary number theory or theory of specific cellular automata—may have sparser networks with more tendrils.

And such differences will be reflected in proofs that can be given. For example, in a sparser network the proof of a particular theorem may not contain many pieces that can be used in proving other theorems. But in a more compact network there may be intermediate definitions and concepts that can be used in a whole range of different theorems.

Indeed, in an extreme case it might even be possible to do the analog of what has been done, say, in the computation of symbolic integrals, and to set up some kind of uniform procedure for finding a proof of essentially any short theorem.

And in general whenever there are enough repeated elements within a single proof or between different proofs this indicates the presence of computational reducibility. Yet while this means that there is in effect less new information in each theorem that is proved, it turns out that in most areas of mathematics these theorems are usually the ones that are considered interesting.

The presence of universality implies that there must at some level be computational irreducibility—and thus that there must be theorems that cannot be reached by any short procedure. But the point is that mathematics has tended to ignore these, and instead to concentrate just on what are in effect limited patches of computational reducibility in the network of all possible theorems.

Yet in a sense this is no different from what has happened, say, in physics, where the phenomena that have traditionally been studied are mostly just those ones that show enough computational reducibility to allow analysis by traditional methods of theoretical physics.

But whereas in physics one has only to look at the natural world to see that other more complex phenomena exist, the usual approaches to mathematics provide almost no hint of anything analogous.

Yet with the new approach based on explicit experimentation used in this book it now becomes quite clear that phenomena such as computational irreducibility occur in abstract mathematical systems.

And indeed the Principle of Computational Equivalence implies that such phenomena should be close at hand in almost every direction: it is merely that—despite its reputation for generality—mathematics has in the past implicitly tended to define itself to avoid them.

So what this means is that in the future, when the ideas and methods of this book have successfully been absorbed, the field of mathematics as it exists today will come to be seen as a small and surprisingly uncharacteristic sample of what is actually possible.

Intelligence in the Universe

Whether or not we as humans are the only examples of intelligence in the universe is one of the great unanswered questions of science.

Just how intelligence should be defined has never been quite clear. But in recent times it has usually been assumed that it has something to do with an ability to perform sophisticated computations.

And with traditional intuition it has always seemed perfectly reasonable that it should take a system as complicated as a human to exhibit such capabilities—and that the whole elaborate history of life on Earth should have been needed to generate such a system.

With the development of computer technology it became clear that many features of intelligence could be achieved in systems that are not biological. Yet our experience has still been that to build a computer requires sophisticated engineering that in a sense exists only because of human biological and cultural development.

But one of the central discoveries of this book is that in fact nothing so elaborate is needed to get sophisticated computation. And indeed the Principle of Computational Equivalence implies that a vast range of systems—even ones with very simple underlying rules—should be equivalent in the sophistication of the computations they perform.

So in as much as intelligence is associated with the ability to do sophisticated computations it should in no way require billions of years of biological evolution to produce—and indeed we should see it all over the place, in all sorts of systems, whether biological or otherwise.

And certainly some everyday turns of phrase might suggest that we do. For when we say that the weather has a mind of its own we are in effect attributing something like intelligence to the motion of a fluid. Yet surely, one might argue, there must be something fundamentally more to true intelligence of the kind that we as humans have.

So what then might this be?

Certainly one can identify all sorts of specific features of human intelligence: the ability to understand language, to do mathematics, solve puzzles, and so on. But the question is whether there are more general features that somehow capture the essence of true intelligence, independent of the particular details of human intelligence.

Perhaps it could be the ability to learn and remember. Or the ability to adapt to a wide range of different and complex situations. Or the ability to handle abstract general representations of data.

At first, all of these might seem like reasonable indicators of true intelligence. But as soon as one tries to think about them independent of the particular example of human intelligence, it becomes much less clear. And indeed, from the discoveries in this book I am now quite certain that any of them can actually be achieved in systems that we would normally never think of as showing anything like intelligence.

Learning and memory, for example, can effectively occur in any system that has structures that form in response to input, and that can persist for a long time and affect the behavior of the system. And this can happen even in simple cellular automata—or, say, in a physical system like a fluid that carves out a long-term pattern in a solid surface.

Adaptation to all sorts of complex situations also occurs in a great many systems. It is well recognized when natural selection is present. But at some level it can also be thought of as occurring whenever a constraint ends up getting satisfied—even say that a fluid flowing around a complex object minimizes the energy it dissipates.

Handling abstraction is also in a sense rather common. Indeed, as soon as one thinks of a system as performing computations one can immediately view features of those computations as being like abstract representations of input to the system.

So given all of this is there any way to define a general notion of true intelligence? My guess is that ultimately there is not, and that in fact any workable definition of what we normally think of as intelligence will end up having to be tied to all sorts of seemingly rather specific details of human intelligence.

And as it turns out this is quite similar to what happens if one tries to define the seemingly much simpler notion of life.

There was a time when it was thought that practically any system that moves spontaneously and responds to stimuli must be alive. But with the development of machines having even the most primitive sensors it became clear that this was not correct.

Work in the field of thermodynamics led to the idea that perhaps living systems could be defined by their ability to take disorganized material and spontaneously organize it—usually to incorporate it into their own structure. Yet all sorts of non-living systems—from crystals to flames—also do this. And Chapter 6 showed that self-organization is actually extremely common even among systems with simple rules.

For a while it was thought that perhaps life might be defined by its ability for self-reproduction. But in the 1950s abstract computational systems were constructed that also had this ability. Yet it seemed that they needed highly complex rules—not unlike those found in actual living cells. But in fact no such complexity is really necessary. And as one might now expect from the intuition in this book, even systems like the one below with remarkably simple rules can still manage to show self-reproduction—despite the fact that they bear almost no other resemblance to ordinary living systems.

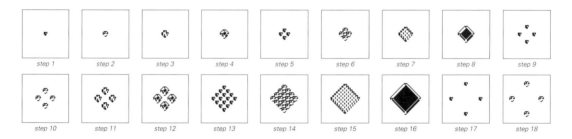

A two-dimensional cellular automaton that exhibits an almost trivial form of self-reproduction, in which multiple copies of any initial pattern appear every time the number of steps of evolution doubles. The rule used is additive, and takes a cell to be black whenever an odd number of its neighbors were black on the step before (outer totalistic code 204). The same basic self-reproduction phenomenon occurs in elementary rule 90, as well as in essentially any other additive rule, in any number of dimensions.

If one looks at typical living systems one of their most obvious features is great apparent complexity. And for a long time it has been thought that such complexity must somehow be unique to living systems—perhaps requiring billions of years of biological evolution to develop. But what I have shown in this book is that this is not the case, and that in fact a vast range of systems—including ones with very simple underlying rules—can generate at least as much complexity as we see in the components of typical living systems.

Yet despite all this, we do not in our everyday experience typically have much difficulty telling living systems from non-living ones. But the reason for this is that all living systems on Earth share an immense number of detailed structural and chemical features—reflecting their long common history of biological evolution.

So what about extraterrestrial life? To be able to recognize this we would need some kind of general definition of life, independent of the details of life on Earth. But just as in the case of intelligence, I believe that no reasonable definition of this kind can actually be given.

Indeed, following the discoveries in this book I have come to the conclusion that almost any general feature that one might think of as characterizing life will actually occur even in many systems with very simple rules. And I have little doubt that all sorts of such systems can be identified both terrestrially and extraterrestrially—and certainly require nothing like the elaborate history of life on Earth to produce.

But most likely we would not consider these systems even close to being real examples of life. And in fact I expect that in the end the only way we would unquestionably view a system as being an example of life is if we found that it shared many specific details with life on Earth—probably down, say, to being made of gelatinous materials and having components analogous to proteins, enzymes, cell membranes and so on—and perhaps even down to being based on specific chemical substances like water, sugars, ATP and DNA.

So what then of extraterrestrial intelligence? To what extent would it have to show the same details as human intelligence—and perhaps even the same kinds of knowledge—for us to recognize it as a valid example of intelligence?

Already just among humans it can in practice be somewhat difficult to recognize intelligence in the absence of shared education and culture. Indeed, in young children it remains almost completely unclear at what stage different aspects of intelligence become active.

And when it comes to other animals things become even more difficult. If one specifically tries to train an animal to solve mathematical puzzles or to communicate using human language then it is usually possible to recognize what intelligence it shows.

But if one just observes the normal activities of the animal it can be remarkably difficult to tell whether they involve intelligence. And so as a typical example it remains quite unclear whether there is intelligence associated with the songs of either birds or whales.

To us these songs may sound quite musical—and indeed they even seem to show some of the same principles of organization as human music. But do they really require intelligence to generate?

Particularly for birds it has increasingly been possible to trace the detailed processes by which songs are produced. And it seems that at least some of their elaborate elements are just direct consequences of the complex patterns of air flow that occur in the vocal tracts of birds.

But there is definitely also input from the brain of the bird. Yet within the brain some of the neural pathways responsible are known. And one might think that if all such pathways could be found then this would immediately show that no intelligence was involved.

Certainly if the pathways could somehow be seen to support only simple computations then this would be a reasonable conclusion. But just using definite pathways—or definite underlying rules—does not in any way preclude intelligence. And in fact if one looks inside a human brain—say in the process of generating speech—one will no doubt also see definite pathways and definite rules in use.

So how then can we judge whether something like a bird song, or a whale song—or, for that matter, an extraterrestrial signal—is a reflection of intelligence? The fundamental criterion we tend to use is whether it has a meaning—or whether it communicates anything.

Everyday experience shows us that it can often be very hard to tell. For even if we just hear a human language that we do not know it can be almost impossible for us to recognize whether what is being said is meaningful or not. And the same is true if we pick up data of any kind that is encoded in a format we do not know.

We might start by trying to use our powers of perception and analysis to find regularities in the data. And if we found too many regularities we might conclude that the data could not represent enough information to communicate anything significant—and indeed perhaps this is the case for at least some highly repetitive bird songs.

But what if we could find no particular regularities? Our everyday experience with human language might make us think that the data could then have no meaning. But there is nothing to say that it might not be a perfectly meaningful message—even one in human language—that just happens to have been encrypted or compressed to a point where it shows no detectable regularities.

And indeed it is sobering to notice that if one just listens even to bird songs and whale songs there is little that fundamentally seems to distinguish them from what can be generated by all sorts of processes in nature—say the motion of chimes blowing in the wind or of plasma in the Earth's magnetosphere.

One might imagine that one could find out whether a meaningful message had been communicated in a particular case by looking for correlations it induces between the actions of sender and receiver. But it is extremely common in all sorts of natural systems to see effects that propagate from one element to another. And when it comes even to whale songs it turns out that no clear correlations have ever in the end been identified between senders and receivers.

But what if one were to notice some event happen to the sender? If one were somehow to see a representation of this in what the sender produced, would it not be evidence for meaningful communication?

Once again, it need not be. For there are a great many cases in which systems generate signals that reflect what happens to them. And so, for example, a drum that is struck in a particular pattern will produce a sound that reflects—and in effect represents—that pattern.

Yet on the other hand even among humans different training or culture can lead to vastly different responses to a given event. And for animals there is the added problem of emphasis on different forms of perception. For presumably dogs can sense the detailed pattern of smell in their environment, and dolphins the detailed pattern of fluid motion around them. Yet we as humans would almost certainly not recognize descriptions presented in such terms.

So if we cannot identify intelligence by looking for meaningful communication, can we perhaps at least tell for a given object whether intelligence has been involved in producing it?

For certainly our everyday experience is that it is usually quite easy to tell whether something is an artifact created by humans.

But a large part of the reason for this is just that most artifacts we encounter in practice have specific elements that look rather similar. Yet presumably this is for the most part just a reflection of the historical development of engineering—and of the fact that the same basic geometrical and other forms have ended up being used over and over again.

So are there then more general ways to recognize artifacts?

A fairly good way in practice to guess whether something is an artifact is just to look and see whether it appears simple. For although there are exceptions—like crystals, bubbles and animal horns—the majority of objects that exist in nature have irregular and often very intricate forms that seem much more complex than typical artifacts.

And indeed this fact has often been taken to show that objects in nature must have been created by a deity whose capabilities go beyond human intelligence. For traditional intuition suggests that if one sees more complexity it must always in a sense have more complex origins.

But one of the main discoveries of this book is that in fact great complexity can arise even in systems with extremely simple underlying rules, so that in the end nothing with rules even as elaborate as human intelligence—let alone beyond it—is needed to explain the kind of complexity we see in nature.

But the question then remains why when human intelligence is involved it tends to create artifacts that look much simpler than objects that just appear in nature. And I believe the basic answer to this has to do with the fact that when we as humans set up artifacts we usually need to be able to foresee what they will do—for otherwise we have no way to tell whether they will achieve the purposes we want.

Yet nature presumably operates under no such constraint. And in fact I have argued that among systems that appear in nature a great many exhibit computational irreducibility—so that in a sense it becomes irreducibly difficult to foresee what they will do.

Yet at least with its traditional methodology engineering tends to rely on computational reducibility. For typically it operates by building systems up in such a way that the behavior of each element can always readily be predicted by something like a simple mathematical formula.

And the result of this is that most systems created by engineering are forced in some sense to seem simple—in mechanical cases for example typically being based only on simple repetitive motion.

But is simplicity a necessary feature of artifacts? Or might artifacts created by extraterrestrial intelligence—or by future human technology—seem to show no signs of simplicity?

As soon as we say that a system achieves a definite purpose this means that we can summarize at least some part of what the system does just by describing this purpose. So if we have a simple description of the purpose it follows that we must be able to give a simple summary of at least some part of what the system does.

But does this then mean that the whole behavior of the system must be simple? Traditional engineering might tend to make one think so. For typically our experience is that if we are able to get a particular kind of system to generate a particular outcome at all, then normally the behavior involved in doing so is quite simple.

But one of the results of this book is that in general things need not work like this. And so for example at the end of Chapter 5 we saw several systems in which a simple constraint of achieving a particular outcome could in effect only be satisfied with fairly complex behavior.

And as I will discuss in the next section I believe that in the effort to optimize things it is almost inevitable that even to achieve comparatively simple purposes more advanced forms of technology will make use of systems that have more and more complex behavior.

So this means that there is in the end no reason to think that artifacts with simple purposes will necessarily look simple.

And so if we are just presented with something, how then can we tell if it has a purpose? Even with things that we know were created by humans it can already be difficult. And so, for example, there are many archeological structures—such as Stonehenge—where it is at best unclear which features were intended to be purposeful.

And even in present-day situations, if we are exposed to objects or activities outside the areas of human endeavor with which we happen to be familiar, it can be very hard for us to tell which features are immediately purposeful, and which are unintentional—or have, say, primarily ornamental or ceremonial functions.

Indeed, even if we are told a purpose we will often not recognize it. And the only way we will normally become convinced of its validity is by understanding how some whole chain of consequences can lead to purposes that happen to fit into our own specific personal context.

So given this how then can we ever expect in general to recognize the presence of purpose—say as a sign of extraterrestrial intelligence?

And as an example if we were to see a cellular automaton how would we be able to tell whether it was created for a purpose?

Of the cellular automata in this book—especially in Chapter 11—a few were specifically constructed to achieve particular purposes. But the vast majority originally just arose as part of my investigation of what happens with the simplest possible underlying rules.

And at first I did not think of most of them as achieving any particular purposes at all. But gradually as I built up the whole context of the science in this book I realized that many of them could in fact be thought of as achieving very definite purposes.

Systems like rule 110 shown on the left have a kind of local coherence in their behavior that reminds one of the operation of traditional engineering systems—or of purposeful human activity. But the same is not true of systems like rule 30. For although one can see that such systems have a lot going on, one tends to assume that somehow none of it is coherent enough to achieve any definite purpose.

Yet in the context of the ideas in this book, a system like rule 30 can be viewed as achieving the purpose of performing a fairly sophisticated computation. And indeed we know that this computation is useful in practice for generating sequences that appear random.

But of course it is not necessary for us to talk about purpose when we describe the behavior of rule 30. We can perfectly well instead talk only about mechanism, and about the way in which the underlying rules for the cellular automaton lead to the behavior we see.

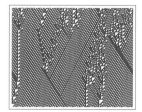

rule 110

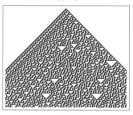

rule 30

Cellular automata whose behavior does and does not give the impression of being purposeful.

And indeed this is true of any system. But as a practical matter we often end up describing what systems do in terms of purpose when this seems to us simpler than describing it in terms of mechanism.

And so for example if we can identify some simple constraint that a system always tries to satisfy it is not uncommon for us to talk of this as being the purpose of the system. And in fact we do this even in cases like minimization of energy in physical systems or natural selection for fitness in biological systems where nothing that we ordinarily think of as intelligence is involved.

So the fact that we may be able to interpret a system as achieving some purpose does not necessarily mean that the system was really created with that purpose in mind. And indeed just looking at the system we will never ultimately be able to tell for sure that it was.

But we can still often manage to guess. And given a particular supposed purpose one potential criterion to use is that the system in a sense not appear to do too much that is extraneous to that purpose.

And so, for example, in looking at the pictures on the right it would normally seem much more plausible that rule 254 might have been set up for the purpose of generating a uniformly expanding pattern than that rule 30 might have been. For while rule 30 does generate such a pattern, it also does a lot else that appears irrelevant to this purpose.

So what this might suggest is that perhaps one could tell that a system was set up for a given purpose if the system turns out to be in a sense the minimal one that achieves that purpose.

But an immediate issue is that in traditional engineering we normally do not come even close to getting systems that are minimal. Yet it seems reasonable to suppose that as technology becomes more advanced it should become more common that the systems it sets up for a given purpose are ones that are minimal.

So as an example of all this consider cellular automata that achieve the purpose of doubling the width of the pattern given in their input. Case (a) in the picture on the next page is a cellular automaton one might construct for this purpose by using ideas from traditional engineering.

But while this cellular automaton seems to have little extraneous going on, it operates in a slow and sequential way, and its underlying

rule 254

rule 30

If the purpose is to generate a uniformly expanding pattern it seems more plausible that the top cellular automaton should have been the one created for this purpose.

831

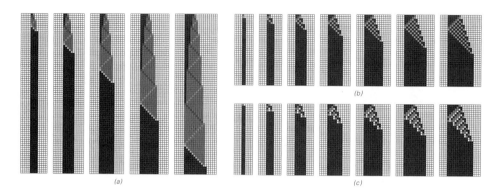

Examples of cellular automata that can be viewed as achieving the purpose of doubling the width of the pattern given in their input. Rule (a) involves 6 colors, and works sequentially, much as a typical traditional engineering system might. Rule (b) involves 4 colors, and works in parallel. Rule (c) was found by a large search, and involves only 3 colors. It takes the fewest steps of any 3-color rule to generate its result. Its rule number is 5407067979.

rules turn out to be far from minimal. For case (b) gets its results much more quickly—in effect by operating in parallel—and its rules involve four possible colors rather than six.

But is case (b) really the minimal cellular automaton that achieves the purpose of doubling its input? Just thinking about it, one might not be able to come up with anything better. But if one in effect explicitly searches all 8 trillion or so rules that involve less than four colors, it turns out that one can find 4277 three-color rules that work.

The pictures on the facing page show a few typical examples.

Each uses at least a slightly different scheme, but all achieve the same purpose of doubling their input. Yet often they operate in ways that seem considerably more complex than most familiar artifacts. And indeed some of the examples might look to us more like systems that just occur in nature than like artifacts.

But the point is that with sufficiently advanced technology one might expect that doubling of input would be implemented using a rule that is in some sense optimal. Different criteria for optimality could lead to different rules, but usually they will be rules like those on the facing page—and sometimes rules with quite complex behavior.

But now the question is if one were just to encounter such a rule, would one be able to guess that it was created for a purpose? After all,

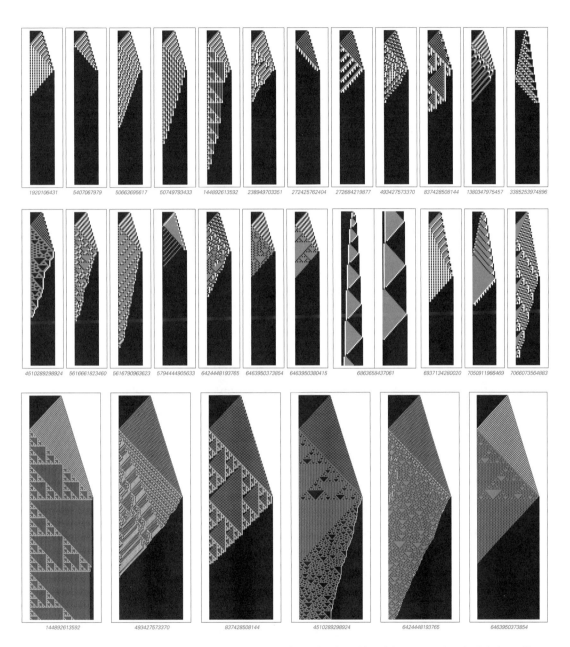

Examples of rules with three colors that achieve the purpose of doubling the width of the pattern given in their input. These examples are taken from the 4277 found in effect by searching exhaustively all 7,625,597,484,987 possible rules with three colors. In most cases the number of steps to generate the final pattern increases roughly linearly with the width of the input—although in the case of the fourth-to-last rule on the second row it is $2(n^2 - n + 1)$ for width n.

there are all sorts of features in the behavior of these rules that could in principle represent a possible purpose. But what is special about rules like those on the previous page is that they are the minimal ones that exhibit the particular feature of doubling their input.

And in general if one sees some feature in the behavior of a system then finding out that the rule for the system is the minimal or optimal one for producing that feature may make it seem more likely that at least with sufficiently advanced technology the system might have specifically been created for the purpose of exhibiting that feature.

Computational irreducibility implies that it can be arbitrarily difficult to find minimal or optimal rules. Yet given any procedure for trying to do this it is certainly always possible that the procedure could just occur in nature without any purpose or intelligence being involved.

And in fact one might consider this not all that unlikely for the kind of fairly straightforward exhaustive searches that I ended up using to find the cellular automaton rules in the pictures on the previous page.

So what does all this mean for extraterrestrial intelligence?

Extrapolating from our own development we might expect that given sufficiently advanced technology it would be almost inevitable for artifacts to be constructed on an astronomical scale—perhaps for example giant machines with objects like stars as components.

Yet we do not believe that we have ever seen any such artifacts.

But how do we know for sure? For certainly our astronomical observations have revealed all sorts of phenomena for which we do not yet have any very satisfactory explanations. And indeed until just a few centuries ago most such unexplained phenomena would routinely have been attributed to some kind of divine intelligence.

But in more recent times it has become almost universally assumed that they must instead be the result of physical processes in which nothing like intelligence is involved.

Yet what the discoveries in this book have shown is that even such physical processes can often correspond to computations that are at least as sophisticated as any that we as humans perform.

But what we believe is that somehow none of the phenomena we see have any sense of purpose analogous to typical human artifacts.

Occasionally we do see evidence of simple geometrical shapes like those familiar from human artifacts—or visible on the Earth from space. But normally our explanations for these end up being short enough that they seem to leave no room for anything like intelligence. And when we see elaborate patterns, say in nebulas or galaxies, we assume that these can have no purpose—even though they may remind us to some extent of human art.

So if we do not recognize any objects that seem to be artifacts, what about signals that might correspond to messages?

If we looked at the Earth from far away the most obvious signs of human intelligence would probably be found in radio signals.

And in fact in the past it was often assumed that just to generate radio signals at all must require intelligence and technology. So when complex radio signals not of human origin were discovered in the early 1900s it was at first thought that they must be coming from extraterrestrial intelligence. But it was eventually realized that in fact the signals were just produced by effects in the Earth's magnetosphere.

And then again in the 1960s when the intense and highly regular signals of pulsars were discovered it was briefly thought that they too must come from extraterrestrial intelligence. But it was soon realized that these signals could actually be produced just by ordinary physical processes in the magnetospheres of rapidly rotating neutron stars.

So what might a real signal from extraterrestrial intelligence be like? Human radio signals currently tend to be characterized by the presence of sharply defined carrier frequencies, corresponding in effect to almost perfect small-scale repetition. But such regularity greatly reduces the rate at which information can be transmitted. And as technology advances less and less regularity needs to be present.

But in practice essentially all serious searches for extraterrestrial intelligence made so far have been based on using radio telescopes to look for signals with sharply defined frequencies. And indeed no such signals have been found. But as we saw in Chapter 10 even signals that are nested rather than purely repetitive cannot reliably be recognized just by looking for peaks in frequency spectra.

And there is certainly in general no lack of radio signals that we receive from around our galaxy and beyond. But the point is that these signals typically seem to us quite random. And normally this has made us assume that they must in effect just be some kind of radio noise that is being produced by one of several simple physical processes.

But could it be that some of these signals instead come from extraterrestrial intelligence—and are in fact meaningful messages?

Ongoing communications between extraterrestrials seem likely to be localized to regions of space where they are needed, and therefore presumably not accessible to us. And even if some signals involved in such communications are broadcast, my guess is that they will exhibit essentially no detectable regularities. For any such regularity represents in a sense a redundancy or inefficiency that can be removed by the sender and receiver both using appropriate data compression.

But if there are beacons that are intended to be noticed even if one does not already know that they are there, then the signals these produce must necessarily have recognizable distinguishing features, and thus regularities that can be detected, at least by their potential users.

So perhaps the problem is just that the methods of perception and analysis that we as humans have are not powerful enough. And perhaps if we could only find the appropriate new method it would suddenly be clear that some of what we thought was random radio noise is actually the output of beacons set up by extraterrestrial intelligence.

For as we saw in Chapter 10 most of the methods of perception and analysis that we currently use can in general do little more than recognize repetition—and sometimes nesting. Yet in the course of this book we have seen a great many examples where data that appears to us quite random can in fact be produced by very simple underlying rules.

And although I somewhat doubt it, one could certainly imagine that if one were to show data like the center column of rule 30 or the digit sequence of π to an extraterrestrial then they would immediately be able to deduce simple rules that can produce these.

But even if at some point we were to find that some of the seemingly random radio noise that we detect can be generated by simple rules, what would this mean about extraterrestrial intelligence?

In many respects, the simpler the rules, the more likely it might seem that they could be associated with ordinary physical processes, without anything like intelligence being involved.

Yet as we discussed above, if one could actually determine that the rules used in a given case were the simplest possible, then this might suggest that they were somehow set up on purpose. But in practice if one just receives a signal one normally has no way to tell which of all possible rules for producing it were in fact used.

So is there then any kind of signal that could be sent that would unambiguously communicate the presence of intelligence?

In the past, one might have thought that it would be enough for the production of the signal to involve sophisticated computation. But the discoveries in this book have made it clear that in fact such computation is quite common in all sorts of systems that do not show anything that we would normally consider intelligence.

And indeed it seems likely that for example an ordinary physical process like fluid turbulence in the gas around a star should rather quickly do more computation than has by most measures ever been done throughout the whole course of human intellectual history.

In discussions of extraterrestrial intelligence it is often claimed that mathematical constructs—such as the sequence of primes— somehow serve as universal signs of intelligence.

But from the results in this book it is clear that this is not correct.

For while in the past it might have seemed that the only way to generate primes was by using intelligence, we now know that the rather straightforward computations required can actually be carried out by a vast range of different systems—with no apparent need for intelligence.

One might nevertheless imagine that any sufficiently advanced intelligence would somehow at least consider the primes significant.

But here again I do not believe that this is correct. For very little even of current human technology depends on ideas about primes. And I am also fairly sure that not much can be deduced from the fact that primes happen to be popular in present-day human mathematics.

For despite its reputation for generality I argued at length in the previous section that the whole field of mathematics that we as humans have historically developed ultimately covers only a tiny fraction of what is possible—notably leaving out the vast majority of systems that I have studied in this book.

And if one identifies a feature—such as repetition or nesting—that is common to many possible systems, then it becomes inevitable that this feature will appear not only when intelligence or mathematics is involved, but also in all sorts of systems that just occur in nature.

So what about trying to set up a signal that gives evidence of somehow having been created for a purpose? I argued above that if the rules for a system are as simple as they can be, then this may suggest the presence of purpose. But such a criterion relies on seeing not only a signal but also the mechanism by which the signal was produced.

So what about a signal on its own? One might imagine that one could set something up—say the solution to a difficult mathematical problem—that was somehow easy to describe in terms of a constraint or purpose, but difficult to explain in terms of an explicit mechanism.

But in a sense such a thing cannot exist. For given a constraint, it is always in principle simple to set up an exhaustive search that provides a mechanism for finding what satisfies the constraint.

However, this may still take a lot of computational effort. But we cannot use that alone as a criterion. For as we have seen, many systems that just occur in nature actually end up doing more computation than typical systems that we explicitly set up for a purpose.

So even if we cannot find an abstract way to give evidence of purpose or intelligence, what about using the practical fact that both the sender and receiver of a signal exist in the same physical universe? Can one perhaps use a signal that is a representation of actual data in, say, astronomy, physics or chemistry?

As I discussed earlier, the more direct the representation the more easily an ordinary physical process can be expected to generate it, and the less there will be any indication of intelligence—just as, for example, something like a photograph can be produced essentially just by projecting light, while a diagram or a painting requires more.

But as soon as there is interpretation of data, it can become very difficult to recognize the results. For different forms of perception and different experiences and contexts can cause vastly different features to be emphasized. And thus, for example, the fact that we can readily recognize pictures of animals in cave paintings made by Stone Age humans depends greatly on the fact that our visual system still picks out the same specific features.

But what about more abstract art?

Although one has the feeling that this involves more human input, it rapidly becomes extremely difficult to tell what has been created on purpose. And so, for example, if one sees a splash of paint it is almost impossible to know without detailed cultural background and context whether it is intended to be purposeful art.

So what does all this mean about extraterrestrial intelligence?

My main conclusion is rather similar to my conclusion about artificial intelligence in Chapter 10: that the basic issue is not finding systems that perform sophisticated enough computations, but rather finding ones whose details happen to be similar enough to us as humans that we recognize what they do as showing intelligence.

And there is perhaps some analogy to recognizing the capability for sophisticated computation in the first place. For while this is undoubtedly very common say in cellular automata, the most immediate suggestions of it are in class 4 systems like rule 110 that in effect happen to do their computations in a way that looks at least somewhat similar to the way we as humans are used to doing them.

So should we expect that somehow recognizable extraterrestrial intelligence will occur at a level of a few percent—like class 4 systems?

There is clearly more to the phenomenon of intelligence than this. But if we require something that follows too many of the details of us as humans there is already evidence that it does not exist. For if such intelligence had ever arisen in the past, then extrapolating from our own history we would expect that some of it would long ago have colonized our galaxy—at least with signals, if not with physical objects.

But I suspect that if we generalize even quite modestly our definition of intelligence then there will be examples that can be found—at least with sufficiently powerful methods of perception and analysis. Yet it seems likely that they will behave in some ways that are as bizarrely different from human intelligence as many of the simple programs in this book are different from the systems that have traditionally been studied in human mathematics and science.

Implications for Technology

My main purpose in this book has been to build a new kind of basic science. But I expect that in time what I have done will also have many implications for technology. No doubt there will be all sorts of specific applications of particular results and ideas. But in the long run probably the most important consequence will be to introduce a vast new range of systems and processes that can be used for technology.

And indeed one of the things that emerges from this book is that traditional engineering has actually considered only a tiny and quite unrepresentative fraction of all the kinds of systems and processes that are in principle possible.

Presumably the reason—as I have mentioned several times in this book—is that its whole methodology has tended to be based on setting up systems whose behavior is simple enough that almost every aspect of them can always readily be predicted. But doing this has immediately excluded many of the systems that I have studied in this book—or for that matter that occur in nature. And no doubt this is why systems created by engineering have in the past usually ended up looking so much simpler than typical systems in nature.

And with traditional intuition it has normally been assumed that the only way to create systems that show a higher degree of complexity is somehow to build this complexity into their underlying rules.

But one of the central discoveries of this book is that this is not the case, and that in fact it is perfectly possible for systems even with extremely simple underlying rules to produce behavior that has immense complexity—and that looks like what one sees in nature.

And I believe that if one uses such systems it is almost inevitable that a vast amount of new technology will become possible.

There are some places where just the abstract ability to produce complexity from simple rules is already important. One example discussed in Chapter 10 is cryptography. Other examples include all sorts of practical processes in which bias or deadlock can be avoided by using randomness, or in which one wants to generate behavior that is somehow too complex for an adversary to predict.

Being able to produce complexity that is even roughly like what we see in nature also has immediate consequences—say in generating realistic textures and computer graphics or in producing artistic images that we abstractly perceive as having features familiar from nature.

The phenomenon of computational irreducibility implies that to find out what some specific system with complex behavior will do can require explicit simulation that involves an irreducible amount of computational work. But as a practical matter, if one can set up a model that is based on sufficiently simple rules then it becomes more likely that one will be able to make designs and build control devices that work even with some system in nature that shows complex behavior.

So what about computers? Although the components used have shifted from vacuum tubes to semiconductors the fundamental rules by which computers operate have changed very little in half a century.

But what the Principle of Computational Equivalence implies is that there are actually a vast range of very different kinds of rules that all lead to exactly the same computational capabilities—and so can all in principle be used as a basis for making computers.

Traditional intuition suggests that to be able to do sophisticated computations one would inevitably need a system with complicated underlying rules. But what I have shown in this book is that this is not the case, and that in fact even systems with extremely simple rules—like the rule 110 cellular automaton—can often be universal, and thus be capable of doing computations as sophisticated as any other system.

And the fact that the underlying rules can be so simple vastly expands the kinds of components that can realistically be used to implement them. For while it is quite implausible that some simple chemical process could successfully assemble a traditional computer out of atoms, it seems quite plausible that this could be done for something like a rule 110 cellular automaton.

Indeed, it seems likely that a system could be set up in which just one or a few atoms would correspond to a cell in a system like a cellular automaton. And one thing this would mean is that doing computations would then translate almost directly into building actual physical structures out of atoms.

In the past biology—with all its details of DNA, proteins, ribosomes and so on—has provided our only example of programmable construction on an atomic scale. But the discoveries in this book suggest that there are vastly simpler systems that could also be used.

And indeed my guess is that the essential features of all sorts of intricate structures that are seen in living systems can actually be reproduced with remarkably simple rules—making it for example possible to use technology to repair or replace a whole new range of functions of biological tissues and organs.

But given some form of perhaps complex behavior, how can one find rules that will manage to generate it? The traditional engineering approach—if it works at all—will almost inevitably give rules that are in effect at least as complicated as the behavior one is trying to get.

At first biology seems to do better by repeatedly making random modifications to genetic programs, and then applying natural selection. But while this process does quite often yield programs with complex behavior, I argued earlier in this book that it does not usually manage to mold anything but fairly simple aspects of this behavior.

So what then can one do? Occasionally some kind of iterative or directed search may work. But in my experience there are so many different and unexpected things that can happen with simple programs that ultimately the only way to find what one wants is essentially just to do an exhaustive search of all possibilities.

And with computers as they are today one can already often look at trillions of cases—as on page 833. But while this is enough to see a tremendous range of behavior, there is no guarantee that one will in fact run across whatever specific features one is looking for.

Yet in a sense this is a familiar problem. For especially early in their history many branches of technology have ended up searching the natural world for ingredients or systems that serve particular purposes—whether for making light bulb filaments or drugs. And in some sense the only difference here is that in the abstract world of simple programs doing a search becomes much more systematic.

But while traditional engineering has usually ended up finding ways to avoid searches for the limited kinds of systems it considers, the phenomenon of computational irreducibility makes it inevitable that if one considers all possible simple programs then finding particular forms of behavior can require doing searches that involve irreducibly large amounts of computational work.

And in a sense this means that if one tries directly to produce specific pieces of technology one can potentially always get stuck. So in practice a better approach will often be in effect just to do basic science—and much as I have done in this book to try to build up a body of abstract knowledge about how all sorts of simple programs behave.

In chemistry for example one might start by studying the basic science of how all sorts of different substances behave. But having developed a library of results one is then in a position to pick out substances that might be relevant for a specific technological purpose.

And I believe much the same will happen with simple programs. Indeed, in my experience it is remarkable just how often even elementary cellular automata like rule 90 and rule 30 can be applied in one way or another to technological situations.

In general one can think of technology as trying to take systems that exist in nature or elsewhere and harness them to achieve human purposes. But history suggests that it is often difficult even to imagine a purpose without having seen at least something that achieves it.

And indeed a vast quantity of current technology is in the end based on trying to set up our own systems to emulate features that we have noticed exist in ordinary biological or physical systems.

But inevitably we tend to notice only those features that somehow fit into the whole conceptual framework we use. And insofar as that framework is based even implicitly on traditional science it will tend to miss much of what I have discussed in this book.

So in the decades to come, when the science in this book has been absorbed, it is my expectation that it will not only suggest many new ways to achieve existing technological purposes but will also suggest many new purposes that technology can address.

Historical Perspectives

It would be most satisfying if science were to prove that we as humans are in some fundamental way special, and above everything else in the universe. But if one looks at the history of science many of its greatest advances have come precisely from identifying ways in which we are not special—for this is what allows science to make ever more general statements about the universe and the things in it.

Four centuries ago we learned for example that our planet does not lie at a special position in the universe. A century and a half ago we learned that there was nothing very special about the origin of our species. And over the past century we have learned that there is nothing special about our various physical, chemical and other constituents.

Yet in Western thought there is still a strong belief that there must be something fundamentally special about us. And nowadays the most common assumption is that it must have to do with the level of intelligence or complexity that we exhibit. But building on what I have discovered in this book, the Principle of Computational Equivalence now makes the fairly dramatic statement that even in these ways there is nothing fundamentally special about us.

For if one thinks in computational terms the issue is essentially whether we somehow show a specially high level of computational sophistication. Yet the Principle of Computational Equivalence asserts that almost any system whose behavior is not obviously simple will tend to be exactly equivalent in its computational sophistication.

So this means that there is in the end no difference between the level of computational sophistication that is achieved by humans and by all sorts of other systems in nature and elsewhere.

For my discoveries imply that whether the underlying system is a human brain, a turbulent fluid, or a cellular automaton, the behavior it exhibits will correspond to a computation of equivalent sophistication.

And while from the point of view of modern intellectual thinking this may come as quite a shock, it is perhaps not so surprising at the level of everyday experience. For there are certainly many systems in nature whose behavior is complex enough that we often describe it in human terms. And indeed in early human thinking it is very common to encounter the idea of animism: that systems with complex behavior in nature must be driven by the same kind of essential spirit as humans.

But for thousands of years this has been seen as naive and counter to progress in science. Yet now essentially this idea—viewed in computational terms through the discoveries in this book—emerges as crucial. For as I discussed earlier in this chapter, it is the computational equivalence of us as observers to the systems in nature that we observe that makes these systems seem to us so complex and unpredictable.

And while in the past it was often assumed that such complexity must somehow be special to systems in nature, what my discoveries and the Principle of Computational Equivalence now show is that in fact it is vastly more general. For what we have seen in this book is that even when their underlying rules are almost as simple as possible, abstract systems like cellular automata can achieve exactly the same level of computational sophistication as anything else.

It is perhaps a little humbling to discover that we as humans are in effect computationally no more capable than cellular automata with very simple rules. But the Principle of Computational Equivalence also implies that the same is ultimately true of our whole universe.

So while science has often made it seem that we as humans are somehow insignificant compared to the universe, the Principle of Computational Equivalence now shows that in a certain sense we are at the same level as it is. For the principle implies that what goes on inside us can ultimately achieve just the same level of computational sophistication as our whole universe.

But while science has in the past shown that in many ways there is nothing special about us as humans, the very success of science has tended to give us the idea that with our intelligence we are in some way above the universe. Yet now the Principle of Computational Equivalence implies that the computational sophistication of our intelligence should in a sense be shared by many parts of our universe— an idea that perhaps seems more familiar from religion than science.

Particularly with all the successes of science, there has been a great desire to capture the essence of the human condition in abstract scientific terms. And this has become all the more relevant as its replication with technology begins to seem realistic. But what the Principle of Computational Equivalence suggests is that abstract descriptions will never ultimately distinguish us from all sorts of other systems in nature and elsewhere. And what this means is that in a sense there can be no abstract basic science of the human condition—only something that involves all sorts of specific details of humans and their history.

So while we might have imagined that science would eventually show us how to rise above all our human details what we now see is that in fact these details are in effect the only important thing about us.

And indeed at some level it is the Principle of Computational Equivalence that allows these details to be significant. For this is what leads to the phenomenon of computational irreducibility. And this in turn is in effect what allows history to be significant—and what implies that something irreducible can be achieved by the evolution of a system.

Looking at the progress of science over the course of history one might assume that it would only be a matter of time before everything would somehow be predicted by science. But the Principle of Computational Equivalence—and the phenomenon of computational irreducibility—now shows that this will never happen.

There will always be details that can be reduced further—and that will allow science to continue to show progress. But we now know that there are some fundamental boundaries to science and knowledge.

And indeed in the end the Principle of Computational Equivalence encapsulates both the ultimate power and the ultimate weakness of science. For it implies that all the wonders of our universe can in effect be captured by simple rules, yet it shows that there can be no way to know all the consequences of these rules, except in effect just to watch and see how they unfold.

General Notes

■ **Website.** A large amount of additional material related to this book and these notes will progressively be made available through the website www.wolframscience.com. (See also the copyright page at the beginning of the book.)

■ **The role of these notes.** The material in these notes is intended to be complementary to the main text, and is not always self-contained on its own. It is thus important to read these notes in parallel with the sections of the main text to which they refer, since some necessary points may be made only in the main text. Captions to pictures in the main text also often contain details that are not repeated in these notes.

■ **Writing style.** This book was not easy to write, not least because it contains many complex intellectual arguments presented in plain language. And in order to make these arguments as easy to understand as possible, I have had to adopt some rhetorical devices. Perhaps most annoying to those with a copyediting orientation will be my predilection for starting sentences with conjunctions. The main reason I have done this is to break up what would otherwise be extremely long sentences. For the points that I make are often sufficiently complex to require quite long explanations. And to make what I have written more readable than, say, a typical classic work of philosophy, I have broken these explanations into several sentences, necessarily with conjunctions at the beginning of each. Also annoying to some will be my widespread use of short paragraphs. In the main text I normally follow the principle that any paragraph should communicate just one basic idea. And my hope is then that after reading each paragraph readers will pause a moment to absorb each idea before going on to the next one. (This book introduces the third major distinct style of writing that I have used in publications. The first I developed for scientific papers; the second for documents like *The Mathematica Book*.)

■ **Billions.** Following standard American usage, billion in this book means 10^9, trillion 10^{12}, and so on.

■ **Clarity and modesty.** There is a common style of understated scientific writing to which I was once a devoted subscriber. But at some point I discovered that more significant results are usually incomprehensible if presented in this style. For unless one has a realistic understanding of how important something is, it is very difficult to place or absorb it. And so in writing this book I have chosen to explain straightforwardly the importance I believe my various results have. Perhaps I might avoid some criticism by a greater display of modesty, but the cost would be a drastic reduction in clarity.

■ **Explaining ideas.** In presenting major new ideas in a book such as this, there is a trade-off between trying to explain these ideas directly on their own, and using previous ideas to provide a context. For some readers there is a clear short-term benefit in referring to previous ideas, and in discussing to what extent they are right and wrong. But for other readers this approach is likely just to introduce confusion. And over the course of time the ideas that typical readers know will tend to shift. So to make this book as broadly accessible as possible what I mostly do is in the main text to discuss ideas as directly as I can—but then in these notes to outline their historical context. Occasionally in the main text I do mention existing ideas—though I try hard to avoid fads that I expect will not be widely remembered within a few years. Throughout the book my main goal is to explain new ideas, not to criticize ones from the past. Sometimes clarity demands that I say explicitly that something from the past is wrong, but generally I try to avoid this, preferring instead just to state whatever I now believe is true. No doubt this book will draw the ire of some of those with whose ideas its results do not agree, but much as I might like to do so, I cannot realistically avoid this just by the way I present what I have discovered.

■ **Technology references.** In an effort to make the main text of this book as timeless as possible, I have generally avoided

849

referring to everyday systems whose character or name I expect will change as technology advances. Inevitably, however, I do discuss computers, even though I fully expect that some of the terms and concepts I use in connection with them will end up seeming dated in a matter of a few decades.

■ **Whimsy.** Cellular automata and most of the other systems in this book readily admit various kinds of whimsical descriptions. The rule 30 cellular automaton, for example, can be described as follows. Imagine a stadium full of people, with each person having two cards: one black and one white. Make the person in the middle of the top row of seats hold up a black card, and make everyone else in that row hold up a white card. Now each successive person in each successive row determines the color of the card they hold up by looking at the person directly above them, and above them immediately to their left and right, and then applying the simple rule on page 27. A photograph of the stadium will then show the pattern produced by rule 30. Descriptions like this may make abstract systems seem more connected to at least artificial everyday situations, but if the goal is to focus on fundamental ideas, as in this book, then such whimsy is, in my experience, normally just a major distraction.

■ **Timeline of writing.** I worked on the writing of this book with few breaks for a little over ten years, beginning in June 1991, and ending in January 2002. The chapters were written roughly as follows: Chapter 1: 1991, 1999, 2001; Chapter 2: 1991–2; Chapter 3: 1992; Chapter 4: 1992–3; Chapter 5: 1993; Chapter 6: 1992–3; Chapter 7: 1994–6; Chapter 8: 1994–5, 1997; Chapter 9: 1995–8, 2001; Chapter 10: 1998–9; Chapter 11: 1995; Chapter 12: 1999–2001. Some sections of chapters (usually later ones) were added well after the rest. These notes were also sometimes written well after the main text of a given chapter.

■ **Identifying new material.** The vast majority of results in this book have never appeared in published form before. A few were however included—implicitly or explicitly—in publications of mine from the early 1980s (see page 881). Whenever I am aware of antecedents to major material in the main text I have indicated this in the notes. Within the notes themselves, results that are given without historical discussion and without statements such as "it is known that" are generally new to this book. Researchers seeking further information should consult the website for the book.

■ **Citations and references.** In developing the ideas described in this book I have looked at many thousands of books, papers and websites—and have interacted with hundreds of people (see page xiii). But rather than trying to give a huge list of specific references, I have instead included in these notes historical information tracing key contributions. From the names of concepts and people that I mention, it is straightforward to do web or database searches that give a vastly more complete picture of available references than could possibly fit in a book of manageable size—or than could be created correctly without immense scholarship. Note that while most current works of science tend to refer mainly just to very recent material, this book often refers to material that is centuries or even millennia old—in some ways more in the tradition of fields like philosophy.

■ **Historical notes.** I have included extensive historical notes in this book in part out of respect for what has gone before, in part to provide context for ideas (and to see how current beliefs came to be as they are) and in part because the steps one goes through in understanding things may track steps that were gone through historically. Often in the book my conclusions in a particular field differ in a fundamental way from what has been traditional, and it has been important to me in confirming my understanding to study history and see how the conclusions I have reached were missed before. My discussion of science in this book is generally quite precise, being based among other things on computer experiments that can readily be reproduced. But my discussion of history is inevitably less precise. And while I have gone to considerable effort to ensure that its main elements are correct, ultimate objective confirmation is usually impossible. I have always tried to read original writings—for I have often found that later characterizations drop elements crucial for my purposes, or recast history to simplify pedagogy. But even for pieces of history where the people involved are still alive there are often no primary written records, leaving me to rely on secondary sources and recollections extracted in personal interviews—which are inevitably colored by later ideas and understanding. And while with sufficient effort it is usually possible to give fairly simple explanations for fundamental ideas in science, the same may not be true of their history. Looking at the historical notes in this book one striking feature is how often individuals of significant fame are mentioned—but not for the reason they are usually famous. And perhaps the explanation for this is in part that most of those who one can now see made contributions to the kinds of foundational issues I address were capable enough to have been successful at something—but without the whole context of this book they tended to view the types of results I discuss largely as curiosities, and so never tried to do much with them. Note that in mentioning people in connection with ideas and results, I have tried to concentrate on those who seemed to make the most essential contributions for my purposes—even when this does not entirely agree with traditions or criteria in particular academic fields.

■ **Dates.** Rather than following the usual academic practice of giving years when the discoveries were first published in books or journals, I have when possible given years when discoveries were first made. Note that I use a form like 1880s to refer to a decade, and 1800s to refer to a whole century.

■ **Autobiographical elements.** Every discovery in this book has some kind of specific personal story associated with it. Sometimes the story is quite straightforward; sometimes it is convoluted and colorful. But much as I enjoy recounting such stories, I have chosen not to make them part of this book.

■ **Cover image.** The image on the cover of this book is derived from the first 440 or so steps (with perhaps 10 at each end cut off by trimming) of the pattern generated by evolution according to the rule 110 cellular automaton discussed on page 32, with an initial condition consisting of repeats of ⬜⬜⬛⬛⬛ followed by repeats of ⬛⬛⬛⬜⬜. The picture on the right shows 3000 steps in this evolution. The central region grows by 1 cell every 2 steps on the left and 22 cells every 340 steps on the right. Many persistent structures emanate from the right-hand edge of the region. After just 29 steps, this edge takes on a form that repeats every 1700 steps. During each such cycle, a total of 65 persistent structures are produced, of 11 of the 15 kinds from page 292, and their interactions make the full repetition period 6800 steps.

■ **Endpapers.** The goldenrod pages inside the front cover show the center 900 or so cells of the first 500 or so steps in the evolution of the rule 30 cellular automaton of page 29 from a single black cell. The pages inside the back cover show the next 500 or so steps.

■ **Using color.** Aside from practicalities of printing, what made me decide not to use color in this book were issues of visual perception. For much as it is easier to read text in black and white, so also it is easier to assimilate detailed pictures if they are just in black and white. And in fact many types of images in this book show quite misleading features in color. In human visual perception the color of something tends to seem different depending on what is around it—so that for example a red element tends to look purple or pink if the elements around it are respectively blue or white. And particularly if there are few colors arranged in ways that are not visually familiar it is typical for this effect to make all sorts of spurious patterns appear.

■ **Pictures in the book.** All the diagrammatic pictures in this book were created using *Mathematica*. (The photographs were also laid out and image-processed using *Mathematica*.) The ability of *Mathematica* to manipulate graphics in a symbolic

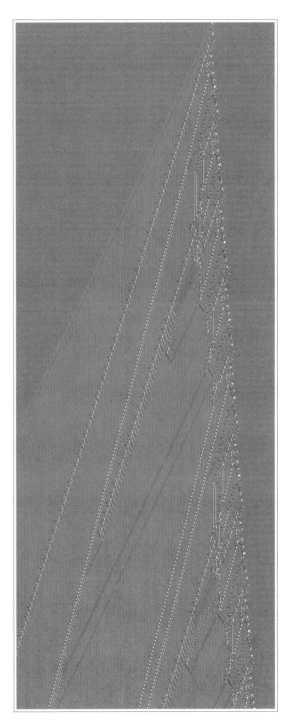

way was crucial—and was what ultimately made it possible for the book to have so many elaborate pictures.

To those familiar with book layout it may seem surprising that I was able to include so many pictures of so many different shapes and sizes without having to resort to a device like figure numbers. And indeed it required solving innumerable small geometrical puzzles to do so. But what ultimately made it possible was that the *Mathematica* programs for generating the pictures were almost always general enough that it was straightforward for me to get, say, a picture with a different number of cells or steps.

■ **Hyphenation.** An unusual feature of the text in this book is that it almost never uses hyphenation; from seeing so much word-wrapped text on computers I at least have come to view hyphenation as an ugly and misleading device.

■ **Book production system.** Beyond its actual content, the production of this book was a highly complex process that relied on the methodology for software releases developed at my company over the past fifteen years. Had I been starting the book now I would likely have authored all of it directly in *Mathematica* and *Publicon*. But a decade ago I made the decision to compose all the original source for the book in FrameMaker. This source was then processed by an elaborate automated procedure much like a standard software build. The first step involved converting a MIF version of the complete source into a *Mathematica* symbolic expression. Then within *Mathematica* various transformations and tests were done on this expression—with for example every program in these notes being formatted and broken into lines using rules similar to *Mathematica StandardForm*. The resulting symbolic expressions were then converted back to MIF, formatted in FrameMaker, and automatically output as PDF. (Note that special characters in programs are rendered using the new Mathematica-Sans font specifically created for the book.) (See also the colophon at the very end of the book.)

■ **Printing.** Many of the pictures in this book have a rather different character from things that are normally printed. For unlike traditional diagrams consisting of separate visible elements—or photographs involving smooth gradations of color—they often for example contain hundreds of cells per inch, each in effect independently black or white. And to capture this properly required careful sheet-fed printing on paper smooth enough to avoid significant spreading of ink. (See also the colophon at the very end of the book.)

■ **Index.** In the index to this book I have tried to cater both to those who have already read the book in detail, and to those who have not. My approach has generally been to include any term that might realistically come to mind when thinking

of a given topic—or remembering what the book says about that topic. And this means that even if the book mentions a term only in passing, I have tended to include it if for one reason or another I think it is likely to be memorable to people with certain experience or interests. Note that looking up *Mathematica* functions used in connection with some issue is often a good way to identify related issues. In the actual building of the index in this book, sorting, processing and checking were done using a variety of automated *Mathematica* procedures, operating on a symbolic representation of the full text and index of the book. Often it is possible by reading an index to identify the important issues in a book. And to some extent that is possible here, though often the presence of more subentries just reflects material being more spread out, not more important.

■ **People in the index.** Conventions for personal names vary considerably with culture and historical period. I have tried in the index to give all names in the form they might be used on standardized documents in the modern U.S. I have done standard transliterations from non-Latin character sets. I give in full those forenames that I believe are or were most commonly used by a particular individual; for other forenames (including for example Russian patronymics) I give only initials. I normally give formal versions of forenames—though for individuals I have personally known I give in the text the form of forenames I would normally use in addressing them. I have dropped all honorifics or titles, except when they significantly alter a name. When there are several versions of a name, I normally use the one that was current closest to the time of work I mention. For each person in the index I list the country or countries where that person predominantly worked. Note that this may not reflect where the person was born, educated, did military service, or died. Rather, it tries to indicate where the person did the majority of their work, particularly as it relates to this book. I generally refer to countries or regions by the names of their closest present-day approximations, as these might appear in postal addresses. When borders have changed, I tend to favor the country whose language is what the person normally speaks or spoke. I usually list countries in the order that a person has worked in them, ignoring repeats. Note that while many of the people listed are well known, extensive research (often through personal contacts, as well as institutional and government records) was required to track down quite a few of them. (Ending dates are obviously not included for people who died after the writing of this book was finished in January 2002.)

■ **Notation.** In the main text, I have almost entirely avoided any kind of formal symbolic notation—usually relying instead on diagrammatic pictures. In these notes, however, it will often be convenient to use such notation to give precise and compact representations of objects and operations. In the past, essentially the only large-scale notation available for theoretical science has been traditional mathematical notation. But on its own this would do me little good—for I need to represent not only traditional mathematics, but also more general rules and programs, as well as procedures and algorithms. But one of the reasons I created the *Mathematica* language was precisely to provide a much more general notation. So in these notes I use this language throughout as my notation. And this has many important advantages—and indeed it is hard to imagine that I would ever have been able to write these notes without it. One point is that it is completely uniform and standardized: there can never be any hidden assumptions or ambiguity about what a particular piece of notation means, since ultimately it is defined by the actual *Mathematica* software system and its documentation (see below). In cases where there is traditional mathematical notation for something, the corresponding *Mathematica* notation is normally almost identical—though occasionally a few details are changed to avoid ambiguity. The concept that everything is a symbolic expression allows *Mathematica* notation, however, to represent essentially any kind of abstract object. And when it comes to procedures and algorithms, the primitives in the *Mathematica* language are chosen to make typical steps easy to represent—with the result that a single line of *Mathematica* can often capture what would otherwise require many paragraphs of English text (and large amounts of pseudocode, or lower-level computer language code). Another very important practical feature of *Mathematica* notation is that by now a large number of people are familiar with it—certainly more than are for example familiar with sophisticated traditional notation in, say, mathematical logic. And the final and very critical advantage of *Mathematica* notation is that one can not only read it, but also actually execute it on a computer, and interact with it. And this makes it both vastly easier to apply and build on, and also easier to analyze and understand.

■ **Mathematica.** I created *Mathematica* to be an integrated language and environment for computing in general, and technical computing in particular. Following its release in 1988, *Mathematica* has become very widely used in science, technology, education and elsewhere. (It is now also increasingly used as a component inside other software systems.)

Mathematica is available from Wolfram Research for all standard computer systems; much more information about it can be found on the web, especially from www.wolfram.com.

There are many books about *Mathematica*—the original one being my *The Mathematica Book*.

The core of *Mathematica* is its language—which is based on the concept of symbolic programming. This language supports most traditional programming paradigms, but considerably generalizes them with the ideas of symbolic programming that I developed for it. In recent years there has started to be increasing use of the language component of *Mathematica* for all sorts of applications outside the area of technical computing where *Mathematica* as a whole has traditionally been most widely used.

The programs in these notes were created for *Mathematica* 4.1 (released 2000). They should run without any change in all subsequent versions of *Mathematica*, and the majority will also run in prior versions, all the way back to *Mathematica* 1 (released 1988) or *Mathematica* 2 (released 1990). Most of the programs require only the language component of *Mathematica*—and not its mathematical knowledge base—and so should run in all software systems powered by *Mathematica*, in which language capabilities are enabled.

Here are examples of how some of the basic *Mathematica* constructs used in the notes in this book work:

- Iteration

  $Nest[f, x, 3] \longrightarrow f[f[f[x]]]$

  $NestList[f, x, 3] \longrightarrow \{x, f[x], f[f[x]], f[f[f[x]]]\}$

  $Fold[f, x, \{1, 2\}] \longrightarrow f[f[x, 1], 2]$

  $FoldList[f, x, \{1, 2\}] \longrightarrow \{x, f[x, 1], f[f[x, 1], 2]\}$

- Functional operations

  $Function[x, x + k][a] \longrightarrow a + k$

  $(\# + k \, \&)[a] \longrightarrow a + k$

  $(r[\#1] + s[\#2] \, \&)[a, b] \longrightarrow r[a] + s[b]$

  $Map[f, \{a, b, c\}] \longrightarrow \{f[a], f[b], f[c]\}$

  $Apply[f, \{a, b, c\}] \longrightarrow f[a, b, c]$

  $Select[\{1, 2, 3, 4, 5\}, EvenQ] \longrightarrow \{2, 4\}$

  $MapIndexed[f, \{a, b, c\}] \longrightarrow \{f[a, \{1\}], f[b, \{2\}], f[c, \{3\}]\}$

- List manipulation

  $\{a, b, c, d\}[[3]] \longrightarrow c$

  $\{a, b, c, d\}[[\{2, 4, 3, 2\}]] \longrightarrow \{b, d, c, b\}$

  $Take[\{a, b, c, d, e\}, 2] \longrightarrow \{a, b\}$

  $Drop[\{a, b, c, d, e\}, -2] \longrightarrow \{a, b, c\}$

  $Rest[\{a, b, c, d\}] \longrightarrow \{b, c, d\}$

  $ReplacePart[\{a, b, c, d\}, x, 3] \longrightarrow \{a, b, x, d\}$

  $Length[\{a, b, c\}] \longrightarrow 3$

  $Range[5] \longrightarrow \{1, 2, 3, 4, 5\}$

  $Table[f[i], \{i, 4\}] \longrightarrow \{f[1], f[2], f[3], f[4]\}$

Table[f[i, j], {i, 2}, {j, 3}]→
  {{f[1, 1], f[1, 2], f[1, 3]}, {f[2, 1], f[2, 2], f[2, 3]}}
Array[f, {2, 2}]→*{{f[1, 1], f[1, 2]}, {f[2, 1], f[2, 2]}}*

Flatten[{{a, b}, {c}, {d, e}}]→*{a, b, c, d, e}*

Flatten[{{a, {b, c}}, {{d}, e}}, 1]→*{a, {b, c}, {d}, e}*

Partition[{a, b, c, d}, 2, 1]→*{{a, b}, {b, c}, {c, d}}*

Split[{a, a, a, b, b, a, a}]→*{{a, a, a}, {b, b}, {a, a}}*

ListConvolve[{a, b}, {1, 2, 3, 4, 5}]→
  {2 a + b, 3 a + 2 b, 4 a + 3 b, 5 a + 4 b}

Position[{a, b, c, a, a}, a]→*{{1}, {4}, {5}}*

RotateLeft[{a, b, c, d, e}, 2]→*{c, d, e, a, b}*

Join[{a, b, c}, {d, b}]→*{a, b, c, d, b}*

Union[{a, a, c, b, b}]→*{a, b, c}*

- Transformation rules

  {a, b, c, d} /. b → p→*{a, p, c, d}*

  {f[a], f[b], f[c]} /. f[a] → p→*{p, f[b], f[c]}*

  {f[a], f[b], f[c]} /. f[x_] → p[x]→*{p[a], p[b], p[c]}*

  {f[1], f[b], f[2]} /. f[x_Integer] → p[x]→*{p[1], f[b], p[2]}*

  {f[1, 2], f[3], f[4, 5]} /. f[x_, y_] → x + y→*{3, f[3], 9}*

  {f[1], g[2], f[2], g[3]} /. f[1] | g[_] → p→*{p, p, f[2], p}*

- Numerical functions

  Quotient[207, 10]→*20*

  Mod[207, 10]→*7*

  Floor[1.45]→*1*

  Ceiling[1.45]→*2*

  IntegerDigits[13, 2]→*{1, 1, 0, 1}*
  IntegerDigits[13, 2, 6]→*{0, 0, 1, 1, 0, 1}*

  DigitCount[13, 2, 1]→*3*

  FromDigits[{1, 1, 0, 1}, 2]→*13*

The *Mathematica* programs in these notes are formatted in *Mathematica StandardForm*. The following table specifies how to enter these programs in *Mathematica InputForm*, using only ordinary keyboard characters:

π	Pi	∞	Infinity	e	E	i	I
$x°$	x Degree	x^y	x ∧ y	$\sqrt{x}$	Sqrt[x]	$x \to y$	x -> y
$x \neq y$	x != y	$x \leq y$	x <= y	$\partial_x y$	D[y, x]	$\neg x$	!x
$x \wedge y$	x && y	$x \vee y$	x || y	$x \veebar y$	Xor[x, y]	$x \barwedge y$	Nand[x, y]

- **About the programs.** Like other aspects of the exposition in this book, I have gone to considerable effort to make the programs in these notes as clear and concise as possible. And I believe the final programs will be useful both to execute, and to read and study—if necessary without a computer. Most of the programs involve only built-in *Mathematica* functions, and so can be run in *Mathematica* without setting up any further definitions. (Many programs nevertheless contain variables that need to be assigned their values before the programs are run—as can be done for example with *Block[{k = 2}, program]*. When subsidiary functions are used, these functions also typically need to be defined before the programs are run—even though in these notes I often show the necessary definitions after the programs. Note that most of the programs do not explicitly do input checking or error generation. Only occasionally do the programs significantly sacrifice efficiency for elegance.) A good first step in understanding any program is to run it on a few inputs. The symbolic character of the *Mathematica* language also allows programs to be taken apart, so that their pieces can be run and analyzed separately. Careful study of the various programs in these notes should provide good background not only for implementing what I discuss in the book, but also for doing high-level programming of any kind. Many of the programs use several of the programming paradigms available in *Mathematica*—making it essentially impossible to capture their essence in any lower-level language. Note that a given program can essentially always be written in *Mathematica* in many different ways—though often other ways end up being vastly longer than the ones presented here. Material about the programs should be available at the book website—including for example some of the automated tests run to check the programs, as well as annotations about how the programs work.

- **Computer experiments.** Essentially all the computer experiments for this book were done using *Mathematica* running on a standard workstation-class computer, and later PC (initially on a 33 MHz NeXTstation, then on a 100 MHz HP 700 running NeXTSTEP, then on a 200 MHz P6 PC running Windows 95, and finally on 450 MHz, 700 MHz and faster PCs running Windows 95, and later Windows NT—with a Linux fileserver). For some larger searches earlier in the project, I wrote special-purpose C programs connected to *Mathematica* via *MathLink*. (Increasing computer speed and greater efficiency in successive versions of *Mathematica* have gradually almost eliminated my use of C.) In some cases I have run programs for many days or weeks, sometimes distributed via *MathLink* across a few hundred computers in my company's network. So far in my life the primary computer hardware systems I have used have been: Elliott 903 (1973–6); IBM 370 (1976–8); CDC 7600 (1978–9); VAX 11/780 (1980–2); Sun-1, 2, Ridge 32 (1982–4); CM-1 (1985); Sun-3 (1985–8); SPARC (1988–91); NeXT (1991–4); HP 700 (1995–6); PC (1996–). The primary languages have been: assembler (1973–6); FORTRAN (1976–9); C (1979–~1994); SMP (1980–6); *Mathematica* (1987–). (See also page 899.)

■ **Educational issues.** The new kind of science in this book represents a unique educational opportunity. For it touches an immense range of important and compelling everyday phenomena and issues in science, yet to understand its key ideas requires no prior scientific or technical education. So this means that it is potentially realistic to use as the basis for an overall introduction to the ideas of science. And indeed having understood its basic elements, it becomes vastly easier to understand many aspects of traditional science, and to see how they fit into the whole framework of knowledge.

No doubt there will at first be a tendency to follow the progression of scientific history and to present the ideas of this book only at an advanced stage in the educational process, after teaching many aspects of traditional science. But it is fairly clear that it is vastly easier to explain much of what is in this book than to explain many ideas in traditional science. For among other things the new kind of science in this book does not rely on elaborate abstract concepts from traditional mathematics; instead it is based mostly just on pictures, and on ideas that have become increasingly familiar from practical use of computers. And in fact, in my experience, with good presentation, surprisingly young children are able to grasp many key ideas in this book—even if their knowledge of mathematics does not go beyond the simplest operations on numbers.

Over the past fifty or so years traditional mathematics has become a core part of education. And while its more elementary aspects are certainly crucial for everyday modern life, beyond basic algebra its central place in education must presumably be justified more on the basis of promoting overall patterns of thinking than in supplying specific factual knowledge of everyday relevance. But in fact I believe that the basic aspects of the new kind of science in this book in many ways provide more suitable material for general education than traditional mathematics. They involve some of the same kinds of precise thinking, but do not rely on abstract concepts that are potentially very difficult to communicate. And insofar as they involve the development of technical expertise, it is in the direction of computing—which is vastly more relevant to modern life than advanced mathematics.

The new kind of science in this book connects in all sorts of ways with mathematics and the existing sciences—and it can be used at an educational level to place some of the fundamental ideas in these areas in a clearer context. In computer science it can also be used as a rich source of basic examples—much as physics is used as a source of basic examples in traditional mathematics education.

A remarkable feature of the new kind of science in this book is that it makes genuine research accessible to people with almost no specific technical knowledge. For it is almost certain that experiments on, say, some specific cellular automaton whose rule has been picked at random from a large set will never have been done before. To conclude anything interesting from such experiments nevertheless requires certain scientific methodology and judgement—but from an educational point of view this represents a uniquely accessible environment in which to develop such skills.

In many fields, advanced education seems useful only if one intends to pursue those specific fields. But a few fields such as physics are notable for being sources of individuals with broadly applicable skills. I believe that the new kind of science in this book will in time serve a similar role.

■ **Reading this book.** This is a long book densely packed with ideas and results, and to read all of it carefully is a major undertaking. The first section of Chapter 1 provides a basic—though compressed—overview of some of key ideas. Chapter 2 describes some of the basic results that led me to develop the new kind of science in the book. Every subsequent chapter in one way or another builds on earlier ones. Some people will probably find the sweeping conclusions of the final chapter of the book the most interesting; others will probably be more interested in specific results and applications in earlier chapters.

These notes are never necessary for the basic flow of any of the arguments I make in the book—though they often provide context and important supporting information, as well as considerable amounts of new primary material. Specialists in particular fields should be sure to read the notes that relate to their fields before they draw any final conclusions about what I have to say.

I have written this book with considerable care, and I believe that to those seriously interested in its contents, it will repay careful and repeated reading. Note that in the main text I have tried to emphasize important points by various kinds of stylistic devices. But in packing as much as possible into these notes I have often been unable to do this. And in general these notes have a high enough information density that it will be rare that everything they say can readily be assimilated in just one reading, even if it is quite careful.

■ **Learning the new kind of science.** There will, I hope, be many who want to learn about what is in this book, whether out of general intellectual interest, to apply it in some way or another, or to participate in its further development. But regardless of the purpose, the best first step will certainly be to read as much of this book as possible with care. In time there will doubtless also be all sorts of additional material and educational options available. But ultimately the key to a real understanding is to experience ideas for oneself. And for the new kind of science in this book this is in a sense unprecedentedly easy, for all it requires is a standard computer on which to do computer experiments.

At first the best thing is probably just to repeat some of the experiments I describe in this book—using the software and resources described at the website, or perhaps just by typing in some of the programs in these notes. And even if one can already see the result of an experiment in a picture in this book, it has been my consistent observation that one internalizes results of experiments much better if one gets them by running a program oneself than if one just sees them printed in a book. To get a deeper understanding, however, one invariably needs to try formulating experiments for oneself. One might wonder, for example, what would happen if some particular system were run for more steps than I show in this book. Would the system go on doing what one sees in the book, or might it start doing something quite different? With the appropriate setup, one can immediately run a program to find out. Often one will have some kind of guess about what the answer should be. At first—if my own experience is a guide—this guess will quite often be wrong. But gradually, after seeing what happens in enough cases, one will begin to develop a correct and robust new intuition. Realistically this seems to take several months even for the most talented and open-minded people. But as the new intuition matures, ideas in this book like the Principle of Computational Equivalence, that may at first seem hard to believe, will slowly come to seem almost obvious.

For someone to assimilate all of the new kind of science I describe in this book will take a very significant time. Indeed, in a traditional educational setting I expect that it will require an investment of years comparable to learning an area like physics. How long it will take a given individual to get to the point of being able to do something specific with the new kind of science in this book will depend greatly on their background and particular goals. But in almost any case a crucial practical step—if it has not already been taken—will be to learn well *Mathematica* and the language it embodies. For although most simple programs can be implemented in almost any computational environment, not using the capabilities of *Mathematica* will be an immediate handicap—which, for example, would certainly have prevented me from discovering the vast majority of what is now in this book.

■ **Developing the new kind of science.** Up to this point in its history the science in this book has essentially been just my personal project. But now that the book is out, all sorts of other people can begin to participate—adding their own personal achievements to the development of the intellectual structure that I have built in this book.

The first obvious but crucial thing to do is to explain and interpret what is already in the book. For although this is a long book that I have tried to write as clearly as possible, there is immensely more that can and should be said—in many different ways—about almost all the ideas and results it contains. Sometimes a more technical presentation may be useful; sometimes a less technical one. Sometimes it will be helpful to make more connections to some existing area of thought or scholarship. And sometimes particular ideas and results in this book will just benefit from the emphasis of having a whole paper or book or website devoted to them.

One of my goals in this book has been to answer the most obvious questions about each of the subjects I address. And at this I believe I have been moderately successful. But the science I have developed in this book opens up an area so vast that the twenty years I have spent investigating it have allowed me to explore only tiny parts. And indeed from almost every page of this book there are all sorts of new questions that emerge. In fact, even about systems that I have studied as extensively as cellular automata I am always amazed at just how easy it is to identify worthwhile questions that have not yet been addressed. And in general the ideas and methods of this book seem to yield an unending stream of important questions of a remarkable range of different kinds.

On the website associated with this book I plan to maintain a list of questions that I believe are of particular interest. The questions will be of many kinds and at many levels. Some it will be possible to address just by fairly straightforward but organized computer experimentation, while others will benefit from varying levels of technical skill and knowledge from existing areas of science, mathematics or elsewhere.

Like any serious intellectual pursuit, doing well the new kind of science in this book is not easy. In writing the book I have put great effort into explaining things in straightforward ways. But the fact that in some particular case I may have succeeded does not mean that the underlying science was easy. And in fact my uniform experience has been that to make progress in the kind of science I describe in this book requires at a raw intellectual level at least as much as any traditional area of science. The kind of extensive detailed technical knowledge that characterizes most traditional areas of science is usually not needed—though it can be helpful. But if anything, greater clarity and organization of thought is needed than in areas where there is existing technical formalism to fall back on. At a practical level the most important basic skill is probably *Mathematica* programming. For it is crucial to be able to try out new ideas and experiments quickly—and in my experience it is also important to have the discipline of formulating things in the precise language of *Mathematica*.

One feature of this book is that it covers a broad area and comes to very broad conclusions. But to get to the point of being able to do this has taken me twenty years of gradually building up from specific detailed results and ideas. And I have no doubt that in the future essentially all significant contributions will also be made by building on foundations of specific detailed facts. And indeed, what I expect to be the mainstay of the science that develops from this book is the gradual accumulation of more and more knowledge of a variety of detailed concrete kinds.

I have tried in this book to lead by example in defining the way I believe things should be done. Probably the single most important principle that I have followed is just to try to keep everything as simple as possible. Study the simplest systems. Ask the most obvious questions. Search for the most straightforward explanations. For among other things, this is ultimately how the most useful and powerful results are obtained. Not that it is easy to do this. For while in the end it may be possible to get to something simple and elegant, it often takes huge intellectual effort to see just how this can be done. And without great tenacity there is a tremendous tendency to stop before one has gone far enough.

In most existing fields of science there are so many technicalities to learn and keep current on that it is rare for anyone but a professional scientist to be able to make any significant contribution. But in the new kind of science that I describe in this book I believe that at least at first there will be opportunities for a much broader range of people to make contributions. In existing fields of science their largely closed communities tend to maintain standards of quality mostly through direct institutional and personal contact. Yet particularly when there are technical aspects to a field it is also comparatively easy for practitioners to assess a piece of work just from the overall way it handles and presents its technicalities. And in fact there are obvious analogs of this in the new kind of science that I describe in this book. First, there is the issue of whether tools like computers are used in effective ways. But in many ways more central is whether there is a certain basic level of clarity and simplicity to a piece of work. Often it is difficult to achieve this. But the point is that the skills necessary to do so correspond rather directly to the ones necessary to carry out the actual science itself well.

■ **Applications.** At the core of this book is a body of ideas and results that define a new kind of basic science. And I have no doubt that in time this will yield a remarkably broad range of applications. And sometimes—particularly in technology— these applications may be quite straightforward and direct. But if the objective is to develop a model for some specific system in nature or elsewhere it is almost inevitable that this will not be easy. For while I believe that the basic science that I develop in this book provides a remarkably powerful new framework, coming up with an actual model requires all sorts of detailed work and analysis. Certainly it would be wonderful if one could just take the ideas and results in this book and somehow immediately use them to create models for all sorts of systems. And indeed—particularly from the examples I give in Chapter 8—there will probably be at least a few cases where this can be done. But most of the time nothing like it will be possible. And instead—just as in any other framework—there will be no choice but first to learn all sorts of details of a system, and then to use judgement and creativity to see which of them are really essential to a model and which are not. (See also page 364.)

The Foundations for a New Kind of Science

An Outline of Basic Ideas

■ **Mathematics in science.** The main event usually viewed as marking the beginning of the modern mathematical approach to science was the publication of Isaac Newton's 1687 book *Mathematical Principles of Natural Philosophy* (the *Principia*). The idea that mathematics might be relevant to science nevertheless had long precursors in both practical and philosophical traditions. Before 500 BC the Babylonians were using arithmetic to describe and predict astronomical data. And by 500 BC the Pythagoreans had come to believe that all natural phenomena should somehow be reducible to relationships between numbers. Many Greek philosophers then discussed the general concept that nature should be amenable to abstract reasoning of the kind used in mathematics. And at a more practical level, the results and methodology of Euclid's work on geometry from around 300 BC became the basis for studies in astronomy, optics and mechanics, notably by Archimedes and Ptolemy. In medieval times there were some doubts about the utility of mathematics in science, and in the late 1200s, for example, Albertus Magnus made the statement that "many of the geometer's figures are not found in natural bodies, and many natural figures, particularly those of animals and plants, are not determinable by the art of geometry". Roger Bacon nevertheless wrote in 1267 that "mathematics is the door and key to the sciences", and by the 1500s it was often believed that for science to be meaningful it must somehow follow the systematic character of mathematics. (Typical of the time was the statement of Leonardo da Vinci that "no human inquiry can be called science unless it pursues its path through mathematical exposition and demonstration".) Around the end of the 1500s Galileo began to develop more explicit connections between concepts in mathematics and in physics, and concluded that the universe could be understood only in the "language of mathematics", whose "characters are triangles, circles and other geometric figures".

What Isaac Newton then did was in effect to suggest that natural systems are at some fundamental level actually governed by purely abstract laws that can be specified in terms of mathematical equations. This idea has met with its greatest success in physics, where for the past three centuries essentially every major theory has been formulated in terms of mathematical equations. Starting in the mid-1800s, it has also had increasing success in chemistry. And in the past century, it has had a few scattered successes in dealing with simpler phenomena in fields like biology and economics. But despite the vast range of phenomena in nature that have never successfully been described in mathematical terms, it has become quite universally assumed that, as David Hilbert put it in 1900, "mathematics is the foundation of all exact knowledge of natural phenomena". There continue to be theories in science that are not explicitly mathematical—examples being continental drift and evolution by natural selection—but, as for example Alfred Whitehead stated in 1911, it is generally believed that "all science as it grows toward perfection becomes mathematical in its ideas".

■ **Definition of mathematics.** When I use the term "mathematics" in this book what I mean is that field of human endeavor that has in practice traditionally been called mathematics. One could in principle imagine defining mathematics to encompass all studies of abstract systems, and indeed this was in essence the definition that I had in mind when I chose the name *Mathematica*. But in practice mathematics has defined itself to be vastly narrower, and to include, for example, nothing like the majority of the programs that I discuss in this book. Indeed, in many respects, what is called mathematics today can be seen as a direct extension of the particular notions of arithmetic and geometry that apparently arose in Babylonian times. Typical dictionary definitions reflect this by describing mathematics as the study of number and space, together with their abstractions and generalizations. And even logic—an abstract system that dates from antiquity—is not normally considered part of mainstream mathematics. Particularly over the past century the defining characteristic of research in mathematics has increasingly been the use of theorem and proof methodology. And while some generalization has occurred in the types of systems being studied, it has usually been much limited by the desire to maintain the validity of some set of theorems (see page 793). This emphasis on theorems has also led to a focus on equations that statically state facts rather than on rules that define actions, as in most of the systems in this book. But despite all these issues, many mathematicians implicitly tend to assume that somehow mathematics as it is practiced is universal, and that any possible abstract system will be covered by some area of mathematics or another. The results of this book, however, make it quite clear that this is not the case, and that in fact traditional mathematics has reached only a tiny fraction of all the kinds of abstract systems that can in principle be studied.

■ **Reasons for mathematics in science.** It is not surprising that there should be issues in science to which mathematics is relevant, since until about a century ago the whole purpose of mathematics was at some level thought of as being to provide abstract idealizations of aspects of physical reality (with the consequence that concepts like dimensions above 3 and transfinite numbers were not readily accepted as meaningful even in mathematics). But there is absolutely no reason to think that the specific concepts that have arisen so far in the history of mathematics should cover all of science, and indeed in this book I give extensive evidence that they do not. At times the role of mathematics in science has been used in philosophy as an indicator of the ultimate power of human thinking. In the mid-1900s, especially among physicists, there was occasionally some surprise expressed about the effectiveness of mathematics in the natural sciences. One explanation advanced by Albert Einstein was that the only physical laws we can recognize are ones that are easy to express in our system of mathematics.

■ **History of programs and nature.** Given the idea of using programs as a basis for describing nature, one can go back in history and find at least a few rough precursors of this idea. Around 100 AD, for example, following earlier Greek thinking, Lucretius made the somewhat vague suggestion that the universe might consist of atoms assembled according to grammatical rules like letters and words in human language. From the Pythagoreans around 500 BC through Ptolemy around 150 AD to the early work of Johannes Kepler around 1595 there was the notion that the planets might follow definite geometrical rules like the elements of a mechanical clock. But following the work of Isaac Newton in the late 1600s it increasingly came to be believed that systems

could only meaningfully be described by the mathematical equations they satisfy, and not by any explicit mechanism or rules. The failure of the concept of ether and the rise of quantum mechanics in the early 1900s strengthened this view to the point where at least in physics mechanistic explanations of any kind became largely disreputable. (Starting in the 1800s systems based on very simple rules were nevertheless used in studies of genetics and heredity.) With the advent of electronics and computers in the 1940s and 1950s, models like neural networks and cellular automata began to be introduced, primarily in biology (see pages 876 and 1099). But in essentially all cases they were viewed just as approximations to models based on traditional mathematical equations. In the 1960s and 1970s there arose in the early computer hacker community the general idea that the universe might somehow operate like a program. But attempts to engineer explicit features of our universe using constructs from practical programming were unsuccessful, and the idea largely fell into disrepute (see page 1026). Nevertheless, starting in the 1970s many programs were written to simulate all sorts of scientific and technological systems, and often these programs in effect defined the models used. But in almost all cases the elements of the models were firmly based on traditional mathematical equations, and the programs themselves were highly complex, and not much like the simple programs I discuss in this book. (See also pages 363 and 992.)

■ **Extensions of mathematics.** See page 793.

■ **The role of logic.** In addition to standard mathematics, the formal system most widely discussed since antiquity is logic (see page 1099). And starting with Aristotle there was in fact a long tradition of trying to use logic as a framework for drawing conclusions about nature. In the early 1600s the experimental method was suggested as a better alternative. And after mathematics began to show extensive success in describing nature in the late 1600s no further large-scale efforts to do this on the basis of logic appear to have been made. It is conceivable that Gottfried Leibniz might have tried in the late 1600s, but when his work was followed up in the late 1800s by Gottlob Frege and others the emphasis was on building up mathematics, not natural science, from logic (see page 1149). And indeed by this point logic was viewed mostly as a possible representation of human thought—and not as a formal system relevant to nature. So when computers arose it was their numerical and mathematical rather than logical capabilities that were normally assumed relevant for natural science. But in the early 1980s the cellular automata that I studied I often characterized as being based on logical rules, rather than traditional mathematical ones. However, as we will see on page 806, traditional logic is in fact in many ways very narrow compared to the whole range of rules based on simple programs that I actually consider in this book.

■ **Complexity and theology.** Both complexity and order in the natural world have been cited as evidence for an intelligent creator (compare page 1195). Early mythologies most often assume that the universe started in chaos, with a supernatural being adding order, then creating a series of specific complex natural systems. In Greek philosophy it was commonly thought that the regularities seen in astronomy and elsewhere (such as the obvious circular shapes of the Sun and Moon) were reflections of perfect mathematical forms associated with divine beings. About complexity Aristotle did note that what nature makes is "finer than art", though this was not central to his arguments about causes of natural phenomena. By the beginning of the Christian era, however, there is evidence of a general belief that the complexity of nature must be the work of a supernatural being—and for example there are statements in the Bible that can be read in this way. Around 1270 Thomas Aquinas gave as an argument for the existence of God the fact that things in nature seem to "act for an end" (as revealed for example by always acting in the same way), and thus must have been specifically designed with that end in mind. In astronomy, as specific natural laws began to be discovered, the role of God began to recede somewhat, with Isaac Newton claiming, for example, that God must have first set the planets on their courses, but then mathematical laws took over to govern their subsequent behavior. Particularly in biology, however, the so-called "argument by design" became ever more popular. Typical was John Ray's 1691 book *The Wisdom of God Manifested in the Works of the Creation,* which gave a long series of examples from biology that it claimed were so complex that they must be the work of a supernatural being. By the early 1800s, such ideas had led to the field of natural theology, and William Paley gave the much quoted argument that if it took a sophisticated human watchmaker to construct a watch, then the only plausible explanation for the vastly greater complexity of biological systems was that they must have been created by a supernatural being. Following the publication of Charles Darwin's *Origin of Species* in 1859 many scientists began to argue that natural selection could explain all the basic phenomena of biology, and although some religious groups maintained strong resistance, it was widely assumed by the mid-1900s that no other explanation was needed. In fact, however, just how complexity arises was never really resolved, and in the end I believe that it is only with the ideas of this book that this can successfully be done.

■ **Artifacts and natural systems.** See page 828.

■ **Complexity and science.** Ever since antiquity science has tended to see its main purpose as being the study of regularities—and this has meant that insofar as complexity is viewed as an absence of regularities, it has tended to be ignored or avoided. There have however been occasional discussions of various general aspects of complexity and what can account for them. Thus, for example, by 200 BC the Epicureans were discussing the idea that varied and complex forms in nature could be made up from arrangements of small numbers of types of elementary atoms in much the same way as varied and complex written texts are made up from small numbers of types of letters. And although its consequences were remarkably confused, the notion of a single underlying substance that could be transmuted into anything—living or not—was also a centerpiece of alchemy. Starting in the 1600s successes in physics and discoveries like the circulation of blood led to the idea that it should be possible to explain the operation of almost any natural system in essentially mechanical terms—leading for example René Descartes to claim in 1637 that we should one day be able to explain the operation of a tree just like we do a clock. But as mathematical methods developed, they seemed to apply mainly to physical systems, and not for example to biological ones. And indeed Immanuel Kant wrote in 1790 that "it is absurd to hope that another Newton will arise in the future who will make comprehensible to us the production of a blade of grass according to natural laws". In the late 1700s and early 1800s mathematical methods began to be used in economics and later in studying populations. And partly influenced by results from this, Charles Darwin in 1859 suggested natural selection as the basis for many phenomena in biology, including complexity. By the late 1800s advances in chemistry had established that biological systems were made of the same basic components as physical ones. But biology still continued to concentrate on very specific observations—with no serious theoretical discussion of anything as general as the phenomenon of complexity. In the 1800s statistics was increasingly viewed as providing a scientific approach to complex processes in practical social systems. And in the late 1800s statistical mechanics was then used as a basis for analyzing complex microscopic processes in physics. Most of the advances in physics in the late 1800s and early 1900s in effect avoided complexity by concentrating on properties and systems simple enough to be described by explicit mathematical formulas. And when other fields tried in the early and mid-1900s to imitate successes in physics, they too generally tended to concentrate on issues that seemed amenable to explicit mathematical formulas. Within mathematics itself—especially in number theory and the three-body problem—there were calculations that yielded results that seemed complex. But normally this complexity was viewed just as something to be overcome—either by looking at things in a different way, or by proving more powerful theorems—and not as something to be studied or even much commented on in its own right.

In the 1940s, however, successes in the analysis of logistical and electronic systems led to discussion of the idea that it might be possible to set up some sort of general approach to complex systems—especially biological and social ones. And by the late 1940s the cybernetics movement was becoming increasingly popular—with Norbert Wiener emphasizing feedback control and stochastic differential equations, and John von Neumann and others emphasizing systems based on networks of elements often modelled after neurons. There were spinoffs such as control theory and game theory, but little progress was made on core issues of complexity, and already by the mid-1950s what began to dominate were vague discussions involving fashionable issues in areas such as psychiatry and anthropology. There also emerged a tradition of robotics and artificial intelligence, and a few of the systems that were built or simulated did show some complexity of behavior (see page 879). But in most cases this was viewed just as something to be overcome in order to achieve the engineering objectives sought. Particularly in the 1960s there was discussion of complexity in large human organizations—especially in connection with the development of management science and the features of various forms of hierarchy—and there emerged what was called systems theory, which in practice typically involved simulating networks of differential equations, often representing relationships in flowcharts. Attempts were for example made at worldwide models, but by the 1970s their results—especially in economics—were being discredited. (Similar methods are nevertheless used today, especially in environmental modelling.)

With its strong emphasis on simple laws and measurements of numbers, physics has normally tended to define itself to avoid complexity. But from at least the 1940s, issues of complexity were nevertheless occasionally mentioned by physicists as important, most often in connection with fluid turbulence or features of nonlinear differential equations. Questions about pattern formation, particularly in biology and in relation to thermodynamics, led to a sequence of studies of reaction-diffusion equations, which by the 1970s were being presented as relevant to general issues of complexity, under names like self-organization, synergetics and dissipative structures. By the late 1970s the work of

Benoit Mandelbrot on fractals provided an important example of a general approach to addressing a certain kind of complexity. And chaos theory—with its basis in the mathematics of dynamical systems theory—also began to become popular in the late 1970s, being discussed particularly in connection with fluid turbulence. In essentially all cases, however, the emphasis remained on trying to find some aspect of complex behavior that could be summarized by a single number or a traditional mathematical equation.

As discussed on pages 44–50, there were by the beginning of the 1980s various kinds of abstract systems whose rules were simple but which had nevertheless shown complex behavior, particularly in computer simulations. But usually this was considered largely a curiosity, and there was no particular sense that there might be a general phenomenon of complexity that could be of central interest, say in natural science. And indeed there remained an almost universal belief that to capture any complexity of real scientific relevance one must have a complex underlying model. My work on cellular automata in the early 1980s provided strong evidence, however, that complex behavior very much like what was seen in nature could in fact arise in a very general way from remarkably simple underlying rules. And starting around the mid-1980s it began to be not uncommon to hear the statement that complex behavior can arise from simple rules—though often there was great confusion about just what this was actually saying, and what, for example, should be considered complex behavior, or a simple rule.

That complexity could be identified as a coherent phenomenon that could be studied scientifically in its own right was something I began to emphasize around 1984. And having created the beginnings of what I considered to be the necessary intellectual structure, I started to try to develop an organizational structure to allow what I called complex systems research to spread. Some of what I did had fairly immediate effects, but much did not, and by late 1986 I had started building *Mathematica* and decided to pursue my own scientific interests in a more independent way (see page 20). By the late 1980s, however, there was widespread discussion of what was by then being called complexity theory. (I had avoided this name to prevent confusion with the largely unrelated field of computational complexity theory). And indeed many of the points I had made about the promise of the field were being enthusiastically repeated in popular accounts—and there were starting to be quite a number of new institutions devoted to the field. (A notable example was the Santa Fe Institute, whose orientation towards complexity seems to have been a quite direct consequence of my efforts.)

But despite all this, no major new scientific developments were forthcoming—not least because there was a tremendous tendency to ignore the idea of simple underlying rules and of what I had discovered in cellular automata, and instead to set up computer simulations with rules far too complicated to allow them to be used in studying fundamental questions. And combined with a predilection for considering issues in the social and biological sciences that seem hard to pin down, this led to considerable skepticism among many scientists—with the result that by the mid-1990s the field was to some extent in retreat—though the statement that complexity is somehow an important and fundamental issue has continued to be emphasized especially in studies of ecological and business systems.

Watching the history of the field of complexity theory has made it particularly clear to me that without a major new intellectual structure complexity cannot realistically be studied in a meaningful scientific way. But it is now just such a structure that I believe I have finally been able to set up in this book.

Relations to Other Areas

■ **Page 7 · Mathematics.** I discuss the implications of this book for the foundations of mathematics mainly on pages 772–821 and in the rather extensive corresponding notes. With a sufficiently general definition of mathematics, however, the whole core of the book can in fact be viewed as a work of experimental mathematics. And even with a more traditional definition, this is at least true of much of my discussion of systems based on numbers in Chapter 4. The notes to almost all chapters of the book contain a great many new mathematical results, mostly emerging from my analysis of some of the simpler behavior considered in the book. Pages 606–620 and 737–750 discuss in general the capabilities of mathematical analysis, while pages 588–597 address the foundations of statistics. Note that some ideas and results highly relevant to current frontiers in mathematics appear in some rather unexpected places in the book. Specific examples include the parameter space sets that I discuss in connection with shapes of plant leaves on page 407, and the minimal axioms for logic that I discuss on page 810. A more general example is the issue of smooth objects arising from combinatorial data that I discuss in Chapter 9 in connection with the nature of space in fundamental physics.

■ **Page 8 · Physics.** I discuss general mechanisms and models relevant for physical systems in Chapter 7, specific types of everyday physical systems in Chapter 8, and applications to basic foundational problems in physics in Chapter 9. I

mention some further fundamental issues in physics around page 730 and in chemistry on page 1193.

■ **Page 8 · Biology.** The main place I discuss applications to biology is on pages 383–429 of Chapter 8, where I consider first general questions about biology and evolution, and then more specific issues about growth and pattern in biological organisms. I consider visual and auditory perception on pages 577–588, and the operation of brains on pages 620–631. I also discuss the definition of life on pages 823 and 1178, as well as mentioning protein folding and structure on pages 1003 and 1184.

■ **Page 9 · Social and related sciences.** I discuss the particular example of financial systems on pages 429–432, and make some general comments on page 1014. The end of Chapter 10, as well as some parts of Chapter 12, also discuss various issues that can be viewed as foundational questions.

■ **Page 10 · Computer science.** Chapter 11 as well as parts of Chapter 12 (especially pages 753–771) address foundational issues in computer science. Chapter 3 uses standard computer science models such as Turing machines and register machines as examples of simple programs. In many places in the book—especially these notes—I discuss all sorts of specific problems and issues of direct relevance to current computer science. Examples include cryptography (pages 598–606), Boolean functions (pages 616–619 and 806–814), user interfaces (page 1102) and quantum computing (page 1147).

■ **Page 10 · Philosophy.** Chapter 12 is the main place I address traditional philosophical issues. On pages 363–369 of Chapter 8, however, I discuss some general issues of modelling, and in Chapter 10 I consider at length not only practical but also foundational questions about perception and to some extent general thinking and consciousness. (See page 1196.)

■ **Page 11 · Technology.** The notes to this book mention many specific technological connections, and I expect that many of the models and methods of analysis that I use in the book can be applied quite directly for technological purposes. I discuss foundational questions about technology mainly on pages 840–843.

■ **Scope of existing sciences.** One might imagine that physics would for example concern itself with all aspects of physical systems, biology with all aspects of biological systems, and so on. But in fact as they are actually practiced most of the traditional sciences are much narrower in scope. Historically what has typically happened is that in each science a certain way of thinking has emerged as the most successful. And then over the course of time, the scope of the science itself has come to be defined to encompass just those issues that this way of thinking is able to address. So when a new phenomenon is observed, a particular science will typically tend to focus on just those aspects of the phenomenon that can be studied by whatever way of thinking has been adopted in that science. And when the phenomenon involves substantial complexity, what has in the past usually happened is that simpler and simpler aspects are investigated until one is found that is simple enough to analyze using the chosen way of thinking.

The Personal Story of the Science in This Book

▪ **Page 17 · Statistical physics cover.** The pictures show disks representing idealized molecules bouncing around in a box, and the book claims that as time goes on there is almost inevitably increasing randomization. The pictures were made in about 1964 by Berni Alder and Frederick Reif from oscilloscope output from the LARC computer at what was then Lawrence Radiation Laboratory. A total of 40 disks were started with positions and velocities determined by a middle-square random number generator (see page 975), and their motion was followed for about 10 collision times—after which roundoff errors in the 64-bit numbers used had grown too big. From the point of view of this book the randomization seen in these pictures is in large part just a reflection of the fact that a random sequence of digits were used in the initial conditions. But what the discoveries in this book show is that such randomness can also be generated

without any such random input—finally clarifying some very basic issues in statistical physics. (See page 441.)

▪ **Page 17 · My 1973 computer experiments.** I used a British Elliott 903 computer with 8 kilowords of 18-bit ferrite core memory. The assembly language program that I wrote filled up a fair fraction of the memory. The system that I looked at was a 2D cellular automaton with discrete particles colliding on a square grid. Had I not been concerned with physics-like conservation laws, or had I used something other than a square grid, the teleprinter output that I generated would have shown randomization. (See page 999.)

▪ **Page 19 · Computer printouts.** The printouts show a series of elementary cellular automata started from random initial conditions (see page 232). I generated them in 1981 using a C program running on a VAX 11/780 computer with an early version of the Unix operating system. (See also page 880.)

▪ **Timeline.** Major periods in my work have been:

▪ 1974–1980: particle physics and cosmology

▪ 1979–1981: developing SMP computer algebra system

▪ 1981–1986: cellular automata etc.

▪ 1986–1991: intensive *Mathematica* development

▪ 1991–2001: writing this book

(Wolfram Research, Inc. was founded in 1987; *Mathematica* 1.0 was released June 23, 1988; the company and successive versions of *Mathematica* continue to be major parts of my life.)

▪ **Detailed history.** See pages 880–882.

The Crucial Experiment

How Do Simple Programs Behave?

■ **Implementing cellular automata.** It is convenient to represent the state of a cellular automaton at each step by a list such as {0, 0, 1, 0, 0}, where 0 corresponds to a white cell and 1 to a black cell. An initial condition consisting of n white cells with one black cell in the middle can then be obtained with the function (see below for comments on this and other *Mathematica* functions)

```
CenterList[n_Integer] :=
    ReplacePart[Table[0, {n}], 1, Ceiling[n/2]]
```

For cellular automata of the kind discussed in this chapter, the rule can also be represented by a list. Thus, for example, rule 30 on page 27 corresponds to the list {0, 0, 0, 1, 1, 1, 1, 0}. (The numbering of rules is discussed on page 53.) In general, the list for a particular rule can be obtained with the function

```
ElementaryRule[num_Integer] := IntegerDigits[num, 2, 8]
```

Given a rule together with a list representing the state a of a cellular automaton at a particular step, the following simple function gives the state at the next step:

```
CAStep[rule_List, a_List] :=
    rule[[8 - (RotateLeft[a] + 2 (a + 2 RotateRight[a]))]]
```

A list of states corresponding to evolution for t steps can then be obtained with

```
CAEvolveList[rule_, init_List, t_Integer] :=
    NestList[CAStep[rule, #] &, init, t]
```

Graphics of this evolution can be generated using

```
CAGraphics[history_List] := Graphics[
    Raster[1 - Reverse[history]], AspectRatio → Automatic]
```

And having set up the definitions above, the *Mathematica* input

```
Show[CAGraphics[CAEvolveList[
    ElementaryRule[30], CenterList[103], 50]]]
```

will generate the image:

The description just given should be adequate for most cellular automaton simulations. In some earlier versions of *Mathematica* a considerably faster version of the program can be created by using the definition

```
CAStep = Compile[{{rule, _Integer, 1}, {a, _Integer, 1}},
    rule[[8 - (RotateLeft[a] + 2 (a + 2 RotateRight[a]))]]]
```

In addition, in *Mathematica* 4 and above, one can use

```
CAStep[rule_, a_] := rule[[8 - ListConvolve[{1, 2, 4}, a, 2]]]
```

or directly in terms of the rule number num

```
Sign[BitAnd[2 ^ ListConvolve[{1, 2, 4}, a, 2], num]]
```

(In versions of *Mathematica* subsequent to the release of this book the built-in *CellularAutomaton* function can be used, as discussed on page 867.) It is also possible to have *CAStep* call the following external C language program via *MathLink*—though typically with successive versions of *Mathematica* the speed advantage obtained will be progressively less significant:

```
#include "mathlink.h"

main(argc, argv)
int argc; char *argv[];
{
MLMain(argc, argv);
}

void casteps(revrule, rlen, a, n, steps)
int *revrule, rlen, *a, n, steps;
{
int i, *ap, t, tp;

for (i = 0; i <steps; i++)
  {
  a[0] = a[n-2]; /* right boundary */
  a[n-1] = a[1]; /* left boundary */

  t = a[0];
  for (ap = a+1; ap <= a+n-2; ap++)
    {
    tp = ap[0];
    ap[0] = revrule[ap[1]+2*(tp + 2*t)];
    t = tp;
    }
  }

MLPutIntegerList(stdlink, a, n);
}
```

The linkage of this external program to the *Mathematica* function *CAStep* is achieved with the following *MathLink* template (note the optional third argument which allows

CAStep to perform several steps of cellular automaton evolution at a time):

```
:Begin:
:Function: casteps
:Pattern: CAStep[rule_List, a_List, steps_Integer:1]
:Arguments: {Reverse[rule], a, steps}
:ArgumentTypes: {IntegerList, IntegerList, Integer}
:ReturnType: Manual
:End:
```

There are a couple of tricky issues in the C program above. First, cellular automaton rules are always defined to use the old values of neighbors in determining the new value of any particular cell. But since the C program explicitly updates values sequentially from left to right, the left-hand neighbor of a particular cell will already have been given its new value when one tries to updates the cell itself. As a result, it is necessary to store the old value of the left-hand neighbor in a temporary variable in order to make it available for updating the cell itself. (Another approach to this problem is to maintain two copies of the array of cells, and to interchange pointers to them after every step in the cellular automaton evolution.)

Another tricky point in cellular automaton programs concerns boundary conditions. Since in a practical computer one can use only a finite array of cells, one must decide how the cellular automaton rule is to be applied to the cells at each end of the array. In both the *Mathematica* and the C programs above, we effectively use a cyclic array, in which the left neighbor of the leftmost cell is taken to be rightmost cell, and vice versa. In the C program, this is implemented by explicitly copying the value of the leftmost cell to the rightmost position in the array, and vice versa, before updating the values in the array. (In a sense there is a bug in the program in that the update only puts new values into $n - 2$ of the n array elements.)

■ **Comments on *Mathematica* functions.** *CenterList* works by first creating a list of n 0's, then replacing the middle 0 by a 1. (In *Mathematica* 4 and above *PadLeft[{1}, n, 0, Floor[n/2]]* can be used instead.) *ElementaryRule* works by converting *num* into a base 2 digit sequence, padding with zeros on the left so as to make a list of length 8. The scheme for numbering rules works so that if the value of a particular cell is q, the value of its left neighbor is p, and the value of its right neighbor is r, then the element at position $8 - (r + 2(q + 2p))$ in the list obtained from *ElementaryRule* will give the new value of the cell.

CAStep uses the fact that *Mathematica* can manipulate all the elements in a list at once. *RotateLeft[a]* and *RotateRight[a]* make shifted versions of the original list of cell values *a*. Then when these lists are added together, their corresponding elements are combined, as in

$\{p, q, r\} + \{s, t, u\} \rightarrow \{p + s, q + t, r + u\}$. The result is that a list is produced which specifies for each cell which element of the rule applies to that cell. The actual list of new cell values is then generated by using the fact that $\{i, j, k\}[[\{2, 1, 1, 3, 2\}]] \rightarrow \{j, i, i, k, j\}$. Note that by using *RotateLeft* and *RotateRight* one automatically gets cyclic boundary conditions.

CAEvolveList applies *CAStep* t times. Many other evolution functions in these notes use the same mechanism. In general $NestList[s[r, \#] \&, i, 2] \rightarrow \{i, s[r, i], s[r, s[r, i]]\}$, etc.

■ **Bitwise optimizations.** The C program above stores each cell value in a separate element of an integer array. But since every value must be either 0 or 1, it can in fact be encoded by just a single bit. And since integer variables in practical computers typically involve 32 or 64 bits, the values of many cells can be packed into a single integer variable. The main point of this is that typical machine instructions operate in parallel on all the bits in such a variable. And thus for example the values of all cells represented by an integer variable *a* can be updated in parallel according to rule 30 by the single C statement

```
a = a>>1 ^ (a | a<<1);
```

This statement, however, will only update the specific block of cells encoded in *a*. Gluing together updates to a sequence of such blocks requires slightly intricate code. (It is much easier to implement in *Mathematica*—as discussed above—since there functions like *BitXor* can operate on integers of any length.) In general, bitwise optimizations require representing cellular automaton rules not by simple look-up tables but rather by Boolean expressions, which must be derived for each rule and can be quite complicated (see page 869). Applying the rules can however be made faster by using bitslicing to avoid shift operations. The idea is to store the cellular automaton configuration in, say, m variables $w[i]$ whose bits correspond respectively to the cell values $\{a_1, a_{m+1}, a_{2m+1}, \ldots\}$, $\{a_2, a_{m+2}, a_{2m+2}, \ldots\}$, $\{a_3, \ldots\}$, etc. This then makes the left and right neighbors of the jth bit in $w[i]$ be the jth bits in $w[i - 1]$ and $w[i + 1]$—so that for example a step of rule 30 evolution can be achieved just by $w[i] = w[i - 1] \wedge (w[i] | w[i + 1])$ with no shift operations needed (except in boundary conditions on $w[0]$ and $w[m - 1]$). If many steps of evolution are required, it is sufficient just to pack all cell values at the beginning, and unpack them at the end.

■ **More general rules.** The programs given so far are for cellular automata with rules of the specific kind described in this chapter. In general, however, a 1D cellular automaton rule can be given as a set of explicit replacements for all possible blocks of cells in each neighborhood (see page 60). Thus, for example, rule 30 can be given as

$\{\{1, 1, 1\} \to 0, \{1, 1, 0\} \to 0, \{1, 0, 1\} \to 0, \{1, 0, 0\} \to 1,$
$\{0, 1, 1\} \to 1, \{0, 1, 0\} \to 1, \{0, 0, 1\} \to 1, \{0, 0, 0\} \to 0\}$

To use rules in this form, *CAStep* can be rewritten as

CAStep[rule_, a_List] :=
   Transpose[{RotateRight[a], a, RotateLeft[a]}] /. rule

or

CAStep[rule_, a_List] := Partition[a, 3, 1, 2] /. rule

The rules that are given can now contain patterns, so that rule 90, for example, can be written as

$\{\{1, \_, 1\} \to 0, \{1, \_, 0\} \to 1, \{0, \_, 1\} \to 1, \{0, \_, 0\} \to 0\}$

But how can one set up a program that can handle rules in several different forms? A convenient approach is to put a "wrapper" around each rule that specifies what form the rule is in. Then, for example, one can define

CAStep[ElementaryCARule[rule_List], a_List] :=
   rule[[8 - (RotateLeft[a] + 2 (a + 2 RotateRight[a]))]]

CAStep[GeneralCARule[rule_, r_Integer : 1], a_List] :=
   Partition[a, 2 r + 1, 1, r + 1] /. rule

CAStep[FunctionCARule[f_, r_Integer : 1], a_List] :=
   Map[f, Partition[a, 2 r + 1, 1, r + 1]]

Note that the second two definitions have been generalized to allow rules that involve r neighbors on each side. In each case, the use of *Partition* could be replaced by *Transpose[Table[RotateLeft[a, i], {i, -r, r}]]*. For efficiency in early versions of *Mathematica*, explicit rule lists in the second definition can be preprocessed using *Dispatch[rules]*, and functions in the third definition preprocessed using *Compile[{{x, _Integer, 1}}, body]*.

I discuss the implementation of totalistic cellular automata on page 886, and of higher-dimensional cellular automata on page 927.

■ **Built-in cellular automaton function.** Versions of *Mathematica* subsequent to the release of this book will include a very general function for cellular automaton evolution. The description is as follows (see also page 886):

CellularAutomaton[rnum, init, t] generates a list representing the evolution of cellular automaton rule *rnum* from initial condition *init* for t steps.

CellularAutomaton[rnum, init, t, {off$_1$, off$_x$ ... }] keeps only the parts of the evolution list with the specified offsets.

Possible settings for *rnum* are:

n	$k = 2, r = 1$, elementary rule
$\{n, k\}$	general nearest-neighbor rule with k colors
$\{n, k, r\}$	general rule with k colors and range r
$\{n, k, \{r_1, r_2, \ldots,$	d-dimensional rule with $(2 r_1 + 1) \times (2 r_2 + 1)$
$\quad r_d\}\}$	$\times \ldots \times (2 r_d + 1)$ neighborhood
$\{n, k, \{\{off_1\}, \{off_2\}, \ldots, \{off_s\}\}\}$	
	rule with neighbors at specified offsets
$\{n, \{k, 1\}\}$	k-color nearest-neighbor totalistic rule

$\{n, \{k, 1\}, r\}$	k-color range r totalistic rule
$\{n, \{k, \{wt_1, wt_2, \ldots \}\}, rspec\}$	
	rule in which neighbor i is assigned weight wt_i
$\{fun, \{\}, rspec\}$	applies the function *fun* to each list of neighbors, with a second argument of the step number

■ *CellularAutomaton[{n, k}, ...]* is equivalent to *CellularAutomaton[{n, {k, {k^2, k, 1}}}, ...]*. ■ Common forms for 2D cellular automata include:

$\{n, \{k, 1\}, \{1, 1\}\}$	9-neighbor totalistic rule
$\{n, \{k, \{\{0, 1, 0\}, \{1, 1, 1\}, \{0, 1, 0\}\}\}, \{1, 1\}\}$	
	5-neighbor totalistic rule
$\{n, \{k, \{\{0, k, 0\}, \{k, 1, k\}, \{0, k, 0\}\}\}, \{1, 1\}\}$	
	5-neighbor outer totalistic rule
$\{n + k^5 (k - 1), \{k, \{\{0, 1, 0\}, \{1, 4k + 1, 1\}, \{0, 1, 0\}\}\}, \{1, 1\}\}$	
	5-neighbor growth rule

■ Normally, all elements in *init* and the evolution list are integers between 0 and k-1. ■ But when a general function is used, the elements of *init* and the evolution list do not have to be integers. ■ The second argument passed to *fun* is the step number, starting at 0. ■ Initial conditions are constructed from *init* as follows:

$\{a_1, a_2, \ldots \}$	explicit list of values a_i, assumed cyclic
$\{\{a_1, a_2, \ldots \}, b\}$	values a_i superimposed on a b background
$\{\{a_1, a_2, \ldots \}, \{b_1, b_2, \ldots \}\}$	
	values a_i superimposed on a background of repetitions of $b_1, b_2, \ldots$
$\{\{\{a_{11}, a_{12}, \ldots \}, off_1\}, \{a_{21}, \ldots \}, off_2\}, \ldots \}, bspec\}$	
	values a_{ij} at offsets off_i on a background
$\{\{a_{11}, a_{12}, \ldots \}, \{a_{21}, \ldots \}, \ldots \}$	
	explicit list of values in two dimensions
$\{aspec, bspec\}$	values in d dimensions with d-dimensional padding

■ The first element of *aspec* is superimposed on the background at the first position in the positive direction in each coordinate relative to the origin. This means that *bspec[[1,1,...]]* is aligned with *aspec[[1, 1,...]]*. ■ Time offsets *off$_t$* are specified as follows:

All	all steps 0 through t (default)
u	steps 0 through u
-1	last step (step t)
$\{u\}$	step u
$\{u_1, u_2\}$	steps u_1 through u_2
$\{u_1, u_2, du\}$	steps $u_1, u_1 + du, \ldots$

■ *CellularAutomaton[rnum, init, t]* generates an evolution list of length t+1. ■ The initial condition is taken to have offset 0. ■ Space offsets *off$_x$* are specified as follows:

All	all cells that can be affected by the specified initial condition
Automatic	all cells in the region that differs from the background
0	cell aligned with beginning of *aspec*
x	cells at offsets up to x on the right
$-x$	cells at offsets up to x on the left
$\{x\}$	cell at offset x to the right
$\{-x\}$	cell at offset x to the left
$\{x_1, x_2\}$	cells at offsets x_1 through x_2
$\{x_1, x_2, dx\}$	cells $x_1, x_1 + dx, \ldots$

■ In one dimension, the first element of *aspec* is taken by default to have space offset 0. ■ In any number of dimensions, *aspec[[1, 1, ...]]* is taken by default to have space offset $\{0, 0, 0, \ldots\}$. ■ Each element of the evolution list produced by *CellularAutomaton* is always the same size. ■ With an initial condition specified by an *aspec* of width w, the region that can be affected after t steps by a cellular automaton with a rule of range *r* has width $w + 2rt$. ■ If no *bspec* background is specified, space offsets of *All* and *Automatic* will include every cell in *aspec*. ■ A space offset of *All* includes all cells that can be affected by the initial condition. ■ A space offset of *Automatic* can be used to trim off background from the sides of a cellular automaton pattern. ■ In working out how wide a region to keep, *Automatic* only looks at results on steps specified by off_t.

Some examples include:

This gives the array of values obtained by running rule 30 for 3 steps, starting from an initial condition consisting of a single 1 surrounded by 0's.

In[1]: = *CellularAutomaton[30, {{1}, 0}, 3]*

Out[1]= {{0, 0, 0, 1, 0, 0, 0}, {0, 0, 1, 1, 1, 0, 0}, {0, 1, 1, 0, 0, 1, 0}, {1, 1, 0, 1, 1, 1, 1}}

This runs rule 30 for 50 steps and makes a picture of the result.

In[2]: = *Show[RasterGraphics[CellularAutomaton[30, {{1}, 0}, 50]]]*

If all values in the initial condition are given explicitly, they are in effect assumed to continue cyclically. The runs rule 30 with 5 cells for 3 steps.

In[3]: = *CellularAutomaton[30, {1, 0, 0, 1, 0}, 3]*

Out[3]= {{1, 0, 0, 1, 0}, {1, 1, 1, 1, 0}, {1, 0, 0, 0, 0}, {1, 1, 0, 0, 1}}

This starts from {1,1} on an infinite background of repeating {1,0,1,1} blocks. By default, only the region of the pattern affected by the {1,1} is given.

In[4]: = *Show[RasterGraphics[CellularAutomaton[30, {{1, 1}, {1, 0, 1, 1}}, 50]]]*

This gives all cells that could possibly be affected, whether or not they are.

In[5]: = *Show[RasterGraphics[CellularAutomaton[30, {{1, 1}, {1, 0, 1, 1}}, 50, {All, All}]]]*

This places blocks in the initial conditions at offsets -10 and 20.

In[6]: = *Show[RasterGraphics[CellularAutomaton[30, {{{1}, {-10}}, {{1, 1}, {20}}}, 0}, 50]]]*

This gives only the last row after running for 10 steps.

In[7]: = *CellularAutomaton[30, {{1}, 0}, 10, -1]*

Out[7]= {{1, 1, 0, 0, 1, 0, 0, 0, 0, 1, 0, 1, 1, 1, 1, 0, 1, 1, 0, 0, 1, 0}}

This runs for 5 steps, giving the cells on the 3 center columns at each step.

In[8]: = *CellularAutomaton[30, {{1}, 0}, 5, {All, {-1, 1}}]*

Out[8]= {{0, 1, 0}, {1, 1, 1}, {1, 0, 0}, {0, 1, 1}, {0, 1, 0}, {1, 1, 1}}

This picks out every other cell in space and time, starting 200 cells to the left.

In[9]: = *Show[RasterGraphics[CellularAutomaton[30, {{1}, 0}, 100, {{1, 100, 2}, {-200, 200, 2}}]]]*

This runs the general *k* = 3, *r* = 1 rule with rule number 921408.

In[10]: = *Show[RasterGraphics[CellularAutomaton[{921408, 3, 1}, {{1}, 0}, 100]]]*

This runs the totalistic *k* = 3, *r* = 1 rule with code 867.

In[11]: = *Show[RasterGraphics[CellularAutomaton[{867, {3, 1}, 1}, {{1}, 0}, 50]]]*

This uses a rule based on applying a function to each neighborhood of cells.

In[12]: = *Show[RasterGraphics[CellularAutomaton[{Mod[Apply[Plus, #], 4] &, {}, 1}, {{1}, 0}, 50]]]*

This runs 2D 9-neighbor totalistic code 3702 for 25 steps, giving the results for the last 5 steps.

In[13]: = *Show[GraphicsArray[Map[RasterGraphics, CellularAutomaton[{3702, {2, 1}, {1, 1}}, {{{1}}, 0}, 25, -5]]]]*

■ **Special-purpose hardware.** The simple structure of cellular automata makes it natural to think of implementing them with special-purpose hardware. And indeed from the 1950s on, a sequence of special-purpose machines have been built to implement 1D, 2D and sometimes 3D cellular automata. Two basic ideas have been used: parallelism and pipelines. Both ideas rely on the local nature of cellular automaton rules.

In the parallel approach, the machine has many separate processors, each dedicated to handling a single cell or a small group of cells. In the pipelined approach, there is just a single processor (or perhaps a few processors) through which the data on different cells is successively piped. The key point, however, is that at every stage it is easy to know what data will be needed, so this data can be prefetched, potentially through a specially built memory system.

In general, the speed increases that can be achieved depend on many details of memory and communications architecture. The increases have tended to become less significant over the years, as the on-chip memories of microprocessors have become larger, and the time necessary to send data from one chip to another has become proportionately more important.

In the future, however, new technologies may change the trade-offs, and indeed cellular automata are obvious candidates for early implementation in both nanotechnology and optical computing. (See also page 841.)

■ **Audio representation.** A step in the evolution of a cellular automaton can be represented as a sound by treating each cell like a key on a piano, with the key taken to be pressed if the cell is black. This yields a chord such as

Play[Evaluate[Apply[Plus, Flatten[Map[Sin[1000 # t] &,
N[2^{1/12}]^Position[list, 1]]]]], {t, 0, 0.2}]

A sequence of such chords can sometimes provide a useful representation of cellular automaton evolution. (See also page 1080.)

■ **Cellular automaton rules as formulas.** The value *a[t, i]* for a cell on step *t* at position *i* in any of the cellular automata in this chapter can be obtained from the definition

a[t_, i_] := f[a[t - 1, i - 1], a[t - 1, i], a[t - 1, i + 1]]

Different rules correspond to different choices of the function *f*. For example, rule 90 on page 25 corresponds to

f[1, _, 1] = 0; f[0, _, 1] = 1; f[1, _, 0] = 1; f[0, _, 0] = 0

One can specify initial conditions for example by

a[0, 0] = 1; a[0, _] = 0

(the cell on step 0 at position 0 has value 1, but all other cells on that step have value 0). Then just asking for *a[4, 0]* one will immediately get the value after 4 steps of the cell at position 0. (For efficiency, the main definition should in practice be given as

a[t_, i_] := a[t, i] = f[a[t - 1, i - 1], a[t - 1, i], a[t - 1, i + 1]]

so that all intermediate values which are computed are automatically stored.)

The definition of the function *f* for rule 90 that we gave above is essentially just a look-up table. But it is also possible to define this function in an algebraic way

f[p_, q_, r_] := Mod[p + r, 2]

Algebraic definitions can also be given for other rules:

- Rule 254 (page 24): *1 - (1 - p)(1 - q)(1 - r)*
- Rule 250 (page 25): *p + r - p r*
- Rule 30 (page 27): *Mod[p + q + r + q r, 2]*
- Rule 110 (page 32): *Mod[(1 + p) q r + q + r, 2]*

In these definitions, we represent the values of cells by the numbers 1 or 0. If values +1 and -1 are used instead, different formulas are obtained; rule 90, for example, corresponds to *p r*. It is also possible to represent values of cells as *True* and *False*. And in this case cellular automaton rules become logic expressions:

- Rule 254: *Or[p, q, r]*
- Rule 250: *Or[p, r]*
- Rule 90: *Xor[p, r]*
- Rule 30: *Xor[p, Or[q, r]]*
- Rule 110: *Xor[Or[p, q], And[p, q, r]]*

(Note that *Not[p]* corresponds to *1 - p*, *And[p, q]* to *p q*, *Xor[p, q]* to *Mod[p + q, 2]* and *Or[p, q]* to *Mod[p q + p + q, 2]*.)

Given either the algebraic or logical form of a cellular automaton rule, it is possible at least in principle to generate symbolic formulas for the results of cellular automaton evolution. Thus, for example, one can use initial conditions

a[0, -1] = p; a[0, 0] = q; a[0, 1] = r; a[0, _] = 0

to generate a formula for the value of a cell that holds for any choice of values for the three initial center cells. In practice, however, most such formulas rapidly become very complicated, as discussed on page 618.

■ **Mathematical interpretation of cellular automata.** In the context of pure mathematics, the state space of a 1D cellular automaton with an infinite number of cells can be viewed as a Cantor set. The cellular automaton rule then corresponds to a continuous mapping of this Cantor set to itself (continuity follows from the locality of the rule). (Compare page 959.)

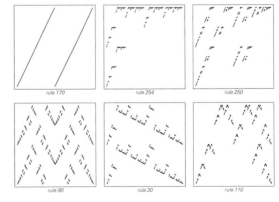

rule 170   rule 254   rule 250

rule 90   rule 30   rule 110

The pictures above show representations of the mappings corresponding to various rules, obtained by plotting *Sum[a[t + 1, i] 2^{-i}, {i, -n, n}]* against *Sum[a[t, i] 2^{-i}, {i, -n, n}]* for all possible choices of the *a[t, i]*. (Periodic boundary conditions are used, so that the *a[t, i]* can be viewed as corresponding precisely to digits of rational numbers.) Rule 170 is the classic shift map which shifts all cell values one position to the left without changing them. In the pictures below, this map has the form *Mod[2 x, 1]* (compare page 153).

■ **Page 26 · Pascal's triangle and rule 90.** As shown on page 611 the pattern produced by rule 90 is exactly Pascal's triangle of binomial coefficients reduced modulo 2: black cells correspond to odd binomial coefficients.

The number of black cells on row *t* is given by $2 \wedge DigitCount[t, 2, 1]$, where *DigitCount[t, 2, 1]* is plotted on page 902. The positions of the black cells are given by (and this establishes the connection with the picture on page 117)

Fold[Flatten[{{#1 - #2, #1 + #2}} &, {0}, 2 ^ DigitPositions[t]]]

DigitPositions[n_] :=
    Flatten[Position[Reverse[IntegerDigits[n, 2]], 1]] - 1

The actual pattern generated by rule 90 corresponds to the coefficients in $PolynomialMod[Expand[(1/x + x)^t], 2]$ (see page 1091); the color of a particular cell is thus given by *Mod[Binomial[t, (n + t)/2], 2] /; EvenQ[n + t]*.

Mod[Binomial[t, n], 2] yields a distorted pattern that is the one produced by rule 60 (see page 58). In this pattern, the color of a particular cell can be obtained directly from the digit sequences for *t* and *n* by *1 - Sign[BitAnd[-t, n]]* or (see page 583)

With[{d = Ceiling[Log[2, Max[t, n] + 1]]}, If[FreeQ[
    IntegerDigits[t, 2, d] - IntegerDigits[n, 2, d], -1], 1, 0]]

■ **Self-similarity.** The pattern generated by rule 90 after a given number of steps has the property that it is identical to what one would get by going twice as many steps, and then keeping only every other row and column. After 2^m steps the triangular region outlined by the pattern contains altogether 4^m cells, but only 3^m of these are black. In the limit of an infinite number of steps one gets a fractal known as a Sierpiński pattern (see page 934), with fractal dimension $Log[2, 3] \approx 1.59$ (see page 933). Nesting occurs in all cellular automata with additive rules (see page 955).

■ **Another initial condition.** Inserting a single ■ in a background of ■□ blocks in rule 90 yields the pattern below in which both the white and striped regions have fractal dimension 2.

■ **More colors.** The pictures below show generalizations of rule 90 to *k* possible colors using the rule

CAStep[k_Integer, a_List] :=
    Mod[RotateLeft[a] + RotateRight[a], k]

or equivalently *Mod[ListCorrelate[{1, 0, 1}, a, 2], k]*. The number of cells that are not white on row *t* in this case is given by *Apply[Times, 1 + IntegerDigits[t, k]]*. (For non-prime *k*, the patterns are obtained by superimposing the patterns corresponding to the factors of *k*.) A related result is that *IntegerExponent[Binomial[t, n], k]* is given by the number of borrows in the base *k* subtraction of *n* from *t*. *Mod[Binomial[t, n], k]* is given for prime *k* by

With[{d = Ceiling[Log[k, Max[t, n] + 1]]},
    Mod[Apply[Times, Apply[Binomial, Transpose[
        {IntegerDigits[t, k, d], IntegerDigits[n, k, d]}], {1}]], k]]

The patterns obtained for any *k* are nested. For prime *k* the total number of non-white cells down to step k^m is $(1/2 k (k + 1))^m$ and the patterns have fractal dimension $1 + Log[k, (k + 1)/2]$ (see page 955). These are examples of additive rules, discussed further on page 952. (See also page 922 for the continuous case.)

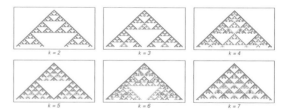

k = 2   *k = 3*   *k = 4*
k = 5   *k = 6*   *k = 7*

■ **History.** Pascal's triangle probably dates from antiquity; it was known in China in the 1200s, and was discussed in some detail by Blaise Pascal in 1654, particularly in connection with probability theory. The digit-based approach to finding binomial coefficients modulo *k* has been invented independently many times since the mid-1800s, notably by Edouard Lucas in 1877 and James Glaisher in 1899. The fact that the odd binomial coefficients form a nested geometrical pattern had apparently not been widely noticed before I emphasized it in 1982.

Binomial[m,n]   *Multinomial[m,n]*   *StirlingS1[m,n]*   *StirlingS2[m,n]*

■ **Other integer functions.** The pictures above show patterns produced by reducing several integer functions modulo 2. With *d* arguments *Multinomial* yields a nested pattern in *d* dimensions. Note that *GCD[m, n]* yields a more complicated pattern (see page 613), as do *JacobiSymbol[m, 2n - 1]* (see page 1081) and various combinations of functions (see page 747).

■ **Bitwise functions.** Bitwise functions typically yield nested patterns. (As discussed above, any cellular automaton rule can be represented as an appropriate combination of bitwise functions.) Note that *BitOr[x, y] + BitAnd[x, y] == x + y* and *BitOr[x, y] - BitAnd[x, y] == BitXor[x, y]*.

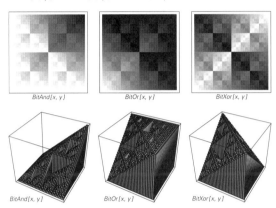

| BitAnd[x, y] | BitOr[x, y] | BitXor[x, y] |

The patterns below show where *BitXor[x, y] == t* for successive *t* and correspond to steps in the "munching squares" program studied on the PDP-1 computer in 1962.

Nesting is also seen in curves obtained by applying bitwise functions to *n* and *2n* for successive *n*. Note that *2n* has the same digits as *n*, but shifted one position to the left.

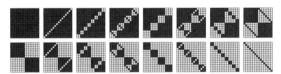

| BitAnd[n, 2n] | BitOr[n, 2n] | BitXor[n, 2n] |

■ **Page 28 · Tests of randomness.** The statistical tests that I have performed include the eight listed on page 1084.

■ **Page 29 · Rule 30.** The left-hand side of the pattern shown has an obvious repetitive character. In general, if one looks along a diagonal *n* cells in from either edge of the pattern, then the period of repetition can be at most 2^n. On the right-hand edge, the first few periods that are seen are {1, 2, 2, 4, 8, 8, 16, 32, 32, 64, 64, 64, 64, 64, 128, 256} and in general the period seems to increase exponentially with depth. On the left-hand edge, the period increases only

extremely slowly: period 2 is first achieved at depth 3, period 4 at depth 8, 8 at 29, 16 at 400, 32 at 87,867, 64 at 2,107,985,255 or more, and so on. (Each period doubling turns out to occur exactly when a diagonal in the pattern eventually becomes a white stripe, and the diagonal to its left has an odd number of black cells in each repeating block.) The boundary that separates repetition on the left from randomness on the right moves an average of about 0.252 cells to the left at every step (compare page 949). The picture below shows the fluctuations around this average.

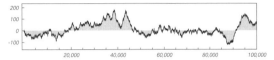

Complete pattern. All possible blocks appear to occur eventually (see page 725). The probability for a block of *n* adjacent white cells (corresponding to a row in a white triangle) seems quite accurately to approach 2^{-n}, with the first length 10 such block occurring at step 67 and the first length 20 one occurring at step 515.

Center column. The pictures below show the excess of black over white cells in the center column. Out of the first 100,000 cells, a total of 50,098 are black, and out of the first million 500,768 are. The longest run of identical colors in the first 100,000 cells consists of 21 black cells, and in the first million elements 22 black cells. The first *n* elements can be found efficiently using

Module[{a = 1}, Table[First[IntegerDigits[
a, a = BitXor[a, BitOr[2a, 4a]]; 2, i]], {i, n}]]

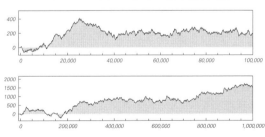

The sequence does not repeat in at least its first million steps, and I would amazed if it ever repeats, but as of now I know of no rigorous proof of this. (Erica Jen showed in 1986 that no pair of columns can ever repeat, and the arguments on page 1087 suggest that neither can the center column together with occasional neighboring cells.)

■ **Page 32 · Rule 110.** Many more details of rule 110 are discussed on pages 229 and 675. Localized structures that can occur are shown on page 292. Note that of the 8 cases in the basic rule for rule 110, only one differs from rule 102—which is a simple additive rule obtained by reflecting rule 60.

The Need for a New Intuition

■ **Reactions of scientists.** Many scientists find the complexity of the pictures in this chapter so surprising that at first they assume it cannot be real. Typically they imagine that while the pictures may look complicated, they would actually seem simple if only they were subjected to the appropriate kind of analysis. In Chapter 10 I will give extensive evidence that this is not the case. But suffice it to say here that when it comes to finding regularities even the most advanced methods from mathematics and statistics tend to be no more powerful than our eyes. And whatever formal definition one may use for complexity (see page 557), the fact that our eyes perceive it in the systems discussed in this chapter is already very significant.

■ **Intuition from practical computing.** Everyday experience with computers and programming leads to observations like the following:

- General-purpose computers and general-purpose programming languages can be built.

- Different programs for doing all sorts of different things can be set up.

- Any given program can be implemented in many ways.

- Programs can behave in complicated and seemingly random ways—particularly when they are not working properly.

- Debugging a program can be difficult.

- It is often difficult to foresee what a program can do by reading its code.

- The lower the level of representation of the code for a program the more difficult it tends to be to understand.

- Some computational problems are easy to state but hard to solve.

- Programs that simulate natural systems are among the most computationally expensive.

- It is possible for people to create large programs—at least in pieces.

- It is almost always possible to optimize a program more, but the optimized version may be more difficult to understand.

- Shorter programs are sometimes more efficient, but optimizations often require many cases to be treated separately, making programs longer.

- If programs are patched too much, they typically stop working at all.

■ **Applications to design.** Many of the pictures in this book look strikingly similar to artistic designs of various styles. Probably this reflects not so much a similarity in underlying rules, but rather similarity in features that are most noticeable to the human visual system. Note that square grids of colored cells as in the cellular automata in this chapter can be used quite directly as weaving patterns. (See also page 929.)

Why These Discoveries Were Not Made Before

■ **Page 43 · Ornamental art.** Almost all major cultural periods are associated with certain characteristic forms of ornament. Often the forms of ornament used on particular kinds of objects probably arose as idealized imitations of earlier or more natural forms for such objects—so that, for example, imitations of weaving, bricks and various plant forms are common. Large-scale purely abstract patterns were also central to art in such cultural traditions as Islam where natural forms were considered works of God that must not be shown directly. Once established, styles of ornament tend to be repeated extensively as a way of providing certain comfort and familiarity—especially in architecture. The vast majority of elaborate ornament seems to have been created by artisans with little or no formal theoretical discussion, although particularly since the 1800s there have been various attempts to find systematic ways to catalog forms of ornament, sometimes based on analogies with grammar. (Issues of proportion have however long been the subject of considerable theoretical discussion.) It is notable that whereas repetitive patterns have been used extensively in ornament, even nesting is rather rare. And even though for example elaborate symmetry rules have been devised, nothing like cellular automaton rules appear to have ever arisen. The results in this book now show that such rules can capture the essence of many complex processes that occur in nature—so that even though they lack historical context such rules can potentially provide a basis for forms of ornament that are familiar as idealizations of nature. (Compare page 929.)

The pictures in the main text show a sequence of early examples of various characteristic forms of ornament.

22,000 BC (Paleolithic). Mammoth ivory bracelet from Mezin, Ukraine. Similar zig-zag designs are seen in other objects from the same period. In the example shown, it is notable that the angle of the zig-zags is comparable to the angle of the Schreger lines that occur naturally in mammoth dentin.

3000 BC (Sumerian). Columns with three colors of clay pegs set in mud from a wall of the Eanna temple in Uruk, Mesopotamia (Warka, Iraq)—perhaps mentioned in the Epic of Gilgamesh. (Now in the Staatliche Museum, Berlin.) This is the earliest known explicit example of mosaic.

1200 BC (Greek). The back of a clay accounting tablet from Pylos, Greece. The pattern was presumably made by the procedure shown below. Legend has it that it was the plan for the labyrinth housing the minotaur in the palace at Knossos, Crete, and that it was designed by Daedalus. It is also said that it was a logo for the city of Troy—or perhaps the plan of some of its walls. The pattern—in either its square or rounded form—has appeared with remarkably little variation in a huge variety of places all over the world—from Cretan coins, to graffiti at Pompeii, to the floor of the cathedral at Chartres, to carvings in Peru, to logos for aboriginal tribes. For probably three thousand years, it has been the single most common design used for mazes.

900 BC (Phoenician). Ivory carving presumably from the Mediterranean area. (Now in the British Museum.) This was a common decorative pattern, formed by drawing circles centered at holes arranged in a triangular array. It is also found in Egyptian and other art. Such patterns were discussed by Euclid and later Leonardo da Vinci in connection with the theory of lunes.

1st century BC (Celtic). The back of the so-called Desborough Mirror—a bronze mirror from Desborough, England made in the Iron Age sometime between 50 BC and 50 AD. (Now in the British Museum.) The engraved pattern is made of parts of circles that just touch each other, as in the picture below.

2nd century AD (Roman). A mosaic from a complex in Rome, Italy. (Now in the National Museum, Rome.) The geometrical pattern was presumably made by first constructing 48 regularly spaced spokes by repeated angle bisection, as in the first picture below, then drawing semicircles centered at the end of each spoke, and finally adding concentric circles through the intersection points. Similar rosette patterns may have been used in Greece around 350 BC; they became popular in churches in the 1500s.

8th century (Islamic). A detail on the outside wall of the Great Mosque of Córdoba, Spain, built around 785 AD.

8th century (Celtic). An area less than 2 inches square from inside the letter ρ on the extremely elaborate chi-rho page of the Book of Kells, an illuminated gospel manuscript created over a period of years at various monasteries, probably starting around 800 AD at the Irish monastery on the island of Iona, Scotland. Even on this one page there are perhaps a dozen other very similar nested structures.

12th century (Italian). A window in the Palatine Chapel in Palermo, Sicily, presumably built around 1140 AD. The chapel is characteristic of so-called Arab-Norman style.

13th century (English). The Dean's Eye rose window of the Lincoln cathedral in England, built around 1225 AD. Similar tree-like patterns are seen in many Gothic windows from the same general period.

13th century (Italian) (4 pictures). Marble mosaics on the floor of the cathedral at Anagni, Italy, made around 1226 AD by Cosmas of the Cosmati group. (The fourth picture is a close-up of the third.) The third picture—particularly the part magnified in the fourth picture—shows an approximate nested structure, presumably created as in the pictures below. The triangles are all equilateral, with the result that at a given step several different sizes of triangles occur—though the basic structure of the pattern is still the same as from the rule 90 cellular automaton. (Compare the Apollonian packing of page 986.) The Cosmati group—mostly four generations of one family—made elaborate geometrical and other mosaics with a mixture of Byzantine, Islamic and other influences from about 1190 to 1300, mostly in and around Rome, but also for example in Westminster Abbey in England. Triangular shapes with one level of nesting are quite common in their work; three levels of nesting as shown here are rare. It is notable that in later imitations of Cosmati mosaics, these kinds of patterns were almost never used.

14th century (Islamic). Wall decoration in the Pir-i-Bakran mausoleum in Linjan, Iran, built around 1299–1312. The pattern is square Kufi calligraphy for a widely quoted verse of the Koran. The pictures below illustrate its relation to standard cursive Arabic writing. The basic Kufi style was already in use as a variant by 700 AD—with the square form being seen in architectural ornament by about 1100 AD.

14th century (Islamic). Tiled wall in the Alcázar of Seville, Spain, built in 1364. (The same pattern was used at about the same time in the Alhambra in Granada, Spain.) The pattern can be made by starting with a grid of triangles, then consistently pushing in or out the sides of each one. (Notable uses of such patterns were made by Maurits Escher starting in the 1930s.)

Other cases. The cases that are known inevitably tend to be ones created out of stone or ceramic materials that survive; no doubt there were others created for example with wood or textiles. One case with wood is Chinese lattice. What has survived mostly shows repetitive patterns, but the ice-ray style, probably going back to 100 AD, has approximate nesting, though with many random elements. The patterns shown are all basically two-dimensional. An example of 1D ornamental patterns are molding profiles. Ever since antiquity these have often been quite elaborate, and it is conceivable that they can sometimes be interpreted as showing nesting.

■ **Recognition of art.** One bizarre possibility is that forms like those from rule 30 could have been created as art long ago but not be recognized now. For while it is easy to tell that a cave painting of an animal is a piece of purposeful art, dots carved into a rock in an approximate rule 30 pattern might not even be noticed as something of human origin. But although there are many seemingly random painted patterns in caves from perhaps 30,000 BC, I would be amazed if any of them were actually produced by definite simple rules. (See page 839.)

■ **The concept of rules.** Processes based on rules occur in a great many areas of human endeavor. Sometimes the rules serve mainly as a constraint. But it is not uncommon for them to be used—like in a cellular automaton—as a way of specifying how structures should be built up. Almost without exception, however, the rules have in the past been chosen to yield only rather specific and simple results. Beyond ornamental art, examples with long histories include:

Architecture. Structures such as ziggurats and pyramids were presumably constructed by assembling collections of stones according to simple rules. The Great Pyramid in Egypt was built around 2500 BC and contains about two million large stones. (By comparison, the pictures of rule 30 on pages 29 and 30 contain a total of about a million cells.) Starting perhaps as long ago as 1000 BC Hindu temples were constructed with similar elements on different scales, yielding a form of approximate nesting. In Roman and later architecture, rooms in buildings have quite often been arranged in roughly nested patterns (an extreme example being the Castel del Monte from the 1200s). From the Middle Ages many Persian gardens (such as those of the Taj Mahal from around 1650) have had fairly regular nested structures obtained by a few successive fourfold subdivisions. And starting in the early 1200s, Gothic windows were often constructed with levels of roughly tree-like nested forms (see above). Nesting does not appear to have been used in physical city plans (except to a small extent in Vauban star fortifications), though it is common in organizational structures. (As indicated above, architectural ornament has also often in effect been constructed using definite rules.)

Textile making. Since early in human history there appear to have been definite rules used for weaving. But insofar as the purpose is to produce fabric the basic arrangement of threads is normally always repetitive.

Rope. Since at least 3000 BC rope has been made by twisting together strands themselves made by twisting, yielding cross-sections with some nesting, as in the second picture below. (Since the development of wire rope in the 1870s precise designs have been used, including at least recently the 7×7×7 one shown last below.)

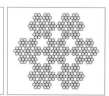

Knots and string figures. For many thousands of years definite rules have been used for tying knots and presumably also for making string figures. But when the rules have more than a few steps they tend to be repetitive.

Paperfolding. Although paperfolding has presumably been practiced for at least 2000 years, even the nested form on page 892 seems to have been noticed only very recently.

Mathematics. Ever since Babylonian times arithmetic has been done by repeatedly applying simple rules to digits in numbers. And ever since ancient Greek times iterative methods have been used to construct geometrical figures. In the late 1600s the idea also emerged that mathematical proofs could be thought of as consisting of repeated applications of definite rules. But the idea of studying possible simple rules independent of their purpose in generating results seems never to have arisen. And as mathematics began to focus on continuous systems the notion of enumerating possible rules became progressively more difficult.

Logic. Rules of logic have been used since around 400 BC. But beyond forms like syllogisms little seems to have been studied in the way of generating identifiable patterns from them. (See page 1099.)

Grammar. The idea that human language is constructed from words according to definite grammatical rules has existed since at least around perhaps 500 BC when Panini gave a grammar for Sanskrit. (Less formal versions of the idea were also common in ancient Greek times.) But for the most part it was not until about the 1950s that rules of grammar began to be viewed as specifications for generating structures, rather than just constraints. (See page 1103.)

Poetry. Definite rules for rhythm in poetry were already well developed in antiquity—and by perhaps 200 BC Indian work on enumerating their possible forms appears to have led to both Pascal's triangle and Fibonacci numbers. Patterns of rhyme involving iterated length-6 permutations (sestina) and interleaved repetitive sequences (terza rima) were in use by the 1300s, notably by Dante.

Music. Simple progressions and various forms of repetition have presumably been used in music since at least the time of Pythagoras. Beginning in the 1200s more complex forms of interleaving such as those of canons have occasionally been used. And in the past century a few composers have implicitly or explicitly used structures based on simple Fibonacci and other substitution systems. Note that rules such as those of counterpoint are used mainly as constraints, not as ways of generating structure.

Military drill. The notion of using definite rules to organize and maneuver formations of soldiers appears to have existed in Babylonian and Assyrian times, and to be well codified by Roman times. Fairly elaborate cases were described for example by Niccolò Machiavelli in 1521, but all were set up to yield only rather simple behavior, such as a column of soldiers being rearranged into lines. (See the firing squad problem on page 1035.)

Games. Games are normally based on definite rules, but are set up so that at each step they involve choosing one of many possibilities, either by skill or randomness. The game of Go, which originated before 500 BC and perhaps as early as 2300 BC, is a case where particularly simple rules manage to allow remarkably complex patterns of play to occur. (Go involves putting black and white stones on a grid, making it visually similar to a cellular automaton.)

Puzzles. Geometric and arithmetic puzzles surprisingly close to those common today seem to have existed since as long ago as 2000 BC. Usually they are based on constraints, and occasionally they can be thought of as providing evidence that simple constraints can have complicated solutions.

Cryptography. Rules for encrypting messages have been used since perhaps 2000 BC, with non-trivial repetitive schemes becoming common in the 1500s, but more complex schemes not appearing until well into the 1900s. (See page 1085.)

Maze designs. From antiquity until about the 1500s the majority of mazes followed a small number of designs—most often based directly on the one shown on page 873, or with subunits like it. (It is now known that there are many other designs that are also possible.)

Rule-based pictures. It is rather common for geometric doodles to be based on definite rules, but it is rare for the rules to be carried far, or for the doodles to be preserved. Some of Leonardo da Vinci's planned book on "Geometrical Play" from the early 1500s has, however, survived, and shows elaborate patterns satisfying particular constraints. Various attempts to enumerate all possible patterns of particular simple kinds have been made—a notable example being Sébastien Truchet in 1704 drawing 2D patterns formed by combining ◣, ◢, ◤, ◥ in various possible ways.

■ **Page 44 · Understanding nature.** In Greek times it was noted that simple geometrical rules could explain many features of astronomy—the most obvious being the apparent revolution of the stars and the circular shapes of the Sun and Moon. But it was noted that with few exceptions—like beehives—natural objects that occur terrestrially did not appear to follow any simple geometrical rules. (The most complicated curves in Greek geometry were things like cissoids and conchoids.) So from this it was concluded that only certain supposedly perfect objects like the heavenly bodies could be expected to be fully amenable to human understanding. What rules for natural objects might in effect have been tried in the Judeo-Christian tradition is less clear—though for example the Book of Job does comment on the difficulty of "numbering the clouds by wisdom". And with the notable exception of the alchemists it continued to be believed throughout the Middle Ages that the wonders of nature were beyond human understanding.

■ **Atomism.** The idea that everything might be made up from large numbers of discrete elements was discussed around perhaps 450 BC by Leucippus and Democritus. Sometime later the Epicureans then suggested that a few types of elements might suffice, and an analogy was made (notably by Lucretius around 100 AD) to the fact that different configurations of letters can make up all the words in a language. But only some schools of Greek philosophy ever supported atomism, and it soon fell out of favor. It was revived in the late 1600s, when corpuscular theories of both light and matter began to be widely discussed. In the early 1800s arguments based on atoms led to success in chemistry, and in the late 1800s statistical mechanics of large assemblies of atoms were used to explain properties of matter (see page 1019). With the rise of quantum theory in the early 1900s it became firmly established that physical systems contain discrete particles. But it was normally assumed that one should think only about explicit particles with realistic mechanical properties—so that abstract idealizations like cellular automata did not arise. (See also pages 1027 and 1043.)

■ **History of cellular automata.** Despite their very simple construction, nothing like general cellular automata appear to have been considered before about the 1950s. Yet in the 1950s—inspired in various ways by the advent of electronic computers—several different kinds of systems equivalent to cellular automata were independently introduced. A variety of precursors can be identified. Operations on sequences of digits had been used since antiquity in doing arithmetic. Finite difference approximations to differential equations began to emerge in the early 1900s and were fairly well known by the 1930s. And Turing machines invented in 1936 were based on thinking about arbitrary operations on sequences of discrete elements. (Notions in physics like the Ising model do not appear to have had a direct influence.)

The best-known way in which cellular automata were introduced (and which eventually led to their name) was through work by John von Neumann in trying to develop an abstract model of self-reproduction in biology—a topic which had emerged from investigations in cybernetics. Around 1947—perhaps based on chemical engineering—von Neumann began by thinking about models based on 3D

factories described by partial differential equations. Soon he changed to thinking about robotics and imagined perhaps implementing an example using a toy construction set. By analogy to electronic circuit layouts he realized however that 2D should be enough. And following a 1951 suggestion from Stanislaw Ulam (who may have already independently considered the problem) he simplified his model and ended up with a 2D cellular automaton (he apparently hoped later to convert the results back to differential equations). The particular cellular automaton he constructed in 1952–3 had 29 possible colors for each cell, and complicated rules specifically set up to emulate the operations of components of an electronic computer and various mechanical devices. To give a mathematical proof of the possibility of self-reproduction, von Neumann then outlined the construction of a 200,000 cell configuration which would reproduce itself (details were filled in by Arthur Burks in the early 1960s). Von Neumann appears to have believed—presumably in part from seeing the complexity of actual biological organisms and electronic computers—that something like this level of complexity would inevitably be necessary for a system to exhibit sophisticated capabilities such as self-reproduction. In this book I show that this is absolutely not the case, but with the intuition he had from existing mathematics and engineering von Neumann presumably never imagined this.

Two immediate threads emerged from von Neumann's work. The first, mostly in the 1960s, was increasingly whimsical discussion of building actual self-reproducing automata—often in the form of spacecraft. The second was an attempt to capture more of the essence of self-reproduction by mathematical studies of detailed properties of cellular automata. Over the course of the 1960s constructions were found for progressively simpler cellular automata capable of self-reproduction (see page 1179) and universal computation (see page 1115). Starting in the early 1960s a few rather simple general features of cellular automata thought to be relevant to self-reproduction were noticed—and were studied with increasingly elaborate technical formalism. (An example was the so-called Garden of Eden result that there can be configurations in cellular automata that arise only as initial conditions; see page 961.) There were also various explicit constructions done of cellular automata whose behavior showed particular simple features perhaps relevant to self-reproduction (such as so-called firing squad synchronization, as on page 1035).

By the end of the 1950s it had been noted that cellular automata could be viewed as parallel computers, and particularly in the 1960s a sequence of increasingly detailed and technical theorems—often analogous to ones about

Turing machines—were proved about their formal computational capabilities. At the end of the 1960s there then began to be attempts to connect cellular automata to mathematical discussions of dynamical systems—although as discussed below this had in fact already been done a decade earlier, with different terminology. And by the mid-1970s work on cellular automata had mostly become quite esoteric, and interest in it largely waned. (Some work nevertheless continued, particularly in Russia and Japan.) Note that even in computer science various names for cellular automata were used, including tessellation automata, cellular spaces, iterative automata, homogeneous structures and universal spaces.

As mentioned in the main text, there were by the late 1950s already all sorts of general-purpose computers on which simulations of cellular automata would have been easy to perform. But for the most part these computers were used to study traditional much more complicated systems such as partial differential equations. Around 1960, however, there were a couple of simulations related to 2D cellular automata done. Stanislaw Ulam and others used computers at Los Alamos to produce a handful of examples of what they called recursively defined geometrical objects—essentially the results of evolving generalized 2D cellular automata from single black cells (see page 928). Especially after obtaining larger pictures in 1967, Ulam noted that in at least one case fairly simple growth rules generated a complicated pattern, and mentioned that this might be relevant to biology. But perhaps because almost no progress was made on this with traditional mathematical methods, the result was not widely known, and was never pursued. (Ulam tried to construct a 1D analog, but ended up not with a cellular automaton, but instead with the sequences based on numbers discussed on page 908.) Around 1961 Edward Fredkin simulated the 2D analog of rule 90 on a PDP-1 computer, and noted its self-reproduction properties (see page 1179), but was generally more interested in finding simple physics-like features.

Despite the lack of investigation in science, one example of a cellular automaton did enter recreational computing in a major way in the early 1970s. Apparently motivated in part by questions in mathematical logic, and in part by work on "simulation games" by Ulam and others, John Conway in 1968 began doing experiments (mostly by hand, but later on a PDP-7 computer) with a variety of different 2D cellular automaton rules, and by 1970 had come up with a simple set of rules he called "The Game of Life", that exhibit a range of complex behavior (see page 249). Largely through popularization in *Scientific American* by Martin Gardner, Life became widely known. An immense amount of effort was spent finding special initial conditions that give particular forms of repetitive or other behavior, but virtually no systematic scientific work was done (perhaps in part because even Conway treated the system largely as a recreation), and almost without exception only the very specific rules of Life were ever investigated. (In 1978 as a possible 1D analog of Life easier to implement on early personal computers Jonathan Millen did however briefly consider what turns out to be the code 20 $k = 2$, $r = 2$ totalistic rule from page 283.)

Quite disconnected from all this, even in the 1950s, specific types of 2D and 1D cellular automata were already being used in various electronic devices and special-purpose computers. In fact, when digital image processing began to be done in the mid-1950s (for such applications as optical character recognition and microscopic particle counting) 2D cellular automaton rules were usually what was used to remove noise. And for several decades starting in 1960 a long line of so-called cellular logic systems were built to implement 2D cellular automata, mainly for image processing. Most of the rules used were specifically set up to have simple behavior, but occasionally it was noted as a largely recreational matter that for example patterns of alternating stripes ("custering") could be generated.

In the late 1950s and early 1960s schemes for electronic miniaturization and early integrated circuits were often based on having identical logical elements laid out on lines or grids to form so-called cellular arrays. In the early 1960s there was for a time interest in iterative arrays in which data would be run repeatedly through such systems. But few design principles emerged, and the technology for making chips with more elaborate and less uniform circuits developed rapidly. Ever since the 1960s the idea of making array or parallel computers has nevertheless resurfaced repeatedly, notably in systems like the ILLIAC IV from the 1960s and 1970s, and systolic arrays and various massively parallel computers from the 1980s. Typically the rules imagined for each element of such systems are however immensely more complicated than for any of the simple cellular automata I consider.

From at least the early 1940s, electronic or other digital delay lines or shift registers were a common way to store data such as digits of numbers, and by the late 1940s it had been noted that so-called linear feedback shift registers (see page 974) could generate complicated output sequences. These systems turn out to be essentially 1D additive cellular automata (like rule 90) with a limited number of cells (compare page 259). Extensive algebraic analysis of their behavior was done starting in the mid-1950s, but most of it concentrated on issues like repetition periods, and did not even explicitly uncover nested patterns. (Related analysis of linear recurrences over finite fields had been done in a few cases in the 1800s, and in some detail in the 1930s.) General 1D cellular automata are related to nonlinear feedback shift registers, and some explorations of these—including ones surprisingly close to rule 30 (see page 1088)—were made using special-purpose hardware by Solomon Golomb in 1956–9 for applications in jamming-resistant radio control—though again concentrating on issues like repetition periods. Linear feedback shift registers quickly became widely used in communications applications. Nonlinear feedback shift registers seem to have been used extensively for military cryptography, but despite persistent rumors the details of what was done continue to be secret.

In pure mathematics, infinite sequences of 0's and 1's have been considered in various forms since at least the late 1800s. Starting in the 1930s the development of symbolic dynamics (see page 960) led to the investigation of mappings of such sequences to themselves. And by the mid-1950s studies were being made (notably by Gustav Hedlund) of so-called shift-commuting block maps—which turn out to be exactly 1D cellular automata (see page 961). In the 1950s and early 1960s there was work in this area (at least in the U.S.) by a number of distinguished pure mathematicians, but since it was in large part for application to cryptography, much of it was kept secret. And what was published was mostly abstract theorems about features too global to reveal any of the kind of complexity I discuss.

Specific types of cellular automata have also arisen—usually under different names—in a vast range of situations. In the late 1950s and early 1960s what were essentially 1D cellular automata were studied as a way to optimize circuits for arithmetic and other operations. From the 1960s onward simulations of idealized neural networks sometimes had neurons connected to neighbors on a grid, yielding a 2D cellular automaton. Similarly, various models of active media—particularly heart and other muscles—and reaction-diffusion processes used a discrete grid and discrete excitation states, corresponding to a 2D cellular automaton. (In physics, discrete idealizations of statistical mechanics and dynamic versions of systems like the Ising model were sometimes close to cellular automata, except for the crucial difference of having randomness built into their underlying rules.) Additive cellular automata such as rule 90 had implicitly arisen in studies of binomial coefficient modulo primes in the 1800s (see page 870), but also appeared in various settings such as the "forests of stunted trees" studied around 1970.

Yet by the late 1970s, despite all these different directions, research on systems equivalent to cellular automata had largely petered out. That this should have happened just around the time when computers were first becoming widely available for exploratory work is ironic. But in a sense it was fortunate, because it allowed me when I started working on cellular automata in 1981 to define the field in a new way (though somewhat to my later regret I chose—in an attempt to recognize history—to use the name "cellular automata" for the systems I was studying). The publication of my first paper on cellular automata in 1983 (see page 881) led to a rapid increase of interest in the field, and over the years since then a steadily increasing number of papers (as indicated by the number of source documents in the Science Citation Index shown below) have been published on cellular automata—almost all following the directions I defined.

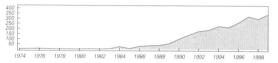

■ **Close approaches.** The basic phenomena in this chapter have come at least somewhat close to being discovered many times in the past. The historical progression of primary examples of this seem to be as follows:

- 500s–200s BC: Simply-stated problems such as finding primes or perfect numbers are presumably seen to have complicated solutions, but no general significance is attached to this (see pages 132 and 910).

- 1200s: Fibonacci sequences, Pascal's triangle and other rule-based numerical constructions are studied, but are found to show only simple behavior.

- 1500s: Leonardo da Vinci experiments with rules corresponding to simple geometrical constraints (see page 875), but finds only simple forms satisfying these constraints.

- 1700s: Leonhard Euler and others compute continued fraction representations for numbers with simple formulas (see pages 143 and 915), noting regularity in some cases, but making no comment in other cases.

- 1700s and 1800s: The digits of π and other transcendental numbers are seen to exhibit apparent randomness (see page 136), but the idea of thinking about this randomness as coming from the process of calculation does not arise.

- 1800s: The distribution of primes is studied extensively—but mostly its regularities, rather than its irregularities, are considered. (See page 132.)

- 1800s: Complicated behavior is found in the three-body problem, but it is assumed that with better mathematical techniques it will eventually be resolved. (See page 972.)

- 1880s: John Venn and others note the apparent randomness of the digits of π, but somehow take it for granted.

- 1906: Axel Thue studies simple substitution systems (see page 893) and finds behavior that seems complicated—though it turns out to be nested.

- 1910s: Gaston Julia and others study iterated maps, but concentrate on properties amenable to simple description.

- 1920: Moses Schönfinkel introduces combinators (see page 1121) but considers mostly cases specifically constructed to correspond to ordinary logical functions.

- 1921: Emil Post looks at a simple tag system (see page 894) whose behavior is difficult to predict, but failing to prove anything about it, goes on to other problems.

- 1920: The Ising model is introduced, but only statistics of configurations, and not any dynamics, are studied.

- 1931: Kurt Gödel establishes Gödel's Theorem (see page 782), but the constructions he uses are so complicated that he and others assume that simple systems can never exhibit similar phenomena.

- Mid-1930s: Alan Turing, Alonzo Church, Emil Post, etc. introduce various models of computation, but use them in constructing proofs, and do not investigate the actual behavior of simple examples.

- 1930s: The $3n+1$ problem (see page 904) is posed, and unpredictable behavior is found, but the main focus is on proving a simple result about it.

- Late 1940s and 1950s: Pseudorandom number generators are developed (see page 974), but are viewed as tricks whose behavior has no particular scientific significance.

- Late 1940s and early 1950s: Complex behavior is occasionally observed in fairly simple electronic devices built to illustrate ideas of cybernetics, but is usually viewed as something to avoid.

- 1952: Alan Turing applies computers to studying biological systems, but uses traditional mathematical models rather than, say, Turing machines.

- 1952–1953: John von Neumann makes theoretical studies of complicated cellular automata, but does not try looking at simpler cases, or simulating the systems on a computer.

- Mid-1950s: Enrico Fermi and collaborators simulate simple systems of nonlinear springs on a computer, but do not notice that simple initial conditions can lead to complicated behavior.

- Mid-1950s to mid-1960s: Specific 2D cellular automata are used for image processing; a few rules showing slightly complex behavior are noticed, but are considered of purely recreational interest.

- Late 1950s: Computer simulations of iterated maps are done, but concentrate mostly on repetitive behavior. (See page 918.)

- Late 1950s: Ideas from dynamical systems theory begin to be applied to systems equivalent to 1D cellular automata, but details of specific behavior are not studied except in trivial cases.

- Late 1950s: Idealized neural networks are simulated on digital computers, but the somewhat complicated behavior seen is considered mainly a distraction from the phenomena of interest, and is not investigated. (See page 1099.)

- Late 1950s: Berni Alder and Thomas Wainwright do computer simulations of dynamics of hard sphere idealized molecules, but concentrate on large-scale features that do not show complexity. (See page 999.)

- 1956–1959: Solomon Golomb simulates nonlinear feedback shift registers—some with rules close to rule 30—but studies mainly their repetition periods not their detailed complex behavior. (See page 1088.)

- 1960, 1967: Stanislaw Ulam and collaborators simulate systems close to 2D cellular automata, and note the appearance of complicated patterns (see above).

- 1961: Edward Fredkin simulates the 2D analog of rule 90 and notes features that amount to nesting (see above).

- Early 1960s: Students at MIT try running many small computer programs, and in some cases visualizing their output. They discover various examples (such as "munching foos") that produce nested behavior (see page 871), but do not go further.

- 1962: Marvin Minsky and others study many simple Turing machines, but do not go far enough to discover the complex behavior shown on page 81.

- 1963: Edward Lorenz simulates a differential equation that shows complex behavior (see page 971), but concentrates on its lack of periodicity and sensitive dependence on initial conditions.

- Mid-1960s: Simulations of random Boolean networks are done (see page 936), but concentrate on simple average properties.

- 1970: John Conway introduces the Game of Life 2D cellular automaton (see above).

- 1971: Michael Paterson considers a class of simple 2D Turing machines that he calls worms and that exhibit complicated behavior (see page 930).

- 1973: I look at some 2D cellular automata, but force the rules to have properties that prevent complex behavior (see page 864).

- Mid-1970s: Benoit Mandelbrot develops the idea of fractals (see page 934), and emphasizes the importance of computer graphics in studying complex forms.

- Mid-1970s: Tommaso Toffoli simulates all 4096 2D cellular automata of the simplest type, but studies mainly just their stabilization from random initial conditions.

- Late 1970s: Douglas Hofstadter studies a recursive sequence with complicated behavior (see page 907), but does not take it far enough to conclude much.

- 1979: Benoit Mandelbrot discovers the Mandelbrot set (see page 934) but concentrates on its nested structure, not its overall complexity.

- 1981: I begin to study 1D cellular automata, and generate a small picture analogous to the one of rule 30 on page 27, but fail to study it.

- 1984: I make a detailed study of rule 30, and begin to understand the significance of it and systems like it.

- **The importance of explicitness.** Looking through this book, one striking difference with most previous scientific accounts is the presence of so many explicit pictures that show how every element in a system behaves. In the past, people have tended to consider it more scientific to give only numerical summaries of such data. But most of the phenomena I discuss in this book could not have been found without such explicit pictures. (See also page 108.)

- **My work on cellular automata.** I began serious work on cellular automata in the middle of 1981. I had been thinking for some time about how complicated patterns could arise in natural systems—in apparent violation of the Second Law of Thermodynamics. I had been particularly interested in self-gravitating gases where the basic physics seemed clear, but where complex phenomena like galaxy formation seemed to occur. I had also been interested in neural networks, where there had been fairly simple models developed by Warren McCulloch and Walter Pitts in the 1940s. I came up with cellular automata as an attempt to capture the essential features of a range of systems, from self-gravitating gases to neural networks. I wanted to find models that had a simple structure like the Ising model in statistical mechanics (studied since the 1920s), but which had definite rules for time evolution and could easily be simulated on a computer. Ironically enough, while cellular automata are good for many things, they turn out to be rather unsuitable for modelling either self-gravitating gases or neural networks. (See page 1021). But by the time I realized this, it was clear that cellular automata were of great interest for many other purposes.

I did my first major computer experiments on cellular automata late in 1981 (see page 19). Two features initially struck me most. First, that starting from random initial conditions, cellular automata could organize themselves to produce complex patterns. And second, that in cases like rule 90 simple initial conditions led to nested or fractal patterns. During the first half of 1982, I worked hard to analyze the behavior of cellular automata using ideas from statistical mechanics, dynamical systems theory and discrete mathematics. And in June 1982, I finished my first paper on cellular automata, entitled "Statistical Mechanics of Cellular Automata". Published in the journal *Reviews of Modern Physics* in July 1983, this paper already presents in raw form many of the key ideas that led to the development of the science described in this book. It discusses the fact that by not using traditional mathematical equations, simple models can potentially be made to reproduce complex phenomena, and it mentions some of the consequences of viewing models like cellular automata as computational systems. The paper also contained a small picture of rule 30 started from a single black cell. But at the time, I did not study this picture in detail, and I tacitly assumed that whenever I saw randomness it must come from the random initial conditions that I used. (See page 112.)

It was some time in the fall of 1981 that I first found out (at a dinner with some then-young MIT computer scientists) that a version of the systems I had invented had been studied before under the name of "cellular automata". (I had been aware of the Game of Life, but its recreational emphasis had put me off studying it.) Knowing the name cellular automata, I was able to track down quite a number of relevant papers from the 1950s and 1960s. But I found that active research on what had been called cellular automata had more or less petered out (with the slight exception of a group at MIT at that time mainly concerned with building special-purpose hardware for 2D cellular automata). By late 1982 preprints of my paper on cellular automata had created quite a stir, and I got involved in organizing a conference held in March 1983 at Los Alamos to bring together many people newly interested in cellular automata with earlier workers in the field.

As part of preparing for that conference, I decided to use the graphics capabilities of the new workstation computer I had just obtained (a very early unit from Sun Microsystems) to investigate in a systematic way the behavior of a large collection of different cellular automata. And after spending several weeks looking at screen after screen of patterns—and trying to analyze their properties—I came to the conclusion that one could identify in the behavior of cellular automata with random initial conditions just four basic classes, each with its own characteristic features (see page 231).

In 1982 and early 1983, my efforts to analyze cellular automata were mainly based on ideas from discrete mathematics and dynamical systems theory. In the course of 1983, I also began to make serious use of formal language theory and the theory of computation. But for the most part I concentrated on characterizing behavior obtained from all possible initial conditions. And in fact I still vaguely assumed that if simple initial conditions were used, only fairly simple behavior would be obtained. Several of my papers had actually shown quite detailed pictures where this was not the case. I had noticed them, but they had never been among the examples I had studied in depth, partly for the superficial reason that the rules they involved were not symmetrical, or inevitably led to patterns that were otherwise not convenient for display. I do not know exactly what made me start looking more carefully at simple initial conditions, though I believe that I first systematically generated high-resolution pictures of all the $k = 2$, $r = 1$ cellular automata as an exercise for an early laserprinter— probably at the beginning of 1984. And I do know that for example on June 1, 1984 I printed out pictures of rule 30, rule 110 and $k = 2$, $r = 2$ totalistic code 10 (see note below), took them with me on a flight from New York to London, and a few days later was in Sweden talking about randomness in rule 30 and its potential significance.

A month or so later, writing an article for *Scientific American*—nominally on the subject of software in science and mathematics—led me to think more carefully about basic issues of computation and modelling, and to describe for the first time the idea of computational irreducibility (see page 737). In the fall of 1984 I began to investigate some of the implications of what I had discovered about cellular automata for foundational questions in science. And by early 1985 I had written what I consider to be my two most fundamental (if excessively short) papers from the period: one on undecidability and intractability in theoretical physics, and the other on intrinsic randomness generation and the origins of randomness in physical systems.

In the early summer of 1985 I was doing consulting at a startup company called Thinking Machines Corporation, which had developed a massively parallel computer called the Connection Machine that was fairly well suited to cellular automaton simulation. Partly as an application for this computer I then ended up making a detailed study of rule 30 and its randomness—among other things proposing it as a practical random sequence generator and cryptosystem.

I had always thought that cellular automata could be a way to get at foundational questions in thermodynamics and hydrodynamics. And in mid-1985, partly in an attempt to find uses for the Connection Machine, I devised a practical scheme for doing fluid mechanics with cellular automata (see page 378). Then over the course of that winter and the following spring I analyzed the scheme and worked out its correspondence to the traditional continuum approach.

By 1986, however, I felt that I had answered at least the first round of obvious questions about cellular automata, and it increasingly seemed that it would not be easier to go further with the computational tools available. In June 1986 I organized one last conference on cellular automata—then in August 1986 essentially left the field to begin the development of *Mathematica*.

Over the years, I have come back to look at cellular automata again and again, and every time I have been amazed and delighted by the richness of the phenomena they exhibit. As I argue in this book, a vast range of systems must in the end show the same basic phenomena. But cellular automata— and especially 1D ones—make the phenomena particularly clear, which is why even after investigating all sorts of other systems 1D cellular automata are still the most common examples that I use in this book.

■ **My papers.** The primary papers that I published about cellular automata and other issues related to this book were (the dates indicate when I finished my work on each paper; the papers were actually published 6–12 months later):

- "Statistical mechanics of cellular automata" (June 1982) (introducing 1D cellular automata and studying many of their properties)

- "Algebraic properties of cellular automata" (with Olivier Martin and Andrew Odlyzko) (February 1983) (analyzing additive cellular automata such as rule 90)

- "Universality and complexity in cellular automata" (April 1983) (classifying cellular automaton behavior)

- "Computation theory of cellular automata" (November 1983) (characterizing behavior using formal language theory)

- "Two-dimensional cellular automata" (with Norman Packard) (October 1984) (extending results to two dimensions)

- "Undecidability and intractability in theoretical physics" (October 1984) (introducing computational irreducibility)

- "Origins of randomness in physical systems" (February 1985) (introducing intrinsic randomness generation)

- "Random sequence generation by cellular automata" (July 1985) (a detailed study of rule 30)

- "Thermodynamics and hydrodynamics of cellular automata" (with James Salem) (November 1985) (continuum behavior from cellular automata)

- "Approaches to complexity engineering" (December 1985) (finding systems that achieve specified goals)

- "Cellular automaton fluids: Basic theory" (March 1986) (deriving the Navier-Stokes equations from cellular automata)

The ideas in the first five and the very last of these papers have been reasonably well absorbed over the past fifteen or so years. But those in the other five have not, and indeed seem to require the whole development of this book to be able to present in an appropriate way.

Other significant publications of mine providing relevant summaries were (the dates here are for actual publication—sometimes close to writing, but sometimes long delayed):

- "Computers in science and mathematics" (September 1984) (*Scientific American* article about foundations of the computational approach to science and mathematics)

- "Cellular automata as models of complexity" (October 1984) (*Nature* article introducing cellular automata)

- "Geometry of binomial coefficients" (November 1984) (additive cellular automata and nested patterns)

- "Twenty problems in the theory of cellular automata" (1985) (a list of unsolved problems to attack—most now finally resolved in this book)

- "Tables of cellular automaton properties" (June 1986) (features of elementary cellular automata)

- "Cryptography with cellular automata" (1986) (using rule 30 as a cryptosystem)

- "Complex systems theory" (1988) (1984 speech suggesting the research direction for the new Santa Fe Institute)

■ **Code 10.** Rule 30 is by many measures the simplest cellular automaton that generates randomness from a single black initial cell. But there are other simple examples—that historically I noticed slightly earlier than rule 30, though did not study—that occur in $k = 2$, $r = 2$ totalistic rules. And indeed among the 64 such rules, 13 show randomness. An example shown below is code 10, which specifies that if 1 or 3 cells out of 5 are black then the next cell is black; otherwise it is white.

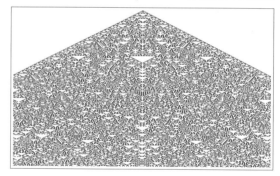

The World of Simple Programs

More Cellular Automata

■ **Page 53 · Numbering scheme.** I introduced the numbering scheme used here in the 1983 paper where I first discussed one-dimensional cellular automata (see page 881). I termed two-color nearest-neighbor cellular automata "elementary" to reflect the idea that their rules are as simple as possible.

■ **Page 55 · Rule equivalences.** The table below gives basic equivalences between elementary cellular automaton rules. In each block the second entry is the rule obtained by interchanging black and white, the third entry is the rule obtained by interchanging left and right, and the fourth entry the rule obtained by applying both operations. (The smallest rule number is given in boldface.) For a rule with number *n* the two operations correspond respectively to computing *1 - Reverse[list]* and *list[[{1, 5, 3, 7, 2, 6, 4, 8}]]* with *list = IntegerDigits[n, 2, 8]*.

■ **Special rules.** Rule 51: complement; rule 170: left shift; rule 204: identity; rule 240: right shift. These rules only ever depend on one cell in each neighborhood.

■ **Rule expressions.** The table on the next page gives Boolean expressions for each of the elementary rules. The expressions

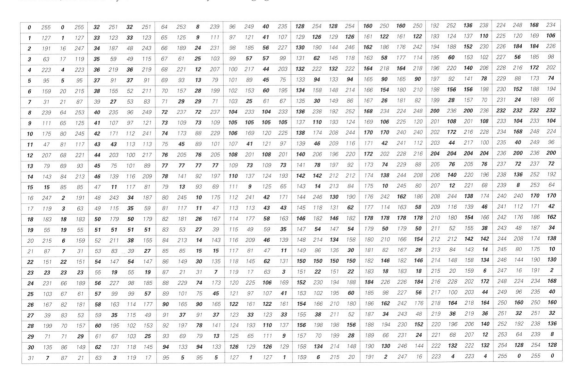

0	255	0	255	**32**	251	32	251	64	253	**8**	239	96	249	**40**	235	**128**	254	128	254	**160**	250	160	250	192	252	**136**	238	224	248	**168**	234
1	127	1	127	**33**	123	33	123	65	125	**9**	111	97	121	**41**	107	129	126	129	126	161	122	161	122	193	124	137	**110**	225	120	169	**106**
2	191	16	247	**34**	187	48	243	66	189	**24**	231	98	185	**56**	227	**130**	190	144	246	**162**	186	176	242	194	188	**152**	230	226	**184**	184	226
3	63	17	119	**35**	59	49	115	67	61	**25**	103	99	**57**	57	99	131	**62**	145	118	163	**58**	177	114	195	**60**	153	102	227	**56**	185	98
4	223	4	223	**36**	219	36	219	68	221	**12**	207	100	217	**44**	203	**132**	222	132	222	**164**	218	164	218	196	220	**140**	206	228	216	**172**	202
5	95	5	95	**37**	91	37	91	69	93	**13**	79	101	89	**45**	75	133	94	133	94	165	90	165	90	197	92	141	**78**	229	88	173	**74**
6	159	20	215	**38**	155	52	211	70	157	**28**	199	102	153	**60**	195	**134**	158	148	214	**166**	154	180	210	198	**156**	156	198	230	**152**	188	194
7	31	21	87	**39**	27	53	83	71	**29**	29	71	103	**25**	61	67	135	**30**	149	86	167	**26**	181	82	199	**28**	157	70	231	**24**	189	66
8	239	64	253	**40**	235	96	249	**72**	237	72	237	**104**	233	104	233	**136**	238	192	252	**168**	234	224	248	**200**	236	200	236	**232**	232	232	232
9	111	65	125	**41**	107	97	121	**73**	109	73	109	**105**	105	105	105	137	**110**	193	124	169	**106**	225	120	201	**108**	201	108	233	**104**	233	104
10	175	80	245	**42**	171	112	241	74	173	**88**	229	106	169	**120**	225	**138**	174	208	244	**170**	170	240	240	202	**172**	216	228	234	**168**	248	224
11	47	81	117	**43**	43	113	113	75	**45**	89	101	107	**41**	121	97	139	**46**	209	116	171	**42**	241	112	203	**44**	217	100	235	**40**	249	96
12	207	68	221	**44**	203	100	217	**76**	205	76	205	**108**	201	108	201	**140**	206	196	220	**172**	202	228	216	**204**	204	204	204	**236**	200	236	200
13	79	69	93	**45**	75	101	89	**77**	77	77	77	**109**	73	109	73	141	**78**	197	92	173	**74**	229	88	205	**76**	205	76	237	**72**	237	72
14	143	84	213	**46**	139	116	209	78	141	**92**	197	110	137	**124**	193	**142**	142	212	212	174	**138**	244	208	206	**140**	220	196	238	**136**	252	192
15	**15**	85	85	47	**11**	117	81	79	**13**	93	69	111	**9**	125	65	143	**14**	213	84	175	**10**	245	80	207	**12**	221	68	239	**8**	253	64
16	247	**2**	191	48	243	**34**	187	80	245	**10**	175	112	241	**42**	171	144	246	**130**	190	176	242	**162**	186	208	244	**138**	174	240	240	**170**	170
17	119	**3**	63	49	115	**35**	59	81	117	**11**	47	113	113	**43**	43	145	118	**131**	62	177	114	**163**	58	209	116	**139**	46	241	112	**171**	42
18	183	18	183	**50**	179	50	179	82	181	**26**	167	114	177	**58**	163	**146**	182	146	182	**178**	178	178	178	210	180	**154**	166	242	176	**186**	162
19	55	19	55	**51**	51	51	51	83	53	**27**	39	115	49	**59**	35	147	54	147	54	179	50	179	50	211	52	155	**38**	243	48	187	**34**
20	215	**6**	159	52	211	**38**	155	84	213	**14**	143	116	209	**46**	139	148	214	**134**	158	180	210	166	154	212	212	**142**	142	244	208	174	**138**
21	87	**7**	31	53	83	**39**	27	85	85	**15**	15	117	81	**47**	11	149	86	**135**	30	181	82	167	26	213	84	143	**14**	245	80	175	**10**
22	151	22	151	**54**	147	54	147	86	149	**30**	135	118	145	**62**	131	**150**	150	150	150	182	146	182	146	214	148	158	**134**	246	144	190	**130**
23	23	23	23	**55**	19	55	19	87	21	**31**	7	119	17	**63**	3	151	22	151	22	183	18	183	18	215	20	159	**6**	247	16	191	**2**
24	231	66	189	**56**	227	98	185	88	229	**74**	173	120	225	**106**	169	**152**	230	194	188	**184**	226	226	184	216	228	202	**172**	248	224	234	**168**
25	103	67	61	**57**	99	99	57	89	101	**75**	45	121	97	**107**	41	153	102	195	**60**	185	98	227	**56**	217	100	203	**44**	249	96	235	**40**
26	167	82	181	**58**	163	114	177	**90**	165	90	165	**122**	161	122	161	154	166	210	180	186	**162**	242	176	218	**164**	218	164	250	**160**	250	160
27	39	83	53	**59**	35	115	49	**91**	37	91	37	**123**	33	123	33	155	**38**	211	52	187	**34**	243	48	219	**36**	219	36	251	**32**	251	32
28	199	70	157	**60**	195	102	153	92	197	**78**	141	124	193	**110**	137	**156**	198	198	156	188	194	230	**152**	220	196	206	**140**	252	192	238	**136**
29	71	71	29	**61**	67	103	25	93	69	79	**13**	125	65	111	**9**	157	70	199	**28**	189	66	231	**24**	221	68	207	**12**	253	64	239	**8**
30	135	86	149	**62**	131	118	145	**94**	133	94	133	**126**	129	126	129	158	**134**	214	148	190	**130**	246	144	222	**132**	222	132	254	**128**	254	128
31	**7**	87	21	63	**3**	119	17	95	**5**	95	5	127	**1**	127	1	159	**6**	215	20	191	**2**	247	16	223	**4**	223	4	255	**0**	255	0

rule 0 : 0	rule 64 : p ∧ q ∧ (¬r)	rule 128 : p ∧ q ∧ r	rule 192 : p ∧ q
rule 1 : ¬(p ∨ q ∨ r)	rule 65 : ¬((p ∨ q) ∨ r)	rule 129 : ¬((p ⊻ q) ∨ (p ⊻ r))	rule 193 : p ⊻ (p ∨ q ∨ (¬r)) ⊻ q
rule 2 : (¬p) ∧ (¬q) ∧ r	rule 66 : (p ⊻ r) ∧ (q ⊻ r)	rule 130 : (p ⊻ q ⊻ r) ∧ r	rule 194 : p ⊻ (p ∨ q ∨ r) ⊻ q
rule 3 : ¬(p ∨ q)	rule 67 : p ⊻ (p ∧ q ∧ r) ⊻ (¬q)	rule 131 : p ⊻ (p ∧ q ∧ (¬r)) ⊻ (¬q)	rule 195 : p ⊻ (¬q)
rule 4 : (¬(p ∨ r)) ∧ q	rule 68 : q ∧ (¬r)	rule 132 : (p ⊻ q ⊻ r) ∧ q	rule 196 : (p ∨ (¬r)) ∧ q
rule 5 : ¬(p ∨ r)	rule 69 : ((¬p) ∨ q ∨ r) ⊻ r	rule 133 : p ⊻ (p ∧ (¬q) ∧ r) ⊻ (¬r)	rule 197 : (¬(p ∨ (q ⊻ r))) ∨ q
rule 6 : (¬p) ∧ (q ⊻ r)	rule 70 : ((p ∧ r) ⊻ q) ⊻ r	rule 134 : (p ∧ (q ⊻ r)) ⊻ q ⊻ r	rule 198 : (p ∧ r) ⊻ q ⊻ r
rule 7 : ¬(p ∨ (q ∧ r))	rule 71 : ((p ⊻ (¬r)) ∨ q) ⊻ r	rule 135 : (¬p) ⊻ (q ∧ r)	rule 199 : p ⊻ (p ∨ (¬q) ∨ r) ⊻ q
rule 8 : (¬p) ∧ q ∧ r	rule 72 : (p ∧ q) ⊻ (q ∧ r)	rule 136 : q ∧ r	rule 200 : (p ∨ r) ∧ q
rule 9 : ¬(p ∨ (q ⊻ r))	rule 73 : ¬((p ∧ r) ∨ (p ⊻ q ⊻ r))	rule 137 : ((¬p) ∨ q ∨ r) ⊻ q ⊻ r	rule 201 : (¬(p ∨ r)) ⊻ q
rule 10 : (¬p) ∧ r	rule 74 : (p ∧ (q ∨ r)) ⊻ r	rule 138 : (p ∧ (¬q) ∧ r) ⊻ r	rule 202 : (p ∧ (q ⊻ r)) ⊻ r
rule 11 : p ⊻ (p ∨ (¬q) ∨ r)	rule 75 : p ⊻ ((¬q) ∨ r)	rule 139 : ¬((p ∨ q) ∧ (q ∧ r))	rule 203 : (p ⊻ (¬q)) ∨ (q ∧ r)
rule 12 : (p ∧ q ∧ r) ⊻ q	rule 76 : (p ∧ q ∧ r) ⊻ q	rule 140 : (p ∨ q ∧ r) ⊻ q	rule 204 : q
rule 13 : p ⊻ (p ∨ q ∨ (¬r))	rule 77 : p ⊻ ((p ∨ q) ∨ (p ⊻ (¬r)))	rule 141 : p ⊻ ((p ⊻ q) ∨ (¬r))	rule 205 : (¬(p ∨ r)) ∨ q
rule 14 : p ⊻ (p ∨ q ∨ r)	rule 78 : p ⊻ ((p ⊻ q) ∨ r)	rule 142 : p ⊻ ((p ∨ q) ∨ (p ⊻ r))	rule 206 : ((¬p) ∧ r) ∨ q
rule 15 : ¬p	rule 79 : (¬p) ∨ (q ∧ (¬r))	rule 143 : (¬p) ∨ (q ∧ r)	rule 207 : ¬(p ∧ (¬q))
rule 16 : p ∧ (¬q) ∧ (¬r)	rule 80 : p ∧ (¬r)	rule 144 : p ∧ (q ⊻ r)	rule 208 : p ∧ (q ∨ (¬r))
rule 17 : ¬(q ∨ r)	rule 81 : (p ∨ (¬q) ∨ r) ⊻ r	rule 145 : ((¬p) ∧ q ∧ r) ⊻ q ⊻ (¬r)	rule 209 : ¬((p ∧ q) ⊻ (q ∨ r))
rule 18 : (p ⊻ q ⊻ r) ∧ (¬q)	rule 82 : (p ∨ (q ∧ r)) ⊻ r	rule 146 : p ⊻ ((p ∨ r) ∧ q) ⊻ r	rule 210 : p ⊻ (q ∧ r) ⊻ r
rule 19 : ¬((p ∧ r) ∨ q)	rule 83 : (p ∨ (q ⊻ (¬r))) ⊻ r	rule 147 : (p ∧ r) ⊻ (¬q)	rule 211 : p ⊻ ((¬p) ∨ q ∨ r) ⊻ q
rule 20 : (p ⊻ q) ∧ (¬r)	rule 84 : (p ∨ q ∧ r) ⊻ r	rule 148 : p ⊻ ((p ∨ q) ∧ r) ⊻ q	rule 212 : ((p ∨ q) ⊻ (p ∨ r)) ⊻ r
rule 21 : ¬((p ∧ q) ∨ r)	rule 85 : ¬r	rule 149 : (p ∧ q) ⊻ (¬r)	rule 213 : (p ∧ q) ∨ (¬r)
rule 22 : p ⊻ (p ∧ q ∧ r) ⊻ q ⊻ r	rule 86 : (p ∨ q) ⊻ r	rule 150 : p ⊻ q ⊻ r	rule 214 : (p ∧ r) ∨ (p ⊻ q ⊻ r)
rule 23 : p ⊻ ((p ⊻ (¬q)) ∨ (q ⊻ r))	rule 87 : ¬((p ∨ q) ∧ r)	rule 151 : p ⊻ (¬(p ∨ q ∨ r)) ⊻ q ⊻ r	rule 215 : ¬((p ⊻ q) ∧ r)
rule 24 : (p ⊻ q) ∧ (p ⊻ r)	rule 88 : p ⊻ ((p ∨ q) ∧ r)	rule 152 : (p ∧ q ∨ r) ⊻ q ⊻ r	rule 216 : p ⊻ ((p ⊻ q) ∧ r)
rule 25 : (p ∧ q ∧ r) ⊻ q ⊻ (¬r)	rule 89 : (p ∨ (¬q)) ⊻ r	rule 153 : q ⊻ (¬r)	rule 217 : (p ∧ q) ∨ (q ⊻ (¬r))
rule 26 : p ⊻ ((p ∧ q) ∨ r)	rule 90 : p ⊻ r	rule 154 : p ⊻ (p ∧ q) ⊻ r	rule 218 : p ⊻ (p ∧ q ∧ r) ⊻ r
rule 27 : p ⊻ ((p ⊻ (¬q)) ∨ r)	rule 91 : p ⊻ (¬(p ∨ q ∨ r)) ⊻ r	rule 155 : (p ∨ q ∨ (¬r)) ⊻ q ⊻ r	rule 219 : (p ⊻ r) ∨ (p ⊻ (¬q))
rule 28 : p ⊻ ((p ∧ r) ∨ q)	rule 92 : (p ∨ (q ⊻ r)) ⊻ r	rule 156 : p ⊻ (p ∧ r) ⊻ q	rule 220 : (p ∧ (¬r)) ∨ q
rule 29 : p ⊻ ((p ⊻ (¬r)) ∨ q)	rule 93 : ¬((p ∨ (¬q)) ∧ r)	rule 157 : (p ∨ (¬q) ∨ r) ⊻ q ⊻ r	rule 221 : q ∨ (¬r)
rule 30 : p ⊻ (q ∨ r)	rule 94 : (p ∧ r) ⊻ (p ∨ q ∨ r)	rule 158 : (p ⊻ q ⊻ r) ∨ (q ∧ r)	rule 222 : (p ⊻ q ⊻ r) ∨ q
rule 31 : ¬(p ∧ (q ∨ r))	rule 95 : ¬(p ∧ r)	rule 159 : ¬(p ∧ (q ⊻ r))	rule 223 : ¬(p ∧ (¬q) ∧ r)
rule 32 : p ∧ (¬q) ∧ r	rule 96 : p ∧ (q ⊻ r)	rule 160 : p ∧ r	rule 224 : p ∧ (q ∨ r)
rule 33 : ¬((p ⊻ q ⊻ r) ∨ q)	rule 97 : p ⊻ ((p ∨ q ∨ r) ∨ (q ∧ r))	rule 161 : p ⊻ (p ∨ (¬q) ∨ r) ⊻ r	rule 225 : p ⊻ (¬(q ∨ r))
rule 34 : (¬q) ∧ r	rule 98 : ((p ∨ r) ∧ q) ⊻ r	rule 162 : (p ∨ (¬q)) ∧ r	rule 226 : (p ∧ q) ⊻ (q ∨ r) ⊻ r
rule 35 : ((¬p) ∨ q ∨ r) ⊻ q	rule 99 : ((¬p) ∨ r) ⊻ q	rule 163 : ((¬p) ∨ (q ⊻ r)) ∨ q	rule 227 : (p ∧ r) ∨ (p ⊻ (¬q))
rule 36 : (p ⊻ q) ∧ (q ⊻ r)	rule 100 : ((p ∨ q) ∧ r) ⊻ q	rule 164 : p ⊻ (p ∨ q ∨ r) ⊻ r	rule 228 : ((p ⊻ q) ∧ r) ∨ q
rule 37 : p ⊻ (p ∧ q ∧ r) ⊻ (¬r)	rule 101 : p ⊻ (p ∧ q) ⊻ (¬r)	rule 165 : p ⊻ (¬r)	rule 229 : (p ∧ q) ∨ (p ⊻ (¬r))
rule 38 : ((p ∧ q) ∨ r) ⊻ q	rule 102 : q ⊻ r	rule 166 : (p ∧ q) ⊻ q ⊻ r	rule 230 : (p ∧ q ∧ r) ⊻ q ⊻ r
rule 39 : ((p ⊻ (¬q)) ∨ r) ⊻ q	rule 103 : (¬(p ∨ q ∨ r)) ⊻ q ⊻ r	rule 167 : p ⊻ (p ∨ q ∨ (¬r)) ⊻ r	rule 231 : (p ⊻ (¬q)) ∨ (q ⊻ r)
rule 40 : (p ⊻ q) ∧ r	rule 104 : p ⊻ (p ∨ q ∨ r) ⊻ q ⊻ r	rule 168 : (p ∨ q) ∧ r	rule 232 : (p ∧ q) ∨ ((p ∨ q) ∧ r)
rule 41 : ¬((p ∧ q) ∨ (p ⊻ q ⊻ r))	rule 105 : p ⊻ q ⊻ (¬r)	rule 169 : (¬(p ∨ q)) ⊻ r	rule 233 : p ⊻ (p ∧ q ∧ r) ⊻ q ⊻ (¬r)
rule 42 : (p ∧ q ∧ r) ⊻ r	rule 106 : (p ∧ q) ⊻ r	rule 170 : r	rule 234 : (p ∧ q) ∨ r
rule 43 : p ⊻ ((p ⊻ r) ∨ (p ⊻ (¬q)))	rule 107 : p ⊻ (p ∨ q ∨ (¬r)) ⊻ q ⊻ r	rule 171 : (¬(p ∨ q)) ∨ r	rule 235 : (p ⊻ (¬q)) ∨ r
rule 44 : (p ∧ (q ∨ r)) ⊻ q	rule 108 : (p ∧ r) ⊻ q	rule 172 : (p ∧ (q ⊻ r)) ⊻ q	rule 236 : (p ∧ r) ∨ q
rule 45 : p ⊻ (q ∨ (¬r))	rule 109 : p ⊻ (p ∨ (¬q) ∨ r) ⊻ q ⊻ r	rule 173 : (p ⊻ (¬r)) ∨ (q ∧ r)	rule 237 : (p ⊻ (¬r)) ∨ q
rule 46 : (p ∧ q) ⊻ (q ∨ r)	rule 110 : (p ∧ q ∧ r) ⊻ q ⊻ r	rule 174 : (p ∧ q) ∨ r	rule 238 : q ∨ r
rule 47 : (¬q) ∨ ((¬q) ∧ r)	rule 111 : (¬p) ∨ (q ⊻ r)	rule 175 : (¬p) ∨ r	rule 239 : (¬p) ∨ q ∨ r
rule 48 : p ∧ (¬q)	rule 112 : p ⊻ (p ∧ q ∧ r)	rule 176 : p ∧ ((¬q) ∨ r)	rule 240 : p
rule 49 : (p ∨ q ∨ (¬r)) ⊻ q	rule 113 : p ⊻ (¬((p ∨ q) ∨ (p ⊻ r)))	rule 177 : p ⊻ (¬((p ∧ q) ∨ r))	rule 241 : p ∨ (¬(q ∨ r))
rule 50 : (p ∨ q ∨ r) ⊻ q	rule 114 : ((p ∨ q) ∧ r) ⊻ r	rule 178 : ((p ∨ q) ∧ r) ⊻ q	rule 242 : p ∨ ((¬q) ∧ r)
rule 51 : ¬q	rule 115 : (p ∧ (¬r)) ∨ (¬q)	rule 179 : (p ∧ r) ∨ (¬q)	rule 243 : p ∨ (¬q)
rule 52 : (p ∨ (q ∧ r)) ⊻ q	rule 116 : (p ∨ q) ⊻ (q ∧ r)	rule 180 : p ⊻ q ⊻ (q ∧ r)	rule 244 : p ∨ (q ∧ (¬r))
rule 53 : (p ∨ (q ⊻ (¬r))) ⊻ q	rule 117 : (p ∧ (¬q)) ∨ (¬r)	rule 181 : p ⊻ ((¬p) ∨ q ∨ r) ⊻ r	rule 245 : p ∨ (¬r)
rule 54 : (p ∨ r) ⊻ q	rule 118 : (p ∨ r) ⊻ (q ∧ r)	rule 182 : (p ∧ r) ⊻ (p ∨ q ∨ r)	rule 246 : p ∨ (q ⊻ r)
rule 55 : ¬((p ∨ r) ∧ q)	rule 119 : ¬(q ∧ r)	rule 183 : (p ⊻ q ⊻ r) ∨ (¬q)	rule 247 : p ∨ (¬q) ∨ (¬r)
rule 56 : p ⊻ ((p ∨ r) ∧ q)	rule 120 : p ⊻ (q ∧ r)	rule 184 : p ⊻ (p ∧ q) ⊻ (q ∧ r)	rule 248 : p ∨ (q ∧ r)
rule 57 : (p ∨ (¬r)) ⊻ q	rule 121 : p ⊻ ((¬p) ∨ q ∨ r) ⊻ q ⊻ r	rule 185 : (p ∧ r) ∨ (q ⊻ (¬r))	rule 249 : p ∨ (q ⊻ (¬r))
rule 58 : (p ∨ (q ⊻ r)) ⊻ q	rule 122 : p ⊻ (p ∧ (¬q) ∧ r)	rule 186 : (p ∧ (¬q)) ∨ r	rule 250 : p ∨ r
rule 59 : ((¬p) ∧ r) ∨ (¬q)	rule 123 : ¬((p ⊻ q ⊻ r) ∧ q)	rule 187 : (¬q) ∨ r	rule 251 : p ∨ (¬q) ∨ r
rule 60 : p ⊻ q	rule 124 : p ⊻ (p ∧ q ∧ (¬r)) ⊻ q	rule 188 : p ⊻ (p ∧ q ∧ r) ⊻ q	rule 252 : p ∨ q
rule 61 : p ⊻ (p ∨ q ∨ r) ⊻ (¬q)	rule 125 : (p ∨ q) ⊻ (¬r)	rule 189 : (p ∧ q) ∨ (p ⊻ (¬r))	rule 253 : p ∨ q ∨ (¬r)
rule 62 : (p ∧ q) ⊻ (p ∨ q ∨ r)	rule 126 : (p ⊻ q) ∨ (p ⊻ r)	rule 190 : (p ⊻ q) ∨ r	rule 254 : p ∨ q ∨ r
rule 63 : ¬(p ∧ q)	rule 127 : ¬(p ∧ q ∧ r)	rule 191 : (¬p) ∨ (¬q) ∨ r	rule 255 : 1

use the minimum possible number of operators; when there are several equivalent forms, I give the most uniform and symmetrical one. Note that $\veebar$ stands for *Xor*.

■ **Rule orderings.** The fact that successive rules often show very different behavior does not appear to be affected by using alternative orderings such as Gray code (see page 901.)

■ **Page 58 · Algebraic forms.** The rules here can be expressed in algebraic terms (see page 869) as follows:

- Rule 22: *Mod[p + q + r + p q r, 2]*
- Rule 60: *Mod[p + q, 2]*
- Rule 105: *Mod[1 + p + q + r, 2]*
- Rule 129: *Mod[1 + p + q + r + p q + q r + p r, 2]*
- Rule 150: *Mod[p + q + r, 2]*
- Rule 225: *Mod[1 + p + q + r + q r, 2]*

Note that rules 60, 105 and 150 are additive, like rule 90.

■ **Rule 150.** This rule can be viewed as an analog of rule 90 in which the values of three cells, rather than two, are added modulo 2. Corresponding to the result on page 870 for rule 90, the number of black cells at row t in the pattern from rule 150 is given by

$Apply[Times, Map[(2^{\#+2} - (-1)^{\#+2})/3\ \&,$
$\quad Cases[Split[IntegerDigits[t, 2]], k : \{(1)..\} :\to Length[k]]]]$

There are a total of 2^m *Fibonacci*[m + 2] black cells in the pattern obtained up to step 2^m, implying fractal dimension $Log[2, 1 + \sqrt{5}]$. (See also page 956.)

The value at step t in the column immediately adjacent to the center is the nested sequence discussed on page 892 and given by *Mod[IntegerExponent[t, 2], 2]*. The cell at position n on row t turns out to be given by *Mod[GegenbauerC[n, -t, -1/2], 2]*, as discussed on page 612.

■ **Rule 225.** The width of the pattern after t steps varies between $Sqrt[3/2]\sqrt{t}$ (achieved when $t = 3 \times 2^{2n+1}$) and $Sqrt[9/2]\sqrt{t}$ (achieved when $t = 2^{2n+1}$). The pattern scales differently in the horizontal and vertical direction, corresponding to fractal dimensions $Log[2, 5]$ and $Log[4, 5]$ respectively. Note that with more complicated initial conditions rule 225 often no longer yields a regular nested pattern, as shown on page 951. The resulting patterns typically grow at a roughly constant average rate.

■ **Rule 22.** With more complicated initial conditions the pattern is often no longer nested, as shown on page 263.

■ **Page 59 · Algebraic forms.** The rules here can be expressed in algebraic terms (see page 869) as follows:

- Rule 30: *Mod[p + q + r + q r, 2]*
- Rule 45: *Mod[1 + p + r + q r, 2]*
- Rule 73: *Mod[1 + p + q + r + p r + p q r, 2]*

■ **Rule 45.** The center column of the pattern appears for practical purposes random, just as in rule 30. The left edge of the pattern moves 1 cell every 2 steps; the boundary between repetition and randomness moves on average 0.17 cells per step.

■ **Rule 73.** The pattern has a few definite regularities. The center column of cells is repetitive, alternating between black and white on successive steps. And in all cases black cells appear only in blocks that are an odd number of cells wide. (Any block in rule 73 consisting of an even number of black cells will evolve to a structure that remains fixed forever, as mentioned on page 954.) The more complicated central region of the pattern grows 4 cells every 7 steps; the outer region consists of blocks that are 12 cells wide and repeat every 3 steps.

■ **Alternating colors.** The pictures below show rules 45 and 73 with the colors of cells on alternate steps reversed.

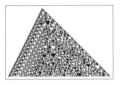 

■ **Two-cell neighborhoods.** By having cells on successive steps be arranged like hexagons or staggered bricks, as in the pictures below, one can set up cellular automata in which the new color of each cell depends on the previous colors of two rather than three neighboring cells.

With k possible colors for each cell, there are a total of k^{k^2} possible rules of this type, each specified by a k^2-digit number in base k (7743 for the rule shown above). For $k = 2$, there are 16 possible rules, and the most complicated pattern obtained is nested like the rule 90 elementary cellular automaton. With $k = 3$, there are 19,683 possible rules, 1734 of which are fundamentally inequivalent, and many more complicated patterns are seen, as in the pictures at the top of the next page.

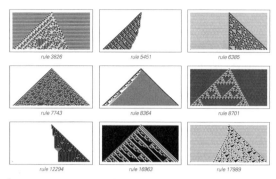

rule 3826 · rule 5451 · rule 6385
rule 7743 · rule 8364 · rule 8701
rule 12294 · rule 16963 · rule 17989

With *rule* given by *IntegerDigits[num, k, k²]* a single step of evolution can be implemented as

CAStep[{k_, rule_}, a_List] := rule[[k² - RotateLeft[a] - k a]]

■ **Page 60 · Numbers of rules.** Allowing k possible colors for each cell and considering r neighbors on each side, there are $k^{k^{2r+1}}$ possible cellular automaton rules in all, of which $k^{1/2 k^{r+1} (1+k^r)}$ are symmetric, and $k^{1+(k-1)(2r+1)}$ are totalistic. (For $k = 2$, $r = 1$ there are therefore 256 possible rules altogether, of which 16 are totalistic. For $k = 2$, $r = 2$ there are 4,294,967,296 rules in all, of which 64 are totalistic. And for $k = 3$, $r = 1$ there are 7,625,597,484,987 rules in all, with 2187 totalistic ones.) Note that for $k > 2$, a particular rule will in general be totalistic only for a specific assignment of values to colors. I first introduced totalistic rules in 1983.

■ **Implementation of general cellular automata.** With k colors and r neighbors on each side, a single step in the evolution of a general cellular automaton is given by

CAStep[CARule[rule_List, k_, r_], a_List] :=
rule[[-1 - ListConvolve[k ^ Range[0, 2 r], a, r + 1]]]

where *rule* is obtained from a rule number *num* by *IntegerDigits[num, k, k²ʳ⁺¹]*. (See also page 927.)

■ **Implementation of totalistic cellular automata.** To handle totalistic rules that involve k colors and nearest neighbors, one can add the definition

CAStep[TotalisticCARule[rule_List, 1], a_List] :=
rule[[-1 - (RotateLeft[a] + a + RotateRight[a])]]

to what was given on page 867. The following definition also handles the more general case of r neighbors:

CAStep[TotalisticCARule[rule_List, r_Integer], a_List] :=
rule[[-1 - Sum[RotateLeft[a, i], {i, -r, r}]]]

One can generate the representation of totalistic rules used by these functions from code numbers using

ToTotalisticCARule[num_Integer, k_Integer, r_Integer] :=
TotalisticCARule[IntegerDigits[num, k, 1 + (k - 1) (2 r + 1)], r]

■ **Common framework.** The *Mathematica* built-in function *CellularAutomaton* discussed on page 867 handles general and

totalistic rules in the same framework by using *ListConvolve[w, a, r + 1]* and taking the weights w to be respectively k ^ *Table[i - 1, {i, 2 r + 1}]* and *Table[1, {2 r + 1}]*.

■ **Page 63 · Mod 3 rule.** Code 420 is an example of an additive rule, and yields a pattern corresponding to Pascal's triangle modulo 3, as discussed on page 870.

■ **Compositions of cellular automata.** One way to construct more complicated rules is from compositions of simpler rules. One can, for example, consider each step applying first one elementary cellular automaton rule, then another. The result is in effect a $k = 2$, $r = 2$ rule. Usually the order in which the two elementary rules are applied will matter, and the overall behavior obtained will have no simple relationship to that of either of the individual rules. (See also page 956.)

■ **Rules based on algebraic systems.** If the values of cells are taken to be elements of some finite algebraic system, then one can set up a cellular automaton with rule

a[t_, i_] := f[a[t - 1, i - 1], a[t - 1, i]]

where f is the analog of multiplication for the system (see also page 1094). The pattern obtained after t steps is then given by

NestList[f[RotateRight[#], #] &, init, t]

The pictures below show results with f being *Times*, and cells having values (a) $\{1, -1\}$, (b) the unit complex numbers $\{1, î, -1, -î\}$, (c) the unit quaternions.

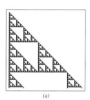

(a) · (b) · (c)

In general, with n elements f can be specified by an $n \times n$ "multiplication table". For $n = 2$, the patterns obtained are at most nested. Pictures (a) and (b) below however correspond to the $n = 3$ multiplication tables $\{\{1, 1, 3\}, \{3, 3, 2\}, \{2, 2, 1\}\}$ and $\{\{3, 1, 3\}, \{1, 3, 1\}, \{3, 1, 2\}\}$. Note that for (b) the table is symmetric, corresponding to a commutative multiplication operation.

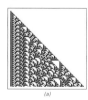

(a) · (b) · (c)

If f is associative (flat), so that $f[f[i, j], k] == f[i, f[j, k]]$, then the algebraic system is known as a semigroup. (See also page 805.) With a single cell seed, no pattern more complicated than nested can be obtained in such a system. And with any seed, it appears to require a semigroup with at least six elements to obtain a more complicated pattern.

If f has an identity element, so that $f[1, i] == i$ for all i, and has inverses, so that $f[i, j] == 1$ for some j, then the system is a group. (See page 945.) If the group is Abelian, so that $f[i, j] == f[j, i]$, then only nested patterns are ever produced (see page 955). But it turns out that the very simplest possible non-Abelian group yields the pattern in (c) above. The group used is S_3, which has six elements and multiplication table

$\{\{1, 2, 3, 4, 5, 6\}, \{2, 1, 5, 6, 3, 4\}, \{3, 4, 1, 2, 6, 5\},$
$\{4, 3, 6, 5, 1, 2\}, \{5, 6, 2, 1, 4, 3\}, \{6, 5, 4, 3, 2, 1\}\}$

The initial condition contains $\{5, 6\}$ surrounded by 1's.

Mobile Automata

■ **Implementation.** The state of a mobile automaton at a particular step can conveniently be represented by a pair $\{list, n\}$, where $list$ gives the values of the cells, and n specifies the position of the active cell (the value of the active cell is thus $list[[n]]$). Then, for example, the rule for the mobile automaton shown on page 71 can be given as

$\{\{1, 1, 1\} \to \{0, 1\}, \{1, 1, 0\} \to \{0, 1\},$
$\{1, 0, 1\} \to \{1, -1\}, \{1, 0, 0\} \to \{0, -1\}, \{0, 1, 1\} \to \{0, -1\},$
$\{0, 1, 0\} \to \{0, 1\}, \{0, 0, 1\} \to \{1, 1\}, \{0, 0, 0\} \to \{1, -1\}\}$

where the left-hand side in each case gives the value of the active cell and its left and right neighbors, while the right-hand side consists of a pair containing the new value of the active cell and the displacement of its position. (In analogy with cellular automata, this rule can be labelled $\{35, 57\}$ where the first number refers to colors, and the second displacements.) With a rule given in this form, each step in the evolution of the mobile automaton corresponds to the function

$MAStep[rule\_, \{list\_List, n\_Integer\}] /; 1 < n < Length[list] :=$
  $Apply[\{ReplacePart[list, \#1, n], n + \#2\} \&,$
    $Replace[Take[list, \{n - 1, n + 1\}], rule]]$

The complete evolution for many steps can then be obtained with

$MAEvolveList[rule\_, init\_List, t\_Integer] :=$
  $NestList[MAStep[rule, \#] \&, init, t]$

(The program will run more efficiently if $Dispatch$ is applied to the rule before giving it as input.)

For the mobile automaton on page 73, the rule can be given as

$\{\{1, 1, 1\} \to \{\{0, 0, 0\}, -1\}, \{1, 1, 0\} \to \{\{1, 0, 1\}, -1\},$
$\{1, 0, 1\} \to \{\{1, 1, 1\}, 1\}, \{1, 0, 0\} \to \{\{1, 0, 0\}, 1\},$
$\{0, 1, 1\} \to \{\{0, 0, 0\}, 1\}, \{0, 1, 0\} \to \{\{0, 1, 1\}, -1\},$
$\{0, 0, 1\} \to \{\{1, 0, 1\}, 1\}, \{0, 0, 0\} \to \{\{1, 1, 1\}, 1\}\}$

and $MAStep$ must be rewritten as

$MAStep[rule\_, \{list\_List, n\_Integer\}] /; 1 < n < Length[list] :=$
  $Apply[\{Join[Take[list, \{1, n - 2\}], \#1, Take[list, \{n + 2, -1\}]],$
    $n + \#2\} \&, Replace[Take[list, \{n - 1, n + 1\}], rule]]$

■ **Compressed evolution.** An alternative compression scheme for mobile automata is discussed on page 488.

■ **Page 72 · Distribution of behavior.** The pictures below show the distributions of transient and of period lengths for the 65,318 mobile automata of the type described here that yield ultimately repetitive behavior. Rule (f) has a period equal to the maximum of 16.

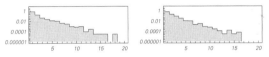

■ **Page 75 · Active cell motion.** The pictures below show the positions of the active cell for 20,000 steps of evolution in various mobile automata. (a), (b) and (c) correspond respectively to the rules on pages 73, 74 and 75. (c) has an outer envelope whose edges grow at rates $\{-1.5, 0.3\} \sqrt{t}$. (d) yields logarithmic growth as shown on page 496 (like Turing machine (f) on page 79). In most cases where the behavior is ultimately repetitive, transients and periods seem to follow the same approximate exponential distribution as in the note above. (g) however suddenly yields repetitive behavior with period 4032 after 405,941 steps. (h) does not appear to evolve to strict repetition or nesting, but does show progressively longer patches with fairly orderly behavior. (c) shows no obvious deviation from randomness in at least the first billion steps (after which the pattern it produces is 57,014 cells wide).

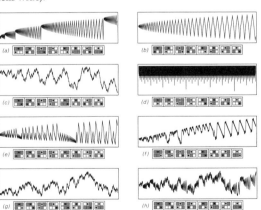

■ **Implementation of generalized mobile automata.** The state of a generalized mobile automaton at a particular step can be specified by *{list, nlist}*, where *list* gives the values of the cells, and *nlist* is a list of the positions of active cells. The rule can be given by specifying a list of cases such as *{0, 0, 0} → {1, {1, -1}}*, where in each case the second sublist specifies the new relative positions of active cells. With this setup successive steps in the evolution of the system can be obtained from

GMAStep[rules_, {list_, nlist_}] := Module[{a, na}, {a, na} = Transpose[Map[Replace[Take[list, {# - 1, # + 1}], rules] &, nlist]]; {Fold[ReplacePart[#1, Last[#2], First[#2]] &, list, Transpose[{nlist, a}]], Union[Flatten[nlist + na]]}]

Turing Machines

■ **Implementation.** The state of a Turing machine at a particular step can be represented by the triple *{s, list, n}*, where *s* gives the state of the head, *list* gives the values of the cells, and *n* specifies the position of the head (the cell under the head thus has value *list[[n]]*). Then, for example, the rule for the Turing machine shown on page 78 can be given as

{{1, 0} → {3, 1, -1}, {1, 1} → {2, 0, 1}, {2, 0} → {1, 1, 1}, {2, 1} → {3, 1, 1}, {3, 0} → {2, 1, 1}, {3, 1} → {1, 0, -1}}

where the left-hand side in each case gives the state of the head and the value of the cell under the head, and the right-hand side consists of a triple giving the new state of the head, the new value of the cell under the head and the displacement of the head.

With a rule given in this form, a single step in the evolution of the Turing machine can be implemented with the function

TMStep[rule_List, {s_, a_List, n_}] /; 1 ≤ n ≤ Length[a] := Apply[{#1, ReplacePart[a, #2, n], n + #3} &, Replace[{s, a[[n]]}, rule]]

The evolution for many steps can then be obtained using

TMEvolveList[rule_, init_List, t_Integer] := NestList[TMStep[rule, #] &, init, t]

An alternative approach is to represent the complete state of the Turing machine by *MapAt[{s, #} &, list, n]*, and then to use

TMStep[rule_, c_] := Replace[c, {a___, x_, h_List, y_, b___} :⟩ Apply[{{a, x, #2, {#1, y}, b}, {a, {#1, x}, #2, y, b}}[[#3]] &, h /. rule]]

The result of *t* steps of evolution from a blank tape can also be obtained from (see also page 1143)

s = 1; a[_] = 0; n = 0;
Do[{s, a[n], d} = {s, a[n]} /. rule; n += d, {t}]

■ **Number of rules.** With *k* possible colors for each cell and *s* possible states, there are a total of $(2sk)^{sk}$ possible Turing machine rules. Often many of these rules are immediately equivalent, or can show only very simple behavior (see page 1120).

■ **Numbering scheme.** One can number Turing machines and get their rules using

Flatten[MapIndexed[{1, -1}#2 + {0, k} → {1, 1, 2} Mod[Quotient[#1, {2 k, 2, 1}], {s, k, 2}] + {1, 0, -1} &, Partition[IntegerDigits[n, 2 s k, s k], k], {2}]]

The examples on page 79 have numbers 3024, 982, 925, 1971, 2506 and 1953.

■ **Page 79 · Counter machine.** Turing machine (f) operates like a base 2 counter: at steps where its head is at the leftmost position, the colors of the cells correspond to the reverse of the base 2 digit sequences of successive numbers. All possible arrangements of colors are thus eventually produced. The overall pattern attains width *j* after $2^j - j$ steps.

■ **Page 80 · Distribution of behavior.** With 2 possible states and 2 possible colors for each cell, starting from a blank tape, the maximum repetition period obtained is 9 steps, and 12 out of the 4096 possible rules (or about 0.29%) yield non-repetitive behavior. With 3 states and 2 colors, the maximum period is 24, and about 0.37% of rules yield non-repetitive behavior, always nested. (Usually I have not found more complicated behavior in such rules even with initial conditions in which there are both black and white cells, though see page 761.) With 2 states and 3 colors, the maximum repetition period is again 24, about 0.65% of rules yield non-repetitive behavior, and the 14 rules discussed on page 709 yield more complex behavior. With more colors or more states, the percentage of rules that yield non-repetitive behavior steadily increases, as shown below, roughly like *0.28 (s - 1)(k - 1)*. (Compare page 1120.)

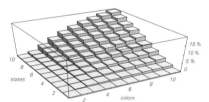

■ **Page 81 · Head motion.** The picture below shows the motion of the head for the first million steps. After about 20,000 steps, the width of the pattern produced grows at a rate close to $\sqrt{t}$.

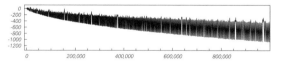

■ **Localized structures.** Even when the overall behavior of a Turing machine is complicated, it is possible for simple localized structures to exist, much as in cellular automata

such as rule 110. What can happen is that with certain specific repetitive backgrounds, the head can move in a simple repetitive way, as shown in the pictures below for the Turing machine from page 81.

■ **History.** Turing machines were invented by Alan Turing in 1936 to serve as idealized models for the basic processes of mathematical calculation (see page 1128). As discussed on page 1110, Turing's main interest was in showing what his machines could in principle be made to do, not in finding out what simple examples of them actually did. Indeed, so far as I know, even though he had access to the necessary technology, Turing never explicitly simulated any Turing machine on a computer.

Since Turing's time, Turing machines have been extensively used as abstract models in theoretical computer science. But in almost no cases has the explicit behavior of simple Turing machines been considered. In the early 1960s, however, Marvin Minsky and others did work on finding the simplest Turing machines that could exhibit certain properties. Most of their effort was devoted to finding ingenious constructions for creating appropriate machines (see page 1119). But around 1961 they did systematically study all 4096 2-state 2-color machines, and simulated the behavior of some simple Turing machines on a computer. They found repetitive and nested behavior, but did not investigate enough examples to discover the more complex behavior shown in the main text.

As an offshoot of abstract studies of Turing machines, Tibor Radó in 1962 formulated what he called the Busy Beaver Problem: to find a Turing machine with a specified number of states that "keeps busy" for as many steps as possible before finally reaching a particular "halt state" (numbered 0 below). (A variant of the problem asks for the maximum number of black cells that are left when the machine halts.) By 1966 the results for 2, 3 and 4 states had been found: the maximum numbers of steps are 6, 21 and 107, respectively, with 4, 5 and 13 final black cells. Rules achieving these bounds are:

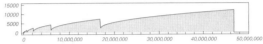

The result for 5 states is still unknown, but a machine taking 47,176,870 steps and leaving 4098 black cells was found by Heiner Marxen and Jürgen Buntrock in 1990. Its rule is:

The pictures below show (a) the first 500 steps of evolution, (b) the first million steps in compressed form and (c) the

number of black cells obtained at each step. Perhaps not surprisingly for a system optimized to run as long as possible, the machine operates in a rather systematic and regular way. With 6 states, a machine is known that takes about 3.002×10^{1730} steps to halt, and leaves about 1.29×10^{865} black cells. (See also page 1144.)

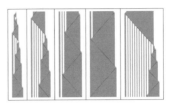

Substitution Systems

■ **Implementation.** The rule for a neighbor-independent substitution system such as the first one on page 82 can conveniently be given as $\{1 \rightarrow \{1, 0\}, 0 \rightarrow \{0, 1\}\}$. And with this representation, the evolution for t steps is given by

```
SSEvolveList[rule_, init_List, t_Integer] :=
    NestList[Flatten[# /. rule] &, init, t]
```

where in the first example on page 82, the initial condition is $\{1\}$.

An alternative approach is to use strings, representing the rule by $\{"B" \rightarrow "BA", "A" \rightarrow "AB"\}$ and the initial condition by $"B"$. In this case, the evolution can be obtained using

```
SSEvolveList[rule_, init_String, t_Integer] :=
    NestList[StringReplace[#, rule] &, init, t]
```

For a neighbor-dependent substitution system such as the first one on page 85 the rule can be given as

$$\{\{1, 1\} \rightarrow \{0, 1\}, \{1, 0\} \rightarrow \{1, 0\}, \{0, 1\} \rightarrow \{0\}, \{0, 0\} \rightarrow \{0, 1\}\}$$

And with this representation, the evolution for t steps is given by

```
SS2EvolveList[rule_, init_List, t_Integer] :=
    NestList[Flatten[Partition[#, 2, 1] /. rule] &, init, t]
```

where the initial condition for the first example on page 85 is $\{0, 1, 1, 0\}$.

■ **Page 83 · Properties.** The examples shown here all appear in quite a number of different contexts in this book. Note that each of them in effect yields a single sequence that gets progressively longer at each step; other rules make the colors of elements alternate on successive steps.

(a) (*Successive digits sequence*) The sequence produced is repetitive, with the element at position n being black for n

odd and white for n even. There are a total of 2^t elements after t steps. The complete pattern formed by looking at all the steps together has the same structure as the arrangement of base 2 digits in successive numbers shown on page 117.

(b) *(Thue-Morse sequence)* The color $s[n]$ of the element at position n is given by $1 - Mod[DigitCount[n - 1, 2, 1], 2]$. These colors satisfy $s[n\_] := If[EvenQ[n], 1 - s[n/2], s[(n + 1)/2]]$ with $s[1] = 1$. There are a total of 2^t elements in the sequence after t steps. The sequence on step t can be obtained from $Nest[Join[\#, 1 - \#]\ \&, \{1\}, t - 1]$. The number of black and white elements at each step is always the same. All four possible pairs of successive elements occur, though not with equal frequency. Runs of three identical elements never occur, and in general no block of elements can ever occur more than twice. The first 2^m elements in the sequence can be obtained from (see page 1081)

$(CoefficientList[Product[1 - z^{2^s}, \{s, 0, m - 1\}], z] + 1)/2$

The first n elements can also be obtained from (see page 1092)

$Mod[CoefficientList[Series[(1 + Sqrt[(1 - 3x)/(1 + x)])/$
$(2(1 + x)), \{x, 0, n - 1\}], x], 2]$

The sequence occurs many times in this book; it can for example be derived from a column of values in the rule 150 cellular automaton pattern discussed on page 885.

(c) *(Fibonacci-related sequence)* The sequence at step t can be obtained from $a[t\_] := Join[a[t - 1], a[t - 2]]; a[1] = \{0\}; a[2] = \{0, 1\}$. This sequence has length $Fibonacci[t + 1]$ (or approximately 1.618^{t+1}) (see note below). The color of the element at position n is given by $2 - (Floor[(n + 1)\ GoldenRatio] - Floor[n\ GoldenRatio])$ (see page 904), while the position of the kth white element is given by the so-called Beatty sequence $Floor[k\ GoldenRatio]$. The ratio of the number of white elements to black at step t is $Fibonacci[t - 1]/Fibonacci[t - 2]$, which approaches $GoldenRatio$ for large t. For all $m \le Fibonacci[t - 1]$, the number of distinct blocks of m successive elements that actually appear out of the 2^m possibilities is $m + 1$ (making it a so-called Sturmian sequence as discussed on page 1084).

(d) *(Cantor set)* The color of the element at position n is given by $If[FreeQ[IntegerDigits[n - 1, 3], 1], 1, 0]$, which turns out to be equivalent to

$If[OddQ[n], Sign[Mod[Binomial[n - 1, (n - 1)/2], 3]], 0, 1]$

There are 3^t elements after t steps, of which 2^t are black. The picture below shows the number of black cells that occur before position n. The resulting curve has a nested form, with envelope $n ^\wedge Log[3, 2]$.

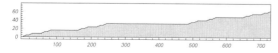

■ **Growth rates.** The total number of elements of each color that occur at each step in a neighbor-independent substitution system can be found by forming the matrix m where $m[[i, j]]$ gives the number of elements of color $j + 1$ that appear in the block that replaces an element of color $i + 1$. For case (c) above, $m = \{\{1, 1\}, \{1, 0\}\}$. A list that gives the number of elements of each color at step t can then be found from $init . MatrixPower[m, t]$, where $init$ gives the initial number of elements of each color—$\{1, 0\}$ for case (c) above. For large t, the total number of elements typically grows like λ^t, where λ is the largest eigenvalue of m; the relative numbers of elements of each color are given by the corresponding eigenvector. For case (c), λ is $GoldenRatio$, or $(1 + \sqrt{5})/2$. There are exceptional cases where $\lambda == 1$, so that the growth is not exponential. For the rule $\{0 \to \{0, 1\}, 1 \to \{1\}\}$, $m = \{\{1, 1\}, \{0, 1\}\}$, and the number of elements at step t starting with $\{0\}$ is just t. For $\{0 \to \{0, 1\}, 1 \to \{1, 2\}, 2 \to \{2\}\}$, $m = \{\{1, 1, 0\}, \{0, 1, 1\}, \{0, 0, 1\}\}$, and the number of elements starting with $\{0\}$ is $(t^2 - t + 2)/2$. For neighbor-independent rules, the growth for large t must follow an exponential or an integer power less than the number of possible colors. For neighbor-dependent rules, any form of growth can in principle be obtained.

■ **Fibonacci numbers.** The Fibonacci numbers $Fibonacci[n]$ ($f[n]$ for short) can be generated by the recurrence relation

$f[n\_] := f[n] = f[n - 1] + f[n - 2]$

$f[1] = f[2] = 1$

The first few Fibonacci numbers are: 1, 1, 2, 3, 5, 8, 13, 21, 34, 55, 89, 144, 233, 377. For large n the ratio $f[n]/f[n - 1]$ approaches $GoldenRatio$ or $(1 + \sqrt{5})/2 \approx 1.618$.

$Fibonacci[n]$ can be obtained in many ways:

■ $(GoldenRatio^n - (-GoldenRatio)^{-n})/\sqrt{5}$

■ $Round[GoldenRatio^n/\sqrt{5}]$

■ $2^{1-n} Coefficient[(1 + \sqrt{5})^n, \sqrt{5}]$

■ $MatrixPower[\{\{1, 1\}, \{1, 0\}\}, n - 1][[1, 1]]$

■ $Numerator[NestList[1/(1 + \#)\ \&, 1, n]]$

■ $Coefficient[Series[1/(1 - t - t^2), \{t, 0, n\}], t^{n-1}]$

■ $Sum[Binomial[n - i - 1, i], \{i, 0, (n - 1)/2\}]$

■ $2^{n-2} - Count[IntegerDigits[Range[0, 2^{n-2}], 2], \{\_\_\_, 1, 1, \_\_\_\}]$

A fast method for evaluating $Fibonacci[n]$ is

$First[Fold[f, \{1, 0, -1\}, Rest[IntegerDigits[n, 2]]]]$

$f[\{a\_, b\_, s\_\}, 0] = \{a(a + 2b), s + a(2a - b), 1\}$

$f[\{a\_, b\_, s\_\}, 1] = \{-s + (a + b)(a + 2b), a(a + 2b), -1\}$

Fibonacci numbers appear to have first arisen in perhaps 200 BC in work by Pingala on enumerating possible patterns of poetry formed from syllables of two lengths. They were independently discussed by Leonardo Fibonacci in 1202 as solutions to a mathematical puzzle concerning rabbit breeding, and by Johannes Kepler in 1611 in connection with approximations to the pentagon. Their recurrence relation appears to have been understood from the early 1600s, but it has only been in the past very few decades that they have in general become widely discussed.

For $m > 1$, the value of n for which $m == Fibonacci[n]$ is $Round[Log[GoldenRatio, \sqrt{5} \, m]]$.

The sequence $Mod[Fibonacci[n], k]$ is always purely repetitive; the maximum period is $6k$, achieved when $k = 10 \, 5^m$ (compare page 975).

$Mod[Fibonacci[n], n]$ has the fairly complicated form shown below. It appears to be zero only when n is of the form 5^m or $12q$, where q is not prime ($q > 5$).

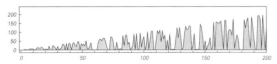

The number *GoldenRatio* appears to have been used in art and architecture since antiquity. *1/GoldenRatio* is the default *AspectRatio* for *Mathematica* graphics. In addition:

- *GoldenRatio* is the solution to $x == 1 + 1/x$ or $x^2 == x + 1$

- The right-hand rectangle in ▭ is similar to the whole rectangle when the aspect ratio is *GoldenRatio*

- $Cos[\pi/5] == Cos[36°] == GoldenRatio/2$

- The ratio of the length of the diagonal to the length of a side in a regular pentagon is *GoldenRatio*

- The corners of an icosahedron are at coordinates
  $Flatten[Array[NestList[RotateRight,$
  $\quad \{0, (-1)^{\#1} \, GoldenRatio, (-1)^{\#2} \}, 3] \&, \{2, 2\}], 2]$

- $1 + FixedPoint[N[1/(1 + \#), k] \&, 1]$ approximates *GoldenRatio* to k digits, as does
  $FixedPoint[N[Sqrt[1 + \#], k] \&, 1]$

- A successive angle difference of *GoldenRatio* radians yields points maximally separated around a circle (see page 1006).

■ **Lucas numbers.** Lucas numbers *Lucas[n]* satisfy the same recurrence relation $f[n\_] := f[n - 1] + f[n - 2]$ as Fibonacci numbers, but with the initial conditions $f[1] = 1; f[2] = 3$. Among the relations satisfied by Lucas numbers are:

- $Lucas[n\_] := Fibonacci[n - 1] + Fibonacci[n + 1]$

- $GoldenRatio^n == (Lucas[n] + Fibonacci[n] \sqrt{5})/2$

■ **Generalized Fibonacci sequences.** Any linear recurrence relation yields sequences with many properties in common with the Fibonacci numbers—though with *GoldenRatio* replaced by other algebraic numbers. The Perrin sequence $f[n\_] := f[n - 2] + f[n - 3]; f[0] = 3; f[1] = 0; f[2] = 2$ has the peculiar property that $Mod[f[n], n] == 0$ mostly but not always only for n prime. (For more on recurrence relations see page 128.)

■ **Connections with digit sequences.** In a sequence generated by a neighbor-independent substitution system the color of the element at position n turns out always to be related to the digit sequence of the number n in an appropriate base. The basic reason for this is that as shown on page 84 the evolution of the substitution system always yields a tree, and the successive digits in n determine which branch is taken at each level in order to reach the element at position n. In cases (a) and (b) on pages 83 and 84, the tree has two branches at every node, and so the base 2 digits of n determine the successive left and right branches that must be taken. Given that a branch with a certain color has been reached, the color of the branch to be taken next is then determined purely by the next digit in the digit sequence of n. For case (b) on pages 83 and 84, the rule that gives the color of the next branch in terms of the color of the current branch and the next digit is $\{\{0, 0\} \to 0, \{0, 1\} \to 1, \{1, 0\} \to 1, \{1, 1\} \to 0\}$. In terms of this rule, the color of the element at position n is given by

$\quad Fold[Replace[\{\#1, \#2\}, rule] \&, 1, IntegerDigits[n - 1, 2]]$

The rule used here can be thought of as a finite automaton with two states. In general, the behavior of any neighbor-independent substitution system where each element is subdivided into exactly k elements can be reproduced by a finite automaton with k states operating on digit sequences in base k. The nested structure of the patterns produced is thus a direct consequence of the nesting seen in the patterns of these digit sequences, as shown on page 117.

Note that if the rule for the finite automaton is represented for example as $\{\{1, 2\}, \{2, 1\}\}$ where each sublist corresponds to a particular state, and the elements of the sublist give the successor states with inputs $Range[0, k - 1]$, then the nth element in the output sequence can be obtained from

$\quad Fold[rule[[\#1, \#2]] \&, 1, IntegerDigits[n - 1, k] + 1] - 1$

while the first k^m elements can be obtained from

$\quad Nest[Flatten[rule[[\#]]] \&, 1, m] - 1$

To treat examples such as case (c) where elements can subdivide into blocks of several different lengths one must generalize the notion of digit sequences. In base k a number is constructed from a digit sequence $a[r], ..., a[1], a[0]$ (with $0 \le a[i] < k$) according to $Sum[a[i] k^i, \{i, 0, r\}]$. But given a sequence of digits that are each 0 or 1, it is also possible for example to construct numbers according to

Sum[a[i] Fibonacci[i + 2], {i, 0, r}]. (As discussed on page 1070, this representation is unique so long as one does not allow any pairs of adjacent 1's in the digit sequence.) It then turns out that if one expresses the position n as a generalized digit sequence of this kind, then the color of the corresponding element in substitution system (c) is just the last digit in this sequence.

■ **Connections with square roots.** Substitution systems such as (c) above are related to projections of lines with quadratic irrational slopes, as discussed on page 904.

■ **Spectra of substitution systems.** See page 1080.

■ **Representation by paths.** An alternative to representing substitution systems by 1D sequences of black and white squares is to use 2D paths consisting of sequences of left and right turns. The paths obtained at successive steps for rule (b) above are shown below.

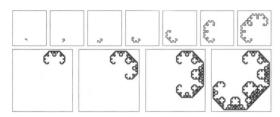

The pictures below show paths obtained with the rule *{1 → {1}, 0 → {0, 0, 1}},* starting from *{0}.* Note the similarity to the 2D system shown on page 190.

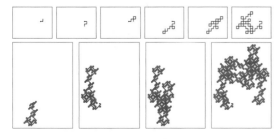

When the paths do not cross themselves, nested structure is evident. But in a case like the rule *{1 → {0, 0, 1}, 0 → {1, 0}}* starting with *{1},* the presence of many crossings tends to hide such regularity, as in the pictures below.

■ **Paperfolding sequences.** The sequence of up and down creases in a strip of paper that is successively folded in half is given by a substitution system; after t steps the sequence turns out to be *NestList[Join[#, {0}, Reverse[1 - #]] &, {0}, t].* The corresponding path (effectively obtained by making each crease a right angle) is shown below. (See page 189.)

■ **2D representations.** Individual sequences from 1D substitution systems can be displayed in 2D by breaking them into a succession of rows. The pictures below show results for the substitution systems on page 83. In case (b), with rows chosen to be 2^i elements in length, the leftmost column will always be identical to the beginning of the sequence, and in addition every interior element will be black exactly when the cell at the top of its column has the same color as the one at the beginning of its row. In case (c), stripes appear at angles related to *GoldenRatio.*

(a) (b) (c) (d)

■ **Page 84 · Other examples.**

(a) *(Period-doubling sequence)* After t steps, there are a total of 2^t elements, and the sequence is given by *Nest[MapAt[1 - # &, Join[#, #], -1] &, {0}, t].* It contains a total of *Round[2^t/3]* black elements, and if the last element is dropped, it forms a palindrome. The nth element is given by *Mod[IntegerExponent[n, 2], 2].* As discussed on page 885, the sequence appears in a vertical column of cellular automaton rule 150. The Thue-Morse sequence discussed on page 890 can be obtained from it by applying

1 - Mod[Flatten[Partition[FoldList[Plus, 0, list], 1, 2]], 2]

(b) The nth element is simply *Mod[n, 2].*

(c) Same as (a), after the replacement *1 → {1, 1}* in each sequence. Note that the spectra of (a) and (c) are nevertheless different, as discussed on page 1080.

(d) The length of the sequence at step t satisfies $a[t] == 2 a[t - 1] + a[t - 2]$, so that $a[t] = Round[(1 + \sqrt{2})^{t-1}/2]$ for $t > 1$. The number of white elements at step t is then *Round[a[t]/$\sqrt{2}$].* Much like example (c) on page 83 there are $m + 1$ distinct blocks of length m, and with $f = Floor[(1 - 1/\sqrt{2})(\# + 1/\sqrt{2})]$ & the nth element of the sequence is given by $f[n + 1] - f[n]$ (see page 903).

(e) For large t the number of elements increases like λ^t with $\lambda = (\sqrt{13} + 1)/2$; there are always λ times as many white elements as black ones.

(f) The number of elements at step t is $Round[(1 + \sqrt{2})^t/2]$, and the nth element is given by $Floor[\sqrt{2}\ (n + 1)] - Floor[\sqrt{2}\ n]$ (see page 903).

(g) The number of elements is the same as in (f).

(h) The number of black elements is 2^{t-1}; the total number of elements is $2^{t-2}\ (t + 1)$.

(i) and (j) The total number of elements is 3^{t-1}.

■ **History.** In their various representations, 1D substitution systems have been invented independently many times for many different purposes. (For the history of fractals and 2D substitution systems see page 934.) Viewed as generators of sequences with certain combinatorial properties, substitution systems such as example (b) on page 83 appeared in the work of Axel Thue in 1906. (Thue's stated purpose in this work was to develop the science of logic by finding difficult problems with possible connections to number theory.) The sequence of example (b) was rediscovered by Marston Morse in 1917 in connection with his development of symbolic dynamics—and in finding what could happen in discrete approximations to continuous systems. Studies of general neighbor-independent substitution systems (sometimes under such names as sequence homomorphisms, iterated morphisms and uniform tag systems) have continued in this context to this day. In addition, particularly since the 1980s, they have been studied in the context of formal language theory and the so-called combinatorics of words. (Period-doubling phenomena also led to contact with physics starting in the late 1970s.)

Independent of work in symbolic dynamics, substitution systems viewed as generators of sequences were reinvented in 1968 by Aristid Lindenmayer under the name of L systems for the purpose of constructing models of branching plants (see page 1005). So-called 0L systems correspond to my neighbor-independent substitution systems; 1L systems correspond to the neighbor-dependent substitution systems on page 85. Work on L systems has proceeded along two quite different lines: modelling specific plant systems, and investigating general computational capabilities. In the mid-1980s, particularly through the work of Alvy Ray Smith, L systems became widely used for realistic renderings of plants in computer graphics.

The idea of constructing abstract trees such as family trees according to definite rules presumably goes back to antiquity.

The tree representation of rule (c) from page 83 was for example probably drawn by Leonardo Fibonacci in 1202.

The first six levels of the specific pattern in example (a) on page 83 correspond exactly to the segregation diagram for the I Ching that arose in China as early as 2000 BC. Black regions represent yin and white ones yang. The elements on level six correspond to the 64 hexagrams of the I Ching. At what time the segregation diagram was first drawn is not clear, but it was almost certainly before 1000 AD, and in the 1600s it appears to have influenced Gottfried Leibniz in his development of base 2 numbers.

Viewed in terms of digit sequences, example (d) from page 83 was discussed by Georg Cantor in 1883 in connection with his investigations of the idea of continuity. General relations between digit sequences and sequences produced by neighbor-independent substitution systems were found in the 1960s. Connections of sequences such as (c) to algebraic numbers (see page 903) arose in precursors to studies of wavelets.

Paths representing sequences from 1D substitution systems can be generated by 2D geometrical substitution systems, as on page 189. The "C" curve shown on the facing page and on page 190 was for example described by Paul Lévy in 1937, and was rediscovered as the output of a simple computer program by William Gosper in the 1960s. Paperfolding or so-called dragon curves (as shown above) were discussed by John Heighway in the mid-1960s, and were analyzed by Chandler Davis, Donald Knuth and others. These curves have the property that they eventually fill space. Space-filling curves based on slightly more complicated substitution systems were already discussed by Giuseppe Peano in 1890 and by David Hilbert in 1891 in connection with questions about the foundations of calculus.

Sequences from substitution systems have no doubt appeared over the years as incidental features of great many pieces of mathematical work. As early as 1851, for example, Eugène Prouhet showed that if sequences of integers were partitioned according to sequence (b) on page 83, then sums of powers of these integers would be equal: thus $Apply[Plus, Flatten[Position[s, i]]^k]$ is equal for $i = 0$ and $i = 1$ if s is a sequence of the form (b) on page 83 with length 2^m, $m > k$. The optimal solution to the Towers of Hanoi puzzle invented in 1883 also turns out to be an example of a substitution system sequence.

Sequential Substitution Systems

■ **Implementation.** Sequential substitution systems can be implemented quite directly by using *Mathematica*'s standard mechanism for applying transformation rules to symbolic expressions. Having made the definition

    Attributes[s] = Flat

the state of a sequential substitution system at a particular step can be represented by a symbolic expression such as s[1, 0, 1, 0]. The rule on page 82 can then be given simply as

    s[1, 0] → s[0, 1, 0]

while the rule on page 85 becomes

    {s[0, 1, 0] → s[0, 0, 1], s[0] → s[0, 1, 0]}

The *Flat* attribute of *s* makes these rules apply not only for example to the whole sequence s[1, 0, 1, 0] but also to any subsequence such as s[1, 0]. (With *s* being *Flat*, s[s[1, 0], 1, s[0]] is equivalent to s[1, 0, 1, 0] and so on. A *Flat* function has the mathematical property of being associative.) And with this setup, *t* steps of evolution can be found with

    SSSEvolveList[rule_, init_s, t_Integer] :=
       NestList[# /. rule &, init, t]

Note that as an alternative to having *s* be *Flat*, one can explicitly set up rules based on patterns such as s[x___, 1, 0, y___] → s[x, 0, 1, 0, y]. And by using rules such as s[x___, 1, 0, y___] :→ {s[x, 0, 1, 0, y], Length[s[x]]} one can keep track of the positions at which substitutions are made. (*StringReplace* replaces all occurrences of a given substring, not just the first one, so cannot be used directly as an alternative to having a flat function.)

■ **Capabilities.** Even with the single rule {s[1, 0] → s[0, 1]}, a sequential substitution system can sort its initial conditions so that all 0's occur before all 1's. (See also page 1113.)

■ **Order of replacements.** For many sequential substitution systems the evolution effectively stops because a string is produced to which none of the replacements given apply. In most sequential substitution systems there is more than one possible replacement that can in principle apply at a particular step, so the order in which the replacements are tried matters. (Multiway systems discussed on page 497 are what result if all possible replacements are performed at each step.) There are however special sequential substitution systems (those with the so-called confluence property discussed on page 1036) in which in a certain sense the order of replacements does not matter.

■ **History.** Sequential substitution systems are closely related to the multiway systems discussed on page 938, and are often considered examples of production systems or string rewriting systems. In the form I discuss here, they seem to have arisen first under the name "normal algorithms" in the work of Andrei Markov in the late 1940s on computability and the idealization of mathematical processes. Starting in

the 1960s text editors like TECO and ed used sequential substitution system rules, as have string-processing languages such as SNOBOL and perl. *Mathematica* uses an analog of sequential substitution system rules to transform general symbolic expressions. The fact that new rules can be added to a sequential substitution system incrementally without changing its basic structure has made such systems popular in studies of adaptive programming.

Tag Systems

■ **Implementation.** With the rules for case (a) on page 94 given for example by

    {2, {{0, 0} → {1, 1}, {1, 0} → {}, {0, 1} → {1, 0}, {1, 1} → {0, 0, 0}}}

the evolution of a tag system can be obtained from

    TSEvolveList[{n_, rule_}, init_, t_] := NestList[If[Length[#] <
       n, {}, Join[Drop[#, n], Take[#, n] /. rule]] &, init, t]

An alternative implementation is based on applying to the list at each step rules such as

    {{0, 0, s___} → {s, 1, 1}, {1, 0, s___} → {s},
       {0, 1, s___} → {s, 1, 0}, {1, 1, s___} → {s, 0, 0, 0}}

There are a total of $((k^{r+1} - 1)/(k - 1))^{k^n}$ possible rules if blocks up to length *r* can be added at each step and *k* colors are allowed. For *r* = 3, *k* = 2 and *n* = 2 this is 50,625.

■ **Page 94 · Randomness.** To get some idea of the randomness of the behavior, one can look at the sequence of first elements produced on successive steps. In case (a), the fraction of black elements fluctuates around 1/2; in (b) it approaches 3/4; in (d) it fluctuates around near 0.3548, while in (e) and (f) it does not appear to stabilize.

■ **History.** The tag systems that I consider are generalizations of those first discussed by Emil Post in 1920 as simple idealizations of certain syntactic reduction rules in Alfred Whitehead and Bertrand Russell's *Principia Mathematica* (see page 1149). Post's tag systems differ from mine in that his allow the choice of block that is added at each step to depend only on the very first element in the sequence at that step (see however page 670). (The lag systems studied in 1963 by Hao Wang allow dependence on more than just the first element, but remove only the first element.) It turns out that in order to get complex behavior in such systems, one needs either to allow more than two possible colors for each element, or to remove more than two elements from the beginning of the sequence at each step. Around 1921, Post apparently studied all tag systems of his type that involve removal and addition of no more than two elements at each step, and he concluded that none of them produced complicated behavior. But then he looked at rules that remove three elements at each step, and he discovered the rule {3, {{0, _, _} → {0, 0}, {1, _, _} → {1, 1, 0, 1}}}. As he noted, the behavior of this rule varies considerably with the initial conditions used. But at least for all the initial conditions up to length 28, the rule eventually just leads to behavior that repeats with a period of 1, 2, 6, 10, 28 or 40. With more than two colors, one finds that rules of Post's type which remove just two elements at each step can yield complex behavior, even starting from an initial condition such as {0, 0}. An example is {2, {{0, _} → {2, 1}, {1, _} → {0}, {2, _} → {0, 2, 1, 2}}}. (See also pages 1113 and 1141.)

Cyclic Tag Systems

▪ **Implementation.** With the rules for the cyclic tag system on page 95 given as {{1, 1}, {1, 0}}, the evolution can be obtained from

    CTEvolveList[rules_, init_, t_] :=
        Map[Last, NestList[CTStep, {rules, init}, t]]
    CTStep[{{r_, s___}, {0, a___}}] := {{s, r}, {a}}
    CTStep[{{r_, s___}, {1, a___}}] := {{s, r}, Join[{a}, r]}
    CTStep[{u_, {}}] := {u, {}}

The leading elements on many more than t successive steps can be obtained directly from

    CTList[rules_, init_, t_] :=
        Flatten[Map[Last, NestList[CTListStep, {rules, init}, t]]]
    CTListStep[{rules_, list_}] :=
        {RotateLeft[rules, Length[list]], Flatten[rules[[
            Mod[Flatten[Position[list, 1]], Length[rules], 1]]]]}

▪ **Page 95 · Generalizations.** The implementation above immediately allows cyclic tag systems which cycle through a list of more than two blocks. (With just one block the behavior is always repetitive.) Cyclic tag systems which allow any value for each element can be obtained by adding the rule

    CTStep[{{r_, s___}, {n_, a___}}] :=
        {{s, r}, Flatten[{a, Table[r, {n}]}]}

The leading elements in this case can be obtained using

    CTListStep[{rules_, list_}] :=
        {RotateLeft[rules, Length[list]], With[{n = Length[rules]},
            Flatten[Apply[Table[#1, {#2}] &, Map[Transpose[
            {rules, #}] &, Partition[list, n, n, 1, 0]], {2}]]]}

▪ **Mechanical implementation.** Cyclic tag systems admit a particularly straightforward mechanical implementation. Black and white balls are kept in a trough as in the picture below. At each step the leftmost ball in the trough is released, and if this ball is black (as determined, for example, by size) a mechanism causes a new block of balls to be added at the right-hand end of the trough. This mechanism can work in

several ways; typically it will involve a rotary element that determines which case of the rule to use at each step. Rule (e) from the main text allows a particularly simple supply of new balls. Note that the system will inevitably fail if the trough overflows with balls.

▪ **Page 96 · Properties.** Assuming that black and white elements occur in an uncorrelated way, then the sequences in a cyclic tag system with n blocks should grow by an average of Count[Flatten[rules], 1]/n - 1 elements at each step. With n = 2 blocks, this means that growth can occur only if the total number of black elements in both blocks is more than 3. Rules such as {{1, 0}, {0, 1}} and {{1, 1}, {0}} therefore yield repetitive behavior with sequences of limited length.

Note that if all blocks in a cyclic tag system with n blocks have lengths divisible by n, then one can tell in advance on which steps blocks will be added, and the overall behavior obtained must correspond to a neighbor-independent substitution system. The rules for the relevant substitution system may however depend on the initial conditions for the cyclic tag system.

    Flatten[{1, 0, CTList[{{1, 0, 0, 1}, {0, 1, 1, 0}}, {0, 1}, t]}]

gives for example the Thue-Morse substitution system {1 → {1, 0}, 0 → {0, 1}}.

In example (a), the elements are correlated, so that slower growth occurs than in the estimate above. In example (c), the elements are again correlated: the growth is by an average of ($\sqrt{5}$ - 1)/2 ≈ 0.618 elements at each step, and the first elements on alternate steps form the same nested sequence as obtained from the substitution system {1 → {1, 0}, 0 → {1}}. In example (d), the frequency of 1's among the first elements of sequence is approximately 3/4; {0, 0} never occurs, and the frequency of {1, 1} is approximately 1/2. In example (e), the frequency of 1's is again about 3/4, but now {0, 0} occurs with frequency 0.05, {1, 1} occurs with frequency 0.55, while {0, 0, 0} and {0, 1, 0} cannot occur.

▪ **History.** Cyclic tag systems were studied by Matthew Cook in 1994 in connection with working on the rule 110 cellular automaton for this book. The sequence {1, 2, 2, 1, 1, 2, ...} defined by the property list == Map[Length, Split[list]] was suggested as a mathematical puzzle by William Kolakoski in 1965 and is equivalent to

    Join[{1, 2}, Map[First, CTEvolveList[{{1}, {2}}, {2}, t]]]

It is known that this sequence does not repeat, contains no more than two identical consecutive blocks, and has at least very close to equal numbers of 1's and 2's. Replacing 2 by 3 yields a sequence which has a fairly simple nested form.

Register Machines

▪ Implementation. The state of a register machine at a particular step can be represented by the pair *{n, list}*, where *n* gives the position in the program of current instruction being executed (the "program counter") and *list* gives the values of the registers. The program for the register machine on page 99 can then be given as

   {i[1], d[2, 1], i[2], d[1, 3], d[2, 1]}

where *i[_]* represents an increment instruction, and *d[_, _]* a decrement jump.

With this setup, the evolution of any register machine can be implemented using the functions (a typical initial condition is *{1, {0, 0}}*)

   RMStep[prog_, {n_Integer, list_List}] := If[n > Length[prog],
   *   {n, list}, RMExecute[prog[[n]], {n, list}]]*

   RMExecute[i[r_], {n_, list_}] := {n + 1, MapAt[# + 1 &, list, r]}

   RMExecute[d[r_, m_], {n_, list_}] :=
   *   If[list[[r]] > 0, {m, MapAt[# - 1 &, list, r]}, {n + 1, list}]*

   RMEvolveList[prog_, init : {_Integer, _List}, t_Integer] :=
   *   NestList[RMStep[prog, #] &, init, t]*

The total number of possible programs of length *n* using *k* registers is $(k (1 + n))^n$. Note that by prepending suitable *i[r]* instructions one can effectively set up initial conditions with arbitrary values in registers.

▪ Halting. It is sometimes convenient to think of register machines as going into a special halt state if they try to execute instructions beyond the end of their program. (See page 1137.) The fraction of possible register machines that do this starting from initial condition *{1, {0, 0}}* decreases steadily with program length *n*, reaching about 0.76 for *n = 8*. The most common number of steps before halting is always *n*, while the maximum numbers of steps for *n* up to 8 is *{1, 3, 5, 10, 16, 37, 215, 1280}* where in the last case this is achieved by

   {i[1], d[2, 7], d[2, 1], i[2], i[2], d[1, 4], i[1], d[2, 3]}

▪ Page 101 · Extended instruction sets. One can consider also including instructions such as

   RMExecute[eq[r1_, r2_, m_], {n_, list_}] :=
   *   If[list[[r1]] == list[[r2]], {m, list}, {n + 1, list}]*

   RMExecute[add[r1_, r2_], {n_, list_}] :=
   *   {n + 1, ReplacePart[list, list[[r1]] + list[[r2]], r1]}*

   RMExecute[jmp[r1_], {n_, list_}] := {list[[r1]], list}

Note that by being able to add and subtract only 1 at each step, the register machines shown in the main text necessarily operate quite slowly: they always take at least *n* steps to build up a number of size *n*. But while extending the instruction set can increase the speed of operations, it does not appear to yield a much larger density of machines with complex behavior.

▪ History. Register machines (also known as counter machines and program machines) are a fairly obvious idealization of practical computers, and have been invented in slightly different forms several times. Early uses of them were made by John Shepherdson and Howard Sturgis around 1959 and Marvin Minsky around 1960. Somewhat similar constructs were part of Kurt Gödel's 1931 work on representing logic within arithmetic (see page 1158).

▪ Page 102 · Random programs. See page 1182.

Symbolic Systems

▪ Implementation. The evolution for *t* steps of the first symbolic system shown can be implemented simply by

   NestList[# /. e[x_][y_] → x[x[y]] &, init, t]

▪ Symbolic expressions. Expressions like *Log[x]* and *f[x]* that give values of functions are familiar from mathematics and from typical computer languages. Expressions like *f[g[x]]* giving compositions of functions are also familiar. But in general, as in *Mathematica*, it is possible to have expressions in which the head *h* in *h[x]* can itself be any expression—not just a single symbol. Thus for example *f[g][x]*, *f[g[h]][x]* and *f[g][h][x]* are all possible expressions. And these kinds of expressions often arise in *Mathematica* when one manipulates functions as a whole before applying them to arguments. ($\partial_{xx} f[x]$ for example gives *f″[x]* which is *Derivative[2][f][x]*.) (In principle one can imagine representing all objects with forms such as *f[x, y]* by so-called currying as *f[x][y]*, and indeed I tried this in the early 1980s in SMP. But although this can be convenient when *f* is a discrete function such as a matrix, it is inconsistent with general mathematical and other usage in which for example *Gamma[x]* and *Gamma[a, x]* are both treated as values of functions.)

▪ Representations. Among the representations that can be used for expressions are:

functional	a[b[c[d]]]	a[b][c[d]]	a[b[c][d]]	a[b][c][d]
Polish	{∘, a, ∘, b, ∘, c, d}	{∘, ∘, a, b, ∘, c, d}	{∘, a, ∘, ∘, b, c, d}	{∘, ∘, ∘, a, b, c, d}
operator	a ∘ (b ∘ (c ∘ d))	(a ∘ b) ∘ (c ∘ d)	a ∘ ((b ∘ c) ∘ d)	((a ∘ b) ∘ c) ∘ d
tree	{a, {b, {c, d}}}	{{a, b}, {c, d}}	{a, {{b, c}, d}}	{{{a, b}, c}, d}

Typical transformation rules are non-local in all these representations. Polish representation (whose reverse form has been used in HP calculators) for an expression can be obtained using (see also page 1173)

   Flatten[expr //. x_[y_] → {∘, x, y}]

The original expression can be recovered using

First[Reverse[list] //. {w___, x_, y_, o, z___} → {w, y[x], z }]

(Pictures of symbolic system evolution made with Polish notation differ in detail but look qualitatively similar to those made as in the main text with functional notation.)

The tree representation of an expression can be obtained using *expr //. x_[y_] → {x, y}*, and when each object has just one argument, the tree is binary, as in LISP.

If only a single symbol ever appears, then all that matters is the overall structure of an expression, which can be captured as in the main text by the sequence of opening and closing brackets, given by

Flatten[Characters[ToString[expr]]] /.
   { "[" → 1, "]" → 0, "e" → {} }]

■ **Possible expressions.** *LeafCount[expr]* gives the number of symbols that appear anywhere in an expression, while *Depth[expr]* gives the number of closing brackets at the end of its functional representation—equal to the number of levels in the rightmost branch of the tree representation. (The maximum number of levels in the tree can be computed from *expr /. _Symbol → 1 //. x_[y_] → 1 + Max[x, y].*)

With a list *s* of possible symbols, *c[s, n]* gives all possible expressions with *LeafCount[expr] == n*:

c[s_, 1] = s; c[s_, n_] := Flatten[
   Table[Outer[#1[#2] &, c[s, n – m], c[s, m]], {m, n – 1}]]

There are a total of *Binomial[2 n – 2, n – 1] Length[s]^n/n* such expressions. When *Length[s] == 1* the expressions correspond to possible balanced sequences of opening and closing brackets (see page 989).

■ **Page 103 · Properties.** All initial conditions eventually evolve to expressions of the form *Nest[e, e, m]*, which then remain fixed. The quantity *expr //. {e → 0, x_[y_] → 2^x + y }* turns out to remain constant through the evolution, so this gives the final value of *m* for any initial condition. The maximum is *Nest[2$^\#$ &, 0, n]* (compare page 906), achieved for initial conditions of the form *Nest[#[e] &, e, n]*. (By analogy with page 1122 any *e* expression can be interpreted as a Church numeral *u = expr //. {e → 2, x_[y_] → y^x } = 2$^{2^m}$*, so that *expr[a][b]* evolves to *Nest[a, b, u].*) During the evolution the rule can apply only to the inner part *FixedPoint[Replace[#, e[x_] → x] &, expr]* of an expression. The depth of this inner part for initial condition *e[e][e][e][e][e]* is shown below. For all initial conditions this depth seems at first to increase linearly, then to decrease in a nested way according to

FoldList[Plus, 0, Flatten[Table[
   {1, 1, Table[-1, {IntegerExponent[i, 2] + 1}]}, {i, m}]]]

This quantity alternates between value *1* at position *2^i* and value *j* at position *2^i – j + 1*. It reaches a fixed point as soon as the depth reaches 0. For initial conditions of size *n*, this occurs after at most *Sum[Nest[2$^\#$ &, 0, i] – 1, {i, n}] + 1* steps. (See also page 1145.)

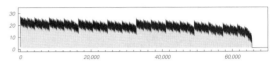

■ **Other rules.** If only a single variable appears in the rule, then typically only nested behavior can be generated—though in an example like *e[x_][_] → e[x[e[e][e]][e]]* it can be quite complex. The left-hand side of each rule can consist of any expression; *e[e[x_]][y_]* and *e[e][x_[y_]]* are two possibilities. However, at least with small initial conditions it seems easier to achieve complex behavior with rules based on *e[x_][y_]*. Note that rules with no explicit *e*'s on the left-hand side always give trees with regular nested structures; *x_[y_] → x[y][x[y]]* (or *x_ → x[x]* in *Mathematica*), for example, yields balanced binary trees.

■ **Long halting times.** Symbolic systems with rules of the form *e[x_][y_] → Nest[x, y, r]* always evolve to fixed points— though with initial conditions of size *n* this can take of order *Nest[r$^\#$ &, 0, n]* steps (see above). In general there will be symbolic systems where the number of steps to evolve to a fixed point grows arbitrarily rapidly with *n* (see page 1145), and indeed I suspect that there are even systems with quite simple rules where proving that a fixed point is always reached in a finite number of steps is beyond, for example, the axiom system for arithmetic (see page 1163).

■ **Trees.** The rules given on pages 103 and 104 correspond to the transformations on trees shown below.

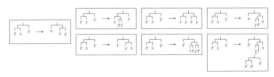

The first few steps in evolution from two initial conditions of the system on page 103 correspond to the sequences of trees below.

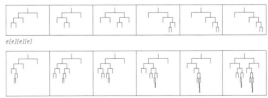

■ **Order dependence.** The operation *expr /. lhs → rhs* in *Mathematica* has the effect of scanning the functional representation of *expr* from left to right, and applying rules whenever possible while avoiding overlaps. (Standard evaluation in *Mathematica* is equivalent to *expr //. rules* and uses the same ordering, while *Map* uses a different order.) One can have a rule be applied only once using

Module[{i = 1}, expr /. lhs :→ rhs /; i++ == 1]

Many symbolic systems (including the one on page 103) have the so-called Church-Rosser property (see page 1036) which implies that if a fixed point is reached in the evolution of the system, this fixed point will be the same regardless of the order in which rules are applied.

■ **History.** Symbolic systems of the general type I discuss here seem to have first arisen in 1920 in the work of Moses Schönfinkel on what became known as combinators. As discussed on page 1121 Schönfinkel introduced certain specific rules that he suggested could be used to build up functions defined in logic. Beginning in the 1930s there were a variety of theoretical studies of how logic and mathematics could be set up with combinators, notably by Haskell Curry. For the most part, however, only Schönfinkel's specific rules were ever used, and only rather specific forms of behavior were investigated. In the 1970s and 1980s there was interest in using combinators as a basis for compilation of functional programming languages, but only fairly specific situations of immediate practical relevance were considered. (Combinators have also been used as logic recreations, notably by Raymond Smullyan.)

Constructs like combinators appear to have almost never been studied in mainstream pure mathematics. Most likely the reason is that building up functions on the basis of the structure of symbolic expressions has never seemed to have much obvious correspondence to the traditional mathematical view of functions as mappings. And in fact even in mathematical logic, combinators have usually not been considered mainstream. Most likely the reason is that ever since the work of Bertrand Russell in the early 1900s it has generally been assumed that it is desirable to distinguish a hierarchy of different types of functions and objects—analogous to the different types of data supported in most programming languages. But combinators are set up not to have any restrictions associated with types. And it turns out that among programming languages *Mathematica* is almost unique in also having this same feature. And from experience with *Mathematica* it is now clear that having a symbolic system which—like combinators—has no built-in notion of types allows great generality and flexibility. (One can always set up the analog of types by having rules only for expressions whose heads have particular structures.)

■ **Operator systems.** One can generalize symbolic systems by having rules that define transformations for any *Mathematica* pattern. Often these can be thought of as one-way versions of axioms for operator systems (see page 1172), but applied only once per step (as */.* does), rather than in all possible ways (as in a multiway system)—so that the evolution is just given by *NestList[# /. rule &, init, t]*. The rule *x_ → x∘x* then for example generates a balanced binary tree. The pictures below show the patterns of opening and closing parentheses obtained from operator system evolution rules in a few cases.

x_ → x∘x   x_∘y_ → (y∘x)∘y   x_∘y_ → (y∘y)∘(x∘x)   x_∘y_ → y∘(x∘x)

■ **Network analogs.** The state of a symbolic system can always be viewed as corresponding to a tree. If a more general network is allowed then rules based on analogs of network substitution systems from page 508 can be used. (One can also construct an infinite tree from a general network by following all its possible paths, as on page 277, but in most cases there will be no simple way to apply symbolic system rules to such a tree.)

How the Discoveries in This Chapter Were Made

■ **Page 109 · Repeatability and numerical analysis.** The discrete nature of the systems that I consider in most of this book makes it almost inevitable that computer experiments on them will be perfectly repeatable. But if, as in the past, one tries to do computer experiments on continuous mathematical systems, then the situation can be different. For in such cases one must inevitably make discrete approximations for the underlying representation of numbers and for the operations that one performs on them. And in many practical situations, one relies for these approximations on "machine arithmetic"—which can differ from one computer system to another.

■ **Page 109 · Studying simple systems.** Over the years, I have watched with disappointment the continuing failure of most scientists and mathematicians to grasp the idea of doing computer experiments on the simplest possible systems. Those with physical science backgrounds tend to add features to their systems in an attempt to produce some kind of presumed realism. And those with mathematical backgrounds tend to add features to make their systems fit in with complicated and abstract ideas—often related to continuity—that exist in modern mathematics. The result of all this has been that remarkably few truly meaningful computer experiments have ended up ever being done.

THE WORLD OF SIMPLE PROGRAMS | NOTES FOR CHAPTER 3

■ **Page 111 · The relevance of theorems.** Following traditional mathematical thinking, one might imagine that the best way to be certain about what could possibly happen in some particular system would be to prove a theorem about it. But in my experience, proofs tend to be subject to many of the same kinds of problems as computer experiments: it is easy to end up making implicit assumptions that can be violated by circumstances one cannot foresee. And indeed, by now I have come to trust the correctness of conclusions based on simple systematic computer experiments much more than I trust all but the simplest proofs.

■ **Attitudes of mathematicians.** Mathematicians often seem to feel that computer experimentation is somehow less precise than their standard mathematical methods. It is true that in studying questions related to continuous mathematics, imprecise numerical approximations have often been made when computers are used (see above). But discrete or symbolic computations can be absolutely precise. And in a sense presenting a particular object found by experiment (such as a cellular automaton whose evolution shows some particular property) can be viewed as a constructive existence proof for such an object. In doing mathematics there is often the idea that proofs should explain the result they prove—and one might not think this could be achieved if one just presents an object with certain properties. But being able to look in detail at how such an object works will in many cases provide a much better understanding than a standard abstract mathematical proof. And inevitably it is much easier to find new results by the experimental approach than by the traditional approach based on proofs.

■ **History of experimental mathematics.** The general idea of finding mathematical results by doing computational experiments has a distinguished, if not widely discussed, history. The method was extensively used, for example, by Carl Friedrich Gauss in the 1800s in his studies of number theory, and presumably by Srinivasa Ramanujan in the early 1900s in coming up with many algebraic identities. The Gibbs phenomenon in Fourier analysis was noticed in 1898 on a mechanical computer constructed by Albert Michelson. Solitons were rediscovered in experiments done around 1954 on an early electronic computer by Enrico Fermi and collaborators. (They had been seen in physical systems by John Scott Russell in 1834, but had not been widely investigated.) The chaos phenomenon was noted in a computer experiment by Edward Lorenz in 1962 (see page 971). Universal behavior in iterated maps (see page 921) was discovered by Mitchell Feigenbaum in 1975 by looking at examples from an electronic calculator. Many aspects of fractals were found by Benoit Mandelbrot in the 1970s using computer graphics. In the 1960s and 1970s a variety of algebraic identities were found using computer algebra, notably by William Gosper. (Starting in the mid-1970s I routinely did computer algebra experiments to find formulas in theoretical physics—though I did not mention this when presenting the formulas.) The idea that as a matter of principle there should be truths in mathematics that can only be reached by some form of inductive reasoning—like in natural science—was discussed by Kurt Gödel in the 1940s and by Gregory Chaitin in the 1970s. But it received little attention. With the release of *Mathematica* in 1988, mathematical experiments began to emerge as a standard element of practical mathematical pedagogy, and gradually also as an approach to be tried in at least some types of mathematical research, especially ones close to number theory. But even now, unlike essentially all other branches of science, mainstream mathematics continues to be entirely dominated by theoretical rather than experimental methods. And even when experiments are done, their purpose is essentially always just to provide another way to look at traditional questions in traditional mathematical systems. What I do in this book—and started in the early 1980s—is, however, rather different: I use computer experiments to look at questions and systems that can be viewed as having a mathematical character, yet have never in the past been considered in any way by traditional mathematics.

■ **Page 113 · Practicalities.** The investigations described in this chapter were done using *Mathematica*, mostly in 1992. For larger searches, I sometimes created optimized C programs that were controlled via *MathLink* from within *Mathematica*—though with the versions of *Mathematica* that exist today this would now be unnecessary. For my very largest searches, I used *Mathematica* to dispatch programs to a large number of different computers on a network, then had the computers send me email whenever they found interesting results. (See also page 854.)

Systems Based on Numbers

The Notion of Numbers

■ **Implementation of digit sequences.** A whole number n can be converted to a sequence of digits in base k using *IntegerDigits[n, k]* or (see also page 1094)

Reverse[Mod[NestWhileList[Floor[#/k] &, n, # ≥ k &], k]]

and from a sequence of digits using *FromDigits[list, k]* or

Fold[k #1 + #2 &, 0, list]

For a number x between 0 and 1, the first m digits in its digit sequence in base k are given by *RealDigits[x, k, m]* or

Floor[k NestList[Mod[k #, 1] &, x, m - 1]]

and from these digits one can reconstruct an approximation to the number using *FromDigits[{list, 0}, k]* or

Fold[#1/k + #2 &, 0, Reverse[list]]/k

■ **Gray code.** In looking at digit sequences, it is sometimes useful to consider ordering numbers by a criterion other than their size. An example is Gray code ordering, in which successive numbers are arranged to differ in only one digit. One possible such ordering for numbers with a total of m digits is

*GrayCode[m_] :=
Nest[Join[#, Length[#] + Reverse[#]] &, {0}, m]*

The succession of sizes and digit sequences of numbers ordered in this way are shown below. (Note that the digit sequence picture is turned on its side relative to those in the main text). The number which appears at position i is given by *BitXor[i, Floor[i/2]]*. (Iterating the related function *BitXor[i, 2 i]* yields numbers whose digit sequences correspond to the rule 60 cellular automaton).

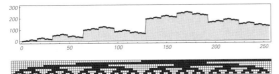

■ **A note for mathematicians.** Some mathematicians will at first find what I say in this chapter quite bizarre. It may help

however to point out that the traditional view of numbers already shows signs of breaking down in many studies of dynamical systems done over the past few decades. Thus for example, instead of getting results in terms of continuous functions, Cantor sets very often appear. Indeed, the symbolic dynamics approach that is often used in dynamical systems theory is quite close to the digit sequence approach I use here—Markov partitions in dynamical systems theory are essentially just generalizations of digit expansions.

However, in the cases that are analyzed in dynamical systems theory, only shifts and other very simple operations are typically performed on digit sequences. And as a result, most of the phenomena that I discuss in this chapter have not been seen in work done in dynamical systems theory.

■ **History of numbers.** Numbers were probably first used many thousands of years ago in commerce, and initially only whole numbers and perhaps rational numbers were needed. But already in Babylonian times, practical problems of geometry began to require square roots. Nevertheless, for a very long time, and despite some development of algebra, only numbers that could somehow in principle be constructed mechanically were ever considered. The invention of fluxions by Isaac Newton in the late 1600s, however, introduced the idea of continuous variables—numbers with a continuous range of possible sizes. But while this was a convenient and powerful notion, it also involved a new level of abstraction, and it brought with it considerable confusion about fundamental issues. In fact, it was really only through the development of rigorous mathematical analysis in the late 1800s that this confusion finally began to clear up. And already by the 1880s Georg Cantor and others had constructed completely discontinuous functions, in which the idea of treating numbers as continuous variables where only the size matters was called into question. But until almost the 1970s, and the emergence of fractal geometry and chaos theory, these functions were largely considered as mathematical curiosities, of no practical relevance. (See also page 1168.)

Independent of pure mathematics, however, practical applications of numbers have always had to go beyond the abstract idealization of continuous variables. For whether one does calculations by hand, by mechanical calculator or by electronic computer, one always needs an explicit representation for numbers, typically in terms of a sequence of digits of a certain length. (From the 1930s to 1960s, some work was done on so-called analog computers which used electrical voltages to represent continuous variables, but such machines turned out not to be reliable enough for most practical purposes.) From the earliest days of electronic computing, however, great efforts were made to try to approximate a continuum of numbers as closely as possible. And indeed for studying systems with fairly simple behavior, such approximations can typically be made to work. But as we shall see later in this chapter, with more complex behavior, it is almost inevitable that the approximation breaks down, and there is no choice but to look at the explicit representations of numbers. (See also page 1128.)

■ **History of digit sequences.** On an abacus or similar device numbers are in effect represented by digit sequences. In antiquity however most systems for writing numbers were like the Roman one and not based on digit sequences. An exception was the Babylonian base 60 system (from which hours:minutes:seconds notation derives). The Hindu-Arabic base 10 system in its modern form probably originated around 600 AD, and particularly following the work of Leonardo Fibonacci in the early 1200s, became common by the 1400s. Base 2 appears to have first been considered explicitly in the early 1600s (notably by John Napier in 1617), and was studied in detail by Gottfried Leibniz starting in 1679. The possibility of arbitrary bases was stated by Blaise Pascal in 1658. Various bases were used in puzzles, but rarely in pure mathematics (work by Georg Cantor in the 1860s being an exception). The first widespread use of base 2 was in electronic computers, starting in the late 1940s. Even in the 1980s digit sequences were viewed by most mathematicians as largely irrelevant for pure mathematical purposes. The study of fractals and nesting, the appearance of many algorithms involving digit sequences and the routine use of long numbers in *Mathematica* have however gradually made digit sequences be seen as more central to mathematics.

Elementary Arithmetic

■ **Page 117 · Substitution systems.** There are many connections between digit sequences and substitution systems, as discussed on page 891. The pattern shown here is essentially a rotated version of the pattern generated by the first substitution system on page 83.

■ **Page 117 · Digit counts.** The number of black squares on row n in the pattern shown here is given by $DigitCount[n, 2, 1]$ and is plotted below. This function appeared on page 870 in the discussion of binomial coefficients modulo 2, and will appear again in several other places in this book. Note the inequality $1 \leq DigitCount[n, 2, 1] \leq Log[2, n]$. Formulas for $DigitCount[n, 2, 1]$ include $n - IntegerExponent[n!, 2]$ and

$$2n - Log[2, Denominator[Derivative[n][(1 - \#)^{-1/2} \&][0]/n!]]$$

Straightforward generalizations of *DigitCount* can be defined for integer and non-integer bases and by looking not only at the total number of digits but also at correlations between digits. In all cases the analogs of the picture below have a nested structure.

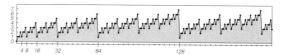

■ **Negative bases.** Given a suitable list of digits from 0 to $k - 1$ one can obtain any positive or negative number using $FromDigits[list, -k]$. The picture below shows the digit sequences of successive numbers in base -2; the row j from the bottom turns out to consist of alternating black and white blocks of length 2^j. (In ordinary base 2 a number $-n$ can be represented as on a typical electronic computer by complementing each digit, including leading 0's.) (See also page 1093.)

■ **Non-power bases.** One can consider representing numbers by $Sum[a[n] f[n], \{n, 0, \infty\}]$ where the $f[n]$ need not be k^n. So long as $f[n]$ grows less rapidly than 2^n (as when $f = Fibonacci$ or $f = Prime$), digits 0 and 1 will suffice, though the representation is not generally unique. (See page 1070.)

■ **Multiplicative digit sequences.** One can consider generalizations of digit sequences in which numbers are broken into parts combined not by addition but by multiplication. Since numbers can be factored uniquely into products of powers of primes, a number can be specified by a list in which 1's appear at the positions of the appropriate $Prime[m]^n$ (which can be sorted by size) and 0's appear elsewhere, as shown below. Note that unlike the case of ordinary additive digits, far more than $Log[m]$ digits are required to specify a number m.

Page 120 · Powers of three in base 2. The nth row in the pattern shown can be obtained simply as *IntegerDigits[3^n, 2]*. Even such individual rows seem in many respects random. The picture below shows the fraction of 1's that appear on successive rows. The fraction seems to tend to 1/2.

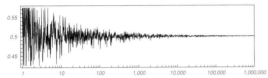

If one looks only at the rightmost s columns of the pattern, one sees repetition—but the period of the repetition grows like 2^s. Typical vertical columns have one obvious deviation from randomness: it is twice as probable for the same colors to occur on successive steps than for opposite colors. (For multiplier m in base k, the relative frequencies of pairs $\{i, j\}$ are given by *Quotient[a i - j - 1 + m, k] - Quotient[m i - j - 1, k]*.)

The sequence *Mod[3^n, 2^s]* obtained from the rightmost s digits corresponds to a simple linear congruential pseudorandom number generator. Such generators are widely used in practical computer systems, as discussed further on page 974. (Note that in the particular case used here, pairs of numbers *Mod[{3^n, 3^{n+1}}, 2^s]* always lie on lines; with multipliers other than 3, such regularities may occur for longer blocks of numbers.)

Note that if one uses base 6 rather than base 2, then as shown on page 614 powers of 3 still yield a complicated pattern, but all operations are strictly local, and the system corresponds to a cellular automaton with 6 possible colors for each cell and rule *{a_, b_, c_} → 3 Mod[b, 2] + Floor[c/2]* (see page 1093).

Leading digits. In base b the leading digits of powers are not equally probable, but follow the logarithmic law from page 914.

Page 122 · Powers of 3/2. The nth value shown in the plot here is *Mod[$(3/2)^n$, 1]*. Measurements suggest that these values are uniformly distributed in the range 0 to 1, but despite a fair amount of mathematical work since the 1940s, there has been no substantial progress towards proving this.

In base 6, $(3/2)^n$ is a cellular automaton with rule

$\{a_-, b_-, c_-\} \to 3 \, Mod[a + Quotient[b, 2], 2] +$
$\quad Quotient[3 \, Mod[b, 2] + Quotient[c, 2], 2]$

(Note that this rule is invertible.) Looking at $u (3/2)^n$ then corresponds to studying the cellular automaton with an initial

condition given by the base 6 digits of u. It is then possible to find special values of u (an example is 0.166669170371...) which make the first digit in the fractional part of $u (3/2)^n$ always nonzero, so that *Mod[u (3/2)^n, 1] > 1/6*. In general, it seems that *Mod[u (3/2)^n, 1]* can be kept as large as about 0.3 (e.g. with $u = 0.38906669065$ ...) but no larger.

General powers. It has been known in principle since the 1930s that *Mod[h^n, 1]* is uniformly distributed in the range 0 to 1 for almost all values of h. However, no specific value of h for which this is true has ever been explicitly found. (Some attempts to construct such values were made in the 1970s.) Exceptions are known to include so-called Pisot numbers such as *GoldenRatio*, $\sqrt{2} + 1$ and *Root[$\#^3 - \# - 1$ &, 1]* (the numerically smallest of all Pisot numbers) for which *Mod[h^n, 1]* becomes 0 or 1 for large n. Note that *Mod[x h^n, 1]* effectively extracts successive digits of x in base h (see pages 149 and 919).

Multiples of irrational numbers. Instead of powers one can consider successive multiples *Mod[h n, 1]* of a number h. The pictures below show results obtained as a function of n for various choices of h. (These correspond to positions of a particle bouncing around in an idealized box, as discussed on pages 971 and 1022.)

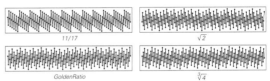

When h is a rational number, the sequence always repeats. But in all other cases, the sequence does not repeat, and in fact it is known that a uniform distribution of values is obtained. (The average difference of successive values is maximized for $h =$ *GoldenRatio*, as mentioned on page 891.)

Relation to substitution systems. Despite the uniform distribution result in the note above, the sequence *Floor[(n + 1) h] - Floor[n h]* is definitely not completely random, and can in fact be generated by a sequence of substitution rules. The first m rules (which yield far more than m elements of the original sequence) are obtained for any h that is not a rational number from the continued fraction form (see page 914) of h by

Map[({0 → Join[#, {1}], 1 → Join[#, {1, 0}]} &)[Table[0,
{# - 1}]] &, Reverse[Rest[ContinuedFraction[h, m]]]]

Given these rules, the original sequence is given by

Floor[h] + Fold[Flatten[#1 /. #2] &, {0}, rules]

If h is the solution to a quadratic equation, then the continued fraction form is repetitive, and so there are a limited number of different substitution rules. In this case, therefore, the original sequence can be found by a neighbor-independent substitution system of the kind discussed on page 82. For $h = GoldenRatio$ the substitution system is $\{0 \to \{1\}, 1 \to \{1, 0\}\}$ (see page 890), for $h = \sqrt{2}$ it is $\{0 \to \{0, 1\}, 1 \to \{0, 1, 0\}\}$ (see page 892) and for $h = \sqrt{3}$ it is $\{0 \to \{1, 1, 0\}, 1 \to \{1, 1, 0, 1\}\}$. (The presence of nested structure is particularly evident in $FoldList[Plus, 0, Table[Mod[h\,n, 1] - 1/2, \{n, max\}]].$) (See also pages 892, 916, 932 and 1084.)

■ **Other uniformly distributed sequences.** Cases in which $Mod[a[n], 1]$ is uniformly distributed include $\sqrt{n}$, $n\,Log[n]$, $Log[Fibonacci[n]]$, $Log[n!]$, $h\,n^2$ and $h\,Prime[n]$ (h irrational) and probably $n\,Sin[n]$. (See also page 914.)

■ **Page 122 · Implementation.** The evolution for t steps of the system at the top of the page can be computed simply by
$NestList[If[EvenQ[\#], 3\#/2, 3(\# + 1)/2] \&, 1, t]$

■ **Page 122 · The *3n+1* problem.** The system described here is similar to the so-called $3\,n + 1$ problem, in which one looks at the rule $n \to If[EvenQ[n], n/2, (3\,n + 1)/2]$ and asks whether for any initial value of n the system eventually evolves to 1 (and thereafter simply repeats the sequence 1, 2, 1, 2, ...). It has been observed that this happens for all initial values of n up to at least 10^{16}, but despite a fair amount of mathematical effort since the problem was first posed in the 1930s, no general proof for all values of n has ever been found. (For negative initial n, the evolution appears always to reach -1, -5 or -17, and then repeat with periods 1, 3 or 11 respectively.) An alternative formulation is to ask whether for all n
$FixedPoint[(3\#/2 \land IntegerExponent[\#, 2] + 1)/2 \&, n] == 2$

With the rule $n \to If[EvenQ[n], 5n/2, (n + 1)/2]$ used in the main text, the sequence produced repeats if n ever reaches 2, 4 or 40 (and possibly higher numbers). But with initial values of n up to 10,000, this happens in only 642 cases, and with values up to 100,000 it happens in only 2683 cases. In all other cases, the values of n in the sequence appear to grow forever.

To get some idea about the origin of this behavior, one can assume that successive values of n are randomly even and odd with equal probability. And with this assumption, n should increase by a factor of $5/2$ half the time, and decrease by a factor close to $1/2$ the rest of the time—so that after t steps it should be multiplied by an overall factor of about $(\sqrt{5}/2)^t$. Starting with $n = 6$, the effective exponents for $t = 10 \land Range[6]$ are $\{39.6, 245.1, 1202.8, 9250.7, 98269.8, 1002020.4\}$. One reason that all sequences do not grow forever is that even with perfect randomness, there will be fluctuations, and occasionally n will reach a low value that makes it get stuck in a repetitive sequence.

If one applies the same kind of argument to the standard $3\,n + 1$ problem, then one concludes that n should on average decrease by a factor of $\sqrt{3}/2$ at each step, making it unsurprising that at least in most cases n eventually reaches the value 1. Indeed, averaging over many initial values of n, there is good quantitative agreement between the predictions of the randomness approximation and the actual $3\,n + 1$ problem. But since there is no fundamental basis for the randomness approximation, it is still conceivable that a particular value of n exists that does not follow its predictions.

The pictures below show how many steps are needed to reach value 1 starting from different values of n. Case (a) is the standard $3\,n + 1$ problem. Cases (b) and (c) use somewhat different rules that yield considerably simpler behavior. In case (b), the number of steps is equal to the number of base 2 digits in n, while in case (c) it is determined by the number of 1's in the base 2 digit sequence of n.

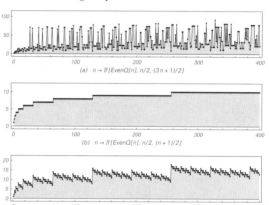

(a) $n \to If[EvenQ[n], n/2, (3\,n + 1)/2]$

(b) $n \to If[EvenQ[n], n/2, (n + 1)/2]$

(c) $n \to If[EvenQ[n], n/2, n + 1]$

■ ***3n+1* problem as cellular automaton.** If one writes the digits of n in base 6, then the rule for updating the digit sequence is a cellular automaton with 7 possible colors (color 6 works as an end marker that appears to the left and right of the actual digit sequence):
$\{a\_, b\_, c\_\} \to If[b == 6, If[EvenQ[a], 6, 4],$
$3\,Mod[a, 2] + Quotient[b, 2]] /. 0 :\to 6 /; a == 6]$

The $3\,n + 1$ problem can then be viewed as a question about the existence of persistent structure in this cellular automaton.

■ **Reconstructing initial conditions.** Given a particular starting value of n, it is difficult to predict what precise sequence of even and odd values will be obtained in the system on page 122. But given t steps in this sequence as a list of 0's and 1's, the following function will reconstruct the rightmost t digits in the starting value of n:

IntegerDigits[First[Fold[{Mod[If[OddQ[#2], 2 First[#1] - 1, 2 First[#1] PowerMod[5, -1, Last[#1]]], Last[#1]], 2 Last[#1]} &, {0, 2}, Reverse[list]]], 2, Length[list]]

■ **A reversible system.** In both the ordinary $3n + 1$ problem and in the systems discussed in the main text different numbers often evolve to the same value so that there is no unique way to reverse the evolution. However, with the rule

n → If[EvenQ[n], 3 n/2, Round[3 n/4]]

it is always possible to go backwards by the rule

n → If[Mod[n, 3] == 0, 2 n/3, Round[4 n/3]]

The picture shows the number of base 10 digits in numbers obtained by backward and forward evolution from $n = 8$. For $n < 8$, the system always enters a short cycle. Starting at $n = 44$, there is also a length 12 cycle. But apart from these cycles, the numbers produced always seem to grow without bound at an average rate of $3/(2\sqrt{2})$ in the forward direction, and $2 \, 4^{1/3}/3$ in the backward direction (at least all numbers up to 10,000 grow to above 10^{100}). Approximately one number in 20 has the property that evolution either backward or forward from it never leads to a smaller number.

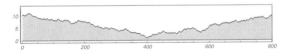

■ **Page 125 · Reversal-addition systems.** The operation that is performed here is

n → n + FromDigits[Reverse[IntegerDigits[n, 2]], 2]

After a few steps, the digit sequence obtained is typically reversal symmetric (a generalized palindrome) except for the interchange of 0 and 1, and for the presence of localized structures. The sequence expands by at least one digit every two steps; more rapid expansion is typically correlated with increased randomness. For most initial n, the overall pattern obtained quickly becomes repetitive, with an effective period of 4 steps. But with the initial condition $n = 512$, no repetition occurs for at least a million steps, at which point n has 568418 base 2 digits. The plot below shows the lengths of the successive regions of regularity visible on the right-hand edge of the picture on page 126 over the course of the first million steps.

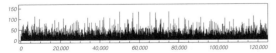

If one works directly with a digit sequence of fixed length, dropping any carries on the left, then a repetitive pattern is typically obtained fairly quickly. If one always includes one

new digit on the left at every step, even when it is 0, then a rather random pattern is produced.

■ **History.** Systems similar to the one described here (though often in base 10) were mentioned in the recreational mathematics literature at least as long ago as 1939. A few small computer experiments were done around 1970, but no large-scale investigations seem to have previously been made.

■ **Digit reversal.** Sequences of the form

Table[FromDigits[
Reverse[IntegerDigits[n, k, m]], k], {n, 0, k^m - 1}]

shown below appear in algorithms such as the fast Fourier transform and, with different values of k for different coordinates, in certain quasi-Monte Carlo schemes. (See pages 1073 and 1085.) Such sequences were considered by Johannes van der Corput in 1935.

$k = 2, m = 7$ $k = 2, m = 10$ $k = 3, m = 6$

■ **Iterated run-length encoding.** Starting say with $\{1\}$ consider repeatedly replacing *list* by (see page 1070)

Flatten[Map[{Length[#], First[#]} &, Split[list]]]

The resulting sequences contain only the numbers 1, 2 and 3, but otherwise at first appear fairly random. However, as noticed by John Conway around 1986, the sequences can actually be obtained by a neighbor-independent substitution system, acting on 92 subsequences, with rules such as $\{3, 1, 1, 3, 3, 2, 2, 1, 1, 3\} → \{\{1, 3, 2\}, \{1, 2, 3, 2, 2, 2, 1, 1, 3\}\}$. The system thus in the end produces patterns that are purely nested, though formed from rather complicated elements. The length of the sequence at the nth step grows like λ^n, where $\lambda \simeq 1.3$ is the root of a degree 71 polynomial, corresponding to the largest eigenvalue of the transition matrix for the substitution system.

■ **Digit count sequences.** Starting say with $\{1\}$ repeatedly replace *list* by

Join[list, IntegerDigits[Apply[Plus, list], 2]]

The resulting sequences grow in length roughly like $n \, Log[n]$. The picture below shows the fluctuations around $m/2$ of the cumulative number of 1's up to position m in the sequence obtained at step 1000. A definite nested structure similar to picture (c) on page 130 is evident.

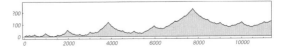

■ **Iterated bitwise operations.** The pictures below show digit sequences generated by repeatedly applying combinations of bitwise and arithmetic operations. The first example corresponds to elementary cellular automaton rule 60. Note that any cellular automaton rule can be reproduced by some appropriate combination of bitwise and arithmetic operations.

BitXor[2 n, n]   BitXor[3 + 2 n, n]   BitXor[3 n, n]   BitXor[6 n, n]   BitOr[2 n, n]   BitOr[6 n, n]

Recursive Sequences

■ **Page 128 · Recurrence relations.** The rules for the sequences given here all have the form of linear recurrence relations. An explicit formula for the nth term in each sequence can be found by solving the algebraic equation obtained by applying the replacement $f[m\_] \to t^m$ to the recurrence relation. (In case (e), for example, the equation is $t^n == -t^{n-1} + t^{n-2}$.) Note that (d) is the Fibonacci sequence, discussed on page 890.

Standard examples of recursive sequences that do not come from linear recurrence relations include factorial

$f[1] := 1; f[n\_] := n \, f[n-1]$

and Ackermann functions (see below). These two sequences both grow rapidly, but smoothly.

A recurrence relation like

$f[0] := x; f[n\_] := a \, f[n-1] \, (1 - f[n-1])$

corresponds to an iterated map of the kind discussed on page 920, and has complicated behavior for many rational x.

■ **Ackermann functions.** A convenient example is

$f[1, n\_] := n; f[m\_, 1] := f[m-1, 2]$

$f[m\_, n\_] := f[m-1, f[m, n-1] + 1]$

The original function constructed by Wilhelm Ackermann around 1926 is essentially

$f[1, x\_, y\_] := x + y;$
$f[m\_, x\_, y\_] := Nest[f[m-1, x, \#] \&, x, y-1]$

or

$f[m\_, x\_, y\_] :=$
$\quad Nest[Function[z, Nest[\#1, x, z-1]] \&, x + \# \&, m-1][y]$

For successive m (following the so-called Grzegorczyk hierarchy) this is $x + y$, $x \, y$, x^y, $Nest[x^\# \&, 1, y]$, ... $f[4, x, y]$ can also be written $Array[x \& , y, 1, Power]$ and is sometimes called tetration and denoted $x \uparrow \uparrow y$.

■ **Page 129 · Computation of sequences.** It is straightforward to compute the various sequences given here, but to avoid a rapid increase in computer time, it is essential to store all the

values of $f[n]$ that one has already computed, rather than recomputing them every time they are needed. This is achieved for example by the definitions

$f[n\_] := f[n] = f[n - f[n-1]] + f[n - f[n-2]]$

$f[1] = f[2] = 1$

The question of which recursive definitions yield meaningful sequences can depend on the details of how the rules are applied. For example, $f[-1]$ may occur, but if the complete expression is $f[-1] - f[-1]$, then the actual value of $f[-1]$ is irrelevant. The default form of evaluation for recursive functions implemented by all standard computer languages (including *Mathematica*) is the so-called leftmost innermost scheme, which attempts to find explicit values for each $f[k]$ that occurs first, and will therefore never notice if $f[k]$ in fact occurs only in the combination $f[k] - f[k]$. (The SMP system that I built around 1980 allowed different schemes—but they rarely seemed useful and were difficult to understand.)

■ **Page 131 · Properties of sequences.** Sequence (d) is given by

$f[n\_] := (n + g[IntegerDigits[n, 2]])/2$

$g[\{(1)..\}] = 1; g[\{1, (0)..\}] = 0$

$g[\{1, s\_\_\}] := 1 + g[IntegerDigits[FromDigits[\{s\}, 2] + 1, 2]]$

The list of elements in the sequence up to value m is given by

$Flatten[Table[Table[n, \{IntegerExponent[n, 2] + 1\}], \{n, m\}]]$

The differences between the first $2 \, (2^k - 1)$ of these elements is

$Nest[Replace[\#, \{x\_\_\_\} \to \{x, 1, x, 0\}] \&, \{\}, k]$

The largest n for which $f[n] == m$ is given by $2 \, m + 1 - DigitCount[m, 2, 1]$ or $IntegerExponent[(2 \, m)!, 2] + 1$ (this satisfies $h[1] = 2; h[m\_] := h[Floor[m/2]] + m$).

The form of sequence (c) is similar to that obtained from concatenation numbers on page 913. Hump m in the picture of sequence (c) shown is given by

$FoldList[Plus, 0, Flatten[Nest[Delete[NestList[Rest, \#,$
$\quad Length[\#] - 1], 2] \&, Append[Table[1, \{m\}], 0], m]] - 1/2$

The first 2^m elements in the sequence can also be generated in terms of reordered base 2 digit sequences by

$FoldList[Plus, 1, Map[Last[Last[\#]] \&,$
$\quad Sort[Table[\{\{Length[\#], Apply[Plus, \#], 1 - \#\} \&\}[$
$\quad\quad IntegerDigits[i, 2]], \{i, 2^m\}]]]]$

Note that the positive and negative fluctuations in sequence (f) are not completely random: although the probability for individual fluctuations in each direction seems to be the same, the probability for two positive fluctuations in a row is smaller than for two negative fluctuations in a row.

In the sequences discussed here, $f[n\_]$ always has the form $f[p[n]] + f[q[n]]$. The plots at the top of the next page show $p[n]$ and $q[n]$ as a function of n.

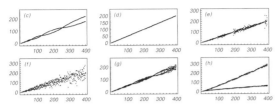

The process of evaluating $f[n]$ for a particular n can be thought of as yielding a tree where each node is a particular $f[k]$ which has two successors, $f[p[k]]$ and $f[q[k]]$. The distinct nodes reached starting from $f[12]$ for sequence (f) are then for example $\{\{12\}, \{3, 7\}, \{1, 2, 4\}, \{1, 2\}, \{1\}\}$. The total lengths of these chains (corresponding to the depth of the evaluation tree) seem to increase roughly like $Log[n]$ for all the rules on this page. For the Fibonacci sequence, it is instead $n - 1$. The maximum number of distinct nodes at any level in the tree has large fluctuations but its peaks seem to increase roughly linearly for all the rules on this page (in the Fibonacci case it is $Ceiling[n/2]$).

■ **History.** The idea of sequences in which later terms are deduced from earlier ones existed in antiquity, notably in the method of induction and in various approximation schemes (compare page 918). The Fibonacci sequence also appears to have arisen in antiquity (see page 890). A fairly clear idea of integer recurrence relations has existed since about the 1600s, but until very recently mainstream mathematics has almost never investigated them. In the late 1800s and early 1900s issues about the foundations of mathematics (see note below) led to the formal definition of so-called recursive functions. But almost without exception the emphasis was on studying what such functions could in principle do, not on looking at the actual behavior of particular ones. And indeed, despite their simple forms, recursive sequences of the kind I discuss here do not for the most part ever appear to have been studied before—although sequence (c) was mentioned in lectures by John Conway around 1988, and the first 17 terms of sequence (e) were given by Douglas Hofstadter in 1979.

■ **Primitive recursive functions.** As part of trying to formalize foundations of arithmetic Richard Dedekind began around 1888 to discuss possible functions that could be defined using recursion (induction). By the 1920s there had then emerged a definite notion of primitive recursive functions. The proof of Gödel's Theorem in 1931 made use of both primitive and general recursive functions—and by the mid-1930s emphasis had shifted to discussion of general recursive functions.

Primitive recursive functions are defined to deal with non-negative integers and to be set up by combining the basic functions $z = 0$ & (zero), $s = \# + 1$ & (successor) and

$p[i\_] := Slot[i]$ & (projection) using the operations of composition and primitive recursion

$f[0, y\_\_\_Integer] := g[y]$

$f[x\_Integer, y\_\_\_Integer] := h[f[x - 1, y], x - 1, y]$

Plus and *Times* can then for example be defined as

$plus[0, y\_] = y; plus[x\_, y\_] := s[plus[x - 1, y]]$

$times[0, y\_] = 0; times[x\_, y\_] := plus[times[x - 1, y], y]$

Most familiar integer mathematical functions also turn out to be primitive recursive—examples being *Power*, *Mod*, *Binomial*, *GCD* and *Prime*. And indeed in the early 1900s it was thought that perhaps any function that could reasonably be computed would be primitive recursive (see page 1125). But the construction in the late 1920s of the Ackermann function $f[m, x, y]$ discussed above showed that this was not correct. For any primitive recursive function can grow for large x at most like $f[m, x, x]$ with fixed m. Yet $f[x, x, x]$ will always eventually grow faster than this—demonstrating that the whole Ackermann function cannot be primitive recursive. (See page 1162.)

A crucial feature of primitive recursive functions is that the number of steps they take to evaluate is always limited, and can always in effect be determined in advance, since the basic operation of primitive recursion can be unwound simply as

$f[x\_, y\_\_\_] := Fold[h[\#1, \#2, y] \&, g[y], Range[0, x - 1]]$

And what this means is that any computation that for example fundamentally involves a search that might not terminate cannot be implemented by a primitive recursive function. General recursive functions, however, also allow

$\mu[f\_] = NestWhile[\# + 1 \&, 0, Function[n, f[n, \#\#1] \neq 0]]$ &

which can perform unbounded searches. (Ordinary primitive recursive functions are always total functions, that give definite values for every possible input. But general recursive functions can be partial functions, that do not terminate for some inputs.) As discussed on page 1121 it turns out that general recursive functions are universal, so that they can be used to represent any possible computable function. (Note that any general recursive function can be expressed in the form $c[f, \mu[g]]$ where f and g are primitive recursive.)

In enumerating recursive functions it is convenient to use symbolic definitions for composition and primitive recursion

$c[g\_, h\_\_\_] = Apply[g, Through[\{h\}[\#\#]]]$ &

$r[g\_, h\_] =$
    $If[\#1 == 0, g[\#\#2], h[\#0[\#1 - 1, \#\#2], \#1 - 1, \#\#2]]$ &

where the more efficient unwound form is

$r[g\_, h\_] = Fold[Function[\{u, v\}, h[u, v, \#\#2]],$
            $g[\#\#2], Range[0, \# - 1]]$ &

And in terms of these, for example, $plus = r[p[1], s]$.

The total number of recursive functions grows roughly exponentially in the size (*LeafCount*) of such expressions, and roughly linearly in the number of arguments.

Most randomly selected primitive recursive functions show very simple behavior—either constant or linearly increasing when fed successive integers as arguments. The smallest examples that show other behavior are:

- *r[z, r[s, s]]*, which is *1/2 # (# + 1) &*, with quadratic growth

- *r[z, r[s, c[s, s]]]*, which is $2^{#+1} - # - 2$ *&*, with exponential growth

- *r[z, r[s, p[2]]]*, which is *2 ^ Ceiling[Log[2, # + 2]] - # - 2 &*, which shows very simple nesting

- *r[z, r[c[s, z], z]]*, which is *Mod[#, 2] &*, with repetitive behavior

- *r[z, r[s, r[s, s]]]* which is *Fold[1/2 #1 (#1 + 1) + #2 &, 0, Range[#]] &*, growing like 2^{2^x}.

r[z, r[s, r[s, r[s, p[2]]]]] is the first function to show significantly more complex behavior, and indeed as the picture below indicates, it already shows remarkable randomness. From its definition, the function can be written as

Fold[Fold[2 ^ Ceiling[Log[2, Ceiling[(#1 + 2)/(#2 + 2)]]] (#2 + 2) - 2 - #1 &, #2, Range[#1]] &, 0, Range[#]] &

Its first zeros are at *{4, 126, 813, 966, 1166, 1177, 1666, 1897}*.

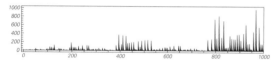

Each zero is immediately followed by a maximum equal to *x*, and as picture below shows, values tend to accumulate for example on lines of the form $\pm x/2^u \pm (2m + 1)2^v$.

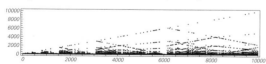

Note that functions of the form *Nest[r[c[s, z], #] &, c[s, s], n]* are given in terms of the original Ackermann function in the note above by *f[n + 1, 2, # + 1] - 1 &*.

Before the example above one might have thought that primitive recursive functions would always have to show rather simple behavior. But already an immediate counterexample is *Prime*. And it turns out that if they never sample values below *f[0]* the functions in the main text are also all primitive recursive. (Their definitions have a

primitive recursive structure, but to operate correctly they must be given integers that are non-negative.)

Among functions with simple explicit definitions, essentially the only examples known fundamentally to be not primitive recursive are ones closely related to the Ackermann function. But given an enumeration of primitive recursive functions (say ordered first by *LeafCount*, then with *Sort*) in which the mth function is *w[m]* diagonalization (see page 1128) yields the function *w[x][x]* shown below which cannot be primitive recursive. It is inevitable that the function shown must eventually grow faster than any primitive recursive function (at *x = 356* its value is 63190, while at *x = 1464* it is 1073844). But by reducing the results modulo 2 one gets a function that does not grow—and has seemingly quite random behavior—yet is presumably again not primitive recursive.

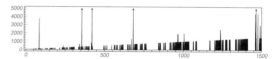

(Note that multiple arguments to a recursive function can be encoded as a single argument using functions like the *β* of page 1120—though the irregularity of such functions tends to make it difficult then to tell what is going on in the underlying recursive function.)

- **Ulam sequences.** Slightly more complicated definitions in terms of numbers yield all sorts of sequences with very complicated forms. An example suggested by Stanislaw Ulam around 1960 (in a peculiar attempt to get a 1D analog of a 2D cellular automaton; see pages 877 and 928) starts with *{1, 2}*, then successively appends the smallest number that is the sum of two previous numbers in just one way, yielding

{1, 2, 3, 4, 6, 8, 11, 13, 16, 18, 26, 28, 36, 38, 47, 48, 53, 57, ...}

With this initial condition, the sequence is known to go on forever. At least up to $n = 10^6$ terms, it increases roughly like *13.5 n*, but as shown below the fluctuations seem random.

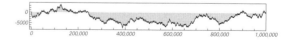

The Sequence of Primes

- **History of primes.** Whether the Babylonians had the notion of primes is not clear, but before 400 BC the Pythagoreans had introduced primes as numbers of objects that can be arranged only in a single line, and not in any other rectangular array. Around 300 BC Euclid discussed various properties of primes in his *Elements*, giving for example a proof that there are an infinity of primes. The sieve of Eratosthenes was described in 200 BC, apparently following ideas of Plato. Then starting in the early 1600s various methods for factoring were developed, and conjectures about formulas for primes were made. Pierre Fermat suggested $2^{2^n} + 1$ as a source for primes and Marin Mersenne $2^{\text{^}}Prime[n] - 1$ (see page 911). In 1752 Christian Goldbach showed that no ordinary polynomial could generate only primes, though as pointed out by Leonhard Euler $n^2 - n + 41$ does so for $n < 40$. (With *If* or *Floor* included there are at least complicated cases known where polynomial-like formulas can be set up whose evaluation corresponds to explicit prime-generating procedures—see page 1162.) Starting around 1800 extensive work was done on analytical approximations to the distribution of primes (see below). There continued to be slow progress in finding specific large primes; $2^{31} - 1$ was found prime around 1750 and $2^{127} - 1$ in 1876. ($2^{2^5} + 1$ was found composite in 1732, as have now all $2^{2^n} + 1$ for $n \le 32$.) Then starting in the 1950s with the use of electronic computers many new large primes were found. The number of digits in the largest known prime has historically increased roughly exponentially with time over the past two decades, with a prime of over 4 million digits ($2^{13466917} - 1$) now being known (see page 911).

■ **Page 132 · Finding primes.** The sieve of Eratosthenes shown in the picture is an appropriate procedure if one wants to find every prime, but testing whether an individual number is prime can be done much more efficiently, as in *PrimeQ[n]* in *Mathematica*, for example by using Fermat's so-called little theorem that $Mod[a^{p-1}, p] == 1$ whenever p is prime. The nth prime *Prime[n]* can also be computed fairly efficiently using ideas from analytic number theory (see below).

■ **Decimation systems.** A somewhat similar system starts with a line of cells, then at each step removes every k^{th} cell that remains, as in the pictures below. The number of steps for which a cell at position n will survive can be computed as

Module[{q = n + k - 1, s = 1},
  While[Mod[q, k] ≠ 0, q = Ceiling[(k - 1) q/k]; s++]; s]

If a cell is going to survive for s steps, then it turns out that this can be determined by looking at the last s digits in the base k representation of its position. For $k = 2$, a cell survives for s steps if these digits are all 0 (so that s==*IntegerExponent[n, k]*). But for $k > 2$, no such simple characterization appears to exist.

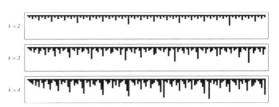

If the cells are arranged on a circle of size n, the question of which cell is removed last is the so-called Josephus problem. The solution is *Fold[Mod[#1 + k, #2, 1] &, 0, Range[n]]*, or *FromDigits[RotateLeft[IntegerDigits[n, 2]], 2]* for $k = 2$.

■ **Page 132 · Divisors.** The picture below shows as black squares the divisors of each successive number (which correspond to the gray dots in the picture in the main text). Primes have divisors 1 and n only. (See also pages 902 and 747.)

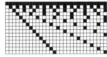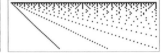

■ **Page 133 · Results about primes.** *Prime[n]* is given approximately by $n\,Log[n] + n\,Log[Log[n]]$. (*Prime[$10^9$]* is 22,801,763,489 while the approximation gives 2.38×10^{10}.) A first approximation to *PrimePi[n]* is $n/Log[n]$. A somewhat better approximation is *LogIntegral[n]*, equal to *Integrate[1/Log[t], {t, 2, n}]*. This was found empirically by Carl Friedrich Gauss in 1792, based on looking at a table of primes. (*PrimePi[10^9]* is 50,847,534 while *LogIntegral[10^9]* is about 50,849,235.) A still better approximation is obtained by subtracting *Sum[LogIntegral[n^{r_i}], {i, -∞, ∞}]* where the r_i are the complex zeros of the Riemann zeta function *Zeta[s]*, discussed on page 918. According to the Riemann Hypothesis, the difference between *PrimePi[n]* and *LogIntegral[n]* is of order $\sqrt{n}\,Log[n]$. More refined analytical estimates of *PrimePi[n]* are good enough that they are used by *Mathematica* to compute *Prime[n]* for large n.

It is known that the ratio of the number of primes of the form $4k + 1$ and $4k + 3$ asymptotically approaches 1, but almost nothing has been proved about the fluctuations.

The gap between successive primes *Prime[n] - Prime[n - 1]* is thought to grow on average at most like $Log[Prime[n]]^2$. It is known that for sufficiently large n a gap of any size must exist. It is believed but not proved that there are an infinite number of "twin primes" with a gap of exactly 2.

■ **History of number theory.** Most areas of mathematics go from inception to maturity within at most a century. But in number theory there are questions that were formulated more than 2000 years ago (such as whether any odd perfect numbers exist) that have still not been answered. Of the principles that have been established in number theory, a great many were first revealed by explicit experiments. From its inception in classical times, through its development in the 1600s to 1800s, number theory was largely separate from other fields of mathematics. But starting at the end of the 1800s, increasing connections were found to other areas of both continuous and discrete mathematics. And through these connections, sophisticated proofs of such results as Fermat's Last Theorem—open for 350 years—have been constructed. Long considered a rather esoteric branch of mathematics, number theory has in recent years grown in practical importance through its use in areas such as coding theory, cryptography and statistical mechanics. Properties of numbers and certain elementary aspects of number theory have also always played a central role in amateur and recreational mathematics. And as this chapter indicates, number theory can also be used to provide many examples of the basic phenomena discussed in this book.

■ **Page 134 · Tables of primes.** No explicit tables of primes appear to have survived from antiquity, but it seems likely that all primes up to somewhere between 5000 and 10000 were known. (In 348 BC, Plato mentioned divisors of 5040, and by 100 AD there is evidence that the fifth perfect number was known, requiring the knowledge that 8191 is prime.) In 1202 Leonardo Fibonacci explicitly gave as an example a list of primes up to 100. And by the mid-1600s there were printed tables of primes up to 100,000, containing as much data as in plots (c) and (d). In the 1700s and 1800s many tables of number factorizations were constructed; by the 1770s there was a table up to 2 million, and by the 1860s up to 100 million. A table of primes up to a trillion could now be generated fairly easily with current computer technology—though for most purposes computation of specific primes is more useful.

■ **Page 134 · Numbers of primes.** The fact that curve (c) must cross the axis was proved by John Littlewood in 1914, and it is known to have at least one crossing below 10^{317}. Somewhat related to the curves shown here is the function *MoebiusMu[n]*, equal to 0 if *n* has a repeated prime factor and otherwise *(-1)^Length[FactorInteger[n]]*. The quantity *FoldList[Plus, 0, Table[MoebiusMu[i], {i, n}]]* behaves very much like a random walk. The so-called Mertens Conjecture from 1897 stated that the magnitude of this quantity is less than $\sqrt{n}$. But this was disproved in 1983, although the necessary *n* is not known explicitly.

■ **Relative primes.** A single number is prime if it has no non-trivial factors. Two numbers are said to be relatively prime if they share no non-trivial factors. The pattern formed by numbers with this property is shown on page 613.

■ **Page 135 · Properties.** (a) The number of divisors of *n* is given by *DivisorSigma[0, n]*, equal to *Length[Divisors[n]]*. For large *n* this number is on average of order *Log[n] + 2 EulerGamma - 1*.

(b) (*Aliquot sums*) The quantity that is plotted is *DivisorSigma[1, n] - 2 n*, equal to *Apply[Plus, Divisors[n]] - 2 n*. This quantity was considered of great significance in antiquity, particularly by the Pythagoreans. Numbers were known as abundant, deficient or perfect depending on whether the quantity was positive, negative or zero. (See notes on perfect numbers below.) For large *n*, *DivisorSigma[1, n]* is known to grow at most like *Log[Log[n]] n Exp[EulerGamma]*, and on average like $\pi^2 n/6$ (see page 1093). As discovered by Srinivasa Ramanujan in 1918 its fluctuations (see below) can be obtained from the formula

$$1/6 \ \pi^2 \ n \ Sum[Apply[Plus, Cos[2 \ \pi \ n \ Select[$$
$$Range[s], GCD[s, \#] == 1 \ \&]]/s]]/s^2, \{s, \infty\}]$$

(c) Squares are taken to be of positive or negative integers, or zero. The number of ways of expressing an integer *n* as the sum of two such squares is *4 Apply[Plus, Im[i^Divisors[n]]]*. This is nonzero when all prime factors of *n* of the form *4 k + 3* appear with even exponents. There is no known simple formula for the number of ways of expressing an integer as a sum of three squares, although part of the condition in the main text for integers to be expressible in this way was established by René Descartes in 1638 and the rest by Adrien Legendre in 1798. Note that the total number of integers less than *n* which can be expressed as a sum of three squares increases roughly like *5 n/6*, with fluctuations related to *IntegerDigits[n, 4]*. It is known that the directions of all vectors *{x, y, z}* for which $x^2 + y^2 + z^2 == n$ are uniformly distributed in the limit of large *n*.

The total number of ways that integers less than *n* can be expressed as a sum of *d* squares is equal to the number of integer lattice points that lie inside a sphere of radius $\sqrt{n}$ in *d*-dimensional space. For *d = 2*, this approaches πn for large *n*, with an error of order n^c, where $1/4 < c \leq 0.315$.

(d) All numbers *n* can be expressed as the sum of four squares, in exactly *8 Apply[Plus, Select[Divisors[n], Mod[#, 4] ≠ 0 &]]* ways, as established by Carl Jacobi in 1829. Edward Waring stated in 1770 that any number can be expressed as a sum of at most 9 cubes and 19 fourth powers. Seven cubes appear to suffice for all but 17 numbers, the last of which is 455; four cubes may suffice for all but 113936676 numbers, the last of which is 7373170279850. (See also page 1166.)

(e) Goldbach's Conjecture has been verified for all even numbers up to 4×10^{14}. In 1973 it was proved that any even number can be written as the sum of a prime and a number that has at most two prime factors, not necessarily distinct. The number of ways of writing an integer n as a sum of two primes can be calculated explicitly as *Length[Select[n - Table[Prime[i], {i, PrimePi[n]}], PrimeQ]]*. This quantity was conjectured by G. H. Hardy and John Littlewood in 1922 to be proportional to

$$2\, n\, \text{Apply[Times, Map[(\# - 1)/(\# - 2) \&,}$$
$$\text{Map[First, Rest[FactorInteger[n]]]]]}/\text{Log[n]}^2$$

It was proved in 1937 by Ivan Vinogradov that any large odd integer can be expressed as a sum of three primes.

■ **Trapezoidal primes.** If one lays out n objects in an $a \times b$ rectangular array, then n is prime if either a or b must be 1. Following the Pythagorean idea of figurate numbers one can instead consider laying out objects in an array of b rows, containing successively a, $a - 1$, ... objects. It turns out all numbers except powers of 2 can be represented this way.

■ **Other integer functions.** *IntegerExponent[n, k]* gives nested behavior as for decimation systems on page 909, while *MultiplicativeOrder[k, n]* and *EulerPhi[n]* yield more complicated behavior, as shown on pages 257 and 1093.

■ **Spectra.** The pictures below show frequency spectra obtained from the sequences in the main text. Some regularity is evident, and in cases (a) and (b) it can be understood from trigonometric sum formulas of Ramanujan discussed above (see also pages 586 and 1081).

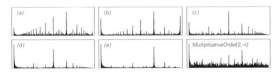

■ **Perfect numbers.** Perfect numbers with the property that *Apply[Plus, Divisors[n]] == 2 n* have been studied since at least the time of Pythagoras around 500 BC. The first few perfect numbers are *{6, 28, 496, 8128, 33550336}* (a total of 39 are currently known). It was shown by Euclid in 300 BC that $2^{n-1}\,(2^n - 1)$ is a perfect number whenever $2^n - 1$ is prime. Leonhard Euler then proved around 1780 that every even perfect number must have this form. The values of n for the known Mersenne primes $2^n - 1$ are shown below. These values can be found using the so-called Lucas-Lehmer test *Nest[Mod[#² - 2, 2ⁿ - 1] &, 4, n - 2] == 0*, and in all cases n itself must be prime.

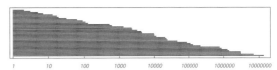

Whether any odd perfect numbers exist is probably the single oldest unsolved problem in mathematics. It is known that any odd perfect number must be greater than 10^{300}, must have a factor of at least 10^6, and must be less than 4^{4^s} if it has only s prime factors. Looking at curve (b) on page 135, however, it does not seem inconceivable that an odd perfect number could exist. For odd n up to 500 million the only values near 0 that appear in the curve are *{-6, -5, -4, -2, -1, 6, 18, 26, 30, 36}*, with, for example, the first 6 occurring at $n = 8925$ and last 18 occurring at $n = 159030135$. Various generalizations of perfect numbers have been considered, requiring for example *IntegerQ[DivisorSigma[1, n]/n]* (pluperfect) or *Abs[DivisorSigma[1, n] - 2 n] < r* (quasiperfect).

■ **Iterated aliquot sums.** Related to case (b) above is a system which repeats the replacement $n \rightarrow$ *Apply[Plus, Divisors[n]] - n* or equivalently $n \rightarrow$ *DivisorSigma[1, n] - n*. The fixed points of this procedure are the perfect numbers (see above). Other numbers usually evolve to perfect numbers, or to short repetitive sequences of numbers. But if one starts, for example, with the number 276, then the picture below shows the number of base 10 digits in the value obtained at each step.

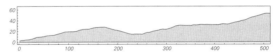

After 500 steps, the value is the 53-digit number
39448887705043893375102470161238803295318090278129552
The question of whether such values can increase forever was considered by Eugène Catalan in 1887, and has remained unresolved since.

Mathematical Constants

■ **Page 137 · Digits of pi.** The digits of π shown here can be obtained in less than a second from *Mathematica* on a typical current computer using *N[π, 7000]*. Historically, the number of decimal digits of π that have been computed is roughly as follows: 2000 BC (Babylonians, Egyptians): 2 digits; 200 BC (Archimedes): 5 digits; 1430 AD: 14 digits; 1610: 35 digits; 1706: 100 digits; 1844: 200 digits; 1855: 500 digits; 1949 (ENIAC computer): 2037 digits; 1961: 100,000 digits (IBM 7090); 1973: 1 million; 1983: 16 million; 1989: 1 billion; 1997: 50 billion; 1999: 206 billion. In the first 200 billion digits, the frequencies of 0 through 9 differ from 20 billion by

$\{30841, -85289, 136978, 69393, -78309,$
$-82947, -118485, -32406, 291044, -130820\}$

An early approximation to π was

$4 \, Sum[(-1)^k /(2k+1), \{k, 0, m\}]$

30 digits were obtained with

$2 \, Apply[Times, 2/Rest[NestList[Sqrt[2+\#] \&, 0, m]]]$

An efficient way to compute π to n digits of precision is

$(\#[\![2]\!]^2 /\#[\![3]\!] \&)[NestWhile[Apply[Function[\{a, b, c, d\},$
$\{(a+b)/2, Sqrt[a\,b], c-d\,(a-b)^2, 2\,d\}], \#] \&,$
$\{1, 1/Sqrt[N[2, n]], 1/4, 1/4\}, \#[\![1]\!] \neq \#[\![2]\!] \&]]$

This requires about $Log[2, n]$ steps, or a total of roughly $n \, Log[n]^2$ operations (see page 1134).

■ **Computing n^{th} digits directly.** Most methods for computing mathematical constants progressively generate each additional digit. But following work by Simon Plouffe and others in 1995 it became clear that it is sometimes possible to generate, at least with overwhelming probability, the nth digit without explicitly finding previous ones. As an example, the nth digit of $Log[2]$ in base 2 is formally given by $Round[FractionalPart[2^n \, Sum[2^{-k}/k, \{k, \infty\}]]]$. And in practice the nth digit can be found just by computing slightly over n terms of the sum, according to

$Round[FractionalPart[$
$Sum[FractionalPart[PowerMod[2, n-k, k]/k], \{k, n\}] +$
$Sum[2^{n-k}/k, \{k, n+1, n+d\}]]]$

where several values of d can be tried to check that the result does not change. (Note that with finite-precision arithmetic, some exponentially small probability exists that truncation of numbers will lead to incorrect results.) The same basic approach as for $Log[2]$ can be used to obtain base 16 digits in π from the following formula for π:

$Sum[16^{-k} \, (4/(8k+1) - 2/(8k+4) -$
$1/(8k+5) - 1/(8k+6)), \{k, 0, \infty\}]$

A similar approach can also be used for many other constants that can be viewed as related to values of $PolyLog$.

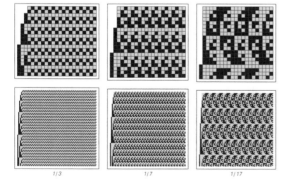

1/3   1/7   1/17

■ **Page 139 · Rational numbers.** The pictures above show the base 2 digit sequences of numbers m/n for successive m.

The digits of $1/n$ in base b repeat with period

$MultiplicativeOrder[b, FixedPoint[\#/GCD[\#, b] \&, n]]$

which is equal to $MultiplicativeOrder[b, n]$ for prime n, and is at most $n-1$. Each repeating block of digits typically seems quite random, and has properties such as all possible subblocks of digits up to a certain length appearing (see page 1084).

■ **Page 139 · Digit sequence properties.** Empirical evidence for the randomness of the digit sequences of $\sqrt{n}$, π, etc. has been accumulating since early computer experiments in the 1940s. The evidence is based on applying various standard statistical tests of randomness, and remains somewhat haphazard. (Already in 1888 John Venn had noted for example that the first 707 digits of π lead to an apparently typical 2D random walk.) (See page 1089.)

The fact that $\sqrt{2}$ is not a rational number was discovered by the Pythagoreans. Numbers that arise as solutions of polynomial equations are called algebraic; those that do not are called transcendental. e and π were proved to be transcendental in 1873 and 1882 respectively. It is known that $Exp[n]$ and $Log[n]$ for whole numbers n (except 0 and 1 respectively) are transcendental. It is also known for example that $Gamma[1/3]$ and $BesselJ[0, n]$ are transcendental. It is not known for example whether $EulerGamma$ is even irrational.

A number is said to be "normal" in a particular base if every digit and every block of digits of any length occur with equal frequency. Note that the fact that a number is normal in one base does not imply anything about its normality in another base (unless the bases are related for example by both being powers of 2). Despite empirical evidence, no number expressed just in terms of standard mathematical functions has ever been rigorously proved to be normal. It has nevertheless been known since the work of Emile Borel in 1909 that numbers picked randomly on the basis of their value are almost always normal. And indeed with explicit constructions in terms of digits, it is quite straightforward to get numbers that are normal. An example of this is the number 0.1234567891011121314... obtained by concatenating the digits of successive integers in base 10 (see below). This number was discussed by David Champernowne in 1933, and is known to be transcendental. A few other results are also known. One based on gradual extension of work by Richard Stoneham from 1971 is that numbers of the form $Sum[1/(p^n \, b^{p^n}), \{n, \infty\}]$ for prime $p > 2$ are normal in base b (for $GCD[b, p] == 1$), and are transcendental.

■ **Page 141 · Square roots.** A standard way to compute $\sqrt{n}$ is Newton's method (actually used already in 2000 BC by the Babylonians), in which one takes an estimate of the value x and then successively applies the rule $x \to 1/2\,(x + n/x)$. After t steps, this method yields a result accurate to about t^2 digits.

Another approach to computing square roots is based on the fact that the ratio of successive terms in for example the sequence $f[i] = 2\,f[i-1] + f[i-2]$ with $f[1] = f[2] = 1$ tends to $1 + \sqrt{2}$. This method yields about $2.5\,t$ base 2 digits after t steps.

The method of computing square roots shown in the main text is less efficient (it computes t digits in t steps), but illustrates more of the mechanisms involved. The basic idea is at every step t to maintain the relation $s^2 + 4\,r == 4^t\,n$, keeping r as small as possible so as to make $s \le 2^t\,\sqrt{n} < s + 4$. Note that the method works not only for integers, but for any rational number n for which $1 \le n < 4$.

■ **Nested digit sequences.** The number obtained from the substitution system $\{1 \to \{1, 0\}, 0 \to \{0, 1\}\}$ is approximately 0.587545966 in base 10. It is certainly conceivable that a quantity such as Feigenbaum's constant (approximately 4.6692016091) could have a digit sequence with this kind of nested structure.

From the result on page 890, the number whose digits are obtained from $\{1 \to \{1, 0\}, 0 \to \{1\}\}$ is given by *Sum[2 ^ (-Floor[n GoldenRatio]), {n, ∞}]*. This number is known to be transcendental. The nth term in its continued fraction representation turns out to be *2 ^ Fibonacci[n - 2]*.

The fact that nested digit sequences do not correspond to algebraic numbers follows from work by Alfred van der Poorten and others in the early 1980s. The argument is based on showing that an algebraic function always exists for which the coefficients in its power series correspond to any given nested sequence when reduced modulo some p. (See page 1092.) But then there is a general result that if a particular sequence of power series coefficients can be obtained from an algebraic (but not rational) function modulo a particular p, then it can only be obtained from transcendental functions modulo any other p—or over the integers.

■ **Concatenation sequences.** One can consider forming sequences by concatenating digits of successive integers in base k, as in *Flatten[Table[IntegerDigits[i, k], {i, n}]]*. In the limit, such sequences contain with equal frequency all possible blocks of any given length, but as shown on page 597, they exhibit other obvious deviations from randomness. The picture below shows the $k = 2$ sequence chopped into length 256 blocks.

Applying *FoldList[Plus, 0, 2 list - 1]* to the whole sequence yields the pattern shown below.

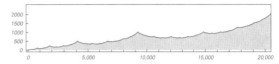

The systematic increase is a consequence of the leading 1 in each concatenated sequence. Dropping this 1 yields the pattern below.

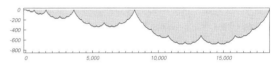

This is similar to picture (c) on page 131, and is a digit-by-digit version of

    FoldList[Plus, 0,
        Table[Apply[Plus, 2 Rest[IntegerDigits[i, 2]] - 1], {i, n}]]

Note that although the picture above has a nested structure, the original concatenation sequences are not nested, and so cannot be generated by substitution systems. The element at position n in the first sequence discussed above can however be obtained in about *Log[n]* steps using

    ((IntegerDigits[#3 + Quotient[#1, #2], 2][[
        Mod[#1, #2] + 1]] &)[n - (# - 2) 2^{#-1} - 2, #,
        2^{#-1}] &)[NestWhile[# + 1 &, 0, (# - 1) 2^# + 1 < n &]]

where the result of the *NestWhile* can be expressed as

    Ceiling[1 + ProductLog[1/2 (n - 1) Log[2]]/Log[2]]

Following work by Maxim Rytin in the late 1990s about k^{n+1} digits of a concatenation sequence can be found fairly efficiently from

    k/(k - 1)^2 -
        (k - 1) Sum[k^{(k^s-1)(1+s-s k)/(k-1)} (1/((k - 1)(k^s - 1)^2) -
            k/((k - 1)(k^{s+1} - 1)^2) + 1/(k^{s+1} - 1)), {s, n}]

Concatenation sequences can also be generated by joining together digits from other representations of numbers; the picture below shows results for the Gray code representation from page 901.

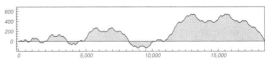

■ **Specially constructed transcendental numbers.** Numbers known to be transcendental include ones whose digit sequences contain 1's only at positions $n!$, 2^n or $Fibonacci[n]$. Concatenation sequences, as well as generalizations formed by concatenating values of polynomials at successive integer points, are also known to yield numbers that are transcendental.

■ **Runs of digits.** One can consider any base 2 digit sequence as consisting of successive runs of 0's and 1's, constructed from the list of run lengths by

    Fold[Join[#1, Table[1 - Last[#1], {#2}]] &, {0}, list]

This representation is related to so-called surreal numbers (though with the first few digits different). The number with run lengths corresponding to successive integers (so that the nth digit is $Mod[Floor[1/2 + Sqrt[2n]], 2]$) turns out to be $(1 - 2^{1/4} EllipticTheta[2, 0, 1/2] + EllipticTheta[3, 0, 1/2])/2$, and appears at least not to be algebraic.

■ **Leading digits.** Even though in individual numbers generated by simple mathematical procedures all possible digits often appear to occur with equal frequency, leading digits in sequences of numbers typically do not. Instead it is common for a leading digit s in base b to occur with frequency $Log[b, (s + 1)/s]$ (so that in base 10 1's occur 30% of the time and 9's 4.5%). This will happen whenever $FractionalPart[Log[b, a[n]]]$ is uniformly distributed, which, as discussed on page 903, is known to be true for sequences such as r^n (with $Log[b, r]$ irrational), n^n, $n!$, $Fibonacci[n]$, but not $r n$, $Prime[n]$ or $Log[n]$. A logarithmic law for leading digits is also found in many practical numerical tables, as noted by Simon Newcomb in 1881 and Frank Benford in 1938.

■ **Page 143 · Continued fractions.** The first n terms in the continued fraction representation for a number x can be found from the built-in *Mathematica* function *ContinuedFraction*, or from

    Floor[NestList[1/Mod[#, 1] &, x, n - 1]]

A rational approximation to the number x can be reconstructed from the continued fraction using *FromContinuedFraction* or by

    Fold[1/#1 + #2 &, Last[list], Rest[Reverse[list]]]

The pictures below show the digit sequences of successive iterates obtained from *NestList[1/Mod[#, 1] &, x, n]* for several numbers x.

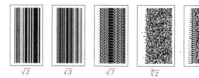

$\sqrt{2}$ $\sqrt{3}$ $\sqrt{7}$ $\sqrt[3]{2}$ e π

Unlike ordinary digits, the individual terms in a continued fraction can be of any size. In the continued fraction for a randomly chosen number, the probability to find a term of size s is $Log[2, (1 + 1/s)/(1 + 1/(s + 1))]$, so that the probability of getting a 1 is about 41.50%, and the probability of getting a large term falls off like $1/s^2$. If one looks at many terms, then their geometric mean is finite, and approaches Khinchin's constant $Khinchin \approx 2.68545$.

In the first 1000 terms of the continued fraction for π, there are 412 1's, and the geometric mean is about 2.6656. The largest individual term is the 432th one, which is equal to 20,776. In the first million terms, there are 414,526 1's, the geometric mean is 2.68447, and the largest term is the 453,294th one, which is 12,996,958.

Note that although the usual continued fraction for π looks quite random, modified forms such as

    4/(Fold[#2/#1 + 2 &, 2, Reverse[Range[1, n, 2]^2]] - 1)

can be very regular.

The continued fractions for $Exp[2/k]$ and $Tan[k/2]$ have simple forms (as discussed by Leonhard Euler in the mid-1700s); other rational powers of e and tangents do not appear to. The sequence of odd numbers gives the continued fraction for $Coth[1]$; the sequence of even numbers for $BesselI[0, 1]/BesselI[1, 1]$. In general, continued fractions whose n^{th} term is $a n + b$ correspond to numbers given by $BesselI[b/a, 2/a]/BesselI[b/a + 1, 2/a]$. Numbers whose continued fraction terms are polynomials in n can presumably also be represented in terms of suitably generalized hypergeometric functions. (All so-called Hurwitz numbers have continued fractions that consist of interleaved polynomial sequences—a property left unchanged by $x \rightarrow (a x + b)/(c x + d)$.)

As discovered by Jeffrey Shallit in 1979, numbers of the form $Sum[1/k^{2^i}, \{i, 0, \infty\}]$ that have nonzero digits in base k only at positions 2^i turn out to have continued fractions with terms of limited size, and with a nested structure that can be found using a substitution system according to

    {0, k - 1, k + 2, k, k, k - 2, k, k + 2, k - 2, k}[[
      Nest[Flatten[{{1, 2}, {3, 4}, {5, 6}, {7, 8}, {5, 6}, {3, 4},
        {9, 10}, {7, 8}, {9, 10}, {3, 4}}[[#]]] &, 1, n]]]

The continued fractions for square roots are always periodic; for higher roots they never appear to show any significant regularities. The first million terms in the continued fraction for $2^{1/3}$ contain 414,983 1's, have geometric mean 2.68505, and have largest term 4,156,269 at position 484,709. Terms of any size presumably in the end always occur in continued fractions for higher roots, though this is not known for certain. Fairly large terms are sometimes seen quite early: in $5^{1/3}$ term 19 is 3052, while in $Root[10 + 8 # - #^3 \&, 1]$ term 34 is 1,501,790. The presence of a large term indicates a close approximation to a rational number. In a few known cases simple formulas yield numbers that are close but not equal to integers. An example discovered by Srinivasa Ramanujan around 1913 is $Exp[\pi\sqrt{163}]$, which is an integer to one part in 10^{30}, and has second continued fraction term 1,333,462,407,511. (This particular example can be understood from the fact that as d increases $Exp[\pi\sqrt{d}]$ becomes extremely close to $-1728\,KleinInvariantJ[(1+\sqrt{-d})/2]$, which turns out to be an integer whenever there is unique factorization of numbers of the form $a+b\sqrt{-d}$ —and $d=163$ is the largest of the 9 cases for which this is so.) Other less spectacular examples include $Exp[\pi]-\pi$ and $163/Log[163]$.

Numbers with digits given by concatenation sequences in any base k (see note above) seem to have unusual continued fractions, in which most terms are fairly small, but some are extremely large. Thus with $k=2$, term 30 is 4,534,532, term 64 is 4,682,854,730,443,938, term 152 is about 2×10^{34} and term 669,468 is about 2×10^{78902}. (For the $k=10$ case of the original Champernowne number, even term 18 is already about 5×10^{165}.) The plots below of the numbers of digits in successive terms turn out to have patterns of peaks that show some signs of nesting.

In analogy to digits in a concatenation sequence the terms in the sequence

$Flatten[Table[Rest[ContinuedFraction[a/b]],$
$\{b, 2, n\}, \{a, b-1\}]]$

are known to occur with the same frequencies as they would in the continued fraction representation for a randomly chosen number.

The pictures below show as a function of n the quantity

$With[\{r = FromContinuedFraction[ContinuedFraction[x, n]]\},$
$-Log[Denominator[r], Abs[x-r]]]$

which gives a measure of the closeness of successive rational approximations to x. For any irrational number this quantity cannot be less than 2, while for algebraic irrationals Klaus Roth showed in 1955 that it can only have finitely many peaks that reach above any specified level.

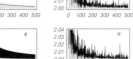

■ **History.** Euclid's algorithm states that starting from integers $\{a, b\}$ iterating $\{a\_, b\_\} :\to If[a > b, \{a-b, b\}, \{a, b-a\}]$ eventually leads to $\{GCD[a, b], 0\}$. (See page 1093.) The pictures below show how this works. The numbers of successively smaller squares (corresponding to the numbers of steps in the algorithm) turn out to be exactly $ContinuedFraction[a/b]$.

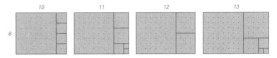

It was discovered in antiquity that Euclid's algorithm starting with $\{x, 1\}$ terminates only when x is rational. In all cases, however, the relationship with continued fractions remains, as below.

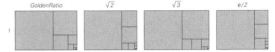

Infinite continued fractions appear to have first been explicitly written down in the mid-1500s, and to have become popular in many problems in number theory by the 1700s. Leonhard Euler studied many continued fractions, while Joseph Lagrange seems to have thought that it might be possible to recognize any algebraic number from its continued fraction. The periodicity of continued fractions for quadratic irrationals was proved by Evariste Galois in 1828. From the late 1800s interest in continued fractions as such waned; it finally increased again in the 1980s in connection with problems in dynamical systems theory.

■ **Egyptian fractions.** Following the ancient Egyptian number system, rational numbers can be represented by sums of reciprocals, as in $3/7 == 1/3 + 1/11 + 1/231$. With suitable distinct integers $a[n]$ one can represent any number by $Sum[1/a[n], \{n, \infty\}]$. The representation is not unique; $a[n] = 2^n$, $n(n+1)$ and $(n+1)!/n$ all yield 1. Simple choices for $a[n]$ yield many standard transcendental numbers: $n!$: $e-1$; $n!^2$: $BesselI[0, 2]-1$; $n\,2^n$: $Log[2]$; n^2: $\pi^2/6$; $(2n-1)(2n-3)$: $\pi\sqrt{3}/9$; $3-16n+16n^2$: $\pi/8$; $n\,n!$: $ExpIntegralEi[1] - EulerGamma$. (See also page 902.)

■ **Nested radicals.** Given a list of integers acting like digits one can consider representing numbers in the form $Fold[Sqrt[\#1 + \#2]\&, 0, Reverse[list]]$. A sequence of identical digits d then corresponds to the number $(1 + Sqrt[4d+1])/2$. (Note that $Nest[Sqrt[\# + 2]\&, 0, n] == 2\,Cos[\pi/2^{n+1}]$.) Repeats of a digit block b give numbers that solve $Fold[\#1^2 - \#2\&, x, b] == x$. It appears that digits 0, 1, 2 are sufficient to represent uniquely all numbers between 1 and 2. For any number x the first n digits are given by

Ceiling[NestList[(2 - Mod[-#, 1])² &, x², n - 1] - 2]

Even rational numbers such as 3/2 do not yield simple digit sequences. For random x, digits 0, 1, 2 appear to occur with limiting frequencies Sqrt[2 + d] - Sqrt[1 + d].

■ **Digital slope representation.** One can approximate a line of any slope h as in the picture below by a sequence of segments on a square grid (such as a digital display device). The vertical distance moved at the nth horizontal position is Floor[n h] - Floor[(n - 1) h], and the sequence obtained from this (which contains only terms Floor[h] and Floor[h] + 1) provides a unique representation for h. As discussed on page 903 this sequence can be generated by applying substitution rules derived from the continued fraction form of h. If h is rational, the sequence is repetitive, while if h is a quadratic irrational, it is nested. Given a sequence of length n, an approximation to h can be reconstructed using

Max[MapIndexed[#1/First[#2] &,
FoldList[Plus, First[list], Rest[list]]]]

The fractional part of the result obtained is always an element of the Farey sequence

Union[Flatten[Table[a/b, {b, n}, {a, 0, b}]]]

(See also pages 892, 932 and 1084.)

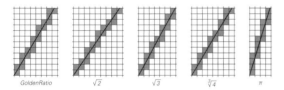

GoldenRatio   √2   √3   ∛4   π

■ **Representations for integers.** See page 560.

■ **Operator representations.** Instead of repeatedly applying an operation to a sequence of digits one can consider forming integers (or other numbers) by performing trees of operations on a single constant. Thus, for example, any integer m can be obtained by a tree of $m - 1$ additions of 1's such as $(1 + (1 + 1)) + 1$. Another operator that can be used to generate any integer is $a \circ b = 2a + b - 1$. In this case 6 is $(1 \circ (1 \circ 1)) \circ 1$, and an integer m can be obtained by Tr[1 + IntegerDigits[m, 2]] - 2 or at most Log[2, m] applications of $\circ$. The operator $k a + b - k + 1$ can be used for any k. It also turns out that BitXor[2a, b] + 1 works, though in this case even for 2 the smallest representation is $(1 \circ 1) \circ (1 \circ ((1 \circ 1) \circ 1))$. (For BitOr[2a, b] - 1 the number of applications needed is With[{i = IntegerDigits[m, 2]}, Tr[i + 1] + i[[2]] (1 + i[[3]]) - 1].) The pictures below show the smallest number of operator applications required for successive integers. With the pair of operators $a + b$ and $a \times b$ (a case considered in recreational

mathematics for n-ary operators) numbers of the form 3^s have particularly small representations. Note that in all cases the size of the smallest representation must at some level increase like Log[m] (compare pages 1067 and 1070), but there may be some "algorithmically simple" integers that have shorter representations.

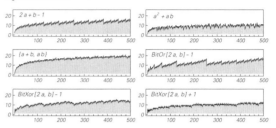

■ **Number classification.** One can imagine classifying real numbers in terms of what kinds of operations are needed to obtain them from integers. Rational numbers require only division (or solving linear equations), while algebraic numbers require solving polynomial equations. Rather little is known about numbers that require solving transcendental equations—and indeed it can even be undecidable (see page 1138) whether two equations can yield the same number. Starting with integers and then applying arithmetic operations and fractional powers one can readily reproduce all algebraic numbers up to degree 4, but not beyond. The sets of numbers that can be obtained by applying elementary functions like Exp, Log and Sin seem in various ways to be disjoint from algebraic numbers. But if one applies multivariate elliptic or hypergeometric functions it was established in the late 1800s and early 1900s that one can in principle reach any algebraic number. One can also ask what numbers can be generated by integrals (or by solving differential equations). For rational functions $f[x]$, Integrate[f[x], {x, 0, 1}] must always be a linear function of Log and ArcTan applied to algebraic numbers ($f[x] = 1/(1 + x^2)$ for example yields $\pi/4$). Multiple integrals of rational functions can be more complicated, as in

Integrate[1/(1 + x² + y²), {x, 0, 1}, {y, 0, 1}] ==
HypergeometricPFQ[{1/2, 1, 1}, {3/2, 3/2}, 1/9]/6 +
1/2 π ArcSinh[1] - Catalan

and presumably often cannot be expressed at all in terms of standard mathematical functions. Integrals of rational functions over regions defined by polynomial inequalities have recently been discussed under the name "periods". Many numbers associated with Zeta and Gamma can readily be generated, though apparently for example e and EulerGamma cannot. One can also consider numbers obtained from infinite sums (or by solving recurrence equations). If $f[n]$ is a rational function, $Sum[f[n], \{n, \infty\}]$ must just be a linear combination of *PolyGamma* functions, but again the multivariate case can be much more complicated.

Mathematical Functions

■ **Page 145 · Mathematical functions.** (See page 1091.) *BesselJ[0, x]* goes like $Sin[x]/\sqrt{x}$ for large x while *AiryAi[-x]* goes like $Sin[x^{3/2}]/x^{1/4}$. Other standard mathematical functions that oscillate at large x include *JacobiSN* and *MathieuC*. Most hypergeometric-type functions either increase or decrease exponentially for large arguments, though in the directions of Stokes lines in the complex plane they can oscillate sinusoidally. (For *AiryAi[x]* the Stokes lines are in directions $(-1)\wedge(\{1, 2, 3\}/3)$.)

■ **Lissajous figures.** Plotting multiple sine functions each on different coordinate axes yields so-called Lissajous or Bowditch figures, as illustrated below. If the coefficients inside all the sine functions are rational, then going from $t = 0$ to $t = 2\pi\, Apply[LCM, Map[Denominator, list]]$ yields a closed curve. Irrational ratios of coefficients lead to curves that never close and eventually fill space uniformly.

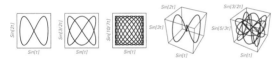

■ **Page 146 · Two sine functions.** $Sin[a\,x] + Sin[b\,x]$ can be rewritten as $2\,Sin[1/2\,(a+b)\,x]\,Cos[1/2\,(a-b)\,x]$ (using *TrigFactor*), implying that the function has two families of equally spaced zeros: $2\pi\,n/(a+b)$ and $2\pi\,(n+1/2)/(b-a)$.

■ **Differential equations.** The function $Sin[x] + Sin[\sqrt{2}\,x]$ can be obtained as the solution of the differential equation $y''[x] + 2\,y[x] - Sin[x] == 0$ with the initial conditions $y[0] == 0$, $y'[0] == 2$.

■ **Musical chords.** In a so-called equal temperament scale the 12 standard musical notes that make up an octave have a progression of frequencies $2^{n/12}$. Most schemes for musical tuning use rational approximations to these numbers. Until the past century, and since at least the 1300s, diminished fifth or tritone chords that consist of two notes (such as C and G♭) with frequency ratio $\sqrt{2}$ have generally been avoided as sounding discordant. (See also page 1079.)

■ **Page 146 · Three sine functions.** All zeros of the function $Sin[a\,x] + Sin[b\,x]$ lie on the real axis. But for $Sin[a\,x] + Sin[b\,x] + Sin[c\,x]$, there are usually zeros off the

real axis (even say for $a = 1$, $b = 3/2$, $c = 5/3$), as shown in the pictures below.

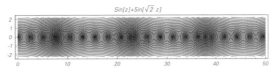

$Sin[z] + Sin[\sqrt{2}\,z]$

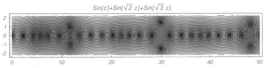

$Sin[z] + Sin[\sqrt{2}\,z] + Sin[\sqrt{3}\,z]$

If a, b and c are rational, $Sin[a\,x] + Sin[b\,x] + Sin[c\,x]$ is periodic with period $2\pi/GCD[a, b, c]$, and there are a limited number of different spacings between zeros. But in a case like $Sin[x] + Sin[\sqrt{2}\,x] + Sin[\sqrt{3}\,x]$ there is a continuous distribution of spacings between zeros, as shown on a logarithmic scale below. (For $0 < x < 10^6$ there are a total of 448,494 zeros, with maximum spacing $\simeq 4.6$ and minimum spacing $\simeq 0.013$.)

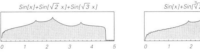

$Sin[x] + Sin[\sqrt{2}\,x] + Sin[\sqrt{3}\,x]$

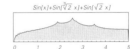

$Sin[x] + Sin[\sqrt[3]{2}\,x] + Sin[\sqrt{2}\,x]$

■ **Page 147 · Substitution systems.** $Cos[a\,x] - Cos[b\,x]$ has two families of zeros: $2\pi\,n/(a+b)$ and $2\pi\,n/(b-a)$. Assuming $b > a > 0$, the number of zeros from the second family which appear between the nth and $n + 1^{th}$ zero from the first family is

$$(Floor[(n+1)\#] - Floor[n\#] \&)[(b-a)/(a+b)]$$

and as discussed on page 903 this sequence can be obtained by applying a sequence of substitution rules. For $Sin[a\,x] + Sin[b\,x]$ a more complicated sequence of substitution rules yields the analogous sequence in which $-1/2$ is inserted in each *Floor*.

■ **Many sine functions.** Adding many sine functions yields a so-called Fourier series (see page 1074). The pictures below show $Sum[Sin[n\,x]/n, \{n, k\}]$ for various numbers of terms k. Apart from a glitch that gets narrower with increasing k (the so-called Gibbs phenomenon), the result has a simple triangular form. Other so-called Fourier series in which the coefficient of $Sin[m\,x]$ is a smooth function of m for all integer m yield similarly simple results.

The pictures below show $Sum[Sin[n^2\,x]/n^2, \{n, k\}]$, where in effect all coefficients of $Sin[m\,x]$ other than those where m is a perfect square are set to zero. The result is a much more complicated curve. Note that for x of the form $p\,\pi/q$, the $k = \infty$ sum is just

$$(\pi/(2\,q))^2 \; Sum[Sin[n^2\, p\, \pi/q]/Sin[n\, \pi/(2\,q)]^2, \{n, q-1\}]$$

2 terms   5 terms   25 terms

The pictures below show $Sum[Cos[2^n\, x], \{n, k\}]$ (as studied by Karl Weierstrass in 1872). The curves obtained in this case show a definite nested structure, in which the value at a point x is essentially determined directly from the base 2 digit sequence of x. (See also page 1080.)

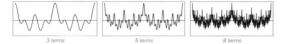

3 terms   5 terms   8 terms

The curves below are approximations to $Sum[Cos[2^n\, x]/2^{a\,n}, \{n, \infty\}]$. They can be thought of as having dimensions $2 - a$ and smoothed power spectra $\omega^{-(1+2\,a)}$.

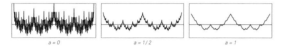

a = 0   a = 1/2   a = 1

▪ **FM synthesis.** More complicated curves can be obtained for example using FM synthesis, as discussed on page 1079.

▪ **Page 148 · Zeta function.** For real s the Riemann zeta function $Zeta[s]$ is given by $Sum[1/n^s, \{n, \infty\}]$ or $Product[1/(1 - Prime[n]^s), \{n, \infty\}]$. The zeta function as analytically continued for complex s was studied by Bernhard Riemann in 1859, who showed that $PrimePi[n]$ could be approximated (see page 909) up to order $\sqrt{n}$ by $LogIntegral[n] - Sum[LogIntegral[n \wedge r[i]], \{i, -\infty, \infty\}]$, where the $r[i]$ are the complex zeros of $Zeta[s]$. The Riemann Hypothesis then states that all $r[i]$ satisfy $Re[r[i]] == 1/2$, which implies a certain randomness in the distribution of prime numbers, and a bound of order $\sqrt{n}\, Log[n]$ on $PrimePi[n] - LogIntegral[n]$. The Riemann Hypothesis is also equivalent to the statement that a bound of order $\sqrt{n}\, Log[n]^2$ exists on $Abs[Log[Apply[LCM, Range[n]]] - n]$.

The picture in the main text shows $RiemannSiegelZ[t]$, defined as $Zeta[1/2 + i\,t]\, Exp[i\, RiemannSiegelTheta[t]]$, where
$RiemannSiegelTheta[t_] = $
$Arg[Gamma[1/4 + i\, t/2]] - 1/2\, t\, Log[\pi]$

The first term in an approximation to $RiemannSiegelZ[t]$ is $2\, Cos[RiemannSiegelTheta[t]]$; to get results to a given precision requires summing a number of terms that

increases like $\sqrt{t}$, making routine computation possible up to $t \sim 10^{10}$.

It is known that:

▪ The average spacing between zeros decreases like $1/Log[t]$.

▪ The amplitude of wiggles grows with t, but more slowly than $t^{0.16}$.

▪ At least the first 10 billion zeros have $Re[s] == 1/2$.

The statistical distribution of zeros was studied by Andrew Odlyzko and others starting in the late 1970s (following ideas of David Hilbert and George Pólya in the early 1900s), and it was found that to a good approximation, the spacings between zeros are distributed like the spacings between eigenvalues of random unitary matrices (see page 977).

In 1972 Sergei Voronin showed that $Zeta[z + (3/4 + i\,t)]$ has a certain universality in that there always in principle exists some t (presumably in practice usually astronomically large) for which it can reproduce to any specified precision over say the region $Abs[z] < 1/4$ any analytic function without zeros.

Iterated Maps and the Chaos Phenomenon

▪ **History of iterated maps.** Newton's method from the late 1600s for finding roots of polynomials (already used in specific cases in antiquity) can be thought of as a smooth iterated map (see page 920) in which a rational function is repeatedly applied (see page 1101). Questions of convergence led in the late 1800s and early 1900s to interest in iteration theory, particularly for rational functions in the complex plane (see page 933). There were occasional comments about complicated behavior (notably by Arthur Cayley in 1879) but no real investigation seems to have been made. In the 1890s Henri Poincaré studied so-called return maps giving for example positions of objects on successive orbits. Starting in the 1930s iterated maps were sometimes considered as possible models in fields like population biology and business cycle theory—usually arising as discrete annualized versions of continuous equations like the Verhulst logistic differential equation from the mid-1800s. In most cases the most that was noted was simple oscillatory behavior, although for example in 1954 William Ricker iterated empirical reproduction curves for fish, and saw more complex behavior—though made little comment on it. In the 1950s Paul Stein and Stanislaw Ulam did an extensive computer study of various iterated maps of nonlinear functions. They concentrated on questions of convergence, but nevertheless noted complicated behavior. (Already in the late 1940s John von Neumann had suggested using $x \to 4x(1-x)$ as a random number generator, commenting on its extraction of initial condition digits, as mentioned on page 921.) Some detailed analytical studies of logistic maps of the form $x \to ax(1-x)$ were done in the late 1950s and early 1960s—and in the mid-1970s iterated maps became popular, with much analysis and computer experimentation on them being done. But typically studies have concentrated on repetition, nesting and sensitive dependence on initial conditions—not on more general issues of complexity.

In connection with his study of continued fractions Carl Friedrich Gauss noted in 1799 complexity in the behavior of the iterated map $x \to FractionalPart[1/x]$. Beginning in the late 1800s there was number theoretical investigation of the sequence $FractionalPart[a^n x]$ associated with the map $x \to FractionalPart[ax]$ (see page 903), notably by G. H. Hardy and John Littlewood in 1914. Various features of randomness such as uniform distribution were established, and connections to smooth iterated maps emerged after the development of symbolic dynamics in the late 1930s.

■ **History of chaos theory.** See page 971.

■ **Page 150 · Exact iterates.** For any integer a the nth iterate of $x \to FractionalPart[ax]$ can be written as $FractionalPart[a^n x]$, or equivalently $1/2 - ArcTan[Cot[a^n \pi x]]/\pi$. In the specific case $a = 2$ the iterates of $If[x < 1/2, ax, a(1-x)]$ have the form $ArcCos[Cos[2^n \pi x]]/\pi$. (See pages 903 and 1098.)

■ **Page 151 · Problems with computer experiments.** The defining characteristic of a system that exhibits chaos is that on successive steps the system samples digits which lie further and further to the right in its initial condition. But in a practical computer, only a limited number of digits can ever be stored. In *Mathematica*, one can choose how many digits to store (and in the pictures shown in the main text, enough digits were used to avoid the problems discussed in this note). But a low-level language such as FORTRAN, C or Java always stores a fixed number of digits, typically around 53, in its standard double-precision floating-point representation of numbers.

So what happens when a system one is simulating tries to sample digits in its initial conditions beyond the ones that are stored? The answer depends on the way that arithmetic is handled in the computer system one uses.

When doing high-precision arithmetic, *Mathematica* follows the principle that it should only ever give digits that are known to be correct on the basis of the input that was provided. This means that in simulating chaotic systems, the numbers produced will typically have progressively fewer digits: later digits cannot be known to be correct without more precise knowledge of this initial condition.

(An example is $NestList[Mod[2 \#, 1] \&, N[\pi/4, 40], 200]$; $Map[Precision, list]$ gives the number of significant digits of each element in the list.)

But most current languages and hardware systems follow a rather different approach. (For low-precision machine arithmetic, *Mathematica* is also forced to follow this approach.) What they do is to give a fixed number of digits as the result of every computation, whether or not all those digits are known to be correct. It is then the task of numerical analysis to establish that in a particular computation, the final results obtained are not unduly affected by digits that are not known to be correct. And in practice, for many kinds of computations, this is to a large extent the case. But whenever chaos is involved, it is inevitably not.

As an example, consider the iterated map $x \to Mod[2x, 1]$ discussed in the main text. At each step, this map shifts all the base 2 digits in x one position to the left. But if the computer gives a fixed number of digits at each step, then additional digits must be filled in on the right. On most computers, these additional digits are always 0. And so after some number of steps, all the digits in x are 0, and thus the value of x is simply 0.

But it turns out that a typical pocket calculator gives a different result. For pocket calculators effectively represent numbers in base 10 (actually so-called binary-coded decimal) not base 2, and fill in unknown digits with 0 in base 10. (Base 10 is used so that multiplying for example 1/3 by 3 gives exactly 1 rather than the more confusing result 0.9999... obtained with base 2.)

Pictures (a) and (c) below show simulations of the shift map on a typical computer, while pictures (b) and (d) show corresponding simulations on a pocket calculator. (Starting with initial condition x the digit sequence at step n is essentially

   $IntegerDigits[Mod[2^n Floor[2^{53} x], 2^{53}], 2, 53]$

on the computer, and

   $Flatten[IntegerDigits[IntegerDigits[$
     $Mod[2^n Floor[10^{12} x], 10^{12}], 10, 12], 2, 4]]$

on the calculator. In both cases the limited number of digits implies behavior that ultimately repeats—but only long after the other effects we discuss have occurred.)

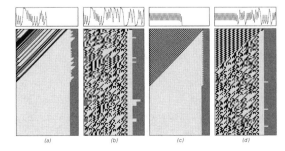

(a)   (b)   (c)   (d)

For the first several steps, the results as shown at the top of each corresponding picture agree. But as soon as the effect of sampling beyond the digits explicitly stored in the initial condition becomes important, the results are completely different. The computer gives simply 0, but the pocket calculator yields apparently random sequences—which turn out to be analogous to those discussed on page 319.

Other chaotic systems have a similar sensitivity to the details of computer arithmetic. But the simple behavior of the shift map turns out to be rather rare: in most cases—such as the multiplication by 3/2 shown in the pictures below—apparent randomness is produced, even on a typical computer.

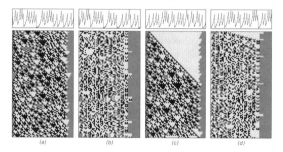

It is important to realize however that this randomness has little to do with the details of the initial conditions. Instead, just as in other examples in this book, the randomness arises from an intrinsic process that occurs even with the simple repetitive initial condition shown in pictures (c) and (d) above.

Computer simulations of chaotic systems have been done since the 1950s. And it has often been observed that the sequences generated in these simulations look quite random. But as we now see, such randomness cannot in fact be a consequence of the chaos phenomenon and of sensitive dependence on initial conditions.

Nevertheless, confusingly enough, even though it does not come from sensitive dependence on initial conditions, such randomness is what makes the overall properties of simulations typically follow the idealized mathematical predictions of chaos theory. The point is that the presence of randomness makes the system behave on different steps as if it were evolving from slightly different initial conditions. But statistical averages over different initial conditions typically yield essentially the results one would get by evolution from a single initial condition containing an infinite number of randomly chosen digits.

■ **Page 152 · Mathematical perspectives.** Mathematicians may be confused by my discussion of complexity in iterated maps.

The first point to make is that the issues I am studying are rather different from the ones that are traditionally studied in the mathematics of these systems. The next point is that I have specifically chosen not to make the idealizations about numbers and operations on numbers that are usually made in mathematics.

In particular, it is usually assumed that performing some standard mathematical operation, such as taking a square root, cannot have a significant effect on the system one is studying. But in trying to track down the origins of complex behavior, the effects of such operations can be significant. Indeed, as we saw on page 141, taking square roots can for example generate seemingly random digit sequences.

Many mathematicians may object that digit sequences are just too fragile an entity to be worth studying. They may argue that it is only robust and invariant concepts that are useful. But robustness with respect to mathematical operations is a different issue from robustness with respect to computational operations. Indeed, we will see later in this book that large classes of digit sequences can be considered equivalent with respect to computational operations, but these classes are quite different ones from those that are considered equivalent with respect to mathematical operations.

■ **Information content of initial conditions.** Common sense suggests that it is a quite different thing to specify a simple initial condition containing, say, a single black cell on a white background, than to specify an initial condition containing an infinite sequence of randomly chosen cells. But in traditional mathematics no distinction is usually made between these kinds of specifications. And as a result, mathematicians may find it difficult to understand my distinction between randomness generated intrinsically by the evolution of a system and randomness from initial conditions (see page 299). The distinction may seem more obvious if one considers, for example, sequential substitution systems or cyclic tag systems. For such systems cannot meaningfully be given infinite random initial conditions, yet they can still perfectly well generate highly random behavior. (Their initial conditions correspond in a sense to integers rather than real numbers.)

■ **Smooth iterated maps.** In the main text, all the functions used as mappings consist of linear pieces, usually joined together discontinuously. But the same basic phenomena seen with such mappings also occur when smooth functions are used. A particularly well-studied example (see page 918) is the so-called logistic map $x \to a x (1 - x)$. The base 2 digit sequences obtained with this map starting from $x = 1/8$ are shown below for various values of a. The quadratic nature of the map typically causes the total number of digits to double at each step. But at least for small a, progressively more digits on the left show purely repetitive behavior. As a increases, the repetition period goes through a series of doublings. The detailed behavior is different for every value of a, but whenever the repetition period is 2^j, it turns out that with any initial condition the leftmost digit always eventually follows a sequence that consists of repetitions of step j in the evolution of the substitution system $\{1 \rightarrow \{1, 0\}, 0 \rightarrow \{1, 1\}\}$ starting either from $\{0\}$ or $\{1\}$. As a approaches 3.569946, the period doublings get closer and closer together, and eventually a point is reached at which the sequence of leftmost digits is no longer repetitive but instead corresponds to the nested pattern formed after an infinite number of steps in the evolution of the substitution system. (An important result discovered by Mitchell Feigenbaum in 1975 is that this basic setup is universal to all smooth maps whose functions have a single hump.) When a is increased further, there is usually no longer repetitive or nested behavior. And although there are typically some constraints, the behavior obtained tends to depend on the details of the digit sequence of the initial conditions. In the special case $a = 4$, it turns out that replacing x by $Sin[\pi u]^2$ makes the mapping become just $u \rightarrow FractionalPart[2u]$, revealing simple shift map dependence on the initial digit sequence. (See pages 1090 and 1098.)

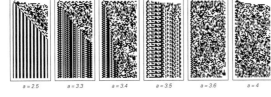

a = 2.5   a = 3.3   a = 3.4   a = 3.5   a = 3.6   a = 4

■ **Higher-dimensional generalizations.** One can consider so-called Anosov maps such as $\{x, y\} \rightarrow Mod[m . \{x, y\}, 1]$ where m is a matrix such as $\{\{2, 1\}, \{1, 1\}\}$. Any initial condition containing only rational numbers will then yield repetitive behavior, much as in the shift map. But as soon as m itself contains rational numbers, complicated behavior can be obtained even with an initial condition such as $\{1, 1\}$.

■ **Distribution of chaotic behavior.** For iterated maps, unlike for discrete systems such as cellular automata, one can get continuous ranges of rules by varying parameters. With maps based on piecewise linear functions the regions of parameters in which chaotic behavior occurs typically have simple shapes; with maps based, say, on quadratic

functions, however, elaborate nested shapes can occur. (See page 934.)

■ **Page 155 · Lyapunov exponents.** The number of new digits that are affected at each step by a small change in initial conditions gives the so-called Lyapunov exponent λ for the evolution. After t steps, the difference in size resulting from the change in initial conditions will be multiplied by approximately $2^{\lambda t}$—at least until this difference is of order 1. (See page 950.)

■ **Chaos in nature.** See page 304.

■ **Bitwise operations.** Cellular automata can be thought of as analogs of iterated maps in which bitwise operations such as $BitXor$ are used instead of ordinary arithmetic ones. (See page 906.)

Continuous Cellular Automata

■ **Implementation.** The state of a continuous cellular automaton at a particular step can be represented by a list of numbers, each lying between 0 and 1. This list can then be updated using

```
CCAEvolveStep[f_, list_List] :=
    Map[f, (RotateLeft[list] + list + RotateRight[list])/3]
CCAEvolveList[f_, init_List, t_Integer] :=
    NestList[CCAEvolveStep[f, #] &, init, t]
```

where for the rule on page 157 f is $FractionalPart[3\#/2]$ & while for the rule on page 158 it is $FractionalPart[\# + 1/4]$ &.

Note that in the definitions above, the elements of *list* can be either exact rational numbers, or approximate numbers obtained using N. For rough calculations, standard machine-precision numbers may sometimes suffice, but for detailed calculations exact rational numbers are essential. Indeed, the presence of exponentially increasing errors would make the bottom of the picture on page 157 qualitatively wrong if just 64-bit double-precision numbers had been used. On page 160 the effect is much larger, and almost all the pictures would be completely wrong—with the notable exception of the one that shows localized structures.

■ **History.** Continuous cellular automata have been introduced independently several times, under several different names. In all cases the rules have been at least slightly more complicated than the ones I consider here, and behavior starting from simple initial conditions does not appear to have been studied before. Versions of continuous cellular automata arose in the mid-1970s as idealizations of coupled ordinary differential equations for arrays of nonlinear oscillators, and implicitly in finite difference approximations to partial differential equations. They began to be studied with extensive computer simulations in the early 1980s, probably following my work on ordinary cellular automata. Most often considered, notably by Kunihiko Kaneko and co-workers, were so-called "coupled map lattices" or "lattice dynamical systems" in which an iterated map (typically a logistic map) was applied at each step to a combination of neighboring cell value. A transition from regular class 2 to irregular class 3 behavior, with class 4 behavior involving localized structures in between, was observed, and was studied in detail by Hugues Chaté and Paul Manneville, starting in the late 1980s.

■ **Page 158 · Properties.** At step t the background is *FractionalPart[a t]*. For rational a this always repeats, cycling through *Denominator[a]* possible values (compare page 255). In most patterns generated from initial conditions containing say a single black cell most cells whose values are not forced to be the same end up being at least slightly different—even in cases like $a = 0.375$. Note that in cases like $a = 0.475$ there is some trace of a pattern at every step— but it only becomes obvious when it makes values wrap around from 1 to 0. The pictures below show successive colors of (a) the background (compare page 950) and (b) the center cell for each $a = n/500$ from 0 to 1 for the systems on page 159. (Compare page 243.)

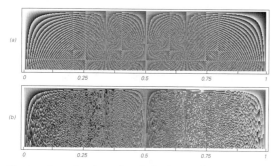

If a is not a rational number the background never repeats, but the main features of patterns obtained seem similar.

■ **Additive rules.** In the case $a = 0$ the systems on page 159 are purely additive. A simpler example is the rule

Mod[RotateLeft[list] + RotateRight[list], 1]

With a single nonzero initial cell with value $1/k$ the pattern produced is just Pascal's triangle modulo k. If k is a rational number only a limited set of values appear, and the pattern has a nested form analogous to those shown on page 870. If k is irrational then equidistribution of *Mod[Binomial[t, x], k]* implies that all possible values eventually appear; the corresponding patterns seem fairly irregular, as shown below. (Compare pages 953 and 1092.)

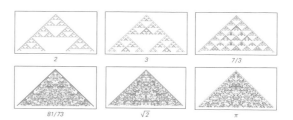

■ **Probabilistic cellular automata.** As an alternative to having continuous values at each cell, one can consider ordinary cellular automata with discrete values, but introduce probabilities for, say, two different rules to be applied at each cell. Examples of probabilistic cellular automata are shown on page 591; their behavior is typically quite similar to continuous cellular automata.

Partial Differential Equations

■ **Ordinary differential equations.** It is also possible to set up systems which have a finite number of continuous variables (say $a[t]$, $b[t]$, etc.) that change continuously with time. The rules for such systems correspond to ordinary differential equations. Over the past century, the field of dynamical systems theory has produced many results about such systems. If all equations are of the form $a'[t] == f[a[t], b[t], ...]$, etc. then it is known for example that it is necessary to have at least three equations in order to get behavior that is not ultimately fixed or repetitive. (The Lorenz equations are an example.) If the function f depends explicitly on time, then two equations suffice. (The van der Pol equations are an example.)

Just as in iterated maps, a small change in the initial values $a[0]$ etc. can often lead to an exponentially increasing difference in later values of $a[t]$, etc. But as in iterated maps, the main part of this process that has been analyzed is simply the excavation of progressively less significant digits in the number $a[0]$.

(Note that numerical simulations of ODEs on computers must approximate continuous time by discrete steps, making the system essentially an iterated map, and often yielding spurious complicated behavior.)

■ **Klein-Gordon equation.** The behavior of the Klein-Gordon equation $\partial_{tt} u[t, x] == \partial_{xx} u[t, x] - u[t, x]$ is visually very similar to that shown for the sine-Gordon equation. For the Klein-Gordon equation, however, there is an exact solution:

$u[t, x] = If[x^2 > t^2, 0, BesselJ[0, Sqrt[t^2 - x^2]]]$

■ **Origins of the equations.** The diffusion equation arises in physics from the evolution of temperature or of gas density.

The wave equation represents the propagation of linear waves, for example along a compressible spring. The sine-Gordon equation represents nonlinear waves obtained for example as the limit of a very large number of pendulums all connected to a spring. The traditional name of the equation is a pun on the Klein-Gordon equation that appears in relativistic quantum mechanics and in describing strings in elastic media. It is notable that unlike with ODEs, essentially all PDEs that have been widely studied come quite directly from physics. My PDE on page 165 is however an exception.

■ **Nonlinearity.** The pictures below show behavior with initial conditions containing two Gaussians (and periodic boundary conditions). The diffusion and wave equations are linear, so that results are linear sums of those with single Gaussians. The sine-Gordon equation is nonlinear, but its solutions satisfy a generalized linear superposition principle. The equation from page 165 shows no such simple superposition principle. Note that even with a linear equation, fairly complicated patterns of behavior can sometimes emerge as a result of boundary conditions.

| wave equation | sine-Gordon equation | my equation |

■ **Higher dimensions.** The pictures below show as examples the solution to the wave equation in 1D, 2D and 3D starting from a stationary square pulse.

In each case a 1D slice through the solution is shown, and the solution is multiplied by r^{d-1}. For the wave equation, and for a fair number of other equations, even and odd dimensions behave differently. In 1D and 3D, the value at the origin quickly becomes exactly 0; in 2D it is given by $1 - t/Sqrt[t^2 - 1]$, which tends to zero only like $-1/(2t^2)$ (which means that a sound pulse cannot propagate in a normal way in 2D).

■ **Page 164 · Singular behavior.** An example of an equation that yields inconsistent behavior is the diffusion equation with a negative diffusion constant:

$$\partial_t u[t, x] == -\partial_{xx} u[t, x]$$

This equation makes any variation in u as a function of x eventually become infinitely rapid.

Many equations used in physics can lead to singularities: the Navier-Stokes equations for fluid flow yield shock waves, while the Einstein equations yield black holes. At a physical level, such singularities usually indicate that processes not captured by the equations have become important. But at a mathematical level one can simply ask whether a particular equation always has solutions which are at least as regular as its initial conditions. Despite much work, however, only a few results along these lines are known.

■ **Existence and uniqueness.** Unlike systems such as cellular automata, PDEs do not have a built-in notion of "evolution" or "time". Instead, as discussed on page 940, a PDE is essentially just a constraint on the values of a function at different times or different positions. In solving a PDE, one is usually interested in determining values that satisfy this constraint inside a particular region, based on information about values on the edges. It is then a fundamental question how much can be specified on the edges in order to obtain a unique solution. If too little is specified, there may be many possible solutions, while if too much is specified there may be no consistent solution at all. For some very simple PDEs, the conditions for unique solutions are known. So-called hyperbolic equations (such as the wave equation, the sine-Gordon equation and my equation) work a little like cellular automata in that in at least one dimension information can propagate only at a limited speed, say c. The result is that in such equations, giving values for $u[t, x]$ at $t = 0$ for $-s < x < s$ will uniquely determine $u[t, x]$ at larger t for $-s + ct < x < s - ct$. In other PDEs, such as so-called elliptic ones, there is no such limit on the rate of information propagation, and as a result, it is immediately necessary to know values of $u[t, x]$ at all x, and on the boundaries of the region, in order to determine $u[t, x]$ for any $t > 0$.

■ **Page 165 · Field equations.** Any equation of the form

$$\partial_{tt} u[t, x] == \partial_{xx} u[t, x] + f[u[t, x]]$$

can be thought of as a classical field equation for a scalar field. Defining

$$v[u] = -Integrate[f[u], u]$$

the field then has Lagrangian density

$$((\partial_t u)^2 - (\partial_x u)^2)/2 - v[u]$$

and conserves the Hamiltonian (energy function)

$$Integrate[((\partial_t u)^2 + (\partial_x u)^2)/2 + v[u], \{x, -\infty, \infty\}]$$

With the choice for $f[u]$ made here (with $a \geq 0$), $v[u]$ is bounded from below, and as a result it follows that no singularities ever occur in $u[t, x]$.

▪ Equation for the background. If $u[t, x]$ is independent of x, as it is sufficiently far away from the main pattern, then the partial differential equation on page 165 reduces to the ordinary differential equation

$$u''[t] == (1 - u[t]^2)(1 + a u[t])$$

$$u[0] == u'[0] == 0$$

For $a = 0$, the solution to this equation can be written in terms of Jacobi elliptic functions as

$$\sqrt{3}\; JacobiSN[t/3^{1/4}, 1/2]^2/(1 + JacobiCN[t/3^{1/4}, 1/2]^2)$$

In general the solution is

$$b\, d\, JacobiSN[r\, t, s]^2/(b - d\, JacobiCN[r\, t, s]^2)$$

where

$$r = -Sqrt[1/8\, a\, c\, (b - d)]$$

$$s = d\, (c - b)/(c\, (d - b))$$

and b, c, d are determined by the equation

$$(x - b)(x - c)(x - d) == -(12 + 6\, a\, x - 4\, x^2 - 3\, a\, x^3)/(3\, a)$$

In all cases (except when $-8/3 < a < -1/\sqrt{6}$), the solution is periodic and non-singular. For $a = 0$, the period is $2\, 3^{1/4}\, EllipticK[1/2] \approx 4.88$. For $a = 1$, the period is about 4.01; for $a = 2$, it is about 3.62; while for $a = 4$, it is about 3.18. For $a = 8/3$, the solution can be written without Jacobi elliptic functions, and is given by

$$3\, Sin[Sqrt[5/6]\, t]^2/(2 + 3\, Cos[Sqrt[5/6]\, t]^2)$$

▪ Numerical analysis. To find numerical solutions to PDEs on a digital computer one has no choice but to make approximations. In the typical case of the finite difference method one sets up a system with discrete cells in space and time that is much like a continuous cellular automaton, and then hopes that when the cells in this system are made small enough its behavior will be close to that of the continuous PDE.

Several things can go wrong, however. The pictures below show as one example what happens with the diffusion equation when the cells have size dt in time and dx in space. So long as the so-called Courant condition $dt/dx < 1/2$ is satisfied, the results are correct. But when dt/dx is made larger, an instability develops, and the discrete approximation yields completely different results from the continuous PDE.

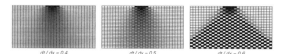

dt/dx = 0.4   dt/dx = 0.5   dt/dx = 0.6

Many methods beyond finite differences have been invented over the past 30 years for finding numerical solutions to PDEs. All however ultimately involve discretization, and can suffer from difficulties that are similar—though often more insidious—to those for finite differences.

For equations where one can come at least close to having explicit algebraic formulas for solutions, it has often been possible to prove that a certain discretization procedure will yield correct results. But when the form of the true solution is more complicated, such proofs are typically impossible.

And indeed in practice it is often difficult to tell whether complexity that is seen is actually a consequence of the underlying PDE, or is instead merely a reflection of the discretization procedure. I strongly suspect that many equations, particularly in fluid dynamics, that have been studied over the past few decades exhibit highly complex behavior. But in most publications such behavior is never shown, presumably because the authors are not sure whether the behavior is a genuine consequence of the equations they are studying.

▪ Implementation. All the numerical solutions shown were found using the *NDSolve* function built into *Mathematica*. In general, finite difference methods, the method of lines and pseudospectral methods can be used. For equations of the form

$$\partial_{tt}\, u[t, x] == \partial_{xx}\, u[t, x] + f[u[t, x]]$$

one can set up a simple finite difference method by taking f in the form of pure function and creating from it a kernel with space step dx and time step dt:

```
PDEKernel[f_, {dx_, dt_}] := Compile[{a, b, c, d},
    Evaluate[(2 b - d) + ((a + c - 2 b)/dx^2 + f[b]) dt^2]]
```

Iteration for n steps is then performed by

```
PDEEvolveList[ker_, {u0_, u1_}, n_] :=
    Map[First, NestList[PDEStep[ker, #] &, {u0, u1}, n]]
PDEStep[ker_, {u1_, u2_}] := {u2, Apply[ker, Transpose[
    {RotateLeft[u2], u2, RotateRight[u2], u1}], {1}]}
```

With this approach an approximation to the top example on page 165 can be obtained from

```
PDEEvolveList[PDEKernel[
    (1 - #^2)(1 + #) &, {0.1, 0.05}], Transpose[
    Table[{1, 1} N[Exp[-x^2]], {x, -20, 20, 0.1}]], 400]
```

For both this example and the middle one the results converge rapidly as dx decreases. But for the bottom example, the pictures below show that convergence is not so rapid, and indeed, as is typical in working with PDEs, despite having used large amounts of computer time I do not know whether the details of the picture in the main text are really correct. The energy function (see above) is at least roughly conserved, but it seems quite likely that the "shocks" visible are merely a consequence of the discretization procedure used.

dx = 0.5   dx = 0.2   dx = 0.05

■ **Different powers.** The equations

$$\partial_{tt} u[t, x] == \partial_{xx} u[t, x] + (1 - u[t, x])^n) (1 + a u[t, x])$$

with $n = 4$, 6, 8, etc. appear to show similar behavior to the $n = 2$ equation in the main text.

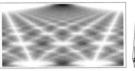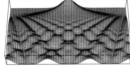

Burger's equation: $\partial_t u[t, x] = \partial_{xx} u[t, x] - u[t, x] \partial_x u[t, x]$

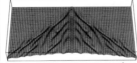

nonlinear Schrödinger equation: $i\, \partial_t u[t, x] = -\partial_{xx} u[t, x] + 4\, Abs[u[t, x]]^2 u[t, x]$

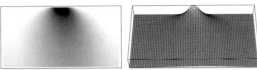

Kuramoto-Sivashinsky equation: $\partial_t u[t, x] = -\partial_{xx} u[t, x] - 1/2\, \partial_{xxxx} u[t, x] + (\partial_x u[t, x])^2$

■ **Other PDEs.** The pictures above show three PDEs that have been studied in recent years. All are of the so-called parabolic type, so that, unlike my equation, they have no limit on the rate of information propagation, and thus a solution in any region immediately depends on values on the boundary—which in the pictures below is taken to be periodic. (The deterministic Kardar-Parisi-Zhang equation $\partial_t u[t, x] == a\, \partial_{xx} u[t, x] + 1/2\, b\, (\partial_x u[t, x])^2$ yields behavior like Burger's equation, but symmetrical. Note that $Abs[u]$ is plotted in the second picture, while for the last equation a common less symmetrical form replaces the last term by $u[t, x] \partial_x u[t, x]$.)

Continuous Versus Discrete Systems

■ **History.** From the late 1600s when calculus was invented it took about two centuries before mathematicians came to terms with the concepts of continuity that it required. And to do so it was necessary to abandon concrete intuition, and instead to rely on abstract mathematical theorems. (See page 1149.) The kind of discrete systems that I consider in this book allow a return to a more concrete form of mathematics, without the necessity for such abstraction.

■ **"Calculus".** It is an irony of language that the word "calculus" now associated with continuous systems comes from the Latin word which means a small pebble of the kind used for doing discrete calculations (same root as "calcium").

Two Dimensions and Beyond

Introduction

■ **Other lattices.** See page 929.

■ **Page 170 · 1D phenomena.** Among the phenomena that cannot occur in one dimension are those associated with shape, winding and knotting, as well as traditional phase transitions with reversible evolution rules (see page 981).

Cellular Automata

■ **Implementation.** An $n \times n$ array of white squares with a single black square in the middle can be generated by

PadLeft[{{1}}, {n, n}, 0, Floor[{n, n}/2]]

For the 5-neighbor rules introduced on page 170 each step can be implemented by

CAStep[rule_, a_] := Map[rule[[10 - #]] &,
  ListConvolve[{{0, 2, 0}, {2, 1, 2}, {0, 2, 0}}, a, 2], {2}]

where *rule* is obtained from the *code* number by *IntegerDigits[code, 2, 10]*.

For the 9-neighbor rules introduced on page 177

CAStep[rule_, a_] := Map[rule[[18 - #]] &,
  ListConvolve[{{2, 2, 2}, {2, 1, 2}, {2, 2, 2}}, a, 2], {2}]

where *rule* is given by *IntegerDigits[code, 2, 18]*.

In d dimensions with k colors, 5-neighbor rules generalize to $(2d+1)$-neighbor rules, with

CAStep[{rule_, d_}, a_] :=
  Map[rule[[-1 - #]] &, a + k AxesTotal[a, d], {d}]
AxesTotal[a_, d_] := Apply[Plus, Map[RotateLeft[a, #] +
  RotateRight[a, #] &, IdentityMatrix[d]]]

with *rule* given by *IntegerDigits[code, k, k (2 d (k - 1) + 1)]*.

9-neighbor rules generalize to 3^d-neighbor rules, with

CAStep[{rule_, d_}, a_] :=
  Map[rule[[-1 - #]] &, a + k FullTotal[a, d], {d}]
FullTotal[a_, d_] :=
  Array[RotateLeft[a, {##}] &, Table[3, {d}], -1, Plus] - a

with *rule* given by *IntegerDigits[code, k, k ((3^d - 1) (k - 1) + 1)]*.

In 3 dimensions, the positions of black cells can conveniently be displayed using

Graphics3D[Map[Cuboid[-Reverse[#]] &, Position[a, 1]]]

■ **General rules.** One can specify the neighborhood for any rule in any dimension by giving a list of the offsets for the cells used to update a given cell. For 1D elementary rules the list is {{-1}, {0}, {1}}, while for 2D 5-neighbor rules it is {{-1, 0}, {0, -1}, {0, 0}, {0, 1}, {1, 0}}. In this book such offset lists are always taken to be in the order given by *Sort*, so that for range r rules in d dimensions the order is the same as *Flatten[Array[List, Table[2 r + 1, {d}], -r], d - 1]*. One can specify a neighborhood configuration by giving in the same order as the offset list the color of each cell in the neighborhood. With offset list *os* and k colors the possible neighborhood configurations are

Reverse[Table[IntegerDigits[i - 1,
  k, Length[os]], {i, k^Length[os]}]]

(These are shown on page 53 for elementary rules and page 941 for 5-neighbor rules.) If a cellular automaton rule takes the new color of a cell with neighborhood configuration *IntegerDigits[i, k, Length[os]]* to be *u[[i + 1]]*, then one can define its rule number to be *FromDigits[Reverse[u], k]*. A single step in evolution of a general cellular automaton with state *a* and rule number *num* is then given by

Map[IntegerDigits[num, k, k^Length[os]][[-1 - #]] &,
  Apply[Plus, MapIndexed[k^(Length[os] - First[#2])
    RotateLeft[a, #1] &, os]], {-1}]

or equivalently by

Map[IntegerDigits[num, k, k^Length[os]][[-# - 1]] &,
  ListCorrelate[Fold[ReplacePart[k #1, 1, #2 + r + 1] &,
    Array[0 &, Table[2 r + 1, {d}]], os], a, r + 1], {d}]

■ **Numbers of possible rules.** The table below gives the total number of 2D rules of various types with two possible colors for each cell. Given an initial pattern with a certain symmetry, a rule will maintain that symmetry if the rule is such that every neighborhood equivalent under the symmetry yields the same color of cell. Rules are considered rotationally symmetric in the table below if they preserve any possible rotational symmetry consistent with the underlying arrangement of cells. Totalistic rules depend only on the total number of black cells in a neighborhood; outer totalistic rules (as in the previous note) also depend on the color of the center cell. Growth totalistic rules make any cell that becomes black remain black forever.

In such a rule, given a list of how many neighbors around a given cell (out of s possible) make the cell turn black the outer totalistic code for the rule can be obtained from

Apply[Plus, 2 ^ Join[2 list, 2 Range[s + 1] - 1]]

	5 - neighbor square	9 - neighbor square	hexagonal
general	$2^{32} \approx 4 \times 10^9$	$2^{512} \approx 10^{154}$	$2^{128} \approx 3 \times 10^{38}$
rotationally symmetric	$2^{12} \approx 4096$	$2^{140} \approx 10^{42}$	$2^{28} \approx 3 \times 10^8$
completely symmetric	$2^{12} \approx 4096$	$2^{102} \approx 5 \times 10^{30}$	$2^{26} \approx 7 \times 10^7$
outer totalistic	$2^{10} = 1024$	$2^{18} \approx 3 \times 10^5$	$2^{14} = 16384$
totalistic	$2^6 = 64$	$2^{10} = 1024$	$2^8 = 256$
growth totalistic	$2^5 = 32$	$2^9 = 512$	$2^7 = 128$

■ **Symmetric 5-neighbor rules.** Among the 32 possible 5-cell neighborhoods shown for example on page 941 there are 12 classes related by symmetries, given by

s = {{1}, {2, 3, 9, 17}, {4, 10, 19, 25},
  {5}, {6, 7, 13, 21}, {8, 14, 23, 29}, {11, 18},
  {12, 20, 26, 27}, {15, 22}, {16, 24, 30, 31}, {28}, {32}}

Completely symmetric 5-neighbor rules can be numbered from 0 to 4095, with each digit specifying the new color of the cell for each of these symmetry classes of neighborhoods. Such rule numbers can be converted to general form using

FromDigits[Map[Last, Sort[Flatten[Map[Thread,
  Thread[{s, IntegerDigits[n, 2, 12]}]], 1]], 2]

■ **Growth rules.** The pictures below show examples of rules in which a cell becomes black if it has exactly the specified numbers of black neighbors (the initial conditions used have the minimal number of black cells for growth). The code numbers in these cases are given by $2/3 (4^n - 1) + Apply[Plus, 4^{list}]$ where n is the number of neighbors, here 5. (See also the 9-neighbor examples on page 373.)

(1)   (1, 2)   (1, 3)   (1, 4)   (1, 3, 4)

■ **Page 171 · Code 942 slices.** The following is the result of taking vertical slices through the pattern with a sequence of offsets from the center:

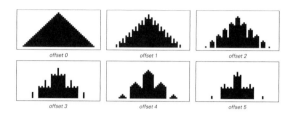

offset 0   offset 1   offset 2

offset 3   offset 4   offset 5

■ **History.** As indicated on pages 876–878, 2D cellular automata were historically studied more extensively than 1D ones—though rarely with simple initial conditions. The 5-cell neighborhood on page 170 was considered by John von Neumann in 1952; the 9-cell one on page 177 by Edward Moore in 1962. (Both are also common in finite difference approximations in numerical analysis.) (The 7-cell hexagonal neighborhood of page 369 was considered for image processing purposes by Marcel Golay in 1959.) Ever since the invention of the Game of Life around 1970 a remarkable number of hardware and software simulators have been built to watch its evolution. But until after my work in the 1980s simulators for more general 2D cellular automata were rare. A sequence of hardware simulators were nevertheless built starting in the mid-1970s by Tommaso Toffoli and later Norman Margolus. And as mentioned on page 1077, going back to the 1950s some image processing systems have been based on particular families of 2D cellular automaton rules.

■ **Ulam systems.** Having formulated the system around 1960, Stanislaw Ulam and collaborators (see page 877) in 1967 simulated 120 steps of the process shown below, with black cells after t steps occurring at positions

Map[First,
  First[Nest[p[q[r[#1], #2]] &, {{1, 0}, {0, 1}, {-1, 0},
    {0, -1}}, #] &, ({#, #} &)[{{{0, 0}, {0, 0}}}], t]]]
UStep[f_, os_, {a_, b_}] := ({Join[a, #], #} &)[f[Flatten[
  Outer[{#1 + #2, #1} &, Map[First, b], os, 1], 1], a]]
r[c_] := Map[First, Select[Split[Sort[c]],
  First[#1] == First[#2] &], Length[#] == 1 &]]
q[c_, a_] := Select[c,
  Apply[And, Map[Function[u, qq[#1, u, a]], a]] &]
p[c_] := Select[c,
  Apply[And, Map[Function[u, pp[#1, u]], c]] &]
pp[{x_, u_}, {y_, v_}] := Max[Abs[x - y]] > 1 || u == v
qq[{x_, u_}, {y_, v_}, a_] := x == y || Max[Abs[x - y]] > 1 ||
  u == y || First[Cases[a, {u, z_} → z]] == y

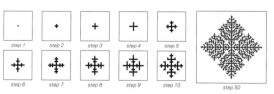

step 1   step 2   step 3   step 4   step 5

step 6   step 7   step 8   step 9   step 10   step 50

These rules are fairly complicated, and involve more history than ordinary cellular automata. But from the discoveries in this book we now know that much simpler rules can also yield very complicated behavior. And as the pictures below show, this is true even just for parts of the rules above (*s* alone yields outer totalistic code 686 in 2D, and rule 90 in 1D).

Ulam also in 1967 considered the pure 2D cellular automaton with outer totalistic code 12 (though he stated its rule in a complicated way). As shown in the pictures below, when started from blocks of certain sizes this rule yields complex patterns—although nothing like this was noted in 1967.

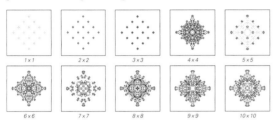

■ **Limiting shapes.** When growth occurs at the maximum rate the outer boundaries of a cellular automaton pattern reflect the neighborhood involved in its underlying rule (in rough analogy to the Wulff construction for shapes of crystals). When growth occurs at a slower rate, a wide range of polygonal and other shapes can be obtained, as illustrated in the main text.

■ **Additive rules.** See page 1092.

■ **Page 174 · Cellular automaton art.** 2D cellular automata can be used to make a wide range of designs for rugs, wallpaper, and similar objects. Repeating squares of pattern can be produced by using periodic boundary conditions. Rules with more than two colors will sometimes be appropriate. For rugs, it is typically desirable to have each cell correspond to more than one tuft, since otherwise with most rules the rug looks too busy. (Compare page 872.)

■ **Page 177 · Code 175850.** See also page 980.

■ **Page 178 · Code 746.** The pattern generated is not perfectly circular, as discussed on page 979. Its interior is mostly fixed, but there are scattered small regions that cycle with a variety of periods.

■ **Page 181 · Code 174826.** The pictures below show the upper-right quadrant for more steps. Most of the lines visible are 8

cells across, and grow by 4 cells every 12 steps. They typically survive being hit by more complicated growth from the side. But occasionally runners 3 cells wide will start on the side of a line. And since these go 2 cells every 3 steps they always catch up with lines, producing complicated growth, often terminating the lines.

■ **Page 183 · Projections from 3D.** Looking from above, with closer cells shown darker, the following show patterns generated after 30 steps, by (a) the rule at the top of page 183, (b) the rule at the bottom of page 183, (c) the rule where a cell becomes black if exactly 3 out of 26 neighbors were black and (d) the same as (c), but with a $3 \times 3 \times 1$ rather than a $3 \times 1 \times 1$ initial block of black cells:

■ **Other geometries.** Systems like cellular automata can readily be set up on any geometrical structure in which a limited number of types of cells can be identified, with every cell of a given type having a similar neighborhood.

In the simplest case, the cells are all identical, and are laid out in the same orientation in a repetitive array. The centers of the cells form a lattice, with coordinates that are integer multiples of some set of basis vectors. The possible complete symmetries of such lattices are much studied in crystallography. But for the purpose of nearest-neighbor cellular automaton rules, what matters is not detailed geometry, but merely what cells are adjacent to a given cell. This can be determined by looking at the Voronoi region (see page 987) for each point in the lattice. In any given dimension, this region (variously known as a Dirichlet domain or Wigner-Seitz cell, and dual to the primitive cell, first Brillouin zone or Wulff shape) has a limited number of possible overall shapes. The most symmetrical versions of these shapes in 2D are the square (4 neighbors) and hexagon (6) and in 3D (as found by Evgraf Fedorov in 1885) the cube (6), hexagonal prism (8), rhombic dodecahedron (12) (e.g.

face-centered cubic crystals), rhombo-hexagonal or elongated dodecahedron (12) and truncated octahedron or tetradecahedron (14) (e.g. body-centered cubic crystals), as shown below. (In 4D, 8, 16 and 24 nearest neighbors are possible; in higher dimensions possibilities have been investigated in connection with sphere packing.) (Compare pages 1029 and 986.)

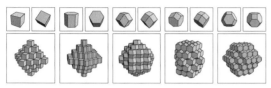

In general, there is no need for individual cells in a cellular automaton to have the same orientation. A triangular lattice is one example where they do not. And indeed, any tiling of congruent figures can readily be used to make a cellular automaton, as illustrated by the pentagonal example below. (Outer totalistic codes specify rules; the first rule makes a particular cell black when any of its five neighbors are black and has code 4094. Note that even though individual cells are pentagonal, large-scale cellular automaton patterns usually have 2-, 4- or 8-fold symmetry.)

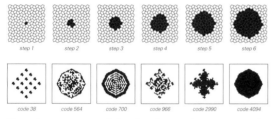

| step 1 | step 2 | step 3 | step 4 | step 5 | step 6 |

| code 38 | code 564 | code 700 | code 966 | code 2990 | code 4094 |

There is even no need for the tiling to be repetitive; the picture below shows a cellular automaton on a nested Penrose tiling (see page 932). This tiling has two different shapes of tile, but here both are treated the same by the cellular automaton rule, which is given by an outer totalistic code number. The first example is code 254, which makes a particular cell become black when any of its three neighbors are black. (Large-scale cellular automaton patterns here can have 5-fold symmetry.) (See also page 1027.)

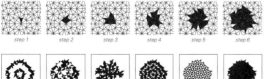

| step 1 | step 2 | step 3 | step 4 | step 5 | step 6 |

| code 22 | code 54 | code 174 | code 214 | code 220 | code 254 |

■ Networks. Cellular automata can be set up so that each cell corresponds to a node in a network. (See page 936.) The only requirement is that around each node the network must have the same structure (or at least a limited number of possible structures). For nearest-neighbor rules, it suffices that each node has the same number of connections. For longer-range rules, the network must satisfy constraints of the kind discussed on page 483. (Cayley graphs of groups always have the necessary homogeneity.) If the connections at each node are not labelled, then only totalistic cellular automaton rules can be implemented. Many topological and geometrical properties of the underlying network can affect the overall behavior of a cellular automaton on it.

Turing Machines

■ Implementation. With rules represented as a list of elements of the form $\{s, a\} \rightarrow \{sp, ap, \{dx, dy\}\}$ (s is the state of the head and a the color of the cell under the head) each step in the evolution of a 2D Turing machine is given by

```
TM2DStep[rule_, {s_, tape_, r : {x_, y_}}] :=
   Apply[{#1, ReplacePart[tape, #2, {r}], r + #3} &,
      {s, tape[[x, y]]} /. rule]
```

■ History. At a formal level 2D Turing machines have been studied since at least the 1950s. And on several occasions systems equivalent to specific simple 2D Turing machines have also been constructed. In fact, much as for cellular automata, more explicit experiments have been done on 2D Turing machines than 1D ones. A tradition of early robotics going back to the 1940s—and leading for example to the Logo computer language—involved studying idealizations of mobile turtles. And in 1971 Michael Paterson and John Conway constructed what they described as an idealization of a prehistoric worm, which was essentially a 2D Turing machine in which the state of the head records the direction of the motion taken at each step. Michael Beeler in 1973 used a computer at MIT to investigate all 1296 possible worms with rules of the simplest type on a hexagonal grid, and he found several with fairly complex behavior. But this discovery does not appear to have been followed up, and systems equivalent to simple 2D Turing machines were reinvented again, largely independently, several times in the mid-1980s: by Christopher Langton in 1985 under the name "vants"; by Rudy Rucker in 1987 under the name "turmites"; and by Allen Brady in 1987 under the name "turning machines". The specific 4-state rule

$$\{s_, c_\} :\rightarrow With[\{sp = s (2 c - 1) i\},$$
$$\{sp, 1 - c, \{Re[sp], Im[sp]\}\}]$$

has been called Langton's ant, and various studies of it were done in the 1990s.

■ **Visualization.** The pictures below show the 2D position of the head at 500 successive steps for the rules on page 185.

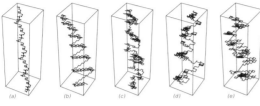

Some 2D Turing machines exhibit elements of randomness at some steps, but then fill in every so often to form simple repetitive patterns. An example is the 3-state rule

■ **Rules based on turning.** The rules used in the main text specify the displacement of the head at each step in terms of fixed directions in the underlying grid. An alternative is to specify the turns to make at each step in the motion of the head. This is how turtles in the Logo computer language are set up. (Compare the discussion of paths in substitution systems on page 892.)

■ **2D mobile automata.** Mobile automata can be generalized just like Turing machines. Even in the simplest case, however, with only four neighbors involved there are already $(4k)^{k^5}$ possible rules, or nearly 10^{29} even for $k = 2$.

Substitution Systems and Fractals

■ **Implementation.** With the rule on page 187 given for example by $\{1 \to \{\{1, 0\}, \{1, 1\}\}, 0 \to \{\{0, 0\}, \{0, 0\}\}\}$ the result of t steps in the evolution of a 2D substitution system from a initial condition such as $\{\{1\}\}$ is given by

```
SS2DEvolve[rule_, init_, t_] :=
    Nest[Flatten2D[# /. rule] &, init, t]

Flatten2D[list_] :=
    Apply[Join, Map[MapThread[Join, #] &, list]]
```

■ **Connection with digit sequences.** Just as in the 1D case discussed on page 891, the color of a cell at position $\{i, j\}$ in a 2D substitution system can be determined using a finite automaton from the digit sequences of the numbers i and j. At step n, the complete array of cells is

```
Table[If[FreeQ[Transpose[IntegerDigits[{i, j}, k, n]], form],
    1, 0], {i, 0, k^n - 1}, {j, 0, k^n - 1}]
```

where for the pattern on page 187, $k = 2$ and $form = \{0, 1\}$. For patterns (a) through (f) on page 188, $k = 3$ and $form$ is given respectively by (a) $\{1, 1\}$, (b) $\{0 | 2, 0 | 2\}$, (c)

$\{0 | 2, 0 | 2\} | \{1, 1\}$, (d) $\{i_-, j_-\} /; j > i$, (e) $\{0, 2\} | \{1, 1\} | \{2, 0\}$, (f) $\{0, 2\} | \{1, 1\}$. Note that the excluded pairs of digits are in exact correspondence with the positions of which squares are 0 in the underlying rules for the substitution systems. (See pages 608 and 1091.)

■ **Page 187 · Sierpiński pattern.** Other ways to generate step n of the pattern shown here in various orientations include:

- $Mod[Array[Binomial, \{2, 2\}^n, 0], 2]$ (see pages 611 and 870)

- $1 - Sign[Array[BitAnd, \{2, 2\}^n, 0]]$ (see pages 608 and 871)

- $NestList[Mod[RotateLeft[\#] + \#, 2] \&,$
  $PadLeft[\{1\}, 2^n], 2^n - 1]$
  (see page 870)

- $NestList[Mod[ListConvolve[\{1, 1\}, \#, -1], 2] \&,$
  $PadLeft[\{1\}, 2^n], 2^n - 1]$
  (see page 870)

- $IntegerDigits[NestList[BitXor[2\#, \#] \&, 1, 2^n - 1], 2, 2^n]$ (see page 906)

- $NestList[Mod[Rest[FoldList[Plus, 0, \#]], 2] \&,$
  $Table[1, \{2^n\}], 2^n - 1]$
  (see page 1034)

- $Table[PadRight[$
  $Mod[CoefficientList[(1 + x)^{t-1}, x], 2], 2^n - 1], \{t, 2^n\}]$
  (see pages 870 and 951)

- $Reverse[Mod[CoefficientList[Series[1/(1 - (1 + x)y),$
  $\{x, 0, 2^n - 1\}, \{y, 0, 2^n - 1\}], \{x, y\}], 2]]$
  (see page 1091)

- $Nest[Apply[Join, MapThread[$
  $Join, \{\{\#, \#\}, \{0\#, \#\}\}, 2]] \&, \{\{1\}\}, n]$
  (compare page 1073)

The positions of black squares can be found from:

- $Nest[Flatten[2\# /. \{x_-, y_-\} \to \{\{x, y\}, \{x + 1, y\}, \{x, y + 1\}\},$
  $1] \&, \{\{0, 0\}\}, n]$

- $(Transpose[\{Re[\#], Im[\#]\}] \&)[$
  $Flatten[Nest[\{2\#, 2\# + 1, 2\# + ii\} \&, \{0\}, n]]]$
  (compare page 1005)

- $Position[Map[Split, NestList[Sort[Flatten[\{\#, \# + 1\}]] \&,$
  $\{0\}, 2^n - 1]], \_?(OddQ[Length[\#]] \&), \{2\}]$
  (see page 358)

- $Flatten[Table[Map[\{t, \#\} \&,$
  $Fold[Flatten[\{\#1, \#1 + \#2\}] \&, 0, Flatten[2 ^ (Position[$
  $Reverse[IntegerDigits[t, 2]], 1] - 1)]]], \{t, 2^n - 1\}], 1]$
  (see page 870)

- $Map[Map[FromDigits[\#, 2] \&, Transpose[Partition[\#, 2]]] \&,$
  $Position[Nest[\{\{\#, \#\}, \{\#\}\} \&, 1, n], 1] - 1]$
  (see page 509)

A formatting hack giving the same visual pattern is

DisplayForm[Nest[SubsuperscriptBox[#, #, #] &, "1", n]]

■ **Non-white backgrounds.** The pictures below show substitution systems in which white squares are replaced by blocks which contain black squares. There is still a nested structure but it is usually not visually as obvious as before. (See page 583.)

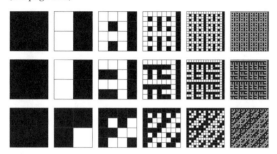

■ **Higher-dimensional generalizations.** The state of a d-dimensional substitution system can be represented by a nested list of depth d. The evolution of the system for t steps can be obtained from

SSEvolve[rule_, init_, t_, d_Integer] :=
  Nest[FlattenArray[# /. rule, d] &, init, t]

FlattenArray[list_, d_] :=
  Fold[Function[{a, n}, Map[MapThread[Join, #, n] &,
    a, -{d + 2}]], list, Reverse[Range[d] - 1]]

The analog in 3D of the 2D rule on page 187 is

{1 → Array[If[LessEqual[##], 0, 1] &, {2, 2, 2}],
  0 → Array[0 &, {2, 2, 2}]}

Note that in d dimensions, each black cell must be replaced by at least $d + 1$ black cells at each step in order to obtain an object that is not restricted to a dimension $d - 1$ hyperplane.

■ **Other shapes.** The systems on pages 187 and 188 are based on subdividing squares into smaller squares. But one can also set up substitution systems that are based on subdividing other geometrical figures, as shown below.

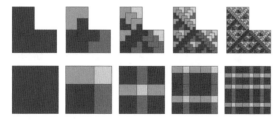

The second example involves two distinct shapes: a square and a *GoldenRatio* aspect ratio rectangle. Labelling each shape and

orientation with a different color, the behavior of this system can be reproduced with equal-sized squares using the rule $\{3 → \{\{1, 0\}, \{3, 2\}\}, 2 → \{\{1\}, \{3\}\}, 1 → \{\{3, 2\}\}, 0 → \{\{3\}\}\}$ starting from initial condition $\{\{3\}\}$.

■ **Penrose tilings.** The nested pattern shown below was studied by Roger Penrose in 1974 (see page 943).

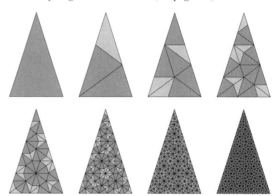

The arrangement of triangles at step t can be obtained from a substitution system according to

With[{φ = GoldenRatio}, Nest[# /. a[p_, q_, r_] :→
  With[{s = (p + φ q) (2 - φ)}, {a[r, s, q], b[r, s, p]}] /.
  b[p_, q_, r_] :→ With[{s = (p + φ r) (2 - φ)}, {a[p, s, s], b[
  r, s, q]}] &, a[{1/2, Sin[2 π/5] φ}, {1, 0}, {0, 0}], t]]

This pattern can be viewed as generalizations of the pattern generated by the 1D Fibonacci substitution system (c) on page 83. As discussed on page 903, this 1D sequence can be obtained by looking at how a line with *GoldenRatio* slope cuts through a 2D lattice of squares. Penrose tilings can be obtained by looking at how a 2D plane with slopes based on *GoldenRatio* cuts through a lattice of hypercubes in 5D. The tilings turn out to have approximate 5-fold symmetry. (See also page 943.)

In general, projections onto any regular lattice in any number of dimensions from hyperplanes with any quadratic irrational slopes will yield nested patterns that can be generated by subdividing some shape or another according to a substitution system. Despite some confusion in the literature, however, this procedure can reproduce only a tiny fraction of all possible nested patterns.

■ **Page 189 · Dragon curve.** The pattern shown here can be obtained in several related ways, including from numbers in base $i - 1$ (see below) and from a doubled version of the paths generated by 1D paperfolding substitution systems (see page 892). Its boundary has fractal dimension $2 \, Log[2, Root[2 + \#1^2 - \#1^3, 1]] \simeq 1.52$.

■ **Implementation.** The most convenient approach is to represent each pattern by a list of complex numbers, with the center of each square being given in terms of each complex number z by $\{Re[z], Im[z]\}$. The pattern after n steps is then given by $Nest[Flatten[f[\#]] \&, \{0\}, n]$, where for the rule on page 189 $f[z\_] = 1/2 (1 - i)\{z + 1/2, z - 1/2\}$ ($f[z\_] = (1 - i)\{z + 1, z\}$ gives a transformed version). For the rule on page 190, $f[z\_] = 1/2 (1 - i)\{i z + 1/2, z - 1/2\}$. For rules (a), (b) and (c) (Koch curve) on page 191 the forms of $f[z\_]$ are respectively:

$(0.296 - 0.57 i) z - 0.067 i - \{1.04, 0.237\}$

$N[1/40 \{17 (\sqrt{3} - i) z, -24 + 14 z\}]$

$N[(1/2 (1/\sqrt{3} - 1) (i + \{1, -1\}) - i - (1 + \{i, -i\}/\sqrt{3}) z)/2]$

■ **Connection with digit sequences.** Patterns after t steps can be viewed as containing all t-digit integers in an appropriate complex base. Thus the patterns on page 189 can be formed from t-digit integers in base $i - 1$ containing only digits 0 and 1, as given by

$Table[FromDigits[IntegerDigits[s, 2, t], i - 1], \{s, 0, 2^t - 1\}]$

In the particular case of base $i - q$ with digits 0 through q^2, it turns out that for sufficiently large t any complex integer can be represented, and will therefore be part of the pattern. (Compare page 1094.)

■ **Visualization.** The 3D pictures below show successive steps in the evolution of each of the geometric substitution systems from the main text.

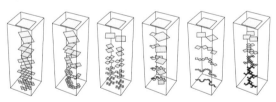

■ **Parameter space sets.** See pages 407 and 1006 for a discussion of varying parameters in geometrical substitution systems.

■ **Affine transformations.** Any set of so-called affine transformations that take the vector for each point, multiply it by a fixed matrix and then add a fixed vector, will yield nested patterns similar to those shown in the main text. Linear operations on complex numbers of the kind discussed above correspond geometrically to rotations, translations and rescalings. General affine transformations also allow reflection and skewing. In addition, affine transformations can readily be generalized to any number of dimensions, while complex numbers represent only two dimensions.

■ **Complex maps.** Many kinds of nonlinear transformations on complex numbers yield nested patterns. Sets of so-called Möbius transformations of the form $z \to (a z + b)/(c z + d)$ always yield such patterns (and correspond to so-called modular groups when $a d - b c == 1$). Transformations of the form $z \to \{Sqrt[z - c], -Sqrt[z - c]\}$ yield so-called Julia sets which form nested patterns for many values of c (see note below). In fact, a fair fraction of all possible transformations based on algebraic functions will yield nested patterns. For typically the continuity of such functions implies that only a limited number of shapes not related by limited variations in local magnification can occur at any scale.

■ **Fractal dimensions.** Certain features of nested patterns can be characterized by so-called fractal dimensions. The pictures below show five patterns with three successively finer grids superimposed. The dimension of a pattern can be computed by looking at how the number of grid squares that have any gray in them varies with the length a of the edge of each grid square. In the first case shown, this number varies like $(1/a)^1$ for small a, while in the last case, it varies like $(1/a)^2$. In general, if the number varies like $(1/a)^d$, one can take d to be the dimension of the pattern. And in the intermediate cases shown, it turns out that d has non-integer values.

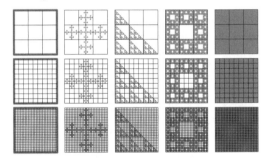

The grid in the pictures above fits over the pattern in a very regular way. But even when this does not happen, the limiting behavior for small a is still $(1/a)^d$ for any nested pattern. This form is inevitable if the underlying pattern effectively has the same structure on all scales. For some of the more complex patterns encountered in this book, however, there continues to be different structure on different scales, so that the effective value of d fluctuates as the scale changes, and may not converge to any definite value. (Precise definitions of dimension based for example on the maximum ever achieved by d will often in general imply formally non-computable values, as in the discussion of page 1138.)

Fractal dimensions characterize some aspects of nested patterns, but patterns with the same dimension can often look very different. One approach to getting better characterizations is to look at each grid square, and to ask not just whether there is any gray in it, but how much. Quantities derived from the mean, variance and other moments of the probability distribution can serve as generalizations of fractal dimension. (Compare page 959.)

■ **History of fractals.** The idea of using nested 2D shapes in art probably goes back to antiquity; some examples were shown on page 43. In mathematics, nested shapes began to be used at the end of the 1800s, mainly as counterexamples to ideas about continuity that had grown out of work on calculus. The first examples were graphs of functions: the curve on page 918 was discussed by Bernhard Riemann in 1861 and by Karl Weierstrass in 1872. Later came geometrical figures: example (c) on page 191 was introduced by Helge von Koch in 1906, the example on page 187 by Wacław Sierpiński in 1916, examples (a) and (c) on page 188 by Karl Menger in 1926 and the example on page 190 by Paul Lévy in 1937. Similar figures were also produced independently in the 1960s in the course of early experiments with computer graphics, primarily at MIT. From the point of view of mathematics, however, nested shapes tended to be viewed as rare and pathological examples, of no general significance. But the crucial idea that was developed by Benoit Mandelbrot in the late 1960s and early 1970s was that in fact nested shapes can be identified in a great many natural systems and in several branches of mathematics. Using early raster-based computer display technology, Mandelbrot was able to produce striking pictures of what he called fractals. And following the publication of Mandelbrot's 1975 book, interest in fractals increased rapidly. Quantitative comparisons of pure power laws implied by the simplest fractals with observations of natural systems have had somewhat mixed success, leading to the introduction of multifractals with more parameters, but Mandelbrot's general idea of the importance of fractals is now well established in both science and mathematics.

■ **The Mandelbrot set.** The pictures below show Julia sets produced by the procedure of taking the transformation $z \to \{Sqrt[z - c], -Sqrt[z - c]\}$ discussed above and iterating it starting at $z = 0$ for an array of values of c in the complex plane.

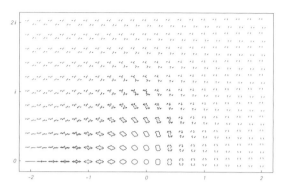

The Mandelbrot set introduced by Benoit Mandelbrot in 1979 is defined as the set of values of c for which such Julia sets are connected. This turns out to be equivalent to the set of values of c for which starting at $z = 0$ the inverse mapping $z \to z^2 + c$ leads only to bounded values of z. The Mandelbrot set turns out to have many intricate features which have been widely reproduced for their aesthetic value, as well as studied by mathematicians. The first picture below shows the overall form of the set; subsequent pictures show successive magnifications of the regions indicated. All parts of the Mandelbrot set are known to be connected. The whole set is not self-similar. However, as seen in the third and fourth pictures, within the set are isolated small copies of the whole set. In addition, as seen in the last picture, near most values of c the boundary of the Mandelbrot set looks very much like the Julia set for that value of c.

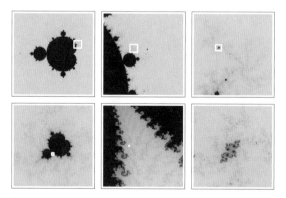

On pages 407 and 1006 I discuss parameter space sets that are somewhat analogous to the Mandelbrot set, but whose properties are in many respects much clearer. And from this discussion there emerges the following interpretation of the Mandelbrot set that appears not to be well known but which I find most illuminating. Look at the array of Julia sets and ask for each c whether the Julia set includes the point $z = 0$.

The set of values of c for which it does corresponds exactly to the boundary of the Mandelbrot set. The pictures below show a generalization of this idea, in which gray level indicates the minimum distance $Abs[z - z_0]$ of any point z in the Julia set from a fixed point z_0. The first picture shows the case $z_0 = 0$, corresponding to the usual Mandelbrot set.

$z_0 = 0$ $z_0 = 1$ $z_0 = i$

■ **Page 192 · Neighbor-dependent substitution systems.** Given a list of individual replacement rules such as $\{\{\_, 1\}, \{0, 1\}\} \rightarrow \{\{1, 0\}, \{1, 1\}\}$, each step in the evolution shown corresponds to

Flatten2D[Partition[list, {2, 2}, 1, -1] /. rule]

One can consider rules in which some replacements lead to subdivision of elements but others do not. However, unlike for the 1D case, there will in general in 2D be an arbitrarily large set of different possible neighborhood configurations around any given cell.

■ **Page 192 · Space-filling curves.** One can conveniently scan a finite 2D grid just by going along each successive row in turn. One can scan a quadrant of an infinite grid using the σ function on page 1127, or one can scan a whole grid by for example going in a square spiral that at step t reaches position

$(1/2 (-1)^{\#} (\{1, -1\} (Abs[\#^2 - t] - \#) + \#^2 - t - Mod[\#, 2]) \&)[$
$Round[\sqrt{t}\,]]$

Network Systems

■ **Implementation.** The nodes in a network system can conveniently be labelled by numbers 1, 2, $\ldots n$, and the network obtained at a particular step can be represented by a list of pairs, where the pair at position i gives the numbers corresponding to the nodes reached by following the above and below connections from node i. With this setup, a network consisting of just one node is $\{\{1, 1\}\}$ and a 1D array of n nodes can be obtained with

CyclicNet[n_] := RotateRight[
Table[Mod[{i - 1, i + 1}, n] + 1, {i, n}]]

With above connections represented as 1 and the below connections as 2, the node reached by following a succession s of connections from node i is given by

Follow[list_, i_, s_List] := Fold[list[[#1]][[#2]] &, i, s]

The total number of distinct nodes reached by following all possible succession of connections up to length d is given by

NeighborNumbers[list_, i_Integer, d_Integer] :=
Map[Length, NestList[Union[Flatten[list[[#]]]] &,
Union[list[[i]]], d - 1]]

For each such list the rules for the network system then specify how the connections from node i should be rerouted. The rule $\{2, 3\} \rightarrow \{\{2, 1\}, \{1\}\}$ specifies that when *NeighborNumbers* gives $\{2, 3\}$ for a node i, the connections from that node should become $\{Follow[list, i, \{2, 1\}], Follow[list, i, \{1\}]\}$. The rule $\{2, 3\} \rightarrow \{\{\{2, 1\}, \{1, 1\}\}, \{1\}\}$ specifies that a new node should be inserted in the above connection, and this new node should have connections $\{Follow[list, i, \{2, 1\}], Follow[list, i, \{1, 1\}]\}$. With rules set up in this way, each step in the evolution of a network system is given by

NetEvolveStep[{depth_Integer, rule_List}, list_List] := Block[
{new = {}}, Join[Table[Map[NetEvolveStep1[#, list, i] &,
Replace[NeighborNumbers[list, i, depth],
rule]], {i, Length[list]}], new]]

NetEvolveStep1[s : {___Integer}, list_, i_] := Follow[list, i, s]

NetEvolveStep1[{s1 : {___Integer}, s2 : {___Integer}},
list_, i_] := Length[list] + Length[
AppendTo[new, {Follow[list, i, s1], Follow[list, i, s2]}]]

The set of nodes that can be reached from node i is given by

ConnectedNodes[list_, i_] :=
FixedPoint[Union[Flatten[{#, list[[#]]}]] &, {i}]

and disconnected nodes can be removed using

RenumberNodes[list_, seq_] :=
Map[Position[seq, #][[1, 1]] &, list[[seq]], {2}]

The sequence of networks obtained on successive steps by applying the rules and then removing all nodes not connected to node number 1 is given by

NetEvolveList[rule_, init_, t_Integer] :=
NestList[(RenumberNodes[#, ConnectedNodes[#, 1]] &)[
NetEvolveStep[rule, #]] &, init, t]

Note that the nodes in each network are not necessarily numbered in the order that they appear on successive lines in the pictures in the main text. Additional information on the origin of each new node must be maintained if this order is to be found.

■ **Rule structure.** For depth 1, the possible results from *NeighborNumbers* are $\{1\}$ and $\{2\}$. For depth 2, they are $\{1, 1\}$, $\{1, 2\}$, $\{2, 1\}$, $\{2, 2\}$, $\{2, 3\}$ and $\{2, 4\}$. In general, each successive element in a list from *NeighborNumbers* cannot be more than twice the previous element.

■ **Undirected networks.** Networks with connections that do not have definite directions are discussed at length in Chapter 9, mainly as potential models for space in the universe. The rules for updating such networks turn out to be somewhat more difficult to apply than those for the network systems discussed here.

■ **Page 199 · Computer science.** The networks discussed here can be thought of as very simple analogs of data structures in practical computer programs. The connections correspond to pointers between elements of these data structures. The fact that there are two connections coming from each node is reminiscent of the LISP language, but in the networks considered here there are no leaves corresponding to atoms in LISP. Note that the process of dropping nodes that become disconnected is analogous to so-called "garbage collection" for data structures. The networks considered here are also related to the combinator systems discussed on page 1121.

■ **Page 202 · Properties.** Random behavior seems to occur in a few out of every thousand randomly selected rules of the kind shown here. In case (c), the following gives a list of the numbers of nodes generated up to step t:

FoldList[Plus, 1, Join[{1, 4, 12, 10, −20, 6, 4},
    Map[d, IntegerDigits[Range[4, t − 5], 2]]]]

$d[\{\_\_\_, 1\}] = 1$

$d[\{1, p : ((0)..), 0\}] :=$
    −Apply[Plus, 4 Range[Length[{p}]] − 1] + 6

$d[\{\_\_, 1, p : ((0)..), 0\}] := d[\{1, p, 0\}] − 7$

$d[\{\_\_\_, p : ((1)..), q : ((0)...), 1, 0\}] :=$
    4 Length[{p}] + 3 Length[{q}] + 2

$d[\{\_\_\_, p : ((1)..), 1, 0\}] := 4 Length[{p}] + 2$

■ **Sequential network systems.** In the network systems discussed in the main text, every node is updated in parallel at each step. It is however also possible to consider systems in which there is only a single active node, and operations are performed only on that node at any particular step. The active node can move by following its above or below connections, in a way that is determined by a rule which depends on the local structure of the network. The pictures below show examples of sequential network systems; the path of the active node is indicated by a thick black line.

It is rather common for the active node eventually to get stuck at a particular position in the network; the picture below shows the effect of this on the total number of nodes in the last case illustrated above. The rule for this system is

{{1, 1} → {{{{}, {1, 1}}, {2}}, 2}, {1, 2} → {{{2, 2}, {{}, {2, 2}}}, 2},
    {2, 1} → {{{}, {2, 2}}, 2}, {2, 2} → {{{1, 2}, {{1}, {2}}}, 1},
    {2, 3} → {{{{1, 2}, {1}}, {{2}, {2, 1}}}, 2},
    {2, 4} → {{{2, 2}, {2, 1}, {}}}, 1}}

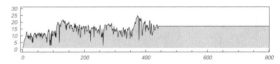

■ **Dimensionality of networks.** As discussed on page 479, if a sufficiently large network has a d-dimensional form, then by following r connections in succession from a given node, one should reach about r^d distinct nodes. The plots below show the actual numbers of nodes reached as a function of r for the systems on pages 202 and 203 at steps 1, 10, 20, ..., 200.

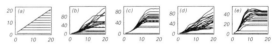

■ **Cellular automata on networks.** The cellular automata that we have considered so far all have cells arranged in regular arrays. But one can also set up generalizations in which the cells correspond to nodes in arbitrary networks. Given a network of the kind discussed in the main text of this section, one can assign a color to each node, and then update this color at each step according to a rule that depends on the colors of the nodes to which the connections from that node go. The behavior obtained depends greatly on the form of the network, but with networks of finite size the results are typically like those obtained for other finite size cellular automata of the kind discussed on page 259.

■ **Implementation.** Given a network represented as a list in which element i is {a, i, b}, where a is the node reached by the above connection from node i, and b is the node reached by the below connection, each step corresponds to

NetCAStep[{rule_, net_}, list_] :=
    Map[Replace[#, rule] &, list[[net]]]

■ **Boolean networks.** Several lines of development from the cybernetics movement (notably in immunology, genetics and management science) led in the 1960s to a study of random Boolean networks—notably by Stuart Kauffman and Crayton Walker. Such systems are like cellular automata on networks, except for the fact that when they are set up each node has a rule that is randomly chosen from all 2^{2^s} possible ones with s inputs. With $s = 2$ class 2 behavior (see Chapter 6) tends to dominate. But for $s > 2$, the behavior one sees quickly approaches what is typical for a random mapping in which the network representing the evolution of the 2^m states of the m underlying nodes is itself connected essentially randomly (see page 963). (Attempts were made in the 1980s to study phase transitions as a function of s in analogy to ones in percolation and spin glasses.) Note that in almost all work on random Boolean networks averages are in effect taken over possible configurations, making it impossible to see anything like the kind of complex behavior that I discuss in cellular automata and many other systems in this book.

Multiway Systems

■ **Implementation.** It is convenient to represent the state of a multiway system at each step by a list of strings, where an individual string is for example "ABBAAB". The rules for the multiway system can then be given for example as

$\{$"AAB" → " BB", " BA" → " ABB"$\}$

The evolution of the system is given by the functions

MWStep[rule_List, slist_List] := Union[Flatten[
   Map[Function[s, Map[MWStep1[#, s] &, rule]], slist]]]

MWStep1[p_String → q_String, s_String] :=
   Map[StringReplacePart[s, q, #] &, StringPosition[s, p]]

MWEvolveList[rule_, init_List, t_Integer] :=
   NestList[MWStep[rule, #] &, init, t]

An alternative approach uses lists instead of strings, and in effect works by tracing the internal steps that *Mathematica* goes through in trying out possible matchings. With the rule from above written as

$\{\{x\_\_\_, 0, 0, 1, y\_\_\_\} → \{x, 1, 1, y\},$
$\{x\_\_\_, 1, 0, y\_\_\_\} → \{x, 0, 1, 1, y\}\}$

MWStep can be rewritten as

MWStep[rule_List, slist_List] :=
   Union[Flatten[Map[ReplaceList[#, rule] &, slist], 1]]

The case shown on page 206 is

$\{$"AB" → "", "ABA" → "ABBAB", "ABABBB" → "AAAAABA"$\}$

starting with $\{$"ABABAB"$\}$. Note that the rules are set up so that a string for which there are no applicable replacements at a given step is simply dropped.

■ **General properties.** The merging of states (as done above by *Union*) is crucial to the behavior seen. Note that the pictures shown indicate only which states yield which states—not for example in how many ways the rules can be applied to a given state to yield a given new state.

If there was no merging, then if a typical state yielded more than one new state, then inevitably the total number of states would increase exponentially. But when there is merging, this need not occur—making it difficult to give probabilistic estimates of growth rates. Note that a given rule can yield very different growth rates with different initial conditions. Thus, for example, the growth rate for $\{$"A" → "AA", "AB" → "BA", "BA" → "AB"$\}$ is t^{n+1}, where n is the number of initial B's. With most rules, states that appear at one step can disappear at later steps. But if "A" → "A" and its analogs are part of the rule, then every state will always be kept, almost inevitably leading to overall nesting in pictures like those on page 208.

In cases where all strings that appear both in rules and initial conditions are sorted—so that for example A's appear before B's—any string generated will also be sorted, so it can be specified just by giving a list of how many A's and how many B's appear in it. The rule for the system can then be stated in terms of a difference vector—which for $\{$"BA" → "AAA", "BAA" → "BBBA"$\}$ is $\{\{2, -1\}, \{-1, 2\}\}$. Given a list of string specifications, a step in the evolution of the multiway system corresponds to

Select[Union[Flatten[Outer[Plus, diff, list, 1], 1]],
   Abs[#] == # &]

■ **Page 206 · Properties.** The total number of strings grows approximately quadratically; its differences repeat (offset by 1) with period 1071. The number of new strings generated at successive steps grows approximately linearly; its differences repeat with period 21. The third element of the rule is at first used only on some steps—but after step 50 it appears to be used somewhere in every step.

The pictures below show in stacked form (as on page 208) all sequences generated at various steps of evolution. Note that after just a few steps, the sequences produced always seem to consist of white elements followed by black, with possibly one block of black in the white region. Without this additional block of black, only the first case in the rule can ever apply.

step 100   step 200   step 300   step 400

In analogy with page 796 the picture below shows when different strings with lengths up to 10 are reached in the evolution of the system.

Different initial conditions for this multiway system lead to behavior that either dies out (as for *"ABA"*), or grows exponentially forever (as for *"ABAABABA"*).

■ **Frequency of behavior.** Among multiway systems with randomly chosen rules, one finds about equal numbers that grow rapidly and die out completely. A few percent exhibit repetitive behavior, while only one in several million exhibit more complex behavior. One common form of more complex behavior is quadratic growth, with essentially periodic fluctuations superimposed—as on page 206.

■ **History.** Versions of multiway systems have been invented many times in a variety of contexts. In mathematics specific examples of them arose in formal group theory (see below) around the end of the 1800s. Axel Thue considered versions with two-way rules (analogous to semigroups, as discussed below) in 1912, leading to the name semi-Thue systems sometimes being used for general multiway systems. Other names for multiway systems have included string and term rewrite systems, production systems and associative calculi. From the early 1900s various generalizations of multiway systems were used as idealizations of mathematical proofs (see page 1150); multiway systems with explicit pattern variables (such as s_-) were studied under the name canonical systems by Emil Post starting in the 1920s. Since the 1950s, multiway systems have been widely used as generators of formal languages (see below). Simple analogs of multiway systems have also been used in genetic analysis in biology and in models for particle showers and other branching processes in physics and elsewhere.

■ **Semigroups and groups.** The multiway systems that I discuss can be viewed as representations for generalized versions of familiar mathematical structures. Semigroups are obtained by requiring that rules come in pairs: with each rule such as *"ABB" → "BA"* there must also be the reversed rule *"BA" → "ABB"*. Such pairs of rules correspond to relations in the semigroup, specifying for example that *"ABB"* is equivalent to *"BA"*. (The operation in the semigroup is concatenation of strings; *""* acts as an identity element, so in fact a monoid is always obtained.) Groups require that not only rules but also symbols come in pairs. Thus, for example, in addition to a symbol *A*, there must be an inverse symbol *a*, with the rules *"Aa" → ""*, *"aA" → ""* and their reversals.

In the usual mathematical approach, the objects of greatest interest for many purposes are those collections of sequences that cannot be transformed into each other by any of the rules given. Such collections correspond to distinct elements of the group or semigroup, and in general many different choices of underlying rules may yield the same elements with the same

properties. In terms of multiway systems, each of the elements corresponds to a disconnected part of the network formed from all possible sequences.

Given a particular representation of a group or semigroup in terms of rules for a multiway system, an object that is often useful is the so-called Cayley graph—a network where each node is an element of the group, and the connections show what elements are reached by appending each possible symbol to the sequences that represent a given element. The so-called free semigroup has no relations and thus no rules, so that all strings of generators correspond to distinct elements, and the Cayley graph is a tree like the ones shown on page 196. The simplest non-trivial commutative semigroup has rules *"AB" → "BA"* and *"BA" → "AB"*, so that strings of generators with *A*'s and *B*'s in different orders are equivalent and the Cayley graph is a 2D grid.

For some sets of underlying rules, the total number of distinct elements in a group or semigroup is finite. (Compare page 945.) A major mathematical achievement in the 1980s was the complete classification of all possible so-called simple finite groups that in effect have no factors. (For semigroups no such classification has yet been made.) In each case, there are many different choices of rules that yield the same group (and similar Cayley graphs). And it is known that even fairly simple sets of rules can yield large and complicated groups. The icosahedral group A_5 defined by the rules $x^2 == y^3 == (xy)^5 == 1$ has 60 elements. But in the most complicated case a dozen rules yield the Monster Group, where the number of elements is

  808017424794512875886459904961710757005754368000000000
(See also pages 945 and 1032.)

Following work in the 1980s and 1990s by Mikhael Gromov and others, it is also known that for groups with randomly chosen underlying rules, the Cayley graph is usually either finite, or has a rapidly branching tree-like structure. But there are presumably also marginal cases that exhibit complex behavior analogous to what we saw in the main text. And indeed for example, despite conjectures to the contrary, it was found in the 1980s by Rostislav Grigorchuk that complicated groups could be constructed in which growth intermediate between polynomial and exponential can occur. (Note that different choices of generators can yield Cayley graphs with different local subgraphs; but the overall structure of a sufficiently large graph for a particular group is always the same.)

■ **Formal languages.** The multiway systems that I discuss are similar to so-called generative grammars in the theory of formal languages. The idea of a generative grammar is that all possible expressions in a particular formal language can be produced by applying in all possible ways the set of replacement rules given by the grammar. Thus, for example, the rules {"x" → "xx", "x" → "(x)", "x" → "()"} starting with "x" will generate all expressions that consist of balanced sequences of parentheses. (Final expressions correspond to those without the "non-terminal" symbol x.) The hierarchy described by Noam Chomsky in 1956 distinguishes four kinds of generative grammars (see page 1104):

Regular grammars. The left-hand side of each rule must consist of one non-terminal symbol, and the right-hand side can contain only one non-terminal symbol. An example is {"x" → "xA", "x" → "yB", "y" → "xA"} starting with "x" which generates sequences in which no pair of B's ever appear together. Expressions in regular languages can be recognized by finite automata of the kind discussed on page 957.

Context-free grammars. The left-hand side of each rule must consist of one non-terminal symbol, but the right-hand side can contain several non-terminal symbols. Examples include the parenthesis language mentioned above, {"x" → "AxA", "x" → "B"} starting with "x", and the syntactic definitions of *Mathematica* and most other modern computer languages. Context-free languages can be recognized by a computer using only memory on a single last-in first-out stack. (See pages 1091 and 1103.)

Context-sensitive grammars. The left-hand side of each rule is no longer than the right, but is otherwise unrestricted. An example is {"Ax" → "AAxx", "xA" → "BAA", "xB" → "Bx"} starting with "AAxBA", which generates expressions of the form Table["A", {n}] <> Table["B", {n}] <> Table["A", {n}].

Unrestricted grammars. Any rules are allowed.

(See also page 944.)

■ **Multidimensional multiway systems.** As a generalization of multiway systems based on 1D strings one can consider systems in which rules operate on arbitrary blocks of elements in an array in any number of dimensions. Still more general network substitution systems are discussed on page 508.

■ **Limited size versions.** One can set up multiway systems of limited size by applying transformations cyclically to strings.

■ **Multiway tag systems.** See page 1141.

■ **Multiway systems based on numbers.** One can consider for example the rule n → {n + 1, 2 n} implemented by

  NestList[Union[Flatten[{# + 1, 2 #}]] &, {0}, t]

In this case there are *Fibonacci[t + 2]* distinct numbers obtained at step *t*. In general, rules based on simple arithmetic operations yield only simple nested structures. If the numbers *n* are allowed to have both real and imaginary parts then results analogous to those discussed for substitution systems on page 933 are obtained. (Somewhat related systems based on recursive sequences are discussed on page 907. Compare also sorted multiway systems on page 937.)

■ **Non-deterministic systems.** Multiway systems are examples of what are often in computer science called non-deterministic systems. The general idea of a non-deterministic system is to have rules with several possible outcomes, and then to allow each of these outcomes to be followed. Non-deterministic Turing machines are a common example. For most types of systems (such as Turing machines) such non-deterministic versions do not ultimately allow any greater range of computations to be performed than deterministic ones. (But see page 766.)

■ **Fundamental physics.** See page 504.

■ **Game systems.** One can think of positions or configurations in a game as corresponding to nodes in a large network, and the possible moves in the game as corresponding to connections between nodes. Most games have rules which imply that if certain states are reached one player can be forced in the end to lose, regardless of what specific moves they make. And even though the underlying rules in the game may be simple, the pattern of such winning positions is often quite complex. Most games have huge networks whose structure is difficult to visualize (even the network for tic-tac-toe, for example, has 5478 nodes). One example that allows easy visualization is a simplification of several common games known as nim. This has *k* piles of objects, and on alternate steps each of two players takes as many objects as they want from any one of the piles. The winner is the player who manages to take the very last object. With just two piles one player can force the other to lose by arranging that after each of their moves the two piles have equal heights. With more than two piles it was discovered in 1901 that one player can in general force the other to lose by arranging that after each of their moves *Apply[BitXor, h] == 0*, where *h* is the list of heights. For *k > 1* this yields a nested pattern, analogous to those shown on page 871. If one allows only specific numbers of objects to be taken at each step a nested pattern is again obtained. With more general rules it seems almost inevitable that much more complicated patterns will occur.

Systems Based on Constraints

■ **The notion of equations.** In the mathematical framework traditionally used in the exact sciences, laws of nature are usually represented not by explicit rules for evolution, but rather by abstract equations. And in general what such equations do is to specify constraints that systems must satisfy. Sometimes these constraints just relate the state of a system at one time to its state at a previous time. And in such cases, the constraints can usually be converted into explicit evolution rules. But if the constraints relate different features of a system at one particular time, then they cannot be converted into evolution rules. In computer programs and other kinds of discrete systems, explicit evolution rules and implicit constraints usually work very differently. But in traditional continuous mathematics, it turns out that these differences are somewhat obscured. First of all, at a formal level, equations corresponding to these two cases can look very similar. And secondly, the equations are almost always so difficult to deal with at all that distinctions between the two cases are not readily noticed.

In the language of differential equations—the most widely used models in traditional science—the two cases we are discussing are essentially so-called initial value and boundary value problems, discussed on page 923. And at a formal level, the two cases are so similar that in studying partial differential equations one often starts with an equation, and only later tries to work out whether initial or boundary values are needed in order to get either any solution or a unique solution. For the specific case of second-order equations, it is known in general what is needed. Elliptic equations such as the Laplace equation need boundary values, while hyperbolic and parabolic equations such as the wave equation and diffusion equation need initial values. But for higher-order equations it can be extremely difficult to work out what initial or boundary values are needed, and indeed this has been the subject of much research for many decades.

Given a partial differential equation with initial or boundary values, there is then the question of solving it. To do this on a computer requires constructing a discrete approximation. But it turns out that the standard methods used (such as finite difference and finite element) involve extremely similar computations for initial and for boundary value problems, leaving no trace of the significant differences between these cases that are so obvious in the discrete systems that we discuss in most of this book.

■ **Linear and nonlinear systems.** A vast number of different applications of traditional mathematics are ultimately based on linear equations of the form $u == m \cdot v$ where u and v are vectors (lists) and m is a matrix (list of lists), all containing ordinary continuous numbers. If v is known then such equations in essence provide explicit rules for computing u. But if only u is known, then the equations can instead be thought of as providing implicit constraints for v. However, it so happens that even in this case v can still be found fairly straightforwardly using *LinearSolve[m, u]*. With vectors of length n it generically takes about n^2 steps to compute u given v, and a little less than n^3 steps to compute v given u (the best known algorithms—which are based on matrix multiplication—currently involve about $n^{2.4}$ steps). But as soon as the original equation is nonlinear, say $u == m_1 \cdot v + m_2 \cdot v^2$, the situation changes dramatically. It still takes only about n^2 steps to compute u given v, but it becomes vastly more difficult to compute v given u, taking perhaps 2^{2^n} steps. (Generically there are 2^n solutions for v, and even for integer coefficients in the range $-r$ to $+r$ already in 95% of cases there are 4 solutions with $n = 2$ as soon as $r \geq 6$.)

■ **Explanations based on constraints.** In some areas of science it is common to give explanations in terms of constraints rather than mechanisms. Thus, for example, in physics there are so-called variational principles which state that physical systems will behave in ways that minimize or maximize certain quantities. One such principle implies that atoms in molecules will tend to arrange themselves so as to minimize their energy. For simple molecules, this is a useful principle. But for complicated molecules of the kind that are common in living systems, this principle becomes much less useful. In fact, in finding out what configuration such molecules actually adopt, it is usually much more relevant to know how the molecule evolves in time as it is created than which of its configurations formally has minimum energy. (See pages 342 and 1185.)

■ **Page 211 · 1D constraints.** The constraints in the main text can be thought of as specifying that only some of the k^n possible blocks of cells of length n (with k possible colors for each cell) are allowed. To see the consequences of such constraints consider breaking a sequence of colors into blocks of length n, with each block overlapping by $n-1$ cells with its predecessor, as in *Partition[list, n, 1]*. If all possible sequences of colors were allowed, then there would be k possibilities for what block could follow a given block, given by *Map[Rest, Table[Append[list, i], {i, 0, k-1}]]*. The possible sequences of length n blocks that can occur are conveniently represented by possible paths by so-called de Bruijn networks, of the kind shown for $k = 2$ and $n = 2$ through 5 below.

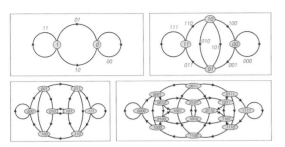

Given the network for a particular n, it is straightforward to see what happens when only certain length n blocks are allowed: one just keeps the arcs in the network that correspond to allowed blocks, and drops all other ones. Then if one can still form an infinite path by going along the arcs that remain, this path will correspond to a pattern that satisfies the constraints. Sometimes there will be a unique such path; in other cases there will be choices that can be made along the path. But the crucial point is that since there are only k^{n-1} nodes in the network, then if any infinite path is possible, there must be such a path that visits the same node and thus repeats itself after at most k^{n-1} cells. The constraint on page 210 has $k = 2$ and $n = 3$; the pattern that satisfies it repeats with period 4, thus saturating the bound. (See also page 266.)

■ **1D cellular automata.** In a cellular automaton with k colors and r neighbors, configurations that are left invariant after t steps of evolution according to the cellular automaton rule are exactly the ones which contain only those length $2r + 1$ blocks in which the center cell is the same before and after the evolution. Such configurations therefore obey constraints of the kind discussed in the main text. As we will see on page 225 some cellular automata evolve to invariant configurations from any initial conditions, but most do not. (See page 954.)

■ **Dynamical systems theory.** Sets of sequences in which a finite collection of blocks are excluded are sometimes known as finite complement languages, or subshifts of finite type. (See page 958.)

■ **Page 215 · 2D constraints.** The constraints shown here are minimal, in the sense that in each case removing any of the allowed templates prevents the constraint from ever being satisfied. Note that constraints which differ only by overall rotation, reflection or interchange of black and white are not explicitly shown. The number of allowed templates out of the total of 32 possible varies from 1 to 15 for the constraints shown, with 12 being the most common. Smaller sets of allowed templates typically seem to lead to constraints that can be satisfied by visually simpler patterns.

■ **Numbering scheme.** The constraint numbered n allows the templates at *Position[IntegerDigits[n, 2, 32], 1]* in the list below. (See also page 927.)

■ **Identifying the 171 patterns.** The number of constraints to consider can be reduced by symmetries, by discarding sets of templates that are supersets of ones already known to be satisfiable, and by requiring that each template in the set be compatible with itself or with at least one other in each of the eight immediately adjacent positions. The remaining constraints can then be analyzed by attempting to build up explicit patterns that satisfy them, as discussed below.

■ **Checking constraints.** A set of allowed templates can be specified by a *Mathematica* pattern of the form $t_1 | t_2 | t_3$ etc. where the t_i are for example {{_, 1, _}, {0, 0, 1}, {_, 0, _}}. To check whether an array *list* contains only arrangements of colors corresponding to allowed templates one can then use

```
SatisfiedQ[list_, allowed_] :=
  Apply[And, Map[MatchQ[#, allowed] &,
    Partition[list, {3, 3}, {1, 1}], {2}], {0, 1}]
```

■ **Representing repetitive patterns.** Repetitive patterns are often most conveniently represented as tessellations of rectangles whose corners overlap. Pattern (a) on page 213 can be specified as

{{2, -1, 2, 3}, {{0, 0, 0, 0}, {1, 1, 0, 0}, {1, 0, 0, 0}}}

Given this, a complete nx by ny array filled with this pattern can be constructed from

```
c[{d1_, d2_, d3_, d4_}, {x_, y_}] :=
  With[{d = d1 d2 + d1 d4 + d3 d4},
    Mod[{{d2 x + d4 x + d3 y, d4 x - d1 y}}/d, 1]]

Fill[{dlist_, data_}, {nx_, ny_}] :=
  Array[c[dlist, {##}] &, {nx, ny}] /. Flatten[MapIndexed[
    c[dlist, Reverse[#2]] → #1 &, Reverse[data], {2}], 1]
```

■ **Searching for patterns.** The basic approach to finding a pattern which satisfies a particular constraint on an infinite array of cells is to start with a pattern which satisfies the constraint in a small region, and then to try to extend the pattern. Often the constraint will immediately force a unique extension of the pattern, at least for some distance. But eventually there will normally be places where the pattern is not yet uniquely determined, and so a series of choices have to be made. The procedure used to find the results in this book attempts to extend patterns along a square spiral, making whatever choices are needed, and backtracking if these turn out to be inconsistent with the constraint. At every step in the procedure, regularities are tested for that would imply the possibility of an infinite repetitive pattern. In addition, whenever there is a choice, the first cases to be tried are set up to be ones that tend to extend whatever regularity has developed so far. And when backtracking is needed, the procedure always goes back to the most recent choice that actually affected whatever inconsistency was discovered. And in addition it remembers what has already been worked out, so as to avoid, for example, unnecessarily working out the pattern on the opposite side of the spiral again.

■ **Undecidability.** The general problem of whether an infinite pattern exists that satisfies a particular constraint is formally undecidable (see page 1139). This means that in general there can be no upper bound on the size of region for which the constraints can be satisfied, even if they are not satisfiable for the complete infinite grid.

■ **NP completeness.** The problem of whether a pattern can be found that satisfies a constraint even in a finite region is NP-complete. (See page 1145.) This suggests that to determine whether a repetitive pattern with repeating blocks of size n exists may in general take a number of steps which grows more rapidly than any polynomial in n.

■ **Enumerating patterns.** Compare page 959.

■ **Page 219 · Non-periodic pattern.** The color at position x,y in the pattern is given by

$a[x\_, y\_] := Mod[y + 1, 2] /; x + y > 0$

$a[x\_, y\_] := 0 /; Mod[x + y, 2] == 1$

$a[x\_, y\_] :=$
$\quad Mod[Floor[(x - y) 2^{(x+y-6)/4}], 2] /; Mod[x + y, 4] == 2$

$a[x\_, y\_] := 1 - Sign[Mod[x - y + 2, 2^{(-x-y+8)/4}]]$

The origin of the x,y coordinates is the only freedom in this pattern. The nested structure is like the progression of base 2 digit sequences shown on page 117. Negative numbers are effectively represented by complements of digit sequences, much as in typical practical computers. With the procedure described above for finding patterns that satisfy a constraint, generating the pattern shown here is straightforward once the appropriate constraint is identified.

■ **Other types of constraints.** Constraints based on smaller templates simply require smaller numbers of repetitive patterns: ▦:4; ▦:7; ▦:17; ▦:11; ▦:12. To extend the class of systems considered in the main text, one can increase the size of the templates, or increase the number of possible colors for each cell. For 3×3 templates with two colors extensive randomized searches have failed to discover examples where non-repetitive patterns are forced to occur. Another extension of the constraints in the main text is to require that not just a single template, but every template in the set, must occur somewhere in the pattern. Searches of such systems have also failed to discover examples of forced non-repetitive patterns beyond the one shown in the text.

■ **Forcing nested patterns.** It is straightforward to find constraints that allow nested patterns; the challenge is to find ones that force such patterns to occur. Many nested patterns (such as the one made by rule 90, for example) contain large areas of uniform white, and it is typically difficult to prevent pure repetition of that area. One approach to finding constraints that can be satisfied only by nested patterns is nevertheless to start from specific nested patterns, look at what templates occur, and then see whether these templates are such that they do not allow any purely repetitive patterns. A convenient way to generate a large class of nested patterns is to use 2D substitution systems of the kind discussed on page 188. But searching all 4 billion or so possible such systems with 2×2 blocks and up to four colors one finds not a single case in which a nested pattern is forced to occur. It can nevertheless be shown that with a sufficiently large number of extra colors any nested pattern can be forced to occur. And it turns out that a result from the mid-1970s by Robert Ammann for a related problem of tiling (see below) allows one to construct a specific system with 16 colors in which constraints of the kind discussed here force a nested pattern to occur. One starts from the substitution system with rules

$\{1 \rightarrow \{\{3\}\}, 2 \rightarrow \{\{13, 1\}, \{4, 10\}\}, 3 \rightarrow \{\{15, 1\}, \{4, 12\}\},$
$\quad 4 \rightarrow \{\{14, 1\}, \{2, 9\}\}, 5 \rightarrow \{\{13, 1\}, \{4, 12\}\}, 6 \rightarrow \{\{13, 1\}, \{8, 9\}\},$
$\quad 7 \rightarrow \{\{15, 1\}, \{4, 10\}\}, 8 \rightarrow \{\{14, 1\}, \{6, 10\}\}, 9 \rightarrow \{\{14\}, \{2\}\},$
$\quad 10 \rightarrow \{\{16\}, \{7\}\}, 11 \rightarrow \{\{13\}, \{8\}\}, 12 \rightarrow \{\{16\}, \{3\}\},$
$\quad 13 \rightarrow \{\{5, 11\}\}, 14 \rightarrow \{\{2, 9\}\}, 15 \rightarrow \{\{3, 11\}\}, 16 \rightarrow \{\{6, 10\}\}\}$

This yields the nested pattern below which contains only 51 of the 65,536 possible 2×2 blocks of cells with 16 colors. It then turns out that with the constraint that the only 2×2 arrangements of colors that can occur are ones that match these 51 blocks, one is forced to get the nested pattern below.

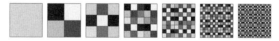

■ **Relation to 2D cellular automata.** The kind of constraints discussed are exactly those that must be satisfied by configurations that remain unchanged in the evolution of a 2D cellular automaton. The argument for this is similar to the one on pages 941 and 954 for 1D cellular automata. The point is that of the 32 5-cell neighborhoods involved in the 2D cellular automaton rule, only some subset will have the property that the center cell remains unchanged after applying the rule. And any configuration which does not change must involve only these subsets. Using the results of this section it then follows that in the evolution of all 2D cellular automata of the type discussed on page 170 there exist purely repetitive configurations that remain unchanged.

■ **Relation to 1D cellular automata.** A picture that shows the evolution of a 1D cellular automaton can be thought of as a 2D array of cells in which the color of each cell satisfies a constraint that relates it to the cells above according to the cellular automaton rule. This constraint can then be represented in terms of a set of allowed templates; the set for rule 30 is as follows:

To reproduce an ordinary picture of cellular automaton evolution, one would have to specify in advance a whole line of black and white cells. Below this line there would then be a unique pattern corresponding to the application of the cellular automaton rule. But above the line, except for reversible rules, there is no guarantee that any pattern satisfying the constraints can exist.

If one specifies no cells in advance, or at most a few cells, as in the systems discussed in the main text, then the issue is different, however. And now it is always possible to construct a repetitive pattern which satisfies the constraints simply by finding repetitive behavior in the evolution of the cellular automaton from a spatially repetitive initial condition.

■ **Non-computable patterns.** It is known to be possible to set up constraints that will force patterns in which finding the color of a particular cell can require doing something like solving a halting problem—which cannot in general be done by any finite computation. (See also page 1139.)

■ **Tiling.** The constraints discussed here are similar to those encountered in covering the plane with tiles of various shapes. Of regular polygons, only squares, triangles and hexagons can be used to do this, and in these cases the tilings are always repetitive. For some time it was believed that any set of tiles that could cover the plane could be arranged to do so repetitively. But in 1964 Robert Berger demonstrated that this was not the case, and constructed a set of about 20,000 tiles that could cover the plane only in a nested fashion. Later Berger reduced the number of tiles needed to 104. Then Raphael Robinson in 1971 reduced the number tiles to six, and in 1974 Roger Penrose showed that just two tiles were necessary. Penrose's tiles can cover the plane only in a nested pattern that can be constructed from a substitution system that successively subdivides each tile, as shown on page 932. (Note that various dissections of these tiles can also be used. The edges of the particular shapes shown should strictly be distinguished in order to prevent trivial periodic arrangements.) The triangles in the construction have angles

which are multiples of $\pi/5$, so that the whole tiling has an approximate 5-fold symmetry (see page 994). Repetitive tilings of the plane can only have 3-, 4- or 6-fold symmetry.

No single shape is known which has the property that it can tile the plane only non-repetitively, although one strongly suspects that one must exist. In 3D, John Conway has found a single biprism that can fill space only in a sequence of layers with an irrational rotation angle between each layer.

In addition, in no case has a simple set of tiles been found which force a pattern more complicated than a nested one. The results on page 221 in this book can be used to constructed a complicated set of tiles with this property, but I suspect that a much simpler set could be found.

(See also page 1139.)

■ **Polyominoes.** An example of a tiling problem that is in some respects particularly close to the grid-based constraint systems discussed in the main text concerns covering the plane with polyominoes that are formed by gluing collections of squares together. Tiling by polyominoes has been investigated since at least the late 1950s, particularly by Solomon Golomb, but it is only very recently that sets of polyominoes which force non-periodic patterns have been found. The set (a) below was announced by Roger Penrose in 1994; the slightly smaller set (b) was found by Matthew Cook as part of the development of this book.

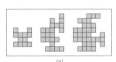 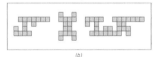

(a)   (b)

Both of these sets yield nested patterns. Steps in the construction of the pattern for set (b) are shown below. At stage n the number of polyominoes of each type is $Fibonacci[2n - \{2, 0, 1\}]/\{1, 2, 1\}$. Set (a) works in a roughly similar way, but with a considerably more complicated recursion.

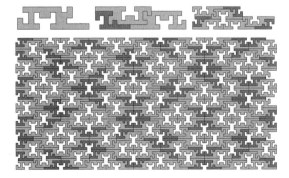

■ **Ground states of spin systems.** The constraints discussed in the main text are similar to those that arise in the physics of 2D spin systems. An example of such a system is the so-called Ising model discussed on page 981. The idea in all such systems is to have an array of spins, each of which can be either up or down. The energy associated with each spin is then given by some function which depends on the configuration of neighboring spins. The ground state of the system corresponds to an arrangement of spins with the smallest total energy. In the ordinary Ising model, this ground state is simply all spins up or all spins down. But in generalizations of the Ising model with more complicated energy functions, the conditions to get a state of the lowest possible energy can correspond exactly to the constraints discussed in the main text. And from the results shown one sees that in some cases random-looking ground states should occur. Note that a rather different way to get a somewhat similar ground state is to consider a spin glass, in which the standard Ising model energy function is used, but multiplied by -1 or +1 at random for each spin.

■ **Correspondence systems.** For a discussion of a class of 1D systems based on constraints see page 757.

■ **Sequence equations.** Another way to set up 1D systems based on constraints is by having equations like *Flatten[{x, 1, x, 0, y}]* === *Flatten[{0, y, 0, y, x}]*, where each variable stands for a list. Fairly simple such equations can force fairly complicated results, although as discussed on page 1141 there are known to be limits to this complexity.

■ **Pattern-avoiding sequences.** As another form of constraint one can require, say, that no pair of identical blocks ever appear together in a sequence, so that the sequence does not match *{___, x__, x__, ___}*. With just two possible elements, no sequence above length 3 can satisfy this constraint. But with $k = 3$ possible elements, there are infinite nested sequences that can, such as the one produced by the substitution system *{0 → {0, 1, 2}, 1 → {0, 2}, 2 → {1}}*, starting with *{0}*. One can find the sequences of length n that work by using

Nest[DeleteCases[Flatten[Map[Table[Append[#, i – 1],
{i, k}] &, #], 1], {___, x__, x__, ___}]] &, {{}}, n]

and the number of these grows roughly like $3^{n/4}$.

The constraint that no triple of identical blocks appear together turns out to be satisfied by the Thue-Morse nested sequence from page 83—as already noted by Axel Thue in 1906. (The number of sequences that work seems to grow roughly like $2^{n/2}$.)

For any given k, many combinations of blocks will inevitably occur in sufficiently long sequences (compare page 1068). (For example, with $k = 2$, *{___, x__, y__, x__, y__, ___}* always

matches any sequence with length more than 18.) But some patterns of blocks can be avoided. And for example it is known that for $k \geq 2$ any pattern with length 6 or more (excluding the ___'s) and only two different variables (say $x__$ and $y__$) can always be avoided. But it also known that among the infinite sequences which do this, there are always nested ones (sometimes one has to iterate one substitution rule, then at the end apply once a different substitution rule). With more variables, however, it seems possible that there will be patterns that can be avoided only by sequences with a more complicated structure. And a potential sign of this would be patterns for which the number of sequences that avoid them varies in a complicated way with length.

■ **Formal languages.** Formal languages of the kind discussed on page 938 can be used to define constraints on 1D sequences. The constraints shown on page 210 correspond to special cases of regular languages (see page 940). For both regular and context-free languages the so-called pumping lemmas imply that if any finite sequences satisfy the constraints, then so must an essentially repetitive infinite sequence.

■ **Diophantine equations.** Any algebraic equation—such as $x^3 + x + 1 == 0$—can readily be solved if one allows the variables to have any numerical value. But if one insists that the variables be whole numbers, then the problem is more analogous to the discrete constraints in the main text, and becomes much more difficult. And in fact, even though such so-called Diophantine equations have been studied since well before the time of Diophantus around perhaps 250 AD, only limited results about them are known.

Linear Diophantine equations such as $ax == by + c$ yield simple repetitive results, as in the pictures below, and can be handled essentially just by knowing *ExtendedGCD[a, b]*.

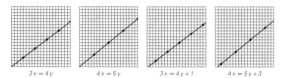

| $3x = 4y$ | $4x = 5y$ | $3x = 4y + 1$ | $4x = 5y + 3$ |

Even the simplest quadratic Diophantine equations can already show much more complex behavior. The equation $x^2 == a y^2$ has no solution except when a is a perfect square. But the Pell equation $x^2 == a y^2 + 1$ (already studied in antiquity) has infinitely many solutions whenever a is positive and not a perfect square. The smallest solution for x is given by

Numerator[FromContinuedFraction[
ContinuedFraction[$\sqrt{a}$, (If[EvenQ[#], #, 2 #] &)[
Length[Last[ContinuedFraction[$\sqrt{a}$]]]]]]]

This is plotted below; complicated variation and some very large values are seen (with $a = 61$ for example $x == 1766319049$).

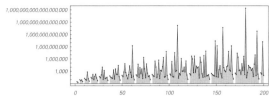

In three variables, the equation $x^2 + y^2 == z^2$ yields so-called Pythagorean triples $\{3, 4, 5\}$, $\{5, 12, 13\}$, etc. And even in this case the set of possible solutions for x and y in the pictures below looks fairly complicated—though after removing common factors, they are in fact just given by $\{x == r^2 - s^2, y == 2\,r\,s, z == r^2 + s^2\}$. (See page 1078.)

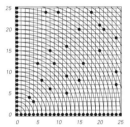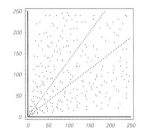

The pictures below show the possible solutions for x and y in various Diophantine equations. As in other systems based on numbers, nested patterns are not common—though page 1160 shows how they can in principle be achieved with an equation whose solutions satisfy $Mod[Binomial[x, y], 2] == 1$. (The equation $(2x + 1)y == z$ also for example has solutions only when z is not of the form 2^i.)

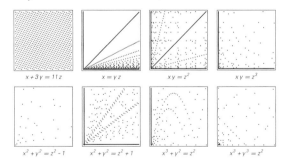

$x + 3y = 11z$ $x = yz$ $xy = z^2$ $xy = z^3$

$x^2 + y^2 = z^2 - 1$ $x^2 + y^2 = z^2 + 1$ $x^3 + y^2 = z^2$ $x^3 + y^3 = z^2$

Many Diophantine equations have at most very sparse solutions. And indeed for example Fermat's Last Theorem states that $x^n + y^n == z^n$ can never be satisfied for $n > 2$. With four variables one has for example $3^3 + 4^3 + 5^3 == 6^3$, $1^3 + 6^3 + 8^3 == 9^3$—but with fourth powers the smallest result is $95800^4 + 217519^4 + 414560^4 == 422481^4$.

(See pages 791 and 1164.)

■ **Matrices satisfying constraints.** One can consider for example magic squares, Latin squares (quasigroup multiplication tables), and matrices having the Hadamard property discussed on page 1073. One can also consider matrices whose powers contain certain patterns. (See also page 805.)

■ **Finite groups and semigroups.** Any finite group or semigroup can be thought of as defined by having a multiplication table which satisfies the constraints given on page 887. The total number of semigroups increases faster than exponentially with size in a seemingly quite uniform way. But the number of groups varies in a complicated way with size, as in the picture below. (The peaks are known to grow roughly like $n^{(2/27\,Log[2, n]^2)}$—intermediate between polynomial and exponential.) As mentioned on page 938, through major mathematical effort, a complete classification of all finite so-called simple groups that in effect have no factors is known. Most such groups come in families that are easy to characterize; a handful of so-called sporadic ones are much more difficult to find. But this classification does not immediately provide a practical way to enumerate all possible groups. (See also pages 938 and 1032.)

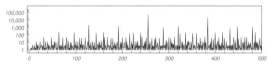

■ **Constraints on formulas.** Many standard problems of algebraic computation can be viewed as consisting in finding formulas that satisfy certain constraints. An example is exact solution of algebraic equations. For quadratic equations the standard formula gives solutions for arbitrary coefficients in terms of square roots. Similar formulas in terms of nth roots have been known since the 1500s for equations with degrees n up to 4, although their *LeafCount* starting at $n = 1$ increases like 6, 25, 183, 718. For higher degrees it is known that such general formulas must involve other functions. For degrees 5 and 6 it was shown in the late 1800s that *EllipticTheta* or *Hypergeometric2F1* are sufficient, although for degrees 5 and 6 respectively the necessary formulas have a *LeafCount* in the billions. (Sharing common subexpressions yields a *LeafCount* in the thousands.) (See also page 1129.)

Starting from Randomness

The Emergence of Order

■ **Page 226 · Properties of patterns.** For a random initial condition, the average density of black cells is exactly 1/2. For rule 126, the density after many steps is still 1/2. For rule 22, it is approximately 0.35095. For rule 30 and rule 150 it is exactly 1/2, while for rule 182 it is 3/4. And insofar as rule 110 converges to a definite density, the density is 4/7. (See page 953 for a method of estimating these densities.)

Even after many steps, individual lines in the patterns produced by rules 30 and 150 remain in general completely random. But in rule 126, black cells always tend to appear in pairs, while in rule 182, every white cell tends to be surrounded by black ones. And in rule 22, there are more complicated conditions involving blocks of 4 cells.

The density of triangles of size n goes roughly like 2^{-n} for rules 126, 30 (see also page 871), 150 and 182 and roughly like 1.3^{-n} for rule 22.

In the algebraic representation discussed on page 869, rule 22 is $Mod[p + q + r + p\,q\,r, 2]$, rule 126 is $Mod[(p + q)(q + r) + (p + r), 2]$, rule 150 is $Mod[p + q + r, 2]$ and rule 182 is $Mod[p\,r\,(1 + q) + (p + q + r), 2]$.

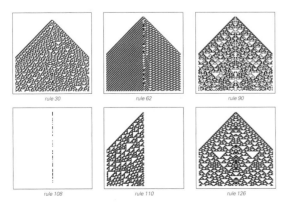

rule 30   rule 62   rule 90

rule 108   rule 110   rule 126

■ **Continual injection of randomness.** In the main text we discuss what happens when one starts from random initial conditions and then evolves according to a definite cellular automaton rule. As an alternative one can consider starting with very simple initial conditions, such as all cells white, and then at each step randomly changing the color of the center cell. Some examples of what happens are shown at the bottom of the previous column. The results are usually very similar to those obtained with random initial conditions.

■ **History.** The fact that despite initial randomness processes like friction can make systems settle down into definite configurations has been the basis for all sorts of engineering throughout history. The rise of statistical mechanics in the late 1800s emphasized the idea of entropy increase and the fundamental tendency for systems to become progressively more disordered as they evolve to thermodynamic equilibrium. Theories were nevertheless developed for a few cases of spontaneous pattern formation—notably in convection, cirrus clouds and ocean waves. When the study of feedback and stability became popular in the 1940s, there were many results about how specific simple fixed or repetitive behaviors in time could emerge despite random input. In the 1950s it was suggested that reaction-diffusion processes might be responsible for spontaneous pattern formation in biology (see page 1012)—and starting in the 1970s such processes were discussed as prime examples of the phenomenon of self-organization. But in their usual form, they yield essentially only rather simple repetitive patterns. Ever since around 1900 it tended to be assumed that any fundamental theory of systems with many components must be based on statistical mechanics. But almost all work in the field of statistical mechanics concentrated on systems in or very near thermal equilibrium—in which in a sense there is almost complete disorder. In the 1970s there began to be more discussion of phenomena far from equilibrium, although typically it got no further than to consider how external forces could lead to reaction-diffusion-like phenomena. My own work on cellular automata in 1981 emerged in part from thinking about self-gravitating systems (see page 880) where it seemed conceivable that there might be very basic rules quite different from those usually studied in statistical mechanics. And when I first generated pictures of the behavior of arbitrary cellular automaton rules, what struck me most was the order that emerged even from random initial conditions. But while it was immediately clear that most cellular automata do not have the kind of reversible underlying rules assumed in traditional statistical mechanics, it still seemed initially very surprising that their overall behavior could be so elaborate—and so far from the complete orderlessness one might expect on the basis of traditional ideas of entropy maximization.

Four Classes of Behavior

■ **Different runs.** The qualitative behavior seen with a given cellular automaton rule will normally look exactly the same for essentially all different large random initial conditions—just as it does for different parts of a single initial condition. And as discussed on page 597 any obvious differences could in effect be thought of as revealing deviations from randomness in the initial conditions.

■ **Page 232 · Elementary rules.** The examples shown have rule numbers n for which $IntegerDigits[n, 2, 8]$ matches $\{\_, i\_, \_, j\_, i\_, \_, j\_, 0\}$.

■ **Page 235 · States of matter.** As suggested by pages 944 and 1193, working out whether a particular substance at a particular temperature will be a solid, liquid or gas may in fact be computationally comparable in difficulty to working out what class of behavior a particular cellular automaton will exhibit.

■ **Page 235 · Class 4 rules.** Other examples of class 4 totalistic rules with $k = 3$ colors include 357 (page 282), 438, 600, 792, 924, 1038, 1041, 1086, 1329 (page 282), 1572, 1599 (see page 70), 1635 (see page 67), 1662, 1815 (page 236), 2007 (page 237) and 2049 (see page 68).

■ **Frequencies of classes.** The pie charts below show results for 1D totalistic cellular automata with k colors and range r. Class 3 tends to become more common as the number of elements in the rule increases because as soon as any of these elements yield class 3 behavior, that behavior dominates the system.

$k = 2, r = 1$ $k = 2, r = 2$ $k = 2, r = 3$ $k = 3, r = 1$

■ **History.** I discovered the classification scheme for cellular automata described here late in 1983, and announced it in January 1984. Much work has been done by me and others on ways to make the classification scheme precise. The notion that class 4 can be viewed as intermediate between class 2 and class 3 was studied particularly by Christopher Langton, Wentian Li and Norman Packard in 1986 for ordinary cellular automata, by Hyman Hartman in 1985 for probabilistic cellular automata and by Hugues Chaté and Paul Manneville in 1990 for continuous cellular automata.

■ **Subclasses within class 4.** Different class 4 systems can show localized structures with strikingly similar forms, and this may allow subclasses within class 4 to be identified. In addition, class 4 systems show varying levels of activity, and it is possible that there may be discrete transitions—perhaps analogous to percolation—that can be used to define boundaries between subclasses.

■ **Page 240 · Undecidability.** Almost any definite procedure for determining the class of a particular rule will have the feature that in borderline cases it can take arbitrarily long, often formally showing undecidability, as discussed on page 1138. (An example would be a test for class 1 based on checking that no initial pattern of any size can survive. Including probabilities can help, but there are still always borderline cases and potential undecidability.)

■ **Page 244 · Continuous cellular automata.** In ordinary cellular automata, going from one rule to the next in a sequence involves some discrete change. But in continuous cellular automata, the parameters of the rule can be varied smoothly. Nevertheless, it still turns out that there are discrete transitions in the overall behavior that is produced. In fact, there is often a complicated set of transitions that depends more on the digit sequence of the parameter than its size. And between these transitions there are usually ranges of parameter values that yield definite class 4 behavior. (Compare page 922.)

■ **Nearby cellular automaton rules.** In a range r cellular automaton the new color of a particular cell depends only on cells at most a distance r away. One can make an equivalent cellular automaton of larger range by having a rule in which cells at distance more than r have no effect. One can then define nearby cellular automata to be those where the differences in the rule involve only cells close to the edge of the range. With larger and larger ranges one can then construct closer approximations to continuous sequences of cellular automata.

■ **2D class 4 cellular automata.** No 5- or 9-neighbor totalistic rules nor 5-neighbor outer totalistic ones appear to yield class 4 behavior with a white background. But among 9-neighbor outer totalistic rules there are examples with codes 224 (Game of Life), 226, 4320 (sometimes called HighLife), 5344, 6248, 6752, 6754 and 8416, etc. It turns out that the simplest moving structures are the same in codes 224, 226 and 4320.

■ **Page 249 · Game of Life.** Invented by John Conway around 1970 (see page 877), the Life 2D cellular automaton has been much studied in recreational computing, and as described on page 964 many localized structures in it have been identified. Each step in its evolution can be implemented using

```
LifeStep[a_List] :=
  MapThread[If[#1 == 1 && #2 == 4 || #2 == 3, 1, 0] &,
    {a, Sum[RotateLeft[a, {i, j}], {i, -1, 1}, {j, -1, 1}]}, 2]
```

A more efficient implementation can be obtained by operating not on a complete array of black and white cells but rather just on a list of positions of black cells. With this setup, each step then corresponds to

```
LifeStep[list_] :=
  With[{p = Flatten[Array[List, {3, 3}, -1], 1]},
    With[{u = Split[Sort[Flatten[Outer[Plus, list, p, 1], 1]]]},
      Union[Cases[u, {x_, _, _} → x],
        Intersection[Cases[u, {x_, _, _, _} → x], list]]]]
```

(A still more efficient implementation is based on finding runs of length 3 and 4 in *Sort[u]*.)

■ **3D class 4 rules.** With a cubic lattice of the type shown on page 183, and with updating rules of the form

```
LifeStep3D[{p_, q_, r_}, a_List] := MapThread[If[
  #1 == 1 && p ≤ #2 ≤ q || #2 == r, 1, 0] &, {a, Sum[RotateLeft[
  a, {i, j, k}], {i, -1, 1}, {j, -1, 1}, {k, -1, 1}] - a}, 3]
```

Carter Bays discovered between 1986 and 1990 the three examples {5, 7, 6}, {4, 5, 5}, and {5, 6, 5}. The pictures below show successive steps in the evolution of a moving structure in the second of these rules.

■ **Random initial conditions in other systems.** Whenever the initial conditions for a system can involve an infinite sequence of elements these elements can potentially be chosen at random. In systems like mobile automata and Turing machines the colors of initial cells can be random, but the active cell must start at a definite location, and depending on the behavior only a limited region of initial cells near this location may ever be sampled. Ordinary substitution systems can operate on infinite sequences of elements chosen at random. Sequential substitution systems, however, rely on scanning limited sequences of elements,

and so cannot readily be given infinite random initial conditions. The same is true of ordinary and cyclic tag systems. Systems based on continuous numbers involve infinite sequences of digits which can readily be chosen at random (see page 154). But systems based on integers (including register machines) always deal with finite sequences of digits, for which there is no unique definition of randomness. (See however the discussion of number representations on page 1070.) Random networks (see pages 963 and 1038) can be used to provide random initial conditions for network systems. Multiway systems cannot meaningfully be given infinite random initial conditions since these would typically lead to an infinite number of possible states. Systems based on constraints do not have initial conditions. (See also page 920.)

Sensitivity to Initial Conditions

■ **Page 251 · Properties.** In rule 126, the outer edges of the region of change always expand by exactly one cell per step. The same is true of the right-hand edge in rule 30—though the left-hand edge in this case expands only about 0.2428 cells on average per step. In rule 22, both edges expand about 0.7660 cells on average per step.

The motion of the right-hand edge in rule 30 can be understood by noting that with this rule the color of a particular cell will always change if the color of the cell to its left is changed on the previous step (see page 601). Nothing as simple is true for the left-hand edge, and indeed this seems to execute an essentially random walk—with an average motion of about 0.2428 cells per step. Note that in the approximation that the colors of all cells in the pattern are assumed completely independent and random there should be motion by 0.25 cells per step. Curiously, as discussed on page 871, the region of non-repetitive behavior in evolution from a single black cell according to rule 30 seems to grow at a similar but not identical rate of about 0.252 cells per step. (For rule 45, the left-hand edge of the difference pattern moves about 0.1724 cells per step; for rule 54 both edges move about 0.553 cells per step.)

■ **Difference patterns.** The maximum rate at which a region of change can grow is determined by the range of the underlying cellular automaton rule. If the rule involves up to r nearest neighbors, then at each step a change in the color of a given cell can affect cells up to r away—so that the edge of the region of change can move by r cells.

For most class 3 rules, once one is inside the region of change, the colors of cells usually become essentially uncorrelated.

However, for additive rules the pattern of differences is just exactly the pattern that would be obtained by evolution from an initial condition consisting only of the changes made. In general the pattern of probabilities for changes can be thought of as being somewhat like a Green's function in mathematical physics—though the nonadditivity of most cellular automata makes this analogy less useful. (Note that the pattern of differences between two initial conditions in a rule with k possible colors can always be reproduced by looking at the evolution from a single initial condition of a suitable rule with $2k$ colors.) In 2D class 3 cellular automata, the region of change usually ends up having a roughly circular shape—a result presumably related to the Central Limit Theorem (see page 976).

For any additive or partially additive class 3 cellular automaton (such as rule 90 or rule 30) any change in initial conditions will always lead to expanding differences. But in other rules it sometimes may not. And thus, for example, in rule 22, changing the color of a single cell has no effect after even one step if the cell has a ■ block on either side. But while there are a few other initial conditions for which differences can die out after several steps most forms of averaging will say that the majority of initial conditions lead to growing patterns of differences.

■ **Lyapunov exponents.** If one thinks of cells to the right of a point in a 1D cellular automaton as being like digits in a real number, then linear growth in the region of differences associated with a change further to the right is analogous to the exponentially sensitive dependence on initial conditions shown on page 155. The speed at which the region of differences expands in the cellular automaton can thus be thought of as giving a Lyapunov exponent (see page 921) that characterizes instability in the system.

Systems of Limited Size and Class 2 Behavior

■ **Page 255 · Cyclic addition.** After t steps, the dot will be at position $Mod[mt, n]$ where n is the total number of positions, and m is the number of positions moved at each step. The repetition period is given by $n/GCD[m, n]$. The picture on page 613 shows the values of m and n for which this is equal to n.

An alternative interpretation of the system discussed here involves arranging the possible positions in a circle, so that at each step the dot goes a fraction m/n of the way around the circle. The repetition period is maximal when m/n is a fraction in lowest terms. The picture below shows the repetition periods as a function of the numerical size of the quantity m/n.

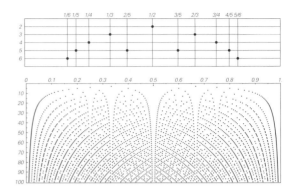

■ **Page 257 · Cyclic multiplication.** With multiplication by k at each step the dot will be at position $Mod[k^t, n]$ after t steps. If k and n have no factors in common, there will be a t for which $Mod[k^t, n] == 1$, so that the dot returns to position 1. The smallest such t is given by $MultiplicativeOrder[k, n]$, which always divides $EulerPhi[n]$ (see page 1093), and has a value between $Log[k, n]$ and $n-1$, with the upper limit being attained only if n is prime. (This value is related to the repetition period for the digit sequence of $1/n$ in base k, as discussed on page 912). When $GCD[k, n] == 1$ the dot can never visit position 0. But if $n == k^s$, the dot reaches 0 after s steps, and then stays there. In general, the dot will visit position $m = k \wedge IntegerExponent[n, k]$ every $MultiplicativeOrder[k, n/m]$ steps.

■ **Page 260 · Maximum periods.** A cellular automaton with n cells and k colors has k^n possible states, but if the system has cyclic boundary conditions, then the maximum repetition period is smaller than k^n. The reason is that different states of the cellular automaton have different symmetry properties, and thus cannot be on the same cycle. In particular, if a state of a cellular automaton has a certain spatial period, given by the minimum positive m for which $RotateLeft[list, m] == list$, then this state can never evolve to one with a larger spatial period. The number of states with spatial period m is given by

$$s[m\_, k\_] := k^m - Apply[Plus, Map[s[\#, k] \&, Drop[Divisors[m], -1]]]$$

or equivalently

$$s[m\_, k\_] := Apply[Plus, (MoebiusMu[m/\#] k^\# \&)[Divisors[m]]]$$

In a cellular automaton with a total of n cells, the maximum possible repetition period is thus $s[n, k]$. For $k = 2$, the maximum periods for n up to 10 are: $\{2, 2, 6, 12, 30, 54, 126, 240, 504, 990\}$. In all cases, $s[n, k]$ is divisible by n. For prime n, $s[n, k]$ is $k^n - k$. For large n, $s[n, k]$ oscillates between about $k^n - k^{n/2}$ and $k^n - k$. (See page 963.)

■ **Additive cellular automata.** In the case of additive rules such as rule 90 and rule 60, a mathematical analysis of the repetition periods can be given (as done by Olivier Martin, Andrew Odlyzko and me in 1983). One starts by converting the list of cell colors at each step to a polynomial *FromDigits[list, x]*. Then for the case of rule 60 with *n* cells and cyclic boundary conditions, the state obtained after *t* steps is given by

PolynomialMod[(1 + x)^t z, {x^n - 1, 2}]

where *z* is the polynomial representing the initial state, and *z = 1* for a single black cell in the first position. The state *z = 1* evolves after one step to the state *z = 1 + x*, and for odd *n* this latter state always eventually appears again. Using the result that $1 + x^{2^m} == (1 + x)^{2^m}$ modulo 2 for any *m*, one then finds that the repetition period always divides the quantity *p[n] = 2 ^ MultiplicativeOrder[2, n] - 1*, which in turn is at most $2^{n-1} - 1$. The actual periods are often smaller than *p[n]*, with the following ratios occurring:

n	11	13	19	25	27	29	37	41	43	53
ratio	3	5	27	41	19	565	21255	25	3	1266205

There appears to be no case for *n > 5* where the period achieves the absolute maximum $2^{n-1} - 1$.

In the case of rule 90 a similar analysis can be given, with the *1 + x* used at each step replaced by *1/x + x*. And now the repetition period for odd *n* divides

q[n] = 2 ^ MultiplicativeOrder[2, n, {1, -1}] - 1

The exponent here always lies between *Log[k, n]* and *(n - 1)/2*, with the upper bound being attained only if *n* is prime. Unlike for the case of rule 60, the period is usually equal to *q[n]* (and is assumed so for the picture on page 260), with the first exception occurring at *n = 37*.

■ **Rules 30 and 45.** Maximum periods are often achieved with initial conditions consisting of a single black cell. Particularly for rule 30, however, there are quite a few exceptions. For *n = 13*, for example, the maximum period is 832 but the period with a single black cell is 260. For rule 45, the maximum possible period discussed above is achieved for *n = 9*, but does not appear to be achieved for any larger *n*. (See page 962.)

■ **Comparison of rules.** Rules 45, 30 and 60, together with their conjugates and reflections, yield the longest repetition periods of all elementary rules (see page 1087). The picture below compares their periods as a function of *n*.

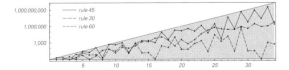

■ **Implementing boundary conditions.** In the bitwise representation discussed on page 865, 0's outside of a width *n* can be implemented by applying *BitAnd[a, 2^n - 1]* at each step. Cyclic boundary conditions can be implemented efficiently in assembler on computers that support cyclic shift instructions.

Randomness in Class 3 Systems

■ **Page 263 · Rule 22.** Randomness is obtained with initial conditions consisting of two black squares *4 m* positions apart for any *m ≥ 2*. The base 2 digit sequences for 19, 25, 37, 39, 41, 45, 47, 51, 57, 61, … also give initial conditions that yield randomness. Despite its overall randomness there are some regularities in the pattern shown at the bottom of the page. The overall density of black cells is not 1/2 but is instead approximately 0.35, just as for random initial conditions. And if one looks at the center cell in the pattern one finds that it is never black on two successive steps, and the probability for white to follow white is about twice the probability for black to follow white. There is also a region of repetitive behavior on each side of the pattern; the random part in the middle expands at about 0.766 cells per step—the same speed that we found on page 949 that changes spread in this rule.

■ **Rule 225.** With initial conditions consisting of a single black cell, this class 3 rule yields a regular nested pattern, as shown on page 58. But with the initial condition ■■■, it yields the much more complicated pattern shown below. With a background consisting of repetitions of the block ■□, insertion of a single initial white cell yields a largely random pattern that expands by one cell per step. Rule 225 can be expressed as ¬ p ∪ (q ∨ r).

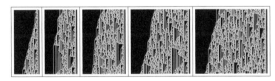

■ **Rule 94.** With appropriate initial conditions this class 2 rule can yield both nested and random behavior, as shown below.

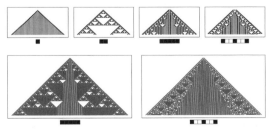

▪ **Rule 218.** If pairs of adjacent black cells appear anywhere in its initial conditions this class 2 rule gives uniform black, but if none do it gives a rule 90 nested pattern.

▪ **Additive rules.** Of the 256 elementary cellular automata 8 are additive: {0, 60, 90, 102, 150, 170, 204, 240}. All of these are either trivial or essentially equivalent to rules 90 or 150.

Of all $k^{k^{2r+1}}$ rules with k colors and range r it turns out that there are always exactly k^{2r+1} additive ones—each obtained by taking the cells in the neighborhood and adding them modulo k with weights between 0 and $k-1$. As discussed on page 955, any rule based on addition modulo k must yield a nested pattern, and it therefore follows that any rule that is additive must give a nested pattern, as in the examples below. (See also page 870.)

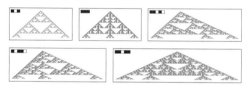

Note that each step in the evolution of any additive cellular automaton can be computed as

$Mod[ListCorrelate[w, list, Ceiling[Length[w]/2]], k]$

(See page 1087 for a discussion of partial additivity.)

▪ **Page 264 · Generalized additivity.** In general what it means for a system to be additive is that some addition operation ⊕ can be used to combine any set of evolution histories to yield another possible evolution history. If ϕ is the rule for the system, this then requires for any states u and v the distributive property

$\phi[u \oplus v] == \phi[u] \oplus \phi[v]$

(In mathematical terms this is equivalent to the statement that ϕ is conjugate to itself under the action of ⊕—or alternatively that ϕ defines a homomorphism with respect to the ⊕ operation.) In the usual case, $u \oplus v$ is just $Mod[u + v, k]$, yielding say for rule 90 the results below.

| $\phi[u]$ | $\phi[v]$ | $\phi[u \oplus v]$ | $\phi[u] \oplus \phi[v]$ |

But it turns out that some elementary rules show additivity with respect to other addition operations. An example as shown below is rule 250 with $u \oplus v$ taken as $Max[u, v]$ (Or).

| $\phi[u]$ | $\phi[v]$ | $\phi[u \oplus v]$ | $\phi[u] \oplus \phi[v]$ |

If a system is additive it means that one can work out how the system will behave from any initial condition just by combining the patterns ("Green's functions") obtained from certain basic initial conditions—say ones containing a single black cell. To get all the familiar properties of additivity one needs an addition operation that is associative (*Flat*) and commutative (*Orderless*), and has an identity element (white or *0* in the cases above)—so that it defines a commutative monoid. (Usually it is also convenient to be able to get all possible elements by combining a small number of basic generator elements.)

The inequivalent commutative monoids with up to $k = 4$ colors are (in total there are 1, 2, 5, 19, 78, 421, 2637, ... such objects):

| 6 | 14 | 4017 | 8229 | 13008 | 19569 | 19650 |

For $k = 2$, $r = 1$ the number of rules additive with respect to these is respectively: {8, 9}; for $k = 2$, $r = 2$: {32, 33}; for $k = 3$, $r = 1$: {28, 27, 35, 244, 28}; for $k = 4$, $r = 1$:

{1001, 65, 540, 577, 126, 4225, 540, 9065,
   757, 408, 65, 133, 862, 224, 72, 72, 91, 4096, 64}

It turns out to be possible to show that any rules ϕ additive with respect to some addition operation ⊕ must work by applying that operation to values associated with cells in their neighborhood. The values are obtained by applying to cells at each position one of the unary operations (endomorphisms) σ that satisfy $\sigma[a \oplus b] == \sigma[a] \oplus \sigma[b]$ for individual cell values a and b. (For *Xor*, there are 2 possible σ, while for *Or* there are 3.)

The basic examples are then rules of the form *RotateLeft[a]* ⊕ *RotateRight[a]*—analogs of rule 90, but with other addition operations (compare page 886). The σ can be used to give analogs of the weights that appear in the note above. And rules that involve more than two cells can be obtained by having several instances of ⊕—which can always be flattened. But in all cases the general results for associative rules on page 956 show that the patterns obtained must be at most nested.

If instead of an ordinary cellular automaton with a limited number of possible colors one considers a system in which every cell can have any integer value then additivity with respect to ordinary addition becomes just traditional linearity. And the only way to achieve this is to have a rule in which the new value of a cell is given by a linear form such as $ax + by$. If the values of cells are allowed to be any real number then linear forms such as $ax + by$ again yield additivity with respect to ordinary addition. But in general one can apply to each cell value any function σ that obeys the so-called Cauchy functional equation $\sigma[x + y] == \sigma[x] + \sigma[y]$. If $\sigma[x]$ is required to be continuous, then the only form it can have is cx. But if one allows σ to be discontinuous then there can be some other exotic possibilities. It is inevitable that within any rationally related set of values x one must have $\sigma[x] = cx$ with fixed c. But if one assumes the Axiom of Choice then in principle it becomes possible to construct $\sigma[x]$ which have different c for different sets of x values. (Note however that I do not believe that such σ could ever actually be constructed in any explicit way by any real computational system—or in fact by any system in our universe.)

In general $\oplus$ need not be ordinary addition, but can be any operation that defines a commutative monoid—including an infinite one. An example is ordinary numbers modulo an irrational. And indeed a cellular automaton whose rule is based on $Mod[x + y, \pi]$ will show additivity with respect to this operation (see page 922). If $\oplus$ has an inverse, so that it defines a group, then the only continuous (Lie group) examples turn out to be combinations of ordinary addition and modular addition (the group U(1)). This assumes, however, that the underlying cellular automaton has discrete cells. But one can also imagine setting up systems whose states are continuous functions of position. ϕ then defines a mapping from one such function to another. To be analogous to cellular automata one can then require this mapping to be local, in which case if it is continuous it must be just a linear differential operator involving $Derivative[n]$—and at some level its behavior must be fairly simple. (Compare page 161.)

■ **Probabilistic estimates.** One way to get estimates for density and other properties of class 3 cellular automata is to make the assumption that the color of each cell at each step is completely random. And with this assumption, if the overall density of black cells at a particular step is p, then each cell at that step should independently have probability p to be black. This means that for example the probability to find a black cell followed by two white cells is $p(1-p)^2$. And in general, the probabilities for all 8 possible combinations of 3 cells are given by

    probs = Apply[Times, Table[IntegerDigits[8 - i, 2, 3],
        {i, 8}] /. {1 → p, 0 → 1 - p}, {1}]

In terms of these probabilities the density at the next step in the evolution of cellular automaton with rule number m is then given by

    Simplify[probs . IntegerDigits[m, 2, 8]]

For rule 22, for example, this means that if the density at a particular step is p, then the density on the next step should be $3p(1-p)^2$, and the densities on subsequent steps should be obtained by iterating this function. (At least for the 256 elementary cellular automata this iterated map is never chaotic.) The stable density after many steps is then given by $Solve[3p(1-p)^2 == p, p]$, so that $p \to 1 - 1/\sqrt{3}$ or approximately 0.42. The actual density for rule 22 is however 0.35095. The reason for the discrepancy is that the probabilities for different cells are in fact correlated. One can systematically include more such correlations by looking at more steps of evolution at once. For two steps, one must consider probabilities for all 32 combinations of 5 cells, and for rule 22 the function becomes $p(1-p)^2(2 + 3p^2)$, yielding density 0.35012; for three steps it is $p(1-p)^2(p^4 - 18p^3 + 41p^2 - 22p + 6)$ yielding density 0.379. The plot below shows what happens with more steps: the results seem to converge slowly to the exact result indicated by the gray line.

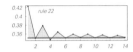
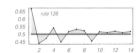

(For rules 90 and 30 the functions obtained after one step are respectively $2p(1-p)$ and $p(2p^2 - 5p + 3)$, both of which turn out to imply correct final densities of $1/2$.)

Probabilistic approximation schemes like this are often used in statistical physics under the name of mean field theories. In general, such approximations tend to work better for systems in larger numbers of dimensions, where correlations tend to be less important.

Probabilistic estimates can also be used for other quantities, such as growth rates of difference patterns (see page 949). In most cases, however, buildup of correlations tends to prevent systematic improvement of such approximations.

■ **Density in rule 90.** From the superposition principle above and the number of black cells at step t in a pattern starting from a single black cell (see page 870) one can compute the density after t steps in the evolution of rule 90 with initial conditions of density p to be (see also page 602)

    1/2 (1 - (1 - 2p)) ^ (2 ^ DigitCount[t, 2, 1])

■ **Densities in other rules.** The pictures below show how the densities on successive steps depend on the initial density. Densities are indicated by gray levels. Initial densities are shown across each picture. Successive steps are shown down the page. Rule 236 is class 2, and the density retains a memory of its initial value. But in the class 3 rules 126 and 30, the densities converge quickly to a fixed value.

Page 339 shows a cellular automaton with very different behavior.

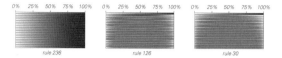

rule 236 *rule 126* *rule 30*

▪ **Density oscillations in rule 73.** Although there are always some fluctuations, most rules yield densities that converge more or less uniformly to their final values. One exception is rule 73, which yields densities that continue to oscillate with a period of 3 steps forever. The origin of this phenomenon is that with completely random initial conditions rule 73 evolves to a collection of independent regions, as in the picture below, and many of these regions contain patterns that repeat with period 3. The boundaries between regions come from blocks of even numbers of black cells in the initial conditions, and if one does not allow any such blocks, the density oscillations no longer occur. (See also page 699.)

Special Initial Conditions

▪ **Page 267 · Repeating blocks.** The discussion in the main text is mostly about repetition strictly every p steps, and no sooner. (If a system repeats for example every 3 steps, then it is inevitable that it will also repeat in the same way every 6, 9, 12, 15, etc. steps.) Finding configurations in a 1D cellular automaton that repeat with a particular period is equivalent to satisfying the kind of constraints we discussed on page 211. And as described there, if such constraints can be satisfied at all, then it must be possible to satisfy them with a configuration that consists of a repetition of identical blocks. Indeed, for period p, the length of blocks required is at most 2^{2p} (or 2^{2pr} for range r rules).

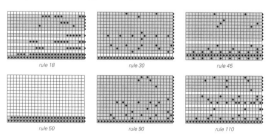

rule 18 *rule 30* *rule 45*

rule 50 *rule 90* *rule 110*

The pictures at the bottom of the previous column summarize which periods can be obtained with various rules. Periods from 1 to 15 are represented by different rows, with period 1 at the bottom. Within each row a gray bar indicates that a particular period can be obtained with blocks of some length. The black dots indicate specific block sizes up to 25 that work.

In rule 90 (as well as other additive rules such as 60 and 150) any period can occur, but all configurations that repeat must consist of a sequence of identical blocks. For periods up to 10, examples of such blocks in rule 90 are given by the digits of

{0, 40, 24, 2176, 107904, 640, 96, 8421376, 7566031296234863392, 15561286137}

For period 1 the possible blocks are □ and ■□; for period 2 ■■□□ and ■■■□. The total number of configurations in rule 90 that repeat with any period that divides p is always 4^p.

Rules 30 and 45 (as well as other one-sided additive rules) also have the property that all configurations that repeat must consist of a sequence of identical blocks. The total number of configurations in rule 30 that repeat with periods that divide 1 through 10 are {3, 3, 15, 10, 8, 99, 18, 14, 30, 163}. In general for one-sided additive rules the number of such configurations increases for large p like $k^{h_{tx}p}$, where h_{tx} is the spacetime entropy of page 960. (This is the analog of a standard result in dynamical systems theory about expansive homeomorphisms.)

For rules that do not show at least one-sided additivity there can be an infinite number of configurations that repeat with a given period. To find them one considers all possible blocks of length $2pr+1$ and picks out those that after p steps evolve so that their center cell ends up the same color as it was originally. The possible configurations that repeat with period p then correspond to the finite complement language (see page 958) obtained by stringing together these blocks. For $p = 2$, rule 18 leaves 20 of the 32 possible length 5 blocks invariant, but these blocks can only be strung together to yield repetitions of {a, b, 0, 0}, where now a and b are not fixed, but in every case can each be either {1} or {0, 1}.

(See also page 700.)

▪ **Localized structures.** See pages 281 and 1118.

▪ **2D cellular automata.** As expected from the discussion of constraints on page 942, the problem of finding repeating configurations is much more difficult in two dimensions than in one dimension. Thus for example unlike in 1D there is no guarantee in 2D that among repeating configurations of a particular period there is necessarily one that consists just of a repetitive array of fixed blocks. Indeed, as discussed on page 1139, it is in a sense possible that the only repeating configurations are arbitrarily complex. Note that if one considers configurations in 2D that consist only of infinitely long stripes, then the problem reduces again to the 1D case. (See also page 349.)

■ **Systems based on numbers.** An iterated map of the kind discussed on page 150 with rule $x \to Mod[a\,x, 1]$ (with rational a) will yield repetitive behavior when its initial condition is a rational number. The same is true for higher-dimensional generalizations such as so-called Anosov maps $\{x, y\} \to Mod[m \cdot \{x, y\}, 1]$. The continued fraction map $x \to Mod[1/x, 1]$ discussed on page 914 becomes repetitive whenever its initial condition is a solution to a quadratic equation.

For a map $x \to f[x]$ where $f[x]$ is a polynomial such as $a\,x\,(1-x)$ the real initial conditions that yield period p are given by

$$Select[x \,/.\, Solve[Nest[f, x, p] == x, x], Im[\#] == 0 \,\&]$$

For $x \to a\,x\,(1-x)$ the results usually cannot be expressed in terms of explicit radicals beyond period 2. (See page 961.)

■ **Sarkovskii's theorem.** For any iterated map based on a continuous function such as a polynomial it was shown in 1962 that if an initial condition exists that gives period 3, then other initial conditions must exist that give any other period. In general, if a period m is possible then so must all periods n for which $p = \{m, n\}$ satisfies

$$OrderedQ[(Transpose[If[MemberQ[p/\#, 1], Map[Reverse,$$
$$\{p/\#, \#\}], \{\#, p/\#\}]] \,\&)[2 \hat{\,} IntegerExponent[p, 2]]]$$

Extensions of this to other types of systems seem difficult to find, but it is conceivable that when viewed as continuous mappings on a Cantor set (see page 869) at least some cellular automata might exhibit similar properties.

■ **Page 269 · Rule emulations.** See pages 702 and 1118.

■ **Renormalization group.** The notion of studying systems by seeing the effect of changing the scale on which one looks at them has been widely used in physics since about 1970, and there is some analogy between this and what I do here with cellular automata. In the lattice version in physics one typically considers what happens to averages over all possible configurations of a system if one does a so-called blocking transformation that replaces blocks of elements by individual elements. And what one finds is that in certain cases—notably in connection with nesting at critical points associated with phase transitions (see page 981)—certain averages turn out to be the same as one would get if one did no blocking but just changed parameters ("coupling constants") in the underlying rules that specify the weighting of different configurations. How such effective parameters change with scale is then governed by so-called renormalization group differential equations. And when one looks at large scales the versions of these equations that arise in practice essentially always show fixed points, whose properties do not depend much on details of the equations—leading to certain universal results across many different underlying systems (see page 983).

What I do in the main text can be thought of as carrying out blocking transformations on cellular automata. But only rarely do such transformations yield cellular automata whose rules are of the same type one started from. And in most cases such rules will not suffice even if one takes averages. And indeed, so far as I can tell, only in those cases where there is fairly simple nested behavior is any direct analog of renormalization group methods useful. (See page 989.)

■ **Page 271 · Self-similarity of additive rules.** The fact that rule 90 can emulate itself can be seen fairly easily from a symbolic description of the rule. Given three cells $\{a_1, a_2, a_3\}$ the rule specifies that the new value of the center cell will be $Mod[a_1 + a_3, 2]$. But given $\{a_1, 0, a_2, 0, a_3, 0\}$ the value after one step is $\{Mod[a_1 + a_2, 2], 0, Mod[a_2 + a_3, 2], 0\}$ and after two steps is again $\{Mod[a_1 + a_3, 2], 0\}$. It turns out that this argument generalizes (by interspersing $k - 1$ 0's and going for k steps) to any additive rule based on reduction modulo k (see page 952) so long as k is prime. And it follows that in this case the pattern generated after a certain number of steps from a single non-white cell will always be the same as one gets by going k times that number of steps and then keeping only every k^{th} row and column. And this immediately implies that the pattern must always have a nested form. If k is not prime the pattern is no longer strictly invariant with respect to keeping only every k^{th} row and column—but is in effect still a superposition of patterns with this property for factor of k. (Compare page 870.)

■ **Fractal dimensions.** The total number of nonzero cells in the first t rows of the pattern generated by the evolution of an additive cellular automaton with k colors and weights w (see page 952) from a single initial 1 can be found using

$$g[w\_, k\_, t\_] := Apply[Plus, Sign[NestList[Mod[$$
$$ListCorrelate[w, \#, \{-1, 1\}, 0] \,\&, \{1\}, t - 1]], \{0, 1\}]$$

The fractal dimension of this pattern is then given by the large m limit of

$$Log[k, g[w, k, k^{m+1}]/g[w, k, k^m]]$$

When k is prime it turns out that this can be computed as

$$d[w\_, k\_ : 2] := Log[k, Max[Abs[Eigenvalues[With[$$
$$\{s = Length[w] - 1\}, (Map[Function[u, Map[Count[u, \#] \,\&,$$
$$\#]], Map[Flatten[Map[Partition[Take[\#, k + s - 1], s, 1] \,\&,$$
$$NestList[Mod[ListConvolve[w, \#], k] \,\&, \#, k - 1]], 1] \,\&,$$
$$Map[Flatten[Map[\{Table[0, \{k - 1\}], \#\} \,\&, Append[\#,$$
$$0]]] \,\&, \#]] \,\&)[Array[IntegerDigits[\#, k, s] \,\&, k^s - 1]]]]]]$$

For rule 90 one gets $d[\{1, 0, 1\}] = Log[2, 3] \simeq 1.58$. For rule 150 $d[\{1, 1, 1\}] = Log[2, 1 + \sqrt{5}\,] \simeq 1.69$. (See page 58.) For the other rules on page 952:

$d[\{1, 1, 0, 1, 0\}] = $
  $Log[2, Root[4 + 2\# - 2\#^2 - 3\#^3 + \#^4 \&, 2]] \simeq 1.72$

$d[\{1, 1, 0, 1, 1\}] = $
  $Log[2, Root[-4 + 4\# + \#^2 - 4\#^3 + \#^4 \&, 2]] \simeq 1.8$

Other cases include (see page 870):

$d[\{1, 0, 1\}, k] = 1 + Log[k, (k + 1)/2]$

$d[\{1, 1, 1\}, 3] = Log[3, 6] \simeq 1.63$

$d[\{1, 1, 1\}, 5] = Log[5, 19] \simeq 1.83$

$d[\{1, 1, 1\}, 7] = Log[7, Root[-27136 + 23280\# - $
  $7288\#^2 + 1008\#^3 - 59\#^4 + \#^5 \&, 1]] \simeq 1.85$

■ **General associative rules.** With a cellular automaton rule in which the new color of a cell is given by $f[a_1, a_2]$ (compare page 886) it turns out that the pattern generated by evolution from a single non-white cell is always nested if the function f has the property of being associative or *Flat*. In fact, for a system involving k colors the pattern produced will always be essentially just one of the patterns obtained from an additive rule with k or less colors. In general, the pattern produced by evolution for t steps is given by

NestList[
  Inner[f, Prepend[#, 0], Append[#, 0], List] &, {a}, t]

so that the first few steps yield

{a}
{f[0, a], f[a, 0]}
{f[0, f[0, a]], f[f[0, a], f[a, 0]], f[f[a, 0], 0]}
{f[0, f[0, f[0, a]]], f[f[0, f[0, a]], f[f[0, a], f[a, 0]]],
  f[f[f[0, a], f[a, 0]], f[f[a, 0], 0]], f[f[f[a, 0], 0], 0]}

If f is *Flat*, however, then the last two lines here become

{f[0, 0, a], f[0, a, a, 0], f[a, 0, 0]}
{f[0, 0, 0, a], f[0, 0, a, 0, a, a, 0],
  f[0, a, a, 0, a, 0, 0], f[a, 0, 0, 0]}

and in general the number of a's that appear in a particular element is given as in Pascal's triangle by a binomial coefficient. If f is commutative (*Orderless*) then all that can ever matter to the value of an element is its number of a's. Yet since there are a finite set of possible values for each element it immediately follows that the resulting pattern must be essentially Pascal's triangle modulo some integer. And even if f is not commutative, the same result will hold so long as $f[0, a] == a$ and $f[a, 0] == a$—since then any element can be reduced to $f[a, a, a, ...]$. The result can also be generalized to cellular automata with basic rules involving more than two elements—since if f is *Flat*, $f[a_1, a_2, a_3]$ is always just $f[f[a_1, a_2], a_3]$.

If one starts from more than a single non-0 element, then it is still true that a nested pattern will be produced if f is both associative and commutative. And from the discussion on page 952 this means that any rule that shows generalized additivity must always yield a nested pattern. But if f is not commutative, then even if it is associative, non-nested patterns can be produced. And indeed page 887 shows an example of this based on the non-commutative group S_3. (In general f can correspond to an almost arbitrary semigroup, but with a single initial element only a cyclic subgroup of it is ever explored.)

■ **Nesting in rule 45.** As illustrated on page 701, starting from a single black cell on a background of repeated ■□ blocks, rule 45 yields a slanted version of the nested rule 90 pattern.

■ **Uniqueness of patterns.** Starting from a particular initial condition, different rules can often yield the same pattern. The picture below shows in sorted order the configurations obtained at each successive step in the evolution of all 256 elementary cellular automata starting from a single black cell. After a large number of steps, between 94 and 105 distinct individual configurations are obtained, together with 143 distinct complete patterns. (Compare page 1186.)

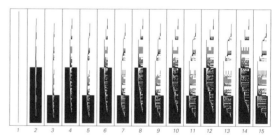

■ **Square root of rule 30.** Although rule 30 cannot apparently be decomposed into other $k = 2$, $r = 1$ cellular automata, it can be viewed as the square of the $k = 3$, $r = 1/2$ cellular automata with rule numbers 11736, 11739 and 11742.

■ **Page 272 · Nested initial conditions.** The pictures below show patterns generated by rule 90 starting from the nested sequences on page 83. (See page 1091.)

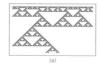
(a)

(b)

(c)

The Notion of Attractors

■ **Page 275 · Discrete systems.** In traditional mathematics mechanical and other systems are assumed continuous, so that for example a pendulum may get exponentially close to the attractor state where it has stopped, but it will never strictly reach this attractor. In discrete systems like cellular automata, however, there is no problem in explicitly reaching at least simple attractors.

■ **Implementation.** One can represent a network by a list such as $\{\{1 \to 2\}, \{0 \to 3, 1 \to 2\}, \{0 \to 3, 1 \to 1\}\}$ where each element represents a node whose number corresponds to the position of the element, and for each node there are rules that specify to which nodes arcs with different values lead. Starting with a list of nodes, the nodes reached by following arcs with value *a* for one step are given by

```
NetStep[net_, i_, a_] :=
    Union[ReplaceList[a, Flatten[net[[i]]]]]
```

A list of values then corresponds to a path in the network starting from any node if

```
Fold[NetStep[net, #1, #2] &,
    Range[Length[net]], list] =!= {}
```

Given a set of sequences of values represented by a particular network, the set obtained after one step of cellular automaton evolution is given by

```
NetCAStep[{k_, r_, rtab_}, net_] := Flatten[
    Map[Table[# /. (a_ → s_) :> rtab[[i k + a + 1]] → k^{2 r} (s - 1) +
        1 + Mod[i k + a, k^{2 r}], {i, 0, k^{2 r} - 1}] &, net], 1]
```

where here elementary rule 126 is specified for example by $\{2, 1, Reverse[IntegerDigits[126, 2, 8]]\}$. Starting from the set of all possible sequences, as given by

```
AllNet[k_ : 2] := {Thread[Range[k] - 1 → 1]}
```

this then yields for rule 126 the network

$\{\{0 \to 1, 1 \to 2\}, \{1 \to 3, 1 \to 4\}, \{1 \to 1, 1 \to 2\}, \{1 \to 3, 0 \to 4\}\}$

It is always possible to find a minimal network that represents a set of sequences. This can be done by first creating a "deterministic" network in which at most one arc of each value comes out of each node, then combining equivalent nodes. The whole procedure can be performed using

```
MinNet[net_, k_ : 2] := Module[{d = DSets[net, k], q, b},
    If[First[d] =!= {}, AllNet[k], q = ISets[b = Map[Table[
        Position[d, NetStep[net, #, a]][[1, 1]], {a, 0, k - 1}] &, d]];
    DeleteCases[MapIndexed[#2[[2]] - 1 → #1 &, Rest[
        Map[Position[q, #][[1, 1]] &, Transpose[Map[#[[Map[
        First, q]]] &, Transpose[b]], {2}] - 1, {2}], _ → 0, {2}]]]
```

```
DSets[net_, k_ : 2] :=
    FixedPoint[Union[Flatten[Map[Table[NetStep[net, #, a],
        {a, 0, k - 1}] &, #], 1]] &, {Range[Length[net]]}]
```

```
ISets[list_] := FixedPoint[Function[g, Flatten[Map[
    Map[Last, Split[Sort[Transpose[{Map[Position[g, #][[1,
        1]] &, list, {2}], Range[Length[list]]}]][[#]], First[#1] ==
    First[#2] &], {2}] &, g], 1]], {{1}, Range[2, Length[list]]}]]
```

If *net* has *q* nodes, then in general *MinNet[net]* can have as many as $2^q - 1$ nodes. The form of *MinNet* given here can take

up to about n^2 steps to generate a result with *n* nodes; an *n Log[n]* procedure is known. The result from *MinNet* for rule 126 is $\{\{1 \to 3\}, \{0 \to 2, 1 \to 1\}, \{0 \to 2, 1 \to 3\}\}$.

In general *MinNet* will yield a network with the property that any allowed sequence of values corresponds to a path which starts from node 1. In the main text, however, the networks allow paths that start at any node. To obtain such trimmed networks one can apply the function

```
TrimNet[net_] :=
    With[{m = Apply[Intersection, Map[FixedPoint[
        Union[#, Flatten[Map[Last, net[[#]], {2}]]] &,
        #] &, Map[List, Range[Length[net]]]]]},
    net[[m]] /. Table[(a_ → m[[i]]) → a → i, {i, Length[m]}]]
```

■ **Finite automata.** The networks discussed in the main text can be viewed as finite automata (also known as finite state machines). Each node in the network corresponds to a state in the automaton, and each arc represents a transition that occurs when a particular value is given as input. *NetCAStep* above in general produces a non-deterministic finite automaton (NDFA) for which a particular sequence of values does not determine a unique path through the network. *MinNet* creates an equivalent DFA, then minimizes this. The Myhill-Nerode theorem ensures that a unique minimal DFA can always be found (though to do so is in general a PSPACE-complete problem).

The total number of distinct minimal finite automata with $k = 2$ possible labels for each arc grows with the number of nodes as follows: 3, 7, 78, 1388, … (The simple result $(n + 1)^{nk}$ based on the number of ways to connect up *n* nodes is a significant overestimate because of equivalence between automata with different patterns of connections.)

■ **Regular languages.** The set of sequences obtained by following possible paths through a finite network is often called a regular language, and appears in studies of many kinds of systems. (See page 939.)

■ **Regular expressions.** The sequences in a regular language correspond to those that can be matched by *Mathematica* patterns that use no explicit pattern names. Thus for example $\{(0 | 1) ...\}$ corresponds to all possible sequences of 0's and 1's, while $\{1, 1, (1) ..., 0, (0) ...\} ...$ corresponds to the sequences that can occur after 2 steps in rule 126 and $\{(0) ..., 1, \{0, (0) ..., 1, 1\} | \{1, (1) ..., 0\}\} ...$ to those that can occur after 2 steps in rule 110 (see page 279).

■ **Generating functions.** The sequences in a regular language can be thought of as corresponding to products of non-commuting variables that appear as coefficients in a formal power series expansion of a generating function. A basic result is that for regular languages this generating function is always rational. (Compare the discussion of entropies below.)

■ **History.** Simple finite automata have implicitly been used in electromechanical machines for over a century. A formal version of them appeared in 1943 in McCulloch-Pitts neural network models. (An earlier analog had appeared in Markov chains.) Intensive work on them in the 1950s (sometimes under the name sequential machines) established many basic properties, including interpretation as regular languages and equivalence to regular expressions. Connections to formal power series and to substitution systems (see page 891) were studied in the 1960s. And with the development of the Unix operating system in the 1970s regular expressions began to be widely used in practical computing in lexical analysis (lex) and text searching (ed and grep). Regular languages also arose in dynamical systems theory in the early 1970s under the name of sofic systems.

■ **Page 278 · Network properties.** The number of nodes and connections at step $t > 1$ are: rule 108: 8, 13; rule 128: $2t$, $2t + 2$; rule 132: $2t + 1$, $3t + 3$; rule 160: $(t + 1)^2$, $(t + 1)(t + 3)$; rule 184: $2t$, $3t + 1$. For rule 126 the first few cases are

$$\{\{1, 2\}, \{3, 5\}, \{13, 23\}, \{106, 196\}, \{2866, 5474\}\}$$

and for rule 110 they are

$$\{\{1, 2\}, \{5, 9\}, \{20, 38\}, \{206, 403\}, \{1353, 2666\}\}$$

The maximum size of network that can possibly be generated after t steps of cellular automaton evolution is $2^{k^{2rt}} - 1$. For $t = 1$ the maximum of 15 (with 29 connections) is achieved for 16 out of the 256 possible elementary rules, including 22, 37, 73, 94, 104, 122, 146 and 164. For $t = 2$, rule 22 gives the largest network, with 280 nodes and 551 arcs. The $k = 2$, $r = 2$ totalistic rule with code 20 gives a network with 65535 nodes after just 1 step. Note that rules which yield maximal size networks are in a sense close to allowing all possible sequences. (The shortest excluded block for code 20 is of length 36.)

■ **Excluded blocks.** As the evolution of a cellular automaton proceeds, the set of sequences that can appear typically shrinks, with progressively more blocks being excluded. In some cases the set of allowed sequences forms a so-called finite complement language (or subshift of finite type) that can be characterized completely just by saying that some finite set of blocks are excluded. But whenever the overall behavior is at all complex, there tend to be an infinite set of blocks excluded, making it necessary to use a network of the kind discussed in the main text. If there are n nodes in such a network, then if any blocks are excluded, the shortest one of them must be of length less than n. And if there are going to be an infinite number of excluded blocks, there must be additional excluded blocks with lengths

between n and $2n$. In rule 126, the lengths of the shortest newly excluded blocks on successive steps are 0, 3, 12, 13, 14, 14, 17, 15. It is common to see such lengths progressively increase, although in principle they can decrease by as much as $2r$ from one step to the next. (As an example, in rule 54 they decrease from 9 to 7 between steps 4 and 5.)

■ **Entropies and dimensions.** There are 2^n sequences possible for n cells that are each either black or white. But as we have seen, in most cellular automata not all these sequences can occur except in the initial conditions. The number of sequences s_n of length n that can actually occur is given by

$$Apply[Plus, Flatten[MatrixPower[m, n]]]$$

where the adjacency matrix m is given by

$$MapAt[1 + \# \&, Table[0, \{Length[net]\}, \{Length[net]\}],$$
$$Flatten[MapIndexed[\{First[\#2], Last[\#1]\} \&, net, \{2\}], 1]]$$

For rule 32, for example, s_n turns out to be $Fibonacci[n + 3]$, so that for large n it is approximately $GoldenRatio^n$. For any rule, s_n for large n will behave like κ^n, where κ is the largest eigenvalue of m. For rule 126 after 1 step, the characteristic polynomial for m is $x^3 - 2x^2 + x - 1$, giving $\kappa \simeq 1.755$. After 2 steps, the polynomial is

$$x^{13} - 4x^{12} + 6x^{11} - 5x^{10} + 3x^9 - 3x^8 +$$
$$5x^7 - 3x^6 - x^5 + 4x^4 - 2x^3 + x^2 - x + 1$$

giving $\kappa \simeq 1.732$. Note that κ is always an algebraic number—or strictly a so-called Perron number, obtained from a polynomial with leading coefficient 1. (Note that any possible Perron number can be obtained for example from some finite complement language.)

It is often convenient to fit s_n for large n to the form 2^{hn}, where h is the so-called spatial (topological) entropy (see page 1084), given by $Log[2, \kappa]$. The value of this for successive t never increases; for the first 3 steps in rule 126 it is for example approximately 1, 0.811, 0.793. The exact value of h after more steps tends to be very difficult to find, and indeed the question of whether its limiting value after infinitely many steps satisfies a given bound—say even being nonzero—is in general undecidable (see page 1138).

If one associates with each possible sequence of length n a number $Sum[a_i 2^{-i}, \{i, n\}]$, then the set of sequences that actually occur at a given step form a Cantor set (see note below), whose Hausdorff dimension turns out to be exactly h.

■ **Cycles and zeta functions.** The number of sequences of n cells that can occur repeatedly, corresponding to cycles in the network, is given in terms of the adjacency matrix m by $Tr[MatrixPower[m, n]]$. These numbers can also be obtained as the coefficients of x^n in the series expansion of

$x\,\partial_x\,Log[\zeta[m,x]]$, with the so-called zeta function, which is always a rational function of x, given by

$\zeta[m\_,\,x\_] := 1/Det[IdentityMatrix[Length[m]] - m\,x]$

and corresponds to the product over all cycles of $1/(1-x^n)$.

■ **2D generalizations.** Above 1D no systematic method seems to exist for finding exact formulas for entropies (as expected from the discussion at the end of Chapter 5). Indeed, even working out for large n how many of the 2^{n^2} possible configurations of a $n \times n$ grid of black and white squares contain no pair of adjacent black cells is difficult. Fitting the result to $2^{h\,n^2}$ one finds $h \simeq 0.589$, but no exact formula for h has ever been found. With hexagonal cells, however, the exact solution of the so-called hard hexagon lattice gas model in 1980 showed that $h \simeq 0.481$ is the logarithm of the largest root of a degree 12 polynomial. (The solution of the so-called dimer problem in 1961 also showed that for complete coverings of a square grid by 2-cell dominoes $h = Catalan/(\pi\,Log[2]) \simeq 0.421$.)

■ **Probability-based entropies.** This section has concentrated on characterizing what sequences can possibly occur in 1D cellular automata, with no regard to their probability. It turns out to be difficult to extend the discussion of networks to include probabilities in a rigorous way. But it is straightforward to define versions of entropy that take account of probabilities—and indeed the closest analog to the usual entropy in physics or information theory is obtained by taking the probabilities $p[i]$ for the k^n blocks of length n (assuming k colors), then constructing

$-Limit[Sum[p[i]\,Log[k,\,p[i]],\,\{i,\,k^n\}]/n,\,n \to \infty]$

I have tended to call this quantity measure entropy, though in other contexts, it is often just called entropy or information, and is sometimes called information dimension. The quantity

$Limit[Sum[UnitStep[p[i]],\,\{i,\,k^n\}]/n,\,n \to \infty]$

is the entropy discussed in the notes above, and is variously called set entropy, topological entropy, capacity and fractal dimension. An example of a generalization is the quantity given for blocks of size n by

$h[q\_,\,n\_] := Log[k,\,Sum[p[i]^q,\,\{i,\,k^n\}]]/(n\,(q-1))$

where $q = 0$ yields set entropy, the limit $q \to 1$ measure entropy, and $q = 2$ so-called correlation entropy. For any q the maximum $h[q,\,n] == 1$ occurs when all $p[i] == k^{-n}$. It is always the case that $h[q+1,\,n] \le h[q,\,n]$. The $h[q]$ have been introduced in almost identical form several times, notably by Alfréd Rényi in the 1950s as information measures for probability distributions, in the 1970s as part of the thermodynamic formalism for dynamical systems, and in the 1980s as generalized dimensions for multifractals. (Related objects have also arisen in connection with Hölder exponents for discontinuous functions.)

■ **Entropy estimates.** Entropies $h[n]$ computed from blocks of size n always decrease with n; the quantity $n\,h[n]$ is always convex (negative second difference) with respect to n. At least at a basic level, to compute topological entropy one needs in effect to count every possible sequence that can be generated. But one can potentially get an estimate of measure entropy just by sampling possible sequences. One problem, however, is that even though such sampling may give estimates of probabilities that are unbiased (and have Gaussian errors), a direct computation of measure entropy from them will tend to give a value that is systematically too small. (A potential way around this is to use the theory of unbiased estimators for polynomials just above and below $p\,Log[p]$.)

■ **Nested structure of attractors.** Associating with each sequence of length n (and k possible colors for each element) a number $Sum[a[i]\,k^{-i},\,\{i,\,n\}]$, the set of sequences that occur in the limit $n \to \infty$ forms a Cantor set. For $k = 3$, the set of sequences where the second color never occurs corresponds to the standard middle-thirds Cantor set. In general, whenever the possible sequences correspond to paths through a finite network, it follows that the Cantor set obtained has a nested structure. Indeed, constructing the Cantor set in levels by considering progressively longer sequences is effectively equivalent to following successive steps in a substitution system of the kind discussed on page 83. (To see the equivalence first set up s kinds of elements in the substitution system corresponding to the s nodes in the network.) Note that if the possible sequences cannot be described by a network, then the Cantor set obtained will inevitably not have a strictly nested form.

■ **Surjectivity and injectivity.** One can think of a cellular automaton rule as a mapping (endomorphism) from the space of possible states of the cellular automaton to itself. (See page 869.) Usually this mapping is contractive, so that not all the states which appear as input to the mapping can also appear as output. But in some cases, the mapping is surjective or onto, meaning that any state which appears as input can also appear as output. Among $k = 2$, $r = 1$ elementary cellular automata it turns out that this happens precisely for those 30 rules that are additive with respect to at least the first or last position on which they depend (see pages 601 and 1087); this includes both rules 90 and 150 and rules 30 and 45. With $k = 2$, $r = 2$ there are a total of 4,294,967,296 possible rules. Out of these 141,884 are onto— and 11,388 of these turn out not to be additive with respect to any position. The easiest way to test whether a particular rule is onto seems to be essentially just to construct the minimal finite automaton discussed on page 957. The onto

$k = 2$, $r = 2$ rules were found in 1961 in a computer study by Gustav Hedlund and others; they later apparently provided input in the design of S-boxes for DES cryptography (see page 1085).

Even when a cellular automaton mapping is surjective, it is still often many-to-one, in the sense that several input states can yield the same output state. (Thus for example additive rules such as 90 and 150, as well as one-sided additive rules such as 30 and 45 are always 4-to-1.) But some surjective rules also have the property of being injective, so that different input states always yield different output states. And in such a case the cellular automaton mapping is one-to-one or bijective (an automorphism). This is equivalent to saying that the rule is reversible, as discussed on page 1017.

(In 2D such properties are in general undecidable; see page 1138.)

■ **Temporal sequences.** So far we have considered possible sequences of cells that can occur at a particular step in the evolution of a cellular automaton. But one can also consider sequences formed from the color of a particular cell on a succession of steps. For class 1 and 2 cellular automata, there are typically only a limited number of possible sequences of any length allowed. And when the length is large, the sequences are almost always either just uniform or repetitive. For class 3 cellular automata, however, the number of sequences of length n typically grows rapidly with n. For additive rules such as 60 and 90, and for partially additive rules such as 30 and 45, any possible sequence can occur if an appropriate initial condition is given. For rule 18, it appears that any sequence can occur that never contains more than one adjacent black cell. I know of no general characterization of temporal sequences analogous to the finite automaton one used for spatial sequences above. However, if one defines the entropy or dimension h_t for temporal sequences by analogy with the definition for spatial sequences above, then it follows for example that $h_t \leq 2\lambda h_x$, where λ is the maximum rate at which changes grow in the cellular automaton. The origin of this inequality is indicated in the picture below. The basic idea is that the size of the region that can affect a given cell in the course of t steps is $2\lambda t$. But for large sizes x the total number of possible configurations of this region is $k^{h_x x}$. (Inequalities between entropies and Lyapunov exponents are also common in dynamical systems based on numbers, but are more difficult to derive.) Note that in effect, h_x gives the information content of spatial sequences in units of bits per unit distance, while h_t gives the corresponding quantity for temporal sequences in units of bits per unit time. (One can also define directional entropies based on sequences at different slopes; the values of such entropies tend to change discontinuously when the slope crosses λ.)

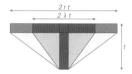

Different classes of cellular automata show characteristically different entropy values. Class 1 has $h_x = 0$ and $h_t = 0$. Class 2 has $h_x \neq 0$ but $h_t = 0$. Class 3 has $h_x \neq 0$ and $h_t \neq 0$. Class 4 tends to show fluctuations which prevent definite values of h_x and h_t from being found.

■ **Spacetime patches.** One can imagine defining entropies and dimensions associated with regions of any shape in the spacetime history of a cellular automaton. As an example, one can consider patches that extend x cells across in space and t cells down in time. If the color of every cell in such a patch could be chosen independently then there would be $k^{t x}$ possible configurations of the complete patch. But in fact, having just specified a block of length $x + 2rt$ in the initial conditions, the cellular automaton rule then uniquely determines the color of every cell in the patch, allowing a total of at most $s[t, x] = k^{x+2rt}$ configurations. One can define a topological spacetime entropy h_{tx} as

$Limit[Limit[Log[k, s[t, x]]/t, t \to \infty], x \to \infty]$

and a measure spacetime entropy h_{tx}^{μ} by replacing s with $p\,Log[p]$. In general, $h_t \leq h_{tx} \leq 2\lambda h_x$ and $h \leq 2r h_t$. For additive rules like rule 90 and rule 150 every possible configuration of the initial block leads to a different configuration for the patch, so that $h_{tx} = 2r = 2$. But for other rules many different configurations of the initial block can lead to the same configuration for the patch, yielding potentially much smaller values of h_{tx}. Just as for most other entropies, when a cellular automaton shows complicated behavior it tends to be difficult to find much more than upper bounds for h_{tx}. For rule 30, $h_{tx}^{\mu} < 1.155$, and there is some evidence that its true value may actually be 1. For rule 18 it appears that $h_{tx}^{\mu} = 1$, while for rule 22 $h_{tx}^{\mu} < 0.915$ and for rule 54 $h_{tx}^{\mu} < 0.25$.

■ **History.** The analysis of cellular automata given in this section is largely as I worked it out in the early 1980s. Parts of it, however, are related to earlier investigations, particularly in dynamical systems theory. Starting in the 1930s the idea of symbolic dynamics began to emerge, in which one partitions continuous values in a system into bins represented by discrete symbols, and then looks at the sequences of such symbols that can be produced by the evolution of the system. In connection with early work on chaos theory, it was noted that there are some systems that act like "full shifts", in the sense that the set of sequences they generate includes all possibilities—and corresponds to what one would get by starting with any possible number, then successively shifting digits to the left, and at each step picking off the leading digit. It was noted that some systems could also yield various kinds of subshifts that are subsets of full shifts. But since—unlike in cellular automata—the symbol sequences being studied were obtained by rather arbitrary partitionings of continuous values, the question arose of what effect using different partitionings would have. One approach was to try to find invariants that would remain unchanged in different partitionings—and this is what led, for example, to the study of topological entropy in the 1960s. Another approach was to look at actual possible transformations between partitionings, and this led from the late 1950s to various studies of so-called shift-commuting block maps (or sliding-block codes)—which turn out to be exactly 1D cellular automata (see page 878). The locality of cellular automaton rules was thought of as making them the analog for symbol sequences of continuous functions for real numbers (compare page 869). Of particular interest were invertible (reversible) cellular automaton rules, since systems related by these were considered conjugate or topologically equivalent.

In the 1950s and 1960s—quite independent of symbolic dynamics—there was a certain amount of work done in connection with ideas about self-reproduction (see page 876) on the question of what configurations one could arrange to produce in 1D and 2D cellular automata. And this led for example to the study of so-called Garden of Eden states that can appear only in initial conditions—as well as to some general discussion of properties such as surjectivity.

When I started working on cellular automata in the early 1980s I wanted to see how far one could get by following ideas of statistical mechanics and dynamical systems theory and trying to find global characterizations of the possible behavior of individual cellular automata. In the traditional symbolic dynamics of continuous systems it had always been assumed that meaningful quantities must be invariant under continuous invertible transformations of symbol sequences. It turns out that the spacetime (or "invariant") entropy defined in the previous note has this property. But the spatial and temporal entropies that I introduced do not—and indeed in studying specific cellular automata there seems to be no particular reason why such a property would be useful.

■ **Attractors in systems based on numbers.** Particularly for systems based on ordinary differential equations (see page 922) a geometrical classification of possible attractors exists. There are fixed points, limit cycles and so-called strange attractors. (The first two of these were identified around the end of the 1800s; the last with clarity only in the 1960s.) Fixed points correspond to zero-dimensional subsets of the space of possible states, limit cycles to one-dimensional subsets (circles, solenoids, etc.). Strange attractors often have a nested structure with non-integer fractal dimension. But even in cases where the behavior obtained with a particular random initial condition is very complicated the structure of the attractor is almost invariably quite simple.

■ **Iterated maps.** For maps of the form $x \to a\,x\,(1-x)$ discussed on page 920 the attractor for small a is a fixed point, then a period 2 limit cycle, then period 4, 8, 16, etc. There is an accumulation of limit cycles at $a \simeq 3.569946$ where the system has a special nested structure. (See pages 920 and 955.)

■ **Attractors in Turing machines.** In theoretical studies Turing machines are often set up so that if their initial conditions follow a particular formal grammar (see page 938) then they evolve to "accept" states—which can be thought of as being somewhat like attractors.

■ **Systems of limited size.** For any system with a limited total number of states, it is possible to create a finite network that gives a global representation of the behavior of the system. The idea of this network (which is very different from the finite automata networks discussed above) is to have each node represent a complete state of the system. At each step in the evolution of the system, every state evolves to some new state, and this process is represented in the network by an arc that joins each node to a new node. The picture below gives the networks obtained for systems of the kind shown on page 255. Each node is labelled by a possible position for the dot. In the first case shown, starting for example at position 4 the dot then visits positions 5, 0, 1, 2 and so on, at each step going from one node in the network to the next.

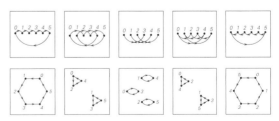

The pictures below give networks obtained from the system shown on page 257 for various values of n. For odd n, the networks consist purely of cycles. But for even n, there are also trees of states that lead to these cycles.

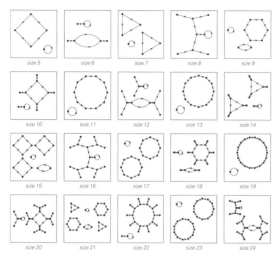

In general, any network that represents the evolution of a system with definite rules will have the same basic form. There are cycles which contain states that are visited repeatedly, and there can also be trees that represent transient states that can each only ever occur at most once in the evolution of the system.

The picture below shows the network obtained from a class 1 cellular automaton (rule 254) with 4 cells and thus 16 possible states. All but one of these 16 states evolve after at most two steps to state 15, which corresponds to all cells being black.

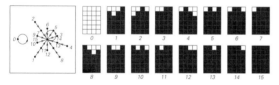

The pictures below show networks obtained when more cells are included in the cellular automaton above. The same convergence to a single fixed point is observed.

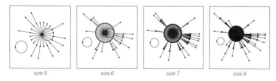

The pictures below give corresponding results for a class 2 cellular automaton (rule 132). The number of distinct cycles now increases with the size of the system. (As discussed below, identical pieces of the network are often related by symmetries of the underlying cellular automaton system.)

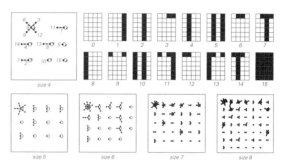

In class 3, larger cycles are usually obtained, and often the whole network is dominated by a single largest cycle. The second set of pictures below summarize the results for some larger cellular automata. Each distinct region corresponds to a disjoint part of the network, with the area of the region being proportional to the number of nodes involved. The dark blobs represent cycles. (See page 1087.)

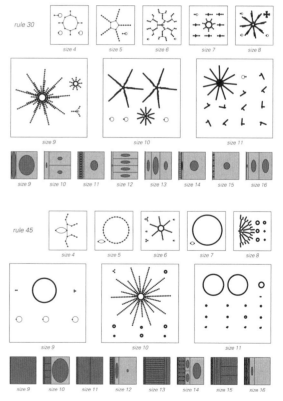

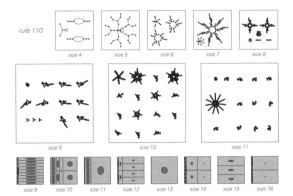

rule 110

size 4	size 5	size 6	size 7	size 8

size 9	size 10	size 11

size 9	size 10	size 11	size 12	size 13	size 14	size 15	size 16

For large sizes there is a rough correspondence with the infinite size case, but many features are still different. (To recover correct infinite size results one must increase size while keeping the number of steps of evolution fixed; the networks shown above, however, effectively depend on arbitrarily many steps of evolution.)

■ **Symmetries.** Many of the networks above contain large numbers of identical pieces. Typically the reason is that the states in each piece are shifted copies of each other, and in such cases the number of pieces will be a divisor of n. (See page 950.) If the underlying cellular automaton rule exhibits an invariance—say under reflection in space or permutation of colors—this will also often lead to the presence of identical pieces in the final network, corresponding to cosets of the symmetry transformation.

■ **Shift rules.** The pictures below show networks obtained with rule 170, which just shifts every configuration one position to the left at each step. With any shift rule, all states lie on cycles, and the lengths of these cycles are the divisors of the size n. Every cycle corresponds in effect to a distinct necklace with n beads; with k colors the total number of these is

Apply[Plus, (EulerPhi[n/#] k# &)[Divisors[n]]]/n

The number of cycles of length exactly m is $s[m, k]/m$, where $s[m, k]$ is defined on page 950. For prime k, each cycle (except all 0's) corresponds to a term in the product Factor[x^{k^n-1} - 1, Modulus → k]. (See page 975.)

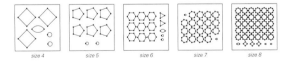

size 4	size 5	size 6	size 7	size 8

■ **Additive rules.** The pictures below show networks obtained for the additive cellular automata with rules 60 and 90. The networks are highly regular and can be

analyzed by the algebraic methods mentioned on page 951. The lengths of the longest cycles are given on page 951; all other cycles must have lengths which divide these. Rooted at every state on each cycle is an identical structure. When the number of cells n is odd this structure consists of a single arc, so that half of all states lie on cycles. When n is even, the structure is a balanced tree of depth $2^{IntegerExponent[n, 2]}$ and degree 2 for rule 60, and depth $2^{IntegerExponent[n/2, 2]}$ and degree 4 for rule 90. The total fraction of states on cycles is in both cases $2^{(-2^{IntegerExponent[n, 2]})}$. States with a single black cell are always on the longest cycles. The state with no black cells always forms a cycle of length 1.

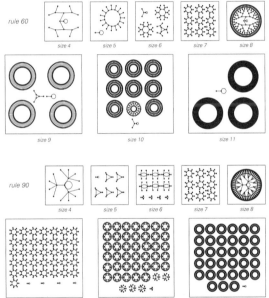

rule 60

size 4	size 5	size 6	size 7	size 8

size 9	size 10	size 11

rule 90

size 4	size 5	size 6	size 7	size 8

size 9	size 10	size 11

■ **Random networks.** The pictures below show networks in which each of a set of n nodes has as its successor a node that is chosen at random from the set. The total number of possible such networks is n^n. For large n, the average number of distinct cycles in all such networks is $Sqrt[\pi/2] Log[n]$, and the average length of these cycles is $Sqrt[\pi n/8]$. The average fraction of nodes that have no predecessor is $(1 - 1/n)^n$ or $1/e$ in the limit $n \to \infty$. Note that processes such as cellular automaton evolution do not yield networks whose properties are particularly close to those of purely random ones.

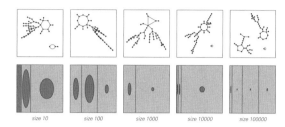

| size 10 | size 100 | size 1000 | size 10000 | size 100000 |

Structures in Class 4 Systems

■ **Page 283 · Survival data.** The number of steps for which the pattern produced by each of the first 1000 initial conditions in code 20 survive are indicated in the picture below. 72 of these initial conditions lead to persistent structures. Among the first million initial conditions, 60,171 lead to persistent structures and among the first billion initial conditions the number is 71,079,205.

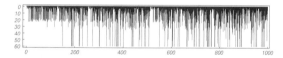

■ **Page 290 · Background.** At every step the background pattern in rule 110 consists of repetitions of the block $b = \{1, 0, 0, 1, 1, 0, 1, 1, 1, 1, 1, 0, 0, 0\}$, as shown in the picture below. On step t the color of a cell at position x is given by $b[\![Mod[x + 4t, 14] + 1]\!]$.

■ **Page 292 · Structures.** The persistent structures shown can be obtained from the following $\{n, w\}$ by inserting the sequences $IntegerDigits[n, 2, w]$ between repetitions of the background block b:

$\{\{152, 8\}, \{183, 8\}, \{18472955, 25\}, \{732, 10\}, \{129643, 18\}, \{0, 5\}, \{152, 13\}, \{39672, 21\}, \{619, 15\}, \{44, 7\}, \{334900605644, 39\}, \{8440, 15\}, \{248, 9\}, \{760, 11\}, \{38, 6\}\}$

The repetition periods and distances moved in each period for the structures are respectively

$\{\{4, -2\}, \{12, -6\}, \{12, -6\}, \{42, -14\}, \{42, -14\}, \{15, -4\}, \{15, -4\}, \{15, -4\}, \{15, -4\}, \{30, -8\}, \{92, -18\}, \{36, -4\}, \{7, 0\}, \{10, 2\}, \{3, 2\}\}$

Note that the periodicity of the background forces all rule 110 structures to have periods and distances given by $\{4, -2\}r + \{3, 2\}s$ where r and s are non-negative integers. Extended versions of structures (d)–(i) can be obtained by collisions with (a). Extended versions of (b) and (c) can be obtained from

$Flatten[\{IntegerDigits[1468, 2], Table[\ IntegerDigits[102524348, 2], \{n\}], IntegerDigits[v, 2]\}]$

where n is a non-negative integer and v is one of $\{1784, 801016, 410097400, 13304, 6406392, 3280778648\}$

Note that in most cases multiple copies of the same structure can travel next to each other, as seen on page 290.

■ **Page 293 · Glider gun.** The initial conditions shown correspond to $\{n, w\} = \{1339191737336, 41\}$.

■ **Page 294 · Collisions.** A fundamental result is that the sum of the widths of all persistent structures involved in an interaction must be conserved modulo 14.

■ **The Game of Life.** The 2D cellular automaton described on page 949 supports a whole range of persistent structures, many of which have been given quaint names by its enthusiasts. With typical random initial conditions the most common structures to occur are:

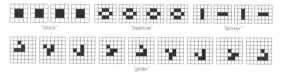

"block" *"beehive"* *"blinker"*

"glider"

The next most common moving structure is the so-called "spaceship":

The complete set of structures with less than 8 black cells that remain unchanged at every step in the evolution are:

More complicated repetitive and moving structures are shown in the pictures below. If one looks at the history of a single row of cells, it typically looks much like the complete histories we have seen in 1D class 4 cellular automata.

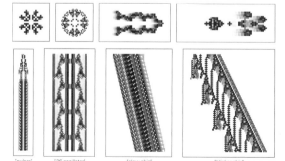

"pulsar" *"26 oscillator"* *"slow ship"* *"blinker ship"*

Structures with all repetition periods up to 18 have been found in Life; examples are shown in the pictures below.

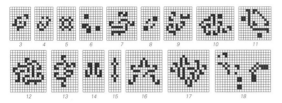

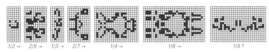

Persistent structures with various speeds in the horizontal and vertical direction have also been found, as shown below.

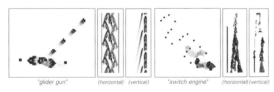

The first example of unbounded growth in Life was the so-called "glider gun", discovered by William Gosper in 1970 and shown below. This object emits a glider every 30 steps. The simplest known initial condition which leads to a glider gun contains 21 black cells. The so-called "switch engine" discovered in 1971 generates unbounded growth by leaving a trail behind when it moves; it is now known that it can be obtained from an initial condition with 10 black cells, or black cells in just a 5×5 or 39×1 region. It is also known that from less than 10 initial black cells no unbounded growth is ever possible.

"glider gun"   (horizontal) (vertical)   "switch engine"   (horizontal)(vertical)

Many more elaborate structures similar to the glider gun were found in the 1970s and 1980s; two are illustrated below.

"pulsar puffer"   "spaceship gun"

A simpler kind of unbounded growth occurs if one starts from an infinite line of black cells. In that case, the evolution is effectively 1D, and turns out to follow elementary rule 22, thus producing the infinitely growing nested pattern shown on page 263.

For a long time it was not clear whether Life would support any kind of uniform unbounded growth from a finite initial region of black cells. However, in 1993 David Bell found starting from 206 black cells the "spacefiller" shown below. This object is closely analogous to those shown for code 1329 on page 287.

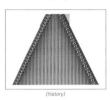

step 5   step 50   (history)

As in other class 4 cellular automata, there are structures in Life which take a very long time to settle down. The so-called "puffer train" below which starts from 23 black cells becomes repetitive with period 140 only after more than 1100 steps.

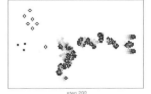

step 200   step 200   step 500

step 500

■ **Other 2D cellular automata.** The general problem of finding persistent structures is much more difficult in 2D than in 1D, and there is no completely general procedure, for example, for finding all structures of any size that have a certain repetition period.

■ **Structures in Turing machines.** See page 888.

Mechanisms in Programs and Nature

Universality of Behavior

■ **History.** That very different natural and artificial systems can show similar forms has been noted for many centuries. Informal studies have been done by a whole sequence of architects interested both in codifying possible forms and in finding ways to make structures fit in with nature and with our perception of it. Beginning in the Renaissance the point has also been noted by representational and decorative artists, most often in the context of developing a theory of the types of forms to be studied by students of art. The growth of comparative anatomy in the 1800s led to attempts at more scientific treatments, with analogies between biological and physical systems being emphasized particularly by D'Arcy Thompson in 1917. Yet despite all this, the phenomenon of similarity between forms remained largely a curiosity, discussed mainly in illustrated books with no clear basis in either art or science. In a few cases (such as work by Peter Stevens in 1974) general themes were however suggested. These included for example symmetry, the golden ratio, spirals, vortices, minimal surfaces, branching patterns, and—since the 1980s—fractals. The suggestion is also sometimes made that we perceive a kind of harmony in nature because we see only a limited number of types of forms in it. And particularly in classical architecture the idea is almost universally used that structures will seem more comfortable to us if they repeat in ornament or otherwise forms with which we have become familiar from nature. Whenever a scientific model has the same character for different systems this means that the systems will tend to show similar forms. And as models like cellular automata capable of dealing with complexity have become more widespread it has been increasingly popular to show that they can capture similar forms seen in very different systems.

Three Mechanisms for Randomness

■ **Page 299 · Definition.** How randomness can be defined is discussed at length on page 552.

■ **History.** In antiquity, it was often assumed that all events must be governed by deterministic fate—with any apparent randomness being the result of arbitrariness on the part of the gods. Around 330 BC Aristotle mentioned that instead randomness might just be associated with coincidences outside whatever system one is looking at, while around 300 BC Epicurus suggested that there might be randomness continually injected into the motion of all atoms. The rise of emphasis on human free will (see page 1135) eroded belief in determinism, but did not especially address issues of randomness. By the 1700s the success of Newtonian physics seemed again to establish a form of determinism, and led to the assumption that whatever randomness was actually seen must reflect lack of knowledge on the part of the observer— or particularly in astronomy some form of error of measurement. The presence of apparent randomness in digit sequences of square roots, logarithms, numbers like π, and other mathematical constructs was presumably noticed by the 1600s (see page 911), and by the late 1800s it was being taken for granted. But the significance of this for randomness in nature was never recognized. In the late 1800s and early 1900s attempts to justify both statistical mechanics and probability theory led to ideas that perfect microscopic randomness might somehow be a fundamental feature of the physical world. And particularly with the rise of quantum mechanics it came to be thought that meaningful calculations could be done only on probabilities, not on individual random sequences. Indeed, in almost every area where quantitative methods were used, if randomness was observed, then either a different system was studied, or efforts were made to remove the randomness by averaging or some other statistical method. One case where there was occasional discussion of origins of randomness from at least the early 1900s was fluid turbulence (see page 997). Early theories tended to concentrate on superpositions of repetitive motions, but by the 1970s ideas of chaos theory began to dominate. And in fact the widespread assumption emerged that between randomness in the environment, quantum randomness and chaos theory almost any observed randomness in nature could be accounted for. Traditional mathematical models of natural systems are often expressed in terms of probabilities, but do not normally involve anything one can explicitly consider as randomness. Models used in computer simulations, however, do very often use explicit randomness. For not knowing about the phenomenon of intrinsic randomness generation, it has normally been assumed that with the kinds of discrete elements and fairly simple rules common in such models, realistically complicated behavior can only ever be obtained if explicit randomness is continually introduced.

■ **Applications of randomness.** See page 1192.

■ **Sources of randomness.** Two simple mechanical methods for generating randomness seem to have been used in almost every civilization throughout recorded history. One is to toss an object and see which way up or where it lands; the other is to select an object from a collection mixed by shaking. The first method has been common in games of chance, with polyhedral dice already existing in 2750 BC. The second—often called drawing lots—has normally been used when there is more at stake. It is mentioned several times in the Bible, and even today remains the most common method for large lotteries. (See page 969.) Variants include methods such as drawing straws. In antiquity fortune-telling from randomness often involved looking say at growth patterns of goat entrails or sheep shoulder blades; today configurations of tea leaves are sometimes considered. In early modern times the matching of fracture patterns in broken tally sticks was used to identify counterparties in financial contracts. Horse races and other events used as a basis for gambling can be viewed as randomness sources. Children's games like musical chairs in effect generate randomness by picking arbitrary stopping times. Games of chance based on wheels seem to have existed in Roman times; roulette developed in the 1700s. Card shuffling (see page 974) has been used as a source of randomness since at least the 1300s. Pegboards (as on page 312) were used to demonstrate effects of randomness in the late 1800s. An explicit table of 40,000 random digits was created in 1927 by Leonard Tippett from details of census data. And in 1938 further tables were generated by Ronald Fisher from digits of logarithms. Several tables based on physical processes were produced, with the RAND Corporation in 1955 publishing a table of a million random

digits obtained from an electronic roulette wheel. Beginning in the 1950s, however, it became increasingly common to use pseudorandom generators whenever long sequences were needed—with linear feedback shift registers being most popular in standalone electronic devices, and linear congruential generators in programs (see page 974). There nevertheless continued to be occasional work done on mechanical sources of randomness for toys and games, and on physical electronic sources for cryptography systems (see page 969).

Randomness from the Environment

■ **Page 301 · Stochastic models.** The mechanism for randomness discussed in this section is the basis for so-called stochastic models now widely used in traditional science. Typically the idea of these models is to approximate those elements of a system about which one does not know much by random variables. (See also page 588.) In the early work along these lines done by James Clerk Maxwell and others in the 1880s, analytical formulas were usually worked out for the probabilities of different outcomes. But when electronic computers became available in the 1940s, the so-called Monte Carlo method became increasingly popular, in which instead explicit simulations are performed with different choices of random variables, and then statistical averages are found. Early uses of the Monte Carlo method were mostly in physics, particularly for studies of neutron diffusion and particle shower generation in high-energy collisions. But by the 1980s the Monte Carlo method had also become common in other fields, and was routinely used in studying for example message flows in communication networks and pricing processes in financial markets. (See also page 1192.)

■ **Page 301 · Ocean surfaces.** See page 1001.

■ **Page 302 · Random walks.** See page 328.

■ **Page 302 · Electronic noise.** Three types of noise are commonly observed in typical devices:

Shot noise. Electric currents are not continuous but are ultimately made up from large numbers of moving charge carriers, typically electrons. Shot noise arises from statistical fluctuations in the flow of charge carriers: if a single bit of data is represented by 10,000 electrons, the magnitude of the fluctuations will typically be about 1%. When looked at as a waveform over time, shot noise has a flat frequency spectrum.

Thermal (Johnson) noise. Even though an electric current may have a definite overall direction, the individual charge carriers within it will exhibit random motions. In a material at nonzero temperature, the energy of these motions and thus the intensity of the thermal noise they produce is essentially proportional to temperature. (At very low temperatures, quantum mechanical fluctuations still yield random motion in most materials.) Like shot noise, thermal noise has a flat frequency spectrum.

Flicker (1/f) noise. Almost all electronic devices also exhibit a third kind of noise, whose main characteristic is that its spectrum is not flat, but instead goes roughly like *1/f* over a wide range of frequencies. Such a spectrum implies the presence of large low-frequency fluctuations, and indeed fluctuations are often seen over timescales of many minutes or even hours. Unlike the types of noise described above, this kind of noise can be affected by details of the construction of individual devices. Although seen since the 1920s its origins remain somewhat mysterious (see below).

■ **Power spectra.** Many random processes in nature show power spectra $Abs[Fourier[data]]^2$ with fairly simple forms. Most common are white noise uniform in frequency and $1/f^2$ noise associated with random walks. Other pure power laws $1/f^\alpha$ are also sometimes seen; the pictures below show some examples. (Note that the correlations in such data in some sense go like $t^{\alpha-1}$.) Particularly over the past few decades all sorts of examples of "$1/f$ noise" have been identified with $\alpha \simeq 1$, including flicker noise in resistors, semiconductor devices and vacuum tubes, as well as thunderstorms, earthquake and sunspot activity, heartbeat intervals, road traffic density and some DNA sequences. A pure $1/f^\alpha$ spectrum presumably reflects some form of underlying nesting or self-similarity, although exactly what has usually been difficult to determine. Mechanisms that generally seem able to give $\alpha \simeq 1$ include random walks with exponential waiting times, power-law distributions of step sizes (Lévy flights), or white noise variations of parameters, as well as random processes with exponentially distributed relaxation times (as from Boltzmann factors for uniformly distributed barrier heights), fractional integration of white noise, intermittency at transitions to chaos, and random substitution systems. (There was confusion in the late 1980s when theoretical studies of self-organized criticality failed correctly to take squares in computing power spectra.) Note that the Weierstrass function of page 918 yields a $1/f$ spectrum, and presumably suitable averages of spectra from any substitution system should also have $1/f^\alpha$ forms (compare page 586).

1 $1/f^{1/2}$ $1/f$ $1/f^{3/2}$ $1/f^2$

■ **Page 303 · Spark chambers.** The sensitivity of sparks to microscopic details of the environment is highlighted by the several devices which essentially use them to detect the passage of individual elementary particles such as protons. Such particles leave a tiny trail of ionized gas, which becomes the path of the spark. This principle was used in Geiger counters, and later in spark chambers and wire chambers.

■ **Physical randomness generators.** It is almost universally assumed that at some level physical processes must be the best potential sources of true randomness. But in practice their record has actually been very poor. It does not help that unlike algorithms physical devices can be affected by their environment, and can also not normally be copied identically. But in almost every case I know where detailed analysis has been done substantial deviations from perfect randomness have been found. This has however typically been attributed to engineering mistakes—or to sampling data too quickly—and not to anything more fundamental that is for example worth describing in publications.

■ **Mechanical randomness.** It takes only small imperfections in dice or roulette wheels to get substantially non-random results (see page 971). Gaming regulations typically require dice to be perfect cubes to within one part in a few thousand; casinos normally retire dice after a few hundred rolls.

In processes like stirring and shaking it can take a long time for correlations to disappear—as in the phenomenon of long-time tails mentioned on page 999. One notable consequence were traces of insertion order among the 366 capsules used in the 1970 draft lottery in the U.S. But despite such problems mixing of objects remains by far the most common way to generate randomness when there is a desire for the public to see randomization occur. And so for example all the state lotteries in the U.S. are currently based on mixing between 10 and 54 balls. (Numbers games were instead sometimes based on digits of financial data in newspapers.)

There have been a steady stream of inventions for mechanical randomness generation. Some are essentially versions of dice. Others involve complicated cams or linkages, particularly for mechanical toys. And still others involve making objects like balls bounce around as randomly as possible in air or other fluids.

■ **Electronic randomness.** Since the 1940s a steady stream of electronic devices for producing randomness have been invented, with no single one ever becoming widely used. An early example was the ERNIE machine from 1957 for British national lottery (premium bond) drawings, which worked by sampling shot noise from neon discharge tubes—and perhaps because it extracted only a few digits per second no deviations from randomness in its output were found. (U.S. missiles apparently used a similar method to produce randomly spaced radar pulses for determining altitude.) Since the 1970s electronic randomness generators have typically been based on features of semiconductor devices—sometimes thermal noise, but more often breakdown, often in back-biased zener diodes. All sorts of schemes have been invented for getting unbiased output from such systems, and acceptable randomness can often be obtained at kilohertz rates, but obvious correlations almost always appear at higher rates. Macroscopic thermal diffusion undoubtedly underestimates the time for good microscopic randomization. For in addition to *1/f* noise effects, solitons and other collective lattice effects presumably lead to power-law decay of correlations. It still seems likely however that some general inequalities should exist between the rate and quality of randomness that can be extracted from a system with particular thermodynamic properties.

▪ **Quantum randomness.** It is usually assumed that even if all else fails a quantum process such as radioactive decay will yield perfect randomness. But in practice the most accurate measurements show phenomena such as *1/f* noise, presumably as a result of features of the detector and perhaps of electromagnetic fields associated with decay products. Acceptable randomness has however been obtained at rates of tens of bits per second. Recent attempts have also been made to produce quantum randomness at megahertz rates by detecting paths of single photons. (See also page 1064.)

▪ **Randomness in computer systems.** Most randomness needed in practical computer systems is generated purely by programs, as discussed on page 317. But to avoid having a particular program give exactly the same random sequence every time it is run, one usually starts from a seed chosen on the basis of some random feature of the environment. Until the early 1990s this seed was most often taken from the exact time of day indicated by the computer's clock at the moment when it was requested. But particularly in environments where multiple programs can start almost simultaneously other approaches became necessary. Versions of the Unix operating system, for example, began to support a virtual device (typically called /dev/random) to maintain a kind of pool of randomness based on details of the computer system. Most often this uses precise timings between interrupts generated by keys being pressed, a mouse being moved, or data being delivered from a disk, network, or other device. And to prevent the same state being reached every time a computer is

rebooted, some information is permanently maintained in a file. At the end of the 1990s standard microprocessors also began to include instructions to sample thermal noise from an on-chip resistor. (Any password or encryption key made up by a human can be thought of as a source of randomness; some systems look at details of biometric data, or scribbles drawn with a mouse.)

▪ **Randomness in biology.** Thermal fluctuations in chemical reactions lead to many kinds of microscopic randomness in biological systems, sometimes amplified when organisms grow. For example, small-scale randomness in embryos can affect large-scale pigmentation patterns in adult organisms, as discussed on page 1013. Random changes in single DNA molecules can have global effects on the development of an organism. Standard mitotic cell division normally produces identical copies of DNA—with random errors potentially leading for example to cancers. But in sexual reproduction genetic material is rearranged in ways normally assumed by classical genetics to be perfectly random. One reason is that which sperm fertilizes a given egg is determined by random details of sperm and fluid motion. Another reason is that egg and sperm cells get half the genetic material of an organism, somewhat at random. In most cells, say in humans, there are two versions of all 23 chromosomes—one from the father and one from the mother. But when meiosis forms egg and sperm cells they get only one version of each. There is also exchange of DNA between paternal and maternal chromosomes, typically with a few crossovers per chromosome, at positions that seem more or less randomly distributed among many possibilities (the details affect regions of repeating DNA used for example in DNA fingerprinting).

In the immune system blocks of DNA—and joins between them—are selected at random by microscopic chemical processes when antibodies are formed.

Most animal behavior is ultimately controlled by electrical activity in nerve cells—and this can be affected by details of sensory input, as well as by microscopic chemical processes in individual cells and synapses (see page 1011).

Flagellated microorganisms can show random changes in direction as a result of tumbling when their flagella counter-rotate and the filaments in them flail around.

(See also page 1011.)

Chaos Theory and Randomness from Initial Conditions

▪ **Page 305 · Spinning and tossing.** Starting with speed v, the speed of the ball at time t is simply $v - at$, where a is the deceleration produced by friction. The ball thus stops at time

v/a. The distance gone by the ball at a given time is $x = v\,t - a\,t^2/2$, and its orientation is $Mod[x, 2\,\pi\,r]$. For dice and coins there are some additional detailed effects associated with the shapes of these objects and the way they bounce. (Polyhedral dice have become more common since Dungeons & Dragons became popular in the late 1970s.) Note that in practice a coin tossed in the air will typically turn over between ten and twenty times while a die rolled on a table will turn over a few tens of times. A coin spun on a table can rotate several hundred times before falling over and coming to rest.

■ **Billiards.** A somewhat related system is formed by a billiard ball bouncing around on a table. The issue of which sequence of horizontal and vertical sides the ball hits depends on the exact slope with which the ball is started (in the picture below it is $1/\sqrt{2}$). In general, it is given by the successive terms in the continued fraction form (see page 914) of this slope, and is related to substitution systems (see page 903). (See also page 1022.)

2 bounces   5 bounces   10 bounces   50 bounces   100 bounces

■ **Fluttering.** If one releases a stationary piece of paper in air, then unlike a coin, it does not typically maintain the same orientation as it falls. Small pieces of paper spin in a repetitive way; but larger pieces of paper tend to flutter in a seemingly random way (as discussed, among others, by James Clerk Maxwell in 1853). A similar phenomenon can be seen if one drops a coin in water. I suspect that in these cases the randomness that occurs has an intrinsic origin, rather than being the result of sensitive dependence on initial conditions.

■ **History of chaos theory.** The idea that small causes can sometimes have large effects has been noted by historians and others since antiquity, and captured for example in "for want of a nail … a kingdom was lost". In 1860 James Clerk Maxwell discussed how collisions between hard sphere molecules could lead to progressive amplification of small changes and yield microscopic randomness in gases. In the 1870s Maxwell also suggested that mechanical instability and amplification of infinitely small changes at occasional critical points might explain apparent free will (see page 1135). (It was already fairly well understood that for example small changes could determine which way a beam would buckle.) In 1890 Henri Poincaré found sensitive dependence on initial conditions in a particular case of the

three-body problem (see below), and later proposed that such phenomena could be common, say in meteorology. In 1898 Jacques Hadamard noted general divergence of trajectories in spaces of negative curvature, and Pierre Duhem discussed the possible general significance of this in 1908. In the 1800s there had been work on nonlinear oscillators—particularly in connection with models of musical instruments—and in 1927 Balthazar van der Pol noted occasional "noisy" behavior in a vacuum tube oscillator circuit presumably governed by a simple nonlinear differential equation. By the 1930s the field of dynamical systems theory had begun to provide characterizations of possible forms of behavior in differential equations. And in the early 1940s Mary Cartwright and John Littlewood noted that van der Pol's equation could exhibit solutions somehow sensitive to all digits in its initial conditions. The iterated map $x \to 4\,x\,(1 - x)$ was also known to have a similar property (see page 918). But most investigations centered on simple and usually repetitive behavior—with any strange behavior implicitly assumed to be infinitely unlikely. In 1962, however, Edward Lorenz did a computer simulation of a set of simplified differential equations for fluid convection (see page 998) in which he saw complicated behavior that seemed to depend sensitively on initial conditions—in a way that he suggested was like the map $x \to FractionalPart[2\,x]$. In the mid-1960s, notably through the work of Steve Smale, proofs were given that there could be differential equations in which such sensitivity is generic. In the late 1960s there began to be all sorts of simulations of differential equations with complicated behavior, first mainly on analog computers, and later on digital computers. Then in the mid-1970s, particularly following discussion by Robert May, studies of iterated maps with sensitive dependence on initial conditions became common. Work by Robert Shaw in the late 1970s clarified connections between information content of initial conditions and apparent randomness of behavior. The term "chaos" had been used since antiquity to describe various forms of randomness, but in the late 1970s it became specifically tied to the phenomenon of sensitive dependence on initial conditions. By the early 1980s at least indirect signs of chaos in this sense (see note below) had been seen in all sorts of mechanical, electrical, fluid and other systems, and there emerged a widespread conviction that such chaos must be the source of all important randomness in nature. So in 1985 when I raised the possibility that intrinsic randomness might instead be a key phenomenon this was greeted with much hostility by some younger proponents of chaos theory. Insofar as what they had to say was of a scientific nature, their main point was that somehow what I had seen in cellular automata must be specific to discrete systems, and would not occur in the continuous systems assumed to be relevant in nature. But from many results in this book it is now clear that this is not correct. (Note that James Gleick's 1987 popular book *Chaos* covers somewhat more than is usually considered chaos theory—including some of my results on cellular automata from the early 1980s.)

■ **Information content of initial conditions.** See page 920.

■ **Recognizing chaos.** Any system that depends sensitively on digits in its initial conditions must necessarily be able to show behavior that is not purely repetitive (compare page 955). And when it is said that chaos has been found in a particular system in nature what this most often actually means is just that behavior with no specific repetition frequency has been seen (compare page 586). To give evidence that this is not merely a reflection of continual injection of randomness from the environment what is normally done is to show that at least some aspect of the behavior of the system can be fit by a definite simple iterated map or differential equation. But inevitably the fit will only be approximate, so there will always be room for effects from randomness in the environment. And in general this kind of approach can never establish that sensitive dependence on initial conditions is actually the dominant source of randomness in a given system—say as opposed to intrinsic randomness generation. (Attempts are sometimes made to detect sensitive dependence directly by watching whether a system can do different things after it appears to return to almost exactly the same state. But the problem is that it is hard to be sure that the system really is in the same state—and that there are not all sorts of large differences that do not happen to have been observed.)

■ **Instability.** Sensitive dependence on initial conditions is associated with a kind of uniform instability in systems. But vastly more common in practice is instability only at specific critical points—say bifurcation points—combined with either intrinsic randomness generation or randomness from the environment. (Note that despite its widespread use in discussions of chaos theory, this is also what usually seems to happen with the weather; see page 1177.)

■ **Page 313 · Three-body problem.** The two-body problem was analyzed by Johannes Kepler in 1609 and solved by Isaac Newton in 1687. The three-body problem was a central topic in mathematical physics from the mid-1700s until the early 1900s. Various exact results were obtained—notably the existence of stable equilateral triangle configurations corresponding to so-called Lagrange points. Many

approximate practical calculations, particularly on the Earth-Moon-Sun system, were done using series expansions involving thousands of algebraic terms. (It is now possible to get most results just by direct numerical computation using for example *NDSolve*.) From its basic setup the three-body system conserves standard mechanical quantities like energy and angular momentum. But it was thought it might also conserve other quantities (or so-called integrals of the motion). In 1887, however, Heinrich Bruns showed that there could be no such quantities expressible as algebraic functions of the positions and velocities of the bodies (in standard Cartesian coordinates). In the mid-1890s Henri Poincaré then showed that there could also be no such quantities analytic in positions, velocities and mass ratios. And from these results the conclusion was drawn that the three-body problem could not be solved in terms of algebraic formulas and integrals. In 1912 Karl Sundman did however find an infinite series that could in principle be summed to give the solution—but which converges exceptionally slowly. And even now it remains conceivable that the three-body problem could be solved in terms of more sophisticated standard mathematical functions. But I strongly suspect that in fact nothing like this will ever be possible and that instead the three-body problem will turn out to show the phenomenon of computational irreducibility discussed in Chapter 12 (and that for example three-body systems are universal and in effect able to perform any computation). (See also page 1132.)

In Henri Poincaré's study of the collection of possible trajectories for three-body systems he identified sensitive dependence on initial conditions (see above), noted the general complexity of what could happen (particularly in connection with so-called homoclinic tangles), and developed topology to provide a simpler overall description. With appropriate initial conditions one can get various forms of simple behavior. The pictures below show some of the possible repetitive orbits of an idealized planet moving in the plane of a pair of stars that are in a perfect elliptical orbit.

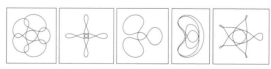

The pictures below show results for a fairly typical sequence of initial conditions where all three bodies interact. (The two bodies at the bottom are initially at rest; the body at the top is given progressively larger rightward velocities.) What generically happens is that one of the bodies escapes from the other two (like t or sometimes $t^{2/3}$). Often this happens quickly, but sometimes all three bodies show complex and apparently random behavior for quite a while. (The delay before escaping is reminiscent of resonant scattering.)

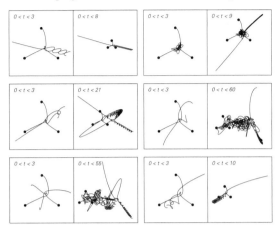

■ **Page 314 · Simple case.** The position of the idealized planet in the case shown satisfies the differential equation

$$\partial_{tt} z[t] == -z[t]/(z[t]^2 + (1/2\,(1 + e\,Sin[2\,\pi\,t]))^2)^{3/2}$$

where e is the eccentricity of the elliptical orbit of the stars ($e = 0.1$ in the picture). (Note that the physical situation is unstable: if the planet is perturbed so that there is a difference between its distance to each star, this will tend to increase.) Except when $e = 0$, the equation has no solution in terms of standard mathematical functions. It can be solved numerically in *Mathematica* using *NDSolve*, although a working precision of 40 decimal digits was used to obtain the results shown. Following work by Kirill Sitnikov in 1960 and by Vladimir Alekseev in 1968, it was established that with suitably chosen initial conditions, the equation yields any sequence $Floor[t[i + 1] - t[i]]$ of successive zero-crossing times $t[i]$. The pictures below show the dependence of $z[t]$ on t and $z[0]$. As t increases, $z[t]$ typically begins to vary more rapidly with $z[0]$—reflecting sensitive dependence on initial conditions.

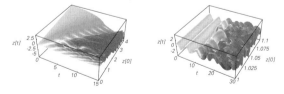

■ **Page 314 · Randomness in the solar system.** Most motion observed in the solar system on human timescales is highly regular—though sometimes intricate, as in the sequence of numbers of days between successive new moons shown

below. In the mid-1980s, however, work by Jack Wisdom and others established that randomness associated with sensitive dependence on initial conditions could occur in certain current situations in the solar system, notably in the orbits of asteroids. Various calculations suggest that there should also be sensitive dependence on initial conditions in the orbits of planets in the solar system—with effects doubling every few million years. But there are so far no observational signs of randomness resulting from this, and indeed the planets—at least now—mostly just seem to have orbits that are within a few percent of circles. If a planet moved in too random a way then it would tend to collide or escape from the solar system. And indeed it seems quite likely that in the past there may have been significantly more planets in our solar system—with only those that maintained regular orbits now being left. (See also page 1021.)

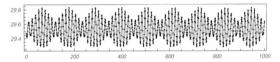

The Intrinsic Generation of Randomness

■ **Autoplectic processes.** In the 1985 paper where I introduced intrinsic randomness generation I called processes that show this autoplectic, while I called processes that transcribe randomness from outside homoplectic.

■ **Page 316 · Algorithmic randomness.** The idea of there being no simple procedure that can generate a particular sequence can be stated more precisely by saying that there is no program shorter than the sequence itself which can be used to generate the sequence, as discussed in more detail on page 1067.

■ **Page 317 · Randomness in *Mathematica*.** *SeedRandom[n]* is the function that sets up the initial conditions for the cellular automaton. The idea of using this kind of system in general and this system in particular as a source of randomness was described in my 1987 U.S. patent number 4,691,291.

■ **Page 321 · Cellular automata.** From the discussion here it should not be thought that in general there is necessarily anything better about generating randomness with cellular automata than with systems based on numbers. But the point is that the specific method used for making practical linear congruential generators does not yield particularly good randomness and has led to some incorrect intuition about the generation of randomness. If one goes beyond the specifics of linear congruential generators, then one can find many features of systems based on numbers that seem to be perfectly random, as discussed in Chapter 4. In addition, one should recognize that while the complete evolution of the cellular automaton may effectively generate perfect randomness, there may be deviations from randomness introduced when one constructs a practical random number generator with a limited number of cells. Nevertheless, no such deviations have so far been found except when one looks at sequences whose lengths are close to the repetition period. (See however page 603.)

■ **Page 321 · Card shuffling.** Another rather poor example of intrinsic randomness generation is perfect card shuffling. In a typical case, one splits the deck of cards in two, then carefully riffles the cards so as to make alternate cards come from each part of the deck. Surprisingly enough, this simple procedure, which can be represented by the function

```
s[list_] := Flatten[
    Transpose[Reverse[Partition[list, Length[list]/2]]]]
```

with or without the *Reverse*, is able to produce orderings which at least in some respects seem quite random. But by doing *Nest[s, Range[52], 26]* one ends up with a simple reversal of the original deck, as in the pictures below.

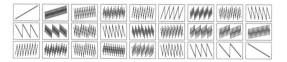

■ **Random number generators.** A fairly small number of different types of random number generators have been used in practice, so it is possible to describe all the major ones here.

Linear congruential generators. The original suggestion made by Derrick Lehmer in 1948 was to take a number n and at each step to replace it by $Mod[a\,n, m]$. Lehmer used $a = 23$ and $m = 10^8 + 1$. Most subsequent implementations have used $m = 2^j$, often with $j = 31$. Such choices are particularly convenient on computers where machine integers are represented by 32 binary digits. The behavior of the linear congruential generator depends greatly on the exact choice of a. Starting with the so-called RANDU generator used on mainframe computers in the 1960s, a common choice made was $a = 65539$. But as shown in the main text, this choice leads to embarrassingly obvious regularities. Starting in the mid-1970s, another common choice was $a = 69069$. This was also found to lead to regularities, but only in six or more dimensions. (Small values of a also lead to an excess of runs of identical digits, as mentioned on page 903.)

The repetition period for a generator with rule $n \to Mod[a\,n, m]$ is given (for a and m relatively prime) by *MultiplicativeOrder[a, m]*. If m is of the form 2^j, this implies a maximum period for any a of $m/4$, achieved when *MemberQ[{3, 5}, Mod[a, 8]]*. In general the maximum period is *CarmichaelLambda[m]*, where the value $m - 1$ can be achieved for prime m.

As illustrated in the main text, when $m = 2^j$ the right-hand base 2 digits in numbers produced by linear congruential generators repeat with short periods; a digit k positions from the right will typically repeat with period no more than 2^k. When $m = 2^j - 1$ is prime, however, even the rightmost digit repeats only with period $m - 1$ for many values of a.

More general linear congruential generators use the basic rule $n \to Mod[a\,n + b, m]$, and in this case, $n = 0$ is no longer special, and a repetition period of exactly m can be achieved with appropriate choices of a, b and m. Note that if the period is equal to its absolute maximum of m, then every possible n is always visited, whatever n one starts from. Page 962 showed diagrams that represent the evolution for all possible starting values of n.

Each point in the 2D plots in the main text has coordinates of the form $\{n[i], n[i + 1]\}$ where $n[i + 1] = Mod[a\,n[i], m]$. If one could ignore the *Mod*, then the coordinates would simply be $\{n[i], a\,n[i]\}$, so the points would lie on a single straight line with slope a. But the presence of the *Mod* takes the points off this line whenever $a\,n[i] \geq m$. Nevertheless, if a is small, there are long runs of $n[i]$ for which the *Mod* is never important. And that is why in the case $a = 3$ the points in the plot fall on obvious lines.

In the case $a = 65539$, the points lie on planes in 3D. The reason for this is that

$$n[i + 2] == Mod[65539^2\,n[i], 2^{31}] ==$$
$$Mod[6\,n[i + 1] - 9\,n[i], 2^{31}]$$

so that in computing $n[i + 2]$ from $n[i + 1]$ and $n[i]$ only small coefficients are involved.

It is a general result related to finding short vectors in lattices that for some d the quantity $n[i + d]$ can always be written in terms of the $n[i + k]\,/; k < d$ using only small coefficients. And as a consequence, the points produced by any linear congruential generator must lie on regular hyperplanes in some number of dimensions.

(For cryptanalysis of linear congruential generators see page 1089.)

Linear feedback shift registers. Used since the 1950s, particularly in special-purpose electronic devices, these systems are effectively based on running additive cellular automata such as rule 60 in registers with a limited number of cells and with a certain type of spiral boundary conditions. In a typical case, each cell is updated using

    LFSRStep[list_] :=
      Append[Rest[list], Mod[list⟦1⟧ + list⟦2⟧, 2]]

with a step of cellular automaton evolution corresponding to the result of updating all cells in the register. As with additive cellular automata, the behavior obtained depends greatly on the length n of the register. The maximal repetition period of $2^n - 1$ can be achieved only if *Factor[1 + x + x^n, Modulus → 2]* finds no factors. (For $n < 512$, this is true when $n = 1, 2, 3, 4, 6, 7, 9, 15, 22, 28, 30, 46, 60, 63, 127, 153, 172, 303$ or 471. Maximal period is assured when in addition *PrimeQ[$2^n - 1$].*) The pictures below show the evolution obtained for $n = 30$ with

    NestList[Nest[LFSRStep, #, n] &,
      Append[Table[0, {n - 1}], 1], t]

Like additive cellular automata as discussed on page 951, states in a linear feedback shift register can be represented by a polynomial *FromDigits[list, x]*. Starting from a single 1, the state after t steps is then given by

    PolynomialMod[x^t, {1 + x + x^n, 2}]

This result illustrates the analogy with linear congruential generators. And if the distribution of points generated is studied with the Cantor set geometry, the same kind of problems occur as in the linear congruential case (compare page 1094).

In general, linear feedback shift registers can have "taps" at any list of positions on the register, so that their evolution is given by

    LFSRStep[taps_List, list_] :=
      Append[Rest[list], Mod[Apply[Plus, list⟦taps⟧], 2]]

(With taps specified by the positions of 1's in a vector of 0's, the inside of the *Mod* can be replaced by *vec . list* as on page 1087.) For a register of size n the maximal period of $2^n - 1$ is obtained whenever $x^n + Apply[Plus, x^{taps-1}]$ is one of the *EulerPhi[$2^n - 1$]/n* primitive polynomials that appear in *Factor[Cyclotomic[$2^n - 1$, x], Modulus → 2].* (See pages 963 and 1084.)

One can also consider nonlinear feedback shift registers, as discussed on page 1088.

Generalized Fibonacci generators. It was suggested in the late 1950s that the Fibonacci sequence $f[n_] := f[n-1] + f[n-2]$

modulo 2^k might be used with different choices of $f[0]$ and $f[1]$ as a random number generator (see page 891). This particular idea did not work well, but generalizations based on the recurrence $f[n_] := Mod[f[n-p] + f[n-q], 2^k]$ have been studied extensively, for example with $p = 24$, $q = 55$. Such generators are directly related to linear feedback shift registers, since with a list of length q, each step is simply

    Append[Rest[list], Mod[list⟦1⟧ + list⟦q - p + 1⟧, 2^k]]

Cryptographic generators. As discussed on page 598, so-called stream cipher cryptographic systems work essentially by generating a repeatable random sequence. Practical stream cipher systems can thus be used as random number generators. Starting in the 1980s, the most common example has been the Data Encryption Standard (DES) introduced by the U.S. government (see page 1085). Unless special-purpose hardware is used, however, this method has not usually been efficient enough for practical random number generation applications.

Quadratic congruential generators. Several generalizations of linear congruential generators have been considered in which nonlinear functions of n are used at each step. In fact, the first known generator for digital computers was John von Neumann's "middle square method"

    $n → FromDigits[Take[IntegerDigits[n^2, 10, 20], {5, 15}], 10]$

In practice this generator has too short a repetition period to be useful. But in the early 1980s studies of public key cryptographic systems based on number theoretical problems led to some reinvestigation of quadratic congruential generators. The simplest example uses the rule

    $n → Mod[n^2, m]$

It was shown that for $m = pq$ with p and q prime the sequence $Mod[n, 2]$ was in a sense as difficult to predict as the number m is to factor (see page 1090). But in practice, the period of the generator in such cases is usually too short to be useful. In addition, there has been the practical problem that if n is stored on a computer as a 32-bit number, then n^2 can be 64 bits long, and so cannot be stored in the same way. In general, the period divides *CarmichaelLambda[CarmichaelLambda[m]]*. When m is a prime, this implies that the period can then be as long as $(m - 3)/2$. The largest m less than 2^{16} for which this is true is 65063, and the sequence generated in this case appears to be fairly random.

Cellular automaton generators. I invented the rule 30 cellular automaton random number generator in 1985. Since that time the generator has become quite widely used for a variety of applications. Essentially all the other generators discussed here have certain linearity properties which allow for fairly complete analysis using traditional mathematical methods. Rule 30 has no such properties. Empirical studies, however, suggest that the repetition period, for example, is about $2^{0.63 n}$, where n is the number of cells (see page 260). Note that rule 45 can be used as an alternative to rule 30. It has a somewhat longer period, but does not mix up nearby initial conditions as quickly as rule 30. (See also page 603.)

■ **Unequal probabilities.** Given a sequence a of n equally probable 0's and 1's, the following generates a single 0 or 1 with probabilities approximating $\{1-p, p\}$ to n digits:

Fold[{BitAnd, BitOr}[[1 + First[#2]]][#1, Last[#2]] &, 0,
    Reverse[Transpose[{First[RealDigits[p, 2, n, -1]], a}]]]

This can be generalized to allow a whole sequence to be generated with as little as an average of two input digits being used for each output digit.

■ **Page 323 · Sources of repeatable randomness.** In using repeatability to test for intrinsic randomness generation, one must avoid systems in which there is essentially some kind of static randomness in the environment. Sources of this include the profile of a rough solid surface, or the detailed patterns of grains inside a solid.

■ **Page 324 · Probabilistic rules.** There appears to be a discrete transition as a function of the size of the perturbations, similar to phase transitions seen in the phenomenon of directed percolation. Note that if one just uses the original cellular automata rules, then with any nonzero probability of reversing the colors of cells, the patterns will be essentially destroyed. With more complicated cellular automaton rules, one can get behavior closer to the continuous cellular automata shown here. (See also page 591.)

■ **Page 325 · Noisy cellular automata.** In correspondence with electronics, the continuous cellular automata used here can be thought of as analog models for digital cellular automata. The specific form of the continuous generalization of the modulo 2 function used is

$\lambda[x\_] := Exp[-10(x-1)^2] + Exp[-10(x-3)^2]$

Each cell in the system is then updated according to $\lambda[a + c]$ for rule 90, and $\lambda[a + b + c + b c]$ for rule 30. Perturbations of size δ are then added using $v + Sign[v - 1/2]$ Random[] δ.

Note that the basic approach used here can be extended to allow discrete cellular automata to be approximated by partial differential equations where not only color but also space and time are continuous. (Compare page 464.)

■ **Page 326 · Repeatably random experiments.** Over the years, I have asked many experimental scientists about repeatability in seemingly random data, and in almost all cases they have told me that they have never looked for such a thing. But in a few cases they say that in fact on thinking about it they remember various forms of repeatability.

Examples where I have seen evidence of repeatable randomness as a function of time in published experimental data include temperature differences in thermal convection in closed cells of liquid helium, reaction rates in oxidation of carbon monoxide on catalytic surfaces, and output voltages from firings of excited single nerve cells. Typically there are quite long periods of time where the behavior is rather accurately repeatable—even though it may wiggle tens or hundreds in a seemingly random way—interspersed with jumps of some kind. In most cases the only credible models seem to be ones based on intrinsic randomness generation. But insofar as there is any definite model, it is inevitable that looking in sufficient detail at sufficiently many components of the system will reveal regularities associated with the underlying mechanism.

The Phenomenon of Continuity

■ **Discreteness in computer programs.** The reason for discreteness in computer programs is that the only real way we know how to construct such programs is using discrete logical structures. The data that is manipulated by programs can be continuous, as can the elements of their rules. But at some level one always gives discrete symbolic descriptions of the logical structure of programs. And it is then certainly more consistent to make both data and programs involve only discrete elements. In Chapter 12 I will argue that this approach is not only convenient, but also necessary if we are to represent our computations using processes that can actually occur in nature.

■ **Central Limit Theorem.** Averages of large collections of random numbers tend to follow a Gaussian or normal distribution in which the probability of getting value x is

$Exp[-(x - \mu)^2/(2\sigma^2)]/(Sqrt[2\pi]\sigma)$

The mean μ and standard deviation σ are determined by properties of the random numbers, but the form of the distribution is always the same. The only conditions are that the random numbers should be statistically independent, and that their distribution should have bounded variance, so that, for example, the probability for very large numbers is rapidly damped. (The limit of an infinite collection of numbers gives $\sigma \to 0$ in accordance with the law of large numbers.) The pictures at the top of the next page show how averages of successively larger collections of uniformly distributed numbers converge to a Gaussian distribution.

The Central Limit Theorem leads to a self-similarity property for the Gaussian distribution: if one takes n numbers that follow Gaussian distributions, then their average should also follow a Gaussian distribution, though with a standard deviation that is $1/\sqrt{n}$ times smaller.

■ **History.** That averages of random numbers follow bell-shaped distributions was known in the late 1600s. The formula for the Gaussian distribution was derived by Abraham de Moivre around 1733 in connection with theoretical studies of gambling. In the late 1700s Pierre-Simon Laplace did this again to predict the distribution of comet orbits, and showed that the same results would be obtained for other underlying distributions. Carl Friedrich Gauss made connections to the distribution of observational errors, and the relevance of the Gaussian distribution to biological and social systems was noted. Progressively more general proofs of the Central Limit Theorem were given from the early 1800s to the 1930s. Many natural systems were found to exhibit Gaussian distributions—a typical example being height distributions for humans. (Weight distributions are however closer to lognormal; compare page 1003.) And when statistical methods such as analysis of variance became established in the early 1900s it became increasingly common to assume underlying Gaussian distributions. (Gaussian distributions were also found in statistical mechanics in the late 1800s.)

■ **Related results.** Gaussian distributions arise when large numbers of random variables get added together. If instead such variables (say probabilities) get multiplied together what arises is the lognormal distribution

$Exp[-(Log[x] - \mu)^2/(2\sigma^2)]/(Sqrt[2\pi] x \sigma)$

For a wide range of underlying distributions the extreme values in large collections of random variables follow the Fisher-Tippett distribution

$Exp[(x - \mu)/\beta] Exp[-Exp[(x - \mu)/\beta]]/\beta$

related to the Weibull distribution used in reliability analysis.

For large symmetric matrices with random entries following a distribution with mean 0 and bounded variance the density of normalized eigenvalues tends to Wigner's semicircle law

$2 Sqrt[1 - x^2] UnitStep[1 - x^2]/\pi$

while the distribution of spacings between tends to

$1/2 (\pi x) Exp[1/4 (-\pi) x^2]$

The distribution of largest eigenvalues can often be expressed in terms of Painlevé functions.

(See also *1/f* noise on page 969.)

■ **Page 328 · Random walks.** In one dimension, a random walk with t steps of length 1 starting at position 0 can be generated from

$NestList[\# + (-1)^{\wedge}Random[Integer] \&, 0, t]$

or equivalently

$FoldList[Plus, 0, Table[(-1)^{\wedge}Random[Integer], \{t\}]]$

A generalization to d dimensions is then

$FoldList[Plus, Table[0, \{d\}], Table[RotateLeft[PadLeft[$
$\{(-1)^{\wedge}Random[Integer]\}, d], Random[Integer, d - 1]], \{t\}]]$

A fundamental property of random walks is that after t steps the root mean square displacement from the starting position is proportional to $\sqrt{t}$. In general, the probability distribution for the displacement of a particle that executes a random walk is

$With[\{\sigma = 1\}, (d/(2\pi\sigma t))^{d/2} Exp[-d r^2/(2\sigma t)]]$

The same results are obtained, with a different value of σ, for other random microscopic rules, so long as the variance of the distribution of step lengths is bounded (as in the Central Limit Theorem).

As mentioned on page 1082, the frequency spectrum $Abs[Fourier[list]]^2$ for a 1D random walk goes like $1/\omega^2$.

The character of random walks changes somewhat in different numbers of dimensions. For example, in 1D and 2D, there is probability 1 that a particle will eventually return to its starting point. But in 3D, this probability (on a simple cubic lattice) drops to about 0.341, and in d dimensions the probability falls roughly like $1/(2d)$. After a large number of steps t, the number of distinct positions visited will be proportional to t, at least above 2 dimensions (in 2D, it is proportional to $t/Log[t]$ and in 1D $\sqrt{t}$). Note that the outer boundaries of patterns like those on page 330 formed by n random walks tend to become rougher when t is much larger than $Log[n]$.

To make a random walk on a lattice with k directions in two dimensions, one can set up

$e = Table[\{Cos[2\pi s/k], Sin[2\pi s/k]\}, \{s, 0, k - 1\}]$

then use

$FoldList[Plus, \{0, 0\}, Table[e[[Random[Integer, \{1, k\}]]], \{t\}]]$

It turns out that on any regular lattice, in any number of dimensions, the average behavior of a random walk is always isotropic. As discussed in the note below, this can be viewed as a consequence of the fact that the probability distribution in a random walk depends only on

$Sum[Outer[Times, e[[s]], e[[s]]], \{s, Length[e]\}]$

and not on products of more of the $e[[s]]$.

There are nevertheless some properties of random walks that are not isotropic. The picture below, for example, shows the so-called extreme value distribution of positions furthest from the origin reached after 10 steps and 100 steps by random walks on various lattices.

| 4 directions | 6 directions | 4 directions | 5 directions | 6 directions |

In the pictures in the main text, all particles start out at a particular position, and progressively spread out from there. But in general, one can consider sources that emit new particles every step, or absorbers and reflectors of particles. The average distribution of particles is given in general by the diffusion equation shown on page 163. The solutions to this equation are always smooth and continuous.

A physical example of an approximation to a random walk is the spreading of ink on blotting paper.

■ **Self-avoiding walks.** Any walk where the probabilities for a given step depend only on a fixed number of preceding steps gives the same kind of limiting Gaussian distribution. But imposing the constraint that a walk must always avoid anywhere it has been before (as for example in an idealized polymer molecule) leads to correlations over arbitrary times. If one adds individual steps at random then in 2D one typically gets stuck after perhaps a few tens of steps. But tricks are known for generating long self-avoiding walks by combining shorter walks or successively pivoting pieces starting with a simple line. The pictures below show some 1000-step examples. They look in many ways similar to ordinary random walks, but their limiting distribution is no longer strictly Gaussian, and their root mean square displacement after t steps varies like $t^{3/4}$. (In $d \leq 4$ dimensions the exponent is close to the Flory mean field theory value $3/(2 + d)$; for $d > 4$ the results are the same as without self-avoidance.)

| 1 particle | 20 particles | 1000 particles |

■ **Page 331 · Basic aggregation model.** This model appears to have first been described by Murray Eden in 1961 as a way of studying biological growth, and was simulated by him on a computer for clusters up to about 32,000 cells. By the mid-1980s clusters with a billion cells had been grown, and a very surprising slight anisotropy had been observed. The pictures below show which cells occur in more than 10% of 1000 randomly grown clusters. There is a 2% or so anisotropy that appears to remain essentially fixed for clusters above perhaps a million cells, tucking them in along the diagonal directions. The width of the region of roughness on the surface of each cluster varies with the radius of the cluster approximately like $r^{1/3}$. The most extensive use of the model in practice has been for studying tumor growth: currently a typical tumor at detection contains about a billion cells, and it is important to predict what protrusions there will be that can break off and form additional tumors elsewhere.

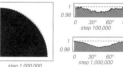

| step 10,000 | step 100,000 | step 1,000,000 |

■ **Implementation.** One way to represent a cluster is by giving a list of the coordinates at which each black cell occurs. Then starting with a single black cell at the origin, represented by {{0, 0}}, the cluster can be grown for t steps as follows:

    AEvolve[t_] := Nest[AStep, {{0, 0}}, t]

    AStep[c_] := (If[! MemberQ[c, #], Append[c, #],
        AStep[c]] &)[f[c] + f[{{1, 0}, {0, 1}, {-1, 0}, {0, -1}}]]

    f[a_] := a[[Random[Integer, {1, Length[a]}]]]

This implementation can easily be extended to any type of lattice and any number of dimensions. Even with various additional optimizations, it is remarkable how much slower it is to grow a cluster with a model that requires external random input than to generate similar patterns with models such as cellular automata that intrinsically generate their own randomness.

The implementation above is a so-called type B Eden model in which one first selects a cell in the cluster, then randomly selects one of its neighbors. One gets extremely similar results with a type A Eden model in which one just randomly selects a cell from all the ones adjacent to the cluster. With a grid of cells set up in advance, each step in this type of Eden model can be achieved with

    AStep[a_] := ReplacePart[a, 1, (#[[Random[
        Integer, {1, Length[#]}]]] &)[Position[(1 - a) Sign[
        ListConvolve[{{0, 1, 0}, {1, 0, 1}, {0, 1, 0}}, a, {2, 2}]], 1]]]

This implementation can readily be extended to generalized aggregation models (see below).

■ **Page 332 · Generalized aggregation models.** One can in general have rules in which new cells can be added only at positions whose neighborhoods match specific templates (compare page 213). There are 32 possible symmetric such rules with just 4 immediate neighbors—of which 16 lead to growth (from any seed), and all seem to yield at least approximately circular clusters (of varying densities). Without symmetry, all sorts of shapes can be obtained, as in the pictures below. (The rule numbers here follow the scheme on page 927 with offsets {{-1, 0}, {0, -1}, {0, 1}, {1, 0}}). Note that even though the underlying rule involves randomness definite geometrical shapes can be produced. An extreme case is rule 2, where only a single neighborhood with a single black cell is allowed, so that growth occurs along a single line.

| 4531 | 10779 | 15320 | 64881 | 65415 |

If one puts conditions on where cells can be added one can in principle get clusters where no further growth is possible. This does not seem to happen for rules that involve 4 neighbors, but with 8 neighbors there are cases in which clusters can get fairly large, but end up having no sites where further cells can be added. The pictures below show examples for a rule that allows growth except when there are exactly 1, 3 or 4 neighbors (totalistic constraint 242).

| 6 steps | 14 steps | 109 steps | 219 steps | 787 steps | 6795 steps |

The question of what ultimate forms of behavior can occur with any sequence of random choices, starting from a given configuration with a given rule, is presumably in general undecidable. (It has some immediate relations to tiling problems and to halting problems for non-deterministic Turing machines.) With the rule illustrated above, however, those clusters that do successfully grow exhibit complicated and irregular shapes, but nevertheless eventually seem to take on a roughly circular shape, as in the pictures below.

| step 100 | step 1000 | step 10,000 | step 100,000 | step 1,000,000 |

At some level the basic aggregation model of page 331 has a deterministic outcome: after sufficiently many steps every cell will be black. But most generalized aggregation models do not have this property: instead, the form of their internal patterns depends on the sequence of random choices made. Particularly with more than two colors it is however possible to arrange that the internal pattern always ends up being the same, or at least has patches that are the same—essentially by

using rules with the confluence property discussed on page 1036.

The pictures below show 1D generalized aggregation systems with various templates. The second one is the analog of the system from page 331.

■ Page 333 · Diffusion-limited aggregation (DLA). While many 2D cellular automata produce intricate nested shapes, the aggregation models shown here seem to tend to simple limiting shapes. Most likely there are some generalized aggregation models for which this is not the case. And indeed this phenomenon has been seen in other systems with randomness in their underlying rules. An example studied extensively in the 1980s is diffusion-limited aggregation (DLA). The idea of this model is to add cells to a cluster one at a time, and to determine where a cell will be added by seeing where a random walk that starts far from the cluster first lands on a square adjacent to the cluster. An example of the behavior obtained in this model is shown below:

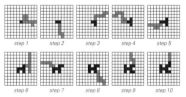

| step 1 | step 2 | step 3 | step 4 | step 5 | |
| step 6 | step 7 | step 8 | step 9 | step 10 | step 1000 |

The lack of smooth overall behavior in this case can perhaps be attributed to the global probing of the cluster that is effectively done by each incoming random walk. (See also page 994.)

■ Page 334 · Code 746. Much as in the aggregation model above, the pictures below show that there is a slight deviation from perfect circular growth, with an anisotropy that appears to remain roughly fixed at perhaps 4% above a few thousand steps (corresponding to patterns with a few million cells).

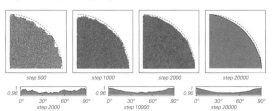

■ **Other rules.** The pictures below show patterns generated after 10,000 steps with several rules, starting respectively from rows of 7, 6, 7 and 11 cells (compare pages 177 and 181). The outer boundaries are somewhat smooth, though definitely not circular. In the second rule shown, the interior of the pattern always continues to change; in the others it remains essentially fixed.

code 746   code 29408   code 175850   code 174826

■ **Isotropy.** Any pattern grown from a single cell according to rules that do not distinguish different directions on a lattice must show the same symmetry as the lattice. But we have seen that in fact many rules actually yield almost circular patterns with much higher symmetry. One can characterize the symmetry of a pattern by taking the list v of positions of cells it contains, and looking at tensors of successive ranks n:

> Apply[Plus,
>   Map[Apply[Outer[Times, ##]] &, Table[#, {n}]] &, v]]

For circular or spherical patterns that are perfectly isotropic in d dimensions these tensors must all be proportional to

> $(d - 2)!!$ Array[Apply[Times, Map[(1 - Mod[#, 2])(# - 1)!! &,
>   Table[Count[{##}, i], {i, d}]]] &, Table[d, {n}]]/(d + n - 2)!!

For odd n this is inevitably true for any lattice with mirror symmetry. But for even n it can fail. For a square lattice, it still nevertheless always holds up to $n = 2$ (so that the analogs of moments of inertia satisfy $I_{xx} == I_{yy}$, $I_{xy} == I_{yx} == 0$). And for a hexagonal lattice it holds up to $n = 4$. But when $n = 4$ isotropy requires the $\{1, 1, 1, 1\}$ and $\{1, 1, 2, 2\}$ tensor components to have ratio $\beta = 3$—while square symmetry allows these components to have any ratio. (In general there will be more than one component unless the representation of the lattice symmetry group carried by the rank n tensor is irreducible.) In 3D no regular lattice forces isotropy beyond $n = 2$, while in 4D the SO(8) lattice works up to $n = 4$, in 8D the E_8 lattice up to $n = 6$, and in 24D the Leech lattice up to $n = 10$. (Lattices that give dense sphere packings tend to show more isotropy.) Note that isotropy can also be characterized using analogs of multipole moments, obtained in 2D by summing $r_i Exp[i n \theta_i]$, and in higher dimensions by summing appropriate *SphericalHarmonicY* or *GegenbauerC* functions. For isotropy, only the $n = 0$ moment can be nonzero. On a 2D lattice with m directions, all moments are forced to be zero except when m divides n. (Sums of squares of moments of given order in general provide rotationally

invariant measures of anisotropy—equal to pair correlations weighted with *LegendreP* or *GegenbauerC* functions.)

Even though it is not inevitable from lattice symmetry, one might think that if there is some kind of effective randomness in the underlying rules then sufficiently large patterns would still often show some sort of average isotropy. And at least in the case of ordinary random walks, they do, so that for example, the ratio averaged over all possible walks of $n = 4$ tensor components after t steps on a square lattice is $\beta = 3 + 2/(t - 1)$, converging to the isotropic value 3, and the ratio of $n = 6$ components is $5 - 4/(t - 1) + 32/(3 t - 4)$. For the aggregation model of page 331, β also decreases with t, reaching 4 around $t = 10$, but now its asymptotic value is around 3.07.

In continuous systems such as partial differential equations, isotropy requires that coordinates in effect appear only in ∇. In most finite difference approximations, there is presumably isotropy in the end, but the rates of convergence are almost inevitably rather different in different directions relative to the lattice.

■ **Page 336 · Domains.** Some of the effective rules for interfaces between black and white domains are easy to state. Given a flat interface, the layer of cells immediately on either side of this interface behaves like the rule 150 1D cellular automaton. On an infinitely long interface, protrusions of cells with one color into a domain of the opposite color get progressively smaller, eventually leaving only a certain pattern of cells in the layer immediately on one side of the interface. 90° corners in an otherwise flat interface effectively act like reflective boundary conditions for the layer of cells on top of the interface.

The phenomenon of domains illustrated here is also found in various 2D cellular automata with 4-neighbor rather than 8-neighbor rules. One example is totalistic code 52, which is a direct analog in the 4-neighbor case of the rule illustrated here. Other examples are outer totalistic codes 111, 293, 295 and 920. The domain boundaries in these cases, however, are not as clear as for the 8-neighbor totalistic rule with code 976 that is shown here.

■ **Spinodal decomposition.** The separation into progressively larger black and white regions seen in the cellular automata shown here is reminiscent of the phenomena that occur for example in the separation of randomly mixed oil and water. Various continuous models of such processes have been proposed, notably the Cahn-Hilliard equation from 1958. One feature often found is that the average radius of "droplets" increases with time roughly like $t^{1/3}$.

Origins of Discreteness

■ **Page 339 · 1D transitions.** There are no examples of the phenomenon shown here among the 256 rules with two possible colors and depending only on nearest neighbors. Among the 4,294,967,296 rules that depend on next-nearest neighbors, there are a handful of examples, including rules with numbers 4196304428, 4262364716, 4268278316 and 4266296876. The behavior obtained with the first of these rules is shown below. An example that depends on three neighbors on each side was discovered by Peter Gacs, Georgii Kurdyumov and Leonid Levin in 1978, following work on how reliable electronic circuits can be built from unreliable components by Andrei Toom:

{a1_, a2_, a3_, a4_, a5_, a6_, a7_} →
    If[If[a4 == 1, a1 + a3 + a4, a4 + a5 + a7] ≥ 2, 1, 0]

The 4-color rule shown in the text is probably the clearest example available in one dimension. It has rule number 294869764523995749814890097794812493824.

| 40% black | 45% black | 55% black | 60% black |

■ **Page 340 · 2D transitions.** The simplest symmetrical rules (such as 4-neighbor totalistic code 56) which make the new color of a cell be the same as the majority of the cells in its neighborhood do not exhibit the discrete transition phenomenon, but instead lead to fixed regions of black and white. The 4-neighbor rule with totalistic code 52 can be used as an alternative to the second rule shown here. A probabilistic version of the first rule shown here was discussed by Andrei Toom in 1980.

■ **Phase transitions.** The discrete transitions shown in cellular automata in this section are examples of general phenomena known in physics as phase transitions. A phase transition can be defined as any discontinuous change that occurs in a system with a large number of components when a parameter associated with that system is varied. (Some physicists might argue for a somewhat narrower definition that allows only discontinuities in the so-called partition function of equilibrium statistical mechanics, but for many of the most interesting applications, the definition I use is the appropriate one.) Standard examples of phase transitions include boiling, melting, sublimation (solids such as dry ice turning into gases), loss of magnetization when a ferromagnet is heated, alignment of molecules in liquid crystals above a certain electric field (the basis for liquid crystal displays), and the onset of superconductivity and superfluidity at low temperatures.

It is conventional to distinguish two kinds of phase transitions, often called first-order and higher-order. First-order transitions occur when a system has two possible states, such as liquid and gas, and as a parameter is varied, which of these states is the stable one changes. Boiling and melting are both examples of first-order transitions, as is the phenomenon shown in the cellular automaton in the main text. Note that one feature of first-order transitions is that as soon as the transition is passed, the whole system always switches completely from one state to the other.

Higher-order transitions are in a sense more gradual. On one side of the transition, a system is typically completely disordered. But when the transition is passed, the system does not immediately become completely ordered. Instead, its order increases gradually from zero as the parameter is varied. Typically the presence of order is signalled by the breaking of some kind of symmetry—say of rotational symmetry by the spontaneous selection of a preferred direction.

■ **The Ising model.** The 2D Ising model is a prototypical example of a system with a higher-order phase transition. Introduced by Wilhelm Lenz in 1920 as an idealization of ferromagnetic materials (and studied by Ernst Ising) it involves a square array s of spins, each either up or down (+1 or -1), corresponding to two orientations for magnetic moments of atoms. The magnetic energy of the system is taken to be

e[s_] := -1/2 Apply[Plus, s ListConvolve[
    {{0, 1, 0}, {1, 0, 1}, {0, 1, 0}}, s, 2], {0, 1}]

so that each pair of adjacent spins contributes -1 when they are parallel and +1 when they are not. The overall magnetization of the system is given by m[s_] := Apply[Plus, s, {0, 1}].

In physical ferromagnetic materials what is observed is that at high temperature, corresponding to high internal energy, there is no overall magnetization. But when the temperature goes below a critical value, spins tend to line up, and an overall magnetization spontaneously develops. In the context of the 2D Ising model this phenomenon is associated with the fact that those configurations of a large array of spins that have high total energy are overwhelmingly likely to have near zero overall magnetization, while those that have low total energy are overwhelmingly likely to have nonzero overall magnetization. For an $n \times n$ array s of spins there are a total of 2^{n^2} possible configurations. The pictures below show the results of picking all configurations with a given energy $e[s]$ (cyclic boundary conditions are assumed) and then working out their distribution of magnetization values $m[s]$. Even for small n the pictures demonstrate that for large $e[s]$ the magnetization $m[s]$ is likely to be close to zero, but for smaller $e[s]$ two branches approaching +1 and -1 appear. In the limit $n \to \infty$ the distribution of magnetization values becomes sharp, and a definite discontinuous phase transition is observed.

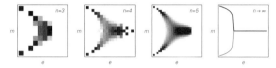

Following the work of Lars Onsager around 1944, it turns out that an exact solution in terms of traditional mathematical functions can be found in this case. (This seems to be true only in 2D, and not in 3D or higher.) Almost all spin configurations with $e[s] > -\sqrt{2}$ (where here and below all quantities are divided by the total number of spins, so that $-2 \leq e[s] \leq 2$ and $-1 \leq m[s] \leq +1$) yield $m[s] == 0$. But for smaller $e[s]$ one can show that

$Abs[m[s]] == (1 - Sinh[2\beta]^{-4})^{1/8}$

where β can be deduced from

$e[s] == -(Coth[2\beta](1 + 2 EllipticK[4 Sech[2\beta]^2 Tanh[2\beta]^2]$
$(-1 + 2 Tanh[2\beta]^2)/\pi))$

This implies that just below the critical point $e_0 = -\sqrt{2}$ (which corresponds to $\beta = Log[1 + \sqrt{2}]/2$) $Abs[m] \sim (e_0 - e)^{1/8}$, where here 1/8 is a so-called critical exponent. (Another analytical result is that for $e \sim e_0$ correlations between pairs of spins can be expressed in terms of Painlevé functions.)

Despite its directness, the approach above of considering sets of configurations with specific energies $e[s]$ is not how the Ising model has usually been studied. Instead, what has normally been done is to take the array of spins to be in thermal equilibrium with a heat bath, so that, following standard statistical mechanics, each possible spin configuration occurs with probability $Exp[-\beta e[s]]$, where β is inverse temperature. It nevertheless turns out that in the limit $n \to \infty$ this so-called canonical ensemble approach yields the same results for most quantities as the microcanonical approach that I have used; β simply appears as a parameter, as in the formulas above.

About actual spin systems evolving in time the Ising model itself does not make any statement. But whenever the evolution is ergodic, so that all states of a given energy are visited with equal frequency, the average behavior obtained

will at least eventually correspond to the average over all states discussed above.

In Monte Carlo studies of the Ising model one normally tries to sample states with appropriate probabilities by randomly flipping spins according to a procedure that can be thought of as emulating interaction with a heat bath. But in most actual physical spin systems it seems unlikely that there will be so much continual interaction with the environment. And from my discussion of intrinsic randomness generation it should come as no surprise that even a completely deterministic rule for the evolution of spins can make the system visit possible states in an effectively random way.

Among the simplest possible types of rules all those that conserve the energy $e[s]$ turn out to have behavior that is too simple and regular. And indeed, of the 4096 symmetric 5-neighbor rules, only identity and complement conserve $e[s]$. Of the 2^{32} general 5-neighbor rules 34 conserve $e[s]$—but all have only very simple behavior. (Compositions of several such rules can nevertheless yield complex behavior. Note that as indicated on page 1022, 34 of the 256 elementary 1D rules conserve the analog of $e[s]$.) Of the 262,144 9-neighbor outer totalistic rules the only ones that conserve $e[s]$ are identity and complement. But among all 2^{512} 9-neighbor rules, there are undoubtedly examples that show effectively random behavior. One marginally more complicated case effectively involving 13 neighbors is

```
IsingEvolve[list_, t_Integer] :=
    First[Nest[IsingStep, {list, Mask[list]}, t]]
IsingStep[{a_, mask_}] := {MapThread[
    If[#2 == 2 && #3 == 1, 1 - #1, #1] &, {a, ListConvolve[
        {{0, 1, 0}, {1, 0, 1}, {0, 1, 0}}, a, 2], mask}, 2], 1 - mask}
```

where

```
Mask[list_] := Array[Mod[#1 + #2, 2] &, Dimensions[list]]
```

is set up so that alternating checkerboards of cells are updated on successive steps.

One can see a phase transition in this system by looking at the dependence of behavior on conserved total energy $e[s]$. If there are no correlations between spins, and a fraction p of them are +1, then $m[s] == p$ and $e[s] == -2(1 - 2p)^2$. And since the evolution conserves $e[s]$ changing the initial value of p allows one to sample different total energies. But since the evolution does not conserve $m[s]$ the average of this after many steps can be expected to be typical of all possible states of given $e[s]$.

The pictures at the top of the next page show the values of $m[s]$ (densities of +1 cells) after 0, 10, 100 and 1000 steps for a 500×500 system as a function of the initial values of $m[s]$ and $e[s]$. Also shown is the result expected for an infinite system at infinite time. (The slow approach to this limit can be viewed as being a consequence of smallness of finite size scaling exponents in Ising-like systems.)

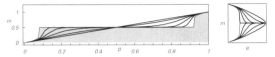

The phase transition in the Ising model is associated with a lack of smoothness in the dependence of the final m value on e or the initial value p of m in limiting cases of the pictures above. The transition occurs at $e = -\sqrt{2}$, corresponding to $p = (1 \pm 2^{-1/4})/2$. The pictures show typical configurations generated after 1000 steps from various initial densities, as well as slices through their evolution.

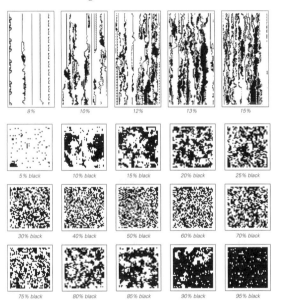

And what one sees at least roughly is that right around the phase transition there are patches of black and white of all sizes, forming an approximately nested random pattern. (See also pages 989 and 1149.)

■ **General features of phase transitions.** To reproduce the Ising model, a cellular automaton must have several special properties. In addition to conserving energy, its evolution must be reversible in the sense discussed on page 435. And with the constraint of reversibility, it turns out that it is impossible to get a non-trivial phase transition in any 1D system with the kind of short-range interactions that exist in a cellular automaton. But in systems whose evolution is not reversible, it is possible for phase transitions to occur in 1D, as the examples in the main text show.

One point to notice is that the sharp change which characterizes any phase transition can only be a true discontinuity in the limit of an infinitely large system. In the case of the system on page 339, for example, it is possible to find special configurations with a finite total number of cells which lead to behavior opposite to what one expects purely on the basis of their initial density of black cells. When the total number of cells increases, however, the fraction of such configurations rapidly decreases, and in the infinite size limit, there are no such configurations, and a truly discontinuous transition occurs exactly at density 1/2.

The discrete nature of phase transitions was at one time often explained as a consequence of changes in the symmetry of a system. The idea is that symmetry is either present or absent, and there is no continuous variation of level of symmetry possible. Thus, for example, above the transition, the Ising model treats up and down spins exactly the same. But below the transition, it effectively makes a choice of one spin direction or the other. Similarly, when a liquid freezes into a crystalline solid, it effectively makes a choice about the alignment of the crystal in space. But in boiling, as well as in a number of model examples, there is no obvious change of symmetry. And from studying phase transitions in cellular automata, it does not seem that an interpretation in terms of symmetry is particularly useful.

A common feature of phase transitions is that right at the transition point, there is competition between both phases, and some kind of nested structure is typically formed, as discussed on page 273 and above. The overall form and fractal dimension of this nested structure is typically independent of small-scale features of the system, making it fairly universal, and amenable to analysis using the renormalization group approach (see page 955).

■ **Percolation.** A simple example of a phase transition studied extensively since the 1950s involves taking a square lattice and filling in at random a certain density of black cells. In the limit of infinite size, there is a discrete transition at a density of about 0.592746, with zero probability below the transition to find a connected "percolating" cluster of black cells spanning the lattice, and unit probability above. (For a triangular lattice the critical density is exactly 1/2.) One can also study directed percolation in which one takes account of the connectivity of cells only in one direction on the lattice. (Compare the probabilistic cellular automata on pages 325 and 591. Note that the evolution of such systems is also analogous to the process of applying transfer matrices in studies of spin systems like Ising models.)

■ **Page 341 · Rate equations.** In standard chemical kinetics one assumes that molecules are uniformly distributed in space, so that the rates for particular reactions are proportional to the products of the densities of the molecules that react in them. Conditions for equilibrium where rates balance thus tend to be polynomial equations for densities—with discontinuous jumps in solutions sometimes occurring as parameters are changed. Analogous equations arise in probabilistic approximations to systems like cellular automata, as on page 953. But here—as well as in fast chemical reactions—correlations in spatial arrangements of elements tend to be important, invalidating simple probabilistic approaches. (For the cellular automaton on page 339 the simple condition for equilibrium is $p == p^2 (3 - 2p)$, which correctly implies that 0, 1/2 and 1 are possible equilibrium densities.)

■ **Discreteness in space.** Many systems with continuous underlying rules generate discrete cellular structures in space. One common mechanism is for a wave of a definite wavelength to form (see page 988), and then for some feature of each cycle of this wave to be picked out, as in the picture below. In Chladni figures of sand on vibrating plates and in cloud streets in the atmosphere what happens is that material collects at points of zero displacement. And when a stream of water breaks up into discrete drops what happens is that oscillation minima yield necks that break.

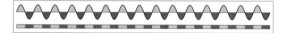

Superpositions of waves at different angles can lead to various 2D cellular structures, as in the pictures below (compare page 1078).

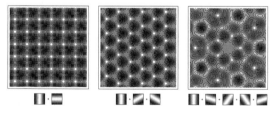

Various forms of focusing and accumulation can also lead to discreteness in continuous systems. The first picture below shows a caustic or catastrophe in which a continuous distribution of light rays are focused by a circular reflector onto a discrete line with a cusp. The second picture shows a shock wave produced by an accumulation of circular waves emanating from a moving object—as seen in wakes of ships, sonic booms from supersonic aircraft, and Cerenkov light from fast-moving charged particles.

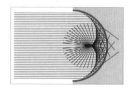 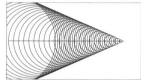

The Problem of Satisfying Constraints

■ **Rules versus constraints.** See page 940.

■ **NP completeness.** Finding 2D patterns that satisfy the constraints in the previous section is in general a so-called NP-complete problem. And this means that no known algorithm can be expected to solve this problem exactly for a size n array (say with given boundaries) in much less than 2^n steps (see page 1145). The same is true even if one allows a small fraction of squares to violate the constraints. However, the 1D version of the problem is not NP-complete, and in fact there is a specific rather efficient algorithm described on page 954 for solving it. Nevertheless, the procedures discussed in this section do not manage to make use of such specific algorithms, and in fact typically show little difference between problems that are and are not formally NP-complete.

■ **Page 343 · Distribution.** The distribution shown here rapidly approaches a Gaussian. (Note that in a 5×5 array, there are 10 interior squares that are subject to the constraints, while in a 10×10 array there are 65.) Very similar results seem to be obtained for constraints in a wide range of discrete systems.

■ **Page 346 · Implementation.** The number of squares violating the constraint used here is given by

$Cost[list\_] := Apply[Plus, Abs[list - RotateLeft[list]]]$

When applied to all possible patterns, this function yields a distribution with Gaussian tails, but with a sharp point in the middle. Successive steps in the iterative procedure used on this page are given by

$Move[list\_] := (If[Cost[\#] < Cost[list], \#, list] \&)[$
$\quad MapAt[1 - \# \&, list, Random[Integer, \{1, Length[list]\}]]]$

while those in the procedure on page 347 have $\leq$ in place of $<$. The third curve shown on page 346 is obtained from

$Table[Cost[IntegerDigits[i, 2, n]], \{i, 0, 2^n - 1\}]$

There is no single ordering that makes all states which can be reached by changing a single square be adjacent. However, the ordering defined by *GrayCode* from page 901 does do this for one particular sequence of single square changes. The resulting curve is very similar to what is already shown.

■ **Page 347 · Iterative improvement.** The borders of the regions of black and white in the picture shown here essentially follow random walks and annihilate in pairs so that their number decreases with time like $1/\sqrt{t}$. In 2D the regions are more complicated and there is no such simple behavior. Indeed starting from a particular state it is for example not clear whether it is ever possible to reach all other states.

■ **Gradient descent.** A standard method for finding a minimum in a smooth function $f[x]$ is to use

$FixedPoint[\# - a\,f'[\#]\,\&,\,x_0]$

If there are local minima, then which one is reached will depend on the starting point x_0. It will not necessarily be the one closest to x_0 because of potentially complicated overshooting effects associated with the step size a. Newton's method for finding zeros of $f[x]$ is related and is given by

$FixedPoint[\# - f[\#]/f'[\#]\,\&,\,x_0]$

■ **Combinatorial optimization.** The problem of coming as close as possible to satisfying constraints in an arrangement of black and white squares is a simple example of a combinatorial optimization problem. In general, such problems involve minimization of a quantity that is determined by the arrangement of some set of discrete elements. A typical example is finding a placement of components in a 2D circuit so that the total length of wire necessary to the connect these components is minimized (related to the so-called travelling salesman problem). In using iterative procedures to solve combinatorial optimization problems, one issue is what kind of changes should be made at each step. In the main text we considered changing just one square at a time. But one can also change larger numbers of squares, or, for example, interchange whole blocks of squares. In general, the larger the changes made, the faster one can potentially approach a minimum, but the greater the chance is of overshooting. In the main text, we assumed that at each step we should always move closer to the minimum, or at least not get further away. But in trying to get over the kind of bumps shown in the third curve on page 346 it is sometimes better also to allow some probability of moving away from the minimum at a particular step. One approach is simulated annealing, in which one starts with this probability being large, and progressively decreases it. The notion is that at the beginning, one wants to move easily over the coarse features of a jagged curve, but then later home in on details. If the curve has a nested form, which appears to be the case in some combinatorial optimization problems, then this scheme can be expected to be at least somewhat effective. For the problems considered in the main text, simulated annealing provides some improvement but not much.

■ **Biologically motivated schemes.** The process of biological evolution by natural selection can be thought of as an iterative procedure for optimization. Usually, however, what is being optimized is some aspect of the form or behavior of an organism, which represents a very complicated constraint on the underlying genetic material. (It is as if one is defining constraints on the initial conditions for a cellular automaton by looking at the pattern generated by the cellular automaton after a long time.) But the strategies of biological evolution can also be used in trying to satisfy simpler constraints. Two of the most important strategies are maintaining a whole population of individuals, not just the single best result so far, and using sex to produce large-scale mixing. But once again, while these strategies may in some cases lead to greater efficiency, they do not usually lead to qualitative differences. (See also page 1105.)

■ **History.** Work on combinatorial optimization started in earnest in the late 1950s, but by the time NP completeness was discovered in 1971 (see page 1143) it had become clear that finding exact solutions would be very difficult. Approximate methods tended to be constructed for specific problems. But in the early 1980s, simulated annealing was suggested by Scott Kirkpatrick and others as one of the first potentially general approaches. And starting in the mid-1980s, extensive work was done on biologically motivated so-called genetic algorithms, which had been advocated by John Holland since the 1960s. Progress in combinatorial optimization is however often difficult to recognize, because there are almost no general results, and results that are quoted are often sensitive to details of the problems studied and the computer implementations used.

■ **Page 349 · 2D cellular automata.** The rule numbers are specified as on page 927.

■ **Page 349 · Circle packings.** Hexagonal packing of equal circles has been known since early antiquity (e.g. the fourth picture on page 43). It fills a fraction $\pi/\sqrt{12} \simeq 0.91$ of area—which was proved maximal for periodic packings by Carl Friedrich Gauss in 1831 and for any packing by Axel Thue in 1910 and László Fejes Tóth in 1940. Much has been done to study densest packings of limited numbers of circles into various shapes, as well as onto surfaces of spheres (as in golf balls, pollen grains or radiolarians). Typically it has been found that with enough circles, patches of hexagonal packing always tend to form. (See page 987.)

For circles of unequal sizes rather little has been done. A procedure analogous to the one on page 350 was introduced by Charles Bennett in 1971 for 3D spheres (relevant for binary alloys). The picture below shows the network of contacts between circles in the cases from page 350. Note that with the procedure used, each new circle added must immediately touch two existing ones, though subsequently it may get touched by varying numbers of other circles.

ratio 1:1   ratio 1:0.9   ratio 1:0.8   ratio 1:0.7   ratio 1:0.5

The distribution of numbers of circles that touch a given circle changes with the ratio of circle sizes, as in the picture below. The total filling fraction seems to vary fairly smoothly with this ratio, though I would not be surprised if some small-scale jumps were present.

ratio 1:1   ratio 1:0.9   ratio 1:0.8   ratio 1:0.7   ratio 1:0.5

Note that even a single circle of different size in the center can have a large-scale effect on the results of the procedure, as illustrated in the pictures below.

ratio 1:1   ratio 1:1.1   ratio 1:1.2   ratio 1:1.3   ratio 1:1.4

Finding densest packings of n circles is in general like solving quadratic programming problems with about n^2 constraints. But at least for many size ratios I suspect that the final result will simply involve each kind of circle forming a separated hexagonally-packed region. This will not happen, however, for size ratios $\leq 2/\sqrt{3} - 1 \approx 0.15$, since then the small circles can fit into the interstices of an ordinary hexagonal pattern, yielding a filling fraction $1/18\,(17\sqrt{13} - 24)\,\pi \approx 0.95$. The picture below shows what happens if one repeatedly inserts circles to form a so-called Apollonian packing derived from the problem studied by Apollonius of finding a circle that touches three others. At step t, 3^{t-1} circles are added for each original circle, and the network of tangencies among circles is exactly example (a) from page 509. Most of the circles added at a given step are not the same size, however, making the overall geometry not straightforwardly nested. (The total numbers of different sizes of circles for the first few steps are {2, 3, 5, 10, 24, 63, 178, 521}. At step 3, for example, the new circles have radii $(25 - 12\sqrt{3})/193$ and $(19 - 6\sqrt{3})/253$. In general, the radius of a circle inscribed between three other touching circles that have radii p, q, r is $p\,q\,r/(p\,q + p\,r + q\,r + 2\,Sqrt[p\,q\,r\,(p + q + r)])$.) In the limit of an infinite number of steps the filling fraction tends to 1, while

the region left unfilled has a fractal dimension of about 1.3057.

step 1   step 2   step 3   step 4 step 8 step 12

To achieve filling fraction 1 requires arbitrarily small circles, but there are many different arrangements of circles that will work, some not even close to nested. When actual granular materials are formed by crushing, there is probably some tendency to generate smaller pieces by following essentially substitution system rules, and the result may be a nested distribution of sizes that allows an Apollonian-like packing.

Apollonian packings turn out to correspond to limit sets invariant under groups of rational transformations in the complex plane. Note that as on page 1007 packings can be constructed in which the sizes of circles vary smoothly with position according to a harmonic function.

■ **Sphere packings.** The 3D face-centered cubic (fcc) packing shown in the main text has presumably been known since antiquity, and has been used extensively for packing fruit, cannon balls, etc. It fills space with a density $\pi/\sqrt{18} \approx 0.74$, which Johannes Kepler suggested in 1609 might be the maximum possible. This was proved for periodic packings by Carl Friedrich Gauss in 1831, and for any packing by Thomas Hales in 1998. (By offsetting successive layers hexagonal close packing (hcp) can be obtained; this has the same density as fcc, but has a trapezoid-rhombic dodecahedron Voronoi diagram—see note below and page 929—rather than an ordinary rhombic dodecahedron.)

Random packings of spheres typically have densities around 0.64 (compared to 0.74 for fcc). Many of their large pores appear to be associated with poor packing of tetrahedral clusters of 4 spheres. (Note that individual such clusters—as well as for example 13-sphere approximate icosahedra—represent locally dense packings.)

It is common for shaking to cause granular materials (such as coffee or sand grains) to settle and pack at least a few percent better. Larger objects normally come to the top (as with mixed nuts, popcorn or pebbles and sand), essentially because the smaller ones more easily fall through interstices.

■ **Higher dimensions.** In no dimension above 3 is it known for certain what configuration of spheres yields the densest packing. Cases in which spheres are arranged on repetitive lattices are related to error-correcting codes and groups. Up to 8D, the densest packings of this type are known to be ones obtained by successively adding layers individually optimized in each dimension. And in fact up to 26D (with the exception of 11 through 13) all the densest packings known so far are lattices that work like this. In 8D and 24D these lattices are known to be ones in which each sphere touches the maximal number of others (240 and 196560 respectively). (In 8D the lattice also corresponds to the root vectors of the Lie group E_8; in 24D it is the Leech lattice derived from a Golay code, and related to the Monster Group). In various dimensions above 10 packings in which successive layers are shifted give slightly higher densities than known lattices. In all examples found so far the densest packings can always be repetitive; most can also be highly symmetrical—though in high dimensions random lattices often do not yield much worse results.

■ **Discrete packings.** The pictures below show a discrete analog of circle packing in which one arranges as many circles as possible with a given diameter on a grid. (The grid is assumed to wrap around.)

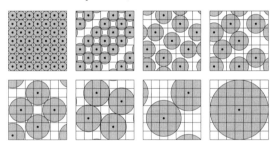

The pictures show all the distinct maximal cases that exist for a 7×7 grid, corresponding to possible circles with diameters $Sqrt[m^2 + n^2]$. Already some of these are difficult to find. And in fact in general finding such packings is an NP-complete problem: it is equivalent to the problem of finding the maximum clique (completely connected set) in the graph whose vertices are joined whenever they correspond to grid points on which non-overlapping circles could be centered.

On large grids, optimal packings seem to approach rational approximations to hexagonal packings. But what happens if one generalizes to allow circles of different sizes is not clear.

■ **Voronoi diagrams.** The Voronoi diagram for a set of points shows the region around each point in which one is closer to that point than to any other. (The edges of the regions are thus like watersheds.) The pictures below show a few examples. In 2D the regions in a Voronoi diagram are always polygons, and in 3D polyhedra. If all the points lie on a repetitive lattice each region will always be the same, and is often known as a Wigner-Seitz cell or a Dirichlet domain. For a simple cubic lattice the regions are cubes with 6 faces. For

an fcc lattice they are rhombic dodecahedra with 12 faces and for a bcc lattice they are truncated octahedra (tetradecahedra) with 14 faces. (Compare page 929.)

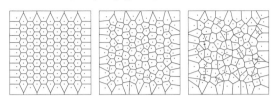

Voronoi diagrams for irregularly distributed points have found many applications. In 2D they are used in studies of animal territories, retail store utilization and municipal districting. In 3D they are used as simple models of foams, grains in solids, assemblies of biological cells and self-gravitating regions in primordial galaxy formation. Voronoi diagrams are relevant whenever there is growth in all directions at an identical speed from a collection of seed points. (In high dimensions they also appear immediately in studying error-correcting codes.)

Modern computational geometry has provided efficient algorithms for constructing Voronoi diagrams, and has allowed them to be used in mesh generation, point location, cluster analysis, machining plans and many other computational tasks.

■ **Discrete Voronoi diagrams.** The $k = 3$, $r = 1$ cellular automaton
$$\{\{0 \mid 1, n : (0 \mid 1), 0 \mid 1\} \to n, \{\_, 0, \_\} \to 2, \{\_, n\_, \_\} \to n - 1\}$$
is an example of a system that generates discrete 1D Voronoi diagrams by having regions that grow from every initial black cell, but stop whenever they meet, as shown below.

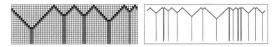

Analogous behavior can also be obtained in 2D, as shown for a 2D cellular automaton in the pictures below.

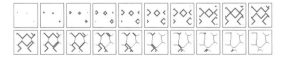

■ **Brillouin zones.** A region in an ordinary Voronoi diagram shows where a given point is closest. One can also consider higher-order Voronoi diagrams in which each region shows where a given point is the kth closest. The total area of each region is the same for every k, but some complexity in shape is seen, though for large k they always in a sense approximate circles. 3D versions of such regions have been encountered in studies of quantum mechanical properties of crystals since the 1930s.

■ **Packing deformable objects.** If one pushes together identical deformable objects in 2D they tend to arrange themselves in a regular hexagonal array—and this configuration is known to minimize total boundary length. In 3D the arrangement one gets is typically not very regular—although as noted at various times since the 1600s individual objects often have pentagonal faces suggestive of dodecahedra. (The average number of faces for each object depends on the details of the random process used to pack them, but is typically around 14. Note that for a 3D Voronoi diagram with randomly placed points, the average number of faces for each region is $2 + 48\pi^2/35 \simeq 15.5$.) It was suggested by William Thomson (Kelvin) in 1887 that an array of 14-faced tetradecahedra on a bcc lattice might yield minimum total face area. But in 1993 Denis Weaire and Robert Phelan discovered a layered repetitive arrangement of 12- and 14-faced polyhedra (average 13.5) that yields 0.003 times less total area. It seems likely that there are polyhedra which fill space in a less regular way and yield still smaller total area. (Note that if the surfaces minimize area like soap films they are slightly curved in all these cases. See also pages 1007 and 1039.)

■ **Page 351 · Protein folding.** When the molecular structure of proteins was first studied in the 1950s it was assumed that given their amino acid sequences pure minimization of energy would determine their often elaborate overall shapes. But by the 1990s it was fairly clear that in fact many details of the actual processes by which proteins are assembled can greatly affect their specific pattern of folding. (Examples include effects of chaperone molecules and prions.) (See pages 1003 and 1184.)

Origins of Simple Behavior

■ **Previous approaches.** Before the discoveries in this book, nested and sometimes even repetitive behavior were quite often considered complex, and it was assumed that elaborate theories were necessary to explain them. Most of the theories that have been proposed are ultimately equivalent to what I discuss in this section, though they are usually presented in vastly more complicated ways.

■ **Uniformity in frequency.** As shown on page 587, a completely random sequence of cells yields a spectrum that is essentially uniform in frequency. Such uniformity in frequency is implied by standard quantum theory to exist in

the idealized zero-point fluctuations of a free quantum field—with direct consequences for such semiclassical phenomena as the Casimir effect and Hawking radiation. (See page 1062.)

■ **Repetition in numbers.** A common source of repetition in systems involving numbers is the almost trivial fact that in a sequence of successive integers there is a repetitive pattern of cases at which a particular divisor occurs. Other examples include the repetitive structure of digits in rational numbers (see page 138) and continued fraction terms in square roots (see page 144).

■ **Repetition in continuous systems.** A standard approach to partial differential equations (PDEs) used for more than a century is so-called linear stability analysis, in which one assumes that small fluctuations around some kind of basic solution can be treated as a superposition of waves of the form $Exp[i k x] Exp[i \omega t]$. And at least in a linear approximation any given PDE then typically implies that ω is connected to the wavenumber k by a so-called dispersion relation, which often has a simple algebraic form. For some k this yields a value of ω that is real—corresponding to an ordinary wave that maintains the same amplitude. But for some k one often finds that ω has an imaginary part. The most common case $Im[\omega] > 0$ yields exponential damping. But particularly when the original PDE is nonlinear one often finds that $Im[\omega] < 0$ for some range of k—implying an instability which causes modes with certain spatial wavelengths to grow. The mode with the most negative $Im[\omega]$ will grow fastest, potentially leading to repetitive behavior that shows a particular dominant spatial wavelength. Repetitive patterns with this type of origin are seen in a number of situations, especially in fluids (and notably in connection with Kelvin-Helmholtz, Rayleigh-Taylor and other well-studied instabilities). Examples are ripples and swell on an ocean (compare page 1001), Bénard convection cells, cloud streets and splash coronas. Note that modes that grow exponentially inevitably soon become too large for a linear approximation—and when this approximation breaks down more complicated behavior with no sign of simple repetitive patterns is often seen.

■ **Examples of nesting.** Examples in which a single element splits into others include branching in plants, particle showers, genealogical trees, river deltas and crushing of rocks. Examples in which elements merge include river tributaries and some cracking phenomena.

■ **Page 358 · Nesting in numbers.** Chapter 4 contains several examples of systems based on numbers that exhibit nested behavior. Ultimately these examples can usually be traced to nesting in the pattern of digits of successive integers, but significant translation is often required.

■ **Nested lists.** One can think of structures that annihilate in pairs as being like parentheses or other delimiters that come in pairs, as in the picture below.

A string of balanced parentheses is analogous to a nested *Mathematica* list such as *{{{}, {{}}}, {}}*. The *Mathematica* expression tree for this list then has a structure analogous to the nested pattern in the picture.

The set of possible strings of balanced parentheses forms a context-free language, as discussed on page 939. The number of such strings containing $2n$ characters is the nth Catalan number *Binomial[2n, n]/(n + 1)* (as obtained from the generating function *(1 - Sqrt[1 - 4x])/(2x)*). The number of strings of depth d (and thus taking d steps to annihilate completely) is given by *c[{n, n}, d] - c[{n, n}, d - 1]* where

c[{_, _}, -1] = 0; c[{0, 0}, _] = 1; c[{m_, n_}, _] := 0 /; n > m;

c[{m_, n_}, d_] :=
  Sum[c[{i, j}, d], {i, 0, m - 1}, {j, m - d, n - 1}]

Several types of structures are equivalent to strings of balanced parentheses, as illustrated below.

■ **Phase transitions.** Nesting in systems like rule 184 (see page 273) is closely related to the phenomenon of scaling studied in phase transitions and critical phenomena since the 1960s. As discussed on page 983 ordinary equilibrium statistical mechanics effectively samples configurations of systems like rule 184 after large numbers of steps of evolution. But the point is that when the initial number of black and white cells is exactly equal—corresponding to a phase transition point— a typical configuration of rule 184 will contain domains with a nested distribution of sizes. The properties of such configurations can be studied by considering invariance under rescalings of the kind discussed on page 955, in analogy to renormalization group methods. A typical result is that correlations between colors of different cells fall off like a power of distance—with the specific power depending only on general features of the nested patterns formed, and not on most details of the system.

■ **Self-organized criticality.** The fact that in traditional statistical mechanics nesting had been encountered only at the precise locations of phase transitions led in the 1980s to the notion that despite its ubiquity in nature nesting must somehow require fine tuning of parameters. Already in the early 1980s, however, my studies on simple additive and other cellular automata (see page 26) had for example made it rather clear that this is not the case. But in the late 1980s it became popular to think that in many systems nesting (as well as the largely unrelated phenomenon of *1/f* noise) might be the result of fine tuning of parameters achieved through some automatic process of self-regulation. Computer experiments on various cellular automata and related systems were given as examples of how this might work. But in most of these experiments mistakes and misinterpretations were found, and in the end little of value was learned about the origins of nesting (or *1/f* noise). Nevertheless, a number of interesting systems did emerge, the best known being the idealized sandpile model from the 1987 work of Per Bak, Chao Tang and Kurt Wiesenfeld. This is a $k = 8$ 2D cellular automaton in which toppling of sand above a critical slope is captured by updating an array of relative sand heights s according to the rule

SandStep[s_] := s + ListConvolve[
  {{0, 1, 0}, {1, -4, 1}, {0, 1, 0}}, UnitStep[s - 4], 2, 0]

Starting from any initial condition, the rule eventually yields a fixed configuration with all values less than 4, as in the picture below. (With an $n \times n$ initial block of 4's, stabilization typically takes about $0.4n^2$ steps.).

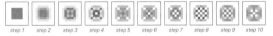

step 1   step 2   step 3   step 4   step 5   step 6   step 7   step 8   step 9   step 10

To model the pouring of sand into a pile one can consider a series of cycles, in which at each cycle one first adds 4 to the value of the center cell, then repeatedly applies the rule until a new fixed configuration *FixedPoint[SandStep, s]* is obtained. (The more usual version of the model adds to a random cell.) The picture below shows slices through the evolution at several successive cycles. Avalanches of different sizes occur, yielding activity that lasts for varying numbers of steps.

cycle 50   cycle 51   cycle 52   cycle 53   cycle 54   cycle 55   cycle 56   cycle 57   cycle 58

The pictures at the top of the next page show some of the final fixed configurations, together with the number of steps needed to reach them. (The total value of s at cycle t is $4t$; the radius of the nonzero region is about $0.74\sqrt{t}$.) The behavior one sees is fairly complicated—a fact which in the past resulted in much confusion and some bizarre claims, but which in the light of the discoveries in this book no longer seems surprising.

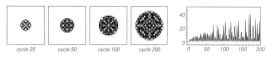

cycle 25   cycle 50   cycle 100   cycle 200

The system can be generalized to d dimensions as a $k = 4d$ cellular automaton with $2d$ final values. The total value of s is always conserved. In 1D, the update rule is simply

```
SandStep[s_]:=
  s + ListConvolve[{1, -2, 1}, UnitStep[s - 2], 2, 0]
```

In this case the evolution obtained if one repeatedly adds to the center cell (as in the first picture below) is always quite simple. But as the pictures below illustrate, evolution from typical initial conditions yields behavior that often looks a little like rule 184. With a total initial s value of m, the number of steps before a fixed point is reached seems to increase roughly like m^2.

When $d > 1$, more complicated behavior is seen for evolution from at least some initial conditions, as indicated above.

■ **Random walks.** It is a consequence of the Central Limit Theorem that the pattern of any random walk with steps of bounded length (see page 977) must have a certain nested or self-similar structure, in the sense that rescaled averages of different numbers of steps will always yield patterns that look qualitatively the same. As emphasized by Benoit Mandelbrot in connection with a variety of systems in nature, the same is also true for random walks whose step lengths follow a power-law distribution, but are unbounded. (Compare page 969.)

■ **Structure of algorithms.** The two most common overall frameworks that have traditionally been used in algorithms in computer science are iteration and recursion—and these correspond quite directly to having operations performed respectively in repetitive and nested ways. But while iteration is generally viewed as being quite easy to understand, until recently even recursion was usually considered rather difficult. No doubt the methods of this book will in the future lead to all sorts of algorithms based on much more complex patterns of behavior. (See page 1142.)

■ **Origins of localized structures.** Much as with other features of behavior, one can identify several mechanisms that can lead to localized structures. In 1D, localized structures sometimes arise as defects in largely repetitive behavior, or more generally as boundaries between states with different properties—such as the different phases of the repetitive background in rule 110. In higher dimensions a common source—especially in systems that show some level of continuity—are point, line or other topological defects (see page 1045), of which vortices are a typical example.

Implications for Everyday Systems

Issues of Modelling

■ **Page 363 · Uncertainties of this chapter.** In earlier chapters of this book what I have said can mostly be said with absolute certainty, since it is based on observations about the behavior of purely abstract systems that I have explicitly constructed. But in this chapter, I study actual systems that exist in nature, and as a result, most of what I say cannot be said with any absolute certainty, but instead must involve a significant component of hypothesis. For I no longer control the basic rules of the systems I am studying, and instead I must just try to deduce these rules from observation—with the potential that despite my best efforts my deductions could simply be incorrect.

■ **Experiences of modelling.** Over the course of the past 25 years I have constructed an immense number of models for a wide range of scientific, technical and business purposes. But while these models have often proved extremely useful in practice, I have usually considered them intellectually quite unsatisfactory. For being models, they are inevitably incomplete, and it is never in any definitive sense possible to establish their validity.

■ **Page 363 · Notes on this chapter.** Much of this book is concerned with topics that have never been discussed in any concrete form before, so that between the main text and these notes I have been able to include a large fraction of everything that is known about them. But in this chapter (as well as some of the ones that follow) the systems I consider have often had huge amounts written about them before, making any kind of complete summary quite impossible.

■ **Material for this chapter.** Like the rest of this book, this chapter is strongly based on my personal work and observations. For almost all of the systems discussed I have personally collected extensive data and samples, often over the course of many years, and sometimes in quite unlikely and amusing circumstances. I have also tried to study the existing scientific literature, and indeed in working on this chapter I have looked at many thousands of papers and books—even though the vast majority of them tend to ignore overall issues, and instead concentrate on details of often excruciating specificity.

■ **Page 365 · Models versus experiments.** In modern science it is usually said that the ultimate test of any model is its agreement with experiment. But this is often interpreted to mean that if an experiment ever disagrees with a model, then the model must be wrong. Particularly when the model is simple and the experiment is complex, however, my personal experience has been that it is quite common for it to be the experiment, rather than the model, that is wrong. When I started doing particle physics in the mid-1970s I assumed—like most theoretical scientists—that the results of experiments could somehow always be treated as rigid constraints on models. But in 1977 I worked on constructing the first model based on QCD for heavy particle production in high-energy proton-proton collisions. The model predicted a certain rate for the production of such particles. But an experiment which failed to see any of these particles implied that the rate must be much lower. And on the basis of this I spent great effort trying to see what might be wrong with the model—only to discover some time later that in fact the methodology of the experiment was flawed and its results were wrong. At first I thought that perhaps this was an isolated incident. But soon I had seen many examples where the stated results of physics experiments were incorrect, either through straightforward mistakes or through subtly prejudiced analysis. And outside of physics, I have tended to find still less reliability in the results of complex experiments.

■ **Page 366 · Models versus reality.** Questions about the correspondence between models and reality have been much debated in the philosophy of science for many centuries, and were, for example, central to the disagreement between Galileo and the church in the early 1600s. Many successful models are in practice first introduced as convenient calculational devices, but later turn out to have a direct correspondence to reality. Two examples are planets orbiting the Sun, and quarks being constituents of particles. It remains to be seen whether such models as the imaginary time statistical mechanics formalism for quantum mechanics (see page 1061) turn out to have any direct correspondence to reality.

■ **History of modelling.** Creation myths can in a sense be viewed as primitive models. Early examples of models with more extensive structure included epicycles. Traditional mathematical models of the modern type originated in the 1600s. The success of such models in physics led to attempts to imitate them in other fields, but for the most part these did not succeed. The idea of modelling intricate patterns using programs arose to some extent in the study of fractals in the late 1970s. And the notion of models based on simple programs such as cellular automata was central to my work in the early 1980s. But despite quite a number of fairly well-known successes, there is even now surprisingly little understanding among most scientists of the idea of models based on simple programs. Work in computer graphics—with its emphasis on producing pictures that look right—has made some contributions. And it seems likely that the possibility of computerized and especially image-based data taking will contribute further. (See also page 860.)

■ **Page 367 · Finding models.** Even though a model may have a simple form, it may not be at all easy to find. Indeed, many of the models in this chapter took me a very long time to find. By far my most common mistake was trying to build too much into the basic structure of the model. Often I was sure that some feature of the behavior of a system must be built into the underlying model—yet I could see no simple way to do it. But eventually what happened was that I tried a few other very simple models, and to my great surprise one of them ended up showing the behavior I wanted, even though I had in no way explicitly built it in.

■ **Page 369 · Consequences of models.** Given a program it is always possible to run the program to find out what it will do. But as I discuss in Chapter 12, when the behavior is complex it may take an irreducible amount of computational work to answer any given question about it. However, this is not a sign of imperfection in the model; it is merely a fundamental feature of complex behavior.

■ **Universality in models.** With traditional models based on equations, it is usually assumed that there is a unique correct version of any model. But in the previous chapter we saw that it is possible for quite different programs to yield

essentially the same large-scale behavior, implying that with programs there can be many models that have the same consequences but different detailed underlying structure.

The Growth of Crystals

■ **Page 369 · Nucleation.** In the absence of container walls or of other objects that can act as seeds, liquids and gases can typically be supercooled quite far below their freezing points. It appears to be extremely unlikely for spontaneous microscopic fluctuations to initiate crystal growth, and natural snowflakes, for example, presumably nucleate around dust or other particles in the air. Snowflakes in man-made snow are typically nucleated by synthetic materials. In this case and in experiments on cloud seeding it has been observed that the details of seeds can affect the overall shapes of crystals that grow from them.

■ **Page 369 · Implementation.** One can treat hexagonal lattices as distorted square lattices, updated according to

$CAStep[rule\_List, a\_] := Map[rule[[14 - \#]] \&,$
$\quad a + 2\ ListConvolve[\{\{1, 1, 0\}, \{1, 0, 1\}, \{0, 1, 1\}\}, a, 2], \{2\}]$

where $rule = IntegerDigits[code, 2, 14]$. On this page the rule used is code 16382; on page 371 it is code 10926. The centers of an array of regular hexagons are given by $Table[\{i\sqrt{3}, j\}, \{i, 1, m\}, \{j, Mod[i, 2], n, 2\}]$.

■ **Page 372 · Identical snowflakes.** The widespread claim that no two snowflakes are alike is not in practice true. It is however the case that as a result of turbulent air currents a collection of snowflakes that fall to the ground in a particular region will often have come from very different regions of a cloud, and therefore will have grown in different environments. Note that the reason that the six arms of a single snowflake usually look the same is that all of them have grown in essentially the same environment. Deviations are usually the result of collisions between falling snowflakes.

■ **History of snowflake studies.** Rough sketches of snowflakes were published by Olaus Magnus of Uppsala around 1550. Johannes Kepler made more detailed pictures and identified hexagonal symmetry around 1611. Over the course of the next few centuries, following work by René Descartes, Robert Hooke and others, progressively more accurate pictures were made and correlations between weather conditions and snowflake forms were found. Thousands of photographs of snowflakes were taken by Wilson Bentley over the period 1884–1931. Beginning in 1932 an extensive study of snowflakes was made by Ukichiro Nakaya, who in 1936 also produced the first artificial snowflakes. Most of the fairly small amount of more recent work on snowflakes has been done as part of more general studies on dendritic crystal growth. Note that tree-like snowflakes are what make snow fluffy, while simple hexagons make it denser and more slippery. The proportion of different types of snowflakes is important in understanding phenomena such as avalanches.

■ **History of crystal growth.** The vast majority of work done on crystal growth has been concerned with practical methods rather than with theoretical analyses. The first synthetic gemstones were made in the mid-1800s, and methods for making high-quality crystals of various materials have been developed over the course of the past century. Since the mid-1970s such crystals have been crucial to the semiconductor industry. Systematic studies of the symmetries of crystals with flat facets began in the 1700s, and the relationship to internal structure was confirmed by X-ray crystallography in the 1920s. The many different possible external forms of crystals have been noted in mineralogy since Greek times, but although classification schemes have been given, these forms have apparently still not been studied in a particularly systematic way.

■ **Models of crystal growth.** There are two common types of models for crystal growth: ones based on the physics of individual atoms, and ones based on continuum descriptions of large collections of atoms. In the former category, it was recognized in the 1940s that a single atom is very unlikely to stick to a completely flat surface, so growth will always tend to occur at steps on a crystal surface, often associated with screw dislocations in the crystal structure. In practice, however, as scanning tunnelling microscopes have revealed, most crystal surfaces that are not grown at an extremely slow rate tend to be quite rough at an atomic scale—and so it seems that for example the aggregation model from page 331 may be more appropriate. In snowflakes and other crystals features such as the branches of tree-like structures are much larger than atomic dimensions, so a continuum description can potentially be used. It is possible to write down a nonlinear partial differential equation for the motion of the solidification front, taking into account basic thermodynamic effects. The first result (discovered by William Mullins and Robert Sekerka in 1963) is that if every part of the front is at the same temperature, then any deviations from planarity in the front will tend to grow. The shape of the front is presumably stabilized by the Gibbs-Thomson effect, which implies that the freezing temperature is lower when the front is more curved. The characteristic length for deformations of the front turns out to be the geometric mean of a microscopic length associated with surface energy and a macroscopic length associated with diffusion. It is this characteristic

length that presumably determines the size of an individual cell in the cellular automaton model.

Dendritic crystals are commonly seen in ice formations on windows, and in pieces of aluminum of the kind found at typical hardware stores.

■ **Hopper crystals.** When a pool of molten bismuth solidifies it tends to form crystals like those in the first two pictures below. What seems to give these crystals their characteristic "hoppered" shapes is that there is more rapid growth at the edges of each face than at the center. (Spirals are probably associated with underlying screw dislocations.) Hoppering has not been much studied for scientific purposes, but has been noticed in many substances, including galena, rose quartz, gold, calcite, salt and ice.

■ **Page 373 · Other models.** There are many ways to extend the simple cellular automata shown here. One possibility is to allow dependence on next-nearest as well as nearest neighbors. In this case it turns out that non-convex as well as convex faceted shapes can be obtained. Another possibility is to allow cells that have become black to turn white again. In this case all the various kinds of patterns that we saw in Chapter 5 can occur. A general feature of cellular automaton rules is that they are fundamentally local. Some models of crystal growth, however, call for long-range effects such as a temperature field which changes throughout the crystal in an effectively instantaneous way. It turns out, however, that many seemingly long-range effects can actually be captured quite easily in cellular automata. In a typical case, this can be done by introducing a third possible color for each cell, and then having rapidly changing arrangements of this color.

■ **Polycrystalline materials.** When solids with complicated forms are seen, it has usually been assumed that they must be aggregates of many separate crystals, with each crystal having a simple faceted shape. But the results given here indicate that in fact individual crystals can yield highly complex shapes. There will nevertheless be cases however where multiple crystals are involved. These can be modelled by having a cellular automaton in which one starts from several separated seeds. Sometimes the regions associated with different seeds may have different characteristics; the boundaries between these regions then form a Voronoi diagram (see page 1038).

■ **Quasicrystals.** In some special materials it was discovered in 1984 that atoms are arranged not on a purely repetitive grid, but instead in a pattern with the nested type of structure discussed on page 932. A characteristic feature of such patterns is that they can have approximate pentagonal or icosahedral symmetry, which is impossible for purely repetitive patterns. It has usually been assumed that the arrangement of atoms in a quasicrystal is determined by satisfying a constraint analogous to minimization of energy. And as we saw on page 932 it is indeed possible to get nested patterns by requiring that certain constraints be satisfied. But another explanation for such patterns is that they are the result of growth processes that are some kind of cross between those on pages 373 and 659.

■ **Amorphous materials.** When solidification occurs fairly slowly, atoms have time to arrange themselves in a regular crystalline way. But if the cooling is sufficiently rapid, amorphous solids such as glasses are often formed. And in such cases, the packing of atoms is quite random—except that locally there is often approximate icosahedral structure, analogous to that discussed on page 943. (See also page 986.)

■ **Diffusion-limited aggregation (DLA).** DLA is a model for a variety of natural growth processes that was invented by Thomas Witten and Leonard Sander in 1981, and which at first seems quite different from a cellular automaton. The basic idea of DLA is to build up a cluster of black cells by starting with a single black cell and then successively introducing new black cells far away that undergo random walks and stick to the cluster as soon as they come into contact with it. The patterns that are obtained by this procedure turn out for reasons that are still not particularly clear to have a random but on average nested form. (Depending on precise details of the underlying model, very large clusters may sometimes not have nested forms, at least in 2D.) The basic reason that DLA patterns are not very dense is that once arms have formed on the outside of the cluster, they tend to catch new cells before these cells have had a chance to go inside. It turns out that at a mathematical level DLA can be reproduced by solving the Laplace equation at each step with a constant boundary condition on the cluster, and then using the result to give the probability for adding a new cell at each point on the cluster. To construct a cellular automaton analog of DLA one can introduce gray as well as black and white cells, and then have the gray cells represent pieces of solid that have not yet become permanently attached to the main cluster. Rapid rearrangement of gray cells on successive steps can then have a similar effect to the random walks that occur in the usual DLA model. Whether a pattern with all the properties expected in DLA is produced

seems to depend in some detail on the rules for the gray cells. But so long as there is effective randomness in the successive positions of these cells, and so long as the total number of them is conserved, then it appears that DLA-like results are usually obtained. No doubt there are also simpler cellular automaton rules that yield similar results. (See also page 979.)

■ **Boiling.** The boiling of a liquid such as water involves a kind of growth inhibition that is in some ways analogous to that seen in dendritic crystal growth. When a particular piece of liquid boils—forming a bubble of gas—a certain latent heat is consumed, reducing the local temperature, and inhibiting further boiling. In the pictures below the liquid is divided into cells, with each cell having a temperature from 0 to 1, corresponding exactly to a continuous cellular automaton of the kind discussed on page 155. At each step, the temperature of every cell is given by the average of its temperature and the temperatures of its neighbors, representing the process of heat diffusion, with a constant amount added to represent external heating. If the temperature of any cell exceeds 1, then only the fractional part is kept, as in the systems on page 158, representing the consumption of latent heat in the boiling process. The pictures below illustrate the kind of seemingly random pattern of bubble formation that can be heard in the noise produced by boiling water.

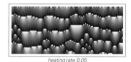 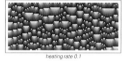

heating rate 0.05   heating rate 0.1

The Breaking of Materials

■ **Phenomenology of microscopic fracture.** Different materials show rather different characteristics depending on how ductile or brittle they are. Ductile materials—such as taffy or mild steel—bend and smoothly neck before breaking. Brittle materials—such as chalk or glass—do not deform significantly before catastrophic failure. Ductile materials in effect flow slightly before breaking, and as a result their fracture surfaces tend to be less jagged. In addition, in response to stresses in the material, small voids often form—perhaps nucleating around imperfections—yielding a pockmarked surface. In brittle materials, the beginning of the fracture surface typically looks quite mirror-like, then it starts to look misty, and finally, often at a sharply defined point, it begins to look complex and hackled. (This sequence is qualitatively not unlike the initiation of randomness in turbulent fluid flow and many other systems.) Cracks in brittle materials typically seem to start slowly, then accelerate to about half the Rayleigh speed at which small deformation waves on the surface would propagate. Brittle fracture involves violent breaking of atomic bonds; it usually leaves a jagged surface, and can lead to emission of both high-frequency sound as well as light. Directly around a crack complex patterns of stress are typically produced, though away from the crack they resolve quickly to a fairly smooth and simple form. It is known that ultrasound can affect the course of cracks, suggesting that crack propagation is affected by local stresses. There are many different detailed geometries for fracture, associated with snapping, tearing, shattering, pulling apart, and so on. In many situations, individual cracks will split into multiple cracks as they propagate, sometimes producing elaborate tree-like structures. The statistical properties of fracture surfaces have been studied fairly extensively. There is reasonable evidence of self-similarity, typically associated with a fractal dimension around 0.8 or slightly smaller.

■ **Models of microscopic fracture.** Two kinds of models have traditionally been studied: ones based on looking at arrays of atoms, and ones based on continuum descriptions of materials. At the atomic level, a simple model suggested fairly recently is that atoms are connected by bonds with a random distribution of strengths, and that cracks follow paths that minimize the total strength of bonds to be broken. It is not clear why in a crystal bonds should be of different strengths, and there is some evidence that this model yields incorrect predictions for the statistical properties of actual cracks. A slightly better model, related to the one in the main text, is that the bonds between atoms are identical, and act like springs which break when they are stretched too far. In recent years, computer simulations with millions of atoms have been carried out—usually with realistic but complicated interatomic force laws—and some randomness has been observed, but its origins have not been isolated. A set of nonlinear partial differential equations known as the Lamé equations are commonly used as a continuum description of elastic materials. Various instabilities have been found in these equations, but the equations are based on small deformations, and presumably cannot be relied upon to provide information about fracture.

■ **History.** Fracture has been a critical issue throughout the history of engineering. Its scientific study was particularly stimulated by failures of various types of ships and aircraft in the 1940s and 1950s, and many quantitative empirical results were obtained, so that by the 1960s ductile fracture as an engineering issue became fairly well understood. In the 1980s, ideas about fractals suggested new interpretations of

fracture surfaces, and in the past few years, various models of fracture based on ideas from statistical physics have been tried. Atomic-level computer experiments on fracture began in earnest in the late 1980s, but only very recently has it been possible to include enough atoms to even begin addressing questions about the structure of cracks.

■ **Page 375 · Experimental data.** To investigate the model in the main text requires looking not only at the path of a crack, but also at dislocations of atoms near it. To do this dynamically is difficult, but in a perfect crystal final patterns of dislocations that remain at the edge of a region affected by fracture can be seen for example by electron diffraction. And it turns out that these often look remarkably like patterns made by 1D class 3 cellular automata. (Similar patterns may perhaps also be seen in recent detailed simulations of fracture processes in arrays of idealized atoms.)

■ **Large-scale fractures.** It is remarkable to what extent very large-scale fractures can look like small-scale ones. If the path of a crack were, say, a perfect random walk, then one might imagine that large-scale cracks could simply be combinations of many small-scale segments. But when one looks at geological systems, for example, the smallest relevant scales for the cracks one sees are certainly no smaller than particles of soil. And as a result, one needs a more general mechanism, not just one that just relates to atoms and molecules.

■ **Alternate models.** It is straightforward to set up 3-color cellular automata with the same basic idea as in the main text, but in which there is no need for a special cell to represent the crack. In addition, instead of modelling the displacement of atoms, one can try to model directly the presence or absence of atoms at particular positions. And then one can start from a repetitive array of cells, with a perturbation to represent the beginning of the crack.

■ **Electric breakdown.** Somewhat related to fracture is the process of electric breakdown, visible for example in lightning, Lichtenberg figures or plasma-filled glass globes used as executive toys. At least in the case of lightning, there is some evidence that small inhomogeneities in the atmosphere can be important in producing at least some aspects of the apparent randomness that is seen. (With electric potential thought of like a diffusion field, models based on diffusion-limited aggregation are sometimes used.)

■ **Crushing.** For a rather wide range of cases it appears that in crushed solids such as rocks the probability of a particular fragment having a diameter larger than r is given approximately by $r^{-2.5}$. It seems likely that the origin of this is that each rock has a certain probability to break into, say, two smaller rocks at each stage in the crushing process, much as in a substitution system.

■ **Effects of microscopic roughness.** The two most obvious features that are affected by the microscopic roughness of materials are visual appearance and sliding friction. A perfectly flat surface will reflect light like a mirror. Roughness will lead to more diffuse reflection, although the connection between observed properties of rough surfaces and typical parametrizations used in computer graphics is not clear.

The friction force that opposes sliding is usually assumed to be proportional purely to the force with which surfaces are pressed together. Presumably at least the beginning of the explanation for this slightly bizarre fact is that most of the friction force is associated with microscopic peaks in rough surfaces, and that the number of these peaks that come into close contact increases as surfaces are pushed together.

■ **Crinkling.** A question somewhat related to fracture concerns the generation of definite creases in crumpled or wrinkled objects such as pieces of paper or fabric. It is not too difficult to make various statements about details of the particular arrangements of creases that can occur, but nothing seems to be known about the origin of the overall randomness that is almost universally seen.

Fluid Flow

■ **Page 376 · Reynolds numbers.** If a system is to act like a continuum fluid, then almost by definition its behavior can involve only a limited number of macroscopic quantities, such as density and velocity. And from this it follows that patterns of flow should not depend separately on absolute speeds and sizes. Instead, the character of a flow should typically be determined by a single Reynolds number, $Re = U L/v$, where U is the characteristic speed of the flow (measured say in cm/sec), L is a characteristic size (measured say in cm), and v is the kinematic viscosity of the fluid. For water, $v = 0.01$, for air $v = 0.15$, and for glycerine $v = 10000$, all in units of cm^2/sec. In flow past a cylinder it is conventional to take L to be the diameter of the cylinder. But the fact that the form of flow should depend only on Reynolds number means that in the pictures in the main text for example it is not necessary to specify absolute sizes or speeds: one need only know the product $U L$ that appears in the Reynolds number. In practice, moving one's finger slowly through water gives a Reynolds number of about 100 (so that a regular array of dimples corresponding to eddies are visible

behind one's finger), walking in air about 10,000, a boat in the millions, and a large airplane in the billions.

The Reynolds number roughly measures the ratio of inertial to viscous effects. When the Reynolds number is small the viscous damping dominates, and the flow is laminar and smooth. When the Reynolds number is large, inertia associated with fluid motions dominates, and the flow is turbulent and complicated.

In different systems, the characteristic length used typically in the definition of Reynolds number is different. In most cases, however, the transition from laminar to turbulent flow occurs at Reynolds numbers around a hundred.

In some situations, however, Reynolds number alone does not appear to be sufficient to determine when a flow will become turbulent. Indeed, modern experiments on streams of dye in water (or rising columns of smoke) typically show a transition to turbulence at a significantly lower Reynolds number than the original experiments on these systems done by Osborne Reynolds in the 1880s. Presumably the reason for this is that the transition point can be lowered by perturbations from the environment, and such perturbations are more common in the modern mechanized world. If perturbations are indeed important, it implies that a traditional fluid description is not adequate. I suspect, however, that even though perturbations may determine the precise point at which turbulence begins, intrinsic randomness generation will dominate once turbulence has been initiated.

■ **Navier-Stokes equations.** The traditional model of fluids used in physics is based on a set of partial differential equations known as the Navier-Stokes equations. These equations were originally derived in the 1840s on the basis of conservation laws and first-order approximations. But if one assumes sufficient randomness in microscopic molecular processes they can also be derived from molecular dynamics, as done in the early 1900s, as well as from cellular automata of the kind shown on page 378, as I did in 1985 (see below). For very low Reynolds numbers and simple geometries, it is often possible to find explicit formulas for solutions to the Navier-Stokes equations. But even in the regime of flow where regular arrays of eddies are produced, analytical methods have never yielded complete explicit solutions. In this regime, however, numerical approximations are fairly easy to find. Since about the 1960s computers have been powerful enough to allow computations at least nominally to be extended to considerably higher Reynolds numbers. And indeed it has become increasingly common to see numerical results given far into the turbulent regime—leading sometimes to the assumption that turbulence has somehow been derived from the Navier-Stokes equations. But just what such numerical results actually have to do with detailed solutions to the Navier-Stokes equations is not clear. For in particular it ends up being almost impossible to distinguish whatever genuine instability and apparent randomness may be implied by the Navier-Stokes equations from artifacts that get introduced through the discretization procedure used in solving the equations on a computer. One of the key advantages of my cellular automaton approach to fluids is precisely that it does not require any such approximations.

At a mathematical level analysis of the Navier-Stokes has never established the formal uniqueness and existence of solutions. Indeed, there is even some evidence that singularities might almost inevitably form, which would imply a breakdown of the equations, and perhaps a need to account for underlying molecular processes.

In turbulent flow at higher Reynolds numbers there begin to be eddies with a wide range of sizes. And to capture all these eddies in a computation eventually involves prohibitively large amounts of information. In practice, therefore, semi-empirical models of turbulence tend to be used—often "eddy viscosities"—with no direct relation to the Navier-Stokes equations. In airflow past an airplane there is however typically only a one-inch layer on each surface where such issues are important; the large-scale features of the remainder of the flow, which nevertheless accounts for only about half the drag on the airplane, can usually be studied without reference to turbulence.

The Navier-Stokes equations assume that all speeds are small compared to the speed of sound—and thus that the Mach number giving the ratio of these speeds is much less than one. In essentially all practical situations, Mach numbers close to one occur only at extremely high Reynolds numbers—where turbulence in any case would make it impossible to work out the detailed consequences of the Navier-Stokes equations. Nevertheless, in the case of cellular automaton fluids, I was able in 1985 to work out the rather complicated next order corrections to the Navier-Stokes equations.

Above the speed of sound, fluids form shocks where density or velocity change over very small distances (see below). And by Mach 4 or so, shocks are typically so sharp that changes occur in less than the distance between molecular collisions—making it essential to go beyond the continuum fluid approximation, and account for molecular effects.

■ **Models of turbulence.** Traditional models typically view turbulence as consisting of some form of cascade of eddies.

This notion was already suggested in pictures by Leonardo da Vinci from around 1510, and in Japanese pictures (notably by Katsushika Hokusai) from around 1800 showing ocean waves breaking into precisely nested tongues of water. The theoretical study of turbulence began in earnest in the early 1900s, with emphasis on issues such as energy transfer among eddies and statistical correlations between velocities. Most published work became increasingly mathematical, but particularly following the ideas of Lewis Richardson in the 1920s, the underlying physical notion was that a large eddy, formed say by fluid flowing around an object, would be unstable, and would break up into smaller eddies, which in turn would break up into still smaller eddies, until eventually the eddies would be of such a size as to be readily damped by viscosity. An important step was taken in 1941 by Andrei Kolmogorov who argued that if the eddies in such a cascade were in a statistical equilibrium, then dimensional analysis would effectively imply that the spectrum of velocity fluctuations associated with the eddies must have a $k^{-5/3}$ distribution, with k being wavenumber. This result has turned out to be in respectable agreement with a range of experimental data, but its physical significance has remained somewhat unclear. For there appear to be no explicit entities in fluids that can be directly identified as cascades of eddies. One possibility might be that an eddy could correspond to a local patch of vorticity or rotation in the fluid. And it is a general feature of fluids that interfaces between regions of different velocity are unstable, typically first becoming wavy and then breaking into separate pieces. But physical experiments and simulations in the past few years have suggested that vorticity in turbulent fluids in practice tends to become concentrated on a complicated network of lines that stretch and twist. Perhaps some interpretation can be made involving eddies existing only in a fractal region, or interacting with each other as well as branching. And perhaps new forms of definite localized structures can be identified. But no clear understanding has yet emerged, and indeed most of the analysis that is done—which tends to be largely statistical in nature—is not likely to shed much light on the general question of why there is so much apparent randomness in turbulence.

■ **Chaos theory and turbulence.** The full Navier-Stokes equations for fluid flow are far from being amenable to traditional mathematical analysis. But some simplified ordinary differential equations which potentially approximate various situations in fluid flow can be more amenable to analysis—and can exhibit the chaos phenomenon. Work in the 1950s by Lev Landau, Andrei Kolmogorov and others focused on equations with periodic and quasiperiodic behavior. But in 1962 Edward Lorenz discovered more complicated behavior in computer experiments on equations related to fluid flow (see page 971). Analysis of this behavior was closely linked to the chaos phenomenon of sensitive dependence on initial conditions. And by the late 1970s it had become popular to believe that the randomness in fluid turbulence was somehow associated with this phenomenon.

Experiments in very restricted situations showed correspondence with iterated maps in which the chaos phenomenon is seen. But the details of the connection with true turbulence remained unclear. And as I argue in the main text, the chaos phenomenon in the end seems quite unlikely to explain most of the randomness we see in turbulence. The basic problem is that a complex pattern of flow in effect involves a huge amount of information—and to extract this information purely from initial conditions would require for example going to a submolecular level, far below where traditional models of fluids could possibly apply.

Even within the context of the Lorenz equations there are already indications of difficulties with the chaos explanation. The Lorenz equations represent a first-order approximation to certain Navier-Stokes-like equations, in which viscosity is ignored. And when one goes to higher orders progressively more account is taken of viscosity, but the chaos phenomenon becomes progressively weaker. I suspect that in the limit where viscosity is fully included most details of initial conditions will simply be damped out, as physical intuition suggests. Even within the Lorenz equations, however, one can see evidence of intrinsic randomness generation, in which randomness is produced without any need for randomness in initial conditions. And as it turns out I suspect that despite subsequent developments the original ideas of Andrei Kolmogorov about complicated behavior in ordinary differential equations were probably more in line with my notion of intrinsic randomness generation than with the chaos phenomenon.

■ **Flows past objects.** By far the most experimental data has been collected for flows past cylinders. The few comparisons that have been done indicate that most results are extremely similar for plates and other non-streamlined or "bluff" objects. For spheres at infinitesimal Reynolds numbers a fairly simple exact analytical solution to the Navier-Stokes equations was found by George Stokes in 1851, giving a drag coefficient of $6\pi/R$. For a cylinder, there are difficulties with boundary conditions at infinity, but the drag coefficient was nevertheless calculated by William Oseen in 1915 to be $8\pi/(R(1/2 + Log[8/R] - EulerGamma))$. At infinitesimal Reynolds number the flow around a

symmetrical object is always symmetrical. As the Reynolds number increases, it becomes progressively more asymmetrical, and at $R \simeq 6$ for a cylinder, closed eddies begin to appear behind the object. The length of the region associated with these eddies is found to grow almost perfectly linearly with Reynolds number. At $R \simeq 30-40$ for a cylinder, oscillations are often seen in the eddies, and at $R \simeq 46-49$, a vortex street forms. Increasingly accurate numerical calculations based on direct approximations to the Navier-Stokes equations have been done in the regime of attached eddies since the 1930s. For a vortex street no analytical solution has ever been found, and indeed it is only recently that the general paths of fluid elements have even been accurately deduced. A simple model due to Theodore von Kármán from 1911 predicts a relative spacing of $\pi/Log[1 + \sqrt{2}\,]$ between vortices, and bifurcation theory analyses have provided some justification for some such result. Over the range $50 \lesssim R \lesssim 150$ vortices are found to be generated at a cylinder with almost perfect periodicity at a dimensionless frequency (Strouhal number) that increases smoothly from about 0.12 to 0.19. But even though successive vortices are formed at fixed intervals, irregularities can develop as the array of vortices goes downstream, and such irregularities seem to occur at lower Reynolds numbers for flows past plates than cylinders. Some direct calculations of interactions between vortices have been done in the context of the Navier-Stokes equations, but the cellular automaton approach of page 378 seems to provide essentially the first reliable global results. In both calculations and experiments, there is often sensitivity to details of whatever boundary conditions are imposed on the fluid, even if they are far from the object. Results can also be affected by the history of the flow. In general, the early way the flow develops over time typically mirrors quite precisely the long-time behavior seen at successively greater Reynolds numbers. In experiments, the process of vortex generation at a cylinder first becomes irregular somewhere between $R = 140$ and $R = 194$. After this surprisingly few qualitative changes are seen even up to Reynolds numbers as high as 100,000. There is overall periodicity much like in a vortex street, but the detailed motion of the fluid is increasingly random. Typically the scale of the smallest eddies gets smaller in rough correspondence with the $R^{-3/4}$ prediction of Kolmogorov's general arguments about turbulence. In flow past a cylinder, there are various quite sudden changes in the periodicity, apparently associated with 3D phenomena in which the flow is not uniform along the axis of the cylinder. The drag coefficient remains almost constant at a value around 1 until $R \simeq 3 \times 10^5$, at which point it drops precipitously for a while.

This phenomenon is associated with details of flow close to the cylinder. At lower Reynolds numbers, the flow is still laminar when it first comes around the cylinder; but there is a transition to turbulence in this boundary layer after which the fluid can in effect slide more easily around the cylinder. When the speed of the flow passes the speed of sound in the fluid, shocks appear. Usually they form simple geometrical patterns (see below), and have the effect of forcing the turbulent wake behind the cylinder to become narrower.

■ **2D fluids.** The cellular automaton shown in the main text is purely two-dimensional. Experiments done on soap films since the 1980s indicate, however, that at least up to Reynolds numbers of several hundred, the patterns of flow around objects such as cylinders are almost identical to those seen in ordinary 3D fluids. The basic argument for Kolmogorov's $k^{-5/3}$ result for the spectrum of turbulence is independent of dimension, but there are reasons to believe that in 2D eddies will tend to combine, so that after sufficiently long times only a small number of large eddies will be left. There is some evidence for this kind of process in the Earth's atmosphere, as well as in such phenomena as the Red Spot on Jupiter. At a microscopic level, there are some not completely unrelated issues in 2D about whether perturbations in a fluid made up of discrete molecules damp quickly enough to lead to ordinary viscosity. Formally, there is evidence that the Navier-Stokes equations in 2D might have a $\nabla^2 \text{Log}[\nabla^2]$ viscosity term, rather than a ∇^2 one. But this effect, even if it is in fact present in principle, is almost certainly irrelevant on the scales of practical experiments.

■ **Cellular automaton fluids.** A large number of technical issues can be studied in connection with cellular automaton fluids. Many were already discussed in my original 1985 paper. Others have been covered in some of the many papers that have appeared since then. Of particular concern are issues about how rotation and translation invariance emerge at the level of fluid processes even though they are absent in the underlying cellular automaton structure. The very simplest rules turn out to have difficulties in these regards (see page 1024), which is why the model shown in the main text, for example, is on a hexagonal rather than a square grid (compare page 980). The model can be viewed as a block cellular automaton of the type discussed on page 460, but on a 2D hexagonal grid. In general a block cellular automaton works by making replacements for overlapping blocks of cells on alternating steps. In the 1D case of page 460, the blocks that are replaced consist of pairs of adjacent cells with two different alignments. On a 2D square grid, one can use overlapping 2×2 square blocks. But on a 2D hexagonal grid,

one must instead alternate on successive steps between hexagons and their dual triangles.

■ **Vorticity-based models.** As an alternative to models of fluids based on elements with discrete velocities, one can consider using elements with discrete vorticities.

■ **History of cellular automaton fluids.** Following the development of the molecular model for gases in the late 1800s (see page 1019), early mathematical derivations of continuum fluid behavior from underlying molecular dynamics were already complete by the 1920s. More streamlined approaches with the same basic assumptions continued to be developed over the next several decades. In the late 1950s Berni Alder and Thomas Wainwright began to do computer simulations of idealized molecular dynamics of 2D hard spheres—mainly to investigate transitions between solids, liquids and gases. In 1967 they observed so-called long-time tails not expected from existing calculations, and although it was realized that these were a consequence of fluid-like behavior not readily accounted for in purely microscopic approximations, it did not seem plausible that large-scale fluid phenomena could be investigated with molecular dynamics. The idea of setting up models with discrete approximations to the velocities of molecules appears to have arisen first in the work of James Broadwell in 1964 on the dynamics of rarefied gases. In the 1960s there was also interest in so-called lattice gases in which—by analogy with spin systems like the Ising model—discrete particles were placed in all possible configurations on a lattice subject to certain local constraints, and average equilibrium properties were computed. By the early 1970s more dynamic models were sometimes being considered, and for example Yves Pomeau and collaborators constructed idealized models of gases in which both positions and velocities of molecules were discrete. As it happens, in 1973, as one of my earliest computer programs, I created a simulation of essentially the same kind of system (see page 17). But it turned out that this particular kind of system, set up as it was on a square grid, was almost uniquely unable to generate the kind of randomness that we have seen so often in this book, and that is needed to obtain standard large-scale fluid behavior. And as a result, essentially no further development on discrete models of fluids was then done until after my work on cellular automata in the early 1980s. I had always viewed turbulent fluids as an important potential application for cellular automata. And in 1984, as part of work I was doing on massively parallel computing, I resolved to develop a practical approach to fluid mechanics based on cellular automata. I initiated discussions with various members of the fluid dynamics community, who strongly discouraged me from pursuing my ideas. But I persisted, and by the summer of 1985 I had managed to produce pictures like those on page 378. Meanwhile, however, some of the very same individuals who had discouraged me had in fact themselves pursued exactly the line of research I had discussed. And by late 1985, cellular automaton fluids were generating considerable interest throughout the fluid mechanics community. Many claims were made that existing computational methods were necessarily far superior. But in practice over the years since 1985, cellular automaton methods have grown steadily in popularity, and are now widely used in physics and engineering. Yet despite all the work that has been done, the fundamental issues about the origins of turbulence that I had originally planned to investigate in cellular automaton fluids have remained largely untouched.

■ **Computational fluid dynamics.** From its inception in the mid-1940s until the invention of cellular automaton fluids in the 1980s, essentially all computational fluid dynamics involved taking the continuum Navier-Stokes equations and then approximating these equations using some form of discrete mesh in space and time, and arguing that when the mesh becomes small enough, correct results would be obtained. Cellular automaton fluids start from a fundamentally discrete system which can be simulated precisely, and thus avoid the need for any such arguments. One issue however is that in the simplest cellular automaton fluids molecules are in effect counted in unary: each molecule is traced separately, rather than just being included as part of a total number that can be manipulated using standard arithmetic operations. A variety of tricks, however, maintain precision while in effect allowing a large number of molecules to be handled at the same time.

■ **Sound waves and shocks.** Sound waves in a fluid correspond to periodic variations in density. The pictures below show how a density perturbation leads to a sound wave in a cellular automaton fluid. The sound wave turns out to travel at a fraction $1/\sqrt{2}$ of the microscopic particle speed.

| step 1 | step 50 | step 100 | step 150 |

When the speed of a fluid relative to an object becomes comparable to the speed of sound, the fluid will inevitably show variations in density. Typically shocks develop at the front and back of an object, as illustrated below.

| step 100 | step 500 | step 1000 |

It turns out that when two shocks meet, they usually have little effect on each other, and when there are boundaries, shocks are usually reflected in simple ways. The result of this is that in most situations patterns of shocks generated have a fairly simple geometrical structure, with none of the randomness of turbulence.

■ **Splashes.** Particularly familiar everyday examples of complex fluid behavior are splashes made by objects falling into water. When a water drop hits a water surface, at first a symmetrical crater forms. But soon its rim becomes unstable, and several peaks (often with small drops at the top) appear in a characteristic coronet pattern. If the original drop was moving quickly, a whole hemisphere of water then closes in above. But in any case a peak appears at the center, sometimes with a spherical drop at the top. If a solid object is dropped into water, the overall structure of the splash made can depend in great detail on its shape and surface roughness. Splashes were studied using flash photography by Arthur Worthington around 1900 (as well as Harold Edgerton in the 1950s), but remarkably little theoretical investigation of them has ever been made.

■ **Generalizations of fluid flow.** In the simplest case the local state of a fluid is characterized by its velocity and perhaps density. But there are many situations where there are also other quantities relevant, notably temperature and chemical composition. And it turns out to be rather straightforward to generalize cellular automaton fluids to handle these.

■ **Convection.** When there is a temperature difference between the top and bottom of a fluid, hot fluid tends to rise, and cold fluid then comes down again. At low temperature differences (characterized by a low dimensionless Rayleigh number) a regular pattern of hexagonal Bénard convection cells is formed (see page 377). But as the temperature difference increases, a transition to turbulence is seen, with most of the same characteristics as in flow past an object. A cellular automaton model can be made by allowing particles with more than one possible energy: the average particle energy in a region corresponds to fluid temperature.

■ **Atmospheric turbulence.** Convection occurs because air near the ground is warmer than air at higher altitudes. On a clear night over flat terrain, air flow can be laminar near the ground. Usually, however, it is turbulent near the ground—producing, for example, random gusting in wind—but becomes laminar at higher altitudes. Turbulent convection nevertheless occurs in most clouds, leading to random billowing shapes. The "turbulence" that causes bumps in airplanes is often associated with clouds, though sometimes with larger-scale wave-like fluid motions such as the jet stream.

■ **Ocean surfaces.** At low wind speeds, regular ripples are seen; at higher wind speeds, a random pattern of creases occurs. It seems likely that randomness in the wind has little to do with the behavior of the ocean surface; instead it is the intrinsic dynamics of the water that is most important.

■ **Granular materials.** Sand and other granular materials show many phenomena seen in fluids. (Sand dunes are the rough analog of ocean waves.) Vortices have recently been seen, and presumably under appropriate conditions turbulence will eventually also be seen.

■ **Geological structures.** Typical landscapes on Earth are to a first approximation formed by regions of crust being uplifted through tectonic activity, then being sculpted by progressive erosion (and redeposition of sediment) associated with the flow of water. (Visually very different special cases include volcanos, impact craters and wind-sculpted deserts.) Eventually erosion and deposition will in effect completely smooth out a landscape. But at intermediate times one will see all sorts of potentially dramatic gullies that reflect the pattern of drainage, and the formation of a whole tree of streams and rivers. (Such trees have been studied since at least the early 1900s, with typical examples of concepts being Horton stream order, equal to *Depth* for trees given as *Mathematica* expressions.) If one imagines a uniform slope with discrete streams of water going randomly in each direction at the top, and then merging whenever they meet, one immediately gets a simple tree structure a little like in the pictures at the top of page 359. (More complicated models based for example on aggregation, percolation and energy minimization have been proposed in recent years—and perhaps because most random spanning trees are similar, they tend to give similar results.) As emphasized by Benoit Mandelbrot in the 1970s and 1980s, topography and contour lines (notably coastlines) seem to show apparently random structure on a wide range of scales—with definite power laws being measured in quite a few cases. And presumably at some level this is the result of the nested patterns in which erosion occurs. (An unrelated effect is that as a result of the

dynamics of flow in it, even a single river on a featureless landscape will typically tend to increase the curvature of its meanders, until they break off and form oxbow lakes.)

Fundamental Issues in Biology

■ **Page 383 · History.** The origins of biological complexity have been debated since antiquity. For a long time it was assumed that the magnitude of the complexity was so great that it could never have arisen from any ordinary natural process, and therefore must have been inserted from outside through some kind of divine plan. However, with the publication of Charles Darwin's *Origin of Species* in 1859 it became clear that there were natural processes that could in fact shape features of biological organisms. There was no specific argument for why natural selection should lead to the development of complexity, although Darwin appears to have believed that this would emerge somewhat like a principle in physics. In the century or so after the publication of *Origin of Species* many detailed aspects of natural selection were elucidated, but the increasing use of traditional mathematical methods largely precluded serious analysis of complexity. Continuing controversy about contradictions with religious accounts of creation caused most scientists to be adamant in assuming that every aspect of biological systems must be shaped purely by natural selection. And by the 1980s natural selection had become firmly enshrined as a force of practically unbounded power, assumed—though without specific evidence—to be capable of solving almost any problem and producing almost any degree of complexity.

My own work on cellular automata in the early 1980s showed that great complexity could be generated just from simple programs, without any process like natural selection. But although I and others believed that my results should be relevant to biological systems there was still a pervasive belief that the level of complexity seen in biology must somehow be uniquely associated with natural selection. In the late 1980s the study of artificial life caused several detailed computer simulations of natural selection to be done, and these simulations reproduced various known features of biological evolution. But from looking at such simulations, as well as from my own experiments done from 1980 onwards, I increasingly came to believe that almost any complexity being generated had its origin in phenomena similar to those I had seen in cellular automata—and had essentially nothing to do with natural selection.

■ **Attitudes of biologists.** Over the years, I have discussed versions of the ideas in this section with many biologists of different kinds. Most are quick to point out at least anecdotal cases in which features of organisms do not seem to have been shaped by natural selection. But if asked about complexity—either in specific examples or in general—the vast majority soon end up trying to give explanations based on natural selection. Those with a historical bent often recognize that the origins of complexity have always been somewhat mysterious in biology, and indeed sometimes state that this has laid the field open to many attacks. But generally my experience has been that the further one goes from those involved with specific molecular or other details of biological systems the more one encounters a fundamental conviction that natural selection must be the ultimate origin of any important feature of biological systems.

■ **Page 383 · Genetic programs.** Genetic programs are encoded as sequences of four possible nucleotide bases on strands of DNA or RNA. The simplest known viruses have programs that are a few thousand elements in length; bacteria typically have programs that are a few million elements; fruit flies a few hundred million; and humans around four billion. There is not a uniform correspondence between apparent sophistication of organisms and lengths of genetic programs: different species of amphibians, for example, have programs that can differ in length by a factor of a hundred, and can be as many as tens of billions of elements long. Genetic programs are normally broken into sections, many of which are genes that provide templates for making particular proteins. In humans, there are perhaps around 40,000 genes, specifying proteins for about 200 distinct cell types. Many of the low-level details of how proteins are produced is now known, but higher-level issues about organization into different cell types remain somewhat mysterious. Note that although most of the information necessary to construct an organism is encoded in its genetic program, other material in the original egg cell or the environment before birth can probably also sometimes be relevant.

■ **Page 386 · Tricks in evolution.** Among the tricks used are: sexual reproduction, causing large-scale mixing of similar programs; organs, suborganisms, symbiosis and parasitism, allowing different parts of programs to be optimized separately; mutation rate enzymes, allowing parts that need change to be searched more quickly; learnability in individual organisms, allowing larger local deviations from optimality to be tried.

■ **Page 387 · Belief in optimality.** The notion that features of biological organisms are always somehow optimized for a particular purpose has become extremely deep seated—and indeed it has been discussed since antiquity. Most modern biologists at least pay lip service to historical accidents and

developmental constraints, but if pressed revert surprisingly quickly to the notion of optimization for a purpose.

■ **Page 390 · Studying natural selection.** From the basic description of natural selection one might have thought that it would correspond to a unique simple program. But in fact there are always many somewhat arbitrary details, particularly centering around exactly how to prune less fit organisms. And the consequence of this is that in my experience it is essentially impossible to come up with precise definitive conclusions about natural selection on the basis of specific simple computer experiments. Using the Principle of Computational Equivalence discussed in Chapter 12, however, I suspect that it will nevertheless be possible to develop a general theory of what natural selection typically can and cannot do.

■ **Page 391 · Other models.** Sequential substitution systems are probably more realistic than cellular automata as models of genetic programs, since elements can explicitly be added to their rules at will. As a rather different approach, one can consider a fixed underlying rule—say a class 4 cellular automaton—with modifications in initial conditions. The notion of universality in Chapter 11 implies that under suitable conditions this should be equivalent to modifications in rules. As an alternative to modelling individual organisms, one can also consider substitution systems which directly generate genealogical trees for populations of organisms, somewhat like Leonardo Fibonacci's original model of a rabbit population.

■ **Page 391 · Adaptive value of complexity.** One might think that the reason complexity is not more widespread in biology is that somehow it is too sensitive to perturbations. But in fact, as discussed in Chapter 7, randomness and complexity tend to lead to more, rather than less, robustness in overall behavior. Indeed, many even seemingly simple biological processes appear to be stabilized by randomness—leading, for example, to random fluctuations in interbeat intervals for healthy hearts. And some biological processes rely directly on complex or random phenomena—for example, finding good paths for foraging for food, avoiding predators or mounting suitable immune responses. (Compare page 1192.)

■ **Page 393 · Genetic algorithms.** As mentioned on page 985, it is straightforward to apply natural selection to computer programs, and for certain kinds of practical tasks with appropriate continuity properties this may be a useful approach.

■ **Page 394 · Smooth variables.** Despite their importance in understanding natural selection both in biology and in potential computational applications, the fundamental origins of smooth variables or so-called quantitative traits seem to have been investigated rather little. Within populations of organisms such traits are often found to have Gaussian distributions (as, for example, in heights of humans), but this gives little clue as to their origin. (Weights of humans nevertheless have closer to a lognormal distribution.) It is generally assumed that smooth variables must be associated with so-called polygenes that effectively include a large number of individual discrete genes. In pre-Mendelian genetics, observations on smooth variables are presumably what led to the theory that traits of offspring are determined by smoothly mixing the blood of their parents.

■ **Page 395 · Species.** One feature of biological organisms is that they normally occur in discrete species, with distinct differences between different species. It seems likely that the existence of such discreteness is related to the discreteness of underlying genetic programs. Currently there are a few million species known. Most are distinguished just by their habitats, visual appearance or various simple numerical characteristics. Sometimes, however, it is known that members of different species have the traditional defining characteristic that they cannot normally mate, though this may well be more a matter of the mechanics of mating and development than a fundamental feature.

■ **Defining life.** See pages 823 and 1178.

■ **Page 397 · Analogies with thermodynamics.** Over the past century there have been a number of attempts to connect the development of complexity in biological systems with the increase of entropy in thermodynamic systems. In fact, when it was first introduced the very term "entropy" was supposed to suggest an analogy with biological evolution. But despite this, no detailed correspondence between thermodynamics and evolution has ever been forthcoming. However, my statement here that complexity in biology can occur because natural selection cannot control complex behavior is rather similar to my statement in Chapter 9 that entropy can increase because physical experiments in a sense also cannot control complex behavior.

■ **Page 398 · Major new features.** Traditional groupings of living organisms into kingdoms and phyla are typically defined by the presence of major new features. Standard examples from higher animals include regulation of body temperature and internal gestation of young. Important examples from earlier in the history of life include nuclear membranes, sexual reproduction, multicellularity, protective shells and photosynthesis.

Trilobites are a fairly clear example of organisms where over the course of a few hundred million years the fossil record shows increases in apparent morphological complexity, followed by decreases. Something similar can be seen in the historical evolution of technological systems such as cars.

■ **Software statistics.** Empirical analysis of the million or so lines of source code that make up *Mathematica* suggests that different functions—which are roughly analogous to different genes—rather accurately follow an exponential distribution of sizes, with a slightly elevated tail.

■ **Proteins.** At a molecular level much of any living cell is made up of proteins formed from chains of tens to thousands of amino acids. Of the thousands of proteins now known some (like keratin and collagen) are fibrous, and have a simple repetitive underlying structure. But many are globular, and have at least a core in which the 3D packing of amino acids seems quite random. Usually there are some sections that consist of simple α helices, β sheets, or combinations of these. But other parts—often including sites important for function—seem more like random walks. At some level the 3D shapes of proteins (tertiary structure) are presumably determined by energy minimization. But in practice very different shapes can probably have almost identical energies, so that in as much as a given protein always takes on the same shape this must be associated with the dynamics of the process by which the protein folds when it is assembled. (Compare page 988.) One might expect that biological evolution would have had obvious effects on proteins. But as mentioned on page 1184 the actual sequences of amino acids in proteins typically appear quite random. And at some level this is presumably why there seems to be so much randomness in their shapes. (Biological evolution may conceivably have selected for proteins that fold reliably or are more robust with respect to changes in single amino acids, but there is currently no clear evidence for this.)

Growth of Plants and Animals

■ **History.** The first steps towards a theory of biological form were already taken in Greek times with attempts—notably by Aristotle—to classify biological organisms and to understand their growth. By the 1600s extensive classification had been done, and many structural features had been identified as in common between different organisms. But despite hopes on the part of René Descartes, Galileo and others that biological processes might follow the same kind of rigid clockwork rules that were beginning to emerge in physics, no general principles were forthcoming. Rough analogies between the forms and functions of biological and non-biological systems were fairly common among both artists and scientists, but were rarely thought to have much scientific significance. In the 1800s more detailed analogies began to emerge, sometimes as offshoots of the field of morphology named by Johann Goethe, and sometimes with mathematical interpretations, and in 1917 D'Arcy Thompson published the first edition of his book *On Growth and Form* which used mathematical methods—mostly from analytical geometry—to discuss a variety of biological processes, usually in analogy with ones in physics. But emphasis on evolutionary rather than mechanistic explanations for a long time caused little further work to be done along these lines. Much additional data was obtained, particularly in embryology, and by the 1930s it seemed fairly clear that at least some aspects of growth in the embryo were controlled by chemical messengers. In 1951 Alan Turing worked out a general mathematical model of this based on reaction-diffusion equations, and suggested that such a model might account for many pigmentation and structural patterns in biological systems (see page 1012). For nearly twenty years, however, no significant follow-up was done on this idea. There were quite a few attempts—often misguided in my opinion—to use traditional ideas from physics and engineering to derive forms of biological organisms from constraints of mechanical or other optimality. And in the late 1960s, René Thom made an important attempt to use sophisticated methods from topology to develop a general theory of biological form. But the mathematics of his work was inaccessible to most natural scientists, and its popularized version, known as catastrophe theory, largely fell into disrepute.

The idea of comparing systems in biology and engineering dates back to antiquity, but for a long time it was mainly thought of just as an inspiration for engineering. In the mid-1940s, however, mostly under the banner of cybernetics, tools from the analysis of electrical systems began to be used for studying biological systems. And partly from this—with much reinforcement from the discovery of the genetic code—there emerged the idea of thinking about biological systems in purely abstract logical or computational terms. This led to an early introduction of 2D cellular automata (see page 876), but the emphasis was on ambitious general questions rather than specific models. Little progress was made, and by the 1960s most work along these lines had petered out. In the late 1970s, however, fractals and L systems (see below) began to provide examples where simple rules could be seen to yield biological-like branching behavior. And in the 1980s, interest in non-equilibrium physical processes, and in phenomena such as diffusion-limited aggregation, led to renewed interest in reaction-diffusion equations, and to

somewhat more explicit models for various biological processes. My own work on cellular automata in the early 1980s started a number of new lines of computational modelling, some of which became involved in the rise and fall of the artificial life movement in the late 1980s and early 1990s.

■ **Page 400 · Growth in plants.** At the lowest level, the growth of any organism proceeds by either division or expansion of cells, together with occasional formation of cavities between cells. In plants, cells typically expand—normally through intake of water—only for a limited period, after which the cellulose in their walls crystallizes to make them quite rigid. In most plants—at least after the embryonic stage—cells typically divide only in localized regions known as meristems, and each division yields one cell that can divide again, and one that cannot. Often the very tip of a stem consists of a single cell in the shape of an inverted tetrahedron, and in lower plants such as mosses this is essentially the only cell that divides. In flowering plants, cell division normally occurs around the edge of a region of size 0.2–1 mm containing many tens of cells. (Hearts of palm in palm trees can however be much larger.) The details of how cell division works in plants remain largely unknown. There is some evidence that orientation of new cells is in part controlled by microscopic fibers. Various small molecules that can diffuse between cells (such as so-called auxins) are known to affect growth and production of new stems (see below).

■ **Page 401 · Branching in plants.** Almost all kinds of plants exhibit some form of branching, and particularly in smaller plants the branching is often extremely regular. In a plant as large as a typical tree—particularly one that grows slowly—different conditions associated with the growth of different branches may however destroy some of the regularity of branching. Among algae and more primitive plants such as whisk ferns, repeated splitting of a single branch into two is particularly common. Ferns and conifers both typically exhibit three-way branching. Among flowering plants so-called dicotyledons exhibit branching throughout the plant. Monocotyledons—of which palms and grasses are two examples—typically have only one primary site of growth, and thus do not exhibit repeated branching. (In grasses the growth site is at the bottom of the stem, and in bamboos there are multiple growth sites up the stem.)

The forms of branching in plants have been used as means of classification since antiquity. Alexander von Humboldt in 1808 identified 19 overall types of branching which have been used, with some modifications, by plant geographers and botanists ever since. Note that in the vast majority of cases, branches do not lie in a plane; often they are instead arranged in a spiral, as discussed on page 408. But when projected into two dimensions, the patterns obtained still look similar to those in the main text.

■ **Page 402 · Implementation.** It is convenient to represent the positions of all tips by complex numbers. One can take the original stem to extend from the point -1 to 0; the rule is then specified by the list b of complex numbers corresponding to the positions of the new tip obtained after one step. And after n steps the positions of all tips generated are given simply by

Nest[Flatten[Outer[Times, 1 + #, b]] &, {0}, n]

■ **Mathematical properties.** If an element c of the list b is real, so that there is a stem that goes straight up, then the limiting height of the center of the pattern is obtained by summing a geometric series, and is given by $1/(1-c)$. The overall limiting pattern will be finite so long as $Abs[c] < 1$ for all elements of b. After n steps the total length of all stems is given by $Apply[Plus, Abs[b]]^n$. (See page 1006 for other properties.)

■ **Page 402 · Simple geometries.** Page 357 shows how some of the nested patterns commonly seen in this book can be produced by the growth processes shown here.

■ **History of branching models.** The concept of systematic rules for the way that stems—particularly those carrying flowers—are connected in a plant seems to have been clearly understood among botanists by the 1800s. Only with the advent of computer graphics in the 1970s, however, does the idea appear to have arisen of varying angles to get different forms. An early example was the work of Hisao Honda in 1970 on the structure of trees. Pictures analogous to the bottom row on page 402 were also generated by Benoit Mandelbrot in connection with his development of fractals. Starting in 1967 Aristid Lindenmayer emphasized the use of substitution or L systems (see page 893) as a way of modelling patterns of connections in plants. And beginning in the early 1980s—particularly through work by Alvy Ray Smith and later Przemyslaw Prusinkiewicz—models based on L systems and fractals became routinely used for producing images of plants in practical computer graphics. Around the same time Michael Barnsley also used so-called iterated function systems to make pictures of ferns—but he appears to have viewed these more as a curiosity than a contribution to botany. Over the past decade or so, a few mentions have been made of using complicated models based on L systems to reproduce shapes of specific types of leaves, but so far as I can tell, nothing like the simple model that I describe in the main text has ever been considered before.

■ **Page 404 · Leaf shapes.** Leaves are usually put into categories like the ones below, with names mostly derived from Latin words for similar-looking objects.

Some classification of leaf shapes was done by Theophrastus as early as 300 BC, and classifications similar to those above were in use by the early Renaissance period. (They appear for example in the first edition of the *Encyclopedia Britannica* from 1768.) Leaf shapes have been widely used since antiquity as a way of identifying plants—initially particularly for medicinal purposes. But there has been very little general scientific investigation of leaf shapes, and most of what has been done has concentrated on the expansion of leaves once they are out of their buds. Already in 1724 Stephen Hales looked at the motion of grids of marks on fig leaves, and noted that growth seemed to occur more or less uniformly throughout the leaf. Similar but increasingly quantitative studies have been made ever since, and have reported a variety of non-uniformities in growth. For a long time it was believed that after leaves came out of their buds growth was due mainly to cell expansion, but in the 1980s it became clear that many cell divisions in fact occur, both on the boundary and the interior. At the earliest stages, buds that will turn into leaves start as bumps on a plant stem, with a structure that is essentially impossible to discern. Surgically modifying such buds when they are as small as 0.1 mm can have dramatic effects on final leaf shape, suggesting that at least some aspects of the shape are already determined at that point. On a single plant different leaves can have somewhat different shapes—sometimes for example those lower on a tree are smoother, while those higher are pointier. It may nevertheless be that leaves on a single plant initially have a discrete set of possible shapes, with variations in final shape arising from differences in environmental conditions during expansion. My model for leaf shapes is presumably most relevant for initial shapes.

Traditional evolutionary explanations have not had much to say about detailed questions of leaf shape; one minor claim is that the pointed tips at the ends of many tropical leaves exist to allow moisture to drip off the leaves. The fossil record suggests that leaves first arose roughly 400 million years ago, probably when collections of branches which lay in a plane became joined by webbing. Early plants such as ferns have compound leaves in which explicit branching structure is still seen. Extremely few models for shapes of individual leaves appear to have ever been proposed. In 1917 D'Arcy Thompson mentioned that leaves might have growth rates that are simple functions of angle, and drew the first of the pictures shown below.

Cos[θ/2]   *Cos[2θ/3]*   *Sin[2θ]*   *Abs[θ]*   *Abs[θ]²*

With new tip positions as on page 400 given by $\{p\,Exp[i\,\theta],\,p\,Exp[-i\,\theta],\,q\}$, rough $\{p, q, \theta\}$ for at least some versions of some common plants include: wild carrot (Queen Anne's lace) $\{0.4, 0.7, 30°\}$, cypress $\{0.4, 0.7, 45°\}$, coralbells $\{0.5, 0.4, 0°\}$, ivy $\{0.5, 0.6, 0°\}$, grape $\{0.5, 0.6, 15°\}$, sycamore $\{0.5, 0.6, 15°\}$, mallow $\{0.5, 0.6, 30°\}$, goosefoot $\{0.55, 0.8, 30°\}$, willow $\{0.55, 0.8, 80°\}$, morning glory $\{0.7, 0.8, 0°\}$, cucumber $\{0.7, 0.8, 15°\}$, ginger $\{0.65, 0.6, 15°\}$.

■ **Page 404 · Self-limiting growth.** It is often said that in plants, unlike animals, there is no global control of growth. And one feature of the simple branching processes I describe is that for purely mathematical reasons, their rules always produce structures that are of limited size. Note that in fact it is known that there is some global control of growth even in plants: for example hormones produced by leaves can affect growth of roots.

■ **Page 407 · Parameter space sets.** Points in the space of parameters can conveniently be labelled by a complex number c, where the imaginary direction is taken to increase to the right. The pattern corresponding to each point is the limit of $Nest[Flatten[1 + \{c\#, Conjugate[c]\#\}] \&, \{1\}, n]$ when $n \to \infty$. Such a limiting pattern exists only within the unit circle $Abs[c] < 1$. It then turns out that the limiting pattern is either completely connected or completely disconnected; which it is depends on whether it contains any points on the vertical axis $Im[c] == 0$. Every point in the pattern must correspond to some list of left and right branchings, represented by 0's and 1's respectively; in terms of this list the position of the point is given by $Fold[1 + \{c, Conjugate[c]\}[[1 + \#2]]\#1 \&, 1, Reverse[list]]$. Patterns are disconnected if there is a gap between the parts obtained from lists starting with 0 and with 1. The magnitude of this gap turns out to be given by

$$With[\{d = Conjugate[c], r = 1 - Abs[c]^2\},$$
$$Which[Im[c] < 0, d, Im[c] == 0, 0,$$
$$Re[c] > 0, With[\{n = Ceiling[\pi/2/Arg[c]]\},$$
$$Im[c(1 - d^n)/(1 - d)] + Im[c\,d^n(1 + d)]/r], Arg[c] >$$
$$3\pi/4, Im[c + c^2]/r, True, Im[c] + Im[c^2 + c^3]/r]]$$

The picture below shows the region for which the gap is positive, corresponding to trees which are not connected. (This region was found by Michael Barnsley and others in

the late 1980s.) The overall maximum gap occurs at $c = 1/2\,Sqrt[5 - \sqrt{17}\,]i$. The bottom boundary of the region lies along $Re[c] = -1/2$; the extremal point on the edge of the gap in this case corresponds to $\{0, 0, 1, 0, 1, 0, 1, ...\}$ where the last two elements repeat forever. The rest of the boundary consists of a sequence of algebraic curves, with almost imperceptible changes in slope in between; the first corresponds to $\{0, 0, 0, 1, 0, 1, 0, 1, ...\}$, while subsequent ones correspond to $\{0, 1, 1, 1, 0, 1, 0, 1, 0, 1, ...\}$, $\{0, 1, 1, 1, 1, 0, 1, 0, 1, 0, 1, ...\}$, etc.

In the pictures in the main text, the black region is connected wherever it does not protrude into the shaded region, which corresponds to disconnected patterns, in the pictures above. And in general it turns out that near any particular value of c the sets shown in black in the main text always look at sufficient magnification like the pattern that would be obtained for that value of c. The reason for this is that if c changes only slightly, then the pattern to a first approximation deforms only slightly, so that the part seen through the peephole just shifts, and in a small region of c values the peephole in effect simply scans over different parts of the pattern.

A simple way to approximate the pictures in the main text would be to generate patterns by iterating the substitution system a fixed number of times. In practice, however, it is essential to prune the tree of points at each stage. And at least for $Abs[c]$ not too close to 1, this can be done by discarding points that are so far away from the peephole that their descendents could not possibly return to it.

The parameter space sets discussed here are somewhat analogous to the Mandelbrot set discussed on page 934, though in many ways easier to understand.

(See also the discussion of universal objects on page 1127.)

■ **Page 409 · Mathematics of phyllotaxis.** A rotation by $GoldenRatio == (1 + \sqrt{5})/2$ turns is equivalent to a rotation by $2 - GoldenRatio == GoldenRatio^{-2} \approx 0.38$ turns, or $137.5°$. Successive approximations to this number are given by $Fibonacci[n - 2]/Fibonacci[n]$, so that elements numbered $Fibonacci[n]$ (i.e. 1, 2, 3, 5, 8, 13, ...) will be the ones that come closest to being a whole number of turns apart, and thus to being lined up on the stem. As mentioned on page 891, having $GoldenRatio$ turns between elements makes them in a sense as evenly distributed as possible, given that they are added sequentially.

■ **History of phyllotaxis.** The regularities of phyllotaxis were presumably noticed in antiquity, and were certainly recognized in the 1400s, notably by Leonardo da Vinci. By the 1800s various mathematical features of phyllotaxis were known, and in 1837 Louis and Auguste Bravais identified the presence of a golden ratio angle. In 1868 Wilhelm Hofmeister proposed that new elements form in the largest gap left by previous elements. And in 1913 Johannes Schoute argued that diffusion of a chemical creates fields of inhibition around new elements—a model in outline equivalent to mine. In the past century features of phyllotaxis have been rediscovered surprisingly many times, with work being done quite independently both in abstract mathematical settings, and in the context of specific models (most of which are ultimately very similar). One development in the 1990s is the generation of phyllotaxis-like patterns in superconductors, ferrofluids and other physical systems.

■ **Observed phyllotaxis.** Many spiral patterns in actual plants converge to within a degree or less of 137.5 °, though just as in the model in the main text, there are usually deviations for the first few elements produced. The angles are particularly accurate in, for example, flower heads—where it is likely the positions of elements are adjusted by mechanical forces after they are originally generated. Other examples of phyllotaxis-like patterns in biology include the scales of pangolins and surfaces of tooth-like structures in certain kinds of rays and sharks.

■ **Projections of patterns.** The literature of phyllotaxis is full of baroque descriptions of the features of projections of patterns with golden ratio angles. In the pictures below, the nth point has position $(\sqrt{n}\ \{Sin[\#], Cos[\#]\}\ \&)[2\ \pi\ n\ GoldenRatio]$, and in such pictures regular spirals or parastichies emanating from the center are seen whenever points whose numbers differ by $Fibonacci[m]$ are joined. Note that the tips of many growing stems seem to be approximately paraboloidal, making the nth point a distance $\sqrt{n}$ from the center.

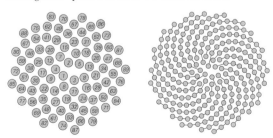

■ **Page 410 · Implementation.** It is convenient to consider a line of discrete cells, much as in a continuous cellular automaton. With a concentrations list c, the position p of a new element is given by $Position[c, Max[c], 1, 1][[1, 1]]$, while the new list of concentrations is $\lambda\ c + RotateRight[f, p]$ where f is a list of depletions associated with addition of a new element at position 1. In the main text a Gaussian form is used for f. Other smooth functions typically nevertheless yield identical results. Note that in order to get an accurate approximation to a golden ratio angle there must be a fairly large number of cells.

■ **Shapes of cells.** Many types of cells are arranged like typical 3D packings of deformable objects (see page 988)—with considerable apparent randomness in individual shapes and positions, but definite overall statistical properties. Cells arranged on a surface—as in the retina or in skin—or that are intrinsically elongated—as in muscle—tend again to be arranged like typical packings, but now in 2D, where a regular hexagonal grid is formed.

■ **Page 412 · Symmetries.** Biological systems often show definite discrete symmetry. (In monocotyledon plants there is usually 3-fold symmetry; in dicotyledons 4- or 5-fold. Animals like starfish often have 5-fold symmetry; higher animals usually only 2-fold symmetry. There are fossils with 7- and 9-fold symmetry. At microscopic levels there are sometimes other symmetries: cilia of eukaryotic cells can for example show 9- and 13-fold symmetry. In the phyllotaxis process discussed in the main text one new element is produced at a time. But if several elements are produced together the same basic mechanism will tend to make these elements be equally spaced in angle—leading to overall discrete symmetry. (Individual proteins sometimes also arrange themselves into overall structures that have discrete symmetries—which can then be reflected in shapes of cells or larger objects.) (See also page 1011.)

■ **Page 412 · Locally isotropic growth.** A convenient way to see what happens if elements of a surface grow isotropically is to divide the surface into a collection of very small circles, and then to expand the circle at each point by a factor $h[x, y]$. If the local curvature of the surface is originally $c[x, y]$, then after such growth, the curvature turns out to be $(c[x, y] + Laplacian[Log[h[x, y]]])/h[x, y]$ where $Laplacian[f\_] := \partial_{xx} f + \partial_{yy} f$. In order for the surface to stay flat its growth rate $Log[h[x, y]]$ must therefore solve Laplace's equation, and hence must be a harmonic function $Re[f[x + i\ y]]$. This is equivalent to saying that the growth must correspond to a conformal mapping which locally preserves angles. The pictures below show results for several growth rate functions; in the last case, the function is not harmonic, and the surface cannot be drawn in the plane without tearing. Note that if the elements of a surface are allowed to change shape, then the surface can always remain flat, as in the top row of pictures on page 412. Harmonic growth rate functions can potentially be obtained from the large-time effects of a chemical subject to diffusion. And this may perhaps be related to the flatness observed in the growth of leaves. (See also page 1010.)

1 x $x^2 - y^2$ $-\sqrt{x^2 + y^2}$

■ **Page 413 · Branching in animals.** Capillaries, bronchioles and kidney ducts in higher animals typically seem to form trees in which each tip as it extends repeatedly splits into two branches. (In human lungs, for example, there are about 20 levels of branching.) The same kind of structure is seen in the digestive systems of lower animals—as visible externally, for example, in the arms of a basket star.

■ **Page 413 · Antlers.** Like stems of plants antlers grow at their tips, and can thus exhibit branching. This is made possible by the fact that antlers, unlike horns, have a layer of soft tissue on the outside—which delivers the nutrients needed for growth to occur on the outer surface of the bone at their tips.

■ **Page 414 · Shells.** Shells grow through the secretion of rigid material from the soft lip or mantle of the animal inside, and over periods of months to years they form coiled structures that normally follow rather accurate equiangular spirals, typically right-handed. The number of turns or whorls varies widely, from less than one in a typical bivalve, to more than thirty in a highly pointed univalve such as a screw shell. Usually the coiled structure is obvious from looking at the apex on the outside of the shell, but in cowries, for example, it is made less obvious by the fact that later whorls completely cover earlier ones, and at the opening of the shell some dissolving and resculpting of material occurs. In addition to smooth coiled overall structures, some shells exhibit spines. These are associated with tentacles of tissue which secrete shell material at their tips as they grow. Inside shells such as nautiluses, there are a sequence of sealed chambers, with septa between them laid down perhaps once a month. These septa in present-day species are smooth, but in fossil ammonites they can be highly corrugated. Typically the corrugations are accurately symmetrical, and I suspect that they in effect represent slices through a lettuce-leaf-like structure formed from a surface with tree-like internal growth.

■ **Shell model.** The center of the opening of a shell is taken to trace out a helix whose $\{x, y, z\}$ coordinates are given as a function of the total angle of revolution t by $a^t \{Cos[t], Sin[t], b\}$. On row (a) of page 415 the parameter a varies from 1.05 to 1.65, while on row (b) b varies from 0 to 6. The complete surface of the shell is obtained by varying both t and θ in

$$a^t \{Cos[t] (1 + c (Cos[e] Cos[\theta] + d Sin[e] Sin[\theta])),$$
$$Sin[t] (1 + c (Cos[e] Cos[\theta] + d Sin[e] Sin[\theta])),$$
$$b + c (Cos[\theta] Sin[e] - d Cos[e] Sin[\theta])\}$$

where c varies from 0.4 to 1.6 on row (c), d from 1 to 4 on row (d) and e from 0 to 1.2 on row (e). For many values of parameters the surface defined by this formula intersects itself. However, in an actual shell material can only be added on the outside of what already exists, and this can be represented by restricting θ to run over only part of the range $-\pi$ to π. The effect of this on internal structure can be seen in the slice of the cone shell on row (b) of page 414. Most real shells follow the model described here with remarkable accuracy. There are, however, deviations in some species, most often as a result of gradual changes in parameters during the life of the organism. As the pictures in the main text show, shells of actual molluscs (both current and fossil) exist throughout a large region of parameter space. And in fact it appears that the only parameter values that are not covered are ones where the shell could not easily have been secreted by an animal because its shape is degenerate and leaves little useful room for the animal. Some regions of parameter space are more common than others, and this may be a consequence either of natural selection or of the detailed molecular biology of mollusc growth. Shells where successive whorls do not touch (as in the first picture on row (c) of page 415) appear to be significantly less common than others, perhaps because they have lower mechanical rigidity. They do however occur, though sometimes as internal rather than external shells.

■ **History.** Following Aristotle's notion of gnomon figures that keep the same shape when they grow, equiangular spirals were discussed by René Descartes in 1638, and soon thereafter Christopher Wren noted their relation to shells. A clear mathematical model of shell growth based on equiangular spirals was given by Henry Moseley in 1838, and the model used here is a direct extension of his. Careful studies from the mid-1800s to mid-1900s validated Moseley's basic model for a wide variety of shells, though an increasing emphasis was placed on shells that showed deviations from the model. In the mid-1960s David Raup used early computer graphics to generate pictures for various ranges of parameters, but perhaps because he considered only specific classes of molluscs there emerged from his work the belief that parameters of shells are greatly constrained—with explanations being proposed based on optimization of such features as strength, relative volume, and stability when falling through water. But as discussed in the main text I strongly suspect that in fact there are no such global constraints, and instead almost all reasonable values of parameters from the simple model used do actually occur in real molluscs. In the past few decades, increasingly complex models for shells have been constructed, typically focusing on fairly specific or unusual cases. Most of these models have far more parameters than the simple one used here, and by varying these parameters it is almost always possible to get forms that probably do not correspond to real shells. And presumably the reason for this is just that such models represent processes that do not occur in the growth of actual molluscs. One widespread issue concerns the orientation of the opening to a shell. The model used here assumes that this opening always stays vertical—which appears to be what happens most often in practice. But following the notion of Frenet frames in differential geometry, it has often come to be supposed that the opening to a shell instead typically lies in a plane perpendicular to the helix traced out by the growth of the shell. This idea, however, leads to twisted shapes like those shown below that occur rarely, if ever, in actual shells. And in fact, despite elaborate efforts of computer graphics it has proved rather difficult with parametrizations based on Frenet frames to produce shells that have a reasonable range of realistic shapes.

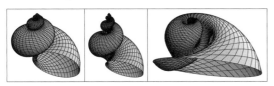

■ **Page 417 · Discrete folding.** See page 892.

■ **Page 418 · Intrinsically defined curves.** With curvature given by a function $f[s]$ of the arc length s, explicit coordinates $\{x[s], y[s]\}$ of points are obtained from (compare page 1048)

$$NDSolve[\{x'[s] == Cos[\theta[s]], y'[s] == Sin[\theta[s]], \theta'[s] == f[s], x[0] == y[0] == \theta[0] == 0\}, \{x, y, \theta\}, \{s, 0, s_{max}\}]$$

For various choices of $f[s]$, formulas for $\{x[s], y[s]\}$ can be found using *DSolve*:

$f[s] = 1$: $\{Sin[\theta], Cos[\theta]\}$

$f[s] = s$: $\{FresnelS[\theta], FresnelC[\theta]\}$

$f[s] = 1/\sqrt{s}$: $\sqrt{\theta}\ \{Sin[\sqrt{\theta}], Cos[\sqrt{\theta}]\}$

$f[s] = 1/s$: $\theta\{Cos[Log[\theta]], Sin[Log[\theta]]\}$

$f[s] = 1/s^2$: $\theta\{Sin[1/\theta], Cos[1/\theta]\}$

$f[s] = s^n$: result involves $Gamma[1/n, \pm i\,\theta^n/n]$

$f[s] = Sin[s]$: result involves $Integrate[Sin[Sin[\theta]], \theta]$, expressible in terms of generalized Kampé de Fériet hypergeometric functions of two variables.

When $s_{max} \to \infty$, $f[s] = a\,s\,Sin[s]$ yields 2D shapes that are basically nested, with pieces overlapping for $Abs[a] < 1$.

The general idea of so-called natural equations for obtaining curves from local curvature appears to have been first considered by Leonhard Euler in 1736. Many examples with fairly simple behavior were studied in the 1800s. The case of $f[s] = a\,Sin[b\,s]$ was studied by Eduard Lehr in 1932. Cases related to $f[s] = s\,Sin[s]$ were studied by Alfred Gray around 1992 using *Mathematica*.

■ **Multidimensional generalizations.** Curvatures for surfaces and higher-dimensional objects can be defined in terms of the principal axes of approximating ellipsoids at each point. There are combinations of these curvatures—in 2D Gaussian curvature and mean curvature—which are independent of the coordinate system used. (Compare page 1049.) Given such curvatures, a surface can in principle be obtained by solving certain partial differential equations. But even in the case of zero mean curvature, which corresponds to minimal surfaces of the kind followed by an idealized soap film, this is already a mathematical problem of significant difficulty.

If one looks at projections of surfaces, it is common to see lines of discontinuity at which a surface goes, say, from having three sheets to one. Catastrophe theory provides a classification of such discontinuities—the simplest being a cusp. And as emphasized by René Thom in the 1960s, it is possible that some structures seen in animals may be related to such discontinuities.

■ **Page 419 · Embryo development.** Starting from a single egg cell, embryos first exhibit a series of geometrically quite precise cell divisions corresponding, I suspect, to a simple neighbor-independent substitution system. When the embryo consists of a definite number of cells—from tens to tens of thousands depending on species—the phenomenon of gastrulation occurs, and the hollow sphere of cells that has been produced folds in on itself so as to begin to form more tubular structures. In organisms with a total of just a few thousand cells, the final position and type of every cell seems to be determined directly by the genetic program of the organism; most likely what happens is that each cell division leads to some modification in genetic material, perhaps through rules like those in a multiway system. Beyond a few thousand cells, however, individual cells seem to be less relevant, and instead what appears to happen is that chemicals such as retinoic acid (a derivative of vitamin A) produced by particular cells diffuse to affect all cells in a region a tenth of a millimeter or so across. Probably as a result of chemical concentration gradients, different so-called homeobox genes are then activated in different parts of the region. Each of these genes—out of a total of 38 in humans—yields proteins which then in turn switch on or off large banks of genes, allowing different forms of behavior for cells in different places.

■ **History of embryology.** General issues of embryology were already discussed in Greek times, notably by Hippocrates and Aristotle. But even in the 1700s it was still thought that perhaps every embryo started from a very small version of a complete organism. In the 1800s, however, detailed studies revealed the progressive development of complexity in the growth of an embryo. At the end of the 1800s experiments based on removing or modifying parts of early embryos began, and by the 1920s it had been discovered that there were definite pieces of embryos that were responsible for inducing various aspects of development to occur. That concentrations of diffusing chemicals might define where in an embryo different elements would form was first suggested in the early 1900s, but it was not until the 1970s and 1980s—after it was emphasized by Lewis Wolpert in 1969 under the name "positional information"—that there was clear experimental investigation of this idea. From the 1930s and before, it was known that different genes are involved in different aspects of embryo development. And with the advent of gene manipulation methods in the 1970s and 1980s, it became possible to investigate the genetic control of development in organisms such as fruit flies in tremendous detail. Among the important discoveries made were the homeobox genes (see note above).

■ **Page 420 · Bones.** Precursors of bones can be identified quite early in the growth of most vertebrate embryos. Typically the cells involved are cartilage, with bone subsequently forming around them. In hardened bones growth normally occurs by replication of cartilage cells in plates perhaps a millimeter thick, with bone forming by a somewhat complicated process involving continual dissolving and redeposition of already hardened material. The rate at which bone grows depends on the pressure exerted on it, and presumably this allows feedback that for example prevents coiling. Quite how the complicated collection of tens of bones that make up a typical skull manage to grow so as to stay connected—often with highly corrugated suture lines—remains fairly mysterious.

■ **General constraints on growth.** Given a system made from material with certain overall properties, one can ask what distributions of growth are consistent with those properties, and what kinds of shapes can be produced. With material

that is completely rigid growth can occur only at boundaries. With material where every part can deform arbitrarily any kind of growth can occur. With material where parts can locally expand, but cannot change their shape, page 1007 showed that a 2D surface will remain flat if the growth rate is a harmonic function. The Riemann mapping theorem of complex analysis then implies that even in this case, any smooth initial shape can grow into any other such shape with a suitable growth rate function. In a 3D system with locally isotropic growth the condition to avoid tearing is that the Ricci scalar curvature must vanish, and this is achieved if the local growth rate satisfies a certain partial differential equation. (See also page 1049.)

■ **Parametrizations of growth.** The idea that different objects—say different human bodies or faces—can be related by changing a small number of geometrical parameters was used by artists such as Albrecht Dürer in the 1500s, and may have been known to architects and others in antiquity. (In modern times this idea is associated for example with the notion that just a few measurements are sufficient to specify the fitting of clothes.) D'Arcy Thompson in 1917 suggested that shapes in many different species could also be related in this way. In the case of shells and horns he gave a fairly precise analysis, as discussed above. But he also drew various pictures of fishes and skulls, and argued that they were related by deformations of coordinates. Largely from this grew the field of morphometrics, in which the relative positions of features such as eyes or tips of fins are compared in different species. And although statistical significance is reduced by considering only discrete features, some evidence has emerged that different species do indeed have shapes related by changes in fairly small numbers of geometrical parameters. Such changes could be accounted for by changes in growth rates, but it is noteworthy that my results above on branching and folding make it clear that in general changes in growth rates can have much more dramatic effects.

As emphasized by D'Arcy Thompson, even a single organism will change shape if its parts grow at different rates. And in the 1930s and 1940s it became popular to study differential growth, typically under the name of allometry. Exponential growth was usually assumed, and there was much discussion about the details and correctness of this. Practical applications were made to farm animals, and later to changes in facial bone structure during childhood. But despite some work in the past twenty years using models based on fluids, solid mechanics and networks of rigid elements, much about differential growth remains unclear. (A better approach may be one similar to general relativity.)

■ **Schemes for growth.** After the initial embryonic stage, many general features of the growth of different types of organisms can be viewed as consequences of the nature of the elements that make the organisms rigid. In plants, as we have discussed, essentially all cells have rigid cellulose walls. In vertebrate animals, rigidity comes mainly from bones that are internal to the organism. In arthropods and some other invertebrates, an exoskeleton is typically the main source of rigidity. Growth in such organisms usually then proceeds by adding soft tissue on the inside, then periodically moulting the exoskeleton. In a first approximation, the mechanical pressure of internal tissue will typically make the shape of the exoskeleton form an approximate minimal surface.

■ **Tumors.** In both plants and animals tumors seem to grow mainly by fairly random addition of cells to their surface—much as in the aggregation models shown on page 332.

■ **Pollen.** The grains of pollen produced by different species of plants have a remarkable range of different forms. Produced in groups of four, each grain is effectively a single cell (with two nuclei) between a few and few hundred microns across. At an overall level most grains seem to have regular polyhedral shapes, though often with bulges or dents. Perhaps such forms arise through grains effectively being made with small numbers of roughly spherical elements being either as tightly or loosely packed as possible. The outer walls of pollen grains are often covered with a certain density of tiny columns that can form spikes, or can have plates on top that can form cross-linkages and can join together to appear as patches.

■ **Radiolarians.** The silicate skeletons of single-cell plankton organisms such as radiolarians and diatoms have been used for well over a century as examples of complex microscopic forms in biology. (See page 385.) Most likely their overall shapes are determined before they harden through minimization of area by surface tension. Their pores and cross-linkages presumably reflect packings of many roughly spherical elements on the surface during formation (as seen in the mid-1990s in aluminophosphates).

■ **Self-assembly.** Some growth—particularly at a microscopic level—seems to be based on objects with particular shapes or affinities sticking together only in specific ways—much as in the systems based on constraints discussed on page 210 (and especially the network constraint systems of page 483). (See also page 1193.)

■ **Animal behavior.** Simple repetitive behavior is common, as in circadian and brain rhythms, as well as peristalsis and walking. (In a millipede there are, for example, typically just two modes of locomotion, both simple, involving opposite legs moving either together or oppositely.) Many structures built by animals have repetitive forms, as in beehives and spider webs; the more complex structures made for example by termites can perhaps be understood in terms of generalized aggregation systems (see page 978). (Typical models involve the notion of stigmergy: that elements are added at a particular point based only on features immediately around them; see also page 1184.) Nested patterns may occur in flocks of birds such as geese. Fairly regular nested space-filling curves are sometimes seen in the eating paths of caterpillars. Apparent randomness is common in physiological processes such as twitchings of muscles and microscopic eye motions, as well as in random walks executed during foraging. My suspicion is that just as there appear to be small collections of cells—so-called central pattern generators—that generate repetitive behavior, so also there will turn out to be small collections of cells that generate intrinsically random behavior.

Biological Pigmentation Patterns

■ **Collecting shells.** The shells I show in this section are mostly from my fairly small personal collection, obtained at shops and markets around the world. (A few of the ones on page 416 are from the Field Museum.) The vast majority of shells on typical beaches do not have especially elaborate patterns. The Philippines are the largest current source of collectible shells: when molluscs intended as food are caught in nets interesting-looking shells are sometimes picked out before being discarded. Shell collecting as a hobby probably had its greatest popularity in the late 1700s and 1800s. In recent times one reason for studying animals that live in cone shells is that they produce potent neurotoxins that show promise as pain-control drugs.

■ **Shell patterns.** The so-called mantle of soft tissue which covers the animal inside the shell is what secretes the shell and produces the pattern on it. Some species deposit material in a highly regular way every day; others seem to do it intermittently over periods of months or years. In many species the outer surface of the shell is covered by a kind of skin known as the periostracum, and in most cases this skin is opaque, thereby obscuring the patterns underneath until long after the animal has died. Note that if one makes a hole in a shell, the pattern is usually quite unaffected, suggesting that the pattern is primarily a consequence of features of the underlying mantle. In addition, patterns are often divided into three or four large bands, presumably in correspondence with features of the anatomy of the mantle. Sometimes physical ridges exist on shells in correspondence with their pigmentation patterns. It is not clear whether multiple kinds of shell patterns can occur within one species, or whether they are always associated with genetically different species.

■ **Cowries.** In cowries the outside of the shell is covered by the mantle of the animal. The patterns on the shell typically involve spots, and are typical of those obtained from 2D cellular automata of the kind shown on page 428. The mantle is normally in two parts; the boundary between them shows up as a discontinuity in the shell pattern.

■ **History.** Elaborate patterns on shells have been noticed since antiquity, and have featured in a number of well-known works of art and literature. Since the late 1600s they have also been extensively used in classifying molluscs. But almost no efforts to understand the origins of such patterns seem to ever have been made. One study was done in 1969 by Conrad Waddington and Russell Cowe in which patterns on one particular kind of shell were reproduced by a specific computer simulation based on the idea of diverging waves of pigment. In 1982 I noticed that the patterns I had generated with 1D cellular automata looked remarkably similar to patterns on shells. I used this quite widely as an illustration of how cellular automata might be relevant to modelling natural systems. And I also made some efforts to do actual biological experiments, but I gave up when it seemed that the species of molluscs I wanted to study were difficult, if not impossible, to keep in captivity. Following my work, various other studies of shell patterns were done. Bard Ermentrout, John Campbell and George Oster constructed a model based on the idea that pigment-producing cells might act like nerve cells with a certain degree of memory. And Hans Meinhardt has constructed progressively more elaborate models based on reaction-diffusion equations.

■ **Page 426 · Animals shown.** Flatworm, cuttlefish, honeycomb moray, spotted moray, foureye butterfly fish; emperor angelfish, suckermouth catfish, ornate cowfish, clown triggerfish, poison-dart frog; ornate horned frog, marbled salamander, spiny softshell, gila monster, ball python; gray-banded kingsnake, guinea fowl, peacock, ring-tailed lemur, panda; cheetah, ocelot, leopard, tiger, spotted hyena; western spotted skunk, civet, zebra, brazilian tapir, giraffe.

■ **Animal coloration.** Coloration can arise either directly through the presence of visible colored cells such as those in freckles, or indirectly by virtue of cells such as hair follicles imparting pigments to the non-living elements such as fur, feathers and scales that grow from them. In many cases such elements are arranged in a highly regular way, often in a repetitive hexagonal pattern. Evolutionary optimization is often used to explain observed pigmentation patterns—with

varying degrees of success. The notion that for example the stripes of a zebra are for camouflage may at first seem implausible, but there is some evidence that dramatic stripes do make it harder for a predator to recognize the overall shape of the zebra. Many of the pigments used by animals are by-products of metabolism, suggesting that at least at first pigmentation patterns were probably often incidental to the operation of the animal.

■ **Page 427 · Implementation.** Given a 2D array of values a and a list of weights w, each step in the evolution of the system corresponds to

```
WeightedStep[w_List, a_] := Map[If[# > 0, 1, 0] &,
    Sum[w[[1 + i]] Apply[Plus, Map[RotateLeft[a, #] &,
        Layer[i]]], {i, 0, Length[w] - 1}], {2}]
Layer[n_] := Layer[n] = Select[Flatten[Table[{i, j},
    {i, -n, n}, {j, -n, n}], 1], MemberQ[#, n | -n] &]
```

■ **Features of the model.** The model is a totalistic 2D cellular automaton, as discussed on page 927. It shows class 2 behavior in which information propagates only over limited distances, so that except when the total size of the system is comparable to the range of the rule, boundary conditions are not crucial.

Similar models have been considered before. In the early 1950s (see below) Alan Turing used a model which effectively differed mainly in having continuous color levels. In 1979 Nicholas Swindale constructed a model with discrete levels to investigate ocular dominance stripes in the brain (see below). And following my work on cellular automata in the early 1980s, David Young in 1984 considered a model even more similar to the one I use here.

There are simple cellular automata—such as 8-neighbor outer totalistic code 196623—which eventually yield maze-like patterns even when started from simple initial conditions. The rule on page 336 gives dappled patterns with progressively larger spots.

■ **Reaction-diffusion processes.** The cellular automaton in the main text can be viewed as a discrete idealization of a reaction-diffusion process. The notion that diffusion might be important in embryo development had been suggested in the early 1900s (see page 1004), but it was only in 1952 that Alan Turing showed how it could lead to the formation of definite patterns. Diffusion of a single chemical always tends to smooth out distributions of concentration. But Turing pointed out that with two chemicals in which each can be produced from the other it is possible for separated regions to develop. If $c = \{u[t, x], v[t, x]\}$ is a vector of chemical concentrations, then for suitable values of parameters even the standard linear diffusion equation $\partial_t c == d \cdot \partial_{xx} c + m \cdot c$

can exhibit an instability which causes disturbances with certain spatial wavelengths to grow (compare page 988). In his 1952 paper Turing used a finite difference approximation to a pair of diffusion equations to show that starting from a random distribution of concentration values dappled regions could develop in which one or the other chemical was dominant. With purely linear equations, any instability will always eventually lead to infinite concentrations, but Turing noted that this could be avoided by using realistic nonlinear chemical rate equations. In the couple of years before his death in 1954, Turing appears to have tried to simulate such nonlinear equations on an early digital computer, but my cursory efforts to understand his programs—written as they are in a 32-character machine code—were not successful.

Following Turing's work, the fact that simple reaction-diffusion equations can yield spatially inhomogeneous patterns has been rediscovered—with varying degrees of independence—many times. In the early 1970s Ilya Prigogine termed the patterns dissipative structures. And in the mid-1970s, Hermann Haken considered the phenomenon a cornerstone of what he called synergetics.

Many detailed mathematical analyses of linear reaction-diffusion equations have been done since the 1970s; numerical solutions to linear and occasionally nonlinear such equations have also often been found, and in recent years explicit pictures of patterns—rather than just curves of related functions—have commonly been generated. In the context of biological pigmentation patterns detailed studies have been done particularly by Hans Meinhardt and James Murray.

■ **Scales of patterns.** The visual appearance of a pattern on an actual animal depends greatly on the scale of the pattern relative to the whole animal. Pandas and anteaters, for example, typically have just a few regions of different color, while other animals can have hundreds of regions. Studies based on linear reaction-diffusion equations sometimes assume that patterns correspond to stationary modes of the equations, which inevitably depend greatly on boundary conditions. But in more realistic models patterns emerge from long time behavior with generic initial conditions, making boundary conditions—and effects such as changes in them associated with growth of an embryo—much less important.

■ **Excitable media.** In many physical situations effects become decreasingly important as they propagate further away. But in active or excitable media such as heart, muscle and nerve tissue an effect can maintain its magnitude as it propagates, leading to the formation of a variety of spatial structures. An

early model of such media was constructed in 1946 by Norbert Wiener and Arturo Rosenblueth, based on a discrete array of continuous elements. Models with discrete elements were already considered in the 1960s, and in 1977 James Greenberg and Stuart Hastings introduced a simple 2D cellular automaton with three colors. The pictures below show what is probably the most complex feature of this cellular automaton and related systems: the formation of spiral waves. Such spiral waves were studied in 2D and 3D in the 1970s and 1980s, particularly by Arthur Winfree and others; they are fairly easy to observe in both inorganic chemical reactions (see below) and slime mold colonies.

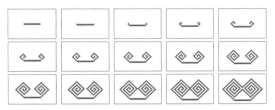

■ **Examples in chemistry.** Overall concentrations in chemical reactions can be described by nonlinear ordinary differential equations. Reactions with oscillatory behavior were predicted by Alfred Lotka in 1910 and observed experimentally by William Bray in 1917, but for some reason they were not further investigated at that time. An example was found experimentally by Boris Belousov in 1951 and extensive investigations of it were begun by Anatol Zhabotinsky around 1960. In the early 1970s spiral waves were seen in the spatial distribution of concentrations in this reaction, and by the end of the 1970s images of such waves were commonly used as icons of the somewhat ill-defined notion of self-organization.

■ **Maze-like patterns.** Maze-like patterns occur in several quite different kinds of systems. Cases in which the underlying mechanism is probably similar to that discussed in the main text include brain coral, large-scale vegetation bands seen in tropical areas, patterns of sand dunes, patterns in pre-turbulent fluid convection, and ocular dominance stripes consisting of regions of brain tissue that get marked when different dye is introduced into nerves from left and right eyes. Cases in which the underlying mechanism is probably more associated with folding of fixed amounts of material include human fingerprint patterns and patterns in ferrofluids consisting of suspensions of magnetic particles.

■ **Origins of randomness.** The model in the main text assumes that randomness enters through initial conditions. If the two parts of a single animal—say opposite wings on a butterfly—

form together, then these initial conditions can be expected to be the same. But usually even the two sides of a single animal are never physically together, and they normally end up having quite uncorrelated random features. In cases such as fingerprints and zebra stripes there is some correlation between different sides, suggesting an intrinsic component to the randomness that occurs. (The fingerprints of identical twins are typically similar but not identical; iris patterns are quite different.) Note that at least sometimes random initial patterns are formed by cells that have the same type, but different lineages—as in cells expressing genes from the two different X chromosomes in a female animal such as a typical tortoiseshell cat. (In general, quite a few traits—particularly related to aging—can show significant variation in strains of organisms that are genetically identical.)

Financial Systems

▪ **Laws of human behavior.** Over the past century there have been a fair number of quantitative laws proposed for features of human behavior. Some are presumably a direct reflection of human biological construction. Thus for example, Weber's law that the perceived strength of a stimulus tends to vary logarithmically with its actual strength seems likely to be related to the electrochemistry of nerve cells. Of laws for more complicated cognitive or social phenomena the vast majority are statistical in nature. And of those that withstand scrutiny, most in my experience turn out to be transformed versions of statements that some quantity or another can be approximated by perfect randomness. Gaussian distributions typically arise when measurements involve sums of random quantities; other common distributions are obtained from products or other simple combinations of random quantities, or from the results of simple processes based on random quantities. Exponential distributions (as seen, for example, in learning curves) and power-law distributions (as in Zipf's law below) are both, for example, very easy to obtain. (Note that particularly in economics there are also various laws derived from calculus and game theory that are viewed as being quite successful, and are not fundamentally statistical.)

▪ **Zipf's law.** To a fairly good approximation the nth most common word in a large sample of English text occurs with frequency $1/n$, as illustrated in the first picture below. This fact was first noticed around the end of the 1800s, and was attributed in 1949 by George Zipf to a general, though vague, Principle of Least Effort for human behavior. I suspect that in fact the law has a rather simple probabilistic origin. Consider generating a long piece of text by picking at random from k letters and a space. Now collect and rank all the "words"

delimited by spaces that are formed. When $k = 1$, the nth most common word will have frequency c^{-n}. But when $k \geq 2$, it turns out that the nth most common word will have a frequency that approximates c/n. If all k letters have equal probabilities, there will be many words with equal frequency, so the distribution will contain steps, as in the second picture below. If the k letters have non-commensurate probabilities, then a smooth distribution is obtained, as in the third picture. If all letter probabilities are equal, then words will simply be ranked by length, with all k^m words of length m occurring with frequency p^m. The normalization of probabilities then implies $p = 1/(2k)$, and since the word at rank roughly k^m then has probability $1/(2k)^m$, Zipf's law follows.

▪ **Motion of people and cars.** To a first approximation crowds of people seem to show aggregate fluid-like behavior similar to what is seen in gases. Fronts of people—as occur in riots or infantry battles—seem to show instabilities perhaps analogous to those in fluids. Road traffic that is constrained to travel along a line exhibits stop-start instabilities when its overall rate is reduced, say by an obstruction. This appears to be a consequence of the delay before one driver responds to changes in speed of cars in front of them. Fairly accurate cellular automaton models of this phenomenon were developed in the early 1990s.

▪ **Growth of cities.** In the absence of geographical constraints, such as terrain or oceans, cities typically have patchy, irregular, shapes. At first an aggregation system (see page 331) might seem to be an obvious model for their growth: each new development gets added to the exterior of the city at a random position. But actual cities look much more irregular. Most likely the reason is that embedded within the cities is a network of transportation routes, and these tend to have a tree- or vein-like structure (though not necessarily with a single center)—with major freeways etc. as trunks. The result of following this structure is to produce a much more irregular boundary.

▪ **Randomness in markets.** After the somewhat tricky process of correcting for overall trends, empirical price data from a wide range of markets seem to a first approximation to follow random walks and thus to exhibit Gaussian fluctuations, as noted by Louis Bachelier in 1900. However, particularly on timescales less than a day, it has in the past decade become clear that, as suggested by Benoit Mandelbrot in the early 1960s, large price fluctuations are significantly more common than a Gaussian distribution would imply.

Such an effect is easy to model with the approach used in the main text if different entities interact in clumps or herds—which can be forced if they are connected in a hierarchical network rather than just a line.

The observed standard deviation of a price—or essentially so-called volatility or beta—can be considered as a measure of the risk of fluctuations in that price. The Capital Asset Pricing Model proposed in the early 1960s suggested that average rates of price increases should be proportional to such variances. And the Black-Scholes model from 1973 implies that prices of suitably constructed options should depend in a sense only on such variances. Over the past decade various corrections to this model have been developed based on non-Gaussian distributions of prices.

■ **Speculative markets.** Cases of markets that seem to operate almost completely independent of objective value have occurred many times in economic history, particularly in connection with innovations in technology or finance. Examples range from tulip bulbs in the mid-1630s to railroads in the mid-1800s to internet businesses in the late 1990s. (Note however that in any particular case it can be claimed that certain speculation was rational, even if it did not work out—but usually it is difficult to get convincing evidence for this, and often effects are obscured by generalized money supply or bankruptcy issues.)

■ **Properties of markets.** Issues of how averaging is done and how irrelevant trends are removed turn out to make unequivocal tests of almost any quantitative hypothesis about prices essentially impossible. The rational expectations theory that prices reflect discounted future earnings has for example been subjected to many empirical tests, but has never been convincingly proved or disproved.

■ **Efficient markets.** In its strong form the so-called Efficient Market Hypothesis states that prices immediately adjust to reflect all possible information, so that knowing a particular piece of information can never be used to make a profit. It is now widely recognized—even in academia—that this hypothesis is a fairly poor representation of reality.

■ **Details of trading.** Cynics might suggest that much of the randomness in practical markets is associated with details of trading. For much of the money actually made from markets on an ongoing basis comes from commissions on trades. And if prices quickly settled down to their final values, fewer trades would tend to be made. (Different entities would nevertheless still often need liquidity at different times.)

■ **Models of markets.** When serious economic theory began in the 1700s arguments tended to be based purely on common sense. But with the work of Léon Walras in the 1870s mathematical models began to become popular. In the early 1900s, common sense again for a while became dominant. But particularly with the development of game theory in the 1940s the notion became established, at least in theoretical economics, that prices represent equilibrium points whose properties can be derived mathematically from requirements of optimality. In practical trading, partly as an outgrowth of theories of business cycles, there had emerged all sorts of elaborate so-called technical analysis in which patterns of price movements were supposed—often on the basis of almost mystical theories—to be indicators of future behavior. In the late 1970s, particularly after the work of Fischer Black and Myron Scholes on options pricing, new models of markets based on methods from statistical physics began to be used, but in these models randomness was taken purely as an assumption. In another direction, it was noticed that dynamic versions of game theory could yield iterated maps and ordinary differential equations which would lead to chaotic behavior in prices, but connections with randomness in actual markets were not established. By the mid-1980s, however, it began to be clear that the whole game-theoretical idea of thinking of markets as collections of rational entities that optimize their positions on the basis of complete information was quite inadequate. Some attempts were made to extend traditional mathematical models, and various highly theoretical analyses were done based on treating entities in the market as universal computers. But by the end of the 1980s, the idea had emerged of doing explicit computer simulations with entities in the market represented by practical programs. (See also page 1105.) Often these programs used fairly sophisticated algorithms intended to mimic human traders, but in competitions between programs simpler algorithms have never seemed to be at much of a disadvantage. The model in the main text is in a sense an ultimate idealization along these lines. It follows a sequence of efforts that I have made since the mid-1980s—though have never considered very satisfactory—to find minimal but accurate models of financial processes.

Fundamental Physics

The Notion of Reversibility

■ **Page 437 · Testing for reversibility.** To show that a cellular automaton is reversible it is sufficient to check that all configurations consisting of repetitions of different blocks have different successors. This can be done for blocks up to length n in a 1D cellular automaton with k colors using

```
ReversibleQ[rule_, k_, n_] := Catch[Do[
    If[Length[Union[Table[CAStep[rule, IntegerDigits[i, k, m]],
        {i, 0, k^m - 1}]]] ≠ k^m, Throw[False]], {m, n}]; True]
```

For $k = 2$, $r = 1$ it turns out that it suffices to test only up to $n = 4$ (128 out of the 256 rules fail at $n = 1$, 64 at $n = 2$, 44 at $n = 3$ and 14 at $n = 4$); for $k = 2$, $r = 2$ it suffices to test up to $n = 15$, and for $k = 3$, $r = 1$, up to $n = 9$. But although these results suggest that in general it should suffice to test only up to $n = k^{2r}$, all that has so far been rigorously proved is that $n = k^{2r}(k^{2r} - 1) + 2r + 1$ (or $n = 15$ for $k = 2$, $r = 1$) is sufficient.

For 2D cellular automata an analogous procedure can in principle be used, though there is no upper limit on the size of blocks that need to be tested, and in fact the question of whether a particular rule is reversible is directly equivalent to the tiling problem discussed on page 213 (compare page 942), and is thus formally undecidable.

■ **Numbers of reversible rules.** For $k = 2$, $r = 1$, there are 6 reversible rules, as shown on page 436. For $k = 2$, $r = 2$ there are 62 reversible rules, in 20 families inequivalent under symmetries, out of a total of 2^{32} or about 4 billion possible rules. For $k = 3$, $r = 1$ there are 1800 reversible rules, in 172 families. For $k = 4$, $r = 1$, some of the reversible rules can be constructed from the second-order cellular automata below. Note that for any k and r, no non-trivial totalistic rule can ever be reversible.

■ **Inverse rules.** Some reversible rules are self-inverse, so that applying the same rule twice yields the identity. Other rules come in distinct pairs. Most often a rule that involves r neighbors has an inverse that also involves at most r neighbors. But for both $k = 2$, $r = 2$ and $k = 3$, $r = 1$ there turn out to be reversible rules whose inverses involve larger

numbers of neighbors. For any given rule one can define the neighborhood size s to be the largest block of cells that is ever needed to determine the color of a single new cell. In general $s \le 2r + 1$, and for a simple identity or shift rule, $s = 1$. For $k = 2$, $r = 1$, it then turns out that all the reversible rules and their inverses have $s = 1$. For $k = 2$, $r = 2$, the reversible rules have values of s from 1 to 5, but their inverses have values $\bar{s}$ from 1 to 6. There are only 8 rules (the inequivalent ones being 16740555 and 3327051468) where $\bar{s} > s$, and in each case $\bar{s} = 6$ while $s = 5$. For $k = 3$, $r = 1$, there are a total of 936 rules with this property: 576, 216 and 144 with $\bar{s} = 4$, 5 and 6, and in all cases $s = 3$. Examples with $\bar{s} = 3$, 4, 5 and 6 are shown below. For arbitrary k and r, it is not clear what the maximum $\bar{s}$ can be; the only bound rigorously established so far is $\bar{s} \le r + 1/2 k^{2r+1}(k^{2r} - 1)$.

2828556973047   3762560660157   538556225233   3066231781977

■ **Surjectivity and injectivity.** See page 959.

■ **Directional reversibility.** Even if successive time steps in the evolution of a cellular automaton do not correspond to an injective map, it is still possible to get an injective map by looking at successive lines at some angle in the spacetime evolution of the system. Examples where this works include the surjective rules 30 and 90.

■ **Page 437 · Second-order cellular automata.** Second-order elementary rules can be implemented using

```
CA2EvolveList[rule_List, {a_List, b_List}, t_Integer] :=
    Map[First, NestList[CA2Step[rule, #] &, {a, b}, t]]
CA2Step[rule_List, {a_, b_}] := {b, Mod[a + rule[[
        8 - (RotateLeft[b] + 2 (b + 2 RotateRight[b]))]], 2]}
```

where *rule* is obtained from the rule number using `IntegerDigits[n, 2, 8]`.

The combination *Drop[list, -1] + 2 Drop[list, 1]* of the result from *CA2EvolveList* corresponds to evolution according to a first-order $k = 4$, $r = 1$ rule.

■ **History.** The concept of getting reversibility in a cellular automaton by having a second-order rule was apparently first suggested by Edward Fredkin around 1970 in the context of 2D systems—on the basis of an analogy with second-order differential equations in physics. Similar ideas had appeared in numerical analysis in the 1960s in connection with so-called symmetric or self-adjoint discrete approximations to differential equations.

■ **Page 438 · Properties.** The pattern from rule 67R with simple initial conditions grows irregularly, at an average rate of about 1 cell every 5 steps. The right-hand side of the pattern from rule 173R consists three triangles that repeat progressively larger at steps of the form $2(9^s - 1)$. Rule 90R has the property that of the diamond of cells at relative positions $\{\{-n, 0\}, \{0, -n\}, \{n, 0\}, \{0, n\}\}$ it is always true for any n that an even number are black.

■ **Page 439 · Properties.** The initial conditions used here have a single black cell on two successive initial steps. For rule 150R, however, there is no black cell on the first initial step. The pattern generated by rule 150R has fractal dimension $Log[2, 3 + \sqrt{17}] - 1$ or about 1.83. In rule 154R, each diagonal stripe is followed by at least one 0; otherwise, the positions of the stripes appear to be quite random, with a density around 0.44.

■ **Generalized additive rules.** Additive cellular automata of the kind discussed on page 952 can be generalized by allowing the new value of each cell to be obtained from combinations of cells on s previous steps. For rule 90 the combination c can be specified as $\{\{1, 0, 1\}\}$, while for rule 150R it can be specified as $\{\{0, 1, 0\}, \{1, 1, 1\}\}$. All generalized additive rules ultimately yield nested patterns. Starting with a list of the initial conditions for s steps, the configurations for the next s steps are given by

    Append[Rest[list],
      Map[Mod[Apply[Plus, Flatten[c#]], 2] &, Transpose[
        Table[RotateLeft[list, {0, i}], {i, -r, r}], {3, 2, 1}]]]]

where $r = (Length[First[c]] - 1)/2$.
Just as for ordinary additive rules on page 1091, an algebraic analysis for generalized additive rules can be given. The objects that appear are solutions to linear recurrences of order s, and in general involve s^{th} roots. For rule 150R, the configuration at step t as shown in the picture on page 439 is given by $(u^t - v^t)/Sqrt[4 + h^2]$, where $\{u, v\} = z /. Solve[z^2 == h z + 1]$ and $h = 1/x + 1 + x$. (See also page 1078.)

■ **Page 440 · Rule 37R.** Complicated structures are fairly easy to get with this rule. The initial condition $\{1, 0, 1\}$ with all cells 0 on the previous step yields a structure that repeats but only every 666 steps. The initial condition $\{\{0, 1, 1\}, \{1, 0, 0\}\}$ yields a pattern that grows sporadically for 3774 steps, then breaks into two repetitive structures. The typical background repeats every 3 steps.

■ **Classification of reversible rules.** In a reversible system it is possible with suitable initial conditions to get absolutely any arrangement of cells to appear at any step. Despite this, however, the overall spacetime pattern of cells is not arbitrary, but is instead determined by the underlying rules. If one starts with completely random initial conditions then class 2 and class 3 behavior are often seen. Class 1 behavior can never occur in a reversible system. Class 4 behavior can occur, as in rule 37R, but is typically obvious only if one starts say with a low density of black cells.

For arbitrary rules, difference patterns of the kind shown on page 250 can get both larger and smaller. In a reversible rule, such patterns can grow and shrink, but can never die out completely.

■ **Emergence of reversibility.** Once on an attractor, any system—even if it does not have reversible underlying rules—must in some sense show approximate reversibility. (Compare page 959.)

■ **Other reversible systems.** Reversible examples can be found of essentially all the types of systems discussed in this book. Reversible mobile automata can for instance be constructed using

    Table[[IntegerDigits[i, 2, 3] → If[First[#] == 0, {#, -1},
      {Reverse[#], 1}] &)[IntegerDigits[perm[[i]], 2, 3]], {i, 8}]

where *perm* is an element of *Permutations[Range[8]]*. An example that exhibits complex behavior is:

Systems based on numbers are typically reversible whenever the mathematical operations they involve are invertible. Thus, for example, the system on page 121 based on successive multiplication by 3/2 is reversible by using division by 3/2. Page 905 gives another example of a reversible system based on numbers.

Multiway systems are reversible whenever both $a \to b$ and $b \to a$ are present as rules, so that the system corresponds mathematically to a semigroup. (See page 938.)

■ **Reversible computation.** Typical practical computers—and computer languages—are not even close to reversible: many inputs can lead to the same output, and there is no unique way to undo the steps of a computation. But despite early confusion (see page 1020), it has been known since at least the 1970s that there is nothing in principle which prevents computation from being reversible. And indeed—just like with the cellular automata in this section—most of the systems in Chapter 11 that exhibit universal computation can readily be made reversible with only slight overhead.

Irreversibility and the Second Law of Thermodynamics

■ **Time reversal invariance.** The reversibility of the laws of physics implies that given the state of a physical system at a particular time, it is always possibly to work out uniquely both its future and its past. Time reversal invariance would further imply that the rules for going in each direction should be identical. To a very good approximation this appears to be true, but it turns out that in certain esoteric particle physics processes small deviations have been found. In particular, it was discovered in 1964 that the decay of the K^0 particle violated time reversal invariance at the level of about one part in a thousand. In current theories, this effect is not attributed any particularly fundamental origin, and is just assumed to be associated with the arbitrary setting of certain parameters. K^0 decay was for a long time the only example of time reversal violation that had explicitly been seen, although recently examples in B particle decays have probably also been seen. It also turns out that the only current viable theories of the apparent preponderance of matter over antimatter in the universe are based on the idea that a small amount of time reversal violation occurred in the decays of certain very massive particles in the very early universe.

The basic formalism used for particle physics assumes not only reversibility, but also so-called CPT invariance. This means that same rules should apply if one not only reverses the direction of time (T), but also simultaneously inverts all spatial coordinates (P) and conjugates all charges (C), replacing particles by antiparticles. In a certain mathematical sense, CPT invariance can be viewed as a generalization of relativistic invariance: with a speed faster than light, something close to an ordinary relativistic transformation is a CPT transformation.

Originally it was assumed that C, P and T would all separately be invariances, as they are in classical mechanics. But in 1957 it was discovered that in radioactive beta decay, C and P are in a sense each maximally violated: among other things, the correlation between spin and motion direction is exactly opposite for neutrinos and for antineutrinos that are emitted. Despite this, it was still assumed that CP and T

would be true invariances. But in 1964 these too were found to be violated. Starting with a pure beam of K^0 particles, it turns out that quantum mechanical mixing processes lead after about 10^{-8} seconds to a certain mixture of $\overline{K}^0$ particles—the antiparticles of the K^0. And what effectively happens is that the amount of mixing differs by about 0.1% in the positive and negative time directions. (What is actually observed is a small probability for the long-lived component of a K^0 beam to decay into two rather than three pions. Some analysis is required to connect this with T violation.) Particle physics experiments so far support exact CPT invariance. Simple models of gravity potentially suggest CPT violation (as a consequence of deviations from pure special relativistic invariance), but such effects tend to disappear when the models are refined.

■ **History of thermodynamics.** Basic physical notions of heat and temperature were established in the 1600s, and scientists of the time appear to have thought correctly that heat is associated with the motion of microscopic constituents of matter. But in the 1700s it became widely believed that heat was instead a separate fluid-like substance. Experiments by James Joule and others in the 1840s put this in doubt, and finally in the 1850s it became accepted that heat is in fact a form of energy. The relation between heat and energy was important for the development of steam engines, and in 1824 Sadi Carnot had captured some of the ideas of thermodynamics in his discussion of the efficiency of an idealized engine. Around 1850 Rudolf Clausius and William Thomson (Kelvin) stated both the First Law—that total energy is conserved—and the Second Law of Thermodynamics. The Second Law was originally formulated in terms of the fact that heat does not spontaneously flow from a colder body to a hotter. Other formulations followed quickly, and Kelvin in particular understood some of the law's general implications. The idea that gases consist of molecules in motion had been discussed in some detail by Daniel Bernoulli in 1738, but had fallen out of favor, and was revived by Clausius in 1857. Following this, James Clerk Maxwell in 1860 derived from the mechanics of individual molecular collisions the expected distribution of molecular speeds in a gas. Over the next several years the kinetic theory of gases developed rapidly, and many macroscopic properties of gases in equilibrium were computed. In 1872 Ludwig Boltzmann constructed an equation that he thought could describe the detailed time development of a gas, whether in equilibrium or not. In the 1860s Clausius had introduced entropy as a ratio of heat to temperature, and had stated the Second Law in terms of the increase of this quantity. Boltzmann then showed that his equation implied the so-called H Theorem, which states that a quantity equal to entropy in equilibrium must always increase with time. At first, it seemed that Boltzmann had successfully proved the Second Law. But then it was noticed that since molecular collisions were assumed reversible, his derivation could be run in reverse, and would then imply the opposite of the Second Law. Much later it was realized that Boltzmann's original equation implicitly assumed that molecules are uncorrelated before each collision, but not afterwards, thereby introducing a fundamental asymmetry in time. Early in the 1870s Maxwell and Kelvin appear to have already understood that the Second Law could not formally be derived from microscopic physics, but must somehow be a consequence of human inability to track large numbers of molecules. In responding to objections concerning reversibility Boltzmann realized around 1876 that in a gas there are many more states that seem random than seem orderly. This realization led him to argue that entropy must be proportional to the logarithm of the number of possible states of a system, and to formulate ideas about ergodicity. The statistical mechanics of systems of particles was put in a more general context by Willard Gibbs, beginning around 1900. Gibbs introduced the notion of an ensemble—a collection of many possible states of a system, each assigned a certain probability. He argued that if the time evolution of a single state were to visit all other states in the ensemble—the so-called ergodic hypothesis—then averaged over a sufficiently long time a single state would behave in a way that was typical of the ensemble. Gibbs also gave qualitative arguments that entropy would increase if it were measured in a "coarse-grained" way in which nearby states were not distinguished. In the early 1900s the development of thermodynamics was largely overshadowed by quantum theory and little fundamental work was done on it. Nevertheless, by the 1930s, the Second Law had somehow come to be generally regarded as a principle of physics whose foundations should be questioned only as a curiosity. Despite neglect in physics, however, ergodic theory became an active area of pure mathematics, and from the 1920s to the 1960s properties related to ergodicity were established for many kinds of simple systems. When electronic computers became available in the 1950s, Enrico Fermi and others began to investigate the ergodic properties of nonlinear systems of springs. But they ended up concentrating on recurrence phenomena related to solitons, and not looking at general questions related to the Second Law. Much the same happened in the 1960s, when the first simulations of hard sphere gases were led to concentrate on the specific phenomenon of long-time tails. And by the 1970s, computer experiments were mostly oriented towards ordinary

differential equations and strange attractors, rather than towards systems with large numbers of components, to which the Second Law might apply. Starting in the 1950s, it was recognized that entropy is simply the negative of the information quantity introduced in the 1940s by Claude Shannon. Following statements by John von Neumann, it was thought that any computational process must necessarily increase entropy, but by the early 1970s, notably with work by Charles Bennett, it became accepted that this is not so (see page 1018), laying some early groundwork for relating computational and thermodynamic ideas.

■ **Current thinking on the Second Law.** The vast majority of current physics textbooks imply that the Second Law is well established, though with surprising regularity they say that detailed arguments for it are beyond their scope. More specialized articles tend to admit that the origins of the Second Law remain mysterious. Most ultimately attribute its validity to unknown constraints on initial conditions or measurements, though some appeal to external perturbations, to cosmology or to unknown features of quantum mechanics.

An argument for the Second Law from around 1900, still reproduced in many textbooks, is that if a system is ergodic then it will visit all its possible states, and the vast majority of these will look random. But only very special kinds of systems are in fact ergodic, and even in such systems, the time necessary to visit a significant fraction of all possible states is astronomically long. Another argument for the Second Law, arising from work in the 1930s and 1940s, particularly on systems of hard spheres, is based on the notion of instability with respect to small changes in initial conditions. The argument suffers however from the same difficulties as the ones for chaos theory discussed in Chapter 6 and does not in the end explain in any real way the origins of randomness, or the observed validity of the Second Law.

With the Second Law accepted as a general principle, there is confusion about why systems in nature have not all dissipated into complete randomness. And often the rather absurd claim is made that all the order we see in the universe must just be a fluctuation—leaving little explanatory power for principles such as the Second Law.

■ **My explanation of the Second Law.** What I say in this book is not incompatible with much of what has been said about the Second Law before; it is simply that I make more definite some key points that have been left vague before. In particular, I use notions of computation to specify what kinds of initial conditions can reasonably be prepared, and what kinds of measurements can reasonably be made. In a sense what I do is just to require that the operation of coarse graining correspond to a computation that is less sophisticated than the actual evolution of the system being studied. (See also Chapters 10 and 12.)

■ **Biological systems and Maxwell's demon.** Unlike most physical systems, biological systems typically seem capable of spontaneously organizing themselves. And as a result, even the original statements of the Second Law talked only about "inanimate systems". In the mid-1860s James Clerk Maxwell then suggested that a demon operating at a microscopic level could reduce the randomness of a system such as a gas by intelligently controlling the motion of molecules. For many years there was considerable confusion about Maxwell's demon. There were arguments that the demon must use a flashlight that generates entropy. And there were extensive demonstrations that actual biological systems reduce their internal entropy only at the cost of increases in the entropy of their environment. But in fact the main point is that if the evolution of the whole system is to be reversible, then the demon must store enough information to reverse its own actions, and this limits how much the demon can do, preventing it, for example, from unscrambling a large system of gas molecules.

■ **Self-gravitating systems.** The observed existence of structures such as galaxies might lead one to think that any large number of objects subject to mutual gravitational attraction might not follow the Second Law and become randomized, but might instead always form orderly clumps. It is difficult to know, however, what an idealized self-gravitating system would do. For in practice, issues such as the limited size of a galaxy, its overall rotation, and the details of stellar collisions all seem to have major effects on the results obtained. (And it is presumably not feasible to do a small-scale experiment, say in Earth orbit.) There are known to be various instabilities that lead in the direction of clumping and core collapse, but how these weigh against effects such as the transfer of energy into tight binding of small groups of stars is not clear. Small galaxies such as globular clusters that contain less than a million stars seem to exhibit a certain uniformity which suggests a kind of equilibrium. Larger galaxies such as our own that contain perhaps 100 billion stars often have intricate spiral or other structure, whose origin may be associated with gravitational effects, or may be a consequence of detailed processes of star formation and explosion. (There is some evidence that older galaxies of a given size tend to develop more regularities in their structure.) Current theories of the early universe tend to assume that galaxies originally began to form as a result of density fluctuations of non-gravitational origin (and reflected

in the cosmic microwave background). But there is evidence that a widespread fractal structure develops—with a correlation function of the form $r^{-1.8}$—in the distribution of stars in our galaxy, galaxies in clusters and clusters in superclusters, perhaps suggesting the existence of general overall laws for self-gravitating systems. (See also page 973.)

As mentioned on page 880, it so happens that my original interest in cellular automata around 1981 developed in part from trying to model the growth of structure in self-gravitating systems. At first I attempted to merge and generalize ideas from traditional areas of mathematical physics, such as kinetic theory, statistical mechanics and field theory. But then, particularly as I began to think about doing explicit computer simulations, I decided to take a different tack and instead to look for the most idealized possible models. And in doing this I quickly came up with cellular automata. But when I started to investigate cellular automata, I discovered some very remarkable phenomena, and I was soon led away from self-gravitating systems, and into the process of developing the much more general science in this book. Over the years, I have occasionally come back to the problem of self-gravitating systems, but I have never succeeded in developing what I consider to be a satisfactory approach to them.

■ **Cosmology and the Second Law.** In the standard big bang model it is assumed that all matter in the universe was initially in completely random thermal equilibrium. But such equilibrium implies uniformity, and from this it follows that the initial conditions for the gravitational forces in the universe must have been highly regular, resulting in simple overall expansion, rather than random expansion in some places and contraction in others. As I discuss on page 1026 I suspect that in fact the universe as a whole probably had what were ultimately very simple initial conditions, and it is just that the effective rules for the evolution of matter led to rapid randomization, whereas those for gravity did not.

■ **Alignment of time in the universe.** Evidence from astronomy clearly suggests that the direction of irreversible processes is the same throughout the universe. The reason for this is presumably that all parts of the universe are expanding—with the local consequence that radiation is more often emitted than absorbed, as evidenced by the fact that the night sky is dark. Olbers' paradox asks why one does not see a bright star in every direction in the night sky. The answer is that locally stars are clumped, and light from stars further away is progressively red-shifted to lower energy. Focusing a larger and larger distance away, the light one sees was emitted longer and longer ago. And eventually one sees light emitted when the universe was filled with hot opaque gas—now red-shifted to become the 2.7K cosmic microwave background.

■ **Poincaré recurrence.** Systems of limited size that contain only discrete elements inevitably repeat their evolution after a sufficiently long time (see page 258). In 1890 Henri Poincaré established the somewhat less obvious fact that even continuous systems also always eventually get at least arbitrarily close to repeating themselves. This discovery led to some confusion in early interpretations of the Second Law, but the huge length of time involved in a Poincaré recurrence makes it completely irrelevant in practice.

■ **Page 446 · Billiards.** The discrete system I consider here is analogous to continuous so-called billiard systems consisting of circular balls in the plane. The simplest case involves one ball bouncing around in a region of a definite shape. In a rectangular region, the position is given by $Mod[a\,t, \{w, h\}]$ and every point will be visited if the parameters have irrational ratios. In a region that contains fixed circular obstructions, the motion can become sensitively dependent on initial conditions. (This setup is similar to a so-called Lorentz gas.) For a system of balls in a region with cyclic boundaries, a complicated proof due to Yakov Sinai from the 1960s purports to show that every ball eventually visits every point in the region, and that certain simple statistical properties of trajectories are consistent with randomness. (See also page 971.)

■ **Page 449 · Entropy of particles in a box.** The number of possible states of a region of m cells containing q particles is $Binomial[m, q]$. In the large size limit, the logarithm of this can be approximated by $q\,Log[m/q]/m$.

■ **Page 457 · Periods in rule 37R.** With a system of size n, the maximum possible repetition period is 2^{2n}. In actuality, however, the periods are considerably shorter. With all cells 0 on one step, and a block of nonzero cells on the next step, the periods are for example: $\{1\}$: 21; $\{1, 1\}$: $3n-8$; $\{1, 0, 1\}$: 666; $\{1, 1, 1\}$: $3n-8$; $\{1, 0, 0, 1\}$: irregular ($< 24n$; peaks at $6j+1$); $\{1, 0, 0, 1, 0, 1\}$: irregular ($\lesssim 2^n$; 857727 for $n=26$; 13705406 for $n=100$). With completely random initial conditions, there are great fluctuations, but a typical period is around $2^{n/3}$.

Conserved Quantities and Continuum Phenomena

■ **Physics.** The quantities in physics that so far seem to be exactly conserved are: energy, momentum, angular momentum, electric charge, color charge, lepton number (as well as electron number, muon number and τ lepton number) and baryon number.

■ **Implementation.** Whether a k-color cellular automaton with range r conserves total cell value can be determined from

```
Catch[Do[
  (If[Apply[Plus, CAStep[rule, #] - #] ≠ 0, Throw[False]] &)[
   IntegerDigits[i, k, m]], {m, w}, {i, 0, k^m - 1}]; True]
```

where w can be taken to be k^{2r}, and perhaps smaller. Among the 256 elementary cellular automata just 5 conserve total cell value. Among the 2^{32} $k=2$, $r=2$ rules 428 do, and of these 2 are symmetric, and 6 are reversible, and all these are just shift and identity rules.

■ **More general conserved quantities.** Some rules conserve not total numbers of cells with given colors, but rather total numbers of blocks of cells with given forms—or combinations of these. The pictures below show the simplest quantities of these kinds that end up being conserved by various elementary rules.

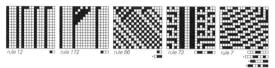

rule 12   rule 172   rule 56   rule 73   rule 7

Among the 256 elementary rules, the total numbers that have conserved quantities involving at most blocks of lengths 1 through 10 are $\{5, 38, 66, 88, 102, 108, 108, 114, 118, 118\}$.

Rules that show complicated behavior usually do not seem to have conserved quantities, and this is true for example of rules 30, 90 and 110, at least up to blocks of length 10.

One can count the number of occurrences of each of the k^b possible blocks of length b in a given state using

```
BC[list_] :=
  With[{z = Map[FromDigits[#, k] &, Partition[list, b, 1, 1]]},
   Map[Count[z, #] &, Range[0, k^b - 1]]]
```

Conserved quantities of the kind discussed here are then of the form $q \cdot BC[a]$ where q is some fixed list. A way to find candidates for q is to compute

```
NullSpace[Table[With[{u = Table[Random[Integer,
  {0, k - 1}], {m}]}, BC[CAStep[u]] - BC[u]], {s}]]
```

for progressively larger m and s, and to see what lists continue to appear. For block size b, k^{b-1} lists will always appear as a result of trivial conserved quantities. (With $k=2$, for $b=1$, $\{1, 1\}$ represents conservation of the total number of cells, regardless of color, while for $b=2$, $\{1, 1, 1, 1\}$ represents the same thing, while $\{0, 1, -1, 0\}$ represents the fact that in going along in any state the number of black-to-white transitions must equal the number of white-to-black ones.) If more than k^{b-1} lists appear, however, then some must correspond to genuine non-trivial conserved quantities. To identify any such quantity with certainty, it turns out to be enough to look at the k^{b+2r-1} states where no block of length

$b + 2r - 1$ appears more than once (and perhaps even just some fairly small subset of these).

(See also page 981.)

▪ **Other conserved quantities.** The conserved quantities discussed so far can all be thought of as taking values assigned to blocks of different kinds in a given state and then just adding them up as ordinary numbers. But one can also imagine using other operations to combine such values. Addition modulo n can be handled by inserting *Modulus → n* in *NullSpace* in the previous note. And doing this shows for example that rule 150 conserves the total number of black cells modulo 2. But in general not many additional conserved quantities are found in this way. One can also consider combining values of blocks by the multiplication operation in a group—and seeing whether the conjugacy class of the result is conserved.

▪ **PDEs.** In the early 1960s it was discovered that certain nonlinear PDEs support an infinite number of distinct conserved quantities, associated with so-called integrability and the presence of solitons. Systematic methods now exist to find conserved quantities that are given by integrals of polynomials of any given degree in the dependent variables and their derivatives. Most randomly chosen PDEs appear, however, to have no such conserved quantities.

▪ **Local conservation laws.** Whenever a system like a cellular automaton (or PDE) has a global conserved quantity there must always be a local conservation law which expresses the fact that every point in the system the total flux of the conserved quantity into a particular region must equal the rate of increase of the quantity inside it. (If the conserved quantity is thought of like charge, the flux is then current.) In any 1D $k = 2$, $r = 1$ cellular automaton, it follows from the basic structure of the rule that one can tell what the difference in values of a particular cell on two successive steps will be just by looking at the cell and its immediate neighbor on each side. But if the number of black cells is conserved, then one can compute this difference instead by defining a suitable flux, and subtracting its values on the left and right of the cell. What the flux should be depends on the rule. For rule 184, it can be taken to be 1 for each ▪□ block, and to be 0 otherwise. For rule 170, it is 1 for both □□ and ▪□. For rule 150, it is 1 for □□ and ▪▪, with all computations done modulo 2. In general, if the global conserved quantity involves blocks of size b, the flux can be computed by looking at blocks of size $b + 2r - 1$. What the values for these blocks should be can be found by solving a system of linear equations; that a solution must exist can be seen by looking at the de Bruijn network (see page 941), with nodes labelled by size $b + 2r - 1$ blocks,

and connections by value differences between size b blocks at the center of the possible size $b + 2r$ blocks. (Note that the same basic kind of setup works in any number of dimensions.)

▪ **Block cellular automata.** With a rule of the form $\{\{1, 1\} \rightarrow \{1, 1\}, \{1, 0\} \rightarrow \{1, 0\}, \{0, 1\} \rightarrow \{0, 0\}, \{0, 0\} \rightarrow \{0, 1\}\}$ the evolution of a block cellular automaton with blocks of size n can be implemented using

```
BCAEvolveList[{n_Integer, rule_}, init_, t_] :=
    FoldList[BCAStep[{n, rule}, #1, #2] &, init, Range[t]] /;
    Mod[Length[init], n] == 0
BCAStep[{n_, rule_}, a_, d_] := RotateRight[
    Flatten[Partition[RotateLeft[a, d], n]] /. rule], d]
```

Starting with a single black cell, none of the $k = 2$, $n = 2$ block cellular automata generate anything beyond simple nested patterns. In general, there are k^{nk^n} possible rules for block cellular automata with k colors and blocks of size n. Of these, $k^n!$ are reversible. For $k = 2$, the number of rules that conserve the total number of black cells can be computed from $q = Binomial[n, Range[0, n]]$ as $Apply[Times, q^q]$. The number of these rules that are also reversible is $Apply[Times, q!]$. In general, a block cellular automaton is reversible only if its rule simply permutes the k^n possible blocks.

Compressing each block into a single cell, and n steps into one, any block cellular automaton with k colors and block size n can be translated directly into an ordinary cellular automaton with k^n colors and range $r = n/2$.

▪ **Page 461 · Block rules.** These pictures show the behavior of rule (c) starting from some special initial conditions.

The repetition period with a total of n cells can be 3^n steps. With random initial conditions, the period is typically up to about $3^{n/2}$. Starting with a block of q black cells, the period can get close to this. For $n = 20$, $q = 17$, for example, it is 31,300.

Note that even in rule (b) wraparound phenomena can lead to repetition periods that increase rapidly with n (e.g. 4820 for $n = 20$, $q = 15$), but presumably not exponentially.

In rule (d), the repetition periods can typically be larger than in rule (c): e.g. 803,780 for $n = 20$, $q = 13$.

▪ **Page 464 · Limiting procedures.** Several different limiting procedures all appear to yield the same continuum behavior for the cellular automata shown here. In the pictures on this page a large ensemble of different initial conditions is considered, and the density of each individual cell averaged over this ensemble is computed. In a more direct analogy to actual physical systems, one would consider instead a very large number of cells, then compute the density in a single state of the system by averaging over regions that contain many cells but are nevertheless small compared to the size of the whole system.

■ **PDE approximations.** Cellular automaton (d) in the main text can be viewed as minimal discrete approximations to the diffusion equation. The evolution of densities in the ensemble average is analogous to a traditional finite difference method with a real number at each site. The cellular automaton itself uses in effect a distributed representation of the density.

■ **Diffusion equation.** In an appropriate limit the density distribution for cellular automaton (d) appears to satisfy the usual diffusion equation $\partial_t f[x, t] == c\, \partial_{xx} f[x, t]$ discussed on page 163. The solution to this equation with an impulse initial condition is $Exp[-x^2/t]$, and with a block from $-a$ to a it is $(Erf[(a-x)/\sqrt{t}\,] + Erf[(a+x)/\sqrt{t}\,])/a$.

■ **Derivation of the diffusion equation.** With some appropriate assumptions, it is fairly straightforward to derive the usual diffusion equation from a cellular automaton. Let the density of black cells at position x and time t be $f[x, t]$, where this density can conveniently be computed by averaging over many instances of the system. If we assume that the density varies slowly with position and time, then we can make series expansions such as

$$f[x + dx, t] == f[x, t] + \partial_x f[x, t]\, dx + 1/2\, \partial_{xx} f[x, t]\, dx^2 + \ldots$$

where the coordinates are scaled so that adjacent cells are at positions $x-dx$, x, $x+dx$, etc. If we then assume perfect underlying randomness, the density at a particular position must be given in terms of the densities at neighboring positions on the previous step by

$$f[x, t+dt] == p_1 f[x-dx, t] + p_2 f[x, t] + p_3 f[x+dx, t]$$

Density conservation implies that $p_1 + p_2 + p_3 == 1$, while left-right symmetry implies $p_1 == p_3$. And from this it follows that

$$f[x, t+dt] == c\, (f[x-dx, t] + f[x+dx, t]) + (1-2\,c) f[x, t]$$

Performing a series expansion then yields

$$f[x, t] + dt\, \partial_t f[x, t] == f[x, t] + c\, dx^2\, \partial_{xx} f[x, t]$$

which in turn gives exactly the usual 1D diffusion equation $\partial_t f[x, t] == \xi\, \partial_{xx} f[x, t]$, where ξ is the diffusion coefficient for the system. I first gave this derivation in 1986, together with extensive generalizations.

■ **Page 464 · Non-standard diffusion.** To get ordinary diffusion behavior of the kind that occurs in gases—and is described by the diffusion equation—it is in effect necessary to have perfect uncorrelated randomness, with no structure that persists too long. But for example in the rule (a) picture on page 463 there is in effect a block of solid that persists in the middle—so that no ordinary diffusion behavior is seen. In rule (c) there is considerable apparent randomness, but it turns out that there are also fluctuations that last too long to yield ordinary diffusion. And thus for example whenever there is a structure containing s identical cells (as on page 462), this typically takes about s^2 steps to decay away. The result is that on page 464 the limiting form of the average behavior does not end up being an ordinary Gaussian.

■ **Conservation of vector quantities.** Conservation of the total number of colored cells is analogous to conservation of a scalar quantity such as energy or particle number. One can also consider conservation of a vector quantity such as momentum which has not only a magnitude but also a direction. Direction makes little sense in 1D, but is meaningful in 2D. The 2D cellular automaton used as a model of an idealized gas on page 446 provides an example of a system that can be viewed as conserving a vector quantity. In the absence of fixed scatterers, the total fluxes of particles in the horizontal and the vertical directions are conserved. But in a sense there is too much conservation in this system, and there is no interaction between horizontal and vertical motions. This can be achieved by having more complicated underlying rules. One possibility is to use a hexagonal rather than square grid, thereby allowing six particle directions rather than four. On such a grid it is possible to randomize microscopic particle motions, but nevertheless conserve overall momenta. This is essentially the model used in my discussion of fluids on page 378.

Ultimate Models for the Universe

■ **History of ultimate models.** From the earliest days of Greek science until well into the 1900s, it seems to have often been believed that an ultimate model of the universe was not far away. In antiquity there were vague ideas about everything being made of elements like fire and water. In the 1700s, following the success of Newtonian mechanics, a common assumption seems to have been that everything (with the possible exception of light) must consist of tiny corpuscles with gravity-like forces between them. In the 1800s the notion of fields—and the ether—began to develop, and in the 1880s it was suggested that atoms might be knotted vortices in the ether (see page 1044). When the electron was discovered in 1897 it was briefly thought that it might be the fundamental constituent of everything. And later it was imagined that perhaps electromagnetic fields could underlie everything. Then after the introduction of general relativity for the gravitational field in 1915, there were efforts, especially in the 1930s, to introduce extensions that would yield unified field theories of everything (see page 1028). By the 1950s, however, an increasing number of subatomic particles were being found, and most efforts at unification became considerably more modest. In the 1960s the quark model began to explain many of the particles that were seen. Then in the 1970s work in quantum field theory encouraged the use of gauge theories and by the late 1970s the so-called Standard Model had emerged, with the Weinberg-Salam $SU(2) \otimes U(1)$ gauge theory for weak interactions and electromagnetism, and the QCD $SU(3)$ gauge theory for strong interactions. The discoveries of the c quark, τ lepton and b quark were largely unexpected, but by the late 1970s there was widespread enthusiasm for the idea of a single "grand unified" gauge theory, based say on $SU(5)$, that would explain all forces except gravity. By the mid-1980s failure to observe expected proton decay cast doubts on simple versions of such models, and various possibilities based on supersymmetry and groups like $SO(10)$ were considered. Occasional attempts to construct quantum theories of gravity had been made since the 1930s, and in the late 1980s these began to be pursued more vigorously. In the mid-1980s the discovery that string theory could be given various mathematical features that were considered desirable made it emerge as the main hope for an ultimate "theory of everything". But despite all sorts of elegant mathematical work, the theory remains rather distant from observed features of our universe. In some parts of particle physics, it is still sometimes claimed that an ultimate theory is not far away, but outside it generally seems to be assumed that physics is somehow instead an endless frontier—that will continue to yield a stream of surprising and increasingly complex discoveries forever—with no ultimate theory ever being found.

■ **Theological implications.** Some may view an ultimate model of the universe as "leaving no room for a god", while others may view it as a direct reflection of the existence of a god. In any case, knowing a complete and ultimate model does make it impossible to have miracles or divine interventions that come from outside the laws of the universe—though working out what will happen on the basis of these laws may nevertheless be irreducibly difficult.

■ **Origins of physical models.** Considering the reputation of physics as an empirical science, it is remarkable how many significant theories were in fact first constructed on largely aesthetic grounds. Notable examples include Maxwell's equations for electromagnetism (1880s), general relativity (1915), the Dirac equation for relativistic electrons (1928), and QCD (early 1970s). This history makes it seem more plausible that one might be able to come up with an ultimate model of physics on largely aesthetic grounds, rather than mainly by working from detailed experimental observations.

■ **Simplicity in scientific models.** To curtail absurdly complicated early scientific models Occam's razor principle that "entities should not be multiplied beyond necessity" was introduced in the 1300s. This principle has worked well in physics, where it has often proven to be the case, for example, that out of all possible terms in an equation the only ones that actually occur are the very simplest. But in a field like biology, the principle has usually been regarded as much less successful. For many complicated features are seen in biological organisms, and when there have been guesses of simple explanations for them, these have often turned out to be wrong. Much of what is seen is probably a reflection of complicated details of the history of biological evolution. But particularly after the discoveries in this book it seems likely that at least some of what appears complicated may actually be produced by very simple underlying programs—which perhaps occur because they were the first to be tried, or are the most efficient or robust. Outside of natural science, Occam's principle can sometimes be useful—typically because simplicity is a good assumption in some aspect of human behavior or motivation. In looking at well-developed technological systems or human organizations simplicity is also quite often a reasonable assumption—since over the course of time parts that are complicated or difficult to understand will tend to have been optimized away.

■ **Numerology.** Ever since the Pythagoreans many attempts to find truly ultimate models of the universe have ended up centering on derivations of numbers that are somehow thought to be characteristic of the universe. In the past century, the emphasis has been on physical constants such as the fine structure constant $\alpha \simeq 1/137.0359896$, and usually the idea is that such constants arise directly from counting objects of some specified type using traditional discrete mathematics. A notable effort along these lines was made by Arthur Eddington in the mid-1930s, and certainly over the past twenty or so years I have received a steady stream of mail presenting such notions with varying degrees of obscurity and mysticism. But while I believe that every feature of our universe does indeed come from an ultimate discrete model, I would be very surprised if the values of constants which happen to be easy for us to measure in the end turn out to be given by simple traditional mathematical formulas.

■ **Emergence of simple laws.** In statistical physics it is seen that universal and fairly simple overall laws often emerge even in systems whose underlying molecular or other structure can be quite complicated. The basic origin of this phenomenon is the averaging effect of randomness discussed in Chapter 7 (technically, it is the survival only of leading operators at renormalization group fixed points). The same phenomenon is also seen in quantum field theory, where it is essentially a consequence of the averaging effect of quantum fluctuations, which have a direct mathematical analog to statistical physics.

■ **Apparent simplicity.** Given any rules it is always possible to develop a form of description in which these rules will be considered simple. But what is interesting to ask is whether the underlying rules of the universe will seem simple—or special, say in their elegance or symmetry—with respect to forms of description that we as humans currently use.

■ **Mechanistic models.** Until quite recently, it was generally assumed that if one were able to get at the microscopic constituents of the universe they would look essentially like small-scale analogs of objects familiar from everyday life. And so, for example, the various models of atoms from the end of the 1800s and beginning of the 1900s were all based on familiar mechanical systems. But with the rise of quantum mechanics it came to be believed throughout mainstream physics that any true fundamental model must be abstract and mathematical—and never ultimately amenable to any kind of direct mechanistic description. Occasionally there have been mechanistic descriptions used—as in the parton and bag models, and various continuum models of high-energy collisions—but they have typically been viewed only as convenient rough approximations. (Feynman diagrams may also seem superficially mechanistic, but are really just representations of quite abstract mathematical formulas.) And indeed since at least the 1960s mechanistic models have tended to carry the stigma of uninformed amateur science.

With the rise of computers there began to be occasional discussion—though largely outside of mainstream science—that the universe might have a mechanism related to computers. Since the 1950s science fiction has sometimes featured the idea that the universe or some part of it—such as the Earth—could be an intentionally created computer, or that our perception of the universe could be based on a computer simulation. Starting in the 1950s a few computer scientists considered the idea that the universe might have components like a computer. Konrad Zuse suggested that it could be a continuous cellular automaton; Edward Fredkin an ordinary cellular automaton (compare page 1027). And over the past few decades—normally in the context of amateur science—there have been a steady stream of systems like cellular automata constructed to have elements

reminiscent of observed particles or forces. From the point of view of mainstream physics, such models have usually seemed quite naive. And from what I say in the main text, no such literal mechanistic model can ever in the end realistically be expected to work. For if an ultimate model is going to be simple, then in a sense it cannot have room for all sorts of elements that are immediately recognizable in terms of everyday known physics. And instead I believe that what must happen relies on the phenomena discovered in this book—and involves the emergence of complex properties without any obvious underlying mechanistic set up. (Compare page 860.)

■ **The Anthropic Principle.** It is sometimes argued that the reason our universe has the characteristics it does is because otherwise an intelligence such as us could not have arisen to observe it. But to apply such an argument one must among other things assume that we can imagine all the ways in which intelligence could conceivably operate. Yet as we have seen in this book it is possible for highly complex behavior—ultimately not dissimilar to intelligence—to arise from simple programs in ways that we never came even close to imagining. And indeed, as we discuss in Chapter 12, it seems likely that above a fairly low threshold the vast majority of underlying rules can in fact in some way or another support arbitrarily complex computations—potentially allowing something one might call intelligence in a vast range of very different universes. (See page 822.)

■ **Physics versus mathematics.** Theoretical physics can be viewed as taking physical input in the form of models and then using mathematics to work out the consequences. If I am correct that there is a simple underlying program for the universe, then this means that theoretical physics must at some level have only a very small amount of true physical input—and the rest must in a sense all just be mathematics.

■ **Initial conditions.** To find the behavior of the universe one potentially needs to know not only its rule but also its initial conditions. Like the rule, I suspect that the initial conditions will turn out to be simple. And ultimately there should be traces of such simplicity in, say, the distribution of galaxies or the cosmic microwave background. But ideas like those on page 1055—as well as inflation—tend to suggest that we currently see only a tiny fraction of the whole universe, making it very difficult for example to recognize overall geometrical regularities. And it could also be that even though there might ultimately have been simple initial conditions, the current phase of our universe might be the result of some sequence of previous phases, and so effectively have much more complicated initial conditions. (Proposals discussed in quantum cosmology since the 1980s that for example just involve requiring the universe to satisfy final but not initial boundary condition constraints do not fit well into my kinds of models.)

■ **Consequences of an ultimate model.** Even if one knows an ultimate model for the universe, there will inevitably be irreducible difficulty in working out all its consequences. Indeed, questions like "does there exist a way to transmit information faster than light?" may boil down to issues analogous to whether it is possible to construct a configuration that has a certain property in, say, the rule 110 cellular automaton. And while some such questions may be answered by fairly straightforward computational or mathematical means, there will be no upper bound on the amount of effort that it could take to answer any particular question.

■ **Meaning of the universe.** If the whole history of our universe can be obtained by following definite simple rules, then at some level this history has the same kind of character as a construct such as the digit sequence of π. And what this suggests is that it makes no more or less sense to talk about the meaning of phenomena in our universe as it does to talk about the meaning of phenomena in the digit sequence of π.

The Nature of Space

■ **History of discrete space.** The idea that matter might be made up of discrete particles existed in antiquity (see page 876), and occasionally the notion was discussed that space might also be discrete—and that this might for example be a way of avoiding issues like Zeno's paradox. In 1644 René Descartes proposed that space might initially consist of an array of identical tiny discrete spheres, with motion then occurring through chains of these spheres going around in vortices—albeit with pieces being abraded off. But with the rise of calculus in the 1700s all serious fundamental models in physics began to assume continuous space. In discussing the notion of curved space, Bernhard Riemann remarked in 1854 that it would be easier to give a general mathematical definition of distance if space were discrete. But since physical theories seemed to require continuous space, the necessary new mathematics was developed and almost universally used—though for example in 1887 William Thomson (Kelvin) did consider a discrete foam-like model for the ether (compare page 988). Starting in 1930, difficulties with infinities in quantum field theory again led to a series of proposals that spacetime might be discrete. And indeed by the late 1930s this notion was fairly widely discussed as a possible inevitable feature of quantum mechanics. But there were problems with relativistic invariance, and after ideas of renormalization developed in the 1940s, discrete space seemed unnecessary, and has been out of favor ever since. Some non-standard versions of quantum field theory involving discrete space did however continue to be investigated into the 1960s, and by then a few isolated other initiatives had arisen that involved discrete space. The idea that space might be defined by some sort of causal network of discrete elementary quantum events arose in various forms in work by Carl von Weizsäcker (ur-theory), John Wheeler (pregeometry), David Finkelstein (spacetime code), David Bohm (topochronology) and Roger Penrose (spin networks; see page 1055). General arguments for discrete space were also sometimes made—notably by Edward Fredkin, Marvin Minsky and to some extent Richard Feynman—on the basis of analogies to computers and in particular the idea that a given region of space should contain only a finite amount of information. In the 1980s approximation schemes such as lattice gauge theory and later Regge calculus (see page 1054) that take space to be discrete became popular, and it was occasionally suggested that versions of these could be exact models. There have been a variety of continuing initiatives that involve discrete space, with names like combinatorial physics—but most have used essentially mechanistic models (see page 1026), and none have achieved significant mainstream acceptance. Work on quantum gravity in the late 1980s and 1990s led to renewed interest in the microscopic features of spacetime (see page 1054). Models that involve discreteness have been proposed—most often based on spin networks—but there is usually still some form of continuous averaging present, leading for example to suggestions very different from mine that perhaps this could lead to the traditional continuum description through some analog of the wave-particle duality of elementary quantum mechanics. I myself became interested in the idea of completely discrete space in the mid-1970s, but I could not find a plausible framework for it until I started thinking about networks in the mid-1980s.

■ **Planck length.** Even in existing particle physics it is generally assumed that the traditional simple continuum description of space must break down at least below about the Planck length $Sqrt[\hbar\, G/c^3] \simeq 2 \times 10^{-35}$ meters—since at this scale dimensional analysis suggests that quantum effects should be comparable in magnitude to gravitational ones.

■ **Page 472 · Symmetry.** A system like a cellular automaton that consists of a large number of identical cells must in effect be arranged like a crystal, and therefore must exhibit one of the limited number of possible crystal symmetries in any particular dimension, as discussed on page 929. And even a generalized cellular automaton constructed say on a Penrose tiling still turns out to have a discrete spatial symmetry.

■ **Page 474 · Space and its contents.** A number of somewhat different ideas about space were discussed in antiquity. Around 375 BC Plato vaguely suggested that the universe might consist of large numbers of abstract polyhedra. A little later Aristotle proposed that space is set up so as to provide a definite place for everything—and in effect to force it there. But in geometry as developed by Euclid there was at least a mathematical notion of space as a kind of uniform background. And by sometime after 300 BC the Epicureans developed the idea of atoms of matter existing in a mostly featureless void of space. In the Middle Ages there was discussion about how the non-material character of God might fit in with ideas about space. In the early 1600s the concept of inertia developed by Galileo implied that space must have a certain fundamental uniformity. And with the formulation of mechanics by Isaac Newton in 1687 space became increasingly viewed as something purely abstract, quite different in character from material objects which exist in it. Philosophers had meanwhile discussed matter—as opposed to mind—being something characterized by having spatial extent. And for example in 1643 Thomas Hobbes suggested that the whole universe might be made of the same continuous stuff, with different densities of it corresponding to different materials, and geometry being just an abstract idealization of its properties. But in the late 1600s Gottfried Leibniz suggested instead that everything might consist of discrete monads, with space emerging from the pattern of relative distances between them. Yet with the success of Newtonian mechanics such ideas had by the late 1700s been largely forgotten—leading space almost always to be viewed just in simple abstract geometrical terms. The development of non-Euclidean geometry in the mid-1800s nevertheless suggested that even at the level of geometry space could in principle have a complicated structure. But in physics it was still assumed that space itself must have a standard fixed Euclidean form—and that everything in the universe must just exist in this space. By the late 1800s, however, it was widely believed that in addition to ordinary material objects, there must throughout space be a fluid-like ether with certain mechanical and electromagnetic properties. And in the 1860s it was even suggested that perhaps atoms might just correspond to knots in this ether (see page 1044). But this idea soon fell out of favor, and when relativity theory was introduced in 1905 it emphasized relations between material objects and in effect always treated space as just some kind of abstract background, with no real structure of its own. But in 1915 general relativity

introduced the idea that space could actually have a varying non-Euclidean geometry—and that this could represent gravity. Yet it was still assumed that matter was something different—that for example had to be represented separately by explicit terms in the Einstein equations. There were nevertheless immediate thoughts that perhaps at least electromagnetism could be like gravity and just arise from features of space. And in 1918 Hermann Weyl suggested that this could happen through local variations of scale or "gauge" in space, while in the 1920s Theodor Kaluza and Oskar Klein suggested that it could be associated with a fifth spacetime dimension of invisibly small extent. And from the 1920s to the 1950s Albert Einstein increasingly considered the possibility that there might be a unified field theory in which all matter would somehow be associated with the geometry of space. His main specific idea was to allow the metric of spacetime to be non-symmetric (see page 1052) and perhaps complex—with its additional components yielding electromagnetism. And he then tried to construct nonlinear field equations that would show no singularities, but would have solutions (perhaps analogous to the geons discussed on page 1054) that would exhibit various discrete features corresponding to particles—and perhaps quantum effects. But with the development of quantum field theory in the 1920s and 1930s most of physics again treated space as fixed and featureless—though now filled with various types of fields, whose excitations were set up to correspond to observed types of particles. Gravity has never fit very well into this framework. But it has always still been expected that in an ultimate quantum theory of gravity space will have to have a structure that is somehow like a quantum field. But when quantum gravity began to be investigated in earnest in the 1980s (see page 1054) most efforts concentrated on the already difficult problem of pure gravity—and did not consider how matter might enter. In the development of ordinary quantum field theories, supergravity theories studied in the 1980s did nominally support particles identified with gravitons, but were still formulated on a fixed background spacetime. And when string theory became popular in the 1980s the idea was again to have strings propagating in a background spacetime—though it turned out that for consistency this spacetime had to satisfy the Einstein equations. Consistency also typically required the basic spacetime to be 10-dimensional—with the reduction to observed 4D spacetime normally assumed to occur through restriction of the other dimensions to some kind of so-called Calabi-Yau manifold of small extent, associated excitations with various particles through an analog of the Kaluza-Klein mechanism. It has always been hoped that this kind of seemingly arbitrary setup would somehow automatically emerge from the underlying theory. And in the late 1990s there seemed to be some signs of this when dualities were discovered in various generalized string theories—notably for example between quantum particle excitations and gravitational black hole configurations. So while it remains impossible to work out all the consequences of string theories, it is conceivable that among the representations of such theories there might be ones in which matter can be viewed as just being associated with features of space.

Space as a Network

■ **Page 476 · Trivalent networks.** With n nodes and 3 connections at each node a network must always have an even number of nodes, and a total of $3n/2$ connections. Of all possible such networks, most large ones end up being connected. The number of distinct such networks for even n from 2 to 10 is $\{2, 5, 17, 71, 388\}$. If no self connections are allowed then these numbers become $\{1, 2, 6, 20, 91\}$, while if neither self nor multiple connections are allowed (yielding what are often referred to as cubic or 3-regular graphs), the numbers become $\{0, 1, 2, 5, 19, 85, 509, 4060, 41301, 510489\}$, or asymptotically $(6n)!/((3n)!(2n)!288^n e^2)$. (For symmetric graphs see page 1032.) If one requires the networks to be planar the numbers are $\{0, 1, 1, 3, 9, 32, 133, 681, 3893, 24809, 169206\}$. If one looks at subnetworks with dangling connections, the number of these up to size 10 is $\{2, 5, 7, 22, 43, 141, 373, 1270, 4053, 14671\}$, or $\{1, 1, 2, 6, 10, 29, 64, 194, 531, 1733\}$ if no self or multiple connections are allowed (see also page 1039).

■ **Properties of networks.** Over the past century or so a variety of global properties of networks have been studied. Typical ones include:

- Edge connectivity: the minimum number of connections that must be removed to make the network disconnected.

- Diameter: the maximum distance between any two nodes in the network. The pictures below show the largest planar trivalent networks with diameters 1, 2 and 3, and the largest known ones with diameters 4, 5 and 6.

- Circumference: the length of the longest cycle in the network. Although difficult to determine in particular cases, many networks allow so-called Hamiltonian cycles that include every node. (Up to 8 nodes, all 8 trivalent networks have this property; up to 10 nodes 25 of 27 do.)

- Girth: the length of the shortest cycle in the network. The pictures below show the smallest trivalent networks with girths 3 through 8 (so-called cages). Girth can be relevant in seeing whether a particular cluster can ever occur in network.

- Chromatic number: the minimum of colors that can be assigned to nodes so that no adjacent nodes end up the same color. It follows from the Four-Color Theorem that the maximum for planar networks is 4. It turns out that for all trivalent networks the maximum is also 4, and is almost always 3.

■ **Regular polytopes.** In 3D, of the five regular polyhedra, only the tetrahedron, cube and dodecahedron have three edges meeting at each vertex, corresponding to a trivalent network. (Of the 13 additional Archimedean solids, 7 yield trivalent networks.) In 4D the six regular polytopes have 4, 4, 6, 8, 4 and 12 edges meeting at each vertex, and in higher dimensions the simplex ($d + 1$ vertices) and hypercube (2^d vertices) have d edges meeting at each vertex, while the co-cube ($2d$ vertices) has $2(d-1)$. (See also symmetric graphs on page 1032, and page 929.)

■ **Page 476 · Generalizations.** Almost any kind of generalized network can be emulated by a trivalent network just by introducing more nodes. As indicated in the main text, networks with more than three connections at each node can be emulated by combining nodes into groups, and looking only at the connections between groups. Networks with colored nodes can be emulated by representing each color of node by a fixed group of nodes. Going beyond ordinary networks, one can consider hypernetworks in which connections join not just pairs of nodes, but larger numbers of nodes. Such hypernetworks are specified by adjacency tensors rather than adjacency matrices. But it is possible to emulate any hypernetwork by having each generalized connection correspond to a group of connections in an ordinary trivalent network.

■ **Maintaining simple rules.** An important reason for considering models based solely on trivalent networks is that they allow simpler evolution rules to be maintained (see page 508). If nodes can have more than three connections, then they will often be able to evolve to have any number of connections—in which case one must give what is in effect an infinite set of rules to specify what to do for each number of connections.

■ **Page 477 · 3D network.** The 3D network (c) can be laid out in space using $Array[x[8\{\#\#\}] \&, \{n, n, n\}]$ where

$$x[m:\{\_, \_, \_\}] := \{x_1[m], x_1[m+4],$$
$$x_2[m+\{4, 2, 0\}], x_2[m+\{0, 6, 4\}]\}$$
$$x_1[m:\{\_, \_, \_\}] := Line[Map[\# + m \&, \{\{1, 0, 0\}, \{1, 1, 1\},$$
$$\{0, 2, 1\}, \{1, 1, 1\}, \{3, 1, 3\}, \{3, 0, 4\}, \{3, 1, 3\}, \{4, 2, 3\}\}]]$$
$$x_2[\{i\_, j\_, k\_\}] :=$$
$$x_1[\{-i-4, -j-2, k\}] /. \{a\_, b\_, c\_\} \rightarrow \{-a, -b, c\}$$

The resulting structure is a cubic array of blocks with each block containing 8 nodes. The shortest cycle that returns to a particular node turns out to involve 10 edges. The structure does not correspond to the way that chemical bonds are arranged in any common crystalline materials, probably because it would be likely to be mechanically unstable.

■ **Continuum limits.** For all everyday purposes a region in a network with enough nodes and an appropriate pattern of connections can act just like ordinary continuous space. But at a formal mathematical level this can happen rigorously only in an infinite limit. And in general, there is no reason to expect that all properties of the system (notably for example the existence of particles) will be preserved by taking such a limit. But in understanding the structure of space and comparing to ordinary continuous space it is convenient to imagine taking such a limit. Inevitably there are several scales involved, and one can only expect continuum behavior if one looks at scales intermediate between individual connections in the underlying network and the overall size of the whole network. Yet as I will discuss on pages 534 and 1050 even at such scales it is far from straightforward to see how all the various well-studied properties of ordinary continuous space (as embodied for example in the theory of manifolds) can emerge from discrete underlying networks.

■ **Page 478 · Definitions of distance.** Any measure of distance—whether in ordinary continuous space or elsewhere—takes a pair of points and yields a number. Several properties are normally assumed. First, that if the points are identical the distance is zero, and if they are different, it is a positive number. Second, that the distance between points A and B is the same as between B and A. And third, that the so-called triangle inequality holds, so that the distance AC is no greater than the sum of the distances AB and BC. With distance on a network defined as the length of shortest path between nodes one immediately gets all three of these properties. And even though all distances defined this way will be integers, they still make any network formally correspond in mathematical terms to a metric space (or strictly a path metric space). If the connections on the underlying network are one-way (as in causal networks) then one no longer necessarily gets the second property, and when

a continuum limit exists it can correspond to a (perhaps discontinuous) section through a fiber bundle rather than to a manifold. Note that as discussed on page 536 physical measures of distance will always end up being based not just on single paths in a network, but on the propagation of something like a particle, which typically in effect requires the presence of many paths. (See page 1048.)

■ **Page 478 · Definitions of dimension.** The most obvious way to define the dimension of a space is somehow to ask how many parameters—or coordinates—are needed to specify a point in it. But starting in the 1870s the discovery of constructs like space-filling curves (see page 1127) led to investigation of other definitions. And indeed there is some reason to believe that around 1884 Georg Cantor may have tried developing a definition based on essentially the idea that I use here of looking at growth rates of volumes of spheres (balls). But for standard continuous spaces this definition is hard to make robust—since unlike in discrete networks where one can define volume just by counting nodes, defining volume in a continuous space requires assigning a potentially arbitrary density function. And as a result, in the late 1800s and early 1900s other definitions of dimension were developed. What emerged as most popular is topological dimension, in which one fills space with overlapping balls, and asks what the minimum number that ever have to overlap at any point will be. Also considered was so-called Hausdorff dimension, which became popular in connection with fractals in the 1980s (see page 933), and which can have non-integer values. But for discrete networks the standard definitions for both topological and Hausdorff dimension give the trivial result 0. One can get more meaningful results by thinking about continuum limits, but the definition of dimension that I give in the main text seems much more straightforward. Even here, there are however some subtleties. For example, to find a definite volume growth rate one does still need to take some kind of limit—and one needs to avoid sampling too many or too few nodes in the network. And just as with fractal dimensions discussed on page 933 there are issues about whether a definite power law for the growth rate will emerge, and how one should average over results for different parts of the network. There are some alternative approaches to defining dimension in which some of these issues at least become less explicit. For example, one can imagine not just forming a ball on the network, but instead growing something like a cellular automaton, and seeing how big a pattern it produces after some number of steps. And similarly, one can for example look at the statistics of random walks on the network. A slightly different but still related approach is to study the density of eigenvalues of the Laplace operator—which can also be thought of as measuring the number of solutions to equations giving linear constraints on numbers assigned to connected nodes. More sophisticated versions of this involve looking at invariants studied in topological field theory. And there are potentially also definitions based for example on considering geodesics and seeing how many linearly independent directions can be defined with them. (Note that given explicit coordinates, one can check whether one is in d or more dimensions by asking for all possible points

$Det[Table[(x[i] - x[j]) . (x[i] - x[j]), \{i, d + 3\}, \{j, d + 3\}]] == 0$

and this should also work for sufficiently separated points on networks. Still another related approach is to consider coloring the edges of a network: if there are $d + 1$ possible colors, all of which appear at every node, then it follows that d coordinates can consistently be assigned to each node.)

■ **Page 478 · Counting of nodes.** The number of nodes reached by going out to network distance r (with $r > 1$) from any node in the networks on page 477 is (a) $4r - 4$, (b) $3r^2/2 - 3r/2 + 1$, and (c)

$First[Select[4r^3/9 + 2r^2/3 +$
$\{2, 5/3, 5/3\}r - \{10/9, 1, -4/9\}, IntegerQ]]$

In any trivalent network, the quantity $f[r]$ obtained by adding up the numbers of nodes reached by going distance r from each node must satisfy $f[0] = n$ and $f[1] = 3n$, where n is the total number of nodes in the network. In addition, the limit of $f[r]$ for large r must be n^2. The values of $f[r]$ for all other r will depend on the pattern of connections in the network.

■ **Page 479 · Cycle lengths.** The lengths of the shortest cycles (girths) of the networks on page 479 are (a) 3, (b) 5, (c) 4, (d) 4, (e) 3, (f) 5, (g) 6, (h) 10, (i) ∞, (j) 3. Note that rules of the kind discussed on page 508 which involve replacing clusters of nodes can only apply when cycles in the cluster match those in the network.

■ **Page 479 · Volumes of spheres.** See page 1050.

■ **Page 480 · Implementation.** Networks are conveniently represented by assigning a number to each node, then having lists of rules which specify what nodes the connection from a particular node go to. The tetrahedron network from page 476 is for example given in this representation by

$\{1 \to \{2, 3, 4\}, 2 \to \{1, 3, 4\}, 3 \to \{1, 2, 4\}, 4 \to \{1, 2, 3\}\}$

The list of nodes reached by following up to n connections from node i are then given by

$NodeLists[g\_, i\_, n\_] :=$
$\quad NestList[Union[Flatten[\# /. g]] \&, \{i\}, n]$

The network distance corresponding to the length of the shortest path between two nodes is given by

$Distance[g\_, \{i\_, j\_\}] := Length[NestWhileList[$
$\quad Union[Flatten[\# /. g]] \&, \{i\}, ! MemberQ[\#, j] \&]] - 1$

■ **Finding layouts.** One way to lay out a network g so that network distances in it come as close as possible to ordinary distances in d-dimensional space, is just to search for values of the $x[i, k]$ which minimize a quantity such as

$With[\{n = Length[g]\}, Apply[Plus,$
$\quad Flatten[(Table[Distance[g, \{i, j\}], \{i, n\}, \{j, n\}]^2 - Table[$
$\quad\quad Sum[(x[i, k] - x[j, k])^2, \{k, d\}], \{i, n\}, \{j, n\}])^2]]]$

using for example *FindMinimum* starting say with $x[1, \_] \to 0$ and all the other $x[\_, \_] \to Random[]$. Rarely is there a unique minimum that can be found, but the approach nevertheless seems to work fairly well whenever a good layout exists in a particular number of dimensions. One can imagine weighting different network distances differently, but usually I have found that equal weightings work best. If one ignores all constraints beyond network distance 1, then one is in effect just trying to build the network out of identical rigid rods. It turns out that this is almost always possible even in 2D (though not in 1D); the only exception is the tetrahedron network. And in fact very few trivalent structures are rigid, in the sense the angles between rods are uniquely determined. (In 3D, for example, this is true only for the tetrahedron.)

■ **Hamming distances.** In the so-called loop switching method of routing messages in communications systems one lays out a network on an m-dimensional Boolean hypercube so that the distance on the hypercube (equal to Hamming distance) agrees with distance in the network. It is known that to achieve this exactly, m must be at the least the number of either positive or negative eigenvalues of the distance matrix for the network, and can need to be as much as $n - 1$, where n is the total number of nodes.

■ **Continuous mathematics.** Even though networks are discrete, it is conceivable that network-based models can also be formulated in terms of continuous mathematics, with a network-like structure emerging for example from the pattern of singularities or topology of continuous surfaces or functions.

The Relationship of Space and Time

■ **History.** The idea of representing time graphically like space has a long history—and was used for example by Nicholas Oresme in the mid-1300s. In the 1700s and 1800s the idea of position and time as just two coordinates was widespread in mathematical physics—and this then led to notions like "travelling in time" in H. G. Wells's 1895 *The Time Machine*. The mathematical framework developed for relativity theory in the early 1900s (see page 1042) treated space and time very symmetrically, leading popular accounts of the theory to emphasize a kind of fundamental equivalence between them and to try to make this seem inevitable through rather confusing thought experiments on such topics as idealized trains travelling near the speed of light.

In the context of traditional mathematical equations there has never been much reason to consider the possibility that space and time might be fundamentally different. For typically space and time are both just represented by abstract symbolic variables, and the formal process of solving equations as a function of position in space and as a function of time is essentially identical. But as soon as one tries to construct more explicit models of space and time one is immediately led to consider the possibility that they may be quite different.

■ **Page 482 · Discreteness in time.** In present-day physics, time, like space, is always assumed to be perfectly continuous. But experiments—the most direct of which are based on looking for quantization in the measured decay times of very short-lived particles—have only demonstrated continuity on scales longer than about 10^{-26} seconds, and there is nothing to say that on shorter scales time is not in fact discrete. (The possibility of a discrete quantum of time was briefly discussed in the 1920s when quantum mechanics was first being developed.)

■ **Page 483 · Network constraint systems.** Cases (a), (f) and (p) allow all networks that do not contain respectively cycles of length 1 (self-loops), cycles of length 3 or less, and cycles of length 5 or less. In cases where an infinite sequence of networks is allowed, there are typically particular subnetworks that can occur any number of times, making the sizes of allowed networks form arithmetic progressions. In cases (m), (n) and (o) respectively triangle, pentagon and square subnetworks can be repeated.

The main text excludes templates that have no dangling connections, and are thus themselves already complete networks. There are 5 such templates involving nodes out to distance one, but of these only 3 correspond to networks that satisfy the constraint that around each node the network has the same form as the template. Among templates involving nodes out to distance two there are 106 that have no dangling connections, and of these only 8 satisfy the constraints.

The main text considers only constraints based on a single template. One can also allow each node to have a neighborhood that corresponds to any of a set of templates. For templates involving nodes out to distance one, there are 13 minimal sets in the sense of page 941, of which only 6 contain just one template, 6 contain two and 1 contains three.

If one does allow dangling connections to be joined within a single template, the results are similar to those discussed so far. There are 52 possible templates involving nodes out to distance two, of which 12 allow complete networks to be formed, none forced to be larger than 12 nodes. There are 46 minimal sets, with the largest containing 4 templates, but none forcing a network larger than 16 nodes.

■ **Symmetric graphs.** The constraints in a network constraint system require that the structure around each node agrees with a template that contains some number of nodes. A symmetric graph satisfies the same type of constraint, but with the template being the whole network. The pictures below show the smallest few symmetric graphs with 3 connections at each node (with up to 100 nodes there are still only 37 such graphs; compare page 1029).

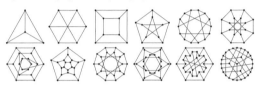

■ **Cayley graphs.** As discussed on page 938, the structure of a group can be represented by a Cayley graph where nodes correspond to elements in the group, and connections specify results of multiplying by generators. The transitivity of group multiplication implies that Cayley graphs always have the property of being symmetric (see above). The number of connections at each node is fixed, and given by the number of distinct generators and inverses. In cases such as the tetrahedral group A_4 there are 3 connections at each node. The relations among the generators of a group can be thought of as constraints defining the Cayley graph. As mentioned on page 938, there are finite groups that have simple relations but at least very large Cayley graphs. For infinite groups, it is known (see page 938) that in most cases Cayley graphs are locally like trees, and so do not have finite dimension. It appears that only when the group is nilpotent (so that certain combinations of elements commute much as they do on a lattice) is there polynomial growth in the Cayley graph and thus finite dimension.

■ **Page 485 · Spacetime symmetric rules.** With $k = 2$ and the neighborhoods shown here, only the additive rules 90R, 105R, 150R and 165R are space-time symmetric. For larger k and larger neighborhoods, there presumably begin to be non-additive rules with this property.

Time and Causal Networks

■ **Causal networks.** The idea of using networks to represent interdependencies of events seems to have developed with the systematization of manufacturing in the early 1900s—

notably in the work of Frank and Lillian Gilbreth—and has been popular since at least the 1940s. Early applications included switching circuits, logistics planning, decision analysis and general flowcharting. In the last few decades causal networks have been widely used in system specification methods such as Petri nets, as well as in schemes for medical and other diagnosis. Since at least the 1960s, causal networks have also been discussed as representations of connections between events in spacetime, particularly in quantum mechanics (see page 1027).

Causal networks like mine that are ultimately associated with some evolution or flow of activity always have certain properties. In particular, they can never contain loops, and thus correspond to directed acyclic graphs. And from this it follows for example that even the most circuitous path between two nodes must be of finite length.

Causal networks can also be viewed as Hasse diagrams of partially ordered sets, as discussed on page 1040.

■ **Implementation.** Given a list of successive positions of the active cell, as from *Map[Last, MAEvolveList[rule, init, t]]* (see page 887), the network can be generated using

MAToNet[list_] := Module[{u, j, k}, u[_] = ∞; Reverse[
  Table[j = list[[i]]; k = {u[j - 1], u[j], u[j + 1]}; u[j - 1] =
  u[j] = u[j + 1] = i; i → k, {i, Length[list], 1, -1}]]]

where nodes not yet found by explicit evolution are indicated by ∞.

■ **Page 488 · Mobile automata.** The special structure of mobile automata of the type used here leads to several special features in the causal networks derived from them. One of these is that every node always has exactly 3 incoming and 3 outgoing connections. Another feature is that there is always a path of doubled connections (associated with the active cell) that visits every node in some order. And in addition, the final network must always be planar—as it is whenever it is derived from the evolution of a local underlying 1D system.

■ **Computational compression.** In the model for time described here, it is noteworthy that in a sense an arbitrary amount of underlying computation can take place between successive moments in perceived time.

■ **Page 496 · 2D mobile automata.** As in 2D random walks, active cells in 2D mobile automata often do not return to positions they have visited before, with the result that no causal connections end up being created.

The Sequencing of Events in the Universe

■ **Implementation.** Sequential substitution systems in which only one replacement is ever done at each step can just be implemented using /. as described on page 893. Substitution systems in which all replacements are done that are found to fit in a left-to-right scan can be implemented as follows

GSSEvolveList[rule_, s_, n_] :=
  NestList[GSSStep[rule, #] &, s, n]
GSSStep[rule_, s_] :=
  g[rule, s, f[StringPosition[s, Map[First, rule]]]]
f[{}] = {}; f[s_] := Fold[If[Last[Last[#1]] ≥ First[#2],
  #1, Append[#1, #2]] &, {First[s]}, Rest[s]]
g[rule_, s_, {}] := s; g[rule_, s_, pos_] := StringReplacePart[
  s, Map[StringTake[s, #] &, pos] /. rule, pos]

with rules given as *{"ABA" → "BAAB", "BBBB" → "AA"}*.

■ **Generating causal networks.** If every element generated in the evolution of a generalized substitution system is assigned a unique number, then events can be represented for example by *{4, 5} → {11, 12, 13}*—and from a list of such events a causal network can be built up using

With[{u = Map[First, list]}, MapIndexed[Function[
  {e, i}, First[i] → Map[(If[# === {}, ∞, #[[1, 1]]] &)[
  Position[u, #]] &, Last[e]]]], list]]

■ **The sequential limit.** Even when the order of applying rules does not matter, using the scheme of a sequential substitution system will often give different results. If there is a tree of possible replacements (as in *"A" → "AA"*), then the sequential substitution system in a sense does depth-first recursion in the infinite tree, never returning from the single path it takes. Other schemes are closer to breadth-first recursion.

■ **Page 502 · Rule (b).** The maximum number of steps for which the rule can be applied occurs with initial conditions consisting of a white element followed by n black elements, and in this case the number of steps is $2^n + n$.

■ **String theory.** The sequences of symbols I call strings here have absolutely no direct connection to the continuous deformable 1D objects known as strings in string theory.

■ **String overlaps.** The total numbers of strings with length n and k colors that cannot overlap themselves are given by

a[0] = 1; a[n_] := k a[n - 1] - If[EvenQ[n], a[n/2], 0]

Up to reversal and interchange of A and B, the first few overlap-free strings with 2 colors are A, AB, AAB, $AAAB$, $AABB$.

The shortest pairs of strings of 2 elements with no self- or mutual overlaps are *{"A", "B"}*, *{"AABB", "AABAB"}*, *{"AABB", "ABABB"}*; there are a total of 13 such pairs with strings up to length 5, and 85 with strings up to length 6.

The shortest non-overlapping triple of strings is *{"AAABB", "ABABB", "ABAABB"}* and its variants. There are a total of 36 such triples with no string having length more than 6.

■ **Simulating mobile automata.** Given a mobile automaton like the one from page 73 with rules in the form used on page

887—and behavior of any complexity—the following will yield a causal-invariant substitution system that emulates it:

Map[StringJoin, Map[{"AAABB", "ABABB", "ABAABB"}[[
    # + 1]] &, Map[Insert[#[[1]], 2, 2] →
    Insert[#[[2, 1]], 2, 2 + #[[2, 2]]] &, rule], {2}], {2}]

■ **Sequential cellular automata.** Ordinary cellular automata are set up so that every cell is updated in parallel at each step, based on the colors of neighboring cells on the previous step. But in analogy with generalized substitution systems, one can also consider sequential cellular automata, in which cells are updated sequentially rather than in parallel. The behavior of such systems is usually very different from that of corresponding ordinary cellular automata, mainly because in sequential cellular automata the new color of a particular cell can depend on new rather than old colors of neighboring cells.

The pictures below show the behavior of several sequential cellular automata with $k = 2$, $r = 1$ elementary rules. In the top picture of each pair every individual update is indicated by a black dot. In the bottom picture each line represents one complete step of evolution, including one update of each cell. Note that in this representation, effects can propagate all the way across the system in a single step.

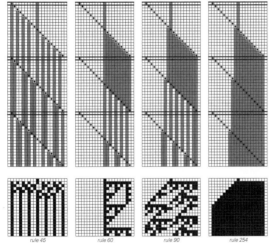

rule 45   rule 60   rule 90   rule 254

Size dependence. Because effects can propagate all the way across the system in a single step, the overall size, as well as boundary conditions, for the system can be significant after just a few steps, as illustrated in the pictures of rule 60 below.

size 49   size 50   size 51

Additive rules. Among elementary sequential cellular automata, those with additive rules turn out to yield some of the most complex behavior, as illustrated below. The top row shows evolution with the boundary forced to be white; the bottom row shows cyclic boundary conditions. Even though the basic rule is additive, there seems to be no simple traditional mathematical description of the results.

rule 60   rule 90   rule 165

Updating orders. Somewhat different results are typically obtained if one allows different updating orders. For each complete update of a rule 90 sequential cellular automaton, the pictures below show results with (a) left-to-right scan, (b) random ordering of all cells, the same for each pass through the whole system, (c) random ordering of all cells, different for different passes, (d) completely random ordering, in which a particular cell can be updated twice before other cells have even been updated once.

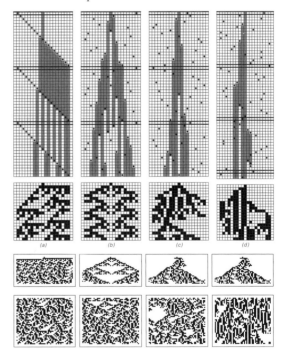

(a)   (b)   (c)   (d)

History. Sequential cellular automata have a similar relationship to ordinary cellular automata as implicit updating schemes in finite difference methods have to explicit ones, or as infinite impulse response digital filters have to finite ones. There were several studies of sequential or asynchronous cellular automata done following my work on ordinary cellular automata in the early 1980s.

Implementation. The following will update triples of cells in the specified order by using the function *f* :

OrderedUpdate[f_, a_, order_] := Fold[ReplacePart[
    #1, f[Take[#1, {#2 - 1, #2 + 1}]], #2] &, a, order]

A random ordering of *n* cells corresponds to a random permutation of the form

Fold[Insert[#1, #2, Random[Integer, Length[#1]] + 1] &,
    {}, Range[n]]

■ **Intrinsic synchronization in cellular automata.** Taking the rules for an ordinary cellular automaton and applying them sequentially will normally yield very different results. But it turns out that there are variants on cellular automata in which the rules can be applied in any order and the overall behavior obtained—or at least the causal network—is always the same. The picture below shows how this works for a simple block cellular automaton. The basic idea is that to each cell is added an arrow, and any pair of cells is updated only when their arrows point at each other. This in a sense forces cells to wait to be updated until the data they need is ready. Note that the rules can be thought of as replacements such as *"A><B" → "<AB>"* for blocks of length 4 with 4 colors.

 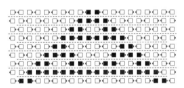

■ **"Firing squad" synchronization.** By choosing appropriate rules it is possible to achieve many forms of synchronization directly within cellular automata. One version posed as a problem by John Myhill in 1957 consists in setting up a rule in which all cells in a region go into a special state after exactly the same number of steps. The problem was first solved in the early 1960s; the solution using 6 colors and a minimal number of steps shown on the right below was found in 1988 by Jacques Mazoyer, who also determined that no similar 4-color solutions exist. Note that this solution in effect constructs a nested pattern of any width (it does this by optionally including or excluding one additional cell at each nesting level, using a mechanism related to the decimation systems of page 909). If one drops the requirement of cells

going into a special state, then even the 2-color elementary rule 60 shown on the left can be viewed as solving the problem—but only for widths that are powers of 2.

width 32   width 10   width 25   width 50

width 35

■ **Distributed computing.** Many of the basic issues about the progress of time in a universe consisting of many separate elements have analogs in the progress of computations that are distributed across many separate computing elements. In practice, such computations are most often done by requiring explicit synchronization of all elements at appropriate points, and implementing this using a mechanism that is outside of the computation. But more theoretical investigations of formal concurrent systems, temporal logics, dataflow systems, Petri nets and so on have led to ideas about distributed computing that are somewhat closer to the ones I discuss here for the universe. And, as it happens, in the mid-1980s I tried hard, though at the time without much success, to use updating rules for networks as the basis for a new kind of programming language intended for massively parallel computers.

Uniqueness and Branching in Time

■ **Page 506 · String transformations.** An example of a rule that allows one to go from any string of *A*'s and *B*'s to any other is

{"A" → "AA", "AA" → "A", "A" → "B", "B" → "A"}

(Compare page 1038.)

■ **Parallel universes.** The idea of parallel universes which somehow interact with each other has been much explored in science fiction. And one might think that if the history of each universe corresponds to one path in a multiway system then the convergence of paths might represent interactions between universes. But in fact, much as in the case of time travel, such connections do not represent additional observable effects; they simply imply consistency conditions, in this case between universes whose paths converge.

■ **Many-worlds models.** The notion of "many-figured time" has been discussed since the 1950s in the context of the many-worlds interpretation of quantum mechanics. There are some similarities to the multiway systems that I consider here. But an important difference is that while in the many-worlds approach, branchings are associated with possible observation or measurement events, what I suggest here is that they could be an intrinsic feature of even the very lowest-level rules for the universe. (See also page 1063.)

■ **Spacetime networks from multiway systems.** The main text considers models in which the steps of evolution in a multiway system yield a succession of events in time. An alternative kind of model, somewhat analogous to the ones based on constraints on page 483, is to take the pattern of evolution of a multiway system to define directly a complete spacetime network. Instead of looking separately at strings produced at each step, one instead maintains just a single copy of each distinct string ever produced, and makes that correspond to a node in the network. Each node is then connected to the nodes associated with the strings reached by one application of the multiway rule, as on page 209.

It is fairly straightforward to generate in this way networks of any dimension. For example, starting with n A's the rule $\{"A" \to "AB", "AB" \to "A"\}$ yields a regular n-dimensional grid, as shown below.

If each node in a network is associated with a point in spacetime, then one slightly peculiar feature is that every such point would have an associated string—something like an encoded position coordinate. And it then becomes somewhat difficult to understand why different regions of spacetime seem to behave so similarly—and do not, for example, seem to depend on the details of their coordinates.

■ **Page 507 · Commuting operations.** If replacements on strings are viewed as mathematical operations, then when the replacements give the same result if applied in any order, the corresponding operations commute.

■ **Conditions for convergence.** One way to guarantee that there is convergence after one step is to require as in the previous section that blocks to be replaced cannot overlap with themselves or each other. And of the 196 possible rules involving two colors and blocks of length at most three, 112 have this property. But there are also an additional 20 rules which allow some overlap but which nevertheless yield convergence after one step. Examples are $"AAA" \to "A"$ and $"AA" \to "ABA"$. In these rules some of the elements essentially just supply context, but are not affected by the replacement. These elements can then overlap while not affecting the

result. Note that unless one excludes the context elements from events, paths in the multiway system will converge, but the causal networks on these paths will be locally slightly different.

Much as in the previous section, even if paths do not converge for every possible string, it can still be true that paths converge for all strings that are actually generated from a particular initial string.

In general, one can consider convergence after any number of steps, requiring that any two strings which have a common ancestor must at some point also have a common successor. Note that a rule such as $\{"A" \to "B", "A" \to "C", "B" \to "A", "B" \to "D"\}$ exhibits convergence for all paths that have diverged for only one step, but not for all those that have diverged for longer. In general it is formally undecidable whether a particular multiway system will eventually exhibit convergence of all paths.

■ **Confluence.** As mentioned on page 938, multiway systems have been studied in mathematical logic, typically under names such as rewrite systems, since the early 1900s. The property of path convergence discussed in the main text has been considered since the 1930s, usually under the name of confluence, or sometimes the Church-Rosser property. (Also considered is strong confluence—that paths can always converge in at most one step, and local confluence—that paths can converge after diverging for one step but not necessarily more. Early in its history confluence was most often studied for symbolic systems and lambda calculus rather than ordinary multiway systems.)

Confluence is important in defining a notion of equivalence for strings. One can say that two strings are equivalent if they can both be transformed to the same string by using the rules of the multiway system. And with such a definition, confluence is what is needed to obtain transitivity for equality, so that $p == q$ and $q == r$ implies $p == r$.

Most often confluence is studied in the context of terminating multiway systems—multiway systems in which eventually strings are produced to which no further replacements apply. If a terminating multiway system has the confluence property, then this implies that regardless of the path taken, a given string will always evolve to a unique string that can be thought of as giving a canonical or normal form for the original string. Examples (a) through (c) below have this property; (d) does not. In example (a), the canonical form is all elements black; in (b) it is a single black element, and in (c) all elements are black, except the last one, which is white if there were any initial white elements. Note that the first example on page 507 has a canonical form consisting of a sorted string.

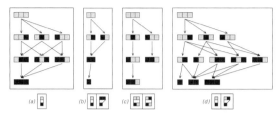

(a) (b) (c) (d)

The process of evaluation in mathematics or in a computer language such as *Mathematica* can be thought of as involving the application of a sequence of replacement rules. Only if these rules have the confluence property will the results always be unique, and independent of the order of rule application.

The evaluation of functions with attribute *Flat* in *Mathematica* provides an example of confluence. If *f* is *Flat*, then in evaluating *f[a, b, c]* one can equally well start with *f[f[a, b], c]* or *f[a, f[b, c]]*. Showing only the arguments to *f*, the pictures below illustrate how the flat functions *Xor* and *And* are confluent, while the non-flat function *Implies* is not.

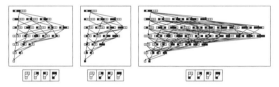

■ **Completion.** If one has a multiway system that terminates but is not confluent then it turns out often to be possible to make it confluent by adding a finite set of new rules. Given a string *p* which gets transformed either to *q* or *r* by the original rules, one can always imagine adding a new rule *q → r* or *r → q* that makes the paths from *p* immediately converge. To do this explicitly for all possible *p* that can occur would however entail having infinitely many new rules. But as noted by Donald Knuth and Peter Bendix in 1970 it turns out often to be sufficient just iteratively to add new rules only for each so-called critical pair *q, r* that is obtained from strings *p* that represent minimal overlaps in the left-hand sides of the rules one has. To decide whether to add *q → r* or *r → q* in each case one can have some kind of ordering on strings. For the procedure to work this ordering must be such that the strings generated on successive steps in every possible evolution of the multiway system follow the ordering. A number of variations of the basic procedure—using different orderings and with different schemes for dropping redundant rules—have been proposed for systems arising in different kinds of applications. The original Knuth-Bendix procedure was for equations (of the form *a ↔ b*) had

the feature that it could terminate yet not give a confluent multiway system. But in the 1980s so-called unfailing completion algorithms (see page 1158) were developed that—if they terminate—guarantee to give confluent systems. (The question of whether any procedure of this type will terminate in a particular case is nevertheless in general undecidable.)

The basic idea of so-called critical pair completion procedures has arisen several times—notably in the Gröbner basis approach of Bruno Buchberger from 1965 to finding canonical forms for systems of polynomials.

■ **Relationships between types of networks.** Each arrow on each path in a multiway system corresponds to a node in a causal network. Each element in each string in a multiway system corresponds to a connection in a causal network. Each complete string in a multiway system corresponds to a possible slice that goes through all connections across a causal network. Such a slice can be considered in traditional physics terms as a spacelike hypersurface (see page 1041).

Evolution of Networks

■ **Page 509 · Neighbor-independent rules.** Even though the same replacement is performed at each node at each step, the networks produced are not homogeneous. In the first case shown, the picture produced after *t* steps has $4 \times 3^{t-k-1}$ regions with 3×2^k edges. In the limit $t \to \infty$, the picture has the geometrical form of an Apollonian circle packing (see page 986). The number of nodes at distance up to *r* from a given node is at most $1 + Sum[c[i] + c[i-1], \{i, n\}]$ where $c[i\_] := 2 \wedge DigitCount[i, 2]$. In practice this number fluctuates greatly with *r*, making pictures like those on page 479 not exhibit smooth profiles. Averaged over all nodes, however, the number of nodes at distance up to *r* approximates $r \wedge Log[2, 3]$, implying an effective dimension of $Log[2, 3]$. Note that there is no upper limit on the dimension that can be obtained with appropriate neighbor-independent rules.

■ **Implementation.** For many practical purposes the best representation for networks is the one given on page 1031. But in updating networks a particularly straightforward implementation of one scheme can be obtained if one uses instead a more explicit symbolic representation such as

$u[1 \to v[2, 3, 4], 2 \to v[1, 3, 4], 3 \to v[1, 2, 4], 4 \to v[1, 2, 3]]$

This allows one to capture the basic character of networks by

$Attributes[u] = \{Flat, Orderless\}; Attributes[v] = Orderless$

Updating rules can then be written in terms of ordinary *Mathematica* patterns. A slight complication is that the patterns have to include all nodes whose connections go to nodes whose labels are changed by the update. The rule at the top of page 509 must therefore be written out as

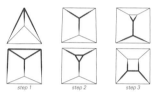

and this corresponds to the *Mathematica* rule

$u[i1\_ \to v[i2\_, i3\_, i4\_], i3\_ \to v[i1\_, i5\_, i6\_],$
$\quad i4\_ \to v[i1\_, i7\_, i8\_]] :\to u[i1 \to v[i2, new[1], new[2]],$
$\quad new[1] \to v[i1, new[2], i3], new[2] \to v[i1, new[1], i4],$
$\quad i3 \to v[new[1], i5, i6], i4 \to v[new[2], i7, i8]]$

(Strictly there also need to be additional rules to cover where for example nodes 3 and 4 are actually the same.) With rules in this form the network update is simply

$NetStep[rule\_, net\_] := Block[\{new\},$
$\quad net /. rule /. new[n\_] \to n + Apply[Max, Map[First, net]]]$

Note that just as we discussed for strings on page 1033 the direct use of $/.$ here corresponds to a particular scheme for applying the update rule.

■ **Identifying subnetworks.** The problem of finding where in a network a given subnetwork can occur turns out in general to be computationally difficult. For strings the analogous problem is straightforward, since in a string of length n one can ultimately just try each of the n possible starting points for the substring and see for which of them a match occurs. But for a network with n nodes, a similar procedure would require one to check n^k possible configurations in order to find out where a subnetwork of size k occurs. In practice, however, for fixed subnetworks, one can devise fairly efficient procedures. But the general problem of so-called subgraph isomorphism is formally NP-complete.

■ **Page 509 · Number of replacements.** The total number of distinct replacements that maintain planarity, involve clusters with up to five nodes and have from 3 to 7 dangling connections is $\{16, 8, 125, 24, 246\}$. Not maintaining planarity, the numbers are $\{14, 5, 13, 2, 2\}$. (See page 1039.)

■ **Cycles in networks.** See page 1031.

■ **Planar networks.** One feature of a planar network is that it is always possible to identify definite regions or faces bounded by connections in the network. And from Euler's formula $f + n = e + 2$, it then follows that the average number of edges of each face is always $6(1 - 2/f)$, where f is the total number of faces. Note that with my definition of dimension for networks, the fact that a network is planar does not necessarily mean that it has be two-dimensional—and for example the networks on page 509 are not.

■ **Arbitrary transformations.** By applying the string transformation rules on page 1035 at appropriate locations, it is possible to transform any string of A's and B's to any other. And the analog of this for networks is that by applying the rules shown below at appropriate locations it is possible to transform any network into any other. These rules correspond to the moves invented by James Alexander in 1923 in connection with transforming one knot into another. (Note that the first two rules suffice for all planar networks, and are sometimes called respectively T2 and T1.)

As an example, the pictures below show how a tetrahedron network can be transformed into a cube.

■ **Random networks.** One way to generate the connections for a "completely random" trivalent network with n nodes is just to apply a random permutation:

$RandomNetwork[n\_?EvenQ] := Partition[$
$\quad Fold[Insert[\#1, \#2, Random[Integer, Length[\#1]] + 1] \&,$
$\quad \{\}, Floor[Range[1, n + 2/3, 1/3]]], 2]$

Networks obtained in this way are usually connected, but will almost always contain self-loops and multiple edges. Properties of random networks are discussed on page 963. A convenient way to get somewhat random planar networks is from 2D Voronoi diagrams of the kind discussed on page 987.

■ **Random replacements.** As indicated in the note above, applying the second rule (T1, shown as (b) on page 511) at an appropriate sequence of positions can transform one planar network into any other with the same number of nodes. The pictures below show what happens if this rule is repeatedly applied at random positions in a network. Each time it is applied, the rule adds two edges to one face, and removes them from another. After many steps the pictures below show that faces with large numbers of edges appear. The average number of edges must always be 6 (see note above), but in a sufficiently large network the probability for a face to have n edges eventually approaches an equilibrium value of $8(n-2)(2n-3)!!(3/8)^n/n!$. (For large n this is approximately λ^n with $\lambda = 3/4$; if 1- and 2-edged regions are allowed then $\lambda = (3 + \sqrt{3})/6 \approx 0.79$.) There may be some easy way to derive such results, but so far it has only been done using fairly sophisticated techniques from quantum field theory developed in the late 1970s. The starting point is to look at a

ϕ^3 field theory with SU(n) internal symmetry and to note that in the limit $n \to \infty$ what dominates are Feynman diagrams that have the structure of planar trivalent networks (see page 1040). And it then turns out that in zero spacetime dimensions the complete path integral for the theory can be evaluated exactly—yielding in effect a generating function for the number of possible networks. Parametric differentiation (to yield n-point correlation functions) then gives results for n-sided regions. Another result that has been derived is that the average total number $m[n]$ of edges of all faces around a given face with n edges is $7n + 3 + 9/(n + 1)$. Note that the networks obtained always have dimension 2 according to my definitions.

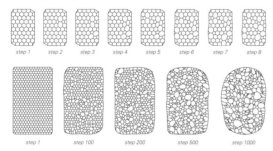

step 1 step 2 step 3 step 4 step 5 step 6 step 7 step 8

step 1 step 100 step 200 step 500 step 1000

■ **Cellular structures.** There are many systems in nature that consist of assemblies of discrete regions—and the lines that define the interfaces between these regions form networks. In many cases the regions are fixed once established (compare page 988). But in other cases there is continuing evolution, as for example in soap and other foams and froths, grains in metals and perhaps some biological tissues. In 2D situations the lines between regions generically form a trivalent planar network. In a soap foam, the geometrical layout of this network is determined by surface tension forces—with connections meeting at 120° at each node, though being slightly curved and of different lengths. Pressure differences lead to diffusion of gas and on average to von Neumann's Law that the area of an n-sided region changes linearly with time, at a rate proportional to $n - 6$. Typically the network topology of a foam continually rearranges itself through cascades of seemingly random T1 processes (rule (b) from page 511), with regions that reach zero size disappearing through T2 processes (reversed rule (a)). And as noted for example by Cyril Smith in the early 1950s there is a characteristic coarsening that occurs. Something similar is already visible in the pure T1 pictures in the note above. But results such as the so-called Aboav-Weaire law that $m[n]$ from the note above is in practice about $5n + c$ suggest that T2 processes are also important. (Processes like cell division

in 2D biological tissue in effect directly add connections to a network. But this can again be thought of as a combination of T1 and T2 processes, and in appropriate idealizations can lead to very similar results.)

■ **Page 514 · Cluster numbers.** The following tables give the total numbers of distinct clusters—with number of nodes going across the page, and number of dangling connections going down. (See also page 1038.)

	1	2	3	4	5	6	7	8	9	10
0	0	0	0	1	0	2	0	5	0	19
1	0	0	0	0	1	0	4	0	19	0
2	0	0	0	1	0	5	0	23	0	132
3	1	0	1	0	3	0	15	0	91	0
4	0	1	0	2	0	9	0	54	0	390
5	0	0	1	0	4	0	22	0	166	0
6	0	0	0	2	0	9	0	63	0	551

	1	2	3	4	5	6	7	8	9	10
7	0	0	0	0	2	0	17	0	157	0
8	0	0	0	0	0	4	0	38	0	424
9	0	0	0	0	0	0	6	0	80	0
10	0	0	0	0	0	0	0	11	0	180
11	0	0	0	0	0	0	0	0	18	0
12	0	0	0	0	0	0	0	0	0	37

■ **Page 515 · Non-overlapping clusters.** The picture shows all distinct clusters with 3 dangling connections and 9 nodes that are not self-overlapping. The only smaller cluster with the same property is the trivial one with just a single node.

Most clusters that can overlap will be able to do so in an infinite number of possible networks. (One can see this by noting that they can overlap inside clusters with dangling connections, not just closed networks.) But there are some clusters that can overlap only in a few small networks. The pictures below show examples where this happens. The pictures in the main text still treat such clusters as non-overlapping.

 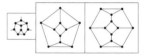

If two clusters overlap, then this means that there is some network in which there are copies of these clusters that involve some of the same nodes. And it is possible to search for such a network by starting from a single node and then sequentially trying to take corresponding pieces from the two clusters.

■ **1- and 2-connection clusters.** Clusters with just one or two dangling connections can always in effect be thought of just as adding extra structure to single connections in a network. But this extra structure can be important in the application of other rules—and can for example emulate something like having multiple colors of connections.

■ **Connectedness.** It is not clear whether a network that represents the universe must remain globally connected, or whether pieces can break off. But any replacements that take connected clusters and yield connected clusters must always maintain the connectedness of any network.

■ **Reversibility.** By including both forward and backward versions of every transformation it is straightforward to set up reversible rules for network evolution. It is not clear, however, whether the basic rules for the universe are really reversible. It could well be that the apparent reversibility we see arises because the universe is effectively on an attractor, as discussed on page 1018. Note that if pieces of the universe can break off, but cannot reconnect, then there will inevitably be an irreversible loss of information.

■ **1/n expansion.** If there are n possible colors for each connection in a network, then for large n it turns out that the vast majority of networks will be planar. This idea was used in the 1980s as a way of simplifying the Feynman diagrams to consider in QCD and other quantum field theories. (See page 1039.)

■ **Feynman diagrams.** In the standard approach to particle physics, possible interaction processes are represented by networks in which each node corresponds to an elementary interaction, and the nodes are joined by connections which correspond to the propagation of particles in spacetime. I can see no direct physical relationship between such diagrams and the networks I consider. However, at a mathematical level, the set of trivalent networks with n nodes formally corresponds to the set of nth order Feynman diagrams in a ϕ^3 field theory. (Compare page 1039.)

■ **Chemical analogy.** The evolution of a network can be thought of as an idealized version of a chemical process in which molecules are networks of bonds. (See page 1193.)

■ **Symbolic representations.** Expressions in which common subexpressions are shared correspond to networks, as do collections of relations between objects representing nodes.

■ **Graph grammars.** The notion of generalizing substitutions for strings to the case of networks has been discussed in computer science since the 1960s—and a fair amount of formal work has been done on so-called graph grammars for specifying formal languages whose elements are networks. Even a good analog of regular languages has, however, not yet been found. But applications to constructing or verifying practical network-based system description schemes are quite often discussed. In mathematics rather little is usually done with anything but very trivial network substitutions. In mathematics, rather little is usually done with network substitutions, though the proof of the Four-Color Theorem in 1976 was for example based on showing that 300 or so possible replacement rules—if applied in an appropriate sequence—can transform any graph to have one of 1936 smaller subgraphs that require the same number of colors. (32 rules and 633 subgraphs are now known to be sufficient.)

■ **Network mobile automata.** The analog of a mobile automaton can be defined for networks by setting up a single active node, then having rules which replace clusters of nodes around this active node, and move its position. The pictures below show two simple examples.

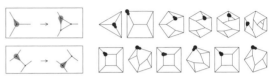

The total number of replacements that can be used in the rules of a network mobile automaton and which involve clusters with up to four nodes and have from 1 to 4 dangling connections is {14, 10, 2727, 781}. Despite looking at several hundred thousand cases I have not been able to find network mobile automata with especially complicated behavior.

Note that by having a cluster of nodes with a unique form it is possible to emulate a network mobile automaton using an ordinary network substitution system.

■ **Directed network systems.** If one adds directionality to the connections in a network it becomes particularly easy to set up rules for clusters of nodes that cannot overlap. For no two clusters whose dangling connections all point inwards can ever overlap, at least so long as neither of these clusters themselves contain subclusters whose dangling connections similarly all point inwards. The pictures below show a few examples of such clusters. Note that in a random network of n nodes, about $n/8$ such clusters typically occur.

Space, Time and Relativity

■ **Page 516 · Posets.** The way I set things up, collections of events can be thought of as partially ordered sets (posets). If all events occurred in a definite sequence in time, this would define a total linear ordering for them. But with the setup I use, there is only a partial ordering of events, defined by causal connections. The causal networks I draw are so-called Hasse or order diagrams of the posets of events. If a connection goes directly from x to y in this network then x is said to cover y. And in general if there is a path from x to y then one writes $x > y$. The collection of all events that will lead to a given set of events (the union of their past light cones) is known as the filter of that set. Within a poset, there can be sequences of elements that are totally ordered, and these are called chains. (The maximum length of any chain is sometimes called the dimension of a poset, but this is unrelated to the notions of dimension I consider.) There can also be sets of elements between which no ordering relations at all are defined, and these are called antichains.

Standard examples of posets include subsets of a set ordered by the subset relation, complex numbers ordered by magnitude, and integers ordered by divisibility. Posets first arose as general concepts in the late 1800s in connection with the development of mathematical logic, and to some extent abstract algebra. They became somewhat popular in the mid-1900s, both as formal generalizations in lattice theory, and as structures in various combinatorics applications. It was already noted in the 1920s that events in relativity theory formed posets.

The pictures below show the first few distinct possible Hasse diagrams for posets. For successive numbers of elements the total numbers of these are 1, 2, 5, 16, 63, 318, 2045, 16999, ...

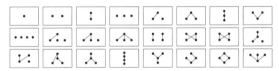

■ **Page 517 · Spacelike slices.** The definition of spacelike slices used here is directly analogous to what is used in traditional relativity theory (typically under names like spacelike hypersurfaces and Cauchy surfaces). There will normally be many different possible choices of spacelike slices, but in all cases a particular such slice is set up to represent what can consistently be thought of as all of space at a given time. One definition of a spacelike slice is then a maximal set of points in which no pair are causally related (corresponding to a maximal antichain in a poset). Another definition (equivalent for any connected causal network) is that spacelike slices are what consistently divide a causal network into a past and a future. And an intermediate definition is that a spacelike slice contains points that are not themselves causally related, but which appear in either the past or the future of every other point. Given a spacelike slice in a causal network, it is always possible to construct another such slice by finding all those points whose immediate predecessors are all included either in the original slice or its predecessors.

■ **Page 518 · Speed of light.** In a vacuum the speed of light is 299,792,458 meters/second (and this is actually what is taken to define a meter). In materials light mostly travels

slower—basically because there are delays when it is absorbed and reemitted by atoms. In a first approximation, the slowdown factor is the refractive index. But particularly in materials which can amplify light a whole sequence of peculiar effects have been observed—and it is fairly subtle to account correctly for incoming and outgoing signals, and to show that at least no energy or information is transmitted faster than c. The standard mathematical framework of relativity theory implies that any massless particle must propagate at c in a vacuum—so that not only light but also gravitational waves presumably go at this speed (and the same is at least approximately true of neutrinos). The effective mass for massive particles increases by a factor $1/Sqrt[1 - v^2/c^2]$ at speed v, making it take progressively more energy to increase v. At a formal mathematical level it is possible to imagine tachyons which always travel faster than c. But the structure of modern physics would find it difficult to accommodate interactions between these and ordinary particles.

■ **Page 522 · History of relativity.** (See also page 1028.) The idea that mechanical processes should work the same regardless of how fast one is moving was expressed by Galileo in the early 1600s, particularly in connection with the motion of the Earth—and was incorporated in the laws of mechanics formulated by Isaac Newton in 1687. But when the wave theory of light finally became popular in the mid-1800s it seemed to imply that no similar principle could be true for light. For it was generally assumed that waves of light must correspond to explicit disturbances in a medium or ether that fills space. And it was thus expected that for example the apparent speed of light would depend on how fast one was moving with respect to this ether. And indeed in particular this was what the equations for electromagnetism developed by James Maxwell in the 1860s seemed to suggest. But in 1881 an experiment by Albert Michelson (repeated more accurately in 1887 as the Michelson-Morley experiment and now done to the 10^{-20} level) showed that in fact this was not correct. Already in 1882 George FitzGerald and Hendrik Lorentz noted that if there was a contraction in length by a factor $Sqrt[1 - v^2/c^2]$ in any object moving at speed v (with c being the speed of light) then this would explain the result. And in 1904 Lorentz pointed out that Maxwell's equations are formally invariant under a so-called Lorentz transformation of space and time coordinates (see note below). Then in 1905 Albert Einstein proposed his so-called special theory of relativity—which took as its basic postulates not only that the laws of mechanics and electrodynamics are independent of how fast one is moving, but that this is also true of the speed of light.

And while at first these postulates might seem incompatible, what Einstein showed was that they are not—at least if modifications are made to the basic laws of mechanics. In the few years that followed, various formulations of this result were given, with Hermann Minkowski in 1908 showing that it could be derived if one just assumes that space and time enter all physical laws together in a certain kind of 4D vector. In the late 1800s Ernst Mach had emphasized the idea of formulating science and particularly mechanics in terms only of concepts that can actually be measured by observers. And in this framework Einstein and others gave what seemed to be almost purely deductive arguments for relativity theory—with the result that it generally came to be assumed that there was no meaningful sense in which one could ever imagine deriving relativity from anything more fundamental. Yet as I discussed earlier in the chapter, if a complete theory of physics is to be as simple as possible, then most things like relativity theory must in effect be derived from more basic features of the theory—as I start to try to do in the main text of this section.

■ **Standard treatment.** In a standard treatment of relativity theory one way to begin is to consider setting up a square grid of points in space and time—and then to ask what kind of transformed grid corresponds to this same set of points if one is moving at some velocity v. At first one might assume that the answer would just be a grid that has been sheared by the simple transformation $\{t, x\} \rightarrow \{t, x - v t\}$, as in the first row of pictures below. And indeed for purposes of Newtonian mechanics this so-called Galilean transformation is exactly what is needed. But as the pictures below illustrate, it implies that light cones tip as v increases, so that the apparent speed of light changes, and for example Maxwell's equations must change their form. But the key point is that with an appropriate transformation that affects both space and time, the speed of light can be left the same. The necessary transformation is the so-called Lorentz transformation

$$\{t, x\} \rightarrow \{t - v x/c^2, x - v t\}/Sqrt[1 - v^2/c^2]$$

And from this the time dilation factor $1/Sqrt[1 - v^2/c^2]$ shown on page 524 follows, as well as the length contraction factor $Sqrt[1 - v^2/c^2]$. An important feature of the Lorentz transformation is that it preserves the quantity $c^2 t^2 - x^2$—with the result that as v changes in the pictures below a given point in the grid traces out a hyperbola whose asymptotes lie on a light cone. Note that on a light cone $c^2 t^2 - x^2$ always vanishes. Note also that the intersection of the past and future light cones for two events separated by a distance x in space and t in time always has a volume proportional exactly to $c^2 t^2 - x^2$.

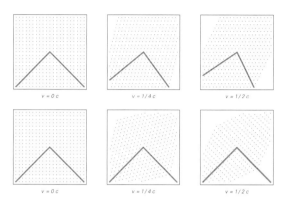

$v = 0 c$ $v = 1/4 c$ $v = 1/2 c$

$v = 0 c$ $v = 1/4 c$ $v = 1/2 c$

■ **Inferences from relativity.** The pictures on page 524 show that an idealized clock based on bouncing light between mirrors will exhibit relativistic time dilation. And from such derivations it is often assumed that the same result must hold for any possible clock system. But as a practical matter it does not. And indeed for example the clocks in GPS satellites are specifically set up so as to remove the effects of time dilation. And in the twin paradox one can certainly imagine that each twin could have an accelerometer whose readings they use to correct their clocks. Indeed, even when it comes to individual particles there are subtle effects associated with acceleration and radiation (see page 1062)—so that in the end not entirely clear that something like a biological system would actually in practice exhibit just standard time dilation.

One feature of relativity is that it implies that only relative motion is ultimately ever detectable. (This was also implied by Newtonian mechanics for purely mechanical systems.) And from this it is often concluded that there can be nothing like an ether that one can consider as defining an absolute state of rest in the universe. But in fact the cosmic microwave background in effect does exactly this. For in standard cosmological models it fills the universe, but is everywhere at rest relative to the global center of mass of the universe. And from the anisotropies we have observed in the microwave background it is thus possible to conclude that the Earth is moving at an absolute speed of about $c/10^3$ relative to the center of mass of the universe. In particle physics standard models also in effect introduce things that are assumed to be at rest relative to the center of mass of the universe. One example is the Higgs condensate discussed in connection with particle masses (see page 1047). Other possible examples include zero-point fluctuations in quantum fields.

Outside of science, relativity theory is sometimes given as evidence for various general ideas of cultural relativism (compare page 1131)—which have existed since well before relativity theory in physics, and seem in the end to have no meaningful connection to it.

■ **Particle physics.** Relativity theory was originally formulated just for mechanics and electromagnetism. But its predictions like $E = m c^2$ were immediately applied for example to radioactivity, and soon it came to be assumed that the theory would work for any system at all—unless it involved gravity. So this has meant that in particle physics $c^2 t^2 - x^2 - y^2 - z^2$ is at some level the only quantity that ever appears. And to make mathematical work easier, what is very often done is to carry out the so-called Wick rotation $t \to i t$—so relativistic invariance is just independence on 4D orientation. (See page 1061.) But except in rather simple cases there is practically no evidence that results obtained after Wick rotation have anything to do with physical reality—and certainly the transformation removes some very basic phenomena such as particle propagation. One feature of it, however, is that it maps the equation for quantum mechanical time evolution into the equation for probabilities in statistical mechanics, with imaginary time corresponding to inverse temperature. And while it is conceivable that this mapping may have some deep significance, none has so far ever been identified.

■ **Time travel.** The idea that space and time are similar suggests that it might be possible to move backwards and forwards in time just like it is possible to move backwards and forwards in space. And indeed in the partial differential equations that define general relativity, it is formally possible for the motion of particles to achieve this, at least when there is sufficient negative energy density from matter or a cosmological constant. But even in this case there is no real progression in which one travels backwards in time. Instead, the possibility of motion that leads to earlier times simply implies a requirement of consistency between behavior at earlier and later times.

Elementary Particles

■ **Note for physicists.** My goal in the remainder of this chapter is not to present a specific ultimate model for physics, but rather to discuss at a fairly general level some features that I believe such a model will have, given the overall discoveries of this book, and the specific results I have described in this chapter. I am certainly aware that many physicists will want to know more details. But particularly in making contact with existing physics it is almost inevitable that all sorts of technical formalism will be needed—and to maintain balance in this book I have not included this here. (Given my own personal background in theoretical physics it will come as no

surprise that I have often used such formalism in the process of working out what I describe in these sections.)

■ **Page 525 · Types of particles.** Current particle physics identifies three basic types of known elementary particles: leptons, quarks and gauge bosons. The known leptons are the electron (e), muon (μ) and tau lepton (τ), and their corresponding neutrinos (v_e, v_μ, v_τ). Quarks exist inside hadrons like the proton and pion, but never seem to occur as ordinary free particles. Six types are known: u, d, c (charm), s (strange), t (top), b. Gauge bosons are associated with forces. Those currently known are the photon (γ) for electromagnetism (QED), W and Z for so-called weak interactions, and the gluon (g) for QCD interactions between quarks. Gravitons associated with gravitational forces presumably also exist. In ordinary matter, the only particles that contribute in direct ways to everyday physical, chemical and even nuclear properties are electrons, photons and effectively u and d quarks, and gluons. (These, together presumably with some type of neutrino, are the only types of particles that never seem to decay.) The first reasonably direct observations of the various types of particles were as follows (some were predicted in advance): e (1897), γ (~1905), u, d (1914/~1970), μ (1937), s (1946), v_e (1956), v_μ (1962), c (1974), τ, v_τ (1975), b (1977), g (~1979), W (1983), Z (1983), t (1995).

Most particles exist in several variations. Apart from the photon (and graviton), all have distinct antiparticles. Each quark has 3 possible color configurations; the gluon has 8. Most particles also have multiple spin states. Quarks and leptons have spin 1/2, yielding 2 spin states (neutrinos could have only 1 if they were massless). Gauge bosons normally have spin 1 (the graviton would have spin 2) yielding 3 spin states for massive ones. Real massless ones such as the photon always have just 2. (See page 1046.)

In the Standard Model the idea of spontaneous symmetry breaking (see page 1047) allows particles with different masses to be viewed as manifestations of single particles, and this is effectively done for W, Z, γ, as well as for each of the 3 so-called families of quarks and leptons: u, d; c, s; t, b and e, v_e; μ, v_μ; τ, v_τ. Grand unified models typically do this for all known gauge bosons (except gravitons) and for corresponding families of quarks and leptons—and inevitably imply the existence of various additional particles more massive than those known, but with properties that are somehow intermediate. Some models also unify different families, and supersymmetric models unify quarks and leptons with gauge bosons.

■ **History.** The idea that matter—and light—might be made up of discrete particles was already discussed in antiquity (see page 876). But it was only in the mid-1800s that there started to be real evidence for the existence of some kind of discrete atoms of matter. Yet at the time, the idea of fields was popular, and it was believed that the universe must be filled with a continuous fluid-like ether responsible at least for light and other electromagnetic phenomena. So for example following ideas of William Rankine from 1849 William Thomson (Kelvin) in 1867 suggested that perhaps atoms might be like knotted stable vortex rings in the ether—with different knots corresponding to different chemical elements. But though it initiated the mathematical classification of knots, and now has certain conceptual similarities to what I discuss in this book, the details of this model did not work out—and it had been largely abandoned even before the electron was discovered in 1897. Ernest Rutherford's work in the 1910s on scattering from atoms introduced the idea of an atomic nucleus, and after the discovery of the neutron in 1932 it became clear that the main constituents of nuclei were protons and neutrons. The positron and the muon were discovered in cosmic rays in the 1930s, followed in the 1940s by a handful of other particles. By the 1960s particle accelerators were finding large numbers of new particles every year. And the hypothesis was then suggested that all these particles might actually be composed of just three more fundamental particles that became known as quarks. An alternative so-called democratic or bootstrap hypothesis was also suggested: that somehow any particle could just be viewed as a composite of all others with the same overall properties—with everything being determined by consistency in the web of interactions between particles, and no particles in a sense being more fundamental than others. But by the early 1970s experiments on so-called deep inelastic scattering had given increasingly direct evidence for point-like constituents inside particles like protons—and by the mid-1970s these were routinely identified with quarks.

As soon as the electron was discovered there were questions about its possible size. For if its charge was distributed over a sphere of radius r, this was expected to lead to electrostatic repulsion energy proportional to $1/r$. And although it was suggested around 1900 that effects associated with this might account for the mass of the electron, this ran into problems with relativity theory, and it also remained mysterious just what might hold the electron together. (A late suggestion made in 1953 by Hendrik Casimir was that it could be forces associated with zero-point fluctuations in quantum fields—but at least with the simplest setup these turned out to have wrong sign.)

The development of quantum theory in the 1920s showed that discrete particles will inevitably exhibit continuous

wave-like features in their spatial distribution of probability amplitudes. But traditional quantum mechanics and quantum field theory are both normally formulated with the assumption that the basic particles they describe have zero intrinsic spatial size. Sometimes nonzero size is taken into account by inserting additional interaction parameters—as done in the 1950s with magnetic moments and form factors of protons and neutrons. But for example in quantum electrodynamics the definite assumption is made that electrons are intrinsically of zero size. Quantum fluctuations make any particle in an interacting field theory effectively be surrounded by virtual particles. Yet not unlike in classical electrodynamics having zero intrinsic size for the electron still immediately suggests that an electron should have infinite self-energy. In the 1930s ideas about avoiding this centered around modifying basic laws of electrodynamics or the structure of spacetime (see page 1027). But the development of renormalization in the 1940s showed that these infinities could in effect just be factored out. And by the 1960s a long series of successes in the predictions of QED had led to the almost universal belief that its assumption of point-like electrons must be correct. It was occasionally suggested that the muon might be some kind of composite object. But experiments seemed to indicate that it was in every way identical to the electron, except in mass. And although no reasonable explanation for its existence was found, it came to be generally assumed by the 1970s that it was just another point-like particle. And indeed—apart from few rare suggestions to the contrary—the same is now assumed throughout mainstream practical particle physics for all of the basic particles that appear in the Standard Model. (Actual experiments based on high-energy scattering and precision magnetic moment measurements have shown only that electrons and muons must have sizes smaller than about $\hbar c/(10\,TeV) \simeq 10^{-20}\,m$—or about 10^{-5} times the size of a proton. One can make arguments that composite particles this small should have masses much larger than are observed—but it is easy to find theories that avoid these.)

In the 1980s superstring theory introduced the idea that particles might actually be tiny 1D strings—with different types of particles corresponding essentially just to strings in different modes of vibration. Since the 1960s it has been noted in many simplified quantum field theories that there can be a kind of duality in which a soliton or other extended field configuration in one representation becomes what acts like an elementary particle in another representation. And in the late 1990s there were indications that such phenomena could occur in generalized string theories—leading to suggestions of at least an abstract correspondence between for example particles like electrons and gravitational configurations like black holes.

■ **Page 526 · Topological defects.** An idealized vortex in a 2D fluid involves velocity vectors that in effect wind around a point—and can never be unwound by making a series of small local perturbations. The result is a certain kind of stability that can be viewed as being of topological origin. One can classify forms of stability like this in terms of the mathematics of homotopy. Most common are point and line defects in vector fields, but more complicated defects can occur, notably in liquid crystals, models of condensates in the early universe, and certain nonlinear field theories. Analogs of homotopy can presumably be devised to represent certain forms of stability in systems like the networks I consider.

■ **Page 527 · Kuratowski's theorem.** Any network can be laid out in 3D space. (This is related to the Whitney embedding theorem that any d-dimensional manifold can be embedded in $(2d+1)$-dimensional space.) When one says that a network is planar what one means is that it can be laid out in ordinary 2D space without any lines crossing. Kuratowski's theorem that planarity is associated with the absence of specific subgraphs in a network is an important result in graph theory established in the late 1920s. A subgraph is formally defined to be what one gets by selecting just some subset of connections in a network—and with this definition Kuratowski's theorem must allow extensions of K_5 and $K_{3,3}$ where extra nodes have been inserted in the middle of connections. (K_5 and $K_{3,3}$ are examples of so-called complete graphs, obtained by taking sets of specified numbers of nodes and connecting them in all possible ways.) Another approach is to consider reducing whole networks to so-called minors by deleting connections or merging connected nodes, and in this case Wagner's theorem shows that any non-planar network must be exactly reducible to either K_5 or $K_{3,3}$.

One can generalize the question of planarity to asking whether networks can be laid out on 2D surfaces with various topological structures—and in fact the genus of a graph can be defined to be the number of handles that must be added to a plane to embed the graph without crossings. But even on a torus it turns out that there is no finite set of (extended) subgraphs whose absence guarantees that a network can successfully be laid out. Nevertheless, if one considers minors a finite list does suffice—though for example on a torus it is known that at least 800 (and perhaps vastly more) are needed. (There is in fact a general theorem established since the 1980s that absolutely any list of networks—say for example ones that cannot be laid on a given surface—must actually in effect always all be reducible

to some finite list of minors.) Note that finding the genus for a particular trivalent network is in general NP-complete.

■ **Page 527 · Gauge invariance.** It is often convenient to define quantities for which only differences or derivatives matter. In classical physics an example is electric potential, which can be shifted by any constant amount without affecting voltage differences or the electric field given by its gradient. In the mid-1800s the idea emerged of a vector potential whose curl gives the magnetic field, and it was soon recognized—notably by James Clerk Maxwell—that any function whose curl vanishes (and that can therefore normally be written as a gradient) could be added to the vector potential without affecting the magnetic field. By the end of the 1800s the general conditions on electromagnetic potentials for invariance of fields were known, though were not thought particularly significant. In 1918 Hermann Weyl tried to reproduce electromagnetism by adding the notion of an arbitrary scale or gauge to the metric of general relativity (see page 1028)—and noted the "gauge invariance" of his theory under simultaneous transformation of electromagnetic potentials and multiplication of the metric by a position-dependent factor. Following the introduction of the Schrödinger equation in quantum mechanics in 1926 it was almost immediately noticed that the equations for a charged particle in an electromagnetic field were invariant under gauge transformations in which the wave function was multiplied by a position-dependent phase factor. The idea then arose that perhaps some kind of gauge invariance could also be used as the basis for formulating theories of forces other than electromagnetism. And after a few earlier attempts, Yang-Mills theories were introduced in 1954 by extending the notion of a phase factor to an element of an arbitrary non-Abelian group. In the 1970s the Standard Model then emerged, based entirely on such theories. In mathematical terms, gauge theories can be viewed as describing fiber bundles in which connections between values of group elements in fibers at neighboring spacetime points are specified by gauge potentials—and curvatures correspond to gauge fields. (General relativity is in effect a special case in which the group elements are themselves related to spacetime coordinates.)

■ **Page 527 · Identifying particles.** In something like a class 4 cellular automaton it is quite straightforward to start enumerating possible persistent structures—as we saw in Chapter 6. But in a network system it can be much more difficult. Ultimately what one wants to do is to find what possible types of forms for local regions are inequivalent under the application of the underlying rules. But in general it may be undecidable even whether two such forms are actually equivalent (compare the notes below and on page

1051)—since to tell this one might need to be able to apply the rules infinitely many times. In specific cases, however, generalizations of concepts like planarity and homotopy may provide useful guides. And a first step may be to look at small closed networks and try to determine which of these can be transformed into each other by a given set of rules.

■ **Knot theory.** Somewhat analogous to the problem in the note above is the problem of classifying knots. The pictures below show some of the simplest distinct knots. But given presentations of two knots, no finite procedure is known that determines in general whether the knots are equivalent (or constructs a sequence of Reidemeister moves that transform one into the other). Quite probably this is in general undecidable, though since the 1920s a few polynomial invariants have been discovered—with recent ones being related to ideas from quantum field theory—that have allowed some progress to be made. (Even the problem of determining whether a knot specified by line segments is trivial is known to be NP-complete.)

■ **Page 528 · Charge quantization.** It is an observed fact that the electric and other charges of all particles are simple rational multiples of each other. In the context of electromagnetism alone, there would be no particular reason to expect this (unless magnetic monopoles exist). But as soon as different particles are related by a non-Abelian symmetry group, then the discreteness of the representations of such a group immediately implies that all charges must be rational multiples of each other.

■ **Spin.** Even when they appear to be of zero size, particles exhibit intrinsic angular momentum known as spin. The total spin is always a fixed multiple of the basic unit $\hbar$: $1/2$ for quarks and leptons, 1 for photons and other ordinary gauge bosons, 2 for gravitons, and in theory 0 for Higgs particles. (Observed mesons have spins up to perhaps 5 and nuclei up to more than 50.) Particles of higher spin in effect require more information to specify their orientation (or polarization or its analog). And in the context of network models it could be that spin is somehow related to something as simple as the number of places at which the core of a particle is attached to the rest of the network. Spin values can be thought of as specifying which irreducible representation of the group of symmetries of spacetime is needed to describe a particle after momentum has been factored out. For ordinary massive

particles in d-dimensional space the group is Spin(d), while for massless particles it is $E(d - 1)$ (the Euclidean group). (For tachyons, it would be fundamentally non-compact, forcing continuous spin values.) For small transformations, Spin(d) is just the ordinary rotation group SO(d), but globally it is its universal cover, or SU(2) in 3D. And this can be thought of as what allows half-integer spins, which must be described by spinors rather than vectors or tensors. Such objects have the property that they are not left invariant by 360° rotations, but only by 720° ones—a feature potentially fairly easy to reproduce with networks, perhaps even without definite integer dimensions. In the standard formalism of quantum field theory it can be shown that (above 2D) half-integer spins must always be associated with fermions (which for example satisfy the exclusion principle), and integer spins with bosons. (This spin-statistics connection also seems to hold for various kinds of objects defined by extended field configurations.)

■ **Page 528 · Particle masses.** The measured masses of known elementary particles in units of GeV (roughly equal to the proton mass) are: photon: 0, electron: 0.000510998902; muon: 0.1056583569; τ lepton: 1.77705; W: 80.4; Z: 91.19. Recent evidence suggests a mass of about 10^{-11} GeV for at least one type of neutrino. Quarks and gluons presumably never occur as free particles, but still act in many ways as if they have definite masses. For all of them their confinement contributes perhaps 0.3 GeV of effective mass. Then there is also a direct mass: gluons 0; u: ~0.005; d ~0.01; s: ~0.2; c: 1.3; b: 4.4; t: 176 GeV. Note that among sets of particles that have the same quantum numbers—like d, s, b or γ, Z—mixing occurs that makes states of definite mass—that would propagate unchanged as free particles—differ by a unitary transformation from states that are left unchanged by interactions. When one sets up a quantum field theory one can typically in effect insert various mass parameters for particles. Self-interactions normally introduce formally infinite corrections—but if a theory is renormalizable then this means that there are only a limited number of independent such corrections, with the result that relations between masses of different particles are preserved. In quantum field theory any particle is always surrounded by a kind of cloud of virtual particles interacting with it. And following the Uncertainty Principle phenomena involving larger momentum scales will then to probe progressively smaller parts of this cloud—yielding different effective masses. (The masses tend to go up or down logarithmically with momentum scale—following so-called renormalization group equations.)

The Standard Model starts off with certain symmetries that force the masses of all ordinary particles to be zero. But then one assumes that nonzero masses are generated by spontaneous symmetry breaking. One starts by taking each particle to be coupled to a so-called Higgs field. Then one introduces self-interactions in this field so as to make its stable state be one that has constant nonzero value throughout the universe. But this means that as particles propagate, their interactions with the background give them an effective mass. And by having Higgs couplings be proportional to observed particle masses, it becomes inevitable that these will be the masses of particles. One prediction of the usual version of this mechanism for mass is that a definite Higgs particle should exist—which in the minimal Standard Model experiments should observe fairly soon. At times there have been hopes of so-called dynamical symmetry breaking giving the same effective results as the Higgs mechanism, but without an explicit Higgs field— perhaps through something similar to various phenomena in condensed matter physics. String theory, like the Standard Model, tends to start with zero mass particles—and then hopes that an appropriate Higgs-like mechanism will generate nonzero ones.

■ **More particles.** To produce more massive particles requires higher-energy particle collisions, and today's accelerators only allow one to search up to masses of perhaps 200 GeV. (Sufficiently stable particles could have survived from the early universe, and a few cosmic ray interactions in principle give higher energies—but are normally too rare to be useful.) I am not sure whether in my approach one should expect an infinite series of progressively more massive particles. The example of nonplanarity might suggest not, but even in the class 4 cellular automata discussed in Chapter 6 it is not clear whether fundamentally different progressively larger structures will appear forever. In quantum field theory particles of any mass can always in principle exist for short times in virtual form. But normally their effects decrease like powers of their mass—making them hard to measure. In two kinds of cases, however, this does not happen: one is so-called anomalies, the other interactions with the Higgs field, in which couplings are proportional to mass. In the minimal Standard Model it turns out to be impossible to get quarks or leptons with masses much above about 200 GeV without destabilizing the vacuum (a fact pointed out by David Politzer and me in 1979). But with more complicated models one can avoid this constraint. In supersymmetric models— and string theory—there are typically also all sorts of other types of particles, assumed to have high masses since they have not been observed. There is evidence against any more

than the three known generations of quarks and leptons in that the decay process $Z^0 \to \nu\,\bar\nu$ has a rate that rather accurately agrees with what is expected from just three types of low-mass neutrinos.

■ **Page 530 · Expansion of the universe.** See page 1055.

The Phenomenon of Gravity

■ **History.** With the Earth believed to be the center of the universe, gravity did not seem to require much explanation: it was just a force bringing things to a natural place. But with the advent of Copernican astronomy in the 1500s something more was needed. In the early 1600s Galileo noted that the force of gravity seems to depend only on the mass of an object, and not on any of its other features. In 1687 Isaac Newton then suggested a universal inverse square law of gravity between objects. In the 1700s and 1800s all sorts of celestial mechanics was done on the basis of this—with occasional observational anomalies being resolved for example by the discovery of new planets. Starting in the mid-1800s there were attempts to formulate gravity in the same way as electromagnetism—and in 1900 it was for example suggested that gravitational effects might propagate at the speed of light. Following his introduction of relativity theory in 1905, Albert Einstein began to seek a theory of gravity that would fit in with it. Ordinary special relativity has the feature that it assumes that systems behave the same regardless of their overall velocity—but not regardless of their acceleration. In 1907 Einstein then suggested the equivalence principle that gravity always locally has the same effect as an acceleration. (This principle requires only slightly more than Galileo's idea of the equivalence of gravitational and inertial mass, which has now been verified to the 10^{-12} level.) But by 1912 Einstein realized that if the effective laws of physics were somehow to remain the same in systems with different accelerations (or in different gravitational fields) then this would require a change in their perceived geometry. And building on ideas of differential geometry and tensor calculus from the late 1800s Einstein then began to formulate the concept that gravity is associated with curvature of space. In the late 1800s Ernst Mach had argued that phenomena like acceleration and rotation could ultimately be defined only relative to matter in the universe. And partly on this basis Einstein used the idea that curvature in space must be like a field produced by matter—leading eventually to his formulation in 1915 of the standard Einstein equations for general relativity. An immediate prediction of these was a deviation from the inverse square law, explaining an observed precession in the orbit of Mercury. After a dramatic verification in 1919 of predicted bending of light by the Sun, general relativity began to be widely accepted. In the 1920s expansion of the universe was discovered, and this was seen to be consistent with general relativity. In the 1940s study of the evolution of stars then led to discussion of what became known as black holes. But for the most part general relativity was still viewed as being highly elegant though of little practical relevance. In the 1960s, however, more work began to be done on it. The discovery of the cosmic microwave background in 1965 led to increasing interest in cosmology. Precision tests—particularly with spacecraft—were designed. In calculations it was sometimes difficult to tell what was a genuine effect, and what was just a feature of the particular coordinates used. But a variety of increasingly abstract mathematical methods were developed, leading notably to general theorems about inevitability of singularities. Detailed calculations tended to require complicated symbolic tensor manipulation (with some associated problems being NP-complete), but with the development of computer algebra this gradually became more feasible—and by the mid-1970s approximate numerical methods were also being used. Various alternative formulations of general relativity were proposed, based for example on tetrads, spinors and twistors (and more recently on connection, loop and non-commutative geometry methods)—but none led to any great simplification. Meanwhile, there continued to be ever more accurate experimental tests of general relativity in the solar system— and at least in the weak gravitational fields available there (with metrics differing from the identity by at most one part in 10^6), all have worked out to around the 10^{-3} level. Starting in the 1960s, more and more ambitious gravitational wave detectors have been built—although none as yet have actually observed anything. Measurements done on a binary pulsar system are nevertheless consistent at a 10^{-3} level with the emission of gravitational radiation in a fairly strong gravitational field at the rate implied by general relativity. And since the 1980s there has been increasing conviction that at least indirect effects of black holes associated with very strong gravitational fields are being observed.

Over the years, some variants of general relativity have been proposed. At least when formulated in terms of tensors, none have quite the simplicity of the original theory—but some lead to rather different predictions, such as an absence of singularities like black holes. Ever since quantum theory began in the early 1900s there has been discussion of quantum gravity—and almost every major method developed for handling other quantum phenomena has been tried on gravity. Starting in the 1980s a variety of methods more specific to quantum gravity were also pursued, but none have yet had convincing success. (See page 1054.)

■ **Differential geometry.** Standard descriptions of properties like curvature—as used for example in general relativity— are normally based on differential geometry. In its usual formulation this assumes that space is continuous, and can always effectively be treated as some kind of deformed version of ordinary Euclidean space—thus forming what is known as a manifold. The result of this is that points in space can always be specified by lists of coordinates—although historically one of the objectives of differential geometry has been to find ways to define properties like curvature so that they do not depend on the choice of such coordinates. The geometrical properties of a space are in general specified by its so-called metric—and this metric allows one to compute quantities based on lengths and angles from coordinates. The metric can be written as a matrix g, defined so that the analog for infinitesimal vectors u and v of $u \cdot v$ in ordinary Euclidean space is $u \cdot g \cdot v$. (This is essentially equivalent to saying that infinitesimal arc length is related to infinitesimal coordinate distances by $ds^2 = g_{i,j} \, dx_i \, dx_j$.) In d dimensions the metric g for a so-called Riemannian space can in general be any $d \times d$ positive-definite symmetric matrix—and can vary with position. But for ordinary flat Euclidean space it is always just *IdentityMatrix[d]* (at least with Cartesian coordinates). Within say a surface whose points $\{x_1, x_2, ...\}$ are obtained by evaluating an expression e as a function of parameters p (so that for example $e = \{x, y, f[x, y]\}$, $p = \{x, y\}$ for a *Plot3D* surface) the metric turns out to be given by

(Transpose[#] . # &)[Outer[D, e, p]]

In ordinary Euclidean space a defining feature of geometry is that the shortest path between two points is a straight line. But in an arbitrary space things can be more complicated, and in general such a path will be a geodesic (see note below) which can have a more complicated form. If the coordinates along a path are given by an expression s (such as $\{t, 1 + t, t^2\}$) that depends on a parameter t, and the metric at position p is $g[p]$, then the length of a path turns out to be

Integrate[Sqrt[$\partial_t s$. g[s] . $\partial_t s$], {t, t_1, t_2}]

and geodesics then correspond to paths that extremize this quantity. In ordinary Euclidean space, such paths are straight lines, so that the length of a path between points with lists of coordinates a and b is just the ordinary Euclidean distance *Sqrt[(a − b) . (a − b)]*. But in general, even though geodesics are not straight lines their lengths can still be used to define a so-called geodesic distance—which turns out to have all the various properties of a distance discussed on page 1030.

If one draws a circle of radius r on a page, then the smaller r is, the more curved the circle will be—and one can define the circle to have a constant curvature equal to $1/r$. If one draws a more general curve on a page, one can define its curvature at every point by seeing what size of circle fits it best at that point—or equivalently what the coefficients are in a quadratic approximation. (Compare page 418.) With a 2D surface in ordinary 3D space, one can imagine fitting quadrics (generalized ellipsoids). But these are now specified by two radii, yielding two principal curvatures. And in general these curvatures depend on the way the surface is laid out in 3D space. But a crucial point noted by Carl-Friedrich Gauss in the 1820s is that the product of such curvatures—the so-called Gaussian curvature—is always independent of how the surface is laid out, and can thus be viewed as intrinsic to the surface itself, and for example determined purely from the metric for the 2D space corresponding to the surface.

In a 2D space, intrinsic curvature is completely specified just by Gaussian curvature. In higher-dimensional spaces, there are more components, but in general they are all part of the so-called Riemann tensor—a rank-4 tensor introduced by Bernhard Riemann in 1854. (In *Mathematica*, the explicit form of such a tensor can be represented as a nested list for which $TensorRank[list] == 4$.) Several descriptions of the Riemann tensor can be given. One is based on looking at infinitesimal vectors u, v and w and asking how much w differs when transported two ways around the edges of a parallelogram, from x to $x + u + v$ via $x + u$ and via $x + v$. In ordinary flat space there is no difference, but in general the difference is a vector that is defined to be $Riemann . u . v . w$. (The $Riemann$ that appears here is formally $R_{ijk}{}^l$.) Another description of the Riemann tensor is based on geodesics. In flat Euclidean space any two geodesics that start parallel always remain so. But a defining feature of general non-Euclidean spaces is that this is not in general so. And it turns out that the Riemann tensor is what determines the rate at which geodesics deviate from being parallel. Still another description of the Riemann tensor is as the coefficient of the quadratic terms in an expansion of the metric about a particular point, using so-called normal coordinates set up to make linear terms vanish. In general the Riemann tensor can always be computed from the metric, though it is somewhat complicated. If p is a list of coordinate parameters that appear in a d-dimensional metric g, then

$Riemann = Table[\partial_{p[[j]]} \Gamma[[i, k]] - \partial_{p[[i]]} \Gamma[[j, k]] +$
$\quad \Gamma[[i, k]] . \Gamma[[j]] - \Gamma[[j, k]] . \Gamma[[i]], \{i, d\}, \{j, d\}, \{k, d\}]$

where the so-called Christoffel symbol $\Gamma_{ij}{}^k$ is

$\Gamma = With[\{gi = Inverse[g]\}, Table[Sum[$
$\quad gi[[l, k]] (\partial_{p[[j]]} g[[i, l]] + \partial_{p[[i]]} g[[j, l]] - \partial_{p[[l]]} g[[i, j]]),$
$\quad \{l, d\}], \{i, d\}, \{j, d\}, \{k, d\}]]/2$

There are d^4 elements in the nested lists for $Riemann$, but symmetries and the so-called Bianchi identity reduce the

number of independent components to $1/12\, d^2\, (d^2 - 1)$—or 20 for $d = 4$. One can then compute the Ricci tensor ($R_{ik} = R_{ijk}{}^j$) using

$RicciTensor = Map[Tr, Transpose[Riemann, \{1, 3, 2, 4\}], \{2\}]$

and this has $1/2\, d\, (d + 1)$ independent components in $d > 2$ dimensions. (The parts of the Riemann tensor not captured by the Ricci tensor correspond to the so-called Weyl tensor; for $d = 2$ the Ricci tensor has only one independent component, equal to the negative of the Gaussian curvature.) Finally, the Ricci scalar curvature is given by

$RicciScalar = Tr[RicciTensor . Inverse[g]]$

■ **Page 531 · Geodesics.** On a sphere all geodesics are arcs of great circles. On a surface of constant negative curvature (like (c)) geodesics diverge exponentially, as noted in early work on chaos theory (see page 971). The path of a geodesic can in general be found by requiring that the analog of acceleration vanishes for it. In the case of a surface defined by $z == f[x, y]$ this is equivalent to solving

$x''[t] == -(f^{(1,0)}[x[t], y[t]] (y'[t]^2 f^{(0,2)}[x[t], y[t]] +$
$\quad 2 x'[t] y'[t] f^{(1,1)}[x[t], y[t]] + x'[t]^2 f^{(2,0)}[x[t], y[t]]))/$
$\quad (1 + f^{(0,1)}[x[t], y[t]]^2 + f^{(1,0)}[x[t], y[t]]^2)$

together with the corresponding equation for y'', as already noted by Leonhard Euler in 1728 in connection with his development of the calculus of variations.

■ **Page 532 · Spherical networks.** One can construct networks of constant positive curvature by approximating the surface of a sphere—starting with a dodecahedron and adding hexagons. (Euler's theorem implies that at any stage there must always be exactly 12 pentagonal faces.) The following are examples with 20, 60, 80, 180 and 320 nodes:

The object with 60 nodes is a truncated icosahedron—the shape of a standard soccer ball, as well the shape of the fullerene molecule C_{60}. (Note that in C_{60} one of the connections at each node is always a double chemical bond, since carbon has valence 4.) Geodesic domes are typically duals of such networks—with three edges on each face.

■ **Hyperbolic networks.** Any surface that always has positive curvature must eventually close up to form something like a sphere. But a surface that has negative curvature (and no holes) must in some sense be infinite—more like cases (c) and (d) on page 412. Yet even in such a case one can always define coordinates that nominally allow the surface to be drawn in a finite way—and the Poincaré disk model used in the pictures below is the standard way of doing this. In ordinary flat space, regular polygons with more than 6 sides can never form a tessellation. But in a space with negative curvature this is possible for polygons with arbitrarily many sides—and the networks that result have been much studied as Cayley graphs of Fuchsian groups. One feature of these networks is that the number of nodes reached in them by following r connections always grows like 2^r. But if one intersperses hexagons in the networks (as in the main text) then one finds that for small r the number of nodes just grows like r^2—as one would expect for something like a 2D surface. But if one tries to look at growth rates on scales that are not small compared to characteristic lengths associated with curvature then one again sees exponential growth—just as in the case of a uniform tessellation without hexagons.

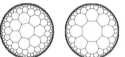

■ **Page 533 · Sphere volumes.** In ordinary flat Euclidean space the area of a 2D circle is πr^2, and the volume of a 3D sphere $4\pi r^3/3$. In general, the volume of a sphere in d-dimensional Euclidean space is $s[d]r^d$ where $s[d] = \pi^{d/2}/(d/2)!$ (the surface area is $d\,s[d]r^{d-1}$). (The function $s[d]$ has a maximum around $d = 5.26$, then decreases rapidly with d.)

If instead of flat space one considers a space defined by the surface of a 3D sphere—say with radius a—one can ask about areas of circles in this space. Such circles are no longer flat, but instead are like caps on the sphere—with a circle of radius r containing all points that are geodesic (great circle) distance less than r from its center. Such a circle has area

$$2\pi a^2(1 - Cos[r/a]) = \pi r^2(1 - r^2/(12\,a^2) + r^4/(360\,a^4) - ...)$$

In the d-dimensional space corresponding to the surface of a $(d+1)$-dimensional sphere of radius a, the volume of a d-dimensional sphere of radius r is similarly given by

$$d\,s[d]a^d\,Integrate[Sin[\theta]^{d-1}, \{\theta, 0, r/a\}] =$$
$$s[d]r^d(1 - d(d-1)r^2/((6(d+2))a^2) +$$
$$(d(5d^2 - 12d + 7))r^4/((360(d+4))a^4) + ...)$$

where

$$Integrate[Sin[x]^{d-1}, x] = -Cos[x]$$
$$Hypergeometric2F1[1/2, (2-d)/2, 3/2, Cos[x]^2]$$

In an arbitrary d-dimensional space the volume of a sphere can depend on position, but in general it is given by

$$s[d]r^d(1 - RicciScalar\,r^2/(6(d+2)) + ...)$$

where the Ricci scalar curvature is evaluated at the position of the sphere. (The space corresponding to a $(d+1)$-dimensional sphere has $RicciScalar = d(d-1)/a^2$.) The $d = 2$ version of this formula was derived in 1848; the general case in 1917 and 1939. Various derivations can be given. One can

start from the fact that the volume density in any space is given in terms of the metric by $Sqrt[Det[g]]$. But in normal coordinates the first non-trivial term in the expansion of the metric is proportional to the Riemann tensor, yet the symmetry of a spherical volume makes it inevitable that the Ricci scalar is the only combination of components that can appear at lowest order. To next order the result is

$$s[d]r^d(1 - RicciScalar\,r^2/(6(d+2)) +$$
$$(5\,RicciScalar^2 - 3\,RiemannNorm + 8\,RicciNorm -$$
$$18\,Laplacian[RicciScalar])r^4/(360(d+2)(d+4)) + ...)$$

where the new quantities involved are

$$RicciNorm = Norm[RicciTensor, \{g, g\}]$$
$$RiemannNorm = Norm[Riemann, \{g, g, g, Inverse[g]\}]$$
$$Norm[t\_, gl\_] := Tr[Flatten[t\,Dual[t, gl]]]$$
$$Dual[t\_, gl\_] := Fold[Transpose[\#1 . Inverse[\#2], RotateLeft[$$
$$Range[TensorRank[t]]]] \&, t, Reverse[gl]]$$
$$Laplacian[f\_] := Inner[D, Sqrt[Det[g]]$$
$$(Inverse[g] . Map[\partial_\# f \&, p]), p]/Sqrt[Det[g]]$$

In general the series in r may not converge, but it is known that at least in most cases only flat space can give a result that shows no correction to the basic r^d form. It is also known that if the Ricci tensor is non-negative, then the volume never grows faster than r^d.

■ **Cylinder volumes.** In any d-dimensional space, the volume of a cylinder of length x and radius r whose direction is defined by a unit vector v turns out to be given by

$$s[d-1]r^{d-1}x$$
$$(1 - (d-1)(RicciScalar - RicciTensor . v . v)r^2/(d+1) + ...)$$

Note that what determines the volume of the cylinder is curvature orthogonal to its direction—and this is what leads to the combination of Ricci scalar and tensor that appears.

■ **Page 533 · Discrete spaces.** Most work with surfaces done on computers—whether for computer graphics, computer-aided design, solving boundary value problems or otherwise—makes use of discrete approximations. Typically surfaces are represented by collections of patches—with a simple mesh of triangles often being used. The triangles are however normally specified not so much by their network of connections as by the explicit coordinates of their vertices. And while there are various triangulation methods that for example avoid triangles with small angles, no standard method yields networks analogous to the ones I consider in which all triangle edges are effectively the same length.

In pure mathematics a basic idea in topology has been to look for finite or discrete ways to capture essential features of continuous surfaces and spaces. And as an early part of this Henri Poincaré in the 1890s introduced the concept of approximating manifolds by cell complexes consisting of collections of generalized polyhedra. By the 1920s there was then extensive work on so-called combinatorial topology, in which spaces are thought of as being decomposed into abstract complexes consisting say of triangles, tetrahedra and higher-dimensional simplices. But while explicit coordinates and lengths are not usually discussed, it is still imagined that one knows more information than in the networks I consider: not only how vertices are connected by edges, but also how edges are arranged around faces, faces around volumes, and so on. And while in 2D and 3D it is possible to set up such an approximation to any manifold in this way, it turns out that at least in 5D and above it is not. Before the 1960s it had been hoped that in accordance with the Hauptvermutung of combinatorial topology it would be possible to tell whether a continuous mapping and thus topological equivalence exists between manifolds just by seeing whether subdivisions of simplicial complexes for them could be identical. But in the 1960s it was discovered that at least in 5D and above this will not always work. And largely as a result of this, there has tended to be less interest in ideas like simplicial complexes.

And indeed a crucial point for my discussion in the main text is that in formulating general relativity one actually does not appear to need all the structure of a simplicial complex. In fact, the only features of manifolds that ultimately seem relevant are ones that in appropriate limits are determined just from the connectivity of networks. The details of the limits are mathematically somewhat intricate (compare page 1030), but the basic approach is straightforward. One can find the volume of a sphere (geodesic ball) in a network just by counting the number of nodes out to a given network distance from a certain node. And from the limiting growth rate of this one can immediately get the Ricci scalar curvature—just as in the continuous case discussed above. To get the Ricci tensor one also needs a direction. But one can get this from a geodesic—which is in effect the analog of a straight line in the network. Note that unlike in a continuous space there is however usually no obvious way to continue a geodesic in a network. And in general, some—but not all—of the standard constructions used in continuous spaces can also immediately be used in networks. So for example it is straightforward to construct a triangle in a network: one just starts from a particular node, follows geodesics to two others, then joins these with a geodesic. But to extend the triangle into a parallelogram is not so easy—since there is no immediate notion of parallelism in the network. And this means that neither the Riemann tensor, nor a so-called Schild ladder for parallel transport, can readily be constructed.

Since the 1980s there has been increasing interest in formulating notions of continuous geometry for objects like Cayley graphs of groups—which are fundamentally discrete but have infinite limits analogous to continuous systems. (Compare page 938.)

■ **Manifold undecidability.** Given a particular set of network substitution rules there is in general no finite way to decide whether any sequence of such rules exists that will transform particular networks into each other. (Compare undecidability in multiway systems on page 779.) And although one might not expect it on the basis of traditional mathematical intuition, there is an analog of this even for topological equivalence of ordinary continuous manifolds. For the fundamental groups that represent how basic loops can be combined must be equivalent for equivalent manifolds. Yet it turns out that in 4D and above the fundamental group can have essentially any set of generators and relations—so that the undecidability of the word problem for arbitrary groups (see page 1141) implies undecidability of equivalence of manifolds. (In 2D it is straightforward to decide equivalence, and in 3D it is known that only some fundamental groups can be obtained—roughly because not all networks can be embedded in 2D—and it is expected that it will ultimately be possible to decide equivalence.)

■ **Non-integer dimensions.** Unlike in traditional differential geometry (and general relativity) my formulation of space as a network potentially allows concepts like curvature to be defined even outside of integers numbers of dimensions.

■ **Page 534 · Lorentzian spaces.** In ordinary Euclidean space distance is given by $Sqrt[x^2 + y^2 + z^2]$. In setting up relativity theory it is convenient (see page 1042) to define an analog of distance (so-called proper time) in 4D spacetime by $Sqrt[c^2 t^2 - x^2 - y^2 - z^2]$. And in terms of differential geometry such Minkowski space can be specified by the metric $DiagonalMatrix[\{+1, -1, -1, -1\}]$ (now taking $c = 1$). To set up general relativity one then considers not Riemannian manifolds but instead Lorentzian ones in which the metric is not positive definite, but instead has the signature of Minkowski space.

In such Lorentzian spaces, however, there is no useful immediate analog of a sphere. For given any point, even the light cone that corresponds to points at zero spacetime distance from it has an infinite volume. But with an appropriate definition one can still set up cones that have finite volume. To do this in general one starts by picking a vector e in a timelike direction, then normalizes it to be a unit vector so that $e \cdot g \cdot e == -1$. Then one defines a cone of height t whose apex is a given point to be those points whose displacement vector v satisfies $0 > e \cdot g \cdot v > -t$ (and $0 > v \cdot g \cdot v$). And the volume of such a cone then turns out to be

$s[d] t^{d+1} (1 - t^2 (d + 1) (d \, RicciScalar + 2 (d + 1) (RicciTensor \cdot e \cdot e))/((d + 2)(d + 3)) + ...)/(d + 1)$

■ **Torsion.** In standard geometry, one assumes that the distance from one point to another is the same as the distance back, so that the metric tensor can be taken to be symmetric, and there is zero so-called torsion. But in for example a causal network, connections have definite directions, and there is in general no such symmetry. And if one looks at the volume of a cone this can then introduce a correction proportional to r. But as soon as there is enough uniformity to define a reasonable notion of static space, it seems that this effect must vanish. (Note that in pure mathematics there are several different uses of the word "torsion". Here I use it to refer to the antisymmetric parts of the metric tensor.)

■ **Random causal networks.** If one assumes that there are events at random positions in continuous spacetime, then one can construct an effective causal network for them by setting up connections between each event and all events in its future light cone—then deleting connections that are redundant in the sense that they just provide shortcuts to events that could otherwise be reached by following multiple connections. The pictures below show examples of causal networks obtained in this way. The number of connections generally increases faster than linearly with the number of events. Most links end up being at angles that are close to the edge of the light cone.

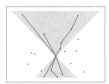

■ **Page 534 · Einstein equations.** In the absence of matter, the standard statement of the Einstein equations is that all components of the Ricci tensor—and thus also the Ricci scalar—must be zero (or formally that $R_{ij} = 0$). But since the vanishing of all components of a tensor must be independent of the coordinates used, it follows that the vacuum Einstein equations are equivalent to the statement $RicciTensor \cdot e \cdot e == 0$ for all timelike unit vectors e—a statement that can readily be applied to networks of the kind I consider in the main text. (A related statement is that the 3D Ricci scalar curvature of all spacelike hypersurfaces must vanish wherever these have vanishing extrinsic curvature.)

Another way to state the Einstein equations—already discussed by David Hilbert in 1915—is as the constraint that the integral of $RicciScalar \, Sqrt[Det[g]]$ (the so-called Einstein-Hilbert action) be an extremum. (An idealized soap film or other minimal surface extremizes the integral of the intrinsic volume element $Sqrt[Det[g]]$, without a $RicciScalar$ factor.) In the discrete Regge calculus that I mention on page 1054 this variational principle turns out to have a rather simple form.

The Einstein-Hilbert action—and the Einstein equations—can be viewed as having the simplest forms that do not ultimately depend on the choice of coordinates. Higher-order terms—say powers of the Ricci scalar curvature—could well arise from underlying network systems, but would not contribute noticeably except in very high gravitational fields.

Various physical interpretations can be given of the vanishing of the Ricci tensor implied by the ordinary vacuum Einstein equations. Closely related to my discussion of the absence of t^2 terms in volume growth for 4D spacetime cones is the statement that if one sets up a small 3D ball of comoving test particles then the volume it defines must have zero first and second derivatives with time.

Below 4D the vanishing of the Ricci tensor immediately implies the vanishing of all components of the Riemann tensor—so that the vacuum Einstein equations force space at least locally to have its ordinary flat form. (Even in 2D there can nevertheless still be non-trivial global topology—for example with flat space having its edges identified as on a torus. In the Euclidean case there were for a long time no non-trivial solutions to the Einstein equations known in any number of dimensions, but in the 1970s examples were found, including large families of Calabi-Yau manifolds.)

In the presence of matter, the typical formal statement of the full Einstein equations is $R_{\mu\nu} - R g_{\mu\nu}/2 = 8 \pi \, G \, T_{\mu\nu}/c^4$, where $T_{\mu\nu}$ is the energy-momentum (stress-energy) tensor for matter and G is the gravitational constant. (An additional so-called cosmological term $\lambda g_{\mu\nu}$ is sometimes added on the right to adjust the effective overall energy density of the universe, and thus its expansion rate. Note that the equation can also be written $R_{\mu\nu} = 8 \pi \, G (T_{\mu\nu} - 1/2 \, T_\mu^\mu \, g_{\mu\nu})/c^4$.) The μ , ν component of $T_{\mu\nu}$ gives the flux of the μ component of 4-momentum (whose components are energy and ordinary 3-momentum) in the ν direction. The fact that T_{00} is energy density implies that for static matter (where $E = m c^2$) the equation is in a sense a minimal extension of Poisson's equation of Newtonian gravity theory. Note that conservation of energy and momentum implies that $T_{\mu\nu}$ must have zero divergence—a result guaranteed in the Einstein equations by the structure of the left-hand side.

In the variational approach to gravity mentioned above, the *RicciScalar* plays the role of a Lagrangian density for pure gravity—and in the presence of matter the Lagrangian density for matter must be added to it. At a physical level, the full Einstein equations can be interpreted as saying that the volume v of a small ball of comoving test particles satisfies

$$\partial_{tt} v[t]/v[t] == -1/2\,(\rho + 3\,p)$$

where ρ is the total energy density and p is the pressure averaged over all space directions.

To solve the full Einstein equations in any particular physical situation requires a knowledge of $T_{\mu\nu}$—and thus of properties of matter such as the relation between pressure and energy density (equation of state). Quite a few global results about the formation of singularities and the absence of paths looping around in time can nevertheless be obtained just by assuming certain so-called energy conditions for $T_{\mu\nu}$. (A fairly stringent example is $0 \leq p \leq \rho/3$—and whether this is actually true for non-trivial interacting quantum fields remains unclear.)

In their usual formulation, the Einstein equations are thought of as defining constraints on the structure of 4D spacetime. But at some level they can also be viewed as defining how 3D space evolves with time. And indeed the so-called initial value formulations constructed in the 1960s allow one to start with a 3D metric and various extrinsic curvatures defined for a 3D spacelike hypersurface, and then work out how these change on successive hypersurfaces. But at least in terms of tensors, the equations involved show nothing like the simplicity of the usual 4D Einstein equations. One can potentially view the causal networks that I discuss in the main text as providing another approach to setting up an initial value formulation of the Einstein equations.

■ **Page 536 · Pure gravity.** In the absence of matter, the Einstein equations always admit ordinary flat Minkowski space as a solution. But they also admit other solutions that in effect represent configurations of pure gravitational field. And in fact the 4D vacuum Einstein equations are already a sophisticated set of nonlinear partial differential equations that can support all sorts of complex behavior. Several tens of families of solutions to the equations have been found—some with obvious physical interpretations, others without.

Already in 1916 Karl Schwarzschild gave the solution for a spherically symmetric gravitational field. He imagined that this field itself existed in a vacuum—but that it was produced by a mass such as a star at its center. In its original form the metric becomes singular at radius $2\,G\,m/c^2$ (or $3\,m$ km with m in solar masses). At first it was assumed that this would always be inside a star, where the vacuum Einstein equations

would not apply. But in the 1930s it was suggested that stars could collapse to concentrate their mass in a smaller radius. The singularity was then interpreted as an event horizon that separates the interior of a black hole from the ordinary space around it. In 1960 it was realized, however, that appropriate coordinates allowed smooth continuation across the event horizon—and that the only genuine singularity was infinite curvature at a single point at the center. Sometimes it was said that this must reflect the presence of a point mass, but soon it was typically just said to be a point at which the Einstein equations—for whatever reason—do not apply. Different choices of coordinates led to different apparent locations and forms of the singularity, and by the late 1970s the most common representation was just a smooth manifold with a topology reflecting the removal of a point—and without any specific reference to the presence of matter.

Appealing to ideas of Ernst Mach from the late 1800s it has often been assumed that to get curvature in space always eventually requires the presence of matter. But in fact even the vacuum Einstein equations for complete universes (with no points left out) have solutions that show curvature. If one assumes that space is both homogeneous and isotropic then it turns out that only ordinary flat Minkowski space is allowed. (When matter or a cosmological term is present one gets different solutions—that always expand or contract, and are much studied in cosmology.) If anisotropy is present, however, then there can be all sorts of solutions—classified for example as having different Bianchi symmetry types. And a variety of inhomogeneous solutions with no singularities are also known—an example being the 1962 Ozsváth-Schücking rotating vacuum. But in all cases the structure is too simple to capture much that seems relevant for our present universe.

One form of solution to the vacuum Einstein equations is a gravitational wave consisting of a small perturbation propagating through flat space. No solutions have yet been found that represent complete universes containing emitters and absorbers of such waves (or even for example just two massive bodies). But it is known that combinations of gravitational waves can be set up that will for example evolve to generate singularities. And I suspect that nonlinear interactions between such waves will also inevitably lead to the analog of turbulence for pure gravity. (Numerical simulations often show all sorts of complex behavior—but in the past this has normally been attributed just to the approximations used. Note that for example Bianchi type IX solutions for a complete universe show sensitive dependence on initial conditions—and no doubt this can also happen with nonlinear gravitational waves.)

As mentioned on page 1028, Albert Einstein considered the possibility that particles of matter might somehow just be localized structures in gravitational and electromagnetic fields. And in the mid-1950s John Wheeler studied explicit simple examples of such so-called geons. But in all cases they were found to be unstable—decaying into ordinary gravitational waves. The idea of having purely gravitational localized structures has also occasionally been considered—but so far no stable field configuration has been found. (And no purely repetitive solutions can exist.)

The equivalence principle (see page 1047) might suggest that anything with mass—or energy—should affect the curvature of space in the same way. But in the Einstein equations the energy-momentum tensor is not supposed to include contributions from the gravitational field. (There are alternative and seemingly inelegant theories of gravity that work differently—and notably do not yield black holes. The setup is also somewhat different in recent versions of string theory.) The very definition of energy for the gravitational field is not particularly straightforward in general relativity. But perhaps a definition could be found that would allow localized structures in the gravitational field to make effective contributions to the energy-momentum tensor that would mimic those from explicit particles of matter. Nevertheless, there are quite a few phenomena associated with particles that seem difficult to reproduce with pure gravity—at least say without extra dimensions. One example is parity violation; another is the presence of long-range forces other than gravity.

▪ **Quantum gravity.** That there should be quantum effects in gravity was already noted in the 1910s, and when quantum field theory began to develop in the 1930s, there were immediately attempts to apply it to gravity. The first idea was to represent gravity as a field that exists in flat spacetime, and by analogy with photons in quantum electrodynamics to introduce gravitons (at one point identified with neutrinos). By the mid-1950s a path integral (see page 1061) based on the Einstein-Hilbert action had been constructed, and by the early 1960s Feynman diagram rules had been derived, and it had been verified that tree diagrams involving gravitons gave results that agreed with general relativity for small gravitational fields. But as soon as loop diagrams were considered, infinities began to appear. And unlike for quantum electrodynamics there did not seem to be only a finite number of these—that could be removed by renormalization. And in fact by 1973 gravity coupled to matter had been shown for certain not to be renormalizable—and the same was finally shown for pure gravity in 1986. There was an attempt in the 1970s and early 1980s to look

directly at the path integral—without doing an expansion in terms of Feynman diagrams. But despite the fact that at least in Euclidean spacetime a variety of seemingly relevant field configurations were identified, many mathematical difficulties were encountered. And in the late-1970s there began to be interest in the idea that supersymmetric field theories might make infinities associated with gravitons be cancelled by ones associated with other particles. But in the end this did not work out. And then in the mid-1980s one of the great attractions of string theory was that it seemed to support graviton excitations without the problem of infinities seen in point-particle field theories. But it had other problems, and to avoid these, supersymmetry had to be introduced, leading to the presence of many other particles that have so far not been observed. (See also page 1029.)

Starting in the 1950s a rather different approach to quantum gravity involved trying to find a representation of the structure of spacetime in which a quantum analog of the Einstein equations could be obtained by the formal procedure of canonical quantization (see page 1058). Yet despite a few signs of progress in the 1960s there was great difficulty in finding appropriately independent variables to use. In the late 1980s, however, it was suggested that variables could be used corresponding roughly to gravitational fluxes through loops in space. And in terms of these loop variables it was at least formally possible to write down a version of quantum gravity. Yet while this was found in the 1990s to have a correspondence with spin networks (see below), it has remained impossible to see just how it might yield ordinary general relativity as a limit.

Even if one assumes that spacetime is in a sense ultimately continuous one can imagine investigating quantum gravity by doing some kind of discrete approximation. And in 1961 Tullio Regge noted that for a simplicial complex (see page 1050) the Einstein-Hilbert action has a rather simple form in terms of angles between edges. Starting in the 1980s after the development of lattice gauge theories, simulations of random surfaces and higher-dimensional spaces set up in this way were done—often using so-called dynamic triangulation based on random sequences of generalized Alexander moves from page 1038. But there were difficulties with Lorentzian spaces, and when large-scale average behavior was studied, it seemed difficult to reproduce observed smooth spacetime. Analytical approaches (that happened to be like 0D string theory) were also found for 2D discrete spacetimes (compare page 1038)—but they were not successfully extended to higher dimensions.

Over the years, various attempts have been made to derive quantum gravity from fundamentally discrete models of spacetime (compare page 1027). In recent times the most widely discussed have been spin networks—which despite their name ultimately seem to have fairly little to do with the systems I consider. Spin networks were introduced in 1964 by Roger Penrose as a way to set up an intrinsically quantum mechanical model of spacetime. A simple analog involves a 2D surface made out of triangles whose edges have integer lengths j_i. If one computes the product of $Exp[i(j_1 + j_2 - j_3)]$ for all triangles, then it turns out for example that this quantity is extremized exactly when the whole surface is flat. In 3D one imagines breaking space into tetrahedra whose edge lengths correspond to discrete quantum spin values. And in 1968 Tullio Regge and Giorgio Ponzano suggested—almost as an afterthought in technical work on $6j$ symbols—that the quantum probability amplitude for any form of space might perhaps be given by the product of $6j$ symbols for the spins on each tetrahedron. The $SixJSymbol[\{j_1, j_2, j_3\}, \{j_4, j_5, j_6\}]$ are slightly esoteric objects that correspond to recoupling coefficients for the 3D rotation group SO(3), and that arose in 1940s studies of combinations of three angular momenta in atomic physics— and were often represented graphically as networks. For large j_i they are approximated by $Cos[\theta + \pi/4]/Sqrt[12 \pi v]$, where v is the volume of the tetrahedron and θ is a deficit angle. And from this it turns out that limits of products of $6j$ symbols correspond essentially to $Exp[is]$, where s is the discrete form of the Einstein-Hilbert action—extremized by flat 3D space. (The picture below shows for example $Abs[SixJSymbol[\{j, j, j\}, \{j, j, j\}]]$. Note that for any j the $6j$ symbols can be given in terms of $HypergeometricPFQ$.)

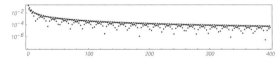

In the early 1990s there was again interest in spin networks when the Turaev-Viro invariant for 3D spaces was discovered from a topological field theory involving triangulations weighted with $6j$ symbols of the quantum group $SU(2)_q$— and it was seen that invariance under Alexander moves on the triangulation corresponded to the Biedenharn-Elliott identity for $6j$ symbols. In the mid-1990s it was then found that states in 3D loop quantum gravity (see above) could be represented in terms of spin networks—leading for example to quantization of all areas and volumes. In attempting extensions to 4D, spin foams have been introduced—and variously interpreted in terms of simplified Feynman diagrams, constructs in multidimensional category theory, and possible evolutions of spin networks. In all cases, however, spin networks and spin foams seem to be viewed

just as calculational constructs that must be evaluated and added together to get quantum amplitudes—quite different from my idea of associating an explicit evolution history for the universe with the evolution of a network.

■ **Cosmology.** On a large scale our universe appears to show a uniform expansion that makes progressively more distant galaxies recede from us at progressively higher speeds. In general relativity this is explained by saying that the initial conditions must have involved expansion—and that there is not enough in the way of matter or gravitational fields to produce the gravity to slow down this expansion too much. (Note that as soon as objects get gravitationally bound—like galaxies in clusters—there is no longer expansion between them.) The standard big bang model assumes that the universe starts with matter at what is in effect an arbitrarily high temperature. One issue much discussed in cosmology since the late 1970s is how the universe manages to be so uniform. Thermal equilibrium should eventually lead to uniformity— but different parts of the universe cannot come to equilibrium until there has at least been time for effects to propagate between them. Yet there seems for example to be overall uniformity in what we see if we look in opposite directions in the sky—even though extrapolating from the current rate of expansion there has not been enough time since the beginning of the universe for anything to propagate from one side to the other. But starting in the early 1980s it has been popular to think that early in its history the universe must have undergone a period of exponential expansion or so-called inflation. And what this would do is to take just a tiny region and make it large enough to correspond to everything we can now see in the universe. But the point is that a sufficiently tiny region will have had time to come to thermal equilibrium— and so will be approximately uniform, just as the cosmic microwave background is now observed to be. The actual process of inflation is usually assumed to reflect some form of phase transition associated with decreasing temperature of matter in the universe. Most often it is assumed that in the present universe a delicate balance must exist between energy density from a background Higgs field (see page 1047) and a cosmological term in the Einstein equations (see page 1052). But above a critical temperature thermal fluctuations should prevent the background from forming—leading to at least some period in which the universe is dominated by a cosmological term which yields exponential expansion. There tend to be various detailed problems with this scenario, but at least with a sufficiently complicated setup it seems possible to get results that are consistent with observations made so far.

In the context of the discoveries in this book, my expectation is that the universe started from a simple small network, then progressively added more and more nodes as it evolved, until eventually on a large scale something corresponding to 4D spacetime emerged. And with this setup, the observed uniformity of the universe becomes much less surprising. Intrinsic randomness generation always tends to lead to a certain uniformity in networks. But the crucial point is that this will not take long to happen throughout any network if it is appropriately connected. Traditional models tend to assume that there are ultimately a fixed number of spacetime dimensions in the universe. And with this assumption it is inevitable that if the universe in a sense expands at the speed of light, then regions on opposite sides of it can essentially never share any common history. But in a network model the situation is different. The causal network always captures what happens. And in a case like page 518—with spacetime always effectively having a fixed finite dimension—points that are a distance t apart tend to have common ancestors only at least t steps back. But in a case like (a) on page 514—where spacetime has the structure of an exponentially growing tree—points a distance t apart typically have common ancestors just $Log[t]$ steps back. And in fact many kinds of causal networks—say associated with early randomly connected space networks—will inevitably yield common ancestors for distant parts of the universe. (Note that such phenomena presumably occur at around the Planck scale of 10^{19} GeV rather than at the 10^{15} GeV or lower scale normally discussed in connection with inflation. They can to some extent be captured in general relativity by imagining an effective spacetime dimension that is initially infinite, then gradually decreases to 4.)

Quantum Phenomena

■ **History.** In classical physics quantities like energy were always assumed to correspond to continuous variables. But in 1900 Max Planck noticed that fits to the measured spectrum of electromagnetic radiation produced by hot objects could be explained if there were discrete quanta of electromagnetic energy. And by 1910 work by Albert Einstein, notably on the photoelectric effect and on heat capacities of solids, had given evidence for discrete quanta of energy in both light and matter. In 1913 Niels Bohr then made the suggestion that the discrete spectrum of light emitted by hydrogen atoms could be explained as being produced by electrons making transitions between orbits with discrete quantized angular momenta. By 1920 ideas from celestial mechanics had been used to develop a formalism for quantized orbits which successfully explained various features of atoms and chemical elements. But it was not clear

how to extend the formalism say to a problem like propagation of light through a crystal. In 1925, however, Werner Heisenberg suggested a new and more general formalism that became known as matrix mechanics. The original idea was to imagine describing the state of an atom in terms of an array of amplitudes for virtual oscillators with each possible frequency. Particular conditions amounting to quantization were then imposed on matrices of transitions between these, and the idea was introduced that only certain kinds of amplitude combinations could ever be observed. In 1923 Louis de Broglie had suggested that just as light—which in optics was traditionally described in terms of waves—seemed in some respects to act like discrete particles, so conversely particles like electrons might in some respects act like waves. In 1926 Erwin Schrödinger then suggested a partial differential equation for the wave functions of particles like electrons. And when effectively restricted to a finite region, this equation allowed only certain modes, corresponding to discrete quantum states—whose properties turned out to be exactly the same as implied by matrix mechanics. In the late 1920s Paul Dirac developed a more abstract operator-based formalism. And by the end of the 1920s basic practical quantum mechanics was established in more or less the form it appears in textbooks today. In the period since, increasing computational capabilities have allowed coupled Schrödinger equations for progressively more particles to be solved (reasonably accurate solutions for hundreds of particles can now be found), allowing ever larger studies in atomic, molecular, nuclear and solid-state physics. A notable theoretical interest starting in the 1980s was so-called quantum chaos, in which it was found that modes (wave functions) in regions like stadiums that did not yield simple analytical solutions tended to show complicated and seemingly random forms.

Basic quantum mechanics is set up to describe how fixed numbers of particles behave—say in externally applied electromagnetic or other fields. But to describe things like fields one must allow particles to be created and destroyed. In the mid-1920s there was already discussion of how to set up a formalism for this, with an underlying idea again being to think in terms of virtual oscillators—but now one for each possible state of each possible one of any number of particles. At first this was just applied to a pure electromagnetic field of non-interacting photons, but by the end of the 1920s there was a version of quantum electrodynamics (QED) for interacting photons and electrons that is essentially the same as today. To find predictions from this theory a so-called perturbation expansion was made, with successive terms representing progressively more interactions, and each having a higher power of the so-called coupling constant $\alpha \simeq 1/137$. It was immediately noticed, however, that self-interactions of particles would give rise to infinities, much as in classical electromagnetism. At first attempts were made to avoid this by modifying the basic theory (see page 1044). But by the mid-1940s detailed calculations were being done in which infinite parts were just being dropped—and the results were being found to agree rather precisely with experiments. In the late 1940s this procedure was then essentially justified by the idea of renormalization: that since in all possible QED processes only three different infinities can ever appear, these can in effect systematically be factored out from all predictions of the theory. Then in 1949 Feynman diagrams were introduced (see note below) to represent terms in the QED perturbation expansion—and the rules for these rapidly became what defined QED in essentially all practical applications. Evaluating Feynman diagrams involved extensive algebra, and indeed stimulated the development of computer algebra (including my own interest in the field). But by the 1970s the dozen or so standard processes discussed in QED had been calculated to order α^2—and by the mid-1980s the anomalous magnetic moment of the electron had been calculated to order α^4, and nearly one part in a trillion (see note below).

But despite the success of perturbation theory in QED it did not at first seem applicable to other issues in particle physics. The weak interactions involved in radioactive beta decay seemed too weak for anything beyond lowest order to be relevant—and in any case not renormalizable. And the strong interactions responsible for holding nuclei together (and associated for example with exchange of pions and other mesons) seemed too strong for it to make sense to do an expansion with larger numbers of individual interactions treated as less important. So this led in the 1960s to attempts to base theories just on setting up simple mathematical constraints on the overall so-called S matrix defining the mapping from incoming to outgoing quantum states. But by the end of the 1960s theoretical progress seemed blocked by basic questions about functions of several complex variables, and predictions that were made did not seem to work well.

By the early 1970s, however, there was increasing interest in so-called gauge or Yang-Mills theories formed in essence by generalizing QED to operate not just with a scalar charge, but with charges viewed as elements of non-Abelian groups. In 1972 it was shown that spontaneously broken gauge theories of the kind needed to describe weak interactions were renormalizable—allowing meaningful use of perturbation theory and Feynman diagrams. And then in 1973 it was discovered that QCD—the gauge theory for quarks and gluons with SU(3) color charges—was asymptotically free (it was known to be renormalizable), so that for processes probing sufficiently small distances, its effective coupling was small enough for perturbation theory. By the early 1980s first-order calculations of most basic QCD processes had been done—and by the 1990s second-order corrections were also known. Schemes for adding up all Feynman diagrams with certain very simple repetitive or other structures were developed. But despite a few results about large-distance analogs of renormalizability, the question of what QCD might imply for processes at larger distances could not really be addressed by such methods.

In 1941 Richard Feynman pointed out that amplitudes in quantum theory could be worked out by using path integrals that sum with appropriate weights contributions from all possible histories of a system. (The Schrödinger equation is like a diffusion equation in imaginary time, so the path integral for it can be thought of as like an enumeration of random walks. The idea of describing random walks with path integrals was discussed from the early 1900s.) At first the path integral was viewed mostly as a curiosity, but by the late 1970s it was emerging as the standard way to define a quantum field theory. Attempts were made to see if the path integral for QCD (and later for quantum gravity) could be approximated with a few exact solutions (such as instantons) to classical field equations. By the early 1980s there was then extensive work on lattice gauge theories in which the path integral (in Euclidean space) was approximated by randomly sampling discretized field configurations. But—I suspect for reasons that I discuss in the note below—such methods were never extremely successful. And the result is that beyond perturbation theory there is still no real example of a definitive success from standard relativistic quantum field theory. (In addition, even efforts in the context of so-called axiomatic field theory to set up mathematically rigorous formulations have run into many difficulties—with the only examples satisfying all proposed axioms typically in the end being field theories without any real interactions. In condensed matter physics there are nevertheless cases like the Kondo model where exact solutions have been found, and where the effective energy function for electrons happens to be roughly the same as in a relativistic theory.)

As mentioned on page 1044, ordinary quantum field theory in effect deals only with point particles. And indeed a recurring issue in it has been difficulty with constraints and redundant degrees of freedom—such as those associated with extended objects. (A typical goal is to find variables in which one can carry out what is known as canonical quantization: essentially applying the same straightforward transformation of equations that happens to work in ordinary elementary quantum mechanics.) One feature of string theory and its generalizations is that they define presumably consistent quantum field theories for excitations of extended objects—though an analog of quantum field theory in which whole strings can be created and destroyed has not yet been developed.

When the formalism of quantum mechanics was developed in the mid-1920s there were immediately questions about its interpretation. But it was quickly suggested that given a wave function ψ from the Schrödinger equation $Abs[\psi]^2$ should represent probability—and essentially all practical applications have been based on this ever since. From a conceptual point of view it has however often seemed peculiar that a supposedly fundamental theory should talk only about probabilities. Following the introduction of the uncertainty principle and related formalism in the 1920s one idea that arose was that—in rough analogy to relativity theory—it might just be that there are only certain quantities that are observable in definite ways. But this was not enough, and by the 1930s it was being suggested that the validity of quantum mechanics might be a sign that whole new general frameworks for philosophy or logic were needed—a notion supported by the apparent need to bring consciousness into discussions about measurement in quantum mechanics (see page 1063). The peculiar character of quantum mechanics was again emphasized by the idealized experiment of Albert Einstein, Boris Podolsky and Nathan Rosen in 1935. But among most physicists the apparent lack of an ordinary mechanistic way to think about quantum mechanics ended up just being seen as another piece of evidence for the fundamental role of mathematical formalism in physics.

One way for probabilities to appear even in deterministic systems is for there to be hidden variables whose values are unknown. But following mathematical work in the early 1930s it was usually assumed that this could not be what was going on in quantum mechanics. In 1952 David Bohm did however manage to construct a somewhat elaborate model based on hidden variables that gave the same results as ordinary quantum mechanics—though involved infinitely fast propagation of information. In the early 1960s John Bell then showed that in any hidden variables theory of a certain general type there are specific inequalities that combinations of probabilities must satisfy (see page 1064). And by the early 1980s experiments had shown that such inequalities were indeed violated in practice—so that there were in fact correlations of the kind suggested by quantum mechanics. At first these just seemed like isolated esoteric effects, but by the mid-1990s they were being codified in the field of quantum

information theory, and led to constructions with names like quantum cryptography and quantum teleportation.

Particularly when viewed in terms of path integrals the standard formalism of quantum theory tends to suggest that quantum systems somehow do more computation in their evolution than classical ones. And after occasional discussion as early as the 1950s, this led by the late 1980s to extensive investigation of systems that could be viewed as quantum analogs of idealized computers. In the mid-1990s efficient procedures for integer factoring and a few other problems were suggested for such systems, and by the late 1990s small experiments on these were beginning to be done in various types of physical systems. But it is becoming increasingly unclear just how the idealizations in the underlying model really work, and to what extent quantum mechanics is actually in the end even required—as opposed, say, just to classical wave phenomena. (See page 1147.)

Partly as a result of discussions about measurement there began to be questions in the 1980s about whether ordinary quantum mechanics can describe systems containing very large numbers of particles. Experiments in the 1980s and 1990s on such phenomena as macroscopic superposition and Bose-Einstein condensation nevertheless showed that standard quantum effects still occur with trillions of atoms. But inevitably the kinds of general phenomena that I discuss in this book will also occur—leading to all sorts of behavior that at least cannot readily be foreseen just from the basic rules of quantum mechanics.

■ **Quantum effects.** Over the years, many suggested effects have been thought to be characteristic of quantum systems:

- Basic quantization (1913): mechanical properties of particles in effectively bounded systems are discrete;

- Wave-particle duality (1923): objects like electrons and photons can be described as either waves or particles;

- Spin (1925): particles can have intrinsic angular momentum even if they are of zero size;

- Non-commuting measurements (1926): one can get different results doing measurements in different orders;

- Complex amplitudes (1926): processes are described by complex probability amplitudes;

- Probabilism (1926): outcomes are random, though probabilities for them can be computed;

- Amplitude superposition (1926): there is a linear superposition principle for probability amplitudes;

- State superposition (1926): quantum systems can occur in superpositions of measurable states;

- Exclusion principle (1926): amplitudes cancel for fermions like electrons to go in the same state;

- Interference (1927): probability amplitudes for particles can interfere, potentially destructively;

- Uncertainty principle (1927): quantities like position and momenta have related measurement uncertainties;

- Hilbert space (1927): states of systems are represented by vectors of amplitudes rather than individual variables;

- Field quantization (1927): only discrete numbers of any particular kind of particle can in effect ever exist;

- Quantum tunnelling (1928): particles have amplitudes to go where no classical motion would take them;

- Virtual particles (1932): particles can occur for short times without their usual energy-momentum relation;

- Spinors (1930s): fermions show rotational invariance under SU(2) rather than SO(3);

- Entanglement (1935): separated parts of a system often inevitably behave in irreducibly correlated ways;

- Quantum logic (1936): relations between events do not follow ordinary laws of logic;

- Path integrals (1941): probabilities for behavior are obtained by summing contributions from many paths;

- Imaginary time (1947): statistical mechanics is like quantum mechanics in imaginary time;

- Vacuum fluctuations (1948): there are continual random field fluctuations even in the vacuum;

- Aharanov-Bohm effect (1959): magnetic fields can affect particles even in regions where they have zero strength;

- Bell's inequalities (1964): correlations between events can be larger than in any ordinary probabilistic system;

- Anomalies (1969): virtual particles can have effects that violate the original symmetries of a system;

- Delayed choice experiments (1978): whether particle or wave features are seen can be determined after an event;

- Quantum computing (1980s): there is the potential for fundamental parallelism in computations.

All of these effects are implied by the standard mathematical formalism of quantum theory. But it has never been entirely clear which of them are in a sense true defining features of quantum phenomena, and which are somehow just details. It does not help that most of the effects—at least individually— can be reproduced by mechanisms that seem to have little to do with the usual structure of quantum theory. So for example there will tend to be quantization whenever the

underlying elements of a system are discrete. Similarly, features like the uncertainty principle and path integrals tend to be seen whenever things like waves are involved. And probabilistic effects can arise from any of the mechanisms for randomness discussed in Chapter 7. Complex amplitudes can be thought of just as vector quantities. And it is straightforward to set up rules that will for example reproduce the detailed evolution of amplitudes according say to the Schrödinger equation (see note below). It is somewhat more difficult to set up a system in which such amplitudes will somehow directly determine probabilities. And indeed in recent times consequences of this—such as violations of Bell's inequalities—are what have probably most often been quoted as the most unique features of quantum systems. It is however notable that the vast majority of traditional applications of quantum theory do not seem to have anything to do with such effects. And in fact I do not consider it at all clear just what is really essential about them, and what is in the end just a consequence of the extreme limits that seem to need to be taken to get explicit versions of them.

- **Reproducing quantum phenomena.** Given molecular dynamics it is much easier to see how to reproduce fluid mechanics than rigid-body mechanics—since to get rigid bodies with only a few degrees of freedom requires taking all sorts of limits of correlations between underlying molecules. And I strongly suspect that given a discrete underlying model of the type I discuss here it will similarly be much easier to reproduce quantum field theory than ordinary quantum mechanics. And indeed even with traditional formalism, it is usually difficult to see how quantum mechanics can be obtained as a limit of quantum field theory. (Classical limits are slightly easier: they tend to be associated with stationary features or caustics that occur at large quantum numbers—or coherent states that represent eigenstates of raising or particle creation operators. Note that the exclusion principle makes classical limits for fermions difficult—but crucial for the stability of bulk matter.)

- **Discrete quantum mechanics.** While there are many issues in finding a complete underlying discrete model for quantum phenomena, it is quite straightforward to set up continuous cellular automata whose limiting behavior reproduces the evolution of probability amplitudes in standard quantum mechanics. One starts by assigning a continuous complex number value to each cell. Then given the list of such values the crucial constraint imposed by the standard formalism of quantum mechanics is unitarity: that the quantity $Tr[Abs[list]^2]$ representing total probability should be conserved. This is in a sense analogous to conservation of total density in diffusion processes. From the discussion of page 1024 one can reproduce the 1D diffusion equation with a continuous block cellular automaton in which the new value of each block is given by $\{\{1 - \xi, \xi\}, \{\xi, 1 - \xi\}\} . \{a_1, a_2\}$. So in the case of quantum mechanics one can consider having each new block be given by $\{\{Cos[\theta], i\,Sin[\theta]\}, \{i\,Sin[\theta], Cos[\theta]\}\} . \{a_1, a_2\}$. The pictures below show examples of behavior obtained with this rule. (Gray levels represent magnitude for each cell, and arrows phase.) And it turns out that in suitable limits one generally gets essentially the behavior expected from either the Dirac or Klein-Gordon equations for relativistic particles, or the Schrödinger equation for non-relativistic particles. (Versions of this were noticed by Richard Feynman in the 1940s in connection with his development of path integrals, and were pointed out again several times in the 1980s and 1990s.)

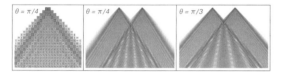

One might hope to be able to get an ordinary cellular automaton with a limited set of possible values by choosing a suitable θ. But in fact in non-trivial cases most of the cells generated at each step end up having distinct values. One can generalize the setup to more dimensions or to allow $n \times n$ matrices that are elements of SU(n). Such matrices can be viewed in the context of ordinary quantum formalism as S matrices for elementary evolution events—and can in general represent interactions. (Note that all rules based on matrices are additive, reflecting the usual assumption of linearity at the level of amplitudes in quantum mechanics. Non-additive unitary rules can also be found. The analog of an external potential can be introduced by progressively changing values of certain cells at each step. Despite their basic setup the systems discussed here are not direct analogs of standard quantum spin systems, since these normally have local Hamiltonians and non-local evolution functions, while the systems here have local evolution functions but seem always to require non-local Hamiltonians.)

■ **Page 540 · Feynman diagrams.** The pictures below show a typical set of Feynman diagrams used to do calculations in QED—in this case for so-called Compton scattering of a photon by an electron. The straight lines in the diagrams represent electrons; the wavy ones photons. At some level each diagram can be thought of as representing a process in which an electron and photon come in from the left, interact in some way, then go out to the right. The incoming and

outgoing lines correspond to real particles that propagate to infinity. The lines inside each diagram correspond to virtual particles that in effect propagate only a limited distance, and have a distribution of energy-momentum and polarization properties that can differ from real particles. (Exchanges of virtual photons can be thought of as producing familiar electromagnetic forces; exchanges of virtual electrons as yielding an analog of covalent forces in chemistry.)

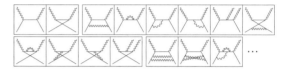

To work out the total probability for a process from Feynman diagrams, what one does is to find the expression corresponding to each diagram, then one adds these up, and squares the result. The first two blocks of pictures above show all the diagrams for Compton scattering that involve 2 or 3 photons—and contribute through order α^3. Since for QED $\alpha \simeq 1/137$, one might expect that this would give quite an accurate result—and indeed experiments suggest that it does. But the number of diagrams grows rapidly with order, and in fact the kth order term can be about $(-1)^k \alpha^k (k/2)!$, yielding a series that formally diverges. In simpler examples where exact results are known, however, the first few terms typically still seem to give numerically accurate results for small α. (The high-order terms often seem to be associated with asymptotic series for things like $Exp[-1/\alpha]$.)

The most extensive calculation made so far in QED is for the magnetic moment of the electron. Ignoring parts that depend on particle masses the result (derived in successive orders from 1, 1, 7, 72, 891 diagrams) is

$$2 (1 + \alpha/(2\,\pi) + (3\,Zeta[3]/4 - 1/2\,\pi^2\,Log[2] + \pi^2/12 + 197/144) (\alpha/\pi)^2 + (83/72\,\pi^2\,Zeta[3] - 215\,Zeta[5]/24 - 239\,\pi^4/2160 + 139\,Zeta[3]/18 + 25/18\,(24\,PolyLog[4, 1/2] + Log[2]^4 - \pi^2\,Log[2]^2) - 298/9\,\pi^2\,Log[2] + 17101\,\pi^2/810 + 28259/5184) (\alpha/\pi)^3 - 1.4\,(\alpha/\pi)^4 + ...)$$

or roughly

$$2. + 0.32\,\alpha - 0.067\,\alpha^2 + 0.076\,\alpha^3 - 0.029\,\alpha^4 + ...$$

The comparative simplicity of the symbolic forms here (which might get still simpler in terms of suitable generalized polylogarithm functions) may be a hint that methods much more efficient than explicit Feynman diagram evaluation could be used. But it seems likely that there would be limits to this, and that in the end QED will exhibit the kind of computational irreducibility that I discuss in Chapter 12.

Feynman diagrams in QCD work at the formal level very much like those in QED—except that there are usually many more of them, and their numerical results tend to be larger, with expansion parameters often effectively being $\alpha \pi$ rather than α/π. For processes with large characteristic momentum transfers in which the effective α in QCD is small, remarkably accurate results are obtained with first and perhaps second-order Feynman diagrams. But as soon as the effective α becomes larger, Feynman diagrams as such rapidly seem to stop being useful.

■ **Quantum field theory.** In standard approaches to quantum field theory one tends to think of particles as some kind of small perturbations in a field. Normally for calculations these perturbations are on their own taken to be plane waves of definite frequency, and indeed in many ways they are direct analogs of waves in classical field theories like those of electromagnetism or fluid mechanics. To investigate collisions between particles, one thus looks at what happens with multiple waves. In a system described by linear equations, there is always a simple superposition principle, and waves just pass through each other unchanged. But what in effect leads to non-trivial interactions between particles is the presence of nonlinearities. If these are small enough then it makes sense to do a perturbation expansion in which one approximates field configurations in terms of a succession of arrangements of ordinary waves—as in Feynman diagrams. But just as one cannot expect to capture fully turbulent fluid flow in terms of a few simple waves, so in general as soon as there is substantial nonlinearity it will no longer be sufficient just to do perturbation expansions. And indeed for example in QCD there are presumably many cases in which it is necessary to look at something closer to actual complete field configurations—and correlations in them.

The way the path integral for a quantum field theory works, each possible configuration of the field is in effect taken to make a contribution $Exp[i\,s/\hbar]$, where s is the so-called action for the field configuration (given by the integral of the Lagrangian density—essentially a modified energy density), and $\hbar$ is a basic scale factor for quantum effects (Planck's constant divided by 2π). In most places in the space of all possible field configurations, the value of s will vary quite quickly between nearby configurations. And assuming this variation is somehow random, the contributions of these nearby configurations will tend to cancel out. But inevitably there will be some places in the space where s is stationary (has zero variational derivative) with respect to changes in fields. And in some approximation the field configurations in these places can be expected to dominate the path integral. But it turns out that these field configurations are exactly the ones that satisfy the partial differential equations for the classical version of the field theory. (This is analogous to what happens for example in classical diffraction theory,

where there is an analog of the path integral—with $\hbar$ replaced by inverse frequency—whose stationary points correspond through the so-called eikonal approximation to rays in geometrical optics.) In cases like QED and QCD the most obvious solutions to the classical equations are ones in which all fields are zero. And indeed standard perturbation theory is based on starting from these and then looking at the expansion of $Exp[i\,s/\hbar]$ in powers of the coupling constant. But while this works for QED, it is only adequate for QCD in situations where the effective coupling is small. And indeed in other situations it seems likely that there will be all sorts of other solutions to the classical equations that become important. But apart from a few special cases with high symmetry, remarkably little is known about solutions to the classical equations even for pure gluon fields. No doubt the analog of turbulence can occur, and certainly there is sensitive dependence on initial conditions (even non-Abelian plane waves involve iterated maps that show this). Presumably much like in fluids there are various coherent structures such as color flux tubes and glueballs. But I doubt that states involving organized arrangements of these are common. And in general when there is strong coupling the path integral will potentially be dominated by large numbers of configurations not close to classical solutions.

In studying quantum field theories it has been common to consider effectively replacing time coordinates t by $i\,t$ to go from ordinary Minowski space to Euclidean space (see page 1043). But while there is no problem in doing this at a formal mathematical level—and indeed the expressions one gets from Feynman diagrams can always be analytically continued in this way—what general correspondence there is for actual physical processes is far from clear. Formally continuing to Euclidean space makes path integrals easier to define with traditional mathematics, and gives them weights of the form $Exp[-\beta\,s]$—analogous to constant temperature systems in statistical mechanics. Discretizing yields lattice gauge theories with energy functions involving for example $Cos[\theta_i - \theta_j]$ for color directions at adjacent sites. And Monte Carlo studies of such theories suggest all sorts of complex behavior, often similar in outline from what appears to occur in the corresponding classical field theories. (It seems conceivable that asymptotic freedom could lead to an analog of damping at small scales roughly like viscosity in turbulent fluids.)

One of the apparent implications of QCD is the confinement of quarks and gluons inside color-neutral hadrons. And at some level this is presumably a reflection of the fact that QCD forces get stronger rather than weaker with increasing distance. The beginnings of this are visible in perturbation theory in the increase of the effective coupling with distance associated with asymptotic freedom. (In QED effective couplings decrease slightly with distance because fields get screened by virtual electron-positron pairs. The same happens with virtual quarks in QCD, but a larger effect is virtual gluon pairs whose color magnetic moments line up with a color field and serve to increase it.) At larger distances something like color flux tubes that act like elastic strings may form. But no detailed way to get confinement with purely classical gluon fields is known. In the quantum case, a sign of confinement would be exponential decrease with spacetime area of the average phase of color flux through so-called Wilson loops—and this is achieved if there is in a sense maximal randomness in field configurations. (Note that it is not inconceivable that the formal problem of whether quarks and gluons can ever escape to infinity starting from some given class of field configurations may in general be undecidable.)

■ **Vacuum fluctuations.** As an analog of the uncertainty principle, one of the implications of the basic formalism of quantum theory is that an ordinary quantum field can in a sense never maintain precisely zero value, but must always show certain fluctuations—even in what one considers the vacuum. And in terms of Feynman diagrams the way this happens is by virtual particle-antiparticle pairs of all types and all energy-momenta continually forming and annihilating at all points in the vacuum. Insofar as such vacuum fluctuations are always exactly the same, however, they presumably cannot be detected. (In the formalism of quantum field theory, they are usually removed by so-called normal ordering. But without this every mode of any quantum system will show a zero-point energy $\hbar\omega/2$—positive in sign for bosons and negative for fermions, cancelling for perfect supersymmetry. Quite what gravitational effects such zero-point energy might have has never been clear.) If one somehow changes the space in which a vacuum exists, there can be directly observable effects of vacuum fluctuations. An example is the 1948 Casimir effect—in which the absence of low-energy (long wavelength) virtual particle pairs in the space between two metal plates (but not in the infinite space outside) leads to a small but measurable force of attraction between them. The different detailed patterns of modes of different fields in different spaces can lead to very different effective vacuum energies—often negative. And at least with the idealization of impermeable classical conducting boundaries one predicts (based on work of mine from 1981) the peculiar effect that closed cycles can be set up that systematically extract energy from vacuum fluctuations in a photon field.

If one has moving boundaries it turns out that vacuum fluctuations can in effect be viewed as producing real particles. And as known since the 1960s, the same is true for expanding universes. What happens in essence is that the modes of fields in different background spacetime structures differ to the point where zero-point excitations seem like actual particle excitations to a detector or observer calibrated to fields in ordinary fixed flat infinite spacetime. And in fact just uniform acceleration turns out to make detectors register real particles in a vacuum—in this case with a thermal spectrum at a temperature proportional to the acceleration. (Uniform rotation also leads to real particles, but apparently with a different spectrum.) As expected from the equivalence principle, a uniform gravitational field should produce the same effect. (Uniform electric fields lead in a formally similar way to production of charged particles.) And as pointed out by Stephen Hawking in 1974, black holes should also generate thermal radiation (at a temperature $\hbar c^3/(8\pi G k M)$). A common interpretation is that the radiated particles are somehow ones left behind when the other particle in a virtual pair goes inside the event horizon. (A similar explanation can be given for uniform acceleration—for which there is also an event horizon.) There has been much discussion of the idea that Hawking radiation somehow shows pure quantum states spontaneously turning into mixed ones, more or less as in quantum measurements. But presumably this is just a reflection of the idealization involved in looking at quantum fields in a fixed background classical spacetime. And indeed work in string theory in the mid-1990s may suggest ways in which quantum gravity configurations of black hole surfaces could maintain the information needed for the whole system to act as a pure state.

■ **Page 542 · Quantum measurement.** The basic mathematical formalism used in standard quantum theory to describe pure quantum processes deals just with vectors of probability amplitudes. Yet our everyday experience of the physical world is that we observe definite things to happen. And the way this is normally captured is by saying that when an observation is made the vector of amplitudes is somehow replaced by its projection s into a subspace corresponding to the outcome seen—with the probability of getting the outcome being taken to be determined by s . Conjugate[s].

At the level of pure quantum processes, the standard rules of quantum theory say that amplitudes should be added as complex numbers—with the result that they can for example potentially cancel each other, and generally lead to wave-like interference phenomena. But after an observation is made, it is in effect assumed that a system can be described by ordinary real-number probabilities—so that for example no interference is possible. (At a formal level, results of pure quantum processes are termed pure quantum states, and are characterized by vectors of probability amplitudes; results of all possible observations are termed mixed states, and are in effect represented as mixtures of pure states.)

Ever since the 1930s there have been questions about just what should count as an observation. To explain everyday experience, conscious perception presumably always must. But it was not clear whether the operation of inanimate measuring devices of various kinds also should. And a major apparent problem was that if everything—including the measuring device—is supposed to be treated as part of the same quantum system, then all of it must follow the rules for pure quantum processes, which do not explicitly include any reduction of the kind supposed to occur in observations.

One approach to getting around this suggested in the late 1950s is the many-worlds interpretation (see page 1035): that there is in a sense a universal pure quantum process that involves all possible outcomes for every conceivable observation, and that represents the tree of all possible threads of history—but that in a particular thread, involving a particular sequence of tree branches, and representing a particular thread of experience for us, there is in effect a reduction in the pure quantum process at each branch point. Similar schemes have been popular in quantum cosmology since the early 1990s in connection with studying wave functions for the complete universe.

A quite different—and I think much more fruitful—approach is to consider analyzing actual potential measurement processes in the context of ordinary quantum mechanics. For even if one takes these processes to be pure quantum ones, what I believe is that in almost all cases appropriate idealized limits of them will reproduce what are in effect the usual rules for observations in quantum theory. A key point is that for one to consider something a reasonable measurement it must in a sense yield a definitive result. And in the context of standard quantum theory this means that somehow all the probability amplitudes associated with the measuring device must in effect be concentrated in specific outcomes—with no significant interference between different outcomes.

If one has just a few quantum particles—governed say by an appropriate Schrödinger equation—then presumably there can be no such concentration. But with a sufficiently large number of particles—and appropriate interactions—one expects that there can be. At first this might seem impossible. For the basic rules for pure quantum processes are entirely reversible (unitary). So one might think that if the evolution of a system leads to concentration of amplitudes, then it

should equally well lead to the reverse. But the crucial point is that while this may in principle be possible, it may essentially never happen in practice—just like classical reversible systems essentially never show behavior that goes against the Second Law of thermodynamics. As suggested by the main text, the details in the quantum measurement case are slightly more complicated—since to represent multiple outcomes measuring devices typically have to have the analogs of multiple equilibrium states. But the basic phenomena are ultimately very similar—and both are in effect based on the presence of microscopic randomness. (In a quantum system the randomness serves to give collections of complex numbers whose average is essentially always zero.)

This so-called decoherence approach was discussed in the 1930s, and finally began to become popular in the 1980s. But to make it work there needs to be some source of appropriate randomness. And almost without exception what has been assumed is that this must come through the first mechanism discussed in Chapter 7: that there is somehow randomness present in the environment that always gets into the system one is looking at. Various different specific mechanisms for this have been suggested, including ones based on ambient low-frequency photons, background quantum vacuum fluctuations and background spacetime metric fluctuations. (A somewhat related proposal involves quantum gravity effects in which irreversibility is assumed to be generated through analogs of the black hole processes mentioned in the previous note.) And indeed in recent practical experiments where simple pure quantum states have carefully been set up, they seem to be destroyed by randomness from the environment on timescales of at most perhaps microseconds. But this does not mean that in more complicated systems more characteristic of real measuring devices there may not be other sources of randomness that end up dominating.

One might imagine that a possibility would be the second mechanism for randomness from Chapter 7, based on ideas of chaos theory. For certainly in the standard formalism, quantum probability amplitudes are taken to be continuous quantities in which an arbitrary number of digits can be specified. But at least for a single particle, the Schrödinger equation is in all ways linear, and so it cannot support any kind of real sensitivity to initial conditions, or even to parameters. But when many particles are involved the situation can presumably be different, as it definitely can be in quantum field theory (see page 1061).

I suspect, however, that in fact the most important source of randomness in most cases will instead be the phenomenon of intrinsic randomness generation that I first discovered in systems like the rule 30 cellular automaton. Just like in so many other areas, the emphasis on traditional mathematical methods has meant that for the most part fundamental studies have been made only on quantum systems that in the end turn out to have fairly simple behavior. Yet even within the standard formalism of quantum theory there are actually no doubt many closed systems that intrinsically manage to produce complex and seemingly random behavior even with very simple parameters and initial conditions. And in fact some clear signs of this were already present in studies of so-called quantum chaos in the 1980s—although most of the specific cases actually considered involved time-independent constraint satisfaction, not explicit time evolution. Curiously, what the Principle of Computational Equivalence suggests is that when quantum systems intrinsically produce apparent randomness they will in the end typically be capable of doing computations just as sophisticated as any other system—and in particular just as sophisticated as would be involved in conscious perception.

As a practical matter, mechanisms like intrinsic randomness generation presumably allow systems involving macroscopic numbers of particles to yield behavior in which interference becomes astronomically unlikely. But to reproduce the kind of exact reduction of probability amplitudes that is implied by the standard formalism of quantum theory inevitably requires taking the limit of an infinite system. Yet the Principle of Computational Equivalence suggests that the results of such a limit will typically be non-computable. (Using quantum field theory to represent infinite numbers of particles presumably cannot help; after appropriate analysis of the fairly sophisticated continuous mathematics involved, exactly the same computational issues should arise.)

It is often assumed that quantum systems should somehow easily be able to generate perfect randomness. But any sequence of bits one extracts must be deduced from a corresponding sequence of measurements. And certainly in practice—as mentioned on pages 303 and 970—correlations in the internal states of measuring devices between successive measurements will tend to lead to deviations from randomness. Whatever generates randomness and brings measuring devices back to equilibrium will eventually damp out such correlations. But insofar as measuring devices must formally involve infinite numbers of particles this process will formally require infinitely many steps. So this means that in effect an infinite computation is actually being done to generate each new bit. But with this amount of computation there are many ways to generate random bits. And in fact an infinite computation could even in principle produce algorithmic randomness (see page 1067) of the kind that is implicitly suggested by the

traditional continuous mathematical formalism of quantum theory. So what this suggests is that there may in the end be no clear way to tell whether randomness is coming from an underlying quantum process that is being measured, or from the actual process of measurement. And indeed when it comes to more realistic finite measuring devices I would not be surprised if most of the supposed quantum randomness they measure is actually more properly attributed to intrinsic randomness generation associated with their internal mechanisms.

■ **Page 543 · Bell's inequalities.** In classical physics one can set up light waves that are linearly polarized with any given orientation. And if these hit polarizing ("anti-glare") filters whose orientation is off by an angle θ, then the waves transmitted will have intensity $Cos[\theta]^2$. In quantum theory the quantization of particle spin implies that any photon hitting a polarizing filter will always either just go through or be absorbed—so that in effect its spin measured relative to the orientation of the polarizer is either +1 or -1. A variety of atomic and other processes give pairs of photons that are forced to have total spin 0. And in what is essentially the Einstein-Podolsky-Rosen setup mentioned on page 1058 one can ask what happens if such photons are made to hit polarizers whose orientations differ by angle θ. In ordinary quantum theory, a straightforward calculation implies that the expected value of the product of the two measured spin values will be $-Cos[\theta]$. But now imagine instead that when each photon is produced it is assigned some "hidden variable" ϕ that in effect explicitly specifies the angle of its polarization. Then assume that a polarizer oriented at $0°$ will measure the spin of such a photon to have value $f[\phi]$ for some fixed function f. Now the expected value of the product of the two measured spin values is found just by averaging over ϕ as

$$Integrate[f[\phi] f[\theta - \phi], \{\phi, 0, 2\pi\}]/(2\pi)$$

A version of Bell's inequalities is then that this integral can decrease with θ no faster than $\theta/(2\pi) - 1$—as achieved when $f = Sign$. (In 3D ϕ must be extended to a sphere, but the same final result holds.) Yet as mentioned on page 1058, actual experiments show that in fact the decrease with θ is more rapid—and is instead consistent with the quantum theory result $-Cos[\theta]$. So what this means is that there is in a sense more correlation between measurements made on separated photons than can apparently be explained by the individual photons carrying any kind of explicit hidden property. (In the standard formalism of quantum theory this is normally explained by saying that the two photons can only meaningfully be considered as part of a single "entangled" state. Note that because of the probabilistic nature of the correlations it turns out to be impossible to use them to do anything that would normally be considered communicating information faster than the speed of light.)

A basic assumption in deriving Bell's inequalities is that the choice of polarizer angle for measuring one photon is not affected by the choice of angle for the other. And indeed experiments have been done which try to enforce this by choosing the angles for the polarizers only just before the photons reach them—and too close in time for a light signal to get from one to the other. Such experiments again show violations of Bell's inequalities. But inevitably the actually devices that work out choices of polarizer angles must be in causal contact as part of setting up the experiment. And although it seems contrived, it is thus at least conceivable that with a realistic model for their time evolution such devices could end up operating in just such a way as to yield observed violations of Bell's inequalities.

Another way to get violations of Bell's inequalities is to allow explicit instantaneous propagation of information. But traditional models involving for example a background quantum potential again seem quite contrived, and difficult to generalize to relativistic cases. The approach I discuss in the main text is quite different, in effect using the idea that in a network model of space there can be direct connections between particles that do not in a sense ever have to go through ordinary intermediate points in space.

When set up for pairs of particles, Bell's inequalities tend just to provide numerical constraints on probabilities. But for triples of particles, it was noticed in the late 1980s that they can give constraints that force probabilities to be 0 or 1, implying that with the assumptions made, certain configurations of measurement results are simply impossible.

In quantum field theory the whole concept of measurement is much less developed than in quantum mechanics—not least because in field theory it is much more difficult to factor out subsystems, and so to avoid having to give explicit descriptions of measuring devices. But at least in axiomatic quantum field theory it is typically assumed that one can somehow measure expectation values of any suitably smeared product of field operators. (It is possible that these could be reconstructed from combinations of idealized scattering experiments). And to get a kind of analog of Bell's inequalities one can look at correlations defined by such expectation values for field operators at spacelike-separated points (too close in time for light signals to get from one to another). And it then turns out that even in the vacuum state the vacuum fluctuations that are present show nonzero such correlations—an analog of ordinary quantum mechanical entanglement. (In a non-interacting approximation these correlations turn out to be as large as is mathematically possible, but fall off exponentially outside the light cone, with exponents determined by the smallest particle mass or the measurement resolution.) In a sense, however, the presence of such correlations is just a reflection of the idealized way in which the vacuum state is set up—with each field mode determined all at once for the whole system.

Processes of Perception and Analysis

Defining the Notion of Randomness

■ **Page 554 · Algorithmic information theory.** A description of a piece of data can always be thought of as some kind of program for reproducing the data. So if one could find the shortest program that works then this must correspond to the shortest possible description of the data—and in algorithmic information theory if this is no shorter than the data itself then the data is considered to be algorithmically random.

How long the shortest program is for a given piece of data will in general depend on what system is supposed to run the program. But in a sense the program will on the whole be as short as possible if the system is universal (see page 642). And between any two universal systems programs can differ in length by at most a constant: for one can always just add a fixed interpreter program to the programs for one system in order to make them run on the other system.

As mentioned in the main text, any data generated by a simple program can by definition never be algorithmically random. And so even though algorithmic randomness is often considered in theoretical discussions (see note below) it cannot be directly relevant to the kind of randomness we see in so many systems in this book—or, I believe, in nature.

If one considers all 2^n possible sequences (say of 0's and 1's) of length n then it is straightforward to see that most of them must be more or less algorithmically random. For in order to have enough programs to generate all 2^n sequences most of the programs one uses must themselves be close to length n. (In practice there are subtleties associated with the encoding of programs that make this hold only for sufficiently large n.) But even though one knows that almost all long sequences must be algorithmically random, it turns out to be undecidable in general whether any particular sequence is algorithmically random. For in general one can give no upper limit to how much computational effort one might have to expend in order to find out whether any given short

program—after any number of steps—will generate the sequence one wants.

But even though one can never expect to construct them explicitly, one can still give formal descriptions of sequences that are algorithmically random. An example due to Gregory Chaitin is the digits of the fraction Ω of initial conditions for which a universal system halts (essentially a compressed version—with various subtleties about limits—of the sequence from page 1127 giving the outcome for each initial condition). As emphasized by Chaitin, it is possible to ask questions purely in arithmetic (say about sequences of values of a parameter that yield infinite numbers of solutions to an integer equation) whose answers would correspond to algorithmically random sequences. (See page 786.)

As a reduced analog of algorithmic information theory one can for example ask what the simplest cellular automaton rule is that will generate a given sequence if started from a single black cell. Page 1186 gives some results, and suggests that sequences which require more complicated cellular automaton rules do tend to look to us more complicated and more random.

■ **History.** Randomness and unpredictability were discussed as general notions in antiquity in connection both with questions of free will (see page 1135) and games of chance. When probability theory emerged in the mid-1600s it implicitly assumed sequences random in the sense of having limiting frequencies following its predictions. By the 1800s there was extensive debate about this, but in the early 1900s with the advent of statistical mechanics and measure theory the use of ensembles (see page 1020) turned discussions of probability away from issues of randomness in individual sequences. With the development of statistical hypothesis testing in the early 1900s various tests for randomness were proposed (see page 1084). Sometimes these were claimed to have some kind of general significance, but mostly they were just viewed as simple practical methods. In many fields outside of statistics, however, the idea persisted even to the 1990s that block frequencies (or flat frequency spectra) were somehow the only ultimate tests for randomness. In 1909 Emile Borel had formulated the notion of normal numbers (see page 912) whose infinite digit sequences contain all blocks with equal frequency. And in the 1920s Richard von Mises—attempting to capture the observed lack of systematically successful gambling schemes—suggested that randomness for individual infinite sequences could be defined in general by requiring that "collectives" consisting of elements appearing at positions specified by any procedure should show equal frequencies. To disallow procedures say specially set up to pick out all the infinite number of 1's in a sequence Alonzo Church in 1940 suggested that only procedures corresponding to finite computations be considered. (Compare page 1021 on coarse-graining in thermodynamics.) Starting in the late 1940s the development of information theory began to suggest connections between randomness and inability to compress data, but emphasis on $p\,Log[p]$ measures of information content (see page 1071) reinforced the idea that block frequencies are the only real criterion for randomness. In the early 1960s, however, the notion of algorithmic randomness (see note above) was introduced by Gregory Chaitin, Andrei Kolmogorov and Ray Solomonoff. And unlike earlier proposals the consequences of this definition seemed to show remarkable consistency (in 1966 for example Per Martin-Löf proved that in effect it covered all possible statistical tests)—so that by the early 1990s it had become generally accepted as the appropriate ultimate definition of randomness. In the 1980s, however, work on cryptography had led to the study of some slightly weaker definitions of randomness based on inability to do cryptanalysis or make predictions with polynomial-time computations (see page 1089). But quite what the relationship of any of these definitions might be to natural science or everyday experience was never much discussed. Note that definitions of randomness given in dictionaries tend to emphasize lack of aim or purpose, in effect following the common legal approach of looking at underlying intentions (or say at physical construction of dice) rather than trying to tell if things are random from their observed behavior.

■ **Inevitable regularities and Ramsey theory.** One might have thought that there could be no meaningful type of regularity that would be present in all possible data of a given kind. But through the development since the late 1920s of Ramsey theory it has become clear that this is not the case. As one example, consider looking for runs of m equally spaced squares of the same color embedded in sequences of black and white squares of length n. The pictures below show results with $m = 3$ for various n. For $n < 9$ there are always some sequences in which no runs of length 3 exist. But it turns out that for $n \geq 9$ every single possible sequence contains at least one run of length 3. For any m the same is true for sufficiently large n; it is known that $m = 4$ requires $n \geq 35$ and $m = 5$ requires $n \geq 178$. (In problems like this the analog of n often grows extremely rapidly with m.) If one has a sufficiently long sequence, therefore, just knowing that a run of equally spaced identical elements exists in it does not narrow down at all what the sequence actually is, and can so cannot ultimately be considered a useful regularity.

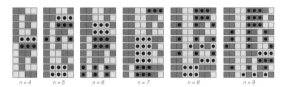

$n = 4$ $n = 5$ $n = 6$ $n = 7$ $n = 8$ $n = 9$

(Compare pattern-avoiding sequences on page 944.)

Defining Complexity

■ **Page 557 · History.** There have been terms for complexity in everyday language since antiquity. But the idea of treating complexity as a coherent scientific concept potentially amenable to explicit definition is quite new: indeed this became popular only in the late 1980s—in part as a result of my own efforts. That what one would usually call complexity can be present in mathematical systems was for example already noted in the 1890s by Henri Poincaré in connection with the three-body problem (see page 972). And in the 1920s the issue of quantifying the complexity of simple mathematical formulas had come up in work on assessing statistical models (compare page 1083). By the 1940s general comments about biological, social and occasionally other systems being characterized by high complexity were common, particularly in connection with the cybernetics movement. Most often complexity seems to have been thought of as associated with the presence of large numbers of components with different types or behavior, and typically also with the presence of extensive interconnections or interdependencies. But occasionally—especially in some areas of social science—complexity was instead thought of as being characterized by somehow going beyond what human minds can handle. In the 1950s there was some discussion in pure mathematics of notions of complexity associated variously with sizes of axioms for logical theories, and with numbers of ways to satisfy such axioms. The development of information theory in the late 1940s—followed by the discovery of the structure of DNA in 1953—led to the idea that perhaps complexity might be related to information content. And when the notion of algorithmic information content as the length of a shortest program (see page 1067) emerged in the 1960s it was suggested that this might be an appropriate definition for complexity. Several other definitions used in specific fields in the 1960s and 1970s were also based on sizes of descriptions: examples were optimal orders of models in systems theory, lengths of logic expressions for circuit and program design, and numbers of factors in Krohn-Rhodes decompositions of semigroups. Beginning in the 1970s computational complexity theory took a somewhat different direction, defining what it called complexity in terms of resources needed to perform computational tasks. Starting in the 1980s with the rise of complex systems research (see page 862) it was considered important by many physicists to find a definition that would provide some kind of numerical measure of complexity. It was noted that both very ordered and very disordered systems normally seem to be of low complexity, and much was made of the observation that systems on the border between these extremes—particularly class 4 cellular automata—seem to have higher complexity. In addition, the presence of some kind of hierarchy was often taken to indicate higher complexity, as was evidence of computational capabilities. It was also usually assumed that living systems should have the highest complexity—perhaps as a result of their long evolutionary history. And this made informal definitions of complexity often include all sorts of detailed features of life (see page 1178). One attempt at an abstract definition was what Charles Bennett called logical depth: the number of computational steps needed to reproduce something from its shortest description. Many simpler definitions of complexity were proposed in the 1980s. Quite a few were based just on changing $p_i \, Log[p_i]$ in the definition of entropy to a quantity vanishing for both ordered and disordered p_i. Many others were based on looking at correlations and mutual information measures—and using the fact that in a system with many interdependent and potentially hierarchical parts this should go on changing as one looks at more and more. Some were based purely on fractal dimensions or dimensions associated with strange attractors. Following my 1984 study of minimal sizes of finite automata capable of reproducing states in cellular automaton evolution (see page 276) a whole series of definitions were developed based on minimal sizes of descriptions in terms of deterministic and probabilistic finite automata (see page 1084). In general it is possible to imagine setting up all sorts of definitions for quantities that one chooses to call complexity. But what is most relevant for my purposes in this book is instead to find ways to capture everyday notions of complexity—and then to see how systems can produce these. (Note that since the 1980s there has been interest in finding measures of complexity that instead for example allow maintainability and robustness of software and management systems to be assessed. Sometimes these have been based on observations of humans trying to understand or verify systems, but more often they have just been based for example on simple properties of networks that define the flow of control or data—or in some cases on the length of documentation needed.) (The kind of complexity discussed here has nothing directly to do with complex numbers such as $\sqrt{-1}$ introduced into mathematics since the 1600s.)

Data Compression

■ **Practicalities.** Data compression is important in making maximal use of limited information storage and transmission capabilities. One might think that as such capabilities increase, data compression would become less relevant. But so far this has not been the case, since the volume of data always seems to increase more rapidly than capabilities for storing and transmitting it. In the future, compression is always likely to remain relevant when there are physical constraints—such as transmission by electromagnetic radiation that is not spatially localized.

■ **History.** Morse code, invented in 1838 for use in telegraphy, is an early example of data compression based on using shorter codewords for letters such as "e" and "t" that are more common in English. Modern work on data compression began in the late 1940s with the development of information theory. In 1949 Claude Shannon and Robert Fano devised a systematic way to assign codewords based on probabilities of blocks. An optimal method for doing this was then found by David Huffman in 1951. Early implementations were typically done in hardware, with specific choices of codewords being made as compromises between compression and error correction. In the mid-1970s, the idea emerged of dynamically updating codewords for Huffman encoding, based on the actual data encountered. And in the late 1970s, with online storage of text files becoming common, software compression programs began to be developed, almost all based on adaptive Huffman coding. In 1977 Abraham Lempel and Jacob Ziv suggested the basic idea of pointer-based encoding. In the mid-1980s, following work by Terry Welch, the so-called LZW algorithm rapidly became the method of choice for most general-purpose compression systems. It was used in programs such as PKZIP, as well as in hardware devices such as modems. In the late 1980s, digital images became more common, and standards for compressing them emerged. In the early 1990s, lossy compression methods (to be discussed in the next section) also began to be widely used. Current image compression standards include: FAX CCITT 3 (run-length encoding, with codewords determined by Huffman coding from a definite distribution of run lengths); GIF (LZW); JPEG (lossy discrete cosine transform, then Huffman or arithmetic coding); BMP (run-length encoding, etc.); TIFF (FAX, JPEG, GIF, etc.). Typical compression ratios currently achieved for text are around 3:1, for line diagrams and text images around 3:1, and for photographic images around 2:1 lossless, and 20:1 lossy. (For sound compression see page 1080.)

■ **Page 560 · Number representations.** The sequence of 1's and 0's representing a number *n* are obtained as follows:

(a) *Unary.* Table[0, {n}]. (Not self-delimited.)

(b) *Ordinary base 2.* IntegerDigits[n, 2]. (Not self-delimited.)

(c) *Length prefixed.* Starting with an ordinary base 2 digit sequence, one prepends a unary specification of its length, then a specification of that length specification, and so on:

(Flatten[{Sign[-Range[1 - Length[#], 0]], #}] &)[
    Map[Rest, IntegerDigits[Rest[Reverse[NestWhileList[
        Floor[Log[2, #]] &, n + 1, # > 1 &]]], 2]]]

(d) *Binary-coded base 3.* One takes base 3 representation, then converts each digit to a pair of base 2 digits, handling the beginning and end of the sequence in a special way.

Flatten[IntegerDigits[
    Append[2 - With[{w = Floor[Log[3, 2 n]]},
        IntegerDigits[n - (3^{w+1} - 1)/2, 3, w]], 3], 2, 2]]

(e) *Fibonacci encoding.* Instead of decomposing a number into a sum of powers of an integer base, one decomposes it into a sum of Fibonacci numbers (see page 902). This decomposition becomes unique when one requires that no pair of 1's appear together.

Apply[Take, RealDigits[(N[#, N[Log[10, #]] + 3]] &)[
    n √5 /GoldenRatio² + 1/2], GoldenRatio]]

The representations of all the first *Fibonacci[n]* - 1 numbers can be obtained from (the version in the main text has Rest[RotateLeft[Join[#, {0, 1}]]] & applied)

Apply[Join, Map[Last,
    NestList[{#[[2]], Join[Map[Join[{1, 0}, Rest[#]] &, #[[2]]],
        Map[Join[{1, 0}, #] &, #[[1]]]]} &, {{}, {{1}}}, n - 3]]]

■ **Lengths of representations.** (a) *n*, (b) Floor[Log[2, n] + 1], (c) Tr[FixedPointList[Max[0, Ceiling[Log[2, #]]] &, n + 2]] - n - 3, (d) 2 Ceiling[Log[3, 2 n + 1]], (e) Floor[Log[GoldenRatio, √5 (n + 1/2)]]. Large *n* approximations:

(a) *n*, (b) *Log[2, n]*, (c) *Log[2, n] + Log[2, Log[2, n]] + ...*, (d) 2 *Log[3, n]*, (e) *Log[GoldenRatio, n]*.

Shown on a logarithmic scale, representations (b) through (e) (given here for numbers 1 through 500) all grow roughly linearly:

■ **Completeness.** If one successively reads 0's and 1's from an infinite sequence then the representations (c), (d) and (e) have the property that eventually one will always accumulate a valid representation for some number or another. The pictures below show which sequences of 0's and 1's correspond to complete numbers in these representations. Every vertical column is a possible sequence of 0's and 1's, and the column is shown to terminate when a complete number is obtained.

With an infinite random sequence of 0's and 1's, different number representations yield different distributions of sizes of numbers. Representation (b), for example, is more weighted towards large numbers, while (c) is more weighted towards small numbers. Maximal compression for a sequence of numbers with a particular distribution of sizes is obtained by choosing a representation that yields a matching such distribution. (See also page 949.)

■ **Practical computing.** Numbers used for arithmetic in practical computing are usually assumed to have a fixed length of, say, 32 bits, and thus do not need to be self-delimiting. In *Mathematica*, where integers can be of essentially any size, a representation closer to (b) above is used.

■ **Page 561 · Run-length encoding.** Data can be converted to run lengths by Map[Length, Split[data]]. Each number is then replaced by its representation.

With completely random input, the output will on average be longer by a factor Sum[2^{-(n+1)} r[n], {n, 1, ∞}] where r[n] is the length of the representation for *n*. For the Fibonacci encoding used in the main text, this factor is approximately 1.41028. (In base 2 this number has 1's essentially at positions *Fibonacci[n]*; as discussed on page 914, the number is transcendental.)

■ **Page 563 · Huffman coding.** From a list *p* of probabilities for blocks, the list of codewords can be generated using

    Map[Drop[Last[#], -1] &, Sort[
     Flatten[MapIndexed[Rule, FixedPoint[Replace[Sort[#],
      {{p0_, i0_}, {p1_, i1_}, pi___} → {{p0 + p1, {i0, i1}},
       pi}} &, MapIndexed[List, p]][[1, 2]], {-1}]]]]] - 1

Given the list of codewords *c*, the sequence of blocks that occur in encoded data *d* can be uniquely reconstructed using

    First[{{}, d} //. MapIndexed[
     {{r___}, Flatten[{#1, s___}]} → {{r, #2[[1]]}, {s}} &, c]]

Note that the encoded data can consist of any sequence of 0's and 1's. If all 2^b possible blocks of length *b* occur with equal probability, then the Huffman codewords will consist of blocks equivalent to the original ones. In an opposite extreme, blocks with probabilities $1/2$, $1/4$, $1/8$, ... will yield codewords of lengths 1, 2, 3, ...

In practical applications, Huffman coding is sometimes extended to allow the choice of codewords to be updated dynamically as more data is read.

■ **Maximal block compression.** If one has data that consists of a long sequence of blocks, each of length *b*, and each independently chosen with probability $p[i]$ to be of type *i*, then as argued by Claude Shannon in the late 1940s, it turns out that the minimum number of base 2 bits needed on average to represent each block in such a sequence is $h = -Sum[p[i] Log[2, p[i]], \{i, 2^b\}]$. If all blocks occur with an equal probability of 2^{-b}, then *h* takes on its maximum possible value of *b*. If only one block occurs with nonzero probability then $h == 0$. Following Shannon, the quantity *h* (whose form is analogous to entropy in physics, as discussed on page 1020) is often referred to as "information content". This name, however, is very misleading. For certainly *h* does not in general give the length of the shortest possible description of the data; all it does is to give the shortest length of description that is obtained by treating successive blocks as if they occur with independent probabilities. With this assumption one then finds that maximal compression occurs if a block of probability $p[i]$ is represented by a codeword of length $-Log[2, p[i]]$. Huffman coding with a large number of codewords will approach this if all the $p[i]$ are powers of $1/2$. (The self-delimiting of codewords leads to deviations for small numbers of codewords.) For $p[i]$ that are not powers of $1/2$, non-integer length codewords would be required. The method of arithmetic coding provides an alternative in which the output does not consist of separate codewords concatenated together. (Compare algorithmic information content discussed on pages 554 and 1067.)

■ **Arithmetic coding.** Consider dividing the interval from 0 to 1 into a succession of bins, with each bin having a width equal to the probability for some sequence of blocks to occur.

The idea of arithmetic coding is to represent each such bin by the digit sequence of the shortest number within the bin—after trailing zeros have been dropped. For any sequence *s* this can be done using

    Module[{c, m = 0},
     Map[c[#] = {m, m += Count[s, #]/Length[s]} &, Union[s]];
     Function[x, (First[RealDigits[2^# Ceiling[2^-# Min[x]],
      2, -#, -1]] &)[Floor[Log[2, Max[x] - Min[x]]]]][
      Fold[(Max[#1] - Min[#1]) c[#2] + Min[#1] &, {0, 1}, s]]]

Huffman coding of a sequence containing a single 0 block together with *n* 1 blocks will yield output of length about *n*; arithmetic coding will yield length about $Log[n]$. Compression in arithmetic coding still relies, however, on unequal block probabilities, just like in Huffman coding. Originally suggested in the early 1960s, arithmetic coding reemerged in the late 1980s when high-speed floating-point computation became common, and is occasionally used in practice.

■ **Page 565 · Pointer-based encoding.** One can encode a list of data *d* by generating pointers to the longest and most recent copies of each subsequence of length at least *b* using

    PEncode[d_, b_ : 4] := Module[{i, a, u, v},
     i = 2; a = {First[d]}; While[i ≤ Length[d], {u, v} =
      Last[Sort[Table[{MatchLength[d, i, j], j}, {j, i - 1}]]];
      If[u ≥ b, AppendTo[a, p[i - v, u]]; i += u,
       AppendTo[a, d[[i]]]; i++]]; a]
    MatchLength[d_, i_, j_] := With[{m = Length[d] - i}, Catch[
     Do[If[d[[i + k]] =!= d[[j + k]], Throw[k]], {k, 0, m}]; m + 1]]

The process of encoding can be made considerably faster by keeping a dictionary of previously encountered subsequences. One can reproduce the original data using

    PDecode[a_] := Module[{d = Flatten[
     a /. p[j_, r_] :→ Table[p[j], {r}]]}, Flatten[MapIndexed[
      If[Head[#1] === p, d[[#2]] = d[[#2 - First[#1]]], #1] &, d]]]

To get a representation purely in terms of 0 and 1, one can use a self-delimiting representation for each integer that appears. (Knowing the explicit representation one could then determine whether each block would be shorter if encoded literally or using a pointer.) The encoded version of a purely repetitive sequence of length *n* has a length that grows like $Log[n]$. The encoded version of a purely nested sequence grows like $Log[n]^2$. The encoded version of a sufficiently random sequence grows like *n* (with the specific encoding used in the text, the length is about $2n$). Note that any sequence of 0's and 1's corresponds to the beginning of the encoding for some sequence or another.

It is possible to construct sequences whose encoded versions grow roughly like fractional powers of *n*. An example is the sequence $Table[Append[Table[0, \{r\}], 1], \{r, s\}]$ whose encoded version grows like $\sqrt{n} \, Log[n]$. Cyclic tag systems often seem to produce sequences whose encoded versions grow like fractional powers of n. Sequences produced by concatenation sequences are not typically compressed by pointer encoding.

With completely random input, the probability that the length b subsequence which begins at element n is a repeat of a previous subsequence is roughly $1 - (1 - 2^{-b})^{n-1}$. The overall fraction of a length n input that consists of repeats of length at least b is greater than $1 - 2^b/n$ and is essentially

$$1 - Sum[(1 - 2^{-b})^i \, Product[1 + (1 - 2^{-b})^i - (1 - 2^{-b-1})^i,$$
$$\{j, i - b + 1, i - 1\}], \{i, b, n - b\}]/(n - 2b + 1)$$

6   8   10   12   14   16

■ **LZW algorithms.** Practical implementations of pointer-based encoding can maintain only a limited dictionary of possible repeats. Various schemes exist for optimizing the construction, storage and rewriting of such dictionaries.

■ **Page 568 · Recursive subdivision.** In one dimension, encoding can be done using

Subdivide[a_] := Flatten[
  If[Length[a] == 2, a, If[Apply[SameQ, a], {1, First[a]},
   {0, Map[Subdivide, Partition[a, Length[a]/2]]}]]]

In n dimensions, it can be done using

Subdivide[a_, n_] := With[{s = Table[1, {n}]}, Flatten[
  If[Dimensions[a] == 2 s, a, If[Apply[SameQ, Flatten[a]],
   {1, First[Flatten[a]]}, {0, Map[Subdivide[#, n] &,
   Partition[a, 1/2 Length[a] s], {n}]}]]]]

■ **2D run-length encoding.** A simple way to generalize run-length encoding to two dimensions is to scan data one row after another, always finding the largest rectangle of uniform color that starts at each particular point. The pictures below show regions with an area of more than 10 cells found in this way. The presence of so many thin and overlapping regions prevents good compression.

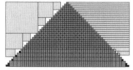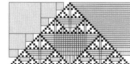

2D run-length encoding can also be done by scanning the data according to a more complicated space-filling curve, of the kind discussed on page 893.

Irreversible Data Compression

■ **History.** The idea of creating sounds by adding together pure tones goes back to antiquity. At a mathematical level, following work by Joseph Fourier around 1810 it became clear by the mid-1800s how any sufficiently smooth function could be decomposed into sums of sine waves with frequencies corresponding to successive integers. Early telephony and sound recording in the late 1800s already used the idea of compressing sounds by dropping high- and low-frequency components. From the early days of television in the 1950s, some attempts were made to do similar kinds of compression for images. Serious efforts in this direction were not made, however, until digital storage and processing of images became common in the late 1980s.

■ **Orthogonal bases.** The defining feature of a set of basic forms is that it is complete, in the sense that any piece of data can be built up by adding the basic forms with appropriate weights. Most sets of basic forms used in practice also have the feature of being orthogonal, which turns out to make it particularly easy to work out the weights for a given piece of data. In 1D, a basic form $a[[i]]$ is just a list. Orthogonality is then the property that $a[[i]] . a[[j]] == 0$ for all $i \neq j$. And when this property holds, the weights are given essentially just by $data . a$.

The concept of orthogonal bases was historically worked out first in the considerably more difficult case of continuous functions. Here a typical orthogonality property is $Integrate[f[r, x] f[s, x], \{x, 0, 1\}] == KroneckerDelta[r, s]$. As discovered by Joseph Fourier around 1810, this is satisfied for basis functions such as $Sin[2 n \pi x]/\sqrt{2}$.

■ **Page 573 · Walsh transforms.** The basic forms shown in the main text are 2D Walsh functions—represented as ± 1 matrices. Each collection of such functions can be obtained from lists of vectors representing 1D Walsh functions by using $Outer[Outer[Times, ##] \&, b, b, 1, 1]$, or equivalently $Map[Transpose, Map[\# b \&, b, \{2\}]]$.

The pictures below show how 1D arrays of data values can be built up by adding together 1D Walsh functions. At each step the Walsh function used is given underneath the array of values obtained so far.

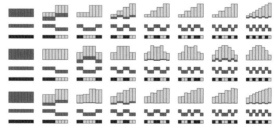

The components of the vectors for 1D Walsh functions can be ordered in many ways. The pictures below show the

complete matrices of basis vectors obtained with three common orderings.

(a) *(b)* *(c)*

The matrices for size $n = 2^s$ can be obtained from

Nest[Apply[Join, f[{Map[Flatten[Map[{#, #} &, #]] &, #],
Map[Flatten[Map[{#, -#} &, #]] &, g[#]]}]] &, {{1}}, s]

with (a) *f = Identity*, *g = Reverse*, (b) *f = Transpose*, *g = Identity*, and (c) *f = g = Identity*. (a) is used in the main text. Known as sequency order, it has the property that each row involves one more change of color than the previous row. (b) is known as natural or Hadamard order. It exhibits a nested structure, and can be obtained as in the pictures below from the evolution of a 2D substitution system, or equivalently from a Kronecker product as in

Nest[Flatten2D[Map[# {{1, 1}, {1, -1}} &, #, {2}]] &, {{1}}, s]

with

Flatten2D[a_] :=
Apply[Join, Apply[Join, Map[Transpose, a], {2}]]

(c) is known as dyadic or Paley order. It is related to (a) by Gray code reordering of the rows, and to (b) by reordering according to (see page 905)

BitReverseOrder[a_] :=
With[{n = Length[a]}, a[[Map[FromDigits[Reverse[#], 2] &,
IntegerDigits[Range[0, n - 1], 2, Log[2, n]]] + 1]]]

It is also given by

Array[Apply[Times, (-1)^(IntegerDigits[#1, 2, s]
Reverse[IntegerDigits[#2, 2, s]])] &, 2^{s, s}, 0]

where (b) is obtained simply by dropping the *Reverse*.

Walsh functions can correspond to nested sequences. The function at position $2/3 (1 + 4^{(-(Floor[s/2] + 1/2)))} 2^s$ in basis (a), for example, is exactly the Thue-Morse sequence (with 0 replaced by -1) from page 83.

Given the matrix m of basis vectors, the Walsh transform is simply *data . m*. Direct evaluation of this for length n takes n^2 steps. However, the nested structure of m in natural order allows evaluation in only about $n \, Log[n]$ steps using

Nest[Flatten[Transpose[Partition[#, 2] . {{1, 1}, {1, -1}}]] &,
data, Log[2, Length[data]]]

This procedure is similar to the fast Fourier transform discussed below. Transforms of 2D data are equivalent to 1D transforms of flattened data.

Walsh functions were used by electrical engineers such as Frank Fowle in the 1890s to find transpositions of wires that minimized crosstalk; they were introduced into mathematics by Joseph Walsh in 1923. Raymond Paley introduced the dyadic basis in 1932. Mathematical connections with harmonic analysis of discrete groups were investigated from the late 1940s. In the 1960s, Walsh transforms became fairly widespread in discrete signal and image processing.

■ **Page 575 · Walsh spectra.** The arrays of absolute values of weights of basic forms for successive images are as follows:

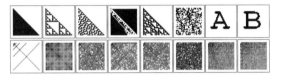

■ **Hadamard matrices.** Hadamard matrices are $n \times n$ matrices with elements -1 and +1, whose rows are orthogonal, so that *m . Transpose[m] == n IdentityMatrix[n]*. The matrices used in Walsh transforms are special cases with $n = 2^s$. There are thought to be Hadamard matrices with every size $n = 4k$ (and for $n > 2$ no other sizes are possible); the number of distinct such matrices for each k up to 7 is 1, 1, 1, 5, 3, 60, 487. The so-called Paley family of Hadamard matrices for $n = 4k = p + 1$ with p prime are given by

PadLeft[Array[JacobiSymbol[#2 - #1, n - 1] &, {n, n} - 1] -
IdentityMatrix[n - 1], {n, n}, 1]

Originally introduced by Jacques Hadamard in 1893 as the matrices with elements $Abs[a] \le 1$ which attain the maximal possible determinant $\pm n^{n/2}$, Hadamard matrices appear in various combinatorial problems, particularly design of exhaustive combinations of experiments and Reed-Muller error-correcting codes.

■ **Image averaging.** Walsh functions yield significantly better compression than simple successive averaging of 2×2 blocks of cells, as shown below.

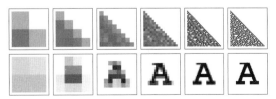

■ **Practical image compression.** Two basic phenomena contribute to our ability to compress images in practice. First, that typical images of relevance tend to be far from random—indeed they often involve quite limited numbers of distinct objects. And second, that many fine details of images go unnoticed by the human visual system (see the next section).

■ **Fourier transforms.** In a typical Fourier transform, one uses basic forms such as $Exp[i\pi r x/n]$ with r running from 1 to n. The weights associated with these forms can be found using *Fourier*, and given these weights the original data can also be reconstructed using *InverseFourier*. The pictures below show what happens in such a so-called discrete cosine transform when different fractions of the weights are kept, and others are effectively set to zero. High-frequency wiggles associated with the so-called Gibbs phenomenon are typical near edges.

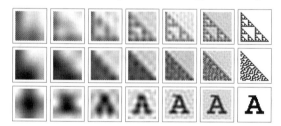

Fourier[data] can be thought of as multiplication by the $n \times n$ matrix $Array[Exp[2\pi i \#1 \#2/n] \&, \{n, n\}, 0]$. Applying *BitReverseOrder* to this matrix yields a matrix which has an essentially nested form, and for size $n = 2^s$ can be obtained from

$Nest[With[\{c = BitReverseOrder[Range[0, Length[\#] - 1]/$
$Length[\#]]\}, Flatten2D[MapIndexed[\#1 \{\{1, 1\},$
$\{1, -1\}(-1)^c[[Last[\#2]]]\} \&, \#, \{2\}]]] \&, \{\{1\}\}, s]$

Using this structure, one obtains the so-called fast Fourier transform which operates in $n\,Log[n]$ steps and is given by

$With[\{n = Length[data]\}, Fold[Flatten[Map[With[$
$\{k = Length[\#]/2\}, \{\{1, 1\}, \{1, -1\}\} . \{Take[\#, k], Drop[$
$\#, k](-1)^{\wedge}(Range[0, k-1]/k)\}] \&, Partition[\#\#]]] \&,$
$BitReverseOrder[data], 2^{\wedge}Range[Log[2, n]]]]/\sqrt{n}\,]$

(See also page 1080.)

■ **JPEG compression.** In common use since the early 1990s JPEG compression works by first assigning color values to definite bins, then applying a discrete Fourier cosine transform, then applying Huffman encoding to the resulting weights. The "quality" of the image is determined by how many weights are kept; a typical default quality factor, used say by *Export* in *Mathematica*, is 75.

■ **Wavelets.** Each basic form in an ordinary Walsh or Fourier transform has nonzero elements spread throughout. With wavelets the elements are more localized. As noted in the late

1980s basic forms can be set up by scaling and translating just a single appropriately chosen underlying shape. The (a) Haar and (b) Daubechies wavelets $\psi[x]$ shown below both have the property that the basic forms $2^{m/2}\,\psi[2^m x - n]$ (whose 2D analogs are shown as on page 573) are orthogonal for every different m and n.

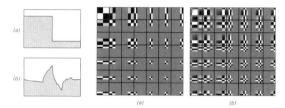

The pictures below show images built up by keeping successively more of these basic forms. Sharp edges have fewer wiggles than with Fourier transforms.

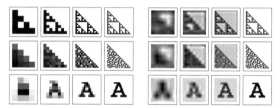

■ **Sound compression.** See page 1080.

Visual Perception

■ **Color vision.** The three types of color-sensitive cone cells on the human retina each have definite response curves as a function of wavelength. The perceived color of light with a given wavelength distribution is basically determined by the three numbers obtained by integrating these responses. For any wavelength distribution it turns out that if one scales these numbers to add up to one, then the chromaticity values obtained must lie within a certain region. Mixing n specific colors in different proportions allows one to reach any point in an n-cornered polytope. For $n = 3$ this polytope comes close to filling the region of all possible colors, but for no n can it completely fill it—which is why practical displays and printing processes can produce only limited ranges of colors.

An important observation, related to the fact that limitations in color ranges are usually not too troublesome, is that the perceived colors of objects stay more or less constant even when viewed in very different lighting, corresponding to very different wavelength distributions. In recent years it has become clear that the origin of this phenomenon is that beyond the original cone cells, most color-sensitive cells in our visual system respond not to absolute color levels, but instead to differences in color levels at slightly different positions. (Responses to nearby relative values rather than absolute values seem to be common in many forms of human perception.)

The fact that white light is a mixture of colors was noticed by Isaac Newton in 1704, and it became clear in the course of the 1700s that three primaries could reproduce most colors. Thomas Young suggested in 1802 that there might be three types of color receptors in the eye, but it was not until 1959 that these were actually identified—though on the basis of perceptual experiments, parametrizations of color space were already well established by the 1930s. While humans and primates normally have three types of cone cells, it has been found that other mammals normally have two, while birds, reptiles and fishes typically have between 3 and 5.

■ **Nerve cells.** In the retina and the brain, nerve cells typically have an irregular tree-like structure, with between a few and a few thousand dendrites carrying input signals, and one or more axons carrying output signals. Nerve cells can respond on timescales of order milliseconds to changes in their inputs by changing their rate of generating output electrical spikes. As has been believed since the 1940s, most often nerve cells seem to operate at least roughly by effectively adding up their inputs with various positive or negative weights, then going into an excited state if the result exceeds some threshold. The weights seem to be determined by detailed properties of the synapses between nerve cells. Their values can presumably change to reflect certain aspects of the activity of the cell, thus forming a basis for memory (see page 1102). In organisms with a total of only a few thousand nerve cells, each individual cell typically has definite connections and a definite function. But in humans with perhaps 100 billion nerve cells, the physical connections seem quite haphazard, and most nerve cells probably develop their function as a result of building up weights associated with their actual pattern of behavior, either spontaneous or in response to external stimuli.

■ **The visual system.** Connected to the 100 million or so light-sensitive photoreceptor cells on the retina are roughly two layers of nerve cells, with various kinds of cross-connections, out of which come the million fibers that form the optic nerve. After essentially one stop, most of these go to the primary visual cortex at the back of the brain, which itself contains more than 100 million nerve cells. Physical connections between nerve cells have usually been difficult to map. But starting in the 1950s it became possible to record electrical activity in single cells, and from this the discovery was made that many cells respond to rather specific visual stimuli. In the retina, most common are center-surround cells, which respond when there is a higher level of light in the center of a roughly circular region and a lower level outside, or vice versa. In the first few layers of the visual cortex about half the cells respond to elongated versions of similar stimuli, while others seem sensitive to various forms of change or motion. In the fovea at the center of the retina, a single center-surround cell seems to get input from just a few nearby photoreceptors. In successive layers of the visual cortex cells seem to get input from progressively larger regions. There is a very direct mapping of positions on the retina to regions in the visual cortex. But within each region there are different cells responding to stimuli at different angles, as well as to stimuli from different eyes. Cells with particular kinds of responses are usually found to be arranged in labyrinthine patterns very much like those shown on page 427. And no doubt the processes which produce these patterns during the development of the organism can be idealized by simple 2D cellular automata. Quite what determines the pattern of illumination to which a given cell will respond is not yet clear, although there is some evidence that it is the result of adaptation associated with various kinds of test inputs. Since the late 1970s, it has been common to assume that the response of a cell can be modelled by derivatives of Gaussians such as those shown below, or perhaps by Gabor functions given by products of trigonometric functions and Gaussians. Experiments have determined responses to these and other specific stimuli, but inevitably no experiment can find all the stimuli to which a cell is sensitive.

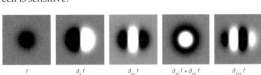

f $\partial_x f$ $\partial_{xx} f$ $\partial_{xx} f + \partial_{yy} f$ $\partial_{xxx} f$

The visual systems of a number of specific higher and lower organisms have now been studied, and despite a few differences (such as cross-connections being behind the photoreceptors on the retinas of octopuses and squids, but in front in most higher animals), the same general features are usually seen. In lower organisms, there tend to be fewer layers of cells, with individual cells more specialized to particular visual stimuli of relevance to the organism.

■ **Feedback.** Most of the lowest levels of visual processing seem to involve only signals going successively from one layer in the eye or brain to the next. But presumably there is at least some feedback to previous layers, yielding in effect iteration of rules like the ones used in the main text. The resulting evolution process is likely to have attractors, potentially explaining the fact that in images such as "Magic Eye" random dot stereograms features can pop out after several seconds or minutes of scrutiny, even without any conscious effort.

■ **Scale invariance.** In a first approximation our recognition of objects does not seem to be much affected by overall size or overall light level. For light level—as with color constancy—this is presumably achieved by responding only to differences between levels at different positions. Probably the same effect contributes to scale invariance by emphasizing only edges and corners. And if one is looking at objects like letters, it helps that one has learned them at many different sizes. But also similar cells most likely receive inputs from regions with a range of different sizes on the retina—making even unfamiliar textures seem the same over at least a certain range of scales. When viewed at a normal reading distance of 12 inches each square in the picture on page 578 covers a region about 5 cells across on the retina. With good lighting and good eyesight the textures in the picture can still be distinguished at a distance of 5 feet, where each square covers only one cell. But if the picture is enlarged by a factor of 3 or more then at normal reading distance it can become difficult to distinguish the textures—perhaps because the squares cover regions larger than the templates used at the lowest levels in our visual system.

■ **History.** Ever since antiquity the visual arts have yielded practical schemes and sometimes also fairly abstract frameworks for determining what features of images will have what impact. In fact, even in prehistoric times it seems to have been known, for example, that edges are often sufficient to communicate visual forms, as in the pictures below.

Visual perception has been used for centuries as an example in philosophical discussions about the nature of experience. Traditional mathematical methods began to be applied to it in the second half of the 1800s, particularly through the development of psychophysics. Studies of visual illusions around the end of the 1800s raised many questions that were not readily amenable to numerical measurement or traditional mathematical analysis, and this led in part to the Gestalt approach to psychology which attempted to formulate various global principles of visual perception.

In the 1940s and 1950s, the idea emerged that visual images might be processed using arrays of simple elements. At a largely theoretical level, this led to the perceptron model of the visual system as a network of idealized neurons. And at a practical level it also led to many systems for image processing (see below), based essentially on simple cellular automata (see page 928). Such systems were widely used by the end of the 1960s, especially in aerial reconnaissance and biomedical applications.

Attempts to characterize human abilities to perceive texture appear to have started in earnest with the work of Bela Julesz around 1962. At first it was thought that the visual system might be sensitive only to the overall autocorrelation of an image, given by the probability that randomly selected points have the same color. But within a few years it became clear that images could be constructed—notably with systems equivalent to additive cellular automata (see below)—that had the same autocorrelations but looked completely different. Julesz then suggested that discrimination between textures might be based on the presence of "textons", loosely defined as localized regions like those shown below with some set of distinct geometrical or topological properties.

In the 1970s, two approaches to vision developed. One was largely an outgrowth of work in artificial intelligence, and concentrated mostly on trying to use traditional mathematics to characterize fairly high-level perception of objects and their geometrical properties. The other, emphasized particularly by David Marr, concentrated on lower-level processes, mostly based on simple models of the responses of single nerve cells, and very often effectively applying *ListConvolve* with simple kernels, as in the pictures below.

In the 1980s, approaches based on neural networks capable of learning became popular, and attempts were made in the context of computational neuroscience to create models combining higher- and lower-level aspects of visual perception.

The basic idea that early stages of visual perception involve extraction of local features has been fairly clear since the 1950s, and researchers from a variety of fields have invented and reinvented implementations of this idea many times. But mainly through a desire to use traditional mathematics, these implementations have tended to be implicitly restricted to using elements with various linearity properties—typically leading to rather unconvincing results. My model is closer to what is often done in practical image processing, and apparently to how actual nerve cells work, and in effect assumes highly nonlinear elements.

■ **Page 581 · Implementation.** The exact matches for a template σ in data containing elements 0 and 1 can be obtained from

Sign[ListCorrelate[2 σ - 1, data] - Count[σ, 1, 2]] + 1

■ **Testing the model.** Although it is difficult to get good systematic data, the many examples I have tried indicate that the levels of discrimination between textures that we achieve with our visual system agree remarkably well with those suggested by my simple model. A practical issue that arises is that if one repeatedly tries experiments with the same set of textures, then after a while one learns to discriminate these particular textures better. Shifting successive rows or even just making an overall rotation seems, however, to avoid this effect.

■ **Related models.** Rather than requiring particular templates to be matched, one can consider applying arbitrary cellular automaton rules. The pictures below show results from a single step of the 16 even-numbered totalistic 5-neighbor rules. The results are surprisingly easy to interpret in terms of feature extraction.

■ **Image processing.** The release of programs like Photoshop in the late 1980s made image processing operations such as smoothing, sharpening and edge detection widely available on general-purpose computers. Most of these operations are just done by applying *ListConvolve* with simple kernels. (Even before computers, such convolutions could be done using the fact that diffraction of light effectively performs Fourier transforms.) Ever since the 1960s all sorts of schemes for nonlinear processing of images have been discussed and used in particular communities. An example originally popular in the earth and environmental sciences is so-called mathematical morphology, based on "dilation" of data consisting of 0's and 1's with a "structuring element" σ according to *Sign[ListConvolve[σ, data, 1, 0]]* (as well as the dual operation of "erosion"). Most schemes like this can ultimately be thought of as picking out templates or applying simple cellular automaton rules.

■ **Real textures.** The textures I consider in the main text are all based on arrays of discrete black and white squares. One can also consider textures associated, say, with surface roughness of physical objects. Models of these are often needed for realistic computer graphics. Common approaches are to assume that the surfaces are random with some frequency spectrum, or can be generated as fractals using substitution systems with random parameters. In recent times, models based on wavelets have also been used.

■ **Statistical methods.** Even though they do not appear to correspond to how the human visual system works, statistical methods are often used in trying to discriminate textures automatically. Correlations, conditional entropies and fractal dimensions are commonly computed. Often it is assumed that different parts of a texture are statistically independent, so that the texture can be characterized by probabilities for local patterns, as in a so-called Markov random field or generalized autoregressive moving average (ARMA) process.

■ **Camouflage.** On both animals and military vehicles it is often important to have patterns that cannot be distinguished from a background by the visual systems of predators. And in most cases this is presumably best achieved by avoiding differences in densities of certain local features. Note that in a related situation almost any fairly random overlaid pattern containing many local features can successfully be used to mask the contents of a paper envelope.

■ **Halftoning.** In printed books like this one, gray levels are usually obtained by printing small dots of black with varying sizes. On displays consisting of fixed arrays of pixels, gray levels must be obtained by having only a certain density of pixels be black. One way to achieve this is to break the array into $2^n \times 2^n$ blocks, then successively to fill in pixels in each block until the appropriate gray level is reached, as in the pictures below, in an order given for example by

Nest[
  Flatten2D[{{4 # + 0, 4 # + 2}, {4 # + 3, 4 # + 1}}] &, {{0}}, n]

An alternative to this so-called ordered dither approach is the Floyd-Steinberg or error-diffusion method invented in 1976. This scans sequentially, accumulating and spreading total gray level in the data, then generating a black pixel whenever a threshold is exceeded. The method can be implemented using

Module[{a = Flatten[data], r, s},
  {r, s} = Dimensions[data]; Partition[Do[
    a[[i + {1, s - 1, s, s + 1}]] += m (a[[i]] - If[a[[i]] < 1/2, 0, 1]),
    {i, r s - s - 1}]; Map[If[# < 1/2, 0, 1] &, a], s]]

In its original version $m = \{7, 3, 5, 1\}/16$, as in the first row of pictures below. But even with $m = \{1, 0, 1, 0\}/2$ the method generates fairly random patterns, as in the second row below. (Note that significantly different results can be obtained if different boundary conditions are used for each row.)

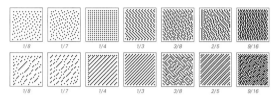

To give the best impression of uniform gray, one must in general minimize features detected by the human visual system. One simple way to do this appears to be to use nested patterns like the ones below.

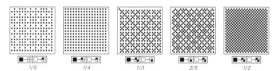

■ **Generating textures.** As discussed on page 217, it is in general difficult to find 2D patterns which at all points match some definite set of templates. With 2×2 templates, there turn out to be just 7 minimal such patterns, shown below. Constructing patterns in which templates occur with definite densities is also difficult, although randomized iterative schemes allow some approximation to be obtained.

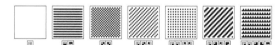

One-dimensional cellular automata are especially convenient generators of distinctive textures. Indeed, as was noticed around 1980, generalizations of additive rules involving cells in different relative locations can produce textures with similar statistics, but different visual appearance, as shown below. (All the examples shown turn out to correspond to ordinary, sequential and reversible cellular automata seen elsewhere in this book.) (See also page 1018.)

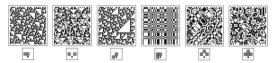

■ **Moire patterns.** The pictures below show moire patterns formed by superimposing grids of points at different angles. Our visual system does not immediately perceive the grids,

but instead mainly picks up features formed from local arrangements of dots. The second picture below is similar to patterns of halftone screens visible in 4-color printing under a magnifying glass.

In the first two pictures below, bands with spacing $1/2\, Csc[\theta/2]$ are visible wherever lines cross. In the second two pictures there is also an apparent repetitive pattern with approximately the same repetition period.

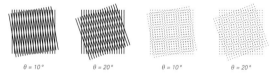

θ = 10°   θ = 20°   θ = 10°   θ = 20°

The patterns are exactly repetitive only when $Tan[\theta] == u/v$, where u and v are elements of a primitive Pythagorean triple (so that u, v and $Sqrt[u^2 + v^2]$ are all integers, and $GCD[u, v] == 1$). This occurs when $u = r^2 - s^2$, $v = 2rs$ (see page 945), and in this case the minimum displacement that leaves the whole pattern unchanged is $\{s, r\}$.

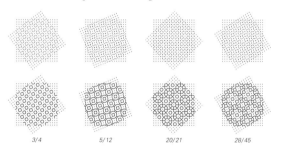

3/4   5/12   20/21   28/45

The second row of pictures illustrates what happens if points closer than distance $1/\sqrt{2}$ are joined. The results appear to capture at least some of the features picked out by our visual system.

■ **Perception and presentation.** In writing this book it has been a great challenge to find graphical representations that make the behavior of systems as clear as possible for the purposes of human visual perception. Even small changes in representation can greatly affect what properties are noticed. As a simple example, the pictures below are identical, except for the fact that the colors of cells on alternate rows have been reversed.

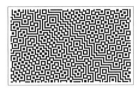 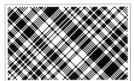

Auditory Perception

■ **Sounds.** The human auditory system is sensitive to sound at frequencies between about 20 Hz and 20 kHz. Middle A on a piano typically corresponds to a frequency of 440 Hz. Each octave represents a change in frequency by a factor of two. In western music there are normally 12 notes identified within an octave. These differ in frequency by successive factors of roughly $2^{1/12}$ —with different temperament schemes using different rational approximations to powers of this quantity.

The perceived character of a sound seems to depend most on the frequencies it contains, but also to be somewhat affected by the way its intensity ramps up with time, as well as the way frequencies change during this ramp up. Many musical instruments produce sound by vibrating strings or air in cylindrical or conical tubes, and in these cases, there is one main frequency, together with roughly equally spaced overtones. In percussion instruments, the spectrum of frequencies is usually much more complicated. In speech, vowels and voiced consonants tend to be characterized by the lowest two or three frequencies of the mouth. In nature, processes such as fluid turbulence and fracture yield a broad spectrum of frequencies. In speech, letters like "s" also yield broad spectra, presumably because they involve fluid turbulence.

Any sound can be specified by giving its amplitude or waveform as a function of time. $Sin[\omega\,t]$ corresponds to a pure tone. Other simple mathematical functions can also yield distinctive sounds. FM synthesis functions such as $Sin[\omega\,(t + a\,Sin[b\,t])]$ can be made to sound somewhat like various musical instruments, and indeed were widely used in early synthesizers.

■ **Auditory system.** Sound is detected by the motion it causes in hair cells in the cochlea of the inner ear. When vibrations of a particular frequency enter the cochlea an active process involving hair cells causes the vibrations to be concentrated at a certain distance down the cochlea. To a good approximation this distance is proportional to the logarithm of the frequency, and going up one octave in frequency corresponds to moving roughly 3.5 mm. Of the 12,000 or so hair cells in the cochlea most seem to be involved mainly with mechanical issues; about 3500 seem to produce outgoing signals. These are collected by about 30,000 nerve fibers which go down the auditory nerve and after several stops reach the auditory cortex. Different nerve cells seem to have rates of firing which are set up to reflect both sound intensity, and below perhaps 300 Hz, actual amplitude peaks in the sound waveform. Much as in both the visual and tactile systems, there seems to be a fairly direct mapping from position on the cochlea to position in the auditory cortex. In animals such as bats it is known that specific nerve cells respond to particular kinds of frequency changes. But in primates, for example, little is known about exactly what features are extracted in the auditory cortex.

The fact that there are a million nerve fibers going from the eye to the brain, but only about 30,000 going from the ear to the brain means that while it takes several million bits per second to transmit video of acceptable quality, a few tens of thousands of bits are adequate for audio (NTSC television is 5 MHz; audio CDs 22 kHz; telephone 8 kHz). Presumably related is also the fact that it is typically much easier to make realistic sound effects than realistic visual ones.

■ **Chords.** Two pure tones played together exhibit beats at the difference of their frequencies—a consequence of the fact that

$$Sin[\omega_1\,t] + Sin[\omega_2\,t] == 2\,Sin[1/2\,(\omega_1 + \omega_2)\,t]\,Cos[1/2\,(\omega_1 - \omega_2)\,t]$$

With $\omega \simeq 500\,Hz$, one can explicitly hear the time variation of the beats if their frequency is below about 15 Hz, and the result is quite pleasant. But between 15 Hz and about 60 Hz, the sound tends to be rather grating—possibly because this frequency range conflicts with that used for signals in the auditory nerve.

In music it is usually thought that chords consisting of tones with frequencies whose ratios have small denominators (such as 3/2, corresponding to a perfect fifth) yield the most pleasing sounds. The mechanics of the ear imply that if two tones of reasonable amplitude are played together, progressively smaller additional signals will effectively be generated at frequencies $Abs[n_1\,\omega_1 \pm n_2\,\omega_2]$. The picture below shows the extent to which such frequencies tend to be in the range that yield grating effects. The minima at values of ω_2/ω_1 corresponding to rationals with small denominators may explain why such chords seem more pleasing. (See also page 917.)

■ **History.** The notion of musical notes and of concepts such as octaves goes back at least five thousand years. Around 550 BC the Pythagoreans identified various potential connections between numbers and the perception of sounds. And over the course of time a wide range of mathematical and aesthetic principles were suggested. But it was not until the 1800s, particularly with the work of Hermann Helmholtz, that the physical basis for the perception of sound began to be seriously investigated. Work on speech sounds by Alexander Graham Bell and others was related to the development of the telephone in the late 1800s. In the past few decades, with better experiments, particularly on the emission of sound by the ear, and with ideas and analysis from electrical engineers and physicists the basic behavior of at least the cochlea is becoming largely understood.

■ **Sonification.** Sound has occasionally been used as a means of understanding scientific data. In the 1950s and 1960s analog computers (and sometimes digital computers) routinely had sound output. And in the 1970s some discoveries about chaos in differential equations were made using such output. In experimental neuroscience sounds are also routinely used to monitor impulses in nerve cells.

■ **Implementation.** *ListPlay[data]* in *Mathematica* generates sound output by treating the elements of *data* as successive samples in the waveform of the sound, typically with a default sample rate of 8000 Hz.

■ **Time variation.** Many systems discussed in this book produce sounds with distinctive and sometimes pleasing time variation. Particularly dramatic are the concatenation systems discussed on page 913, as well as successive rows in nested patterns such as *Flatten[IntegerDigits[NestList[BitXor[#, 2#] &, 1, 500], 2]]* and sequences based on numbers such as *Flatten[Table[If[GCD[i, j] == 0, 1, 0], {i, 1000}, {j, i}]]* (see page 613). The recursive sequences on page 130 yield sounds reminiscent of many natural systems.

■ **Musical scores.** Instead of taking a sequence to correspond directly to the waveform of a sound, one can consider it to give a musical score in which each element represents a note of a certain frequency, played for some specific short time. (One can avoid clicks by arranging the waveform to cross zero at both the beginning and end of each note.) With this setup my experience is that both repetitive and random sequences tend to seem quite monotonous and dull. But nested sequences I have found can quite often generate rather pleasing tunes. (One can either determine frequencies of notes directly from the values of elements, or, say, from cumulative sums of such values, or from heights in paths like those on page 892.) (See also page 869.)

■ **Recognizing repetition.** The curve of the function $Sin[x] + Sin[\sqrt{2}\ x]$ shown on page 146 looks complicated to the eye. But a sound with a corresponding waveform is recognized by the ear as consisting simply of two pure tones. However, if one uses the function to generate a score—say playing a note at the position of each peak—then no such simplicity can be recognized. And this fact is presumably why musical scores normally have notes only at integer multiples of some fixed time interval.

■ **Sound compression.** Sound compression has in practice mostly been applied to human speech. In typical voice coders (vocoders) 64k bits per second of digital data are obtained by sampling the original sound waveform 8000 times per second, and assigning one of 256 possible levels to each sample. (Since the 1960s, so-called mu-law companding has often been used, in which these levels are distributed exponentially in amplitude.) Encoding only differences between successive samples leads to perhaps a factor of 2 compression. Much more dramatic compression can be achieved by making an explicit model for speech sounds. Most common is to assume that within each phoneme-length chunk of a few tens of milliseconds the vocal tract acts like a linear filter excited either by pure tones or randomness. In so-called linear predictive coding (LPC) optimal parameters are found to make each sound sample be a linear combination of, say, 8 preceding samples. The residue from this procedure is then often fitted to a code book of possible forms, and the result is that intelligible speech can be obtained with as little as 3 kbps of data. Hardware implementations of LPC and related methods have been widespread since before the 1980s; software implementations are now becoming common. Music has in the past rarely been compressed, except insofar as it can be specified by a score. But recently the MP3 format associated with MPEG and largely based on LPC methods has begun to be used for compression of arbitrary sounds, and is increasingly applied to music.

■ **Page 586 · Spectra.** The spectra shown are given by *Abs[Fourier[data]]*, where the symmetrical second half of this list is dropped in the pictures. Also of relevance are intensity or power spectra, obtained as the square of these spectra. These are related to the autocorrelation function according to

$$Fourier[list]^2 == $$
$$Fourier[ListConvolve[list, list, \{1, 1\}]]/Sqrt[Length[list]]$$

(See also page 1074.)

■ **Spectra of substitution systems.** Questions that turn out to be related to spectra of substitution systems have arisen in various areas of pure mathematics since the late 1800s. In the 1980s, particularly following discoveries in iterated maps and quasicrystals, studies of such spectra were made in the context of number theory and dynamical systems theory. Some general principles were proposed, but a great many exceptions were always eventually found.

As suggested by the pictures in the main text, spectra such as (b) and (d) in the limit consist purely of discrete Dirac delta function peaks, while spectra such as (a) and (c) also contain essentially continuous parts. There seems to be no simple criterion for deciding from the rule what type of spectrum will be obtained. (In some cases it works to look at whether the limiting ratio of lengths on successive steps is a Pisot number.) One general result, however, is that all so-called Sturmian sequences $Round[(n + 1) a + b] - Round[n a + b]$ with a an irrational number must yield discrete spectra. And as discussed on page 903, if a is a quadratic irrational, then such sequences can be generated by substitution systems.

For any substitution system the spectrum $\phi[i][t, \omega]$ at step t from initial condition i is given by a linear recurrence relation in terms of the $\phi[j][t-1, \omega]$. With k colors each giving a string of the same length s the recurrence relation is

$Thread[Map[\phi[\#][t + 1, \omega] \&, Range[k] - 1] ==$
$Apply[Plus, MapIndexed[Exp[i \omega (Last[\#2] - 1) s^t]$
$\phi[\#1][t, \omega] \&, Range[k] - 1 /. rules, \{-1\}, \{1\}]/\sqrt{s}]$

Some specific properties of the examples shown include:

(a) *(Thue-Morse sequence)* The spectrum is essentially $Nest[Range[2 Length[\#]] Join[\#, Reverse[\#]] \&, \{1\}, t]$. The main peak is at position 1/3, and in the power spectrum this peak contains half of the total. The generating function for the sequence (with 0 replaced by -1) satisfies $f[z] == (1 - z) f[z^2]$, so that $f[z] == Product[1 - z^{2^n}, \{n, 0, \infty\}]$. (Z transform or generating function methods can be applied directly only for substitution systems with rules such as $\{1 \to list, 0 \to 1 - list\}$.) After t steps a continuous approximation to the spectrum is $Product[1 - Exp[2^s i \omega], \{s, t\}]$, which is an example of a type of product studied by Frigyes Riesz in 1918 in connection with questions about the convergence of trigonometric series. It is related to the product of sawtooth functions given by $Product[Abs[Mod[2^s \omega, 2, -1]], \{s, t\}]$. Peaks occur for values of ω such as 1/3 that are not well approximated by numbers of the form $a/2^b$ with small a and b.

(b) *(Fibonacci-related sequence)* This sequence is a Sturmian one. The maximum of the spectrum is at $Fibonacci[t]$. The spectrum is roughly like the markings on a ruler that is recursively divided into $\{GoldenRatio, 1\}$ pieces.

(c) *(Cantor set)* In the limit, no single peak contains a nonzero fraction of the power spectrum. After t steps a continuous approximation to the spectrum is $Product[1 + Exp[3^s 2 i \omega], \{s, t\}]$.

(d) *(Period-doubling sequence)* The spectrum is $(2^\# - (-1)^\# \&)[1 + IntegerExponent[n, 2]]$, almost like the markings on a base 2 ruler.

(See also page 917.)

■ **Flat spectra.** Any impulse sequence $Join[\{1\}, Table[0, \{n\}]]$ will yield a flat spectrum. With odd n the same turns out to be true for sequences $Exp[2 \pi i Mod[Range[n]^2, n]/n]$—a fact used in the design of acoustic diffusers (see page 1183). For sequences involving only two distinct integers flat spectra are rare; with ± 1 those equivalent to $\{1, 1, 1, -1\}$ seem to be the only examples. ($\{r^2, r s, s^2, -r s\}$ works for any r and s, as do all lists obtained working modulo $x^n - 1$ from $p[x]/p[1/x]$ where $p[x]$ is any invertible polynomial.) If one ignores the first component of the spectrum the remainder is flat for a constant sequence, or for a random sequence in the limit of infinite length. It is also flat for maximal length LFSR sequences (see page 1084) and for sequences $JacobiSymbol[Range[0, p - 1], p]$ with prime p (see page 870). By adding a suitable constant to each element one can then arrange in such cases for the whole spectrum to be flat. If $Mod[p, 4] == 1$ $JacobiSymbol$ sequences also satisfy $Fourier[list] == list$. Sequences of 0's and 1's that have the same property are $\{1, 0, 1, 0\}$, $\{1, 0, 0, 1, 0, 0, 1, 0, 0\}$ or in general $Flatten[Table[\{1, Table[0, \{n - 1\}]\}, \{n\}]]$. If -1 is allowed, additional sequences such as $\{0, 1, 0, -1, 0, -1, 0, 1\}$ are also possible. (See also pages 911.)

■ **Nested vibrations.** With an assembly of springs arranged in a nested pattern simple initial excitations can yield motion that shows nested behavior in time. If the standard methodology of mechanics is followed, and the system is analyzed in terms of normal modes, then the spectrum of possible frequencies can look complicated, just as in the examples on page 586. (Similar considerations apply to the motion of quantum mechanical electrons in nested potentials.)

■ **Page 587 · Random block sequences.** Analytical forms for all but the last spectrum are: 1, $u^2/(1 + 8 u^2)$, $1/(1 + 8 u^2)$, u^2, $(1 - 4 u^2)^2/(1 - 5 u^2 + 8 u^4)$, $u^2/(1 - 5 u^2 + 8 u^4)$, $u^2 + 1/36 DiracDelta[\omega - 1/3]$, where $u = Cos[\pi \omega]$, and ω runs from 0 to 1/2 in each plot. Given a list of blocks such as $\{\{1, 1\}, \{0\}\}$ each element of $Flatten[list]$ can be thought of as a state in a finite automaton or a Markov process (see page 1084). The transitions between these states have probabilities given by $m[Map[Length, list]]$ where

$m[s\_] := With[\{q = FoldList[Plus, 0, s]\}, ReplacePart[$
$RotateRight[IdentityMatrix[Last[q]], \{0, 1\}], 1/Length[s],$
$Flatten[Outer[List, Rest[q], Drop[q, -1] + 1], 1]]]$

The average spectrum of sequences generated according to these probabilities can be obtained by computing the correlation function for elements a distance r apart

$$\xi[list\_, r\_] := With[\{w = (\# - Apply[Plus, \#]/Length[\#] \&)[\\ Flatten[list]]\}, w . MatrixPower[\\ m[Map[Length, list]], r] . w/Length[w]]$$

then forming $Sum[\xi[Abs[r]] Cos[2 \pi r \omega], \{r, -n/2, n/2\}]$ and taking the limit $n \to \infty$. If $\xi[r] = \lambda^r$ then the spectrum is $(1 - \lambda^2)/(\lambda^2 - 2 \lambda Cos[2 \pi \omega] + 1) - 1$. For a random walk (see page 977) in which ± 1 occur with equal probability the spectrum is $Csc[\pi \omega]^2/2$, or roughly $1/\omega^2$.

The same basic setup also applies to spectra associated with linear filters and ARMA time series processes (see page 1083), in which elements in a sequence are generated from external random noise by forming linear combinations of the noise with definite configurations of elements in the sequence.

▪ Spectra of cellular automata. When cellular automata have non-trivial attractors as discussed in Chapter 6 the spectra of sequences obtained at particular steps can exhibit a variety of features, as shown below.

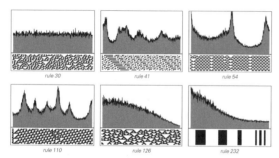

▪ 2D spectra. The pictures below give the 2D Fourier transforms of the nested patterns shown on page 583.

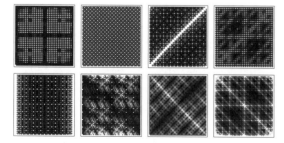

▪ Diffraction patterns. X-ray diffraction patterns give Fourier transforms of the spatial arrangement of atoms in a material. For an ordinary crystal with atoms on a repetitive lattice, the patterns consist of a few isolated peaks. For quasicrystals with generalized Penrose tiling structures the patterns also contain a few large peaks, though as in example (b) on page 586 there are also a hierarchy of smaller peaks present. In general, materials with nested structures do not necessarily yield discrete diffraction patterns. In the early 1990s, experiments were done in which layers a few atoms thick of two different materials were deposited in a Thue-Morse sequence. The resulting object was found to yield X-ray diffraction patterns just like example (a) on page 586.

Statistical Analysis

▪ History. Some computations of odds for games of chance were already made in antiquity. Beginning around the 1200s increasingly elaborate results based on the combinatorial enumeration of possibilities were obtained by mystics and mathematicians, with systematically correct methods being developed in the mid-1600s and early 1700s. The idea of making inferences from sampled data arose in the mid-1600s in connection with estimating populations and developing precursors of life insurance. The method of averaging to correct for what were assumed to be random errors of observation began to be used, primarily in astronomy, in the mid-1700s, while least squares fitting and the notion of probability distributions became established around 1800. Probabilistic models based on random variations between individuals began to be used in biology in the mid-1800s, and many of the classical methods now used for statistical analysis were developed in the late 1800s and early 1900s in the context of agricultural research. In physics fundamentally probabilistic models were central to the introduction of statistical mechanics in the late 1800s and quantum mechanics in the early 1900s. Beginning as early as the 1700s, the foundations of statistical analysis have been vigorously debated, with a succession of fairly specific approaches being claimed as the only ones capable of drawing unbiased conclusions from data. The practical use of statistical analysis began to increase rapidly in the 1960s and 1970s, particularly among biological and social scientists, as computers became more widespread. All too often, however, inadequate amounts of data have ended up being subjected to elaborate statistical analyses whose results are then blindly assumed to represent definitive scientific conclusions. In the 1980s, at least in some fields, traditional statistical analysis began to become less popular, being replaced by more direct examination of data presented graphically by computer. In addition, in the 1990s, particularly in the context of consumer electronics devices, there has been an increasing emphasis on using statistical analysis to make decisions from data, and methods such as fuzzy logic and neural networks have become popular.

■ **Practical statistics.** The vast majority of statistical analysis is in practice done on continuous numerical data. And with surprising regularity it is assumed that random variations in such data follow a Gaussian distribution (see page 976). But while this may sometimes be true—perhaps as a consequence of the Central Limit Theorem—it is rarely checked, making it likely that many detailed inferences are wrong. So-called robust statistics uses for example medians rather than means as an attempt to downplay outlying data that does not follow a Gaussian distribution.

Classical statistical analysis mostly involves trying to use data to estimate parameters in specific probabilistic models. Non-parametric statistics and related methods often claim to derive conclusions without assuming particular models for data. But insofar as a conclusion relies on extrapolation beyond actual measured data it must inevitably in some way use a model for data that has not been measured.

■ **Time series.** Sequences of continuous numerical data are often known as time series, and starting in the 1960s standard models for them have consisted of linear recurrence relations or linear differential equations with random noise continually being added. The linearity of such models has allowed efficient methods for estimating their parameters to be developed, and these are widely used, under slightly different names, in control engineering and in business analysis. In recent years nonlinear models have also sometimes been considered, but typically their parameters are very difficult to estimate reliably. As discussed on page 919 it was already realized in the 1970s that even without external random noise nonlinear models could produce time series with seemingly random features. But confusion about the importance of sensitivity to initial conditions caused the kind of discoveries made in this book to be missed.

■ **Page 588 · Origin of probabilities.** Probabilities are normally assumed to enter for at least two reasons: (a) because of random variation between individuals, and (b) because of random errors in measurement. (a) is particularly common in the biological and social sciences; (b) in the physical sciences. In physics effects of statistical mechanics and quantum mechanics are also assumed to introduce probabilities. Probabilistic models for abstract mathematical systems have in the past been rare, though the results about randomness in this book may make them more common in the future.

■ **Probabilistic models.** A probabilistic model must associate with every sequence a probability that is a number between 0 and 1. This can be done either by giving an explicit procedure for taking sequences and finding probabilities, or by defining a process in which sequences are generated with appropriate probabilities. A typical example of the first approach is the Ising model for spin systems in which relative probabilities of sequences are found by multiplying together the results of applying a simple function to blocks of nearby elements in the sequence. Monte Carlo methods and probabilistic cellular automata provide examples of the second approach.

■ **Page 588 · Binomial distribution.** If black squares appear independently with probability p then the probability that m squares out of n are black is $Binomial[n, m] p^m (1 - p)^{n-m}$.

■ **Page 589 · Estimation of parameters.** One way to estimate parameters in simple probabilistic models is to compute the mean and other moments of the data and then to work out what values of the parameters will reproduce these. More general is the maximum likelihood method in which one finds the values of the parameters which maximize the probability of generating the observed data from the model. (Least squares fits do this for models in which the data exhibits independent Gaussian variations.) Various modifications can be made involving for example weighting with a risk function before maximizing. If one starts with a priori probability distributions for all parameters, then Bayes's Theorem on conditional probabilities allows one to avoid the arbitrariness of methods such as maximum likelihood and explicitly to work out from the observed data what the probability is for each possible choice of parameters in the model. It is rare in practice, however, to be able to get convincing *a priori* probability distributions, although when there are physical or other reasons to expect entropy to be maximized the so-called maximum entropy method may be useful.

■ **Complexity of models.** The pictures at the top of the next page show least squares fits (found using *Fit* in *Mathematica*) to polynomials with progressively higher degrees and therefore progressively more parameters. Which fit should be considered best in any particular case must ultimately depend on external considerations. But since the 1980s there have been attempts to find general criteria, typically based on maximizing quantities such as $-Log[p] - d$ (the Akaike information criterion), where p is the probability that the observed data would be generated from a given model ($-Log[p]$ is proportional to variance in a least squares fit), and d is the number of parameters in the model.

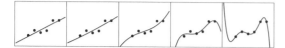

■ **Page 590 · Markov processes.** The networks in the main text can be viewed as representing finite automata (see page 957) with probabilities associated with transitions between nodes or states. Given a vector of probabilities to be in each state, the evolution of the system corresponds to multiplication by the matrix of probabilities for each transition. (Compare the calculation of properties of substitution systems on page 890.) Markov processes first arose in the early 1900s and have been widely studied since the 1950s. In their first uses as models it was typically assumed that each state transition could explicitly be observed. But by the 1980s hidden Markov models were being studied, in which only some of the states or transitions could be distinguished by outside observations. Practical applications were made in speech understanding and text compression. And in the late 1980s, building on work of mine from 1984 (described on page 276), James Crutchfield made a study of such models in which he defined the complexity of a model to be equal to $-p\,Log[p]$ summed over all connections in the network. He argued that the best scientific model is one that minimizes this complexity—which with probabilities 0 and 1 is equivalent to minimizing the number of nodes in the network.

■ **Non-local processes.** It follows from the fact that any path in a finite network must always eventually return to a node where it has been before that any Markov process must be fundamentally local, in the sense that the probabilities it implies for what happens at a given point in a sequence must be independent of those for points sufficiently far away. But probabilistic models based on other underlying systems can yield sequences with long-range correlations. As an example, probabilistic neighbor-independent substitution systems can yield sequences with hierarchical structures that have approximate nesting. And since the mid-1990s such systems (usually characterized as random trees or random context-free languages) have sometimes been used in analyzing data that is expected to have grammatical structure of some kind.

■ **Page 594 · Block frequencies.** In any repetitive sequence the number of distinct blocks of length m must become constant with m for sufficiently large m. In a nested sequence the number must always continue increasing roughly linearly, and must be greater than m for every m. (The differences of successive numbers themselves form a nested sequence.) If exactly $m+1$ distinct blocks occur for every m, then the sequence must be of the so-called Sturmian type discussed

on page 916, and the nth element must be given by $Round[(n+1)a+b]-Round[na+b]$, where a is an irrational number. Up to limited m nested sequences can contain all k^m possible blocks, and can do so with asymptotically equal frequencies. Pictures (b), (c) and (d) show the simplest cases where this occurs (for length 3 $\{1 \to \{1, 1, 1, 0, 0, 0\}, 0 \to \{1, 0\}\}$ also works). Linear feedback shift registers of the type used in picture (e) are discussed below. Concatenation sequences of the type used in picture (f) are discussed on page 913. In both cases equal frequencies of blocks are obtained only for sequences of length exactly 2^j.

■ **LFSR sequences.** Often referred to as pseudonoise or PN sequences, maximal length linear feedback shift register sequences have repetition period $2^n - 1$ and are generated by shift registers that go through all their possible states except the one consisting of all 0's, as discussed on page 974. Blocks in such sequences obtained from $Partition[list, n, 1]$ must all be distinct since they correspond to successive complete states of the shift register. This means that every block with length up to n (except all 0's) must occur with equal frequency. (Note that only a small fraction of all possible sequences with this property can be generated by LFSRs.) The regularity of PN sequences is revealed by looking at the autocorrelation $RotateLeft[(-1)^{list}, m] . (-1)^{list}$. This quantity is -1 for all nonzero m for PN sequences (so that all but the first component in $Abs[Fourier[(-1)^{list}]]^2$ are equal), but has mean 0 for truly random sequences. (Related sequences can be generated from $RealDigits[1/p, 2]$ as discussed on page 912.)

■ **Entropy estimates.** Fitting the number of distinct blocks of length b to the form $k^{h\,b}$ for large b the quantity h gives the so-called topological entropy of the system. The so-called measure entropy is given as discussed on page 959 by the limit of $-Sum[p_i\,Log[k, p_i], \{i, k^b\}]/b$ where the p_i are the probabilities for the blocks. Actually getting accurate estimates of such entropies is however often rather difficult, and typically upper bounds are ultimately all that can realistically be given. Note also that as discussed in the main text having maximal entropy does not by any means imply perfect randomness.

■ **Tests of randomness.** Statistical analysis has in practice been much more concerned with finding regularities in data than in testing for randomness. But over the course of the past century a variety of tests of randomness have been proposed, especially in the context of games of chance and their government regulation. Most often the tests are applied not directly to sequences of 0's and 1's, but instead say to numbers obtained from blocks of 8 elements. A typical collection of tests described by Donald Knuth in 1968 includes: (1) frequency or equidistribution test (possible elements should occur with equal frequency); (2) serial test (pairs of elements should be equally likely to be in descending and ascending order); (3) gap test (runs of elements all greater or less than some fixed value should have lengths that follow a binomial distribution); (4) poker test (blocks corresponding to possible poker hands should occur with appropriate frequencies); (5) coupon collector's test (runs before complete sets of values are found should have lengths that follow a definite distribution); (6) permutation test (in blocks of elements possible orderings of values should occur equally often); (7) runs up test (runs of monotonically increasing elements should have lengths that follow a definite distribution); (8) maximum-of-t test (maximum values in blocks of elements should follow a power-law distribution). With appropriate values of parameters, these tests in practice tend to be at least somewhat independent, although in principle, if sufficient data were available, they could all be subsumed into basic block frequency and run-length tests. Of the sequences on page 594, (a) through (d) as well as (f) fail every single one of the tests, (e) fails only the serial test, while (g) and (h) pass all the tests. (Failure is defined as a value that is as large or small as that obtained from the data occurring below a specified probability in the set of all possible sequences.) Widespread use of tests like these on pseudorandom generators (see page 974) began in the late 1970s, with discoveries of defects in common generators being announced every few years.

In the 1980s simulations in physics had begun to use pseudorandom generators to produce sequences with billions of elements, and by the late 1980s evidence had developed that a few common generators gave incorrect results in such cases as phase transition properties of the 3D Ising model and shapes of diffusion-limited aggregates. (These difficulties provided yet more support for my contention that models with intrinsic randomness are more reliable than those with external randomness.) In the 1990s various idealizations of physics simulations—based on random walks, correlation functions, localization of eigenstates, and so on—were used as tests of pseudorandom generators. These tests mostly seem simpler than those shown on page 597 obtained by running a cellular automaton rule on the data.

Over the years, essentially every proposed statistical test of randomness has been applied to the center column of rule 30. And occasionally people have told me that their tests have found deviations from randomness. But in every single case further investigation showed that the results were somehow incorrect. So as of now, the center column of rule 30 appears to pass every single proposed statistical test of randomness.

■ **Difference tables.** See page 1091.

■ **Randomized algorithms.** Whether a randomized algorithm gives correct answers can be viewed as a test of randomness for whatever supposedly random sequence is provided to it. But in most practical cases such tests are not particularly stringent; linear congruential generators, for example, almost always pass. (There are perhaps exceptions in VLSI testing.) And this is basically why it has so often proved possible to replace randomized algorithms by deterministic ones that are at least as efficient (see page 1192). An example is Monte Carlo integration, where what ultimately matters is uniform sampling of the integrand—which can usually be achieved better by quasi-random irrational number multiple (see page 903) or digit reversal (see page 905) sequences than by sequences one might consider more random.

Cryptography and Cryptanalysis

■ **History.** Cryptography has been in use since antiquity, and has been a decisive factor in a remarkably large number of military and other campaigns. Typical of early systems was the substitution cipher of Julius Caesar, in which every letter was cyclically shifted in the alphabet by three positions, with A being replaced by D, B by E, and so on. Systems based on more arbitrary substitutions were in use by the 1300s. And while methods for their cryptanalysis were developed in the 1400s, such systems continued to see occasional serious use until the early 1900s. Ciphers of the type shown on page 599 were introduced in the 1500s, notably by Blaise de Vigenère; systematic methods for their cryptanalysis were developed in the mid-1800s and early 1900s. By the mid-1800s, however, codes based on books of translations for whole phrases were much more common than ciphers, probably because more sophisticated algorithms for ciphers were difficult to implement by hand. But in the 1920s electromechanical technology led to the development of rotor machines, in which an encrypting sequence with an extremely long period was generated by rotating a sequence of noncommensurate rotors. A notable achievement of cryptanalysis was the 1940 breaking of the German Enigma rotor machine using a mixture of statistical analysis and automatic enumeration of keys. Starting in the 1950s, electronic devices were the primary ones used for cryptography. Linear feedback shift registers and perhaps nonlinear ones seem to have been common, though little is publicly known about military cryptographic systems after World War II. In 1977 the U.S. government introduced the DES data encryption standard, and in the 1980s this became the dominant force in the growing field of commercial cryptography. DES takes 64-bit blocks of data and a 56-bit key, and applies 16 rounds of substitutions and permutations. The S-box that implements each substitution works much like a single step of a cellular automaton. No fast method of cryptanalysis for DES is publicly known, although by now for a single DES system an exhaustive search of keys has become feasible. Two major changes occurred in cryptography in the 1980s. First, cryptographic systems routinely began to be implemented in software rather than in special-purpose hardware, and thus became much more widely available. And second, following the introduction of public-key cryptography in 1975, the idea emerged of basing cryptography not on systems with complicated and seemingly arbitrary construction, but instead on systems derived from well-known mathematical problems. Initially several different problems were considered, but after a while the only ones to survive were those such as the RSA system discussed below based essentially on the problem of factoring integers. Present-day publicly available cryptographic systems are almost all based on variants of either DES (such as the IDEA system of PGP), linear feedback shift registers or RSA. My cellular automaton cryptographic system is one of the very few fundamentally different systems to have been introduced in recent years.

■ **Basic theory.** As was recognized in the 1920s the only way to make a completely secure cryptographic system is to use a so-called one-time pad and to have a key that is as long as the message, and is chosen completely at random separately for each message. As soon as there are a limited number of possible keys then in principle one can always try each of them in turn, looking in each case to see whether they imply an original message that is meaningful in the language in which the message is written. And as Claude Shannon argued in the 1940s, the length of message needed to be reasonably certain that only one key will satisfy this criterion is equal to the length of the key divided by the redundancy of the language in which the message is written—equal to about 0.5 for English (see below).

In a cryptographic system with keys of length n there will typically be a total of k^n possible keys. If one guesses a key it will normally take a time polynomial in n to check whether the key is correct, and thus the problem of cryptanalysis is in the class known in theoretical computer science as NP or non-deterministic polynomial time (see page 1142). It is suspected but not established that there exist at least some problems in NP that cannot be solved in polynomial time, potentially indicating that for an appropriate system it might be impossible to do cryptanalysis in any time polynomial in n. (See page 1089.)

■ **Text.** As the picture below illustrates, English text typically remains intelligible until about half its characters have been deleted, indicating that it has a redundancy of around 0.5. Most other languages have slightly higher redundancies, making documents in those languages slightly longer than their counterparts in English.

```
About half the letters in typical English text are redundant.
About half the letter- in typical Eng--sh text are redun-ant.
Abou- half the -etter- in ty-ical Eng--sh text are redun--nt.
Abou- half the -e-t--- i- ty-ical Eng--sh text are redun--nt.
Abou- half t-e -e-t--- -- ty-ical Eng--sh text ar- red-n--nt.
Abou- h-l- t-e -e----- -- ty-ical Eng--sh text ar- r-d-n--nt.
Abou- h--- --- -e----- -- ty-ical -ng--sh tex- ar- --d-n--nt.
Abou- h--- --- -e----- -- ty-ica- -ng---h tex- ar- --d-n--nt.
A-ou- h--- --- -e----- -- ty---a- -ng--- h te-- --r- --d---n-.
--ou- ---- --- -e----- -- ty---a- -n---- te-- --r- --d----n-.
--o-- ---- --- -e----- -- ty---a- -n---- te-- --r- ---------.
----- ---- --- -e------- -- t------ ------- -e-- -r- --------.
```

Redundancy can in principle be estimated by breaking text into blocks of length b, then looking for the limit of the entropy as $b \to \infty$ (see page 1084). Statistically uniform samples of text do not in practice, however, tend to be large enough to allow more than about $b = 6$ to be reached, and the presence of correlations (even though exponentially damped) between far-separated letters means that computed entropies usually decrease continually with b, making it difficult to estimate their limit (see page 1084). Note that particularly in computer languages higher redundancy is found if one takes account of grammatical structure.

■ **Page 599 · Cryptanalysis.** The so-called Vigenère cipher was thought for several centuries to be unbreakable. The idea of looking for repeats was introduced by Friedrich Kasiski in 1863. A statistical approach based on the fact that frequencies tend to be closer to uniform for longer keys was introduced by William Friedman in the 1920s. The methods described in the main text are fairly characteristic of the mixture between generality and detail that is typical in practical cryptanalysis.

■ **Page 600 · Linear feedback shift registers.** See notes on pages 974 and 1084. LFSR sequences are widely used in radio technology, particularly in the context of spread spectrum applications. Their purpose is usually to provide a way to distinguish or synchronize signals, and sometimes to provide a level of cryptographic security. In CDMA technology for cellular telephones, for example, data is overlaid on LFSR sequences, and sequences other than the one intended for a particular receiver seem like noise which can be ignored. As another example, the Global Positioning System (GPS) works by having 24 satellites each transmit maximal length sequences from different length 10 LFSRs. Position is deduced from the arrival times of signals, as determined by the relative phases of the LFSR sequences received. (GPS P-code apparently uses much longer LFSR sequences and repeats only every 267 days. Before May 2000 it was used to add unpredictable timing errors to ordinary GPS signals.)

■ **LFSR cryptanalysis.** Given a sequence obtained from a length n LFSR (see page 975)

Nest[Mod[Append[#, Take[#, -n] . vec], 2] &, list, t]

the vector of taps *vec* can be deduced from

*LinearSolve[Table[Take[seq, {i, i + n - 1}], {i, n}],
Take[seq, {n + 1, 2 n}], Modulus → 2]*

(An iterative algorithm in n taking about n^2 rather than n^3 steps was given by Elwyn Berlekamp and James Massey in 1968.) The same basic approach can be used to deduce the rule for an additive cellular automaton from vertical sequences.

■ **Page 603 · Rule 30 cryptography.** Rule 30 is known to have many of the properties desirable for practical cryptography. It does not repeat with any short period or show any obvious structure for almost all keys. Small changes in keys typically leads to large changes in the encrypting sequence. The Boolean expressions which determine the encrypting sequence from the key rapidly become highly complex (see page 618). And furthermore the system can be implemented very efficiently, particularly in parallel hardware.

I originally studied rule 30 in the context of basic science, but I soon realized that it could serve as the basis for practical random sequence generation and cryptography, and I analyzed this extensively in 1985. (Most but not all of the results from my original paper are included in this book, together with various new results.) In 1985 and soon thereafter a number of people (notably Richard and Carl Feynman) tried to cryptanalyze rule 30, but without success. From the beginning, computations of spacetime entropies for rule 30 (see page 960) gave indications that for strong cryptography one should not sample all cells in a column, and in 1991 Willi Meier and Othmar Staffelbach described essentially the explicit cryptanalysis approach shown on page 601. Rule 30 has been widely used for random sequence generation, but for a variety of reasons I have not in the past much emphasized its applications in cryptography.

■ **Properties of rule 30.** Rule 30 can be written in the form $p \veebar (q \vee r)$ (see page 869) and thus exhibits a kind of one-sided additivity on the left. This leads to some features that are desirable for cryptography (such as long repetition periods) and to some that are not (such as the sideways evolution of page 601). It implies that every block of length m that occurs at a particular step has exactly 4 immediate predecessor blocks of length $m + 2$ (see page 960). It also implies that all 2^t possible single columns of t cells can be generated from some initial condition. Not all 4^t pairs of adjacent columns can occur, however. There seems to be no simple

characterization, say in terms of paths through networks, of which can, but for successive t the total numbers are

*{4, 12, 32, 80, 200, 496, 1208, 2916, 6964, 16476, 38616,
89844, 207544, 476596, 1089000, 2477236, 5615036}*

or roughly 2.25^t.

Given two complete adjacent columns page 601 shows how all columns any distance to the left can be found. It turns out that this can be done even if the right-hand one of the two adjacent columns is not complete. So for example whenever there is a black cell in the left column it is irrelevant what appears in the right column. Note that the configuration of relevant cells can be repetitive only if the initial conditions were repetitive (see page 871).

In a cellular automaton of limited size n, any column must eventually repeat. There could be 2^n distinct possible columns; in practice, for successive n there are *{2, 3, 7, 14, 30, 60, 101, 245, 497, 972, 1997, 3997}*—within 2% of 2^n already for $n = 12$. This means that for the initial conditions to be determined uniquely, the number of cells that must be given in a column is almost exactly n, as illustrated in the pictures below. Many distinct columns correspond to starting at different points on a single cycle of states. The length of the longest cycle grows roughly like $2^{0.63n}$ (see page 260). The complete cycle structure is illustrated on page 962. Most of the 2^n possible states have unique predecessors; for large n, about $2^{0.76n}$ or $Root[\#^3 - \#^2 - 2 \&, 1]^n$ instead have 0 or 2 predecessors. The predecessors of a given state can be found from

*Cases[Map[Fold[Prepend[#1, If[#2 == 1 ⊻
Take[#1, 2] == {0, 0}, 0, 1]] &, #, Reverse[list]] &, {{0,
0}, {0, 1}, {1, 0}, {1, 1}}], {a_, b_, c___, a_, b_} → {b, c, a}]*

■ **Directional sampling.** One can consider sampling cells not in a vertical column but on lines at any angle. In a rule 30 system of infinite size, it turns out that at 45° clockwise from vertical all possible sequences can occur on any two adjacent lines, probably making cryptanalysis more difficult in this case. (Note that directional sampling is always equivalent to looking at a vertical column in the evolution of a cellular automaton whose basic rule has been composed with an appropriate shift rule.)

■ **Alternative rules.** Among elementary rules, rule 45 is the only plausible alternative to rule 30. It usually yields longer repetition periods (see page 260), but shows slightly slower responses to changes in the key. (Changes expand about 1.24 cells per step in rule 30, and about 1.17 in rule 45.) Rule 45 shares with rule 30 the property of one-sided additivity. With the occasional exception of the additive rule 60, elementary rules not equivalent to 30 or 45 tend to exhibit vastly shorter repetition periods. (The completely non-additive rule with largest typical repetition period is rule 110.) (See page 951.)

If one considers rules that depend on 4 rather than 3 cells, then the results turn out to be surprisingly similar: out of all 65536 possible such rules the ones with longest periods essentially always seem to be variants of rules 45, 30 or 60. In a region of size 15, for example, the longest period is 20460, and this is achieved by rule 13251, which is just rule 45 applied to the first three cells in the neighborhood. (Rule 45 itself has period 6820 in this case.) After a few rules with long periods, the periods obtained drop off rapidly. (In general the number of rules with a given period seems to decrease roughly exponentially with period.) For size 15, the 33 rules with the longest periods are all additive with respect to one position. The pictures below show the first rules that are not additive with respect to any position.

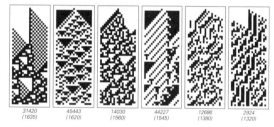

| 31420 (1635) | 45443 (1620) | 14030 (1560) | 44227 (1545) | 12686 (1380) | 2924 (1320) |

Among the 4,294,967,296 $r = 2$ rules which depend on 5 cells, there are again just a few that give long periods, but now only a small fraction of these seem directly related to rules 45 and 30, and perhaps half are not additive with respect to any position. The pictures below show the rules with longest periods for size 15; these same rules also yield the longest periods for many other sizes. The first two are additive with respect to one position, but do not appear to be directly related to rules 45 or 30; the last two are not additive with respect to any position. Formulas for the rules are respectively:

$p \veebar (\neg q \vee r \vee s \wedge \neg t)$

$r \veebar (\neg p \vee q \vee s \wedge \neg t)$

$u = \neg p \wedge \neg q \vee q \wedge t; \neg r \wedge u \vee q \wedge \neg s \wedge (p \vee \neg r) \vee r \wedge s \wedge \neg u$

$s \wedge (q \wedge \neg r \vee p \wedge \neg q \wedge t) \vee \neg (s \vee (p \vee q) \wedge (r \veebar (q \vee t)))$

Note that for size 15 the maximum possible period is 32730 (see page 950).

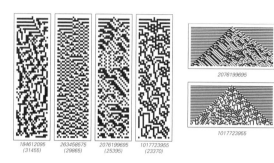

| 184612095 (31455) | 263458575 (29865) | 2076199695 (25395) | 1017723955 (23370) |

2076199695

1017723955

■ **Nonlinear feedback shift registers.** Linear feedback shift registers of the kind discussed on page 974 can be generalized to allow any function f (note the slight analogy with cyclic tag systems):

    NLFSRStep[f_, taps_, list_] :=
        Append[Rest[list], f[list[[taps]]]]

With the choice $f = IntegerDigits[s, 2, 8][[8 - \# . \{4, 2, 1\}]]$ & and $taps = \{1, 2, 3\}$ this is essentially a rule s elementary cellular automaton. With a list of length n, Nest[NLFSRStep[f, taps, #] &, list, n] gives one step in the evolution of the cellular automaton in a register of width n, with a certain kind of spiral boundary condition. The case analogous to rule 30 yields some of the longest repetition periods—usually remarkably close to the absolute maximum of $2^n - 1$ (for $n = 21$ the result is 1999864, 95% of the maximum).

Nonlinear feedback shift registers were apparently studied in the context of military cryptography in the 1950s, but very little about them has made its way into the open literature (see page 878). An empirical investigation of repetition periods in such systems was made by Solomon Golomb in 1959. The main conclusion drawn from extensive data was that nothing like the linear theory applies. One set of computations concerned functions

$f[\{w_, x_, y_, z_\}] := Mod[w + y + z + x y + x z + y z, 2]$

(apparently chosen to have balance between 0's and 1's that would minimize correlations). Tap positions $\{1, 2, 3, 4\}$ were among those studied, but nothing like the pictures below were apparently ever explicitly generated—and nearly three decades passed before I noticed the remarkable behavior of the rule 30 cellular automaton.

Sequences of states in any shift register must correspond to paths through a network of the kind shown on page 941. And as noted by Nicolaas de Bruijn in 1946 there are $2^{2^{n-1}-n}$ such paths with length 2^n, and thus this number of functions f out of the 2^{2^n} possible must yield sequences of maximal length. (For k colors, the number of paths is $k!^{k^{n-1}}/k^n$.)

■ **Backtracking.** If one wants to find out which of the 2^n possible initial conditions of width n evolve to yield a specific column of colors in a system like an elementary cellular automaton one can usually do somewhat better than just testing all possibilities. The picture below illustrates a typical approach, applied to 3 steps of rule 30. The idea is successively to look at each numbered cell, and to make a tree of possibilities representing what happens if one tries to fill in each possible color for each cell. A branch in the resulting tree continues only if it corresponds to a configuration of cell colors whose evolution is consistent with the specified column of colors.

The picture below shows trees obtained for the column ■□■ in various elementary cellular automata. In cases like rules 250 and 254 no initial condition gives the specified column, so all branches eventually die out. In class 2 examples like rule 10 many intermediate configurations are possible. Rules like 90 and to some extent 30 that allow sideways evolution yield comparatively simple trees.

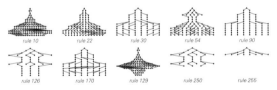

rule 10   rule 22   rule 30   rule 54   rule 90

rule 126   rule 170   rule 129   rule 250   rule 255

If one wants to find just a single initial condition that works then one can set up a recursive algorithm that in effect does a depth-first traversal of the tree. No doubt in many cases the number of nodes that have to be visited eventually increases like 2^t, but many branches usually die off quickly, greatly reducing the typical effort required in practice.

■ **Deducing cellular automaton rules.** Given a complete cellular automaton pattern it is easy to deduce the rule which produced it just by identifying examples of places where each element in the rule was used, as in the picture at the top of the next column. Given an incomplete pattern, deducing the rule in effect requires solving Boolean equations.

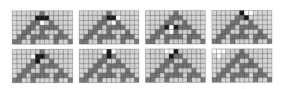

■ **Linear congruential generators.** Cryptanalysis of linear congruential generators is fairly straightforward. Given only an output list *NestList[Mod[a #, m] &, x, n]* parameters $\{a, m\}$ that generate the list can be found for sufficiently large n from

> *With[{α = Apply[#2 . Rest[list]/#1 &, Apply[*
>   *ExtendedGCD, Drop[list, -1]]]}, ({Mod[α, #], #} &)[*
>   *Fold[GCD[#1, If[#1 == 0, #2, Mod[#2, #1]]] &, 0,*
>   *ListCorrelate[{α, -1}, list]]]]*

With slightly more effort both x and $\{a, m\}$ can be found just from *First[IntegerDigits[list, 2, p]]*.

■ **Digit sequence encryption.** One can consider using as encrypting sequences the digit sequences of numbers obtained from standard mathematical functions. As discussed on page 139 such digit sequences often seem locally very random. But in many cases one can immediately tell how a sequence was made just by globally applying appropriate mathematical functions. Thus, for example, given the digit sequence of $\sqrt{s}$ one can retrieve the key s just by squaring the number obtained from early digits in the sequence. Whenever a number x is known to satisfy *Sum[a[i] f[i][x], {i, n}] == 0* with fixed $f[i]$ one can take the early digits of x and use *LatticeReduce* to find integer solutions for the $a[i]$. With $f[i\_] = \#^i$ & this method allows algebraic numbers to be recognized. If no linear equation is satisfied by any combination of known functions of x, however, the method fails, and it seems quite likely that in such cases secure encrypting sequences can be generated, albeit less efficiently than with systems like cellular automata.

■ **Problem-based cryptography.** Particularly following the work of Whitfield Diffie and Martin Hellman in 1976 it became popular to consider cryptography systems based on mathematical problems that are easy to state but have been found difficult to solve. It was at first hoped that the problems could be NP-complete ones, which are universal in the sense that their solution can be used to provide a solution to any problem in the class NP (see page 1086). To date, however, no system has been devised whose cryptanalysis is known to be NP-complete. Indeed, essentially the only problem on which cryptography systems have so far successfully been based is factoring of integers (see below). And while this problem has resisted a fair number of attempts at solution, it is not known to be NP-complete (and indeed its ability to be solved in polynomial time on a formal quantum computer may suggest that it is not).

My cellular automaton cryptography system follows the principle of being based on a problem that is easy to state. And indeed the general problem of finding initial conditions for a cellular automaton is NP-complete (see page 767). But the problem is not known to be NP-complete for the specific case of, say, rule 30. Significantly less work has been done on the problem of finding initial conditions for rule 30 than on the problem of factoring integers. But the greater simplicity of rule 30 might make one already have almost as much confidence in the difficulty of solving this problem as of factoring integers.

■ **Factoring integers.** The difficulty of factoring is presumably related to the irregularity of the pattern of divisors shown on page 909. One approach to factoring a number n is just to try dividing it by each of the numbers up to $\sqrt{n}$. A sequence of much faster methods have however been developed over the past few decades, one simple example that works for most n being the so-called rho method of John Pollard (compare the quadratic residue sequences discussed below):

```
Module[{f = Mod[#² + 1, n] &, a = 2, b = 5, c},
   While[(c = GCD[n, a - b]) == 1, {a, b} = {f[a], f[f[b]]}]; c]
```

Most existing methods depend on facts in number theory that are fairly easy to state, though implementing them for maximum efficiency tends to lead to complex programs. Typical running times for *FactorInteger[n]* in *Mathematica* 4 are shown below for the first 1000 numbers with each of 15 through 30 digits. Different current methods asymptotically require slightly different numbers of steps—but all typically at least $Exp[Sqrt[Log[n]]]$. Nevertheless, to test whether a number is prime (*PrimeQ*) it is known that only a few more than $Log[n]$ steps suffice.

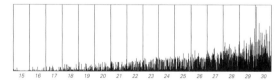

■ **RSA cryptography.** Widely used in practice, the idea is to encode messages using a public key specified by a number n, but to make it so that to decode the messages requires a private key based on the factors of n. An element m in a message is encoded as $c = PowerMod[m, d, n]$. It can then be decoded as $PowerMod[c, e, n]$, where $e = PowerMod[d, -1, EulerPhi[n]]$. But to find $EulerPhi[n]$ (see page 1093) is equivalent in difficulty to finding the factors of n.

■ **Quadratic residue sequences.** As an outgrowth of ideas related to RSA cryptography it was shown in 1982 by Lenore Blum, Manuel Blum and Michael Shub that the sequence

$Mod[NestList[Mod[\#^2, m] \&, x0, n], 2]$

discussed on page 975 has the property that if $m = p\,q$ with p and q primes (congruent to 3 modulo 4) then any systematic regularities detected in the sequence can eventually be used to discover factors of m. What is behind this is that each of the numbers in the basic sequence here must be a so-called quadratic residue of the form $Mod[v^2, m]$, and given any such quadratic residue x the expression $GCD[x + Mod[x^2, m], m]$ turns out always to be a factor of m—and at least sometimes a non-trivial one. So if one could reconstruct sufficiently many complete numbers x from the sequence of $Mod[x, 2]$ values then this would provide a way to factor m (compare the Pollard rho method above). But in practice it is difficult to do this, because without knowing the factors of m one cannot even readily tell whether a given x is a quadratic residue modulo m. The pictures below show as black squares all the quadratic residues for each successive m going down the page (the ordinary squares 1, 4, 9, 16, … show up as vertical black stripes). If m is a prime p, then the simple tests $JacobiSymbol[x, p] == 1$ (see page 1081) or $Mod[x^{(p-1)/2}, p] == 1$ determine whether x is a quadratic residue. But with $m = p\,q$, one has to factor m and find p and q in order to carry out similar tests. The condition $Mod[p, 4] == Mod[q, 4] == 3$ ensures that only one of the solutions $+v$ and $-v$ to $x == Mod[v^2, m]$ is ever a quadratic residue, with the result that the iterated mapping $x \to Mod[x^2, m]$ always has a unique inverse. But unlike in a cellular automaton even given a complete x (the analog of a complete cellular automaton state) it is difficult to invert the mapping and solve for the x on the previous step.

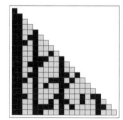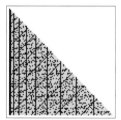

Traditional Mathematics and Mathematical Formulas

■ **Practical empirical mathematics.** In looking for formulas to describe behavior seen in this book I have in practice typically taken associated sequences of numbers and then tested whether obvious regularities are revealed by combinations of such operations as: computing successive differences (see note below), computing running totals, looking for repeated blocks, picking out running maxima, picking out numbers with particular modular residues, and looking at positions of particular values, and at the forms of the digit sequences of these positions.

■ **Difference tables and polynomials.** A common mathematical approach to analyzing sequences is to form a difference table by repeatedly evaluating $d[list_] := Drop[list, 1] - Drop[list, -1]$. If the elements of *list* correspond to values of a polynomial of degree n at successive integers, then $Nest[d, list, n + 1]$ will contain only zeros. If the differences are computed modulo k then the difference table corresponds essentially to the evolution of an additive cellular automaton (see page 597). The pictures below show the results with $k = 2$ (rule 60) for (a) $Fibonacci[n]$, (b) Thue-Morse sequence, (c) Fibonacci substitution system, (d) $(Prime[n] - 1)/2$, (e) digits of π. (See also page 956.)

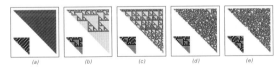

(a)　(b)　(c)　(d)　(e)

■ **Page 607 · Implementation.** The color of a cell at position $\{x, y\}$ in the pattern shown is given by $Extract[\{\{1, 0, 1\}, \{0, 1, 0\}\}, Mod[\{y, x\}, \{2, 3\}] + 1]$.

■ **Page 608 · Nested patterns and numbers.** See page 931.

■ **Page 609 · Implementation.** Given the rules for a substitution system in the form used on page 931 a finite automaton (as on page 957) which yields the color of each cell from the digit sequences of its position is

$Map[Flatten[MapIndexed[\#2 - 1 \to Position[rules, \#1 \to _][[$
$1, 1]] \&, Last[\#], \{-1\}]] \&, rules]$

This works in any number of dimensions so long as each replacement yields a block of the same cuboidal form.

■ **Arbitrary digit operations.** If the operation on digit sequences that determines whether a square will be black can be performed by a finite automaton (see page 957) then the pattern generated must always be either repetitive or nested. The pictures below show examples with more general operations. Picture (a) in effect shows which words in a simple context-free language of parenthesis matching (see page 939) are syntactically correct. Scanning the digit sequences from the left, one starts with 0 open parentheses, then adds 1 whenever corresponding digits in the x and y coordinates differ, and subtracts 1 whenever they are the

same. A square is black if no negative number ever appears. Picture (b) has a black square wherever digits at more than half the possible positions differ between the x and y coordinates. Picture (c) has a black square wherever the maximum run of either identical or different digits has a length which is an odd number. All the patterns shown have the kind of intricate substructure typical of nesting. But none of the patterns are purely nested.

(a)　(b)　(c)

■ **Page 610 · Generating functions.** A convenient algebraic way to describe a sequence of numbers $a[n]$ is to give a generating function $Sum[a[n] x^n, \{n, 0, \infty\}]$. $1/(1 - x)$ thus corresponds to the constant sequence and $1/(1 - x - x^2)$ to the Fibonacci sequence (see page 890). A 2D array can be described by $Sum[a[t, n] x^n y^t, \{n, -\infty, \infty\}, \{t, -\infty, \infty\}]$. The array for rule 60 is then $1/(1 - (1 + x) y)$, for rule 90 $1/(1 - (1/x + x) y)$, for rule 150 $1/(1 - (1/x + 1 + x) y)$ and for second-order reversible rule 150 (see page 439) $1/(1 - (1/x + 1 + x) y - y^2)$. Any rational function is the generating function for some additive cellular automaton.

■ **Page 611 · Pascal's triangle.** See notes on page 870.

■ **Nesting in bitwise functions.** See page 871.

■ **Trinomial coefficients.** The coefficient of x^n in the expansion of $(1 + x + x^2)^t$ is

$Sum[Binomial[n + t - 1 - 3 k, n - 3 k]$
$Binomial[t, k] (-1)^k, \{k, 0, t\}]$

which can be evaluated as

$Binomial[2 t, n] Hypergeometric2F1[-n, n - 2 t, 1/2 - t, 1/4]$

or finally $GegenbauerC[n, -t, -1/2]$. This result follows directly from the generating function formula

$(1 - 2 x z + x^2)^{-m} == Sum[GegenbauerC[n, m, z] x^n, \{n, 0, \infty\}]$

■ **Gegenbauer functions.** Introduced by Leopold Gegenbauer in 1893 $GegenbauerC[n, m, z]$ is a polynomial in z with integer coefficients for all integer n and m. It is a special case of *Hypergeometric2F1* and *JacobiP* and satisfies a second-order ordinary differential equation in z. The $GegenbauerC[n, d/2 - 1, z]$ form a set of orthogonal functions on a d-dimensional sphere. The $GegenbauerC[n, 1/2, z]$ obtained for $d = 3$ are $LegendreP[n, z]$.

■ **Standard mathematical functions.** There are an infinite number of possible functions with integer or continuous arguments. But in practice there is a definite set of standard named mathematical functions that are considered reasonable to include as primitives in formulas, and that are implemented as built-in functions in *Mathematica*. The so-called elementary functions (logarithms, exponentials, trigonometric and hyperbolic functions, and their inverses) were mostly introduced before about 1700. In the 1700s and 1800s another several hundred so-called special functions were introduced. Most arose first as solutions to specific differential equations, typically in physics and astronomy; some arose as products, sums of series or inverses of other functions. In the mid-1800s it became clear that despite their different origins most of these functions could be viewed as special cases of *Hypergeometric2F1[a, b, c, z]*, and that the functions covered the solutions to all linear differential equations of a certain type. (*Zeta* and *PolyLog* are parametric derivatives of *Hypergeometric2F1*; elliptic modular functions are inverses.) Rather few new special functions have been introduced over the past century. The main reason has been that the obvious generalizations seem to yield classes of functions whose properties cannot be worked out with much completeness. So, for example, if there are more parameters it becomes difficult to find continuous definitions that work for all complex values of these parameters. (Typically one needs to generalize formulas that are initially set up with integer numbers of terms; examples include taking *Power[x, y]* to be *Exp[Log[x]y]* and *x!* to be *Gamma[x + 1]*.) And if one modifies the usual hypergeometric equation $y''[x] == f[y[x], y'[x]]$ by making f nonlinear then solutions typically become hard to find, and vary greatly in character with the form of f. (For rational f Paul Painlevé in the 1890s identified just 6 additional types of functions that are needed, but even now series expansions are not known for all of them.) Generalizations of special functions can in principle be used to represent the results of many kinds of computations. Thus, for example, generalized elliptic theta functions represent solutions to arbitrary polynomial equations, while multivariate hypergeometric functions represent arbitrary conformal mappings. In *Mathematica*, however, functions like *Root* provide more convenient ways to access such results.

A variety of standard mathematical functions with integer arguments were introduced in the late 1800s and early 1900s in connection with number theory. A few functions that involve manipulation of digits have also become standard since the use of computers became widespread.

■ **1D sequences.** Generating functions that are rational always lead to sequences which after reduction modulo 2 are purely repetitive. Algebraic generating functions can also lead to nested sequences. (Note that to get only integer sequences such generating functions have to be specially chosen.) *Sqrt[1 - 4 x]/2* yields a sequence with 1's at positions 2^m, as essentially obtained from the substitution system $\{2 \rightarrow \{2, 1\}, 1 \rightarrow \{1, 0\}, 0 \rightarrow \{0, 0\}\}$. *Sqrt[(1 - 3 x)/(1 + x)]/2* yields sequence (a) on page 84. *(1 + Sqrt[(1 - 3 x)/(1 + x)])/(2 (1 + x))* (see page 890) yields the Thue-Morse sequence. (This particular generating function satisfies the equation $(1 + x)^3 f^2 - (1 + x)^2 f + x == 0$.) *(1 - 9 x)^{1/3}* yields almost the Cantor set sequence from page 83. *EllipticTheta[3, π, x]/2* gives a sequence with 1's at positions m^2.

For any sequence with an algebraic generating function and thus for any nested sequence the nth element can always be expressed in terms of hypergeometric functions. For the Thue-Morse sequence the result is

$$1/2 \, (-1)^n + (-3)^n \sqrt{\pi} \; Hypergeometric2F1[3/2, \\ -n, 3/2 - n, -1/3]/(4 \, n! \, Gamma[3/2 - n])$$

■ **Multidimensional additive rules.** The 2D analog of rule 90 yields the patterns shown below. The colors of cells are given essentially by *Mod[Multinomial[t, x, y], 2]*. In d dimensions $(2 d)^{DigitCount[t, 2, 1]}$ cells are black at step t. The fractal dimension of the $(d+1)$-dimensional structure formed from all black cells is *Log[2, 1 + 2 d]*.

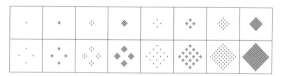

The 2D analog of rule 150 yields the patterns below; the fractal dimension of the structure in this case is *Log[2, (1 + Sqrt[1 + 4/d]) d]*.

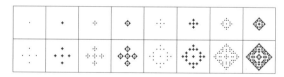

■ **Continuous generalizations.** Functions such as *Binomial[t, n]* and *GegenbauerC[n, -t, -1/2]* can immediately be evaluated for continuous t and n. The pictures on the right below show $Sin[1/2 \, \pi \, a[t, n]]^2$ for these functions (equivalent to *Mod[a[t, n], 2]* for integer $a[t, n]$). The discrete results on the left can be obtained by sampling only where integer grid lines cross. Note that without further conditions the continuous forms cannot be considered unique extensions of the discrete ones. The presence of poles in quantities such as

GegenbauerC[1/2, -t, -1/2] leads to essential singularities in the rightmost picture below. (Compare page 922.)

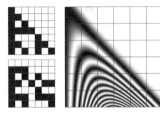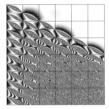

■ **Nested continuous functions.** Most standard continuous mathematical functions never show any kind of nested behavior. Elliptic theta and elliptic modular functions are exceptions. Each of these functions has definite finite values only in a limited region of the complex plane, and on the boundary of this region they exhibit singularities at every single rational point. The picture below shows *Im[ModularLambda[x + i y]]*. Like other elliptic modular functions, *ModularLambda* satisfies $f[z] == f[(a + bz)/(c + dz)]$ with a, b, c, d integers such that $ac - bd == 1$. The function can be obtained as the solution to a second-order nonlinear ordinary differential equation. Nested behavior is also found for example in *EllipticTheta[3, 0, z]*, which is given essentially by $Sum[z^{n^2}, \{n, \infty\}]$.

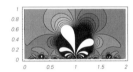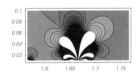

■ **Page 613 · GCD array.** (See also page 950.) There are various deviations from perfect randomness. The density of white squares is asymptotically $6/\pi^2 \simeq 0.61$. (The probability for s randomly chosen integers to be relatively prime is $1/Zeta[s]$.) No 2×2 or larger block of white squares can ever occur. An arrangement of black squares with any list of relative offsets will always eventually occur. (This follows from the Chinese Remainder Theorem.) The first 2×2 block of black squares occurs at $\{14, 20\}$, the first 3×3 block at $\{1274, 1308\}$ and the first 4×4 block at $\{7247643, 10199370\}$. The densities of such blocks are respectively about 0.002, 2×10^{-6} and 10^{-14}. In general the density for an arrangement of white squares with offsets v is given in s dimensions by (no simple closed formula seems to exist except for the 1×1 case)

Product[With[{p = Prime[n]},
*   1 - Length[Union[Mod[v, p]]]/p^s], {n, ∞}]*

White squares correspond to lattice points that are directly visible from the origin at the top left of the picture, so that

lines to them do not pass through any other integer points. On row n the number of white squares encountered before reaching the leading diagonal is *EulerPhi[n]*. This function is shown below. Its computation is known in general to be equivalent in difficulty to factoring n (see page 1090). *GCD* can be computed using Euclid's algorithm as discussed on page 915.

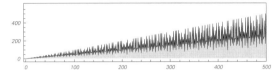

■ **Power cellular automata.** Multiplication by m in base k corresponds to a local cellular automaton operation on digit sequences when every prime that divides m also divides k. The first non-trivial cases for which this is so are $k = 6$, $m = 2^i 3^j$ and $k = 10$, $m = 2^i 5^j$. When m itself divides k, the cellular automaton rule is $\{\_, b\_, c\_\} \rightarrow m\,Mod[b, k/m] + Quotient[c, k/m]$; in other cases the rule can be obtained by composition. A similar result holds for rational m, obtained for example by allowing i and j above to be negative. In all cases the cellular automaton rule, like the original operation on numbers, is invertible. The inverse rule, corresponding to multiplication by $1/m$, can be obtained by applying the rule for multiplication by the integer k^q/m, then shifting right by q positions. (See page 903.)

The condition for locality in negative bases (see page 902) is more stringent. The first non-trivial example is $k = -6$, $m = 8$, corresponding to a rule that depends on four neighboring cells.

Non-trivial examples of multiplication by m in base k all appear to be class 3 systems (see page 250), with small changes in initial conditions growing at a roughly fixed rate.

■ **Page 615 · Computing powers.** The method of repeated squaring (also known as the binary power method, Russian peasant method and Pingala's method) computes the quantity m^t by performing about $Log[t]$ multiplications and building up the sequence

FoldList[#1^2 m^{#2} &, 1, IntegerDigits[t, 2]]

(related to the Horner form for the base 2 representation of t). Given two numbers x and y their product can be computed in base k by (*FromDigits* does the carries)

FromDigits[ListConvolve[IntegerDigits[x, k],
*   IntegerDigits[y, k], {1, -1}, 0], k]*

For numbers with n digits direct evaluation of the convolution would take about n^2 steps. But FFT-related methods reduce this to about $n\,Log[n]$ steps (see also page 1142). And this implies that to find a particular digit of m^t in base k will take altogether about $t\,Log[t]^2$ steps.

One might think that a more efficient approach would be to start with the trivial length t digit sequence for c^t in base c, then to find a particular base k digit just by converting to base k. However, the straightforward method for converting a t-digit number x to base k takes about t divisions, though this can be reduced to around $Log[t]$ by using a recursive method such as

FixedPoint[Flatten[Map[If[# < k, #, With[
    {e = Ceiling[Log[k, #]/2]}, {Quotient[#, k^e], With[
    {s = Mod[#, k^e]}, If[s == 0, Table[0, {e}], {Table[0,
    {e - Floor[Log[k, s]] - 1}], s}]]}]] &, #]] &, {x}]

The pictures below show stages in the computation of 3^{20} (a) by a power tree in base 2 and (b) by conversion from base 3. Both approaches seem to require about the same number of underlying steps. Note that even though one may only want to find a single digit in m^t, I know of no way to do this without essentially computing all the other digits in m^t as well.

■ **Complex powers.** The pictures below show successive powers of complex numbers z with digits extracted according to

(2 d[Re[#], w] + d[Im[#], w] &)[z^t]

d[x_, w_] := If[x < 0, 1 - d[-x, w], IntegerDigits[x, 2, w]]

Non-trivial cases of complex number multiplication never correspond to local cellular automaton operations. (Compare page 933.)

$z = 1 + i$ $z = 2 + i$ $z = 3 + i$ $z = 1 + 2i$

■ **Additive cellular automata.** As discussed on page 951 a step in the evolution of an additive cellular automaton can be thought of as multiplication by a polynomial modulo k. After t steps, therefore, the configuration of such a system is given by $PolynomialMod[poly^t, k]$. This quantity can be computed using power tree methods (see below), though as discussed on page 609, even more efficient methods are also available. (A similar formalism can be set up for any of the cellular automata with generalized additivity discussed on page 952; see also page 886.)

■ **The more general case.** One can think of a single step in the evolution of any system as taking a rule r and state s, and producing a new state $h[r, s]$. Usually the representations that are used for r and s will be quite different, and the

function h will have no special properties. But for both multiplication rules and additive cellular automata it turns out that rules and states can be represented in the same way, and the evolution functions h have the property of being associative, so that $h[a, h[b, c]] == h[h[a, b], c]$. This means that in effect one can always choose to evolve the rule rather than a state. A consequence is that for example 4 steps of evolution can be computed not only as $h[r, h[r, h[r, h[r, s]]]]$ but also as $h[h[h[r, r], h[r, r]], s]$ or $u = h[r, r]; h[h[u, u], s]$—which requires only 3 applications of h. And in general if h is associative the result $Nest[h[r, #] \&, s, t]$ of t steps of evolution can be rewritten for example using the repeated squaring method as

h[Fold[If[#2 == 0, h[#1, #1], h[r, h[#1, #1]]] &,
    r, Rest[IntegerDigits[t, 2]]], s]

which requires only about $Log[t]$ rather than t applications of h.

As a very simple example, consider a system which starts with the integer 1, then at each step just adds 1. One can compute the result of 9 steps of evolution as $1 + 1 + 1 + 1 + 1 + 1 + 1 + 1 + 1 + 1$, but a better scheme is to use partial results and compute successively $1 + 1; 2 + 2; 1 + 4; 5 + 5$—which is what the repeated squaring method above does when $h = Plus$, $r = s = 1$. This same basic scheme can be used with any associative function h—Max, GCD, And, Dot, $Join$ or whatever—so long as suitable forms for r and s are used.

For the multiplication rules discussed in the main text both states and rules can immediately be represented by integers, with $h = Times$, and $r = m$ giving the multiplier. For additive cellular automata, states and rules can be represented as polynomials (see page 951), with $h[a_, b_] := PolynomialMod[a \, b, k]$ and for example $r = 1 + x$ for elementary rule 60. The correspondence between multiplication rules and additive cellular automata can be seen even more directly if one represents all states by integers and computes h in terms of base k digits. In both cases it then turns out that h can be obtained from (see note above)

h[a_, b_] := FromDigits[g[ListConvolve[
    IntegerDigits[a, k], IntegerDigits[b, k], {1, -1}, 0]], k]

where for multiplication rules $g = Identity$ and for additive cellular automata $g = Mod[#, k] \&$. For multiplication rules, there are normally carries (handled by $FromDigits$), but for power cellular automata, these have only limited range, so that $g = Mod[#, k^\sigma] \&$ can be used.

For any associative function h the repeated squaring method allows the result of t steps of evolution to be computed with only about $Log[t]$ applications of h. But to be able to do this some of the arguments given to h inevitably need to be larger.

So whether a speedup is in the end achieved will depend on how fast h can be evaluated for arguments of various sizes. Typically the issue is whether $h[a, b]$ for large a and b can be found with much less effort than it would take to evaluate $h[r, b]$ about a times. If $h = Times$, then as discussed in the note above, the most obvious procedure for evaluating $h[a, b]$ would involve about $m\,n$ operations, where m and n are the numbers of digits in a and b. But when $m \simeq n$ FFT-related methods allow this to be reduced to about $n\,Log[n]$ operations. And in fact whenever h is commutative (*Orderless*) it turns out that such methods can be used, and substantial speedups obtained. But whether anything like this will work in other cases is not clear.

(See also page 886.)

■ **Evaluation chains.** The idea of building up computations like $1 + 1 + 1 + ...$ from partial results has existed since Egyptian times. Since the late 1800s there have been efforts to find schemes that require the absolute minimum number of steps. The method based on *IntegerDigits* in the previous two notes can be improved (notably by power tree methods), but apparently about $Log[t]$ steps are always needed. (Finding the optimal addition chain for given t may be NP-complete.)

One can also consider building up lists of non-identical elements, say by successively using *Join*. In general a length n list can require about n steps. But if the list contains a nested sequence, say generated using a substitution system, then about $Log[n]$ steps should be sufficient. (Compare page 566.)

■ **Boolean formulas.** A Boolean function of n variables can always be specified by an explicit table giving values for all 2^n possible inputs. (Any cellular automaton rule with an n-cell neighborhood corresponds to such a function; digit sequences in rule numbers correspond to explicit tables of values.) Like ordinary algebraic functions, Boolean functions can also be represented by a variety of kinds of formulas. Those on pages 616 and 618 use so-called disjunctive normal form (DNF) $And[...] \lor And[...] \lor ...$, which is common in practice in programmable logic arrays (PLAs). (The addition and multiplication operators in the main text should be interpreted as *Or* and *And* respectively.) In general any given function will allow many DNF representations; minimal ones can be found as described below. Writing a Boolean function in DNF is the rough analog of applying *Expand* to a polynomial. Conjunctive normal form (CNF) $Or[...] \land Or[...] \land ...$ is the rough analog of applying *Factor*. DNF and CNF both involve Boolean formulas of depth 2. As in the note on multilevel formulas below, one can also in effect introduce intermediate

variables to get recursive formulas of larger depth, somewhat analogous to results from *Collect*. (Unbalanced depths in different parts of a formula lead to latencies in a circuit, reducing practical utility.)

■ **DNF minimization.** From a table of values for a Boolean function one can immediately get a DNF representation just by listing cases where the value is 1. For one step in rule 30, for example, this yields $\{\{1, 0, 0\}, \{0, 1, 1\}, \{0, 1, 0\}, \{0, 0, 1\}\}$, as shown on page 616. One can think of this as specifying corners that should be colored on an n-dimensional Boolean hypercube. To reduce the representation, one must introduce "don't care" elements _; in this example the final minimal form consists of the list of 3 so-called implicants $\{\{1, 0, 0\}, \{0, 1, \_\}, \{0, \_, 1\}\}$. In general, an implicant with m _'s can be thought of as corresponding to an m-dimensional hyperplane on the Boolean hypercube. The problem of minimization is then to find the minimal set of hyperplanes that will cover the corners for a particular Boolean function. The first step is to work out so-called prime implicants corresponding to hyperplanes that cannot be contained in higher-dimensional ones. Given an original DNF list s, this can be done using $PI[s, n]$:

$PI[s\_, n\_] := Union[Flatten[$
$\qquad FixedPointList[f[Last[\#], n] \&, \{\{\}, s\}][[All, 1]], 1]]$

$g[a\_, b\_] := With[\{i = Position[Transpose[\{a, b\}], \{0, 1\}]\},$
$\qquad If[Length[i] == 1 \&\& Delete[a, i] === Delete[b, i],$
$\qquad \{ReplacePart[a, \_, i]\}, \{\}]]$

$f[s\_, n\_] := With[$
$\qquad \{w = Flatten[Apply[Outer[g, \#1, \#2, 1] \&, Partition[Table[$
$\qquad Select[s, Count[\#, 1] == i \&], \{i, 0, n\}], 2, 1], \{1\}],$
$\qquad 3]\}, \{Complement[s, w, SameTest \to MatchQ], w\}]$

The minimal DNF then consists of a collection of these prime implicants. Sometimes it is all of them, but increasingly often when $n \geq 3$ it is only some. (For example, in $\{\{0, 0, \_\}, \{0, \_, 1\}, \{\_, 0, 0\}\}$ the first prime implicant is covered by the others, and can therefore be dropped.) Given the original list s and the complete prime implicant list p the so-called Quine-McCluskey procedure can be used to find a minimal list of prime implicants, and thus a minimal DNF:

$QM[s\_, p\_] := First[Sort[Map[p[[\#]] \&,$
$\qquad h[\{\}, Range[Length[s]], Outer[MatchQ, s, p, 1]]]]]$

$h[i\_, r\_, t\_] := Flatten[Map[h[Join[i, r[[\#]]], Drop[r, \#],$
$\qquad Delete[Drop[t, \{\}, \#], Position[t[[All, \#]], \{True\}]]] \&,$
$\qquad First[Sort[Map[Position[\#, True] \&, t]]]], 1]$

$h[i\_, \_, \{\}] := \{i\}$

The number of steps required in this procedure can increase exponentially with the length of p. Other procedures work slightly more efficiently, but in general the problem of finding the minimal DNF for a Boolean function of n

variables is NP-complete (see page 768) and is thus expected to grow in difficulty faster than any polynomial in n. In practice, however, cases up to about $n = 12$ are nevertheless currently handled quite routinely.

■ **Formula sizes.** There are a total of 2^{2^n} possible Boolean functions of n variables. The maximum number of terms needed to represent any of these functions in DNF is 2^{n-1}. The actual numbers of functions which require 0, 1, 2, ... terms is for $n = 2$: {1, 9, 6}; for $n = 3$: {1, 27, 130, 88, 10}, and for $n = 4$: {1, 81, 1804, 13472, 28904, 17032, 3704, 512, 26}. The maximal length turns out always to be realized for the simple parity function Xor, as well as its negation. The reason for this is essentially that these functions are the ones that make the coloring of the Boolean hypercube maximally fragmented. (Other functions with maximal length are never additive, at least for $n \leq 4$.)

■ **Cellular automaton formulas.** See page 869. The maximum length DNF for elementary rules after 1 step is 4, and this is achieved by rules 105, 107, 109, 121, 150, 151, 158, 182, 214 and 233. These rules have behavior of quite varying complexity. Rules 150 and 105 are additive, and correspond to Xor and its negation. After t steps the maximum conceivable DNF would be of length 2^{2t}. In practice, after 2 steps, the maximum length is 9, achieved by rules 107, 121 and 182; after 3 steps, it is 33 achieved by rule 182; after 4 steps, 78 achieved by rule 129; after 5 steps 256 achieved by rules 105 and 150. The distributions of lengths for all elementary rules are shown below.

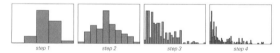

step 1   step 2   step 3   step 4

Note that the length of a minimal DNF representation cannot be considered a reliable measure of the complexity of a function, since among other things, just exchanging the role of black and white can substantially change this length (as in the case of rule 126 versus rule 129).

■ **Primitive functions.** There are several possible choices of primitive functions that can be combined to represent any Boolean function. In DNF And, Or and Not are used. $Nand = Not[And[\#\#]]$ & alone is also sufficient, as shown on page 619 and further discussed on page 807. (It is indicated by $\bar{n}$ in the main text.) The functions And, Xor and Not are equivalent to $Times$, $Plus$ and $1 - \#$ for variables modulo 2, and in this case algebraic functions like $PolynomialReduce$ can be used for minimization. (See also page 1102.)

■ **Multilevel formulas.** DNF formulas always have depth 2. By allowing larger depths one can potentially find smaller formulas

for functions. A major result from the 1980s is that it requires a formula with depth at least $Log[n]/(c + Log[Log[n]])$ to make it possible to represent an Xor of n variables using a polynomial number of And, Or and Not operations. If one chooses an n-variable Boolean function at random out of the 2^{2^n} possibilities, it is typical that regardless of depth a formula involving at least $2^n/n$ operations will be needed to represent it. A formula of polynomial size and logarithmic depth exists only when a function is the computational complexity class NC discussed on page 1149.

Little is known about systematic minimization of Boolean formulas with depths above 2. Nevertheless, some programs for circuit design such as SIS do include a few heuristics. And this for example allows SIS to generate higher depth formulas somewhat smaller than the minimal DNF for the first three steps of rule 30 evolution.

$$b_1 = a_2 + a_3 \cdot \bar{a}_1 \, b_1 + a_1 \, \bar{b}_1$$
$$b_1 = \bar{a}_2 \, a_3 + a_2 \, \bar{a}_3; \, b_2 = a_4 + a_5; \, a_1 \, b_1 + a_1 \, \bar{b}_2 + \bar{a}_1 \, b_1 \, b_2$$
$$b_1 = a_6 + a_7; \, b_2 = a_4 + a_5; \, b_3 = \bar{a}_5 \, b_1 + a_4 \, \bar{b}_1; \, b_4 = \bar{b}_1 + b_2; \, \bar{a}_1 \, \bar{a}_3 \, b_3 + \bar{a}_1 \, a_2 \, \bar{b}_2 +$$
$$a_1 \, \bar{a}_2 \, \bar{a}_3 \, b_3 + \bar{a}_1 \, a_2 \, a_4 \, \bar{b}_3 + a_1 \, a_2 \, \bar{a}_4 \, b_2 + \bar{a}_1 \, \bar{a}_2 \, a_3 \, b_4 + a_1 \, \bar{a}_2 \, a_3 \, \bar{b}_4 + a_1 \, a_2 \, a_3 \, b_4$$

■ **Page 619 · NAND expressions.** If one allows a depth of at most $2n$ any n-input Boolean function can be obtained just by combining 2-input $Nand$ functions. (See page 807.) (Note that unless one introduces an explicit copy operation—or adds variables as in the previous note—there is no way to use the same intermediate result multiple times without recomputing it.)

The pictures below show the distributions of numbers of $Nand$ operations needed for all 2^{2^n} n-input Boolean functions. For $n = 2$, the largest number of such operations is 6, achieved by Nor; for $n = 3$, it is 14, achieved by Xor (rule 150); for $n = 4$, it is 27, achieved by rule 5737, which is $Not[Xor[\#\#]]$ & except when all inputs are $True$. The average number of operations needed when $n = 2$, 3, 4 is about {2.875, 6.09, 12.23}.

n=2   n=3   n=4

The maximum depths for the expressions of minimal size are respectively 4, 6 and 7, always achieved among others for the function taking the most $Nand$ operations. The total numbers of functions involving successive depths are: $n = 2$: {2, 3, 5, 6}, $n = 3$: {3, 6, 22, 99, 72, 54}, $n = 4$: {4, 10, 64, 923, 9663, 54622, 250}, corresponding to averages {2.9, 4.5, 5.8}.

The following generates explicit lists of n-input Boolean functions requiring successively larger numbers of *Nand* operations:

```
Map[FromDigits[#, 2] &, NestWhile[Append[#,
    Complement[Flatten[Table[Outer[1 - Times[##] &,
    #[[i]], #[[-i]], 1], {i, Length[#]}], 2], Flatten[#, 1]]] &,
    {1 - Transpose[IntegerDigits[Range[2^n] - 1, 2, n]]},
    Length[Flatten[#, 1]] < 2^2^n &], {2}]
```

The results for 2-step cellular automaton evolution in the main text were found by a recursive procedure. First, expressions containing progressively more *Nand* operations were enumerated, and those for functions that had not been seen before were kept. It then turned out that this made it possible to get to expressions at least half as large as any needed, so that it could be assumed that remaining expressions could be decomposed as $f[\#\#] \bar{n} g[\#\#]$ &, where f had already been found. The pictures below show some more results obtained in this way.

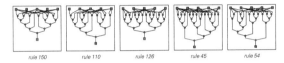

rule 150   rule 110   rule 126   rule 45   rule 54

■ **Cellular automaton formulas.** For 1 step, the elementary cellular automaton rules are exactly the 256 $n = 3$ Boolean functions. For 2 steps, they represent a small subset of the 2^{32} $n = 5$ functions. They require an average of about 11.6 *Nand* operations, and a maximum of 27 (achieved by rules 107 and 121).

For rule 254 the result after t steps (which is always asymmetric, even though the rule is symmetric) is

$$Nest[\{\{\#, \#[[2]] + 1\}, \#[[2]] + 1\} \&, \{\{1, 1\}, \{2, 2\}\}, t - 2]$$

If explicit copy operations were allowed, then the number of *Nand* operations after t steps could not increase faster than t^2 for any rule. But without copy (fanout) operations no corresponding result is immediately clear.

■ **Binary decision diagrams.** One can specify a Boolean function of n variables by giving a finite automaton (and thus a network) in which paths exist only for those lists of values for which the function yields *True*. The resulting so-called binary decision diagram (BDD) can be minimized using the methods of page 957. Out of all possible Boolean functions the number that require BDDs of sizes 1, 2, ... is for $n = 2$: {1, 0, 6, 9} and for $n = 3$: {1, 0, 0, 27, 36, 132, 60}; the absolute maximum grows roughly like 2^n. For cellular automata with simple behavior, the minimal BDD typically grows linearly on successive steps. For rule 254, for example, it is $8t + 2$, while for rule 90 it is $4t + 2$. For cellular automata with more complex behavior, it typically grows roughly exponentially.

Thus for rule 30 it is {7, 14, 29, 60, 129} and for rule 110 {7, 15, 27, 52, 88}. The size of the minimal BDD can depend on the order in which variables are specified; thus for example, just reflecting rule 30 to give rule 86 yields {6, 11, 20, 36, 63}.

In practical system design BDDs have become fairly popular in the past ten years, and by maintaining minimality when logical combinations of functions are formed, cases with millions of nodes have been studied. (Some practical systems are found to yield fairly small BDDs, while others are not.)

■ **History.** Logic has been used as an abstraction of arguments in ordinary language since antiquity. Its serious mathematical formulation began with the work of George Boole in the mid-1800s. (See page 1151.) Concepts of Boolean algebra were applied to electronic switching circuits by Claude Shannon in 1937, and became a standard part of electronic design methodology by the 1950s. DNF had been introduced as part of the development of mathematical logic in the early 1900s, but became particularly popular in the 1970s with the advent of programmable logic arrays (PLAs) used in application-specific integrated circuits (ASICs). Diagrammatic and mechanical methods for minimizing simple logic expressions have existed since at least medieval times. More systematic methods for minimizing complex expressions began to be developed in the early 1950s, but until well into the 1980s a diagrammatic method known as a Karnaugh map was the most commonly used in practice. In the late 1970s there began to be computer programs for large-scale Boolean minimization—the best known being *Espresso*. Only in the 1990s, however, did exact minimization of complex DNF expressions become common. Minimization of Boolean expressions with depth larger than 2 has been considered off and on since the late 1950s, and became popular in the 1990s in connection with the BDDs discussed above. Various forms of Boolean minimization have routinely been used in chip and circuit design since the late 1980s, though often physical and geometrical constraints are now more important than pure logical ones. In addition, theoretical studies of minimal Boolean circuits became increasingly popular starting in the 1980s, as discussed on page 1148.

■ **Reversible logic.** In an ordinary Boolean function with n inputs there is no unique way to tell from its output which of the 2^n possible sets of inputs was given. But as noted in the 1970s, it is possible to set up systems that evaluate Boolean functions, yet operate reversibly. The basic idea is to have m outputs as well as m inputs—with every one of the 2^m possible sets of inputs mapping to a unique set of outputs. Normally one specifies the first n inputs, taking the others to be fixed, and then looks say at the first output, ignoring all others. One can represent the inside of such a system much like a sorting network from page 1142—but with s-input s-output gates instead of pair comparisons. If each such gate is itself reversible, then overall reversibility is guaranteed. With gates that in effect implement $\{p, q\} \to \{p \bar\pi q\}$ and $\{p\} \to \{p, p\}$ (with other inputs constant, and other outputs ignored) one can set up a direct translation of Boolean functions given in the form shown on page 619. Of the 24 possible reversible $s = 2$ gates, none can yield anything other than additive Boolean functions (as formed from *Xor* and *Not*). But of the 40,320 ($8!$) reversible $s = 3$ gates (in 52 distinct classes) it turns out that 38,976 (in 23 classes) can be used to reproduce any possible Boolean function. A simple example of such a universal gate is $\{p\_, q\_, 1\} \to \{q, p, 1\}$—and not allowing permutations of gate inputs (or in effect wire crossings) a simple example is $\{p\_, q\_, q\_\} \to \{q, 1 - p, 1 - p\}$. (Compare pages 1147 and 1173.)

■ **Continuous systems.** The systems I discuss in the main text of this section are mostly discrete. But from experience with traditional mathematics one might have the impression that it would at some basic level be easier to get formulas for continuous systems. I believe, however, that this is not the case, and that the reason for the impression is just that it is usually so much more difficult even to represent the states of continuous systems that one normally tends to work only with ones that have comparatively simple overall behavior—and are therefore more readily described by formulas. (See also pages 167 and 729.)

As an example of what can happen in continuous systems consider iterated mappings $x \to a x (1 - x)$ from page 920. Each successive step in such a mapping can in principle be represented by an algebraic formula. But the table below gives for example the actual algebraic formulas obtained in the case $a = 4$ after applying *FullSimplify*—and shows that these increase quite rapidly in complexity.

x
$4 (1 - x) x$
$16 (1 - 2 x)^2 (1 - x) x$
$64 (1 - 2 x)^2 (1 - x) x (8 (x - 1) x + 1)^2$
$256 (1 - 2 x)^2 (1 - x) x (8 (x - 1) x + 1)^2 (32 (x - 1) x (1 - 2 x)^2 + 1)^2$
$1024 (1 - 2 x)^2 (1 - x) x (8 (x - 1) x + 1)^2 (32 (x - 1) x (1 - 2 x)^2 + 1)^2$
$(128 (1 - 2 x)^2 (x - 1) x (8 (x - 1) x + 1)^2 + 1)^2$

In the specific case $a = 4$, however, it turns out that by allowing more sophisticated mathematical functions one can get a complete formula: the result after any number of steps t can be written in any of the forms

$Sin[2^t ArcSin[\sqrt{x} \,]]^2$

$(1 - Cos[2^t ArcCos[1 - 2 x]])/2$

$(1 - ChebyshevT [2^t, 1 - 2 x])/2$

where these follow from functional relations such as

$Sin[2 x]^2 == 4 Sin[x]^2 (1 - Sin[x]^2)$

$ChebyshevT [m n, x] == ChebyshevT [m, ChebyshevT [n, x]]$

For $a = 2$ it also turns out that there is a complete formula:

$(1 - (1 - 2 x)^{2^t})/2$

And the same is true for $a = -2$:

$1/2 - Cos[1/3 (\pi - (-2)^t (\pi - 3 ArcCos[1/2 - x]))]$

In all these examples t enters essentially only in a^t. And if one assumes that this is a general feature then one can formally derive for any a the result

$1/2 (1 - g[a^t InverseFunction[g][1 - 2 x]])$

where g is a function that satisfies the functional equation

$g[a x] == 1 + 1/2 a (g[x]^2 - 1)$

When $a = 4$, $g[x]$ is $Cosh[Sqrt[2 x]]$. When $a = 2$ it is $Exp[x]$ and when $a = -2$ it is $2 Cos[1/3 (\pi - \sqrt{3} \, x)]$. But in general for arbitrary a there is no standard mathematical function that seems to satisfy the functional equation. (It has long been known that only elliptic functions such as *JacobiSN* satisfy polynomial addition formulas—but there is no immediate analog of this for replication formulas.) Given the functional equation one can find a power series for $g[x]$ for any a. The series has an accumulation of poles on the circle $Abs[a]^2 == 1$; the coefficient of x^m turns out to have denominator

$2 \wedge (m - DigitCount[m, 2, 1]) Apply[Times,$
$\quad Table[Cyclotomic[s, a] \wedge Floor[(m - 1)/s], \{s, m - 1\}]]$

For other iterated maps general formulas also seem rare. But for example $x \to a x + b$ and $x \to 1/(a + b x)$ both give results just involving powers, while $x \to Sqrt[a x + b]$ sometimes yields trigonometric functions, as on page 915. In addition, from a known replication formula for an elliptic or other function one can often construct an iterated map whose behavior can be expressed in terms of that function. (See also page 919.)

Human Thinking

■ **The brain.** There are a total of about 100 billion neurons in a human brain (see page 1075), each with an average of a few thousand synapses connecting it to other cells. On a small scale the arrangement of neurons seems quite haphazard. But on a larger scale the brain seems to be organized into areas with very definite functions. This organization is sometimes revealed by explicitly following nerve fibers. More often it has been deduced by looking at what happens if parts of the brain are disabled or stimulated. In recent times it has also begun to be possible to image local electrical and metabolic activity while the brain is in normal operation. From all these methods it is known that each kind of sensory input is first processed in its own specific area of the brain. Inputs from different senses are integrated in an area that effectively maintains a map of the body; a similar area initiates output to muscles. Certain higher mental functions are known to be localized in definite areas of the brain, though within these areas there is often variability between individuals. Areas are currently known for specific aspects of language, memory (see below) and various cognitive tasks. There is some evidence that thinking about seemingly rather similar things can lead to significantly different patterns of activity.

Most of the action of the brain seems to be associated with local electrical connections between neurons. Some collective electrical activity is however revealed by EEG. In addition, levels of chemicals such as hormones, drugs and neurotransmitters can have significant global effects on the brain.

■ **History.** Ever since antiquity immense amounts have been written about human thinking. Until recent centuries most of it was in the tradition of philosophy, and indeed one of the major themes of philosophy throughout its history has been the elucidation of principles of human thinking. However, almost all the relevant ideas generated have remained forever controversial, and almost none have become concrete enough to be applied in science or technology. An exception is logic, which was introduced in earnest by Aristotle in the 4th century BC as a way to model certain patterns of human reasoning. Logic developed somewhat in medieval times, and in the late 1600s Gottfried Leibniz tried to use it as the foundation for a universal language to capture all systematic thinking. Beginning with the work of George Boole in the mid-1800s most of logic began to become more closely integrated with mathematics and even less convincingly relevant as a model for general human thinking.

The notion of applying scientific methods to the study of human thinking developed largely with the rise of the field of psychology in the mid-1800s. Two somewhat different approaches were taken. The first concentrated on doing fairly controlled experiments on humans or animals and looking at responses to specific stimuli. The second concentrated on trying to formulate fairly general theories based on observations of overall human behavior, initially in adults and later especially in children. Both approaches achieved some success, but by the 1930s many of their positions had become quite extreme, and the identification of phenomena to contradict every simple conclusion reached led increasingly to the view that human thinking would allow no simple explanations.

The idea that it might be possible to construct machines or other inanimate objects that could emulate human thinking

existed already in antiquity, and became increasingly popular starting in the 1600s. It began to appear widely in fiction in the 1800s, and has remained a standard fixture in portrayals of the future ever since.

In the early 1900s it became clear that the brain consists of neurons which operate electrically, and by the 1940s analogies between brains and electrical machines were widely discussed, particularly in the context of the cybernetics movement. In 1943 Warren McCulloch and Walter Pitts formulated a simple idealized model of networks of neurons and tried to analyze it using methods of mathematical logic. In 1949 Donald Hebb then argued that simple underlying neural mechanisms could explain observed psychological phenomena such as learning. Computer simulations of neural networks were done starting in the mid-1950s, but the networks were too small to have any chance to exhibit behavior that could reasonably be identified with thinking. (Ironically enough, as mentioned on page 879, the phenomenon central to this book of complex behavior with simple underlying rules was in effect seen in some of these experiments, but it was considered a distraction and ignored.) And in the 1960s, particularly after Frank Rosenblatt's introduction of perceptrons, neural networks were increasingly used only as systems for specific visual and other tasks (see page 1076).

The idea that computers could be made to exhibit human-like thinking was discussed by Alan Turing in 1950 using many of the same arguments that one would give today. Turing made the prediction that by 2000 a computer would exist that could pass the so-called Turing test and be able to imitate a human in a conversation. (René Descartes had discussed a similar test for machines in 1637, but concluded that it would never be passed.) When electronic computers were first becoming widespread in the 1950s they were often popularly referred to as "electronic brains". And when early efforts to make computers perform tasks such as playing games were fairly successful, the expectation developed that general human-like thinking was not far away. In the 1960s, with extensive support from the U.S. government, great effort was put into the field of artificial intelligence. Many programs were written to perform specific tasks. Sometimes the programs were set up to follow general models of the high-level processes of thinking. But by the 1970s it was becoming clear that in almost all cases where programs were successful (notable examples being chess, algebra and autonomous control), they typically worked by following definite algorithms not closely related to general human thinking.

Occasional work on neural networks had continued through the 1960s and 1970s, with a few definite results being obtained using methods from physics. Then in the early 1980s, particularly following work by John Hopfield, computer simulations of neural networks became widespread. Early applications, particularly by Terrence Sejnowski and Geoffrey Hinton, demonstrated that simple neural networks could be made to learn tasks of at least some sophistication. But by the mid-1990s it was becoming clear that—probably in large part as a consequence of reliance on methods from traditional mathematics—typical neural network models were mostly being successful only in situations where what was needed was a fairly straightforward extension of standard continuous probabilistic models of data.

■ **The future.** To achieve human-like thinking with computers will no doubt require advances in both basic science and technology. I strongly suspect that a key element is to be able to store a collection of experiences comparable to those of a human. Indeed, to succeed even with specific tasks such as speech recognition or language translation seems to require human-like amounts of background knowledge. Present-day computers are beginning to have storage capacities that are probably comparable to those of the brain. From looking at the brain one might guess that parallel or other non-standard hardware might be required to achieve efficient human-like thinking. But I rather suspect that—much as in the analogy between birds and airplanes—it will in the end be possible to set up algorithms that achieve the same basic functions but work satisfactorily even on standard sequential-processing computers.

■ **Sleep.** A common feature of higher organisms is the existence of distinct behavioral states of sleep and wakefulness. There are various theories that sleep is somehow fundamental to the process of thinking. But my guess is that its most important function is quite mundane: just as muscles build up lactic acid waste products, so also I suspect synapses in the brain build up waste products, and these can only safely be cleared out when the brain is not in normal use.

■ **Page 621 · Pointer encoding.** The pointer encoding compression method discussed on page 571 implements a very simple form of memory based on literal repetitions, and already leads to fairly good compression of many kinds of data.

■ **Page 622 · Hashing.** Given data in the form of sequences of numbers between 0 and $k - 1$, a very simple hashing scheme is just to compute $FromDigits[Take[list, n], k]$. But for data corresponding, say, to English words this scheme yields a very nonuniform distribution of hash codes, since, for example, there are many words beginning with "ba", but

none beginning with "bb". The slightly modified but still very simple scheme $Mod[FromDigits[list, k], m]$, where m is usually chosen to be a prime, is what is most often used in practice. For a fair fraction of values of m, the hash codes obtained from this scheme change whenever any element of $list$ is changed. If $m = k^s - 1$ then it turns out that interchanging a pair of adjacent length s blocks in $list$ never affects the result. Out of the many hundreds of times that I have used hashing in practice, I recall only a couple of cases where schemes like the one just described were not adequate, and in these cases the data always turned out to have quite dramatic regularities.

In typical applications hash codes give locations in computer memory, from which actual data is found either by following a chain of pointers, or by probing successive locations until an empty one is reached. In the internals of *Mathematica* the most common way that hashing is used is for recognizing data and finding unique stored versions of it. There are several subtleties associated with setting up hash codes that appropriately handle approximate real numbers and *Mathematica* patterns.

Hashing is a sufficiently simple idea that it has been invented independently many times since at least the 1950s. The main alternative to hashing is to store data with successive elements corresponding to successive levels in a tree. In the past decade, hashing has become widely used not only for searching but also for authentication. The basic idea in this case is to take a document and to compute from it a small hash code that changes when almost any change is made in the document, and for which it is a difficult problem of cryptanalysis to work out what changes in the document will lead to no change in the hash code. Schemes for such hash codes can fairly easily be constructed using rule 30 and other cellular automata.

■ **Page 623 · Similar words.** The soundex system for hashing names according to sound was first used on 1880 U.S. census data, and is still today widely used by telephone information services. The system works essentially by dropping vowels and assigning consonants to six possible groups. More sophisticated systems along the same lines can be set up using finite automata.

Natural language query systems usually work by stripping words to their linguistic roots (e.g. "stripping" → "strip") before looking them up. Spell-checking systems typically find suggested corrections by doing a succession of lookups after applying transformations based on common errors.

Even given two specific words it can be difficult to find out whether they should be considered similar. Fairly efficient algorithms are known for cases such as genetic sequences where small numbers of insertions, deletions and substitutions are expected. But if more complicated transformations are allowed—say corresponding to rules in a multiway system—the problem rapidly becomes intractable (see page 765).

■ **Numerical data.** In situations where pieces of data can be thought of as points in space similarity can often be defined in terms of spatial distance. And this means that around every point corresponding to a piece of data in memory there is a region of points that can be considered more similar to that point than to any other. Picture (a) shows a so-called Voronoi diagram (see page 1038) obtained in this way in two dimensions. Particularly in higher dimensions, it becomes rather difficult in practice to determine for certain which existing point is closest to some new point. But to do it approximately is considerably easier. One approach, illustrated in picture (b), is to use a d-dimensional tree. Another approach, illustrated in picture (c), is to set up a continuous function with minima at the existing points, and then to search for the closest minimum. In most cases, this search will be done using some iterative scheme such as Newton's method; the result is that the boundaries between regions typically take on an intricate nested form. (The case shown corresponds to iteration of the map $z \to z - (z^3 - 1)/(3z^2)$ corresponding to Newton's method for finding the complex roots of $z^3 == 1$.)

(a)   (b)   (c)

The pictures below show how one can build up a kind of memory landscape by successively adding points. In a first approximation, the regions considered similar to a particular minimum are delimited by sharp watersheds corresponding to local maxima in the landscape. But if an iterative scheme for minimization is used, these watersheds are typically no longer sharp, but take on a local nested structure, much as in picture (c) above.

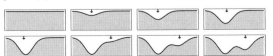

In numbers earlier digits are traditionally considered more important than later ones, and this allows numbers to be arranged in a simple one-dimensional sequence. But in strings where each element is considered equally important, no such layout is possible. A vague approximation, perhaps useful for some applications, is nevertheless to use a space-filling curve (see page 893).

■ **Error-correcting codes.** In many information transmission and storage applications one needs to be able to recover data even if some errors are introduced into it. The standard way to do this is to set up an error-correcting code in which blocks of m original data elements are represented by a codeword of length n that in effect includes some redundant elements. Then—somewhat in analogy to retrieving closest memories—one can take a sequence of length n that one receives and find the codeword that differs from it in the fewest elements. If the codewords are chosen so that every pair differs by at least r elements (or equivalently, have so-called Hamming distance at least r), then this means that errors in up to $Floor[(r - 1)/2]$ elements can be corrected, and finding suitable codewords is like finding packings of spheres in n-dimensional space. It is common in practice to use so-called linear codes which can be analyzed using algebraic methods, and for which the spheres are arranged in a repetitive array. The Hamming codes with $n = 2^s - 1$, $m = n - s$, $r = 3$ are an example, invented by Marcel Golay in 1949 and Richard Hamming in 1950. Defining

$PM[s_] := IntegerDigits[Range[2^s - 1], 2, s]$

blocks of data of length m can be encoded with

$Join[data, Mod[data . Select[PM[s], Count[\#, 1] > 1 \&], 2]]$

while blocks of length n (and at most one error) can be decoded with

$Drop[(If[\# == 0, data, MapAt[1 - \# \&, data, \#]] \&)[$
$\quad FromDigits[Mod[data . PM[s], 2], 2]], -s]$

A number of families of linear codes are known, together with a few nonlinear ones. But in all cases they tend to be based on rather special mathematical structures which do not seem likely to occur in any system like the brain.

■ **Matrix memories.** Many times since the 1950s it has been noted that methods from linear algebra suggest ways to construct associative memories in which data can potentially be retrieved on the basis of some form of similarity. Typically one starts from some list of vectors to be stored, then forms a matrix such as $m = PseudoInverse[list]$. Given a new piece of data corresponding to a vector v, its decomposition in terms of stored vectors can be found by computing $v . m$. And by applying various forms of thresholding one can often pick out at least approximately the stored vector closest to the piece of data given. But such schemes tend to be inefficient in practice, as well as presumably being unrealistic as actual models of the brain.

■ **Neural network models.** The basic rule used in essentially all neural network models is extremely simple. Each neuron is assumed to have a value between -1 and 1 corresponding roughly to a firing rate. Then given a list $s[i]$ of the values of one set of neurons, one finds the values of another set using $s[i + 1] = u[w \cdot s[i]]$, where in early models $u = Sign$ was usually chosen, and now $u = Tanh$ is more common, and w is a rectangular matrix which gives weights—normally assumed to be continuous numbers, often between -1 and +1—for the synaptic connections between the neurons in each set. In the simplest case, studied especially in the context of perceptrons in the 1960s, one has only two sets of neurons: an input layer and an output layer. But with suitable weights one can reproduce many functions. For example, with three inputs and one output, $w = \{\{-1, +1, -1\}\}$ yields essentially the rule for the rule 178 elementary cellular automaton. But out of the 2^{2^n} possible Boolean functions of n inputs, only 14 (out of 16) can be obtained for $n = 2$, 104 (out of 256) for $n = 3$, 1882 for $n = 4$, and 94304 for $n = 5$. (The VC dimension is $n + 1$ for such systems.) The key idea that became popular in the early 1980s was to consider neural networks with an additional layer of "hidden units". By introducing enough hidden units it is then possible—just as in the formulas discussed on page 616—to reproduce essentially any function. Suitable weights (which are typically far from unique) are in practice usually found by gradient descent methods based either on minimization of deviations from desired outputs given particular inputs (supervised learning) or on maximization of some discrimination or other criterion (unsupervised learning).

Particularly in early investigations of neural networks, it was common to consider systems more like very simple cellular automata, in which the $s[i]$ corresponded not to states of successive layers of neurons, but rather to states of the same set of neurons at successive times. For most choices of weights, such a system exhibits typical class 3 behavior and never settles down to give an obvious definite output. But in special circumstances probably not of great biological relevance it can yield class 2 behavior. An example studied by John Hopfield in 1981 is a symmetric matrix w with neuron values being updated sequentially in a random order rather than in parallel.

■ **Memory.** Since the early 1900s it has been suspected that long-term memory is somehow encoded in the strengths of synaptic connections between nerve cells. It is known that at least in specific cases such strengths can remain unchanged for at least hours or more, but can immediately change if connected nerve cells have various patterns of simultaneous excitation. The changes that occur appear to be associated with changes in ionic channels in cell membranes and sometimes with the addition of new synapses between cells.

Observations suggest that in humans there are several different types of memory, with somewhat different characteristics. (Examples include memory for facts and for motor skills.) Usually there is a short-term or so-called working component, lasting perhaps 30 seconds, and typically holding perhaps seven items, and a long-term component that can apparently last a lifetime. Specific parts of the brain (such as the hippocampus) appear necessary for the long-term component to form. In at least some cases there is evidence for specialized areas that handle particular types of memories. When new data is first presented, many parts of the brain are often active in processing it. But once the data has somehow been learned, only parts directly associated with handling it usually appear to be active.

Memories often seem at some level to be built up incrementally, as reflected in smooth learning curves for motor skills. It is not clear whether this is due to actual incremental changes in nerve cells or just to the filling in of progressively more cases that differ in detail.

Experiments on human learning suggest that a particular memory typically involves an association between components from several sensory systems, as well as emotional state.

When several incomplete examples of data are presented, there appears to be some commonality in the character of generalizations that we make. One mathematically convenient but probably unrealistic model studied in recent years in the context of computational learning theory involves building up minimal Boolean formulas consistent with the examples seen.

■ **Child development.** As children get older their thinking becomes progressively more sophisticated, advancing through a series of fairly definite stages that appear to be associated with an increasing ability to handle generalization and abstraction. It is not clear whether this development is primarily associated with physiological changes or with the accumulation of more experiences (or, in effect, with the addition of more layers of software). Nor is it clear how it relates to the fact that the number of items that can be stored in short-term memory seems steadily to increase.

■ **Computer interfaces.** The earliest computer interfaces were essentially just numerical. By the 1960s text-based interfaces were common, and in the decade following the introduction of the Macintosh in 1984 graphical interfaces based on menus and dialogs came to largely dominate consumer software. Such interfaces work well if what one wants is basically to take a single object and apply operations to it. And they can be extended somewhat by using visual block diagrams or flowcharts. But whenever there is neither just a single active data element nor an obvious sequence of independent execution steps—as for many of the programs in this book—my experience has always been that the only viable choice of interface is a computer language like *Mathematica*, based essentially on one-dimensional sequences of word-like constructs. The rule diagrams in this book represent a possible new method for specifying some simpler programs, but it remains to be seen whether such diagrams can readily both be created incrementally by humans and interpreted by computer.

■ **Page 627 · Structure of *Mathematica*.** Beneath all the sophisticated capabilities of *Mathematica* lies a remarkably simple basic structure. The key idea is to represent data of any kind by a symbolic expression of the general form *head[arg₁, arg₂, …]*. ($a + b^2$ is thus *Plus[a, Power[b, 2]]*, *{a, b, c}* is *List[a, b, c]* and *a = b + 1* is *Set[a, Plus[b, 1]]*.) The basic action of *Mathematica* is then to transform such expressions according to whatever rules it knows. Most often these rules are specified in terms of *Mathematica* patterns— expressions in which _ can stand for any expression.

■ **Context-free languages.** The set of valid expressions in a context-free language can be defined recursively by rules such as *"e" → "e + e"* and *"e" → "(e)"* that specify how one expression can be built up from sequences of literal objects or "tokens" and other expressions. (As discussed on page 939, the fact that the left-hand side contains nothing more than *"e"* is what makes the language context free.) To interpret or parse an expression in a context-free language one has to go backwards and find out which rules could be used to generate that expression. (For the built-in syntax of *Mathematica* this is achieved using *ToExpression*.)

It is convenient to think of expressions in a language as having forms such as *s["(", "(", ")", ")"]* with *Attributes[s] = Flat*. Then the rules for the language consisting of balanced runs of parentheses (see page 939) can be written as

{s[e] → s[e, e], s[e] → s["(", e, ")"], s[e] → s["(", ")"]}

Different expressions in the language can be obtained by applying different sequences of these rules, say using (this gives so-called leftmost derivations)

Fold[#1 /. rules[[#2]] &, s[e], list]

Given an expression, one can then use the following to find a list of rules that will generate it—if this exists:

*Parse[rules_, expr_] := Catch[Block[{t = {}}, NestWhile[
    ReplaceList[#, MapIndexed[ReverseRule, rules]] &,
    {{expr, {}}}, # /. {s[e], u_} :→ Throw[u]; # =!= {} &];]]*

*ReverseRule[a_ → b_, {i_}] := {_, {s[x__, b, y__], {u___}},
    ___} :→ {s[x, a, y], {i, u}} /; FreeQ[s[x], s[a]]*

In general, there will in principle be more than one such list, and to pick the appropriate list in a practical situation one normally takes the rules of the language to apply with a certain precedence—which is how, for example, *x + y z* comes to be interpreted in *Mathematica* as *Plus[x, Times[y, z]]* rather than *Times[Plus[x, y], z]*. (Note that in practice the output from a parser for a context-free language is usually represented as a tree—as in *Mathematica FullForm*—with each node corresponding to one rule application.)

Given only the rules for a context-free language, it is often very difficult to find out the properties of the language (compare page 944). Indeed, determining even whether two sets of rules ultimately yield the same set of expressions is in general undecidable (see page 1138).

■ **Languages.** There are about 140 human languages and 15 full-fledged computer languages currently in use by a million people or more. Human languages typically have perhaps 50,000 reasonably common words; computer languages usually have a few hundred at most (*Mathematica*, however, has at least nominally somewhat over 1000). In expressing general human issues, different human languages tend to be largely equivalent—though they often differ when it comes to matters of special cultural or environmental interest to their users. Computer languages are also mostly equivalent in their handling of general programming issues—and indeed among widespread languages the only substantial exception is *Mathematica*, which supports symbolic, functional and pattern-based as well as procedural programming. Human languages have mostly evolved quite haphazardly over the course of many centuries, becoming sometimes simpler, sometimes more complicated. Computer languages are almost always specifically designed once and for all, usually by a single person. New human languages have sometimes been developed—a notable example being Esperanto in the 1890s—but for reasons largely of political history none have in practice become widely used.

Human languages always seem to have fairly definite rules for what is grammatically correct. And in a first approximation these rules can usually be thought of as specifying that every sentence must be constructed from various independent nested phrases, much as in a context-free grammar (see above). But in any given language there are always many exceptions, and in the end it has proved essentially impossible to identify specific detailed features— beyond for example the existence of nouns and verbs—that are convincingly universal across more than just languages with clear historical connections (such as the Indo-European ones). (One obvious general deviation from the context-free model is that in practice subordinate clauses can never be nested too deep if a sentence is expected to be understood.)

All the computer languages that are in widespread use today are based quite explicitly on context-free grammars. And even though the original motivation for this was typically ease of specification or implementation, I strongly suspect that it has also been critical in making it readily possible for people to learn such languages. For in my observation, exceptions to the context-free model are often what confuse users of computer languages the most—even when those users have never been exposed to computer languages before. And indeed the same seems to be true for traditional mathematical notation, where occasional deviations from the context-free model in fields like logic seem to make material particularly hard to read. (A notable feature that I was surprised to discover in designing *Mathematica* 3 is that users of mathematical notation seem to have a remarkably universal view of the precedence of different mathematical operators.)

The idea of describing languages by grammars dates back to antiquity (see page 875). And starting in the 1800s extensive studies were made of the comparative grammars of different languages. But the notion that grammars could be thought of like programs for generating languages did not emerge with clarity until the work of Noam Chomsky beginning in 1956. And following this, there were for a while many efforts to formulate precise models for human languages, and to relate these to properties of the brain. But by the 1980s it became clear—notably through the failure of attempts to automate natural language understanding and translation—that language cannot in most cases (with the possible exception of grammar-checking software) meaningfully be isolated from other aspects of human thinking.

Computer languages emerged in the early 1950s as higher-level alternatives to programming directly in machine code. FORTRAN was developed in 1954 with a syntax intended as a simple idealization of mathematical notation. And in 1958, as part of the ALGOL project, John Backus used the idea of production systems from mathematical logic (see page 1150) to set up a recursive specification equivalent to a context-free grammar. A few deviations from this approach were tried—notably in LISP and APL—but by the 1970s, following the development of automated compiler generators such as yacc, so-called Backus-Naur context-free specifications for computer languages had become quite standard. (A practical enhancement to this was the introduction of two-dimensional grammar in *Mathematica* 3 in 1996.)

■ **Page 631 · Computer language fluency.** It is common that when one knows a human language sufficiently well, one

feels that one can readily "think in that language". In my experience the same is eventually true with computer languages. In particular, after many years of using *Mathematica*, I have now got to the point where I can effectively think directly in *Mathematica*, so that I can start entering a *Mathematica* program even though I may be a long way from being able to explain in English what I want to do.

■ **Brainteasers.** In many puzzles and IQ tests the setup is to give a few elements in some sequence of numbers, strings or pictures, then to ask what the next element would be. The correct answer is normally assumed to be the one that in a sense allows the simplest description of all the data. But despite attempts to remove cultural and other biases such questions in practice seem almost always to rely on being able to retrieve from memory various specific forms and transformations. And I strongly suspect that if one were, for example, to construct similar questions using outputs from many of the simple programs I discuss in this book then unless one had studied almost exactly the cases of such programs used one would never manage to work out the answers.

■ **Human generation of randomness.** If asked to type a random sequence of 0's and 1's, most people will at first produce a sequence with too many alternations between 0 and 1. But with modest learning time my experience is that one can generate sequences with quite good randomness.

■ **Game theory.** Remarkably simple models are often believed to capture features of what might seem like sophisticated decision making by humans, animals and human organizations. A particular case on which many studies have been done is the so-called iterated Prisoner's Dilemma, in which two players make a sequence of choices a and b to "cooperate" (1) or "defect" (2), each trying to maximize their score $m[\![a, b]\!]$ with $m = \{\{1, -1\}, \{2, 0\}\}$. At a single step, standard static game theory from the 1940s implies that a player should always defect, but in the 1960s a folk theorem emerged that if a whole sequence of steps is considered then a possible strategy for perfectly rational players is always to cooperate—in apparent agreement with some observations on human and animal behavior. In 1979 Robert Axelrod tried setting up computer programs as players and found that in tournaments between them the winner was often a simple "tit-for-tat" program that cooperates on the first step, then on subsequent steps just does whatever its opponent did on the previous step. The same winner was also often obtained by natural selection—a fact widely taken to explain cooperation phenomena in evolutionary biology and the social sciences. In the late 1980s similar studies were done on processes such as auctions (cf page 1015), and in the late 1990s on games such as Rock, Paper, Scissors (RoShamBo) (with $m = \{\{0, -1, 1\}, \{1, 0, -1\}, \{-1, 1, 0\}\}$). (A simpler game—certainly played since antiquity—is Penny Matching or Evens and Odds, with $m = \{\{1, -1\}, \{-1, 1\}\}$.) But even though they seemed to capture or better actual human behavior, the programs considered in all these cases typically just used standard statistical or Markov model methods, or matching of specific sequences—making them far too weak to make predictions about the kinds of complex behavior shown in this book. (Note that a program can always win the games above if it can in effect successfully predict each move its opponent will make. In a game between two arbitrary programs it can be undecidable which will win more often over the course of an infinite number of moves.)

■ **Games between programs.** One can set up a game between two programs generating single bits of output by for example taking the input at each step to be the concatenation of the historical sequences of outputs from the two programs. The pictures below show what happens if the programs operate by applying elementary cellular automaton rules t times to $2t + 1$ inputs. The plots on the left show cumulative scores in the Evens and Odds game; the array on the right indicates for each of the 256 possible rules the average number of wins it gets against each of the 256 rules. At some level considerable complexity is evident. But the rules that win most often typically seem to do so in rather simple ways.

Higher Forms of Perception and Analysis

■ **Biological perception.** Animals can process data not only from visual or auditory sources (as discussed on pages 577 and 585), but also from mechanical, thermal, chemical and other sources. Usually special receptors for each type of data convert it into electrical impulses in nerve cells. Mechanical and thermal data are often mapped onto an array of nerve cells in the brain, from which features are extracted similar to those in visual perception. Taste involves data from solids and liquids; smell data from gases. The human tongue has millions of taste buds scattered on its surface, each with many tens of nerve cells. Rather little is currently known about how taste data is processed, and it is not even clear whether the traditional notion that there are just four or so primary tastes is correct. The human nose has several tens of millions of receptors, apparently broken into a few hundred distinct types. Each of these types probably has proteins that form pockets with definite shapes, making it respond to molecules whose shapes fit into these pockets. People typically distinguish a few thousand odors, presumably by comparing responses of different receptor types. (Foods usually contain tens of distinct odors; manufactured scents hundreds.) There is evidence that at the first level of processing in the brain all receptors of a given type excite nerve cells that lie in the same spatial region. But just how different regions are laid out is not clear, and may well differ between individuals. Polymers whose lengths differ by more than one or two repeating units often seem to smell different, and it is conceivable that elaborate general features of shapes of molecules can be perceived. But more likely there is no way to build up sophisticated taste or smell data—and no analog of any properties such as repetition or nesting.

■ **Page 634 · Evolving to predict.** If one thinks that biological evolution is infinitely powerful one might imagine that by emulating it one would always be able to find ways to predict any sequence of data. But in practice methods based, for example, on genetic programming seem to do at best only about as well as all sorts of other methods discussed in this chapter. And typically what limits them seems to be much the same as I argue in Chapter 8 limits actual biological evolution: that incremental changes are difficult to make except when the behavior is fairly simple. (See also page 985.)

It is common for animals to move in apparently random ways when they are trying to avoid predators. Yet I suspect that the randomness they use is often generated by quite simple rules (see page 1011)—so that in principle it could be predictable. So it is then notable that biological evolution has apparently never made predators able to catch their prey by predicting anything that looks to us particularly random; instead strategies tend to be based on tricks that do not require predicting more than at most repetition.

■ **Page 635 · Familiar features.** What makes features familiar to us is that they are common in our typical environment and are readily recognized by our built-in human powers of perception. In the distant past humans were presumably exposed only to features generated by ordinary natural processes. But ever since the dawn of civilization humans have increasingly been exposed to things that were explicitly constructed through engineering, architecture, art, mathematics and other human activities. And indeed as human knowledge and culture have progressed, humans have ended up being exposed to new kinds of features. For example, while repetition has been much emphasized for several millennia, it is only in the past couple of decades that precise nesting has had much emphasis. So this may make one wonder what features will be emphasized in the future. The vast majority of forms created by humans in the past— say in art or architecture—have had basic features that are either directly copied from systems in nature, or are in effect built up by using extremely simple kinds of rules. On the basis of the discoveries in this book I thus tend to suspect that almost any feature that might end up becoming emphasized in the future will already be present—and probably even be fairly common—in the behavior of the kinds of simple programs that I have discussed in this book. (When future technology is routinely able to interact with individual atoms there will presumably quickly be a new class of quantum and other features that become familiar.)

■ **Relativism and postmodernism.** See pages 1131 and 1196.

The Notion of Computation

Computation as a Framework

■ **History of computing.** Even in prehistoric times there were no doubt schemes for computation based for example on making specific arrangements of pebbles. Such schemes were somewhat formalized a few thousand years ago with the invention of the abacus. And by about 200 BC the development of gears had made it possible to create devices (such as the Antikythera device from perhaps around 90 BC) in which the positions of wheels would correspond to positions of astronomical objects. By about 100 AD Hero had described an odometer-like device that could be driven automatically and could effectively count in digital form. But it was not until the 1600s that mechanical devices for digital computation appear to have actually been built. Around 1621 Wilhelm Schickard probably built a machine based on gears for doing simplified multiplications involved in Johannes Kepler's calculations of the orbit of the Moon. But much more widely known were the machines built in the 1640s by Blaise Pascal for doing addition on numbers with five or so digits and in the 1670s by Gottfried Leibniz for doing multiplication, division and square roots. At first, these machines were viewed mainly as curiosities. But as the technology improved, they gradually began to find practical applications. In the mid-1800s, for example, following the ideas of Charles Babbage, so-called difference engines were used to automatically compute and print tables of values of polynomials. And from the late 1800s until about 1970 mechanical calculators were in very widespread use. (In addition, starting with Stanley Jevons in 1869, a few machines were constructed for evaluating logic expressions, though they were viewed almost entirely as curiosities.)

In parallel with the development of devices for digital computation, various so-called analog computers were also built that used continuous physical processes to in effect perform computations. In 1876 William Thomson (Kelvin) constructed a so-called harmonic analyzer, in which an assembly of disks were used to sum trigonometric series and thus to predict tides. Kelvin mentioned that a similar device could be built to solve differential equations. This idea was independently developed by Vannevar Bush, who built the first mechanical so-called differential analyzer in the late 1920s. And in the 1930s, electrical analog computers began to be produced, and in fact they remained in widespread use for finding approximate solutions to differential equations until the late 1960s.

The types of machines discussed so far all have the feature that they have to be physically rearranged or rewired in order to perform different calculations. But the idea of a programmable machine already emerged around 1800, first with player pianos, and then with Marie Jacquard's invention of an automatic loom which used punched cards to determine its weaving patterns. And in the 1830s, Charles Babbage described what he called an analytical engine, which, if built, would have been able to perform sequences of arithmetic operations under punched card control. Starting at the end of the 1800s tabulating machines based on punched cards became widely used for commercial and government data processing. Initially, these machines were purely mechanical, but by the 1930s, most were electromechanical, and had units for carrying out basic arithmetic operations. The Harvard Mark I computer (proposed by Howard Aiken in 1937 and completed in 1944) consisted of many such units hooked together so as to perform scientific calculations. Following work by John Atanasoff around 1940, electronic machines with similar architectures started to be built. The first large-scale such system was the ENIAC, built between 1943 and 1946. The focus of the ENIAC was on numerical computation, originally for creating ballistics tables. But in the early 1940s, the British wartime cryptanalysis group (which included Alan Turing) constructed fairly large electromechanical machines that performed logical, rather than arithmetic, operations.

All the systems mentioned so far had the feature that they performed operations in what was essentially a fixed sequence. But by the late 1940s it had become clear, particularly through the writings of John von Neumann, that it would be convenient to be able to jump around instead of always having to follow a fixed sequence. And with the idea of storing programs electronically, this became fairly easy to do, so that by 1950 more than ten stored-program computers had been built in the U.S. and in England. Speed and memory capacity have increased immensely since the 1950s, particularly as a result of the development of semiconductor chip technology, but in many respects the basic hardware architecture of computers has remained very much the same.

Major changes have, however, occurred in software. In the late 1950s and early 1960s, the main innovation was the development of computer languages such as FORTRAN, COBOL and BASIC. These languages allowed programs to be specified in a somewhat abstract way, independent of the precise details of the hardware architecture of the computer. But the languages were primarily intended only for specifying numerical calculations. In the late 1960s and early 1970s, there developed the notion of operating systems—programs whose purpose was to control the resources of a computer—and with them came languages such as C. And then in the late 1970s and early 1980s, as the cost of computer memory fell, it began to be feasible to manipulate not just purely numerical data, but also data representing text and later pictures. With the advent of personal computers in the early 1980s, interactive computing became common, and as the resolution of computer displays increased, concepts such as graphical user interfaces developed. In more recent years continuing increases in speed have made it possible for more and more layers of software to be constructed, and for many operations previously done with special hardware to be implemented purely in software.

■ **Practical computers.** At the lowest level the hardware of a practical computer consists of digital electronic circuits. In these circuits, lumps of electric charge (in 2001 about half a million electrons each) flow through channels which cross to form various kinds of gates. Each gate performs a simple logic operation; for example, letting charge pass in one channel only if charge is present in the other channel. From circuits containing millions of such gates are built the two main elements of the computer: the processor which actually performs computations, and the memory which stores data. The memory consists of an array of cells, with the presence or absence of a lump of charge at gates in each cell representing a 1 or 0 value for the bit of data associated with that cell.

One of the crucial ideas of a general-purpose computer is that sequences of such bits of data in memory can represent information of absolutely any kind. Numbers for example are typically represented in base 2 by sequences of 32 or more bits. Similarly, characters of text are usually represented by sequences of 8 or more bits. (The character "a" is typically 01100001.) Images are usually represented by bitmaps containing thousands or millions of bits, with each bit specifying for example whether a pixel at a particular location should, say, be black or white. Every possible location in memory has a definite address, independent of its contents. The address is typically represented as a number which itself can be stored in memory.

What makes possible essential universality in a practical computer is that the data which is stored in memory can be a program. At the lowest level, a program consists of a sequence of instructions to be executed by the processor. Any particular kind of processor is built to support a certain fixed set of possible kinds of instructions, each represented by a specific number or opcode. There are typically a few tens of possible instructions, each executed by a certain part of the circuit in the processor. A typical one of these instructions might add two numbers together; a program would specify which numbers to add by giving their addresses in memory.

What practical computers always basically do is to repeat millions of times a second a simple cycle, in which the processor fetches an instruction from memory, then executes the instruction. The address of the instruction to be fetched at each point is specified by the current value of the program counter—a number stored in memory that is incremented by the processor, or can be modified by instruction in the program. At any given time, there are usually several programs stored in the memory of a computer, all organized by an operating system program which determines when other programs should run. Devices like keyboards, mice and microphones convert input into data that is inserted into memory at certain fixed locations. The operating system periodically checks these locations, and if necessary runs programs to respond to the input that is given.

A crucial achievement in practical computing over the past several decades has been the creation of more and more sophisticated software. Often the programs that make up this software are several million instructions long. They usually contain many subprograms that perform parts of their task. Some programs are set up to perform very specific applications, say word processing. But an important class of programs are languages. A language provides a fixed set of constructs that allow one to specify computations. The set of instructions performed by the processor in a computer constitutes a low-level "machine" language. In practice, however, programs are rarely written at such a low level. More often, languages like C, FORTRAN, Java or *Mathematica* are used. In these languages, each construct represents what is often a large number of machine instructions. There are two basic ways that languages can operate: compiled or interpreted. In a compiled language like C or FORTRAN, the source code of the program must always first be translated by a compiler program into object code that essentially consists of machine instructions. Once compiled, a program can be executed any number of times. In an interpreted language, each piece of input effectively causes a fixed subprogram to be executed to perform an operation specified by that input.

■ **Intuition from practical computing.** See page 872.

Computations in Cellular Automata

■ **Page 639 · Other examples.** Rule 152 and rule 144, which effectively compute *Ceiling[n/2]* and *Ceiling[n/4]*, respectively, are shown below with *n = 18* initial black cells.

rule 152   rule 144

As discussed on page 989 rule 184 effectively determines whether its initial conditions correspond to a balanced sequence of open and close parentheses. (Rule 132 can be viewed as being like a syntax checker for a regular language; rule 184 for a context-free language.)

■ **Page 639 · Squaring cellular automaton.** The rules are

$\{\{0, \_, 3\} \rightarrow 0, \{\_, 2, 3\} \rightarrow 3, \{1, 1, 3\} \rightarrow 4, \{\_, 1, 4\} \rightarrow 4, \{1|2, 3, \_\} \rightarrow 5, \{p : (0|1), 4, \_\} \rightarrow 7 - p, \{7, 2, 6\} \rightarrow 3, \{7, \_, \_\} \rightarrow 7, \{\_, 7, p : (1|2)\} \rightarrow p, \{\_, p : (5|6), \_\} \rightarrow 7 - p, \{5|6, p : (1|2), \_\} \rightarrow 7 - p, \{5|6, 0, 0\} \rightarrow 1, \{\_, p : (1|2), \_\} \rightarrow p, \{\_, \_, \_\} \rightarrow 0\}$

and the initial conditions consist of *Append[Table[1, {n}], 3]* surrounded by *0*'s. The rules can be implemented using *GeneralCARule* as given on page 867. (See also page 1186.)

■ **Page 640 · Primes cellular automaton.** The rules are

$\{\{13, 3, 13\} \rightarrow 12, \{6, \_, 4\} \rightarrow 15, \{10, \_, 3|11\} \rightarrow 15, \{13, 7, \_\} \rightarrow 8, \{13, 8, 7\} \rightarrow 13, \{15, 8, \_\} \rightarrow 1, \{8, \_, \_\} \rightarrow 7, \{15, 1, \_\} \rightarrow 2, \{\_, 1, \_\} \rightarrow 1, \{1, \_, \_\} \rightarrow 8, \{2|4|5, \_, \_\} \rightarrow 13, \{15, 2, \_\} \rightarrow 4, \{\_, 4, 8\} \rightarrow 4, \{\_, 4, \_\} \rightarrow 5, \{\_, 5, \_\} \rightarrow 3, \{15, 3, \_\} \rightarrow 12, \{\_, x : (2|3|8), \_\} \rightarrow x, \{\_, x : (11|12), \_\} \rightarrow x - 1, \{11, \_, \_\} \rightarrow 13, \{13, \_, 1|2|3|5|6|10|11\} \rightarrow 15, \{13, 0, 8\} \rightarrow 15, \{14, \_, 6|10\} \rightarrow 15, \{10, 0|9|13, 6|10\} \rightarrow 15, \{6, \_, 6\} \rightarrow 0, \{\_, \_, 10\} \rightarrow 9, \{6|10, 15, 9\} \rightarrow 14, \{\_, 6|10, 9|14|15\} \rightarrow 10, \{\_, 6|10, \_\} \rightarrow 6, \{6|10, 15, \_\} \rightarrow 13, \{13|14, \_, 9|15\} \rightarrow 14, \{13|14, \_, \_\} \rightarrow 13, \{\_, \_, 15\} \rightarrow 15, \{\_, \_, 9|14\} \rightarrow 9, \{\_, \_, \_\} \rightarrow 0\}$

and the initial conditions consist of *{10, 0, 4, 8}* surrounded by *0*'s. The right-hand region in the pattern grows like $\sqrt{t}$. (See also page 132.)

■ **Random initial conditions.** The pictures below show the squaring and primes cellular automata starting from random initial conditions. Note that for both systems the majority of cases in their rules are not used in the specific computations for which they were constructed. Changing these cases can lead to different behavior with random initial conditions.

 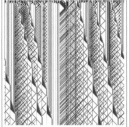

■ **Efficiency of computations.** Present-day practical computers almost always process data in a basically sequential manner. Cellular automata, however, intrinsically operate in parallel, and can thus presumably perform at least some computations in fundamentally fewer steps. (Compare the discussion of P completeness on page 1149.)

■ **Minimal programs for sequences.** See page 1186.

The Phenomenon of Universality

■ **History of universality.** In Greek times it was noted as a philosophical matter that any single human language can be used to describe the same basic range of facts and processes. And with logic introduced as a way to formalize arguments (see page 1099), Gottfried Leibniz in the 1600s considered the idea of setting up a universal language based on logic that would provide a precise description analogous to a mathematical proof of any fact or process. But while Leibniz considered the possibility of checking his descriptions by machine, he apparently did not imagine setting up the analog of a computation in which something is explicitly generated from input that has been given.

The idea of having an abstract procedure that can be fed a range of different inputs had precursors in antiquity in the use of letters to denote objects in geometrical constructions, and in the 1500s in the introduction of symbolic formulas and algebraic variables. But the notion of abstract functions in mathematics reached its modern form only near the end of the 1800s.

At the beginning of the 1800s practical devices such as the player pianos and the Jacquard loom were invented that could in effect be fed different inputs using analogs of punched cards. And in the 1830s Charles Babbage and Ada Lovelace noted that a similar approach could be used to specify the mathematical procedure to be followed by a mechanical calculating machine (see page 1107). But it was somehow assumed that the specification of the procedure must be done quite separately from the specification of the data to which the procedure was to be applied.

Starting in the 1880s attempts to build up both numbers and the operations of arithmetic from logic and set theory began to suggest that both data and procedures could potentially be described in common terms. And in the 1920s work by Moses Schönfinkel on combinators and by Emil Post on string rewriting systems provided fairly concrete examples of this.

In 1930 Kurt Gödel used the same basic idea to set up Gödel numbers to encode logical and other procedures as numbers. (Leibniz had in fact already done this for basic logic expressions in 1679.) But Gödel then took the crucial step of showing that the process of finding outputs from all such procedures could in effect be viewed as equivalent to following relations of logic and arithmetic—thus establishing that these relations are in a certain sense universal (see page 784). This fact, however, was embedded inside the rather technical proof of Gödel's Theorem, and it was at first not at all clear how specific it might be to the particular mathematical systems considered.

But in 1935 Alonzo Church constructed a system in lambda calculus that he showed could be made to emulate any other system in lambda calculus if given appropriate input, and in 1936 Alan Turing did the same thing for Turing machines. As discussed on page 1125, both Church and Turing argued that the systems they set up would be able to perform any reasonable computation. In both cases, their original motivation was to use this fact to construct an argument that the so-called decision problem (Entscheidungsproblem) of mathematical logic was undecidable (see page 1136). But Turing in particular gradually realized that his notion of universality could be applied to practical computers.

Turing's results were used in the 1940s—notably in the work of Warren McCulloch and Walter Pitts—as a basis for the assertion that electric circuit analogs of neural networks could achieve the sophistication of brains, and this appears to have influenced John von Neumann's thinking about the general programmability of electronic computers.

Nevertheless, by the late 1940s, practical computer engineering had also been led to the idea of storing programs—like data—electronically, and in the 1950s it became widely understood that general-purpose practical computers could be viewed as universal systems.

Many theoretical investigations of universality were made in the 1950s and 1960s, but gradually the emphasis shifted more towards issues of languages and algorithms.

■ **Universality in *Mathematica*.** As an example of how different primitive operations can be used to do the same computation, the following are a few ways that the factorial function can be defined in *Mathematica*:

$f[n\_] := n\,!$

$f[n\_] := n\,f[n-1]; f[1] = 1$

$f[n\_] := Product[i, \{i, n\}]$

$f[n\_] := Module[\{t = 1\}, Do[t = t\,i, \{i, n\}]; t]$

$f[n\_] := Module[\{t = 1, i\}, For[i = 1, i \leq n, i++, t *= i]; t]$

$f[n\_] := Apply[Times, Range[n]]$

$f[n\_] := Fold[Times, 1, Range[n]]$

$f[n\_] := If[n == 1, 1, n\,f[n-1]]$

$f[n\_] := Fold[\#2[\#1]\,\&, 1, Array[Function[t, \#1\,t]\,\&, n]]$

$f = If[\#1 == 1, 1, \#1\,\#0[\#1-1]]\,\&$

A Universal Cellular Automaton

■ **Page 648 · Universal cellular automaton.** The rules for the universal cellular automaton are

$\{\{\_, 3, 7, 18, \_\} \to 12, \{\_, 5, 7\,|\,8, 0, \_\} \to 12, \{\_, 3, 10, 18, \_\} \to 16,$
$\{\_, 5, 10\,|\,11, 0, \_\} \to 16, \{\_, 5, 8, 18, \_\} \to 7, \{\_, 5, 14, 0\,|\,18, \_\} \to$
$12, \{\_, \_, 8, 5, \_\} \to 7, \{\_, \_, 14, 5, \_\} \to 12, \{\_, 5, 11, 18, \_\} \to 10,$
$\{\_, 5, 17, 0\,|\,18, \_\} \to 16, \{\_, \_, x : (11\,|\,17), 5, \_\} \to x - 1,$
$\{\_, 0\,|\,9\,|\,18, x : (7\,|\,10\,|\,16), 3, \_\} \to x + 1, \{\_, 0\,|\,9\,|\,18, 12, 3, \_\} \to$
$14, \{\_, \_, 0\,|\,9\,|\,18, 7\,|\,10\,|\,12\,|\,16, x : (3\,|\,5)\} \to 8 - x,$
$\{\_, \_, \_, 8\,|\,11\,|\,14\,|\,17, x : (3\,|\,5)\} \to 8 - x, \{\_, 13, 4, \_, x : (0\,|\,18)\} \to$
$x, \{18, \_, 4, \_, \_\} \to 18, \{\_, \_, 18, \_, 4\} \to 18, \{0, \_, 4, \_, \_\} \to 0,$
$\{\_, \_, 0, \_, 4\} \to 0, \{4, \_, 0\,|\,18, 1, \_\} \to 3, \{4, \_, \_, \_, \_\} \to 4,$
$\{\_, \_, 4, \_, \_\} \to 9, \{\_, 4, 12, \_, \_\} \to 7, \{\_, 4, 16, \_, \_\} \to 10,$
$\{x : (0\,|\,18), \_, 6, \_, \_\} \to x, \{\_, 2, 6, 15, x : (0\,|\,18)\} \to x, \{\_, 12\,|\,16,$
$6, 7, \_\} \to 0, \{\_, 12\,|\,16, 6, 10, \_\} \to 18, \{\_, 9, 10, 6, \_\} \to 16,$
$\{\_, 9, 7, 6, \_\} \to 12, \{9, 15, 6, 7, 9\} \to 0, \{9, 15, 6, 10, 9\} \to 18,$
$\{9, \_, 6, \_, \_\} \to 9, \{\_, 6, 7, 9, 12\,|\,16\} \to 12, \{\_, 6, 10, 9, 12\,|\,16\} \to$
$16, \{12\,|\,16, 6, 7, 9, \_\} \to 12, \{12\,|\,16, 6, 10, 9, \_\} \to 16,$
$\{6, 13, \_, \_, \_\} \to 9, \{6, \_, \_, \_, \_\} \to 6, \{\_, \_, 9, 13, 3\} \to 9,$
$\{\_, 9, 13, 3, \_\} \to 15, \{\_, \_, \_, 15, 3\} \to 3, \{\_, 3, 15, 0\,|\,18, \_\} \to 13,$
$\{\_, 13, 3, \_, 0\,|\,18\} \to 6, \{x : (0\,|\,18), 15, 9, \_, \_\} \to x,$
$\{\_, 6, 13, \_, \_\} \to 15, \{\_, 4, 15, \_, \_\} \to 13, \{\_, \_, \_, 15, 6\} \to 6,$
$\{\_, \_, 2, 6, 15\} \to 1, \{\_, \_, 1, 6, \_\} \to 2, \{\_, 1, 6, \_, \_\} \to 9, \{\_, 3, 2,$
$\_, \_\} \to 1, \{3, 2, \_, \_, \_\} \to 3, \{\_, \_, 3, 2, \_\} \to 3, \{\_, 1, 9, 1, 6\} \to 6,$
$\{\_, \_, 9, 1, 6\} \to 4, \{\_, 4, 2, \_, \_\} \to 1, \{\_, \_, \_, \_, x : (3\,|\,5)\} \to x,$
$\{\_, \_, 3\,|\,5, \_, x : (0\,|\,18)\} \to x, \{\_, \_, x : (1\,|\,2\,|\,7\,|\,8\,|\,9\,|\,10\,|\,11\,|$
$12\,|\,13\,|\,14\,|\,15\,|\,16\,|\,17), \_, \_\} \to x, \{\_, \_, 18, 7\,|\,10, 18\} \to 18,$
$\{\_, \_, 0, 7\,|\,10, 18, \_, \_\} \to 0, \{\_, \_, 0\,|\,18, \_, \_\} \to 9, \{\_, \_, x, \_, \_, \_\} \to x\}$

where the numbers correspond to the icons shown in the main text according to

0 1 2 3 4 5 6 7 8 9 10 11 12 13 14 15 16 17 18

The block in the initial conditions for the universal cellular automaton corresponding to a cell with color a is given by

Flatten[{Transpose[{Join[{4, 18 (1 − a), 6}, Table[9,
{2²ʳ⁺¹ − 3}]], 10 − 3 rtab }], Table[{9, 1}, {r}], 9, 13}]

where r is the range of the rule to be emulated ($r = 1$ for elementary rules) and *rtab* is the list of outcomes for that rule (starting with the outcome for $\{1, 1, (1)...\}$). In general, there are 2^{2r+1} cases in the rule to be emulated; each block in the universal cellular automaton is $2(2^{2r+1} + r + 1)$ cells wide, and each step in the rule to be emulated corresponds to $(3r + 2)2^{2r+1} + 3r^2 + 7r + 3$ steps in the evolution of the universal cellular automaton.

■ **Page 655 · More colors.** Given a rule that involves three colors and nearest neighbors, the following converts each case of the rule to a collection of cases for a rule with two colors:

CA3ToCA2[{a_, b_, c_} → d_] := Union[Flatten[Table[Thread[
Partition[Flatten[{l, a, b, c, r} /. coding], 11, 1]][[{2,
3, 4}]] → (d /. coding)], {l, 0, 2}, {r, 0, 2}], 2]]
coding = {0 → {0, 0, 0}, 1 → {0, 0, 1}, 2 → {0, 1, 1}}

The problem of encoding cells with several colors by blocks of black and white cells is related to standard problems in coding theory (see page 560). One approach is to use $\{1, 1\}$ to indicate the boundary of each block, and then within each block to use all possible digit sequences which do not contain $\{1, 1\}$, as in the Fibonacci number system discussed on page 892. Note that the original rule with k colors and r neighbors involves $Log[2, k^{k^{2r+1}}]$ bits of information; the two-color rule that emulates it involves $Log[2, 2^{2^{2s+1}}]$ bits. As a result, the minimum possible s for $k = 3$, $r = 1$ is about 2.2; in the specific example shown in the main text it is 5.

Emulating Other Systems with Cellular Automata

■ **Page 657 · Mobile automata.** Given a mobile automaton with rules in the form used on page 887, a cellular automaton which emulates it can be constructed using

MAToCA[rules_] :=
Append[Flatten[Map[g, rules]], {_, _, x_, _, _} → x]
g[{a_, b_, c_} → {d_, e_}] := {{_, a, b + 2, c, _} → d, If[e == 1,
{a, b + 2, c, _, _} → c + 2, {_, _, a, b + 2, c} → a + 2]}

This specific definition assumes that the mobile automaton has two possible colors for each cell; it yields a cellular automaton with four possible colors for each cell. An initial

condition with a single 2 surrounded by 0's corresponds to all cells being white in the mobile automaton.

■ **Page 658 · Turing machines.** Given any Turing machine with rules in the form used on page 888 and k possible colors for each cell, a cellular automaton which emulates it can be constructed using

TMToCA[rules_, k_ : 2] :=
Flatten[{Map[g[#, k] &, rules], {_, x_, _} → x}]
g[{s_, a_} → {sp_, ap_, d_}, k_] := {If[d == 1, Identity,
Reverse][{k s + a, x_, _}] → k sp + x, {_, k s + a, _} → ap}

If the Turing machine has s states for its head, then the cellular automaton has $k(s + 1)$ colors for each cell. An initial condition with a single cell of color k surrounded by 0's corresponds to being in state 1 with a blank tape in the Turing machine.

■ **Page 659 · Substitution systems.** Given a substitution system with rules in the form such as $\{1 → \{0\}, 0 → \{0, 1\}\}$ used on page 889, the rules for a cellular automaton which emulates it are obtained from

SSToCA[rules_] := {{b, b, p[x_, _]} → s[x],
{_, s[v : (0 | 1)], p[x_, _]} → p[v, x], {_, p[_, y_], _} → s[y],
{_, s[v : (0 | 1)], _m} → m[v], {s[0 | 1], m[v : (0 | 1)], _} →
s[v], {b, m[v : (0 | 1)], _} → r[v], {_, r[v : (0 | 1)], _} →
(Replace[v, rules] /. {{x_} → s[x], {x_, y_} → p[x, y]}),
{_r, s[v : (0 | 1)], _} → r[v], {_r, b, _} → m[b],
{s[0 | 1], m[b], _} → b, {_, v_, _} → v}

where specific values for cells can be obtained from

{b → 0, s[0] → 1, m[0] → 2, p[0, 0] → 3,
r[0] → 4, p[0, 1] → 5, p[1, 0] → 6, r[1] → 7,
p[1, 1] → 8, m[1] → 9, m[b] → 10, s[1] → 11}

An initial condition consisting of a single element with color i in the substitution system is represented by $m[i]$ surrounded by b's in the cellular automaton. The specific definition given above works for neighbor-independent substitution systems whose elements have two possible colors, and in which each element is replaced at each step by at most two new elements.

■ **Page 660 · Sequential substitution systems.** Given a sequential substitution system with rules in the form used on page 893, the rules for a cellular automaton which emulates it can be obtained from

SSSToCA[rules_] := Flatten[{{v[_, _, _], u, _} → u, {_, v[rn_,
x_, _], u} → r[rn + 1, x], {_, v[_, x_, _], _} → x, MapIndexed[
With[{rn = #2[[1]], rs = #1[[1]], rr = #1[[2]]}, {If[Length[rs] ==
1, {u, r[rn, First[rs]], _} → q[0, rr], {u, r[rn, First[rs]], _} →
v[rn, First[rs], Take[rs, 1]]}, {u, r[rn, x_], _} → v[rn, x, {}],
{v[rn, _, Drop[rs, −1]], Last[rs], _} → q[Length[rs] − 1, rr],
Table[{v[rn, _, Flatten[{___, Take[rs, i − 1]}]], rs[[i]], _} → v[
rn, rs[[i]], Take[rs, i]], {i, Length[rs] − 1, 1, −1}], {v[rn, _, _],
y_, _} → v[rn, y, {}]} &, rules /. s → List], {_, q[0, {x__, _}],

_} → q[0, {x}], {_, q[0, {x_}], _} → r[1, x], {_, q[0, {}], x_} →
r[1, x], {_, q[_, {___, x_}], _} → x, {_, q[_, {}], x_} → x,
{_, x_, q[0, _]} → x, {_, _, q[n_, {}]} → q[n - 1, {}],
{_, _, q[n_, {x___, _}]} → q[n - 1, {x}], {q[_, {}], _, _} → w,
{q[0, {__, x_}], p[y_, _], _} → p[x, y], {q[0, {_, x_}], y_, _} →
p[x, y], {p[_, x_], p[y_, _], _} → p[x, y], {p[_, x_], u, _} → x,
{p[_, x_], y_, _} → p[x, y], {_, p[x_, _], _} → x, {w, u, _} → u,
{w, x_, _} → w, {_, w, x_} → x, {_, r[rn_, x_], _} → x,
{_, u, r[_, _]} → u, {_, x_, r[rn_, _]} → r[rn, x], {_, x_, _} → x}}

The initial condition is obtained by applying the rule
s[x_, y__] → {r[1, x], y} and then padding with u's.

■ **Page 661 · Register machines.** Given the program for a
register machine in the form used on page 896, the rules for a
cellular automaton that emulates it can be obtained from

g[i[1], p_, m_] :=
　{{_, p, _} → p + 1, {_, 0, p} → m + 2, {_, _, p} → m + 3}
g[i[2], p_, m_] :=
　{{_, p, _} → p + 1, {p, 0, _} → m + 5, {p, _, _} → m + 6}
g[d[1, q_], p_, m_] := {{m + 2 | m + 3, p, _} → q, {m + 1,
　p, _} → p, {0, p, _} → p + 1, {_, m + 2 | m + 3, p} → m + 1}
g[d[2, q_], p_, m_] := {{_, p, m + 5 | m + 6} → q, {_, p,
　m + 4} → p, {_, p, 0} → p + 1, {p, m + 5 | m + 6, _} → m + 4}
RMToCA[prog_] := With[{m = Length[prog]}, Flatten[
　{MapIndexed[g[#1, First[#2], m] &, prog], {{0, 0 | m + 1,
　m + 3} → m + 2, {0, m + 1, _} → 0, {0, 0, m + 1} → 0,
　{_, _, x : (m + 1 | m + 3)} → x, {_, m + 1 | m + 3, _} → m + 2,
　{m + 6, 0 | m + 4, 0} → m + 5, {_, m + 4, 0} → 0,
　{m + 4, 0, 0} → 0, {x : (m + 4 | m + 6), _, _} → x,
　{_, m + 4 | m + 6, _} → m + 5, {_, x_, _} → x}}]]]

If m is the length of the register machine program, then the
resulting cellular automaton has m + 7 possible colors for
each cell. If the initial numbers in the two registers are a
and b, then the initial conditions for the cellular automaton
are Join[Table[m + 2, {a}], {1}, Table[m + 5, {b}]] surrounded
by 0's.

■ **Page 661 · Multiplication systems.** The rules for the cellular
automaton shown here are

{{_, 0, 3 | 8} → 5, {_, 0, 2 | 7} → 8, {_, 1, 4 | 9} → 9,
　{_, 1, 3 | 8} → 4, {_, 1, 2 | 7} → 8, {_, 10, 4 | 9} → 3,
　{_, 10, 3 | 8} → 7, {_, 10, 2 | 7} → 2, {5 | 6, 1, 0} → 9,
　{5 | 6, 10, 0} → 3, {5 | 6, 1, _} → 6, {5 | 6, 10, _} → 5,
　{_, 2 | 3 | 4 | 5, _} → 10, {_, 6 | 7 | 8 | 9, _} → 1, {_, x_, _} → x}

and the initial condition consists of a single 3 surrounded by
0's. The idea used is that multiplication by 3 can be achieved
by scanning digits from right to left, adding to each digit the
value of the digit on its immediate right, as well as a carry
that can propagate any distance but cannot be larger than 1.
Note that as discussed on page 614 multiplication by some
multipliers in some bases (such as by 3 in base 6) can be
achieved by a single step in the evolution of a suitable
cellular automaton. After t steps, the width of the pattern
shown here is about Sqrt[Log[2, 3] t]. (See also page 119.)

■ **Continuous systems.** See page 1128.

■ **Page 662 · Logic circuits.** The rules for the cellular automaton
shown here are

{{0, 1, 1 | 3} → 1, {0, 3, 3} → 3, {1, 0, 0 | 1 | 3} → 1,
　{1, 1, 3} → 4, {1, 3, 0} → 3, {1, 3, 3} → 2, {2, 1, 3} → 3,
　{2, 3, 0} → 2, {2, 0, _} → 4, {3, 3, 0} → 3, {4, 0, 0 | 1 | 2 | 4} → 2,
　{4, 3, 3} → 3, {4, 1, 3} → 1, {4, 3, 0} → 4, {_, _, _} → 0}

The initial conditions are given by

Flatten[Block[{And, Or}, Map[{0, 2 (# + 1)} &, expr, {-1}] //.
　{! x_ :→ {0, x, 0}, And[x__] :→ {0, 0, 1, 0, x, 1, 3, 0, 0},
　Or[x__] :→ {0, 0, 1, 0, x, 0, 1, 3, 0}}]]

and in terms of these initial conditions the cellular automaton
must be run for Length[list //. {0, x__} → {x}] - 1 steps in order
to find the result.

■ **Page 663 · RAM.** The rules for the cellular automaton shown
here are

{{2, 4 | 8, 2 | 11, _, _} → 2, {11 | 10, 4 | 8, 2 | 11, _, _} → 11,
　{2, 4 | 8, _, _, _} → 10, {11 | 10, 4 | 8, _, _, _} → 2,
　{2, 0, _, _, _} → 2, {11, 0, _, _, _} → 11,
　{3 | 7 | 6, _, 10, _, _} → 1, {x : (3 | 7 | 6), _, _, _, _} → x,
　{_, _, 6, 4, 10} → 5, {_, _, 6, 8, 10} → 9, {_, 3, _, 10, _} → 4,
　{_, 7, _, 10, _} → 8, {_, _, 1, _, x : (5 | 9)} → x, {1, _, _, _, _} → 1,
　{_, _, 1, _, _} → 1, {_, _, _, _, 1} → 1, {_, _, x : (4 | 8 | 0), _, _} → x}

The initial conditions are divided into two parts: instructions
on the left and memory on the right. Given a list of 0 and 1
values for successive memory locations, the right-hand initial
conditions are Flatten[list /. {1 → {8, 1}, 0 → {4, 1}}]. To access
location n the left-hand initial conditions must contain
Flatten[{0, i, IntegerDigits[n, 2] /. {1 → {0, 11}, 0 → {0, 2}}}]
inserted in a repetitive {0, 1} background. If i is 7, a 1 will be
written to location n; if it is 3, a 0 will be written; and if it is 6,
the contents of location n will be read and sent back to the left.

Emulating Cellular Automata with Other Systems

■ **Page 664 · Mobile automata.** Given the rules for an
elementary cellular automaton in the form used on page 867, the
following will construct a mobile automaton which emulates it:

vals = {x, p[0], q[0, 0], q[0, 1], q[1, 0], q[1, 1], p[1]}

CAToMA[rules_] := Table[(# → Replace[#, {{q[a_, b_], p[c_],
　p[d_]} :→ {q[c, {a, c, d} /. rules], 1}, {q[a_, b_], p[c_], x} :→
　{q[c, {a, c, 0} /. rules], 1}, {q[_, _], x, x} → {p[0], -1},
　{q[_, _], q[_, a_], p[_]} → {p[a], -1}, {x, q[_, a_], p[_]} →
　{p[a], -1}, {x, x, p[_]} → {q[0, 0], 1}, {_, _, _} →
　{x, 0}}] &)[vals[[IntegerDigits[i, 7, 3] + 1]]], {i, 0, 7³ - 1}]

The ordering in vals defines a mapping of symbolic cell
values onto colors. Given a list of initial cell colors for the
cellular automaton, the initial conditions for the mobile
automaton are given by Flatten[{p[0], Map[p, list], p[0]}]
surrounded by x's, with the active cell being placed initially
just before the first p[0].

■ **Page 665 · Turing machines.** Given the rules for an elementary cellular automaton in the form used on page 867, the following will construct a Turing machine which emulates it:

```
CAToTM[rules_] :=
  {{q[a_, b_], c : (0 | 1)} :→ {q[b, c], {a, b, c} /. rules, 1},
   {q[_, _], x} → {p[0], 0, -1}, {p[a_], b : (0 | 1)} →
     {p[b], a, -1}, {p[_], x} → {q[0, 0], 0, 1}}
```

Given a list of initial cell colors for the cellular automaton, the initial tape for the Turing machine consists of *Join[{0, 0}, list, {0, 0}]* surrounded by *x*'s, with the head of the Turing machine on the first *0* in state *q[0, 0]*.

For specific cellular automata it is often possible to construct smaller Turing machines, as on pages 707 and 1119. By combining identical cases in rules and writing rules as compositions of ones with smaller neighborhoods one can for example readily construct Turing machines with 4 states and 3 colors that emulate 166 of the elementary cellular automata.

■ **Page 667 · Sequential substitution systems.** Given the rules for an elementary cellular automaton in the form used on page 867, the following will construct a sequential substitution system which emulates it:

```
CAToSSS[rules_] := Join[rules /.
  ({a_, b_, c_} → d_) → {1, 2 a, 2 b, 2 c} → {2 d, 1, 2 b, 2 c},
  {{1, 0, 0} → {0, 0}, {0} → {1, 0, 0, 0}}]
```

The initial condition *{0, 0, 2, 0, 0}* for the sequential substitution system corresponds to a single black cell surrounded by white cells in the cellular automaton.

■ **Page 667 · Tag systems.** Given the rules for an elementary cellular automaton in the form used on page 867, the following will construct a tag system which emulates it:

```
CAToTS[rules_] := {2, {{s[x_], s[y_]} :→
    {d[x, y], d[x, y]}, {d[w_, x_], d[y_, z_]} :→
    {s[{w, x, y} /. rules], s[{x, y, z} /. rules]},
  {s[x_], d[y_, z_]} :→ {s[0], s[0], s[{0, y, z} /. rules]},
  {d[x_, y_], s[z_]} :→ {s[{x, y, 0} /. rules], s[0], s[0]}}}
```

The initial condition for the tag system that corresponds to a single black cell in the cellular automaton is *{s[0], s[0], s[1], s[0], s[0]}*. Given a list of all steps in the evolution of the tag system, *Cases[list, {__s}]* picks out successive steps in the cellular automaton evolution.

■ **Page 668 · Symbolic systems.** Given the rules for an elementary cellular automaton in the form used on page 867 (with *{0, 0, 0} → 0*), the following will construct a symbolic system which emulates it:

```
Flatten[{{Array[p[x_][#1][#2][#3] →
  p[x[{##}] /. rules]][#2][#3] &, {2, 2, 2}, 0] /. {0 → p, 1 → q},
  {r[x_] → p[r[p]][p]][x], p[x_][p][p][r] → x[p][p][r]}}]
```

The initial condition for the symbolic system is given by

```
Fold[#1[#2] &, r[p][p], init /. {0 → p, 1 → q}][p][p][r]
```

Step *t* in the cellular automaton corresponds to step *t (t + Length[init] + 3)* in the symbolic system.

Note that the succession of states shown here depends on the detailed order in which rules are applied (see page 898). It is also possible to construct symbolic systems with the so-called confluence property, in which results from any fixed number of steps of cellular automaton evolution can be found by applying rules in any possible order (see page 1036).

■ **Page 669 · Cyclic tag systems.** From a tag system which depends only on its first element, with rules given as in the note below, the following constructs a cyclic tag system emulating it:

```
TS1ToCT[{n_, subs_}] := With[{k = Length[subs]},
  Join[Map[v[Last[#], k] &, subs], Table[{}, {k (n - 1)}]]]

u[i_, k_] := Table[If[j == i + 1, 1, 0], {j, k}]

v[list_, k_] := Flatten[Map[u[#, k] &, list]]
```

The initial condition for the tag system can be converted using *v[list, k]*. The list representing the complete history of the resulting cyclic tag system can then be interpreted using

```
Map[Map[Position[#, 1][[1, 1]] - 1 &, Partition[#, k]] &,
  Take[history, {1, -1, n k}]]
```

This construction is relevant to the proof of the universality of rule 110 starting on page 678.

■ **Page 669 · Multicolor Turing machines.** Given rules in the form on page 888 for a Turing machine with *s* states and *k* colors the following yields an equivalent Turing machine with $With[\{c = Ceiling[Log[2, k]]\}, ((3\,2^c) + 2c - 7)s]$ states (always less than $6.03\,k\,s$) and 2 colors:

```
TMToTM2[rule_, s_, k_] := (# /. MapIndexed[
  #1 → First[#2] &, Union[Map[#[[1, 1]] &, #]]] &)[
  With[{b = Ceiling[Log[2, k]] - 1}, Flatten[Table[
  {Table[{Table[{{m, i, n, d}, c} → {{m, Mod[i, 2^{n-1}], n - 1,
    d}, Quotient[i, 2^{n-1}], 1}, {n, 2, b}, {i, 0, 2^n - 1}], Table[
    {{m, i, 1, d}, c} → {{m, -1, 1, d}, i, d}, {i, 0, 1}], Table[
    {{m, -1, n, d}, c} → {{m, -1, n + 1, d}, c, d}, {n, b - 1}],
    {{m, -1, b, d}, c} → {{0, 0, m}, c, d}], {d, -1, 1, 2}],
  Table[{{i, n, m}, c} → {{i + 2^n c, n + 1, m}, c, -1},
    {n, 0, b - 1}, {i, 0, 2^n - 1}], With[{r = 2^b}, Table[
    If[i + r c ≥ k, {}, Cases[rule, ({m, i + r c} → {x_, y_, z_}) →
    {{i, b, m}, c} → {{x, Mod[y, r], b, z}, Quotient[y, r],
    1}]], {i, 0, r - 1}]]}, {m, s}], {c, 0, 1}]]]
```

Some of these states are usually unnecessary, and in the main text such states have been pruned. Given an initial condition *{i, list, n}* the initial condition for the 2-color Turing machine is

```
With[{b = Ceiling[Log[2, k]]},
  {i, Flatten[IntegerDigits[list, 2, b]], b n}]
```

■ **Page 670 · One-element-dependence tag systems.** Writing the rule *{3, {{0, _, _} → {0, 0}, {1, _, _} → {1, 1, 0, 1}}}* from page 895 as *{3, {0 → {0, 0}, 1 → {1, 1, 0, 1}}}* the evolution of a tag system that depends only on its first element is obtained from

```
TS1EvolveList[rule_, init_, t_] :=
   NestList[TS1Step[rule, #] &, init, t]
TS1Step[{n_, subs_}, {}] = {}
TS1Step[{n_, subs_}, list_] :=
   Drop[Join[list, First[list] /. subs], n]
```

Given a Turing machine in the form used on page 888 the following will construct a tag system that emulates it:

```
TMToTS1[rules_] :=
   {2, Union[Flatten[rules /. ({i_, u_} → {j_, v_, r_}):→
     {Map[#[i] → {#[i, 1], #[i, 0]} &, {a, b, c, d}], If[r == 1,
     {a[i, u] → {a[j], a[j]}, b[i, u] → Table[b[j], {4}], c[i, u] →
     Flatten[{Table[b[j], {2 v}], Table[c[j], {2 − u}]}],
     d[i, u] → {d[j]}}, {a[i, u] → Table[a[j], {2 − u}],
     b[i, u] → {b[j]}, c[i, u] → Flatten[{c[j], c[j],
     Table[d[j], {2 v}]}], d[i, u] → Table[d[j], {4}]}]}]]]}
```

A Turing machine in state *i* with a blank tape corresponds to initial condition *{a[i], a[i], c[i]}* for the tag system. The configuration of the tape on each side of the head in the Turing machine evolution can be obtained from the tag system evolution using

```
Cases[history, x : {a[_], ___}:→
   Apply[{#1, Reverse[#2]} &, Map[
   Drop[IntegerDigits[Count[x, #], 2], −1] &, {_b, _d}]]]
```

■ **Page 672 · Register machines.** Given the rules for a Turing machine in the form used on page 888, a register machine program to emulate the Turing machine can be obtained by techniques analogous to those used in compilers for practical computer languages. Here *TMCompile* creates a program segment for each element of the Turing machine rule, and *TMToRM* resolves addresses and links the segments together.

```
TMToRM[rules_] := Module[{segs, adrs}, segs =
   Map[TMCompile, rules]; adrs = Thread[Map[First, rules] →
   Drop[FoldList[Plus, 1, Map[Length, segs]], −1]];
   MapIndexed[#1 /. {dr[r_, n_]:→ d[r, n + First[#2]],
   dm[r_, z_]:→ d[r, z /. adrs]} &, Flatten[segs]]]

TMCompile[_ → z : {_, _, 1}] := f[z, {1, 2}]

TMCompile[_ → z : {_, _, −1}] := f[z, {2, 1}]

f[{s_, a_, _}, {ra_, rb_}] := Flatten[{i[3], dr[ra, −1],
   dr[3, 3], i[ra], i[ra], dr[3, −2], If[a == 1, i[ra], {}], i[3],
   dr[rb, 5], i[rb], dr[3, −1], dr[rb, 1], dm[rb, {s, 0}],
   dr[rb, −6], i[rb], dr[3, −1], dr[rb, 1], dm[rb, {s, 1}]}]
```

A blank initial tape for the Turing machine corresponds to initial conditions *{1, {0, 0, 0}}* for the register machine. (Assuming that the Turing machine starts in state 1, with a 0 under its head, other initial conditions can be encoded just by taking the values of cells on the left and right to give the digits of the numbers that are initially in the first two

registers.) Given the list of successive configurations of the register machine, the steps that correspond to successive steps of Turing machine evolution can be obtained from

```
(Flatten[Partition[Complement[#, # − 1], 1, 2]] &)[
   Position[list, {_, {_, _, 0}}]]
```

The program given above works for Turing machines with any number of states, but it requires some simple extensions to handle more than two possible colors for each cell. Note that for a Turing machine with *s* states, the length of the register machine program generated is between *34 s* and *36 s*.

■ **Register machines with many registers.** It turns out that a register machine with any number of registers can always be emulated by a register machine with just two registers. The basic idea is to encode the list of values of all the registers in the multiregister machine in the single number given by

```
RMEncode[list_] :=
   Product[Prime[j]^list[[j]], {j, Length[list]}]
```

and then to have this number be the value at appropriate steps of the first register in the 2-register machine. The program in the multiregister machine can be converted to a program for the 2-register machine according to

```
RMToRM2[prog_] :=
   Module[{segs, adrs}, segs = MapIndexed[seg, prog];
   adrs = FoldList[Plus, 1, Map[Length, segs]];
   MapIndexed[#1 /. {ds[r_, s_]:→ d[r, adrs[[s]]],
   dr[r_, j_]:→ d[r, j + First[#2]]} &, Flatten[segs]]]

seg[i[r_], {a_}] := With[{p = Prime[r]},
   Flatten[{Table[i[2], {p}], dr[1, −p], i[1],
   dr[2, −1], Table[dr[1, 1], {p + 1}]}]]

seg[d[r_, n_], {a_}] := With[{p = Prime[r]}, Flatten[{i[2], dr[
   1, 5], i[1], dr[2, −1], dr[1, 1], ds[1, n], Table[{If[m == p − 1,
   ds[1, a], dr[1, 3 p + 2 − m]], Table[i[1], {p}], dr[2, −p],
   Table[dr[1, 1], {2 p − m − 1}], ds[1, a + 1]}, {m, p − 1}]}]]
```

The initial conditions for the 2-register machine are given by *{1, {RMEncode[list], 0}}* and the results corresponding to each step in the evolution of the multiregister machine appear whenever register 2 in the 2-register machine is incremented from 0.

■ **Computations with register machines.** As an example, the following program for a 3-register machine starting with initial condition *{n, 0, 0}* will compute *{Round[√n], 0, 0}*:

```
{d[1, 4], i[1], d[1, 15], i[2], d[1, 6], d[1, 11], i[1],
   d[2, 7], d[3, 7], d[1, 15], d[3, 4], d[2, 12], d[3, 4]}
```

■ **Page 673 · Arithmetic systems.** Given the program for a register machine with *nr* registers in the form on page 896, an arithmetic system which emulates it can be obtained from

```
RMToAS[prog_, nr_] := With[{p = Length[prog], g =
   Product[Prime[j], {j, nr}]}, {p g, Sort[Flatten[MapIndexed[
   With[{n = First[#2] − 1}, #1 /. {i[r_]:→ Table[n + j p →
   (1 + n + Prime[r] (−n + #)) &], {j, 0, g − 1}], d[r_, k_]:→
   Table[n + j p → If[Mod[j, Prime[r]] == 0, −1 + k + (−n +
   #)/Prime[r] &, # + 1 &], {j, 0, g − 1}]}] &, prog]]]}]
```

The rules for the arithmetic system are represented so that the system from page 122 becomes for example {2, {0 :→ (3 #/2 &), 1 :→ (3 (# + 1)/2 &)}}. If the register machine starts at instruction *n* with values *regs* in its registers, then the corresponding arithmetic system starts with the number *n* + Table[Prime[i] ^ reg[[i]], {i, nr}] p - 1 where p = Length[prog]. The evolution of the arithmetic system is given by

ASEvolveList[{n_, rules_}, init_, t_] :=
    NestList[(Mod[#, n] /. rules)[#] &, init, t]

Given a value *m* obtained in the evolution of the arithmetic system, the state of the register machine to which it corresponds is

{Mod[m, p] + 1, Map[Last, FactorInteger[
    Product[Prime[i], {i, nr}] Quotient[m, p]]] - 1}

Note that it is possible to have each successive step involve only multiplication, with no addition, at the cost of using considerably larger numbers overall.

■ **History.** The correspondence between arithmetic systems and register machines was established (using a slightly different approach) by Marvin Minsky in 1962. Additional work was done by John Conway, starting around 1971. Conway considered fraction systems based on rules of the form

FSEvolveList[fracs_, init_, t_] :=
    NestList[First[Select[fracs #, IntegerQ, 1]] &, init, t]

With the choice

fracs = {17/91, 78/85, 19/51, 23/38, 29/33, 77/29, 95/
    23, 77/19, 1/17, 11/13, 13/11, 15/14, 15/2, 55/1}

starting at *2* the result for Log[2, list] is as shown below, where Rest[Log[2, Select[list, IntegerQ[Log[2, #]] &]]] gives exactly the primes.

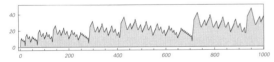

(Compare the discussion of universality in integer equations on page 786.)

■ **Multiway systems.** It is straightforward to emulate a *k*-color multiway system with a 2-color one, just by encoding successive colors by strings like "AAABBB", "AAABAB" and "AABABB" that have no overlaps. (Compare page 1033.)

The Rule 110 Cellular Automaton

■ **History.** The fact that 1D cellular automata can be universal was discussed by Alvy Ray Smith in 1970—who set up an 18-color nearest-neighbor cellular automaton rule capable of emulating Marvin Minsky's 7-state 4-color universal Turing machine (see page 706). (Roger Banks also mentioned in 1970

a 17-color cellular automaton that he believed was universal.) But without any particular reason to think it would be interesting, almost nothing was done on finding simpler universal 1D cellular automata. In 1984 I suggested that cellular automata showing what I called class 4 behavior should be universal—and I identified some simple rules (such as *k* = 2, *r* = 2 totalistic code 20) as explicit candidates. A piece published in *Scientific American* in 1985 describing my interest in finding simple 1D universal cellular automata led me to receive a large number of proofs of the fact (already well known to me) that 1D cellular automata can in principle emulate Turing machines. In 1989 Kristian Lindgren and Mats Nordahl constructed a 7-color nearest-neighbor cellular automaton that could emulate Minsky's 7,4 universal Turing machine, and showed that in general a rule with *s* + *k* + 2 colors could emulate an *s*-state *k*-color Turing machine (compare page 658). Following my ideas about class 4 cellular automata I had come by 1985 to suspect that rule 110 must be universal. And when I started working on the writing of this book in 1991, I decided to try to establish this for certain. The general outline of what had to be done was fairly clear—but there were an immense number of details to be handled, and I asked a young assistant of mine named Matthew Cook to investigate them. His initial results were encouraging, but after a few months he became increasingly convinced that rule 110 would never in fact be proved universal. I insisted, however, that he keep on trying, and over the next several years he developed a systematic computer-aided design system for working with structures in rule 110. Using this he was then in 1994 successfully able to find the main elements of the proof. Many details were filled in over the next year, some mistakes were corrected in 1998, and the specific version in the note below was constructed in 2001. Like most proofs of universality, the final proof he found is conceptually quite straightforward, but is filled with many excruciatingly elaborate details. And among these details it is certainly possible that a few errors still remain. But if so, I believe that they can be overcome by the same general methods that have been used in the proof so far. Quite probably a somewhat simpler proof can be given, but as discussed on page 722 it is essentially inevitable that proofs of universality must be at least somewhat complicated. In the future it should be possible to give a proof in a form that can be checked completely by computer. (The initial conditions in the note below quite soon become too large to run explicitly on any existing computer.) And in addition, with sufficient effort, I believe one should be able to construct an automated system that will allow many universality proofs of this general kind to be found almost entirely by computer (compare page 810).

■ **Page 683 · Initial conditions.** The following takes the rules for a cyclic tag system in the form used on page 895 (with the restrictions in the note below), together with the initial conditions for the tag system, and yields a specification of initial conditions in rule 110 which will emulate it. This specification gives a list of three blocks $\{b_1, b_2, b_3\}$ and the final initial conditions consist of an infinite repetition of b_1 blocks, followed by b_2, followed by an infinite repetition of b_3 blocks. The b_1 blocks act like "clock pulses", b_2 encodes the initial conditions for the tag system and the b_3 blocks encode the rules for the tag system.

```
CTToR110[rules_ /;
  Select[rules, Mod[Length[#], 6] ≠ 0 &] == {}, init_] :=
Module[{g1, g2, g3, nr = 0, x1, y1, sp}, g1 = Flatten[
  Map[If[# === {}, {{{2}}}, {{{1, 3, 5 – First[#]}}, Table[
    {4, 5 – #[[n]]}, {n, 2, Length[#]}]}] &, rules] /. a_Integer :>
  Map[{d[#[[1]], #[[2]]], s[#[[3]]]} &, Partition[c[a], 3]], 4];
  g2 = g1 = MapThread[If[#1 === #2 === {d[22, 11], s3}, {d[
    20, 8], s3}, #1] &, {g1, RotateRight[g1, 6]}]; While[Mod[
  Apply[Plus, Map[#[[1, 2]] &, g2]], 30] ≠ 0, nr ++; g2 = Join[
  g2, g1]]; y1 = g2[[1, 1, 2]] – 11; If[y1 < 0, y1 += 30]; Cases[
  Last[g2][[2]], s[d[x_, y1], _, _, a_]] :> (x1 = x + Length[a]);
  g3 = Fold[sadd, {d[x1, y1], {}, g2]; sp = Ceiling[5 Length[
  g3[[2]]]/(28 nr) + 2; {Join[Fold[sadd, {d[17, 1], {}},
  Flatten[Table[{{d[sp 28 + 6, 1], s[5]}, {d[398, 1], s[5]},
  {d[342, 1], s[5]}, {d[370, 1], s[5]}, {3}, 1]][[2]], bg[
  4, 11]], Flatten[Join[Table[bgi, {sp 2 + 1 + 24 Length[init]}],
  init /. {0 → init0, 1 → init1}, bg[1, 9], bg[6, 60 – g2[[1, 1, 1]] +
  g3[[1, 1]] + If[g2[[1, 1, 2]] < g3[[1, 2]], 8, 0]]]], g3[[2]]}]
```

$s[1] = struct[\{3, 0, 1, 10, 4, 8\}, 2]$;

$s[2] = struct[\{3, 0, 1, 1, 619, 15\}, 2]$;

$s[3] = struct[\{3, 0, 1, 10, 4956, 18\}, 2]$;

$s[4] = struct[\{0, 0, 9, 10, 4, 8\}]$;

$s[5] = struct[\{5, 0, 9, 14, 1, 1\}]$;

```
{c[1], c[2]} = Map[Join[{22, 11, 3, 39, 3, 1}, #] &,
  {{63, 12, 2, 48, 5, 4, 29, 26, 4, 43, 26, 4, 23, 3, 4, 47, 4, 4},
  {87, 6, 2, 32, 2, 4, 13, 23, 4, 27, 16, 4}}];
```

```
{c[3], c[4], c[5]} = Map[Join[#, {4, 17, 22, 4,
  39, 27, 4, 47, 4, 4}] &, {{17, 22, 4, 23, 24, 4, 31, 29},
  {17, 22, 4, 47, 18, 4, 15, 19}, {41, 16, 4, 47, 18, 4, 15, 19}}]
```

```
{init0, init1} = Map[IntegerDigits[216 (# + 432 10⁴⁹), 2] &,
{24600556015465847173551005175056992262806506706 1,
104374616548946685289708983044175655088983470964 5 }]
```

$bgi = IntegerDigits[9976, 2]$

$bg[s_, n_] := Array[bgi[[1 + Mod[\# - 1, 14]]] \&, n, s]$

```
ev[s[d[x_, y_], pl_, pr_, b_]] := Module[{r, pl1, pr1}, r =
  Sign[BitAnd[2 ^ ListConvolve[{1, 2, 4}, Join[bg[pl – 2, 2], b,
  bg[pr, 2]]], 110]]; pl1 = (Position[r – bg[pl + 3, Length[r]],
  1 | –1] /. {} → {{Length[r]}})[[1, 1]]; pr1 = Max[pl1,
  (Position[r – bg[pr + 5 – Length[r], Length[r]], 1 | –1] /. {} →
  {{1}})[[–1, 1]]]; s[d[x + pl1 – 2, y + 1], pl1 + Mod[pl + 2, 14],
  1 + Mod[pr + 4, 14] + pr1 – Length[r], Take[r, {pl1, pr1}]]]
```

```
struct[{x_, y_, pl_, pr_, b_, bl_}, p_Integer : 1] := Module[
  {gr = s[d[x, y], pl, pr, IntegerDigits[b, 2, bl]], p2 = p + 1},
  Drop[NestWhile[Append[#, ev[Last[#]]] &, {gr},
  If[Rest[Last[#]] === Rest[gr], p2––; p2 > 0 &], –1]]
sadd[{d[x_, y_], b_}, {d[dx_, dy_], st_}] :=
  Module[{x1 = dx – x, y1 = dy – y, b2, x2, y2}, While[y1 > 0,
  {x1, y1} += If[Length[st] == 30, {8, –30}, {–2, –3}]];
  b2 = First[Cases[st, s[d[x3_, –y1], pl_, _, sb_]] :>
  Join[bg[pl – x1 – x3, x1 + x3], x2 = x3 + Length[sb];
  y2 = –y1; sb]]]; {d[x2, y2], Join[b, b2]}]
```

CTToR110[{{}, {1}}] yields blocks of lengths $\{7204, 1873, 7088\}$. But even CTToR110[{{0, 0, 0, 0, 0, 0}, {}, {1, 1, 1, 1, 1, 1}, {}, {1}}] already yields blocks of lengths $\{105736, 34717, 95404\}$. The picture below shows what happens if one chops these blocks into rows and arranges these in 2D arrays. In the first two blocks, much of what one sees is just padding to prevent clock pulses on the left from hitting data in the middle too early on any given step. The part of the middle block that actually encodes an initial condition grows like $180\ Length[init]$. The core of the right-hand block grows approximately like $500\ (Length[Flatten[rules]] + Length[rules])$, but to make a block that can just be repeated without shifts, between 1 and 30 repeats of this core can be needed.

■ **Page 689 · Tag systems.** The discussion in the main text and the construction above require a cyclic tag system with blocks that are a multiple of 6 long, and in which at least one block is added at some point in each complete cycle. By inserting $k = 6\ Ceiling[Length[subs]/6]$ in the definition of TS1ToCT from page 1113 one can construct a cyclic tag system of this kind to emulate any one-element-dependence tag system.

Class 4 Behavior and Universality

■ **2-neighbor rules.** Among 3-color 2-neighbor rules class 4 behavior seems to be comparatively rare; the picture at the top of the facing page shows an example with rule number 2144.

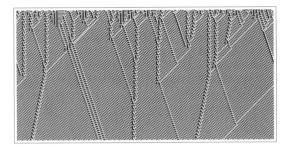

■ **Totalistic rules.** It is straightforward to show that totalistic cellular automata can be universal. Explicit simple candidates include $k = 2$, $r = 2$ rules with codes 20 and 52, as well as the various $k = 3$, $r = 1$ class 4 rules shown in Chapter 3.

■ **Page 693 · 2D cellular automata.** Universality was essentially built in explicitly to the underlying rules for the 2D cellular automaton constructed by John von Neumann in 1952 as a model for self-reproduction. For among the 29 possible states allowed for each cell were ones set up to behave quite directly like components for practical electronic computers like the EDVAC—as well as to grow new memory areas and so on. In the mid-1960s Edgar Codd showed that a system similar to von Neumann's could be constructed with only 8 possible states for each cell. Then in 1970 Roger Banks managed to show that the 2-state 5-neighbor symmetric 2D rule 4005091440 was able to reproduce all the same logical elements. (This system, like rule 110, requires an infinite repetitive background in order to support universality.) Following the invention of the Game of Life, considerable work was done in the early 1970s to identify structures that could be used to make the analog of logic circuits. John Conway worked on an explicit proof of universality based on emulating register machines, but this was apparently never completed. Yet by the 1980s it had come to be generally believed that the Game of Life had in fact been proved universal. No particularly rigorous treatments of the system were given, and the mere existence of configurations that can act for example like logic gates was often assumed immediately to imply universality. From the discoveries I have made, I have no doubt at all that the Game of Life is in the end universal, and indeed I believe that the kind of elaborate behavior needed to support various components is in fact good evidence for this. But the fact remains that a complete and rigorous proof of universality has apparently still never been given for the Game of Life. Particularly in recent years elaborate constructions have been made of for example Turing machines. But so far they have always had

only a fixed number of elements on their tape, which is not sufficient for universality. Extending constructions is often very tricky; much as in rule 110 it is easy for there to be subtle bugs associated with rare mismatches in the placement of structures and timing of interactions. The pictures below nevertheless show a rather simple implementation of a NAND gate in Life. The input comes from the left encoded as the presence or absence of spaceships 92 cells apart. The spaceships are converted to gliders. When only one glider is present, a new spaceship emerges on the right as the output. But when two gliders are present, their collision forms a wall, which prevents output of the spaceship.

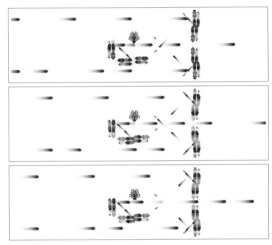

If one considers rules with more than two colors, it becomes straightforward to emulate standard logic circuits. The pictures below show how 1D cellular automata can be implemented in the 4-color WireWorld cellular automaton of Brian Silverman from 1987, whose rules find the new value of a cell from its old value a and the number u of its 8 neighbors that are 1's according to

$$a /. \{0 \to 0, 1 \to 2, 2 \to 3, 3 :\to If[0 < u < 3, 1, 3]\}$$

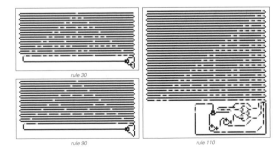

rule 30

rule 90

rule 110

The Threshold of Universality in Cellular Automata

■ **Claims of non-universality.** Over the years, there have been a few erroneous claims of proofs that universality is impossible in particular kinds of simple cellular automata. The basic mistake is usually to make the implicit assumption that computation must be done in some rather specific way—that does not happen to be consistent with the way we have for example seen that it can be done in rule 110.

■ **Page 700 · Rule 73.** ■■■■ on a white background yields a pattern that contains the last structure shown here.

■ **Page 700 · Rule 30.** For the first background shown, no initial region up to size 25 yields a truly localized structure, though for example ▭▭▭■■▭■■■ starts off growing quite slowly.

■ **Rule 41.** Various rules like rule 41 below can perhaps be viewed as having localized structures—though ones that apparently always travel in the same direction at the same speed. None of the first million initial conditions for rule 41 yield unbounded growth, though some can still generate fairly wide patterns, as in the pictures below. (The initial condition consisting ▭▭■■■▭■■▭▭■■■ repeated, followed by ■, followed by ■■▭▭▭ repeated nevertheless yields a region that grows forever.)

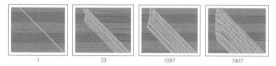

| 1 | 73 | 1097 | 7407 |

■ **Page 702 · Rule emulations.** The network below shows which quiescent symmetric elementary rules can emulate which with blocks of length 8 or less. (Compare page 269.)

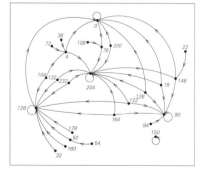

In all cases things are set up so that several steps in one rule emulate a single step in another. The examples shown in detail in the main text all have the feature that the block size b and number of steps t are matched, so that $r\,t = b$ (where

the range $r = 1$ for elementary rules). It is also possible to set up emulations where this equality does not hold—and indeed some of the cases listed in the main text and shown in the picture above are of this type. In those where $r\,t < b$ there are more cells that are in principle determined by a given set of initial blocks—but the outermost of these cells are ignored when the outcome for a particular cell is deduced. In cases where $r\,t > b$ there are more initial cells whose values are specified—but the outermost of these turn out to be irrelevant in determining the outcome for a particular cell. This lack of dependence makes it somewhat inevitable that the only rules that end up being emulated in this way are ones with very simple behavior.

In any 1D cellular automaton the color of a particular cell can always be determined from the colors t steps back of a block of $2\,r\,t + 1$ cells (compare pages 605 and 960). But such a block corresponds in a sense to a horizontal slice through the cone of previous cell colors. And it turns out also to be possible to determine the color of a particular cell from slices at essentially any rational angle corresponding to a propagation speed less than r. So this means that one can consider encodings based on blocks that have a kind of staircase shape—as in the rule 45 example shown.

■ **Encodings.** Generalizing the setup in the main text one can say that a cellular automaton i can emulate j if there is some encoding function ϕ that encodes the initial conditions a_j for j as initial conditions for i, and which has an inverse that decodes the outcome for i to give the outcome for j. With evolution functions f_i and f_j the requirement for the emulation to work is

$$f_j[a_j] == InverseFunction[\phi][f_i[\phi[a_j]]]$$

In the main text the encoding function is taken to have the form *Flatten[a /. rules]*—where *rules* are say {1 → {1, 1}, 0 → {0, 0}}—with the result that the decoding function for emulations that work is *Partition[ā, b] /. Map[Reverse, rules]*.

An immediate generalization is to allow *rules* to have a form like {1 → {1, 1}, 1 → {1, 0}, 0 → {0, 0}} in which several blocks are in effect allowed to serve as possible encodings for a single cell value. Another generalization is to allow blocks at a variety of angles (see above). In most cases, however, introducing these kinds of slightly more complicated encodings does not fundamentally seem to expand the set of rules that a given rule can emulate. But often it does allow the emulations to work with smaller blocks. And so, for example, with the setup shown in the main text, rule 54 can emulate rule 0 only with blocks of length $b = 6$. But if either multiple blocks or $\delta = 1$ are allowed, b can be reduced to 4, with *rules* being {1 → {1, 1, 1, 1}, 0 → {0, 0, 0, 0}, 0 → {0, 1, 1, 1}} and {0 → {0, 1, 0, 0}, 1 → {0, 0, 1, 0}} in the two cases.

Various questions about encoding functions ϕ have been studied over the past several decades in coding theory. The block-based encodings discussed so far here correspond to block codes. Convolutional codes (related to sequential cellular automata) are the other major class of codes studied in coding theory, but in their usual form these do not seem especially useful for our present purposes.

In the most general case the encoding function can involve an arbitrary terminating computation (see page 1126). But types of encoding functions that are at least somewhat powerful yet can realistically be sampled systematically may perhaps include those based on neighbor-dependent substitution systems, and on formal languages (finite automata and generalizations).

■ **Logic operations and universality.** Knowing that the circuits in practical computers use only a small set of basic logic operations—often just *Nand*—it is sometimes assumed that if a particular system could be shown to emulate logic operations like *Nand*, then this would immediately establish its universality. But at least on the face of it, this is not correct. For somehow there also has to be a way to store arbitrarily large amounts of data—and to apply suitable combinations of *Nand* operations to it. Yet while practical computers have elaborate circuits containing huge numbers of *Nand* operations, we now know that for example simple cellular automata that can be implemented with just a few *Nand* operations (see page 619) are enough. And from what I have discovered in this book, it may well be that in fact most systems capable of supporting even a single *Nand* operation will actually turn out to be universal. But the point is that in any particular case this will not normally be an easy matter to demonstrate. (Compare page 807.)

Universality in Turing Machines and Other Systems

■ **Page 706 · Minsky's Turing machine.** The universal Turing machine shown was constructed by Marvin Minsky in 1962. If the rules for a one-element-dependence tag system are given in the form {2, {{0, 1}, {0, 1, 1}}} (compare page 1114), the initial conditions for the Turing machine are

    TagToMTM[{2, rule_}, init_] :=
    With[{b = FoldList[Plus, 1, Map[Length, rule] + 1]},
    Drop[Flatten[{Reverse[Flatten[{1, Map[{Map[
        {1, 0, Table[0, {b[[# + 1]]}]}} &, #], 1} &, rule], 1}]],
        0, 0, Map[{Table[2, {b[[# + 1]]}], 3} &, init]}], -1]]

surrounded by *0*'s, with the head on the leftmost *2*, in state *1*. An element *-1* in the tag system corresponds to halting of the Turing machine. The different cases in the rules for the tag system are laid out on the left in the Turing machine. Each step of tag system evolution is implemented by having the

head of the Turing machine scan as far to the left as it needs to get to the case of the tag system rule that applies—then copy the appropriate elements to the end of the sequence on the right. Note that although the Turing machine can emulate any number of colors in the tag system, it can only emulate directly rules that delete exactly 2 elements at each step. But since we know that at least with sufficiently many colors such tag systems are universal, it follows that the Turing machine is also universal.

■ **History.** Alan Turing gave the first construction for a universal Turing machine in 1936. His construction was complicated and had several bugs. Claude Shannon showed in 1956 that 2 colors were sufficient so long as enough states were used. (See page 669; conversion of Minsky's machine using this method yields a {43, 2} machine.) After Minsky's 1962 result, comparatively little more was published about small universal Turing machines. In the 1980s and 1990s, however, Yurii Rogozhin found examples of universal Turing machines for which the number of states and number of colors were: {24, 2}, {10, 3}, {7, 4}, {5, 5}, {4, 6}, {3, 10}, and {2, 18}. The smallest product of these numbers is 24 (compare note below), and the rule he gave in this case is:

Note that these results concern Turing machines which can halt (see page 1137); the Turing machines that I consider do not typically have this feature.

■ **Page 707 · Rule 110 Turing machines.** Given an initial condition for rule 110, the initial condition for the Turing machine shown here is obtained as *Prepend[4 list, 0]* with *1*'s on the left and *0*'s on the right. The Turing machine

    {{1, 2} → {2, 2, -1}, {1, 1} → {1, 1, -1}, {1, 0} → {3, 1, 1},
     {2, 2} → {4, 0, -1}, {2, 1} → {1, 2, -1}, {2, 0} → {2, 1, -1},
     {3, 2} → {3, 2, 1}, {3, 1} → {3, 1, 1}, {3, 0} → {1, 0, -1},
     {4, 2} → {2, 2, 1}, {4, 1} → {4, 1, 1}, {4, 0} → {2, 2, -1}}

with $s = 4$ states and $k = 3$ possible colors also emulates rule 110 when started from *Prepend[list + 1, 1]* surrounded by *0*'s. The $s = 3$, $k = 4$ Turing machine

    {{1, 0} → {1, 2, 1}, {1, 1} → {2, 3, 1},
     {1, 2} → {1, 0, -1}, {1, 3} → {1, 1, -1}, {2, 0} → {1, 3, 1},
     {2, 1} → {3, 3, 1}, {3, 0} → {1, 3, 1}, {3, 1} → {3, 2, 1}}

started from *Append[list, 0]* with *0*'s on the left and *2*'s on the right generates a shifted version of rule 110. Note that this Turing machine requires only 8 out of the 12 possible cases in its rules to be specified.

■ **Rule 60 Turing machines.** One can emulate rule 60 using the 8-case $s = 3$, $k = 3$ Turing machine (with initial condition *Append[list + 1, 1]* surrounded by *0*'s)

    {{1, 2} → {2, 2, 1}, {1, 1} → {1, 1, 1},
     {1, 0} → {3, 1, -1}, {2, 2} → {2, 1, 1}, {2, 1} → {1, 2, 1},
     {3, 2} → {3, 2, -1}, {3, 1} → {3, 1, -1}, {3, 0} → {1, 0, 1}}

or by using the 6-case $s = 2$, $k = 4$ Turing machine (with initial condition *Append[3 list, 0]* with 0's on the left and 1's on the right)

$\{\{1, 3\} \to \{2, 2, 1\}, \{1, 2\} \to \{1, 3, -1\}, \{1, 1\} \to \{1, 0, -1\},$
$\{1, 0\} \to \{1, 1, 1\}, \{2, 3\} \to \{2, 1, 1\}, \{2, 0\} \to \{1, 2, 1\}\}$

This second Turing machine is directly analogous to the one for rule 110 on page 707. Random searches suggest that among $s = 3$, $k = 3$ Turing machines roughly one in 25 million reproduce rule 60 in the same way as the machines discussed here. (See also page 665.)

■ **Turing machine enumeration.** Of the 4096 $s = 2$, $k = 2$ Turing machines (see page 888) 560 are distinct after taking account of obvious symmetries and equivalences. Ignoring machines which cannot escape from one of their possible states or which yield motion in only one direction or cells of only one color leaves a total of 237 cases. If one now ignores machines that do not allow the head to move more than one step in one of the two directions, that always yield the same color when moving in a particular direction, or that always leave the tape unchanged, one is finally left with just 25 distinct cases.

Of the 2,985,984 $s = 3$, $k = 2$ machines, 125,294 survive after taking account of obvious symmetries and equivalences, while imposing analogs of the other conditions above yields in the end 16,400 distinct cases. For $s = 2$, $k = 3$ machines, the first two numbers are the same, but the final number of distinct cases is 48,505.

■ **States versus colors.** The total number of possible Turing machines depends on the product $s\,k$. The number of distinct machines that need to be considered increases as k increases for given $s\,k$ (see note above). $s = 1$ or $k = 1$ always yield trivial behavior. The fraction of machines that show non-repetitive behavior seems to increase roughly like $(s-1)(k-1)$ (see page 888). More complex behavior—and presumably also universality—seems however to occur slightly more often with larger k than with larger s.

■ **$s=2$, $k=2$ Turing machines.** As illustrated on page 761, even extremely simple Turing machines can have behavior that depends in a somewhat complicated way on initial conditions. Thus, for example, with the rule

$\{\{1, 0\} \to \{1, 1, -1\}, \{1, 1\} \to \{2, 1, 1\},$
$\{2, 0\} \to \{1, 0, -1\}, \{2, 1\} \to \{1, 0, 1\}\}$

the head moves to the right whenever the initial condition consists of odd-length blocks of 1's separated by single 0's; otherwise it stays in a fixed region.

■ **Page 709 · Machine 596440.** For any list of initial colors *init*, it turns out that successive rows in the first t steps of the compressed evolution pattern turn out to be given by

NestList[Join[{0}, Mod[1 + Rest[FoldList[Plus, 0, #]], 2],
{{0}, {1, 1, 0}}[[Mod[Apply[Plus, #], 2] + 1]]] &, init, t]

Inside the right-hand part of this pattern the cell values can then be obtained from an upside-down version of the rule 60 additive cellular automaton, and starting from a sequence of 1's the picture below shows that a typical rule 60 nested pattern can be produced, at least in a limited region.

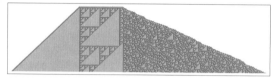

The presence of glitches on the right-hand edge of the whole pattern means, however, that overall there is nothing as simple as nested behavior—making it conceivable that (possibly with analogies to tag systems) behavior complex enough to support universality can occur. The plot below shows the distances between successive outward glitches on the right-hand side; considerable complexity is evident.

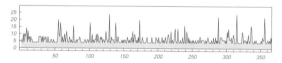

■ **Page 710 · $s=3$, $k=2$ Turing machines.** Compare page 763 and particularly the discussion of machine 600720 on page 1145.

■ **Tag systems.** Marvin Minsky showed in 1961 that one-element-dependence tag systems (see page 670) can be universal. Hao Wang in 1963 constructed an example that deletes just 2 elements at each step and adds at most 3 elements—but has a large number of colors. I suspect that universal examples with blocks of the same size exist with just 3 colors.

■ **Encoding sequences by integers.** In many constructions it is useful to be able to encode a list of integers of any length by a single integer. (See e.g. page 1127.) One way to do this is by using the Gödel number *Product[Prime[i] ^ list[[i]], {i, Length[list]}]*. An alternative is to use the Chinese Remainder Theorem. Given $p = Array[Prime, Length[list], PrimePi[Max[list]] + 1]$ or any list of integers that are all relatively prime and above *Max[list]* (the integers in *list* are assumed positive)

CRT[list_, p_] :=
  With[{m = Apply[Times, p]}, Mod[Apply[Plus,
    MapThread[#1 (m/#2) ^ EulerPhi[#2] &, {list, p}]], m]]

yields a number x such that *Mod[x, p] == list*. Based on this

LE[list_] := Module[{n = Length[list], i = Max[MapIndexed[
  #1 - #2 &, PrimePi[list]]] + 1}, CRT[PadRight[
  list, n + i], Join[Array[Prime[i + #] &, n], Array[Prime, i]]]]

will yield a number *x* that can be decoded into a list of length *n* using essentially the so-called Gödel β function

Mod[x, Prime[Rest[NestList[NestWhile[# + 1 &,
 # + 1, Mod[x, Prime[#]] == 0 &] &, 0, n]]]]

■ **Register machines.** The results of page 100 suggest that with 2 registers and up to 8 instructions no universal register machines (URMs) exist. Using the method of page 672 one can construct a URM with 3 registers and 175 instructions (or 2 registers and 4694 instructions) that emulates the universal Turing machine on page 706. Using work by Ivan Korec from the 1980s and 1990s one can also construct URMs which directly emulate other register machines. An example with 8 registers and 41 instructions is:

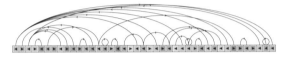

or

{d[4, 40], i[5], d[3, 9], i[3], d[7, 4], d[5, 14], i[6],
d[3, 3], i[7], d[6, 2], i[6], d[5, 11], d[6, 3], d[4, 35],
d[6, 15], i[4], d[8, 16], d[5, 21], i[1], d[3, 1], d[5, 25],
i[2], d[3, 1], i[6], d[5, 32], d[1, 28], d[3, 1], d[4, 28],
i[4], d[6, 29], d[3, 1], d[5, 24], d[2, 28], d[3, 1],
i[8], i[6], d[5, 36], i[6], d[3, 3], d[6, 40], d[4, 3]}

Given any register machine, one first applies the function *RMToRM2* from page 1114, then takes the resulting program and initial condition and finds an initial condition for the URM using

R2ToURM[prog_, init_] := Join[init, With[
{n = Length[prog]}, {1 + LE[Reverse[prog] /. {i[x_] → x,
d[x_, y_] → 4 + 2 n + x - 2 y}], n + 1, 0, 0, 0}]]

For the first example on page 98 this gives *{0, 0, 211680, 3, 0, 0, 0}*. The process of emulation is quite slow, with each emulated step in this example taking about 20 million URM steps.

■ **Recursive functions.** The general recursive functions from page 907 provided an early example of universality (see page 907). That such functions are universal can be demonstrated by showing for example that they can emulate any tag system. With the state of a 2-color tag system encoded as an integer according to *FromDigits[Reverse[list] + 1, 3]* the following takes the rule for any such tag system (in the first form from page 894) and yields a primitive recursive function that emulates a single step in its evolution:

TSToPR[{n_, rule_}] := Fold[Apply[c, Flatten[{#1, Array[p, #
2], c[r[z, c[r[p[1], s], c[r[z, p[2]], c[r[z, r[c[s, z], c[r[c[s,
c[s, z]], z], p[2]]], p[2]]], p[1]]], p[#2]]}]}] &, c[c[r[p[1],
s], p[1], c[r[p[1], r[z, c[s, c[s, s]]]], c[c[r[z, c[r[p[1], s],
c[r[z, c[s, z]], c[r[p[1], r[z, c[r[p[1], s], c[r[z, p[2]], c[
r[z, r[c[s, z], c[r[c[s, c[s, z]], z], p[2]]], p[2]], p[1]]], p[
2], p[3]]], p[1]], p[1], p[1], p[1], p[2]], p[n + 1],

MapIndexed[c[r[z, c[r[p[1], p[4]], p[2], p[3], p[4]]], c[r[z,
r[c[s, z], c[r[c[s, c[s, z]], z], p[2]]]], p[Length[#2] + 1]], #
1[[1]], #1[[2]]] &, Nest[Partition[#, 2] &, Table[Nest[c[s, #] &
z, FromDigits[Reverse[IntegerDigits[i, 2, n]] /. rule] + 1, 3]],
{i, 0, 2^n - 1}], n - 1], {0, n - 1}]], Range[n, 1, -1]]

(For tag system (a) from page 94 this yields a primitive recursive function of size 325.) The result of *t* steps of evolution is in general given in terms of this function *f* by *Nest[f, init, t]*, or equivalently *r[p[1], f][t, init]*. Any fixed number of steps of evolution can thus be emulated by applying a primitive recursive function. But if one wants to find out what happens after an arbitrarily large number of steps, one needs to use the μ operator, yielding a general recursive function. (So for example $\mu[r[p[1], f]][init]$ returns the smallest *t* for which the tag system reaches state *{}*—and never returns if the tag system does not halt.) Note that the same basic approach can be used to emulate Turing machines with recursive functions; the Turing machine configuration *{s, list, n}* can be encoded by a integer such as

2 ^ FromDigits[Reverse[Take[list, n - 1]]]
3 ^ FromDigits[Take[list, {n + 1, -1}]] 5 ^ list[[n]] 7^s

■ **Lambda calculus.** Formulations of recursive function theory from the 1920s and before tended to be based on making explicit definitions like those in the note above. But in the so-called lambda calculus of Alonzo Church from around 1930 what were instead used were pure functions such as *s = Function[x, x + 1]* and *plus = Function[{x, y}, If[x == 0, y, s[plus[x - 1, y]]]]*—of just the kind now familiar from *Mathematica*. Note that the explicit names of ("bound") variables in such pure functions are never significant—which is why in *Mathematica* one can for example use *s = # + 1 &*. (See page 907.)

The definitions in the note above involve both symbolic functions and literal integers. In the so-called pure lambda calculus integers are represented by symbolic expressions. The typical way this is done is to say that a function f_n corresponds to an integer *n* if $f_n[a][b]$ yields *Nest[a, b, n]* (see note below).

■ **Page 711 · Combinators.** After it became widely known in the 1910s that *Nand* could be used to build up any expression in basic logic (see page 1173) Moses Schönfinkel introduced combinators in 1920 with the idea of providing an analogous way to build up functions—and to remove any mention of variables—particularly in predicate logic (see page 898). Given the combinator rules

crules = {s[x_][y_][z_] → x[z][y[z]], k[x_][y_] → x}

the setup was that any function *f* would be written as some combination of *s* and *k*—which Schönfinkel referred to respectively as "fusion" and "constancy"—and then the result of applying the function to an argument *x* would be given by *f[x] //. crules*. (Multiple arguments were handled for example as *f[x][y][z]* in what became known as "currying".) A very simple example of a combinator is *id = s[k][k]*, which corresponds to the identity function, since *id[x] //. crules* yields *x* for any *x*. (In general any combinator of the form *s[k][_]* will also work.) Another example of a combinator is *b = s[k[s]][k]*, for which *b[x][y][z] //. crules* yields *x[y[z]]*.

With the development of lambda calculus in the early 1930s it became clear that given any expression *expr* such as *x[y[x][z]]* with a list of variables *vars* such as *{x, y, z}* one can always find a combinator equivalent to a lambda function such as *Function[x, Function[y, Function[z, x[y[x][z]]]]]*, and it turns out that this can be done simply using

    ToC[expr_, vars_] := Fold[rm, expr, Reverse[vars]]
    rm[v_, v_] = id
    rm[f_[v_], v_] /; FreeQ[f, v] = f
    rm[h_, v_] /; FreeQ[h, v] = k[h]
    rm[f_[g_], v_] := s[rm[f, v]][rm[g, v]]

So this shows that any lambda function can in effect be written in terms of combinators, without anything analogous to variables ever explicitly having to be introduced. And based on the result that lambda functions can represent recursive functions, which can in turn represent Turing machines (see note above), it has been known since the mid-1930s that combinators are universal. The rule 110 combinator on page 713 provides however a much more direct proof of this.

The usual approach to working with combinators involves building up arithmetic constructs from them. This typically begins by using so-called Church numerals (based on work by Alonzo Church on lambda calculus), and defining a combinator *e_n* to correspond to an integer *n* if *e_n[a][b] //. crules* yields *Nest[a, b, n]*. (The *e* on page 103 can thus be considered a Church numeral for 2 since *e[a][b]* is *a[a[b]]*.) This can be achieved by taking *e_n* to be *Nest[inc, zero, n]* where

    zero = s[k]
    inc = s[s[k[s]][k]]

With this setup one then finds

    plus = s[k[s]][s[k[s[k[s]]]][s[k[k]]]]
    times = s[k[s]][k]
    power = s[k[s[k][k]]][k]

(Note that *power[x][y] //. crules* is *y[x]*, and that by analogy *x[x[y]]* corresponds to y^{x^2}, *x[y[x]]* to x^{xy}, *x[y[x]]* to x^{y^x}, and so on.)

Another approach involves representing integers directly as combinator expressions. As an example, one can take *n* to be

represented just by *Nest[s, k, n]*. And one can then convert any Church numeral *x* to this representation by applying *s[s[s[k][k]][k[s]]][k[k]]*. To go the other way, one uses the result that for all Church numerals *x* and *y*, *Nest[s, k, n][x][y]* is also a Church numeral—as can be seen recursively by noting its equality to *Nest[s, k, n − 1][y][x[y]]*, where as above *x[y]* is *power[y][x]*. And from this it follows that *Nest[s, k, n]* can be converted to the Church numeral for *n* by applying

    s[s[s[s[s[k][k]][k[s[s[k][s]][k]][s[k][k]]]]][
    k[s[s[k][s]][k]][s[s[k][s]][k]][s[k][k]]]]][s[s[k][s]][
    s[s[k][s]][s[k[s[s[s[s[k][k]][k[s]]][k][k]]][k[s[
    k][s]][k]][s[k][k]]]]][k[s[s[k][s]][k]][s[s[k][s]][k]][s[k][
    k]]]]][k[s[s[s[k][k]][k[s[s[k][s]][k][s[s[k][s]][k]]]]][s[
    k][k]][s[k[s[s[k][s]][k]]][s[s[k][k]][k[k]]]]]][s[k][k]][s[
    s[k][k]][k[k]]]]]]][k[s[s[s[k][k]][k[s[k]]][k[s[k]]]]]][
    k[s[k]]]]]][s[s[k][s]][k][s[s[k][s]][k]][s[k][k]]]]]]]]][
    k[s[k][k]][s[s[k][s]][k]]]]]]][k[s[k][k]][k[s[k]]]]

Using this one can find from the corresponding results for Church numerals combinator expressions for *plus*, *times* and *power*—with sizes 377, 378 and 382 respectively. It seems certain that vastly simpler combinator expressions will also work, but searches indicate that if *inc* has size less than 4, *plus* must have size at least 8. (Searches based on other representations for integers have also not yielded much. With *n* represented by *Nest[k, s[k][k], n]*, however, *s[s[s[s]][k]][k]* serves as a decrement function, and with *n* represented by *Nest[s[s], s[k], n]*, *s[s[s][k]][k[k[s[s]]]]* serves as a doubling function.)

■ **Page 712 · Combinator properties.** The size of a combinator expression is conveniently measured by its *LeafCount*. If the evolution of a combinator expression reaches a fixed point, then the expression generated is always the same (Church-Rosser property). But the behavior in the course of the evolution can depend on how the combinator rules are applied; here *expr /. crules* is used at each step, as in the symbolic systems of page 896. The total number of combinator expressions of successively greater sizes is *{2, 4, 16, 80, 448, 2688, 16896, 109824, ...}* (or in general 2^n *Binomial[2n − 2, n − 1]/n*; see page 897). Of these, *{2, 4, 12, 40, 144, 544, 2128, 8544, ...}* are themselves fixed points. Of combinator expressions up to size 6 all evolve to fixed points, in at most *{1, 1, 2, 3, 4, 7}* steps respectively (compare case (a)); the largest fixed points have sizes *{1, 2, 3, 4, 6, 10}* (compare case (b)). At size 7, all but 2 of the 16,896 possible combinator expressions evolve to fixed points, in at most 12 steps (case (c)). The largest fixed point has size 41 (case (d)). *s[s[s]][s][s][s][s]* (case (e)) and *s[s][s][s][s]][s][s]* lead to expressions that grow like $2^{t/2}$. The maximum number of levels in these expressions (see page 897) grows roughly linearly, although *Depth[expr]* reaches 14 after 26 and 25 steps, then stays there. At size 8, out of all 109,824 combinator expressions it appears that 49 show exponential growth, and many more show roughly linear growth. *s[s][k][s[s[s]][s]][s]* goes to a fixed point of size 80. *s[s[s]][s][s][s][s][k]* (case (i)) increases rapidly to size 7050 but then repeats with period 3. *s[s[s[s]][s]]][s][s][k]* (case (j)) grows to a maximum size of 1263, but then after 98 steps evolves to a fixed point of size 17. For *s[s][k][s[s[s][k]]][k]* (case (k)) the size at step *t - 7* is given by

$$h[1] = h[2] = h[3] = 12$$

$$h[t\_] := If[Mod[t, 4] == 2, 2, 1] (h[Ceiling[t/2] - 1] + t) + \{3, 5, -7, -1\}[[Mod[t, 4] + 1]]$$

Examples with similar behavior are *s[s[s][k]][s][s[s][k]]*, *s[s[s]][s][s[s][k]][k]* and *s[s[s][s]][s][s[s][k]]*. Among those with roughly exponential growth but seemingly random fluctuations are *s[s[s[s]]][s][s][s][k]*, *s[s[s]][s][s[s][s]][k]* and *s[s[s[s]][s][s]][k][s]*.

■ **Single combinators.** As already noted by Moses Schönfinkel in 1920, it is possible to set up combinator systems with just a single combinator. In such cases, combinator expressions can be viewed as binary trees without labels, equivalent to balanced strings of parentheses (see page 989) or sequences of 0's and 1's. One example of a single combinator system can be found using *{s → j[j], k → j[j[j]]}*, and has combinator rules (whose order matters):

$$\{j[j][x\_][y\_][z\_] \rightarrow x[z][y[z]], j[j[j]][x\_][y\_] \rightarrow x\}$$

The smallest initial conditions in this case that lead to unbounded growth are of size 14; two are versions of those for *s*, *k* combinators above, while the third is *j[j][j[j[j]]][j[j][j]]][j[j][j[j[j]]]]][j[j][j]]*.

The forms *j[j]* and *j[j[j]]* appear to be the simplest that can be used for *s* and *k*; *j* and *j[j]*, for example, do not work.

■ **Page 714 · Cellular automaton combinators.** With *k* and *s[k]* representing respectively cell values *0* and *1*, a combinator *f* for which *f[a$_{-1}$][a$_0$][a$_1$]* gives the new value of a single cell in an elementary cellular automaton with rule number *m* can be constructed as

Apply[p[p[p[#1][#2]][p[#3][#4]]][p[p[#5][#6]][p[#7][#8]]]] /. {0 → k, 1 → s[k]} &, IntegerDigits[m, 2, 8]] //. crules

where

p = ToC[z[y][x], {x, y, z}] //. crules

The resulting combinator has size 61, but for specific rules somewhat smaller combinators can be found—an example for rule 90 is *s[k[k]][s[s][k[s[s[s[k][k]][k[s[k]]]]][k[k]]]]]* with size 16.

To emulate cellular automaton evolution one starts by encoding a list of cell values by the single combinator

p[num[Length[list]]][
Fold[p[Nest[s, k, #2]][#1] &, p[k][k], list]] //. crules

where

num[n_] := Nest[inc, s[k], n]

inc = s[s[k[s]][k]]

One can recover the original list by using

Extract[expr, Map[Reverse[IntegerDigits[#, 2]] &,
3 + 59/15 (16 ^ Range[Depth[expr[s[k]][s][k] //. crules] - 1, 1, -1] - 1)]] /. {k → 0, s[k] → 1}

In terms of the combinator *f* a single complete step of cellular automaton evolution can be represented by

w = cr[p[inc[inc[x[s[k]]]]][
inc[x[s[k]]][cr[p[y[s[k]][k]][p[y[s[k]]][s[k]]]][y[k]]],
{y}]][p[x[s[k]]][cr[p[p[f[y[k][k][k][s[k]]]][
y[k][k][s[k]]][y[k][s[k]]]][y[s[k]]]][y[k][k]], {y}]][
p[p[k][k]][p[k][x[k]]]][s[k]]][p[k][p[k][k]]][k]], {x}]
cr[expr_, vars_] := ToC[expr //. crules, vars]

where there is padding with *0* on either side. With this setup *t* steps of evolution are given simply by *Nest[w, init, t]*. With an initial condition of *n* cells, this then takes roughly *(100 + 35 n) t + 33 t^2* steps of combinator evolution.

■ **Testing universality.** One can tell that a symbolic system is universal if one can find expressions that act like the *s* and *k* combinators, so that, for example, for some expression *e*, *e[x][y][z]* evolves to *x[z][y[z]]*.

■ **Criteria for universality.** See page 1126.

■ **Classes of systems.** This chapter has shown that various individual systems with fixed rules exhibit universality when suitable initial conditions are chosen. One can also consider whole classes of systems in which rules as well as initial conditions can be chosen. And then one can say for example that as a class of systems cellular automata are universal, but neighbor-independent substitution systems are not.

The Principle of Computational Equivalence

Basic Framework

■ **All is computation.** The early history of science includes many examples of attempts to treat all aspects of the universe in a uniform way. Some were more successful than others. "All is fire" was never definite enough to lead to much, but "all is number" can be viewed as an antecedent to the whole application of mathematics to science, and "all is atoms" to the atomic theory of matter and quantum mechanics. My "all is computation" will, I believe, form the basis for a fruitful new direction in science. It should be pointed out, however, that it is wrong to think that once one has described everything as, say, computation, then there is nothing more to do. Indeed, the phenomenon of computational irreducibility discussed in this chapter specifically implies that in many cases irreducible work has to be done in order to find out how any particular system will behave.

Outline of the Principle

■ **Note for mathematicians.** The way I discuss the Principle of Computational Equivalence is in a sense opposite to what would be typical in modern mathematics. For rather than starting with very specific definitions and then expanding from these, I start from general intuition and then use this to come up with more specific results. In the years to come there will no doubt be many attempts to formulate parts of the Principle of Computational Equivalence in ways that are closer to the traditions of modern mathematics. But at least at first, I suspect that huge simplifications will be made, with the result that all sorts of misleading conclusions will probably be reached, perhaps in some cases even seemingly contradicting the principle.

■ **History.** As I discuss elsewhere, aspects of the Principle of Computational Equivalence have many antecedents. But the complete principle is presented for the first time in this book, and is the result of thinking I did in the late 1980s and early 1990s.

■ **Page 717 · Church's Thesis.** The idea that any computation that can be done at all can be done by a universal system such as a universal Turing machine is often referred to as Church's Thesis. Following the introduction of so-called primitive recursive functions (see page 907) in the 1880s, there had by the 1920s emerged the idea that perhaps any reasonable function could be computed using the small set of operations on which primitive recursive functions are based. This notion was supported by the fact that certain modifications to these operations were found to allow only the exact same set of functions. But the discovery of the Ackermann function in the late 1920s (see page 906) showed that there are reasonable functions that are not primitive recursive. The proof of Gödel's Theorem in 1931 made use of so-called general recursive functions (see page 1121) as a way to represent possible functions in arithmetic. And in the early 1930s the two basic idealizations used in foundational studies of mathematical processes were then general recursive functions and lambda calculus (see page 1121). By 1934 these were known to be equivalent, and in 1935 Alonzo Church suggested that either of them could be used to do any mathematical calculation which could effectively be done. (It had been noted that many specific kinds of calculations could be done within such systems—and that processes like diagonalization led to operations of a seemingly rather different character.) In 1936 Alan Turing then introduced the idea of Turing machines, and argued that any mathematical process that could be carried out in practice, say by a person, could be carried out by a Turing machine. Turing proved that his machines were exactly equivalent in their computational capabilities to lambda calculus. By the 1940s Emil Post had shown that the string rewriting systems he had studied were also equivalent, and as electronic computers began to be developed it became quite firmly established that Turing machines provided an appropriate idealization for what computations could be done. From the 1940s to 1960s many different types of systems—almost all mentioned at some point or another in this book—were shown to be equivalent in their computational capabilities. (Starting in the 1970s, as discussed on page 1143, emphasis shifted to studies not of overall equivalence but instead equivalence with respect to classes of transformations such as polynomial time.)

When textbooks of computer science began to be written some confusion developed about the character of Church's Thesis: was it something that could somehow be deduced, or was it instead essentially just a definition of computability? Turing and Post seem to have thought of Church's Thesis as characterizing the "mathematicizing power" of humans, and Turing at least seems to have thought that it might not apply to continuous processes in physics. Kurt Gödel privately discussed the question of whether the universe could be viewed as following Church's Thesis and being "mechanical". And starting in the 1950s a few physicists, notably Richard Feynman, asked about fundamental comparisons between computational and physical processes. But it was not until the 1980s—perhaps particularly following some of my work—that it began to be more widely realized that Church's Thesis should best be considered a statement about nature and about the kinds of computations that can be done in our universe. The validity of Church's Thesis has long been taken more or less for granted by computer scientists, but among physicists there are still nagging doubts, mostly revolving around the perfect continua assumed in space and quantum mechanics in the traditional formalism of theoretical physics (see page 730). Such doubts will in the end only be put to rest by the explicit construction of a discrete fundamental theory along the lines I discuss in Chapter 9.

The Content of the Principle

▪ **Page 719 · Character of principles.** Examples of principles that can be viewed in several ways include the Principle of Entropy Increase (Second Law of Thermodynamics), the Principle of Relativity, Newton's Laws, the Uncertainty Principle and the Principle of Natural Selection. The Principle of Entropy Increase, for example, is partly a law of nature relating to properties of heat, partly an abstract fact about ensembles of dynamical systems, and partly a foundation for the definition of entropy. In this case and in others, however, the most important role of a principle is as a guide to intuition and understanding.

▪ **Page 720 · Oracles.** Following his introduction of Turing machines Alan Turing tried in 1937 to develop models that would somehow allow the ultimate result of absolutely every conceivable computation to be determined. And as a step towards this, he introduced the idea of oracles which would

give results of computations that could not be found by any Turing machine in any limited number of steps. He then noted, for example, that if an oracle were set up that could answer the question for a particular universal system of whether that system would ever halt when given any specific input, then with an appropriate transformation of input this same oracle could also answer the question for any other system that can be emulated by the universal system. But it turns out that this is no longer true if one allows systems which themselves can access the oracle in the course of their evolution. Yet one can then imagine a higher-level oracle for these systems, and indeed a whole hierarchy of levels of oracles—as studied in the theory of degrees of unsolvability. (Note that for example to answer the question of whether or not a given Turing machine always halts can require a second-order oracle, since it is a Π_2 question in the sense of page 1139.)

▪ **Initial conditions.** Oracles are usually imagined as being included in the internal rules for a system. But if there are an infinite number of elements that can be specified in the initial condition—as in a cellular automaton—then a table for an oracle could also be given in the initial conditions.

▪ **Page 722 · Criteria for universality.** To be universal a system must in effect be able to emulate any feature of any system. So at some level any feature can be thought of as a criterion for universality. Some features—like the possibility of information transmission—may be more obvious than others, but despite occasional assertions to the contrary in the scientific literature none is ever the whole story. Since any given universal system must be able to emulate any other universal system it follows that within any such system it must in a sense be possible to find any known universal system. But inevitably the encoding will sometimes be very complicated. And in practice if there are many simple rules that are universal they cannot all be related by simple encodings. (See also the end of Chapter 11.)

▪ **Page 722 · Encodings.** One can prevent an encoding from itself introducing universality by insisting, for example, that it be primitive recursive (see page 907) or always involve only a bounded number of steps. One can also do this—as in the rule 110 proof in the previous chapter—by having programs and data be encoded separately, and appear, say, as distinct parts of the initial conditions for the system one is studying. (See also page 1118.)

▪ **Density of universal systems.** One might imagine that it would be possible to make estimates of the overall density of universal systems, perhaps using arguments like those for the density of primes, or for the density of algorithmically random sequences. But as it turns out I know of no way to make any such estimates. If one has shown that various simple rules are universal, then it follows that rules which generalize these must also be universal. But even from this I do not know, for example, how to prove that the density of universal rules cannot decrease when rules become more complicated.

■ **Page 723 · Proving universality.** The question of whether a system is universal is in general undecidable. Using a specific mathematical axiom system such as Peano arithmetic or set theory it may also be that there is no proof that can be given. (It is straightforward to construct complicated examples where this is the case.) In practice it seems to get more difficult to prove universality when the structure of a system gets simpler. Current proofs of universality all work by showing how to emulate a known universal system. Some level of checking can be done by tracing the emulation of random initial conditions for the universal system. In the future it seems likely that automated theorem-proving methods should help in finding proofs of universality.

■ **Page 724 · History.** There are various precedents in philosophy and mysticism for the idea of encoding all possible knowledge of some kind in a single object. An example in computation theory is the concept emphasized by Gregory Chaitin of a number whose n^{th} digit specifies whether a computation with initial condition n in a particular system will ever halt. This particular number is far from being computable (see page 1128), as a result of the undecidability of the halting problem (see page 754). But a finite version in which one looks at results after a limited number of steps is similar to my concept of a universal object. (See also page 1067.)

■ **Page 725 · Universal objects.** A more direct way to create a universal object is to set up, say, a 4D array in which two of the dimensions range respectively over possible 1D cellular automaton rules and over possible initial conditions, while the other two dimensions correspond to space and time in the evolution of each cellular automaton from each initial condition. (Compare the parameter space sets of page 1006.)

■ **Page 725 · Block occurrences.** The pictures below show at which step each successive block of length up to 8 first appears in evolution according to various cellular automaton rules starting from a single black cell. For rule 30, the numbers of steps needed for each block of lengths 1 through 10 to appear at least once is {1, 2, 4, 12, 22, 24, 33, 59, 69, 113}. (See also page 871.)

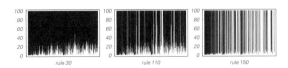

rule 30   rule 110   rule 150

The Validity of the Principle

■ **Page 729 · Continuum and cardinality.** Some notion of a distinction between continuous and discrete systems has existed since antiquity. But in the 1870s the distinction became more precise with Georg Cantor's characterization of the total numbers of possible objects of various types in terms of different orders of infinity (see page 1162). The total number of possible integers corresponds to the smallest level of infinity, usually denoted $\aleph_0$. The total number of possible lists of integers of given finite length—and thus the number of possible rational numbers—turns out also to be $\aleph_0$. The reason is that it is always possible to encode any finite list of integers as a single integer, as discussed on page 1120. (A way to do this for pairs of non-negative integers is to use $\sigma[\{x\_, y\_\}] := 1/2 (x + y)(x + y + 1) + x$.) But for real numbers the story is different. Any real number x can be represented as a set of integers using for example

$Rest[FoldList[Plus, 1, ContinuedFraction[x]]]$

but except when x is rational this list is not finite. Since the number of possible subsets of a set with k elements is 2^k, the number of possible real numbers is $2^{\aleph_0}$. And using Cantor's diagonal argument (see note below) one can then show that this must be larger than $\aleph_0$. (The claim that there are no sets intermediate in size between $\aleph_0$ and $2^{\aleph_0}$ is the so-called continuum hypothesis, which is known to be independent of the standard axioms of set theory, as discussed on page 1155.) Much as for integers, finite lists of real numbers can be encoded as single real numbers—using for example roughly $FromDigits[Flatten[Transpose[RealDigits[list]]]]$—so that the number of such lists is $2^{\aleph_0}$. (Space-filling curves yield a more continuous version of such an encoding.) But unlike for integers the same turns out to be true even for infinite lists of real numbers. (The function σ above can for example be used to specify the order in which to sample elements in $RealDigits[list]$). The total number of possible functions of real numbers is $2^{2^{\aleph_0}}$; the number of continuous such functions (which can always be represented by a list of coefficients for a series) is however only $2^{\aleph_0}$.

In systems like cellular automata, finite arrangements of black cells on a background of white cells can readily be specified by single integers, so the number of them is $\aleph_0$. But infinite configurations of cells are like digit sequences of real numbers (as discussed on page 869 they correspond more precisely to elements in a Cantor set), so the number of them is $2^{\aleph_0}$. Continuous cellular automata (see page 155) also have $2^{\aleph_0}$ possible states.

■ **Computable reals.** The stated purpose of Alan Turing's original 1936 paper on computation was to introduce the notion of computable real numbers, whose n^{th} digit for any n could be found by a Turing machine in a finite number of steps. Real numbers used in any explicit way in traditional mathematics are always computable in this sense. But as Turing pointed out, the overwhelming majority of all possible real numbers are not computable. For certainly there can be no more computable real numbers than there are possible Turing machines. But with his discovery of universality, Turing established that any Turing machine can be emulated by a single universal Turing machine with suitable initial conditions. And the point is that any such initial conditions can always be encoded as an integer.

As examples of non-computable reals that can readily be defined, Turing considered numbers whose successive digits are determined by the eventual behavior after an infinitely long time of a universal system with successive possible initial conditions (compare page 964). With two possible forms of behavior $h[i] = 0$ or 1 for initial condition i, an example of such a number is $Sum[2^{-i} h[i], \{i, \infty\}]$. Closely related is the total probability for each form of behavior, given for example by $Sum[2 \hat{\ } (-Ceiling[Log[2, i]]) h[i], \{i, \infty\}]$. I suspect that many limiting properties of systems like cellular automata in general correspond to non-computable reals. An example is the average density of black cells after an arbitrarily long time. For many rules, this converges rapidly to a definite value; but for some rules it will wiggle forever as more and more initial conditions are included in the average.

■ **Diagonal arguments.** Similar arguments were used by Georg Cantor in 1891 to show that there must be more real numbers than integers and by Alan Turing in 1936 to show that the problem of enumerating computable real numbers is unsolvable. One might imagine that it should be possible to set up a function $f[i, n]$ which if given successive integers i would give the nth base 2 digit in every possible real number. But what about the number whose n^{th} digit is $1 - f[n, n]$? This is still a real number, yet it cannot be generated by $f[i, n]$ for any i—thus showing that there are more real numbers than integers. Analogously, one might imagine that it should be possible to have a function $f[i, n]$ which enumerates all possible programs that always halt, and specifies a digit in their output when given input n. But what about the program with output $1 - f[n, n]$? This program always halts, yet it does not correspond to any possible value of i—even though

universality implies that any program should be encodable by a single integer i. And the only possible conclusion from this is that $f[i, n]$ cannot in fact be implemented as a program that always halts—thus demonstrating that the computable real numbers cannot explicitly be enumerated. (Closely related is the undecidability of the problem discussed on page 1137 of whether a system halts given any particular input.) (See also pages 907 and 1162.)

■ **Continuous computation.** Various models of computation that involve continuous elements have been proposed since the 1930s, and unlike those with discrete elements they have often not proved ultimately equivalent. One general class of models based on the work of Alan Turing in 1936 follow the operation of standard digital computers, and involve looking at real numbers in terms of digits, and using discrete processes to generate these digits. Such models inevitably handle only computable reals (in the sense defined above), and can never do computations beyond those possible in ordinary discrete systems. Functions are usually considered computable in such models if one can take the procedure for finding the digits of x and get a procedure for finding the digits of $f[x]$. And with this definition all standard mathematical functions are computable—even those from chaos theory that excavate digits rapidly. (It seems possible however to construct functions computable in this sense whose derivatives are not computable.) The same basic approach can be used whenever numbers are represented by constructs with discrete elements (see page 143), including for example symbolic formulas.

Several times since the 1940s it has been suggested that models of computation should be closer to traditional continuous mathematics, and should look at real numbers as a whole, not in terms of their digit or other representations. In a typical case, what is done is to generalize the register machines of page 97 to have registers that hold arbitrary real numbers. It is then usually assumed, however, that the primitive operations performed on these registers are just those of ordinary arithmetic, with the result that only a very limited set of functions (not including for example the exponential function) can be computed in a finite number of steps. Introducing other standard mathematical functions as primitives does not usually help much, unless one somehow gives the system the capability to solve any equation immediately (see below). (Other appropriate primitives may conceivably be related to the solubility of Hilbert's Thirteenth Problem and the fact that any continuous function with any number of arguments can be written as a one-argument function of a sum of a handful of fixed one-argument functions applied to the arguments of the original function.)

Most of the types of programs that I have discussed in this book can be generalized to allow continuous data, often just by having a continuous range of values for their elements (see e.g. page 155). But the programs themselves normally remain discrete, typically involving discrete choices made at discrete steps. If one has a table of choices, one can imagine generalizing this to a function of a real number. But to specify this function one normally has no choice but to use some type of finite formula. And to set up any kind of continuous evolution, the most obvious approach is to use traditional mathematical ideas of calculus and differential equations (see page 161). This leads to models in which possible computations are assumed, say, to correspond to combinations of differential equations—as in Claude Shannon's 1941 general-purpose analog computer. And if one assumes—as is usually implicitly done in traditional mathematics—that any solutions that exist to these equations can somehow always be found then at least in principle this allows computations impossible for discrete systems to be done.

■ **Initial conditions.** Traditional mathematics tends to assume that real numbers with absolutely any digit sequence can be set up. And if this were the case, then the digits of an initial condition could for example be the table for an oracle of the kind discussed on page 1126—and even a simple shift mapping could then yield output that is computationally more sophisticated than any standard discrete system. But just as in my discussion of chaos theory in Chapter 7, any reasonably complete theory must address how such an initial condition could have been constructed. And presumably the only way is to have another system that already violates the Principle of Computational Equivalence.

■ **Constructible reals.** Instead of finding successive digits using systems like Turing machines, one can imagine constructing complete real numbers using idealizations of mechanical processes. An example studied since antiquity involves finding lengths or angles using a ruler and compass (i.e. as intersections between lines and circles). However, as was shown in the 1800s, this method can yield only numbers formed by operating on rationals with combinations of *Plus*, *Times* and *Sqrt*. (Thus it is impossible with ruler and compass to construct π and "square the circle" but it is possible to construct 17-gons or other n-gons for which *FunctionExpand[Sin[π/n]]* contains only *Plus*, *Times* and *Sqrt*.) Linkages consisting of rods of integer lengths always trace out algebraic curves (or algebraic surfaces in 3D) and in general allow any algebraic number (as represented by *Root*) to be constructed. (Linkages were used by the late 1800s not only in machines such as steam engines, but also in devices for analog computation. More recently they have appeared in

robotics.) Note that above degree 4, algebraic numbers cannot in general be expressed in radicals involving only *Plus*, *Times* and *Power* (see page 945).

■ **Page 732 · Equations.** For any purely algebraic equation involving real numbers it is possible to find a bound on the size of any isolated solutions it has, and then to home in on their actual values. But as discussed on page 786, nothing similar is true for equations involving only integers, and in this case finding solutions can in effect require following the evolution of a system like a cellular automaton for infinitely many steps. If one allows trigonometric functions, any equation for integers can be converted to one for real numbers; for example $x^2 + y^2 == z^2$ for integers is equivalent to $Sin[\pi x]^2 + Sin[\pi y]^2 + Sin[\pi z]^2 + (x^2 + y^2 - z^2)^2 == 0$ for real numbers.

■ **Page 732 · ODEs.** The method of compressing time using algebraic transformations works not only in partial but also in ordinary differential equations.

■ **Emulating discrete systems.** Despite it often being assumed that continuous systems are computationally more sophisticated than discrete ones, it has in practice proved surprisingly difficult to make continuous systems emulate discrete ones. Some integer functions can readily be obtained by supplying integer arguments to continuous functions, so that for example $Mod[x, 2]$ corresponds to $Sin[\pi x/2]^2$ or $(1 - Cos[\pi x])/2$,

$$Mod[x, 3] \leftrightarrow 1 + 2/3 \, (Cos[2/3 \, \pi \, (x - 2)] - Cos[2 \, \pi \, x/3])$$
$$Mod[x, 4] \leftrightarrow (3 - 2 \, Cos[\pi \, x/2] - Cos[\pi \, x] - 2 \, Sin[\pi \, x/2])/2$$
$$Mod[x, n] \leftrightarrow Sum[j \, Product[(Sin[\pi \, (x - i - j)/n]/$$
$$Sin[\pi \, i/n])^2, \{i, n-1\}], \{j, n-1\}]$$

(As another example, $If[x > 0, 1, 0]$ corresponds to $1 - 1/Gamma[1 - x]$.) And in this way the discrete system $x \rightarrow If[EvenQ[x], 3 \, x/2, 3 \, (x + 1)/2]$ from page 122 can be emulated by the continuous iterated map $x \rightarrow (3 + 6 \, x - 3 \, Cos[\pi \, x])/4$. This approach can then be applied to the universal arithmetic system on page 673, establishing that continuous iterated maps can in principle emulate discrete universal systems. A similar result presumably holds for ordinary and therefore also partial differential equations (PDEs). One might expect, however, that it should be possible to construct a PDE that quite directly emulates a system like a cellular automaton. And to do this approximately is not difficult. For as suggested by the bottom row of pictures on page 732 one can imagine having localized structures whose interactions emulate the rules of the cellular automaton. And one can set things up so that these structures exhibit the analog of attractors, and evolve towards one of a few discrete states. But the problem is that in finite time one cannot expect that they will precisely reach such states. (This is somewhat analogous to the issue of asymptotic particle states in the foundations of quantum field theory.) And this means that the overall state of the system will not be properly prepared for the next step of cellular automaton evolution.

Generating repetitive patterns with continuous systems is straightforward, but generating even nested ones is not. Page 147 showed how $Sin[x] + Sin[\sqrt{2}\,x]$ has nested features, and these are reflected in the distribution of eigenvalues for ODEs containing such functions. Strange attractors for many continuous systems also show various forms of Cantor sets and nesting.

■ **Page 732 · Time and gravity.** General relativity implies that time can be affected by gravitational fields—and that for example a process in a lower gravitational field will seem to be going faster if it is looked at by an observer in a higher gravitational field. (Related phenomena associated with motion in special relativity are more difficult to interpret in a static way.) But presumably there are effects that prevent infinite speedups. For if, say, energy were coming from a process at a constant rate, then an infinite speedup would lead to infinite energy density, and thus presumably to infinite gravitational fields that would change the system.

At least formally, general relativity does nevertheless suggest infinite transformations of time in various cases. For example, to a distant observer, an object falling into a black hole will seem to take an infinite time to cross the event horizon—even though to the object itself only a finite time will seem to have passed. One might have thought that this would imply in reverse that to an observer moving with the object the whole infinite future of the outside universe would in effect seem to go by in a finite time. But in the simplest case of a non-rotating black hole (Schwarzschild metric), it turns out that an object will always hit the singularity at the center before this can happen. In a rotating but perfectly spherical black hole (Kerr metric), the situation is nevertheless different, and in this case the whole infinite future of the outside universe can indeed in principle be seen in the finite time between crossing the outer and inner event horizons. But for the reasons mentioned above, this very fact presumably implies instability, and the whole effect disappears if there is any deviation from perfect spherical symmetry.

Even without general relativity there are already issues with time and gravity. For example, it was shown in 1990 that close encounters in a system of 5 idealized point masses can lead to infinite accelerations which cause one mass to be able to go infinitely far in a finite time.

■ **Page 733 · Human thinking.** The discovery in this book that even extremely simple programs can give rise to behavior vastly more complex than expected casts suspicion on any claim that programs are fundamentally unable to reproduce features of human thinking. But complete evidence that human thinking follows the Principle of Computational Equivalence will presumably come only gradually as practical computer systems manage to emulate more and more aspects of human thinking. (See page 628.)

■ **Page 734 · Intermediate degrees.** As discussed on page 753, an important indication of computational sophistication in a system is for its ultimate behavior to be undecidable, in the sense that a limited number of steps in a standard universal system cannot determine in general what the system will do after an infinite number of steps, and whether, for example, it will ever in some sense halt. Such undecidability is inevitable in any system that is universal. But what about other systems? So long as one only ever looks at the original input and final output it turns out that one can construct a system that exhibits undecidability but is not universal. One trivial way to do so is to take a universal system but modify it so that if it ever halts its output is discarded and, say, replaced by its original input. The lack of meaningful output prevents such a system from being universal, but the question of whether the system halts is still undecidable. Nevertheless, the pattern of this undecidability is just the same as for the underlying universal system. So one can then ask whether it is possible to have a system which exhibits undecidability, but with a pattern that does not correspond to that of any universal system.

As I discuss on page 1137, almost all known proofs of undecidability in practice work by reduction to the halting problem for some universal system—this is, by showing that if one could resolve whatever is supposed to be undecidable then one could also solve the halting problem for a universal system. But in 1956 Richard Friedberg and Albert Muchnik both gave an intricate and abstract construction of a system that has a halting problem which is undecidable but is not reducible to the halting problem of any universal system.

The pictures at the top of the facing page show successive steps in the evolution of an analog of their system. The input is an integer that gives a position in either of the two rows of cells at the bottom of each picture. All these cells are initially white, but some eventually become black—and the system is considered to halt for a particular input if the corresponding cell ever becomes black.

The rules for the system are quite complicated, and in essence work by progressively implementing a generalization of a diagonal argument of the kind discussed on page 1128. Note first that the configuration of cells in the rows at the bottom of each picture can be thought of as successive finite approximations to tables for an oracle (see page 1126) which gives the solution to the halting problem for each possible input to the system. To set up the generalized diagonal argument one needs a way to list all possible programs. Any type of program that supports universality can be used for this purpose; the pictures shown use essentially the register machines from page 97. Each row above the bottom one corresponds in effect to a successive register machine—and shows, if relevant, its output when given as input the integer corresponding to that position in the row, together with the complete bottom row of cells found so far. (A dot indicates that the register machine does not halt.) The way the system works is to put down new black cells in the bottom row in just such a way as to arrange that for any register machine at least the output shown will ultimately not agree with the cells in the bottom row. As indicated by vertical gray lines, there is sometimes temporary agreement, but this is always removed within a finite number of steps.

The fact that no register machine can ever ultimately give output that agrees everywhere with the bottom row of cells then demonstrates that the halting problem for the system—whose results appear in the bottom row—must be undecidable. Yet if this halting problem were reducible to a halting problem for a universal system, then by using its results one should ultimately be able to solve the halting problem for any system. However, even using the complete bottom row of cells on the left it turns out that the construction is such that no register machine can ever yield results after any finite number of steps that agree everywhere with the row of cells on the right—thus demonstrating that the halting problem for the system is not reducible to the halting problem for a universal system.

Note however that this result is extremely specific to looking only at what is considered output from the system, and that inside the system there are all sorts of components that are definitely universal.

Explaining the Phenomenon of Complexity

■ **Definition of complexity.** See page 557.

■ **Ingredients for complexity.** With its emphasis on breaking systems down to find their underlying elements traditional science tends to make one think that any important overall property of a system must be a consequence of some specific feature of its underlying construction. But the results of this section imply that for complexity this is not the case. For as discussed on page 1126 there is no direct structural criterion for sophisticated computation and universality. And indeed most ways of ensuring that these do not occur are in essence equivalent just to saying that the overall behavior exhibits some specific regularity and is therefore not complex.

■ **Relativism and equivalence.** Although the notion has been discussed since antiquity, it has become particularly common in the academic humanities in the past few decades to believe that there can be no valid absolute conclusions about the world—only statements made relative to particular cultural contexts. My emphasis of the importance of perception and analysis might seem to support this view, and to some extent it does. But the Principle of Computational Equivalence implies that in the end essentially any method of perception and analysis that can actually be implemented in our universe must have a certain computational equivalence, and must therefore at least in some respects come to the same absolute conclusions.

Computational Irreducibility

■ **History.** The notion that there could be fundamental limits to knowledge or predictability has been discussed repeatedly since antiquity. But most often it has been assumed that the origin of this must be inadequacy in models, not difficulty in working out their consequences. And indeed already in the 1500s with the introduction of symbolic algebra and the discovery of formulas for solving cubic and quartic equations the expectation began to develop that with sufficient cleverness it should be possible to derive a formula for the solution to any purely mathematical problem. Infinitesimals were sometimes thought to get in the way of finite understanding—but this was believed to be overcome by calculus. And when mathematical models for natural systems became widespread in the late 1600s it was generally assumed that their basic consequences could always be found in terms of formulas or geometrical theorems, perhaps with fairly straightforward numerical calculations required for connection to practical situations. In discussing gravitational interactions between many planets Isaac Newton did however comment in 1684 that "to define these motions by exact laws admitting of easy calculation exceeds, if I am not mistaken, the force of any human mind". But in the course of the 1700s and 1800s formulas were successfully found for solutions to a great many problems in mathematical physics (see note below)—at least when suitable special functions (see page 1091) were introduced. The three-body problem (see page 972) nevertheless continued to resist efforts at general solution. In the 1820s it was shown that quintic equations cannot in general be solved in terms of radicals (see page 1137), and by the 1890s it was known that degree 7 equations cannot in general be solved even if elliptic functions are allowed. Around 1890 it was then shown that the three-body problem could not be solved in general in terms of ordinary algebraic functions and integrals (see page 972). However, perhaps in part because of a shift towards probabilistic theories such as quantum and statistical mechanics there remained the conviction that for relevant aspects of behavior formulas should still exist. The difficulty for example of finding more than a few exact solutions to the equations of general relativity was noted—but a steady stream of results (see note below) maintained the belief that with sufficient cleverness a formula could be found for behavior according to any model.

In the 1950s computers began to be used to work out numerical solutions to equations—but this was seen mostly as a convenience for applications, not as a reflection of any basic necessity. A few computer experiments were done on systems with simple underlying rules, but partly because

Monte Carlo methods were sometimes used, it was typically assumed that their results were just approximations to what could in principle be represented by exact formulas. And this view was strengthened in the 1960s when solitons given by simple formulas were found in some of these systems.

The difficulty of solving equations for numerical weather prediction was noted even in the 1920s. And by the 1950s and 1960s the question of whether computer calculations would be able to outrun actual weather was often discussed. But it was normally assumed that the issue was just getting a better approximation to the underlying equations—or better initial measurements—not something more fundamental.

Particularly in the context of game theory and cybernetics the idea had developed in the 1940s that it should be possible to make mathematical predictions even about complex human situations. And for example starting in the early 1950s government control of economies based on predictions from linear models became common. By the early 1970s, however, such approaches were generally seen as unsuccessful, but it was usually assumed that the reason was not fundamental, but was just that there were too many disparate elements to handle in practice.

The notions of universality and undecidability that underlie computational irreducibility emerged in the 1930s, but they were not seen as relevant to questions arising in natural science. Starting in the 1940s they were presumably the basis for a few arguments made about free will and fundamental unpredictability of human behavior (see page 1135), particularly in the context of economics. And in the late 1950s there was brief interest among philosophers in connecting results like Gödel's Theorem to questions of determinism—though mostly there was just confusion centered around the difficulty of finding countable proofs for statements about the continuous processes assumed to occur in physics.

The development of algorithmic information theory in the 1960s led to discussion of objects whose information content cannot be compressed or derived from anything shorter. But as indicated on page 1067 this is rather different from what I call computational irreducibility. In the 1970s computational complexity theory began to address questions about overall resources needed to perform computations, but concentrated on computations that perform fairly specific known practical tasks. At the beginning of the 1980s, however, it was noted that certain problems about models of spin glasses were NP-complete. But there was no immediate realization that this was connected to any underlying general phenomenon.

Starting in the late 1970s there was increasing interest in issues of predictability in models of physical systems. And it was emphasized that when the equations in such models are nonlinear it often becomes difficult to find their solutions. But usually this was at some level assumed to be associated with sensitive dependence on initial conditions and the chaos phenomenon—even though as we saw on page 1098 this alone does not even prevent there from being formulas.

By the early 1980s it had become popular to use computers to study various models of natural systems. Sometimes the idea was to simulate a large collection of disparate elements, say as involved in a nuclear explosion. Sometimes instead the idea was to get a numerical approximation to some fairly simple partial differential equation, say for fluid flow. Sometimes the idea was to use randomized methods to get a statistical approximation to properties say of spin systems or lattice gauge theories. And sometimes the idea was to work out terms in a symbolic perturbation series approximation, say in quantum field theory or celestial mechanics. With any of these approaches huge amounts of computer time were often used. But it was almost always implicitly assumed that this was necessary in order to overcome the approximations being used, and not for some more fundamental reason.

Particularly in physics, there has been some awareness of examples such as quark confinement in QCD where it seems especially difficult to deduce the consequences of a theory—but no general significance has been attached to this.

When I started studying cellular automata in the early 1980s I was quickly struck by the difficulty of finding formulas for their behavior. In traditional models based for example on continuous numbers or approximations to them there was usually no obvious correspondence between a model and computations that might be done about it. But the evolution of a cellular automaton was immediately reminiscent of other computational processes—leading me by 1984 to formulate explicitly the concept of computational irreducibility.

No doubt an important reason computational irreducibility was not identified before is that for more than two centuries students had been led to think that basic theoretical science could somehow always be done with convenient formulas. For almost all textbooks tend to discuss only those cases that happen to come out this way. Starting in earnest in the 1990s, however, the influence of *Mathematica* has gradually led to broader ranges of examples. But there still remains a very widespread belief that if a theoretical result about the behavior of a system is truly fundamental then it must be possible to state it in terms of a simple mathematical formula.

■ **Exact solutions.** Some notable cases where closed-form analytical results have been found in terms of standard mathematical functions include: quadratic equations (~2000 BC) (*Sqrt*); cubic, quartic equations (1530s) ($x^{1/n}$); 2-body problem (1687) (*Cos*); catenary (1690) (*Cosh*); brachistochrone (1696) (*Sin*); spinning top (1849; 1888; 1888) (*JacobiSN*; *WeierstrassP*; hyperelliptic functions); quintic equations (1858) (*EllipticTheta*); half-plane diffraction (1896) (*FresnelC*); Mie scattering (1908) (*BesselJ*, *BesselY*, *LegendreP*); Einstein equations (Schwarzschild (1916), Reissner-Nordström (1916), Kerr (1963) solutions) (rational and trigonometric functions); quantum hydrogen atom and harmonic oscillator (1927) (*LaguerreL*, *HermiteH*); 2D Ising model (1944) (*Sinh*, *EllipticK*); various Feynman diagrams (1960s–1980s) (*PolyLog*); KdV equation (1967) (*Sech* etc.); Toda lattice (1967) (*Sech*); six-vertex spin model (1967) (*Sinh* integrals); Calogero-Moser model (1971) (*Hypergeometric1F1*); Yang-Mills instantons (1975) (rational functions); hard-hexagon spin model (1979) (*EllipticTheta*); additive cellular automata (1984) (*MultiplicativeOrder*); Seiberg-Witten supersymmetric theory (1994) (*Hypergeometric2F1*). When problems are originally stated as differential equations, results in terms of integrals ("quadrature") are sometimes considered exact solutions—as occasionally are convergent series. When one exact solution is found, there often end up being a whole family—with much investigation going into the symmetries that relate them. It is notable that when many of the examples above were discovered they were at first expected to have broad significance in their fields. But the fact that few actually did can be seen as further evidence of how narrow the scope of computational reducibility usually is. Notable examples of systems that have been much investigated, but where no exact solutions have been found include the 3D Ising model, quantum anharmonic oscillator and quantum helium atom.

■ **Amount of computation.** Computational irreducibility suggests that it might be possible to define "amount of computation" as an independently meaningful quantity— perhaps vaguely like entropy or amount of information. And such a quantity might satisfy laws vaguely analogous to the laws of thermodynamics that would for example determine what processes are possible and what are not. If one knew the fundamental rules for the universe then one way in principle to define the amount of computation associated with a given process would be to find the minimum number of applications of the rules for the universe that are needed to reproduce the process at some level of description.

■ **Page 743 · More complicated rules.** The standard rule for a cellular automaton specifies how every possible block of cells of a certain size should be updated at every step. One can imagine finding the outcome of evolution more efficiently by adding rules that specify what happens to larger blocks of cells after more steps. And as a practical matter, one can look up different blocks using a method like hashing. But much as one would expect from data compression this will only in the end work more efficiently if there are some large blocks that are sufficiently common. Note that dealing with blocks of different sizes requires going beyond an ordinary cellular automaton rule. But in a sequential substitution system—and especially in a multiway system (see page 776)—this can be done just as part of an ordinary rule.

■ **Page 744 · Reducible systems.** The color of a cell at step t and position x can be found by starting with initial condition

Flatten[With[{w = Max[Ceiling[Log[2, {t, x}]]]},
    {2 Reverse[IntegerDigits[t, 2, w]] + 1,
        5, 2 IntegerDigits[x, 2, w] + 2}]]

then for rule 188 running the cellular automaton with rule

{{a : (1 | 3), 1 | 3, _} → a, {_, 2 | 4, a : (2 | 4)} → a,
    {3, 5 | 10, 2} → 6, {1, 5 | 7, 4} → 0, {3, 5, 4} → 7,
    {1, 6, 2} → 10, {1, 6 | 11, 4} → 8, {3, 6 | 8 | 10 | 11, 4} → 9,
    {3, 7 | 9, 2} → 11, {1, 8 | 11, 2} → 9, {3, 11, 2} → 8,
    {1, 9 | 10, 4} → 11, {_, a_ /; a > 4, _} → a, {_, _, _} → 0}

and for rule 60 running the cellular automaton with rule

{{a : (1 | 3), 1 | 3, _} → a, {_, 2 | 4, a : (2 | 4)} → a,
    {1, 5, 4} → 0, {_, 5, _} → 5, {_, _, _} → 0}

■ **Speed-up theorems.** That there exist computations that are arbitrarily computationally reducible was noted in work on the theory of computation in the mid-1960s.

■ **Page 745 · Mathematical functions.** The number of bit operations needed to add two n-digit numbers is of order n. The number of operations $m[n]$ needed to multiply them increases just slightly more rapidly than n (see page 1093). (Even if one can do operations on all digits in parallel it still takes of order n steps in a system like a cellular automaton for the effects of different digits to mix together—though see also page 1149.) The number of operations to evaluate $Mod[a, b]$ is of order n if a has n digits and b is small. Many standard continuous mathematical functions just increase or decrease smoothly at large x (see page 917). The main issue in evaluating those that exhibit regular oscillations at large x is to find their oscillation period with sufficient precision. Thus for example if x is an integer with n digits then evaluating $Sin[x]$ or $FractionalPart[x c]$ requires respectively finding π or c to n-digit precision. It is known how to evaluate π (see page 912) and all standard elementary functions to n-digit precision using about $Log[n] m[n]$ operations. (This can be done by repeatedly making use of functional relations such as $Exp[2 x] == Exp[x]^2$ which express $f[2 x]$ as a polynomial in $f[x]$; such an approach is known to work for elementary, elliptic, modular and other functions associated with $ArithmeticGeometricMean$ and for example $DedekindEta$.) Known methods for high-precision evaluation of special functions—usually based in the end on series

representations—typically require of order $n^{1/s} m[n]$ operations, where s is often 2 or 3. (Examples of more difficult cases include $HypergeometricPFQ[a, b, 1]$ and $StieltjesGamma[k]$, where logarithmic series can require an exponential number of terms. Evaluation of $BernoulliB[x]$ is also difficult.) Any iterative procedure (such as $FindRoot$) that yields a constant multiple more digits at each step will take about $Log[n]$ steps to get n digits. Roots of polynomials can thus almost always be found with $NSolve$ in about $Log[n] m[n]$ operations. If one evaluates $NIntegrate$ or $NDSolve$ by effectively fitting functions to order s polynomials the difficulty of getting results with n-digit precision typically increases like $2^{n/s}$. An adaptive algorithm such as Romberg integration reduces this to about $2^{\wedge} \sqrt{n}$. The best-known algorithms for evaluating $Zeta[1/2 + i x]$ (see page 918) to fixed precision take roughly $\sqrt{x}$ operations—or $2^{n/2}$ operations if x is an n-digit integer. (The evaluation is based on the Riemann-Siegel formula, which involves sums of about $\sqrt{x}$ cosines.) Unlike for continuous mathematical functions, known algorithms for number theoretical functions such as $FactorInteger[x]$ or $MoebiusMu[x]$ typically seem to require a number of operations that grows faster with the number of digits n in x than any power of n (see page 1090).

■ **Formulas.** It is always in principle possible to build up some kind of formula for the outcome of any process of evolution, say of a cellular automaton (see page 618). But for there to be computational reducibility this formula needs to be simple and easy to evaluate—as it is if it consists just of a few standard mathematical functions (see note above; page 1098).

■ **Page 747 · Short computations.** Some properties include:

(a) The regions are bounded by the hyperbolas $x y == Exp[n/2]$ for successive integers n.

(d) There is approximate repetition associated with rational approximations to π (for example with period 22), but never precise repetition.

(e) The pattern essentially shows which x are divisors of y, just as on pages 132 and 909.

(h) $Mod[Quotient[s, 2^n], 2]$ extracts the digit associated with 2^n in the base 2 digit sequence of s.

(i) Like (e), except that colors at neighboring positions alternate.

(l) See page 613.

(m) The pattern can be generated by a 2D substitution system with rule {1 -> {{0, 0}, {0, 1}}, 0 -> {{1, 1}, {1, 0}}} (see page 583).

(See also page 870.)

Even though standard mathematical functions are used, few of the pictures can readily be generalized to continuous values of x and y.

■ **Intrinsic limits in science.** Before computational irreducibility other sources of limits to science that have been discussed include: measurement in quantum mechanics, prediction in chaos theory and singularities in gravitation theory. As it happens, in each of these cases I suspect that the supposed limits are actually just associated with a lack of correct analysis of all elements of the relevant systems. In mathematics, however, more valid intrinsic limits—much closer to computational irreducibility—follow for example from Gödel's Theorem.

The Phenomenon of Free Will

■ **History.** Early in history it seems to have generally been assumed that everything about humans must ultimately be determined by unchangeable fate—which it was sometimes thought could be foretold by astrology or other forms of divination. Most Greek philosophers seem to have believed that their various mechanical or moral theories implied rigid determination of human actions. But especially with the advent of the Christian religion the notion that humans can at some level make free choices—particularly about whether to do good or not—emerged as a foundational idea. (The idea had also arisen in Persian and Hebrew religions and legal systems, and was supported by Roman lawyers such as Cicero.) How this could be consistent with God having infinite power was not clear, although around 420 AD Augustine suggested that while God might have infinite knowledge of the future we as humans could not—yielding what can be viewed as a very rough analog of my explanation for free will. In the 1500s some early Protestants made theological arguments against free will—and indeed issues of free will remain a feature of controversy between Christian denominations even today.

In the mid-1600s philosophers such as Thomas Hobbes asserted that minds operate according to definite mechanisms and therefore cannot exhibit free will. In the late 1700s philosophers such as Immanuel Kant—agreeing with earlier work by Gottfried Leibniz—claimed instead that at least some parts of our minds are free and not determined by definite laws. But soon thereafter scientists like Pierre-Simon Laplace began to argue for determinism throughout the universe based on mathematical laws. And with the increasing success of science in the 1800s it came to be widely believed that there must be definite laws for all human actions—providing a foundation for the development of psychology and the social sciences.

In the early 1900s historians and economists emphasized that there were at least not simple laws for various aspects of human behavior. But it was nevertheless typically assumed that methods based on physics would eventually yield deterministic laws for human behavior—and this was for example part of the inspiration for the behaviorist movement in psychology in the mid-1900s. The advent of quantum mechanics in the 1920s, however, showed that even physics might not be entirely deterministic—and by the 1940s the possibility that this might lead to human free will was being discussed by physicists, philosophers and historians. Around this time Karl Popper used both quantum mechanics and sensitive dependence on initial conditions (see also page 971) to argue for fundamental indeterminism. And also around this time Friedrich Hayek (following ideas of Ludwig Mises in the early 1900s) suggested—presumably influenced by work in mathematical logic—that human behavior might be fundamentally unpredictable because in effect brains can explain only systems simpler than themselves, and can thus never explain their own operation. But while this has some similarity to the ideas of computational irreducibility in this book it appears never to have been widely studied.

Questions of free will and responsibility have been widely discussed in criminal and other law since at least the 1800s (see note below). In the 1960s and 1970s ideas from popular psychology tended to diminish the importance of free will relative to physiology or environment and experiences. In the 1980s, however, free will was increasingly attributed to animals other than humans. Free will for computers and robots was discussed in the 1950s in science fiction and to some extent in the field of cybernetics. But following lack of success in artificial intelligence it has for the most part not been seriously studied. Sometimes it is claimed that Gödel's Theorem shows that humans cannot follow definite rules—but I argue on page 1158 that this is not correct.

■ **Determinism in brains.** Early investigations of internal functioning in the brain tended to suggest considerable randomness—say in the sequence of electrical pulses from a nerve cell. But in recent years, with more extensive measurement methods, there has been increasing evidence for precise deterministic underlying rules. (See pages 976 and 1011.)

■ **Amounts of free will.** In my theory the amount of free will associated with a particular decision is in effect related to the amount of computation required to arrive at it. In conscious thinking we can to some extent scrutinize the processes we use, and assess how much computation they involve. But in unconscious thinking we cannot. And probably often these just involve memory lookups with rather little computation. But other unconscious abilities like intuition presumably involve more sophisticated computation.

■ **Responsibility.** It is often assumed that if there are definite underlying rules for our brains then it cannot be meaningful to say that we have any ultimate moral or legal responsibility for our actions. For traditional ideas lead to the notion that in this case all our actions must somehow be thought of as the direct result of whatever external causes (over which we have no control) are responsible for the underlying rules in our brains and the environment in which we find ourselves. But if the processes in our brains are computationally irreducible then as discussed in the main text their outcome can seem in many respects free of underlying rules, making it reasonable to view the processes themselves as what is really responsible for our actions. And since these processes are intrinsic to us, it makes sense to treat us as responsible for their effects.

Several different theories are used in practical legal systems. The theory popular from the behavioral sciences tends to assume that human actions can be understood from underlying rules for the brain, and that people should be dealt with according to the rules they have—which can perhaps be modified by some form of treatment. But computational irreducibility can make it essentially impossible to find what general behavior will arise from particular rules—making it difficult to apply this theory. The alternative pragmatic theory popular in rational philosophy and economics suggests that behavior in legal matters is determined through calculations based on laws and the deterrents they provide. But here there is the issue that computational irreducibility can make it impossible to foresee what consequences a given law will have. Western systems of law tend to be dominated by the moral theory that people should somehow get what they deserve for choices they made with free will—and my explanation now makes this consistent with the existence of definite underlying rules for the brain.

Young children, animals and the insane are typically held less responsible for their actions. And in a moral theory of law this can be understood in my approach as a consequence of the computations they do being less sophisticated—so that their outcome is less free of the environment and of their underlying rules. (In a pragmatic theory the explanation would presumably be that less sophisticated computations would not be up to the task of handling the elaborate system of incentives that laws had defined.)

■ **Will and purpose.** Things that are too predictable do not normally seem free. But things that are too random also do not normally seem to be associated with the exercise of a will. Thus for example continual random twitching in our muscles is not normally thought to be a matter of human will, even though some of it is the result of signals from our brains. For typically one imagines that if something is to be a genuine reflection of human will then there must be some purpose to it. In general it is very difficult to assess whether something has a purpose (see page 829). But in capturing the most obvious aspects of human will what seems to be most important is at least short-term coherence and consistency of action—as often exists in class 4, but not class 3, systems.

■ **Source of will.** Damage to a human brain can lead to apparent disappearance of the will to act, and there is some evidence that one small part of the brain is what is crucial.

Undecidability and Intractability

■ **History.** In the early 1900s, particularly in the context of the ideas of David Hilbert, it was commonly believed that there should be a finite procedure to decide the truth of any mathematical statement. That this is not the case in the standard theory of arithmetic was in effect established by Kurt Gödel in 1931 (see page 1158). Alonzo Church gave the first explicit example of an undecidable problem in 1935 when he showed that no finite procedure in lambda calculus could guarantee to determine the equivalence of two lambda expressions. (A corollary to Gödel's proof had in fact already supplied another explicit undecidable problem by implying that no finite procedure based on recursive functions could decide whether a given primitive recursive function is identically 0.) In 1936 Alan Turing then showed that the halting problem for Turing machines could not be solved in general in a finite number of steps by any Turing machine. Some similar issues had already been considered by Emil Post in the context of tag and multiway systems starting in the 1920s, and in 1947 Post and Andrei Markov were able to establish that an existing mathematical question—the word problem for semigroups (see page 1141)—was undecidable. By the 1960s undecidability was being found in all sorts of systems, but most of the examples were too complicated to seem of much relevance in practical mathematics or computing. And apart from a few vague mentions in fields like psychology, undecidability was viewed mainly as a highly abstract curiosity of no importance to ordinary science. But in the early 1980s my experiments on cellular automata convinced me that undecidability is vastly more common than had been assumed, and in my 1984 paper

"Undecidability and intractability in theoretical physics" I argued that it should be important in many issues in physics and elsewhere.

■ **Mathematical impossibilities.** It is sometimes said that in the 1800s problems such as trisecting angles, squaring the circle, solving quintics, and integrating functions like $Exp[x^2]$ were proved mathematically impossible. But what was actually done was just to show that these problems could not be solved in terms of particular levels of mathematical constructs—say square roots (as in ruler and compass constructions discussed on page 1129), arbitrary roots, or elementary transcendental functions. And in each case higher mathematical constructs that seem in some sense no less implementable immediately allow the problems to be solved. Yet with undecidability one believes that there is absolutely no construct that can explicitly exist in our universe that allows the problem to be solved in any finite way. And unlike traditional mathematical impossibilities, undecidability is normally formulated purely in terms of ordinary integers—making it in a sense necessary to collapse basic distinctions between finite and infinite quantities if any higher-level constructs are to be included.

■ **Page 755 · Code 1004600.** In cases (c) and (d) steady growth at about 0.035 and 0.039 cells per step (of which 28% on average are non-white) is seen up to at least 20 million steps, though there continue to be fluctuations as shown below.

■ **Halting problems.** A classic example of a problem that is known in general to be undecidable is whether a given Turing machine will ever halt when started from a given initial condition. Halting is usually defined by the head of the Turing machine reaching a special halt state. But other criteria can equally well be used—say the head reaching a particular position (see page 759), or a certain pattern of colors being formed on the tape. And in a system like a cellular automaton a halting problem can be set up by asking whether a cell at a particular position ever turns a particular color, or whether, more globally, the complete state of the system ever reaches a fixed point and no longer changes.

In practical computing, one usually thinks of computational programs as being set up much like the register machines of page 896 and halting when they have finished executing their instructions. User interface and operating system programs are not normally intended to halt in an explicit sense, although without external input they often reach states that

do not change. *Mathematica* works by taking its input and repeatedly applying transformation rules—a process which normally reaches a fixed point that is returned as the answer, but with definitions like $x = x + 1$ (x having no value) formally does not.

■ **Proofs of undecidability.** Essentially the same argument due to Alan Turing used on page 1128 to show that most numbers cannot be computable can also be used to show that most problems cannot be decidable. For a problem can be thought of as an infinite list of solutions for successive possible inputs. But this is analogous to a digit sequence of a real number. And since any program for a universal system can be specified by an integer it follows that there must be many problems for which no such program can be given.

To show that a particular problem like the halting problem is undecidable one typically argues by contradiction, setting up analogs of self-referential logic paradoxes such as "this statement is false". Suppose that one had a Turing machine m that could solve the halting problem, in the sense that it itself would always halt after a finite number of steps, but it would determine whether any Turing machine whose description it was given as input would ever halt. One way to see that this is not possible is to imagine modifying m to make a machine m' that halts if its input corresponds to a machine that does not halt, but otherwise goes into an infinite loop and does not itself halt. For if one considers feeding m' as input to itself there is immediately no consistent answer to the question of whether m' halts—leading to the conclusion that in fact no machine m could ever exist in the first place. (To make the proof rigorous one must add another level of self-reference, say setting up m' to ask m whether a Turing machine will halt when fed its own description as input.) In the main text I argued that undecidability is a consequence of universality. In the proof above universality is what guarantees that any Turing machine can successfully be described in a way that can be fed as input to another Turing machine.

■ **Page 756 · Examples of undecidability.** Once universality exists in a system it is known from Gordon Rice's 1953 theorem and its generalizations that most questions about ultimate behavior will be undecidable unless their answers are always trivially the same. Undecidability has been demonstrated in various seemingly rather different types of systems, most often by reduction to halting (termination) problems for multiway systems.

In formal language theory, questions about regular languages are always decidable, but ones about context-free languages (see page 1103) are already often not. It is decidable whether such a language is finite, but not whether it contains every possible string, is regular, is unambiguous, or is equivalent to a language with a different grammar.

In mathematical logic, it can be undecidable whether statements are provable from a given axiom system—say predicate logic or Peano arithmetic (see page 782). It is also undecidable whether one axiom system is equivalent to another—even for basic logic (see page 1170).

In algebra and related areas of mathematics problems of equivalence between objects built up from elements that satisfy relations are often in general undecidable. Examples are word problems for groups and semigroups (see page 1141), and equivalence of finitely specified 4D manifolds (see page 1051). (Equivalence for 3D manifolds is thought to be decidable.) A related undecidable problem is whether two integer matrices can be multiplied together in some sequence to yield the zero matrix. It is also undecidable whether two sets of relations specify the same group or semigroup.

In combinatorics it is known in general to be undecidable whether a given set of tiles can cover the plane (see page 1139). And from this follows the undecidability of various problems about 2D cellular automata (see note below) and spin systems. Also undecidable are many questions about whether strings exist that satisfy particular constraints (see below).

In number theory it is known to be undecidable whether Diophantine equations have solutions (i.e. whether algebraic equations have integer solutions) (see page 786). And this means for example that it is in general undecidable whether expressions that involve both algebraic and trigonometric functions can be zero for real values of variables, or what the values of integrals are in which such expressions appear as denominators (compare page 916).

In computer science, general problems about verifying the possible behavior of programs tend to be undecidable, usually being directly related to halting problems. It is also for example undecidable whether a given program is the shortest one that produces particular output (see page 1067).

It is in general undecidable whether a given system exhibits universality—or undecidability.

■ **Undecidability in cellular automata.** For 1D cellular automata, almost all questions about ultimate limiting behavior are undecidable, even ones that ask about average properties such as density and entropy. (This results in undecidability in classification schemes, as mentioned on page 948.) Questions about behavior after a finite number of steps, even with infinite initial conditions, tend to be

decidable for 1D cellular automata, and related to regular languages (see page 957). In 2D cellular automata, however, even questions about a single step are often undecidable. Examples include whether any configurations are invariant under the cellular automaton evolution (see page 942), and, as established by Jarkko Kari in the late 1980s, whether the evolution is reversible, or can generate every possible configuration (see page 959).

■ **Natural systems.** Undecidable questions arise even in some traditional classes of models for natural systems. For example, in a generalized Ising model (see page 944) for a spin system the undecidability of the tiling problem implies that it is undecidable whether a given energy function leads to a phase transition in the infinite size limit. Somewhat similarly, the undecidability of equivalence of 4-manifolds implies undecidability of questions about quantum gravity models. In models based both on equations and other kinds of rules the existence of formulas for conserved quantities is in general undecidable. In models that involve continuous quantities it can be more difficult to formulate undecidability. But I strongly suspect that with appropriate definitions there is often undecidability in for example the three-body problem, so that the questions such as whether one of the bodies in a particular scattering process will ever escape to infinity are in general undecidable. In biology formal models for neural processes often involve undecidability, so that in principle it can be undecidable whether, say, there is any particular stimulus that will lead to a given response. Formal models for morphogenesis can also involve undecidability, so that for example it can in principle be undecidable whether a particular organism will ever stop growing, or whether a given structure can ever be formed in some class of organisms. (Compare page 407.)

■ **Undecidability in *Mathematica*.** In choosing functions to build into *Mathematica* I tried to avoid ones that would often encounter undecidability. And this is why for example there is no built-in function in *Mathematica* that tries to predict whether a given program will terminate. But inevitably functions like *FixedPoint*, *ReplaceRepeated* and *FullSimplify* can run into undecidability—so that ultimately they have to be limited by constructs such as *$IterationLimit* and *TimeConstraint*.

■ **Undecidability and sets.** Functions that can be computed in finite time by systems like Turing machines are often called recursive (or effectively computable). Sets are called recursive if there is a recursive function that can test whether or not any given element is in them. Sets are called recursively enumerable if there is a recursive function that can eventually generate any element in them.

The set of initial conditions for which a given Turing machine halts is thus not recursive. But it turns out that this set is recursively enumerable. And the reason is that one can generate the elements in it by effectively maintaining a copy of the Turing machine for each possible initial condition, then following a procedure where for example at step n one updates the one for initial condition $IntegerExponent[n, 2]$, and watches to see if it halts. Note that while the complement of a recursive set is always recursive, the complement of a recursively enumerable set may not be recursively enumerable. (An example is the set of initial conditions for which a Turing machines does not halt.) Recursively enumerable sets are characteristically associated with so-called Σ_1 statements of the form $\exists_t \phi[t]$ (where ϕ is recursive). (Asking whether a system ever halts is equivalent to asking whether there exists a number of steps t at which the system can be determined to be in its halting state.) Complements of recursively enumerable sets are characteristically associated with Π_1 statements of the form $\forall_t \phi[t]$—an example being whether a given system never halts. (Π_1 and Σ_1 statements are such that if they can be shown to be undecidable, then respectively they must be true or false, as discussed on page 1167.) If a statement in minimal form involves n alternations of $\exists$ and $\forall$ it is Σ_{n+1} if it starts with $\exists$ and Π_{n+1} if it starts with $\forall$. The Π_n and Σ_n form the so-called arithmetic hierarchy in which statements with larger n can be constructed by allowing ϕ to access an oracle for statements with smaller n (see page 1126). (Showing that a statement with $n \geq 1$ is undecidable does not establish that it is always true or always false.)

■ **Undecidability in tiling problems.** The question of whether a particular set of constraints like those on page 220 can be satisfied over the whole 2D plane is in general undecidable. For much as on page 943, one can imagine setting up a 1D cellular automaton with the property that, say, the absence of a particular color of cell throughout the 2D pattern formed by its evolution signifies satisfaction of the constraints. But even starting from a fixed line of cells, the question of whether a given color will ever occur in the evolution of a 1D cellular automaton is in general undecidable, as discussed in the main text. And although it is somewhat more difficult to show, this question remains undecidable even if one allows any possible configuration of cells on the starting line. (There are several different detailed formulations; the first explicit proof of undecidability in a tiling problem was given by Hao Wang in 1960; the version with no fixed cells by Robert Berger in 1966 by setting up an elaborate emulation of a register machine.) (See also page 943.)

■ **Page 757 · Correspondence systems.** Given a list of pairs p with $\{u, v\} = Transpose[p]$ the constraint to be satisfied is

$$StringJoin[u[[s]]] == StringJoin[v[[s]]]$$

Thus for example $p = \{\{"ABB", "B"\}, \{"B", "BA"\}, \{"A", "B"\}\}$ has shortest solution $s = \{2, 3, 2, 2, 3, 2, 1, 1\}$. (One can have lists instead of strings, replacing $StringJoin$ by $Flatten$.)

Correspondence systems were introduced by Emil Post in 1945 to give simple examples of undecidability; he showed that the so-called Post Correspondence Problem (PCP) of satisfying their constraints is in general undecidable (see below). With 2 string pairs PCP was shown to be decidable in 1981. It is known to be undecidable when 9 pairs are used, but I strongly suspect that it is also undecidable with just 3 pairs. The undecidability of PCP has been used to establish undecidability of many problems related to groups, context-free languages, and other objects defined by relations (see page 1141). Finding PCP solutions shorter than a given length is known to be an NP-complete problem.

With r string pairs and $n = StringLength[StringJoin[p]]$ there are $2^n\, Binomial[n - 1, 2r - 1]$ possible constraints (assuming no strings of zero length), each being related to at most $8r!$ others by straightforward symmetries (or altogether 4^{n-1} for given n). The number of constraints which yield solutions of specified lengths $Length[s]$ for $r = 2$ and $r = 3$ are as follows (the boxes at the end give the number of cases with no solution):

$r = 2, n = 4$	1:12	4							
$r = 2, n = 5$	1:64	64							
$r = 2, n = 6$	1:208	2:28	404						
$r = 2, n = 7$	1:640	3:32	1888						
$r = 2, n = 8$	1:1680	2:176	4:48	7056					
$r = 2, n = 9$	1:4352	3:112	5:56	24152					
$r = 2, n = 10$	1:10496	2:744	3:80	4:168	6:64	74464			
$r = 3, n = 6$	1:56	8							
$r = 3, n = 7$	1:576	192							
$r = 3, n = 8$	1:3312	2:168	3:84	1812					
$r = 3, n = 9$	1:14592	2:1140	3:192	4:288	5:96	8:48	30:48	44:48	12220
$r = 3, n = 10$	1:55296	2:4752	3:2712	4:372	5:492	6:264	7:216		
	12:24	18:48	24:48	36:48	75:48	78:48	64656		

With $r = 2$, as n increases an exponentially decreasing fraction of possible constraints have solutions; with $r = 3$ it appears that a fraction more than $1/4$ continue to do so. With $r = 2$, it appears that if a solution exists, it must have length $n + 4$ or less. With $r \leq 3$, the longest minimal solution lengths for $n \leq 10$ are given above. (Allowing $r > 3$ yields no greater lengths for these values of n.) With $n = 11$, example (l) yields a solution of length 112. The only possible longer $n = 11$ case is $\{\{"AAB", "B"\}, \{"B", "A"\}, \{"A", "AABB"\}\}$, for which any possible solution must be longer than 200. With *n = 12*, *{{"AABAAB", "B"}, {"B", "A"}, {"A", "AB"}}* has minimal solution length 120 and *{{"A", "AABB"}, {"AAB", "B"}, {"B", "AA"}}* has minimal solution length 132.

A given constraint can fail to have a solution either because the colors of cells at some point cannot be made to match, or because the two strings can never have the same finite length (as in *{{"A", "AA"}}*). To know that a solution exists in a particular case, it is sufficient just to exhibit it. To know that no solution is possible of any length, one must in effect have a proof.

In general, one condition for a solution to exist is that integer numbers of pairs can yield strings of the same length, so that given the length differences *d = Map[StringLength, p, {2}] . {1, -1}* there is a vector *v* of non-negative integers such that *v . d == 0*. If only one color of element ever appears this is the complete condition for a solution—and for *r = 2* solutions exist if *Apply[Times, d] < 0* and are then of length at least *Apply[Plus[##]/GCD[##] &, Abs[d]]*. With two colors of elements additional conditions can be constructed involving counting elements of each color, or various blocks of elements.

The undecidability of PCP can be seen to follow from the undecidability of the halting problem through the fact that the question of whether a tag system of the kind on page 93 with initial sequence *s* ever reaches a halting state (where none of its rules apply) is equivalent to the question of whether there is a way to satisfy the PCP constraint

```
TSToPCP[{n_, rule_}, s_] :=
  Map[Flatten[IntegerDigits[#, 2, 2]] &, Module[{f}, f[u_] :=
    Flatten[Map[{1, #} &, 3 u]]; Join[Map[{f[Last[#]],
      RotateLeft[f[First[#]]]} &, rule], {{f[s], {1}}, Flatten[
    Table[{{1, 2}, Append[RotateLeft[f[IntegerDigits[j, 2,
      i]]], 2]}, {i, 0, n - 1}, {j, 0, 2^i - 1}}, 1]}]], {2}]
```

Any PCP constraint can also immediately be related to the evolution of a multiway tag system of the kind discussed in the note below. Assuming that the upper string is never shorter than the lower one, the rules for the relevant tag system are given simply by

Apply[Append[#2, s___] → Prepend[#1, s] &, p, {1}]

In the case of example (e) the existence of a solution of length 24 can then be seen to follow from the fact that *MWTSEvolve[rule, {{"B"}}, 22]* contains *{"B", "A"}*.

This correspondence with tag systems can be used in practice to search for PCP solutions, though it is usually most efficient to run tag systems that correspond both to moving forward and backward in the string, and to see whether their results ever agree. (In most PCP systems, including all the examples

shown except (a) and (g), one string is always systematically longer than the other.) The tag system approach is normally limited by the number of intermediate strings that may need to be kept.

The pictures below show which possible sequences of up to 6 blocks yield upper and lower strings that agree in each of the PCP systems in the main text. As indicated in the first picture for the case of two blocks, each possible successively longer sequence corresponds to a rectangle in the picture (compare page 594). When a sequence of blocks leads to upper and lower strings that disagree, the rectangle is left white. If the strings agree so far, then the rectangle is colored with a gray that is darker if the strings are closer in length. Rectangles that are black (as visible in cases (a) and (b)) correspond to actual PCP solutions where the strings are the same length. Note that in case (c) the presence of only one color in either block means that strings will always agree so far. In cases (m) through (s) there is ultimately no solution, but as the pictures indicate, in these specific PCP systems there are always strings that agree as far as they have gone—it is just that they never end up the same length.

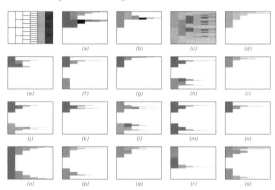

As one example of how one proves that a PCP constraint cannot be satisfied, consider case (s). From looking at the structure of the individual pairs one can see that if there is a solution it must begin with pair 1 or pair 3, and end with pair 1. But in fact it cannot begin with pair 1 because this would mean that the upper string would have to start off being longer, then at some point cross over to being shorter. However, the only way that such a crossover can occur is by pair 3 appearing with its upper *A* aligned with its second lower *A*. Yet starting with pair 1, the upper string is longer by 2 *As*, and the pairs are such that the length difference must always remain even—preventing the crossover from occurring. This means that any solution must begin with pair 3. But this pair must then be followed by another pair 3, which leaves *BAAB* sticking out on the bottom. So how can this *BAAB* be removed? The only way is to use the sequence of pairs 2, 3, 3, 2—yet doing this will just produce another *BAAB* further on. And thus one concludes that there is no way to satisfy these particular PCP constraints.

One can generalize PCP to allow any number of colors, and to require correspondence among any number of strings—though it is fairly easy to translate any such generalization to the 2-string 2-color case.

■ **Multiway tag systems.** As an extension of ordinary multiway systems one can generalize tag systems from page 93 to allow a list of strings at each step. Representing the strings by lists, one can write rules in the form

$\{\{1, 1, s\_\_\_\} \to \{s, 1, 0\}, \{1, s\_\_\_\} \to \{s, 1, 0, 1\}\}$

so that the evolution is given by

MWTSEvolve[rule_, list_, t_] :=
    Nest[Flatten[Map[ReplaceList[#, rule] &, #], 1] &, list, t]

■ **Word problems.** The question of whether a particular string can be generated in a given multiway system is an example of a so-called word problem. An original more specialized version of this was posed by Max Dehn in 1911 for groups and by Axel Thue in 1914 for semigroups. As discussed on page 938 a finitely presented group or semigroup can be viewed as a special case of a multiway system, in which the rules of the multiway system are obtained from relations between strings consisting of products of generators. The word problem then asks if a given product of such generators is equal to the identity element. Following work by Alan Turing in the mid-1930s, it was shown in 1947 by Emil Post from the undecidability of PCP that the word problem for semigroups is in general undecidable. Andrei Markov gave a specific example of this for a semigroup with 13 generators and 33 relations, and by 1966 Gennadií Makanin had found the simpler example

{"CCBB" ↔ "BBCC", "BCCCBB" ↔ "CBBBCC", "ACCBB" ↔ "BBA", "ABCCCBB" ↔ "CBBA", "BBCCBBBBCC" ↔ "BBCCBBBBCCA"}

Using these relations as rules for a multiway system most initial strings yield behavior that either dies out or becomes repetitive. The shortest initial strings that give unbounded growth are "BBBBABB" and "BBBBBBA"—though both of these still eventually yield just exponentially increasing numbers of distinct strings. In 1967 Yuri Matiyasevich constructed a semigroup with 3 complicated relations that has an undecidable word problem. It is not yet known whether undecidability can occur in a semigroup with a single relation. The word problem is known to be decidable for commutative semigroups.

The word problem for groups was shown to be undecidable in the mid-1950s by Petr Novikov and William Boone. There are however various classes of groups for which it is decidable. Abelian groups are one example. Another are so-called automatic groups, studied particularly in the 1980s, in which equivalence of words can be recognized by a finite automaton. (Such groups turn out to have definite geometrical properties, and are associated with spaces of negative curvature.) Even if a group ultimately has only a finite number of distinct elements, its word problem (with elements specified as products of generators) may still be undecidable. Constructions of groups with undecidable word problems have been based on setting up relations that correspond to the rules in a universal Turing machine. With the simplest such machine known in the past (see page 706) one gets a group with 32 generators and 142 relations. But with the universal Turing machine from page 707 one gets a group with 14 generators and 52 relations. (In general $s\,k + 4$ generators and $5\,s\,k + 2$ relations are needed.) From the results in this book it seems likely that there are still much simpler examples—some of which could perhaps be found by setting up groups to emulate rule 110. Note that groups with just one relation were shown always to have decidable word problems by Wilhelm Magnus in 1932.

For ordinary multiway (semi-Thue) systems, an example with an undecidable word problem is known with 2 types of elements and 5 very complicated rules—but I am quite certain that much simpler examples are possible. (1-rule multiway systems always have decidable word problems.)

■ **Sequence equations.** One can ask whether by replacing variables by sequences one can satisfy so-called word or string equations such as

Flatten[{x, 0, x, 0, y}] == Flatten[{y, x, 0, y, 1, 0, 1, 0, 0}]

(with shortest solution $x = \{1, 0, 1, 0, 0, 1, 0, 1, 0, 0, 1, 0, 1, 0\}$, $y = \{1, 0, 1, 0, 0, 1, 0, 1, 0, 0\}$). Knowing about PCP and Diophantine equations one might expect that in general this would be undecidable. But in 1977 Gennadií Makanin gave a complicated algorithm that solves the problem completely in a finite number of steps (though in general triple exponential in the length of the equation).

■ **Fast algorithms.** Most of the fast algorithms now known seem to fall into a few general classes. The most common are ones based on repetition or iteration, classic examples being Euclid's algorithm for *GCD* (page 915), Newton's method for *FindRoot* and the Gaussian elimination method for *LinearSolve*. Starting in the 1960s it began to be realized that fast algorithms could be based on nested or recursive processes, and such algorithms became increasingly popular in the 1980s. In most cases, the idea is recursively to divide data into parts, then to do operations on these parts, and finally reassemble the results. An example is the algorithm of Anatolii Karatsuba from 1961 for finding products of n-digit numbers (with $n = 2^s$) by operating on their digits in the nested pattern of page 608 (see also page 1093) according to

First[f[IntegerDigits[x, 2, n], IntegerDigits[y, 2, n], n/2]]

f[x_, y_, n_] :=
  If[n < 1, x y, g[Partition[x, n], Partition[y, n], n]]
g[{x1_, x0_}, {y1_, y0_}, n_] :=
  With[{z1 = f[x1, y1, n/2], z0 = f[x0, y0, n/2]},
    z1 2^{2n} + (f[x0 + x1, y0 + y1, n/2] - z1 - z0) 2^n + z0]

Other examples include the fast Fourier transform (page 1074) and related algorithms for *ListConvolve*, the quicksort algorithm for *Sort*, and many algorithms in fields such as computational geometry. Starting in the 1980s fast algorithms based on randomized methods (see page 1192) have also become popular. But particularly from the discoveries in this book, it seems likely that the very fastest algorithms for many kinds of problems will not in the end have the type of regular structure that characterizes almost all algorithms currently used.

■ **Sorting networks.** Any list can be sorted using *Fold[PairSort, list, pairs]* by doing a fixed sequence of comparisons of pairs

PairSort[a_, p : {_, _}] := Block[{t = a}, t[[p]] = Sort[t[[p]]]; t]

(Different comparisons often do not interfere and so can be done in parallel.) The pictures below show a few sequences of pair comparisons that sort lists of length $n = 16$.

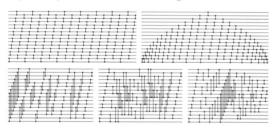

The top two (both with 120 comparisons) have a repetitive structure and correspond to standard sorting algorithms: transposition sort and insertion sort. (Quicksort does not use a fixed sequence of comparisons.) The first one on the bottom (with 63 comparisons) has a nested structure and uses the method invented by Kenneth Batcher in 1964:

Flatten[Reverse[Flatten[With[{m = Ceiling[Log[2, n]] - 1},
  Table[With[{d = If[i == m, 2^t, 2^{t+1} - 2^t]}, Map[
    {0, d} + # &, Select[Range[n - d], BitAnd[# - 1, 2^t] ==
      If[i == m, 0, 2^t] &]]], {t, 0, m}, {i, t, m}]], 1]], 1]

The second one on the bottom also uses 63 comparisons, while the last one is the smallest known for $n = 16$: it uses 60 comparisons and was invented by Milton Green in 1969. For $n \le 16$ the smallest numbers of comparisons known to work

are $\{0, 1, 3, 5, 9, 12, 16, 19, 25, 29, 35, 39, 45, 51, 56, 60\}$. (In general all lists will be sorted correctly if lists of just 0's and 1's are sorted correctly; allowing even just one of these 2^n cases to be wrong greatly reduces the number of comparisons needed.) For $n \le 8$ the Batcher method is known to give minimal length sequences of comparisons (for $n \le 5$ the total numbers of minimal sequences that work are $\{1, 6, 3, 13866\}$). The Batcher method in general requires about $n \, Log[n]^2$ comparisons; it is known that in principle $n \, Log[n]$ are sufficient. Various structures such as de Bruijn and Cayley graphs can be used as the basis for sorting networks, though it is my guess that typically the smallest networks for given n will have no obvious regularity. (See also page 832.)

■ **Page 758 · Computational complexity theory.** Despite its rather general name, computational complexity theory has for the most part been concerned with the quite specific issue of characterizing how the computational resources needed to solve problems grow with input size. From knowing explicit algorithms many problems can be assigned to such classes as:

- NC: can be solved in a number of steps that increases like a polynomial in the logarithm of the input size if processing is done in parallel on a number of arbitrarily connected processors that increases like a polynomial in the input size. (Examples include addition and multiplication.)

- P (polynomial time): can be solved (with one processor) in a number of steps that increases like a polynomial in the input size. (Examples include evaluating standard mathematical functions and simulating the evolution of cellular automata and Turing machines.)

- NP (non-deterministic polynomial time): solutions can be checked in polynomial time. (Examples include many problems based on constraints as well as simulating the evolution of multiway systems and finding initial conditions that lead to given behavior in a cellular automaton.)

- PSPACE (polynomial space): can be solved with an amount of memory that increases like a polynomial in the input size. (Examples include finding repetition periods in systems of limited size.)

Central to computational complexity theory are a collection of hypotheses that imply that NC, P, NP and PSPACE form a strict hierarchy. At each level there are many problems known that are complete at that level in the sense that all other problems at that level can be translated to instances of that problem using only computations at a lower level. (Thus, for example, all problems in NP can be translated to instances of any given NP-complete problem using computations in P.)

■ **History.** Ideas of characterizing problems by growth rates in the computational resources needed to solve them were discussed in the 1950s, notably in the context of operation counts for numerical calculations, sizes of circuits for switching and other applications, and theoretical lengths of proofs. In the 1960s such ideas were increasingly formalized, particularly for execution times on Turing machines, and in 1965 the suggestion was made that one should consider computations feasible if they take times that grow like polynomials in their input size. NP completeness (see below) was introduced by Stephen Cook in 1971 and Leonid Levin around the same time. And over the course of the 1970s a great many well-known problems were shown to be NP-complete. A variety of additional classes of computations— notably ones like NC with various kinds of parallelism, ones based on circuits and ones based on algebraic operations— were defined in the 1970s and 1980s, and many detailed results about them were found. In the 1980s much work was also done on the average difficulty of solving NP-complete problems—both exactly and approximately (see page 985). When computational complexity theory was at its height in the early 1980s it was widely believed that if a problem could be shown, for example, to be NP-complete then there was little chance of being able to work with it in a practical situation. But increasingly it became clear that general asymptotic results are often quite irrelevant in typical problems of reasonable size. And certainly pattern matching with _ in *Mathematica*, as well as polynomial manipulation functions like *GroebnerBasis*, routinely deal with problems that are formally NP-complete.

■ **Lower bounds.** If one could prove for example that P ≠ NP then one would immediately have lower bounds on all NP-complete problems. But absent such a result most of the general lower bounds known so far are based on fairly straightforward information content arguments. One cannot for example sort n objects in less than about n steps since one must at least look at each object, and one cannot multiply two n-digit numbers in less than about n steps since one must at least look at each digit. (As it happens the fastest known algorithms for these problems require very close to n steps.) And if the output from a computation can be of size 2^n then this will normally take at least 2^n steps to generate. Subtleties in defining how big the input to a computation really is can lead to at least apparently exponential lower bounds. An example is testing whether one can match all possible sequences with a regular expression that involves s-fold repetitions. It is fairly clear that this cannot be done in less than about s steps. But this seems exponentially large if s is specified by its digit sequence in the original input regular expression. Similar issues arise in the problem of determining truth or falsity in Presburger arithmetic (see page 1152).

Diagonalization arguments analogous to those on pages 1128 and 1162 show that in principle there must exist functions that can be evaluated only by computations that exceed any given bound. But actually finding examples of such functions that can readily be described as having some useful purpose has in the past seemed essentially impossible.

If one sufficiently restricts the form of the underlying system then it sometimes becomes possible to establish meaningful lower bounds. For example, with deterministic finite automata (see page 957), there are sequences that can be recognized, but only by having exponentially many states. And with DNF Boolean expressions (see page 1096) functions like *Xor* are known to require exponentially many terms, even—as discovered in the 1980s—if any limited number of levels are allowed (see page 1096).

■ **Algorithmic complexity theory.** Ordinary computational complexity theory asks about the resources needed to run programs that perform a given computation. But algorithmic complexity theory (compare page 1067) asks instead about how large the programs themselves need to be. The results of this book indicate however that even programs that are very small—and thus have low algorithmic complexity—can nevertheless perform all sorts of complex computations.

■ **Turing machines.** The Turing machines used here in effect have tapes that extend only to the left, and have no explicit halt states. (They thus differ from the Turing machines which Marvin Minsky and Daniel Bobrow studied in 1961 in the $s = 2$, $k = 2$ case and concluded all had simple behavior.) One can think of each Turing machine as computing a function $f[x]$ of the number x given as its input. The function is total (i.e. defined for all x) if the Turing machine always halts; otherwise it is partial (and undefined for at least some x). Turing machines can be numbered according to the scheme on page 888. The number of steps before a machine with given rule halts can be computed from (see page 888)

Module[{s = 1, a, i = 1, d}, a[_] = 0; MapIndexed[a[#2[[1]]] = #1 &, Reverse[IntegerDigits[x, 2]]]; Do[{s, a[i], d} = {s, a[i]} /. rule; i -= d; If[i == 0, Return[t]], {t, tmax}]]

Of the 4096 Turing machines with $s = 2$, $k = 2$, 748 never halt, 3348 sometimes halt and 1683 always halt. (The most rarely halting are ones like machine 3112 that halt only when $x = 4j - 1$.) The number of distinct functions $f[x]$ that can be computed by such machines is 351, of which 149 are total. 17 machines compute $x + 1$; none compute $x + 2$; 17 compute $x - 1$ and do not halt when $x = 0$—an example being 2575. Most machines compute functions that involve digit manipulations without traditional interpretations as mathematical functions. It is quite common to find machines that compute almost the same function: 1507 and 1511 disagree (where 1507 halts) only for $x \geq 35$. If $t[x]$ is the number of steps to compute $f[x]$ then the number of distinct pairs $\{f[x], t[x]\}$ is 492, or 230 for total $f[x]$. In 164 $t[x]$ does not increase with the number of digits n in x, in 295 it increases linearly, in 27 quadratically, and in 6 exponentially. For total $f[x]$ the corresponding numbers are 84, 136, 7, 3; the 3 machines with exponential growth are 378 (example (f) on page 761), 1953 and 2289; all compute trivial functions. Machine 1447 (example (e)) computes the function which takes the digit sequence of x and replaces its first $3 + IntegerExponent[x + 1, 2]$ 0's by 1's.

Among the 2,985,984 Turing machines with $s = 3$, $k = 2$, at least 2,550,972 sometimes halt, and about 1,271,304 always do. The number of distinct functions that can be computed is about 36,392 (or 75,726 for $\{f[x], t[x]\}$ pairs). 8934 machines compute $x + 1$ (by 25 different methods, including ones like machine 164850 that take exponential steps), 14 compute $x + 2$, and none compute $x + 3$. Those machines that take times that grow precisely like 2^n all tend to compute very straightforward functions which can be computed much faster by other machines.

Among the 2,985,984 Turing machines with $s = 2$, $k = 3$, at least 2,760,721 sometimes halt, and about 974,595 always halt. The number of distinct functions that can be computed is about 315,959 (or 457,508 for $\{f[x], t[x]\}$ pairs). (The fact that there are far fewer distinct functions in the $s = 3$, $k = 2$ case is a consequence of equivalences between states but not colors.)

Among the 2^{32} Turing machines with $s = 4$, $k = 2$ about 80% at least sometimes halt, and about 16% always do. Still none compute $x + 3$. And no Turing machine of any size can directly compute a function like x^2, $2x$ or $Mod[x, 2]$ that involves manipulating all digits in x.

■ **Functions.** The plots below show the values of the functions $f[x]$ for x from 0 to 1023 computed by the Turing machines on pages 761 and 763. Many of the plots use logarithmic scales. Rarely are the values close to their absolute maximum $t[x]$.

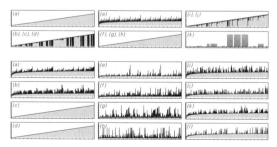

■ **Machine 1507.** This machine shows in some ways the most complicated behavior of any $s = 2$, $k = 2$ Turing machine. As suggested by picture (k) it fails to halt if and only if its configuration at some step matches $\{(0)\ldots, \{1, 1\}, 1, \_\_\}$ (in the alternative form of page 888). For any input x one can test whether the machine will ever halt using

    u[{Reverse[IntegerDigits[x, 2]], 0}]

    u[list_] := v[Split[Flatten[list]]]

    v[{a_, b_ : {}, c_ : {}, d_ : {}, e_ : {}, f_ : {}, g__}] :=
      Which[a == {1} || First[a] == 0, True, c == {}, False,
        EvenQ[Length[b]], u[{a, 1 - b, c, d, e, f, g}],
        EvenQ[Length[c]], u[{a, 1 - b, c, 1, Rest[d], e, f, g, 0}],
        e == {} || Length[d] ≥ Length[b] + Length[a] - 2,
        True, EvenQ[Length[e]], u[{a, b, c, d, f, g}],
        True, u[{a, 1 - b, c, 1 - d, e, 1, Rest[f], g, 0}]]]

This test takes at most $n/3$ recursive steps, even though the original machine can take of order n^2 steps to halt. Among $s = 3$, $k = 2$ machines there are 314 machines that do the same computation as 1507, but none any faster.

■ **Page 763 · Properties.** The maximum numbers of steps increase with input size according to:

(a) $14\,2^{\wedge}Floor[n/2] - 11 + 2\,Mod[n, 2]$

(b) (does not halt for $x = 1$)

(c) $2^n - 1$

(d) $(7\,(1 + Mod[n, 2])\,4^{\wedge}Floor[n/2] + 2\,Mod[n, 2] - 7)/3$

(h) (see note below)

(i) (does not halt for various $x > 53$)

(j) (does not halt for various $x > 39$)

(k) (does not halt for $x = 1$)

(l) $5\,(2^{n-2} - 1)$

■ **Longest halting times.** The pictures below show the largest numbers of steps $t[x]$ that it takes any machine of a particular type to halt when given successive inputs x. For $s = 2$, $k = 2$ the largest results for all inputs of sizes 0 to 4 are $\{7, 17, 31, 49, 71\}$, all obtained with machine 1447. For $n > 4$ the largest results are $2^{n+2} - 3$, achieved for $x = 2^n - 1$ with machines 378 and 1351. For $s = 3$, $k = 2$ the largest results for successive sizes are $\{25, 53, 159, 179, 1021, 5419\}$ (often achieved by machine 600720; see below) and for $s = 2$, $k = 3$ $\{35, 83, 843, 8335\}$ (often achieved by machine 840971). Note the similarity to the busy beaver problem discussed on page 889.

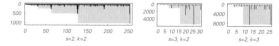

■ **Growth rates.** Some Turing machine can always be found that has halting times that grow at any specified rate. (See page 103 for a symbolic system with halting times that grow like *Nest[2#* &, 0, n].) As discussed on page 1162, if the growth rate is too high then it may not be possible to prove that the machines halt using, say, the standard axioms of arithmetic. The maximum halting times above increase faster than the halting times for any specific Turing machine, and are therefore ultimately not computable by any single Turing machine.

■ **Machine 600720.** (Case (h) of page 763.) The maximum halting times for the first few sizes *n* are

{5, 159, 161, 1021, 5419, 315391,
1978213883, 1978213885, 3018415453261}

These occur for inputs {1, 2, 5, 10, 26, 34, 106, 213, 426} and correspond to outputs (each themselves maximal for given *n*)

2 ^ {3, 23, 24, 63, 148, 1148, 91148, 91149, 3560523} - 1

Such maxima often seem to occur when the input *x* has the form $(20\,4^s - 2)/3$ (and so has digits {1, 1, 0, 1, 0, ..., 1, 0}). The output *f[x]* in such cases is always $2^u - 1$ where

u = Nest[(13 + (6 # + 8) (5/2) ^
IntegerExponent[6 # + 8, 2])/6 &, 1, s + 1]

One then finds that $6\,u + 8$ has the form *Nest[If[EvenQ[#], 5#/2, # + 21]* &, 14, m] for some *m*, suggesting a connection with the number theory systems of page 122. The corresponding halting time *t[x]* is *Last[Nest[h, {8, 4 s + 24}, s]]* - 1 with

h[{i_, j_}] := With[{e = IntegerExponent[3 i + 4, 2]}, {13/6 +
(i + 4/3) (5/2)^{e+1}, ((154 + 75 (i + 4/3) (5/2)^e)^2 -
16321 - 7860 i - 900 i^2 + 3360 e)/3780 + j}]

For *s* > 3 it then turns out that *f[x]* is extremely close to $3560523\,(5/2)^r$, and *t[x]* to $18865098979373\,(5/2)^{2\,r}$, for some integer *r*.

It is very difficult in general to find traditional formulas for *f[x]* and *t[x]*. But if *IntegerDigits[x, 2]* involves no consecutive 0's then for example *f[x]* can be obtained from

2 ^ (b[Join[{1, 1}, #], Length[#]] &)[IntegerDigits[x, 2]] - 1

a[{l_, _}, r_] := ({l + (5 r - 3 #)/2, #} &)[Mod[r, 2]]

a[{l_, 0}, 0] := {l + 1, 0}

a[{l_, 1}, 0] :=
({{13 + # (5/2) ^ IntegerExponent[#, 2]}/6, 0} &)[6 l + 2]

b[list_, i_] := First[Fold[a, {Apply[Plus, Drop[list, -i]], 0},
Apply[Plus, Split[Take[list, -i], #1 == #2 ≠ 0 &], 1]]]

(The corresponding expression for *t[x]* is more complicated.) A few special cases are:

f[4 s] = 4 s + 3

f[4 s + 1] = 2 f[2 s] + 1

f[2^s - 1] = 2^{(10 s + 5 + 3 (-1)^s)/4} - 1

How the halting times behave for large *n* is not clear. It is certainly possible that they could increase like

NestList[#^2 &, 2, n], or 2^{2^n}, although for $x = (20\,4^s - 2)/3$ a better fit for *n* ≲ 200 is just $2^{2.6\,n}$, with outputs increasing like $2^{2^{1.3\,n}}$.

■ **Page 766 · NP completeness.** Among the hundreds of problems known to be NP-complete are:

- Can a non-deterministic Turing machine reach a certain state in a given number of steps?

- Can a multiway system generate a certain string in a given number of steps?

- Is there an assignment of truth values to variables that makes a given Boolean expression true? (Satisfiability; related to minimal Boolean expressions of page 1095.)

- Will a given sequence of pair comparisons correctly sort any list (see page 1142)?

- Will a given pattern of origami folds yield an object that can be made flat?

- Does a network have any parts that match a given subnetwork (see page 1038)?

- Is there a path shorter than some given length that visits all of some set of points in the plane? (Travelling salesman; related to the network layout problem of page 1031.)

- Is there a solution of a certain size to an integer linear programming problem?

- Is there any *x < a* such that $Mod[x^2, b] == c$? (See page 1090.)

- Does a matrix have a permanent of given value?

- Is there a way to satisfy tiling constraints in a finite region? (See page 984.)

- Is there a string of some limited length that solves a correspondence problem?

- Is there an initial condition to a cellular automaton that yields particular behavior after a given number of steps?

(In cases where numbers are involved, it is usually crucial that these be represented by base 2 digit sequences, and not, say, in unary.) Many NP-complete problems at first seem quite unrelated. But often their equivalence becomes clear just by straightforward identification of terms. And so for example the equivalence of satisfiability to problems about networks can be seen by identifying variables and clauses in Boolean expressions respectively with connections and nodes in networks.

One can get an idea of the threshold of NP completeness by looking at seemingly similar problems where one is NP-complete but the other is in P. Examples include:

- Finding a Hamiltonian circuit that visits once every connection in a given network is NP-complete, but finding an Euler circuit that visits once every node is in P.

- Finding the longest path between two nodes in a network is NP-complete, but finding the shortest path is in P.

- Determining satisfiability for a Boolean expression with 3 variables in each clause is NP-complete, but for one with 2 variables is in P. (The latter is like a network with only 2 connections at each node.)

- Solving quadratic Diophantine equations $a x^2 + b y == c$ is NP-complete, but solving linear ones $a x + b y == c$ is in P.

- Finding a minimum energy configuration for a 2D Ising spin glass in a magnetic field is NP-complete, but is in P if there is no magnetic field.

- Finding the permanent of a matrix is NP-complete, but finding its determinant is in P.

It is not known whether problems such as integer factoring or equivalence of networks under relabelling of nodes (graph isomorphism) are NP-complete. It is known that in principle there exist NP problems that are not in P, yet are not NP-complete.

■ **Natural systems.** Finding minimum energy configurations is formally NP-complete in standard models of natural systems such as folding protein and DNA molecules (see page 1003), collections of charges on a sphere (compare page 987), and finite regions of spin glasses (see page 944). As discussed on page 351, however, it seems likely that in nature true minima are very rare, and that instead what is usually seen are just the results of actual dynamical processes of evolution.

In quantum field theory and to a lesser extent quantum mechanics and celestial mechanics, approximation schemes based on perturbation series seem to require computations that grow very rapidly with order. But exactly what this implies about the underlying physical processes is not clear.

■ **P versus NP questions.** Most programs that are explicitly constructed to solve specific problems tend at some level to have rather simple behavior—often just repetitive or nested, so long as appropriate number representations are used. And it is this that makes it realistic to estimate asymptotic growth rates using traditional mathematics, and to determine whether the programs operate in polynomial time. But as the pictures on page 761 suggest, arbitrary computational systems—even Turing machines with very simple rules—can exhibit much more complicated behavior with no clear asymptotic growth rate. And indeed the question of whether

the halting times for a system grow only like a power of input size is in general undecidable. And if one tries to prove a result about halting times using, say, standard axioms of arithmetic or set theory, one may find that the result is independent of those axioms. So this makes it far from clear that the general P = NP question has a definite answer within standard axiom systems of mathematics. If one day someone were to find a provably polynomial time algorithm that solves an NP-complete problem then this would establish that P = NP. But it could well be that the fastest programs for NP-complete problems behave in ways that are too complicated to prove much about using the standard axioms of mathematics.

■ **Non-deterministic Turing machines.** Generalizing rules from page 888 by making each right-hand side a list of possible outcomes, the list of configurations that can be reached after t steps is given by

```
NTMEvolve[rule_, inits_, t_Integer] := Nest[
    Union[Flatten[Map[NTMStep[rule, #] &, #], 1]] &, inits, t]
NTMStep[rule_List, {s_, a_, n_}] /; 1 ≤ n ≤ Length[a] :=
    Apply[{#1, ReplacePart[a, #2, n], n + #3} &,
    Replace[{s, a[[n]]}, rule], {1}]
```

■ **Page 767 · Implementation.** Given a non-deterministic Turing machine with rules in the form above, the rules for a cellular automaton which emulates it can be obtained from

```
NDTMToCA[tm_] := Flatten[{{_, h, _} → h, {s, _c, _} → e, {s,
    _, _} → s, {_, s, c[i_]} → s[i], {_, s, x_} → x, {a[_, _], _s, _} → s,
    {_, a[x_, y_], s[i_]} → a[x, y, i], {x_, _s, _} → x, {_, _, s[i_]} →
    s[i], Map[Table[With[{b = (#[[Min[Length[#], z]]] &)[
    {x, #}/. tm]}, If[Last[b] == -1, {{a[_], a[x, #, z], e} → h, {a[
    _], a[x, #, z], s} → a[x, #, z], {a[_], a[x, #, z], _} → a[b[[2]]],
    {a[x, #, z], a[w_], _} → a[b[[1]], w], {_, a[w_], a[x, #, z]} →
    a[w]}, {{a[_], a[x, #, z], _} → a[b[[2]]], {a[x, #, z], a[w_],
    _} → a[w], {_, a[w_], a[x, #, z]} → a[b[[1]], w]}]], {x,
    Max[Map[#[[1, 1]] &, tm]]}], {z, Max[Map[Length[#[[2]]] &,
    tm]]}]] &, Union[Map[#[[1, 2]] &, tm]]], {_, x_, _} → x}]
```

■ **Page 768 · Satisfiability.** Given variables $s[t, s]$, $a[t, x, a]$, $n[t, n]$ representing whether at step t a non-deterministic Turing machine is in state s, the tape square at position x has color a, and the head is at position n, the following CNF expression represents the assertion that a Turing machine with $stot$ states and $ktot$ possible colors follows the specified rules and halts after at most t steps:

```
NDTMToCNF[rules_, {s_, a_, n_}, t_] :=
{Table[Apply[Or, Table[s[i, j], {j, stot}]], {i, t - 1}],
    Table[! s[i, j] || ! s[i, k], {i, 0, t - 1}, {j, stot}, {k, j + 1, stot}],
    Table[Apply[Or, Table[n[i, j], {j, n + i, Max[0, n - i], -2}]],
    {i, 0, t}], Table[! n[i, j] || ! n[i, k], {i, 0, t}, {j, n + i, Max[0,
    n - i], -2}, {k, j + 2, n + i}], Table[Apply[Or, Table[a[i, j, k],
    {k, 0, ktot - 1}]], {i, 0, t}, {j, Max[1, n - i], n + i}],
    Table[! a[i, j, k] || ! a[i, j, m], {i, 0, t - 1}, {j, Max[1, n - i],
    n + i}, {k, 0, ktot - 1}, {m, k + 1, ktot - 1}], s[0, s],
```

```
Cases[MapIndexed[a[Abs[n - First[#2]], First[#2], #1] &,
  a], a[x_, _, _] /; x < t], Table[a[Abs[n - i], i, 0],
  {i, Length[a] + 1, n + t - 1}], Table[! a[i, j, k] ||
  If[EvenQ[n + i - j], in[i, j], False] || a[i + 1, j, k], {i, 0, t - 2},
  {j, Max[1, n - i], n + i}, {k, 0, ktot - 1}], Table[Map[Function[
  z, Outer[! in[i, j] || ! s[i, z[[1, 1]]] || ! a[i, j, z[[1, 2]]] || ## &,
  Apply[Sequence, Map[If[i < t - 1, {s[i + 1, #[[1]]], in[
    i + 1, j - #[[3]]], a[i + 1, j, #[[2]]]}, {in[i + 1, j - #[[3]]]}] &,
  z[[2]]]]]], rules], {i, 0, t - 1}, {j, n + i, Max[1, n - i], -2}],
  Apply[Or, Table[in[i, 0], {i, n, t, 2}]]}] /. List → And
```

■ **Density of difficult problems.** There are arguments that in an asymptotic sense most instances chosen at random of problems like limited-size PCP or tiling will be difficult to solve. In a problem like satisfiability, however, difficult instances tend to occur only on the boundary between cases where the density of black or white squares implies that there is usually satisfaction or usually not satisfaction. If one looks at simple instances of problems (say PCP with short strings) then my experience is that many are easy to solve. But just as some fraction of cellular automata with very simple rules show immensely complex behavior, so similarly it seems that some fraction of even simple instances of many NP-complete problems also tend to be difficult to solve.

■ **Page 770 · Rule 30 inversion.** The total numbers of sequences for t from 1 to 15 not yielding stripes of heights 1 and 2 are respectively

$\{1, 2, 2, 3, 3, 6, 6, 10, 16, 31, 52, 99, 165, 260\}$

$\{2, 5, 8, 14, 23, 40, 66, 111, 182,$
$316, 540, 921, 1530, 2543, 4122\}$

The sideways evolution of rule 30 discussed on page 601 implies that if one fills cells from the left rather than the right then some sequence of length $t + 1$ will always yield any given stripe of height t.

If the evolution of rule 30 can be set up as on page 704 to emulate any Boolean function then the problem considered here is immediately equivalent to satisfiability.

■ **Systems of limited size.** In the system $x \to Mod[x + m, n]$ from page 255 the repetition period $n/GCD[m, n]$ can be computed using Euclid's algorithm in at most about $Log[GoldenRatio, n]$ steps. In the system $x \to Mod[2x, n]$ from page 257, the repetition period $MultiplicativeOrder[2, n]$ probably cannot always be computed in any polynomial of $Log[n]$ steps, since otherwise $FactorInteger[n]$ could also be computed in about this number of steps. (But see note below.) In a cellular automaton with n cells, the problem of finding the repetition period is in general PSPACE-complete—as follows from the possibility of universality in the underlying cellular automaton. And even in a case like rule 30 I suspect that the period cannot be found much faster than by tracing nearly 2^n steps of evolution. (I know of no way for example

to break the computation into parts that can be done in parallel.) With sufficiently simple behavior, a cellular automaton repetition period can readily be determined in some power of $Log[n]$ steps. But even with an additive rule and nested behavior, the period depends on quantities like $MultiplicativeOrder[2, n]$, which probably take more like n steps to evaluate. (But see note below.)

■ **Page 771 · Quantum computers.** In an ordinary classical setup one typically describes the state of something like a 2-color cellular automaton with n cells just by giving a list of n color values. But the standard formalism of quantum theory (see page 1058) implies that for an analogous quantum system—like a line of n quantum spins each either up or down—one instead has to give a whole vector of probability amplitudes for each of the 2^n possible complete underlying spin configurations. And these amplitudes a_i are assumed to be complex numbers with a continuous range of possible values, subject only to the conventional constraint of unit total probability $Sum[Abs[a_i]^2, \{i, 2^n\}] == 1$. The evolution of such a quantum system can then formally be represented by successive multiplication of the vector of amplitudes by appropriate $2^n \times 2^n$ unitary matrices.

In a classical system like a cellular automaton with n cells a probabilistic ensemble of states can similarly be described by a vector of 2^n probabilities p_i—now satisfying $Sum[p_i, \{i, 2^n\}] == 1$, and evolving by multiplication with $2^n \times 2^n$ matrices having a single 1 in each row. (If the system is reversible—as in the quantum case—then the matrices are invertible.) But even if one assumes that all 2^n states in the ensemble somehow manage to evolve in parallel, it is still fairly clear that to do reliable computations takes essentially as much effort as evolving single instances of the underlying system. For even though the vector of probabilities can formally give outcomes for 2^n different initial conditions, any specific individual outcome could have probability as small as 2^{-n}—and so would take 2^n trials on average to detect.

The idea of setting up quantum analogs of systems like Turing machines and cellular automata began to be pursued in the early 1980s by a number of people, including myself. At first it was not clear what idealizations to make, but by the late 1980s—especially through the work of David Deutsch—the concept had emerged that a quantum computer should be described in terms of a network of basic quantum gates. The idea was to have say n quantum spins (each representing a so-called qubit), then to do computations much like in the reversible logic systems of page 1097 or the sorting networks of page 1142 by applying some appropriate sequence of elementary operations. It was found to be sufficient to do operations on just one and two spins at a time, and in fact it was shown that any $2^n \times 2^n$ unitary matrix can be approximated arbitrarily closely by a suitable sequence of for example underlying 2-spin $\{x, y\} \rightarrow \{x, Mod[x + y, 2]\}$ operations (assuming values 0 and 1), together with 1-spin arbitrary phase change operations. Such phase changes can be produced by repeatedly applying a single irrational rotation, and using the fact that $Mod[h\,s, 2\,\pi]$ will eventually for some s come close to any given phase (see page 903). From the involvement of continuous numbers, one might at first imagine that it should be possible to do fundamentally more computations than can be done say in ordinary discrete cellular automata. But all the evidence is that—just as discussed on page 1128—this will not in fact be possible if one makes the assumption that at some level discrete must be used to set up the initial values of probability amplitudes.

From the fact that the basic evolution of an n-spin quantum system in effect involves superpositions of 2^n spin configurations one might however still imagine that in finite computations exponential speedups should be possible. And as a potential example, consider setting up a quantum computer that evaluates a given Boolean function—with its initial configurations of spins encoding possible inputs to the function, and the final configuration of a particular spin representing the output from the function. One might imagine that with such a computer it would be easy to solve the NP-complete problem of satisfiability from page 768: one would just start off with a superposition in which all 2^n possible inputs have equal amplitude, then look at whether the spin representing the output from the function has any amplitude to be in a particular configuration. But in an actual physical system one does not expect to be able to find values of amplitudes directly. For according to the standard formalism of quantum theory all amplitudes do is to determine probabilities for particular outcomes of measurements. And with the setup described, even if a particular function is ultimately satisfiable the probability for a single output spin to be measured say as up can be as little as 2^{-n}—requiring on average 2^n trials to distinguish from 0, just as in the classical probabilistic case.

With a more elaborate setup, however, it appears sometimes to be possible to spread out quantum amplitudes so as to make different outcomes correspond to much larger probability differences. And indeed in 1994 Peter Shor found a way to do this so as to get quantum computers at least formally to factor integers of size n using resources only polynomial in n. As mentioned in the note above, it becomes straightforward to factor m if one can get the values of $MultiplicativeOrder[a, m]$. But these correspond to periodicities in the list $Mod[a \hat{\ } Range[m], m]$. Given n spins one can imagine using

their 2^n possible configurations to represent each element of $Range[m]$. But now if one sets up a superposition of all these configurations, one can compute $Mod[a^\#, m]\,\&$, then essentially use $Fourier$ to find periodicities—all with a polynomial number of quantum gates. And depending on $FactorInteger[m]$ the resulting amplitudes show fairly large differences which can then be detected in the probabilities for different outcomes of measurements.

In the mid-1990s it was thought that quantum computers might perhaps give polynomial solutions to all NP problems. But in fact only a very few other examples were found—all ultimately based on very much the same ideas as factoring. And indeed it now seems decreasingly likely that quantum computers will give polynomial solutions to NP-complete problems. (Factoring is not known to be NP-complete.)

And even in the case of factoring there are questions about the idealizations used. It does appear that only modest precision is needed for the initial amplitudes. And it seems that perturbations from the environment can be overcome using versions of error-correcting codes. But it remains unclear just what might be needed actually to perform for example the final measurements required.

Simple physical versions of individual quantum gates have been built using particles localized for example in ion traps. But even modestly larger setups have been possible only in NMR and optical systems—which show formal similarities to quantum systems (and for example exhibit interference) but presumably do not have any unique quantum advantage. (There are other approaches to quantum computation that involve for example topology of 4D quantum fields. But it is difficult to see just what idealizations are realistic for these.)

■ **Circuit complexity.** Any function with a fixed size of input can be computed by a circuit of the kind shown on page 619. How the minimal size or depth of circuit needed grows with input size then gives a measure of the difficulty of the computation, with circuit depth growing roughly like number of steps for a Turing machine. Note that much as on page 662 one can construct universal circuits that can be arranged by appropriate choice of parts of their input to compute any function of a given input size. (Compare page 703.)

■ **Page 771 · Finding outcomes.** If one sets up a function to compute the outcome after t steps of evolution from some fixed initial condition—say a single black cell in a cellular automaton—then the input to this function need contain only $Log[2, t]$ digits. But if the evolution is computationally irreducible then to find its outcome will involve explicitly following each of its t steps—thereby effectively finding results for each of the $2 \hat{\ } Log[2, t]$ possible arrangements of digits corresponding to numbers less than t. Note that the computation that is involved is not necessarily in either NP or PSPACE.

■ **P completeness.** If one allows arbitrary initial conditions in a cellular automaton with nearest-neighbor rules, then to compute the color of a particular cell after t steps in general requires specifying as input the colors of all $2t+1$ initial cells up to distance t away (see page 960). And if one always does computations using systems that have only nearest-neighbor rules then just combining $2t+1$ bits of information can take up to t steps—even if the bits are combined in a way that is not computationally irreducible. So to avoid this one can consider systems that are more like circuits in which any element can get data from any other. And given t elements operating in parallel one can consider the class NC studied by Nicholas Pippenger in 1978 of computations that can be done in a number of steps that is at most some power of $Log[t]$. Among such computations are *Plus*, *Times*, *Divide*, *Det* and *LinearSolve* for integers, as well as determining outcomes in additive cellular automata (see page 609). But I strongly suspect that computational irreducibility prevents outcomes in systems like rule 30 and rule 110 from being found by computations that are in NC—implying in effect that allowing arbitrary connections does not help much in computing the evolution of such systems. There is no way yet known to establish this for certain, but just as with NP and P one can consider showing that a computation is P-complete with respect to transformations in NC. It turns out that finding the outcome of evolution in any standard universal Turing machine or cellular automaton is P-complete in this sense, since the process of emulating any such system by any other one is in NC. Results from the mid-1970s established that finding the output from an arbitrary circuit with *And* or *Or* gates is P-complete, and this has made it possible to show that finding the outcome of evolution in various systems not yet known to be universal is P-complete. A notable example due to Cristopher Moore from 1996 is the 3D majority cellular automaton with rule $UnitStep[a + AxesTotal[a, 3] - 4]$ (see page 927); another example is the Ising model cellular automaton from page 982.

Implications for Mathematics and Its Foundations

■ **History.** Babylonian and Egyptian mathematics emphasized arithmetic and the idea of explicit calculation. But Greek mathematics tended to focus on geometry, and increasingly relied on getting results by formal deduction. For being unable to draw geometrical figures with infinite accuracy this seemed the only way to establish anything with certainty.

And when Euclid around 330 BC did his work on geometry he started from 10 axioms (5 "common notions" and 5 "postulates") and derived 465 theorems. Euclid's work was widely studied for more than two millennia and viewed as a quintessential example of deductive thinking. But in arithmetic and algebra—which in effect dealt mostly with discrete entities—a largely calculational approach was still used. In the 1600s and 1700s, however, the development of calculus and notions of continuous functions made use of more deductive methods. Often the basic concepts were somewhat vague, and by the mid-1800s, as mathematics became more elaborate and abstract, it became clear that to get systematically correct results a more rigid formal structure would be needed.

The introduction of non-Euclidean geometry in the 1820s, followed by various forms of abstract algebra in the mid-1800s, and transfinite numbers in the 1880s, indicated that mathematics could be done with abstract structures that had no obvious connection to everyday intuition. Set theory and predicate logic were proposed as ultimate foundations for all of mathematics (see note below). But at the very end of the 1800s paradoxes were discovered in these approaches. And there followed an increasing effort—notably by David Hilbert—to show that everything in mathematics could consistently be derived just by starting from axioms and then using formal processes of proof.

Gödel's Theorem showed in 1931 that at some level this approach was flawed. But by the 1930s pure mathematics had already firmly defined itself to be based on the notion of doing proofs—and indeed for the most part continues to do so even today (see page 859). In recent years, however, the increasing use of explicit computation has made proof less important, at least in most applications of mathematics.

■ **Models of mathematics.** Gottfried Leibniz's notion in the late 1600s of a "universal language" in which arguments in mathematics and elsewhere could be checked with logic can be viewed as an early idealization of mathematics. Starting in 1879 with his "formula language" (*Begriffsschrift*) Gottlob Frege followed a somewhat similar direction, suggesting that arithmetic and from there all of mathematics could be built up from predicate logic, and later an analog of set theory. In the 1890s Giuseppe Peano in his *Formulario* project organized a large body of mathematics into an axiomatic framework involving logic and set theory. Then starting in 1910 Alfred Whitehead and Bertrand Russell in their *Principia Mathematica* attempted to derive many areas of mathematics from foundations of logic and set theory. And although its methods were flawed and its notation obscure this work did much to establish the idea that mathematics could be built up in a uniform way.

Starting in the late 1800s, particularly with the work of Gottlob Frege and David Hilbert, there was increasing interest in so-called metamathematics, and in trying to treat mathematical proofs like other objects in mathematics. This led in the 1920s and 1930s to the introduction of various idealizations for mathematics—notably recursive functions, combinators, lambda calculus, string rewriting systems and Turing machines. All of these were ultimately shown to be universal (see page 784) and thus in a sense capable of reproducing any mathematical system. String rewriting systems—as studied particularly by Emil Post—are close to the multiway systems that I use in this section (see page 938).

Largely independent of mathematical logic the success of abstract algebra led by the end of the 1800s to the notion that any mathematical system could be represented in algebraic terms—much as in the operator systems of this section. Alfred Whitehead to some extent captured this in his 1898 *Universal Algebra*, but it was not until the 1930s that the theory of structures emphasized commonality in the axioms for different fields of mathematics—an idea taken further in the 1940s by category theory (and later by topos theory). And following the work of the Bourbaki group beginning at the end of the 1930s it has become almost universally accepted that structures together with set theory are the appropriate framework for all of pure mathematics.

But in fact the *Mathematica* language released in 1988 is now finally a serious alternative. For while it emphasizes calculation rather than proof its symbolic expressions and transformation rules provide an extremely general way to represent mathematical objects and operations—as for example the notes to this book illustrate.

(See also page 1176.)

■ **Page 773 · Axiom systems.** In the main text I argue that there are many consequences of axiom systems that are quite independent of their details. But in giving the specific axiom systems that have been used in traditional mathematics one needs to take account of all sorts of fairly complicated details.

As indicated by the tabs in the picture, there is a hierarchy to axiom systems in traditional mathematics, with those for basic and predicate logic, for example, being included in all others. (Contrary to usual belief my results strongly suggest however that the presence of logic is not in fact essential to many overall properties of axiom systems.)

As discussed in the main text (see also page 1155) one can think of axioms as giving rules for transforming symbolic expressions—much like rules in *Mathematica*. And at a fundamental level all that matters for such transformations is the structure of expressions. So notation like $a + b$ and $a \times b$, while convenient for interpretation, could equally well be replaced by more generic forms such as $f[a, b]$ or $g[a, b]$ without affecting any of the actual operation of the axioms.

My presentation of axiom systems generally follows the conventions of standard mathematical literature. But by making various details explicit I have been able to put all axiom systems in forms that can be used almost directly in *Mathematica*. Several steps are still necessary though to get the actual rules corresponding to each axiom system. First, the definitions at the top of page 774 must be used to expand out various pieces of notation. In basic logic I use the notation $u = v$ to stand for the pair of rules $u \rightarrow v$ and $v \rightarrow u$. (Note that $=$ has the precedence of $\rightarrow$ not $==$.) In predicate logic the tab at the top specifies how to construct rules (which in this case are often called rules of inference, as discussed on page 1155). $x\_ \wedge y\_ \rightarrow x\_$ is the *modus ponens* or detachment rule (see page 1155). $x\_ \rightarrow \forall_y x\_$ is the generalization rule. $x\_ \rightarrow x\_ \wedge \# \&$ is applied to the axioms given to get a list of rules. Note that while $=$ in basic logic is used in the underlying construction of rules, $==$ in predicate logic is just an abstract operator with properties defined by the last two axioms given.

As is typical in mathematical logic, there are some subtleties associated with variables. In the axioms of basic logic literal variables like a must be replaced with patterns like $a\_$ that can stand for any expression. A rule like $a\_ \wedge (b\_ \vee \neg b\_) \rightarrow a$ can then immediately be applied to part of an expression using *Replace*. But to apply a rule like $a\_ \rightarrow a \wedge (b \vee \neg b)$ requires in effect choosing some new expression for b (see page 1155). And one way to represent this process is just to have the pattern $a\_ \rightarrow a\_ \wedge (b\_ \vee \neg b\_)$ and then to say that any actual rule that can be used must match this pattern. The rules given in the tab for predicate logic work the same way. Note, however, that in predicate logic the expressions that appear on each side of any rule are required to be so-called well-formed formulas (WFFs) consisting of variables (such as a) and constants (such as 0 or $\emptyset$) inside any number of layers of functions (such as $+$, $\cdot$, or Δ) inside a layer of predicates (such as $==$ or $\in$) inside any number of layers of logical connectives (such as $\wedge$ or $\Rightarrow$) or quantifiers (such as $\forall$ or $\exists$). (This setup is reflected in the grammar of the *Mathematica* language, where the operator precedences for functions are higher than for predicates, which are in turn higher than for quantifiers and logical connectives—thus yielding for example few parentheses in the presentation of axiom systems here.)

In basic logic any rule can be applied to any part of any expression. But in predicate logic rules can be applied only to whole expressions, always in effect using *Replace[expr, rules]*. The axioms below (devised by Matthew Szudzik as part of the development of this book) set up basic logic in this way.

$(a \vee b) \vee c = (b \vee a) \vee c$	$a \vee ((b \wedge c) \wedge d) = a \vee ((c \wedge b) \wedge d)$
$((a \vee b) \vee c) \vee d = (a \vee (b \vee c)) \vee d$	$a \vee (((b \wedge c) \wedge d) \wedge e) = a \vee ((b \wedge (c \wedge d)) \wedge e)$
$a \vee (b \wedge (c \wedge \neg c)) = a$	$a \vee (b \wedge (c \vee \neg c)) = a \vee b$
$a \vee (b \vee (c \wedge d)) = a \vee ((b \vee c) \wedge (b \vee d))$	$a \vee (b \wedge (c \vee d)) = a \vee ((b \wedge c) \vee (b \wedge d))$
$a \vee (b \wedge \neg (c \vee d)) = a \vee (b \wedge (\neg c \wedge \neg d))$	$a \vee (b \wedge \neg (c \wedge d)) = a \vee (b \wedge (\neg c \vee \neg d))$
$a \vee (b \wedge c) = a \vee (b \wedge \neg \neg c)$	

■ **Basic logic.** The formal study of logic began in antiquity (see page 1099), with verbal descriptions of many templates for valid arguments—corresponding to theorems of logic—being widely known by medieval times. Following ideas of abstract algebra from the early 1800s, the work of George Boole around 1847 introduced the notion of representing logic in a purely symbolic and algebraic way. (Related notions had been considered by Gottfried Leibniz in the 1680s.) Boole identified *1* with *True* and *0* with *False*, then noted that theorems in logic could be stated as equations in which *Or* is roughly *Plus* and *And* is *Times*—and that such equations can be manipulated by algebraic means. Boole's work was progressively clarified and simplified, notably by Ernst Schröder, and by around 1900, explicit axiom systems for Boolean algebra were being given. Often they included most of the 14 highlighted theorems of page 817, but slight simplifications led for example to the "standard version" of page 773. (Note that the duality between *And* and *Or* is no longer explicit here.) The "Huntington version" of page 773 was given by Edward Huntington in 1933, along with

$$\{ (\neg \neg a) = a, (a \vee \neg (b \vee \neg b)) = a,$$
$$(\neg (\neg (a \vee \neg b) \vee \neg (a \vee \neg c))) = (a \vee \neg (b \vee c)) \}$$

The "Robbins version" was suggested by Herbert Robbins shortly thereafter, but only finally proved correct in 1996 by William McCune using automated theorem proving (see page 1157). The "Sheffer version" based on *Nand* (see page 1173) was given by Henry Sheffer in 1913. The shorter version was devised by David Hillman as part of the development of this book. The shortest version is discussed on page 808. (See also page 1175.)

In the main text each axiom defines an equivalence between expressions. The tradition in philosophy and mathematical logic has more been to take axioms to be true statements from which others can be deduced by the *modus ponens* inference rule $\{x, x \Rightarrow y\} \rightarrow y$ (see page 1155). In 1879 Gottlob Frege

used his diagrammatic notation to set up a symbolic representation for logic on the basis of the axioms

$$\{ a \Rightarrow (b \Rightarrow a), (a \Rightarrow (b \Rightarrow c)) \Rightarrow ((a \Rightarrow b) \Rightarrow (a \Rightarrow c)),$$
$$(a \Rightarrow (b \Rightarrow c)) \Rightarrow (b \Rightarrow (a \Rightarrow c)),$$
$$(a \Rightarrow b) \Rightarrow ((\neg b) \Rightarrow (\neg a)), (\neg \neg a) \Rightarrow a, a \Rightarrow (\neg \neg a) \}$$

Charles Peirce did something similar at almost the same time, and by 1900 this approach to so-called propositional or sentential calculus was well established. (Alfred Whitehead and Bertrand Russell used an axiom system based on *Or* and *Not* in their original 1910 edition of *Principia Mathematica*.) In 1948 Jan Łukasiewicz found the single axiom version

$$\{ ((a \Rightarrow (b \Rightarrow a)) \Rightarrow ((((\neg c) \Rightarrow (d \Rightarrow (\neg e))) \Rightarrow ((c \Rightarrow (d \Rightarrow f)) \Rightarrow$$
$$((e \Rightarrow d) \Rightarrow (e \Rightarrow f)))) \Rightarrow g)) \Rightarrow (h \Rightarrow g) \}$$

equivalent for example to

$$\{ ((\neg a) \Rightarrow (b \Rightarrow (\neg c))) \Rightarrow$$
$$((a \Rightarrow (b \Rightarrow d)) \Rightarrow ((c \Rightarrow b) \Rightarrow (c \Rightarrow d))), a \Rightarrow (b \Rightarrow a) \}$$

It turns out to be possible to convert any axiom system that works with *modus ponens* (and supports the properties of $\Rightarrow$) into a so-called equational one that works with equivalences between expressions by using

Module[{a}, Join[Thread[axioms == a ⇒ a],
{((a ⇒ a) ⇒ b) == b, ((a ⇒ b) ⇒ b) == (b ⇒ a) ⇒ a}]]

An analog of *modus ponens* for *Nand* is $\{x, x \barwedge (y \barwedge z)\} \rightarrow z$, and with this Jean Nicod found in 1917 the single axiom

$$\{ (a \barwedge (b \barwedge c)) \barwedge ((e \barwedge (e \barwedge e)) \barwedge ((d \barwedge b) \barwedge ((a \barwedge d) \barwedge (a \barwedge d)))) \}$$

which was highlighted in the 1925 edition of *Principia Mathematica*. In 1931 Mordechaj Wajsberg found the slightly simpler

$$\{ (a \barwedge (b \barwedge c)) \barwedge (((d \barwedge c) \barwedge ((a \barwedge d) \barwedge (a \barwedge d))) \barwedge (a \barwedge (a \barwedge b))) \}$$

Such an axiom system can be converted to an equational one using

Module[{a}, With[{t = a ⊼ (a ⊼ a), i = #1 ⊼ (#2 ⊼ #2) &},
Join[Thread[axioms == t], {i[t ⊼ (b ⊼ c), c] == t,
i[t, b] == b, i[i[a, b], b] == i[i[b, a], a]}]]]

but then involves 4 axioms.

The question of whether any particular statement in basic logic is true or false is always formally decidable, although in general it is NP-complete (see page 768).

■ **Predicate logic.** Basic logic in effect concerns itself with whole statements (or "propositions") that are each either *True* or *False*. Predicate logic on the other hand takes into account how such statements are built up from other constructs—like those in mathematics. A simple statement in predicate logic is $\forall_x (\forall_y x == y) \vee \forall_x (\exists_y (\neg x == y))$, where $\forall$ is "for all" and $\exists$ is "there exists" (defined in terms of $\forall$ on page 774)—and this particular statement can be proved *True* from the axioms. In general statements in predicate logic can contain arbitrary so-called predicates, say $p[x]$ or $r[x, y]$, that are each either *True* or *False* for given x and y. When predicate logic is used as part of other axiom systems, there are typically axioms which define properties of the predicates. (In real algebra, for example, the predicate $>$ satisfies $a > b \Rightarrow a \neq b$.) But in pure predicate logic the predicates are not assumed to have any particular properties.

Notions of quantifiers like $\forall$ and $\exists$ were already discussed in antiquity, particularly in the context of syllogisms. The first explicit formulation of predicate logic was given by Gottlob Frege in 1879, and by the 1920s predicate logic had become widely accepted as a basis for mathematical axiom systems. (Predicate logic has sometimes also been used as a model for general reasoning—and particularly in the 1980s was the basis for several initiatives in artificial intelligence. But for the most part it has turned out to be too rigid to capture directly typical everyday reasoning processes.)

Monadic pure predicate logic—in which predicates always take only a single argument—reduces in effect to basic logic and is not universal. But as soon as there is even one arbitrary predicate with two arguments the system becomes universal (see page 784). And indeed this is the case even if one considers only statements with quantifiers $\forall \exists \forall$. (The system is also universal with one two-argument function or two one-argument functions.)

In basic logic any statement that is true for all possible assignments of truth values to variables can always be proved from the axioms of basic logic. In 1930 Kurt Gödel showed a similar result for pure predicate logic: that any statement that is true for all possible explicit values of variables and all possible forms of predicates can always be proved from the axioms of predicate logic. (This is often called Gödel's Completeness Theorem, but is not related to completeness of the kind I discuss on page 782 and elsewhere in this section.)

In discussions of predicate logic there is often much said about scoping of variables. A typical issue is that in, say, $\forall_x (\exists_y (\neg x == y))$, x and y are dummy variables whose specific names are not supposed to be significant; yet the names become significant if, say, x is replaced by y. In *Mathematica* most such issues are handled automatically. The axioms for predicate logic given here follow the work of Alfred Tarski in 1962 and use properties of $==$ to minimize issues of variable scoping.

(See also higher-order logics on page 1167.)

▪ **Arithmetic.** Most of the Peano axioms are straightforward statements of elementary facts about arithmetic. The last axiom is a schema (see page 1156) that states the principle of mathematical induction: that if a statement is valid for $a = 0$, and its validity for $a = b$ implies its validity for $a = b + 1$, then

it follows that the statement must be valid for all a. Induction was to some extent already used in antiquity—for example in Euclid's proof that there are always larger primes. It began to be used in more generality in the 1600s. In effect it expresses the idea that the integers form a single ordered sequence, and it provides a basis for the notion of recursion.

In the early history of mathematics arithmetic with integers did not seem to need formal axioms, for facts like $x + y == y + x$ appeared to be self-evident. But in 1861 Hermann Grassmann showed that such facts could be deduced from more basic ones about successors and induction. And in 1891 Giuseppe Peano gave essentially the Peano axioms listed here (they were also given slightly less formally by Richard Dedekind in 1888)—which have been used unchanged ever since. (Note that in second-order logic—and effectively set theory— $+$ and $\times$ can be defined just in terms of Δ; see page 1160. In addition, as noted by Julia Robinson in 1948 it is possible to remove explicit mention of $+$ even in the ordinary Peano axioms, using the fact that if $c == a + b$ then $(\Delta a \times c) \times (\Delta b \times c) == \Delta (c \times c) \times (\Delta a \times b)$. Axioms 3, 4 and 6 can then be replaced by $a \times b == b \times a$, $a \times (b \times c) == (a \times b) \times c$ and $(\Delta a) \times (\Delta a \times b) == \Delta a \times (\Delta b \times (\Delta a))$. See also page 1163.)

The proof of Gödel's Theorem in 1931 (see page 1158) demonstrated the universality of the Peano axioms. It was shown by Raphael Robinson in 1950 that universality is also achieved by the Robinson axioms for reduced arithmetic (usually called Q) in which induction—which cannot be reduced to a finite set of ordinary axioms (see page 1156)—is replaced by a single weaker axiom. Statements like $x + y == y + x$ can no longer be proved in the resulting system (see pages 800 and 1169).

If any single one of the axioms given for reduced arithmetic is removed, universality is lost. It is not clear however exactly what minimal set of axioms is needed, for example, for the existence of solutions to integer equations to be undecidable (see page 787). (It is known, however, that essentially nothing is lost even from full Peano arithmetic if for example one drops axioms of logic such as $\neg \neg a = a$.)

A form of arithmetic in which one allows induction but removes multiplication was considered by Mojzesz Presburger in 1929. It is not universal, although it makes statements of size n potentially take as many as about 2^{2^n} steps to prove (though see page 1143).

The Peano axioms for arithmetic seem sufficient to support most of the whole field of number theory. But if as I believe there are fairly simple results that are unprovable from these axioms it may in fact be necessary to extend the Peano axioms to make certain kinds of progress even in practical number theory. (See also page 1166.)

■ **Algebraic axioms.** Axioms like $a \circ (b \circ c) = (a \circ b) \circ c$ can be used in at least three ways. First, as equations which can be manipulated—like the axioms of basic logic—to establish whether expressions are equal. Second, as on page 773, as statements to be added to the axioms of predicate logic to yield results that hold for every possible system described by the axioms (say every possible semigroup). And third, as definitions of sets whose properties can be studied—and compared—using set theory. High-school algebra typically treats axioms as equations. More advanced algebra often uses predicate logic, but implicitly uses set theory whenever it addresses for example mappings between objects. Note that as discussed on page 1159 how one uses algebraic axioms can affect issues of universality and undecidability. (See also page 1169.)

■ **Groups.** Groups have been used implicitly in the context of geometrical symmetries since antiquity. In the late 1700s specific groups began to be studied explicitly, mainly in the context of permutations of roots of polynomials, and notably by Evariste Galois in 1831. General groups were defined by Arthur Cayley around 1850 and their standard axioms became established by the end of the 1800s. The alternate axioms given in the main text are the shortest known. The first for ordinary groups was found by Graham Higman and Bernhard Neumann in 1952; the second by William McCune (using automated theorem proving) in 1992. For commutative (Abelian) groups the first alternate axioms were found by Alfred Tarski in 1938; the second by William McCune (using automated theorem proving) in 1992. In this case it is known that no shorter axioms are possible. (See page 806.) Note that in terms of the $\bar{\circ}$ operator $1 == a \bar{\circ} a$, $\bar{b} == (a \bar{\circ} a) \bar{\circ} b$, and $a \cdot b == a \bar{\circ} ((a \bar{\circ} a) \bar{\circ} b)$. Ordinary group theory is universal; commutative group theory is not (see page 1159).

■ **Semigroups.** Despite their simpler definition, semigroups have been much less studied than groups, and there have for example been about 7 times fewer mathematical publications about them (and another 7 times fewer about monoids). Semigroups were defined by Jean-Armand de Séguier in 1904, and beginning in the late 1920s a variety of algebraic results about them were found. Since the 1940s they have showed up sporadically in various areas of mathematics—notably in connection with evolution processes, finite automata and category theory.

■ **Fields.** With $\oplus$ being $+$ and $\otimes$ being $\times$ rational, real and complex numbers are all examples of fields. Ordinary

integers lack inverses under $\times$, but reduction modulo a prime p gives a finite field. Since the 1700s many examples of fields have arisen, particularly in algebra and number theory. The general axioms for fields as given here emerged around the end of the 1800s. Shorter versions can undoubtedly be found. (See page 1168.)

■ **Rings.** The axioms given are for commutative rings. With $\oplus$ being $+$ and $\otimes$ being $\times$ the integers are an example. Several examples of rings arose in the 1800s in number theory and algebraic geometry. The study of rings as general algebraic structures became popular in the 1920s. (Note that from the axioms of ring theory one can only expect to prove results that hold for any ring; to get most results in number theory, for example, one needs to use the axioms of arithmetic, which are intended to be specific to ordinary integers.) For non-commutative rings the last axiom given is replaced by $(a \oplus b) \otimes c == a \otimes c \oplus b \otimes c$. Non-commutative rings already studied in the 1800s include quaternions and square matrices.

■ **Other algebraic systems.** Of algebraic systems studied in traditional mathematics the vast majority are special cases of either groups, rings or fields. Probably the most common other examples are those based on lattice theory. Standard axioms for lattice theory are ($\wedge$ is usually called meet, and $\vee$ join)

$$\{a \wedge b == b \wedge a, \ a \vee b == b \vee a, \ (a \wedge b) \wedge c == a \wedge (b \wedge c),$$
$$(a \vee b) \vee c == a \vee (b \vee c), \ a \wedge (a \vee b) == a, \ a \vee a \wedge b == a\}$$

Boolean algebra (basic logic) is a special case of lattice theory, as is the theory of partially ordered sets (of which the causal networks in Chapter 9 are an example). The shortest single axiom currently known for lattice theory has *LeafCount* 79 and involves 7 variables. But I suspect that in fact a *LeafCount* less than about 20 is enough.

(See also page 1171.)

■ **Real algebra.** A notion of real numbers as measures of space or quantity has existed since antiquity. The development of basic algebra gave a formal way to represent operations on such numbers. In the late 1800s there were efforts—notably by Richard Dedekind and Georg Cantor—to set up a general theory of real numbers relying only on basic concepts about integers—and these efforts led to set theory. For purely algebraic questions of the kind that might arise in high-school algebra, however, one can use just the axioms given here. These add to field theory several axioms for ordering, as well as the axiom at the bottom expressing a basic form of continuity (specifically that any polynomial which changes sign must have a zero). With these axioms one can prove results about real polynomials, but not about arbitrary mathematical functions, or integers. The axioms were shown to be complete by Alfred Tarski in the 1930s. The proof was based on setting up a procedure that could in principle resolve any set of real polynomial equations or inequalities. This is now in practice done by *Simplify* and other functions in *Mathematica* using methods of cylindrical algebraic decomposition invented in the 1970s—which work roughly by finding a succession of points of change using *Resultant*. (Note that with n variables the number of steps needed can increase like 2^{2^n}.) (See the note about real analysis below.)

■ **Geometry.** Euclid gave axioms for basic geometry around 300 BC which were used with fairly little modification for more than 2000 years. In the 1830s, however, it was realized that the system would remain consistent even if the so-called parallel postulate was modified to allow space to be curved. Noting the vagueness of Euclid's original axioms there was then increasing interest in setting up more formal axiom systems for geometry. The best-known system was given by David Hilbert in 1899—and by describing geometrical figures using algebraic equations he showed that it was as consistent as the underlying axioms for numbers.

The axioms given here are illustrated below. They were developed by Alfred Tarski and others in the 1940s and 1950s. (Unlike Hilbert's axioms they require only first-order predicate logic.) The first six give basic properties of betweenness of points and congruence of line segments. The second- and third-to-last axioms specify that space has two dimensions; they can be modified for other dimensions. The last axiom is a schema that asserts the continuity of space. (The system is not finitely axiomatizable.)

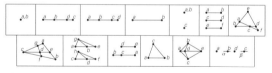

The axioms given can prove most of the results in an elementary geometry textbook—indeed all results that are about geometrical figures such as triangles and circles specified by a fixed finite number of points, but which do not involve concepts like area. The axioms are complete and consistent—and thus not universal. They can however be made universal if axioms from set theory are added.

■ **Category theory.** Developed in the 1940s as a way to organize constructs in algebraic topology, category theory works at the level of whole mathematical objects rather than their elements. In the basic axioms given here the variables represent morphisms that correspond to mappings between objects. (Often morphisms are shown as arrows in diagrams,

and objects as nodes.) The axioms specify that when morphisms are composed their domains and codomains must have appropriately matching types. Some of the methodology of category theory has become widely used in mathematics, but until recently the basic theory itself was not extensively studied—and its axiomatic status remains unclear. Category theory can be viewed as a formalization of operations on abstract data types in computer languages—though unlike in *Mathematica* it normally requires that functions take a single bundle of data as an argument.

■ **Set theory.** Basic notions of finite set theory have been used since antiquity—though became widespread only after their introduction into elementary mathematics education in the 1960s. Detailed ideas about infinite sets emerged in the 1880s through the work of Georg Cantor, who found it useful in studying trigonometric series to define sets of transfinite numbers of points. Several paradoxes associated with infinite sets were quickly noted—a 1901 example due to Bertrand Russell being to ask whether a set containing all sets that do not contain themselves in fact contains itself. To avoid such paradoxes Ernst Zermelo in 1908 suggested formalizing set theory using the first seven axioms given in the main text. (The axiom of infinity, for example, was included to establish that an infinite set such as the integers exists.) In 1922 Abraham Fraenkel noted that Zermelo's axioms did not support certain operations that seemed appropriate in a theory of sets, leading to the addition of Thoralf Skolem's axiom of replacement, and to what is usually called Zermelo-Fraenkel set theory (ZF). (The replacement axiom formally makes the subset axiom redundant.) The axiom of choice was first explicitly formulated by Zermelo in 1904 to capture the idea that in a set all elements can be ordered, so that the process of transfinite induction is possible (see page 1160). The non-constructive character of the axiom of choice has made it always remain somewhat controversial. It has arisen in many different guises and been useful in proving theorems in many areas of mathematics, but it has seemingly peculiar consequences such as the Banach-Tarski result that a solid sphere can be divided into six pieces (each a non-measurable set) that can be reassembled into a solid sphere twice the size. (The nine axioms with the axiom of choice are usually known as ZFC.) The axiom of regularity (or axiom of foundation) formulated by John von Neumann in 1929 explicitly forbids sets which for example can be elements of themselves. But while this axiom is convenient in simplifying work in set theory it has not been found generally useful in mathematics, and is normally considered optional at best.

A few additional axioms have also arisen as potentially useful. Most notable is the Continuum Hypothesis discussed on page 1127, which was proved independent of ZFC by Paul Cohen in 1963. (See also page 1166.)

Note that by using more complicated axioms the only construct beyond predicate logic needed to formulate set theory is $\in$. As discussed on page 1176, however, one cannot avoid axiom schemas in the formulation of set theory given here. (The von Neumann-Bernays-Gödel formulation does avoid these, but at the cost of introducing additional objects more general than sets.)

(See also page 1160.)

■ **General topology.** The axioms given define properties of open sets of points in spaces—and in effect allow issues like connectivity and continuity to be discussed in terms of set theory without introducing any explicit distance function.

■ **Real analysis.** The axiom given is Dedekind's axiom of continuity, which expresses the connectedness of the set of real numbers. Together with set theory it allows standard results about calculus to be derived. But as well as ordinary real numbers, these axioms allow non-standard analysis with constructs such as explicit infinitesimals (see page 1172).

■ **Axiom systems for programs.** (See pages 794 and 1168.)

■ **Page 775 · Implementation.** Given the axioms in the form

$s[1] = (a\_ \barwedge a\_) \barwedge (a\_ \barwedge b\_) \to a;$
$s[2, x\_] := b\_ \to (b \barwedge b) \barwedge (b \barwedge x); s[3] =$
$\quad a\_ \barwedge (a\_ \barwedge b\_) \to a \barwedge (b \barwedge b); s[4] = a\_ \barwedge (b\_ \barwedge b\_) \to a \barwedge (a \barwedge b);$
$s[5] = a\_ \barwedge (a\_ \barwedge (b\_ \barwedge c\_)) \to b \barwedge (b \barwedge (a \barwedge c));$

the proof shown here can be represented by

$\{\{s[2, b], \{2\}\}, \{s[4], \{\}\}, \{s[2, (b \barwedge a) \barwedge ((a \barwedge a) \barwedge (b \barwedge b))],$
$\quad \{2, 2\}\}, \{s[1], \{2, 2, 1\}\}, \{s[2, b \barwedge b], \{2, 2, 2, 2, 2\}\},$
$\quad \{s[5], \{2, 2, 2\}\}, \{s[2, b \barwedge b], \{2, 2, 2, 2, 2, 1\}\},$
$\quad \{s[1], \{2, 2, 2, 2, 2\}\}, \{s[3], \{2, 2, 2\}\},$
$\quad \{s[1], \{2, 2, 2, 2\}\}, \{s[4], \{2, 2, 2\}\}, \{s[5], \{\}\},$
$\quad \{s[2, a], \{2, 2, 1\}\}, \{s[1], \{2, 2\}\}, \{s[3], \{\}\}, \{s[1], \{2\}\}\}$

and applied using

$\mathsf{FoldList}[\mathsf{Function}[\{u, v\},$
$\quad \mathsf{MapAt}[\mathsf{Replace}[\#, v[\![1]\!]] \,\&, u, \{v[\![2]\!]\}]], a \barwedge b, proof]$

■ **Page 776 · Proof structures.** The proof shown is in a sense based on very low-level steps, each consisting of applying a single axiom from the original axiom system. But in practical mathematics it is usual for proofs to be built up in a more hierarchical fashion using intermediate results or lemmas. In the way I set things up lemmas can in effect be introduced as new axioms which can be applied repeatedly during a proof. And in the case shown here if one first proves the lemma

$(a \barwedge (a \barwedge (b \barwedge ((a \barwedge a) \barwedge c)))) = (b \barwedge a)$

and treats it as rule 6, then the main proof can be shortened:

When one just applies axioms from the original axiom system one is in effect following a single line of steps. But when one proves a lemma one is in effect on a separate branch, which only merges with the main proof when one uses the lemma. And if one has nested lemmas one can end up with a proof that is in effect like a tree. (Repeated use of a single lemma can also lead to cycles.) Allowing lemmas can in extreme cases probably make proofs as much as exponentially shorter. (Note that lemmas can also be used in multiway systems.)

In the way I have set things up one always gets from one step in a proof to the next by taking an expression and applying some transformation rule to it. But while this is familiar from algebraic mathematics and from the operation of *Mathematica* it is not the model of proofs that has traditionally been used in mainstream mathematical logic. For there one tends to think not so much about transforming expressions as about taking collections of true statements (such as equations $u == v$), and using so-called rules of inference to deduce other ones. Most often there are two basic rules of inference: *modus ponens* or detachment which uses the logic result $(x \wedge x \Rightarrow y) \Rightarrow y$ to deduce the statement y from statements x and $x \Rightarrow y$, and substitution, which takes statements x and y and deduces $x /. p \to y$, where p is a logical variable in x (see page 1151). And with this approach axioms enter merely as initial true statements, leaving rules of inference to generate successive steps in proofs. And instead of being mainly linear sequences of results, proofs instead become networks in which pairs of results are always combined when *modus ponens* is used. But it is still always in principle possible to convert any proof to a purely sequential one—though perhaps at the cost of having exponentially many more steps.

■ **Substitution strategies.** With the setup I am using each step in a proof involves transforming an expression like $u = v$ using an expression like $s = t$. And for this to happen s or t must match some part w of u or v. The simplest way this can be achieved is for s or t to reproduce w when its variables are replaced by appropriate expressions. But in general one can make replacements not only for variables in s and t, but also for ones in w. And in practice this often makes many more matches possible. Thus for example the axiom $a \circ a = a$ cannot be applied directly to $(p \circ q) \circ (p \circ r) = q \circ r$. But after the replacement $r \to q$, $a \circ a$ matches $(p \circ q) \circ (p \circ r)$ with $a \to p \circ q$, yielding the new theorem $p \circ q = q \circ q$. These kinds of substitutions are used in the proof on page 810. One approach to finding them is so-called paramodulation, which was introduced around 1970 in the context of automated theorem-proving systems, and has been used in many such systems (see page 1157). (Such substitutions are not directly relevant to *Mathematica*, since it transforms expressions rather than theorems or equations. But when I built SMP in 1981, its semantic pattern matching mechanism did use essentially such substitutions.)

■ **One-way transformations.** As formulated in the main text, axioms define two-way transformations. One can also set up axiom systems based on one-way transformations (as in multiway systems). For basic logic, examples of this were studied in the mid-1900s, and with the transformations thought of as rules of inference they were sometimes known as "axiomless formulations".

■ **Axiom schemas.** An axiom like $a + 0 == a$ is a single well-formed formula in the sense of page 1150. But sometimes one needs infinite collections of such individual axioms, and in the main text these are represented by axiom schemas given as *Mathematica* patterns involving objects like x_-. Such schemas are taken to stand for all individual axioms that match the patterns and are well-formed formulas. The induction axiom in arithmetic is an example of a schema. (See the note on finite axiomatizability on page 1176.) Note that as mentioned on page 1150 all the axioms given for basic logic should really be thought of as schemas.

■ **Reducing axiom details.** Traditional axiom systems have many details not seen in the basic structure of multiway systems. But in most cases these details can be avoided—and in the end the universality of multiway systems implies that they can always be made to emulate any axiom system.

Traditional axiom systems tend to be based on operator systems (see page 801) involving general expressions, not just strings. But any expression can always be written as a string using something like *Mathematica FullForm*. (See also page

1169.) Traditional axiom systems also involve symbolic variables, not just literal string elements. But by using methods like those for combinators on page 1121 explicit mention of variables can always be eliminated.

■ **Proofs in practice.** At some level the purpose of a proof is to establish that something is true. But in the practice of modern mathematics proofs have taken on a broader role; indeed they have become the primary framework for the vast majority of mathematical thinking and discourse. And from this perspective the kinds of proofs given on pages 810 and 811—or typically generated by automated theorem proving—are quite unsatisfactory. For while they make it easy at a formal level to check that certain statements are true, they do little at a more conceptual level to illuminate why this might be so. And indeed the kinds of proofs normally considered most mathematically valuable are ones that get built up in terms of concepts and constructs that are somehow expected to be as generally applicable as possible. But such proofs are inevitably difficult to study in a uniform and systematic way (though see page 1176). And as I argue in the main text, it is in fact only for the rather limited kinds of mathematics that have historically been pursued that such proofs can be expected to be sufficient. For in general proofs can be arbitrarily long, and can be quite devoid of what might be considered meaningful structure.

Among practical proofs that show signs of this (and whose mathematical value is thus often considered controversial) most have been done with aid of computers. Examples include the Four-Color Theorem (coloring of maps), the optimality of the Kepler packing (see page 986), the completeness of the Robbins axiom system (see page 1151) and the universality of rule 110 (see page 678).

In the past it was sometimes claimed that using computers is somehow fundamentally incompatible with developing mathematical understanding. But particularly as the use of *Mathematica* has become more widespread there has been increasing recognition that computers can provide crucial raw material for mathematical intuition—a point made rather forcefully by the discoveries in this book. Less well recognized is the fact that formulating mathematical ideas in a *Mathematica* program is at least as effective a way to produce clarity of thinking and understanding as formulating a traditional proof.

■ **Page 778 · Properties.** The second rule shown has the property that black elements always appear before white, so that strings can be specified just by the number of elements of each color that they contain—making the rule one of the sorted type discussed on page 937, based on the difference vector $\{\{2, -1\}, \{-1, 3\}, \{-4, -1\}\}$. The question of whether a given string can be generated is then analogous to finding whether there is a solution with certain positivity properties to a set of linear Diophantine equations.

■ **Page 781 · NAND tautologies.** At each step every possible transformation rule in the axioms is applied wherever it can. New expressions are also created by replacing each possible variable with $x \barwedge y$, where x and y are new variables, and by setting every possible pair of variables equal in turn. The longest tautology at step t is

$Nest[(\# \barwedge \#) \barwedge (\# \barwedge p_t) \&, p \barwedge (p \barwedge p), t-1]$

whose *LeafCount* grows like 3^t. The distribution of sizes of statements generated at each step is shown below.

| 0   10   20 | 0   20   40   60 | 0   50   100   150 | 100   300   500 |
| step 2 | step 3 | step 4 | step 5 |

Even with the same underlying axioms the tautologies are generated in a somewhat different order if one uses a different strategy—say one based on paramodulation (see page 1156). Pages 818 and 1175 discuss the sequence of all NAND theorems listed in order of increasing complexity.

■ **Proof searching.** To find a proof of some statement $p = q$ in a multiway system one can always in principle just start from p, evolve the system until it first generates q, then pick out the sequence of strings on the path from p to q. But doing this will usually involve building up a vast network of strings. And although at some level computational irreducibility and NP completeness (see page 766) imply that in general only a limited amount of this computational work can be saved, there are in practice quite often important optimizations that can be made. For finding a proof of $p = q$ is like searching for a path satisfying the constraint of going from p to q. And just like in the systems based on constraints in Chapter 5 one can usually do at least somewhat better than just to look at every possible path in turn.

For a start, in generating the network of paths one only ever need keep a single path that leads to any particular string; just like in many of my pictures of multiway systems one can in effect always drop any duplicate strings that occur. One might at first imagine that if p and q are both short strings then one could also drop any very long strings that are produced. But as we have seen, it is perfectly possible for long intermediate strings to be needed to get from p to q. Still, it is often reasonable to weight things so that at least at first one looks at paths that involve only shorter strings.

In the most direct approach, one takes a string and at each step just applies the underlying rules or axioms of the

multiway system. But as soon as one knows that there is a path from a string u to a string v, one can also imagine applying the rule $u \to v$ to any string—in effect like a lemma. And one can choose which lemmas to try first by looking for example at which involve the shortest or commonest strings.

It is often important to minimize the number of lemmas one has to keep. Sometimes one can do this by reducing every lemma—and possibly every string—to some at least partially canonical form. One can also use the fact that in a multiway system if $u \to v$ and $r \to s$ then $u <> r \to v <> s$.

If one wants to get from p to q the most efficient thing is to use properties of q to avoid taking wrong turns. But except in systems with rather simple structure this is usually difficult to achieve. Nevertheless, one can for example always in effect work forwards from p, and backwards from q, seeing whether there is any overlap in the sets of strings one gets.

■ **Automated theorem proving.** Since the 1950s a fair amount of work has been done on trying to set up computer systems that can prove theorems automatically. But unlike systems such as *Mathematica* that emphasize explicit computation none of these efforts have ever achieved widespread success in mathematics. And indeed given my ideas in this section this now seems not particularly surprising.

The first attempt at a general system for automated theorem proving was the 1956 Logic Theory Machine of Allen Newell and Herbert Simon—a program which tried to find proofs in basic logic by applying chains of possible axioms. But while the system was successful with a few simple theorems the searches it had to do rapidly became far too slow. And as the field of artificial intelligence developed over the next few years it became widely believed that what would be needed was a general system for imitating heuristics used in human thinking. Some work was nevertheless still done on applying results in mathematical logic to speed up the search process. And in 1963 Alan Robinson suggested the idea of resolution theorem proving, in which one constructs $\neg$ *theorem* $\vee$ *axioms*, then typically writes this in conjunctive normal form and repeatedly applies rules like $(\neg p \vee q) \wedge (p \vee q) \to q$ to try to reduce it to *False*, thereby proving given *axioms* that *theorem* is *True*. But after early enthusiasm it became clear that this approach could not be expected to make theorem proving easy—a point emphasized by the discovery of NP completeness in the early 1970s. Nevertheless, the approach was used with some success, particularly in proving that various mechanical and other engineering systems would behave as intended—although by the mid-1980s such verification was more often done by systematic Boolean function methods (see page 1097). In the 1970s simple versions of the resolution method were incorporated into logic programming languages such as Prolog, but little in the way of mathematical theorem proving was done with them. A notable system under development since the 1970s is the Boyer-Moore theorem prover Nqthm, which uses resolution together with methods related to induction to try to find proofs of statements in a version of LISP. Another family of systems under development at Argonne National Laboratory since the 1960s are intended to find proofs in pure operator (equational) systems (predicate logic with equations). Typical of this effort was the Otter system started in the mid-1980s, which uses the resolution method, together with a variety of ad hoc strategies that are mostly versions of the general ones for multiway systems in the previous note. The development of so-called unfailing completion algorithms (see page 1037) in the late 1980s made possible much more systematic automated theorem provers for pure operator systems—with a notable example being the Waldmeister system developed around 1996 by Arnim Buch and Thomas Hillenbrand.

Ever since the 1970s I at various times investigated using automated theorem-proving systems. But it always seemed that extensive human input—typically from the creators of the system—was needed to make such systems actually find non-trivial proofs. In the late 1990s, however, I decided to try the latest systems and was surprised to find that some of them could routinely produce proofs hundreds of steps long with little or no guidance. Almost any proof that was easy to do by hand almost always seemed to come out automatically in just a few steps. And the overall ability to do proofs—at least in pure operator systems—seemed vastly to exceed that of any human. But as page 810 illustrates, long proofs produced in this way tend to be difficult to read—in large part because they lack the higher-level constructs that are typical in proofs created by humans. As I discuss on page 821, such lack of structure is in some respects inevitable. But at least for specific kinds of theorems in specific areas of mathematics it seems likely that more accessible proofs can be created if each step is allowed to involve sophisticated computations, say as done by *Mathematica*.

■ **Proofs in *Mathematica*.** Most of the individual built-in functions of *Mathematica* I designed to be as predictable as possible—applying transformations in definite ways and using algorithms that are never of fundamentally unknown difficulty. But as their names suggest *Simplify* and *FullSimplify* were intended to be less predictable—and just to do what they can and then return a result. And in many cases these functions end up trying to prove theorems; so for example

FullSimplify[(a + b)/2 ≥ Sqrt[a b], a > 0 && b > 0] must in effect prove a theorem to get the result *True*.

■ **Page 781 · Truth and falsity.** The notion that statements can always be classified as either true or false has been a common idealization in logic since antiquity. But in everyday language, computer languages and mathematics there are many ways in which this idealization can fail. An example is $x + y == z$, which cannot reasonably be considered either true or false unless one knows what x, y and z are. Predicate logic avoids this particular kind of case by implicitly assuming that what is meant is a general statement about all values of any variable—and avoids cases like the expression $x + y$ by requiring all statements to be well-formed formulas (see page 1150). In *Mathematica* functions like *TrueQ* and *IntegerQ* are set up always to yield *True* or *False*—but just by looking at the explicit structure of a symbolic expression.

Note that although the notion of negation seems fairly straightforward in everyday language it can be difficult to implement in computational or mathematical settings. And thus for example even though it may be possible to establish by a finite computation that a particular system halts, it will often be impossible to do the same for the negation of this statement. The same basic issue arises in the intuitionistic approach to mathematics, in which one assumes that any object one handles must be found by a finite construction. And in such cases one can set up an analog of logic in which one no longer takes $\neg \neg a = a$.

It is also possible to assume a specific number $k > 2$ of truth values, as on page 1175, or to use so-called modal logics.

(See also page 1167.)

■ **Page 782 · Gödel's Theorem.** What is normally known as "Gödel's Theorem" (or "Gödel's First Incompleteness Theorem") is the centerpiece of the paper "On Undecidable Propositions of *Principia Mathematica* and Related Systems" published by Kurt Gödel in 1931. What the theorem shows is that there are statements that can be formulated within the standard axiom system for arithmetic but which cannot be proved true or false within that system. Gödel's paper does this first for the statement "this statement is unprovable", and much of the paper is concerned with showing how such a statement can be encoded within arithmetic. Gödel in effect does this by first converting the statement to one about recursive functions and then—by using tricks of number theory such as the beta function of page 1120—to one purely about arithmetic. (Gödel's main achievement is sometimes characterized as the "arithmetization of metamathematics": the discovery that concepts such as provability related to the processes of mathematics can be represented purely as statements in arithmetic.) (See page 784.)

Gödel originally based his theorem on Peano arithmetic (as discussed in the context of *Principia Mathematica*), but expected that it would in fact apply to any reasonable formal system for mathematics—and in later years considered that this had been established by thinking about Turing machines. He suggested that his results could be avoided if some form of transfinite hierarchy of formalisms could be used, and appears to have thought that at some level humans and mathematics do this (compare page 1167).

Gödel's 1931 paper came as a great surprise, although the issues it addressed were already widely discussed in the field of mathematical logic. And while the paper is at a technical level rather clear, it has never been easy for typical mathematicians to read. Beginning in the late 1950s its results began to be widely known outside of mathematics, and by the late 1970s Gödel's Theorem and various misstatements of it were often assigned an almost mystical significance. Self-reference was commonly seen as its central feature, and connections with universality and computation were usually missed. And with the belief that humans must somehow have intrinsic access to all truths in mathematics, Gödel's Theorem has been used to argue for example that computers can fundamentally never emulate human thinking.

The picture on page 786 can be viewed as a modern proof of Gödel's Theorem based on Diophantine equations.

In addition to what is usually called Gödel's Theorem, Kurt Gödel established a second incompleteness theorem: that the statement that the axioms of arithmetic are consistent cannot be proved by using those axioms (see page 1168). He also established what is often called the Completeness Theorem for predicate logic (see page 1152)—though here "completeness" is used in a different sense.

■ **Page 783 · Properties.** The first multiway system here generates all strings that end in ▫■; the third all strings that end in ■. The second system generates all strings where the second-to-last element is white, or the string ends with a run of black elements delimited by white ones.

■ **Page 783 · Essential incompleteness.** If a consistent axiom system is complete this means that any statement in the system can be proved true or false using its axioms, and the question of whether a statement is true can always be decided by a finite procedure. If an axiom system is incomplete then this means that there are statements that cannot be proved true or false using its axioms—and which must therefore be considered independent of those axioms. But even given this it is still possible that a finite procedure

can exist which decides whether a given statement is true, and indeed this happens in the theory of commutative groups (see note below). But often an axiom system will not only be incomplete, but will also be what is called essentially incomplete. And what this means is that there is no finite set of axioms that can consistently be added to make the system complete. A consequence of this is that there can be no finite procedure that always decides whether a given statement is true—making the system what is known as essentially undecidable. (When I use the term "undecidable" I normally mean "essentially undecidable". Early work on mathematical logic sometimes referred to statements that are independent as being undecidable.)

One might think that adding rules to a system could never reduce its computational sophistication. And this is correct if with suitable input one can always avoid the new rules. But often these rules will allow transformations that in effect short-circuit any sophisticated computation. And in the context of axiom systems, adding axioms can be thought of as putting more constraints on a system—thus potentially in effect forcing it to be simpler. The result of all this is that an axiom system that is universal can stop being universal when more axioms are added to it. And indeed this happens when one goes from ordinary group theory to commutative group theory, and from general field theory to real algebra.

■ **Page 784 · Predicate logic.** The universality of predicate logic with a single two-argument function follows immediately from the result on page 1156 that it can be used to emulate any two-way multiway system.

■ **Page 784 · Algebraic axioms.** How universality works with algebraic axioms depends on how those axioms are being used (compare page 1153). What is said in the main text here assumes that they are being used as on page 773—with each variable in effect standing for any object (compare page 1169), and with the axioms being added to predicate logic. The first of these points means that one is concerned with so-called pure group theory—and with finding results valid for all possible groups. The second means that the statements one considers need not just be of the form $\ldots == \ldots$, but can explicitly involve logic; an example is Cayley's theorem

$$a \cdot x == a \cdot y \Rightarrow (x == y \land \exists_z a \cdot z == x) \land$$
$$a \cdot x == b \cdot x \Rightarrow a == b \land (a \cdot b) \cdot x == a \cdot (b \cdot x)$$

With this setup, Alfred Tarski showed in 1946 that any statement in Peano arithmetic can be encoded as a statement in group theory—thus demonstrating that group theory is universal, and that questions about it can be undecidable. This then also immediately follows for semigroup theory and monoid theory. It was shown for ring theory and field theory by Julia Robinson in 1949. But for commutative group theory it is not the case, as shown by Wanda Szmielew around 1950. And indeed there is a procedure based on quantifier elimination for determining in a finite number of steps whether any statement in commutative group theory can be proved. (Commutative group theory is thus a decidable theory. But as mentioned in the note above, it is not complete—since for example it cannot establish the theorem $a == b$ which states that a group has just one element. It is nevertheless not essentially incomplete—and for example adding the axiom $a == b$ makes it complete.) Real algebra is also not universal (see page 1153), and the same is for example true for finite fields—but not for arbitrary fields.

As discussed on page 1141, word problems for systems such as groups are undecidable. But to set up a word problem in general formally requires going beyond predicate logic, and including axioms from set theory. For a word problem relates not, say, to groups in general, but to a particular group, specified by relations between generators. Within predicate logic one can give the relations as statements, but in effect one cannot specify that no other relations hold. It turns out, however, that undecidability for word problems occurs in essentially the same places as universality for axioms with predicate logic. Thus, for example, the word problem is undecidable for groups and semigroups, but is decidable for commutative groups.

One can also consider using algebraic axioms without predicate logic—as in basic logic or in the operator systems of page 801. And one can now ask whether there is then universality. In the case of semigroup theory there is not. But certainly systems of this type can be universal—since for example they can be set up to emulate any multiway system. And it seems likely that the axioms of ordinary group theory are sufficient to achieve universality.

■ **Page 784 · Set theory.** Any integer n can be encoded as a set using for example $Nest[Union[\#, \{\#\}] \&, \{\}, n]$. And from this a statement s in Peano arithmetic (with each variable explicitly quantified) can be translated to a statement in set theory by using

$$Replace[s, \{\forall_{a_-} b_- \rightarrow \forall_a (a \in \mathbb{N} \Rightarrow b),$$
$$\exists_{a_-} b_- \rightarrow \exists_a (a \in \mathbb{N} \wedge b)\}, \{0, \infty\}]$$

and then adding the statements below to provide definitions ($\mathbb{N}$ is the set of non-negative integers, $\langle x, y, z \rangle$ is an ordered triple, and $\updownarrow a$ determines whether each triple in a set a is of the form $\langle x, y, f[x, y] \rangle$ specifying a single-valued function).

$a = \mathbb{N} \Leftrightarrow \forall_b ((\emptyset \in b \wedge \forall_c (c \in b \Rightarrow \cup \{c, \{c\}\} \in b)) \Rightarrow a \subseteq b)$
$a = \Delta b \Leftrightarrow a = \cup \{b, \{b\}\}$
$a = \langle b, c, d \rangle \Leftrightarrow a = \{\{\{b, c\}, \{c\}\}, d\}, \{d\}\}$
$\updownarrow a \Leftrightarrow (\forall_b \forall_c \forall_d ((b, c, d) \in a \Rightarrow \forall_e ((b, c, e) \in a \Rightarrow d = e)) \wedge$ $\forall_b \forall_c ((b \in \mathbb{N} \wedge c \in \mathbb{N}) \Rightarrow \exists_d (d \in \mathbb{N} \wedge \langle b, c, d \rangle \in a)))$
$a = b + c \Leftrightarrow \forall_d ((\updownarrow d \wedge \forall_e \forall_f \forall_g ((\Delta e, f, g) \in d \Rightarrow (e, f, \Delta g) \in d) \wedge$ $\forall_f \forall_g ((\emptyset, f, g) \in d \Rightarrow g = f)) \Rightarrow \langle b, c, a \rangle \in d)$
$a = b \times c \Leftrightarrow \forall_d ((\updownarrow d \wedge \forall_e \forall_f \forall_g ((\Delta e, f, g) \in d \Rightarrow (e, f, f + g) \in d) \wedge$ $\forall_f \forall_g ((\emptyset, f, g) \in d \Rightarrow g = \emptyset)) \Rightarrow \langle b, c, a \rangle \in d)$

This means that set theory can be used to prove any statement that can be proved in Peano arithmetic. But it can also prove other statements—such as Goodstein's result (see note below), and the consistency of arithmetic (see page 1168). An important reason for this is that set theory allows not just ordinary induction over sequences of integers but also transfinite induction over arbitrary ordered sets (see below).

■ **Page 786 · Universal Diophantine equation.** The equation is built up from ones whose solutions are set up to be integers that satisfy particular relations. So for example the equation $a^2 + b^2 == 0$ has solutions that are exactly those integers that satisfy the relation $a == 0 \wedge b == 0$. Similarly, assuming as in the rest of this note that all variables are non-negative, $b == a + c + 1$ has solutions that are exactly those integers that satisfy $a < b$, with c having some allowed value. From various number-theoretical results many relations can readily be encoded as integer equations:

$(a == 0 \vee b == 0) \longleftrightarrow a \, b == 0$

$(a == 0 \wedge b == 0) \longleftrightarrow a + b == 0$

$a < b \longleftrightarrow b == a + c + 1$

$a == Mod[b, c] \longleftrightarrow (b == a + c \, d \wedge a < c)$

$a == Quotient[b, c] \longleftrightarrow (b == a \, c + d \wedge d < c)$

$a == Binomial[b, c] \longleftrightarrow With[\{n = 2^b + 1\},$
$\quad (n + 1)^b == n^c (a + d \, n) + e \wedge e < n^c \wedge a < n]$

$a == b! \longleftrightarrow a == Quotient[c^b, Binomial[c, b]]$

$a == GCD[b, c] \longleftrightarrow (b \, c > 0 \wedge a \, d == b \wedge a \, e == c \wedge a + c \, f == b \, g)$

$a == Floor[b/c] \longleftrightarrow (a \, c + d == b \wedge d < c)$

$PrimeQ[a] \longleftrightarrow (GCD[(a - 1)!, a] == 1 \wedge a > 1)$

$a == BitAnd[c, d] \wedge b == BitOr[c, d] \longleftrightarrow$
$\quad (\sigma[c, a] \wedge \sigma[d, a] \wedge \sigma[b, c] \wedge \sigma[b, d] \wedge a + b == c + d) /.$
$\sigma[x_-, y_-] \rightarrow Mod[Binomial[x, y], 2] == 1$

where the last encoding uses the result on page 608. (Note that any variable a can be forced to be non-negative by including an equation $a == w^2 + x^2 + y^2 + z^2$, as on page 910.)

Given an integer a for which $IntegerDigits[a, 2]$ gives the cell values for a cellular automaton, a single step of evolution according say to rule 30 is given by

$BitXor[a, 2 \, BitOr[a, 2 \, a]]$

where (see page 871)

$BitXor[x, y] == BitOr[x, y] - BitAnd[x, y]$

and a is assumed to be padded with 0's at each end. The corresponding form for rule 110 is

$BitXor[BitAnd[a, 2a, 4a], BitOr[2a, 4a]]$

The final equation is then obtained from

$\{1 + x_4 + x_{12} == 2^{(1+x_3)(x_1+2x_3)}, x_2 + x_{13} == 2^{x_1},$
$1 + x_5 + x_{14} == 2^{x_1}, 2^{x_3} x_5 + 2^{x_1+2x_3} x_6 + 2^{x_1+x_3} x_{15} + x_{16} == x_4,$
$1 + x_{15} + x_{17} == 2^{x_3}, 1 + x_{16} + x_{18} == 2^{x_3},$
$2^{1+x_3}{}^{(1+x_1+2x_3)}(-1+x_2) - x_{10} + x_{11} == 2x_4,$
$x_7 == BitAnd[x_6, 2x_6] \wedge x_8 == BitOr[x_6, 2x_6],$
$x_9 == BitAnd[x_6, 2x_7] \wedge x_{19} == BitOr[x_6, 2x_7],$
$x_{10} == BitAnd[x_9, 2x_8] \wedge x_{11} == BitOr[x_9, 2x_8]\}$

where x_1 through x_4 have the meanings indicated in the main text, and satisfy $x_i \geq 0$. Non-overlapping subsidiary variables are introduced for $BitOr$ and $BitAnd$, yielding a total of 79 variables.

Note that it is potentially somewhat easier to construct Diophantine equations to emulate register machines—or arithmetic systems from page 673—than to emulate cellular automata, but exactly the same basic methods can be used.

In the universal equation in the main text variables appear in exponents. One can reduce such an exponential equation to a pure polynomial equation by encoding powers using integer equations. The simplest known way of doing this (see note below) involves a degree 8 equation with 60 variables:

$a == b^c \leftrightarrow \alpha[d, 4 + be, 1 + z] \wedge \alpha[f, e, 1 + z] \wedge$
$a == Quotient[d, f] \wedge \alpha[g, 4 + b, 1 + z] \wedge e == 16 g (1 + z)$

$\lambda[a\_, b\_, c\_] := Module[\{x\},$
$\quad 2a + x_1 == c \wedge (Mod[b - a, c] == 0 \vee Mod[b + a, c] == 0)]$

$\alpha[a\_, b\_, c\_] := Module[\{x\}, x_1{}^2 - b x_1 x_2 + x_2{}^2 == 1 \wedge$
$x_3{}^2 - b x_3 x_4 + x_4{}^2 == 1 \wedge 1 + x_4 + x_5 == x_3 \wedge Mod[x_3, x_1{}^2] ==$
$0 \wedge 2 x_4 + x_7 == b x_3 \wedge Mod[-b + x_8, x_7] == 0 \wedge$
$Mod[-2 + x_8, x_1] == 0 \wedge x_8 - x_{11} == 3 \wedge x_{12}{}^2 - x_8 x_{12} x_{13} +$
$x_{13}{}^2 == 1 \wedge 1 + 2a + x_{14} == x_1 \wedge \lambda[a, x_{12}, x_7] \wedge \lambda[c, x_{12}, x_1]]$

(This roughly uses the idea that solutions to Pell equations grow exponentially, so that for example $x^2 == 2y^2 + 1$ has solutions $With[\{u = 3 + 2\sqrt{2}\}, (u^n + u^{-n})/2]$.) From this representation of *Power* the universal equation can be converted to a purely polynomial equation with 2154 variables—which when expanded has 1683150 terms, total degree 16 (average per term 6.8), maximum coefficient 17827424 and *LeafCount* 16540206.

Note that the existence of universal Diophantine equations implies that any problem of mathematics—even, say, the Riemann Hypothesis—can in principle be formulated as a question about the existence of solutions to a Diophantine equation. It also means that given any specific enumeration of polynomials, there must be some universal polynomial u which if fed the enumeration number of a polynomial p,

together with an encoding of the values of its variables, will yield the corresponding value of p as a solution to $u == 0$.

■ **Hilbert's Tenth Problem.** Beginning in antiquity various procedures were developed for solving particular kinds of Diophantine equations (see page 1164). In 1900, as one of his list of 23 important mathematical problems, David Hilbert posed the problem of finding a single finite procedure that could systematically determine whether a solution exists to any specified Diophantine equation. The original proof of Gödel's Theorem from 1931 in effect involves showing that certain logical and other operations can be represented by Diophantine equations—and in the end Gödel's Theorem can be viewed as saying that certain statements about Diophantine equations are unprovable. The notion that there might be universal Diophantine equations for which Hilbert's Tenth Problem would be fundamentally unsolvable emerged in work by Martin Davis in 1953. And by 1961 Davis, Hilary Putnam and Julia Robinson had established that there are exponential Diophantine equations that are universal. Extending this to show that Hilbert's original problem about ordinary polynomial Diophantine equations is unsolvable required proving that exponentiation can be represented by a Diophantine equation, and this was finally done by Yuri Matiyasevich in 1969 (see note above).

By the mid-1970s, Matiyasevich had given a construction for a universal Diophantine equation with 9 variables—though with a degree of about 10^{45}. It had been known since the 1930s that any Diophantine equation can be reduced to one with degree 4—and in 1980 James Jones showed that a universal Diophantine equation with degree 4 could be constructed with 58 variables. In 1979 Matiyasevich also showed that universality could be achieved with an exponential Diophantine equation with many terms, but with only 3 variables. As discussed in the main text I believe that vastly simpler Diophantine equations can also be universal. It is even conceivable that a Diophantine equation with 2 variables could be universal: with one variable essentially being used to represent the program and input, and the other the execution history of the program—with no finite solution existing if the program does not halt.

■ **Polynomial value sets.** Closely related to issues of solving Diophantine equations is the question of what set of positive values a polynomial can achieve when fed all possible positive integer values for its variables. A polynomial with a single variable must always yield either be a finite set, or a simple polynomial progression of values. But already the sequence of values for $x^2 y - x y^3$ or even $x(y^2 + 1)$ seem quite complicated. And for example from the fact that $x^2 == y^2 + (xy \pm 1)$ has solutions *Fibonacci[n]* it follows that the positive values of $(2 - (x^2 - y^2 - xy)^2)x$ are just *Fibonacci[n]* (achieved when $\{x, y\}$ is *Fibonacci[{n, n - 1}]*). This is the simplest polynomial giving *Fibonacci[n]*, and there are for example no polynomials with 2 variables, up to 4 terms, total degree less than 4, and integer coefficients between -2 and +2, that give any of 2^n, 3^n or *Prime[n]*. Nevertheless, from the representation for *PrimeQ* in the note above it has been shown that the positive values of a particular polynomial with 26 variables, 891 terms and total degree 97 are exactly the primes. (Polynomials with 42 variables and degree 5, and 10 variables and degree 10^{45}, are also known to work, while it is known that one with 2 variables cannot.) And in general the existence of a universal Diophantine equation implies that any set obtained by any finite computation must correspond to the positive values of some polynomial. The analog of doing a long computation to find a result is having to go to large values of variables to find a positive polynomial value. Note that one can imagine, say, emulating the evolution of a cellular automaton by having the tth positive value of a polynomial represent the tth step of evolution. That universality can be achieved just in the positive values of a polynomial is already remarkable. But I suspect that in the end it will take only a surprisingly simple polynomial, perhaps with just three variables and fairly low degree.

(See also page 1165.)

- **Statements in Peano arithmetic.** Examples include:

- $\sqrt{2}$ is irrational:

  $\neg\, \exists_a\, (\exists_b\, (b \neq 0 \wedge a \times a == (\Delta\Delta 0) \times (b \times b)))$

- There are infinitely many primes of the form $n^2 + 1$:

  $\neg\, \exists_n\, (\forall_c\, (\exists_a\, (\exists_b\, (n + c) \times (n + c) + \Delta 0 == (\Delta\Delta a) \times (\Delta\Delta b))))$

- Every even number (greater than 2) is the sum of two primes (Goldbach's Conjecture; see page 135):

  $\forall_a\, (\exists_b\, (\exists_c\, ((\Delta\Delta 0) \times (\Delta\Delta a) == b + c \wedge \forall_d\, (\forall_e\, (\forall_f\, ((f == (\Delta\Delta d) \times (\Delta\Delta e) \vee f == \Delta 0) \Rightarrow (f \neq b \wedge f \neq c)))))))$

The last two statements have never been proved true or false, and remain unsolved problems of number theory. The picture shows spacings between n for which $n^2 + 1$ is prime.

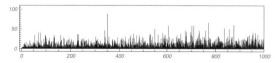

- **Transfinite numbers.** For most mathematical purposes it is quite adequate just to have a single notion of infinity, usually denoted ∞. But as Georg Cantor began to emphasize in the 1870s, it is possible to distinguish different levels of infinity. Most of the details of this have not been widely used in typical mathematics, but they can be helpful in studying foundational issues. Cantor's theory of ordinal numbers is based on the idea that every integer must have a successor. The next integer after all of the ordinary ones—the first infinite integer—is given the name ω. In Cantor's theory $\omega + 1$ is still larger (though $1 + \omega$ is not), as are 2ω, ω^2 and ω^ω. Any arithmetic expression involving ω specifies an ordinal number—and can be thought of as corresponding to a set containing all integers up to that number. The ordinary axioms of arithmetic do not apply, but there are still fairly straightforward rules for manipulating such expressions. In general there are many different expressions that correspond to a given number, though there is always a unique Cantor normal form—essentially a finite sequence of digits giving coefficients of descending powers of ω. However, not all infinite integers can be represented in this way. The first one that cannot is ϵ_0, given by the limit $\omega^{\omega^{\omega^{\cdots}}}$, or effectively $Nest[\omega^\# \&, \omega, \omega]$. ϵ_0 is the smallest solution to $\omega^\epsilon == \epsilon$. Subsequent solutions ($\epsilon_1, ..., \epsilon_\omega, ..., \epsilon_{\epsilon_0}, ...$) define larger ordinals, and one can go on until one reaches the limit $\epsilon_{\epsilon_{\epsilon_\cdots}}$, which is the first solution to $\epsilon_\alpha == \alpha$. Giving this ordinal a name, one can then go on again, until eventually one reaches another limit. And it turns out that in general one in effect has to introduce an infinite sequence of names in order to be able to specify all transfinite integers. (Naming a single largest or "absolutely infinite" integer is never consistent, since one can always then talk about its successor.) As Cantor noted, however, even this only allows one to reach the lowest class of transfinite numbers—in effect those corresponding to sets whose size corresponds to the cardinal number $\aleph_0$. Yet as discussed on page 1127, one can also consider larger cardinal numbers, such as $\aleph_1$, considered in connection with the number of real numbers, and so on. And at least for a while the ordinary axioms of set theory can be used to study the sets that arise.

- **Growth rates.** One can characterize most functions by their ultimate rates of growth. In basic mathematics these might be $n, 2n, 3n, ...$ or $n^2, n^3, ...,$ or $2^n, 3^n, ...,$ or $2^n, 2^{2^n}, 2^{2^{2^n}}, ...$ To go further one begins by defining an analog to the Ackermann function of page 906:

  $f[1][n\_] = 2n;\ f[s\_][n\_] := Nest[f[s - 1], 1, n]$

  $f[2][n]$ is then 2^n, $f[3]$ is iterated power, and so on. Given this one can now form the "diagonal" function

  $f[\omega][n\_] := f[n][n]$

and this has a higher growth rate than any of the $f[s][n]$ with finite s. This higher growth rate is indicated by the transfinite index ω. And in direct analogy to the transfinite numbers discussed above one can then in principle form a hierarchy of functions using operations like

$$f[\omega + s][n\_] := Nest[f[\omega + s - 1], 1, n]$$

together with diagonalization at limit ordinals. In practice, however, it gets more and more difficult to determine that the functions defined in this way actually in a sense halt and yield definite values—and indeed for $f[\epsilon_0]$ this can no longer be proved using the ordinary axioms of arithmetic (see below). Yet it is still possible to define functions with even more rapid rates of growth. An example is the so-called busy beaver function (see page 1144) that gives the maximum number of steps that it takes for any Turing machine of size n to halt when started from a blank tape. In general this function must grow faster than any computable function, and is not itself computable.

■ **Page 787 · Unprovable statements.** After the appearance of Gödel's Theorem a variety of statements more or less directly related to provability were shown to be unprovable in Peano arithmetic and certain other axiom systems. Starting in the 1960s the so-called method of forcing allowed certain kinds of statements in strong axiom systems—like the Continuum Hypothesis in set theory (see page 1155)—to be shown to be unprovable. Then in 1977 Jeffrey Paris and Leo Harrington showed that a variant of Ramsey's Theorem (see page 1068)—a statement that is much more directly mathematical—is also unprovable in Peano arithmetic. The approach they used was in essence based on thinking about growth rates—and since the 1970s almost all new examples of unprovability have been based on similar ideas. Probably the simplest is a statement shown to be unprovable in Peano arithmetic by Laurence Kirby and Jeff Paris in 1982: that certain sequences $g[n]$ defined by Reuben Goodstein in 1944 are of limited length for all n, where

$$g[n\_] := Map[First, NestWhileList[$$
$$\{f[\#] - 1, Last[\#] + 1\} \&, \{n, 3\}, First[\#] > 0 \&]]$$
$$f[\{0, \_\}] = 0; f[\{n\_, k\_\}] := Apply[Plus, MapIndexed[\#1$$
$$k^\wedge f[\{\#2[\![1]\!] - 1, k\}] \&, Reverse[IntegerDigits[n, k - 1]]]]$$

As in the pictures below, $g[1]$ is $\{1, 0\}$, $g[2]$ is $\{2, 2, 1, 0\}$ and $g[3]$ is $\{3, 3, 3, 2, 1, 0\}$. $g[4]$ increases quadratically for a long time, with only element $3 \times 2^{402653211} - 2$ finally being 0. And the point is that in a sense $Length[g[n]]$ grows too quickly for its finiteness to be provable in general in Peano arithmetic.

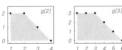

The argument for this as usually presented involves rather technical results from several fields. But the basic idea is

roughly just to set up a correspondence between elements of $g[n]$ and possible proofs in Peano arithmetic—then to use the fact that if one knew that $g[n]$ always terminated this would establish the validity of all these proofs, which would in turn prove the consistency of arithmetic—a result which is known to be unprovable from within arithmetic.

Every possible proof in Peano arithmetic can in principle be encoded as an ordinary integer. But in the late 1930s Gerhard Gentzen showed that if proofs are instead encoded as ordinal numbers (see note above) then any proof can validly be reduced to a preceding one just by operations in logic. To cover all possible proofs, however, requires going up to the ordinal ϵ_0. And from the unprovability of consistency one can conclude that this must be impossible using the ordinary operation of induction in Peano arithmetic. (Set theory, however, allows transfinite induction—essentially induction on arbitrary sets—letting one reach such ordinals and thus prove the consistency of arithmetic.) In constructing $g[n]$ the integer n is in effect treated like an ordinal number in Cantor normal form, and a sequence of numbers that should precede it are found. That this sequence terminates for all n is then provable in set theory, but not Peano arithmetic—and in effect $Length[g[n]]$ must grow like $f[\epsilon_0][n]$.)

In general one can imagine characterizing the power of any axiom system by giving a transfinite number κ which specifies the first function $f[\kappa]$ (see note above) whose termination cannot be proved in that axiom system (or similarly how rapidly the first example of y must grow with x to prevent $\exists_y p[x, y]$ from being provable). But while it is known that in Peano arithmetic $\kappa = \epsilon_0$, quite how to describe the value of κ for, say, set theory remains unknown. And in general I suspect that there are a vast number of functions with simple definitions whose termination cannot be proved not just because they grow too quickly but instead for the more fundamental reason that their behavior is in a sense too complicated.

Whenever a general statement about a system like a Turing machine or a cellular automaton is undecidable, at least some instances of that statement encoded in an axiom system must be unprovable. But normally these tend to be complicated and not at all typical of what arise in ordinary mathematics. (See page 1167.)

■ **Encodings of arithmetic.** Statements in arithmetic are normally written in terms of $+$, $\times$ and Δ (and logical operations). But it turns out also to be possible to encode such statements in terms of other basic operations. This was for example done by Julia Robinson in 1949 with Δ (or $a + 1$) and $Mod[a, b] == 0$. And in the 1990s Ivan Korec and others showed that it could be done just with $Mod[Binomial[a + b, a], k]$ with $k = 6$ or any product of primes—and that it could not be done with k a prime or prime power. These operations can be thought of as finding elements in nested Pascal's triangle patterns produced by k-color additive cellular automata. Korec showed that finding elements in the nested pattern produced by the $k = 3$ cellular automaton with rule $\{\{1, 1, 3\}, \{2, 2, 1\}, \{3, 3, 2\}\}[\![\#1, \#2]\!]\, \&$ (compare page 886) was also enough.

■ **Page 788 · Infinity.** See page 1162.

■ **Page 789 · Diophantine equations.** If variables appear only linearly, then it is possible to use *ExtendedGCD* (see page 944) to find all solutions to any system of Diophantine equations—or to show that none exist. Particularly from the work of Carl Friedrich Gauss around 1800 there emerged a procedure to find solutions to any quadratic Diophantine equation in two variables—in effect by reduction to the Pell equation $x^2 == a\,y^2 + 1$ (see page 944), and then computing *ContinuedFraction*$[\sqrt{a}\,]$. The minimal solutions can be large; the largest ones for successive coefficient sizes are given below. (With size s coefficients it is for example known that the solutions must always be less than $(14\,s)^{5\,s}$.).

1	$1 + x + x^2 + y - x\,y == 0$	$\{x == 2, y == 7\}$
2	$1 + 2x + 2x^2 + 2y + x\,y - 2y^2 == 0$	$\{x == 687, y == 881\}$
3	$2 + 2x + 3x^2 + 3y + x\,y - y^2 == 0$	$\{x == 545759, y == 1256763\}$
4	$-4 - x + 4x^2 - y - 3x\,y - 4y^2 == 0$	$\{x == 251996202018, y == 174633485974\}$

There is a fairly complete theory of homogeneous quadratic Diophantine equations with three variables, and on the basis of results from the early and mid-1900s a finite procedure should in principle be able to handle quadratic Diophantine equations with any number of variables. (The same is not true of simultaneous quadratic Diophantine equations, and indeed with a vector x of just a few variables, a system $m \cdot x^2 == a$ of such equations could quite possibly show undecidability.)

Ever since antiquity there have been an increasing number of scattered results about Diophantine equations involving higher powers. In 1909 Axel Thue showed that any equation of the form $p[x, y] == a$, where $p[x, y]$ is a homogeneous irreducible polynomial of degree at least 3 (such as $x^3 + x\,y^2 + y^3$) can have only a finite number of integer solutions. (He did this by formally factoring $p[x, y]$ into terms $x - \alpha_i\,y$, then looking at rational approximations to the algebraic numbers α_i.) In 1966 Alan Baker then proved an explicit upper bound on such solutions, thereby establishing that in principle they can be found by a finite search procedure. (The proof is based on having bounds for how close to zero $Sum[\alpha_i\,Log[\alpha_j], i, j]$ can be for independent

algebraic numbers α_k.) His bound was roughly $Exp[(c\,s)^{10^5}]$—but later work in essence reduced this, and by the 1990s practical algorithms were being developed. (Even with a bound of 10^{100}, rational approximations to real number results can quickly give the candidates that need to be tested.)

Starting in the late 1800s and continuing ever since a series of progressively more sophisticated geometric and algebraic views of Diophantine equations have developed. These have led for example to the 1993 proof of Fermat's Last Theorem and to the 1983 Faltings theorem (Mordell conjecture) that the topology of the algebraic surface formed by allowing variables to take on complex values determines whether a Diophantine equation has only a finite number of rational solutions—and shows for example that this is the case for any equation of the form $x^n == a\,y^n + 1$ with $n > 3$. Extensive work has been done since the early 1900s on so-called elliptic curve equations such as $x^2 == a\,y^3 + b$ whose corresponding algebraic surface has a single hole (genus 1). (A crucial feature is that given any two rational solutions to such equations, a third can always be found by a simple geometrical construction.) By the 1990s explicit algorithms for such equations were being developed—with bounds on solutions being found by Baker's method (see above). In the late 1990s similar methods were applied to superelliptic (e.g. $x^n == p[y]$) and hyperelliptic (e.g. $x^2 == p[y]$) equations involving higher powers, and it now at least definitely seems possible to handle any two-variable cubic Diophantine equation with a finite procedure. Knowing whether Baker's method can be made to work for any particular class of equations involves, however, seeing whether certain rather elaborate algebraic constructions can be done—and this may perhaps in general be undecidable. Most likely there are already equations of degree 4 where Baker's method cannot be used—perhaps ones like $x^3 == y^4 + x\,y + a$. But in recent years there have begun to be results by other methods about two-variable Diophantine equations, giving, for example, general upper bounds on the number of possible solutions. And although this has now led to the assumption that all two-variable Diophantine equations will eventually be resolved, based on the results of this book I would not be surprised if in fact undecidability and universality appeared in such equations—even perhaps at degree 4 with fairly small coefficients.

The vast majority of work on Diophantine equations has been for the case of two variables (or three for some homogeneous equations). No clear analog of Baker's method is known beyond two variables, and my suspicion is that with three variables undecidability and universality may already be present even in cubic equations.

As mentioned in the main text, proving that even simple specific Diophantine equations have no solutions can be very difficult. Obvious methods involve for example showing that no solutions exist for real variables, or for variables reduced modulo some n. (For quadratic equations Hasse's Principle implies that if no solutions exist for any n then there are no solutions for ordinary integers—but a cubic like $3x^3 + 4y^3 + 5z^3 == 0$ is a counterexample.) If one can find a bound on solutions—say by Baker's method—then one can also try to show that no values below this bound are actually solutions. Over the history of number theory the sophistication of equations for which proofs of no solutions can be given has gradually increased—though even now it is state of the art to show say that $x == y == 1$ is the only solution to $x^2 == 3y^4 - 2$.

Just as for all sorts of other systems with complex behavior, some idea of overall properties of Diophantine equations can be found on the basis of an approximation of perfect randomness. Writing equations in the form $p[x_1, x_2, ..., x_n] == 0$ the distribution of values of p will in general be complicated (see page 1161), but as a first approximation one can try taking it to be purely random. (Versions of this for large numbers of variables are validated by the so-called circle method from the early 1900s.) If p has total degree d then with $x_i < x$ the values of $Abs[p]$ will range up to about x^d. But with n variables the number of different cases sampled for $x_i < x$ will be x^n. The assumption of perfect randomness then suggests that for $d < n$, more and more cases with $p == 0$ will be seen as x increases, so that the equation will have an infinite number of solutions. For $d > n$, on the other hand, it suggests that there will often be no solutions, and that any solutions that exist will usually be small. In the boundary case $d == n$ it suggests that even for arbitrarily large x an average of about one solution should exist—suggesting that the smallest solution may be very large, and presumably explaining the presence of so many large solutions in the $n = d = 2$ and $n = d = 3$ examples in the main text. Note that even though large solutions may be rare when $d > n$ they must always exist in at least some cases whenever there is undecidability and universality in a class of equations. (See also page 1161.)

If one wants to enumerate all possible Diophantine equations there are many ways to do this, assigning different weights to numbers of variables, and sizes of coefficients and of exponents. But with several ways I have tried, it seems that of the first few million equations, the vast majority have no solutions—and this can in most cases be established by fairly elementary methods that are presumably within Peano arithmetic. When solutions do exist, most are fairly small. But as one continues the enumeration there are increasingly a few equations that seem more and more difficult to handle.

■ **Page 790 · Properties.** (All variables are assumed positive.)

• $2x + 3y == a$. There are $Ceiling[a/2] + Ceiling[2a/3] - (a + 1)$ solutions, the one with smallest x being $\{Mod[2a + 2, 3] + 1, 2 Floor[(2a + 2)/3] - (a + 2)\}$. Linear equations like this were already studied in antiquity. (Compare page 915.)

• $x^2 == y^2 + a$. Writing a in terms of distinct factors as $r\,s$, $\{r + s, r - s\}/2$ gives a solution if it yields integers—which happens when $Abs[a] > 4$ and $Mod[a, 4] \neq 2$.

• $x^2 == ay^2 + 1$ (Pell equation). As discussed on page 944, whenever a is not a perfect square, there are always an infinite number of solutions given in terms of $ContinuedFraction[\sqrt{a}\,]$. Note that even when the smallest solution is not very large, subsequent solutions can rapidly get large. Thus for example when $a = 13$, the second solution is already $\{842401, 233640\}$.

• $x^2 == y^3 + a$ (Mordell equation). First studied in the 1600s, a complete theory of this so-called elliptic curve equation was only developed in the late 1900s—using fairly sophisticated algebraic number theory. The picture below shows as a function of a the minimum x that solves the equation. For $a = 68$, the only solution is $x = 1874$; for $a = 1090$, it is $x = 149651610621$. The density of cases with solutions gradually thins out as a increases (for $0 < a \leq 10000$ there are 2468 such cases). There are always only a finite number of solutions (for $0 < a \leq 10000$ the maximum is 12, achieved for $a = 8900$).

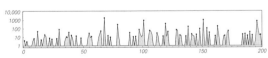

• $x^2 == ay^3 + 1$. Also an elliptic curve equation.

• $x^3 == y^4 + xy + a$. For most values of a (including specifically $a = 1$) the continuous version of this equation defines a surface of genus 3, so there are at most a finite number of integer solutions. (An equation of degree d generically defines a surface of genus $1/2 (d - 1)(d - 2)$.) Note that $x^3 == y^4 + a$ is equivalent to $x^3 == z^2 + a$ by a simple substitution.

• $x^2 == y^5 + ay + 3$. The second smallest solution to $x^2 == y^5 + 5y + 3$ is $\{45531, 73\}$. As for the equations above, there are always at most a finite number of integer solutions.

• $x^3 + y^3 == z^2 + a$. For the homogenous case $a = 0$ the complete solution was found by Leonhard Euler in 1756.

- $x^3 + y^3 == z^3 + a$. No solutions exist when $a = 9n \pm 4$; for $a = n^3$ or $2n^3$ infinite families of solutions are known. Particularly in its less strict form $x^3 + y^3 + z^3 == a$ with x, y, z positive or negative the equation was mentioned in the 1800s and again in the mid-1900s; computer searches for solutions were begun in the 1960s, and by the mid-1990s solutions such as $\{283059965, 2218888517, 2220422932\}$ for the case $a = -30$ had been found. Any solution to the difficult case $x^3 + y^3 == z^3 - 3$ must have $Mod[x, 9] == Mod[y, 9] == Mod[z, 9]$. (Note that $x^2 + y^2 + z^2 == a$ always has solutions except when $a = 4^s (8n + 7)$, as mentioned on page 135.)

- **Large solutions.** A few other 2-variable equations with fairly large smallest solutions are:

  - $x^3 == 3y^3 - xy + 63$: $\{7149, 4957\}$
  - $x^4 == y^3 + 2xy - 2y + 81$: $\{19674, 531117\}$
  - $x^4 == 5y^3 + xy + y - 8x$: $\{69126, 1659072\}$

The equation $x^x y^y == z^z$ is known to have smallest non-trivial solution $\{2985984, 1679616, 4478976\}$.

- **Nearby powers.** One can potentially find integer equations with large solutions but small coefficients by looking say for pairs of integer powers close in value. The pictures below show what happens if one computes x^m and y^n for many x and y, sorts these values, then plots successive differences. The differences are trivially zero when $x = s^n$, $y = s^m$. Often they are large, but surprisingly small ones can sometimes occur (despite various suggestions from the so-called ABC conjecture). Thus, for example, $5853886516781223^3 - 1641843$ is a perfect square, as found by Noam Elkies in 1998. (Another example is $55^5 - 22434^2 == 19$.)

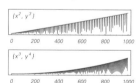
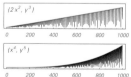

- **Page 791 · Unsolved problems.** Problems in number theory that are simple to state (say in the notation of Peano arithmetic) but that so far remain unsolved include:

  - Is there any odd number equal to the sum of its divisors? (Odd perfect number; 4th century BC) (See page 911.)

  - Are there infinitely many primes that differ by 2? (Twin Prime Conjecture; 1700s?) (See page 909.)

  - Is there a cuboid in which all edges and all diagonals are of integer length? (Perfect cuboid; 1719)

- Is there any even number which is not the sum of two primes? (Goldbach's Conjecture; 1742) (See page 135.)

- Are there infinitely many primes of the form $n^2 + 1$? (Quadratic primes; 1840s?) (See page 1162.)

- Are there infinitely many primes of the form $2^{2^n} + 1$? (Fermat primes; 1844)

- Are there no solutions to $x^m - y^n == 1$ other than $3^2 - 2^3 == 1$? (Catalan's Conjecture; 1844)

- Can every integer not of the form $9n \pm 4$ be written as $a^3 \pm b^3 \pm c^3$? (See note above.)

- How few n^{th} powers need be added to get any given integer? (Waring's Problem; 1770)

(See also Riemann Hypothesis on page 918.)

- **Page 791 · Fermat's Last Theorem.** That $x^n + y^n == z^n$ has no integer solutions for $n > 2$ was suggested by Pierre Fermat around 1665. Fermat proved this for $n = 4$ around 1660; Leonhard Euler for $n = 3$ around 1750. It was proved for $n = 5$ and $n = 7$ in the early 1800s. Then in 1847 Ernst Kummer used ideas of factoring with algebraic integers to prove it for all $n < 37$. Extensions of this method gradually allowed more cases to be covered, and by the 1990s computers had effectively given proofs for all n up to several million. Meanwhile, many connections had been found between the general case and other areas of mathematics—notably the theory of elliptic curves. And finally around 1995, building on extensive work in number theory, Andrew Wiles managed to give a complete proof of the result. His proof is long and complicated, and relies on sophisticated ideas from many areas of mathematics. But while the statement of the proof makes extensive use of concepts from areas like set theory, it seems quite likely that in the end a version of it could be given purely in terms of Peano arithmetic. (By the 1970s it had for example been shown that many classic proofs with a similar character in analytic number theory could at least in principle be carried out purely in Peano arithmetic.)

- **Page 791 · More powerful axioms.** If one looks for example at progressively more complicated Diophantine equations then one can expect that one will find examples where more and more powerful axiom systems are needed to prove statements about them. But my guess is that almost as soon as one reaches cases that cannot be handled by Peano arithmetic one will also reach cases that cannot be handled by set theory or even by still more powerful axiom systems.

Any statement that one can show is independent of the Peano axioms and at least not inconsistent with them one can potentially consider adding as a new axiom. Presumably it is best to add axioms that allow the widest range of new statements to be proved. But I strongly suspect that the set of statements that cannot be proved is somehow sufficiently fragmented that adding a few new axioms will actually make very little difference.

In set theory (see page 1155) a whole sequence of new axioms have historically been added to allow particular kinds of statements to be proved. And for several decades additional so-called large cardinal axioms have been discussed, that in effect state that sets exist larger than any that can be reached with the current axioms of set theory. (As discussed on page 816 any axiom system that is universal must in principle be able to prove any statement that can be proved in any axiom system—but not with the kinds of encodings normally considered in mathematical logic.)

It is notable, however, that if one looks at classic theorems in mathematics many can actually be derived from remarkably weak axioms. And indeed the minimal axioms needed to obtain most of mathematics as it is now practiced are probably much weaker than those on pages 773 and 774.

(If one considers for example theorems about computational issues such as whether Turing machines halt, then it becomes inevitable that to cover more Turing machines one needs more axioms—and to cover all possible machines one needs an infinite set of axioms, that cannot even be generated by any finite set of rules.)

■ **Higher-order logics.** In ordinary predicate—or so-called first-order—logic the objects x that $\forall_x$ and $\exists_x$ range over are variables of the kind used as arguments to functions (or predicates) such as $f[x]$. To set up second-order logic, however, one imagines also being able to use $\forall_f$ and $\exists_f$ where f is a function (say the head of $f[x]$). And then in third-order logic one imagines using $\forall_g$ and $\exists_g$ where g appears in $g[f][x]$.

Early formulations of axiom systems for mathematics made little distinction between first- and second-order logic. The theory of types used in *Principia Mathematica* introduced some distinction, and following the proof of Gödel's Completeness Theorem for first-order logic in 1930 (see page 1152) standard axiom systems for mathematics (as given on pages 773 and 774) began to be reformulated in first-order form, with set theory taking over many of the roles of second-order logic.

In current mathematics, second-order logic is sometimes used at the level of notation, but almost never in its full form beyond. And in fact with any standard computational system it can never be implemented in any explicit way. For even to enumerate theorems in second-order logic is in general impossible for a system like a Turing machine unless one

assumes that an oracle can be added. (Note however that this is possible in Henkin versions of higher-order logic that allow only limited function domains.)

■ **Truth and incompleteness.** In discussions of the foundations of mathematics in the early 1900s it was normally assumed that truth and provability were in a sense equivalent—so that all true statements could in principle be reached by formal processes of proof from fixed axioms (see page 782). Gödel's Theorem showed that there are statements that can never be proved from given axioms. Yet often it seemed inevitable just from the syntactic structure of statements (say as well-formed formulas) that each of them must at some level be either true or false. And this led to the widespread claim that Gödel's Theorem implies the existence of mathematical statements that are true but unprovable—with their negations being false but unprovable. Over the years this often came to be assigned a kind of mystical significance, mainly because it was implicitly assumed that somehow it must still ultimately be possible to know whether any given statement is true or false. But the Principle of Computational Equivalence implies that in fact there are all sorts of statements that simply cannot be decided by any computational process in our universe. So for example, it must in some sense be either true or false that a given Turing machine halts with given input—but according to the Principle of Computational Equivalence there is no finite procedure in our universe through which we can guarantee to know which of these alternatives is correct.

In some cases statements can in effect have default truth values—so that showing that they are unprovable immediately implies, say, that they must be true. An example in arithmetic is whether some integer equation has no solution. For if there were a solution, then given the solution it would be straightforward to give a proof that it is correct. So if it is unprovable that there is no solution, then it follows that there must in fact be no solution. And similarly, if it could be shown for example that Goldbach's Conjecture is unprovable then it would follow that it must be true, for if it were false then there would have to be a specific number which violates it, and this could be proved. Not all statements in mathematics have this kind of default truth value. And thus for example the Continuum Hypothesis in set theory is unprovable but could be either of true or false: it is just independent of the axioms of set theory. In computational systems, showing that it is unprovable that a given Turing machine halts with given input immediately implies that in fact it must not halt. But showing that it is unprovable whether a Turing machine halts with every input (a Π_2 statement in the notation of page 1139) does not immediately imply anything about whether this is in fact true or false.

■ **Page 793 · Generalization in mathematics.** Systems that have evolved from the basic notion of numbers provide a characteristic example of the process of progressive generalization in mathematics. The main such systems and their dates of earliest known reasonably formalized use have been (see also page 901): positive integers (before 10,000 BC), rationals (3000 BC), square roots (2000 BC), other roots (1800 BC), all integers (600 AD, 1600s), decimals (950 AD), complex numbers (1500s, 1800s), polynomials (1591), infinitesimals (1635), algebraic numbers (1744), quaternions (1843), Grassmann algebra (1844), ideals (1844, 1871), octonions (~1845), Boolean algebra (1847), fields (1850s, 1871), matrices (1858), associative algebras (1870), axiomatic real numbers (1872), vectors (1881), transfinite ordinals (1883), transfinite cardinals (1883), operator calculus (1880s), Boolean algebras (1890), algebraic number fields (1893), rings (1897), p-adic numbers (1897), non-Archimedean fields (1899), q-numbers (1926), non-standard integers (1930s), non-standard reals (hyperreals) (1960), interval arithmetic (1968), fuzzy arithmetic (1970s), surreal numbers (1970s). New systems have usually been introduced in connection with extending the domains of particular existing operations. But in almost all cases the systems are set up so as to preserve as many theorems as possible—a notion that was for example made explicit in the Principle of Permanence discussed by George Peacock in 1830 and extended by Hermann Hankel in 1869.

■ **Page 794 · Cellular automaton axioms.** The first 4 axioms are general to one-dimensional cellular automata. The next 8 are specific to rule 110. The final 3 work whenever patterns are embedded in a background of white cells. The universality of rule 110 presumably implies that the axiom system given is universal. (A complete proof would require handling various issues about boundary conditions.)

If the last 2 axioms are dropped any statement can readily be proved true or false essentially just by running rule 110 for a finite number of steps equal to the number of nested ↓ plus ⟨...⟩ in the statement. In practice, a large number of steps can however be required. As an example the statement

$$○ ■ ⇒ (∃_a (∃_b O a ◇ (■ ◇ (■ ◇ (■ ◇ (□ ◇$$
$$(■ ◇ (■ ◇ (■ ◇ (□ ◇ (■ ◇ (■ ◇ (■ ◇ (■ ◇ (■ ◇ (■ ◇ (□ ◇$$
$$(□ ◇ (□ ◇ (■ ◇ (□ ◇ (□ ◇ (■ ◇ (■ ◇ (□ ◇ (■ ◇ (■ ◇ (■ ◇ (■ ◇$$
$$(□ ◇ (□ ◇ (□ ◇ (■ ◇ (□ ◇ (□ ◇ b))))))))))))))))))))))))))))))$$

asserts that a particular localized structure occurs in the evolution of rule 110 from a single black cell. But page 38 shows that this happens for the first time after 2867 steps. (A proof of this without lemmas would probably have to be of length at least 32,910,300.)

The axioms as they are stated apply to any rule 110 evolution, regardless of initial conditions. One can establish that the statement at the bottom on the right cannot be proved either true or false from the axioms by showing that it is true for some initial conditions and false for others. Note from page 279 that the sequence □■■□ cannot occur in rule 110 evolution except as an initial condition. So this means that the statement is false if the initial condition is ■ and true if the initial condition is □■■□.

■ **Practical programs.** Any equivalence between programs in a programming language can be thought of as a theorem. Simple examples in *Mathematica* include:

  First[Prepend[p, q]] === q
  Join[Join[p, q], r] === Join[p, Join[q, r]]
  Partition[Union[p], 1] === Split[Union[p]]

One can set up axiom systems say by combining definitions of programming languages with predicate logic (as done by John McCarthy for LISP in 1963). And for programs whose structure is simple enough it has sometimes been possible to prove theorems useful for optimization or verification. But in the vast majority of cases this has been essentially impossible in practice. And I suspect that this is a reflection of widespread fundamental unprovability. In setting up programs with specific purposes there is inevitably some computational reducibility (see page 828). But I suspect that enough computational irreducibility usually remains to make unprovability common when one asks about all possible forms of behavior of the program.

■ **Page 796 · Rules.** The examples shown here (roughly in order of increasing complexity) correspond respectively to cases (a), (k), (b), (q), (p), (r), (o), (d) on page 798.

■ **Page 797 · Consistency.** Any axiom system that is universal can represent the statement that the system is consistent. But normally such a statement cannot be proved true or false within the system itself. And thus for example Kurt Gödel showed this in 1931 for Peano arithmetic (in his so-called second incompleteness theorem). In 1936, however, Gerhard Gentzen showed that the axioms of set theory imply the consistency of Peano arithmetic (see page 1160). In practical mathematics set theory is always taken to be consistent, but to set up a proof of this would require axioms beyond set theory.

■ **Page 798 · Properties.** For most of the rules shown, there ultimately turn out to be quite easy characterizations of what strings can be produced.

  ■ (a) At step t, the only new string produced is the one containing t black elements.

- (b) All strings of length n containing exactly one black cell are produced—after at most $2n - 1$ steps.

- (c) All strings containing even-length runs of white cells are produced.

- (d) The set of strings produced is complicated. The last length 4 string produced is ▫▫▫■, after 16 steps; the last length 6 one is ▫▫▫▫▫■, after 26 steps.

- (e) All strings that begin with a black element are produced.

- (f) All strings that end with a white element but contain at least one black element, or consist of all white elements ending with black, are produced. Strings of length n take n steps to produce.

- (g) The same strings as in (f) are produced, but now a string of length n with m black elements takes $n + m - 1$ steps.

- (h) All strings appear in which the first run of black elements is of length 1; a string of length n with m black elements appears after $n + m - 1$ steps.

- (i) All strings containing an odd number of black elements are produced; a string of length n with m black cells occurs at step $n + m - 1$.

- (j) All strings that end with a black element are produced.

- (k) Above length 1, the strings produced are exactly those starting with a white element. Those of length n appear after at most $3n - 3$ steps.

- (l) The same strings as in (k) are produced, taking now at most $2n + 1$ steps.

- (m) All strings beginning with a black element are produced, after at most $3n + 1$ steps.

- (n) The set of strings produced is complicated, and seems to include many but not all that do not end with ■▫.

- (o) All strings that do not end in ■▫ are produced.

- (p) All strings are produced, except ones in which every element after the first is white. ▫■■ takes 14 steps.

- (q) All strings are produced, with a string of length n with m white elements taking $n + 2m$ steps.

- (r) All strings are ultimately produced—which is inevitable after the lemmas ■ → ■■ and ■ → □ appear at steps 12 and 13. (See the first rule on page 778.)

■ **Page 800 · Non-standard arithmetic.** Goodstein's result from page 1163 is true for all ordinary integers. But since it is independent of the axioms of arithmetic there must be objects that still satisfy the axioms but for which it is false. It turns out however that any such objects must in effect be infinite. For any set of objects that satisfy the axioms of arithmetic must include all finite ordinary integers, since each of these can be reached just by using Δ repeatedly. And the axioms then turn out to imply that any additional objects must be larger than all these integers—and must therefore be infinite. But for any such truly infinite objects operations like $+$ and $\times$ cannot be computed by finite procedures, making it difficult to describe such objects in an explicit way. Ever since the work of Thoralf Skolem in 1933 non-standard models of arithmetic have been discussed, particularly in the context of ultrafilters and constructs like infinite trees. (See also page 1172.)

■ **Page 800 · Reduced arithmetic.** (See page 1152.) Statements that can be proved with induction but are not provable only with Robinson's axioms are: $x \neq \Delta x$; $x + y == y + x$; $x + (y + z) == (x + y) + z$; $0 + x == x$; $\exists_x (\Delta x + y == z \Rightarrow y \neq z)$; $x \times y == y \times x$; $x \times (y \times z) == (x \times y) \times z$; $x \times (y + z) == x \times y + x \times z$.

■ **Page 800 · Generators and relations.** In the axiom systems of page 773, a single variable can stand for any element—much like a *Mathematica* pattern object such as $x\_$. In studying specific instances of objects like groups one often represents elements as products of constants or generators, and then for example specifies the group by giving relations between these products. In traditional mathematical notation such relations normally look just like ordinary axioms, but in fact the variables that appear in them are now assumed to be literal objects—like x in *Mathematica*—that are generically taken to be unequal. (Compare page 1159.)

■ **Page 801 · Comparison to multiway systems.** Operator systems are normally based on equations, while multiway systems are based on one-way transformations. But for multiway systems where each rule $p \to q$ is accompanied by its reverse $q \to p$, and such pairs are represented say by "AAB" ↔ "BBAA", an equivalent operator system can immediately be obtained either from

    Apply[Equal,
      Map[Fold[#2[#1] &, x, Characters[#]] &, rules, {2}], {1}]

or from (compare page 1172)

    Append[Apply[Equal,
      Map[(Fold[f, First[#], Rest[#]] &)[Characters[#]] &,
      rules, {2}], {1}], f[f[a, b], c] == f[a, f[b, c]]]

where now objects like "A" and "B" are treated as constants—essentially functions with zero arguments. With slightly more effort multiway systems with ordinary one-way rules can also be converted to operator systems. Converting from operator systems to multiway systems is more difficult, though ultimately always possible (see page 1156).

As discussed on page 898, one can set up operator evolution systems similar to symbolic systems (see page 103) that have essentially the same relationship to operator systems as sequential substitution systems do to multiway systems. (See also page 1172.)

■ **Page 802 · Operator systems.** One can represent the possible values of expressions like $f[f[p, q], p]$ by rule numbers analogous to those used for cellular automata. Specifying an operator f (taken in general to have n arguments with k possible values) by giving the rule number u for $f[p, q, ...]$, the rule number for an expression with variables $vars$ can be obtained from

```
With[{m = Length[vars]}, FromDigits[
  Block[{f = Reverse[IntegerDigits[u, k, k^n]][[FromDigits[
    {##}, k] + 1]] &}, Apply[Function[Evaluate[vars], expr],
  Reverse[Array[IntegerDigits[# - 1, k, m] &, k^m]], {1}], k]]
```

■ **Truth tables.** The method of finding results in logic by enumerating all possible combinations of truth values seems to have been rediscovered many times since antiquity. It began to appear regularly in the late 1800s, and became widely known after its use by Emil Post and Ludwig Wittgenstein in the early 1920s.

■ **Page 803 · Proofs of axiom systems.** One way to prove that an axiom system can reproduce all equivalences for a given operator is to show that its axioms can be used to transform any expression to and from a unique standard form. For then one can start with an expression, convert it to standard form, then convert back to any expression that is equivalent. We saw on page 616 that in ordinary logic there is a unique DNF representation in terms of *And*, *Or* and *Not* for any expression, and in 1921 Emil Post used essentially this to give the first proof that an axiom system like the first one on page 773 can completely reproduce all theorems of logic. A standard form in terms of *Nand* can be constructed essentially by direct translation of DNF; other methods can be used for the various other operators shown. (See also page 1175.)

Given a particular axiom system that one knows reproduces all equivalences for a given operator one can tell whether a new axiom system will also work by seeing whether it can be used to derive the axioms in the original system. But often the derivations needed may be very long—as on page 810. And in fact in 1948 Samuel Linial and Emil Post showed that in general the problem is undecidable. They did this in effect by arguing (much as on page 1169) that any multiway system can be emulated by an axiom system of the form on page 803, then knowing that in general it is undecidable whether a multiway system will ever reach some given result. (Note that if an axiom system does manage to reproduce logic in full then as indicated on page 814 its consequences can always be derived by proofs of limited length, if nothing else by using truth tables.)

Since before 1920 it has been known that one way to disprove the validity of a particular axiom system is to show that with $k > 2$ truth values it allows additional operators (see page 805). (Note that even if it works for all finite k this does not establish its validity.) Another way to do this is to look for invariants that should not be present—seeing if there are features that differ between equivalent expressions, yet are always left the same by transformations in the axiom system. (Examples for logic are axiom systems which never change the size of an expression, or which are of the form $\{expr == a\}$ where $Flatten[expr]$ begins or ends with a.)

■ **Junctional calculus.** Expressions are equivalent when $Union[Level[expr, \{-1\}]]$ is the same, and this canonical form can be obtained from the axiom system of page 803 by flattening using $(a \circ b) \circ c == a \circ (b \circ c)$, sorting using $a \circ b == b \circ a$, and removing repeats using $a \circ a == a$. The operator can be either *And* or *Or* (8 or 14). With $k = 3$ there are 9 operators that yield the same results:

$\{13203, 15633, 15663, 16401,$
$17139, 18063, 19539, 19569, 19599\}$

With $k = 4$ there are 3944 such operators (see below). No single axiom can reproduce all equivalences, since such an axiom must of the form $expr == a$, yet $expr$ cannot contain variables other than a, and so cannot for example reproduce $a \circ b = b \circ a$.

■ **Equivalential calculus.** Expressions with variables $vars$ are equivalent if they give the same results for

$Mod[Map[Count[expr, \#, \{-1\}] \&, vars], 2]$

With n variables, there are thus 2^n equivalence classes of expressions (compared to 2^{2^n} for ordinary logic). The operator can be either *Xor* or *Equal* (6 or 9). With $k = 3$ there are no operators that yield the same results; with $k = 4$ $\{458142180, 1310450865, 2984516430, 3836825115\}$ work (see below). The shortest axiom system that works up to $k = 2$ is $\{(a \circ b) \circ a = b\}$. With *modus ponens* as the rule of inference, the shortest single-axiom system that works is known to be $\{(a \circ b) \circ ((c \circ b) \circ (a \circ c))\}$. Note that equivalential calculus describes the smallest non-trivial group, and can be viewed as an extremely minimal model of algebra.

■ **Implicational calculus.** With $k = 2$ the operator can be either 2 or 11 (*Implies*), with $k = 3$ $\{2694, 9337, 15980\}$, and with $k = 4$ any of 16 possibilities. (Operators exist for any k.) No single axiom, at least with up to 7 operators and 4 variables, reproduces all equivalences. With *modus ponens* as the rule of inference, the shortest single-axiom system that works is known to be $\{((a \circ b) \circ c) \circ ((c \circ a) \circ (d \circ a))\}$. Using the method of page 1151 this can be converted to the equational form

$\{((a \circ b) \circ c) \circ ((c \circ a) \circ (d \circ a)) = d \circ d,$
$(a \circ a) \circ b = b, (a \circ b) \circ b = (b \circ a) \circ a\}$

from which the validity of the axiom system in the main text can be established.

■ **Page 803 · Operators on sets.** There is always more than one operator that yields a given collection of equivalences. So for ordinary logic both *Nand* and *Nor* work. And with *k = 4* any of the 12 operators

{1116699, 169585339, 290790239, 459258879,
1090522958, 1309671358, 1430343258, 1515110058,
2184380593, 2575151445, 2863760025, 2986292093}

also turn out to work. One can see why this happens by considering the analogy between operations in logic and operations on sets. As reflected in their traditional notations—and emphasized by Venn diagrams—*And* (∧), *Or* (∨) and *Not* correspond directly to *Intersection* (∩), *Union* (∪) and *Complement*. If one starts from the single-element set *{1}* then applying *Union*, *Intersection* and *Complement* one always gets either *{}* or *{1}*. And applying *Complement[s, Intersection[a, b]]* to these two elements gives the same results and same equivalences as $a \barwedge b$ applied to *True* and *False*. But if one uses instead *s = {1, 2}* then starts with *{1}* and *{2}* one gets any of *{{}, {1}, {2}, {1, 2}}* and in general with *s = Range[n]* one gets any of the 2^n elements in the powerset

    Distribute[Map[{{}, {#}} &, s], List, List, List, Join]

But applying *Complement[s, Intersection[a, b]]* to these elements still always produces the same equivalences as with $a \barwedge b$. Yet now $k = 2^n$. And so one therefore has a representation of Boolean algebra of size 2^n. For ordinary logic based on *Nand* it turns out that there are no other finite representations (though there are other infinite ones). But if one works, say, with *Implies* then there are for example representations of size 3 (see above). And the reason for this is that with *s = {1, 2}* the function *Union[Complement[s, a], b]* corresponding to $a \Rightarrow b$ only ever gets to the 3 elements *{{1}, {2}, {1, 2}}*. Indeed, in general with operators *Implies*, *And* and *Or* one gets to $2^n - 1$ elements, while with operators *Xor* and *Equal* one gets to $2 \char`^ (2 Floor[n/2])$ elements.

(One might think that one could force there only ever to be two elements by adding an axiom like $a == b \lor b == c \lor c == a$. But all this actually does is to force there to be only two objects analogous to *True* and *False*.)

■ **Page 805 · Implementation.** Given an axiom system in the form *{f[a, f[a, a]] = a, f[a, b] = f[b, a]}* one can find rule numbers for the operators *f[x, y]* with *k* values for each variable that are consistent with the axiom system by using

    Module[{c, v}, c = Apply[Function,
    {v = Union[Level[axioms, {-1}]], Apply[And, axioms]}];
    Select[Range[0, k^{k^2} - 1], With[{u = IntegerDigits[#, k, k^2]},
    Block[{f}, f[x_, y_] := u[[-1 - k x - y]];
    Array[c, Table[k, {Length[v]}], 0, And]]] &]]

For *k = 4* this involves checking nearly 16^4 or 4 billion cases, though many of these can often be avoided, for example by using analogs of the so-called Davis-Putnam rules. (In searching for an axiom system for a given operator it is in practice often convenient first to test whether each candidate axiom holds for the operator one wants.)

■ **Page 805 · Properties.** There are k^{k^2} possible forms for binary operators with *k* possible values for each argument. There is always at least some operator that satisfies the constraints of any given axiom system—though in a case like *a = b* it has *k = 1*. Of the 274,499 axiom systems of the form *{... = a}* where *...* involves ∘ up to 6 times, 32,004 allow only operators *{6, 9}*, while 964 allow only *{1, 7}*. The only cases of 2 or less operators that appear with *k = 2* are *{{}, {10}, {12}, {1, 7}, {3, 12}, {5, 10}, {6, 9}, {10, 12}}*. (See page 1174.)

■ **Page 806 · Algebraic systems.** Operator systems can be viewed as algebraic systems of the kind studied in universal algebra (see page 1150). With a single two-argument operator (such as ∘) what one has is in general known as a groupoid (though this term means something different in topology and category theory); with two such operators a ringoid. Given a particular algebraic system, it is sometimes possible—as we saw on page 773—to reduce the number of operators it involves. But the number of systems that have traditionally been studied in mathematics and that are known to require only one 2-argument operator are fairly limited. In addition to basic logic, semigroups and groups, there are essentially only the rather obscure examples of semilattices, with axioms *{a∘(b∘c) = (a∘b)∘c, a∘b = b∘a, a∘a = a}*, central groupoids, with axioms *{(b∘a)∘(a∘c) = b}*, and squags (quasigroup representations of Steiner triple systems), with axioms *{a∘b = b∘a, a∘a = a, a∘(a∘b) = b}* or equivalently *{a∘((b∘(b∘(((c∘c)∘d)∘c)))∘a) = d}*. (Ordinary quasigroups are defined by *{a∘c = b, d∘a = b}* with *c, d* unique for given *a, b*—so that their table is a Latin square; their axioms can be set up with 3 operators as *{a\a∘b = b, a∘b/b = a, a∘(a\b) = b, (a/b)∘b = a}*.)

Pages 773 and 774 indicate that most axiom systems in mathematics involve operators with at most 2 arguments (there are exceptions in geometry). (Constants such as *1* or ∅ can be viewed as 0-argument operators.) One can nevertheless generalize say to polyadic groups, with 3-argument composition and analogs of associativity such as

    f[f[a, b, c], d, e] = f[a, f[b, c, d], e] = f[a, b, f[c, d, e]]

Another example is the cellular automaton axiom system of page 794; see also page 886. (A perhaps important generalization is to have expressions that are arbitrary networks rather than just trees.)

■ **Symbolic systems.** By introducing constants (0-argument operators) and interpreting ∘ as function application one can turn any symbolic system such as $e[x][y] \rightarrow x[x[y]]$ from page 103 into an algebraic system such as $(e \circ a) \circ b = a \circ (a \circ b)$. Doing this for the combinator system from page 711 yields the so-called combinatory algebra $\{((s \circ a) \circ b) \circ c = (a \circ c) \circ (b \circ c), (k \circ a) \circ b = a\}$.

■ **Page 806 · Groups and semigroups.** With k possible values for each variable, the forms of operators allowed by axiom systems for group theory and semigroup theory correspond to multiplication tables for groups and semigroups with k elements. Note that the first group that is not commutative (Abelian) is the group S3 with $k = 6$ elements. The total number of commutative groups with k elements is just

> Apply[Times,
>   Map[PartitionsP[Last[#]] &, FactorInteger[k]]]

(Relabelling of elements makes the number of possible operator forms up to $k!$ times larger.) (See also pages 945, 1153 and 1173.)

■ **Forcing of operators.** Given a particular set of forms for operators one can ask whether an axiom system can be found that will allow these but no others. As discussed in the note on operators on sets on page 1171 some straightforwardly equivalent forms will always be allowed. And unless one limits the number of elements k it is in general undecidable whether a given axiom system will allow no more than a given set of forms. But even with fixed k it is also often not possible to force a particular set of forms. And as an example of this one can consider commutative group theory. The basic axioms for this allow forms of operators corresponding to multiplication tables for all possible commutative groups (see note above). So to force particular forms of operators would require setting up axioms satisfied only by specific commutative groups. But it turns out that given the basic axioms for commutative group theory any non-trivial set of additional axioms can always be reduced to a single axiom of the form $a^n == 1$ (where exponentiation is repeated application of ∘). Yet even given a particular number of elements k, there can be several distinct groups satisfying $a^n == 1$ for a given exponent n. (The groups can be written as products of cyclic ones whose orders correspond to the possible factors of n.) (Something similar is also known in principle to be true for general groups, though the hierarchy of axioms in this case is much more complicated.)

■ **Model theory.** In model theory each form of operator that satisfies the constraints of a given axiom system is called a model of that axiom system. If there is only one inequivalent model the axiom system is said to be categorical—a notion discussed for example by Richard Dedekind in 1887. The Löwenheim-Skolem theorem from 1915 implies that any axiom system must always have a countable model. (For an operator system such a model can have elements which are simply equivalence classes of expressions equal according to the axioms.) So this means that even if one tries to set up an axiom system to describe an uncountable set—such as real numbers—there will inevitably always be extra countable models. Any axiom system that is incomplete must always allow more than one model. The model intended when the axiom system was originally set up is usually called the standard model; others are called non-standard. In arithmetic non-standard models are obscure, as discussed on page 1169. In analysis, however, Abraham Robinson pointed out in 1960 that one can potentially have useful non-standard models, in which there are explicit infinitesimals—much along the lines suggested in the original work on calculus in the late 1600s.

■ **Pure equational logic.** Proofs in operator systems always rely on certain underlying rules about equality, such as the equivalence of $u == v$ and $v == u$, and of $u == v$ and $u == v /. a \rightarrow b$. And as Garrett Birkhoff showed in 1935, any equivalence between expressions that holds for all possible forms of operator must have a finite proof using just these rules. (This is the analog of Gödel's Completeness Theorem from page 1152 for pure predicate logic.) But as soon as one introduces actual axioms that constrain the operators this is no longer true—and in general it can be undecidable whether or not a particular equivalence holds.

■ **Multiway systems.** One can use ideas from operator systems to work out equivalences in multiway systems (compare page 1169). One can think of concatenation of strings as being an operator, in terms of which a string like "ABB" can be written $(a \circ b) \circ b$. (The arguments to ∘ should strictly be distinct constants, but no equivalences are lost by allowing them to be general variables.) Assuming that the rules for a multiway system come in pairs $p \rightarrow q$, $q \rightarrow p$, like "AB" → "AAA", "AAA" → "AB", these can be written as statements about operators, like $a \circ b = (a \circ a) \circ a$. The basic properties of concatenation then also imply that $(a \circ b) \circ c = a \circ (b \circ c)$. And this means that the possible forms for the operator ∘ correspond to possible semigroups. Given a particular such semigroup satisfying axioms derived from a multiway system, one can see whether the operator representations of particular strings are equal—and if they are not, then it follows that the strings can never be reached from each other through evolution of the multiway system. (Such operator representations are a rough analog for multiway systems of truth tables.) As an example, with the multiway system "AB" ↔ "BA" some possible forms of operators are shown below. (In this case these are the commutative semigroups. With $k = 2$, elements 6 out of the total of 8 possible semigroups appear; with $k = 3$, 63 out of 113, and with $k = 4$, 1140 out of 3492—all as shown on page 805.) (See also page 952.)

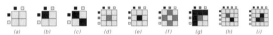
(a)   (b)   (c)   (d)   (e)   (f)   (g)   (h)   (i)

Taking ∘ to be each of these operators, one can work out a representation for any given string like "ABAA" by for example constructing the expression $((a∘b)∘a)∘a$ and finding its value for each of the k^2 possible pairs of values of a and b. Then for each successive operator, the sets of strings where the arrays of values are the same are as shown below.

Ultimately the sets of strings equivalent under the multiway system are exactly those containing particular numbers of black and white elements. But as the pictures above suggest, only some of the distinctions between sets of strings are ever captured when any specific form for the operator is used.

Just as for operator systems, any bidirectional multiway system will allow a certain set of operators. (When there are multiple rules in the multiway system, tighter constraints are obtained by combining them with *And*.) And the pattern of results for simple multiway systems is roughly similar to those on page 805 for operator systems—although, for example, the associativity of concatenation makes it impossible for example to get the operators for *Nand* and basic logic.

■ **Page 806 · Logic in languages.** Human languages always seem to have single words for AND, OR and NOT. A few have distinct words for OR and XOR: examples are Latin with *vel* and *aut* and Finnish with *vai* and *tai*. NOR is somewhat rare, though Dutch has *noch* and Old English *ne*. (Modern English has only the compound form *neither ... nor*.) But remarkably enough it appears that no ordinary language has a single word for NAND. The reason is not clear. Most people seem to find it difficult to think in terms of NAND (NAND is for example not associative, but then neither is NOR). And NAND on the face of it rarely seems useful in everyday situations.

But perhaps these are just reflections of the historical fact that NAND has never been familiar from ordinary languages.

Essentially all computer languages support AND, OR and NOT as ways to combine logical statements; many support AND, OR and XOR as bitwise operations. Circuit design languages like Verilog and VHDL also support NAND, NOR and XNOR. (NAND is the operation easiest to implement with CMOS FETs—the transistors used in most current chips; it was also implemented by pentode vacuum tubes.) Circuit designers sometimes use the linguistic construct "*p* nand *q*".

The Laws of Form presented by George Spencer Brown in 1969 introduce a compact symbolic notation for NAND with any number of arguments and in effect try to develop a way of discussing NAND and reasoning directly in terms of it. (The axioms normally used are essentially the Sheffer ones from page 773.)

■ **Page 806 · Properties.** Page 813 lists theorems satisfied by each function. *{0, 1, 6, 7, 8, 9, 14, 15}* are commutative (orderless) so that $a∘b = b∘a$, while *{0, 6, 8, 9, 10, 12, 14, 15}* are associative (flat), so that $a∘(b∘c) = (a∘b)∘c$. (Compare page 886.)

■ **Notations.** Among those in current use are (highlighted ones are supported directly in *Mathematica*):

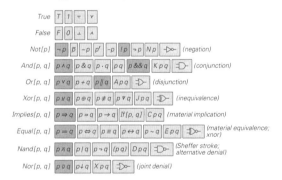

The grouping of terms is normally inferred from precedence of operators (typically ordered $==, ¬, \barπ, ∧, \underline∨, \baru, ∨, ⇒$), or explicitly indicated by parentheses, function brackets, or sometimes nested underbars or dots. So-called Polish notation given second-to-last above avoids all explicit delimiters (see page 896).

■ **Page 807 · Universal logical functions.** The fact that combinations of *Nand* or *Nor* are adequate to reproduce any logical function was noted by Charles Peirce around 1880, and became widely known after the work of Henry Sheffer in 1913. (See also page 1096.) *Nand* and *Nor* are the only 2-input functions universal in this sense. (*{Equal}* can for example reproduce only functions {9, 10, 12, 15}, {Implies} only functions {10, 11, 12, 13, 14, 15}, and {Equal, Implies} only functions {8, 9, 10, 11, 12, 13, 14, 15}.) For 3-input functions, corresponding to elementary cellular automaton rules, 56 of the 256 possibilities turn out to be universal. Of these, 6 are straightforward generalizations of *Nand* and *Nor*. Other universal functions include rules 1, 45 and 202 (*If[a == 1, b, c]*), but not 30, 60 or 110. For large *n* roughly 1/4 of all *n*-input functions are universal. (See also page 1175.)

■ **Page 808 · Searching for logic.** For axiom systems of the form {... = a} one finds:

	2 variables					3 variables				
number of ∘	2	3	4	5	6	2	3	4	5	6
total systems	4	16	80	448	2688	54	405	3402	30618	288684
allow ⊼	0	5	44	168	1532	0	9	124	744	8764
allow only ⊼ etc. for k=2	0	0	2	12	76	0	0	12	84	868
allow only ⊼ etc. for k≤3	0	0	0	0	0	0	0	8	16	296
allow only ⊼ etc. for k≤4	0	0	0	0	0	0	0	0	0	100

{((b∘b)∘a)∘(a∘b) = a} allows the k = 3 operator 15552 for which the NAND theorem (p∘p)∘q = (p∘q)∘q is not true. {(((b∘a)∘c)∘a)∘(a∘c) = a} allows the k = 4 operator 95356335 for which even p∘q = q∘p is not true. Of the 100 cases that remain when k = 4, the 25 inequivalent under renaming of variables and reversing arguments of ∘ are

{(b∘(b∘(a∘a)))∘(a∘(b∘c)),
 (b∘(b∘(a∘a)))∘(a∘(c∘b)), (b∘(b∘(a∘b)))∘(a∘(b∘c)),
 (b∘(b∘(a∘b)))∘(a∘(c∘b)), (b∘(b∘(a∘c)))∘(a∘(c∘b)),
 (b∘(b∘(b∘a)))∘(a∘(b∘c)), (b∘(b∘(b∘a)))∘(a∘(c∘b)),
 (b∘(b∘(c∘a)))∘(a∘(b∘c)), (b∘((a∘b)∘b))∘(a∘(b∘c)),
 (b∘((a∘b)∘b))∘(a∘(c∘b)), (b∘((a∘c)∘b))∘(a∘(c∘b)),
 ((b∘c)∘a)∘(b∘(a∘(b∘a∘b))), ((b∘c)∘a)∘(b∘(b∘(a∘c))),
 ((b∘c)∘a)∘(b∘((a∘a)∘b)), ((b∘c)∘a)∘(b∘((a∘b)∘b)),
 ((b∘c)∘a)∘(b∘((a∘c)∘b)), ((b∘c)∘a)∘(b∘((b∘a)∘b)),
 ((b∘c)∘a)∘(b∘((c∘a)∘b)), ((b∘c)∘a)∘(c∘(c∘(a∘b))),
 ((b∘c)∘a)∘(c∘(c∘(a∘c))), ((b∘c)∘a)∘(c∘((a∘a)∘c)),
 ((b∘c)∘a)∘(c∘((a∘b)∘c)), ((b∘c)∘a)∘(c∘((a∘c)∘c)),
 ((b∘c)∘a)∘(c∘((b∘a)∘c)), ((b∘c)∘a)∘(c∘((c∘a)∘c))}

Of these I was able in 2000—using automated theorem proving—to show that the ones given as (g) and (h) in the main text are indeed axiom systems for logic. (My proof essentially as found by Waldmeister is given on page 810.)

If one adds a∘b = b∘a to any of the other 23 axioms above then in all cases the resulting axiom system can be shown to reproduce logic. But from any of the 23 axioms on their own I have never managed to derive p∘q = q∘p. Indeed, it seems difficult to derive much at all from them—though for example I have found a fairly short proof of (p∘p)∘(p∘q) = p from {(b∘(b∘(b∘a)))∘(a∘(b∘c)) = a}.

It turns out that the first of the 25 axioms allows the k = 6 operator 18857605376550023865453442036 and so cannot be logic. Axioms 3, 19 and 23 allow similar operators, leaving 19 systems as candidate axioms for logic.

It has been known since the 1940s that any axiom system for logic must have at least one axiom that involves more than 2 variables. The results above now show that 3 variables suffice. And adding more variables does not seem to help. The smallest axiom systems with more than 3 variables that work up to k = 2 are of the form {(((b∘c)∘d)∘a)∘(a∘d) = a}. All turn out also to work at k = 3, but fail at k = 4. And with 6 NANDs (as in (g) and (h)) no system of the form {... = a} works even up to k = 4.

For axiom systems of the form {... = a, a∘b = b∘a}:

	2 variables					3 variables				
number of ∘	4	5	6	7	8	4	5	6	7	8
total systems	4	16	80	448	2688	54	405	3402	30618	288684
allow ⊼	0	5	44	168	1532	0	9	124	744	8764
allow only ⊼ etc. for k=2	0	4	20	160	748	0	8	80	736	6248
allow only ⊼ etc. for k≤3	0	0	0	64	16	0	0	32	416	2752
allow only ⊼ etc. for k≤4	0	0	0	48	16	0	0	32	384	2368

With 2 variables the inequivalent cases that remain are
  {(a∘b)∘(a∘(b∘(a∘b))),
   (a∘b)∘(a∘(b∘(b∘b))), (a∘(b∘b))∘(a∘(b∘(b∘b)))}
but all of these allow the k = 6 operator
  1885760537655125429738480884
and so cannot correspond to basic logic. With 3 variables, all 32 cases with 6 NANDs are equivalent to (a∘b)∘(a∘(b∘c)), which is axiom system (f) in the main text. With 7 NANDs there are 8 inequivalent cases:
  {(a∘a)∘(b∘(b∘(a∘c))), (a∘b)∘(a∘(b∘(a∘b))), (a∘b)∘(a∘(b∘(a∘c))),
   (a∘b)∘(a∘(b∘(b∘b))), (a∘b)∘(a∘(b∘(b∘c))),
   (a∘b)∘(a∘(b∘(c∘c))), (a∘b)∘(a∘(c∘(a∘c))), (a∘b)∘(a∘(c∘(c∘c)))}
and of these at least 5 and 6 can readily be proved to be axioms for logic.

Any axiom system must consist of equivalences valid for the operator it describes. But the fact that there are fairly few short such equivalences for *Nand* (see page 818) implies that there can be no axiom system for *Nand* with 6 or less NANDs except the ones discussed above.

■ **Two-operator logic.** If one allows two operators then one can get standard logic if one of these operators is forced to be *Not* and the other is forced to be *And*, *Or* or *Implies*—or in fact any of operators 1, 2, 4, 7, 8, 11, 13, 14 from page 806.

A simple example that allows *Not* and either *And* or *Or* is the Robbins axiom system from page 773. Given the first two axioms (commutativity and associativity) it turns out that no shorter third axiom will work in this case (though ones such as f[g[f[a, g[f[a, b]]]], g[g[b]]] = b of the same size do work).

Much as in the single-operator case, to reproduce logic two pairs of operators must be allowed for k = 2, none for k = 3, 12 for k = 4, and so on. Among single axioms, the shortest that works up to k = 2 is (¬ (¬ (¬ b ∨ a) ∨ ¬ (a ∨ b))) = a. The shortest that works up to $k = 3$ is $(\neg(\neg(a \vee b) \vee \neg b) \vee \neg(\neg a \vee a)) = b$. It is known, however, that at least 3 variables must appear in order to reproduce logic, and an example of a single axiom with 4 variables that has been found recently to work is $\{(\neg(\neg(c \vee b) \vee \neg a) \vee \neg(\neg(\neg d \vee d) \vee \neg a \vee c)) = a\}$.

■ **Page 808 · History.** (See page 1151.) (c) was found by Henry Sheffer in 1913; (e) by Carew Meredith in 1967. Until this book, very little work appears to have been done on finding short axioms for logic in terms of *Nand*. Around 1949 Meredith found the axiom system

$\{(a \circ (b \circ c)) \circ (a \circ (b \circ c)) =$
$\quad ((c \circ a) \circ a) \circ ((b \circ a) \circ a), (a \circ a) \circ (b \circ a) = a\}$

In 1967 George Spencer Brown found (see page 1173)

$\{(a \circ a) \circ ((b \circ b) \circ b) = a,$
$\quad a \circ (b \circ c) = (((c \circ c) \circ a) \circ ((b \circ b) \circ a)) \circ (((c \circ c) \circ a) \circ ((b \circ b) \circ a))\}$

and in 1969 Meredith also gave the system

$\{a \circ (b \circ (a \circ c)) = a \circ (b \circ (b \circ c)), (a \circ a) \circ (b \circ a) = a, a \circ b = b \circ a\}$

■ **Page 812 · Theorem distributions.** The picture below shows which of the possible theorems from page 812 hold for each of the numbered standard mathematical theories from page 805. The theorem close to the right-hand end valid in many cases is $(p \circ p) \circ p = p \circ (p \circ p)$. The lack of regularity in this picture can be viewed as a sign that it is difficult to tell which theorems hold, and thus in effect to do mathematics.

■ **Page 814 · Multivalued logic.** As noted by Jan Łukasiewicz and Emil Post in the early 1920s, it is possible to generalize ordinary logic to allow k values $Range[0, 1, 1/(k-1)]$, say with 0 being *False*, and 1 being *True*. Standard operations in logic can be generalized as $Not[a\_] = 1 - a$, $And[a\_, b\_] = Min[a, b]$, $Or[a\_, b\_] = Max[a, b]$, $Xor[a\_, b\_] = Abs[a - b]$, $Equal[a\_, b\_] = 1 - Abs[a - b]$, $Implies[a\_, b\_] = 1 - UnitStep[a - b](a - b)$. An alternative generalization for *Not* is $Not[a\_] := Mod[(k - 1)a + 1, k]/(k - 1)$. The function $Nand[a\_, b\_] := Not[And[a, b]]$ used in the main text turns out to be universal for any k. Axiom systems can be set up for multivalued logic, but they are presumably more complicated than for ordinary $k = 2$ logic. (Compare page 1171.)

The idea of intermediate truth values has been discussed intermittently ever since antiquity. Often—as in the work of George Boole in 1847—a continuum of values between 0 and 1 are taken to represent probabilities of events, and this is the basis for the field of fuzzy logic popular since the 1980s.

■ **Page 814 · Proof lengths in logic.** As discussed on page 1170 equivalence between expressions can always be proved by transforming to and from canonical form. But with n

variables a DNF-type canonical form can be of size 2^n—and can take up to at least 2^n proof steps to reach. And indeed if logic proofs could in general be done in a number of steps that increases only like a polynomial in n this would mean that the NP-complete problem of satisfiability could also be solved in this number of steps, which seems very unlikely (see page 768).

In practice it is usually extremely difficult to find the absolute shortest proof of a given logic theorem—and the exact length will depend on what axiom system is used, and what kinds of steps are allowed. In fact, as mentioned on page 1155, if one does not allow lemmas some proofs perhaps have to become exponentially longer. The picture below shows in each of the axiom systems from page 808 the lengths of the shortest proofs found by a version of Waldmeister (see page 1158) for all 582 equivalences (see page 818) that involve two variables and up to 3 NANDs on either side.

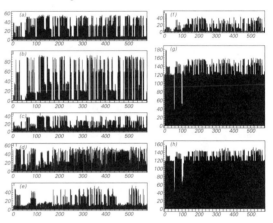

The longest of these are respectively $\{57, 94, 42, 57, 55, 53, 179, 157\}$ and occur for theorems

$\{(((a \barwedge a) \barwedge b) \barwedge b) = (((a \barwedge b) \barwedge a) \barwedge a),$
$\quad (a \barwedge (a \barwedge (a \barwedge a))) = (a \barwedge ((a \barwedge b) \barwedge b)), (((a \barwedge a) \barwedge a) \barwedge a) =$
$\quad (((a \barwedge a) \barwedge b) \barwedge a), (((a \barwedge a) \barwedge b) \barwedge b) = (((a \barwedge b) \barwedge a) \barwedge a),$
$\quad (a \barwedge ((b \barwedge b) \barwedge a)) = (b \barwedge ((a \barwedge a) \barwedge b)), ((a \barwedge a) \barwedge a) = ((b \barwedge b) \barwedge b),$
$\quad ((a \barwedge a) \barwedge a) = ((b \barwedge b) \barwedge b), ((a \barwedge a) \barwedge a) = ((b \barwedge b) \barwedge b)\}$

Note that for systems that do not already have it as an axiom, most theorems use the lemma $(a \barwedge b) = (b \barwedge a)$ which takes respectively $\{6, 1, 8, 49, 8, 1, 119, 118\}$ steps to prove.

■ **Page 818 · NAND theorems.** The total number of expressions with n NANDs and s variables is: $Binomial[2n, n] s^{n+1}/(n+1)$ (see page 897). With $s = 2$ and n from 0 to 7 the number of these *True* for all values of variables is $\{0, 0, 4, 0, 80, 108, 2592, 7296\}$, with the first few distinct ones being (see page 781)

$\{(p \barwedge p) \barwedge p, (((p \barwedge p) \barwedge p) \barwedge p) \barwedge p, (((p \barwedge p) \barwedge p) \barwedge q) \barwedge q\}$

The number of unequal expressions obtained is
{2, 3, 3, 7, 10, 15, 12, 16} (compare page 1096), with the first
few distinct ones being

$$\{p,\ p\barwedge p,\ p\barwedge q,\ (p\barwedge p)\barwedge p,\ (p\barwedge q)\barwedge p,\ (p\barwedge p)\barwedge q\}$$

Most of the axioms from page 808 are too long to appear
early in the list of theorems. But those of system (d) appear at
positions {3, 15, 568} and those of (e) at {855, 4}.

(See also page 1096.)

■ **Page 819 · Finite axiomatizability.** It is known that the axiom
systems (such as Peano arithmetic and set theory) given with
axiom schemas on pages 773 and 774 can be set up only with
an infinite number of individual axioms. But because such
axioms can be described by schemas they must all have
similar forms, so that even though the definition in the main
text suggests that each corresponds to an interesting theorem
these theorems are not in a sense independently interesting.
(Note that for example the theory of specifically finite groups
cannot be set up with a finite number even of schemas—or
with any finite procedure for checking whether a given
candidate axiom should be included.)

■ **Page 820 · Empirical metamathematics.** One can imagine a
network representing some field of mathematics, with nodes
corresponding to theorems and connections corresponding to
proofs, gradually getting filled in as the field develops.
Typical rough characterizations of mathematical results—
independent of their detailed history—might then end up
being something like the following:

- lemma: short theorem appearing at an intermediate stage
  in a proof

- corollary: theorem connected by a short proof to an
  existing theorem

- easy theorem: theorem having a short proof

- difficult theorem: theorem having a long proof

- elegant theorem: theorem whose statement is short and
  somewhat unique

- interesting theorem (see page 817): theorem that cannot
  readily be deduced from earlier theorems, but is well
  connected

- boring theorem: theorem for which there are many others
  very much like it

- useful theorem: theorem that leads to many new ones

- powerful theorem: theorem that substantially reduces the
  lengths of proofs needed for many others

- surprising theorem: theorem that appears in an otherwise
  sparse part of the network of theorems

- deep theorem: theorem that connects components of the
  network of theorems that are otherwise far away

- important theorem: theorem that allows a broad new area
  of the network to be reached.

The picture below shows the network of theorems associated
with Euclid's *Elements*. Each stated theorem is represented by
a node connected to the theorems used in its stated proof.
(Only the shortest connection from each theorem is shown
explicitly.) The axioms (postulates and common notions) are
given in the first column on the left, and successive columns
then show theorems with progressively longer proofs.
(Explicit annotations giving theorems used in proofs were
apparently added to editions of Euclid only in the past few
centuries; the picture below extends the usual annotations in
a few cases.) The theorem with the longest proof is the one
that states that there are only five Platonic solids.

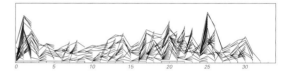

■ **Speedups in other systems.** Multiway systems are almost
unique in being able to be sped up just by adding "results"
already derived in the multiway system. In other systems,
there is no such direct way to insert such results into the rules
for the system.

■ **Character of mathematics.** Since at least the early 1900s
several major schools of thought have existed:

- *Formalism* (e.g. David Hilbert): Mathematics studies formal
  rules that have no intrinsic meaning, but are relevant
  because of their applications or history.

- *Platonism* (e.g. Kurt Gödel): Mathematics involves trying
  to discover the properties of a world of ideal mathematical
  forms, of which we in effect perceive only shadows.

- *Logicism* (e.g. Gottlob Frege, Bertrand Russell):
  Mathematics is an elaborate application of logic, which is
  itself fundamental.

- *Intuitionism* (e.g. Luitzen Brouwer): Mathematics is a
  precise way of handling ideas that are intuitive to the
  human mind.

The results in this book establish a new point of view
somewhere between all of these.

■ **Invention versus discovery in mathematics.** One generally
considers things invented if they are created in a somewhat
arbitrary way, and discovered if they are identified by what

seems like a more inexorable process. The results of this section thus strongly suggest that the basic directions taken by mathematics as currently practiced should mostly be considered invented, not discovered. The new kind of science that I describe in this book, however, tends to suggest forms of mathematics that involve discovery rather than invention.

■ **Ordering of constructs.** One can deduce some kind of ordering among standard mathematical constructs by seeing how difficult they are to implement in various systems—such as cellular automata, Turing machines and Diophantine equations. My experience has usually been that addition is easiest, followed by multiplication, powers, Fibonacci numbers, perfect numbers and then primes. And perhaps this is similar to the order in which these constructs appeared in the early history of mathematics. (Compare page 640.)

■ **Mathematics and the brain.** A possible reason for some constructs to be more common in mathematics is that they are somehow easier for human brains to manipulate. Typical human experience makes small positive integers and simple shapes familiar—so that all human brains are at least well adapted to such constructs. Yet of the limited set of people exposed to higher mathematics, different ones often seem to think in bizarrely different ways. Some think symbolically, presumably applying linguistic capabilities to algebraic or other representations. Some think more visually, using mechanical experience or visual memory. Others seem to think in terms of abstract patterns, perhaps sometimes with implicit analogies to musical harmony. And still others—including some of the purest mathematicians—seem to think directly in terms of constraints, perhaps using some kind of abstraction of everyday geometrical reasoning.

In the history of mathematics there are many concepts that seem to have taken surprisingly long to emerge. And sometimes these are ones that people still find hard to grasp. But they often later seem quite simple and obvious—as with many examples in this book.

It is sometimes thought that people understand concepts in mathematics most easily if they are presented in the order in which they arose historically. But for example the basic notion of programmability seems at some level quite easy even for young children to grasp—even though historically it appeared only recently.

In designing *Mathematica* one of my challenges was to use constructs that are at least ultimately easy for people to understand. Important criteria for this in my experience include specifying processes directly rather than through constraints, the explicitness in the representation of input and output, and the existence of small, memorable,

examples. Typically it seems more difficult for people to understand processes in which larger numbers of different things happen in parallel. (Notably, *FoldList* normally seems more difficult to understand than *NestList*.) Tree structures such as *Mathematica* expressions are fairly easy to understand. But I have never found a way to make general networks similarly easy, and I am beginning to suspect that they may be fundamentally difficult for brains to handle.

■ **Page 821 · Frameworks.** Symbolic integration was in the past done by a collection of ad hoc methods like substitution, partial fractions, integration by parts, and parametric differentiation. But in *Mathematica* *Integrate* is now almost completely systematic, being based on structure theorems for finding general forms of integrals, and on general representations in terms of *MeijerG* and other functions. (In recognizing, for example, whether an expression involving a parameter can have a pole undecidable questions can in principle come up, but they seem rare in practice.) Proofs are essentially always still done in an ad hoc way—with a few minor frameworks like enumeration of cases, induction, and proof by contradiction (reductio ad absurdum) occasionally being used. (More detailed frameworks are used in specific areas; an example are ϵ-δ arguments in calculus.) But although still almost unknown in mainstream mathematics, methods from automated theorem proving (see page 1157) are beginning to allow proofs of many statements that can be formulated in terms of operator systems to be found in a largely systematic way (e.g. page 810). (In the case of Euclidean geometry—which is a complete axiom system— algebraic methods have allowed complete systematization.) In general, the more systematic the proofs in a particular area become, the less relevant they will typically seem compared to the theorems that they establish as true.

Intelligence in the Universe

■ **Page 822 · Animism.** Attributing abstract human qualities such as intelligence to systems in nature is a central part of the idea of animism, discussed on page 1195.

■ **Page 822 · The weather.** Almost all the intricate variations of atmospheric temperature, pressure, velocity and humidity that define the weather we see are in the end determined by fairly simple underlying rules for fluid behavior. (Details of phase changes in water are also important, as are features of topography, ocean currents, solar radiation levels and presumably land use.) Our everyday personal attempts to predict the weather tend to be based just on looking at local conditions and then recalling what happened when we saw these conditions before. But ever since the mid-1800s synoptic weather maps of large areas have been available that summarize conditions in terms of features like fronts and cyclones. And predictions made by looking at simple trends in these features tend at least in some situations to work fairly well. Starting in the 1940s more systematic efforts to predict weather were made by using computers to run approximations to fluid equations. The approximations have improved as larger computers have become available. But even though millions of discrete samples are now used, each one typically still represents something much larger then for example a single cloud. Yet ever since the 1970s, the approach has had at least some success in making predictions up to several days in advance. But although there has been gradual improvement it is usually assumed that—like in the Lorenz equations—the phenomenon of chaos must make forecasts that are based on even slightly different initial measurements eventually diverge exponentially (see page 972). Almost certainly this does indeed happen in at least some critical situations. But it seems that over most of a typical weather map there is no such sensitivity—so that in the end the difficulties of weather prediction are probably much more a result of computational irreducibility and of the sophisticated kinds of computations that the Principle of Computational Equivalence implies should often occur even in simple fluids.

■ **Page 822 · Defining intelligence.** The problem of defining intelligence independent of specific education and culture has been considered important for human intelligence testing since the beginning of the 1900s. Charles Spearman suggested in 1904 that there might be a general intelligence factor (usually called g) associated with all intellectual tasks. Its nature was never very clear, but it was thought that its value could be inferred from performance on puzzles involving numbers, words and pictures. By the 1980s, however, there was increasing emphasis on the idea that different types of human tasks require different types of intelligence. But throughout the 1900s psychologists occasionally tried to give general definitions of intelligence—initially usually in terms of learning or problem-solving capabilities; later more often in terms of adaptation to complex environments.

Particularly starting at the end of the 1800s there was great interest in whether animals other than humans could be considered intelligent. The most common general criterion used was the ability to show behavior based on conceptual or abstract thinking rather than just simple instincts. More specific criteria also included ability to use tools, plan actions, use language, solve logical problems and do arithmetic. But by the mid-1900s it became increasingly clear that it was very difficult to interpret actual observations—

and that unrecognized cues could for example often account for the behavior seen.

When the field of artificial intelligence began in the mid-1900s there was some discussion of appropriate definitions of intelligence (see page 1099). Most focused on mathematical or other problem solving, though some—such as the Turing test—emphasized everyday conversation with humans.

■ **Page 823 · Mimesis.** The notion of inanimate analogs of memory—such as impressions in wax—was discussed for example by Plato in antiquity.

■ **Page 823 · Defining life.** Greek philosophers such as Aristotle defined life by the presence of some form of soul, and the idea that there must be a single unique feature associated with life has always remained popular. In the 1800s the notion of a "life force" was discussed—and thought to be associated perhaps with chemical properties of protoplasm, and perhaps with electricity. The discovery from the mid-1800s to the mid-1900s of all sorts of elaborate chemical processes in living systems led biologists often to view life as defined by its ability to maintain fixed overall structure while achieving chemical functions such as metabolism. When the Second Law of Thermodynamics was formulated in the mid-1800s living systems were usually explicitly excluded (see page 1021), and by the 1930s physicists often considered local entropy decrease a defining feature of life. Among geneticists and soon mathematicians self-reproduction was usually viewed as the defining feature of life, and following the discovery of the structure of DNA in 1953 it came to be widely believed that the presence of self-replicating elements must be fundamental to life. But the recognition that just copying information is fairly easy led in the 1960s to definitions of life based on the large amounts of information encoded in its genetic material, and later to ones based on the apparent difficulty of deriving this information (see page 1069). And perhaps in part reacting to my discoveries about cellular automata it became popular in the 1980s to mention adaptation and essential interdependence of large numbers of different kinds of parts as further necessary characteristics of life. Yet in the end every single general definition that has been given both includes systems that are not normally considered alive, and excludes ones that are. (Self-reproduction, for example, suggests that flames are alive, but mules are not.)

One of the features that defines life on Earth is the presence of DNA, or at least RNA. But as one looks at smaller molecules they become less specific to living systems. It is sometimes thought significant that living systems perpetuate the use of only one chirality of molecules, but actually this can quite easily be achieved by various forms of non-chemical input without life.

The Viking spacecraft that landed on Mars in the 1970s tried specific tests for life on soil samples—essentially whether gases were generated when nutrients were added, whether this behavior changed if the samples were first heated, and whether molecules common in terrestrial life were present. The tests gave confusing results, presumably having to do not with life, but rather with details of martian soil chemistry

■ **Origin of life.** Fossil traces of living cells have been found going back more than 3.8 billion years—to perhaps as little as 700 million years after the formation of the Earth. There were presumably simpler forms of life that preceded the advent of recognizable cells, and even if life arose more than once it is unlikely that evidence of this would remain. (One sees many branches in the fossil record—such as organisms with dominant symmetries other than fivefold—but all seem to have the same ancestry.)

From antiquity until the 1700s it was widely believed that smaller living organisms arise spontaneously in substances like mud, and this was not finally disproved until the 1860s. Controversy surrounding the theory of biological evolution in the late 1800s dissuaded investigation of non-biological origins for life, and at the end of the 1800s it was for example suggested that life on Earth might have arisen from spores of extraterrestrial origin. In the 1920s the idea developed that electrical storms in the atmosphere of the early Earth could lead to production of molecules seen in living systems—and this was confirmed by the experiment of Stanley Miller and Harold Urey in 1953. The molecules obtained were nevertheless still fairly simple—and as it turns out most of them have now also been found in interstellar space. Starting in the 1960s suggestions were made for the chemical and other roles of constituents of the crust as well as atmosphere. Schemes for early forms of self-replication were invented based on molecules such as RNA and on patterns in clay-like materials. (The smallest known system that independently replicates itself is a mycoplasma bacterium with about 580,000 base pairs and perhaps 470 genes. Viroids can be as small as 10,000 atoms but require a host for replication.) In the 1970s it then became popular to investigate complicated cycles of chemical reactions that seemed analogous to ones found in living systems. But with the advent of widespread computer simulations in the 1980s it became clear that all sorts of features normally associated with life were actually rather easy to obtain. (See note above.)

■ **Page 824 · Self-reproduction.** That one can for example make a mold that will produce copies of a shape has been known

since antiquity (see note above). The cybernetics movement highlighted the question of what it takes for self-reproduction to occur autonomously, and in 1952 John von Neumann designed an elaborate 2D cellular automaton that would automatically make a copy of its initial configuration of cells (see page 876). In the course of the 1950s suggestions of several increasingly simple mechanical systems capable of self-reproduction were made—notably by Lionel Penrose. The phenomenon in the main text was noticed around 1961 by Edward Fredkin (see page 877). But while it shows some of the essence of self-reproduction, it lacks many of the more elaborate features common in biological self-reproduction. In the 1980s, however, such features were nevertheless surprisingly often present in computer viruses and worms. (See also page 1092.)

■ **Page 825 · Extraterrestrial life.** Conditions thermally and chemically similar to those on Earth have presumably existed on other bodies in the solar system. Venus, Mars, Europa (a moon of Jupiter) and Titan (a moon of Saturn) have for example all probably had liquid water at some time. But there is so far no evidence for life now or in the past on any of these. Yet if life had arisen one might expect it to have become widespread, since at least on Earth it has managed to spread to many extremes of temperature, pressure and chemical composition. On several occasions structures have been found in extraterrestrial rocks that look somewhat like small versions of microorganism fossils (most notably in 1996 in a meteorite from Mars discovered in Antarctica). But almost certainly these structures have nothing to do with life, and are instead formed by ordinary precipitation of minerals. And although even up to the 1970s it was thought that life might well be found on Mars, it now seems likely that there is nothing quite like terrestrial life anywhere else in our solar system. (Even if life is found elsewhere it might still have originally come from Earth, say via meteorites, since dormant forms such as spores can apparently survive for long periods in space.)

Away from our solar system there is increasing evidence that most stars have planets with a distribution of sizes—so presumably conditions similar to Earth are fairly common. But thus far it has not been possible to see—say in planetary atmospheres—whether there are for example molecules similar to ones characteristically found in life on Earth.

■ **Forms of living systems.** This book has shown that even with underlying rules of some fixed type a vast range of different forms can often be produced. And this makes it reasonable to expect that with appropriate genetic programs the chemical building blocks of life on Earth should in principle allow a vast range of forms. But the comparative weakness of natural selection (see page 391) has meant that only a limited set of such forms have actually been explored. And from the experience of this book I suspect that what others might even be nearby is effectively impossible to foresee. The appearance in engineering of forms somewhat like those in living systems should not be taken to imply that other forms are fundamentally difficult to produce; instead I suspect that it is more a reflection of the copying of living systems for engineering purposes. The overall morphology of living systems on Earth seems to be greatly affected by their basically gelatinous character. So even systems based on solids or gases would likely not be recognized by us as life.

■ **Page 825 · History.** Although Greek philosophers such as Democritus believed that there must be an infinite number of worlds all with inhabitants like us, the prevailing view in antiquity—later supported by theological arguments—was that the Earth is special, and the only abode of life. However, with the development of Copernican ideas in the 1600s it came to be widely though not universally believed, even in theological circles, that other planets—as well as the Moon—must have inhabitants like us. Many astronomers attributed features they saw on the Moon to life if not intelligence, but in the late 1800s, after it was found that the Moon has no atmosphere, belief in life there began to wane. Starting in the 1870s, however, there began to be great interest in life on Mars, and it was thought—perhaps following the emphasis on terrestrial canal-building at the time—that a vast network of canals on Mars had been observed. And although in 1911 the apparent building of new canals on Mars was still being soberly reported by newspapers, there was by the 1920s increasing skepticism. The idea that lichens might exist on Mars and be responsible for seasonal changes in color nevertheless became popular, especially after the discovery of atmospheric carbon dioxide in 1947. Particularly in the 1920s there had been occasional claims of extraterrestrial radio signals (see page 1188), but by the 1950s interest in extraterrestrial intelligence had largely transferred to science fiction (see page 1190). Starting in the late 1940s many sightings were reported of UFOs believed to be alien spacecraft, but by the 1960s these were increasingly discredited. It had been known since the mid-1800s that many other stars are much like the Sun, but it was not until the 1950s that evidence of planets around other stars began to accumulate. Following a certain amount of discussion in the physics community in the 1950s, the first explicit search for extraterrestrial intelligence with a radio telescope was done in 1960 (see page 1189). In the 1960s landings of spacecraft on the Moon confirmed the absence of life there—though returning Apollo astronauts were still quarantined to guard against possible lunar microbes. And despite substantial expectations to the contrary, when spacecraft landed on Mars in 1976 they found no evidence of life there. Some searches for extraterrestrial signals have continued in the radio astronomy community, but perhaps because of its association with science fiction, the topic of extraterrestrial intelligence has generally not been popular with professional scientists. With the rise of amateur science on the web and the availability of low-cost radio telescope components the late 1990s may however have seen a renewal of serious interest.

■ **Page 826 · Bird songs.** Essentially all birds produce calls of some kind, but complex songs are mainly produced by male songbirds, usually in breeding season. Their general form is inherited, but specifics are often learned through imitation during a fixed period of infancy, leading birds in local areas to have distinctive songs. The songs sometimes seem to be associated with attracting mates, and sometimes with defining territory—but often their function is unclear, even when one bird seems to sing in response to another. (There are claims, however, that parrots can learn to have meaningful conversations with humans.) The syrinxes of songbirds have two membranes, which can vibrate independently, in a potentially complex way. A specific region in bird brains appears to coordinate singing; the region contains a few tens of thousands of nerve cells, and is larger in species with more complex songs.

Famous motifs from human music are heard in bird songs probably more often than would be expected by chance. It may be that some common neural mechanism makes the motifs seem pleasing to both birds and humans. Or it could be that humans find them pleasing because they are familiar from bird songs.

■ **Page 826 · Whale songs.** Male whales can produce complex songs lasting tens of minutes during breeding season. The songs often include rhyme-like repeating elements. At a given time all whales in a group typically sing almost the same song, which gradually changes. The function of the song is quite unclear. It has been claimed that its frequencies are optimized for long-range transmission in the ocean, but this appears not to be the case. In dolphins, it is known that one dolphin can produce patterns of sound that are repeated by a specific other dolphin.

■ **Page 826 · Animal communication.** Most animals that live in groups have the capability to produce at least a few specific auditory, visual (e.g. gestures and displays), chemical (e.g. pheromones) or other signals in response to particular situations such as danger. Some animals have also been found to produce much more complex and varied signals.

For example it was discovered in the 1980s that elephants can generate elaborate patterns of sounds—but at frequencies below human hearing. Animals such as octopuses and particularly cuttlefish can show complex and changing patterns of pigmentation. But despite a fair amount of investigation it remains unclear whether these represent more than just simple responses to the environment.

■ **Page 826 · Theories of communication.** Over the course of time the question of what the essential features of communication are has been discussed from many different angles. It appears to have always been a common view that communication somehow involves transferring thoughts from one mind to another. Even in antiquity it was nevertheless recognized that all sorts of aspects of language are purely matters of convention, so that shared conventions are necessary for verbal communication to be possible. In the 1600s the philosophical idea that the only way to get information with certainty is from the senses led to emphasis on observable aspects of communication, and to the conclusion that there is no way to tell whether an accurate transfer of abstract thoughts has occurred between one mind and another. In the late 1600s Gottfried Leibniz nevertheless suggested that perhaps a universal language—modelled on mathematics—could be created that would represent all truths in an objective way accessible to any mind (compare page 1149). But by the late 1800s philosophers like Charles Peirce had developed the idea that communication must be understood purely in terms of its observable features and effects. Three levels of so-called semiotics were then discussed. The first was syntax: the grammatical or other structure of a sequence of verbal or other elements. The second was semantics: the standardized meaning or meanings of the sequence of elements. And the third was pragmatics: the observable effect on those involved in the communication. In the early 1900s, the logical positivism movement suggested that perhaps a universal language or formalism based on logic could be developed that would allow at least scientific truths to be communicated in an unambiguous way not affected by issues of pragmatics—and that anything that could not be communicated like this was somehow meaningless. But by the 1940s it came to be believed—notably by Ludwig Wittgenstein—that ordinary language, with its pragmatic context, could in the end communicate fundamentally more than any formalized logical system, albeit more ambiguously.

Ever since antiquity work has been done to formalize grammatical and other rules of individual human languages. In the early 1900s—notably with the work of Ferdinand de Saussure—there began to be more emphasis on the general question of how languages really operate, and the point was made that the verbal elements or signs in a language should be viewed as somehow intermediate between tangible entities like sounds and abstract thoughts and concepts. The properties of any given sign were recognized as arbitrary, but what was then thought to be essential about a language is the structure of the network of relations between signs—with the ultimate meaning of any given sign inevitably depending on the meanings of signs related to it (as later emphasized in deconstructionism). By the 1950s anthropological studies of various languages—notably by Benjamin Whorf—had encouraged the idea that concepts that did not appear to fit in certain languages simply could not enter the thinking of users of those languages. Evidence to the contrary (notably about past and future among Hopi speakers) eroded this strong form of the so-called Sapir-Whorf hypothesis, so that by the 1970s it was generally believed just that language can have an influence on thinking—a phenomenon definitely seen with mathematical notation and computer languages. Starting in the 1950s, especially with the work of Noam Chomsky, there were claims of universal features in human languages—independent of historical or cultural context (see page 1103). But at least among linguists these are generally assumed just to reflect common aspects of verbal processing in the human brain, not features that must necessarily appear in any conceivable language. (And it remains unclear, for example, to what extent non-verbal forms of communication such as music, gestures and visual ornament show the same grammatical features as ordinary languages.)

The rise of communications technology in the early 1900s led to work on quantitative theories of communication, and for example in 1928 Ralph Hartley suggested that an objective measure of the information content of a message with n possible forms is $Log[n]$. (Similar ideas arose around the same time in statistics, and in fact there had already been work on probabilistic models of written language by Andrei Markov in the 1910s.) In 1948 Claude Shannon suggested using a measure of information based on $p Log[p]$, and there quickly developed the notion that this could be used to find the fundamental redundancy of any sequence of data, independent of its possible meaning (compare page 1071). Human languages were found on this basis to have substantial redundancy (see page 1086), and it has sometimes been suggested that this is important to their operation—allowing errors to be corrected and details of different users to be ignored. (There are also obvious features which reduce redundancy—for example that in most languages common words tend to be short. One can also imagine models of the historical development of languages which will tend to lead to redundancy at the level of Shannon information.)

■ **Mathematical notation.** While it is usually recognized that ordinary human languages depend greatly on history and context, it is sometimes believed that mathematical notation is somehow more universal. But although it so happens that essentially the same mathematical notation is in practice used all around the world by speakers of every ordinary language, I do not believe that it is in any way unique or inevitable, and in fact I think it shows most of the same issues of dependence on history and context as any ordinary language.

As a first example, consider the case of numbers. One can always just use *n* copies of the same symbol to represent an integer *n*—and indeed this idea seems historically to have arisen independently quite a few times. But as soon as one tries to set up a more compact notation there inevitably seem to be many possibilities. And so for example the Greek and Roman number systems were quite different from current Hindu-Arabic base-10 positional notation. Particularly from working with computers it is often now assumed that base-2 positional notation is somehow the most natural and fundamental. But as pages 560 and 916 show, there are many other quite different ways to represent numbers, each with different levels of convenience for different purposes. And it is fairly easy to see how a different historical progression might have ended up making another one of these seem the most natural.

The idea of labelling entities in geometrical diagrams by letters existed in Babylonian and Greek times. But perhaps because until after the 1200s numbers were usually also represented by letters, algebraic notation with letters for variables did not arise until the late 1500s. The idea of having notation for operators emerged in the early 1600s, and by the end of the 1600s, notably with the work of Gottfried Leibniz, essentially all the basic notation now used in algebra and calculus had been established. Most of it was ultimately based on shortenings and idealizations of ordinary language, an important early motivation just being to avoid dependence on particular ordinary languages. Notation for mathematical logic began to emerge in the 1880s, notably with the work of Giuseppe Peano, and by the 1930s it was widely used as the basis for notation in pure mathematics.

In its basic structure of operators, operands, and so on, mathematical notation has always been fairly systematic—and is close to being a context-free language. (In many ways it is like a simple idealization of ordinary language, with operators being like verbs, operands nouns, and so on.) And while traditional mathematical notation suffers from some inconsistencies and ambiguities, it was possible in developing *Mathematica StandardForm* to set up something very close that can be interpreted uniquely in all cases.

Mathematical notation works well for things like ordinary formulas that involve a comparatively small number of basic operations. But there has been no direct generalization for more general constructs and computations. And indeed my goal in designing *Mathematica* was precisely to provide a uniform notation for these (see page 852). Yet to make this work I had to use names derived from ordinary language to specify the primitives I defined.

■ **Computer communication.** Most protocols for exchanging data between computers have in the end traditionally had rather simple structures—with different pieces of information usually being placed at fixed positions, or at least being arranged in predefined sequences—or sometimes being given in name-value pairs. A more general approach, however, is to use tree-structured symbolic expressions of the kind that form the basis for *Mathematica*—and now in essence appear in XML. In the most general case one can imagine directly exchanging a representation of a program, that is run on the computer that receives it, and induces whatever effect one wants. A simple example from 1984 is *PostScript*, which can specify a picture by giving a program for constructing it; a more sophisticated example from the late 1990s is client-side Java. (Advanced forms of data compression can also be thought of as working by sending simple programs.) But a practical problem in exchanging arbitrary programs is the difficulty of guarding against malicious elements like viruses. And although at some level most communications between present-day computers are very regular and structured, this is often obscured by compression or encryption.

When a program is sent between computers it is usually encoded in a syntactically very straightforward way. But computer languages intended for direct use by humans almost always have more elaborate syntax that is a simple idealization of ordinary human language (see page 1103). There are in practice many similarities between different computer languages. Yet except in very low-level languages few of these are necessary consequences of features or limitations of actual computers. And instead most of them must be viewed just as the results of shared history—and the need to fit in with human cognitive abilities.

■ **Meaning in programs.** Many issues about meaning arise for computer languages in more defined versions of the ways they arise for ordinary languages. Input to a computer language will immediately fail to be meaningful if it does not conform to a certain definite syntax. Before the input can have a chance of specifying meaningful action there are often all sorts of issues about whether variables in it refer to entities that can be considered to exist. And even if this is resolved, one can still get something that is in effect nonsense and does not usefully run. In most traditional computer languages it is usually the case that most programs chosen at random will just crash if run, often as a result of trying to write to memory outside the arrays they have allocated. In *Mathematica*, there is almost no similar issue, and programs chosen at random tend instead just to return unchanged. (Compare page 101.)

For the kinds of systems like cellular automata that I have discussed in this book programs chosen at random do very often produce some sort of non-trivial behavior. But as discussed in the main text there is still an issue of when this behavior can reasonably be considered meaningful.

For some purposes a more direct analog of messages is not programs or rules for systems like cellular automata but instead initial conditions. And one might imagine that the very process of running such initial conditions in a system with appropriate underlying rules would somehow be what corresponds to their meaning. But if one was just given a collection of initial conditions without any underlying rules one would then need to find out what underlying rules one was supposed to use in order to determine their meaning. Yet the system will always do something, whatever rules one uses. So then one is back to defining criteria for what counts as meaningful behavior in order to determine—by a kind of generalization of cryptanalysis—what rules one is supposed to use.

■ **Meaning and regularity.** If one considers something to show regularity one may or may not consider it meaningful. But if one considers something random then usually one will also consider it meaningless. For to say that something is meaningful normally implies that one somehow comes to a conclusion from it. And this typically implies that one can find some summary of some aspect of it—and thus some regularity. Yet there are still cases where things that are presumably quite random are considered meaningful— prices in financial markets being one example.

■ **Page 828 · Forms of artifacts.** Much as in biological evolution, once a particular engineering construct has been found to work it normally continues to be used. Examples with characteristic forms include (in rough order of their earliest known use): arrowheads, boomerangs, saws, boxes, stairs, fishhooks, wheels, arches, forks, balls, kites, lenses, springs, catenaries, cogs, screws, chains, trusses, cams, linkages, propellers, clocksprings, parabolic reflectors, airfoils, corrugation, zippers, and geodesic domes. It is notable that not even nested shapes are common, though they appear in cross-sections of rope (see page 874), as well as in address decoder trees on chips—and have recently been used in broadband antennas. (Some self-similarity is also present in standard log-periodic antennas.) When several distinct components are

involved, more complicated structures are not uncommon—as in escapements, and many bearings and joints. More complex shapes for single elements sometimes arise when an analog of area maximization is desired—as with tire treads or fins in devices such as heat exchangers. Quadratic residue sequences $Mod[Range[n]^2, n]$ (see page 1081) are used to give profiles for acoustic diffusers that operate uniformly over a range of frequencies. Musical instruments can have fairly complicated shapes maintained for historical reasons to considerable precision. Some knots can also be thought of as objects with complex forms. It is notable that elaborate types of mechanical motion (and sometimes surprising phenomena in general) are often first implemented in toys. Examples are early mechanical automata and model airplanes, and modern executive toys claiming to illustrate chaos theory through linkages, magnets or fluid systems. Complex trajectories (compare page 972) have sometimes been proposed or used for spacecraft. (See also notes on ornamental art on page 872.)

■ **Page 828 · Recognizing artifacts.** Various situations require picking out artifacts automatically. One example is finding buildings or machines from aerial reconnaissance images; another is finding boat or airplane wreckage on an ocean floor from sonar data. In both these cases the most common approach is to look for straight edges. Outdoor security systems also often need ways to distinguish animals and wind-induced motion from intentional human activity—and tend to have fairly simple procedures for doing this.

To recognize a regular crystal as not being a carefully cut artifact can take specific knowledge. The same can be true of patterns produced by wind on sand or rocks. Lenticular clouds are sometimes mistaken for UFOs on account of their regular shape. The exact cuboid form of the monolith in the movie *2001* was intended to suggest that it was an artifact.

Recognizing artifacts can be a central—and controversial— issue in prehistoric archeology. Sometimes human bones are found nearby. And sometimes chemical analysis suggests controlled fire—as with charcoal or baked clay. But to tell whether for example a piece of rock was formed naturally or was carefully made to be a stone tool can in general be very difficult. And a large part of the way this has been done in practice is just through comparison with known examples that fit into an overall pattern of gradual historical change. In recent decades there has been increasing emphasis on trying to understand and reproduce the whole process of making and using artifacts. And in the field of lithic analysis there are beginning to be fairly systematic ways to recognize for example the effects of the hundreds of orderly impacts needed to make a typical flint arrowhead by knapping. (Sometimes it is also possible to recognize microscopic features characteristic of particular kinds of use or wear—and it is conceivable that in the future analysis of trillions of atomic-scale features could reveal all sorts of details of the history of an object.)

To tell whether or not some arrangement of soil or rocks is an artifact can be extremely difficult—and there are many notorious cases of continuing controversy. Beyond looking for similarities to known examples, a typical approach is just to look for correlations with topographic or other features that might reveal some possible purpose.

■ **Artifacts in data.** In fields like accounting and experimental science it is usually a sign of fraud if primary data is being created for a purpose, rather than merely being reported. If a large amount of numerical data has been made up by a person this can be detectable through statistical deviations from expected randomness—particularly in structural details such as frequency of digits. (So-called artifacts can also be the unintentional result of details of methods used to obtain or process data.)

In numerical computations effects are often called artifacts if they are believed not to be genuine features of an underlying mathematical system, but merely to reflect the computational scheme used. Such effects are usually first noticed through unexpected regularities in some detail of output. But in cases like chaos theory it remains unclear to what extent complex behavior seen in computations is an artifact (see page 920).

■ **Animal artifacts.** Structures like mollusc shells, radiolarian skeletons and to some extent coral are formed through processes of growth like those discussed in Chapter 8. Structures like spider webs, wasp nests, termite mounds, bird nests and beaver dams rely on behavior determined by animal brains. (Even spider webs end up looking quite different if psychoactive drugs are administered to the spider.) And much like human artifacts, many of these structures tend to be distinguished by their comparative geometrical simplicity. In a few cases—particularly with insects—somewhat complicated forms are seen, but it seems likely that these are actually produced by rather simple local rules like those in aggregation systems (see page 1011).

■ **Molecular biology.** DNA sequences of organisms can be thought of as artifacts created by biological evolution, and current data suggests that they contain some long-range correlations not present in typical random sequences. Most likely, however, these have fairly simple origins, perhaps being associated with iterative splicing of subsequences. And in the few thousand proteins currently known, standard statistical tests reveal no significant overall regularities in their sequences of up to a few thousand amino acids. (Some of the 20 standard amino acids do however occur more frequently than others.) Nevertheless, if one looks at overall shapes into which these proteins fold, there is some evidence that the same patterns of behavior are often seen. But probably such patterns would also occur in purely random proteins—at least if their folding happened in the same cellular apparatus. (See page 1003.) Note that the antibodies of the immune system are much like short random proteins—whose range of shapes must be sufficient to match any antigen. (See also page 1194.)

■ **Messages in DNA.** Science fiction has sometimes suggested that an extraterrestrial source of life might have left some form of message in the DNA sequences of all terrestrial organisms, but to get evidence of this would seem to require extensive other knowledge of the source. (See also page 1190.)

■ **Decompilers.** Trying to reverse engineer source code in a programming language like C from machine code output by compilers involves in effect trying to deduce higher-level purposes from lower-level computational steps. And normally this can be done with any reliability only when the machine code represents a fairly direct translation that has not been extensively rearranged or optimized.

■ **Page 828 · Complexity and theology.** See page 861.

■ **Page 829 · Purpose in archeology.** Ideas about the purpose of archeological objects most often ultimately tend to come from comparisons to similar-looking objects in use today. But great differences in typical beliefs and ways of life can make comparisons difficult. And certainly it is now very hard for us to imagine just what range of purposes the first known stone tools from 2.6 million years ago might have been put to—or what purpose the arrays of dots or handprints in cave paintings from 30,000 BC might have had. And even when it comes to early buildings from perhaps 10,000 BC it is still difficult to know just how they were used. Stone circles like Stonehenge from perhaps 3000 BC presumably served some community purpose, but beyond that little can convincingly be said. Definite geographical or astronomical alignments can be identified for many large prehistoric structures, but whether these were actually intentional is almost never clear. After the development of writing starting around 4000 BC, purposes can often be deduced from inscriptions and other written material. But still to work out for example the purpose of the Antikythera device from around 100 BC is very difficult, and depends on being able to trace a long historical tradition of astronomical clocks and orreries.

■ **Dead languages.** Particularly over the past century or so, most of the known written human languages from every point in history have successfully been decoded. But to do this has essentially always required finding a case where there is explicit overlap with a known language—say a

Rosetta stone with the same text in multiple languages, or at least words or proper names that are transliterated. As in cryptanalysis, it is sometimes remarkable how small an amount of text is needed to find a decoding scheme. But usually what is done relies critically on the slowness with which human languages change, and the comparatively limited number of different basic ways in which they work.

■ **Teleology.** There is a common tendency to project human purposes onto natural objects and events—and this is for example almost universally done by young children. Ancient beliefs often held that things in nature are set up by a variety of gods for a variety of purposes. By 400 BC, following ideas of Anaxagoras, Socrates and Plato discussed the notion that things in nature might in effect be optimally designed for coherent purposes by a single mind. Around 350 BC Aristotle claimed that a full explanation of anything should include its purpose (or so-called final cause, or telos)—but said that for systems in nature this is often just to make the final forms of these systems (their so-called formal cause). The rise of monotheistic religions led to the widespread belief that the universe and everything in it was created for definite purposes by a single god. But the development of mathematical science in the 1600s—and its focus on mechanisms ("efficient causes")—led away from ascribing explicit purposes to physical systems. In the mid-1700s David Hume then claimed on philosophical grounds that we fundamentally have no basis for ascribing purposes to any kind of natural system—though in the 1790s Immanuel Kant argued that even though we cannot know whether there really are such purposes, it is still often necessary for us to think in terms of them. And in fact the notion that systems in biology are so complex that they must have been intelligently designed for a purpose remained common. In the late 1800s Darwinian evolution nevertheless suggested that no such purposeful design was necessary—though in a sense it again introduced a notion of purpose associated with optimization of fitness. Ever since the 1700s economics had been discussed in terms of purposeful activities of rational agents. In the early 1900s there were however general attempts to develop mechanistic explanations in the social sciences, but by the mid-1900s purpose was again widely discussed, especially in economics. And in fact, even in physics, a notion of purpose had actually always been quite common. For whenever a physical system satisfies any kind of implicit equation, this defines a constraint that can be viewed as corresponding to some kind of purpose. (See page 940.) That something like a notion of purpose is being used has been more widely recognized for variational principles like the Principle of Least Action in mechanics from the mid-1700s. Results in the

late 1900s in astrophysics and cosmology seemed to suggest that for us to exist our universe must satisfy all sorts of constraints—and to avoid explaining this in terms of purpose the Anthropic Principle was introduced (see page 1026). What I do in this book goes significantly further than traditional science in getting rid of notions of purpose from investigations of nature. For I essentially always consider systems that are based on explicit evolution rules rather than implicit constraints. And in fact I argue that simple programs constructed without known purposes are what one needs to study to find the kinds of complex behavior we see.

■ **Possible purposes.** As part of asking whether the rules for a system are somehow minimal for a given purpose, one can ask what properties the system has that could reasonably be considered a purpose at all. In general one tends to talk of purpose only when doing so allows one to give a simpler description of some aspect of behavior than just describing the behavior directly. But whether one can give a simple description can depend greatly on the framework in which one is operating. And so, for example, while the digits of π have a simple description in terms of traditional mathematics, the results in Chapter 4 suggest that outside of this framework they normally do not. And what this means is that if one saw a system that had the property of generating the digits of π one would be unlikely to think that this could represent a meaningful purpose—unless one happened to be operating in traditional mathematics. And so similarly, one would be unlikely to think that generating the center column from rule 30 could represent any sort of meaningful purpose—unless one was operating within the framework that I have developed in this book.

■ **Page 830 · Purposeful computation.** See page 638.

■ **Page 832 · Doubling rules.** Rule (a) is

$$\{\{0, 2, \_\} \rightarrow 5, \{5, 3, \_\} \rightarrow 5, \{5, \_, \_\} \rightarrow 1,$$
$$\{\_, 5, \_\} \rightarrow 1, \{\_, 2, \_\} \rightarrow 3, \{\_, 3, 2\} \rightarrow 2, \{\_, 1, 2\} \rightarrow 4,$$
$$\{\_, 4, \_\} \rightarrow 3, \{4, 3, \_\} \rightarrow 4, \{4, 0, \_\} \rightarrow 2, \{\_, x\_, \_\} \rightarrow x\}$$

and takes $2n^2 + n$ steps to yield $Table[1, \{2n\}]$ given input $Append[Table[1, \{n-1\}], 2]$. Rule (b) is

$$\{\{\_, 2, \_\} \rightarrow 3, \{\_, 1, 2\} \rightarrow 2, \{3, 0, \_\} \rightarrow 1,$$
$$\{3, \_, \_\} \rightarrow 3, \{\_, 3, \_\} \rightarrow 1, \{\_, x\_, \_\} \rightarrow x\}$$

and takes $3n$ steps. Rule (c) is $k = 3$, $r = 1$ rule 5407067979 and takes $3n-1$ steps.

■ **Page 833 · Searching.** No symmetric $k = 3$, $r = 1$ rule yields doubling. General rules can show subtle bugs; rule 1340716537107 for example first fails at $n = 24$. The total number of $k = 3$, $r = 1$ rules that need to be searched can easily be reduced from 3^{27} to 3^{21}. Several different rules that work can behave identically, since up to 6 of the 27 cases in each rule are not sampled with the initial conditions used. In rules that work, between 8 and 19 cases lead to a change in the color of a cell, with 14 cases being the most common.

■ **Page 833 · Properties.** The number of steps increases irregularly but roughly quadratically with n in rule (a), and roughly linearly in (d) and (e). Rule (b) in the end repeats every 128 steps. The center of the complex pattern in both (d) and (e) emulates $k = 2$ rule 90.

■ **Other functions.** The first three pictures below show rules that yield $3n$ (no $k = 3$ rules yield $4n$, $5n$ or n^2), and the last picture $2n-2$ (corresponding to doubling with initial conditions analogous to page 639).

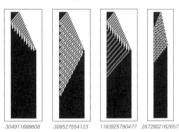

304911688608   308527554123   1183925790477   2672802162657

■ **Page 834 · Minimal cellular automata for sequences.** Given any particular sequence of black and white cells one can look for the simplest cellular automaton which generates that sequence as its center column when evolving from a single black cell (compare page 956). The pictures below show the lowest-numbered cellular automaton rules that manage to generate repetitive sequences containing black cells with successively greater separations s.

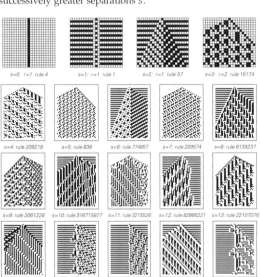

s=0: r=1 rule 4   s=1: r=1 rule 1   s=2: r=1 rule 57   s=3: r=2 rule 15174

s=4: rule 209218   s=5: rule 838   s=6: rule 774857   s=7: rule 209574   s=8: rule 8139237

s=9: rule 2061228   s=10: rule 316715877   s=11: rule 3215526   s=12: rule 82866221   s=13: rule 22107076

14: rule 1006223533   15: rule 37788005   17: rule 72844195   19: rule 273781569   23: rule 22047073

Elementary ($k = 2$, $r = 1$) cellular automata can be found only up to separations $s = 2$. But $k = 2$, $r = 2$ cellular automata can be found for all separations up to 15, as well as 17, 19 and 23. (Note that for example in the $s = 15$ case the lowest-numbered rule exhibits a complex 350-step transient away from the center column.)

The pictures below show the lowest-numbered cellular automata that generate respectively powers of two, squares and the nested Thue-Morse sequence of page 83 (compare rule 150). Of the 4 billion $k = 2$, $r = 2$ cellular automata none turn out to be able to produce for example sequences corresponding to the cubes, powers of 3, Fibonacci numbers, primes, digits of $\sqrt{2}$, or concatenation sequences.

r=1, rule 126   rule 1069090987   rule 69540422

If one looks not just at specific sequences, but instead at all 2^n possible sequences of length n, one can ask how many cellular automaton rules (say with $k = 2$, $r = 2$) one has to go through in order to generate every one of these. The pictures below show on the left the last rules needed to generate any sequence of each successive length—and on the right the form of the sequence (as well as its continuation after length n). Since some different rules generate the same sequences (see page 956) one needs to go through somewhat more than 2^n rules to get every sequence of length n. The sequences shown below can be thought of as being in a sense the ones of each length that are the most difficult to generate—or have the highest algorithmic information content. (Note that the sequence ■■■□ is the first one that cannot be generated by any of the 256 elementary cellular automata; the first sequence that cannot be generated by any $k = 2$, $r = 2$ cellular automata is probably of length 26.)

 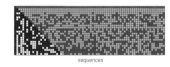

rule numbers   sequences

■ **Other examples.** Minimal systems achieving particular purposes are shown on page 619 for Boolean functions evaluated with NANDs, pages 759 and 889 for Turing machines, page 1142 for sorting networks, and page 1035 for firing squad synchronization.

■ **Page 834 · Minimal theories.** Particularly in fundamental physics it has been found that the correct theory is often the minimal one consistent with basic observations. Yet barring supernatural intervention, the laws of physics embodied in such a theory presumably cannot be considered to have been created for any particular purpose. (See page 1025.)

■ **Page 835 · Earth from space.** Human activity has led to a few large simple geometrical structures that are visually noticeable from space. One is the almost-straight 30-mile railroad causeway built in 1959 that divides halves of the Great Salt Lake in Utah where the water is colored blue and orange. Another is the almost-circular 12-mile-diameter national park created in 1900 that encloses ungrazed vegetation on the Egmont Volcano in New Zealand. On the scale of a few miles, there is also rectilinear arrangement of fields in the U.S. Midwest, as well as straight-line political boundaries with different agriculture on each side. Large geometrical patterns of logging were for example briefly visible after snow in 1961 near Cochrane, Canada—as captured by an early weather satellite. Perfectly straight sections of roads (such as the 90-mile Balladonia-Caiguna road in Australia), as well as the 4-mile-diameter perfectly circular Fermilab accelerator ring are not so easy to see. The Great Wall of China from 200 BC follows local topography and so is not straight.

Some of the most dramatic geometrical structures—such as the dendritic fossil drainage pattern in south Yemen or the bilaterally symmetric coral reefs around islands like Bora Bora—are not artifacts. The same is true of fields of parallel sand dunes, as well as of almost-circular structures such as the 40-mile-diameter impact crater in Manicouagan, Canada (highlighted by an annular lake) and the 30-mile-diameter Richat structure in the Sahara desert of Mauritania. On the Moon, the 50-mile-diameter crater Tycho is also almost circular—and has 1000-mile almost-straight rays coming out from it.

At night, lights of cities are obvious—notably hugging the coast of the Mediterranean—as are fire plumes from oil rigs. In addition, in some areas, sodium streetlamps make the light almost monochromatic. But it would seem difficult to be sure that these were artifacts without more information. In western Kansas there is however a 200-mile square region with light produced by a strikingly regular grid of towns—many at the centers of square counties laid out around 1870 in connection with land grants for railroad development. In addition, there is an isolated 1000-mile straight railroad built in the late 1800s across Kazakhstan between Aktyubinsk and Tashkent, with many towns visible at night along it. There are also 500-mile straight railroads built around the same time between Makat and Nukus, and Yaroslavl and Archangel. All these railroads go through flat empty terrain that previously had only a few nomadic inhabitants—and no settlements to define a route. But in many ways such geometrical forms seem vastly simpler to imagine producing than for example the elaborate pattern of successive lightning strikes visible especially in the tropics from space.

■ **Page 835 · Astronomical objects.** Stars and planets tend to be close to perfect spheres. Lagrange points and resonances often lead to simple geometrical patterns of orbiting bodies. (The orbits of most planets in our solar system are also close to perfect circles; see page 973.) Regular spirograph-like patterns can occur for example in planetary nebulas formed by solar mass exploding stars. Unexplained phenomena that could conceivably be at least in part artifacts include gamma ray bursts and ultra high-energy cosmic rays. The local positions of stars are generally assumed to be random. 88 constellations are usually named—quite a few presumably already identified by the Babylonians and Sumerians around 2000 BC.

■ **Page 835 · Natural radio emissions.** Each of the few million lightning flashes that occur on the Earth each day produce bursts of radio energy. At kilohertz frequencies reflection from the ionosphere allows these signals to propagate up to thousands of miles around the Earth, leading to continual intermittent crackling and popping. Particularly at night such signals can also travel within the ionosphere, but different frequencies travel at different rates, leading to so-called tweeks involving ringing or pinging. Signals can sometimes travel through the magnetosphere along magnetic field lines from one hemisphere to the other, yielding so-called whistlers with frequencies that fall off in a highly regular way with time. (Occasionally the signals can also travel back and forth between hemispheres, giving more complex results.) Radio emission can also occur when charged particles from the Sun excite plasma waves in the magnetosphere. And particularly at dawn or when an aurora is present an elaborate chorus of different elements can be produced—and heard directly on a VLF radio receiver.

Sunspots and solar flares make the Sun the most intense radio source in the solar system. Artificial radio signals from the Earth come next. The interaction of the solar wind with the magnetosphere of Jupiter produces radio emissions that exhibit variations reminiscent of gusting.

Outside the solar system, gas clouds show radio emission at discrete gigahertz frequencies from rotational transitions in molecules and spin-flip transitions in hydrogen atoms. (The narrowest lines come from natural masers and have widths around 1 kHz.) The cosmic microwave background, and processes such as thermal emission from dust, radiation from electrons in ionized gases, and synchrotron radiation from relativistic electrons in magnetic fields yield radio emissions with characteristic continuous frequency spectra. A total of over a million radio sources inside and outside our galaxy have now been catalogued, most with frequency spectra apparently consistent with known natural phenomena. Variations of source properties on timescales of months or years are not uncommon; variations of signals on timescales of tens of minutes can be introduced by propagation through turbulence in the interstellar medium.

Most radio emission from outside the solar system shows little apparent regularity. The almost perfectly repetitive signals from pulsars are an exception. Pulsars appear to be rapidly rotating neutron stars—perhaps 10 miles across—whose magnetic fields trap charged particles that produce radio emissions. When they first form after a supernova pulsars have millisecond repetition rates, but over the course of a few million years they slow to repetition rates of seconds through a series of glitches, associated perhaps with cracking in their solid crusts or perhaps with motion of quantized vortices in their superfluid interiors. Individual pulses from pulsars show some variability, presumably largely reflecting details of plasma dynamics in their magnetospheres.

■ **Page 835 · Artificial radio signals.** In current technology radio signals are essentially always based on carriers of the form $Sin[\omega t]$ with frequencies $\omega/(2\pi)$. When radio was first developed around 1900 information was normally encoded using amplitude modulation (AM) $s[t] Sin[\omega t]$. In the 1940s it also became popular to use frequency modulation (FM) $Sin[(1 + s[t]) \omega t]$, and in the 1970s pulse code modulation (PCM) (pulse trains for $IntegerDigits[s[t], 2]$). All such methods yield signals that remain roughly in the range of frequencies $\{\omega - \delta, \omega + \delta\}$ where δ is the data rate in $s[t]$. But in the late 1990s—particularly for the new generation of cellular telephones—it began to be common to use spread spectrum CDMA methods, in which many signals with the same carrier frequency are combined. Each is roughly of the form $BitXor[u[t], s[t]] Sin[\omega t]$, where $u[t]$ is a pseudonoise (PN) sequence generated by a linear feedback shift register (LFSR) (see page 1084); the idea is that by using a different PN sequence for each signal the corresponding $s[t]$ can be recovered even if thousands are superimposed.

The radio spectrum from about 9 kHz to 300 GHz is divided by national and international legislation into about 460 bands designated for different purposes. And except when spread spectrum methods are used, most bands are then divided into between a few and a few thousand channels in which signals with identical structures but different frequencies are sent.

If one steps through frequencies with an AM radio scanner, one sometimes hears intelligible speech—from radio or TV

broadcasts, or two-way radio communication. But in many frequency bands one hears instead either very regular or seemingly quite random signals. (A few bands allocated for example to distress signals or radio astronomy are normally quiet.) The regular signals come from such sources as navigation beacons, time standards, identification transponders and radars. Most have characteristic almost perfectly repetitive forms (radar pulses, for example, typically have the chirped form $Sin[(1 + \alpha t) \omega t]$)—and some sound uncannily like pulsars. When there are seemingly random signals some arise say from transmission of analog video (though this typically has very rigid overall structure associated with successive lines and frames), but most are now associated with digital data. And when CDMA methods are used there can be spreading over a significant range of frequencies—with regularities being recognizable only if one knows or can cryptanalyze LFSR sequences.

In general to send many signals together one just needs to associate each with a function $f[i, t]$ orthogonal to all other functions $f[j, t]$ (see page 1072). Current electronics (with analog elements such as phase-locked loops) make it easy to handle functions $Sin[\omega t]$, but other functions can yield better data density and perhaps better signal propagation. And as faster digital electronics makes it easier to implement these it seems likely that it will become less and less common to have simple carriers with definite frequencies.

In addition, there is a continuing trend towards greater spatial localization of signals—whether by using phased arrays or by explicitly using technologies like fiber optics.

At present, the most intense overall artificial radio emission from the Earth is probably the 50 or 60 Hz hum from power lines. The most intense directed signals are probably from radars (such as those used for ballistic missile detection) that operate at a few hundred megahertz and put megawatts of power into narrow beams. (Some such systems are however being replaced by lower-power phased array systems.)

■ **Page 835 · SETI.** First claims of extraterrestrial radio signals were made by Nikola Tesla in 1899. More widely believed claims were made by Guglielmo Marconi in 1922, and for several years searches were done—notably by the U.S. military—for signals presumed to be coming from Mars. But it became increasingly accepted that in fact nothing beyond natural radio emissions such as whistlers (see note above) were actually being detected.

When galactic radio emission was first noticed by Karl Jansky in 1931 it seemed too random to be of intelligent origin. And when radio astronomy began to develop it essentially ignored extraterrestrial intelligence. But in 1959

Giuseppe Cocconi and Philip Morrison analyzed the possibility of interstellar radio communication, and in 1960 Frank Drake used a radio telescope to look for explicit signals from two nearby stars.

In 1965 a claim was made that there might be intensity variations of intelligent origin in radio emission from the quasar CTA-102—but this was quickly retracted. Then in 1967 when the first pulsar was discovered it was briefly thought that perhaps its precise 1.33730113-second repetition rate might be of intelligent origin.

Since the 1960s around a hundred different SETI (search for extraterrestrial intelligence) experiments have been done. Most use the same basic scheme: to look for signals that show a narrow band of frequencies—say only 1 Hz wide—perhaps changing in time. (The corresponding waveform is thus required to be an almost perfect sinusoid.) Some concentrate on specific nearby stars, while others look at the whole sky, or test the stream of data from all observations at a particular radio telescope, sometimes scanning for repetitive trains of pulses rather than single frequencies. The best current experiments could successfully detect radio emission at the level now produced on Earth only from about 10 light years away—or from about the nearest 10 stars. The detection distance increases like the square root of the signal strength, covering all 10^{11} stars in our galaxy when the signal uses the total power output of a star.

Most SETI has been done with specially built systems or with existing radio telescopes. But starting in the mid-1990s it became possible to use standard satellite receivers, and there are now plans to set up a large array of these specifically for SETI. In addition, it is now possible to use software instead of hardware to implement SETI signal-processing algorithms—both traditional ones and presumably much more general ones that can for example pick out much weaker signals.

Many SETI experiments look for signals in the so-called "water hole" between the 1420 MHz frequency associated with the 21 cm line of hydrogen and the 1720 MHz frequency associated with hydroxyl (OH). But although there are now practical constraints associated with the fact that on Earth only a few frequency regions have been left clear for radio astronomy I consider this to be a remarkable example of reliance on details of human intellectual development.

Already in the early 1960s it was suggested that lasers instead of radio could be used for interstellar communication, and there have been various attempts to detect interstellar optical pulses. Other suggested methods of communication have included optical solitons, neutrinos and as-yet-unknown faster-than-light quantum effects.

It is sometimes suggested that there must be fundamental limits to detection of radio signals based on such issues as collection areas, noise temperatures and signal degradation. But even existing technology has provided a steady stream of examples where limits like these have been overcome—most often by the use of more sophisticated signal processing.

■ **Detection methods.** Ways to identify computational origins include looking for repeatability in apparently random signals and comparing with output from large collections of possible simple programs. At a practical level, the one-dimensional character of data from radio signals makes it difficult for us to apply our visual systems—which remain our most powerful general-purpose analysis tools.

■ **Higher perception and analysis.** See page 632.

■ **Page 837 · Messages to send.** The idea of trying to send messages to extraterrestrials has existed since at least the early 1800s. The proposed content and medium of the messages has however steadily changed, usually reflecting what seemed to be the most significant human achievements of the time—yet often seeming quaint within just a few decades.

Starting in the 1820s various scientists (notably Carl Friedrich Gauss) suggested signalling the Moon by using such schemes as cutting clearings in a forest to illustrate the Pythagorean theorem or reflecting sunlight from mirrors in different countries placed so as to mimic an observed constellation of stars. In the 1860s, with the rise of telegraphy, schemes for sending flashes of light to Mars were discussed, and the idea developed that mathematics should somehow be the basic language used. In the 1890s radio signals were considered, and were tried by Nikola Tesla in 1899. Discussion in the 1920s led to the idea of sending radio pulses that could be assembled into a bitmap image, and some messages intended for extraterrestrials were probably sent by radio enthusiasts.

There is a long history of attempts to formulate universal languages (see page 1181). The Lincos language of Hans Freudenthal from 1960 was specifically designed for extraterrestrial communication. It was based on predicate logic, and attempted to use this to build up first mathematics, then science, then a general presentation of human affairs.

When the Pioneer 10 spacecraft was launched in 1972 it carried a physical plaque designed by Carl Sagan and others. The plaque is surprisingly full of implicit assumptions based on details of human intellectual development. For example, it has line drawings of humans—whose interpretation inevitably seems very specific to our visual system and artistic culture. It also has a polar plot of the positions of 14 pulsars relative to the Sun, with the pulsars specified by giving their periods as base 2 integers—but with trailing zeros inserted to cover inadequate precision. Perhaps the most peculiar element, however, is a diagram indicating the 21 cm transition in hydrogen—by showing two abstract quantum mechanical spin configurations represented in a way that seems completely specific to the particular details of human mathematics and physics. In 1977 the Voyager spacecraft carried phonograph records that included bitmap images and samples of spoken languages and music.

In 1974 the bitmap image below was sent as a radio signal from the Arecibo radio telescope. At the left-hand end is a version of the pattern of digits from page 117—but distorted so it has no obvious nested structure. There follow atomic numbers for various elements, and bitvectors for components of DNA. Next are idealized pictures of a DNA molecule, a human, and the telescope. All these parts seem to depend almost completely on detailed common conventions—and I suspect that without all sorts of human context their meaning would be essentially impossible to recognize.

In all, remarkably few messages have been sent—perhaps in part because of concerns that they might reveal us to extraterrestrial predators (see page 1191). There has also been a strong tendency to make messages hard even for humans to understand—perhaps on the belief that they must then be more scientific and more universal.

The main text argues that it will be essentially impossible to give definitive evidence of intelligence. Schemes that might however get at least some distance include sending:

- waveforms made of simple underlying elements;

- long complicated sequences that repeat precisely;

- a diversity of kinds of sequences;

- something complicated that satisfies simple constraints.

Examples of the latter include pattern-avoiding sequences (see page 944), magic squares and other combinatorial designs, specifications of large finite groups, and maximal length linear feedback shift register sequences (see page 1084). Notably, the last of these are already being transmitted by GPS satellites and CDMA communications systems. (If cases could be found where the sequences as a whole were forced not to have any obvious regularities, then pattern-avoiding sequences might perhaps be good since they have constraints that are locally fairly easy to recognize.)

Extrapolation of trends in human technology suggest that it will become ever easier to detect weak signals that might be assumed distorted beyond recognition or swamped by noise.

■ **Page 838 · P versus NP.** Given a constraint, it may be an NP-complete problem to find out what object satisfies it. So it may be difficult to generate the object from the constraint. But if one allows oneself to generate the object in any way at all, this may still be easy, even if P ≠ NP.

■ **Science fiction.** Inhabitants of the Moon were described in stories by Lucian around 150 AD and Johannes Kepler in 1634—and in both cases were closely modelled on terrestrial organisms. Interest in fiction about extraterrestrials increased greatly at the end of the 1800s—perhaps because by then few parts of the Earth remained unexplored. And as science fiction developed, accounts of the future sometimes treated extraterrestrials as commonplace—and sometimes did not mention them at all. Most often extraterrestrials have been easy to recognize, being little more than simple combinations of terrestrial animals (and occasionally plants)—though fairly often with extra features like telepathy. Some stories have nevertheless explored extraterrestrial intelligence based for example on solids, gases or energy fields. An example is Fred Hoyle's 1957 *The Black Cloud* in which a large cloud of hydrogen gas achieves intelligence by exchanging electromagnetic signals between rocks whose surface molecular configurations store memories.

The most common fictional scenario for first contact with extraterrestrials is the arrival of spacecraft—often induced by us having passed a technology threshold such as radio, nuclear explosions or faster-than-light travel. Other scenarios sometimes considered include archeological discovery of extraterrestrial artifacts and receipt of radio signals.

In the movie *2001* a black cuboid with side ratios 1:4:9 detected on the Moon through its anomalous magnetic properties sends a radio pulse in response to sunlight. Later there are also a few frames of flashing octahedra, presumably intended to be extraterrestrial artifacts, or perhaps extraterrestrials themselves.

In *The Black Cloud* intelligence is suggested by responsiveness to radio stimuli. Communication is established—as often in science fiction—by the intelligence interpreting material that we supply, and then replying in the same format.

The movie *Contact* centers on a radio signal with several traditional SETI ideas: it is transmitted at *1420 π* MHz, and involves a sequence of primes to draw attention, an amplified TV signal from Earth and a description of a machine to build.

The various *Star Trek* television series depict many encounters with "new life and new civilizations". Sometimes intelligence is seen not associated with something that is considered a lifeform.

Particularly in short stories various scenarios have been explored where it is difficult ever to recognize intelligence. These include one-of-a-kind beings that have nothing to communicate with, as well as beings with inner intellectual activity but no effect on the outside world. When there are extraterrestrials substantially more advanced than humans few efforts have been made to describe their motives and purposes directly—and usually what is emphasized is just their effects on humans.

(See also page 1184.)

■ **Page 839 · Practical arguments.** If extraterrestrials exist at all an obvious question—notably asked by Enrico Fermi in the 1940s—is why we have not encountered them. For there seems no fundamental reason that even spacecraft could not colonize our entire galaxy within just a few million years.

Explanations suggested for apparent absence include:

- Extraterrestrials are visiting, but we do not detect them;
- Extraterrestrials have visited, but not in recorded history;
- Extraterrestrials choose to exist in other dimensions;
- Interstellar travel is somehow infeasible;
- Colonization is somehow ecologically limited;
- Physical travel is not worth it; only signals are ever sent.

Explanations for apparent lack of radio signals include:

- Broadcasting is avoided for fear of conquest;
- There are active efforts to prevent us being contaminated;
- Extraterrestrials have no interest in communicating;
- Radio is the wrong medium;
- There are signals, but we do not understand them.

The so-called Drake equation gives a straightforward upper bound on the number of cases of extraterrestrial intelligence that could have arisen in our galaxy through the same basic chain of circumstances as humans. The result is a product of: rate of formation of suitable stars; fraction with planetary systems; number of Earth-like planets per system; fraction where life develops; fraction where intelligence develops; fraction where technology develops; time communicating civilizations survive. It now seems fairly certain that there are at least hundreds of millions of Earth-like planets in our galaxy. Biologists sometimes argue that intelligence is a rare development—though in the Darwinian approach it certainly

has clear benefit. In addition, particularly in the Cold War period, it was often said that technological civilizations would quickly tend to destroy themselves, but now it seems more likely that intelligence—once developed—will tend to survive indefinitely, at least in machine form.

It is obviously difficult to guess the possible motivations of extraterrestrials, but one might expect that—just as with humans—different extraterrestrials would tend to do different things, so that at least some would choose to send out signals if not spacecraft. Out of about 6 billion humans, however, it is notable that only extremely few choose, say, to explore life in the depths of the oceans—though perhaps this is just because technology has not yet made it easy to do. In human history a key motivator for exploration was trade. But trade requires that there be things of value to exchange; yet it is not clear that with sufficiently advanced technology there would be. For if the fundamental theory of physics is known, then everything about what is possible in our universe can in principle be worked out purely by a computation. Often irreducible work will be required, which one might imagine it would be worthwhile to trade. But as a practical matter, it seems likely that there will be vastly more room to do more extensive computations by using smaller components than by trading and collaborating with even millions of other civilizations. (It is notable that just a couple of decades ago, it was usually assumed that extraterrestrials would inevitably want to use large amounts of energy, and so would eventually for example tap all the output of a star. But seeing the increasing emphasis on information rather than mechanical work in human affairs this now seems much less clear.)

Extrapolating from our development, one might expect that most extraterrestrials would be something like immortal disembodied minds. And what such entities might do has to some extent been considered in the context of the notion of heaven in theology and art. And it is perhaps notable that while such activities as music and thought are often discussed, exploration essentially never is.

■ **Physics as intelligence.** From the point of view of traditional thinking about intelligence in the universe it might seem like an extremely bizarre possibility that perhaps intelligence could exist at a very small scale, and in effect have spread throughout the universe, building as an artifact everything we see. But at least with a broad interpretation of intelligence this is at some level exactly what the Principle of Computational Equivalence suggests has actually happened. For it implies that even at the smallest scales the laws of physics will show the same computational sophistication that we normally associate with intelligence. So in some sense this supports the theological notion that there might be a kind of intelligence that permeates our universe. (See page 1195.)

Implications for Technology

▪ **Covering technology.** In writing this book I have tried to achieve some level of completeness in covering the obvious scientific implications of my ideas. But to cover technological implications at anything like the same level would require at least as long a book again. And in my experience many of the intellectually most interesting aspects of technology emerge only when one actually tries to build technology for real—and they are often in a sense best captured by the technology itself rather than by a book about it.

▪ **Page 840 · Applications of randomness.** Random drawing of lots has been used throughout recorded history as an unbiased way to distribute risks or rewards. Also common have been games of chance (see page 968). Randomness is in general a convenient way to allow local decisions to be made while maintaining overall averages. In biological organisms it is used in determining sex of offspring, as well as in achieving uniform sampling, say in foraging for food. (Especially in antiquity, all sorts of seemingly random phenomena have been used as a basis for fortune telling.)

The notion of taking random samples as a basis for making unbiased deductions has been common since the early 1900s, notably in polling and market research. And in the past few decades explicit randomization has become common as a way of avoiding bias in cases such as clinical trials of drugs.

In the late 1800s it was noted in recreational mathematics that one could find the value of π by looking at randomly dropped needles. In the early 1900s devices based on randomness were built to illustrate statistics and probability (see page 312), and were used for example to find the form of the Student t-distribution. With the advent of digital computers in the mid-1940s Monte Carlo methods (see page 968) were introduced, initially as a way to approximate processes like neutron diffusion. (Similar ideas had been used in 1901 by Kelvin to study the Boltzmann equation.) Such methods became increasingly popular, especially for simulating systems like telephone networks and particle detectors that have many heterogeneous elements—as well as in statistical physics. In the 1970s they also became widely used for high-dimensional numerical integration, notably for Feynman diagram evaluation in quantum electrodynamics. But eventually it was realized that quasi-Monte Carlo methods based on simple sequences could normally do better than ones based on pure randomness (see page 1085).

A convenient way to tell whether expressions are equal is to evaluate them with random numerical values for variables. (Care must be taken with branch cuts and bounding intervals for inexact numbers.) In the late 1970s it was noted that by evaluating *PowerMod[a, n - 1, n] == 1* for several random integers *a* one can with high probability quickly deduce *PrimeQ[n]*. (In the 1960s it had been noted that one can factor polynomials by filling in random integers for variables and factoring the resulting numbers.) And in the 1980s many such randomized algorithms were invented, but by the mid-1990s it was realized that most did not require any kind of true randomness, and could readily be derandomized and made more predictable. (See page 1085.)

There are all sorts of situations where in the absence of anything better it is good to use randomness. Thus, for example, many exploratory searches in this book were done randomly. And in testing large hardware and software systems random inputs are often used.

Randomness is a common way of avoiding pathological cases and deadlocks. (It requires no communication between components so is convenient in parallel systems.) Examples include message routing in networks, retransmission times after ethernet collisions, partitionings for sorting algorithms, and avoiding getting stuck in minimization procedures like simulated annealing. (See page 347.) As on page 333, it is common for randomness to add robustness—as for example in cellular automaton fluids, or in saccadic eye movements in biology.

In cryptography randomness is used to make messages look typical of all possibilities (see page 598). It is also used in roughly the same way in hashing (see page 622). Such randomness must be repeatable. But for cryptographic keys it should not be. And the same is true when one picks unique IDs, say to keep track of repeat web transactions with a low probability of collisions. Randomness is in effect also used in a similar way in the shotgun method for DNA sequencing, as well as in creating radar pulses that are difficult to forge. (In biological organisms random diversity in faces and voices may perhaps have developed for similar reasons.)

The unpredictability of randomness is often useful, say for animals or military vehicles avoiding predators (see page 1105). Such unpredictability can also be used in simulating human or natural processes, say for computer graphics, videogames, or mock handwriting. Random patterns are often used as a way to hide regularities—as in camouflage, security envelopes, and many forms of texturing and distressing. (See page 1077.)

In the past, randomness was usually viewed as a thing to be avoided. But with the spread of computers and consumer electronics that normally operate predictably, it has become increasingly popular as an option.

Microscopic randomness is implicitly used whenever there is dissipation or friction in a system, and generally it adds robustness to the behavior that occurs in systems.

■ **Page 841 · Self-assembly.** Given elements (such as pieces of molecules) that fit together only when certain specified constraints are satisfied it is fairly straightforward to force, say, cellular automaton patterns to be generated, as on page 221. (Notable examples of such self-assembly occur for instance in spherical viruses.)

■ **Page 841 · Nanotechnology.** Popular since the late 1980s, especially through the work of Eric Drexler, nanotechnology has mostly involved investigation of several approaches to making essentially mechanical devices out of small numbers of atoms. One approach extrapolates chip technology, and studies placing atoms individually on solid surfaces using for example scanning probe microscopy. Another extrapolates chemical synthesis—particularly of fullerenes—and considers large molecules made for example out of carbon atoms. And another involves for example setting up fragments of DNA to try to force particular patterns of self-assembly. Most likely it will eventually be possible to have a single universal system that can manufacture almost any rigid atomic-scale structure on the basis of some kind of program. (Ribosomes in biological cells already construct arbitrary proteins from DNA sequences, but ordinary protein shapes are usually difficult to predict.) Existing work has tended to concentrate on trying to make rather elaborate components suitable for building miniature versions of familiar machines. The discoveries in this book imply however that there are much simpler components that can also be used to set up systems that have behavior with essentially any degree of sophistication. Such systems can either have the kind of chemical and mechanical character most often considered in nanotechnology, or can be primarily electronic, for example along the lines of so-called quantum-dot cellular automata. Over the next several decades applications of nanotechnology will no doubt include much higher-capacity computers, active materials of various kinds, and cellular-scale biomedical devices.

■ **Page 842 · Searching for technology.** Many inventions are made by pure ingenuity (sometimes aided by mathematical calculation) or by mimicking processes that go on in nature. But there are also cases where systematic searches are done. Notable examples were the testing of thousands of materials as candidate electric light bulb filaments by Thomas Edison in 1879, and the testing of 606 substances for chemotherapy by Paul Ehrlich in 1910. For at least fifty years it has now

been quite routine to test many hundreds or thousands of substances in looking, say, for catalysts or drugs with particular functions. (Other kinds of systematic searches done include ones for metal alloys, cooking recipes and plant hybrids.) Starting in the late 1980s the methods of combinatorial chemistry (see note below) began to make it possible to do biochemical tests on arrays of millions of related substances. And by the late 1990s, similar ideas were being used for example in materials science: in a typical case an array of different combinations of substances is made by successively spraying through an appropriate sequence of masks, with some physical or chemical test then applied to all the samples.

In the late 1950s maximal length shift register sequences (page 1084) and some error-correcting codes (page 1101) were found by systematic searches of possible polynomials. Most subsequent codes, however, have been found by explicit mathematical constructions. Optimal circuit blocks for operations such as addition and sorting (see page 1142) have occasionally been found by searches, but are more often found by explicit construction, progressive improvement or systematic logic minimization (see page 1097). In some compilers searches are occasionally done for optimal sequences of instructions to implement particular simple functions. And in recent years—notably in the building of *Mathematica*—optimal algorithms for operations such as function evaluation and numerical integration have sometimes been found through searches. In addition, my 1984 identification of rule 30 as a randomness generator was the result of a small-scale systematic search.

Particularly since the 1970s, many systematic methods have been tried for optimizing engineering designs by computer. Usually they are based on iterative improvement rather than systematic search. Some rely on linear programming or gradient descent. Others use methods such as simulated annealing, neural networks and genetic algorithms. But as discussed on page 342, except in very simple cases, the results are usually far from any absolute optimum. (Plant and animal breeding can be viewed as a simple form of randomized search done since the dawn of civilization.)

■ **Page 843 · Methodology in this book.** Much of what is presented in this book comes from systematic enumeration of all possible systems of particular types. However, sometimes I have done large searches for systems (see e.g. page 112). And especially in Chapter 11 I have occasionally explicitly constructed systems that show particular features.

■ **Chemistry.** Chemical compounds are a little like cellular automata and other kinds of programs. For even though the basic physical laws relevant to chemical compounds have been known since the early 1900s, it remains extremely difficult to predict the actual properties of a given compound. And I suspect that the ultimate reason for this—just as in the case of simple programs—is computational irreducibility.

For a single molecule, the minimum energy configuration can presumably always be found by a limited amount of computational work—though potentially increasing rapidly with the number of atoms. But if one allows progressively more molecules computational irreducibility can make it take progressively more computational work to see what will happen. And much as in determining whether constraints like those on page 213 can be satisfied for an infinite region, it can take an infinite amount of computational work to determine bulk properties of an infinite collection of molecules. Thus in practice it has typically been difficult to predict for example boiling and particularly melting points (see note below). So this means in the end that most of chemistry must be based on facts determined experimentally about specific compounds that happen to have been studied.

There are currently about 10 million compounds listed in standard chemical databases. Of these, most were first identified as extracts from biological or other natural systems. In trying to discover compounds that might be useful say as drugs the traditional approach was to search large libraries of compounds, then to study variations on those that seemed promising. But in the 1980s it began to be popular to try so-called rational design in which molecules were created that could at least to some extent specifically be computed to have relevant shapes and chemical functions. Then in the 1990s so-called combinatorial chemistry became popular, in which—somewhat in imitation of the immune system—large numbers of possible compounds were created by successively adding at random several different possible amino acids or other units. But although it will presumably change in the future it remained true in 2001 that half of all drugs in use are derived from just 32 families of compounds.

Doing a synthesis of a chemical is much like constructing a network by applying a specified sequence of transformations. And just like for multiway systems it is presumably in principle undecidable whether a given set of possible transformations can ever be combined to yield a particular chemical. Yet ever since the 1960s there have been computer systems like LHASA that try to find synthesis pathways automatically. But perhaps because they lack even the analog of modern automated theorem-proving methods,

such systems have never in practice been extremely successful.

■ **Interesting chemicals.** The standard IUPAC system for chemical nomenclature assigns a name to essentially any possible compound. But even among hydrocarbons with fairly few atoms not all have ever been considered interesting enough to list in standard chemical databases. Thus for example the following compares the total number of conceivable alkanes (paraffins) to the number actually listed in the 2001 standard Beilstein database:

n	1	2	3	4	5	6	7	8	9	10	11	12	13	14	15	16
total	1	1	1	2	3	5	9	18	35	75	159	355	802	1858	4347	10359
listed	1	1	1	2	3	5	9	18	35	75	68	108	60	60	41	62

Any tree with up to 4 connections at each node can in principle correspond to an alkane with chemical formula C_nH_{2n+2}. The total number of such trees—studied since 1875—increases roughly like $2.79^n\, n^{-5/2}$. If every node has say 4 connections, then eventually one gets dendrimers that cannot realistically be constructed in 3D. But long before this happens one runs into many alkanes that presumably exist, but apparently have never explicitly been studied. The small unbranched ones (methane, ethane, propane, butane, pentane, etc.) are all well known, but ones with more complicated branching are decreasingly known. In coal and petroleum a continuous range of alkanes occur. Branched octanes are used to reduce knocking in car engines. Biological systems contain many specific alkanes— often quite large—that happen to be produced through chemical pathways in biological cells. (The $n = 11$ and $n = 13$ unbranched alkanes are for example known to serve as ant pheromones.)

In general the main way large molecules have traditionally ended up being considered chemically interesting is if they occur in biological systems—or mimic ones that do. Since the 1980s, however, molecules such as the fullerenes that instead have specific regular geometrical shapes have also begun to be considered interesting.

■ **Alkane properties.** The picture on the facing page shows melting points measured for alkanes. (Note that even when alkanes are listed in chemical databases—as discussed above—their melting points may not be given.) Unbranched alkanes yield melting points that increase smoothly for n even and for n odd. Highly symmetrical branched alkanes tend to have high melting points, presumably because they pack well in space. No reliable general method for predicting melting points is however known (see note above), and in fact for large n alkanes tend to form jellies with no clear notion of melting.

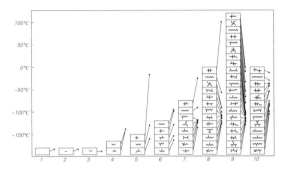

Things appear somewhat simpler with boiling points, and as noticed by Harry Wiener in 1947 (and increasingly discussed since the 1970s) these tend to be well fit as being linearly proportional to the so-called topological index given by the sum of the smallest numbers of connections visited in getting between all pairs of carbon atoms in an alkane molecule.

■ **Page 843 · Components for technology.** The Principle of Computational Equivalence suggests that a vast range of systems in nature can all ultimately be used to make computers. But it is remarkable to what extent even the components of present-day computer systems involve elements of nature originally studied for quite different reasons. Examples include electricity, semiconductors (used for chips), ferrites (used for magnetic storage), liquid crystals (used for displays), piezoelectricity (used for microphones), total internal reflection (used for optical fibers), stimulated emission (used for lasers) and photoconductivity (used for xerographic printing).

■ **Future technology.** The purposes technology should serve inevitably change as human civilization develops. But at least in the immediate future many of these purposes will tend to relate to the current character of our bodies and minds. For certainly technology must interface with these. But presumably as time progresses it will tend to become more integrated, with systems that we have created eventually being able to fit quite interchangeably into our usual biological or mental setup. At first most such systems will probably tend either to be based on standard engineering, or to be quite direct emulations of human components that we see. But particularly by using the ideas and methods of this book I suspect that significant progressive enhancements will be possible. And probably there will be many features that are actually quite easy to take far beyond the originals. One example is memory and the recall of history. Human memory is in many ways quite impressive. Yet for ordinary physical objects we are used to the idea that they remember little of their history, for at a macroscopic level we tend to see only

the coarsest traces. But at a microscopic scale something like the surface of a solid has in at least some form remarkably detailed information about its history. And as technological systems get smaller it should become possible to read and manipulate this. And much as in the discussion at the end of Chapter 10 the ability to interact at such a level will yield quite different experiences, which in turn will tend to suggest different purposes to pursue with technology.

Historical Perspectives

■ **Page 844 · Human uniqueness.** The idea that there is something unique and special about humans has deep roots in Judeo-Christian tradition—and despite some dilution from science remains a standard tenet of Western thought today. Eastern religions have however normally tended to take a different view, and to consider humans as just one of many elements that make up the universe as a whole. (See note below.)

■ **Page 845 · Animism.** Belief in animism remains strong in perhaps several hundred million indigenous people around the world. In its typical form, it involves not only explaining natural phenomena by analogy to human behavior but also assuming that they can be influenced as humans might be, say by offerings or worship. (See also page 1177.)

Particularly since Edward Tylor in 1871 animism has often been thought of as the earliest identifiable form of religion. Polytheism is then assumed to arise when the idea of localized spirits associated with individual natural objects is generalized to the idea of gods associated with types of objects or concepts (as for example in many Roman beliefs). Following their rejection in favor of monotheism by Judaism—and later Christianity and Islam—such ideas have however tended to be considered primitive and pagan. In Europe through the Middle Ages there nevertheless remained widespread belief in animistic kinds of explanations. And even today some Western superstitions center on animism, as do rituals in countries like Japan. Animism is also a key element of the New Age movement of the 1960s, as well as of such ideas as the Gaia Hypothesis.

Particularly since the work of Jean Piaget in the 1940s, young children are often said to go through a phase of animism, in which they interact with complex objects much as if they were alive and human.

■ **Page 845 · Universe as intelligent.** Whether or not something like thinking can be attributed to the universe has long been discussed in philosophy and theology. Theism and the standard Western religions generally attribute thinking to a person-like God who governs the universe but is separate from it. Deism emphasizes that God can govern the universe only according to natural laws—but whether or not this involves thinking is unclear. Pantheism generally identifies the universe and God. In its typical religious form in Eastern metaphysics—as well as in philosophical idealism—the contents of the universe are identified quite directly with the thoughts of God. In scientific pantheism the abstract order of the universe is identified with God (often termed "Nature's God" or "Spinoza's God"), but whether this means that thinking is involved in the operation of the universe is not clear. (See also pages 822 and 1191.)

■ **Non-Western thinking.** Some of my conclusions in this book may seem to resonate with ideas of Eastern thinking. For example, what I say about the fundamental similarity of human thinking to other processes in nature may seem to fit with Buddhism. And what I say about the irreducibility of processes in nature to short formal rules may seem to fit with Taoism. Like essentially all forms of science, however, what I do in this book is done in a rational tradition—with limited relation to the more mystical traditions of Eastern thinking.

■ **Aphorisms.** Particularly from ancient and more fragmentary texts aphorisms have survived that may sometimes seem at least vaguely related to this book. (An example from the pre-Socratics is "everything is full of gods".) But typically it is impossible to see with any definiteness what such aphorisms might really have been intended to mean.

■ **Postmodernism.** Since the mid-1960s postmodernism has argued that science must have fundamental limitations, based on its general belief that any single abstract system must somehow be as limited—and as arbitrary in its conclusions—as the context in which it is set up. My work supports the notion that—despite implicit assumptions made especially in the physical sciences—context can in fact be crucial to the choice of subject matter and interpretation of results in science (see e.g. page 1105). But the Principle of Computational Equivalence suggests at some level a remarkable uniformity among systems, that allows all sorts of general scientific statements to be made without dependence on context. It so happens that some of these statements then imply intrinsic general limitations on science—but even the very fact that such statements can be made is in a sense an example of successful generality in science that goes against the conclusions of postmodernism. (See also page 1131.)

■ **Microcosm.** The notion that a human mind might somehow be analogous to the whole universe was discussed by Plato and others in antiquity, and known in the Middle Ages. But it

was normally assumed that this was something fairly unique to the human mind—and nothing with the generality of the Principle of Computational Equivalence was ever imagined.

■ **Human future.** The Principle of Computational Equivalence and the results of this book at first suggest a rather bleak view of the end point of the development of technology. As I argued in Chapter 10 computers will presumably be able to emulate human thinking. And particularly using the methods of this book one will be able to use progressively smaller physical components as elements of computers. So before too long it will no doubt be possible to implement all the processes of thinking that go on in a single human—or even in billions of humans—in a fairly small piece of material. Each piece of human thinking will then correspond to some microscopic pattern of changes in the atoms of the material. In the past one might have assumed that these changes would somehow show fundamental evidence of representing sophisticated human thinking. But the Principle of Computational Equivalence implies that many ordinary physical processes are computationally just as sophisticated as human thinking. And this means that the pattern of microscopic changes produced by such processes can at some level be just as sophisticated as those corresponding to human thinking. So given, say, an ordinary piece of rock in which there is all sorts of complicated electron motion this may in a fundamental sense be doing no less than some system of the future constructed with nanotechnology to implement operations of human thinking. And while at first this might seem to suggest that the rich history of biology, civilization and technology needed to reach this point would somehow be wasted, what I believe instead is that this just highlights the extent to which such history is what is ultimately the defining feature of the human condition.

■ **Philosophical implications.** The Principle of Computational Equivalence has implications for many issues long discussed in the field of philosophy. Most important are probably those in epistemology (theory of knowledge). In the past, it has usually been assumed that if we could only build up in our minds an adequate model of the world, then we would immediately know whatever we want about the world. But the Principle of Computational Equivalence now implies that even given a model it may be irreducibly difficult to work out its consequences. In effect, computational irreducibility introduces a new kind of limit to knowledge. And it implies that one needs a criterion more sophisticated than immediate predictability to assess a scientific theory—since when computational irreducibility is present this will inevitably be limited. In the past, it has sometimes been assumed that truths that can be deduced purely by operations like those in logic must somehow always be trivial. But computational irreducibility implies that in general they are not. Indeed it implies that even once the basic laws are known there are still an endless series of questions that are worth investigating in science. It is often assumed that one cannot learn much about the world just by studying purely formal systems—and that one has to rely on empirical input. But the Principle of Computational Equivalence implies that at some level there are inevitably common features across both abstract and natural systems. In ontology (theory of being) the Principle of Computational Equivalence implies that special components are vastly less necessary than might have been thought. For it shows that all sorts of sophisticated characteristics can emerge from the very same kinds of simple components. (My discussion of fundamental physics in Chapter 9 also suggests that no separate entities beyond simple rules are needed to capture space, time or matter.) Arguments in several areas of philosophy involve in effect considering fundamentally different intelligences. But the Principle of Computational Equivalence implies that in fact above a certain threshold there is an ultimate equivalence between possible intelligences. In addition, the Principle of Computational Equivalence implies that all sorts of systems in nature and elsewhere will inevitably exhibit features that in the past have been considered unique to intelligence—and this has consequences for the mind-body problem, the question of free will, and recognition of other minds. It has often been thought that traditional logic—and to some extent mathematics—are somehow fundamentally special and provide in a sense unique foundations. But the Principle of Computational Equivalence implies that in fact there are a huge range of other formal systems, equivalent in their ultimate richness, but different in their details, and in the questions to which they naturally lead. In philosophy of science the Principle of Computational Equivalence forces a new methodology based on formal experiments—that is ultimately the foundation for the whole new kind of science that I describe in this book.

Index

Colophon

The original source for this book was created in FrameMaker, processed using an automated build system based on *Mathematica*, and output as PDF. (See also page 852.) The diagrams in the book were created using *Mathematica*, and the text for programs was automatically formatted by *Mathematica*, with both being imported as Encapsulated PostScript. Photographs were enhanced and processed using Photoshop and *Mathematica*. Index manipulation was done using *Mathematica* and IXgen.

The fonts in the book are Trump Mediaeval, Palatino, Univers 45 and Gill Sans, with additional elements in Mathematica, Mathematica-Sans, Optima, Meridien and Janson.

The book was printed on 50-pound Finch VHF paper on a sheet-fed press. It was imaged directly to plates at 2400 dpi, with halftones rendered using a 175-line screen with round dots angled at 45°. The binding was Smythe sewn.

Book data: 1280 pages; 583,313 words (main text: 227,580, notes: 283,751); 2,799,438 characters; 973 illustrations; 1350 notes; 796 *Mathematica* programs; 14,967 index entries.

Book designer: André Kuzniarek

Cover designer: John Bonadies

Additional designers: Jeremy Davis, Jody Jasinski

Layout assistants: Larry Adelston, Richard Miske

Production software developers: Andrew de Laix, Scott Koranda, Patrick Rice, Øyvind Tafjord

Primary graphics finisher: Malgorzata Strzebonska

Additional graphics finishers: Cookie Apichairuk, Hormozd Gahvari, Jay Hawkins,
    Nadya Markin, Jay Warendorff

Custom font designers: Andy Hunt, André Kuzniarek

Proofreaders: Jan Progen, Caroline Small and other members of the
    Wolfram Research Document Quality Assurance group

Book program testers: Daniel Cranston, Bill Landis, Sung-il Pae, Niels Sondergaard

Manufacturing manager: Brenda Skelly

For other credits see pages xii–xiv.

All diagrams and most photographs are original to this book. (Original photographs by the author and Chris Brown, Ian Collier, Matthew Cook, Andrew de Laix, Theodore Gray, André Kuzniarek, Conrad Wolfram.) Additional photographs are licensed from a variety of sources, believed to be in the public domain, or are courtesy of the following: Bildarchiv Preußischer Kulturbesitz; The Board of Trinity College Dublin; The British Museum; National Archaeological Museum, Greece (page 43). A. C. Charters; Yves Couder; P. E. Dimotakis; Peter Freymuth; H. Honji/S. Taneda; E. L. Koschmieder; Fred Landis; MIT Press; Maarten Rutgers Research Group, The Ohio State University; D. Howell Peregrine; Ephraim M. Sparrow (page 377). Ralph Buchsbaum; Jeremy Burgess/Science Photo Library; Photo Researchers; Chip Clark/The Smithsonian Institution; Christian de Duve; Eric Grave/Science Photo Library; Manfred Kage/Peter Arnold, Inc.; Lynn Margulis (page 385). John W. Forsythe/UTMB (page 426). Argos Group (page 993). Calligraphy on page 874 by Mamoun Sakkal.

For legal notices see the copyright page.

Printed by Kromar Printing Ltd, Winnipeg, Canada.